THE DRAMATIC WORKS OF
George Lillo

George Lillo's domestic tragedies provided the impetus for the development of new forms of serious drama during and after the eighteenth century, on the Continent as well as in the English-speaking theatre. The edition makes available for the first time all of the plays known or thought to have been written by the playwright, in reliable old-spelling texts following modern bibliographical principles. Some have not been reprinted since 1810. Even the much-studied *London Merchant* has not previously been published in an edition that recognizes the errors contained in the first edition and the authorial revisions introduced in early reprints. The introduction to each play treats its sources, histories of publication and reception in the theatre, and textual problems. The *apparatus criticus* and historical collations provide full bibliographical detail. Commentary notes discuss the author's use or adaptation of sources and furnish information about links among his own plays, topical background, and literary allusions. The edition makes possible an informed awareness of Lillo's lesser-known plays in a variety of genres, as an enlightening context for further study of these influential domestic dramas.

THE DRAMATIC WORKS OF
George Lillo

Edited by
James L. Steffensen

Including
SILVIA

Edited by
Richard Noble

CLARENDON PRESS · OXFORD
1993

Oxford University Press, Walton Street, Oxford OX2 6DP
Oxford New York Toronto
Delhi Bombay Calcutta Madras Karachi
Kuala Lumpur Singapore Hong Kong Tokyo
Nairobi Dar es Salaam Cape Town
Melbourne Auckland Madrid
and associated companies in
Berlin Ibadan

Oxford is a trade mark of Oxford University Press

Published in the United States
by Oxford University Press Inc., New York

British Library Cataloguing in Publication Data
Data available

Library of Congress Cataloging in Publication Data
Lillo, George, 1693–1739.
[Works. 1992]
The dramatic works of George Lillo / edited by James L.
Steffensen, Richard Noble.
Includes index.
I. Steffensen, James L. II. Noble, Richard, 1958– .
II. Title.
PR3541.L5 1992 822'.5—dc20 91–38854
ISBN 0–19–812714–6

Typeset by Hope Services (Abingdon) Ltd.
Printed in Great Britain
on acid-free paper by
Biddles Ltd.
Guildford and King's Lynn

PREFACE

THIS edition includes all of the extant works for the theatre known or thought to have been written by George Lillo. Some have not been reprinted since 1810; none has previously been published in a critical old-spelling edition. My aim has been to provide reliable texts of Lillo's works—to make them available in editions which represent, as far as can be ascertained, the plays as the author intended them to be read and acted. I hope also to encourage an awareness of Lillo's lesser-known plays of various types as a context for further study of the more familiar domestic tragedies that held a significant place in the development of serious drama during and after the eighteenth century.

The first stage of my work was completed as a doctoral research project for Oxford University. The dissertation included texts and notes for five plays, and a descriptive bibliography of all known editions of these works published in Britain between 1731 and 1775. In preparation for publication, my texts and notes for the five plays have been reviewed and revised. Editions have been completed for the dramas not included in the dissertation: *Silvia*, *Britannia and Batavia*, and *Arden of Feversham*.

My work would not have been possible without sabbatical leaves and research funds granted by Wesleyan University, and additional research support provided by Dartmouth College. During the initial phase of my research at Oxford, I enjoyed the supervision and good counsel of F. W. Bateson. The dissertation was completed under the direction of David Foxon; for his guidance then and later, his bibliographical acumen, and his generosity over many hours spent discussing the minutiae of texts and peculiarities of their editions, I am deeply grateful. A long-standing debt that I can at last acknowledge is owed to Frederick Bracher, in whose class at Pomona College I was introduced to the delights of eighteenth-century drama and first encountered George Lillo.

The staffs of some fifty libraries provided me with assistance and information, graciously and at times at no little expense of time and special effort. First among these helpful people was Wyman Parker, Emeritus Librarian of Wesleyan University, who circulated my check-list of editions among the librarians represented in the Connecticut Valley Libraries Association and entrusted to me for extended periods of time the copies of early editions of Lillo's plays in his charge. I am of course much indebted to the scholars who earlier contributed to the bibliographical, historical, and critical understanding of Lillo's dramatic works. C. F. Burgess, whose helpful study of Lillo's less familiar dramas appeared when I was beginning my own research, encouraged me to edit the plays. Frederick deBoer, my colleague at Wesleyan University, shared the manuscript of his study of Lillo's career and his knowledge of the plays in performance. Joseph F. Reed was regularly generous with his friendship and his expertise in biographical research. I am grateful also for the assistance of my sometime students at Wesleyan, Glen MacLeod and Kenneth Swiger, and for the accuracy, speed, and good humour of Geraldine Cote, who typed many of the most difficult portions of the manuscript. Cornelia B. Wallin of the Williams–Watson Theatre Collection at Dartmouth College has done much to make possible the final stages of my work with the edition. To Peter Saccio, my colleague now at Dartmouth, I owe the example of scholarship and writing that I could at best attempt to emulate, and exemplary friendship that has taken equally in its stride the most dismaying and exhilarating moments of my work.

A particular pleasure in seeing the edition come into print is the opportunity this provides to publish my thanks to those whose consideration, hospitality, and support allowed me to find a second home and a place in scholarship in England and Oxford: Daphne and Robert Levens, Dame Helen Gardner, Mrs L. G. Bickmore, Ann Wolley-Dod, Sir Edgar Williams and his staff at Rhodes House, and the Fellows of Merton College and the former Warden, Robin Harrison.

For more than a decade my research has been aided and scrutinized, and many slips of pen or thought caught and corrected, by Richard Noble, at one time my student and research assistant, now a scholar in his own right. As I planned the edition of *Silvia*, the last of Lillo's plays I took up, it seemed appropriate that we work as collaborators. However, as we discovered the critical significance of the songs and extensive research required to sort out the music, an area of scholarship in which Mr Noble has special expertise, it became clear that he should have primary responsibility for the edition of the ballad opera, while I in turn served to assist and review his research. The edition of *Silvia* is essentially his, the notes about the songs and music are entirely his, and they are so credited. For this special contribution and for his unflagging efforts to ensure the accuracy of all of the collected edition, I am deeply grateful.

I owe my interest in theatre to my mother and father, who introduced me to plays and play-making in my childhood. Their unfailing interest and belief in my own theatrical efforts, whether on stage or in scholarship, I can acknowledge but not repay.

JAMES L. STEFFENSEN, JR.

The Hopkins Center,
Dartmouth College

CONTENTS

LIST OF REPRODUCED TITLE-PAGES

The music for the Airs in *Silvia* is reproduced from a copy of the
first edition by permission of the Bodleian Library (Malone B 38 (5))

LIST OF *SIGLA* FOR EDITIONS CITED IN FOOTNOTES, COMMENTARY, AND HISTORICAL COLLATIONS

Silvia

O   first edition, 1730 ('1731' on title-page)
O2   second issue ('second edition' on title-page), 1731
D   Dublin, 1730
E   Edinburgh, ?1730 ('London, 1731' on title-page)
W1   *Works*, 1775

The London Merchant

G1   first edition, 1731
G2   second edition, 1731
G3   third edition, 1731
G4   fourth edition, 1732
G5   fifth edition, 1735
G6   sixth edition, 1735
G7   seventh edition, 1740
W1   *Works*, 1775

The Christian Hero

G   first edition, 1735
D   Dublin, 1735
W1   *Works*, 1775

Fatal Curiosity

G   first edition, 1737
D   second edition, 1762
W1   *Works*, 1775

Marina

G   first edition, 1738
L   Larpent 9
W1   *Works*, 1775

Elmerick

G   first edition, 1740
L   Larpent 19
L¹   original (early) text of L
L²   revised (inserted) text of L
W1   *Works*, 1775

Britannia and Batavia

G   first edition, 1740
W1 *Works*, 1775

Arden of Feversham

D   first edition, 1762
L   Larpent 160
I   Dublin, 1763
W1 *Works*, 1775

LIST OF ABBREVIATED REFERENCES IN INTRODUCTIONS AND COMMENTARY

Actors, Actresses: Philip A. Highfill, Jr., Kalman A. Burnim, and Edward A. Langhans, eds., *A Biographical Dictionary of Actors, Actresses, Musicians, Dancers, Managers and Other Stage Personnel in London, 1660–1800*, vols. i–xii, Carbondale and Edwardsville, Ill., 1973–87.

Avery: Emmett L. Avery, 'The Shakespeare Ladies Club', *Shakespeare Quarterly*, vii (Spring 1956), 153–8.

Bernbaum: Ernest Bernbaum, *The Drama of Sensibility*, Cambridge, Mass., 1915 (repr. Gloucester, Mass., 1958).

Biographia Dramatica (1764): [David Erskine Baker, ed.,] *The Companion to the Playhouse: or, An Historical Account of All the Dramatic Writers . . . in Great Britain and Ireland . . .*, 2 vols., London, 1764.

Biographia Dramatica (1782): David Erskine Baker, ed., *Biographia Dramatica: or, A Companion to the Playhouse*, rev. by Isaac Reed, 2 vols., London, 1782.

Biographia Dramatica (1812): David Erskine Baker, ed., *Biographia Dramatica: or, A Companion to the Playhouse*, rev. by Isaac Reed, further rev. by Stephen Jones, 2 vols., London, 1812.

Boas: Frederick S. Boas, *An Introduction to Eighteenth-century Drama, 1700–1780*, Oxford, 1953.

Brief Account: Anon., *A Brief Account of the Life and Character of George Castriot, King of Epirus and Albania, Commonly Called, Scanderbeg*, London, 1735.

Burgess: C. F. Burgess, 'Lillo Sans Barnwell, or the Playwright Revisited', *Modern Philology*, lxvi. 1 (Aug. 1968), 5–29.

Charke, *Life*: Charlotte Charke, *A Narrative of the Life of Mrs. Charlotte Charke*, 2nd edn., London, 1755 (repr. Gainesville, Fla., 1969).

Cibber, *Apology*: Colley Cibber, *An Apology for the Life of Colley Cibber*, ed. B. R. S. Fone, Ann Arbor, 1968.

Cibber, *Lives*: Theophilus Cibber, *The Lives of the Poets of Great Britain and Ireland*, 5 vols., London, 1753.

Cokayne, *Baronetage*: G. E. C[okayne], *Complete Baronetage . . .*, 5 vols., Exeter, 1900–6.

Cokayne, *Peerage*: G. E. C[okayne], *The Complete Peerage . . .*, rev. by Vicary Gibbs *et al.*, 13 vols., London, 1910–59.

Davies, *Life*: Thomas Davies, *Some Account of the Life of Mr. George Lillo*, in *The Works of Mr. George Lillo*, ed. Thomas Davies, 2 vols., London, 1775, vol. i, pp. ix–xlviii.

deBoer: Frederik Eugene deBoer, 'George Lillo', unpublished doctoral dissertation, University of Wisconsin, 1965.

DNB: *The Dictionary of National Biography*.

Downer: Alan S. Downer, *The British Drama: A Handbook and Brief Chronicle*, New York, 1950.

Enc. Amer.: *Encyclopedia Americana*, International Edition, Danbury, 1989.

Enc. Brit.: *Encyclopaedia Britannica*, 11th edn., Cambridge, 1910–11.

Fiske: Roger Fiske, *English Theatre Music in the Eighteenth Century*, London, 1973.

Frankland: [Thomas Frankland,] *The Annals of King James and King Charles the First*, London, 1681.

Gagey: Edmund McAdoo Gagey, *Ballad Opera*, New York, 1937.

Garrick, *Correspondence*: *The Private Correspondence of David Garrick With the Most Celebrated Persons of His Time*, [ed. James Boaden,] 2 vols., London, 1831–2.

Garrick, *Letters*: *The Letters of David Garrick*, ed. David M. Little and George M. Kahrl, 3 vols., Cambridge, Mass., 1963.

Genest: John Genest, *Some Account of the English Stage, from . . . 1660 to 1830*, 10 vols., Bath, 1832.

Harris: James Harris, *Philological Inquiries in Three Parts*, London, 1781.

Hoeniger: William Shakespeare, *Pericles*, ed. F. D. Hoeniger, The Arden Shakespeare, London and Cambridge, Mass., 1963.

Johnson, *English Poets*: Samuel Johnson, *The Works of the English Poets, from Chaucer to Cowper*, ed. Alexander Chalmers, 21 vols., London, 1810.

Johnson, *Lives*: Samuel Johnson, *Lives of the English Poets*, ed. George Birkbeck Hill, 3 vols., Oxford, 1905.

Knolles: Richard Knolles, *The Turkish History, from the Original of that Nation to the Growth of the Ottoman Empire*, cont. by Sir Paul Rycaut, 6th edn., 3 vols., London, 1687–1700.

Lavardin: Jacques de Lavardin, *The Historie of George Castriot, Surnamed Scanderbeg, King of Albanie*, trans. Z[achary] I[ones], London, 1596.

London Stage, 1660–1700: William Van Lennep, ed., *The London Stage, 1660–1800*, Part 1: *1660–1700*, Carbondale, Ill., 1965.

London Stage, 1700–1729: Emmett L. Avery, ed., *The London Stage, 1660–1800*, Part 2: *1700–1729*, Carbondale, Ill., 1960.

London Stage, 1729–1747: Arthur H. Scouten, ed., *The London Stage, 1660–1800*, Part 3: *1729–1747*, 2 vols., Carbondale, Ill., 1961.

London Stage, 1747–1776: George Winchester Stone, Jr., ed., *The London Stage, 1660–1800*, Part 4: *1747–1776*, 2 vols., Carbondale, Ill., 1962.

London Stage, 1776–1800: Charles Beecher Hogan, ed., *The London Stage, 1660–1800*, Part 5: *1776–1800*, 3 vols., Carbondale, Ill., 1968.

Lord Lyttelton: *The Works of George Lord Lyttelton*, 3rd edn., 3 vols., London, 1776.

McBurney, *FC*: George Lillo, *Fatal Curiosity*, ed. William H. McBurney, Lincoln, Nebr., 1966.

McBurney, *LM*: George Lillo, *The London Merchant*, ed. William H. McBurney, Lincoln, Nebr., 1965.

Maxwell: William Shakespeare, *Pericles*, ed. J. C. Maxwell, The New Shakespeare, Cambridge, 1956.

Moore: Clement C. Moore, *George Castriot, Surnamed Scanderbeg, King of Albania*, New York, 1850.

Moss: Howard Gene Moss, 'Ballad Opera Songs: A Record of the Ideas Set to Music, 1728–1733', unpublished doctoral dissertation, University of Michigan, 1969.

N & C: George H. Nettleton and Arthur E. Case, eds., *British Dramatists from Dryden to Sheridan*, rev. by George Winchester Stone, Jr., New York, 1969.

Nicoll: Alardyce Nicoll, *A History of English Drama, 1660–1900*, vol. ii, Cambridge, 1952.

Odell: George C. D. Odell, *Shakespeare from Betterton to Irving*, 2 vols., New York, 1920.

OED: *The Oxford English Dictionary*.

Pallette: Drew B. Pallette, 'Notes for a Biography of George Lillo', *Philological Quarterly*, xix. 3 (July 1940), 261–7.

Rosenfeld, *Strolling Players*: Sybil Rosenfeld, *Strolling Players and Drama in the Provinces, 1660–1765*, Cambridge, 1939.

Sanderson: William Sanderson, *A Compleat History of the Lives and Reigns of Mary Queen of Scotland and of . . . James the Sixth*, London, 1656.

Savage: Richard Knolles, *The Turkish History . . . to . . . 1699*, abr. by John Savage, 2 vols., London, 1701.

Scanderbeg the Great: [Anne de La Roche-Guilhem,] *Scanderbeg the Great*, trans. anon., London, 1721.

Vertot: René Aubert de Vertot d'Aubœuf (l'Abbé de Vertot), *The History of the Knights of Malta*, trans. anon., London, 1728.

Ward: George Lillo, *The London Merchant and Fatal Curiosity*, ed. Adolphus William Ward, Boston, 1906.

Wine: *The Tragedy of Master Arden of Faversham*, ed. M. L. Wine, The Revels Plays, London, 1973.

Quotations from primary sources are taken from the following texts:

Arden of Faversham: *The Tragedy of Master Arden of Faversham*, ed. M. L. Wine, The Revels Plays, London, 1973.

Dr. Faustus: Christopher Marlowe, *Doctor Faustus*, ed. John D. Jump, The Revels Plays, London, 1962.

Pericles: William Shakespeare, *Pericles*, ed. F. D. Hoeniger, The Arden Shakespeare, London and Cambridge, Mass., 1963.

Biblical quotations are taken from the Authorized Version of 1611.

Notes

1. When a reference to material from *London Stage* in an introduction or commentary note includes a specific date—as, for example, a date of performance—the item quoted will be found under that date in the part of *London Stage* recorded in the note.

2. Material cited from earlier editions of Lillo's plays (Ward, McBurney, N & C) appears in their notes to the lines in question unless otherwise noted.

INTRODUCTION

GEORGE LILLO spoke to values and sensibilities of the eighteenth century directly and with remarkable effectiveness. Only one of his plays, *The London Merchant*, achieved great success in the theatre, but this unusual tragedy secured for its author the respect of his own generation, was regularly acted throughout the century and well into the next, and was repeatedly reprinted. Received on the Continent as a model for *tragédie domestique et bourgeoise*, it has been accepted as 'the first conscious deliberate effort in the new style'.[1] Lillo's second domestic tragedy, *Fatal Curiosity*, also served as the prototype for a significant new dramatic genre.[2] In the 1780s it was singled out as a modern play reminiscent of the Greek tragedies in form and equal to them in power.[3] Henry Fielding, who produced it, said simply that it gave its author 'Title to be called the best Tragick Poet of his Age'.[4]

Lillo's interests in the theatre were not limited, however, to domestic tragedy. Of the four plays he contributed to the London stage after the initial success of *The London Merchant* in 1731, two were conceived in the heroic tradition: *The Christian Hero*, performed in 1735,[5] and *Elmerick*, first acted in 1740, a few months after the playwright's death. In 1738, in response to the Shakespearian revival, Lillo produced *Marina*, an adaptation of *Pericles*. *Fatal Curiosity*, which Fielding staged in 1736, was domestic in subject but classical in the design of its action and intended effect. Lillo's first work for the stage had been a ballad opera, *Silvia; or, The Country Burial* (1730), a curious mixture of bawdy comedy and morally edifying bucolic romance, and it was said that he also wrote a comedy, *The Regulators*,[6] but no concrete evidence that he did so has been found. *Britannia and Batavia*, his patriotic masque written in 1734 to honour the marriage of the Princess Royal to William, Prince of Orange, was never performed but was printed in 1740. A third domestic tragedy, an adaptation of *Arden of Faversham*, is reported to have been begun, perhaps before 1736,[7] and

---

[1] Nicoll, p. 121.

[2] *Schicksalstragödie*. Association of Lillo's play with this dramatic movement has enhanced its reputation but has also frequently led to misinterpretation of the moral and dramatic bases of his tragedy (see introduction to *Fatal Curiosity*).

[3] Harris, pp. 154–60 and 169–77.

[4] *The Champion*, 26 Feb. 1740.

[5] *The Brief Account of . . . Scanderbeg*, regularly advertised with *The Christian Hero*, almost certainly was not written by Lillo (see introduction to *The Christian Hero*).

[6] *Biographia Dramatica* (David Erskine Baker, ed., rev. by Isaac Reed [London, 1782], ii. 302) reports that the comedy was advertised in proposals for a collected edition of Lillo's plays; 'the intended edition not meeting with encouragement', it did not appear. A note in the reprint (1810) of Davies's collection says that he had made an unsuccessful search for the manuscript.

[7] Davies (*Life*, p. xliii) reports, on the authority of 'Roberts, an old comedian', that the adaptation was written 'before the year 1736'. The actor was probably John Roberts, who acted with Davies in the first performances of *Fatal Curiosity* in 1736. Both he and Davies must have known, if they did

for some reason abandoned; in 1759 the play was performed in a version announced as Lillo's adaptation completed by John Hoadly.

That Lillo took an interest in the theatre and with his first tragedy achieved a brilliant success has been accounted remarkable, because he was not a professional man of the theatre nor at home in literary circles. A goldsmith-jeweller by trade and a Dissenter[8] in his religious convictions, he was born in London, probably in 1693 though perhaps in 1691, of Dutch and English parents and baptized in the Dutch Reform Church called the Austin Friars.[9] He spent his life in London—his childhood probably in Moorfields, his last years in Rotherhithe. At his death in September 1739 he was buried at St Leonard's, Shoreditch, a rather prosperous businessman, possessed of land and houses and able to provide for his heir an income of some sixty pounds a year.[10] Little else is known of him. In 1775, Thomas Davies, hard-pressed to find material for the biography he meant to include in his collection of Lillo's works, sought out, he says, the playwright's business partner, who confirmed that Lillo

not appear in, an unsuccessful production of an adaptation of *Arden of Feversham*, reported to have been written by Eliza Haywood, which Fielding produced at the theatre in Jan. 1736. (*London Stage, 1729–1747*, i. 545 and i, p. cxliii.) No evidence linking Lillo with this adaptation has been found, and had he taken a hand in the writing of it, Fielding would surely have advertised the fact. If Lillo had worked on his version of the play before 1736, the performance and the failure of Mrs Haywood's adaptation might well have discouraged him from pursuing the project. On the other hand, the production, though unsuccessful, could have led him to attempt his own version of the old play. (See introduction to *Arden of Feversham*.)

[8] Cibber (*Lives*, v. 338) asserts that Lillo was educated as a Dissenter. Davies (*Life*, p. xlvii) indicates that the playwright remained a Dissenter throughout his life. C. F. Burgess ('Further Notes for a Biography of George Lillo', *Philological Quarterly*, xlvi [1967], 424–8) suggests that Lillo early became a member of the Church of England, citing his burial at St Leonard's and a record of his mother's remarriage preserved at Lambeth Palace. Burgess does not, however, mention this theory in his study of Lillo's plays, printed in 1968 (see 'Burgess', in the List of Abbreviated References). Frederik deBoer, in his extensive critical consideration of Lillo's works, argues persuasively the essentially Calvinist point of view which informs Lillo's plays.

[9] Cibber, whose *Lives* (v. 338–40) provided the first biography of Lillo, and Davies (*Life*, pp. ix–xlviii), who took much of his biographical information from Cibber, report that Lillo was born on 4 Feb. 1693. The year of his birth appears to be confirmed by information given in the burial register at St Leonard's Church, Shoreditch, which includes the entry, dated 6 Sept. 1739, 'George Lillo from Rotherhithe. Aged 46 years.' However, the record of baptisms at the Dutch Reform Church, Austin Friars, includes among a group of entries apparently referring to Lillo's family a record of the baptism of Joris van Lilloo on 8 Feb. 1691 (W. J. C. Moens, ed., *Dutch Reformed Church Registers* [Lymington, 1884], quoted by Pallette, p. 263; in other entries the family name is spelt 'Lillo'). The contradictions in these church records are discussed by Pallette (pp. 263–5), who first collected this and other evidence which indicates that the records of baptisms do indeed refer to Lillo and his family. In the records of the Dutch Reform Church Lillo's parents are identified as Jacobus van Lillo and Elisabeth Whitehorne; references in his will (see n. 10, below) confirm the playwright's connection with the Whitehorne family. Other documents cited by Pallette indicate that members of the Lillo family dropped the 'van' from their family name and adopted English forms of their given names.

[10] The houses and land are listed among the bequests in Lillo's will, copies of which exist at Somerset House (Pallette, p. 266) and the Bodleian Library (MS Rawl. J fol. 4, item 43); Pallette reports that the two copies vary only in a few minor details. That the income left to Lillo's major legatee was £60 p.a. is reported by Davies (*Life*, p. xlvi), who says that he met the heir, Lillo's nephew John Underwood, 'a jeweller in the city'.

was the son of a Dutch jeweller, brought up in his father's trade, and in character very like the good merchant in his famous tragedy.[11] Fielding, who had worked closely with the playwright during rehearsals of *Fatal Curiosity*, eulogized Lillo's honest manner and lack of worldly ambition, his 'Contempt for all base Means of Application, which . . . restrain'd his Conversation within very narrow Bounds'. He had, said Fielding, 'the Spirit of an old Roman, join'd to the Innocence of a primitive Christian'.[12]

Nothing in the few details known of Lillo's life suggests that he interested himself in writing or associated himself with the theatre during his early years. However, at 37 (or 39), when the first of his dramatic pieces was acted, he was not the unconscious artist he is sometimes described to have been. His writing for the stage reveals not only a sharp awareness of the current theatrical repertoire but familiarity with the conventions of earlier types of drama. The catalogue of the books auctioned off after his death may also indicate his considerable interest in old as well as the most recent plays, though his library was sold intermixed with the books of 'Another Gentleman . . . lately Deceased'[13] and one cannot know for certain which of the items listed in the catalogue actually belonged to the playwright. The books offered for sale included 'the best and scarcest Plays written by Shirley, Massinger, Webster, Middleton, Brome, Marston, Cockain, Chapman, Settle, Crown, [and] Durfey'.[14] The listed items also included a comprehensive collection of the works of Restoration and eighteenth-century dramatists, among them Steele, Cibber, Shadwell, Mrs Behn, Otway, Southerne, Lee, Etheridge, Vanbrugh, Congreve, and Dryden. There were translations of Euripides, Sophocles, and Seneca, and more than 400 unidentified plays sold in bundles. If, as seems likely, many of these items came from Lillo's library, he was a collector deeply interested and uncommonly well read in the literature of the theatre.

Lillo only once published a formal statement of his theories and methods of writing for the stage. Concerned that the 'Novelty' of *The London Merchant* required him to say 'something in its Excuse',[15] he offered in his dedication of the play an explanation of his intentions in writing the tragedy and some comments on the 'Usefulness of Tragedy in general'.[16] He takes a didactic view and a quantitative measure of such plays: 'the more extensively useful the Moral of any Tragedy is, the more excellent that Piece must be of its Kind'.[17] However, to be effective the moral must be dramatized in such a way that the sensibilities of the audience are deeply touched, and because 'Tragedy . . . is more truly august in Proportion to . . . the Numbers that are properly affected by it',[18] Lillo chose not only to make use of the strong appeal of pathos, the

---

[11] *Life*, pp. xlv–xlvi.   [12] *The Champion*, loc. cit.

[13] William McBurney, 'What George Lillo Read: A Speculation', *Huntington Library Quarterly*, xxix (1965–6), 276. McBurney discusses the catalogue (Bodleian Library, Mus. Bibl. III 8° 81) and its possible significance, and provides a selected list of dramatic works included among the items.

[14] Title-page, quoted by McBurney, 'What George Lillo Read . . .', p. 276.

[15] *The London Merchant*, dedication, ll. 64–5.

[16] Ibid., l. 66.   [17] Ibid., ll. 2–3.   [18] Ibid., ll. 12–15.

effectiveness of which had been demonstrated in the work of Otway and his followers, but to draw from the 'Generality of Mankind'[19] characters with whom his audience could easily identify. Lillo allows that tragedies of 'Persons . . . of the highest Rank . . . are [not] without their Use',[20] as long as they provide instructive examples. He himself turned later to stories of kings and conventional heroes as the subjects for three of his plays. But always the useful moral and the appeal to feeling were his conscious aims as he shaped and revised his plays.

In Lillo's view, the lessons to be taught were clear. 'The End of Tragedy', he writes in his dedication, is 'the exciting of the Passions, in order to the correcting such of them as are criminal, either in their Nature, or through their Excess'.[21] Moreover, the theatre can 'inspire [the] Spectators with a just Sense of the Value of Liberty', teaching them to beware tyranny which 'wou'd sacrifice the Constitution of [a] Country, and the Liberties of Mankind, to . . . Ambition or Revenge'.[22] These Protestant and political concerns, the complementary Christian and Roman aspects of Lillo's ethical values, inform the central speeches and direct the ordering of the action of his plays. They are, of course, dimensions of a single morality and implicit in all of Lillo's work, though his emphases vary with individual plays. In *The London Merchant*, for example, he focuses sharply on the danger of indulging the passions, while in *Elmerick* he argues the cause of public liberty and in *The Christian Hero* portrays a virtuous hero in whom self-control and regard for liberty are demonstrated in equal measure.[23]

The care with which Lillo revised his work, developing and making more precise the thematic significance of his characters and situations, is indicated by the adjustments he made in the texts of successive editions of *The London Merchant*. He is reported to have taken an interest in rehearsals, and manuscripts of *Marina* and *Elmerick*, playhouse copies submitted to the Lord Chamberlain's office, help to provide evidence of his revisions before, during, and perhaps after production of his work in the theatre. However, he appears to have been little concerned to oversee the printing of his plays, perhaps because he counted on his publisher to do so.

Silvia was published by John Watts, who issued many books which contained musical notation, including a long list of ballad operas, and was clearly the appropriate publisher to produce an edition which printed the tunes as well as the text. Thereafter, Lillo entrusted the publication of his plays to John Gray, a bookseller who had a shop in the Poultry from about 1728 to 1742.[24] Gray did

---

[19] *The London Merchant*, dedication, ll. 14.
[20] Ibid., ll. 24–5.   [21] Ibid., ll. 6–8.   [22] Ibid., ll. 31–4.
[23] See introductions to these plays.
[24] Gray's name appears on the title-pages of books published as early as 1728 (e.g. *The Life and Works of Joseph Boyse*). Nichols (*Literary Anecdotes of the Eighteenth Century* . . . [London, 1811–15], v. 305) reports that Gray gave up his bookselling business, 'became a Dissenting minister, and afterwards, upon his complying with the terms of admission into the Church of England, rector of a living at Rippon [*sic*] in Yorkshire'. Gray's sale of his rights to *The London Merchant* on 30 Sept. 1742 (British Library, MS Add. 38728, item 128b) may well mark the time of his retirement from

not specialize in plays; his lists are primarily devoted to religious works and a selection of standard items, most of them printed for other booksellers. Lillo may have selected Gray as his publisher because he was a friend. The bookseller is named as an executor in Lillo's will and, like Lillo, is said to have been a Dissenter.[25] He published seven editions of *The London Merchant* between 1731 and 1740, and brought out one edition of each of the other plays acted during the author's lifetime. A few months after the playwright's death, he published *Elmerick* and issued a nonce collection of Lillo's works which included the first printing of *Britannia and Batavia*.

It has been suggested that the popularity of *The London Merchant* on the stage was artificially stimulated by the support of City merchants and others concerned to provide morally instructive entertainment for the young;[26] the printed version of the play, however, seems simply to have found a ready reading public which did not diminish with the years. The play was frequently reprinted, in piratical editions as well as the editions regularly issued by the booksellers who at various times held shares in Gray's old assignment from the author. *Fatal Curiosity* and *The Christian Hero* occasionally appeared in new editions, while the other plays were ignored until 1775, when Thomas Davies published his collection of Lillo's works. In 1762 Davies had issued the first edition of the adaptation of *Arden of Feversham* ascribed to Lillo. A reprint of Davies's collection, published by the Lowndes firm in 1810, is the most recent complete edition of Lillo's plays. In 1906 A. W. Ward provided a modernized edition of *The London Merchant* and *Fatal Curiosity*, laying the groundwork for subsequent editors and making available well-prepared texts which have long proved useful but have been outmoded by the identification of early editions not seen by Ward. William McBurney made a serious bibliographical study of the plays for his modernized editions of *The London Merchant* (1965) and *Fatal Curiosity* (1966), but arrived at some erroneous conclusions, failed to distinguish between the authorized editions and certain piratical reprints of *The London Merchant*, and did not undertake an analysis of the textual variants in the authoritative editions of the play. Of the many modern reprints of *The London Merchant*, only those edited by A. E. Morgan (1935)[27] and Arthur E. Case (1939)[28] are based on precise examinations of the text, and both reprint modernized texts of editions which contain a considerable number of variant readings not introduced by the author.

The bibliographical notes included in the textual introductions of individual plays in the present edition try to identify authoritative and piratical editions of Lillo's plays published during and immediately after his lifetime. In considering

---

the book trade. Advertisements giving extensive lists of books available at Gray's shop are printed in *The Life and Works of Joseph Boyse* and Benjamin Bennet, *The Christian Oratory* . . . (3rd edn., 1732).

[25] See nn. 8 and 10 above.

[26] See the account of first performances in the introduction to *The London Merchant*.

[27] *English Plays 1660–1820* (New York and London, 1935).   [28] N & C.

these early editions, I have been primarily concerned to establish the authority and relationship of texts. Copies of all known later editions of the plays issued before 1776 have also been examined and compared; their textual significance is briefly summarized in the textual introductions, and reference is made to them when it is useful to do so in assessing the continuing interest in Lillo's dramas or in considering particularly problematic details in the authoritative texts.

The present edition tries to provide for modern readers reliable old-spelling texts of Lillo's works in a form which represents, as far as can be ascertained, the author's final intentions for his texts. Multiple copies of first editions and at least one copy of other authoritative editions have been collated, as have Larpent manuscripts of three plays (copies, not holographs, submitted to the Chamberlain's office) and the collected edition of Lillo's works (1775), which has served as the standard edition of the plays and stands as the first effort to correct and edit them as a group. Where there exists a relatively early reprint of the one authoritative edition of a play, the unauthoritative text has been collated as a useful source of eighteenth-century response to confusing or erroneous readings, primarily accidentals, of the first edition.

Basing my decisions on analysis of these collations, I have selected the first edition of each play, with press corrections where they exist, to serve as copy-text for the present edition. However, the edited text of *The London Merchant* includes revisions demonstrably or very possibly authorial, and the text of *Elmerick* includes readings from the Larpent manuscript which are more certainly authoritative than those of the posthumously printed first edition. For *Britannia and Batavia*, the posthumous edition of 1740 is the only early source of the text of a work never performed. The first edition and Larpent manuscript of *Arden of Feversham* represent the minimal authority of a text 'completed by another hand' and not acted or printed until more than two decades after Lillo's death; no earlier or more authentic source for this text is known.

The infrequent occurrence of muddled passages in the first editions indicates that the printers worked from relatively good copy, but very probably the copy for these editions was quite lightly pointed and at times defective or difficult to follow. Certain editions contain errors attributable to careless or hasty production. Pointing seems often to have been supplied by compositors or, in certain reprints of *The London Merchant*, entrusted to an editor. Little evidence of possibly authorial correction of accidentals, and few corrected formes recording author's corrections or revisions of substantive readings, have been found.

The present edition adheres as closely as possible to the copy-text. Obvious errors are corrected, usually with the routine emendations made in eighteenth-century editions, but where necessary with the editor's emendations. Except in certain reprints of *The London Merchant*, the corrections found in early reprints are certainly not authorial, but are accepted if they satisfactorily correct errors. A very few necessary stage directions have been added, when possible adopted from early editions, while others are new to this edition; all are annotated in the textual apparatus and commentary.

The accidentals as well as the substantives of the copy-texts are followed very closely. Punctuation and spelling unlikely to confuse or mislead readers familiar with eighteenth-century texts are retained, as are the irregularities (not errors) and rather idiosyncratic pointing characteristic of some of the copy-texts. Though compositorial punctuation was routine practice in the period, the inconsistencies and errors in certain editions suggest that they were set by compositors uncertain in their habits of pointing. No attempt to normalize this pointing has been made, but where it is misleading I have felt free to emend, noting that emendations made in early reprints indicate that the most awkward pointing of these first editions was no less difficult for eighteenth-century than for modern readers.

The extensive use of dashes in the first editions and Larpent manuscripts may preserve pointing characteristic of the author's manuscripts. Although some of these dashes probably stand in lieu of more precise punctuation, many clearly affect the sense of the lines in which they appear and suggest a kind of histrionic pointing, a guide to interpretation for the actors. Dashes printed in the first editions are retained, of course, but normalized to one em; their appearance in the manuscripts is regularly noted.

Capitalization follows the copy-texts, except for the correction of lower-case letters set at the beginnings of speeches and the capitalization of verbs obviously mistaken for nouns.

The abbreviated speech-headings of the copy-text are retained but have been standardized when more than one spelling or abbreviated form occurs. Character names in stage directions are similarly standardized and routinely spelt out in full. In passages set in roman, proper nouns and the names of persons are regularly italicized, but not accompanying titles such as 'Sir' or 'Lord'. Names that appear in italic passages are set in roman.

Typography and certain accidentals are silently normalized. The edition does not reproduce or note initials and accompanying capitals, factotums, swash italic, letters used in error or shortages, or long *s*. Wrong-font and turned letters are corrected without note, except where turned letters result in apparent misspellings. Single rather than double quotation marks are used throughout, and repeated quotation marks at the start of lines of direct speech are omitted. Act- and scene-headings have been made uniform, following the most frequent practices of the copy-text editions. The typography and position of speech-headings have also been standardized. Stage directions are regularly set in italic, beginning with capitals and ending with periods, and abbreviations have been expanded. Entrances are centred and exits set flush right; directions within speeches are enclosed in brackets and those not properly placed in the copy-texts have been positioned correctly. The layout of extended stage directions that occur between speeches follows the routine styling of the copy-texts.

The lineation of verse passages is silently normalized. Where a speech begins in the middle of a verse line, it has been appropriately set over. Portions of lines overrun in the copy-text are not reproduced or recorded. Hyphenation in such overrun break-lines is retained for compound words, otherwise eliminated, and recorded only in cases of possible ambiguity. Verse lining obviously muddled or incorrect in the copy-text is regularized; such adjustments are noted in the textual introduction or commentary. Rhymed verse is regularly indented. However, the use of roman or italic type for rhymed passages follows the styling of the copy-texts of the individual plays in order to retain the special character of the couplets, set in italics, that occur in *The London Merchant* and their relation to the prose text of the play.

Introductions briefly treat the sources, the early performances, stage history, and critical reception, the early editions and manuscripts (if any), and the textual problems of each play. The primary sources for some of the plays are well known; sources for other plays are here identified. Lillo's familiarity with the drama of his own and earlier periods is clear; echoes of the language of other dramatists and parallels to situations and character types in their plays are regularly to be found in his work. Obvious borrowings are remarked. Plays or playwrights are not cited, however, when their relationship to Lillo's work is tenuous; many of the parallels reflect Lillo's acquaintance with conventions rather than his indebtedness to specific models.

The commentary provides details of the playwright's use or adaptation of material in his sources, cross-reference of significant verbal, thematic, and structural links among his own plays, necessary topical background and identification of obvious literary allusions, glosses of words which the playwright uses in an exceptional sense or which may not be familiar to modern readers of eighteenth-century texts, and explanations of textual decisions about which questions might be expected to arise.

The apparatus criticus records all substantive and semi-substantive emendations and all emended accidentals except the silent normalization described above. All rejections of substantive and semi-substantive alternatives provided by authorized texts other than the first edition or by a Larpent manuscript are also recorded. Variants occurring in the unauthorized texts which have been collated are not recorded, but are remarked in commentary notes if they have served as useful referents in cases in which readings in the copy-text were highly problematic or incorrect.

Historical collations record all emendations, substantive variants, relineation of verse, and variant accidentals except for those silently regularized. Textual information included in the apparatus criticus is recorded also in the historical collations, as is the record of the possibly ambiguous hyphenations that occur at the ends of lines in the copy-text or present edition. Press variants are recorded in tables accompanying the collations. Tables of press variants (but no historical collations) are provided for plays for which there is a single authoritative edition and no Larpent manuscript: *Silvia*, *The Christian Hero*, *Fatal Curiosity*, and

Britannia and Batavia. The record of hyphenations at the ends of lines includes compound words to be found in both the copy-text and present edition and cites all other end-of-line hyphens newly introduced in the present edition.

A list of sigla for editions cited in the apparatus criticus and historical collections will be found on pp. xi–xii. An explanation of symbols and abbreviations used in footnotes and collations precedes the collations, on p. ooo.

Photographic reproductions of the title-pages of first editions precede the texts of each work. For the other authorized editions, quasi-facsimile transcriptions are provided in the textual introductions. Details of typography are recorded as precisely as such transcription allows. Long *s* is reported, as is wrong font. Type printed in red is here underdotted: e.g. Lillo. Angle-brackets ⟨ ⟩ indicate material inferred or omitted because it is missing (usually torn or cropped away) from copies examined. Parentheses are editorial. Square brackets are editorial except when specifically identified as recording brackets that actually appear on the title-pages transcribed.

Quotations from newspaper advertisements, author's or booksellers' notes to the reader, and the like reproduce the capitalization, accidentals, and spelling of items quoted but do not normally report line-breaks or typographical details such as long *s*, large and small capitals, and italic.

Silvia

OR

The Country Burial

INTRODUCTION

SOURCES

GEORGE LILLO began his dramatic career with a play that stands out as an oddity among his works. Ballad opera in general is quite opposite in tone to the serious, even solemn, plays that Lillo was later to write, and *Silvia* was not—for good reason—a success on the stage, in large part because Lillo lacked the lightness of touch and ironic theatricality that had made the form popular. It is nevertheless an interesting failure, for the elements that it has in common with Lillo's later works make it one of the most singular of ballad operas.

Biographia Dramatica dismisses *Silvia* with the statement that it was 'one of the pieces which the general vogue of these ballad operas, occasioned by the success of *The Beggar's Opera*, brought forth into the world'.[1] The vogue was a remarkable one: in the years 1728–30 inclusive just over twenty-five ballad operas were published, of which all but a few were performed. By 1734 the number had nearly trebled. It was therefore quite natural for a playwright to settle on this form in his first attempt to win an audience. It was moreover not only popular but flexible, less a genre unto itself than a catch-all: 'There are satirical ballad-operas; there are pure burlesques; there are farces; there are sentimental dramas; and there are pastorals. That is to say, the ballad-opera, while it provided a new technical form, a new medium, for the writers, did not at the same time provide a fresh atmosphere distinct from the ordinary tones of regular comedy and farce.'[2]

---

[1] *Biographia Dramatica* (1812), iii. 274.   [2] Nicoll, p. 239.

The character types and plot-lines of *Silvia* were accordingly drawn from the stock-in-trade available to any early eighteenth-century playwright. As C. F. Burgess remarks, '*Silvia* is an amalgam of familiar dramatic types, and as such it displays Lillo's knowledge of the theater even at this very early point in his career.'[3]

The most important source that can be directly traced is, however, non-theatrical. The essential element of the main plot, Sir John's immoral proposal and Silvia's indignant refusal of it, was almost certainly suggested by the story of 'Amanda', a 'Scene of Distress in private Life', written by John Hughes, that appeared in *The Spectator*, No. 375.[4] Lillo played very freely with the details of the story, but the basic outline, and especially the moral tone and tear-drawing qualities, are preserved. In Hughes's tale Amanda, the daughter of a ruined but honourable businessman, is sent to live in the country, where the young lord of a nearby manor courts her. She finds him attractive, and realizes that marriage to him could mean the salvation of her family. The young man, having found out her troubles, makes his offer, which leaves Amanda speechless with dismay. He thereupon writes to her father, offering to pay off his debts and settle £400 per annum on Amanda, and urging him to persuade her to overcome her scruples; he is quite open about his non-matrimonial intentions. This letter is intercepted by Amanda's mother, who writes at once to Amanda, urging her not to accept any such terms, while at the same time reporting that the father is now in debtors' prison. The young man in turn intercepts the mother's letter, by which he is greatly impressed. He takes it to Amanda, and seeing her tears upon reading it, repents and writes to her mother to apologize and ask for Amanda's hand in proper fashion. 'To conclude, he Marryed *Amanda*, and enjoyed the double Satisfaction of having restored a worthy Family to their former Prosperity, and of making him self happy by an Alliance to their Virtue.'

The moral atmosphere of Hughes's story comprises a number of elements that are retained in *Silvia*. The young man, like Lillo's Sir John, is 'a Man of great Generosity', but has 'from a loose Education . . . contracted a hearty Aversion to Marriage'. His essential magnanimity is evident in his letter to Amanda's mother:

---

[3] Burgess, p. 7.

[4] *The Spectator*, ed. Donald F. Bond, 5 vols. (Oxford, 1965), is the source for quotations here. Another possible source for Lillo's plot, in addition to *Spectator*, No. 375, is *Spectator*, No. 402, in which 'Dorinda' recounts what passed between her and a 'Gentleman of Greater Fortune' who had long courted her and whom she had come to love. 'As he is very careful of his Fortune, I always thought he lived in a near Manner to lay up what he thought was wanting in my Fortune to make up what he might expect in another.' He proves, however, to have other ideas: '. . . the other Night he with great Frankness and Impudence explained to me, that he thought of me only as a Mistress. I answered this Declaration as it deserved; upon which he only doubled the Terms on which he proposed my Yielding.' She runs to the house of a friend, whose husband insists on hearing her trouble. 'He spoke of the Injury done against the Love he saw I had for the Wretch who would have betrayed me with such Reason and Humanity to my Weakness, that I doubt not of my perseverance. . . . I doubt not but in a small Time Contempt and Hatred will take Place of the Remains of Affection to a Rascal.' The original letter that Steele revised for publication is found in Bond's edition, v. 233–4.

I am full of Shame, and will never forgive my self, if I have not your Pardon for what I lately wrote. It was far from my Intention to add Trouble to the Afflicted; nor could any thing, but my being a Stranger to you, have betrayed me into a Fault, for which if I live I shall endeavour to make you amends, as a Son.[5]

Amanda's refusal of the indecent proposal is quite as instinctive as Silvia's, and, like Silvia, she refuses to read a letter,[6] in this case brought by the suitor himself, who must assure her that it comes from her mother before she will consent to read it. But Amanda, though she is ostensibly the subject of the story, is given nothing to say. Her actions are instead briefly described: she finds the young man attractive and a possible match advantageous, she withdraws speechless to her chamber upon hearing his proposal, she weeps upon reading her mother's letter. Beyond this, we learn only that she 'was in the Bloom of her Youth and Beauty'. It is her mother who is the true moral exemplar, the perfect wife:

a Woman of Sense and Virtue, [who] behaved her self on this occasion with uncommon Decency, and never appeared so amiable in his Eyes as now. Instead of upbraiding him with the ample Fortune she had brought, or the many great Offers she had refused for his Sake, she redoubled all the Instances of her Affection, while her Husband was continually pouring out his Heart to her in Complaints that he had ruined the best Woman in the World. He sometimes came Home at a time when she did not expect him, and surprised her in Tears, which she endeavoured to conceal, and always put on an Air of Cheerfulness to receive him.

Her letter to Amanda is in content and style comparable to many of Silvia's speeches:

Your Father and I have just received a Letter from a Gentleman who pretends to love you, with a Proposal that insults our Misfortunes, and would throw us to a lower Degree of Misery than any thing which is come upon us. How could this barbarous Man think, that the tenderest of Parents would be tempted to supply their Want, by giving up the best of Children to Infamy and Ruin? It is a mean and cruel Artifice to make this Proposal at a time when he thinks our Necessities must compel us to any thing; but we will not eat the Bread of Shame; and therefore we charge thee not to think of us, but to avoid the Snare which is laid for thy Virtue.[7]

There is one telling difference between 'Amanda' and *Silvia*: by all accounts Mrs Welford was the exact opposite of Amanda's mother. An honoured servant, she betrayed her mistress's posterity, and she was so bad a wife to Welford as to leave her son with an entirely degraded view of marriage.[8] She is, as it were, the posthumous villainess of the play. The blame for Silvia's near loss of her birthright and for Welford's moral confusion is squarely placed upon her.[9] Lillo thereby adds a level of complexity and tension to his source, and

---

[5] Cf. II. xv. 13–16.   [6] See II. iv, vii.

[7] Cf. I. iv. 88–9 (in Air IV): 'We're to Ruin and Infamy sold. | The Bird, that beholds the Snares laid.'

[8] See III. xxii. 32–54 and II. xv. 57–65.   [9] See III. xxii. 70–1.

seeks as well a way to incorporate into the family relationships that motivate the plot an old device that usually appears quite gratuitously.

This attention to marital relationships is to some degree borne out in the identification of two ballad operas that may also represent sources for portions of Lillo's work, Essex Hawker's *The Wedding* (1729) and *The Beggar's Wedding* (1729) by Charles Coffey.[10] The first of these concludes with a 'Hudibrastick Skimmington', extraneous to the plot, in which Stitch, a henpecked tailor, and his wife are paraded through the town after a domestic fracas:

> . . . I'll tell thee, t'other day,
> There was at neighbour Stitch's house a fray:
> He being but a Taylor had the worse,
> And the Grey-Mare e'en proved the better horse:
> And that the shrew's great courage may be known,
> They ride to day forsooth a Skimmington.[11]

It seems almost certain that Lillo took these characters to use for his own purposes, which of course differ greatly from Hawker's. It is much less certain that *The Beggar's Wedding* can be regarded as a source. Though it ends, like Lillo's drama, with a discovery of true parentage, the device is too common to be taken as evidence of influence. In both cases, however, it is the father who reveals the truth, which he has known all along, as opposed to the more usual case of surprise all round. It is at any rate notable that both of these earlier ballad operas, especially in their songs, take for granted an irreverent view of marriage that Lillo decidedly opposed. The title-page motto of *The Wedding* is particularly pointed:

> There are no Bargains driv'n,
> Nor Marriages clapp'd up in Heav'n,
> And that's the Reason, as some guess,
> There is no Heav'n in Marriages.[12]

Whatever borrowing there was from these two sources, it was accompanied by a distinct reforming impulse.

Like trade in *The London Merchant*, marriage is in *Silvia* the matrix of virtues that the action of the play is meant to exemplify. The converging plot-lines and character relationships together add up to a theme with variations. The unhappy marriage of the Welfords has a comic counterpart in Timothy and

---

[10] *The Wedding* (also known as *The Country Wedding*) was first performed at Lincoln's Inn Fields, 6 May 1729. *The Beggar's Wedding* was first performed at the New Haymarket Theatre, 29 May 1729. Both plays were quite successful (*London Stage, 1700–1729* and *1729–1747*).

[11] Genest (iii. 244) identifies Hawker's source, *Hudibras*, Part II, Canto ii (ll. 560–844). The name 'Stitch' originates in *The Wedding*. 'Skimmington' is defined in *OED* as 'a ludicrous procession, formerly common in village or country districts, usually intended to bring ridicule or odium upon a woman or her husband in cases where the one was unfaithful to, or ill-treated, the other'. It seems, to judge by the quotations in *OED*, to have been confined to cases of shrewish wives.

[12] *Hudibras*, Part III, Canto i, ll. 545–8.

Dorothy, and the parallel is maintained in the characters of their offspring, Sir John and Lettice. Ned Ploughshare, more a dramatic catalyst than a character in his own right, is the unwanted suitor whom Dorothy would force Lettice to marry. Her dilemma is the opposite of Silvia's, yet both fathers disapprove of forced marriage.[13] Jonathan takes after his master, sidestepping marriage to Betty; in the end he naturally follows the example of his reformed master. Among the village folk the two Gabbles and Goody Costive are negligible, though the former are married, and the latter, a widow, is one more object of Goody Busy's incessant and ill-timed matchmaking.[14] Goody Busy herself is, like Silvia, an outspoken partisan of marriage; her obvious professional interest and unromantic practicality provide a much-needed contrast to Silvia's rhetorical flights.[15] All of this represents an attempt to integrate the play's multiplicity of tone and character type into a single, essentially didactic, thematic scheme.

With this in mind, Lillo's approach to the writing of plays can be clearly seen at the outset of his active involvement in the theatre. C. F. Burgess concludes that the 'emphasis on variety in *Silvia* suggests that Lillo's concern was to make the widest possible appeal and not, as a moral reformer or sentimentalist or middle-class spokesman, to appeal to limited special interests'.[16] Indeed, commenting on the variety of Lillo's work as a whole, Burgess asserts that 'Lillo's chief concern was to write successful plays. He was attached to the stage for its own sake and not because of its potential as a medium of propaganda.'[17] It is Burgess's purpose to correct the exclusive emphasis on didacticism and sentimentality that typifies previous criticism of Lillo's work, most of it based on *The London Merchant* with perhaps secondary reference to *Fatal Curiosity*; but the case is overstated. Lillo had a dual allegiance, to the theatre itself and to a comprehensive morality that informed his work, evidence of which is to be found in the dramatic variety and thematic unity of *Silvia*.

The deeply moral character of the main plot is obvious and, in speech after speech, even overstressed. Equally important is Lillo's treatment of the subplots. His 'low' characters are conventional enough, but they are not, as was common on the stage, taken for granted. With the possible exception of Goody Busy they are not present simply as comic relief, primarily to appeal to the galleries, though Lillo may have hoped to reach the galleries through them; nor do they function as mere expendable counter-examples to the moral development of the main plot. They are important in themselves, and the more serious implications of their actions are not slighted. The play's moral scheme thereby gains a flexibility that takes into account the social realities of those who move in lower spheres of life. Gagey notes what may be the most prominent example: 'Lettice's downfall has convincing motivation, with rather unusual

---

[13] See I. iv. 9–10 and III. xviii. 53–4.   [14] See I. ix. 30–3.
[15] In dramatic terms, Goody Busy and her entourage are the play's chorus, of which she is the leader.
[16] Burgess, p. 7.   [17] Ibid., p. 28.

social consciousness for the time, in her hatred of poverty, work, and confinement.'[18] By drawing both Lettice and Betty into the main plot, Lillo exposes the moral peril into which Sir John has brought them. In the end Lettice is treated with moral as well as material generosity: 'you may yet excell in Virtue many of your Sex, who having never err'd in the manner you have done, look on your Fault as unpardonable'.[19] Though less point is made of the fact, Sir John is also responsible for the corruption of Jonathan, a member of the 'Batchelor's Family'[20] of which he is the head. Even the low comedy of the graveyard scene between Timothy and Dorothy ends with a reconciliation as Timothy's devotion prompts a change of heart in Dorothy, a curious example of a 'sentimental-moral' commonplace introduced into a basically comic context.[21]

Burgess, arguing that the presence of humorous scenes in *Silvia* is evidence of the play's lack of sentimentality, treats humour as simply another distinct element in its dramatic mixture,[22] but the converging structure points in another direction. There is a tendency away from humour for its own sake, segregated from the rest of the play. Timothy, Dorothy, Lettice, and Ned Ploughshare are drawn into the main plot from funny, even mildly bawdy, scenes, through scenes of sorrow or moral endangerment, and at last into a scene in which everyone is happily set to rights. It is unfortunate that the final step in this process—the downright metaphysical Air LXIII[23]—is so unnecessarily forced.

Though Bernbaum believes that the 'improbability of denouement recalls *The Conscious Lovers*',[24] one must take into account the fact that the discovery of Silvia's and Sir John's true parentage is a deliberate disclosure made by a principal character whose moral dilemma can only thereby be resolved. Welford is an unconventionally 'mixed' character, neither tyrannical father nor moral paragon. Similarly, Sir John's emerging consciousness of what he has to lose in offending Silvia—a balancing of gains and losses—culminates, not in one of those almost miraculous reformations that conveniently bring plots to a close, but in his consciousness of a lesson learnt from experience:

I thought, 'till now, the general Love of Women consistent with Generosity, Honour, and Humanity.—False and destructive Principle! By this single Act of mine, how many innocent Persons have I injur'd?[25]

The mention of Bernbaum leads naturally to the question, is *Silvia* a sentimental play? He regards it as such without reservation.[26] Nicoll sees in it 'a union of immoral and sentimental motives', which, without elaboration, he

---

[18] Gagey, p. 97.   [19] III. xxiii. 12–14.   [20] See I. ii. 15–18, III. v. 16–23.

[21] The genuineness of the reconciliation may be undercut, perhaps unintentionally, by Lillo's choice of ballad tunes for Airs XV and XVI (I. x. 45–51 and 59–70; see commentary on music). Benjamin Hoadly, who adapted *Silvia* into two acts, was of the opinion that 'there would be some real true fun in it, if the taylor's sorrow for his drunken wife were made all hypocritical' (see p. 17 below). This would of course add to the comic ramifications of Dorothy's resuscitation in a manner inconsistent with Lillo's apparent purpose.

[22] Burgess, pp. 9–10.   [23] The finale, III. xxiii. 25–45.
[24] Bernbaum, p. 144.   [25] III. xviii. 68–70.
[26] Bernbaum, pp. 143–4.

holds responsible for its failure on the stage.[27] Arthur Sherbo does not discuss the play at all, though he does select passages from *The London Merchant* and *Fatal Curiosity* to illustrate sentimental 'prolongation and repetition' and refinement of emotion.[28] Ira Konigsberg finds 'much evidence of the excessive sentimentality that was to be an essential element in his later works'.[29] Burgess on the other hand argues that *Silvia* contains only touches of sentimentality along with a number of non-sentimental elements that outweigh them.[30] Gagey, refreshingly, does not raise the question and in his discussion, which is consequently rather clear-headed, refers to *Silvia* as 'an object-lesson in morality, driven home by means of a melodramatic plot with the rather strange assistance of sixty-three ballad airs'.[31]

The question must be dealt with briefly. Discussions of sentimentality almost inevitably turn into questions of definition, usually a matter of deciding what qualities should be called 'sentimental' in the eighteenth-century trend towards moral reaction against the 'licence' of the Restoration stage: from the satirical exposure and exploitation of folly, to the positive assertion and exploitation of virtue.[32] Drawing eclectically on the work of Bernbaum and Sherbo, it must be granted that the main plot of *Silvia* is decidedly sentimental in outline and to some degree in its development. Its origin was a story meant, very much in sentimental fashion, to illustrate 'a Noble Saying of *Seneca*[33] the Philosopher, that a Virtuous Person struggling with Misfortunes, and rising above them, is an Object on which the Gods themselves may look down with Delight'.[34] But even if Lillo was basically in sympathy with that tradition, there are signs in *Silvia* of a certain dissatisfaction with its facile treatment of moral themes.

The emotional appeal of sentimental comedy is ultimately founded upon a more or less easy optimism;[35] to the extent that its moral assumptions have a religious basis, its characters move in a world where goodness proceeds from

---

[27] Nicoll, p. 248.

[28] Arthur Sherbo, *English Sentimental Drama* (East Lansing, Mich., 1957), pp. 59–60, 64, 68–9. Discussing *Fatal Curiosity*, arguably an anti-sentimental play, he assumes that Young Wilmot's 'refinement of emotion' is sympathetically portrayed, taking Randal's initial assent to Young Wilmot's plan to conceal his identity from his parents as evidence of Lillo's own attitude (*Fatal Curiosity*, II. ii. 50–7). In fact it becomes clear within a few lines that Randal objects to this 'curiosity', habitual with Young Wilmot, and abets him in it only because he is the servant and Young Wilmot the master.

[29] Ira Konigsberg, 'The Dramatic Background of Richardson's Plots and Characters', *PMLA* lxxxviii. 1 (Mar. 1968), 45. *Silvia* is analysed only in passing, and important aspects of the plot are overlooked in favour of the most 'sentimental' features.

[30] Burgess, pp. 7–10. He raises some interesting points concerning the motives of Silvia and Welford, but rests his case on the quantity of 'ungenteel' humour in the play. His analysis is based on the odd notion that *Silvia* is more closely related to Gay's *The What D'Ye Call It* than to *The Beggar's Opera*. Summing up, he equates the moral with the sentimental and asserts that '*Silvia* is not a sentimental play; its purpose was to amuse and entertain, and the only cause it pleads is that of successful theatre' (p. 10).

[31] Gagey, p. 96.

[32] The question is complicated by the fact that the adjectival form 'sentimental' did not come into use until the 1740s, before which 'sentiment' was restricted to its more technical senses (*OED*).

[33] Cf. *Fatal Curiosity*, II. iii. 1–9. [34] *The Spectator*, No. 375.

[35] The idea of sentimental optimism is developed in Bernbaum, ch. 1 (pp. 1–10).

a diffuse, quasi-religious notion of heaven, a heaven in the goodness of whose image human beings are made. In a way that reflects an over-simplified—and dramatically convenient—Platonic idea, it is assumed that error need but perceive virtue in all its beauty to be immediately won over; or, as Bernbaum puts it, that 'human nature, when not, as in some cases, already perfect, [is] perfectible by an appeal to the emotions'.[36] But the heaven in which Silvia and Welford so fervently believe is of a rather different order:

Sir John. O charming Sounds!—So Heaven cheers a despairing Sinner, with the sweet Voice of Mercy.
Silvia. But Heaven, when it pardons, appears above Reward, by conferring Obligations. That is not in my Power.—To refuse them is, and in that I am determined.—Farewel, for ever.—'Tis hard—but Virtue, Prudence, and my Fame require it. Therefore, farewel for ever.—If your Return to Virtue be sincere, you have a Mistress who will ne'er forsake you; but, ever blooming, crown your Days and Nights with Joy,—when I am Dust.[37]

The obligations conferred by heaven are expressed in the demanding virtue to which Silvia must struggle to remain faithful. That faith is kept by adherence to earthly institutions divinely ordained; that is to say, the bliss of heaven is not to be enjoyed here on earth, where instead the hope of it is kept alive, and love expressed, in duty and obedience.

Marriage, with its corollary responsibilities of parents and children, is the theme of *Silvia*, and is of course such an institution, not—as a more purely sentimental play would imply—an end in itself, a 'Mahomet's Paradise'[38] of endlessly repeated wedding nights.

. . . the World owes its Order, Kingdoms their peaceful regular Succession, and private Families their Domestick Happiness to Marriage.[39]

Not marry, Sir! Why, 'tis a Debt due to your Ancestors—you are the Medium 'twixt them and Posterity, which in you must fail unless prevented by a prudent and timely Choice; and an ample Estate, obtain'd by their Industry, be possess'd by Strangers to their Blood.[40]

If sentimentality is speciously religious and diffuse in its motivation, then Lillo's sentimentality—accepting that his work embraces a good many sentimental qualities—is at least more genuinely religious and realistically articulated in its motivation. That the love of a good, and of course beautiful, woman should act as a vehicle for the reformation of an erring man is a sentimental commonplace. But one of Sir John's lines in the substitute scene printed at the beginning of *Silvia*, uttered at the very moment of his 'conversion', echoes a biblical source for this notion: 'I know not if the Grace of Beauty or the most shining Ornament of thy Sex influences most.'[41] Whether or not Lillo had the passage, from 1 Peter 3, consciously in mind—the biblical flavour of many passages in

---

[36] Bernbaum, p. 10.
[37] III. xxi. 36–43.   [38] See I. iv. 65–7 and Commentary.
[39] I. iv. 46–7.   [40] II. xv. 44–7.   [41] Note on Alterotion's Commentary, ll. 16–17.

his work does at least suggest the possibility—the antithesis can only be explained by reference to it:

> Likewise, ye wives, be in subjection to your own husbands; That, if any obey not the word, they may also without the word be won by the conversation of the wives; While they behold your chaste conversation, coupled with fear. Whose adorning let it not be that outward adorning of plaiting the hair, and of wearing of gold, or of putting on of apparel; but let it be the hidden man of the heart, even the ornament of a meek and quiet spirit, which is in the sight of God of great price. . . . Likewise, ye husbands, dwell with them according to knowledge, giving honour unto the wife, as unto the weaker vessel, and as being heirs together of the grace of life; that your prayers be not hindered.[42]

It is the apparent grounding of Lillo's moral beliefs in something larger than literary fashion that allows for the integration of plot and subplot described earlier; there is no need to protect the one from contamination by the other. However angelic Silvia may be, there is room for Goody Busy, with her earthy, decidedly ungenteel, humour, to uphold marriage in her fashion. The essentially unsentimental notion that virtue entails a lifelong struggle between reason and passion, so strongly developed in the later plays, is less evident in *Silvia*,[43] which ends with a sentimental-sounding optimism: 'What Virtue so bright but Reflection improves, | Or Folly so stubborn but what it removes? | Reflect, be happy, and wise.'[44] Nevertheless, Lillo's emphasis on responsibility and mercy, on moral cause and effect as shown in his evident desire for realistic motivation, at least places his work beyond easy identification with the pure artifice of unalloyed sentiment.

With all this in mind it is still a disappointing experience to read the play. *Silvia* is by no means all bad. The plot depends on an alternation and eventual convergence of a variety of characters, each pursuing a different objective. In this it comes to resemble to some degree the episodic plotting of *The London Merchant*.[45] For the most part, Lillo has succeeded rather well in ordering his scenes, especially in the mid-section of the play (I. viii–II. xv), which easily follows the changing times of day, night, and morning, and without straining credulity separates and regroups characters according to motivations quite natural to them. Equally good are the intrusions of comedy into pathos as Timothy, Goody Busy, and Betty in turn interrupt Silvia's increasingly unhappy

---

[42] I Pet. 3: 1–4, 7. The phrase 'most shining Ornament of thy Sex' would have been less puzzling in Lillo's time, and the biblical influence could be indirect at most; but the use of the word to designate a quality inherent in womanhood, taken together with the context in which it is used—in which 'Grace of Beauty' also has a distinctively religious ring—indicates more direct reference.

[43] Note, however, the epilogue, ll. 21–4:

> A Stranger she to ev'ry modish Game,
> That chills the Blood, or sets it in a Flame;
> When Reason's lost, and raging Passion reigns,
> And the dear Pleasure proves a Hell of Pains.

The imagery indicates that the epilogue and, by its stylistic affinity, the prologue, were Lillo's own compositions.

[44] III. xxiii. 43–5.   [45] See *The London Merchant*, Introduction, p. 115.

meditation, each scene emphasizing a different aspect of her plight: the perfidy of men, the difficulty of finding a husband, and the tortures of jealousy.[46] Act II, scene xv, in which Welford confronts Sir John, is too long, and there is some muddle in Act III, scenes x–xvi, as Sir John struggles in vain to make up his mind while teasing Betty. Both problems are dealt with simultaneously in the printed revision, alterations which may have come about during rehearsal in the theatre. Sir John's change of heart, a climactic moment, is shifted to a more logical point in the action, according to the conventions from which it was derived.[47] Even if Lillo wanted Sir John's prolonged ambivalence to work against the convention, the result had been the lengthening of an already overlong play. Lillo was also working against the grain of another convention, the surprising discovery of parentage, by building it into the plot from the outset. One wonders, however, whether the audience could have perceived what he was about. It is simply not clear, in Welford's opening speech, why Silvia is in need of justice, nor why his own peace of mind should be so closely involved.[48]

Lillo was also capable of creating good characters. Genest singles out Goody Busy,[49] and Gagey remarks on the excellent characterization of Betty and Lettice, noting that 'Lillo does much better with the depiction of sin'.[50] That is the key to the problem. Lillo allows the village characters to speak in their own voices, as it were, and in so doing gives evidence of having had a good 'ear'. But Sir John reformed, Welford, and worst of all Silvia exhibit 'a sententiousness that must have been like a second nature' to Lillo.[51] Burgess, granting that this could be conscious policy, evidence of the 'sententious repetition and prolongation that Arthur Sherbo singles out as one of the distinguishing characteristics of sentimentalism', argues that 'it is equally characteristic of a fledgling dramatist who simply didn't know how to make his characters speak like real people'.[52] It is at any rate a danger that a didactic author courts in dealing with characters who express his own views, to violate dramatic consistency in order to make himself heard. The style that Lillo falls into at such times is not even good sermonizing, with its jerky rhythms and antithetical divisions and subdivisions. Perhaps he was aware of it: in the scene in which Betty comes to denounce Sir John to Silvia she is simply unable to understand Silvia's replies; one sympathizes with her to some extent.[53] Eventually, at any rate, the moralizing bears down upon the comedy, and once the more well-

[46] See II. i–iii, II. xvi–xvii, and III. iii.

[47] The note on alterations refers to 'some Scenes . . . shorten'd, and Airs omitted'. Since a good deal would have depended on factors other than dramatic structure—e.g. which tunes were favourites, which actors were most popular with the audience, etc.—it is difficult to speculate on the nature of these omissions.

[48] Cf. II. xv. 44–7, the irony of which depends upon knowing whose blood is actually involved.

[49] Genest, iii. 303: 'Goody Busy is a good character.'

[50] Gagey, p. 97. Much the same could be said of Millwood in *The London Merchant*, and the Bawd and Bolt in *Marina*.

[51] Burgess, p. 8, quoting Ward, p. xxx.

[52] Burgess, p. 8.   [53] See II. xvi. 32–49, 50–61.

written characters have been drawn into the main plot the play becomes top-heavy with it.

This discussion has so far been conducted without reference to the songs, and yet this is natural in dealing with most examples of ballad opera. As Gagey puts it, 'while the songs may have been the main attraction for the audience, they are not usually the prime concern for the dramatist, and their omission would not incurably ruin the play'.[54] This is certainly true of *Silvia*. Most of the songs simply repeat, in rather stale imagery, what has already been spoken, and some of them are positive obstructions to the action of the play. Above all, there are far too many of them; it would take, by a rough estimate, something over an hour to perform the songs alone.

To judge how well or badly Lillo deployed them, one could look at Charles Johnson's *The Village Opera* (1729), the first and best of the country operas of which *Silvia* is also an example.[55] Johnson's songs almost invariably supplement, rather than merely repeat, the spoken dialogue, and display characters in ways that spoken dialogue could not convey; they often close a scene with a neat summation of what has passed, or carry the action forward within a scene from one discernible phase to the next. In a few cases Lillo has managed to do as much. Airs XX, XXI, and XXII, the last three songs in the graveyard scene between Lettice and Sir John, Jonathan chiming in at the end with a bawdy refrain, advance and maintain the charm of the scene.[56] Air XXIII, which follows immediately in the text, is perhaps the best of all. The song itself is nothing much, but the use of its musical characteristics to bring Timothy on to the stage with Silvia, gracefully merging the comic and the pathetic, is noteworthy.[57] There is a scattering of other songs that function well in the text, but they are not many.

One aspect of the songs sets them apart from those in almost all other ballad operas—Lillo's tendency to adopt a more elevated tone than that of the song originally associated with the tune. The question of association is by far the most difficult element in ballad opera for the modern reader, and it is not often possible to say with confidence how a contemporary audience would have taken Lillo's strategy. Gay's approach in *The Beggar's Opera*, and that of most of the writers, was to lower the tone, parodying the original. Though songs did not

[54] Gagey, p. 7. This must be qualified in the case of the best ballad operas. *The Beggar's Opera* depends on the songs for the exuberance and complexity of its satire. *The Village Opera*, with which *Silvia* is compared below, is characterized by a similar fusion of music and spoken word. Most of its scenes would be unbalanced without their songs, while a good many scenes in *Silvia* would work better without them.

[55] See Gagey, pp. 85–9. First performed at Drury Lane on 6 Feb. 1728/9, it was withdrawn after four performances, the victim of disturbances in the theatre apparently unrelated to the play or the author (*London Stage, 1700–1729*, pp. 1013–14, 1017). Isaac Bickerstaffe reworked it into *Love in a Village*, the first example of comic opera, successor form to ballad opera.

[56] See I. xii. 63–110. Jonathan's songs earlier in the scene (Airs XVIII and XIX) display some ingenuity in the use of associational and musical characteristics of the tunes; see the commentary on music for these and all other airs mentioned in the discussion below.

[57] See II. i.

have to be satirical in this fashion—the ballad-opera literature contains a large number that are to be sung straightforwardly, usually by characters in some state of love—the popularity of ballad opera must have depended in large part on the authors' ability to entertain audiences with this game. In varying the convention Lillo risked losing his audience; whether it was a calculated risk is impossible to say, though the sheer earnestness that characterizes the whole play suggests that it may represent miscalculation. Many of the songs in *Silvia* are, it is true, mildly satirical or bawdy, but these are invariably based on songs that would already have had corresponding associations. When Lillo revises associations, he revises them upwards. Prime examples are Silvia's Air IV, in which 'Tweedside', the most popular of all ballad-opera tunes, and almost always used for love songs, is instead the setting for a reflection on virtuous conduct; Air XXIII, the original of which has a slyly bawdy ending; and Air XXIX, in which the wistful love-song 'Fond Echo' is transformed into a sort of hymn to virtue. Welford twice, in Airs XXVI and XLII, takes rousing street songs and turns them into calls to moral battle that the audience would have had difficulty taking seriously. The reaction of the galleries can perhaps be understood as a matter of disappointed expectations. Awaiting the undemanding entertainment that a ballad opera usually afforded, they were met by Welford, in a state of inexplicable agitation, singing elevated words to a tune of Handel's.[58] Most extraordinary of all, however, is the last song. The chorus, beginning 'Since Truth to the Mind her own Likeness reflects', is set to 'Dutch Skipper', one of the most popular theatre dances of the previous quarter-century and often used for political satire. The complex word-play on 'reflection' is too much for so frivolous a tune to contain, in some ways exemplifying the character of the play as a whole.

Silvia had a short life on the stage, and the book appears to have sold poorly.[59] It may therefore have been the play's intrinsic qualities alone, rather than any notoriety it might have gained, that led Henry Fielding to parody the main plot in the subplot of *The Grub-Street Opera* (1731).[60] In Fielding's play

[58] 'Il tricerbero humiliato', from Handel's *Rinaldo* (1711).

[59] See below pp. 14–22 (performances and text).

[60] Henry Fielding, *The Grub-Street Opera*, ed. Edgar V. Roberts (Lincoln, Nebr., 1968; London, 1969). All quotations are taken from this edition, a modernized text of *The Grub-Street Opera*, with appended scenes from the earlier *Welsh Opera* and *Genuine Grub-Street Opera*. The publishing history of the successive versions and the variations between them are too complex to be dealt with here, and the reader should consult Roberts's edition.

The Welsh Opera, a two-act afterpiece, was the only version that was performed, at the New Theatre in the Haymarket beginning on 22 Apr. 1731 and nine times thereafter (*London Stage, 1729–1747*). Most of the songs that parody Lillo are found in this earlier version, but the treatment of other material from *Silvia* is quite different. Apshones (Welford) does not appear at all, and Molly (Silvia) comes on at the end already married to Owen, her existence having only been hinted at before. As a result the parallel between Owen and Lillo's Sir John is much less clear than it is in *The Grub-Street Opera*. In a scene which does not occur in *The Grub-Street Opera* all the household servants are discovered to be the offspring of rich gentry, the discoverer being a witch, Goody Scratch, who may correspond to Goody Busy. Furthermore, in an aside that Fielding excised in reworking *The Welsh Opera* into *The Grub-Street Opera*, Sir Owen intimates, with a casualness that mocks Welford's spiritual turmoil, that 'this Owen, whom we have bred up as our son, is really the

Lillo's Sir John and Silvia are burlesqued in the characters of Master Owen Apshinken, 'in love with womankind', the son of Sir Owen, 'a gentleman of Wales, in love with tobacco', and Molly, 'a woman of strict virtue', the daughter of Sir Owen's tenant Mr Apshones, who is modelled on Welford.

Fielding's play is a daring satire not only of Walpole and his political associates but also of the royal family: Sir Owen represents George II, as Master Owen does Frederick, Prince of Wales. Harold Gene Moss has argued persuasively that Fielding, reasonably fearing that libel charges might be brought against him, incorporated massive amounts of material from ballad operas to serve as a legal blind. 'Had he been brought to trial, the elements of travesty the work contains would have permitted him to argue that the work was not in fact a satire but rather a travesty of satire, a parodic imitation of what was then in vogue'.[61] *Silvia* was the major victim of Fielding's borrowing, and the only work to be parodied rather than merely imitated, since its subject-matter fitted in so neatly with Fielding's satirical method: 'The opera was writ, sir, with a design to instruct the world in economy. It is a sort of family opera—the husband's *vade mecum*—and is very necessary for all married men to have in their houses.'[62]

The sort of treatment to which Silvia herself is subjected, in the person of Molly, is well represented in this soliloquy:

Oh, unhappy wretch that I am, I must have no husband, or no father. What shall I do—whither shall I turn? Love pleads strong for a husband, duty for a father. Yes, and duty for a husband too. But then what is one who is already so? Well then, I will antedate my duty. I will think him my husband before he is so. But should he prove false, and when I've lost my father, should I lose my husband too—That is impossible; falsehood and he are incompatible.[63]

There is much more of this sort of thing, adding up to thoroughgoing ridicule of Lillo's spotless heroine. Apshones, on the other hand, seems hardly to be burlesqued at all:

I desire you would spare my daughter, sir. I shall take as much care of her as I can. And if you should prevail on her to her ruin, be assured your father's estate should not secure

son of our tenant; and this Molly, who is supposed to be the daughter of our tenant, is really our own daughter. But the discovery of this, and of the reasons which induced me to this, I shall defer till some other oportunity' (Fielding, ed. Roberts, p. 87). In *The Grub-Street Opera*, though the parody of the main plot is much more extensive than it was in *The Welsh Opera*, this element of Lillo's story is entirely ignored.

When Fielding later satirized Richardson's *Pamela* as *Shamela* he was, in a roundabout way, repeating himself. Richardson, like Lillo, seems to have based his story on that of 'Amanda': 'Mr. Richardson's Pamela is no other than the story in [*Spectator*] No. 375. And perhaps it appears with as much advantage in its original brevity, as in its diffused length of a volume' (Nichols, *Literary Anecdotes*, ii. 443, quoted in *Spectator*, ed. Bond, iii. 409).

[61] Harold Gene Moss, 'Satire and Travesty in Fielding's *The Grub-Street Opera*', *Theatre Survey*, xv. 1 (May 1974), 39.

[62] Fielding, ed. Roberts, p. 4 ('Introduction', ll. 43–6).

[63] Ibid., p. 31 (II. i. 69–76).

you from my revenge. You should find that the true spirit of English liberty acknowledges no superior equal to oppression.[64]

Though Fielding may have intended the role to be acted in a ridiculous manner, it is also possible that he found in Welford a character who could be a spokesman for 'the true spirit of English liberty' but could also, if it proved necessary, be represented as merely another element in the travesty of *Silvia*.

Fielding also parodies some of the songs in which Lillo had moralized against the grain of his source.[65] 'Dutch Skipper', the tune of Lillo's finale, is used by Fielding for his Air VII, but in this case the reference is indirect. Rather than parody Lillo, Fielding echoes an elegantly bawdy song by Dryden, 'Sylvia the fair, in the bloom of Fifteen'.[66] Elsewhere he turns a song on its head, as in his Air XX, set to 'Tweedside' and corresponding to Air IV of *Silvia*:

> What woman her virtue would keep,
>   When naught by her virtue she gains?
> While she lulls her soft passions asleep,
>   She's thought but a fool for her pains.
> Since valets, who learn their lords' wit,
>   Our virtue a bauble can call,
> Why should we our ladies' steps quit,
>   Or have any virtue at all?[67]

Fielding was later to become one of Lillo's most admiring friends. He brought on *Fatal Curiosity* at the Haymarket, and may have had a hand in revising it.[68] That he admired this later and perhaps best play of Lillo's, while having lampooned his first effort, is further evidence that in *Silvia* Lillo chose the wrong form in which to realize his own intentions as a playwright. In Edmond Gagey's words, 'the morality rests rather uneasily on a form initiated by the biting wit and cynical satire of Gay'.[69]

PERFORMANCE AND RECEPTION

The stage history of *Silvia* is very brief. It was performed three times at Lincoln's Inn Fields on 10, 11, and 12 November 1730, and once again, reduced to two acts, at Covent Garden on 18 March 1736.[70]

The play ran into trouble on its first night, when 'there appeared a Set of People, who seem'd inclined to damn the whole Performance (if it had been in their Power) by their continual hissing and Cat-Calls; notwithstanding which,

---

[64] Fielding, ed. Roberts, p. 46 (II. vii. 41–6).
[65] See Commentary on the Music, Airs I, IV, X, XXIX, XLIII, L, LXIII.
[66] See Cyrus Lawrence Day, ed., *The Songs of John Dryden* (Cambridge, Mass., 1932), pp. 72, 166. Moss, 'Satire and Travesty', draws the parallel between Fielding's song and Dryden's, but overlooks the oblique reference to *Silvia*.
[67] Fielding, ed. Roberts, p. 28 (I. xii. 21–8).
[68] See General Introduction, p. xvii, and *Fatal Curiosity*, Introduction, pp. 285–6.
[69] Gagey, p. 97.   [70] *London Stage, 1729–1747*.

the same was perform'd with Applause, by the general Approbation of the Pit and Boxes'.[71] No motive is adduced for this behaviour—implied to have been displayed in the gallery—and there may well have been none. By all accounts first-night audiences all too often included 'Parties [who] go to new Plays to make Uproars, which they call by the odious Name of *The Funn of the First Night*'.[72] At times such demonstrations had a political basis, even when the play itself seems to warrant nothing of the kind, but there is no evidence to suggest that such was the case on 10 November 1730.

The second performance was 'By Command of His Royal Highness';[73] but the Prince of Wales was so frequent a patron of the theatre, and of performances of new plays, that nothing much can be read into this instance, though it could reflect the indirect influence of Henrietta Janssen, the play's dedicatee.[74] The third night was, as usual, the author's benefit, and Lillo appears to have cleared about £60, a respectable but by no means spectacular amount.[75]

Lillo had finished the play by 23 January 1729/30, when John Watts bought the copy; and the text of the play was quite possibly printed, though not published, a few months later.[76] From this one could infer that the play had been accepted at the theatre during the season of 1729–30, and perhaps even that production of the work was deferred from that season to the next, owing to the success of the pantomime afterpiece *Perseus and Andromeda*.[77]

The cast that eventually performed *Silvia* was one of the strongest to act in any of Lillo's plays during his lifetime, many of its members having appeared in *The Beggar's Opera* during its first run at Lincoln's Inn Fields in 1728. Mrs Cantrel (or Cantrell) had not then been among them, but she was the current Polly Peachum, her two predecessors having been taken from the stage by the Duke of Bolton and a 'gentleman of fortune'. Though she played a range of non-singing roles—e.g. Mrs Sealand in *The Conscious Lovers*, Lady Wishfort in *The Way of the World*, Alithea in *The Country Wife*—'her forte . . . was comedy and pantomime roles where her singing talents could be used':[78] one of her greatest successes was the title role in John Hippisley's popular ballad opera *Flora* (1729). Sir John was played by Thomas Walker, of whom Thomas Davies wrote that he 'knew no more of music than barely singing in tune; but his

[71] *Daily Courant*, 23 Nov. 1730, quoted in *London Stage, 1729–1747*.

[72] Thomas Whincop, preface to *Scanderbeg* (London, 1747), p. 261, quoted by Nicoll, p. 13.

[73] *London Stage, 1729–1747*.

[74] See commentary on the dedication (Mrs. Harriott Janssen).

[75] *London Stage, 1729–1747*. The figure is arrived at by deducting £40—the usual house charge for the period—from the total receipts of £100. 2s. (money £45. 6s.; tickets £54. 16s.).

[76] See below, The Text, pp. 21–2.

[77] Such was the case with George Jeffrey's tragedy, *Merope*, first performed at Lincoln's Inn Fields on 27 Feb. 1731. According to the theatre's playbill for 16 Apr. 1730, 'The Run of Perseus and Andromeda . . . having postpon'd the Acting of the Tragedy of Merope, this is to inform such Persons who have taken Tickets of the Author, that the same may be returned; or will be taken when the aforesaid Tragedy is acted the ensuing Season.' *Perseus and Andromeda* was first performed on 2 Jan. 1730, and last that season on 12 June (*London Stage, 1729–1747*).

[78] *Actors, Actresses*, iii. 41–2.

singing was supported by his inimitable action, by his speaking to the eye, not charming the ear'.[79] He had been a member of the company for nearly ten years and was well established in a wide variety of roles in tragedy and comedy, examples of the latter being Worthy in *The Recruiting Officer*, Bellmour in *The Old Bachelor*, and Harcourt in *The Country Wife*. He had thus gained a solid reputation as an actor, but his triumph as creator of the role of Macheath had made him a celebrity. John Hippisley, who played Lillo's Jonathan, was one of the most popular low comedians of his day and the original Peachum; his 'performance was much heightened by a distortion of his face, occasioned by an accidental burn in his youth'.[80] Other veterans of the original *Beggar's Opera* were Mrs Martin (Goody Busy; Mrs Peachum and Diana Trapes),[81] Jane Egleton (Betty; Lucy Lockit), Jack Hall (Gaffer Gabble; Lockit), and Mrs Rice (Goody Gabble; Mrs Vixen).

Charles Hulett—Welford—was 'endowed with great Abilities for a Player; but labour'd under the Disadvantage of a Person rather too corpulent for the *Hero*, or the *Lover*'; as for his singing, he had 'a most extraordinary melodious Voice, strong, and clear, and in the Part of *Macheath* . . . he was allow'd to excel the Original'.[82] The role of Lettice Stitch was taken by Mrs Vincent, for the most part a player of comic roles (e.g. Dorinda in *The Beaux' Stratagem*, Isabella in *The Squire of Alsatia*), but also the company's regular Ophelia. Dorothy Stitch was played by Elizabeth Kilby, whose roles generally ran to Abigails and Columbines.

While most ballad-opera performers were actors who could sing, a few were singers turned actors, as were John Laguerre (Timothy Stitch), a baritone, and Thomas Salway (Ned Ploughshare), a tenor.[83] Laguerre's 'first attempt in the dramatic way' after eight years with the company had been the role of Harry Pyefleet in *The Cobler's Opera* (1729).[84] His most popular role was Hob in *Flora*. Salway began his career as a treble at Cannons; at Lincoln's Inn Fields he was a popular entr'acte singer, often appearing in petticoat guise in dialogues with the bass-voiced Richard Leveridge. He was thus the natural choice for the title role in Gay's *Achilles* (1733).[85] As time went on he added occasional minor non-singing roles to his repertoire.

The only subsequent performance of *Silvia* on record took place when the work was mounted as an afterpiece to *The Merry Wives of Windsor* at Covent

[79] Thomas Davies, *Memoirs of the Life of David Garrick, Esq.*, 3rd edn. (London, 1781), i. 24.

[80] *Biographia Dramatica* (1812), i. 348.

[81] In *London Stage, 1729–1747*, pp. cxxvii–cxxviii, this Mrs Martin is confused with Elizabeth Grace—who was not 'Mrs' Martin till 1741—and is thereby unjustly slandered. See *Actors, Actresses*, v. 76–7, s.v. 'Elrington, Mrs. Richard'.

[82] William Rufus Chetwood, *A General History of the Stage* (Dublin), 1749, pp. 174–5 (in the first instance quoting Henry Giffard).

[83] Their vocal ranges are noted in the brief biographies found in Stanley Sadie, ed., *The New Grove Dictionary of Music and Musicians* (London, 1980), x. 362 and xvi. 437.

[84] 17 Mar. 1729 (*London Stage, 1729–1747*).

[85] First performed at Covent Garden, 10 Feb. 1733 (*London Stage, 1729–1747*).

Garden on 18 March 1736, Lacy Ryan's regular benefit night for that season.[86] It was billed as 'A Ballad Opera (not perform'd these Six Years) reduc'd to two short acts'. Walker, Laguerre, Hippisley, Mrs Kilby, and Mrs Martin took their old roles;[87] Silvia was once again played by the company's reigning Polly Peachum, now Hannah Norsa; Betty was also, as before, played by the current Lucy Lockit, Elizabeth Bincks.

The reduction may have been the work of the beneficiary, a leading actor and the under-manager of the company. He himself had written *The Cobler's Opera* (1728), one of the first imitations of *The Beggar's Opera*, and some of his benefits earlier in the decade had included unattributed and unpublished ballad farces.[88] It is, however, just possible that the alterer was Benjamin Hoadly: Garrick had at one time in his possession a manuscript of a two-act version by Hoadly, the return of which was requested by Benjamin's brother John in 1771. According to John Hoadly, Benjamin 'truly thought there would be some real true fun in it, if the taylor's sorrow for his drunken wife were made all hypocritical, and not real as in the original'.[89]

THE TEXT

One authorized edition of *Silvia*, published in 1730 but post-dated 1731, printed on ordinary and fine paper, appeared during Lillo's lifetime. A 'second edition' published in 1731 is actually a reissue of the first edition with partially reprinted preliminaries.

[86] *London Stage, 1729–1747.*

[87] Mrs Forrester, the original Goody Costive, took the role of Goody Gabble. Her former role was not listed in the playbill, and was most likely omitted from the shortened version.

[88] Ryan himself could well have composed or altered these pieces, or, as under-manager—and the company's probable producer of plays (see *London Stage, 1729–1747*, p. xcvii)—he may rather have commissioned them. *The Cobler's Opera* was first performed for Hippisley's benefit on 26 Apr. 1728; it was performed again 'with several Alterations' for Ryan's benefit on 17 Mar. 1729, and first published on that occasion. The afterpiece for Ryan's benefit on 9 Mar. 1730 was *Hudibras: or, Trulla's Triumph*, 'A New Ballad Opera' (anonymous, unpublished). The afterpiece for his benefit on 23 Mar. 1732 was *Tho' Strange, Tis True*, 'a Comic Pastoral Ballad Farce of two short acts' (anonymous, unpublished). For his benefit the following year, 29 Mar. 1733, the afterpiece was *The Stage Coach*, 'Written by Mr. Farquhar. Interspers'd with Variety of Songs to Ballad Tunes'; it is not certain whether this is identical with *The Stage Coach Opera*, first performed for Chetwood's benefit at Drury Lane on 13 May 1730 (see Gagey, pp. 106–7). The afterpiece for Ryan's benefit on 20 Mar. 1735 was *A School for Women*, taken from Molière, 'A Farce, never performed before' (*London Stage, 1700–1729* and *1729–1747*).

[89] Garrick, *Correspondence*, i. 421. For the Hoadly brothers, see Introduction to *Arden of Feversham*, pp. 475–6, 480–3. Garrick had sent a packet of Benjamin's pieces to his widow, from which *The Country Burial*—so it was referred to—was apparently missing, though Garrick was later unable to find it among his own papers (see Garrick, *Letters*, ii. 739–40, and *Correspondence*, i. 433, 542). It is not possible from these sources to date Hoadly's version, nor is there any reference to a performance. John Hoadly's *The Contrast* was acted at Lincoln's Inn Fields on 30 Apr. 1731 (*London Stage, 1729–1747*); and Benjamin Hoadly was evidently acquainted with John Rich in the early 1730s, while John was still at Cambridge. (See Garrick, *Correspondence*, i. 490 (letter dated 2 Nov. 1722): 'I last week burned four acts of a *complete* comedy, and reserved the *first*, to be a memento of the young man's folly and vanity, who could bring it up from Cambridge himself, and send it without a name to John Rich, where by good luck *brother Ben* was, and read it, and found out the ingenious author, and put a stop to his exposing himself.')

First Edition

John Watts registered his copyright of *Silvia* on 13 November 1730. The book had in fact been published three days earlier, at five o'clock on 10 November—the first day of performance—as indicated by an advertisement in the *Daily Post*.[90] All advertisements name both Watts, whose imprint appears on the title-page, and J. Roberts.[91] When the advertisement was repeated in the *Daily Post* of 16 November, Watts added a note:

N.B. It having been industriously reported that I publish'd a spurious Edition of the above-mentioned Opera, Intitled SILVIA: Or, The COUNTRY BURIAL, Written by Mr. George Lillo, I think it incumbent on me, as well for the Satisfaction of the Publick, as in Defence of my Right, in which I am much prejudic'd by such Reports, to declare, That I bought the Copy of the said Opera of the said Mr. Lillo on 23rd of January, 1729, and paid him a very valuable Consideration for the same.

John Watts.

In Justice to Mr. Watts, I think myself oblig'd to acknowledge his Edition to be a true and genuine Copy of the said Opera.

George Lillo.

The origin of these reports is altogether obscure, as is their connection, or lack of it, with the 'Set of People' who tried to disrupt the first performance.[92] It is possible that they were intended to prejudice sales in favour of one of the piratical editions.[93] They may have had something to do with the differences between the printed text and the version actually performed, even though such differences were hardly uncommon and in this case were explicitly noted.[94] Watts's delay in registering his copy may have hurt him. Apart, however, from the question of what prompted the note, there is the confirmation of Lillo's sale of copy to Watts ten months before publication and performance.[95] There is also some evidence, discussed below in the Comments, to suggest that the text

[90] *Daily Post*, 10 Nov. 1730, 'This Day at Five o'Clock will be publish'd . . .'; repeated 12 and 16 Nov., 'This Day is publish'd . . .', and similarly in the *Craftsman*, 14 Nov.

[91] 'Printed for John Watts . . . and sold by J. Roberts in Warwick-Lane.' Roberts was one of the most prolific booksellers of his day; his name occasionally appears in the imprints of other ballad operas printed by Watts.

[92] See above, pp. 14–15.

[93] See below, pp. 23–4. The Edinburgh edition was priced at one shilling, sixpence cheaper than Watts edition; the Dublin edition bears no price on the title-page but was probably sold for a shilling also, if not less.

[94] For a brief survey of 18th-cent. play publication, see Shirley Strum Kenny, 'The Publication of Plays', in Robert D. Hume, ed., *The London Theatre World, 1660–1800* (Carbondale, Ill., 1980), pp. 309–36.

[95] The date of sale given in Watts's advertisement almost certainly refers to the legal year: '1729' is thus 1729/30. The relation between the purchase of Lillo's copy and acceptance of the play at the theatre is discussed above, p. 15. According to A. S. Collins, in his *Authorship in the Age of Johnson* (New York, 1929), p. 262, Watts 'seems to have been very generous' in his dealings with playwrights: 'For two plays by James Millar [*sic*], *The Humours of Oxford* (1729) and *The Mother-in-law* (1733), he gave £80 each, and lists of his payments show him giving from twenty to eighty guineas to very minor writers.'

of the play (sheets B–F) was printed earlier than the preliminaries, perhaps as early as March or April.

The printing-house of John Watts, operated in partnership with the Tonsons, was, according to Plomer,[96] one of the most important in London. Though he was not otherwise a printer of music—his stock did not include music type—he printed and published the first edition of *The Beggar's Opera* with engraved music following the text. In the decade following he printed a large number of ballad operas, most of them, like *Silvia*, in the format he had adopted with the second edition of *The Beggar's Opera*: octavos in which woodcut music was set immediately above the song lyrics.[97] His only other musical venture was the six-volume *Musical Miscellany* (1729–30), in which some of the wood-blocks used for *Silvia* had already appeared.

The 'second edition', a reissue of the first edition with a cancel title, was published *c.*29 October 1731;[98] it was clearly intended to capitalize on the success of *The London Merchant*. Copies of the first issue were included in most copies of John Gray's nonce collection of Lillo's works, *c.*21 June 1740.

First issue (ordinary and fine paper)
For the title-page, see p. 25. In some ordinary copies the price is printed to the right of, rather than below, the date: '[Price 1*s.* 6*d.*]'. No price appears in copies printed on fine paper.

> *Collation*: 8° A⁴ a² B–F⁸ [$4 (−A1,3,4, a2, E3) signed]; 46 leaves, pp. *i–xii* 1
> 2–77 *78–80* ('17' misprinted '71' in some copies)
> *Contents*: A1(*i*) title A1ᵛ(*ii*) blank A2(*iii*)–A3ᵛ(*vi*) dedication A4(*vii*)–A4ᵛ(*viii*)
> table of songs a1(*ix*) dramatis personae a1ᵛ(*x*) blank a2(*xi*) advertisements
> a2ᵛ(*xii*) note on alterations B1(*1*)–F7(77) text (DH: [orn.] | *SILVIA*; | OR,
> THE | COUNTRY BURIAL. | [rule]) F7ᵛ(*78*)–F8ᵛ(*80*) advertisements

Prologue and Epilogue
The only known copies of the prologue and epilogue are printed on the recto and verso respectively of two leaves, almost certainly conjugate, bound into a British Library volume of miscellaneous plays immediately preceding a fine-paper copy of *Silvia*.[99] Both bear a number of manuscript corrections, of which

[96] Henry R. Plomer, *A Dictionary of the Printers and Booksellers Who Were at Work in England, Scotland, and Ireland from 1668 to 1725* (Oxford, 1922), p. 304.

[97] A detailed account of Watts's ballad-opera publications is found in L. J. Morrissey, 'Henry Fielding and the Ballad Opera', *Eighteenth-century Studies*, iv (1971), 386–402. Morrissey overlooks a few of the cases in which other publishers included music with ballad operas, but this does not affect his conclusion that Watts was, for ballad-opera authors, the most desirable publisher.

[98] *Daily Post*, 29 Oct. 1731, '*This Day is Publish'd, (Written by Mr.* LILLO, *Author of the Tragedy of* GEORGE BARNWELL, *or the* LONDON MERCHANT) . . .'; similarly in the *Daily Journal*, 30 Oct.

[99] *Silvia* is the eighth of ten works in the volume (841.d.32.), labelled 'Plays 1717–1738', which also contains a copy of *Fatal Curiosity* marked with extensive deletions and some changes. This copy of *Silvia* is reproduced in *The Ballad Opera*, ed. W. H. Rubsamen (New York, 1974), vol. xvii, where the prologue and epilogue have been repositioned and some marginal annotations and the signature 'a' are omitted.

two are substantive. The paper on which they are printed, rather light in weight and unlike any found in other copies of Watts's edition, contains a watermark (a crowned GR, most likely a countermark) anomalously positioned in the middle of the first (prologue) leaf towards the outer edge. It would appear that these are proof copies printed, according to the usual practice, on an odd scrap of paper. Horizontal creases across the middle of both leaves may have resulted from their being tucked into this copy of *Silvia* before it was included in the present volume. No evidence has been found by which to establish its provenance.

It is not unreasonable to suppose, on the basis of internal evidence, that the prologue and epilogue were both written by Lillo; but their omission from the published edition indicates that they were not recited in the theatre.[100] No other prologue or epilogue has come to light.

'Second edition'

SILVIA; | OR, THE | COUNTRY BURIAL. | AN | OPERA. | As it is Perform'd at the | THEATRE-ROYAL | IN | LINCOLN's-INN FIELDS. | [rule] | Written by | Mr. LILLO, *Author of the Tragedy of* GEORGE | BARNWELL, the *London* MERCHANT. | *With the* MUSICK *prefix'd to each* SONG. | [rule] | The SECOND EDITION, | [double rule] | *LONDON:* | Printed for J. WATTS at the Printing-Office in | *Wild-Court* near *Lincoln's-Inn Fields.* | [short rule] | M DCC XXXI. | [*in square brackets*] [Price One Shilling and Six Pence.]

Notes: Stet comma after 'EDITION'. Thin spaces in date.

Collation: = first issue except A⁴(− A1 + A1.5) instead of A⁴ a²; 45 leaves, pp. *i–x* etc.

Contents: A1(*i*) title A1ᵛ(*ii*) blank A2(*iii*)–A3ᵛ(*vi*) dedication (= first issue) A4(*vii*)–A4ᵛ(*viii*) table of songs (= first issue) A5(*ix*) blank A5ᵛ(*x*) dramatis personae

Note: The order of preliminaries in the collation and contents is an ideal-copy reconstruction. In the one copy seen A2.3 was quired within the newly printed A1.5, with A4 following A5. The reconstruction is based on the fact that the dramatis personae was almost invariably printed to face the first page of the text; since it would have been possible simply to cancel leaf a2, this would seem to be the reason behind the new setting.[101]

---

[100] This copy of *Silvia* coincidentally lacks leaf a2. The rehearsal changes noted on the verso of the leaf and the rejection of the prologue and epilogue may well have come about at roughly the same time, but it is impossible to reconstruct a printing history that would satisfactorily account for the absence of a2 in the presence of physically unrelated proof copies of other matter. The dramatis personae (a1) found in this copy is printed from the same setting of type, including the identically positioned signature 'a', found in all other copies of Watts's edition. The printing of the dramatis personae on a recto page was unusual; it was quite probably so placed to make way for the substitute scene (see below, n. 101).

[101] An analogue of sorts is the rearrangement of preliminaries that took place when Watts printed an altered reimpression of Charles Johnson's *The Village Opera* (1729). Leaf A4 of the first impression contained the dramatis personae on the recto, and on the verso the music and words of a

Comments

Sheets B–F were printed by common octavo imposition, as indicated by the occurrence of tranchefiles in uncut copies. Analysis of running heads reveals no clear evidence of reuse. Adjustment of the inner margins between the printing of copies on ordinary and the larger fine paper resulted in some shifting of type in head and direction lines, but in some instances similar shifting of type is not confined to fine or ordinary copies exclusively. Neither these nor the very few press accidents in the text—there were no press corrections—show conclusively which copies were printed first. A press figure on E8^v, identically positioned in all copies, does at least indicate that all copies of that forme were printed in the same operation. In fine-paper copies A^4, a^2, and B–F^8 respectively were printed on three different lots of paper, evidenced by different watermarks. In ordinary copies A^4 and B–F^8 were printed on a variety of unwatermarked papers. Variations in average widths of chain-lines differentiate at least three moulds, but it is not possible to distinguish the paper used in half-sheet A from some of that used in sheets B–F. Gathering a^2 was printed on a watermarked paper of rather better quality.

Advertisements dated 'November 10, 1730' on a2, and the reference to rehearsals on a2^v, are clear evidence that that gathering was printed very near the time of publication.[102] The three pages of advertisements on F7^v–F8^v are a different matter. Though the advertisements on the first two of these pages were old by November 1730, they were printed from settings of type that were kept standing for use in various books as space allowed, and no very strong conclusion can be drawn from their presence in *Silvia*.[103] It should, however, be noted that the solicitation of pieces for volumes v and vi of the *Musical Miscellany* had been superseded by 24 October, when a notice was printed in the *Craftsman* that those volumes were finished and would be published in about a month's time, in fact two days after the publication of *Silvia*.[104] That publication of these volumes is announced on page a2 of *Silvia* suggests that some time passed between the printing of sheet F and quarter-sheet a. More strongly indicative is the list of recent plays on F8^v, which omits a number of

---

new song in the second act. For the reimpression several songs were taken out of the standing type of the text, while the new song was removed to its proper place. The table of songs was thus shortened by a page, and the preliminaries were reimposed with the dramatis personae on A3^v, the text now beginning on A4 rather than B1. This was not, strictly speaking, a case of reissue: the title-page was reprinted from standing type without alteration.

[102] 'November 10. 1730. *On* Thursday *next* [12 November] *will be Publish'd . . . The* FIFTH *and* SIXTH VOLUMES *of* The MUSICAL MISCELLANY . . . *And on the same Day will be Publish'd . . . The* FIFTH EDITION *of* LETTERS *of* ABELARD *and* HELOISE.'

[103] On F7^v: *Musical Miscellany*, vols. i and ii, '*Lately Publish'd . . .*'; vols. iii and iv, 'Nov. 12, 1729. *This Day was publish'd . . . The* FIFTH and SIXTH Volumes . . . will go to the Press very speedily; therefore all GENTLEMEN and LADIES who are willing to contribute any NEW SONGS to this Collection, are desir'd to send 'em as soon as possible . . .'; *The Fair Circassian*, 4th edn. (dated 1729), '*Just Publish'd . . .*'; F8: A Select Collection of Novels, 2nd edn., '*October* 28, 1729. *This Day was Publish'd . . .*'; Gay's *Fables*, 3rd edn., '*January* 16, 1729. *This Day was Publish'd . . .*'.

[104] *The Craftsman*, 24 Oct. 1730, '*Now Finished, and will be Published the Middle of next Month . . .*'.

books published in the spring and summer of 1730, some of which were advertised in volume vi of the *Musical Miscellany*.[105] Similar lists in books printed soon after the publication of *Silvia* appear to have been kept pretty well up to date; if Watts was consistent in this practice—a point about which one cannot of course be certain—the omissions would indicate that *Silvia* was printed before or at about the same time as the books omitted.

Assuming the earlier printing of the text, it is not certain whether the title gathering was printed at the same time as the text or later. The different paper used for the title gathering in fine-paper copies is evidence of separate printing, and the post-dating of the title-page points to printing relatively late in the year, though later publication could conceivably have been anticipated in the printing of the title.

The three states of the title-page are distinguished only by the price. Fine-paper copies were frequently unpriced, but it is hard to account for the two states of ordinary copies. No other resetting was involved, and there is no evidence in the title gathering by which to establish the order of printing. The numerical price is definitely printed, not stamped: it always occurs in the same position.

For the 'second edition' the title-leaf and gathering a² were cancelled. The new title-page stressed the identity of the author of *The London Merchant*, as did the advertisements, and it was perhaps in deference to Lillo's new-found respectability as a playwright that the note on alterations was suppressed. Its exclusion appears to have been deliberate, in view of the newly printed dramatis personae. Advertisements in Watts's books printed later than October 1731 list *Silvia* without mention of a second edition, and no copies of it have been found in John Gray's 1740 collection. Evidently very few copies were issued in that form and copies of the original edition must have remained in stock and continued to be sold.

Silvia is lacking in two of the copies seen of the nonce collection. It is reasonable to surmise that not enough copies remained, and that Gray did not think it worth the expense to have more printed. Such a short run would have

---

[105] The play-list in the *Musical Miscellany* includes, in addition to *Silvia*, the second edition of *Thom Thumb*, *The Author's Farce*, *The Widow Bewitch'd*, *The Fashionable Lady*, *Patie and Peggy*, *Damon and Phillida*, and *The Chamber-Maid*, all published in 1730 but absent from the play-list in *Silvia*; the list also includes Fielding's *The Coffee-House Politician*, a revision of his own *Rape upon Rape* first performed on 30 Nov. 1730 (*London Stage, 1729–1747*). As part of the same list, the *Musical Miscellany* is advertised as a six-volume set; the third edition of Gay's *Fables* is likewise incorporated in the list. On a separate page the advertisement for the *Select Collection* is printed as it appears in *Silvia*, but without the dateline and headed 'Lately Publish'd . . .'. The advertisements in the *Musical Miscellany* differ not only in content but also in arrangement from the simple list of plays in *Silvia*, and correspond to advertisements found in *The Jovial Crew*, *The Highland Fair*, and *The Devil to Pay*, ballad operas published by Watts in 1731. Comparison shows that the list was kept standing, new books being added as they were published. If F7ᵛ–F8ᵛ of *Silvia* had been printed near the time of performance, the advertisements would almost certainly have been printed as they appear in the *Musical Miscellany*; the advertisements that do appear in *Silvia* strongly indicate printing in late March or early April: the latest play listed there is Thomas Walker's *The Fate of Villainy*, first performed at Goodman's Fields on 24 Feb. 1730 (*London Stage, 1729–1747*).

been uneconomical, and there would have been little hope of selling single copies left over from a longer run.

The edition is neatly printed and nearly free of typographical errors, the most frequent of which involve occasional intermixing of roman and italic punctuation. The printer's copy for the text clearly antedated the final playhouse version, and this is the most likely explanation for the missing, erroneous, or misleading stage directions and scene division in Acts II and III,[106] errors of a kind that a playhouse copyist concerned for details of staging would overlook less easily than a copyist, or author, whose interest centred on the content of the scenes. Most of these errors occur in Act III, a considerable portion of which (scenes x–xiv) was replaced by the new scene printed on a2[v]. The new scene is not divided into French scenes, and a similar departure from the French scene convention in III. viii (III. viii and ix in the present edition) is quite possibly an artefact of alterations made after the scenes had been divided and numbered. The incorrect stage direction at the head of III. viii may perhaps also be related to such alteration.

Punctuation is generally consistent throughout and, within the rather heavy conventions of the period, does not detract from the movement of the lines. Even at its heaviest, in the set speeches of Silvia, Welford, and Sir John, it presents few problems to the modern reader. Capitalization is likewise generally consistent and error-free; its occasional extension to words other than proper or stressed nouns is seldom illogical or distracting. There is some inconsistency in the abbreviation of names in speech-headings, and in the omission of speech-headings in scenes with one character on stage, but no pattern of occurrence points to the work of individual compositors.[107] The book is handsome, though not extravagant, in design, with woodcut ornaments as opposed to composites of printers' flowers.[108] The wood-cut music, almost all competently produced, contributed to the balance of the design; most of the blocks were prepared for this edition.

Later Reprints

Two reprints, of Dublin and Edinburgh origins, followed Watts's edition, most likely printed and published in a matter of days after publication of the latter. The Dublin edition, an octavo dated 1730, was, according to its imprint, printed by S. Powell for George Risk, George Ewing, and William Smith. The Edinburgh edition, a duodecimo dated 1731, bears a spurious Watts imprint, but can be identified as the work of Thomas and Walter Ruddiman on the

---

[106] See textual footnotes and commentary notes to II. xvSD, III. iiSD, III. ii. 7, III. iiiSD, III. vSD, III. viSD, III. viiiSD, III.ix, III. xxiiSD, and III. xxiiiSD.

[107] The one exception is Dorothy Stitch, who is '*Dol.*' in Act I (and 'Dolly' in I. xSD), '*Dor.*' in Act III, an inconsistency that could conceivably be of authorial origin, and is in a way appropriate to the quite different tones of the scenes.

[108] Two flowers are, however, used at the bottom of A4[v], where space would not have allowed for a tailpiece.

evidence of an ornament that similarly identifies a piratical 'second edition' of *The London Merchant*.[109] Both are printed without music, and both incorporate the new scene for the third act without any further alteration apart from renumbering of subsequent scenes, thus identifying Watts's edition as the copy-text. In other respects, both follow Watts as closely as can be expected in such reprints. Variants are mainly confined to accidentals of punctuation, spelling, and capitalization. The few substantive variants, generally erroneous or trivial, are of obviously compositorial origin: there are no signs of systematic editorial intervention, apart from Edinburgh's more complete accommodation of the new scene and corrected numbering of two misnumbered airs. Neither text was set from the other, and neither has any independent authority.

In Thomas Davies's 1775 collected edition of Lillo's works the text, without music, is reprinted as it appears in Watts's edition; the note on alterations is printed at the end of the play, not incorporated into it. The variants that appear in the text, almost all accidental, are clearly a matter of compositorial preference.

Editorial Procedure

Watts's edition serves as copy-text.[110] A necessary stage direction has been added; others have been corrected or revised to specify more accurately which characters are on stage. One scene-division has been corrected, and another scene divided into French scenes to conform with the rest of the text, subsequent scenes being renumbered accordingly. In the few cases where accidentals distort the meaning of the text they have been emended, where possible with reference to the eighteenth-century reprints. Where the reprints provide alternatives to questionable readings retained from the copy-text, reference is made in the commentary. No attempt is made to incorporate the new scene for Act III, since the necessary adjustments to, at least, II. xv would involve only editorial invention. The scene is reprinted, along with the note on unspecified cuts, as it stood in the copy-text. The prologue and epilogue are reprinted, in their normal positions, from the unique British Library copy, adopting the readings indicated in the manuscript corrections. Tune-titles have been added to the table of songs for the convenience of readers principally interested in the music. Stanza divisions of the song lyrics are reproduced as they stand in the copy-text. Editorial treatment of the music is discussed in the headnote to the commentary on the music and historical background of the songs.

[109] See *The London Merchant*, Introduction, p. 142.

[110] Printer's copy for the dedication (A2–A3ᵛ) and text (B1–F7) was a reproduction of CtY, Plays 855 ('second edition'); the table of songs was prepared from the same copy (A4–A4ᵛ). Copy for the dramatis personae (a1) and note on alterations (a2ᵛ) was a reproduction of CLU-C, *PR.3545.L5S5. The prologue and epilogue were prepared from microphotographs of the British Library fine-paper copy, 841.d.32.(8.), incorporating the manuscript corrections found there. Copies collated include: *first edition, ordinary paper*, O (2 copies), L, CtY (2 copies), MH (2 copies), CSmH, ICN, CLU-C; *first edition, fine paper*, O, L; '*second edition*', CtY; *Dublin*, IU, CLU-C; *Edinburgh*, CLU-C; Davies, *Works* (1775), O, L (2 copies), CtMW, CtY (2 copies).

S I L V I A;

OR, THE

COUNTRY BURIAL.

AN

OPERA.

As it is Performed at the

THEATRE-ROYAL

IN

LINCOLN'S-INN FIELDS.

With the MUSICK *prefix'd to each* SONG.

LONDON:

Printed for J. WATTS, at the Printing-Office in
Wild-Court near *Lincolns-Inn Fields.*

MDCCXXXI.

TO
Mrs. *Harriott Janssen.*

MADAM,

To be well Descended, happy in Your Fortune, nobly Ally'd, to be agreeable in Your Person, to have an Understanding solid and extensive, and a Wit at once the most poignant, and yet the most inoffensive and agreeable, may justly raise
5 Admiration and Esteem in others, as they distinguish You in so eminent a manner, and constitute your personal Happiness.

But as it is that easy, graceful manner in which You enjoy them, that Freedom from Vanity, Affectation or Pride, which form your real Character; so the Use You make of Your Fortune, Interest, and good Sense, renders them a
10 general Blessing to all who have the Happiness of being within the Reach of their Influence.

MADAM,

Your Generosity and Condescention in permitting this Address, is an Instance of Both, so much to my Advantage, that I find it impossible, to
15 suppress either my Pride, or Gratitude, on this Occasion; especially when I consider that it is an Honour, that many before have Solicited in vain.

That the Conversation and Friendship of a Lady of your Accomplishments, should be highly Esteemed by Persons of the first Rank both for Dignity and Virtue (not to mention the Noble Lord to whom you are so happily Ally'd) is no
20 more a Wonder, than that there should be among the Nobility, those who are as eminent for their good Sense and fine Taste, as their high Stations.

That You may still continue the Ornament of your own Sex, and the Admiration of ours, must be the sincere Wish of all who are any ways acquainted with your Merit, but of none more than of,

25 *MADAM*,

Your Grateful and Obliged

Humble Servant.

A
TABLE of the SONGS.

1–2 A TABLE of the SONGS.] *In the present edition page-numbers and accidentals within first lines have been silently emended to conform to the text; tune-titles have been added in brackets*

ACT II.

ACT III.

Air 47 *stern*] Ed.; *following text* (III. i. 1); *vain* O

PROLOGUE.

Among the many Candidates for Fame,
How few obtain the Prize—at which all aim.
Since you're the proper Judges in this Cause;
No wonder then, to gain the wish'd Applause,
Each new Advent'rer makes it his Pretence   5
To entertain you—with old English *Sense:*
So wisely tells—what else had ne'er been known,
That by good English *Sense—he means his own.*
Then smartly lashes the dull, tasteless Herd,
Who nought but Show, and Farce, and Song regard.   10
But sure the present Age, and past, he wrongs,
Who grants not English *Sense, in* English *Songs*
In Times remote, when blooming, gay and young,
With gentlest Manners, and harmonious Tongue,
Some reigning Toast grac'd our great Grandsire's Song,   15
Whether with jocund Strains, or graver Airs,
She Mirth excites, or sooths her Lover's Cares;
Whether with decent Pride she does relate
Her Country's Glory, or some Virgin's Fate;
The various Passions, at her Call arise,   20
Glow in the Breast, or trickle from the Eyes.
With sweet, but simple Notes, good Sense convey'd,
Loses no Force, but is the stronger made.
Oh! had our Modern Writers half the Fire,
That did those venerable Bards inspire,   25
They'd force Applause, who now your Patience tire.
Then of their Censure not at all afraid,
We call in Musick to the Muses Aid.
Tho' we the Justness of your Taste maintain,
For well writ Songs—yet think us not so vain   30
As to commend our own—What here is writ,
We to your Judgment humbly do submit.
The Fair, and Brave, we know, small Faults forgive,
And Silvia, if she merits it, shall live.
To ask one Favour only we presume,   35
First hear the Whole, ere you pronounce our Doom.

---

12 *Songs.*] *manuscript correction; punctuation in original setting inked out, but appears to have been a comma*   17 *Lover's*] *manuscript correction; original setting has '*Lovers*'*   25 *those*] *manuscript correction; original setting has '*these*'*   33 *we know*] *manuscript correction; original setting has '*he knows*'*   36 *ere*] *Ed.; original setting has '*e'er*'. See Commentary*

Dramatis Personæ.

MEN

Sir John Freeman,	Mr. *Walker*.
Welford,	Mr. *Hulett*.
Timothy Stitch,	Mr. *Laguerre*.
Gaffer Gabble,	Mr. *Hall*.
Ploughshare,	Mr. *Salway*.
Jonathan,	Mr. *Hippesley*.
Sexton,	Mr. *Ray*.

WOMEN

Silvia,	Mrs. *Cantrel*.
Dorothy Stitch,	Mrs. *Kilby*.
Lettice Stitch,	Mrs. *Vincent*.
Goody Busy,	Mrs. *Martin*.
Goody Gabble,	Mrs. *Rice*.
Goody Costive,	Mrs. *Forrester*.
Betty,	Mrs. *Egleton*.

N. B. Act III, Page 95, for Scene X, XI, XII, XIII, XIV, read as follows:

A Room in Sir John's House.

Sir John discover'd at a Table, reading.

'Tis hard a rooted Love to dispossess;   5
'Tis hard, but you may do it ne'ertheless.
In this your Safety does consist alone:
If possible, or not, it must be done.

A Poem on a Dwarf! what strange stuff is here! Hey ho!—This *Welford's* Daughter has taken so strong hold of my Mind, that Books are useless to me. 10 [*Lays aside the Book.*] O *Silvia, Silvia*! thou hast too strongly possess'd my Heart, ever to be dislodg'd.—The Possession of other Beauties only fires my Imagination with those Joys thou alone art capable to impart.—I have made thee an ungrateful Return to a disinterested Passion, and made thee suffer for what I ought to adore thee.—That Virtue which I endeavour'd to subdue, has 15 made me Captive; and I know not if the Grace of Beauty, or the most shining Ornament of thy Sex, influences most.—I have wrong'd thee, and am—unjust. But I'll acknowledge and repair my Fault.

Enter Jonathan.

Jon. Sir, I have deliver'd your Letter.   20
Sir John. And what Answer?
Jon. Her Eyes deliver'd the Greater Part; but her Tongue said it requir'd none.
Sir John. Ha!—Whither am I going?—whither, but to *Silvia*; the lovely, mournful *Silvia*; to implore her Pardon, to expel her Griefs, to vow eternal Love, eternal Truth.   25

AIR XL. *Draw*, Cupid, *draw*, &c.

Reign, Silvia, *reign, &c.* as in Page 79.   [*Exit.*

☞*This Opera appearing in Rehearsal too long for one Night's Entertainment, some Scenes have been shorten'd, and Airs omitted.*

1 Act] *Ed.*; ~. O   Page 95] *Ed., conforming to present edition*; ~ 61 O   1–2 Scene X … XIII, XIV] *Ed., conforming to present edition*; ~ IX, X, XI, XII, XIII O   27 Page 79] *Ed., conforming to present edition*; ~ 46 O

SILVIA;

OR, THE

COUNTRY BURIAL.

ACT I.

SCENE I.

A Room in Welford's *House.*

Welford.

Now, now's the very Crisis of our Fate.—On this important Hour depends the Happiness, or Ruin, of my dear and only Child, and all my future Peace.—Why am I thus alarm'd! The Event must sure be happy! I have long, with Pleasure, beheld their mutual Love.—The end of all my Hopes and Fears is near—This happy Marriage will restore my long-lost Peace of Mind.—After Marriage, shou'd he prove false, or unkind—what Means are left—what Power on Earth can do her Justice then!—Now my Pains return! thus Joy and Anguish alternately possess my Breast, as Hope or Fear prevails.

AIR I. Since all the World's in Strife.

> The Man, by Foes surrounded,
>   Whilst with himself at Peace,   10
> Dauntless, and unconfounded,
>   Beholds their Rage increase.
> But oh! the torturing Pain,
> That racks his Heart and Brain,
> Who, hourly with himself at War,   15
> The Foe does in his Bosom bear!—
> Shall this Tempest in my Breast
> E'er cease, and I have Rest?
> E'er cease, and I have Rest?

SCENE II.

Welford, *and* Jonathan.

Wel. *Jonathan*, Sir *John* tarries long.

Jon. That is not to be wonder'd at, when he is in such good Company. I know my Master never thinks himself so happy, as when he is with your fair Daughter.

Wel. *Jonathan*, I have observ'd, of all Sir *John*'s Servants, that you, who,   5 indeed, seem best to deserve it, have the greatest share in his Confidence and Favour: Now you are not ignorant of my Friendship for your Master, nor of his Pretensions of Love to my *Silvia*; both which must interest me nearly in every thing that relates to him. I have lately heard some Reflections on his Conduct, that much alarm me. You, if you will, can satisfy my Doubts, without Prejudice   10 to your own Fidelity, or your Master's Honour.

Jon. Ay, dear Sir, I know that any Discoveries, which I might make to you, wou'd be as safe as in my own Bosom, and all the Use you wou'd make of 'em, wou'd be to improve 'em, if possible, to my Master's Advantage, and not at all to my Prejudice. What a wicked, censorious World do we live in! My Master is   15 certainly the most virtuous, sober, modest Gentleman in the Country; and, to say Truth, we are a mighty regular Family. For my part, I am daily edify'd by his good Example.

Wel. This Fellow mocks me. [*Aside.*] The Business of my Farm, and the Care of my Flocks call me hence. Farewel. My best Respects and Service to Sir *John*.   20

(I. ii) 1 *Wel.*] *Ed.; not in* O   5 *Wel.*] *Ed.; Welf.* O. *Silently regularized below: both forms occur*
irregularly throughout O

SCENE III.

Jonathan.

Ha, ha, ha! a pretty Jest truly! discover my Master's Secrets for nothing!—when I'm so well paid for keeping 'em.

AIR II. Gami'orum.

The Servant that betrays his Trust,
    Who's imploy'd in search of Beauty,
To his Master and himself unjust,   5
    Has neither Sense nor Duty.
Priests and Lawyers, by the Throng,
    Are well paid for their Pratling;
What Fool then wou'd use his Tongue,
    Who loses by his Tatling.—   10
Gami—'orum, &c.

SCENE IV.

Another Room in Welford's *House.*

Sir John Freeman, *and* Silvia.

Sil. Urge me no farther—I have said too much. How have you drawn from me the fond Confession?

Sir John. Meerly to say you wou'd obey your Father! is that too much to pay whole Years spent in Adoration of your Charms!

Sil. What can you ask, or what can I say more?   5

Sir John. Can ardent Love be satisfy'd with Duty? You might have said as much to any other Man, who shou'd have gain'd your Father's approbation. You have not yet, my charming Fair, confess'd you love.

Sil. Why will you press me to pass the Bounds of Modesty and Prudence? you know my Father does not force my Will.   10

Sir John. Why then this needless Caution and Reserve? your cruel Coldness chills me to the Heart. You never felt Love's animating Fire; some other Motive, in which Love has no part, must influence you to admit of my Addresses.

Sil. Your Suspicions are as groundless as unkind. There may be Men false, 15 designing, cruel and unjust, who court and flatter only to deceive: wou'd it be therefore just to charge the Crimes of some on all? and, for your constant Love, Truth and Sincerity, return you Doubts, Suspicions and unjust Reproaches? There may be Women too, who, for Wealth or Power, wou'd give their Hands where they refuse their Hearts. If you think me such a one, for my sake, and 20 your own, desist at once: for Love, that is not founded on Esteem, can never yield true Satisfaction, or continue long.

Sir John. Pardon, my dearest *Silvia*, a Fault, caus'd only by Excess of Love— Thou art so great a Blessing, 'twere Presumption to be too secure. Long we suspect, and hardly are convinc'd that the Treasure, on which our Happiness 25 depends, shall ever be attain'd. But now my Fears are husht, and all my Doubts are fled.

AIR III. Blithe *Jockey* young and gay.

Sweet are the Joys of Love,
When Doubts and Fears are past:
Sil. *Virtue does Love improve;*
Truth makes it ever last.
Sir John. *All Virtues in thee shine,*
Sil. *Whate'er I am is thine.*
Both. *Hearts, thus united, prove*
Earth has no Joy like Love.

Sir John. When Love's sincere and constant, how does it bless and how improve Mankind? yet, ambitious Statesmen, and foolish medling Priests, wou'd bind in Fetters the noble free-born Passion. Vain Attempt!—Marriage ne'er yet kindled a mutual Flame, where it was not, but often extinguish'd it where it was; Love is its self its own Security, and needs no other Bonds. 40

Sil. This idle Talk, this common-place Raillery on Marriage, I think, at any Time is best omitted; but sure, Sir *John*, 'tis most improper now. You can't expect that a Maid, who is not weary of her Condition, will take upon her the Defence of a Cause in which she is not concern'd: yet, to pleasure you, who, I presume, delight to hear me talk, tho' I thereby discover my own Simplicity, this 45 I will say, the World owes its Order, Kingdoms their peaceful regular Succession, and private Families their Domestick Happiness to Marriage.

Sir John. The Prejudice of Education only makes you reason thus. I must instruct you better.

Sil. Sir *John*, I understand you not— 50

Sir John. You shall joyn with me, by our Example to convince the World, that Love can subsist without the Marriage Tye.

Sil. Sir *John Freeman*, I have known you long, bred up under one Roof from Infancy together. I don't remember when I knew you not. The innocent Friendship, contracted in our Childhood, in you improv'd to Love, or you have 55 been a thousand Times forsworn. If I have been deceiv'd, when may a Virgin safely believe a Man? I wou'd not wrong your Honour by unjust Suspicions,— but if you have abus'd me—

Sir John. If I love thee not, or if I ever cease to love thee, may I become the most wretched and most accurst of Men.—May I— 60

Sil. Imprecate no more. Wave this Discourse, and I am satisfy'd.

Sir John. 'Tis time, my *Silvia*, to compleat our Joys. [*Takes her by the Hand.*] You must now quit your Father's humble Roof, and shine with me. My Wealth, great as it is, shall be exhausted to support thy Pleasures. Love, only Love, shall be the Priest to joyn us. Enjoyment shall be our Marriage: [*She struggles.*] Each 65 Day I shall a happy Bridegroom be, and you a Bride. *Mahomet*'s Paradise shall be verify'd in us; and all our long Lives shall be but one continu'd Transport.

Sil. Let go my Hand.

Sir John. And lest you shou'd think I mean to deceive and to forsake you, no proud Heiress, that brings a Province for her Portion, shall be joyntur'd as you 70 shall be. Half my Estate shall be settled on thee.

Sil. With brutal Force to compel me to hear thy hated Proposals, is such Insolence.—Thy Breath is blasting, and thy Touch infectious. Oh that my Strength was equal to my Indignation! I'd give my Hand a Ransom for my Body. [*Breaks from him.* 75

Sir John. Stay, my charming angry Fair, and hear me speak.

Sil. Wou'd I had never heard you. Oh that 'twere possible to fly where I might never hear the Voice of Mankind more!—What, set a Price on my Immortal Soul and spotless Fame? Know, thou ungenerous Man, I ne'er was influenced by thy Wealth to hearken to thy Vows; for notwithstanding my 80 humble Birth, and Fortune, I ever scorn'd Riches, when compar'd to Love, as now I do Love and Thee, compar'd to Virtue. She, who capitulates on Terms like these, confesses an Equivalent may be had for Innocence and Fame, and there by forfeits both.

AIR IV. Tweed Side.

By our Weakness we help the Deceit,   85
  If our Virtue we ballanc with Gold.
When Dishonour's propos'd, if we treat,
  We're to Ruin and Infamy sold.
The Bird, that beholds the Snares laid,
  Yet presumptuously plays with the Bait,   90
By its Rashness and Folly betray'd,
  Repents, and grows wiser too late.

SCENE V.

Sir John Freeman.

Jonathan.

SCENE VI.

Sir John Freeman, *and* Jonathan.

Jon. Sir.
Sir John. Order the Groom to bring the Horses to the Gate.

SCENE VII.

Sir John Freeman.

I have made a bold, but unsuccessful Attempt, and by it, perhaps, have lost
her for ever—perhaps not.—I wou'd fain see her once more, methinks.—And
yet there is but little likelyhood of our coming to an Agreement. I am resolv'd
never to marry; and she seems as much resolv'd never to comply without it.
Whatever is the Meaning of it, I find my self more asham'd than angry at the   5
Disappointment. Tho' 'tis certain that I never did, nor ever can, love any other
Woman half so well. I feel a strange Palpitation here! [*Sighing.*] I am not sure
that I don't like her the better for refusing me.—I am sure of nothing—but that
I won't marry—I must e'en have recourse to the general Remedy in these
Cases, a less scrupulous Female. For tho' that won't remove the Cause, yet it is   10
an admirable Opiate, and relieves the Symptoms to a Miracle.

AIR V. Charming is your Face.

(I. v) I O *includes speech-heading: Sir John.*

Wounded by the scornful Fair,
Since she dooms me to Despair,
Let me fly to seek for Rest
On some softer gentler Breast,   15
Whose free Soul no Forms enslave,
But kindly heals the Wounds she gave.

SCENE VIII.

A Country Village.

The Funeral, attended by Timothy Stitch *as chief Mourner,*
Lettice, Ploughshare, *Gaffer* Gabble, *Goody* Busy,
Goody Gabble, *Goody* Costive, *&c. crosses the Stage.*
The Sexton remains.

Sex. A very pretty Fancy this of being buried in her Cloaths. If it were once a Fashion, a Sexton might get as much as an Overseer of the Poor. Every Man is for making the most of his Place. But then there is no Comparison between starving the Living and robbing the Dead, for what shou'd dead Folks do with Cloaths?—But the Truth of it is, in these healthy Countries the Poor live so   5 shamefully long, that Parish-Officers get little now, beside good Eating and Drinking.—But I have heard that formerly such as were past their Labour, used to be provided for at the Expence of the Sheriff,—for then, if Persons were likely to become chargeable to the Parish, the whole Neighbourhood wou'd swear that they were Witches or Wizards; and so they were decently   10 hang'd up, to save Charges.—But in *London*, and other your great Towns, an industrious Man of my Business may make a good Penny of it still,—for there they steal Bodies and all, but here we're forc'd to let them rot in their Graves, because we can't tell what else to do with them.

(I. viii) SD *Gaffer . . . Goody . . . Goody . . . Goody*] *Ed.*; Gaffer . . . Goody . . . Goody . . . Goody O. *Silently normalized below in all* SDs *where these forms occur. See Commentary*   *Sexton*] *Ed.*; Sexton O. *See Commentary*   2 *Sexton*] *Ed.*; Sexton O

AIR VI. There was a Jovial Beggar-Man.

> *Strange Tales some lying Travellers tell,* 15
> *How Men on Men have fed;*
> *Of publick Shambles, where they fell*
> *For Food their Friends when dead.*
> *The Moral of the Fable thus*
> *Men, that are wise, unfold;* 20
> *No matter, so you fill your Purse,*
> *Tho' Living and Dead be sold.*

SCENE IX.

A Church-Yard.

Dorothy Stitch *in the Grave;* Timothy Stitch, Ploughshare,
Gaffer Gabble, Lettice, *Goody* Busy, *Goody*
Gabble, *Goody* Costive, *Sexton, &c.*

AIR VII. Bell Chimes.

> Tim. *Neighbours all, behold with Sorrow,*
> *Whereunto we all must come;*
> *As she to-day, so we to-morrow*
> *May arrive at our long Home.*

G. Busy. Ah. poor *Dorothy Stitch!* Rest her Soul! She was the handsomest 5
Woman in all our Parish. But Beauty is but Skin deep, as the Saying is; and you
see, Neighbours, what we must all come to.

Tim. Oh, my dear Wife! my dear Wife!

Let. Oh, my dear Mother! my dear Mother!

Plough. Don't cry so, *Lettice;* you'll spoil your pretty Face. 10

Let. What's that to you?

(I. viii) 21 *matter,] Ed.;* ~ ₍ₐ₎ O   (I. ix) SD *Sexton] Ed.;* Sexton O   10 *Plough.] Ed.;*
Plou. O. *Silently regularized below: both forms occur irregularly throughout* O

Plough. 'Tis very well, Mrs. *Lettice Stitch*!

Let. So it is, Mr. *Ned Plougshshare*. I ben't afraid of your telling my Mother
now.   [*Goes from him.*

G. Busy. Good *Timothy Stitch*, don't take on so. We did not all come together, 15
nor must we all go together; and our Loss is her Gain, as we all know,
Neighbours.

Omn. Ay, ay, to be sure.

G. Busy. Since we must live by the Living, and not by the Dead, you ought to
thank Heaven, and be contented.   20

AIR VIII. Oh, oh, I've lost my Love.

Tim.   *Whom cruel Death does sever;* Hum, hum.
            Dreadful Thought! they part for ever. Hum, hum.
G. Busy.   *Yet herein still Fortune kind is,* Fara-lall.
            When one's gone, more left behind is, Tara-lall.

A poor Woman, who has lost one Husband, and is unprovided of another, has, 25
indeed, Cause enough of Grief. For tho' she be ever so much afraid to lye
alone, she can't, for very Shame, ask a Man to be her Bed-fellow.

G. Gab. Ay, ay, 'tis very true, Goody *Busy*; tho' 'tis, indeed, a very hard Case.
But Neighbour *Stitch*, here, need but ask and have.

G. Busy. She is in the Right of it. *Timothy Stitch*, we all know what a good 30
Husband you was to your last Wife. Here's Goody *Costive* herself is a Widow.
But I say no more; spare to speak, and spare to speed, all the World over.

AIR IX. *John* of *Bow*.

    Plough. *While you neglect the Living,*
           For the Dead thus grieving,
              Your Sorrows are encreas'd. 35
        Joy to slight for Anguish,
        Fondly thus to languish,
          Is fasting at a Feast.
          You well deserve
           To pine and starve, 40
     Who eat not when you may:
         Each Woman right,
         Or dull, or bright,
         Can give Delight;
          For, in the Night, 45
    Sure ev'ry Cat is Grey.

Tim. How cou'd you name another Wife to me? Where shall I find another like my First? Twenty Winters did we live in Love together, and never quarrell'd once in all our Lives.

G. Busy. What he says is very true, Neighbours; but he may thank himself for 50 that. For let her say or do whatever she wou'd, he wou'd never quarrel with her. Not but that the Woman was a very good Woman in the main.

Omn. Yes, yes; a very good Woman in the main.

G. Gab. Tho' I can't but say she had an ugly way with her, of abusing every Body. 55

G. Cost. Ay, ay; we all know that she was the greatest Scold in the Parish.

G. Gab. And that she swore like a Trooper.

G. Cost. And then she wou'd run in every Body's Debt, and pay no Body, by her Good-will;—as if she had been a Gentlewoman.

G. Busy. Yet, for all that, the Woman was a good Woman in the main. 60

Omn. O yes! a very good Woman in the main.

G. Busy. Tho' she was Proud.

G. Gab. And Lazy.

G. Cost. And Thievish.

1 *Wom.* And Impudent. 65

2 *Wom.* And Whorish.

3 *Wom.* But, above all, a sad Drunkard.

G. Gab. Ah, poor Creature! that was her Death; for we all know she died in her Drink.

G. Cost. Ah, poor Soul! we all lov'd her, to be sure; and wou'd not speak any 70 Harm of her for the World.

G. Busy. Oh, no! to be sure; for it wou'd be a wicked thing of us to speak Ill of the Dead, that cannot answer for themselves.

Gaff. Gab. O yes; a very wicked thing, to be sure. Tho' they do say it is all the Fashion in *London*; the more Shame for 'em, I think.   75

AIR X. Hunt the Squirrel.

G. Busy.   *The Gentlefolks of* London,
                   Infamy scattering,
                   Neighbours bespattering,
                   Care not who are undone,
                   But blast both Living and Dead.   80
Gaff. Gab.   *On high and low*
                   They Scandal throw:
                   Wou'd you the Reason find?
                   'Tis, 'cause they fear
                   Themselves t'appear   85
                   The worst of Humankind.

The Moon is rising, 'tis time to be going home. Let the Sexton fill up the Grave.

Tim. Let the Grave remain uncover'd; I'll take care of that; for here I mean to tarry 'till the Morning. Neighbours, I thank you all: Adieu.—I wish you well to   90
your several Homes.—Good Night.

Gaff. Gab. Stay here in the cold Church-yard all Night, with thy dead Wife!—Why, you are distracted, surely.

G. Gab. If he ben't, that were enough to make him so.

Tim. Nay, never go about to persuade me, for here I will stay, come Life,   95
come Death. Therefore, Neighbours, all go home, and leave me to my self.

AIR XI. Hey ho! who's above?

(I. ix) 94 ben't] D, W1; been't O. *See Commentary*

Gaff. Gab.	*Hey ho! the Man is mad!*	
G. Busy.	*Troth, if he is not, he's as bad.*	
Gaff. Gab.	*Thou'lt dye, ere Morning, too I fear.*	
G. Busy.	*Leave off thy Fooling, and don't stay here.*	100
Tim.	*No, no.*	
Gaff. Gab.⎫ G. Busy. ⎭	*Why, why?*	
Tim.	*I'd rather stay here with my* Dolly, *and dye.*	

G. Busy. This is the strangest Vagary, to pretend to stay here with his Wife, when she's dead; when there are so few Men who care for their Wives 105 Company, while they are alive!

Tim. My Resolution may seem stranger than it is; I will therefore tell you the Reason of it. Some time ago, my Wife was very sick (that cursed *Geneva* often made her so), then I fell sick with Grief; but she soon recovering, I recover'd too. On this Occasion, she told me, if I dy'd first, that she shou'd break her 110 Heart. Yet, she is dead, and I, hard-hearted and ungrateful Wretch, am here alive to speak it.

G. Busy. Poor Heart! he weeps like any rainy Day. But, good *Timothy*, go on with your Tale.

Tim. Let me but dry my Eyes, and then I will. She said that she had heard of 115 People that had been buried alive, and being troubled with Fits, thought, perhaps, that might be her Case.

G. Cost. Ay, ay; we all know what sort of Fits she was troubled withal—But, Mum for that.   [*Aside.*

Tim. And desir'd me, if I out-liv'd her, to let her be buried in her best 120 Cloaths, and to watch the Grave the first Night all alone, nor to let the Body be cover'd 'till the Morning. I promis'd to grant her Request, and now will keep my Word. Nay, tho' the Ghosts of all those whose Bodies have been buried here, should rise to drive me hence, I wou'd not leave the Place 'till Morning.

G. Busy. O terrible! I shake like an old Barn in a windy Day, to hear him talk 125 of it.

AIR XII. Oh that I was, and I wish that I were.

Tim.   *Darkness and Death no Fear alarms,*
          In them who Light and Life despise.
          Will Life restore her to my Arms,
            Or Light reveal her to my Eyes?
          Then Oh, that I were, and I wish that I were,
          In the cold Grave where my true Love lies.

G. Gab. This is downright Madness.

Gaff. Gab. And we shall be as mad as he, to let him have his Will. Therefore, since Persuasion won't do, Force must.

Omn. Ay, ay; let us carry him home by Force.

Gaff. Gab. Here, some of you help to hold him, while others fill up the Grave.

Tim. Hold, hold, Neighbours, and hear me speak: If you fill up the Grave, and force me hence before I have perform'd my Promise, I will never eat, drink, or sleep more.

Let. Oh dear! why that will be the Death of him.

G. Cost. To be sure.

Gaff. Gab. Nay, then I'll have no Hand in it.

G. Gab. Nor I.

G. Cost. Nor I.

G. Busy. Perhaps we may bring our selves into Trouble about it.

G. Gab. I think we are in a worse Quandary now than we were before.

G. Cost. What must we do in this Case?

G. Busy. Pray you now hear me speak.

Omn. Ay, ay, let us hear Goody *Busy* speak.

G. Cost. Ay, ay, she's a notable Woman, and a Midwife, and knows what's fit, as well as any Woman in the Parish.

G. Busy. I say it is dangerous playing with edg'd Tools—and we ought to do as we would be done by—and it is ill medling between a Man and his Wife.—And every honest Man is as good as his Word.—And the Will of the Dead ought to be perform'd.—Therefore, let us leave him to keep his Promise to his Wife.

G. Cost. Ah, dear Heart! there are not many like him. More is the Pity.

Omn. Good Night, *Timothy.* Heaven preserve you! Good Night.

Let. O my dear Father! my dear Father! let me stay with you.   160
Tim. No body shall stay with me. *Lettice*, be a good Girl, and go home.

                                                                    [*Kisses her.*

Plough. Come, you will let me lead you home, sure.
Let. No sure, but I won't. I'll have nothing to say to you, nor shall you have
any thing to do with me. My Father won't make me marry you, for he always   165
us'd to say that it was pity a good-natur'd Girl should be forc'd.

AIR XIII. The Bells shall ring.

Gaff. Gab.   *The Fair and Young, who sigh alone,*
                 Yet are still denying,
              Were Husbands all so constant grown,
                 Wou'd be more complying.   170
G. Busy.   *Priss, Cis, Sue, Marg'ry and* Nan,
                 In the Morning early,
              With us shall come, to cheer the Man,
                 Who lov'd his Wife sincerely.
Chorus.   *The Bells must ring,*   175
                 And the Clerk must sing,
              And the good old Wives must wind us.
                 You and I,
                 And all must dye,
              And leave this World behind us.   180

SCENE X.

Timothy; Dorothy *in the Grave.*

Tim. Now from the Fields the Labourers homeward go; each one to kiss his
Wife, with sweet Content. A good warm Supper, and a loving Spouse, make his
House blest as mine, while *Dolly* liv'd. My House is now like the forsaken Barn,
where the blind Howlet perches all the Day.—The open Air, cold Ground, on
which I sit, with none to talk to but the speechless Dead, is all my Comfort now.   5
I hate my own warm Thatch, Flock-bed and Neighbour's Chat, since *Dolly*, the
Flower of all my Joys, is gone.—Oh, how wretched is the State of Man!

AIR XIV. The State of Man.

 A feeble Life, with Pain began,
  Expos'd to great and numerous Woes:
 Such is the Infant State of Man,   10
  And with his Strength his Sorrow grows.
 'Till his short yet tedious Glass be run;
 Then he ends with Grief, who with Pain begun.

Dor. Oh!   [*Groans in the Grave.*
Tim. Mercy on me!—what Noise was that!—Sure I heard something.—I   15
think I did—perhaps I may hear it again—No no—nothing at all.—All is
still—It was only my Fancy.—I'll return to my Post.—
          [*Dorothy upright in the Grave.*
O dear, O dear! what can be the meaning of this! why do you frighten a Body
so?—Was I not a good Husband to you while living, and am I not performing
my Promise to you now you are Dead?—Why don't you lye still in your   20
Grave?—What is't you'd have?
Dor. Hickup—Not a Drop more,—if you love me.
Tim. It Moves—and Talks!—What will become of me?
Dor. I'm very cold.—Where am I?—Sure this is a Church-yard.—This is a
Grave too.—How came I here?   25
Tim. O dear, O dear!
Dor. Who's that!—*Timothy!*—Come, help me out.

(IX. X) SD Timothy; Dorothy *in the Grave.*] *Ed.*; Timothy. O   1 *Tim.*] *Ed.*; *not in* O
14 *Dor.*] *Ed.*; Dol. O, *which uses only the latter form in this scene, only the former in* III. xviii, xxiii.
Silently regularized below   17+ SD Dorothy] *Ed.*; Dolly O

Tim. No, I thank you, you are Dead, and a Grave is the fittest Place for you.

Dor. I don't believe that.—How came I dead!

Tim. Why you dy'd with Drinking, and was buried to-night.   30

Dor. I don't know any thing of the Matter; but, if I was dead, I am alive again.

Tim. I wish you were.

Dor. I tell you I am. Come hither and feel me. If you wou'd but feel me once, you wou'd be satisfy'd.

Tim. She was always given to lying—I dare not trust her.—Yet if she shou'd   35 be alive again—I have a good Mind to venture. [*Aside, going towards the Grave.*]—Oh, she has me, she has me!

Dor. The Devil have you for a Cowardly, Cabbaging Rogue as you are.— What, are you afraid of your own Wife, Sirrah?

Tim. Nay, now I am sure 'tis my *Dolly* herself, and alive. My dear, dear Jewel,   40 don't be angry. 'Twas only my Fear.

Dor. Yes, yes, you wou'd have had me Dead. You were only afraid I shou'd be alive again.

AIR XV. The 23d of *April*.

So unkind, and so unwilling to receive me again!

    Tim.   *To my Heart the Blood's thrilling, to hear thee complain.*   45

    Dor.   *Will you love me!*

    Tim.   *For ever.*

                Can you doubt me?

    Dor.   *No never.*

    Ambo.   *Oh the Pleasure and Pain!*   50

Dor. I've had a strange Escape! If you hadn't stay'd here, where shou'd I have been by this Time! I can't tell indeed; but I believe 'tis better as it is.

Tim. O my Dear, how can you suspect my Love? I had rather have thee again, than be Lord of the Manor.

Dor. I wou'd not forsake my *Timothy*, to be made a Lady.   55

Tim. Will you go Home with me, and love, and live in Peace; and drink no more Drams, to fright me so?

Dor. Are you as glad as you seem to be! are you willing to take me again!

(I. x)   50 Ambo.] *Ed.*; Amb. O. *See Commentary*

AIR XVI. I live in the Town of *Lynn*.

Tim.   *The Bark in Tempests tost,*
         Will the despairing Crew   60
         Land on some unexpected Coast?
Dor.   *Ay marry, and thank you too.*
         The Maid who dreamt by Night
         Sh' had left her Love so true,
         Will she awake to him and Light?   65
Tim.   *Ay marry, and thank you too.*
         O thou art my happy Coast;
Dor.   *And thou art my Love so true!*
Tim.   *Return my Joy;*
Dor.   *Take me, late lost;*   70
Ambo.   *Ay marry, and thank you too.*

SCENE XI.

Lettice.

   Mercy on me! I'm frighten'd out of my Wits! I dropt the Company going
home, and came back again to see how my poor Father did, and, as sure as any
thing, I saw my Mother's Ghost go over the Style; and but that I know that my
Father's Alive and here, I cou'd have sworn that I had seen his too.—What
shall I do? My Father will be very angry if he shou'd know that I am here; and   5
yet I must speak to him. Father, Father!—Bless me, he is not here. I'm
frighten'd worse now than I was before. Sure he is not fallen into my Mother's
Grave. The Moon shines so directly into it, that I can see him if he be. [*Looks
into the Grave, and shrieks.*] Dear, dear! there's neither Father nor Mother!—
But let me think a little.—If my Mother shou'd be Alive, after all.—Ay marry,   10
that wou'd fright me worse than seeing twenty Ghosts, for she'll force me to
marry *Ned Ploughshare.* I hate Work, Poverty and Confinement; and if I marry
him, I shall have all three.

(I. x)   70 Ambo.] *Ed.*; Amb. O

AIR XVII. As I sat at my Spinning Wheel.

How happy is that Woman's Life,
    Who, fair and free, has Wealth in store!
But oh, how wretched is the Wife,
    That's doom'd to Work, and still be Poor:
To wash, to brew, to card or reel
Or still to turn the Spinning Wheel?

15

SCENE XII.

Sir John, Jonathan, *and* Lettice.

Jon. Sir, you may be as merry as you please with my Cowardice, but I think still we had better have kept on our Horses Backs, and have ventur'd our Necks thro' the Sloughs, than to have come thro' this plaguy Church-yard at this time o' th' Night.

Sir John. Ha, ha, ha!—what, you're afraid of the Dead?

5

Jon. I don't like their Company.—Ah, Laud, a Ghost, a Ghost!

Sir John. Get up, you Cowardly Rascal, or—

Jon. O dear Sir, I can't, I can't. I'm frighten'd to Death.

Sir John. Nay, if that be the Case—you, and the Ghost, if there be one, may be better acquainted presently. I'll not spoil good Company. Farewel.   10

Jon. O Lud, that's worse than t'other. Pray don't leave me, and I will get up.

Sir John. Sure this Fellow's Folly has infected me too; for I think I see some body yonder in White.—Take your Hands from before your Eyes, you Dog, or I'll cut 'em off.

Jon. I will, I will.—O dear, dear Sir, there 'tis again.   15

Sir John. Cease your Impertinence, you Puppy, and let us observe it. It seems to me to be a Woman; if so, she must be in Distress. I'll go and speak to her.

Jon. O dear Sir, don't offer it. 'Tis certainly the Devil, who knowing your Constitution, has turn'd himself into this Shape, on purpose to draw you into his Clutches.   20

Sir John. Away, Fool.   [*Goes to her.*

Jon. Poor Sir *John!*—Poor *Jonathan!*—When the Devil has run away with the Whore-master, what will become of the Pimp! I have follow'd this Master of mine to the Devil, and there will leave him, to go the rest of his Journey with his new Acquaintance, and try to repent and save one.   25

AIR XVIII. The *Oxfordshire* Tragedy.

My Master's Pimp and Favourite too,
In Liv'ry drest of various Hue,
In wanton Pride my Days I've spent,
But now, alas, I must repent.

Methinks I do it very scurvily. If I was sure I was out of the Devil's reach now, I   30
am afraid the Remembrance of my past Sins wou'd give me more Pleasure than Pain. And now I look again, it does not appear so frightful as it did. They are very close.—My Master has it by the Hand, if it shou'd be a Woman after all— as it certainly is—I have made a fine piece of Work on't truly. Now will they strike up a Bargain without me, and I shall lose my Fee for extraordinary   35
Services, my Place as Pimp in ordinary, and my Reputation for ever.

Ay, ay, 'tis so—thus it goes.

(I. xii) 25+ AIR XVIII.] E, W1; ~ XVII. O

AIR XIX. You love and I love.

In a Man's Voice. *Charming, lovely Woman, I am in love with thee;*
In a Woman's.   *Nay Sir, pish Sir, fye Sir, sure that ne'er can be.*
In a Man's.   *You're so fair and charming,*   40
In a Woman's.   *You're so kind and free,*
Alternatively.   *You love, and I love, and you love,*
                 And I am in love with thee.

They are at it still. He palms her, she suffers it; he swears, she lies; he storms,
she yields; *Victoria, Victoria,* huzzah!   45

Sir John. I see and pity your Distress; but, unless you consent to go along with
me, how can I relieve you?

Let. O dear Sir, you are the kindest Gentleman, I shall never have it in my
Power to make you amends.

Sir John. To serve any Person in distress, much more a Woman, rewards   50
itself. And if you are but half so kind as you are fair, you'll always have it in your
Power to lay me under the greatest Obligations in the World.

Let. I don't know what you mean by that, but I shall be very willing to be
instructed, for I hate Ingratitude.

Sir John. I hope you are single, for it is a Principle with me, never to ask any   55
Favour of a married Woman. For he who pays his Liberty for a Woman,
deserves to have her to himself.

Let. Nay, for that matter, I think, the Fools that are married are fit for no body
but one another. For my part, I do, and always did, hate the Thoughts of a
Husband.   60

Sir John. The most beautiful Woman, with the best natured Principles, that
ever I met with in the whole Course of my Life.

Let. How he squeezes my Hand! I understand him—He is a fine
Gentleman.—But I must not seem too forward neither.   [*Aside.*

(I. xii)   37+ AIR XIX.] E, W1; ~ XXI. O   love . . . love] *Ed.*; Love and I Love O

AIR XX. Young I am, and yet unskill'd.

Young I am, and sore afraid: 65
Will you hurt a harmless Maid?
In this Place I fear to stay,
Fear with you to go away.
Tell me, kind Sir, tell me true,
What you will, and I must do: 70
How shall I say, Yes or No?
Can I stay, can I stay, or dare I go?

AIR XXI. Flocks are sporting.

Sir John.   *Faint denying*
                       's half-complying;
               Whilst the Strife 'twixt Love and Shame   75
                       Fans the Fire
                       Of Desire,

(I. xii)   75 *Whilst*] D, E, W1; *Whist* O

Fans the Fire
Of Desire,
'Till it crowns the Lover's Flame,   80
'Till it crowns the Lover's Flame.

Jon. What shou'd you be afraid of, Madam? If you and my Master shou'd
break a Commandment together, there's no manner of harm done; for Sir *John*
has a right to sin scot-free himself, and make his Neighbours pay for it, as he's a
Justice of Peace.   85

Let. A Justice o' Peace! O dear, I'm so afraid now that my Father should
come and spoil my Fortune.   [*Aside.*

Jon. Bear up, Sir, and I warrant we carry her off betwixt us.

Sir John. But what shall we do with her? Let us get off as fast as we can, for it
is certainly the Devil, who, knowing my Constitution, assumes this Shape, as   90
the most likely way to draw me into his Clutches.

Jon. Pox on his Memory.   [*Aside.*

Sir John. Give me leave to lead you to the Style at the end of the Church-
yard, where my Horses wait, and then—

Jon. Mount, Whip, Spur and away. Ha, Sir!   95

Let. O dear Sir!—What am I doing? Whither am I going? Well, well, carry me
where you will, and do with me what you please, for sure you are a civil
Gentleman.

AIR XXII. Once I lov'd a Charming Creature.

O shou'd wanton Fancies move you,
Shou'd you prove a naughty Man,   100
I shall think you never lov'd me;
I shall hate you—if I can.
But for my down, down, derry down,
But for my down, down, derry down.
Sir John. *Shou'd your Charming Beauty move me,*   105
'Twou'd but prove that I'm a Man.

> *You shou'd believe I better lov'd you:*
> *Try, then hate me if you can.*

Jon. *Then for her down, down, derry down,*
      Hey for her down, down, derry down.   11

The End of the First Act.

ACT II.

SCENE I.

Scene *a Grove.*

Silvia.

AIR XXIII. O the Charming Month of *May.*

> *Silent Night yields no Repose,*
> *Silent Night my Anguish knows:*
> *And the gay Morning*
> *Now returning,*
> *Only lights me to new Woes.*

Tim. within. *Only lights me to new Woes.*
Sil.   *Silent Night yields no Repose.*
Tim. within. *Silent Night yields no Repose.*

Sil. Sure Echo's grown enamour'd with my Sorrows, that thus she dwells upon the plaintive Sound.

    Tim. within. *Silent Night yields no Repose.*

Sil. Ha, this is something more! Perhaps, some wretched Maid, like me by Love undone, has chose yon gloomy Thicket to complain in; and kindly joins her sympathizing Notes with mine. I'll try again.

> *Long must I this Torture bear,*
> *Long must I love and despair;*
> *What Life denies us*
> *Death supplies us;*
> *Friendly Death, come end my Care.*

Tim. within. *Friendly Death, come end my Care.*
Sil.   *Long must I this Torture bear.*
Tim. within. *Long must I, &c.*

(II. i)   22 within.] *not in* O

Sil. It seems, indeed, the Voice of one complaining; but one of that false, deceitful Sex, which only seems unhappy, when it wou'd make ours so indeed. Perhaps some busy, prying Wretch, has stole, unheeded, on my Sorrows, and with scornful Repetitions mocks my real Woes. 25

SCENE II.

Timothy, *and* Silvia.

Tim. Forgive, fair Maid, an unhappy Man, who has wandred all the long Night, not knowing where he went, nor where to go. Tir'd with my Misery and fruitless Labour, unable to go farther, I laid me down in yonder Thicket to complain. But, hearing your Voice, I have with much Difficulty crept hither to enquire of you, after my lost Daughter; as I must of all I meet, 'till I have found 5 her.

Sil. Is it a Child you have lost!

Tim. A dearly beloved and loving Child.

Sil. That is a Loss indeed.

Tim. My Wife was buried last Night, and came to Life again, and while I 10 went home with her, my Daughter was carryed away.

Sil. Your Story's very strange.

Tim. But very true.

Sil. I only said that it was strange, not that it was not true. I have heard of People, who, seeming to be dead, have yet reviv'd. That may have been her 15 Case.

Tim. I can't tell—It may be so—My Daughter is about your Age, but not so tall—Have you heard of any such Person?

Sil. No, indeed.

Tim. She's lost for ever, and I am the most miserable Man in the World. 20

AIR XXIV. Parson upon *Dorothy*.

To love my Wife, to lose my Wife,
To find my Wife again,

(II. ii) 20+ *Dorothy*] *Ed.*; Dorothy O   (II. i) 23 *Sil.*] *not in* O

Was Peace and strife,
Was Death and Life,
Was Pleasure and was Pain.   25
In Hopes, and Fears,
In Smiles, and Tears,
Our Days inconstant flow;
But no End I see
Of my Misery,   30
Since Fortune proves my Foe.

Sil. You apprehend your Misery much greater than it is; for, if she be Virtuous, and Prudent, she will find the Means to return.

Tim. She may be kept by Force. She's very handsome—What may she not be forc'd to?   35

Sil. Fear it not. Innocence is the Care of Heaven. Virtue will give her Resolution to resist Temptation, and Strength to oppose Violence should it be offer'd: Duty will teach her such Artifices as will be sufficient to break thro' all Difficulties and Dangers, that Fraud or Force can raise to obstruct her in her Return.—How fare you, Friend? Your Colour changes, and you look not well.   40

Tim. Indeed I'm very sick, and faint.

Sil. Alas, poor Man! lend me your Arm, and let me lead you to yonder Bank; there you may repose your self a while; My Father, who lives at a Farm hard by, will soon be here, who will, I'm sure, assist you with any thing, that his poor House affords, or Power commands.   45

Tim. This Kindness to a Stranger, Heaven will reward.

Sil. Acts of Humanity reward themselves.

Tim. I give you too much Trouble.

Sil. They shew themselves unworthy of their Kind, who seeing their Fellow-Creatures in Distress, take not a Pleasure in relieving them. Are not All expos'd   50
to Time and Chance? there's oft not the distance of an Hour betwixt the height of Happiness and depth of Misery.

AIR XXV. *Polwart* on the Green.

Sil.	*The sweet and blushing Rose*
	Soon withers and decays.
Tim.	*Short are the Joys Life knows,*
	And few our happy Days.
Sil.	*The fairest Day must set in Night;*
Tim.	*Summer in Winter ends;*
Ambo.	*So Anguish still succeeds Delight,*
	And Grief on Joy attends.

SCENE III.

To them, Welford *and Servant.*

Sil. Here is my Father. A good Morning to you, Sir.—Your Blessing.

Wel. Heaven bless my Child.

Sil. Sir, here is an Object, that claims your Pity, and Assistance. An honest Man distrest; so sick and weak he is, that it would be too much trouble to him now to repeat the Tale of his Misfortunes.

Wel. 'Tis enough that you, my *Silvia*, think he needs my Pity, to command all that's in my Power. Come, Friend, accept of this Lad to guide and assist you— I'll follow presently—you shall find a hearty welcome, and all the Assistance I, or my Family, can lend you.

Tim. With many Thanks I accept your Kindness.

SCENE IV.

Welford *and* Silvia.

Wel. Silvia, your Lover tarried late last Night—I have not seen you since till now. Nay, never blush, and turn away—he proposed Marriage, did he not?

Sil. O Father, why did you ever suffer him to talk of Love, or me to hear him?

Wel. There is no Shame in virtuous Love. The most modest Virgin may hear, and may return it too, without a Blush.

Sil. Oh!

Wel. Why weeps my Child? What mean these Sighs, and all these Agonies of Grief, as if thy Heart would burst?

Sil. O, I have cause to weep, despair, and die; for I have heard from the Man, who swore a thousand times he lov'd me, the Man I lov'd, the Man you bid me love, such vile Proposals.—

Wel. O! I am all on Fire—say, *Silvia*, what did he propose?

Sil. What is not fit for you to hear, nor me to speak.

Wel. Then the Villain has dared to attempt thy Innocence and Virtue?

AIR XXVI. Now, now comes on the glorious Year.

> *When tempting Beauty is the Prize,*   15
> *Intemperate Youth, rash and unwise,*
> *Laws human and divine despise,*
> * Not thinking what they're doing;*
> *But did they make the Case their own,*
> *A Child, or Sister thus undone,*   20
> *With Horror struck, they sure would shun,*
> * Nor tempt such dreadful Ruin.*

Sil. Vain of his Wealth, and his superior Birth, with bold, licentious Freedom he rail'd on Marriage; then talk'd to me of Love, Enjoyment, and eternal Truth; endeavouring, by imposing on my Simplicity, to render me vile as his own Ends. 25 More he talk'd of Estates and Settlements, and I know not what; and more he would have talk'd; but I, with just Indignation fired, flew from his hated Presence.

AIR XXVII. One Evening as I lay.

Ah me! unhappy Maid,
  How wretched is my Fate?   30
Deceiv'd thus, and betray'd,
  To love where I should hate.

When Hope has fled our Breast,
  Why should Desire remain?
To rob us of our Rest,   35
  And give incessant Pain.

Wel. I will revenge thee, thou excellent Maid; I will revenge thee on him, my self, and all that ever wrong'd thee.

Sil. Alas! Sir, I want no Revenge; or if I did, what could you do against a Man so powerful?—the Attempt would prove your Ruin.—Let me not see him—let 40
him not insult me with his Presence—by that means to be secur'd from new Injuries, is all the Vengeance I desire.

Wel. He never shall, unless he comes with deep Remorse and humble Penitence to ask your Pardon, and make you Reparation.

Sil. Let him not come at all. The Man, who takes Advantage from a Maid's 45
mean Condition to attempt her Virtue, can never make her Reparation.

Wel. I fear you hate him then.

Sil. Why should you fear it? You methinks should wish it rather. 'Twas long before my Heart was taught to love him, and by the Pain his Cruelty gives me I fear 'twill be much longer ere it will learn to hate him.   50

Wel. I'll go and give Orders that Care be taken of the Stranger, and then I'll see this mighty Man, who, by a vile Abuse of his Power, has dared to wrong me thus. Thou'st Reason indeed for thy Anger; but grieve not, my *Silvia.* I can and will defend thee.

AIR XXVIII. At *Rome* there is a terrible Rout.

For our Poultry and Flocks we oft break our Repose,
To defend them from Foxes and Kites, their known Foes;   5

(II. iv) 50 ere] Wı; e're O

We our Children must guard from worse Vermin than those,
Which no Body can deny, &c.

SCENE V.

Silvia.

My Father bad me not to grieve—happy for me could I in that obey him. In all the height of his Passion he never commanded me to hate the injurious Author of my Woes. Indulgent Parent! He knows that 'tis not in my Power, and wou'dn't impose on me a Task impossible. Answer his Kindness then with equal Fortitude, and bear, without Reproach, those Ills thou canst not cure. To 5 assert the Dignity of injur'd Virtue, tho' in an humble State, be then my Care, and leave the rest to Heaven.

AIR XXIX. Fond Echo.

As wretched and mean, we despise
The Vicious, their Wealth, and high State;
The lowest, in Virtue, may rise,
'Tis Virtue alone makes us great.

10

The hoarse Peacock, tho' gaudy and gay,
  Sweeps the Earth with his Train, tho' so bright;
While the Lark, in his humble Array,
  Soars warbling to Regions of Light.   15

SCENE VI.

A Room in Sir John's *House.*

Enter Betty.

Sir *John* lies beyond his usual Hour—he likes his new Bed-fellow. O the
Impudence of some People!—Here, in his own House—under my Nose, as
'twere—to bring his Trollops. Nay, to oblige me to wait upon her too—warm
the Bed for 'em!—What, make a Bawd of me?—O, I could fire the House, to
be made a Bawd of at these Years. The impudent Creature too—to lie with a
Man the first time he ask'd her.—I wonder Sir *John* isn't asham'd of himself!—
to take up with such a forward Drab—At first, I'm sure, he did not find me so
easy.—Well, I've been a Fool;—but, if it was to do again—

AIR XXX. Young *Philander* woo'd me long.

(II.vi) 1 O *includes speech-heading:* Betty.

Harmless Maids, of Men beware,
  When they're tempting you to Evil;   10
Tho' their Flatt'ries charm the Ear,
  To be forsaken is the Devil.
Un-wed, ne'er consent to do it;
  Trust no false designing Fellow:
Virgins pluckt, like other Fruit,   15
  Lose their Relish, and grow mellow.

SCENE VII.

To her, Jonathan.

Betty. O *Jonathan*! Sir *John* is a barbarous Man to me; but you remember, I hope, before you know what passed, you bid me fear nothing, for you were ready to marry me at any time.

Jon. Ay, ay, very likely, Child. But did Sir *John* promise nothing, before you know what pass'd, but what he has since perform'd?   5

Betty. Yes, he did, to be sure.—He promis'd to love me always. But, what o'that? if he be a Gentleman, and above keeping his Word, I hope that it is no Shame for poor People to be honest?

Jon. The greatest in the World, Child. Why, it would be down-right Impudence in us to pretend to be wiser than our Betters. Besides, you are mine   10 o' course, and must not pretend to talk of Terms now.—I have an equal Right to my Master's cast Cloaths and Mistresses.—You are part of my Perquisites.

AIR XXXI. Great Lord *Frog*, and Lady *Mouse*.

At Table thus my Master feeds;
'Till he has done, I look on;

When the Second Course succeeds,   15
     The first is left, like you.

As I in Love my Master serve,
     Sure, I don't so ill deserve,
Tho' enough remains, to starve?
     I seize you as my Due.   20

Betty. O *Jonathan,* sure you won't use me as my Master has done!

Jon. I can't tell; I'll use you as well as I can; perhaps you may have no reason to repent of the Exchange.

Betty. Because I've been my Master's Fool, do you think I'll be yours?

Jon. Yes.   25

Betty. You're Impudent, and—

Jon. You like me the better for't.

Betty. Now I'm down-right angry with you.

AIR XXXII. Dear *Pickaninny.*

Betty.   *Be gone, Sir, and fly me.*
Jon.   *How can you deny me?*   3
          Be kind, and once try me.
Betty.   *Ne'er talk of it more.*
Jon.   *Come, grant my Desire.*
Betty.   *I your Rudeness admire.*
Jon.   *To your Chamber retire.*   3
Betty.   *Sir, there is the Door.*

[They sing the following Stanza together.]

Jon.   *Come, grant my Desire.*
Betty.   *I'll not grant your Desire.*
Jon.   *I your Beauty admire.*
Betty.   *I your Rudeness admire.*   4
Jon.   *To your Chamber retire.*
Betty.   *By your self, pray, retire.*
Jon.   *Love, there is the Door.*
Betty.   *Sir, there is the Door.*

[Exit *Betty,* on one Side, shutting the Door upon *Jonathan,* who goes off on the other.

SCENE VIII.

Lettice.

AIR XXXIII. Mrs. *Le Gard's* Dance in *Perseus* and *Andromeda.*

When youthful May *adorns the Year,*
The Earth is gay, the Heav'ns are clear,
And the long Days scarce yield to Night:
The Groves with Vernal Musick ring,
Beneath our Feet fresh Odours spring,   5
All Nature revels in Delight:
In Life, Youth is the Bloom of May;
We laugh, we sing, we sport, we play;
And every rolling Hour supplies,
Some new, and some untasted Joys,   10
And all the various Scenes are bright.

How fine I am? All over Lace, and Holland, and Silk, and Silver!—How
pretty I look, too! Nay, I always thought my self too good for a Taylor's
Daughter. And since I find what my Favours are worth, I'll be cunning, and get
as much for 'em as I can, that I may never work, nor be poor again.   15

SCENE IX.

To her, Sir John.

Sir John. Don't you wonder at your own Beauty? Dress'd, or Undress'd,
Night, or Day, you're always charming.

Let. Let me alone: Why do you stare upon a Body so? I can't bear to see you, I
am so asham'd.

Sir John. Kind Innocent, yet charming Creature, that has the Art to please   5
beyond all her Sex, that I ever knew, yet seems to know nothing of it. Last
Night—ye wanton Rogue—

Let. Oh! you're a sad Man.

(II. viii) 1 O *includes speech-heading:* Let.   12 O *includes speech-heading:* Let.

AIR XXXIV. Alas! what mean I, foolish Maid?

O fye! how could you serve me so?
You naughty Man, pray, let me go,
That from you I may run;
But should I go, I fear 'twere vain,
For soon I should return again,
To be by you undone.

Sir John. Never were Tempers better suited. This Girl is as much a Libertine in the Affairs of Love, as my self; only she don't seem so well acquainted with her own Constitution, as to be able to give any Account of the Matter.—It's pure Nature in her; like some lucky Quacks, who, tho' they know nothing of the Theory, yet practise with surprizing Success.

AIR XXXV. Musing, I late on *Windsor* Terras sate.

The lovely, blooming Creature,   20
Charming in ev'ry Feature;
    Loving, moving,
    Joys improving,
When she yields to Nature:
But O! the pleasing Smart,   25
That thrills thro' ev'ry Part,
    When possessing,
    Kissing, pressing,
Passion's improv'd by Art.

SCENE X.

To them, Jonathan.

Jon. Sir, your Honour's Tenant, Farmer *Welford*, is come to wait upon you.
Sir John. Ha! I might well expect him, indeed—I am strangely shock'd.—Yet
I must see him.—Tell him, I am coming down.

SCENE XI.

Sir John *and* Lettice.

Sir John. My Dear, my Affairs force me to leave you for the present; in the
mean time my Servants shall attend you—Your Servants they are now, and as
such command them.
Let. But, will they obey me?
Sir John. Ay, or you shall change them for such as will.   5
Let. Then I shall be a Mistress indeed.
Sir John. Thou art the Mistress of my Life and Fortune; for a Moment, dear
Creature, farewel.
Let. Dear Sir, good by t'ye.

SCENE XII.

Lettice.

I'm now a Lady indeed. A fine House, fine Cloaths, and Servants to
command. And this Sir *John* is the finest, handsomest Gentleman.—Not that I
care for him, any more than I should for any Body else, that would but make a

Gentlewoman of me. But I must take care never to let him know that, for it is
for my Interest that he should love me. Besides, now I am a Gentlewoman, I 5
find, I should like mightily to be admir'd by every body, and care for no body.

AIR XXXVI. When *Cloe* we ply.

> *We Women appear*
> *Now kind, now severe,*
> *As Interest for either doth call;*
> *If we stay, and comply,*
> *If we fly, and deny,*
> *It is all Artifice, all; 'tis Artifice, Artifice all.* 10

SCENE XIII.

Lettice *and* Betty.

Betty. Madam, Breakfast is ready for you.

Let. Is it so, Mrs. *Minks?* but how do you know whether I am ready for that?

Betty. I suppose Sir *John* knows, Madam. He order'd me to get it ready as
soon as I could.

Let. Where is it? How did you know but that I would have had it here in my
own Chamber?

Betty. Nay, if that be all, Madam, I can soon fetch it, for that matter.

Let. Come back; where is the Wench going? You're mighty ready to obey
without Orders, and to run without being sent.

SCENE XIV.

Betty.

My Chamber!—and *Minks*!—How the aukward Trapes takes upon her already? Sir *John* acts like a Gentleman, truly.—To suffer me to be huff'd, and abus'd by this—I don't know what to call her bad enough. I'll not bear it, that's poz. I have let Farmer *Welford* know what a Life my Master leads.—That'll make pure Mischief; for he loves the Daughter so well, that he dares not 5 disoblige the Father. Ay, there's a Girl, who, tho' but the Daughter of a poor Farmer, by her Prudence in keeping the Fellows at a Distance, has as many Admirers as there are Gentlemen in the County. Upon that single Point turns the Happiness or Misery of a Woman's Life. But how few of us have the Wit to find this out 'till it is too late!   10

AIR XXXVII. Room, Room for a Rover.

Frail's the Bliss of Woman,
    Fleeting as a Shade;
While we pity no Man,
    Goddesses we're made:
If our Favours wanting,   15
    To their Wants we're kind;
Ruin'd by our granting,
    We no Favour find.
Birds, for kind complying,
    Love their Females more;   20
We're lov'd for denying,
    Scorn'd when we implore.
    While on ev'ry Tree,
Cherry, Cherry, sing the small Birds;
Terry, Terry, sing the black Birds;   25
    Happier far than we.

SCENE XV.

Another Room in Sir John's *House.*

Sir John *and* Welford.

Wel. Sir *John,* tho' from your late Behaviour I'm convinc'd that you look upon me as a Wretch, whom in the Wantonness of your Wealth and Power you may injure without Danger, yet, I must tell you, that 'tis base to wrong a poor Man, meerly because he is so; and not always so safe as you may imagine.

Sir John. I little expected such an Accusation from any Man, much less, *Welford,* from you; whatever other Faults I may have, Pride and Cruelty, I thank Heav'n, are Strangers to my Nature. If you are uneasy that your Lease is unrenew'd, the Fault is in your self, you might have had it done at any time, upon your applying to me.

Wel. It is not that which I complain of; tho' your refusing it be the Ruining me and my whole Family, yet as it is a Matter of Courtesy, not Right, you are at your Liberty.—But that is not what I now come to speak of.

Sir John. My Love of Pleasure has not so far wasted my Estate, or debauched my Principles, as to tempt me to wrong any Man, much less the Poor. The less they have a Right to, the greater Necessity there is of preserving them in the quiet Possession of that Right.

Wel. Are not our Children the best and dearest Part of our Properties? Is there a Monarch in the Universe that does not esteem an Heir to his Crown dearer than the Crown he wears? Nature is alike in all. The meanest Wretch, who daily labours for the Bread with which he feeds his poor Offspring, loves them as much as the greatest King can his.

AIR XXXVIII. On yonder high Mountain.

(II. xv.) SD *Another . . . House.*] *Ed.; not in* O. *See Commentary*

> *The powerful Law of Nature*
> *Doth Savage Tygers bind;*
> *What fierce or cruel Creature,*
> *But to its Young is kind?*
> *By Hunger strong oppress'd,*
> *They forgoe their needful Prey;*
> *Love confessing,*
> *Still caressing:*
> *Shall Man do less than they?*

25

30

Sir *John*, I have a Daughter.

Sir John. You have, a fair one.

Wel. True, she is fair; but her Beauty is her least Perfection.

Sir John. In the Bloom of Youth she hath Wisdom, Prudence, and Modesty, beyond what I have observ'd in the most venerable Old Age.

35

Wel. And to crown all, an inflexible Virtue, that sets her as much above Temptation from Flattery, Wealth, or Power, as they are beneath her true Value.

Sir John. She is, indeed, the *Phœnix* of her Sex.

Wel. 'Tis no Boasting, but modest Truth in a Father to say she is. Then where is your Judgment, or Gratitude? Have I not preferr'd you to many Gentlemen of superior Merit and Fortune, in your Addresses to my *Silvia*?

40

Sir John. I own the Obligation, and—but that I am resolv'd never to marry.

Wel. Not marry, Sir! Why 'tis a Debt due to your Ancestors—you are the Medium 'twixt them and Posterity, which in you must fail unless prevented by a prudent and timely Choice; and an ample Estate, obtain'd by their Industry, be possess'd by Strangers to their Blood.

45

Sir John. As to my Ancestors, they have had their time, as I now have mine; they liv'd to please themselves, and so will I. As to Posterity, I shall not trouble my self about what I know nothing of, and which may or may not be, notwithstanding all the Care we can take about it.

50

Wel. Since I find, what I hop'd had been only the Warmth of Youth, to be Principles with you, you are justly accountable for their Consequences.

Sir John. Notwithstanding your present Circumstances, I look upon you as a Gentleman. In your Youth, as a Soldier of Fortune, you had Opportunities of knowing the World beyond most Men; which, join'd to your good Sense and just Observation, qualifies you to give Advice the best of any Man I know. And I appeal to your own Experience, whether Marriage be not a state of Life, attended with innumerable Cares, Disappointments, and Inquietudes?

55

Wel. 'Tis true I have found it so; and you, by your living so many Years in my House in your Youth, was frequently an Eye-witness of this sad Truth: And I

60

further confess that my secret Troubles (which were the greater for being so) far exceeded all that ever were visible; but those are not essential to a married State, but might have been prevented by a more prudent Choice. But as it was, one darling Child, not only made them easy, but far o'er-paid them all. (Tho' 65 Heaven knows that Child is now my greatest Trouble.)   [*Aside.*

Sir John. It is not the Lot of every Man to be Father to a *Silvia*. The ill Conveniences of Marriage are certain, the Advantages precarious, therefore I determine to persevere in my Freedom.

AIR XXXIX. A Country Life is sweet.

> *Free from Confinement, and Strife,*   70
> *I'll plow thro' the Ocean of Life,*
> > *To seek new Delights,*
> > *Where Beauty invites,*
> *But ne'er be confin'd to a Wife.*
> > *The Man that is free,*   75
> > *Like a Vessel at Sea,*
> *After Conquest and Plunder may roam;*
> > *But when either's confin'd,*
> > *By Wife, or by Wind,*
> > *Tho' for Glory design'd,*   80
> > *No Advantage they find,*
> *But rot in the Harbour at home.*

Wel. How falsely do you reason? Lewdness is a Gulph which swallows up the Lives and Fortunes of all who venture into it. And such will be your Fate, if you pursue the Course you are now ingag'd in.   8

Sir John. I shall run the Hazard, spite of your wise Admonitions.

Wel. At your own Peril be it then. Have I suppress'd my just Resentment thus long, to expostulate with thee for this? You would be thought a Man of Humanity and Honour—was not your late villanous Attempt upon my

Daughter's Virtue a notorious Instance of both? Nay, Sir, you may start, and 90
frown, and bite your Lips, if you please,—I repeat it again, your villanous
Attempt.

Sir John. Considering who I am, and what you are, supposing I had been to
blame, 'twou'd have become you to have cloath'd your Complaints in softer
Language. 95

Wel. No Words are strong enough to express your Baseness and my Wrongs.

Sir John. Had the worst you seem to apprehend been accomplish'd—

Wel. Confound thy prophane Tongue for such a Supposition.

Sir John. Your Insolence and Outrage would tire the Patience of an Angel. Is
not your Daughter virtuous and chast as ever? 100

Wel. The Excellency of her Virtue, whom you would have ruin'd, but
aggravates thy Guilt.

Sir John. The mighty Ruin you talk of was but to have devoted my Life and
Fortune to her Pleasure, which sure was sufficient to have kept her from
Contempt, and her Beauty would still have been as much admir'd as ever. 105

Wel. After the Loss of Virtue, Beauty and Fortune, like a fair and sumptuous
Monument erected upon a bad Man's Grave, serve only to perpetuate Infamy,
and make it more extensive.

Sir John. What is it that you'd wish your Daughter?

Wel. I wish her Innocence, Peace, Fortune, with Fame on Earth, and 110
Everlasting Happiness hereafter; but you'd make them all impossible to her.

Sir John. She may still be happy.

Wel. And shall, in spite of thee. Fond Fool that I was! I thought to have made
you the happy Instrument to have advanced her to that Lustre and Rank in Life
her Merit claims; but you have render'd your self unworthy of that Happiness 115
and Honour; and notwithstanding all my Dotage on thee, you now force me to
curse the Parent that begot thee, the Womb that bore thee, and the Hour that
gave thee to the Light; for thou hast added to the Wrongs of *Silvia*, hast pierc'd
her Heart with new unthought of Sorrows—I have seen her flowing Tears,
heard her sad Sighs and soft Complaints for thy Ingratitude, unworthy as thou 120
art.

Sir John. O Welford! Father! did she weep and sigh for me? O let me fly to
throw me at her Feet! I cannot bear to hear her Sorrows told. But oh! to see
her—surely I shall die with Tenderness before her! I could not have thought
I had been so happy, or so wretched. 125

AIR XL. Draw, *Cupid*, draw.

(II. xv)   110 Fortune,] W1 (fortune); ~‸ O

Reign, Silvia, Reign;
The Rebel quits his Arms:
  Your Power's compleat,
  And I submit
To your Victorious Charms.   13
    The pleasing Pain,
    The gentle Chain,
That constant Hearts unite,
    Such Joy bestows,
    That Freedom knows   13
No such sincere Delight.

I shiver, and I burn,
I triumph, and I mourn,
    I faint, I die,
    Until I fly   14
Her Passion to return;
    But O, I fear,
    Too fierce to bear
The mighty Joy will be,
    And Love's keen Dart,   14
    Fixt in my Heart,
Prove that of Death to me.

Wel. Whither would you go?

Sir John. Whither but to *Silvia*? to *Silvia* much wrong'd, but more belov'd; to
the loving, mourning *Silvia*.   15

Wel. To what end?

Sir John. To implore her Pardon, to expell her Griefs, to vow eternal Love,
eternal Truth.

Wel. And if she consents to ratify those Vows by marrying—Ha! he starts; a
crimson Blush o'erspreads his guilty Face. Wouldst thou again abuse my fond   15

Credulity? I here renounce all Friendship with thee, and forbid all future
Converse with my *Silvia*. If by my Consent you ever see her Face again, may
Heaven renounce me; if to revenge her Wrongs and punish you, I spare my self,
may—

Sir John. O stop thy Imprecations, thou rash old Man; for know, I cannot,   160
will not live without my *Silvia*'s Sight. Unsay what thou hast sworn—I never
will again abuse my Trust—never again will I repeat my Offence.

Wel. With me you've sinn'd past all Forgiveness.

Sir John. Tho' I ever lov'd thy charming Daughter, yet till this Hour I never
knew how much. Make me not desperate, for if you do, by all the Pains I feel,   165
there's no Revenge so cruel, but I'll pursue, to make thy Misery, if possible, to
equal mine; eject thee from thy Farm; expose thee to Want, and Wretchedness,
and—

Wel. Ha, ha, ha!

Sir John. Fury and Madness! my Submission rejected! my Pains insulted!   170
and my just Resentment laugh'd at!

AIR XLI. *Gillian of Croydon.*

> *Since you despise my Power,*
> > *Tho' doubly press'd with Want and Age,*
> *I'll make you curse the fatal Hour,*
> > *You scorn'd my Love, and urg'd my Rage.*   175
> *Shall I to my Vassal bend?*
> *When the weak with the strong contend,*
> > *On his own Head he plucks the Ruin;*
> > *So I my just Revenge pursuing,*
> *Will crush you, before I end.*   180

(II. xv)   162 Offence.] D, E, W1 (of-|fence D); ~, O

AIR XLII. Heigh Boys up go we.

Wel. *In vain you storm, and threaten high;*
    He's weak, whose Cause is wrong:
    When we your boastive Power shall try,
    You'll find that Right is strong.
        A virtuous Maid,   18
        Wrong'd and betray'd,
    Shall thy Destruction prove;
        There's no Defence,
        Like Innocence,
    Nor Curse like lawless Love.   19

SCENE XVI.

Welford's *House.*

Silvia, *and* Betty.

Betty. Nay, for that matter, I've told your Father already, and he seem'd so little concern'd at it, that it put me out of all Patience. So thought I, perhaps he won't tell Mrs. *Silvia,* and just as I thought, so it happen'd; so thought I, I'll e'en go and tell Mrs. *Silvia* my self.

Sil. Oh!   [*Aside.*

Betty. Madam.

Sil. Alas!

Betty. What did you say?

Sil. Did I say any thing?

Betty. I thought you did.   1

Sil. Not that I know of. Oh! how shall I conceal my Tortures from this busy, prying Creature?   [*Aside.*

Betty. But Mrs. *Silvia,* don't you think this Sir *John* a horrible sort of Man?

Sil. All appear such to me, who fall from Virtue.

Betty. Virtue! Why he minds me no more than we do an old Sweetheart, when   1 we have got a new one.

Sil. The tiresome Impertinent! When shall I have Freedom to complain?

                                                             [*Aside.*

Betty. And then he's so fond of her—Madam must have this, and Madam must have that, and Madam must have t'other; and this isn't good enough, and that isn't fine enough, and t'other isn't rich enough for her. O it would make   20
one distracted to see it! The impudent Strumpet—I could tear her Eyes out.

AIR XLIII. Young *Corydon* and *Phillis*.

> *My Rage is past conceiving;*
> *I storm and curse my Fate,*
> *To think she's still receiving*
> *Such Wealth and Pleasures great,*   25
> *And something else, but what I dare not,*
> *What I dare not, what I dare not name.*

But our *Jonathan*, by the way, is as bad as his Master;—O there's a precious Couple of 'em!—but as I was saying, our *Jonathan*, who is Sir *John*'s Cabinet-Counsellor, says my Master loves no body from his Heart but you; and   30
therefore the best of it is, her Reign is like to be but short.

Sil. When Women do those things, for which upon Reflection they ought to hate themselves, they can't expect that Men will love them long.

Betty. Why as you say, Mrs. *Silvia*, that Woman that a, a—(I don't very well understand her tho', but I suppose that means that Sir *John* should love no body   35
but her self) [*Aside.*]—But what were you saying, Mrs. *Silvia*?

Sil. That she who parts with her Virtue, parts with the only Charm, that makes a Woman truly lovely; and she may well expect, for she deserves, to be despis'd.

Betty. She speaks plain enough now truly. [*Aside.*]—Yes, as you say, one can't   40
hate that impudent Creature too much.

Sil. If she be such, as you have describ'd her, she is miserable, and, whatever she may deserve, as such I sincerely pity her.

AIR XLIV. *Strephon*, when you see me fly.

Where can gentle Pity meet
　　So fit a Subject for her Grief?
Sure that Misery's compleat,
　　When Time, and Death yields no Relief.
Death from lesser Ills may save;
Shame extends beyond the Grave.

45

Betty. Well, I'll stay no longer; she's enough to put one out of Conceit with ones self. [*Aside.*] Mrs. *Silvia*, I hope you believe that what I have told you is nothing but the Truth.

50

Sil. Wou'd I cou'd not. [*Aside.*

Betty. But I beg you to take no manner of Notice.

Sil. You may be assured I never will. May it ever remain unknown; if they are guilty, they may yet repent; which if they do, Heaven innocent and gracious will forgive; the equally guilty World, never will; if they are innocent, what Injury shall I do, what Guilt contract, by propagating Falshood?

55

Betty. Yes, yes, as you say—besides I should be turn'd out of Doors; and you know 'twould vex a body to lose ones Place for such a, a, a—but I've told you what she is, and so, Mrs. *Silvia*, your Servant.—What a way she has of talking? She gives one such Rubs, and yet does not seem to know it neither. I don't like her; but if she does but hold her Tongue I'm safe enough. I've made a pure deal of Mischief, I don't doubt, for I'm sure she's nettled, for all her Gravity.

60

AIR XLV. A Wealthy Merchant's Son.

She who, when she'd please,
　　Finds she's mistaken,
Others Pain gives her Ease,
　　Tho' she's forsaken.

65

(II. xvi) 61 So, Mrs. *Silvia*,] *Ed.*; ~∧ ~∧ O

Since he disdains my Love,
New Beauties courting,   70
His lasting Plague I'll prove,
I'll spoil his Sporting.

SCENE XVII.

Silvia.

She's gone, the busy Impertinent is gone, whose painful Presence check'd my struggling Griefs; and now my swoln Heart, and ready Eyes, may burst with sighing, and o'erflow with Tears! O *Freeman, Freeman*! I thought thy former Baseness, thy vile Attempt upon my injur'd Honour, had giv'n me all the Pains you could inflict, or I endure; but Jealousy, that burning Caustick to a Mind   5 wounded by Love and Injuries before, to Torture adding Torture, Pain to Pain, gives Agonies never to be conceiv'd till they are felt.

AIR XLVI. Whilst I gaze on *Chloe*.

Still to sigh, to pine, and languish,
Still to weep and wish in vain,
Still to bear increasing Anguish,   10
Ever hopeless to complain!

(II. xvii) 1 O *includes speech-heading: Sil.*

Thus to Sorrow never ceasing,
  I a helpless Victim prove;
Ever full, and still increasing,
  Are the Pains of jealous Love.   15

The End of the Second Act.

(II. xvii)   *The End . . . Act.*] *Ed.; not in* O

ACT III.

SCENE I.

SCENE *A Grove.*

Silvia, Welford.

AIR XLVII. Midsummer Wish.

Sil. *When flatt'ring Love, and stern Despair,*
  At once invade the Virgin's Breast,
  The meeting Tydes raise Tempests there,
  The rolling Storm destroys her Rest.
  Bright Innocence, unerring Guide,
  Lead me where Peace serenely reigns;
  If gloomy Death her Mansions hide,
  I'll seek her there, to lose my Pains.

Wel. Still sighing!—Still in Tears!—In soft and gentle Murmurs still complaining! Yet she, innocent even in Thought of any Guilt, that might deserve a Punishment so severe, accuses not the Heavens, nor Me, nor Him,

the cruel Author of her Woes. No Storm of Rage ruffles her lovely Face; no
Thought of Vengeance swells her beating Breast; Virtue, Love, and Grief, so
amply fill her Mind, there is no Room for any ruder Guest. Never did Passion
in a Female Breast run with so deep, so strong, so smooth a Stream.   15

Sil. My Father here!

Wel. Weeping, my *Silvia*! Could'st thou think how deep thy Sorrows wound
me, I know thou would'st endeavour to subdue them.

Sil. I did not know you was so nigh.—I had not else indulg'd this Burst of
Grief: It adds to my Unhappiness, to afflict so tender, and so good a Father.   20

Wel. Thy more than Child-like Duty and Affection, thy yielding Sweetness,
and determin'd Virtue, of which each Hour you give me fresh Examples, do so
affect me, that I am torn 'twixt Joy and Wonder, Sorrow and Remorse, when-
e'er I look upon thee. I, I, wretched as I am, have contributed to all the Wrongs
you suffer.   25

Sil. My dearest Father, do not thus aggravate our common Grief; let not your
Affection for me, cause you to wrong your self. If you have permitted me to
love, and I have been deceiv'd, were not you deceiv'd too?

Wel. Indeed I was; but all shall yet be well; shortly you shall be convinced,
that he's so far unworthy of your Love, that gentle Peace and Joy shall fill your   30
Breast, and he be scorn'd at first, and soon forgot.

AIR XLVIII. How happy are young Lovers.

On some Rock, by Seas surrounded,
　Distant far from Sight of Shore;
When the shipwreck'd Wretch, confounded,
　Hears the bellowing Tempests roar;   35
Hopes of Life do then forsake him,
　When in this deplor'd Extream,
Then his own loud Shrieks awake him,
　And he finds it all a Dream.

Such are your Afflictions; and they, from their excessive Greatness, shall, like   40
some dreadful Vision, find their End.

Sil. Good Man! He knows not that all has been discover'd to me already.
[*Aside.*] Shall I deceive the best of Fathers, and by Hypocrisy make that my
Crime, which is but my Misfortune? No. Whatever Discovery you make of his
Faults, forgive me, if I say, that I must love him still. True, Virtue forbids all   45

Converse with him, and I—obey; his Crimes I hate; his Fall from Virtue I lament; his Person, tho' I never see, nor wish to see again, 'tis still certain I must ever, ever love.

AIR XLIX. One Night, when all the Village slept.

> *You happy Maids, who never knew*
>   *The Pains of constant Love,*   50
> *Be warn'd by me, and never do*
>   *The ling'ring Torture prove.*
>
> *Wisdom, here, brings no Relief,*
>   *And Resolution's vain;*
> *Opposing, we increase our Grief,*   55
>   *And faster bind the Chain.*

SCENE II.

To them, Goody Busy, *Goody* Costive,
and Goody Gabble.

G. Busy. A good Day to you, Mr. *Welford*; I have brought with me all my Neighbours, as you requested; and hearing you were here, with your Daughter, I left them at your House, and chose with Goody *Costive* and Goody *Gabble*, to come to you, that we might have the Pleasure of seeing Mrs. *Silvia*.

Wel. 'Tis kindly done of you; there is my Daughter; I'll leave you with her, 5
and go and bid your Friends welcome.—You may follow at your Leisure.

G. Busy. Do so, do so; I must have a little Talk with her. It is some Years ago since I saw her,—never since she was Christened, as I remember. It is a great

---

(III. ii) SD *To them,*] *Ed.; not in* O   *and Goody* Gabble.] *Ed.; &c.* O. *See Commentary*
7 O *begins* III.iii *with this line. See Commentary*

way, and I (Heaven help me) grow old, I don't use to be so sparing of my Visits
else.   10

SCENE III.

Silvia, *Goody* Busy, *Goody* Costive,
and Goody Gabble.

G. Busy. Dost not know me, pretty one?

Sil. I don't remember to have seen you before; but, as my Father's Friend, I
am pleased to have the Opportunity to know you now.

G. Busy. Pretty Sweetness! thou'rt grown out of my Knowledge too, to be
sure; but we have been better acquainted; I was thy Mother's Midwife.—Let 5
me see—you will be Eighteen come the Time, and not married yet! Now out
upon thy Father, for a naughty Man! it must have been his Fault, for you are so
pretty, that you must have had Offers enow.

Sil. It is soon enough to know Care and Trouble.

G. Busy. Now out upon it! we have never had any good Times since People 10
talk'd so.—Was not I young my self? and don't I know that the most
troublesome and careful Part of a Woman's Life, is from the time that she is fit
for a Husband, till she has got one? Our greatest Care and Trouble is over
then, for the Men, who seldom take any before, are bound to do it then.

AIR L. A Dame of Honour.

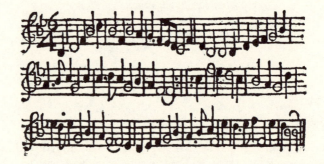

A Maid, tho' beautiful and chaste,
Like a Cypher stands alone;
Man, like a Figure, by her plac'd,
Makes her Worth and Value known.

                                                15

(III. iii) SD *and Goody* Gabble.] *Ed.; &c.* O   1 *G. Busy.* Dost] *Ed.;* —Dost O, *which runs on*
from III. ii. 10 (III. iii. 5 *in* O)

The Tyrant, Man, fast bound for Life,
To rule she takes upon her;   20
Whene'er a Maid is made a Wife,
She becomes a Dame of Honour.

G. Cost. Goody *Busy*, you are always talking to People in praise of Marriage; now I suspect you, being a Midwife, do it for your own Ends.—

G. Busy. Suppose I did, Goody *Costive*, where is the Harm of that? I am sure,   25
Times are so bad, that what with one thing, and what with another, an honest Woman, in my way of Business, can hardly get Bread; and I never expect to see it otherwise, while Matrimony is so much despised as it is; why, the Men are grown so horrible cunning, that few of them will marry at all; and the Women are grown so forward, that they won't stay till they are married.—But you are   30
melancholy, Mrs. *Silvia*.

Sil. A little thoughtful; I hope you'll excuse me.

G. Gabble. Why truly, Neighbour *Busy*, these must needs be great Hardships upon you; for no Marriages, no Lyings-in.

G. Busy. It is not that which I complain of; for, to say the Truth, I don't find   35
but that single People have as many Children as those that are married; but then they are such Infidels, as to let their Children dye without Christening, and what signifies, to the Midwife, a Lying-in, without a Christening?—I had once some Thoughts of going to *London*, but I am informed that it is worse there than here; for there are, it seems, a Number of Women who get their   40
Livelihood by being naught with any Man that will pay them for it, and yet never have any Children at all.

Sil. I can't guess what my Father designs by sending for these People.

[*Aside.*

G. Cost. Good lack-a-day! then they have no need of a Midwife, for certain.

G. Busy. No, no; the Surgeons do all their Business.   45

SCENE IV.

Silvia, *Goody* Busy, *Goody* Costive,
Goody Gabble, *and* Jonathan.

Sil. Jonathan! What comes he for?

Jon. Madam!

Sil. To me?

Jon. Yes, Madam; Sir *John Freeman*, by me, begs your Perusal of this Letter.

Sil. I am sorry Sir *John* has given himself the Trouble, since I am under the   5
Necessity of refusing it.

Jon. My Master commanded me to tell you, that it concern'd the Happiness of your Father.

(III. iii)   **34** Lyings-in] Wı (lyings-in); Lyings-|Inn O. *See Commentary*

Sil. Since such is the Case, I'll this Instant to my Father, and acquaint him of this important Letter—wait you here my Return.   10

SCENE V.

Jonathan, *Goody* Busy, *Goody* Costive, *and Goody* Gabble.

Jon. Well, she's an agreeable Lady, faith. I wonder what Sir *John* means, by employing me in this Affair? If his Design be honourable, he knows I can be of no manner of use to him, 'tis quite out of my way; and if he has any other Thoughts of her, he has less Sense than I imagin'd he had—But who have we here! my old Acquaintance, and former Neighbour, Goody *Busy*!   5

G. Busy. Bless me; Mr. *Jonathan*! is it you! why you are strangely grown; almost out of my Knowledge. But I am glad to see thee, with all my Heart.

Jon. I beg your Pardon, but I must salute you.

G. Busy. 'Tis what we are us'd to at Christenings.—Pray let it go round.

Jon. With all my Heart.   [*Kisses the rest.* 10

G. Cost. A pretty civil young Man truly. I have known some squeamish ill-bred Fellows, refuse to do their Duty by a Woman, because she was in Years.

G. Busy. But where hast been all this while; and what Business dost follow?

Jon. As you see, I serve a Gentleman.

G. Busy. Are you Married?   15

Jon. My Master is a single Man, and won't keep any Body that is married in his Family.

G. Busy. Ay, Shame take these Gentlefolks; they would have every Body as bad as themselves. That must be a sad House, that has never an honest Woman in it.   20

Jon. We live as they do in most Batchelors Families, very lovingly. While my Master is entertaining the House-keeper in his Chamber, I am as civil to the Cook-maid in the Garret.

G. Busy. O sad, O sad! what pity it is that young Men should spend their Time unfruitfully with naughty Women; when, were they honestly married,   25
they might in a lawful way do much good in their Generation. If you have any Thoughts of Marriage, I have a Widow in my Eye, that would do very well for you. She has something to bring you to, and is under Thirty I assure you. While her Husband was in Health, she brought him a Child every Year; but I don't know how it fell out, he grew weary of her, and, as it is suppos'd, thought to   30
have kill'd her with Kindness: but as it always happens in those Cases, he did his own Business instead of hers, he fell into a Consumption—and dy'd about a Month ago.

Jon. No, Goody *Busy*, that will never do for me; a wanton young Widow for a Wife, and a skittish Horse for a long Journey, are two the most troublesome 35 things a Man can meet withal.

G. Busy. Perhaps you would rather have a Maid. Truly they are ticklish things, and I don't much care to meddle or make with 'em. But I do know of a Farmer's Daughter, that will fit you to a Hair. Her Father is a sufficient Man, and will stock a Farm for you. 'Tis true, indeed, she has had one Child; for I am 40 a Woman of Integrity, and would not deceive any Body in these matters for the World. They did not marry her soon enough. But she'll make an excellent stirring Wife, I'll warrant her.

Jon. A Maid that has had a Child, is worse than a Widow that's past it. I don't like any Body that you have propos'd half so well as yourself. 45

G. Busy. Now out upon you, for an idle Pack. Why thou naughty, wanton, young Knave, what wouldst thou do with me? Heaven help me, I am old, and fit for nothing.

Jon. Let me ask you a few Questions, and you'll find you are fit for every thing. 50

G. Busy. Well, come on then.

AIR LI. Canst thou not weave Bonelace.

Jon.	*Thou canst do Housewife's Work!*	
G. Busy.	*Yea, by'r Lady, that I can.*	
Jon.	*Whip and stitch with a Jerk?*	
G. Busy.	*Yea, as well as any one.*	55
Jon.	*Canst thou not bake and brew?*	
G. Busy.	*Yea, by'r Lady, that I can.*	
Jon.	*And do the other thing too?*	
G. Busy.	*Out, you're naughty: get you gone.*	
Jon.	*Thou canst break Jests, and sing?*	60
G. Busy.	*Yea, by'r Lady, that I can.*	
Jon.	*Caper and Dance with a Spring?*	
G. Busy.	*Yea, as well as any one.*	

SCENE VI.

Welford, Silvia, Jonathan, *Goody*
Busy, *Goody* Costive, *and Goody* Gabble.

G. Busy. Come Neighbours, our Friends at Farmer *Welford*'s expect us.—
There is something of Consequence to be done; he would'n't send for us for
nothing.—A Wedding, I hope; old Folks drop off apace, but if the young Ones
would Marry, and be industrious, the World might still be increasing.
         By honest Love alone the World's upheld,   5
         Death can't destroy so fast, as Love can build.

SCENE VII.

Welford, Silvia, *and* Jonathan.

Sil. I have obtained my Father's Leave to receive the Letter you have
brought. Whether the Contents may require or deserve an Answer, I shall take
Time to consider. I have no more to say.

SCENE VIII.

Welford, *and* Silvia.

[Silvia *gives the Letter to* Welford, *who reads it.*]

Wel. See, my *Silvia*, the Picture of a Mind struggling between a Sense of
Virtue, and the Love of Vice. Yet he entreats to see thee in such Terms, as
might move weak Minds to pity him.   [*Gives her the Letter.*
Sil. If Pity be a Weakness, I am, sure, the weakest of my Sex; but yet I fear to
see him.
Wel. His base Attempt on thee, his avow'd Aversion to Marriage, and the
Ruin of the Daughter of that honest Stranger whom we entertain'd, all shew the
Justice of thy Fear.
Sil. That Men should know Vice to be an Evil, by the Pain it gives, and yet
cherish the Monster that destroys their Peace!   1
Wel. I have sworn never to expose thee to be again insulted by that licentious
Man. Yet I cannot but wish he had not render'd himself utterly unworthy of
thee. But I have given him up. You shall have ample Satisfaction for all the
Wrongs you have suffer'd.
Sil. If you can entertain a Thought of Vengeance, how are you chang'd, my 1
Father!
Wel. Hereafter thou wilt know me better.
Sil. Whither have you sent the Stranger and his Wife? whither are you going

(III. vi) SD *and Goody* Gabble.] *Ed.*; *&c.* O   (III. viii) SD Silvia] *Ed.*; Jonathan O

with the People that you sent for? O Sir, forgive my Fears. Urg'd by your Love
for me, you rush on to certain Ruin.   20
 Wel. Whatever becomes of me, you are the Care of Heaven.

SCENE IX.

Silvia.

I never knew him transported thus before. He's going to Sir *John*, and will
certainly provoke him to his Undoing. Instruct me, Heaven, what I shall do to
save him.

AIR LII. When *Flora* she had deck'd.

O gracious Heaven, lend a friendly Ray,
 To guide my Steps, in Darkness lost;   5
From Virtue's Precepts never let me stray,
 But guide me safely thro' this dreary Coast.
  My Love betray'd,
  My Duty paid,
  A spotless Maid,   10
  Let me resign
My useless Breath, into the hands of Death;
For while I live there is no Grief like mine.

SCENE X.

A Room in Sir John's *House.*
Sir John *reading at a Table.*

'Tis hard a rooted Love to dispossess;
'Tis hard, but you may do it ne'ertheless.

SCENE IX. | Silvia.] *Ed.;* O *treats this scene as a continuation of* III. viii, *adding* SD *after*
III. viii. 21: *[Exit. See Commentary* 1 O *runs on from* III. viii. 21, *and includes speech-heading:* Sil.
SCENE X.] *Ed.;* ~ IX. O

In this your Safety does consist alone:
If possible, or not, it must be done.

A Poem on a Dwarf! what strange stuff is here! Hey ho!

SCENE XI.

Sir John, *and* Betty.

Betty. There he sits, poring o'er a Book, which he no more minds, than he does me.—Sir, did you call?   [*Sir* John *throws the Book away.*

Sir John. Who's there; *Betty?* Come hither. Why you look very amiable to-day, *Betty.*

Betty. O Laud, Sir, you make me blush.

Sir John. Betty, fill me some Wine. The large Glass, and fill it up.

Betty. Yes, Sir.

Sir John. My Love to you, *Betty.*

Betty. Thank you, Sir.

Sir John. Fill your self, and pledge me.

Betty. He's coming about again, I see.—Your Health, Sir.—If he would but drink a few more Bumpers; for when he had drank most he always took most notice of me.   [*Aside.*

Sir John. Leave me; and send the Lady that came home with me last Night.

Betty. Sir, cou'd n't I—I—I—

Sir John. What is it you would say!

Betty. Why, Sir, that, that,—I don't know where to find her.

Sir John. Must I be plagu'd with your Impertinence too! go, send her to me, or leave the House your self.

Betty. O Fathers! I can't bear it! I would I could send the Devil to fetch you both.   [*Aside.*

SCENE XII.

Sir John.

AIR LIII. In *Kent,* so fam'd of old.

SCENE XI.] *Ed.;* ~ X. O   SCENE XII.] *Ed.;* ~ XI. O

In vain, in vain I rove,
Wine, Wit, and Women prove,
My Anguish to remove,
   I'm still a Lover.

And if, to ease my Pains,   5
I put on Marriage Chains,
Love, that Constraint disdains,
   Will soon be over.

SCENE XIII.

Sir John, *and* Jonathan.

Jon. Sir, I delivered your Letter to Mrs. *Silvia.*
Sir John. 'Tis well.

SCENE XIV.

Sir John, Jonathan, *and* Betty.

Sir John. You need give your self no farther Trouble to look for the Lady. I'll go and find her my self.

SCENE XV.

Jonathan, *and* Betty.

Betty. How, *Jonathan* here! This Fool loves me however. I'll divert my self, by teazing him.—So Sir.
Jon. So Madam.
Betty. Captain, methinks you look very scurvily after your last Defeat.
Jon. Now I think you look like a Dealer in Second-hand Goods, who having 5
outstood your Market, repents, and wou'd fain be turning the Penny at any rate.
Betty. Ha, ha, how vex'd he is! but it would fret any Man, who going with flying Colours to take possession of a Fort, should find the Gates shut against him.

SCENE XIII.] *Ed.*; ~ XII. O   SCENE XIV.] *Ed.*; ~ XIII. O   SCENE XV] *Ed.*;
~ XIV. O

Jon. Now you want to be attack'd, only for an Excuse to surrender. But you 1c
may keep your tottering Tenement 'till it tumbles about your Ears, for *Jonathan*.

Betty. Poor Fellow! I see he's horrible uneasy. But what Woman can deny
herself the Pleasure of tyrannizing, when she has it in her Power? To be sure,
Jonathan, you can never forget your last Disappointment.

AIR LIV. There was a Knight was drunk with Wine.

> *He seiz'd the Lass, trembling all o'er,*
> *On storming bent, no Doubt, Sir;*
> *But she slipt herself within the Door,*
> *And the Fool was shut without, Sir.*   1

Jon. *But soon repents she e'er said Nay,*
> *And finds herself the Fool, Sir.*   2
> *For she that wou'd not when she may,*
> *She shall not when she wou'd, Sir.*   [Going.

Betty. But *Jonathan, Jonathan.*

Jon. *But she that wou'd not when she may,*
> *She shall not when she wou'd, Sir.*

Betty. Sure you be'nt in Earnest.   2

Jon. *But she that wou'd not when she may,*
> *She shall not when she wou'd, Sir.*

SCENE XVI.

Betty.

O the impudent, pert, conceited Puppy! to leave me before he has had me!
why he's worse than Sir *John*. I am like to have a fine time on't truly, between
'em both!

AIR LV. The Sun was just setting.

SCENE XVI.] *Ed.;* ~XV. O   1 O *includes speech-heading: Betty.*

How kind was I us'd, ere this Lettice *came here!*
But to be refus'd, sure no Woman can bear.   5
By the Master forsaken, I'm scorn'd by the Man;
How was I mistaken in trusting Sir John?
    For he kiss'd me, I grumbl'd,
    He press'd me, I stumbl'd,
    He push'd me, I tumbl'd,   10
     But still he push'd on.

But since that Slut's coming I'm left and undone.
But since, &c.
   But if I don't plague him for serving me so,
   May I be worse tumbl'd, worse push'd, and worse jumbl'd,   15
   Where-ever, where-ever I go.

SCENE XVII.

Another Room in Sir John's *House.*

Sir John, Timothy, Ploughshare, *and* Dorothy.

Sir John. Perhaps it mayn't be agreeable to the Lady, to be expos'd to gratify your Curiosity.

Tim. Sir, the Happiness of our Lives depends on finding our Child. And, as we are inform'd, she is here.

SCENE XVIII.

Sir John, Timothy, Ploughshare,
Dorothy, *and* Lettice *Singing.*

Let. My Father, Mother, and *Ploughshare* here! What will become of me!
Sir John. Stay, Child; whither are you going?

Let. O dear, dear Sir;—

Tim. Ay, here she is; and no doubt but all the rest we have been told is as true.

Plough. Ah *Lettice, Lettice*, what have you been doing? You've spun a fine Thread truly. We shall have the whole Parish ring of you shortly.

Tim. O Child, you'll break my Heart.

Dor. Will she? but I'll break her Neck first.

Let. O dear Sir *John*, save me, save me, or I shall be torn to Pieces.

Plough. How-fine the Slut is! and how familiar with the Justice!

Dor. Ay, ay, 'tis certainly so. Oh you impudent Carrion, I'll be the Death of you.

Tim. To find my Girl ruin'd, is worse than never to have found her at all.

AIR LVI. Hear me weep and wail.

> Welcome endless *Grief*,
>> Farewell my Goose and Sheers forever, ever.
>> Can I find Relief? No never, never.
>> For Grief, from Shame arising,
>> New Pains is still devising:
>>> All Arts must fail,
>>> Distraction prevail,
>> My Brain 'tis now surprizing—prizing.

Sir John. Friends, have Patience. What's past can't be recall'd, but I'm ready to make you any Satisfaction that's in my Power.

Dor. Look ye, Sir, you have utterly ruin'd the Wench. The Blame and Shame must now fall all upon her own Head; whereas, had she been married, you know 'twou'd have fall'n upon her Husband's.

Plough. But who do you think will have her now?

AIR LVII. Send home my long-stray'd Eyes.

Cou'd you return her true and chaste,
I'd meet her with a Bridegroom's Haste;
But since, from you, she's learn'd such Ill,
     To hate her Spouse,
     Or arm his Brows,
Keep her, for me, Sir, keep her still.   30

Let. O dear! what must I do? My Father will break his Heart; my Mother will 35
beat my Brains out; and that Monster, *Ned Ploughshare*, will make me the May-
game of the whole Parish.

Plough. Don't call me Monster: I'm none of your Husband: So keep your
Tongue to your Self.

Let. I won't, 'tis all along of you that this has happen'd. You always knew that 40
I hated you, and yet you would have had me, whether I would or no.

Dor. Yes, Hussy, he would have made an honest Woman of you; but you must
be a Gentlewoman, must you?

AIR LVIII. A Nymph of the Plain.

So true, and so kind,
To whate'er you inclin'd,
To whate'er you inclin'd,
He had never deny'd;
But with Joy had comply'd,
To have made you his Wife,
And obey'd all his Life;
In a manner so soft, so engaging, and sweet,
As well might perswade you his Passion to meet.

Tim. Wife, I never approv'd of your forcing the Girl's Inclinations, and now you see what it's come to.

Sir John. Friend, you seem an honest inoffensive Man, which aggravates my Remorse for having wrong'd you.

AIR LIX. Young *Philoret* and *Celia* met.

Let.	*Regard my Tears, dispel my Fears,*
	I'll ne'er offend you more.
Tim.	*The simple Groom, the Steed being gone,*
	So shuts the Stable Door.
Let.	*Pity my Pain.*
Tim.	*My Pity's vain.*
Let.	*My Folly I deplore.*
Tim.	*Fame that's lost, and Time that's past,*
	What Power can restore?
Ambo.	*Fame that's lost, and Time that's past,*
	What Power can restore?

Sir John. What good-natur'd Man, that was but a Spectator in this Scene, but must be mov'd? I thought, 'till now, the general Love of Women consistent with Generosity, Honour, and Humanity.—False and destructive Principle! By this single Act of mine, how many innocent Persons have I injur'd? The Woman, too—the Easiness with which she gave up her Honour, makes her, tho' pitied, yet despis'd, even by me, the Author of her Ruin.

SCENE XIX.

To them, Jonathan; *whispers*
Sir John.

Sir John. Ha! *Silvia* said you? Sure you mistake!
Jon. No, Sir; she's in the next Room, and desires to see you.
Sir John. Fly then, and conduct her in.—Good People, an Affair of

Consequence obliges me to beg you would leave me for the present. If you please to wait in the next Room, when that's dispatch'd, I'll send for you again. 5

SCENE XX.

Sir John *and* Silvia.

Sir John. She's here, whom most I wish to see; and yet, such is the Power of Guilt, I dare not look upon her. Could I have thought her Sight wou'd ever give me Pain?—But, like a Wretch remov'd at once from impenetrable Darkness, into the mid-day Blaze, I sicken at the cheerful Light, and fain would shun a Brightness, that glads all Eyes but mine. 5

Sil. O Sir! pardon and pity an unhappy Maid: Had Heaven requir'd me to have dy'd, to have shewn my Duty to the best of Parents, the Pain had been far less; but filial Piety commands me to live, and interpose between your Power, and the Weakness of my good, but incens'd Father.

AIR LX. I'm *Ormond* the Brave.

Your heaviest Resentment, ah! let me, let me bear.
   In Pity to his Age, my reverend Father spare:
Toil, Want, and all you can inflict, I will not shun;
   But when I think that he may be, for wretched me, undone,
      Oh, oh!

SCENE XXI.
Sir John, Silvia, *and* Welford.

Wel. O *Silvia*! Never, 'till now, had I Cause to blush for any Act of thine.— Rise, nor offer that Incense to an Idol, which Heaven alone is worthy of, and which, were he not lost to Shame, as well as Honour, he must blush to receive.

SCENE XX.] *Ed.*; ~ XIX. O   SCENE XXI.] *Ed.*; ~XX. O   SD *and*] D, E; AND W1;
amd O

Sil. Condemn me not: Can any Submission be too low to save from Ruin
such a Parent? Still let me kneel.　　　　　　　　　　　　　　　　5

Wel. Heaven, and all that's just on Earth, forbid it.

Sir John. Confounded and amaz'd, I had not Power to raise her from the
Earth.—O *Silvia!*—*Welford!*—cou'd you see my Heart! how deep my
Contrition! how sincere my Sorrow! you would no longer fear, [*To* Silvia.] nor
you be angry. [*To* Welford.] Vice, in all its genuine Deformities, I've just beheld.　10
Virtue, in all its Charms, I see in you—Receive a returning Prodigal to your
Arms; forgive, and make me happy.—Let the Priest, by honourable, holy
Marriage, give me a just Possession of thy Charms, and join me to Virtue, and
to thee, for ever.

Sil. I came to beg your Favour for my Father, not a Husband for my self. You　15
once thought me mean enough to barter my Innocence and Virtue, for your
Wealth; should I now consent to marry you, might it not be justly suspected that
my former Resentment was not from the Love of Virtue, and Contempt of
Riches, but Artifice, to make the better Terms? Virtue is Heaven's best Gift:
Nor have they more than the Appearance of it, who submit to the least　20
Imputation on their Fame, for Wealth or Power, or Love, more tempting to a
generous Mind. Think it not Pride in me, to refuse an Obligation to the Man
who would have robb'd me, of all that distinguish'd me from the vilest of my
Sex.

Sir John. To have my Love and Admiration increas'd, by what gives me　25
Despair, is a Punishment (tho' just) that's insupportable.

AIR LXI. Minuet.

With Pity, gracious Heav'n possess'd,
Taught Mortals how 'twould be address'd:
Celestial Fair,
O sooth my Care!　　　　　　　　　　　　　　　　　　　30
And, as my Heaven on Earth I view thee;
Lovely Creature,
Pride of Nature,
Teach me (like Heaven) how to wooe thee.

(III. xi)　10 angry.] *Ed.*; ~, O　　21 Wealth] *Ed.*; ~, O. *See Commentary*

Sil. I pardon, pity, and I love thee—

Sir John. O charming Sounds!—So Heaven cheers a despairing Sinner, with   35
the sweet Voice of Mercy.

Sil. But Heaven, when it pardons, appears above Reward, by conferring
Obligations. That is not in my Power.—To refuse them is, and in that I am
determined.—Farewel, for ever.—'Tis hard—but Virtue, Prudence, and my   40
Fame require it. Therefore, farewel for ever.—If your Return to Virtue be
sincere, you have a Mistress who will ne'er forsake you; but, ever blooming,
crown your Days and Nights with Joy,—when I am Dust.

Sir John. [*Falling on* Welford*'s Neck.*] O *Welford, Welford*! must I lose her? You
lov'd me once. Is there no Remains of Pity left? Can you behold me sinking, and   45
yet refuse a friendly Hand to save me?

Wel. [*Embracing him.*] Heaven forbids me not to pity, love, and in the Anguish
of my Soul, weep o'er thee, my now dearer than ever, tho' too unhappy Son.

Sir John. Did not you call me Son? O that I were! To be your Son, is all the
Happiness my Soul aspires to.   50

Wel. Too soon you'll find that Name includes the worst of Miseries, certain
Despair.—But, to the Business of my coming.

SCENE XXII.

Sir John, Silvia, Welford, Jonathan, Betty,
Goody Busy, *Goody* Costive, *Goody* Gabble,
Gaffer Gabble, *&c.*

Wel. Goody *Busy*, and the rest of my Friends who came with me, pray, walk
in. Now let all here attend and witness to the Truths I am about to utter; and
you, unhappy Youth, prepare to bear the most surprizing Change of Fortune,
like a Man.—You are not whom you seem, and whom you think your self, Sir
John Freeman, Baronet, and rightful Possessor of a fair Estate, but an innocent   5
Impostor, and Usurper of another's Right, and my unhappy Son indeed.

Sil. What can my Father mean!

G. Busy. This is the strangest Story that ever I heard of.

Sir John. Welford, to invent a Tale so vile, and so absurd, to make me despair
of *Silvia*, as being her Brother, is unworthy of your good Sense and former   10
Probity.

Wel. I will not thank you for your Assent to the Truth of what I affirm. This
excellent Lady is not my Daughter, but the much wrong'd *Angelica Freeman*, the
sole surviving Child of the late Sir *John Freeman*, and Heiress to his large
Estate.—I read Wonder and Surprize in every Face.—You look for Proofs.—   1
Goody *Busy*, you serv'd Sir *John Freeman*'s Lady, and my Wife, as Midwife.

G. Busy. That I did to be sure.

SCENE XXII.] *Ed.*; ~ XXI. O   SD *Sir* John . . . *&c.*] *Ed.*; *Sir* John, Silvia, Welford, Goody
| Busy, Goody Costive, Jonathan, Betty, *&c.* O. *See Commentary*

Wel. How many Children had each?

G. Busy. Two, a Son and a Daughter, I shall never forget it: they lay-in both times together, and your Wife nurs'd both Sir *John*'s Children. 20

Wel. All this is true; but was there any thing remarkable upon the Body of Sir *John*'s Son when born?

G. Busy. No, but yours was mark'd under the left Breast with a bunch of Grapes, the Fruit, Leaves and Stalks all in their proper Shape and Colour, as if they had been growing on the Vine. 25

Sir John. [*Opening his Breast.*] Here is the indelible Mark, visible and fair, as when the Seal of Heaven imprest it first, to distinguish the Impostor from the rightful Heir.

Wel. Too well I know it.

Sil. If this Gentleman be your Son, how could his Birth have been conceal'd 30 so long?

Wel. That—with my own Shame, I am now to discover.—My Wife, while unmarry'd, attended on the Mother of this Lady, then a Virgin, and so far was she honour'd with her Confidence, that she liv'd with her rather as a Sister or Companion than a Servant; after her Marriage to Sir *John*, and my Wife's to 35 me, the Honour of their Friendship was continu'd; for I was happy in Sir *John*'s, as my Wife was in his Lady's.—That we had the same number of Children, and of the same Age and Sex, and that my Wife was entrusted with the Care of theirs, you have heard already.—Soon after the Birth of this Lady, a War breaking out, Sir *John*, who had an honourable Post in the Army, went for 40 *Flanders*: I attended him thither, and (as I had formerly done) serv'd under him as a Voluntier.—In this our Absence, a Fever made dreadful Ravage in this part of the Country.—Of it dy'd Sir *John*'s Lady, and quickly after his Son, (who was then at my House) and my Daughter.—My Wife taking the Advantage of the Lady's Death, and our Absence, reported, that the Son who dy'd was ours; 45 and the surviving one (truly ours) was Sir *John*'s.—Our Daughter who dy'd was bury'd as his; and his, this Lady, was reputed and educated as our own—The Fraud was never so much as suspected by Sir *John*, nor any other Person, my self excepted—I indeed, by Observations, which none else had opportunity to make, soon found it out, and charg'd my Wife with it; she confess'd it, and to 50 my Shame prevail'd upon me to conceal what I could never approve.—She dy'd before Sir *John*, and never liv'd to see her Son possess'd of the Honour and Wealth, which she by such wicked Means had endeavour'd to procure for him.—Thro' Heav'n's Mercy I hope she rests in Peace. But what have been my Tortures e'er since I consented to conceal the guilty Secret!—Stung hourly 55 with Remorse, I attempted to do her Justice and conceal my Shame, by effecting a Marriage between her and my Son; but Heaven, that refus'd the imperfect Satisfaction, and condemn'd the Fraud, has, you see, made vain the

fond Attempt, nor would suffer her to receive that as another's Gift, which is
her own proper Right.   60

Sir John. And long may she enjoy it.—I have not so ill profited by her bright
Example, as to repine at a Change of Fortune, so just, and so much to the
Advantage of this wondrous Pattern of all that's excellent in Womankind.

Sil. Your Justice, and the Moderation of your Son, affects me more than
these unthought of, undesired Riches: can I ever forget your more than paternal 65
Kindness and Affection?

Wel. Spare me the Confusion, that your Goodness gives me; look not so
tenderly, nor speak so kindly, but treat me as your Injuries and my Crimes
deserve.

Sil. The Crime was another's.—Your former Tenderness and present   70
Justice, tho' to the Disadvantage of your Son, is all your own.—If you forsake
me now, I am indeed an Orphan—Riches have Snares, and Youth without a
Guide is expos'd to many Dangers—Be still my Father.

Wel. Thy own worthy Father, were he living, could never love thee more.—
But to be thy Father is impossible.   75

Sil. This is your Son.—Let me be his, and you are still my Father.

Sir John. Do I indeed behold her heavenly Face, all clad in Smiles, and
kindly bent on me? Do I indeed hear her harmonious Voice pronounce me
happy?—Or does my flatt'ring Fancy, to sooth Despair, form Images that have
no real Existence?   80

Wel. Bless her, bless her, Heaven! and as you have made her the best, make
her the happiest of her Sex.—Never did I tast Joys sincere till now.

Sil. This surprizing Discovery unmade,—had I consented to have been
yours,—the Disinterestedness of my Love and Virtue could never have been
known.—Heaven has made our Duty and our Interest one. I may now without   85
Reproach give my Hand, where before I had given my Heart.

[Betty *Weeps.*

Jon. What, in Tears, *Betty*!

Betty. What have I lost for want of reflecting sooner: I'd rather have that
Lady's Virtue, than her Beauty and Estate.

Jon. Poor Girl! Why this is to have it.—I remember on a certain Occasion I   90
made you a Promise of Marriage; if you think it worth claiming, give me your
Hand.

Betty. There it is; if you can forget what's past, you shall have no Reason to
complain of my Conduct for the future.

AIR LXII. Ah how sweet's the cooling Breeze.

(III. xxii)   91 Marriage;] W1 (marriage); ~, O

Sir John.	*Oh how sweet,*	
	All over Charms,	95
	To bless my Arms,	
	Thy generous Virtue all Vice defeating.	
Sil.	*All compleat and pure's my Joy,*	
	Without Alloy;	100
	With Transport unusual my Bosom is beating.	
Sir John.	*Dearest Treasure!*	
Sil.	*O Joy beyond measure!*	
Sir John.	*This truly is Pleasure.*	
	Ye Follies adieu.	105
Both.	*O Dearest!*	
	All compleat and pure's my Joy,	
	Without Alloy;	
	With Transport unusual my Bosom is beating.	
Sil.	*Love gently firing,*	110
	And softly inspiring,	
Sir John.	*Panting, desiring, I'll Virtue pursue.*	
Both.	*Oh Dearest!*	
	All compleat and pure's my Joy,	
	Without Alloy;	115
	White Hours approach, and the black are retreating.	

G. Busy. Ay, this is as it should be—I could even cry for Joy, to see that there is so much honest Love left in the World.

Sir John. Reclaim'd by your Virtue, and restored to Fortune by your Generosity, I hope you'll take it as a Proof of my Sincerity, that I confess my self 120 concern'd for the Distress brought upon an honest Man and his Family by my Folly.

Sil. Your Concern is just and generous, like the Man I hope ever to find you—but have I given my self to you, and not my Fortune? All is yours; dispose of it as you please.   125

Sir John. Jonathan, send *Lettice* and her Friends hither.—O Madam, the longest Life wou'd be too short to pay my Obligation.

SCENE XXIII.

Sir John, Silvia, Welford, Jonathan, Betty,
Goody Busy, *Goody* Costive, *Goody* Gabble,
Gaffer Gabble, *&c.* Timothy, Lettice, Dorothy,
and Ploughshare.

Sir John. Unhappy Girl, I wish it was in my Power to make you ample Satisfaction for the Injury I've done you; but since that is impossible, I will settle something on your Father, in Trust for you, that, managed with Prudence, may secure you from the Fears of Poverty, the Rock on which you split before.— You, Sir, I hope will continue with us.—The Farm lately Tenanted by my Father, with your Consent, Madam, I bestow on this honest Man, for the purposes before-mentioned.

Sil. And may it answer your Intentions, which if it does, we may hereafter give 'em farther Proofs of our regard for their Welfare.

Tim. Dor. Let. Heaven bless you both.

Sir John. Lettice, as I shall never see you more, take this Advice with you.— Keep this Lady's Example in view, and you may yet excell in Virtue many of your Sex, who having never err'd in the manner you have done, look on your Fault as unpardonable.—Nor shall you, *Betty*, or *Jonathan*, be forgot.

Jon. Sir, if you approve of it, *Betty* and I have resolved to take one another for better for worse.

Sir John. That I do approve it, you shall find by the handsome Provision I'll make for you.

Wel. Son, not foreseeing this happy Event, I sent for the Tenants to attend, that upon making the Discovery they might be ready to pay their Duties to this Lady, upon her taking Possession of her Estate.

Sir John. Madam, what think you of inviting 'em in, to partake of the general Joy?

Sil. By all means.

A DANCE.

AIR LXIII. *Dutch* Skipper.

SCENE XXIII.] *Ed.*; ~ XXII. O   sd *Sir* John . . . Ploughshare.] *Ed.*; *Sir* John, Silvia,
Welford, | Goody Busy, Goody Costive, *&c.* Timothy, Let-|tice, Dorothy, *&c.* O

Gaff. Gab.	*Such Virtue possessing,*
	Includes ev'ry Blessing,
	Ev'ry Blessing,
	Our mortal State can know.
Wel.	*Such bright Examples firing,*
	Each gen'rous Soul inspiring,
	Inspiring,
	We scorn the World below.
Plough.	*With Pleasure while we gaze,*
	Transform'd, our Souls we raise,
	For Virtue beheld the Mind renews.
Tim.	*.So the Sun, for ever bright,*
	Communicates his Light,
	And adorns every Object that he views.

25
30
35

CHORUS.

Since Truth to the Mind her own Likeness reflects,
Makes known our Defects, makes known our Defects;
Since Truth to the Mind her own Likeness reflects,
Let none the just Mirror despise.
What Virtue so bright but Reflection improves,
Or Folly so stubborn, but what it removes?
Reflect, be happy, and wise.

40
45

FINIS.

(III. xxiii)   25 Gab.] *Ed.*; Gabb. O

EPILOGUE.

You ever-blooming Belles, *and shining* Beaux,
Known by your forward Airs, and gawdy Cloaths;
Who, in despite of Time, *will still be Young;*
And spite of Nature, *Wits;—with lavish Tongue*
You censure or applause—still vain and loud;   5
The Leaders, and Misleaders of the Croud:
What shall we say to save our Country Maid,
Or poor Sir John, *who has your Cause betray'd?*
Our Rake *repents, and marries—tho' 'tis true,*
When Duns are pressing—so do some of you.   10
You change your State—but never change your Lives—
You wed—but leave Repentance to your Wives.
  Then Silvia, with her musty, moral Speeches,
Her Love of Honour, and Contempt of Riches,
What artful Prude, or vain Coquet can hear,   15
Whose Love is Int'rest, and whose Virtue, Fear?
But then, consider where the Nymph was bred;
She ne'er was at a Ball, *or* Masquerade;
Where lost in Crowds, and in Disguise conceal'd,
The Person's safe—the Crime alone reveal'd.   20
A Stranger she to ev'ry modish Game,
That chills the Blood, or sets it in a Flame;
When Reason's lost, and raging Passion reigns,
And the dear Pleasure proves a Hell of Pains.
At gay Assemblies she was ne'er a Guest,   25
Where murder'd Reputations make the Feast.
So unpolite—to wound another's Name,
Poor Soul!—she thought—wou'd forfeit her own Fame.
Then let her untaught Innocence attone
For Thoughts and Manners—so unlike your own.   30
  But if, remorseless, you deny Applause,
We to the Just and Fair commit our Cause;
Whose Virtues, like their Forms, spotless and bright,
Superior shine with undistinguish'd Light.
With These our Friends—Be the whole Herd our Foes   35
Of Gamesters, Rakes, Coquets and empty Beaux.

---

16 *Fear?*] *manuscript correction; punctuation in original setting inked out, but appears to have been a*
semi-colon   21 *Game,*] *manuscript correction; original setting has* ~ ∧   29 *attone*] *manuscript*
correction; original setting has: atone

London Merchant:

HISTORY

GEORGE BARNWELL.

INTRODUCTION

SOURCES

THE source of Lillo's first tragedy has never been in question. The playwright refers to the old ballad of George Barnwell in his prologue, and from the day of the first performance, when certain wits peddled reprints to the Town, copies of the ballad have been readily available to be compared with the play. However, the dramatic models that may have influenced Lillo have been more difficult to establish. Lillo consciously set out to create a new sort of play: a tragedy 'accommodated to the Circumstances of the Generality of Mankind',[1] written in prose, overtly didactic in purpose, and designed to appeal to the sympathetic emotions of his audience as a means of making effective the moral message. The construction of the play is at least unusual. Its strong assertion of a particular Protestantism and the values of mercantilism is virtually unique. Lillo's choice of a hero 'low, and familiar to Life'[2] has from the first been recognized as truly innovative. However, the playwright's characterizations, certain of his speeches, and his development of the conflict of his tragedy suggest that he was well acquainted with plays of the Restoration and Renaissance as well as the relatively new sentimental drama.

Lillo is thought to have worked on an adaptation of *Arden of Feversham* and may well have known other domestic tragedies of the Elizabethan era.[3] Middle-

---

[1] Dedication, ll. 13–14.

[2] 'Some Remarks on the Play of George Barnwell . . .', *Weekly Register*, 21 Aug. 1731; reprinted by John Loftis, ed., *Essays on the Theatre from Eighteenth Century Periodicals* (Los Angeles, 1960), p. 33.

[3] Davies (*Life*, p. xliii) reports, on the authority of the actor John Roberts, that Lillo worked on the adaptation before 1736 (see Introduction to *Arden of Feversham*). The auction catalogue which

class characters such as Mr Sealand of Steele's *The Conscious Lovers* had become comfortably established on the comic stage in Lillo's own time, and almost certainly he knew Aaron Hill's tragic domestic drama, *The Fatal Extravagance*, which 'in a manner wholly new'[4] attempts to raise 'pity for those woes . . . Which most, who hear, perhaps, too deeply, feel'.[5] In designing to move his audience with pathos, Lillo was following a tradition well established on the English stage, and in his prologue he cites Otway, Southerne, and Rowe as authors of effective tragedies in 'humbler dress'.[6] These playwrights, however, drew their characters from the upper class, even when they eschewed the tragedies of kings. Certain of the conventions of their plays are reflected in *The London Merchant* and in Lillo's other tragedies, but their significance in the study of Lillo's work is largely a matter of tone, an adjustment of dramatic emphasis summed up in Alan Downer's remark about Otway: 'If the action seems of a "certain magnitude," the emotions are domestic, and the emotions are [the playwright's] major concern.'[7] Lillo regularly focuses on private emotion, in his heroic plays as well as his domestic dramas. He does so, however, not merely to exercise his audience's capacity for feeling but to bring them to accept and act upon the moral lessons of his plays.

The ballad of George Barnwell was itself a 'moral Tale'.[8] Published as early as the mid-seventeenth century,[9] and in these early versions called 'A True History', it tells of the seduction of an apprentice, Barnwell, by Sarah Millwood, a 'gallant dainty dame' who observes that the youth is trusted with his master's money, accosts him on the street, and, after some light dalliance to which Barnwell offers no resistance, invites him to her house. Discovering there the 'joys that did abound', the hero of the ballad, unlike Lillo's Barnwell, is eager to repeat the adventure and does so many times, though Millwood's sad tales of distress ensure that his visits are expensive. Forced to run away when his master calls for a review of accounts, the lad comes to Millwood; she turns him out but quickly takes him back when she discovers that he still has money.

---

includes books sold from Lillo's library after his death suggests that he had an extensive collection of early plays (see General Introduction, p. xix).

[4] Title-page (1720), quoted by Bernbaum, p. 129.

[5] *The Fatal Extravagance*, prologue (*The Dramatic Works of Aaron Hill, Esq.* [London, 1760], i. 291). In his tragedy, in part derived from *A Yorkshire Tragedy*, Hill dramatized the downfall of a gambler, 'Nobly *will'd*' but 'Irresolute' (*Works*, i. 296), who ruins his family and loyal friend, murders his villainous creditor, and kills himself. The play was revived at Lincoln's Inn Fields in February 1730 and acted eight times before the end of the season (*London Stage, 1729–1747*, i. 38–59).

[6] ll. 14–16.   [7] p. 256.   [8] Prologue, l. 24.

[9] The ballad was reprinted by Thomas Percy, ed., *Reliques of Ancient English Ballads* (London, 1839 [1st edn. 1765, in which 'George Barnwell' was inserted between pp. 224 and 225 of vol. iii]), pp. 256–60, and by F. J. Child, ed., *English and Scottish Ballads* (Cambridge, 1858), iv. 213–27. Bishop Percy reports that he collated three old copies, printed with intermixed black-letter and roman type, and another copy in the 'Ashmole Collection at Oxford'; an old copy of the ballad is listed in the catalogue of the Bodleian Library but could not be found when I requested it. In Percy's and Child's versions the ballad includes ninety quatrains and is divided into two parts. Quotations in my discussion of the ballad follow Child.

Living with Millwood and now thoroughly luxurious in his tastes, the runaway proposes to steal money from one of his various relations. Advised by Millwood, he chooses his rich uncle, whom he visits in the country, kills, and robs. Barnwell continues his profligate life with Millwood until the stolen money is gone, when she turns on him and calls a constable. The youth escapes by going to sea, and finally feels the 'sting of conscience'. He writes to the Lord Mayor, reporting Millwood's crimes; she is tried and hanged. Barnwell meets the same fate, put to death 'For murder in Polonia', and the ballad concludes with a rephrasing of the moral with which it began: 'All youths of fair England . . . Take heed of harlots.'

Lillo expands the rather limited moral of the ballad and the cast of characters. He establishes that the action takes place in 1588, perhaps because he thought the ballad dated back to that period but very possibly in order to include Thorowgood's account of the British merchants' significant efforts to delay the Spanish Armada.[10] In his plot, he follows the main outline of the ballad, at times compressing the action, elsewhere selecting certain incidents to dramatize, and he frequently recasts the details given in his source. Barnwell's encounter with his uncle, for example, is pared down to the brief episode of the murder, preceded by a monologue that establishes the uncle's admirably Christian view of death. The final events of the tale are revised to bring the hero and the villainess to the gallows at the same time, and, of course, in London. Barnwell's affair with Millwood is dramatized in a few incidents that mark the significant stages in his downfall: the first visit to her house; his succumbing to her wiles a second time, thus signalling his inability to resist her or to reform; her rejection of him after the murder; and, in a scene which Lillo added to the printed text nearly four years after the first performances of the play, the final meeting of Barnwell and Millwood at the gallows.[11] The time scheme is carefully left vague, and Lillo's hero seems to rush directly towards disaster despite the actually episodic plotting of the play.

Barnwell himself is transformed in Lillo's reshaping and fuller definition of the characters of the ballad. Circumstances that would mark him as the instigator of his crimes are altered or eliminated. Millwood proposes sensual adventures, theft, and murder; Barnwell, ever protesting and stung by conscience, acquiesces. The morally admirable characters of the play regularly speak of Barnwell's goodness: 'Never had Youth a higher Sense of Virtue— Justly he thought, and as he thought he practised.'[12] His own words confirm this opinion of his virtuousness. However, Lillo does not portray his hero as the guiltless victim that some commentators have found him to be.[13] In altering the character of the ballad, Lillo intends to pose the situation, paralleled in two of his later plays, of the essentially virtuous man whose passions, stirred beyond control, overwhelm his better, reasoning self.[14] Barnwell is responsible for the

---

[10] I. i. 2–33.   [11] See Textual Introduction, below.
[12] III. iii. 16–17.   [13] Cf. Bernbaum, pp. 153–5.
[14] *The Christian Hero* and *Marina* (see Introductions to these plays).

actions which contradict his moral beliefs, though 'Many less virtuously disposed than [he] . . . have never fallen in the Manner he has done.'[15] The more fortunate many, of course, have not been exposed to Millwood, whose 'powerful Magick of . . . Wit and Form might betray the wisest to simple Dotage, and fire the Blood that Age had froze long since'.[16]

The temptress of the ballad might well have been taken into the play virtually unchanged, and in dramatizing Millwood's bewitching sensuality as well as her methods of manipulating Barnwell, Lillo made full use of material given in his source. But he also added new dimensions to Millwood, and in so doing he created his most original character, a complex and finally tragic figure in many ways advanced beyond her time, and for the actresses who have played her 'one of the greatest female bravura roles'[17] of the English stage. Bernbaum suggests that the playwright 'gave to Millwood almost exactly the same traits as had marked' the male villains of the few serious sentimental dramas that had preceded *The London Merchant.*[18] But many of Millwood's characteristics can surely be traced to the vixens of Restoration comedy, the Marwoods who, in angry resentment against the men who have cheated or scorned them, employ their wit and beauty in vicious scheming.[19] Indeed, in her independence, sensuality, and determination to outwit the world and all men, Millwood echoes the successful witty ladies as well as the thwarted women of Restoration comedy. That Lillo associated her with such characters seems clearly indicated by his having chosen to introduce her to his audience in a comic situation not suggested by the ballad but borrowed from *The Way of the World.*[20] Moreover, Millwood's startlingly effective self-justification of her immorality, the most remarkable element in Lillo's characterization, is rooted in part in the Hobbesian philosophy that underlies the heartless competitions of wit in the old comedies. The realistic exposure of social injustice with which Lillo permits Millwood to jar the comfortable morality of Thorowgood also includes, as McBurney notes,[21] a strong feminist element and a theory, disturbingly persuasive, of economic determinism. Undoubtedly the playwright, like his Thorowgood, had a strong sense of the social ills which Millwood catalogues in

---

[15] v. i. 34–6.

[16] IV. xvi. 63–5. Cf. the ballad (Child, iv. 222):

> So I by wiles bewitcht,
> And snar'd with fancy still,
> Had then no power to 'get' away,
> Or to withstand her will.

[17] deBoer, p. 53.   [18] p. 156.

[19] I am indebted to Prof. Peter Saccio of Dartmouth College (New Hampshire) for allowing me to read his unpublished paper tracing the development of the 'vixen' characters in Restoration and early 18th-cent. plays.

[20] I. iii. 2–3, a clear reference to Lady Wishfort in III. i of Congreve's play. McBurney (*LM*, p. xix) remarks on the probable reference to Lady Wishfort, but also suggests that Lillo's transformation of Millwood 'is prepared for by verbal echoes of' Lady Macbeth and the Cleopatras of Shakespeare and Dryden.

[21] *LM*, p. xxiv.

her defence: 'Truth is Truth, tho' from an Enemy, and spoke in Malice.'[22] It is also conceivable, as deBoer suggests, that this complication of the character of Millwood and of the moral conflict in Lillo's play resulted from the playwright's search for motivation for his villainess, characterization developed not so much for the sake of realism as to explain Millwood's avowed choice of evil as a way of life 'in the face of the overwhelming evidence daily observed by the Protestant of the logic and the material and spiritual advantages of living the upright life'.[23] The playwright's designs entailed a conflict of reason and passion, of good intentions and evil acts, centred in Barnwell and represented by the characters to whom he alternately turns. This design, in which Thorowgood exemplifiies the Christian virtues, required that Millwood be the personification of vice.[24] She is described on occasion as 'Devil', compared to 'Fiends',[25] and in the gallows scene frozen in the apostasy of despair. But such devotion to immorality and pride needed to be explained in the light of the rewards of Protestant virtue stressed in the play.

Thorowgood's character required no such elucidation. Uncharacterized in the ballad, he is developed in the play as the ideal which Barnwell deserts for Millwood, and as the touchstone of values in the play.[26] His predecessors are the worthy gentlemen of sentimental comedy. His charity and his 'tendency to think in homilies' are reiterated in the character of Barnwell's uncle.[27]

The playwright's defence of commerce, 'by mutual Benefits diffusing mutual Love from Pole to Pole'[28] and rightly rewarding its honest practitioners, is one of the strikingly original elements of the play, and no doubt, as many commentators have observed, Lillo was concerned to demonstrate the merits of his own class and to enhance its status.[29] The relationship between the play's assertion of mercantile values and its Protestant moral system is equally important to an understanding of *The London Merchant*. Millwood's sensuality is paralleled by her passion—immoral and unbusinesslike—for 'Riches, no Matter by what Means obtain'd';[30] the defence against such destructive confusion is Thorowgood's 'Method of Merchandize . . . founded in Reason, and the Nature of Things'.[31] For the playwright, certainly, and perhaps for his audience, the alternation between Barnwell's drama and Thorowgood's disquisitions on business involved no discontinuity.[32]

---

[22] IV. xviii. 45.   [23] p. 54.

[24] Nicoll (p. 121) complains that Lillo's 'characters are moulded too much on a kind of morality tradition'.

[25] e.g. IV. xiv. 3 and IV. xviii. 3; IV. xiii. 7.

[26] Lillo's 'double title . . . clearly indicates the ideal and the disastrous deviation from this ideal' (McBurney, *LM*, p. xvi).

[27] deBoer, p. 51.   [28] III. i. 7.

[29] e.g. McBurney, *LM*, p. xvi; Downer, p. 265.

[30] IV. xviii. 14.   [31] III. i. 1–4.

[32] Later audiences may well not have had the benefit of this thematic development of the drama. Editions of the play published during the last two decades of the 18th cent. purport to record passages regularly omitted in performances at the London theatres and indicate that large portions of Thorowgood's more didactic speeches and scenes were cut.

The characters of Maria, Trueman, and Millwood's eventually repentant servants were invented by the playwright. Maria's amiable if somewhat anxious obedience to her father in the question of whom she will marry suggests again the influence of Steele's *Conscious Lovers*; in the anguish she suffers for Barnwell she recalls the distraught wife of the luckless prodigal of Aaron Hill's *Fatal Extravagance* and the pathetic heroines of an earlier period, though Lillo avoids such extremes of pathos as madness and death by heartbreak.[33] Trueman is an unfallen Barnwell, a convenient sounding-board for Thorowgood, but most of all Barnwell's friend; in this he provides a significant clue to the dramatic traditions that may well have influenced Lillo's construction of *The London Merchant*.

In structure the play is something of an oddity—an amalgam of at least two older dramatic forms on which the playwright grafts his new sort of hero and story drawn from common life and his Protestant, mercantile theme. The essential shape is that of the morality debate, reminiscent of *Dr. Faustus*, a drama to which Lillo several times makes reference through verbal echoes in his lines. In the struggle for Barnwell's conscience and life, Millwood as a vice character is pitted against the voices of good, Trueman, Maria, and Thorowgood (friendship, love, and moral strength combined with mercy). However, the sequence of scenes is not developed in terms of a tense conflict within the central character. In the moral system of Lillo's play, the initial surrender to sensuality involves an all but automatic progression to the most terrible crimes. Barnwell's first sexual encounter with Millwood is followed immediately by his theft of his master's money. The playwright neither explains nor details the motivation for this progression from lust to theft; the link is inherent and assumed.[34]

This moral assumption may well account for the unusual construction of *The London Merchant*. No step-by-step progression from lust to theft to murder need be dramatized, and instead Lillo invents a series of scenes which establish and underscore the significance of Barnwell's downfall. Thus he begins his play not with his hero, nor, indeed, with exposition for his plot, but with presentations of the opposing values and attitudes of Thorowgood and Millwood. When Barnwell enters, his situation is already framed by explanation, and in the sequence of brief scenes he meets, attempts to resist, and succumbs to the sensual magic of Millwood. The rest of the play is similarly constructed until plot and comment merge in Act IV as Barnwell, repentant, joins the

---

[33] McBurney (*LM*, p. xviii) suggests that Maria 'resembles Otway's pathetic Belvidera' and that 'the tolling of the death-bell might have been the signal for a scene of fatal madness'. However, the significant aspect of Lillo's characterization is that there is no mad scene, that in evoking pathos he employs the 'natural' rather than the intensely theatrical. Nicoll (pp. 120–1) remarks that Lillo's attempt to create a telling drama 'without an undue infusion of pathetic sentiments' contrasts it with the work of 'Otway and his followers [who] had been too pathetic to secure the true tension of tragedy'.

[34] Cf. deBoer, p. 22. Millwood's servant, Lucy, offers something of a running commentary on the progression; cf. i. v. 71–3 and especially ii. xiii. 5–8.

chorus of explanation.[35] This structure does not prevent the development of considerable intensity in the scenes which frame the Barnwell episodes—the pathos of Maria, for example—and it allows an ironic juxtaposition of scenes as Barnwell's career of crime rushes ahead of the efforts of those who seek to help him. It is a quite original design for a play, if indeed it represents a calculated plan. Certain of Lillo's later plays, though less complex than *The London Merchant*, do follow similar principles of construction.[36]

In development of situation and character relations Lillo clearly borrows from another, well-tried, form of drama. 'The extravagant friendship of the two apprentices', as McBurney observes, 'can hardly be explained except in the terms of the heroic play.'[37] Barnwell's 'first offence'[38] is against friendship; it is followed by his denying, in effect, the other members of Thorowgood's household and the values they represent. The conventional conflict of love and duty is clearly reflected in the situation.[39] It is developed, however, without the complexities of the heroic drama or of a *Venice Preserv'd*, and again without the suspense of plot which hinges on the hero's vacillation between competing loyalties. Barnwell's duty and the illicit love to which he surrenders are unambiguous: 'The law of Heaven . . . requires us to govern our Passions.'[40]

A strong element of ambiguity, however, appears in the playwright's development of his play as a tragedy: the seeming confusion of fatality and personal responsibility as the effective force of the tragic action. This may be taken as evidence that the author was an uncertain craftsman or that he was less concerned about the organization of his play than with the pathos and moral significance of Barnwell's story. But the ambiguity may well stem less from inept dramaturgy than from the Protestant problem of reconciling a Calvinist principle of determinism with the concept of free will. Not only Barnwell's fateful meeting with Millwood but also his rapid downfall and inability to reform have been taken 'to indicate that he is . . . unable to control his own fate, that his destiny has been predetermined'.[41] Millwood says that she herself 'was doom'd before the World began to endless Pains'.[42] At the end of the play, it is

---

[35] This approach to Lillo's development of the play is suggested and detailed by deBoer (pp. 40–1), who further suggests (p. 41) that in passages of couplets at the ends of scenes Lillo consciously breaks the frame of dramatic reality and speaks more directly to his audience. McBurney (*FC*, p. xx) suggests that the couplets in *Fatal Curiosity* have a similar chorus-like quality. It seems more likely, however, that Lillo simply makes use of a rhetorically satisfying convention.

[36] *Fatal Curiosity*, in which the moral situation is established in the first scenes of the drama, and *Marina*, in which thematic material is set into the speeches of the central characters in the play (see Introductions to these plays).

[37] *LM*, p. xviii.   [38] V. v. 22.

[39] Downer (p. 264) and McBurney (loc. cit.) remark on this parallel with the conventional conflicts of Restoration drama, though McBurney, in stressing the parallels with Otway and implying that Maria fills a place in the 'familiar conflicts of love, honor, and friendship', rather forces the comparison.

[40] I. viii. 8–9.   [41] deBoer, pp. 22–3.

[42] V. xi. 39. The statement need not, of course, be accepted as true, given the character and situation. Maria's conclusion that 'it is just and right that Innocence should suffer; for Heaven must be just in all its ways' (IV. i. 5–6) is more persuasive but can be ascribed to her distress and the fact that she does not fully know Barnwell's situation.

strongly suggested that Barnwell was selected and manipulated by providence as an example to teach other youths to avoid his errors. On the basis of such evidence, Bernbaum sees the play as 'firmly rooted in the sentimental tradition', its tragic conclusion 'an accident to virtue', its hero free from responsibility.[43] Emmett L. Avery gives the play as an example of *Schicksalstragödie*.[44] But the assertions of fatality are contradicted, or at least qualified, by other assertions and situations in Lillo's tragedy. 'I now am,—what I've made my self',[45] Barnwell says, and Millwood's immoral life is presented as the result of a combination of social circumstances and personal choice.[46] Moreover, Lillo devotes his fifth act—not suggested in his source and a problem for those who find it extraneous and undramatic—to demonstrating the possibility of redemption through repentance and the Christian hope of mercy. In the prison scenes, Lillo makes it clear that Barnwell, himself responsible for his crimes, can escape damnation through repentance. Millwood's place in the theological scheme is similarly clarified in the gallows scene; posed beside the repentant believer, Barnwell, she—like Marlowe's Faustus—'enacts the "tragic" role of the Christian drama by dying in blasphemous despair'.[47] Certainly the scene is unambiguous in terms of traditional Christian drama. So also is the speech in which Trueman, at the end of the play, urges the audience to avoid as well as to weep for Barnwell's downfall. The dynamics of the tragedy, however, remain paradoxical.

Lillo confronted the problems of fatality and personal responsibility in writing his other tragedies, and in these plays considerably clarified the presentation of his tragic forces and their theological implications. However, with one exception these later plays failed to move his audiences in the way that Barnwell's tragedy did. To these spectators, as probably to the playwright himself, the logic of tragedy or of argument mattered less than the moral example and the evocation of feeling which lent it reality and effectiveness.[48]

PERFORMANCE AND RECEPTION

The London Merchant was first performed at Drury Lane on Tuesday, 22 June 1731.[49] Theophilus Cibber, manager of the summer company, reports that the playwright himself requested the out-of-season production of his play,

---

[43] p. 155. Nicoll (p. 121), in contrast, feels that 'there is not sufficient of that feeling of fate which marked out *The Fatal Extravagance*'.

[44] *London Stage, 1729–1747*, vol. i, p. cxliii.   [45] v. viii. 2.

[46] deBoer (p. 54) suggests that a third factor, inherent evil, also motivates Millwood's immorality. However, the inherent element is that impulsive passion, common to all men but insufficiently controlled by some, which Lillo calls 'inclination', as does Millwood at iv. xviii. 34.

[47] McBurney, *LM*, p. xxiii.

[48] Pope is reported by Joseph Spence to have said of Lillo's method in *The London Merchant*, ''Tis a quality of nature, rather than an effect of judgment, to write so movingly' (S. W. Singer, ed., *Anecdotes, Observations, and Characters of Books and Men* [London, 1820], p. 25, quoted by Malcolm Goldstein, *Pope and the Augustan Stage* [Stanford, 1958], p. 79).

[49] *London Stage, 1729–1747*.

choosing 'rather . . . it should take its fate in the summer, than run the more hazardous fate of encountering the winter critics'.[50] Lillo's ballad opera, *Silvia*, acted three times at Lincoln's Inn Fields in November 1730, had received the 'general Approbation of the Pit and Boxes' but suffered the 'Hissing and Cat-Calls . . . [of] a Set of People, who seem'd inclined to damn the whole Performance',[51] and he may well have been shy of facing a second time the audience that attended first performances during the regular season. In summer, the more sophisticated playgoers were out of town. Cibber considered *The London Merchant* to be 'almost a new species of tragedy, wrote on a very uncommon subject',[52] and seems to have looked on his production as something of a trial run, one of the few such experiments risked by either of the Theatres Royal during this period.[53]

The summer company at Drury Lane included a number of promising young actors, three of whom were Cibbers. Theophilus himself acted Barnwell, while his wife, Jane, played Maria. His sister, Charlotte Charke, just beginning her career in the theatre, was given the part of Lucy. Theophilus was perhaps an unlikely actor for the part of a hapless young apprentice. At twenty-seven and in his eleventh year in the company, he was noted for his Harlequin, fops, and braggish rogues—Pistol was the role with which he was especially identified. But like his father Colley, he regularly undertook a wide range of characters; he was at home in tragedy, had enjoyed success in serious roles, had a following among theatre-goers, and his performance in Lillo's play would certainly have engaged the audience.[54] As Maria, Jane Cibber had the advantages of her charming appearance and manner, and a special talent, singled out for praise by at least one veteran observer of acting in London, to enter so well into her character and feel the emotions so 'sensibly . . . that [a] tender Scene is really heighten'd by her manner of performing it'.[55] Mrs Charke's salary was increased from twenty to thirty shillings a week as the result of her success in the part of Lucy—evidence, perhaps, that this apparently gifted, certainly idiosyncratic, performer entered into her role with the vigour which would later

[50] Cibber, *Lives*, v. 338–9.

[51] *Daily Courant*, 12 Nov. 1730, quoted in *London Stage*, 10 Nov.

[52] *Lives*, loc. cit.   [53] *London Stage, 1729–1747*, vol. i, p. cxliii.

[54] In personal as well as theatrical qualities, Cibber was not a natural Barnwell. He was far from handsome. His reputation as a frequenter of bagnios stood in ironic contradiction to Barnwell's inexperience. However, if the reports of audience response to his production of Lillo's play are accurate, his performance must have been most effective. He continued to play Barnwell at Drury Lane until Dec. 1735, after which the tragedy was omitted from the company's repertoire for several seasons. He seems not to have carried the role with him when he moved to Covent Garden in 1739, nor during the perapatetic career which followed. (*London Stage, 1729–1747*, i. 147–538 [seasons 1730–5]; *Actors, Actresses*, iii. 242–60.)

[55] The first Mrs Theophilus Cibber (Jane Johnson) began her Drury Lane career as Selina in *The Orphan* in 1723. Her parts ranged from Margery in *The Country Wife* and Belinda in *The Man of Mode* to Galatea in *Acis and Galatea*, Melesanda in *Aureng-Zebe*, and Polyxena in *Hecuba*. It was her performance in *Hecuba* that occasioned praise in the anonymous *Reflections upon Reflections* (1726): 'she enters so justly into her Character, and feels so sensibly the Passions at parting from her Mother, that that tender Scene is really heighten'd by her manner of performing it' (*Actors, Actresses*, iii. 260).

carry her to more demanding encounters with *The London Merchant*, as Millwood and several times as Barnwell.[56] Colley Cibber did not act with the summer company. He did contribute an epilogue for Jane to speak, a conventionally shallow piece out of keeping with the tragedy but a gesture in support of the new play.

Trueman was acted by William Mills, another second-generation member of the company at Drury Lane and already well established.[57] Roger Bridgwater, young but steadily building a repertoire of character parts and heavy dramatic roles, played Thorowgood. He continued to act the role at Drury Lane until as late as 1750.[58] Millwood, who would become a favourite of later dramatic actresses, was first acted by Elizabeth Butler. In her fifth year in the company, she had established her claim to a number of choice roles in the regular repertoire, among them Alithea in *The Country Wife*, Belinda in *The Man of Mode*, Emilia in *Othello*, and Regan in *King Lear*. That her talents lent themselves well to an effective characterization of Millwood is suggested by the record of some of the roles which came to her during the next four seasons. These included Gertrude in *Hamlet*, Lady Macbeth, the title role in *Jane Shore*, and Congreve's Marwood and Mrs Frail.[59]

Theophilus Cibber reports that Lillo's play was 'very carefully got up'.[60] Certainly it was well puffed.[61] However, the efforts to promote the play nearly

---

[56] Following the première of Lillo's drama and her accompanying increase in salary, the extraordinary Mrs Charke continued to play Lucy for the 1731–2 season and in the one Drury Lane performance recorded for 1773–4. In the summer of 1734, setting up with a company at the Haymarket, she turned to a more central role: on 1 June she played Barnwell, an apparent highlight in a brief season which also saw her act Macheath, Pistol, Lothario in *The Fair Penitent*, Jack Stocks and Lovemore in *The Lottery*, the title role in *The Mock Doctor*, several other male roles, and a few female roles. Her Barnwell must have achieved some success, for she acted the part again in her benefit, on 22 Aug., 'positively the last Time of the Company's Acting this Season'. On 1 July 1735, continuing her tour through Lillo's cast of characters, she undertook Millwood, to her brother's Barnwell, at Drury Lane. Ten days later she again donned breeches to play George at Lincoln's Inn Fields (*c.* 4 July the patentee of Drury Lane had countermanded summer playing, thus cancelling an announced second performance of the Cibber–Charke production). Mrs Charke appeared as Millwood at least one more time in London (on 1 Oct. 1735 in a performance staged at the theatre in the York Buildings) and once again as Barnwell (at Fielding's Haymarket on 26 Apr. 1736, the single break in a run of *Pasquin* which lasted through the spring). It is not known if the actress played either role during her sporadic, minimally documented, forays into the provinces. Her last recorded association with *The London Merchant* brought her full circle, as Lucy in a production offered by Giffard's company (9 Nov. 1736 and possibly 8 Feb. 1737). Thereafter her interests, or at any rate her performances, shifted to *Fatal Curiosity* (see *Fatal Curiosity*, commentary on the dramatis personae). (Charke, *Life*, p. 59; *London Stage, 1729–1747*, vol. i, *passim*, ii. 613 and 637; *Actors, Actresses*, iii. 167–70.)

[57] Mills's father was the tragedian John Mills, a leading member of the company at Drury Lane (Cibber, *Apology*, p. 342).

[58] Bridgwater's character parts in the regular season, 1731–2, ranged from Banquo and the ghost of Old Hamlet to Worthy in *Greenwich Park* (*London Stage, 1729–1747*, i. 157–222, 1747–1776, i. 229; *Actors, Actresses*, ii. 334).

[59] *London Stage, 1729–1747*, i. 79–222 (seasons 1730–2); *Actors, Actresses*, ii. 450–1.

[60] Cibber, *Lives*, v. 339.

[61] In the *London Evening Post*, 15 June, and *Daily Post*, 16 and 21 June (*London Stage, 1729–1747*, i. 147). The play was originally announced as *The Merchant: or, The True History of George Barnwell*;

brought about an opening-night disaster. Someone reprinted the ballad of George Barnwell, sold copies around the Town, and 'manly gaily-disposed spirits brought the ballad with them to the play, intending to make their pleasant remarks . . . and ludicrous comparisons between the ancient ditty and modern play'.[62] Cibber's much-quoted account of the scoffers who came to laugh but stayed 'to drop their ballads and pull out their handkerchiefs' is confirmed in a review which appeared in the *Weekly Register* on 21 August, the day following the final summer performance of *The London Merchant*:

the Beginning of the first Act occasioned a Sneer in the Audience, as if 'twas impossible they should receive any delicate Pleasure from such an Entertainment; but, before the End of it, the Case was quite alter'd, and most profound Silence argued the deepest Attention, and the sincerest Pleasure imaginable.—This increas'd gradually, as the Plot advanc'd, and new Circumstances of Guilt and Distress aggravated the Concern of the Spectators . . . and I believe there was hardly a Spectator there that did not witness his Approbation by his Tears.[63]

The author of this report was openly concerned to praise the play and, like Cibber, doubtless given to exaggeration in describing its reception. Not everyone applauded the work, and some damned it for bringing to the stage characters 'so low and familiar in life'.[64] Its immediate success in the theatre, however, is indicated by the record of performances: at Drury Lane, seventeen performances during the summer and eleven during the regular season which followed.[65] Interest in the play was such that when it had been printed copies were offered for sale at the theatre.[66] Before they were ready, Queen Caroline requested a manuscript and on 2 July Robert Wilks, one of the co-managers of Drury Lane, carried the copy to Hampton Court.[67] Three days later, the newspapers reported that the play was to be acted at the palace, but the performance did not take place as plans for the theatre at Hampton Court had been delayed.[68] However, on 28 October the Drury Lane company presented *The London Merchant* 'By Their Majesties' Command' and in their presence.[69]

---

the present title was included in advertisements for the third performance (30 June). The tune to which the ballad was sung is called 'The Merchant'.

[62] Cibber, loc. cit. (McBurney, *LM*, p. xii).

[63] Reprinted by Loftis, *Essays on the Theatre* . . . , pp. 33–4.

[64] In reply to such criticism, the commentator in *The Weekly Register* remarked that ''tis the Lowness of Action, not Lowness of Character, that is not allow'd to be there; the Circumstances . . . are all of them of the utmost Importance, and rise as high in the Action, as any we shall meet with in the Stories of more Pomp and Ostentation' (Loftis, loc. cit.).

[65] *London Stage, 1729–1747*, i. 147–221. The performance on 3 Aug. 1731 was advertised as 'the last Time of Acting this Play this Season' (*Daily Post*, 3 Aug.); however, performances resumed on 11 Aug. A special benefit performance given on 21 Aug. is not included in the count for the regular season.

[66] Drury Lane advertisements on 17, 20, and 28 July (*Daily Post*) included the notice that 'Printed Books of GEORGE BARNWELL will be sold at the Theatre'.

[67] *Gentleman's Magazine*, i. 7 (July 1731), 307.

[68] Plans for performances at the palace were announced in the papers early in the summer, but no play was performed there until 18 Oct. (*London Stage, 1729–1747*, vol. i, pp. xxxvii–xxxviii, and i. 146).

[69] *London Stage, 1729–1747*.

By then a production of the play had been given at Bartholomew Fair and another at Southwark Fair, and the enterprising Henry Giffard had staged the tragedy as the initial offering of his first season as manager at Goodman's Fields.[70] Giffard presented the play eleven times before the season was out.[71] On 22 May 1732 yet another production appeared at Lincoln's Inn Fields, and on 1 June, with a performance at the New Haymarket, Lillo's tragedy completed its circuit of every theatre in London then offering plays.[72]

During the forty-five seasons following its première (1731–76), *The London Merchant* was one of the five most popular non-Shakespearian tragedies acted in London. In this regard, Lillo was overshadowed only by Otway and Rowe.[73] Yet a study of the season-by-season record of performances reveals a curious history of sporadic, highly successful revivals alternating with years in which *The London Merchant* virtually disappeared from the stage. The cycles of performances of other plays which became established as 'stock plays' were similarly irregular, often reflecting the needs and ambitions of leading actors as much as the vagaries of public taste, but with Lillo's tragedy this pattern is exaggerated.

In the season following its initial summer production, *The London Merchant* was acted constantly in London; some twenty-five performances are recorded between late September 1731 and the summer of 1732. During the next five seasons (1732–7) the play was scheduled at least as often as the most popular stock plays of the serious dramatists of the Restoration and eighteenth century.[74] However, after June 1737 *The London Merchant* seems not to have been acted at all for two years, and only one performance is recorded for the 1739–40 season. This striking change in the play's fortunes may in part relate to the illnesses and series of tumultuous personal and legal crises which at this time played havoc with Theophilus Cibber's acting schedule. More certainly it reflects the curtailment of theatrical activity which resulted from the enactment of the Licensing Act of 21 June 1737.

While *The London Merchant* was closely associated with Drury Lane, its remarkable record of performances had in large measure stemmed from

---

[70] 26 Aug. at Bartholomew Fair, 8 Sept. at Southwark Fair (*London Stage, 1729–1747*, dates noted and vol. i, p. lxxxii).

[71] *London Stage, 1729–1747*, i. 158–205.   [72] *London Stage, 1729–1747*.

[73] Only during the brief period immediately following the summer première of *The London Merchant* did the play's performance record rival those of Otway's *The Orphan* and Rowe's *Jane Shore*, the era's most popular dramas in this genre. During the earliest and latest decades of the forty-five-year period surveyed, Lillo's play was acted more often than *The Fair Penitent*, which, however, enjoyed a remarkable resurgence in popularity during the 1740s and so stands third among the stock plays of the type. Similarly, *Venice Preserv'd* ranks fourth in total number of performances, but during the first years of the period in question was not scheduled nearly as often as *The London Merchant*; during the late 1760s and early 1770s the performance records of the two plays are virtually the same. (*London Stage, 1729–1747* and *1747–1776, passim*.)

[74] *The London Merchant* was acted 33 times during the seasons 1732–7, an average of 6.6 performances per season. *Jane Shore*, by comparison, was announced an average of 5.5 times per season between 1747 and 1776, the time of the play's greatest popularity during the years surveyed. (*London Stage, 1729–1747, passim*.)

productions offered not only at the patent house but also by Henry Giffard's company at Goodman's Fields, by the occasional companies of independent actors and young hopefuls who turned up briefly at such houses as the New Haymarket and Lincoln's Inn Fields, and by the entrepreneurs of booths at fairs. Drury Lane had presented *The London Merchant* seventeen times during the seasons of 1731–7, but during the same period Giffard had offered the play some eighteen times and there had been at least nineteen performances by irregular companies.[75] Enforcement of the Licensing Act put a stop to virtually all such productions away from the patent houses.

Giffard managed to operate sporadically during 1740–2 and kept Lillo's play alive, offering six of the eight performances recorded for these seasons. His son William, who had acted Barnwell for him for two years, played the part again for two of three performances when, in 1743–4, *The London Merchant* was briefly revived at Drury Lane, which had staged the play only once since 1735.[76] For nearly five years neither of the patent houses performed the play again. William Hallam and his troupe at the New Wells in Goodman's Fields scheduled the play eight times during the seasons of 1744–6.[77] On occasion, performances turned up at fairs.[78]

In 1749 *The London Merchant* found a new place in the Drury Lane repertoire and new life on the London stage. In May a performance was scheduled as a benefit for three members of the company.[79] Perhaps this production revived interest in the play; at any rate, it was offered four times at the beginning of the new season, presented again on Boxing Day, and twice in February.[80] That a Boxing Day performance was also scheduled at Covent Garden, which had not offered the play in a decade, suggests that audiences had welcomed the revival with some enthusiasm.

During the next fifteen years, when the play was acted in London the theatre was Drury Lane, which offered *The London Merchant* as often as three times in a season, but in most years only once or twice, and in two seasons not at all. Performances by irregular companies dwindled in number, then disappeared.[81] Between 1750–1 and 1764–5 only twenty-two London performances are recorded in all, fewer than two per season.[82]

Except for performances in provincial theatres, the play might well have been forgotten, but again a London manager found the old drama useful and audiences responded. In 1765 Garrick required a suitable vehicle to inaugurate the adult acting career of Samuel Cautherly, his protégé and, very probably,

---

[75] Drury Lane performances were only five in number during the seasons 1732–6. (*London Stage, 1729–1747, passim.*)

[76] 4 June 1741.   [77] *London Stage, 1729–1747, passim.*

[78] At Southwark Fair on 27 Sept. 1742, 6 Nov. 1746; at May Fair on 6 June 1744; and at Shepherd's Market, Mayfair, on 28 Aug. 1747. (*London Stage, 1727–1747.*)

[79] 8 May 1749.   [80] *London Stage, 1729–1747, passim.*

[81] The last recorded were at the Blue Boar Inn, Holborn, on 8 Jan. 1750, and at the New Wells, Lemon Street, 20 Nov. 1753 (a benefit for Hallam). (*London Stage, 1747–1776.*)

[82] *London Stage, 1747–1776, passim.*

illegitimate son. The character of Barnwell was, of course, ideal for a young and relatively inexperienced actor; it may also have been peculiarly appropriate to the talents and capacities of Cautherly, who was generally reckoned to be handsome but not notably bright. He made his début in the role on 26 September. Although the puff report which described this event limited its praise to the actor's suitable physical appearance and the 'great simplicity' of his playing, Cautherly was well launched and Lillo's tragedy became a popular attraction for a new generation of London playgoers. Garrick's production was offered eight more times before the end of the season. It was revived only once during the next season, but in 1767–8 Covent Garden staged a new production and effectively took over the play from Drury Lane. Some twenty-eight performances of *The London Merchant* were offered at Covent Garden between 1767–8 and 1775–6; during the same seasons the play appeared fifteen times at Drury Lane.[83]

The cycle of disappearance and revival was repeated once again before the end of the century. Scheduled for two or three performances a season during the 1780s, *The London Merchant* was ignored entirely by the London theatres from 1790 to 1796. But the opportunities which the play provided for striking performances were not forgotten by the actors. Mrs Siddons had played Millwood in Liverpool as early as 1776. Established at Drury Lane, she had revived the reputations of a number of stock plays of the earlier part of the century. In November 1796, with her brother Charles Kemble as Barnwell, she appeared in a new production of *The London Merchant* and scored a triumph. The play was repeated ten times during the season and once in the following year. Thereafter, through the last years of the century, Kemble acted *The London Merchant* at least once a season, assisted by Mrs Powell as Millwood.[84]

The play persisted as a stock drama of the London theatres well into the nineteenth century.[85] Records of performances away from London are not numerous enough to indicate whether or not a continuing tradition of provincial productions influenced revivals in the capital. Dickens's references to *The London Merchant* suggest a lively familiarity with the play among his readers and a devotion to it among actors who roamed the countryside.[86] The publishers' readiness to produce new editions of the text of the play and to include it in popular collections of dramas is evidence that the enthusiasm of an audience of readers continued well past the end of the eighteenth century; an interest in

[83] *London Stage, 1747–1776, passim*; *Actors, Actresses*, iii. 121–7.

[84] *London Stage, 1776–1800, passim*. The Siddons revival was first performed on 28 Nov. 1796. Ward (p. xv) reports that Mrs Siddons selected the play because she thought it would provide an advantageous role for her brother.

[85] Henry Irving frequently played Barnwell at the Theatre Royal, Manchester, during the early years of his career. (Ward, p. xiv.)

[86] Mr Wopsle's edifying reading of George Barnwell—'at once ferocious and maudlin'—to Pip on the eve of his apprenticeship in *Great Expectations* is Dickens's best-known reference to Lillo's play. But Mr Pickwick also is given opportunity to cite the apprentice's regrettable misadventures as a cautionary example for Sam Weller (*Pickwick Papers*, ch. X). Other brief references to the play are found in *Martin Chuzzlewit* (ch. IX) and *Barnaby Rudge* (ch. IV).

seeing a play which had become familiar through reading may also have stimulated new productions in the theatre.

It has been suggested that the apparent popularity of *The London Merchant* was, to no small extent, created through the influence and financial support of persons and groups whose interest was more a matter of public morality than public entertainment.[87] The theatrical record for the years after 1735 provides virtually no support for this explanation of the play's extended if sporadic history of successful performances. Lillo's drama was scheduled when managers felt it would draw audiences sufficient to generate good returns at the box office. It is noteworthy that of the 114 performances recorded as having been presented in London between 1740–1 and 1775–6, only twelve were advertised or otherwise recorded as 'bespoken' (conceivably though not necessarily underwritten), while thirty-one were offered as benefits for members of the theatre companies, whose concern in such events was to increase the evening's income in which they shared. The extent to which actors scheduled the play as a useful vehicle to arouse public interest, establish or re-establish themselves in the London theatre, or repair their fortunes further suggests that in the profession the play was seen as an attraction certain to draw an audience.

During its first year on the stage, but not thereafter, the play was, as Cibber reports, 'frequently bespoke by some eminent merchants and citizens who much approved its moral tendency'.[88] This, no doubt, has been the basis for the

[87] e.g. Bernbaum (p. 158): 'Perhaps one may, in view of the limited vogue of other domestic tragedies, indulge the suspicion that the frequent performance of *George Barnwell* was encouraged by influential citizens, not because they themselves enjoyed it, but because they thought young people should.'

[88] *Lives*, loc. cit. Beginning with the fourth performance at Drury Lane, all performances of *The London Merchant* offered during the summer season and all but four of those presented during the regular season of 1731–2 were advertised as bespoken—normally by 'Persons of Distinction' or 'Persons of Quality', though the 'Eminent Merchants' are mentioned in several announcements. The playwright's second benefit night, 20 July, received their support, and on the following day the *Daily Post* reported that the play was 'perform'd . . . with great Applause, to a crowded Audience, there being present most of the eminent Merchants of the City of London; they appear'd greatly pleased with the Play and Performance.' *The London Merchant* was appropriately scheduled on Lord Mayor's Day, and on 27 Dec. performances at Goodman's Fields as well as Drury Lane began the tradition of presenting the play, as Cibber reports, as a 'proper entertainment for the apprentices'. The number of sponsored performances drops off to two in the 1732–3 season. There were three bespoke performances the following year, two in 1733–4. Thereafter sponsorship was rare. The custom of performances at the Christmas holiday was irregularly maintained, and such scheduling reflects, for the most part, the more general pattern of rise and fall in the play's popularity during the 18th cent. Performances were advertised for 26, 27, or 28 Dec. in 29 of the 69 years surveyed (1731–99). Presentations offered at more than one theatre in the same year bring the total number of holiday performances to 33; of these only four were announced as bespoken, two in 1732, one each in 1733 and 1734. (Cibber, *Lives*, loc. cit.; *London Stage, 1729–1747, 1747–1776,* and *1776–1800, passim.*) Despite this quite sporadic record of Christmas performances, the assumption that the play was regularly offered at times when apprentices would, through scheduling or coercion, be brought to see it persists in anecdote. For example, in a footnote to his essay 'On the Tragedies of Shakespeare', Lamb 'beg[s]' the theatre managers that the play 'should cease to be eternally repeated in the holiday weeks'. (E. W. Lucas, ed., *The Works of Charles and Mary Lamb* [London, 1903], i. 102.) Perhaps the custom was more regularly maintained in provincial theatres, as Ward (p. xiii) suggests in noting holiday performances in Manchester in the latter part of the 19th cent.

assumption that over the years performances of *The London Merchant* were the result of sponsorship by those concerned that apprentices and other young people should see and be instructed by the play. While the eminent merchants who bespoke the early performances may have sought in part to assist the success of a project which one of their own had brought to the theatre, they did undoubtedly find the play edifying and hoped that its moral lesson would prove effective. It was also, however, a play written for them, sympathetically depicting their lives, asserting their values, confirming and congratulating their relatively new standing in society, and not incidentally moving them to tears. It is unlikely that the audience which made *Jane Shore* and *The Orphan* the most popular plays of the era attended *George Barnwell* as a duty. Ultimately the play would be criticized more for its pathos than for its moralizing speeches, a good many of which seem regularly to have been deleted from performance at least as early as the last two decades of the eighteenth century.[89] Lamb would condemn the play for what had come to seem an artificial appeal to the emotions.[90] Thackeray as well as Dickens would find it a ready subject for parody.[91] Yet as late as 1808 Mrs Inchbald could report that, as acted by Charles Kemble, the play 'is an evening's entertainment worthy of the most judicious admirers of the drama'.[92] And in its first seasons respected literary judgement supported the City's high opinion of *The London Merchant*. Pope is reported to have praised it,[93] Lady Mary Wortley Montagu to have admired it. Lady Mary, nicely balancing respect for the playwright's moral intentions with feeling for his pathos, may well have summed up the response of Lillo's first audiences in her reported opinion 'that whoever did not cry at George Barnwell must deserve to be hanged'.[94]

THE TEXT

Lillo's authorized publisher, John Gray, issued six editions of *The London Merchant* during the author's lifetime and a seventh edition a few months after the playwright's death. His first edition provides the primary but not exclusive basis for an authoritative text; reference must also be made to the evidence of author's corrections and alterations recorded in later editions published by

[89] See n. 32 above.

[90] 'They sit and shed tears, because a good sort of young man is tempted by a naughty woman to commit a *trifling peccadillo*, the murder of an uncle or so, that is all, and so comes to an unlucky end, which is *so moving* . . .' Even so, Lamb sought no less a tragic figure than Othello on which to base his contrast with Barnwell. (E. V. Lucas, ed., *The Works of Charles and Mary Lamb*, loc. cit.)

[91] 'George de Barnwell' in *Novels by Eminent Hands*. Thackeray makes use of Lillo to spoof Bulwer-Lytton.

[92] 'Remarks', prefaced to *The London Merchant* in *The British Theatre* (London, 1808), vol. xi.

[93] Cibber reports that Pope attended the first performance and was much pleased by it, remarking that if Lillo 'had erred through the whole play it was only in a few places, where he had unawares let himself into a poetical luxuriancy, affecting to be too elevated for the simplicity of the subject' (Cibber, *Lives* v. 139).

[94] James Archibald Stuart-Wortley-Mackenzie, Lord Wharncliffe, ed., 'Introductory Anecdotes', *The Letters and Works of Lady Mary Wortley Montagu* (Philaldephia, 1837), i. 92.

Gray. The development of the text in this series of reprints can be divided into three stages, each represented by one edition—the second, third, and fifth. In each of these can be observed Lillo's clear but decreasing involvement, and also the quite extensive editorial work of someone other than the author.

At least six unauthorized editions of the play, some of them closely resembling copies of legitimate editions, were published before Lillo's death. These include an early Dublin edition, an early edition printed in Rotterdam with a false London imprint, two spurious second editions (one of them printed in Edinburgh), and false third and fifth editions. None has textual authority.

Later reprints include the series of editions issued with some frequency throughout the eighteenth century by the booksellers who owned or shared the assignment of copy which John Gray sold in 1742, and a succession of piratical editions. The version of the play printed by Thomas Davies in his collection of Lillo's works (1775) followed Gray's seventh edition and served long as the 'standard' text of the play, providing the authority for most editions issued during the nineteenth and early twentieth centuries.

First Edition

Beyond question Lillo authorized John Gray to publish *The London Merchant*. However, the bookseller neglected to enter his copyright in the *Stationers' Register*, an inexplicable oversight that he must have regretted when the popularity of the play encouraged a proliferation of unauthorized editions. Perhaps in an effort to rectify this situation and to confirm Gray's exclusive right to publish the play, Lillo made an assignment of rights to the publisher in November 1735.[95] Whether or not this represents the first formal agreement between publisher and playwright is unclear; Lillo had certainly co-operated with Gray in the preparation of at least some of his early editions of *The London Merchant*, but the assignment signed in 1735 makes no reference to prior agreements and no early assignment has been found. Lillo's choice of the bookseller as one of the executors of his will suggests that John Gray was a friend as well as business acquaintance, and it is possible that publication of the play was arranged without a written agreement.[96]

Advertisements in the *Daily Post* and *Daily Journal* indicate that copies of the first edition were made available at the bookshops of John Gray and John Roberts at five in the afternoon on 14 July 1731. On 20 July, a benefit night for the author, copies also began to be sold at Drury Lane.[97] The booksellers'

---

[95] British Library, MS Add. 38728, item 129.

[96] The assignment grants exclusive rights to John Gray, his heirs and assigns, in return for payment of one hundred guineas. The wording suggests that payment was made at the time the document was signed, but the assignment could of course represent only the formalization in writing of an agreement made when Gray first printed the play.

[97] *Daily Post* and *Daily Journal*, 12 July 1731, 'Tomorrow at 5 in the Evening will be publish'd . . .'; 13 July, 'This Day at Five o'clock in the Evening will be publish'd . . .'; 14 July, 'This Day is publish'd . . .' The announcement of 14 July is repeated in the *Daily Post* on 15, 16, and 17 July, and

advertisements for the edition announce 'a small number printed on a fine Royal Paper', but no fine-paper copies have come to light.

For the title-page, see p. 149.

Collation: 8° A⁶ B–E⁸ F² [$4 (– A1, F2) signed]; 40 leaves, pp. *i–ii* iii–x *xi–xii 1* 2–67 *68* [= 80] [iii centred in parentheses]

Contents: A1(*i*) title A1ᵛ(*ii*) blank A2(iii)–A5ᵛ(x) dedication A6(*xi*) prologue A6ᵛ(*xii*) dramatis personae B1(*1*)–F2(67) text (DH; [double rule] | THE | *London* Merchant: | OR, THE | HISTORY | OF | *GEORGE BARNWELL*. | [rule]) F2ᵛ(*68*) epilogue

Comments

Sheets A and F almost certainly were machined together with A cut and bound as a separate quarter-sheet. Comparison of copies on the Hinman Collator reveals press corrections in A (outer and inner) and F (outer); see Tables of Press Variants.[98] Corrected and uncorrected versions of the cut sheets appear to have been used indiscriminatley when books were made up. Variant states of outer B are marked by the presence of a row of flowers beneath the dropped head in some copies and a plain rule in others; no other changes or corrections appear to have been made and there is no evidence of reimpression.[99]

The text of the edition is relatively clean, but many awkwardnesses in the punctuation and inconsistencies in the settings of stage directions and in the use of speech-headings suggest that the printer's copy was loosely pointed and came to him virtually unedited. That the manuscript was in a few places defective or unclear is indicated by pointing which in a number of lines badly misconstrues the sense.[100]

Inconsistencies in the typographical conventions for setting stage directions suggest that the text was set in haste as well as from unedited copy. This situation is more strongly indicated by the irregular pointing characteristic of the edition—inconsistent at best, frequently awkward or simply incorrect, at times heavy but elsewhere lacking punctuation essential to the meaning of lines

---

in the *Daily Journal* of 16 and 17 July. In the *Daily Post* for 17 and 20 July the Drury Lane advertisements announcing the ninth day of *The London Merchant* (20 July) include the note that 'Printed Books of GEORGE BARNWELL will be sold at the Theatre.' A similar notice appears on 28 and 29 July in advertisements for the performance of 30 July.

[98] When a sheet included a quarter-sheet, it was usual practice to print the outer forme of the quarter-sheet with the inner forme of the three-quarter sheet, and it seems probable that the quarter-sheet for this edition was imposed, and therefore corrected, in this way. Cf. C. Stower, *The Printer's Grammar* (London, 1808), p. 174, and W. Savage, *A Dictionary of the Art of Printing* (London, 1841), p. 339.

[99] McBurney (*LM*, p. 29) records a press correction in inner C (C1ᵛ): II. iii. 12, determines]determine. The present editor has found no copy in which this correction has been made, and it appears that only A and F were issued in uncorrected and corrected states.

[100] The omission of a short but essential speech at the end of II. xii may indicate defective copy; however, the line could simply have been overlooked by the compositor. The incorrect assignment of a speech to Trueman instead of Thorowgood (IV. xviii 7) could well have come about through confusion of similar speech-headings (*Tr.* and *Thor.*) in the copyist's or compositor's copy.

and speeches.[101] The erratic pointing of rhetorical questions is particularly troublesome. No evidence suggests that the author took an interest in the pointing of the printed text, and in the second edition it was of necessity thoroughly revised.

Second Edition

The only authorized second edition was issued on the morning of 30 July 1731.[102] It is to be distinguished from two spurious editions which also announce themselves as 'The Second Edition . . . Printed for J. Gray and sold by John Roberts' (see Early Unauthorized Editions, below).

Title-page
THE | *London* Merchant: | OR, THE | HISTORY | OF | *GEORGE BARNWELL.* | As it is Acted at the | THEATRE-ROYAL | IN | *DRURY-LANE.* | By HIS MAJESTY's Servants. | [rule] | By Mr. *LILLO.* | [rule] | *Learn to be wiſe from others Harm,* | [indent] *And you ſhall do full well.* | [right] Old Ballad of the Lady's Fall. | [rule] | *The* SECOND EDITION. | [rule] | *LONDON:* | Printed for J. GRAY, at the *Croſs-Keys* in the *Poultry*; and | ſold by J. ROBERTS, in *Warwick-Lane.* MDCCXXXI. | *[in square brackets]* [Price One Shilling and Six-pence.]

> *Collation*: 8° A–E⁸ [$4 (– A1) signed]; 40 leaves, pp. *i–ii* iii–x xi–xii *1* 2–67 *68* [iii centred in parentheses]
> *Contents*: A1(*i*) title A1ᵛ(*ii*) blank A2(iii)–A5ᵛ(x) dedication A6(*xi*) prologue A6ᵛ(*xii*) dramatis personae A7(*1*)–E8(67) text (DH: [double rule] | THE | *London* Merchant: | OR, THE | HISTORY | OF | *GEORGE BARNWELL.* | [rule]) E8ᵛ(*68*) epilogue

Comments
The edition follows closely the format of the first edition, except that A is a full octavo gathering and the two-leaf final gathering (F) is therefore not required. The selection of typefaces and the layout of title-pages, heads, and act- and scene-breaks regularly match those of the first edition. The second edition is essentially a new setting, but comparison of copies on the Hinman Collator reveals that some blocks of type originally set for sheets A and F of the first edition were used again for the second edition.[103] Collation of copies of the second edition reveals no press corrections or evidence of reimpression.

---

[101] The inconsistencies in stage directions and punctuation form no pattern which suggests division of work among compositors.

[102] *Daily Post* and *Daily Journal*, 30 July 1731, 'This Morning at Ten will be published . . . The SECOND EDITION . . .'; 31 July, 'This Day is Published . . . The SECOND EDITION . . .'.

[103] Certain passages set in roman type for the dedication (inner forme: A2, A4, A5ᵛ) and the italic type of the epilogue (F2ᵛ) reappear in the second edition. After the run for the first edition, the type was removed from the formes; running heads, titles, and blocks of italic type set for the dedication were removed and set again for the second edition.

The text of the edition was set from a copy of the first edition. However, comparison of the editions reveals some seventy-eight substantive variants and more than four hundred alterations in accidentals. Many, though not all, of the substantive changes were probably introduced by the author, who must have gone over the first edition with some care and provided Gray or the printer with a marked copy or detailed list of adjustments. A number of the new readings, though normally altering only a few words, involve the careful refining of theological points, the slight but significant redefinition of the moral situations of the characters, the elimination of possible ambiguities, and similar changes that clearly bespeak authorial emendation.[104] In several instances, lines that might offend a segment of Lillo's audience are deleted or revised.[105] The order of sentences in an important speech is revised, and a significant piece of stage business is changed.[106] Although a few of the substantive variants are clearly compositorial, nearly half of the new readings are probably author's changes and corrections, and more than twenty others—minor variants, not certainly authorial—may well represent Lillo's reworking of details of his text. A few variants, however, have the look of the work of an editor or meticulous compositor with an eye for verbal nicety, someone who occasionally mistook the sense of a line and was inclined to smooth down the rough edges of the colloquial language that Lillo intended for his play.

Analysis of the variant accidentals makes it clear that the text was indeed heavily edited by someone other than the playwright. Adjusted punctuation includes the routine correction of obvious errors and the regularization of details treated inconsistently in the first edition, but several changes are based on obvious misinterpretations of the text and cannot have been introduced by the author. This erroneous pointing follows a style of punctuation characteristic of the entire second edition, and it seems likely that the publisher, aware of the flaws in his first edition, had the text re-edited or undertook the task himself. The new pointing is generally heavy. Many commas have been added and a good number of semi-colons. Necessary repairs include some twenty-five question marks and exclamation points substituted for confusing semi-colons or full stops printed in the first edition. The regularizing of capitals is probably compositorial, as is the deletion of many dashes. The addition of a few dashes, appropriate and effective in their placement, provides the only evidence that might suggest that the author had any hand in the emended accidentals of the edition.

Third Edition

Gray brought out his third edition of *The London Merchant* on 23 September 1731. The advertisements include a warning to readers to avoid a 'pyrated

---

[104] See Commentary on I. i. 35–6, I. ii. 3, II. iv. 21, III. iii. 50, III. iv. 31–2, III. iv. 106, V. ii. 16.

[105] See Commentary on I. i. 35–6 and I. ii. 3.

[106] V. x. 12–14; V. v. 35.

Edition' of the play.[107] His own new edition, announced as 'Corrected and Improv'd' and issued in a new duodecimo format with an engraved frontispiece, may have been produced to compete in particular with the false 'second edition' in octavo and it seems clearly to have been designed to make obsolete the various piratical editions that had been copied from the legitimate first and second editions. Publication of a new edition at this time may also have been stimulated by the new production of the play at Giffard's theatre in Goodman's Fields, first advertised on 24 September and first performed on 27 Septmeber.[108]

This authorized third edition is to be distinguished from a piratical edition in octavo falsely imprinted as 'The Third Edition . . . Printed for John Gray' (see Early Unauthorized Editions, below).

Title-page

THE | *London* Merchant: | OR, THE | HISTORY | OF | *GEORGE BARNWELL.* | As it is Acted at the | *Theatre-Royal* in *Drury-Lane.* | BY | HIS MAJESTY's Servants. | [rule] | By Mr. *LILLO.* | [rule] | *Learn to be wiſe from others Harm,* | [indent] *And you ſhall do full well.* | [right] Old Ballad of the Lady's Fall. | [rule] | The THIRD EDITION Revis'd. | [rule] | *LONDON:* | Printed for JOHN GRAY, at the *Croſs-Keys* in the | *Poultry.* MDCCXXXI. [*in square brackets*] [*Price* 1 *s.*]

> *Note*: The price may have been printed or stamped after original printing of the title-page.

Collation: 12° (6's) A–F[6] [$3 (− A1, 2) signed]; 36 leaves, pp. *i–v* vi–x *xi–xii 13* 14–71 *72*

Contents: A1(*i*) blank A1[v](*ii*) engraved frontispiece A2(*iii*) title A2[v](*iv*) blank A3(*v*)–A5[v](x) dedication A6(*xi*) prologue A6[v](*xii*) dramatis personae B1(*13*)–F6(71) text (DH: [orn.] | THE | *London* Merchant: | OR, THE | HISTORY | OF | *GEORGE BARNWELL.* | [row of flowers]) F6[v](*72*) epilogue

Comments

Imposition was by half-sheets (work and turn). Collation reveals no press corrections or evidence of reimpression.

The text was set from a copy of Gray's second edition. The shift from octavo to duodecimo format required considerable adjustment to typography. The text is further marked by the elimination of French scene-divisions and contingent adaptation of scene-numbers and stage directions. Again there is evidence of both authorial and editorial emendation, though new readings are not nearly as numerous as in the second edition. Lillo very probably requested certain substantive changes—for example, the lines added at IV. xiv 2–3[109]—but he did not systematically review the entire text. Perhaps as many as twenty of the

---

[107] *Daily Post*, 23 Sept. 1731, 'This Day at Noon will be Publish'd . . .'; 24 Sept., 'This Day is Published . . .'. The announcement of 24 Sept. is repeated in the *Daily Post* on 25 Sept., and in the *Daily Journal* on 1 and 4 Oct.

[108] *London Stage, 1729–1747.*   [109] See also I. iv. 5 and I. v. 8.

thirty-five substantive variants not associated with the altered scene-divisions represent authorial revision. Other, minor variants include compositorial changes and some adjustments which, as in the second edition, reflect an editorial concern for the niceties of grammar and syntax. Punctuation is again adjusted by an editor or compositor, but in this edition emendation of accidentals is directed towards clarifying and simplifying the text; a good many extraneous commas are dropped. Routine regularization of capitals continues, four full dashes are added. In several instances, the alteration of substantive readings and in particular of accidentals works against the meaning of the text. The revision of stage directions, necessitated by the deletion of many scene-headings, is incomplete and at times incorrect. Although Lillo must have agreed to the new style of scene-division, he clearly cannot have supervised the actual revisions. However, it is conceivable if far from certain that he did suggest the inclusion of the few new or expanded directions which are not mere mechanical adjustments but introduce brief descriptions of stage business and properties, details that would seem to have been influenced by production in the theatre.[110]

Fourth Edition

Advertisements indicate that Gray published the edition on 10 February 1732.[111]

Title-page
> THE | *London* Merchant: | OR, THE | HISTORY | OF | *GEORGE BARNWELL*. | As it is Acted at the | *Theatre-Royal* in *Drury-Lane*. | BY | HIS MAJESTY'S Servants. | [rule] | By Mr. *LILLO*. | [rule] | *Learn to be wiſe from others Harm*, | [indent] *And you ſhall do full well*. | [right] Old Ballad of the Lady's Fall. | [rule] | The FOURTH EDITION Revis'd. | [rule] | *LONDON:* | Printed for JOHN GRAY, at the *Croſs-Keys* in the *Poul-|try*, near *Cheapſide*. MDCCXXXII. [*square bracket*] [*Price* 1 *s*.

> *Collation*: 12° (6's) A–F⁶ ($3 (− A1, 2) signed]; 36 leaves, pp. *i–v* vi–x *xi–xii* *13* 14–71 *72*
> *Contents*: A1(*i*) blank A1ᵛ(*ii*) engraved frontispiece A2(*iii*) title A2ᵛ(*iv*) blank A3(*v*)–A5ᵛ(x) dedication A6(*xi*) prologue A6ᵛ(*xii*) dramatis personae B1(*13*)–F6(*71*) text (DH: [orn.] | THE | *London* Merchant: | OR, THE | HISTORY | OF | *GEORGE BARNWELL*. | [row of flowers]) F6ᵛ(*72*) epilogue

Comments
Imposition was in half-sheets (work and turn). The edition was set from a copy of Gray's third edition, which it follows so closely in format and typography that the two editions may on casual examination appear to include the same settings

---

[110] See commentary on I. viiiSD and III. vii. 8+SD, and the text at II. xiiiSD. Directions giving the settings for III. i. and IV. i, omitted from the first and second editions, are supplied in the third edition.
[111] *Daily Journal*, 10 Feb. 1732, 'This Day is Published . . .'; repeated 11 Feb.

of type. Comparison of copies on the Hinman Collator makes it clear that this is not so. Textual collation further distinguishes the two editions. However, the pair of compositors who set the fourth edition followed the third edition so closely that, with one exception, even the italic colons incorrectly set in a number of running heads were reproduced.[112]

No evidence suggests that the author took an interest in the preparation of this edition of his play.

Fifth Edition (Cancel Title: 'Sixth Edition')

The only known copy of the edition includes and presumably was issued with a cancel title-leaf which announces the book as 'The SIXTH EDITION'. An 'Advertisement' printed in the preliminary gathering, consisting of a note from the author concerning a scene added in this edition, identifies the book as 'this Fifth Edition'. Almost certainly the edition was planned and produced as the fifth edition of Lillo's play, and very possibly was issued as such initially. However, the evidence for reconstructing the publication of the edition in its original or altered state is at best suggestive rather than specific.

Gray did not separately advertise publication of a fifth edition of *The London Merchant*. He did, however, promote such an edition in his newspaper advertisements of the publication of the first edition of *The Christian Hero* and in an advertisement printed in the preliminary gathering originally issued with copies of that play. It is clear that the editions of the two plays were closely related in publication and very probably in production, and for both the evidence for assigning dates of publication is contradictory, suggesting that copies were for some reason not available as early as they had been expected to be. Moreover, both editions were reissued with cancel title-pages that altered the edition numbers.[113]

The earliest known reference to an authorized fifth edition of the *Merchant* appears in advertisements published on 23 January 1734/5 to announce the publication 'Next Week' of *The Christian Hero*.[114] It appears that copies of Lillo's new play were not available in late January, and notices run early in the following month identify 6 February as the most likely date of publication; these advertisements again call the readers' attention to a new fifth edition of *The London Merchant*.[115] Both series of advertisements are worded in ways which

---

[112] Collation reveals only four variants that can be called substantive; one of these is a typographical error and another the correction of an error in the third edition. Variant accidentals are few and can be attributed to a conscientious if occasionally careless compositor.

[113] See *The Christian Hero*, Textual Introduction.

[114] *Grub-Street Journal* and *Daily Post and General Advertiser*, 23 Jan. 1734/5, '. . . Where may be had, 1. The London Merchant, or, the History of George Barnwell. The Fifth Genuine Edition; adorned with a beautiful new Frontispiece, taken from an additional Scene never before printed, price 1.s.' The announcement is repeated in the *Daily Post and General Advertiser* on 24 and 25 Jan., and in *The Craftsman* on 1 and 8 Feb.

[115] *Daily Courant*, 5, 6, and 7 Feb. 1734/5; the portion of the advertisement that notes the fifth edition of *The London Merchant* repeats the wording of the announcements printed in January.

suggest that copies of this edition were already available for purchase. However, the advertisement in the title-gathering (first state) of *The Christian Hero* bears the dateline 'Feb. 8, 1734–5', and announces that 'This Day is Published, The Fifth Genuine Edition of The London Merchant'. The editions of both plays bear evidence of some irregularity or haste in production, and it is not unlikely that the new edition of the *Merchant*, like *The Christian Hero*, was delayed, very possibly until 8 February.

There is no uncertainty about the publisher's intentions in bringing out an altered version of the *Merchant*. His newspaper notices and the author's advertisement printed in the edition itself make it clear that the fifth edition was produced specifically to combat the competition of unauthorized editions of the play. A scene not previously published was added, in the words of the author's advertisement, 'to distinguish this Edition from the incorrect, pyrated ones, which the town swarms [*sic*]'.[116] The frontispiece depicting this scene was similarly meant to identify the authorized publication and to make it more appealing than the piratical editions. Several such counterfeit editions were available by 1734, at least three of them purporting to be reprints published by John Gray himself. Moreover, the text of Gray's fourth edition had been reprinted in a 'fifth edition', dated 1733 and 'Printed for J. GREEN', which also included a copy (reversed) of the frontispiece that had identified the authorized third and fourth editions of Lillo's play. Gray's concern to put a new, competitive edition into print is underscored by his doing so before his stock of earlier editions was exhausted: the first advertisements which mention the fifth edition note also that 'An Edition without the new Scene, vastly preferable to any of the pyrated ones, may be had at the same place.'

The cancel, 'sixth edition' title-page very probably represents a further effort to deal with piratical competition, in particular to avoid confusion with the J. Green 'fifth edition'.[117] When this reissue occurred is a matter for conjecture. Gray placed no newspaper advertisements for a sixth edition of *The London Merchant*, though he took the trouble to produce and substitute the new title-page for his fifth edition and later published a proper sixth edition of the play (also dated 1735).

The only evidence for dating the reissued fifth edition relates again to the problematic publication of the two states of *The Christian Hero*. The cancel title-gathering that marks the 'second edition' of that play does include an announcement of the sixth edition of *The London Merchant*, an indication that

---

[116] For the complete text of the author's advertisement, see p. 138.

[117] This plausible hypothesis was put forward by R. H. Griffith, who discovered and first described the only known copy of the fifth edition and its cancel title-page. Griffith's analysis of this and other previously unknown early editions of *The London Merchant* has provided an important and sound foundation for subsequent efforts to reconstruct the history of the play's publication (cf. 'Early Editions of Lillo's *London Merchant*', *Studies in English*, [*University of Texas Bulletin*, No. 3526, 8 July 1935], pp. 23–7). McBurney (*LM*, p. x) has suggested that the fifth edition may never have been issued in its first state. However, the series of advertisements for the edition seems clear evidence that the book was sold in its original form for a time at least.

the altered version of the *Merchant* edition was issued before or, more likely, at about the same time as the second state of the edition of *The Christian Hero*. Evidence relating to production suggests that *The Christian Hero* was reissued very soon after publication of the edition in its original state.[118] This, in turn, suggests that the new edition of the *Merchant* was altered almost immediately after its initial publication.

That only a single example of the fifth edition of the *Merchant* has been found while numerous copies of the other authorized editions of the play survive suggests that relatively few copies of the fifth edition were printed and issued in either state. Certainly it was supplanted by the proper sixth edition before the end of 1735. An advertisement for the 'second edition' of *The Christian Hero*, included in the title-gathering of the proper sixth edition, might be taken to indicate that this new edition of the *Merchant*—a handsomely produced book to replace an edition printed hastily in a short run—was issued early in the year, when Gray was concerned to promote the reissued version of *The Christian Hero*.[119] A cancel title-page could then be explained as a device to make saleable the copies of the fifth edition that remained in stock when the new edition was put on sale. However, such a reconstruction is conjectural at best. It can be argued, on the basis of other evidence, that the proper sixth edition was not issued until as late as November or December of 1735.[120] While it seems likely that the fifth edition was very soon replaced by Gray's next edition of the play, it can be said with some certainty only that the fifth edition was published at about the same time as *The Christian Hero*—probably in early February 1734/5—and was reissued with a 'sixth edition' title-leaf before the end of the year, that is before or at the same time as publication of the proper sixth edition.

Title-page

THE | London Merchant: | OR, THE | HISTORY | OF | GEORGE BARNWELL. | As it is Acted at the | THEATRE-ROYAL in *Drury-Lane.* | BY | HIS MAJESTY's Servants. | [rule] | By Mr. LILLO. | [rule] | *Learn to be wiſe from others Harm,* | *And you ſhall do full well.* | [right] Old Ballad of the Lady's Fall. | [rule] | The SIXTH EDITION. | [rule] | *LONDON:* | Printed for JOHN GRAY, at the *Croſs Keys* in the | *Poultry, near Cheapſide.* | MDCCXXXV.

Collation: 12° (6's) A⁶(± A2) B–F⁶ [\$3 (– A1,2) signed]; 36 leaves, pp. *i–v* vi–x *xi–xii 13* 14–70 *71–2* [misprinting 68 as '98']
Contents: A1(*i*) blank A1ᵛ(*ii*) engraved frontispiece A2(*iii*) title A2ᵛ(*iv*) blank A3(*v*)–A5ᵛ(*x*) dedication A6(*xi*) advertisement A6ᵛ(*xii*) dramatis personae B1(*13*)–F5ᵛ(*70*) text (DH: [orn.] | THE | *London* Merchant: | OR, THE |

---

[118] See *The Christian Hero*, Textual Introduction.
[119] The text of the edition was subject to careful editing, but in design and other aspects of the printing does not match the usual quality of Gray's editions of Lillo's plays (see below).
[120] See the description of the sixth edition, below. The fact that no type set for the title-page of the proper sixth edition was used in printing the cancel title may also be taken as evidence that the second state of the old edition was not issued in conjunction with publication of the new edition.

HISTORY| OF | *GEORGE BARNWELL.* | [row of flowers]) F6(*71*)
prologue F6ᵛ(*72*) epilogue and advertisements

Note: The title-page (A2) is a cancellans attached to the stub of the cancellandum.
The advertisement on A6 identifies the sheets as being of the fifth edition.

Comments

The plate for the engraved frontispiece, which appears for the first time in this
edition, was used again in the proper sixth edition and passed along to Gray's
successors when he sold his interest in the play; the frontispiece reappears in
editions of *The London Merchant* published in the 1740s and 1750s by John
Osborn and Henry Lintot.

The edition is unquestionably legitimate, though the typography and layout
of pages are not of the quality characteristic of Gray's other editions of Lillo's
plays, evidence suggesting some haste in production.

The text is notable for the addition of a scene not previously printed. A final
confrontation of Barnwell and Marwood beneath the gallows, the scene is
clearly Lillo's. He explains his decision to release it in an advertisement
included in the preliminary pages of the edition:

The Scene, added in this Fifth Edition, is | with some Variations, in the Original Copy; |
but by the Advice of some Friends it was left | out in the Representation, and is now
published by | the Advice of others: which are in the Right I shall | not pretend to
determine. There are amongst both-[*sic*]| Gentlemen, whose Judgment I prefer to my
own. | As this Play succeeded on the stage withont [*sic*] it, I | shou'd not, perhaps, have
published it, but to di-|stinguish this Edition from the incorrect, pyrated | ones, which
the Town swarms [*sic*]; to the great Preju-|dice of the Proprietors of the Copy, as well as
to all | the fair Traders, who scorn to incourage such un-|just Practices. | [indent] I cou'd
not but reproach myself with Ingratitude | shou'd I neglect this Opportunity of
confessing my | Obligations and returning my Thanks to the Publick | in general, and my
Friends in Particular, for their | favourable Reception of this Piece. I am very sen-|sible
how much I owe to their Indulgence and wish | I may be able by any future Performance,
if any | shou'd appear to deserve the Continuance of their | Favour.

Except for the new scene, the text of the edition was set from a copy of the
authorized fourth edition and it is clear that Lillo's involvement in the
preparation of the edition was limited to providing copy for the scene and
author's advertisement. He left the editing to his publisher or printer. The new
scene may itself have been set from copy that had been given little or no editing;
in an edition characterized by relatively heavy punctuation, the new material is
remarkable for its simple, at times minimal, pointing. Once again, the
accidentals of reprinted text exhibit the styling of a careful editor, almost
certainly not a compositor or the author. As in the second edition, these
adjustments are meticulous, generally helpful, and extensive. Collation reveals
some four hundred variant accidentals. A number of errors that had passed
unnoticed in earlier editions are corrected, and the editor accurately imitates an
apparent habit of the playwright's in the series of dashes he inserts in the text. A

few misinterpretations and the contrast with the style of pointing characteristic of the new scene identify the altered punctuation as the work of someone other than the author. This editor must also have been responsible for the relatively few substantive changes, which reflect an inclination towards rhetorical and syntactic nicety. None of these substantive variants suggests authorial revision and more than half of the new readings certainly cannot have been contributed by Lillo.

Sixth Edition

No newspaper announcement of the publication of a sixth edition of *The London Merchant* has been found. As noted above, an advertisement for 'The Sixth Genuine Edition' appears in the cancel title-gathering of the 'second edition' of *The Christian Hero*, probably issued in February 1734/5; conceivably this marks publication of the proper sixth edition of the *Merchant* but more likely relates to the reissue of the fifth edition with a cancel title-page.

On 25 November 1735 Lillo signed an agreement granting exclusive copyright to *The London Merchant* to John Gray in return for a payment of one hundred guineas. The agreement mentions no prior assignment of copy and contains no clue as to the reason such an agreement should have been drawn up more than three years after initial publication of the play. Early in 1735 Gray, with Lillo's support, had vigorously asserted his claim to the copyright, which he had neglected to enter in the *Stationers' Register*. Whatever Lillo's original arrangements with the publisher may have been, the assignment made in 1735 was surely intended as a further means to secure Gray's proprietorship of *The London Merchant*.[121] If the agreement was drawn up in expectation of the publication of a new edition of the play, this can only have been the proper sixth edition, which would then have been published in November or December. Gray's next edition was not published until 1740.[122]

Title-page

THE | London Merchant: | OR, THE | HISTORY | OF | GEORGE BARNWELL. | As it is Acted at the | *Theatre-Royal* in *Drury-Lane.* | BY | His

[121] Once or more each week, from 27 June to 17 Oct. 1735, the bookseller Thomas Apsley, 'at the Rose in St. Paul's Church-Yard', ran advertisements in the *Daily Post and General Advertiser* which listed a number of tragedies available at sixpence each. *George Barnwell* is regularly included. The advertisement in Gray's 'second edition' of *The Christian Hero* gives sixpence as the price of the sixth edition of *The London Merchant*, and it is possible that Apsley stocked this or another of the authorized editions of the play. However, it seems more likely that he was selling a piratical edition—an additional stimulus to Gray to obtain Lillo's formal assignment of the copy.

[122] The sixth edition must have remained in stock until at least 1740, when a seventh authorized edition was published. The sixth edition is listed in advertisements announcing publication of *Fatal Curiosity* in 1737, and advertisements for *Marina*, published in the following year, also list *George Barnwell*, though no edition number is noted. Since the seventh edition seems to have been produced primarily to provide copies of the *Merchant* in a format appropriate for binding in Gray's nonce collection of Lillo's works, the sixth edition probably remained current well after 1740. Certainly the eighth edition, produced in 1743 by Gray's successor, John Osborn, derives from the text, format, and typography of the sixth, not the seventh, edition of the play.

MAJESTY's Servants. | [rule] | By Mr. LILLO. | [rule] | *Learn to be wife from others Harm* | *And you fhall do full well.* | [right] Old Ballad of the Lady's Fall. | [rule] | The SIXTH EDITION. | [rule] | *LONDON:* | Printed for JOHN GRAY, at the *Crofs-Keys* in the | *Poultry,* near *Cheapfide.* | MDCCXXXV.

Collation: 12° (6's) A–G⁶ [$3 (– A1, 2) signed]; 42 leaves, pp. *i–v* vi–x *xi–xii 13* 14–80 *81–4*
    Var. 64 page-number omitted (2 copies)
Contents: A1(*i*) blank A1ᵛ(*ii*) engraved frontispiece A2(*iii*) title A2ᵛ(*iv*) blank A3(*v*)–A5ᵛ(x) dedication A6(*xi*) prologue A6ᵛ(*xii*) dramatis personae B1(*13*)–G4ᵛ(80) text (DH: [orn.] | THE | London Merchant: | OR, THE | HISTORY | OF | GEORGE BARNWELL. | [row of flowers]) G5(*81*)–G5ᵛ(*82*) epilogue G6(*83*)–G6ᵛ(*84*) advertisement

Comments

Imposition was by half-sheets (work and turn). Collation reveals no press corrections or evidence of reimpression. The text closely follows that of the fifth edition, but the design of pages, spacing of type, and use of ornaments indicate that the book was more carefully planned and produced than its predecessor. In layout and typography it more closely resembles Gray's third and fourth editions than it does his fifth edition.

The text is a virtual reprint of the fifth edition, routinely corrected and adjusted by the compositor. Of the ten minimal substantive variants, four are typographical errors or misreadings and the others are clearly compositorial changes. The relatively few variations in accidentals also provide no indication of authorial emendation.

The series of later editions published by the booksellers who purchased the assignment of copy originally held by Gray stem from this edition rather than from Gray's final, seventh edition.

Seventh Edition

The first posthumous edition of *The London Merchant* and the last in the series of editions published by John Gray was produced primarily for inclusion in the nonce collection of Lillo's works that the bookseller issued in the summer of 1740. The probable date of the collection is suggested by advertisements printed in the *Craftsman* for 21 and 28 June 1740, which announce publication of the short masque *Britannia and Batavia* and note that 'all Mr. LILLO's other Works' are also available. Published in octavo, the new edition of the *Merchant* could be bound easily with the editions of Lillo's other plays, already in stock and all in octavo, which made up the bulk of the collection. Omission of the dedication and frontispiece also suggests that the new edition was produced primarily to fill out the collection rather than to be sold as a single volume.

Title-page
THE | London Merchant: | OR, THE | HISTORY | OF | GEORGE
BARNWELL. | As it is Acted at the | *Theatre-Royal* in *Drury-Lane*. | By | HIS
MAJESTY's Servants. | By Mr. LILLO. | *Learn to be wife from others Harm,* |
And you fhall do full well. | [right] Old Ballad of the Lady's Fall. | The
SEVENTH EDITION. | *LONDON:* | Printed for JOHN GRAY at the *Crofs-
Keys* in the | *Poultry* near *Cheapfide.* MDCCXL.

Collation: 8° A–E⁸ [$4 (− A1) signed]; 40 leaves, pp. *1–4* 5–79 *80* [5 centred
    in parentheses]
Contents: A1(*1*) title A1ᵛ(*2*) blank A2(*3*) prologue A2ᵛ(*4*) dramatis personae
    A3(5)–E8(79) text (DH: THE | LONDON MERCHANT: | OR, THE |
    HISTORY | OF | GEORGE BARNWELL. | [rule]) E8ᵛ(*80*) epilogue

Comments
The text of the edition was set from a copy of the authorized sixth edition,
which it followed so closely that occasional errors in the copy-text were
reproduced. A very few compositorial corrections were made. Variants are
minimal and without authority.

A copy of the seventh edition served as copy-text for the version of the play
printed in Davies's collected edition of Lillo's works (1775).

Early Unauthorized Editions

The popularity of *The London Merchant* in the theatre was more than matched
by the demand for printed copies of the play. Unauthorized reprints were
published at least as often and nearly as soon as the early editions issued by the
authorized publisher. In Ireland, George Faulkner printed at least two settings
of most of the play, issuing the sheets in various combinations in an edition
bearing a Dublin imprint, dated 1731. Faulkner's use of Gray's first edition as
his copy-text and evidence of hasty printing suggest that every effort was made
to compete with the legitimate London edition as quickly as possible.[123] A
second, probably very early, piratical edition appeared in octavo, bore a London

---

[123] Publication may have concurred with a very early Dublin production of the play. Faulkner
does not reprint the London cast in his list of persons but gives instead the names of another group
of actors, a number of whom were in the company at Dublin's Theatre in Smock Alley in 1731. The
theatre itself is not named, but Thomas Elrington, listed in the part of Barnwell, was manager at
Smock Alley for a number of years, retiring in 1732. Robert Hitchcock, in his *Historical View of the
Irish Stage* (1788), writes that *The London Merchant* was first performed at Smock Alley 'at the
commencement of the season, September 1731' (p. 45). Hitchcock's memory frequently played
him false—he reports, for example, that the *Merchant* was first acted in 1730 at Covent Garden—
and it is possible that this first Dublin production of the play and publication of Faulkner's edition
occurred somewhat earlier than Sept. 1731. It is conceivable also that the Irish edition of the
Merchant went to press before the Smock Alley production actually opened. In Faulkner's later
edition of the play (1751) the list of actors who appeared in the first Dublin performance is altered,
an indication perhaps that copy for the earlier edition was set while the production was still in
rehearsal and before the assignment of roles had been fully settled.

imprint, and was dated 1731. Actually one of a series of English plays produced for Thomas Johnson, it was published in the Netherlands, probably in Rotterdam.[124] Johnson appears to have kept well informed about and often made use of the latest London editions of the plays he chose to reprint; his use of the authorized first edition of Lillo's play as his copy-text suggests that his edition was printed very soon after initial publication of the work, certainly before Gray's third, 'revised' edition appeared in late September 1731. The print order must have been large for copies of the edition remained in stock for some thirty-five years and appeared in collections issued by Johnson's ultimate successor, Hendrik Scheurleer, as late as the 1750s and 1760s. On occasion the edition has been mistaken for the legitimate first edition of *The London Merchant*.[125]

As demand for copies of the play and the activities of piratical publishers brought John Gray to issue new 'revised' editions—and to inveigh against the pirates in his advertisements—some of the purveyors of unauthorized editions adopted his imprint in an effort to pass off their reprints as legitimate editions. At least three such editions, falsely bearing the name of the authorized publisher, have created confusion for editors and bibliographers. One of these—a 'second edition' published in duodecimo, dated 1731 and set from a copy of the legitimate first edition—was probably issued in August or September of 1731. The headpiece printed above the dropped head identifies the edition as printed in Edinburgh by Thomas and Walter Ruddiman.[126] Another false 'second edition' with Gray's imprint, dated 1731, and set from a copy of the genuine second edition, appeared in octavo format. Very probably this is the 'pyrated Edition of this Play . . . incorrectly printed on a bad Paper and Letter' described in the advertisements for his third edition which Gray placed in London newspapers in late September and early October of 1731.[127]

[124] Although best known as a bookseller residing in The Hague, where he was active from *c.*1715, Johnson appears to have operated his business in Rotterdam from 1728 until his death in 1735 (H. L. Ford, *Shakespeare 1700–1740: A Collection of Editions and Separate Plays, with Some Account of T. Johnson and R. Walker* [Oxford, 1935], p. 47).

[125] The edition of *The London Merchant* includes neither of the printer's devices that often serve to identify Johnson editions. It appears, however, that Johnson ceased to use these devices after 1730 (Ford, op. cit., p. 56). In every other respect—in typography, layout, format, and paper—the edition matches editions of plays beyond question printed for Johnson. Ford (Addenda and Corrigenda for p. 56) accepts that the edition, which he found in a copy of a collection issued by Scheurleer in 1750, is Johnson's, and this identification is confirmed by the appearance of the edition in other collections made up exclusively of Johnson plays.

[126] I am indebted to David Foxon for identifying this ornament as one which appears in books printed by the Ruddimans, among them Allen Ramsay's Scots miscellany, *The Ever Green* (vol. i, p. iii), published in Edinburgh in 1724. The imprint identifies this volume as 'Printed by Mr. Thomas Ruddiman'; Walter Ruddiman became his brother's partner in 1715 (H. R. Plomer, *A Dictionary of Printers and Booksellers . . . from 1668–1725* [London, 1922], p. 259).

[127] With the exception of Gray's authorized first and second editions of the play, this 'second edition' is the only known octavo version that can have been in print before publication of the legitimate third edition. Other piratical octavos bear later dates and follow the texts of later authorized editions. The relation of the text of this 'second edition' to the texts of the series of unquestionably authoritative editions provides the most persuasive evidence that it is indeed piratical. Textual collation reveals that the edition can only have been printed after publication of

Gray's imprint was borrowed again for a spurious 'third edition', an octavo dated 1731, which is in fact a reprint of the authorized fourth edition and cannot have been issued before publication of that edition in February 1731/2.[128]

A 'fifth edition', also taken from the authorized fourth edition, bears the probably false imprint of 'J. GREEN, at the *King's-Head*, Cornhill'. Dated 1733, and ornamented with a reversed copy of the frontispiece that had appeared in Gray's third and fourth editions, the unauthorized edition was probably produced before the legitimate fifth edition appeared, with an additional scene and new frontispiece, in February 1734/5.[129]

A unique copy, lacking the first three leaves, may represent another piratical edition issued before Lillo's death. Its text taken from the authorized sixth edition (1735), the reprint was probably issued in the mid-1730s and almost certainly was printed before 1743.[130]

---

the legitimate second edition. However, its variant readings are not reproduced in the authorized third edition—i.e. it did not serve as copy-text for the authorized publisher's next edition, although, as comparison of the seven certainly authoritative editions makes clear, it was Gray's regular practice to have each new edition set from a copy of its most recent predecessor. Moreover, in typography and format this 'second edition' has little more than a surface resemblance to editions published by John Gray. The text is crowded on to the page, the dedication is omitted altogether; a factotum is substituted for the ornamental initial that appears at the head of the text (I. i) in Gray's first, second, third, and fourth editions; and, if not 'incorrectly printed', the book is at best not printed well.

McBurney (*LM*, p. ix) accepts the edition as a second authorized edition. However, the physical characteristics, the relation of the text to the line of editions certainly printed for Gray, and the edition's correspondence with Gray's precisely descriptive advertisements about an illegitimate edition surely mark this 'second edition' as piratical. Possibly it is the version of *The London Merchant* listed in a series of newspaper advertisements for plays placed, between 14 Aug. and 14 Sept. 1731, by pamphlet shops whose rather shadowy proprietors were variously reputed to be involved in piratical activities (cf. *Daily Journal*, 14, 18, and 19 Aug., 11 and 14 Sept.).

[128] Where the texts of Gray's third and fourth editions vary, this edition regularly reproduces the readings of the authorized fourth edition. Independent readings in this 'third edition' indicate also that it cannot have preceded or have been the source of the text of the fourth edition. It lacks the engraved frontispiece that identifies the authorized third and fourth editions. Moreover, the edition is marked by its dissimilarity, in layout and format, to the series of editions published by John Gray, and by a number of omissions from the text, deletions which increase in number and length in the final pages of the play.

McBurney's textual notes identify this as the edition he records as the legitimate third edition (McBurney siglum 'C1'). At times, however, the notes referring to this edition appear to have been conflated with those which refer to the 'third edition revised' (siglum 'C2'), the authorized third edition, which McBurney identifies incorrectly as a second rather than the only legitimate third edition.

[129] The edition was first identified and described by R. H. Griffith (op. cit., p. 24).

[130] The unique copy of the edition, in the Bodleian Library, is bound with a group of Irish editions issued during the latter half of the 18th cent., and the library's catalogue suggests that the edition may have been published in Dublin during the 1760s. However, the text stems from and may well have been set from the authorized sixth edition, published in 1735. Variants separate the edition from the texts of all legitimate editions except the sixth, and from all known lines of piratical texts. It is not impossible that a piratical publisher set a new edition from a copy of a twenty-five-year-old edition which he happened to have about; however, in surveying all known editions of *The London Merchant* issued to 1775, the present editor has found no example of a piratical edition set from the text of a legitimate edition that was more than a few years out of date. Irish and Scottish reprints taken from piratical intermediaries that in turn stem from old editions have been found, but

Other editions purportedly published during the 1730s prove upon close examination to have been published in later decades. The early dates on their title-pages were intended perhaps to allow them to be passed off as old copies still in stock rather than newly printed editions which infringed the copyright claimed by the booksellers who owned or held shares in the assignment of copy purchased from John Gray. Notable examples are a 'seventh edition' and a series of at least four 'eighth editions' 'Printed for J. COOPER at *Shakespear*'s Head in Pall-Mall'. All are dated 1737, but none can have been issued before 1742 and some may have been published as late as 1760.[131]

Later Reprints

Although John Gray had not registered his copyright, his proprietorship of *The London Merchant*, confirmed by Lillo's formal assignment of rights in 1735, was clearly accepted by the well-established, respectable members of the book trade, and while perpetual copyright was disallowed officially, the booksellers' regard for traditional practices was such that the assignment continued to be respected and variously resold late in the century. It first changed hands in September 1742, when Gray sold his interest in the play to John Osborn, who published at least one edition, the eighth (1743), before he reassigned the rights to Henry Lintot in February 1746.[132] Lintot published a series of three 'ninth editions', dated 1747, 1751, and 1754, and a tenth edition, dated 1756. In 1759 Lintot's heirs sold the assignment to a group of four booksellers, two of whom, Thomas Lowndes and Thomas Caslon, held shares in the play as late as 1783.

the use of a piratical edition as copy-text for this edition is improbable. It is likely, therefore, that the incomplete copy represents an edition produced between 1735, when Lillo's publisher issued his sixth edition, and 1743, when that edition was replaced by John Osborn's eighth edition. In its general appearance, the book does not differ markedly from piratical reprints issued in London during the 1730s. The makeshift use of ornaments and the use of flowers to make up headpieces and other ornaments suggest that the edition was produced in a provincial printshop or second-rate printshop in London.

[131] The five reprints are linked not only by their imprints but also by textual details and by ornaments which appear variously in two or more editions in the series. The text of the earliest edition—the 'seventh', dated 1737—frequently parallels that of John Osborn's legitimate eighth edition of 1743 (see below). Of the four Cooper 'eighth editions', the earliest appears to have been set from a copy of the 'seventh' and, in turn, served as copy-text for the next 'eighth edition'; the other two editions follow the text of the legitimate edition published by Henry Lintot in 1754.

[132] Osborn identified his edition as the eighth, properly acknowledging the seven editions published by John Gray. His text stems from the authorized sixth edition, the last of Gray's editions which included the dedication as well as the text of the play. However, comparison of Osborn's text with that of the 'J. Cooper' 'seventh edition' suggests that Osborn's edition may well not have been set directly from a copy of the sixth edition. The Cooper text includes a number of variants seemingly introduced in the Osborn edition, but it fails to reproduce other such readings and instead follows the text of the sixth edition. Collation also makes it clear that the Osborn text cannot have been set from a copy of the piratical 'seventh edition', a procedure which would in any case have been extraordinary for the bookseller who claimed title to the play. The textual evidence is complex but can, in sum, be interpreted only to indicate that the Osborn and Cooper texts stem from an unknown intermediary which was set from Gray's sixth edition. Conceivably Osborn produced an earlier eighth edition—or a seventh—of which no copies have come to light, a not impossible hypothesis given that only two copies of the known Osborn edition have been found.

Five editions issued between 1760 and 1783 bear Lowndes's and Caslon's names along with those of other booksellers who held quarter and sixteenth shares in the play for various periods of time.[133]

Regular publication of new editions by the holders of the assignment and the replacement of frontispiece plates well worn in the production of many copies give some indication of the steady popularity of Lillo's play during the second half of the eighteenth century. The list of piratical editions speaks even more strongly for the persistent popularity of *The London Merchant*. At least eighteen of these reprints were issued between 1740 and 1770. Some took their texts from the most recent editions published by the shareholders, others made use of any text at hand, including old piratical reprints of Gray's earliest editions.[134]

In 1775, when Thomas Davies reprinted *The London Merchant* in his collected edition of Lillo's works, he fortunately chose as his copy-text a copy of Gray's seventh edition. He thus avoided perpetuating the accumulation of minor substantive misreadings and readjusted accidentals that had marked the texts of even the best of the more recent editions. Davies's edition was modernized and regularized, but in the main it is a viable reprint of Gray's last edition of the play and provided a useful and relatively accurate standard text of Lillo's play.

---

[133] The successive sales of copy, 1747–59, are recorded on the back of Lillo's original assignment to John Gray. They can be summarized as follows: 30 Sept. 1742, to John Osborn for £21; 27 Feb. 1746, to Henry Lintot for £7. 14s. 0d; 26 Apr. 1758, to Thomas Lowndes, Thomas Caslon 'and others' for twenty guineas. A sales catalogue identifies the 'others' as J. Robinson and Henry Woodgate, who was for a time in partnership with Samuel Brooks and Stanley Crowder (Longmans, No. 90, lots 15, 16, 17, and 18; Plomer, op. cit., pp. 35 and 67). That piratical competition continued to trouble the booksellers who claimed title to Lillo's play is evidenced by three extant copies of an edition issued with a cancel title-page for the 'eleventh edition', dated 1760. An engraved frontispiece links the edition itself with the J. Cooper piracies (see above), though the text may relate to a piratical edition published in Oxford in 1747 by Robert Walker and William Jackson. The cancel title constitutes the only known issue which bears the names of those who purchased shares in 1759, and the edition in its altered form may represent the partners' effort to realize a profit on their investment by reissuing confiscated copies of a piratical edition. As the 'eleventh edition', the issue maintains the regular sequence of editions sold by the holders of the copyright. Lintot's final edition (1754) was numbered the tenth. The next proper edition known to have been published by the shareholders—Lowndes, Caslon, and a somewhat altered group of partners—appeared in 1763 as the twelfth edition of the play, issued in single copies and in at least two nonce collections of plays sold by Lowndes. A thirteenth edition was published in 1766 and a fourteenth in 1770. While death and bankruptcy occasioned the resale of certain shares, some of them divided into eighths and sixteenths, Lowndes and Caslon held significant interests in the play when a new edition was published in 1782. Caslon died in 1783 and his share was purchased by Lowndes, who continued to produce new editions of *The London Merchant*. Except for the odd 'eleventh edition' reissue, the transmission of the text through the extended series of shareholders' editions was regular; each new edition was set from a copy of its immediate predecessor.

[134] Descriptions of the piratical editions published to 1775 and detailed descriptions of shareholders' editions will be found in the editor's doctoral dissertation, 'The Dramatic Works of George Lillo: An Edition and a Descriptive Bibliography to 1775', vol. iii, on deposit at the Bodleian Library.

Editorial Procedure

Modern editors of *The London Merchant* have recorded the substantive variants of at least some of Gray's series of editions but with very few exceptions have chosen to reprint the first edition, emending only to modernize and to regularize accidentals. The scene added in the fifth edition has been treated variously. A. W. Ward, for example, inserts the scene into a text which otherwise follows the first edition. William McBurney prints the scene in an appendix. Arthur E. Case, having studied a number of early editions of the play, correctly identifies the scene as the author's last revision of his text and therefore adopts the fifth edition as the copy-text for his own edition.

None of these procedures really responds to the relative complexity of the textual evidence, for none of Gray's editions alone can be taken to represent in every respect the author's intentions for the text of his play. Even reprints of the first edition, while they preserve the authenticity of the earliest printed version of the text, perpetuate a series of obvious errors and ignore corrections and authorial revisions introduced in a second edition prepared within two weeks of a hastily printed first edition. The following procedures have therefore been adopted for the present edition:

1. The first edition, including corrections in later states of corrected forms, serves as copy-text.

2. The scene first printed in the fifth edition is adopted.

3. Certainly authoritative readings of the second and third editions are adopted. Variants of uncertain authority found in the second edition are seriously considered and are adopted when no persuasive reason for rejecting them is apparent; indication of editorial nicety is considered reason for rejection, and readings clearly not authorial are, of course, not adopted. Variants of uncertain authority introduced in the third edition are considered but normally rejected. No substantive variant introduced in later editions is adopted.

4. Accidentals of the first edition are retained to the fullest extent commensurate with the requirements of an intelligible text. Obvious errors are corrected, wherever possible with readings of the earliest editions in which viable alternatives appear. Emphatic pointing to identify rhetorical questions, regularized in the second edition, is adopted. A very few dashes introduced in the second and fifth editions are adopted, not as author's revisions but as pointing characteristic of the early editions of Lillo's plays and especially appropriate to the passage concerned.

5. Additions or corrections to stage directions introduced in the second edition are adopted. The few stage directions that describe stage business and properties, added in the third edition, are adopted as conceivably, though not certainly, suggested by the author and as peculiarly helpful to the appreciation of a work intended for performance.

6. The French scene-divisions of the first and second editions are retained. The scene taken from the fifth edition has been given a scene-heading appropriate to its place in the text but has not been subdivided into French scenes; this inconsistency seems preferable to introducing scene-headings and stage directions that would have only the authority of editorial invention.[135]

[135] The copy-text is the first edition, a Yale University copy. Copies collated include: *first edition*, BL, CLU-C, CSmH, CtY (2 copies), DFo, DrU, E, IU, MH, NjP; *second edition*, IU, MH, BM; *third edition*, NN, DFo; *fourth edition*, DFo, CtY; *fifth edition*, TxU; *sixth edition*, CtMW, DFo, CtY; *seventh edition*, CSmH, CtY, NjP; Davies, *Works* (1775), CtMW, O, BL (2 copies), CtY (2 copies). Copies of all unauthorized editions published before 1740 have been collated but variants are not recorded in the apparatus of the edition. Variants recorded by Ward, McBurney, and Case (N & C) have been compared with my collation and their texts consulted in the analysis of disputed passages in the text.

THE
London Merchant:
OR, THE
HISTORY
OF
GEORGE BARNWELL.

As it is Acted at the

THEATRE-ROYAL
IN
DRURY-LANE.

By His Majesty's Servants.

By Mr. LILLO.

Learn to be wise from others Harm,
And you shall do full well.
Old Ballad of the Lady's Fall.

LONDON:

Printed for J. GRAY, at the *Cross-Keys* in the *Poultry*; and
sold by J. ROBERTS, in *Warwick-Lane.* MDCCXXXI.

[Price One Shilling and Six-pence.]

TO
Sir John Eyles, *Bar.*
Member of Parliament for,
and Alderman of the City of
London, and Sub-Governor of
the *South-Sea* Company.

SIR,

If Tragick Poetry be, as Mr. *Dryden* has some where said, the most excellent and most useful Kind of Writing, the more extensively useful the Moral of any Tragedy is, the more excellent that Piece must be of its Kind.

I hope I shall not be thought to insinuate that this, to which I have presumed to prefix your Name, is such; that depends on its Fitness to answer the End of Tragedy, the exciting of the Passions, in order to the correcting such of them as are criminal, either in their Nature, or through their Excess. Whether the following Scenes do this in any tolerable Degree, is, with the Deference, that becomes one who wou'd not be thought vain, submitted to your candid and impartial Judgment.

What I wou'd infer is this, I think, evident Truth; that Tragedy is so far from losing its Dignity, by being accommodated to the Circumstances of the Generality of Mankind, that it is more truly august in Proportion to the Extent of its Influence, and the Numbers that are properly affected by it. As it is more truly great to be the Instrument of Good to many, who stand in need of our Assistance, than to a very small Part of that Number.

If Princes, *&c.* were alone liable to Misfortunes, arising from Vice, or Weakness in themselves, or others, there wou'd be good Reason for confining the Characters in Tragedy to those of superior Rank; but, since the contrary is evident, nothing can be more reasonable than to proportion the Remedy to the Disease.

I am far from denying that Tragedies, founded on any instructive and extraordinary Events in History, or a well-invented Fable, where the Persons introduced are of the highest Rank, are without their Use, even to the Bulk of the Audience. The strong Contrast between a *Tamerlane* and a *Bajazet*, may have its Weight with an unsteady People, and contribute to the fixing of them in the Interest of a Prince of the Character of the former, when, thro' their own Levity, or the Arts of designing Men, they are render'd factious and uneasy, tho' they have the highest Reason to be satisfied. The Sentiments and Example of a *Cato*, may inspire his Spectators with a just Sense of the Value of Liberty, when they see that honest Patriot prefer Death to an Obligation from a Tyrant, who wou'd sacrifice the Constitution of his Country, and the Liberties of Mankind, to his Ambition or Revenge. I have attempted, indeed, to enlarge the Province of the graver Kind of Poetry, and should be glad to see it carried on by some abler Hand. Plays, founded on moral Tales in private Life, may be of admirable Use, by carrying Conviction to the Mind, with such irresistable Force, as to engage all the Faculties and Powers of the Soul in the Cause of Virtue, by stifling Vice in its first Principles. They who imagine this to be too much to be attributed to Tragedy, must be Strangers to the Energy of that noble Species of Poetry. *Shakespear*, who has given such amazing Proofs of his Genius, in that as well as in Comedy, in his *Hamlet*, has the following Lines,

> *Had he the Motive and the Cause for Passion*
> *That I have; he wou'd drown the Stage with Tears*
> *And cleave the general Ear with horrid Speech;*
> *Make mad the Guilty, and appale the Free,*
> *Confound the Ignorant, and amaze indeed*
> *The very Faculty of Eyes and Ears.*

And farther, in the same Speech,

> *I've heard that guilty Creatures at a Play,*
> *Have, by the very cunning of the Scene,*
> *Been so struck to the Soul, that presently*
> *They have proclaim'd their Malefactions.*

Prodigious! yet strictly just. But I shan't take up your valuable Time with my Remarks; only give me Leave just to observe, that he seems so firmly perswaded of the Power of a well wrote Piece to produce the Effect here ascribed to it, as to make *Hamlet* venture his Soul on the Event, and rather trust that, than a Messenger from the other World, tho' it assumed, as he expresses it, his *noble Father's Form*, and assured him, that it was his *Spirit. I'll have*, says *Hamlet*, *Grounds more relative.*

> ———— *The Play's the Thing,*
> *Wherein I'll catch the Conscience of the King.*

Such Plays are the best Answers to them who deny the Lawfulness of the Stage.

Considering the Novelty of this Attempt, I thought it would be expected from me to say something in its Excuse; and I was unwilling to lose the Opportunity of saying something of the Usefulness of Tragedy in general, and what may be reasonably expected from the farther Improvement of this excellent Kind of Poetry.

42 Lines,] *Ed.*; ~. G1–6   46 *appale*] appall G2–6   58–9 *noble Father's Form*] G2–6; noble Father's Form G1   59 *Spirit*] G2–6; Spirit G1   *I'll have*] G2–6; I'll have G1   60 *Grounds more relative*] G2–6; Grounds more | relative G1

Sir, I hope you will not think I have said too much of an Art, a mean Specimen of which I am ambitious enough to recommend to your Favour and Protection. A Mind, conscious of superior Worth, as much despises Flattery, as it is above it. Had I found in my self an Inclination to so contemptible a Vice, I should not have chose Sir JOHN EYLES for my Patron. And indeed the best writ Panegyrick, tho' strictly true, must place you in a Light, much inferior to that in which you have long been fix'd, by the Love and Esteem of your Fellow Citizens; whose Choice of you for one of their Representatives in Parliament, has sufficiently declared their Sense of your Merit. Nor hath the Knowledge of your Worth been confined to the City. The Proprietors in the *South-Sea* Company, in which are included Numbers of Persons, as considerable for their Rank, Fortune, and Understanding, as any in the Kingdom, gave the greatest Proof of their Confidence, in your Capacity and Probity, when they chose you Sub-Governor of their Company, at a Time when their Affairs were in the utmost Confusion, and their Properties in the greatest Danger. Neither is the Court insensible of your Importance. I shall not therefore attempt a Character so well known, nor pretend to add any Thing to a Reputation so well established.

Whatever others may think of a Dedication, wherein there is so much said of other Things, and so little of the Person to whom it is address'd, I have Reason to believe that you will the more easily pardon it on that very Account.

> *I am, SIR,*
> *Your most obedient*
> *humble Servant,*
> GEORGE LILLO.

---

79 Persons,] G2–6; ~; G1   83 Neither] G2–6; Nor G1   84–5 a Character so well known,] G5–6; your | Character, G1–4

PROLOGUE.

Spoke by Mr. CIBBER, *Jun.*

The Tragick Muse, sublime, delights to show
Princes distrest, and Scenes of Royal Woe;
In awful Pomp, Majestick, to relate
The Fall of Nations, or some Heroe's Fate:
That Scepter'd Chiefs may by Example know   5
The strange Vicissitude of Things below:
What Dangers on Security attend;
How Pride and Cruelty in Ruin end:
Hence Providence Supream to know; and own
Humanity adds Glory to a Throne.   10
   In ev'ry former Age, and Foreign Tongue,
With Native Grandure thus the Goddess sung.
Upon our Stage indeed, with wish'd Success,
You've sometimes seen her in a humbler Dress;
Great only in Distress. When she complains   15
In Southern's, Rowe's, or Otway's moving Strains,
The Brillant Drops, that fall from each bright Eye,
The absent Pomp, with brighter Jems, supply.
Forgive us then, if we attempt to show,
In artless Strains, a Tale of private Woe.   20
A London Prentice ruin'd is our Theme,
Drawn from the fam'd old Song, that bears his Name.
We hope your Taste is not so high to scorn
A·moral Tale, esteem'd ere you were born;
Which for a Century of rolling Years,   25
Has fill'd a thousand-thousand Eyes with Tears.
If thoughtless Youth to warn, and shame the Age
From Vice destructive, well becomes the Stage;
If this Example Innocence insure,
Prevent our Guilt, or by Reflection cure;   30
If Millwood's dreadful Crimes, and sad Despair,
Commend the Virtue of the Good and Fair;
Tho' Art be wanting, and our Numbers fail,
Indulge th' Attempt in Justice to the Tale.

Spoke] Spoken G5–7   14 a] an G6–7   16 Rowe's] Row's G6   19 *Forgive*]
G3–7 indent   24 *moral*] mortal G5   ere] G3–7; e'er G1–2. See Commentary   27 *If*]
G2–7 indent   29 insure] G2–7; secure G1   30 Prevent] Prevents G1 (earlier state)
31 Crimes] G2–7; Guilt G1   32 Fair;] G5–7; ~, G1–4   34 *th' Attempt*] the ~ G5–7

Dramatis Personæ.

MEN.

Thorowgood,	Mr. *Bridgwater*.
Barnwell, *Uncle to* George	Mr. *Roberts*.
George Barnwell,	Mr. *Cibber*, Jun.
Trueman,	Mr. *W. Mills*.
Blunt,	Mr. *R. Wetherilt*.

5

WOMEN.

Maria,	Mrs. *Cibber*.
Millwood,	Mrs. *Butler*.
Lucy,	Mrs. *Charke*.

10

Officers with their Attendants, Keeper, and Footmen.

SCENE London, *and an adjacent Village.*

THE
London Merchant:

OR, THE

HISTORY

OF

GEORGE BARNWELL.

ACT I.

SCENE I.

A Room in Thorowgood's *House.*

Thorowgood *and* Trueman.

Tr. Sir, the Packet from *Genoa* is arriv'd.　　　　　　　*[Gives Letters.*
Thor. Heav'n be praised, the Storm that threaten'd our Royal Mistress, pure
Religion, Liberty, and Laws, is for a Time diverted; the haughty and revengeful
Spaniard, disappointed of the Loan on which he depended from *Genoa,* must
now attend the slow return of Wealth from his new World, to supply his empty　5
Coffers, ere he can execute his purpos'd Invasion of our happy Island; by which
means Time is gain'd to make such Preparations on our Part, as may, Heav'n
concurring, prevent his Malice, or turn the meditated Mischief on himself.
Tr. He must be insensible indeed, who is not affected when the Safety of his
Country is concern'd.—Sir, may I know by what means—if I am too bold—　10
Thor. Your Curiosity is laudable; and I gratify it with the greater Pleasure,
because from thence you may learn, how honest Merchants, as such, may
sometimes contribute to the Safety of their Country, as they do at all times to its
Happiness; that if hereafter you should be tempted to any Action that has the
Appearance of Vice or Meanness in it, upon reflecting on the Dignity of our　15
Profession, you may with honest Scorn reject whatever is unworthy of it.

SD　Thorowgood] *Enter* Thorowgood G3–7　　　6　ere] G2–7; e'er G1　　　15　on] upon
G2–7

Tr. Shou'd *Barnwell*, or I, who have the Benefit of your Example, by our ill Conduct bring any Imputation on that honourable Name, we must be left without excuse.

Thor. You complement, young Man.—   [Trueman *bows respectfully.* 20
Nay, I'm not offended. As the Name of Merchant never degrades the Gentleman, so by no means does it exclude him; only take heed not to purchase the Character of Complaisant at the Expence of your Sincerity.—But to answer your Question,—The Bank of *Genoa* had agreed, at excessive Interest and on good Security, to advance the King of *Spain* a Sum of Money sufficient to equip 2
his vast Armado,—of which our peerless *Elizabeth* (more than in Name the Mother of her People) being well informed, sent *Walsingham*, her wise and faithful Secretary, to consult the Merchants of this loyal City, who all agreed to direct their several Agents to influence, if possible, the *Genoese* to break their Contract with the *Spanish* Court. 'Tis done, the State and Bank of *Genoa*, 3
having maturely weigh'd and rightly judged of their true Interest, prefer the Friendship of the Merchants of *London*, to that of a Monarch, who proudly stiles himself King of both *Indies*.

Tr. Happy Success of prudent Councils! What an Expence of Blood and Treasure is here saved?—Excellent Queen! O how unlike those Princes, who 3
make the Danger of foreign Enemies a Pretence to oppress their Subjects, by Taxes great and grievous to be born.

Thor. Not so our gracious Queen, whose richest Exchequer is her Peoples Love, as their Happiness her greatest Glory.

Tr. On these Terms to defend us, is to make our Protection a Benefit worthy her who confers it, and well worth our Acceptance.—Sir, have you any Commands for me at this Time?

Thor. Only look carefully over the Files to see whether there are any Tradesmens Bills unpaid; if there are, send and discharge 'em. We must not let Artificers lose their Time, so useful to the Publick and their Families, in unnecessary Attendance.

SCENE II.

Thorowgood *and* Maria.

Thor. Well, *Maria*, have you given Orders for the Entertainment? I would have it in some measure worthy the Guests. Let there be plenty, and of the best; that the Courtiers may at least commend our Hospitality.

(I. i)   34 Councils!] G2–7; ~. G1   35 those] G2–7; to former G1   36 make] G2–7; made G1   41 —Sir] G5–7; ʌ~ G2–4; *Tr.* Sir G1, *printing as beginning of a new speech.*
See Commentary   43 look] G2–7; to look G1   44 if] G2–7; and if G1   send] G2–7; to send G1   46 Attendance.] *after this line* G3–7 *add* SD: [*Exit* Trueman.   SCENE II.]
G3–7 *omit*   SD Thorowgood *and* Maria.] *Enter* Maria. G3–7 (~.] G5–7, *which run on from*
SD *after* I. i. 46)   1 *Thor.*] G5–7 *omit speech-heading and run on from* SD *above*
3 Courtiers] G3–7; ~, tho' they should deny us Citizens Politeness, G1–2

Ma. Sir, I have endeavoured not to wrong your well-known Generosity by an ill-tim'd Parsimony.

Thor. Nay, 'twas a needless Caution, I have no cause to doubt your Prudence.

Ma. Sir! I find my self unfit for Conversation at present, I should but increase the Number of the Company, without adding to their Satisfaction.

Thor. Nay, my Child, this Melancholy must not be indulged.

Ma. Company will but increase it. I wish you would dispense with my Absence; Solitude best suits my present Temper.

Thor. You are not insensible that it is chiefly on your Account these noble Lords do me the Honour so frequently to grace my Board; shou'd you be absent, the Disappointment may make them repent their Condescension, and think their Labour lost.

Ma. He that shall think his Time or Honour lost in visiting you, can set no real Value on your Daughter's Company, whose only Merit is that she is yours. The Man of Quality, who chuses to converse with a Gentleman and Merchant of your Worth and Character, may confer Honour by so doing, but he loses none.

Thor. Come, come *Maria*, I need not tell you that a young Gentleman may prefer your Conversation to mine, yet intend me no Disrespect at all; for tho' he may lose no Honour in my Company, 'tis very natural for him to expect more Pleasure in yours. I remember the Time, when the Company of the greatest and wisest Man in the Kingdom would have been insipid and tiresome to me, if it had deprived me of an Opportunity of enjoying your Mother's.

Ma. Your's no doubt was as agreeable to her; for generous Minds know no Pleasure in Society but where 'tis mutual.

Thor. Thou know'st I have no Heir, no Child but thee; the Fruits of many Years successful Industry must all be thine; now it would give me Pleasure great as my Love, to see on whom you would bestow it. I am daily solicited by Men of the greatest Rank and Merit for leave to address you, but I have hitherto declin'd it, in hopes that by Observation I shou'd learn which way your Inclination tends; for as I know Love to be essential to Happiness in the Marriage State, I had rather my Approbation should confirm your Choice, than direct it.

Ma. What can I say? How shall I answer, as I ought, this Tenderness, so uncommon, even in the best of Parents: But you are without Example; yet had you been less indulgent, I had been most wretched. That I look on the Croud of Courtiers, that visit here, with equal Esteem, but equal Indifference, you have observed, and I must needs confess; yet had you asserted your Authority, and insisted on a Parent's Right to be obey'd, I had submitted, and to my Duty sacrificed my Peace.

(I. ii) 7 Sir!] ~, G2–7   Conversation] ~; G2–7   at present,] G2–7 *omit. See Commentary*
9 Child,] ~! G5–7   30 thine;] G5–7; ~, G1–4   38 Parents:] ~? G5–7
43 sacrificed] sacrifice G6–7

Thor. From your perfect Obedience in every other Instance, I fear'd as much; and therefore wou'd leave you without a Byass in an Affair wherein your 45 Happiness is so immediately concern'd.

Ma. Whether from a Want of that just Ambition that wou'd become your Daughter, or from some other Cause I know not; but I find high Birth and Titles don't recommend the Man, who owns them, to my Affections.

Thor. I wou'd not that they shou'd, unless his Merit recommends him more. 5(A noble Birth and Fortune, tho' they make not a bad Man good, yet they are a real Advantage to a worthy one, and place his Virtues in the fairest Light.

Ma. I cannot answer for my Inclinations, but they shall ever be submitted to your Wisdom and Authority; and as you will not compel me to marry where I cannot love, so Love shall never make me act contrary to my Duty. Sir, have I 5 your Permission to retire?

Thor. I'll see you to your Chamber.

SCENE III.

A Room in Millwood*'s House.*

Millwood *at her Toilet.* Lucy *waiting.*

Mill. How do I look to Day, *Lucy*?

Lucy. O, killingly, Madam!—A little more Red, and you'll be irresistible!— But why this more than ordinary Care of your Dress and Complexion? What new Conquest are you aiming at?

Mill. A Conquest wou'd be new indeed!

Lucy. Not to you, who make 'em every Day,—but to me.—Well! 'tis what I'm never to expect,—unfortunate as I am:—But your Wit and Beauty—

Mill. First made me a Wretch, and still continue me so.—Men, however generous or sincere to one another, are all selfish Hypocrites in their Affairs with us. We are no otherwise esteemed or regarded by them, but as we 1 contribute to their Satisfaction.

Lucy. You are certainly, Madam, on the wrong Side in this Argument: Is not the Expence all theirs? And I am sure it is our own Fault if we hav'n't our Share of the Pleasure.

Mill. We are but Slaves to Men.

Lucy. Nay, 'tis they that are Slaves most certainly; for we lay them under Contribution.

Mill. Slaves have no Property; no, not even in themselves.—All is the Victors.

Lucy. You are strangely arbitrary in your Principles, Madam.

Mill. I would have my Conquests compleat, like those of the *Spaniards* in the   20
New World; who first plunder'd the Natives of all the Wealth they had, and
then condemn'd the Wretches to the Mines for Life, to work for more.

Lucy. Well, I shall never approve of your Scheme of Government: I should
think it much more politick, as well as just, to find my Subjects an easier
Imployment.   25

Mill. It's a general Maxim among the knowing Part of Mankind, that a
Woman without Virtue, like a Man without Honour or Honesty, is capable of
any Action, tho' never so vile: And yet what Pains will they not take, what Arts
not use, to seduce us from our Innocence, and make us contemptible and
wicked, even in their own Opinions? Then is it not just, the Villains, to their   30
Cost, should find us so?—But Guilt makes them suspicious, and keeps them on
their Guard; therefore we can take Advantage only of the young and innocent
Part of the Sex, who having never injured Women, apprehend no Injury from
them.

Lucy. Ay, they must be young indeed.   35

Mill. Such a one, I think, I have found.—As I've passed thro' the City, I have
often observ'd him receiving and paying considerable Sums of Money; from
thence I conclude he is employ'd in Affairs of Consequence.

Lucy. Is he handsome?

Mill. Ay, ay, the Stripling is well made, and has a good Face.   40

Lucy. About—

Mill. Eighteen—

Lucy. Innocent, Handsome, and about Eighteen.—You'll be vastly happy.—
Why, if you manage well, you may keep him to your self these two or three
Years.   45

Mill. If I manage well, I shall have done with him much sooner. Having long
had a Design on him, and meeting him Yesterday, I made a full Stop, and
gazing wishfully on his Face, ask'd him his Name: He blush'd, and bowing very
low, answer'd, *George Barnwell*. I beg'd his Pardon for the Freedom I had taken,
and told him, that he was the Person I had long wish'd to see, and to whom I   50
had an Affair of Importance to communicate, at a proper Time and Place. He
named a Tavern; I talk'd of Honour and Reputation, and invited him to my
House: He swallow'd the Bait, promis'd to come, and this is the Time I expect
him. [*Knocking at the Door.*] Some Body knocks,—d'ye hear; I am at Home to
no Body to Day, but him.—   55

(I. iii)   31 so?] G5–7; ~. G1–3; ~‸ G4   40 made,] G2–7; ~. G1   and has a good
Face.] G2–7; *not in* G1   43 Eighteen.] ~! G2–7   46 sooner. Having] G5–7; ~,
having G1–4. *See Commentary*   47 him,] G5–7; ~; G1–4   54 him.] G5–7; ~, G1–4
55 him.—] ~.‸ G2–7; *after this line* G3–7 *add* SD: [*Exit* Lucy.] (‸~ *Lucy.*‸ G3; ‸~.‸ G4; *Lucy*
G5–6)

SCENE IV.

Millwood.

Less Affairs must give Way to those of more Consequence; and I am strangely mistaken if this does not prove of great Importance to me and him too, before I have done with him.—Now, after what Manner shall I receive him? Let me consider—what manner of Person am I to receive?—He is young, innocent, and bashful; therefore I must take Care not to put him out of Countenance, at first.—But then, if I have any Skill in Phisiognomy, he is amorous, and, with a little Assistance, will soon get the better of his Modesty.—I'll e'en trust to Nature, who does Wonders in these Matters.—If to seem what one is not, in order to be the better liked for what one really is; if to speak one thing, and mean the direct contrary, be Art in a Woman, I know nothing of Nature.

SCENE V.

[*To her.*] Barnwell *bowing very low.* Lucy *at a Distance.*

Mill. Sir! the Surprize and Joy!—
Barn. Madam.—
Mill. This is such a Favour,—   [*Advancing.*
Barn. Pardon me, Madam,—
Mill. So unhop'd for,—   [*Still advances.*

[Barnwell *salutes her, and retires in Confusion.*]

To see you here.—Excuse the Confusion.—
Barn. I fear I am too bold.—
Mill. Alas, Sir! I may justly apprehend you think me so.—Please, Sir, to sit.—I am as much at a Loss how to receive this Honour as I ought, as I am surpriz'd at your Goodness in confering it.
Barn. I thought you had expected me—I promis'd to come.
Mill. That is the more surprizing; few Men are such religious Observers of their Word.
Barn. All, who are honest, are.

SCENE IV.] G3–7 *omit*   SD Millwood.] G3–7 *omit*   1 G1, 3–4 *include speech-heading: Mill.*; G5–7 *run on from* SD *after* I. iii. 55.   5 put him out of Countenance,] G3–7; shock him G1–2   7 e'en] G3–7; *not in* G1–2   8 one] G7 *omits*   10 Woman,] ~— G3–7
SCENE V.] G3–7 *omit*   SD [*To her.*]] ∧*Enter* ∧∧ G2–7   *low.*] G2–7; ~, G1
2 Madam.] ~∧ G3–4; ~! G5–7   3 Favour,] ~! G5–7   4 Madam,] ~! G5–7
5 for,] ~! G5–6; ~. G7   5+SD–6 *Confusion.*] | To see] *Ed.*; ~.∧ | *Mill.* To see G1–7, *which repeat speech-heading*   6 here.] ~! G5–7   Confusion.] ~! G7   8 I may justly apprehend you think] G3–7; All my Apprehensions proceed from my Fears of your thinking G1–2.
See Commentary

Mill. To one another:—But we simple Women are seldom thought of 15
Consequence enough to gain a Place in your Remembrance.

[Laying her Hand on his, as by Accident.

Barn. Her Disorder is so great, she don't perceive she has laid her Hand on
mine.—Heaven! how she trembles!—What can this mean!   *[Aside.*

Mill. The Interest I have in all that relates to you, (the Reason of which you
shall know hereafter) excites my Curiosity; and, were I sure you would pardon 20
my Presumption, I should desire to know your real Sentiments on a very
particular Subject.

Barn. Madam, you may command my poor Thoughts on any Subject;—I
have none that I would conceal.

Mill. You'll think me bold.   25

Barn. No, indeed.

Mill. What then are your Thoughts of Love?

Barn. If you mean the Love of Women, I have not thought of it at all.—My
Youth and Circumstances make such Thoughts improper in me yet: But if you
mean the general Love we owe to Mankind, I think no one has more of it in his 30
Temper than my self.—I don't know that Person in the World whose
Happiness I don't wish, and wou'd n't promote, were it in my Power.—In an
especial manner I love my Uncle, and my Master, but, above all, my Friend.

Mill. You have a Friend then, whom you love?

Barn. As he does me, sincerely.   35

Mill. He is, no doubt, often bless'd with your Company and Conversation.—

Barn. We live in one House, and both serve the same worthy Merchant.

Mill. Happy, happy Youth!—who e'er thou art, I envy thee, and so must all,
who see and know this Youth.—What have I lost, by being form'd a Woman!—
I hate my Sex, my self.—Had I been a Man, I might, perhaps, have been as 40
happy in your Friendship, as he who now enjoys it:—But as it is,—Oh!—

Barn. I never observ'd Women before, or this is sure the most beautiful of her
Sex. [*Aside.*] ·You seem disorder'd, Madam! May I know the Cause?

Mill. Do not ask me,—I can never speak it, whatever is the Cause;—I wish
for Things impossible:—I wou'd be a Servant, bound to the same Master, to 45
live in one House with you.

Barn. How strange, and yet how kind, her Words and Actions are!—And the
Effect they have on me is as strange.—I feel Desires I never knew before;—I
must be gone, while I have Power to go. [*Aside.*] Madam, I humbly take my
Leave.—   50

Mill. You will not sure leave me so soon!

Barn. Indeed I must.

(I. v)   15 simple] G3–7; silly G1–2   18 Heaven] Heavens G5–7   22 Subject]
G3–7; Affair G1–2. *See Commentary*   28 at] G3–7; *not in* G1–2   37 House] G2–7;
House together G1   43 Sex.] G5–7; ~, G1–4   45 Master] G3–7; Master as you are
G1–2   47 are!] G2–6; ~? G1; ~; G7   49 go.] G5–7; ~, G1–4

Mill. You cannot be so cruel!—I have prepar'd a poor Supper, at which I promis'd my self your Company.

Barn. I am sorry I must refuse the Honour that you design'd me;—But my Duty to my Master calls me hence.—I never yet neglected his Service: He is so gentle, and so good a Master, that should I wrong him, tho' he might forgive me, I never should forgive my self.

Mill. Am I refus'd, by the first Man, the second Favour I ever stoop'd to ask?—Go then thou proud hard-hearted Youth.—But know, you are the only Man that cou'd be found, who would let me sue twice for greater Favours.

Barn. What shall I do!—How shall I go or stay!

Mill. Yet do not,—do not leave me.—I with my Sex's Pride wou'd meet your Scorn:—But when I look upon you,—When I behold those Eyes,— Oh! spare my Tongue, and let my Blushes (this Flood of Tears to that will force its Way) declare what Woman's Modesty should hide.

Barn. Oh, Heavens! she loves me, worthless as I am; her Looks, her Words, her flowing Tears confess it:—And can I leave her then?—Oh, never,— never.—Madam, dry up those Tears.—You shall command me always;—I will stay here for ever, if you'd have me.

Lucy. So! she has wheedled him out of his Virtue of Obedience already, and will strip him of all the rest, one after another, 'till she has left him as few as her Ladyship, or my self.   *[Aside.*

Mill. Now you are kind, indeed; but I mean not to detain you always: I would have you shake off all slavish Obedience to your Master;—but you may serve him still.

Lucy. Serve him still!—Aye, or he'll have no Opportunity of fingering his Cash, and then he'll not serve your End, I'll be sworn.   *[Aside.*

SCENE VI.

[To them.] Blunt.

Blunt. Madam, Supper's on the Table.

Mill. Come, Sir, you'll excuse all Defects.—My Thoughts were too much employ'd on my Guest to observe the Entertainment.

(I. v)   55 that] G2–7 *omit*   63 do not,—do not] G2–4; ~, ˄~, G1; ~,˄ ~˄ G5–7
with] G2–7; wish G1. *See Commentary*   65–6 Blushes (this . . . declare] G2–7 (Blushes—
. . . declare— G5–7); Blushes speak.— | This Flood of Tears to that will force their way, and
declare— G1   69 those] your G2–7   SCENE VI.] G3–7 *omit*   SD [*To them.*]]
˄Enter˄˄ G3–7   2 you'll] G2–7; You'll G1   3 Entertainment.] *after this line* G3–7 *add*
SD: [*Exeunt* Barnwell *and* Millwood.

SCENE VII.

Lucy *and* Blunt.

Blunt. What, is all this Preparation, this elegant Supper, Variety of Wines, and Musick, for the Entertainment of that young Fellow!

Lucy. So it seems.

Blunt. What, is our Mistress turn'd Fool at last! She's in Love with him, I suppose.   5

Lucy. I suppose not,—but she designs to make him in Love with her, if she can.

Blunt. What will she get by that? He seems under Age, and can't be suppos'd to have much Money.

Lucy. But his Master has; and that's the same thing, as she'll manage it.   10

Blunt. I don't like this fooling with a handsome young Fellow; while she's endeavouring to ensnare him, she may be caught her self.

Lucy. Nay, were she like me, that would certainly be the Consequence;—for, I confess, there is something in Youth and Innocence that moves me mightily.

Blunt. Yes, so does the Smoothness and Plumpness of a Patridge move a   15
mighty Desire in the Hawk to be the Destruction of it.

Lucy. Why, Birds are their Prey, as Men are ours; though, as you observ'd, we are sometimes caught our selves:—But that I dare say will never be the Case with our Mistress.

Blunt. I wish it may prove so; for you know we all depend upon her: Should   20
she trifle away her Time with a young Fellow, that there's nothing to be got by, we must all starve.

Lucy. There's no Danger of that, for I am sure she has no View in this Affair, but Interest.

Blunt. Well, and what Hopes are there of Success in that?   25

Lucy. The most promising that can be.—'Tis true, the Youth has his Scruples; but she'll soon teach him to answer them, by stifling his Conscience.—O, the Lad is in a hopeful Way, depend upon't.

SCENE VII.] G3–7 *omit*   SD Lucy *and* Blunt.] G3–7 *omit*   1 What, is] *Ed.*; ~ ∧
~ G1; What's G2–7. *See Commentary*   4 What,] *Ed.*; ~ ∧ G1–7   14 there] their G3
15 Patridge] Partridge G6–7   28 upon't.] *after this line* G3–7 *add* SD: [*Exeunt.* (∧~. G3–5)

SCENE VIII.

Scene draws and discovers Barnwell *and* Millwood
at Supper. An Entertinment of Musick and Singing.
After which they come forward.

Barn. What can I answer!—All that I know is, that you are fair, and I am miserable.

Mill. We are both so, and yet the Fault is in our selves.

Barn. To ease our present Anguish, by plunging into Guilt, is to buy a Moment's Pleasure with an Age of Pain.

Mill. I should have thought the Joys of Love as lasting as they are great: If ours prove otherwise, 'tis your Inconstancy must make them so.

Barn. The Law of Heaven will not be revers'd; and that requires us to govern our Passions.

Mill. To give us Sense of Beauty and Desires, and yet forbid us to taste and be happy, is Cruelty to Nature.—Have we Passions only to torment us!

Barn. To hear you talk,—tho' in the Cause of Vice,—to gaze upon your Beauty,—press your Hand,—and see your Snow-white Bosom heave and fall,—enflames my Wishes;—my Pulse beats high,—my Senses all are in a Hurry, and I am on the Rack of wild Desire;—yet for a Moment's guilty Pleasure, shall I lose my Innocence, my Peace of Mind, and Hopes of solid Happiness?

Mill. Chimeras all,—

—Come on with me and prove,
No Joy's like Woman kind, nor Heav'n like Love.

Barn. I wou'd not,—yet I must on.—

Reluctant thus, the Merchant quits his Ease,
And trusts to Rocks, and Sands, and stormy Seas;
In Hopes some unknown golden Coast to find,
Commits himself, tho' doubtful, to the Wind,
Longs much for Joys to come,—yet mourns those left behind.

The End of the First Act.

SCENE VIII.] G3–7 *omit*   SD *Scene draws . . . come forward.*] G3–7; Barnwell *and*
Millwood *at an Entertainment.* G1–2   11 Cruelty] a cruelty G6–7   15 Desire;—yet]
~.—Yet G2–7   18–19 Chimeras all,— | —Come] Chimeras all!ᴧ Come G5–7, *printing* 18
as beginning of the couplet   20 Woman kind] Woman-kind G6–7   nor] no G2–7
21 I must] must G3–7   26 come,—] G2–7; ~,ᴧ G1   behind.] *after this line* G3–7 *add* SD:
[Exeunt.   The End of the First Act.] G6 *omits*

ACT II.

SCENE I.

A Room in Thorowgood's *House.*

Barnwell.

How strange are all Things round me? Like some Thief, who treads
forbidden Ground, and fain wou'd lurk unseen, fearful I enter each Apartment
of this well known House. To guilty Love, as if that was too little, already have I
added Breach of Trust.—A Thief!—Can I know my self that wretched Thing,
and look my honest Friend and injured Master in the Face?—Tho' Hypocrisy   5
may a while conceal my Guilt, at length it will be known, and publick Shame
and Ruin must ensue. In the mean time, what must be my Life? ever to speak a
Language foreign to my Heart; hourly to add to the Number of my Crimes in
order to conceal 'em.—Sure such was the Condition of the grand Apostate,
when first he lost his Purity; like me disconsolate he wander'd, and while yet in   10
Heaven, bore all his future Hell about him.

SCENE II.

Barnwell *and* Trueman.

Tr. Barnwell! O how I rejoice to see you safe! so will our Master and his
gentle Daughter, who during your Absence often inquir'd after you.
  Barn. Wou'd he were gone, his officious Love will pry into the Secrets of my
Soul.   [*Aside.*
  Tr. Unless you knew the Pain the whole Family has felt on your Account, you   5
can't conceive how much you are belov'd; but why thus cold and silent? when
my Heart is full of Joy for your Return, why do you turn away? why thus avoid
me? what have I done? how am I alter'd since you saw me last? Or rather what
have you done? and why are you thus changed? for I am still the same.
  Barn. What have I done indeed?   [*Aside.* 10
  Tr. Not speak nor look upon me!—
  Barn. By my Face he will discover all I wou'd conceal; methinks already I
begin to hate him.   [*Aside.*
  Tr. I cannot bear this Usage from a Friend, one whom till now I ever found so
loving, whom yet I love, tho' this Unkindness strikes at the Root of Friendship,   15
and might destroy it in any Breast but mine.

  SD Barnwell.] *Enter* Barnwell. G3–7   1 G1, 3–7 *include speech-heading: Barn.*
(*BARNWELL.* G6)   2 and fain wou'd lurk unseen,] G2–7; *not in* G1   3 was] were
G3–7   SCENE II.] G3–7 *omit*   SD Barnwell *and*] *Enter* G3–7   6 belov'd; but] ~:
But G4; ~:—But G5–7   11 speak] ~, G4; ~!—G5–7   me!—] G6–7; ~.ᴧ G1–4;
~;— G5

Barn. I am not well; [*Turning to him.*] Sleep has been a Stranger to these Eyes since you beheld them last.

Tr. Heavy they look indeed, and swoln with Tears;—now they o'erflow;— rightly did my sympathizing Heart forebode last Night when thou wast absent, something fatal to our Peace.

Barn. Your Friendship ingages you too far. My Troubles, whate'er they are, are mine alone, you have no Interest in them, nor ought your Concern for me give you a Moment's Pain.

Tr. You speak as if you knew of Friendship nothing but the Name. Before I saw your Grief I felt it. Since we parted last I have slept no more than you, but pensive in my Chamber sat alone, and spent the tedious Night in Wishes for your Safety and Return; e'en now, tho' ignorant of the Cause, your Sorrow wounds me to the Heart.

Barn. 'Twill not be always thus: Friendship and all Engagements cease, as Circumstances and Occasions vary; and since you once may hate me, perhaps it might be better for us both that now you lov'd me less.

Tr. Sure I but dream! without a Cause would *Barnwell* use me thus?— ungenerous and ungrateful Youth, farewell,—I shall endeavour to follow your Advice,—[*Going.*] Yet stay, perhaps I am too rash, and angry when the Cause demands Compassion. Some unforeseen Calamity may have befaln him too great to bear.

Barn. What Part am I reduc'd to act;—'tis vile and base to move his Temper thus, the best of Friends and Men.

Tr. I am to blame, prithee forgive me *Barnwell*.—Try to compose your ruffled Mind, and let me know the Cause that thus transports you from your Self; my friendly Counsel may restore your Peace.

Barn. All that is possible for Man to do for Man, your generous Friendship may effect; but here even that's in vain.

Tr. Something dreadful is labouring in your Breast, O give it vent and let me share your Grief; 'twill ease your Pain shou'd it admit no cure, and make it lighter by the Part I bear.

Barn. Vain Supposition! my Woes increase by being observ'd, shou'd the Cause be known they wou'd exceed all Bounds.

Tr. So well I know thy honest Heart, Guilt cannot harbour there.

Barn. O Torture insupportable!   [*Aside.*

Tr. Then why am I excluded, have I a Thought I would conceal from you?

Barn. If still you urge me on this hated Subject, I'll never enter more beneath this Roof, nor see your Face again.

Tr. 'Tis strange,—but I have done, say but you hate me not.

Barn. Hate you!—I am not that Monster yet.

(II. ii)   17 well;] G5–7; ~, G1–4   24 give] to give G6–7   30 thus:] *Ed.*; ~, G1–4; ~. G5–7   33 thus?—] G4–7; ~,∧ G1–3   34 Youth,] G3–7; ~∧ G1–2 38 act;—] ~?— G2–4; ~?∧ G5–7   46 Grief;] G5–7; ~, G1–4   cure,] G5–7 (Cure G5–7); ~; G1–4   52 excluded,] ~? G5–7   you?] G2–7; ~. G1

Tr. Shall our Friendship still continue?

Barn. It's a Blessing I never was worthy of, yet now must stand on Terms; and but upon Conditions can confirm it.

Tr. What are they? 60

Barn. Never hereafter, tho' you shou'd wonder at my Conduct, desire to know more than I am willing to reveal.

Tr. 'Tis hard, but upon any Conditions I must be your Friend.

Barn. Then, as much as one lost to himself can be another's, I am yours.

[*Embracing.*

Tr. Be ever so, and may Heav'n restore your Peace. 65

Barn. Will Yesterday return?—We have heard the glorious Sun, that till then incessant roll'd, once stopp'd his rapid Course, and once went back: The Dead have risen; and parched Rocks pour'd forth a liquid Stream to quench a Peoples Thirst: The Sea divided, and form'd Walls of Water, while a whole Nation pass'd in safety thro' its sandy Bosom: Hungry Lions have refus'd their 70 Prey: And Men unhurt have walk'd amidst consuming Flames; but never yet did Time once past, return.

Tr. Tho' the continued Chain of Time has never once been broke, nor ever will, but uninterrupted must keep on its Course, till lost in Eternity it ends there where it first begun; yet as Heav'n can repair whatever Evils Time can bring 75 upon us, we ought never to despair.—But Business requires our Attendance; Business the Youth's best Preservative from ill, as Idleness his worst of Snares. Will you go with me?

Barn. I'll take a little Time to reflect on what has past, and follow you.

SCENE III.

Barnwell.

I might have trusted *Trueman* and ingaged him to apply to my Uncle to repair the Wrong I have done my Master; but what of *Millwood*? must I expose her too? ungenerous and base! then Heav'n requires it not.—But Heaven requires that I forsake her. What! never see her more! Does Heaven require that,—I hope I may see her, and Heav'n not be offended. Presumptuous Hope,—dearly 5 already have I prov'd my Frailty; should I once more tempt Heav'n, I may be left to fall never to rise again.—Yet shall I leave her, for ever leave her, and not

(I. ii) 57 continue?] G2–7; ~. G1   66 return?] G2–7; ~. G1   76 we ought] G2–7; he who trusts Heaven ought G1   despair.—] *Ed.*; ~.ᴧ G1; ~ᴧ— G5–7 77 Snares.] ~— G5–7   79 you.] *after this line* G3–7 *add* SD: [*Exit* Trueman.] (ᴧ~.ᴧ G3; [~.ᴧ G4)   SCENE III.] G3–7 *omit*   SD Barnwell.] G3–7 *omit*   1 G3–4 *add speech-heading: Barn.*; G5–7 *run on from* II. ii. 79   and ingaged him to apply] G3–7; to have applied G1; who wou'd apply G2. *See Commentary*   repair] G2–7; have repaired G1 4 that,] ~? G6–7   7 again.—] G3–7; ~.ᴧ G1; ~—. G2

let her know the Cause? She who loves me with such a boundless Passion;—
can Cruelty be Duty? I judge of what she then must feel, by what I now
indure.—The love of Life and fear of Shame, oppos'd by Inclination strong as   10
Death or Shame, like Wind and Tide in raging Conflict met, when neither can
prevail, keep me in doubt.—How then can I determine?

SCENE IV.

Thorowgood *and* Barnwell.

Thor. Without a Cause assign'd, or Notice given, to absent your self last
Night was a Fault, young Man, and I came to chide you for it, but hope I am
prevented; that modest Blush, the Confusion so visible in your Face, speak
Grief and Shame: When we have offended Heaven, it requires no more; and
shall Man, who needs himself to be forgiven, be harder to appease: If my   5
Pardon or Love be of moment to your Peace, look up secure of both.
Barn. This Goodness has o'er come me. [*Aside.*] O Sir! you know not the
Nature and Extent of my Offence; and I shou'd abuse your mistaken Bounty to
receive 'em. Tho' I had rather die than speak my Shame; tho' Racks could not
have forced the guilty Secret from my Breast, your Kindness has.   10
Thor. Enough, enough, whate'er it be, this Concern shews you're convinc'd,
and I am satisfied. How painful is the Sense of Guilt to an ingenuous Mind;—
some youthful Folly, which it were prudent not to enquire into.—When we
consider the frail Condition of Humanity, it may raise our Pity, not our
Wonder, that Youth should go astray; when Reason, weak at the best when   15
oppos'd to Inclination, scarce form'd, and wholly unassisted by Experience,
faintly contends, or willingly becomes the Slave of Sense. The State of Youth is
much to be deplored; and the more so because they see it not; being then to
danger most expos'd, when they are least prepar'd for their Defence.
                                                                     [*Aside.*
Barn. It will be known, and you recall your Pardon and abhor me.   20
Thor. I never will. Yet be upon your Guard in this gay thoughtless Season of
your Life; now, when the Sense of Pleasure's quick, and Passion high, the
voluptuous Appetites raging and fierce demand the strongest Curb; take heed
of a Relapse: When Vice becomes habitual, the very Power of leaving it is lost.
Barn. Hear me on my Knees confess.   25

(II. iii)   8 Passion;—] G2–4; ~;$_\wedge$ G1; ~.— G5; ~!— G6–7   10 indure.—] G2–3; ~.$_\wedge$
G1; en-|dure$_\wedge$— G4; endure.$_\wedge$ G5–7   12 determine?] G2–7 (~. G7); determines. G1
SCENE IV.] G3–7 *omit*   SD Thorowgood *and* Barnwell.] *Enter* Thorowgood. G3–7
9 'em] it G2–7   12 Mind;—] ~?— G2–7   15–16 best when oppos'd] best, oppos'd
G2–4; best$_\wedge$ opposed G5–7 (oppos-|ed G5). *See Commentary*   18 being] G2–7; they being G1
19 SD [*Aside.*] G2–7; *not in* G1   21 will.] G2–7; ~; so Heav'n confirm to me the Pardon of
my Offences. G1. *See Commentary*   22 now,] G2–7 *omit*   25 me] G2–7; me then G1.
See Commentary

Thor. Not a Syllable more upon this Subject; it were not Mercy, but Cruelty, to hear what must give you such Torment to reveal.

Barn. This Generosity amazes and distracts me.

Thor. This Remorse makes thee dearer to me than if thou hadst never offended; whatever is your Fault, of this I'm certain, 'twas harder for you to offend than me to pardon.   30

SCENE V.

Barnwell.

Villain, Villain, Villain! basely to wrong so excellent a Man: Shou'd I again return to Folly—detested Thought;—but what of *Millwood* then?—Why, I renounce her;—I give her up;—the Struggle's over, and Virtue has prevail'd. Reason may convince, but Gratitude compels. This unlook'd for Generosity has sav'd me from Destruction.   [*Going.* 5

SCENE VI.

[*To him.*] *A Footman.*

Foot. Sir, two Ladies, from your Uncle in the Country, desire to see you.

Barn. Who shou'd they be? [*Aside.*] Tell them I'll wait upon 'em.

SCENE VII.

Barnwell.

Methinks I dread to see 'em.—Now every Thing alarms me.—Guilt what a Coward hast thou made me?

(II. iv)   26 Not a] G2–7; I will not hear a G1   31 pardon.] *after this line* G3–7 *add* SD: [*Exit* Thorowgood. (ʌ~. G3)   SCENE V.] G3–7 *omit*   SD Barnwell.] G3–7 *omit* 1 G1, 3–7 *include speech-heading: Barn.*   Villain, Villain,] ~! ~! G5–7   2 Folly] ~, G2–4; ~? G5–7   SCENE VI.] G3–7 *omit*   SD [*To him.*] *A*] Ed.; ʌ~ʌʌ *a* G1–2; ʌ*Enter*ʌʌ *a* G3–7   2 'em.] *after this line* G3–7 *add* SD: [*Exit Footman.*] (ʌ~. ʌ G3; [~.ʌ G4–6) SCENE VII.] G3–7 *omit*   SD Barnwell.] G3–7 *omit*   1 G1, 3–6 *include speech-heading: Barn.*; G7 *runs on from* SD *after* II. vi. 2   1–2 Now every ... made me?] G3–7 (alarms me,ʌ G4); Guilt, | what a Coward hast thou made me?—Now every | Thing alarms me. G1–2 (made me?ʌ ... ev'ry G2)

SCENE VIII.

Another Room in Thorowgood's *House.*

Millwood *and* Lucy, *and to them a Footman.*

Foot. Ladies, he'll wait upon you immediately.
Mill. 'Tis very well.—I thank you.

SCENE IX.

Barnwell, Millwood, *and* Lucy.

Barn. Confusion! *Millwood.*
Mill. That angry Look tells me that here I'm an unwelcome Guest; I fear'd as much,—the Unhappy are so every where.
Barn. Will nothing but my utter Ruin content you?
Mill. Unkind and cruel! lost my self, your Happiness is now my only Care.
Barn. How did you gain Admission?
Mill. Saying we were desir'd by your Uncle to visit and deliver a Message to you, we were receiv'd by the Family without suspicion, and with much respect conducted here.
Barn. Why did you come at all?   1
Mill. I never shall trouble you more, I'm come to take my Leave for ever. Such is the Malice of my Fate. I go hopeless, despairing ever to return. This Hour is all I have left me. One short Hour is all I have to bestow on Love and you, for whom I thought the longest Life too short.
Barn. Then we are met to part for ever?   1
Mill. It must be so;—yet think not that Time or Absence ever shall put a Period to my Grief, or make me love you less; tho' I must leave you, yet condemn me not.
Barn. Condemn you? No, I approve your Resolution, and rejoice to hear it; 'tis just,—'tis necessary,—I have well weigh'd, and found it so.   2
Lucy. I'm afraid the young Man has more Sense than she thought he had.
                                                                          [*Aside.*
Barn. Before you came I had determin'd never to see you more.
Mill. Confusion!   [*Aside.*
Lucy. Ay! we are all out; this is a Turn so unexpected, that I shall make nothing of my Part, they must e'en play the Scene betwixt themselves.   [*Aside.*

SCENE VIII.] SCENE II. G3–7   SD Millwood *and . . . to them*] Millwood *and* Lucy
discover'd. Enter G3–7 (*discovered* G5–7)   2 you.] *after this line* G3–7 *add* SD: *Exit Footman.*
(*Foot.* G5–6)   SCENE IX.] G3–7 *omit*   SD Barnwell, Millwood, *and* Lucy.] *Enter*
Barnwell. G3–7   1 *Millwood.*] ~! G2–4, 7; ~!— G5–6   9 conducted] G3–7;
directed G1–2   13 left me.] left. G5–7   16 ever shall] shall ever G2–7

Mill. 'Twas some relief to think, tho' absent, you would love me still; but to find, tho' Fortune had been indulgent, that you, more cruel and inconstant, had resolv'd to cast me off.—This, as I never cou'd expect, I have not learnt to bear.

Barn. I am sorry to hear you blame in me a Resolution that so well becomes us both.   30

Mill. I have Reason for what I do, but you have none.

Barn. Can we want a Reason for parting, who have so many to wish we never had met?

Mill. Look on me, *Barnwell*, am I deform'd or old, that Satiety so soon succeeds Enjoyment? nay, look again, am I not she whom Yesterday you 35 thought the fairest and the kindest of her Sex? whose Hand, trembling with Extacy, you prest and moulded thus, while on my Eyes you gazed with such delight, as if Desire increas'd by being fed.

Barn. No more; let me repent my former Follies, if possible, without remembring what they were.   40

Mill. Why?

Barn. Such is my Frailty that 'tis dangerous.

Mill. Where is the Danger, since we are to part?

Barn. The Thought of that already is too painful.

Mill. If it be painful to part, then I may hope at least you do not hate me? 45

Barn. No,—no,—I never said I did,—O my Heart!—

Mill. Perhaps you pity me?

Barn. I do,—I do,—indeed, I do.

Mill. You'll think upon me?

Barn. Doubt it not while I can think at all.   50

Mill. You may judge an Embrace at parting too great a Favour,—though it would be the last? [*He draws back.*] A Look shall then suffice,—farewell,—for ever.

SCENE X.

Barnwell.

If to resolve to suffer be to conquer,—I have conquer'd.—Painful Victory!

(II. ix)   27 indulgent] G2–7; kind G1   29 me] G2–7; ~, G1   33 met?] G6–7; ~.
G1–5   34 me,] G5–7; ~‸ G1–4   39 more;] G5–7; ~, G1–4   51 Favour,—]
G2–7; ~,‸ G1   52 farewell,—] G2–6; ~‸‸ G1; ~,‸ G7   52–3 for ever.] *after this line*
G3–7 *add* SD: [*Exeunt* Millwood *and* Lucy.   SCENE X.] G3–7 *omit*   SD Barnwell.]
G3–7 *omit*   1 G1, 3–7 *include speech-heading:* Barn.   conquer,—] G2–7; ~,‸ G1
conquer'd.—] G2–7; ~.‸ G1

SCENE XI.

Barnwell, Millwood *and* Lucy.

Mill. One thing I had forgot,—I never must return to my own House again. This I thought proper to let you know, lest your Mind should change, and you shou'd seek in vain to find me there. Forgive me this second Intrusion; I only came to give you this Caution, and that perhaps was needless.

Barn. I hope it was, yet it is kind, and I must thank you for it.   5

Mill. My Friend, your Arm. [*To* Lucy.] Now I am gone for ever.   [*Going.*

Barn. One thing more;—sure there's no danger in my knowing where you go? If you think otherwise?—

Mill. Alas!   [*Weeping.*

Lucy. We are right I find, that's my Cue.   [*Aside.* 10
Ah; dear Sir, she's going she knows not whether; but go she must.

Barn. Humanity obliges me to wish you well; why will you thus expose your self to needless Troubles?

Lucy. Nay, there's no help for it: She must quit the Town immediately, and the Kingdom as soon as possible; it was no small Matter you may be sure, that   15
could make her resolve to leave you.

Mill. No more, my Friend; since he for whose dear Sake alone I suffer, and am content to suffer, is kind and pities me. Wheree'er I wander through Wiles and Desarts, benighted and forlorn, that Thought shall give me comfort.

Barn. For my Sake! O tell me how; which way am I so curs'd as to bring such 20
Ruin on thee?

Mill. No matter,—I am contented with my Lot.

Barn. Leave me not in this Incertainty.

Mill. I have said too much.

Barn. How, how am I the Cause of your Undoing?   25

Mill. To know it will but increase your Troubles.

Barn. My Troubles can't be greater than they are.

Lucy. Well, well, Sir, if she won't satisfy you, I will.

Barn. I am bound to you beyond Expression.

Mill. Remember, Sir, that I desir'd you not to hear it.   30

Barn. Begin, and ease my racking Expectation.

Lucy. Why you must know, my Lady here was an only Child; but her Parents dying while she was young, left her and her Fortune, (no inconsiderable one, I assure you) to the Care of a Gentleman, who has a good Estate of his own.

SCENE XI.] G3–7 *omit*   SD Barnwell, Millwood] *Re-enter* Millwood G3–7
8 otherwise?] ~. G5–7   10 Cue] Cure G6   11 Ah;] ~! G5–7   whether] whither
G3–7   18 Wheree'er] Whene'er G2–7   Wiles] Wilds G6–7. *See Commentary*
20 Sake!] ~!— G5–6   22 matter,—] G2–3; ~,ᴧ G1, 4–7   26 To know it will]
G2–7; 'Twill G1

Mill. Ay, ay, the barbarous Man is rich enough;—but what are Riches when 35
compared to Love?

Lucy. For a while he perform'd the Office of a faithful Guardian, settled her
in a House, hir'd her Servants;—but you have seen in what manner she liv'd, so
I need say no more of that.

Mill. How I shall live hereafter, Heaven knows. 40

Lucy. All Things went on as one cou'd wish, till, some Time ago, his Wife
dying, he fell violently in love with his Charge, and wou'd fain have marry'd her:
Now the Man is neither old nor ugly, but a good personable sort of a Man, but I
don't know how it was, she cou'd never endure him; in short, her ill Usage so
provok'd him, that he brought in an Account of his Executorship, wherein he 45
makes her Debtor to him.—

Mill. A Trifle in it self, but more than enough to ruin me, whom, by this
unjust Account, he had stripp'd of all before.

Lucy. Now she having neither Money, nor Friend, except me, who am as
unfortunate as her self, he compell'd her to pass his Account, and give Bond for 50
the Sum he demanded; but still provided handsomely for her, and continued
his Courtship, till being inform'd by his Spies (truly I suspect some in her own
Family) that you were entertain'd at her House, and stay'd with her all Night, he
came this Morning raving, and storming like a Madman; talks no more of
Marriage, so there's no Hopes of making up Matters that Way, but vows her 55
Ruin, unless she'll allow him the same Favour that he supposes she granted
you.

Barn. Must she be ruin'd, or find her Refuge in another's Arms?

Mill. He gave me but an Hour to resolve in, that's happily spent with you;—
and now I go.— 60

Barn. To be expos'd to all the Rigours of the various Seasons, the Summer's
parching Heat, and Winter's Cold; unhous'd to wander Friendless thro' the
unhospitable World, in Misery and Want; attended with Fear and Danger, and
pursu'd by Malice and Revenge; woud'st thou endure all this for me, and can I
do nothing,—nothing to prevent it? 65

Lucy. 'Tis really a Pity, there can be no Way found out.

Barn. O where are all my Resolutions now; like early Vapours, or the
Morning Dew, chas'd by the Sun's warm Beams they're vanish'd and lost, as
tho' they had never been.

Lucy. Now I advis'd her, Sir, to comply with the Gentleman; that wou'd not 70
only put an End to her Troubles, but make her Fortune at once.

(II. xi)   44 was,] G2–7; ~∧ G1   47 this] his G2–7   54 Madman;] G3; Madman∧
G1–2, 4–7   55 Marriage,] *Ed.*; ~; G1–7   61 Seasons,] *Ed.*; ~; G1–7
62 Cold;] G5–7; ~, G1–4   64 Revenge;] G5–7; ~, G1–4   65 nothing,—nothing]
G2–5; ~,∧ ~ G1, 7   67 now;] ~? G2–7   70 Gentleman;] *Ed.*; ~, G1–7

Barn. Tormenting Fiend, away.—I had rather perish, nay, see her perish, than have her sav'd by him; I will my self prevent her Ruin, tho' with my own. A Moment's Patience,—I'll return immediately.

SCENE XII.

Millwood *and* Lucy.

Lucy. 'Twas well you came, or, by what I can perceive, you had lost him.

Mill. That, I must confess, was a Danger I did not foresee; I was only afraid he should have come without Money. You know a House of Entertainment, like mine, is not kept without Expence.

Lucy. That's very true; but then you shou'd be reasonable in your Demands; 'tis pity to discourage a young Man.

Mill. Leave that to me.

SCENE XIII.

Barnwell *with a Bag of Money,* Millwood, *and* Lucy.

Barn. What am I about to do!—Now you, who boast your Reason all-sufficient, suppose your selves in my Condition, and determine for me; whether it's right to let her suffer for my Faults, or, by this small Addition to my Guilt, prevent the ill Effects of what is past.

Lucy. These young Sinners think every Thing in the Ways of Wickedness so strange,—but I cou'd tell him that this is nothing but what's very common; for one Vice as naturally begets another, as a Father a Son:—But he'll find out that himself, if he lives long enough.   [*Aside.*

Barn. Here take this, and with it purchase your Deliverance; return to your House, and live in Peace and Safety.   1

Mill. So I may hope to see you there again.

Barn. Answer me not,—but fly,—least, in the Agonies of my Remorse, I take again what is not mine to give, and abandon thee to Want and Misery.

Mill. Say but you'll come.—

Barn. You are my Fate, my Heaven, or my Hell; only leave me now, dispose   1
of me hereafter as you please.

(II. xi)   74 Patience,—] G2–7; ~,∧ G1   immediately.] G2–7; ~.— G1; *after this line* G3–7 *add* SD*:* [*Exit* Barnwell.   SCENE XII.] G3–7 *omit*   SD Millwood *and* Lucy.] G3–7 *omit*
4 without Expence] G2–7; with no-|thing G1   7 *Mill.* leave . . . to me.] not in G1
SCENE XIII.] G3–7 *omit* SD Barnwell *with . . . and* Lucy.] *Ed.*; Barnwell, Millwood, *and* Lucy.
G1–2 (Millwood∧ G2); *Re-enter* Barnwell, *with a Bag of Money.* G3–7   8 SD [*Aside.*] G3–7;
not in G1–2   11 again.]— G4; ? G6–7   12 least] lest G2–7   16 please.] *after*
this line G3–7 *add* SD*:* [*Exeunt* Millwood *and* Lucy.] ([~.∧ G3–6)

SCENE XIV.

Barnwell.

What have I done?—Were my Resolutions founded on Reason, and sincerely made,—why then has Heaven suffer'd me to fall? I sought not the Occasion; and, if my Heart deceives me not, Compassion and Generosity were my Motives.—Is Virtue inconsistent with it self, or are Vice and Virtue only empty Names? Or do they depend on Accidents, beyond our Power to produce, or to   5 prevent,—wherein we have no Part, and yet must be determin'd by the Event?—But why should I attempt to reason? All is Confusion, Horror, and Remorse;—I find I am lost, cast down from all my late erected Hopes, and plung'd again in Guilt, yet scarce know how or why—

> *Such undistinguish'd Horrors make my Brain,*   10
> *Like Hell, the Seat of Darkness, and of Pain.*

The End of the Second Act.

SCENE XIV.] G3–7 *omit*   SD Barnwell.] G3–7 *omit*   1 G3–6 *add speech-heading:*
Barn.; G7 *runs on from* SD *after* II. xiii. 16   done?] G2–7; ~. G1   2 made,—] ~?∧ G5–7
9 know] known G3   11 *Pain.*] *after this line* G3–7 *add* SD: *[Exit.*

ACT III.

SCENE I.

A Room in Thorowgood*'s House.*

Thorowgood *and* Trueman.

Thor. Methinks I wou'd not have you only learn the Method of Merchandize, and practise it hereafter, merely as a Means of getting Wealth.—'Twill be well worth your Pains to study it as a Science.—See how it is founded in Reason, and the Nature of Things.—How it promotes Humanity, as it has opened and yet keeps up an Intercourse between Nations, far remote from one another in Situation, Customs and Religion; promoting Arts, Industry, Peace and Plenty; by mutual Benefits diffusing mutual Love from Pole to Pole.

Tr. Something of this I have consider'd, and hope, by your Assistance, to extend my Thoughts much farther.—I have observ'd those Countries, where Trade is promoted and encouraged, do not make Discoveries to destroy, but to improve Mankind,—by Love and Friendship, to tame the fierce, and polish the most savage,—to teach them the Advantages of honest Traffick,—by taking from them, with their own Consent, their useless Superfluities, and giving them, in Return, what, from their Ignorance in manual Arts, their Situation, or some other Accident, they stand in need of.

Thor. 'Tis justly observ'd:—The populous East, luxuriant, abounds with glittering Gems, bright Pearls, aromatick Spices, and Health-restoring Drugs: The late found Western World's rich Earth glows with unnumber'd Veins of Gold and Silver Ore.—On every Climate, and on every Country, Heaven has bestowed some good peculiar to it self.—It is the industrious Merchant's Business to collect the various Blessings of each Soil and Climate, and, with the Product of the whole, to enrich his native Country.—Well! I have examin'd your Accounts: They are not only just, as I have always found them, but regularly kept, and fairly enter'd.—I commend your Diligence. Method in Business is the surest Guide. He, who neglects it, frequently stumbles, and always wanders perplex'd, uncertain, and in Danger. Are *Barnwell*'s Accounts ready for my Inspection? he does not use to be the last on these Occasions.

Tr. Upon receiving your Orders he retir'd, I thought in some Confusion.—If you please, I'll go and hasten him.—I hope he has n't been guilty of any Neglect.

Thor. I'm now going to the *Exchange*; let him know, at my Return, I expect to find him ready.

SCENE II.

Maria with a Book sits and reads.

How forcible is Truth? The weakest Mind, inspir'd with Love of that,—fix'd
and collected in it self,—with Indifference beholds—the united Force of Earth
and Hell opposing: Such Souls are rais'd above the Sense of Pain, or so
supported, that they regard it not. The Martyr cheaply purchases his
Heaven.—Small are his Sufferings, great is his Reward;—not so the Wretch,   5
who combats Love with Duty; when the Mind, weaken'd and dissolved by the
soft Passion, feeble and hopeless opposes its own Desires.—What is an Hour, a
Day, a Year of Pain, to a whole Life of Tortures, such as these?

SCENE III.

Trueman and Maria.

Tr. O, *Barnwell!*—O, my Friend, how art thou fallen?
Ma. Ha! *Barnwell!* What of him? Speak, say what of *Barnwell.*
Tr. 'Tis not to be conceal'd.—I've News to tell of him that will afflict your
generous Father, your self, and all who knew him.
Ma. Defend us Heaven!   5
Tr. I cannot speak it.—See there.   [*Gives a Letter*, Maria *reads.*
Ma. Trueman,

*I Know my Absence will surprize my honour'd Master, and your self; and the more,
when you shall understand that the Reason of my withdrawing, is my having
embezzled part of the Cash with which I was entrusted. After this, 'tis needless to*   10
*inform you that I intend never to return again: Though this might have been known, by
examining my Accounts; yet, to prevent that unnecessary Trouble, and to cut off all
fruitless Expectations of my Return, I have left this from the lost*

George Barnwell.

Tr. Lost indeed! Yet how he shou'd be guilty of what he there charges   15
himself withal, raises my Wonder equal to my Grief.—Never had Youth a
higher Sense of Virtue—Justly he thought, and as he thought he practised;
never was Life more regular than his; an Understanding uncommon at his
Years; an open, generous manliness of Temper; his Manners easy, unaffected
and engaging.   20

SCENE II.] G3–7 *omit*   SD Maria] *Enter* Maria G3–7   1 G1, 3–7 *include speech-
heading:* Ma.   SCENE III.] G3–7 *omit*   SD Trueman *and* Maria.] *Enter* Trueman.
G3–7   1 Friend,] ~! G5–7   2 Barnwell.] ~! G5–7   3 I've] G2–7; Iv'e G1
4 knew] know G5–7   6 SD–7 [*Gives . . . reads.* | Trueman,] [Trueman *gives a Letter;* Maria
reads. G6–7, *misprinting salutation of letter as part of* SD (*Gives* G6)   7 Ma.] *Ed.*; G1–7 *do not
include speech-heading*   19 generous] G2–7; ~, G1

Ma. This and much more you might have said with Truth.—He was the delight of every Eye, and Joy of every Heart that knew him.

Tr. Since such he was, and was my Friend, can I support his Loss?—See the fairest and happiest Maid this wealthy City boasts, kindly condescends to weep for thy unhappy Fate, poor ruin'd *Barnwell*! 25

Ma. Trueman, do you think a Soul so delicate as his, so sensible of Shame, can e'er submit to live a Slave to Vice?

Tr. Never, never. So well I know him, I'm sure this Act of his, so contrary to his Nature, must have been caused by some unavoidable Necessity.

Ma. Is there no Means yet to preserve him? 30

Tr. O! that there were.—But few Men recover Reputation lost.—A Merchant never.—Nor wou'd he, I fear, though I shou'd find him, ever be brought to look his injur'd Master in the Face.

Ma. I fear as much,—and therefore wou'd never have my Father know it.

Tr. That's impossible. 35

Ma. What's the Sum?

Tr. 'Tis considerable.—I've mark'd it here, to show it, with the Letter, to your Father, at his Return.

Ma. If I shou'd supply the Money, cou'd you so dispose of that, and the Account, as to conceal this unhappy Mismanagement from my Father? 40

Tr. Nothing more easy:—But can you intend it? Will you save a helpless Wretch from Ruin? Oh! 'twere an Act worthy such exalted Virtue as *Maria*'s.— Sure Heaven, in Mercy to my Friend, inspired the generous Thought.

Ma. Doubt not but I wou'd purchase so great a Happiness at a much dearer Price.—But how shall he be found? 45

Tr. Trust to my Diligence for that.—In the mean time, I'll conceal his Absence from your Father, or find such Excuses for it, that the real Cause shall never be suspected.

Ma. In attempting to save from Shame, one whom we hope may yet return to Virtue, to Heaven and you, the only Witnesses of this Action, I appeal, whether 50 I do any thing misbecoming my Sex and Character.

Tr. Earth must approve the Deed, and Heaven, I doubt not, will reward it.

Ma. If Heaven succeed it, I am well rewarded. A Virgin's Fame is sullied by Suspicion's slightest Breath; and therefore as this must be a Secret from my Father, and the World, for *Barnwell*'s sake, for mine let it be so to him. 55

(III. iii)   26 do] G5–7; Do G1–4   40 Father?] G2–7; ~. G1   42 Virtue] G2–7; ~, G1   50 Heaven] *Ed.*; ~, G1–7   only Witnesses] G3–7; Judges G1–2. *See Commentary* 51 do] G2–7; have done G1   53 succeed] succeeds G2–7   54 slightest] lightest G3–7   55 sake,] G2–4; ~; G1   him.] *after this line* G3–6 *add* SD: [*Exeunt.*

SCENE IV.

Millwood's House.

Lucy *and* Blunt.

Lucy. Well! what do you think of *Millwood's* Conduct now!

Blunt. I own it is surprizing:—I don't know which to admire most, her feign'd, or his real Passion; tho' I have sometimes been afraid that her Avarice wou'd discover her:—But his Youth and want of Experience make it the easier to impose on him.   5

Lucy. No, it is his Love. To do him Justice, notwithstanding his Youth, he don't want Understanding; but you Men are much easier imposed on, in these Affairs, than your Vanity will allow you to believe.—Let me see the wisest of you all, as much in Love with me, as *Barnwell* is with *Millwood*, and I'll engage to make as great a Fool of him.   10

Blunt. And all Circumstances consider'd, to make as much Money of him too.

Lucy. I can't answer for that. Her Artifice in making him rob his Master at first, and the various Stratagems, by which she has obliged him to continue in that Course, astonish even me, who know her so well.—   15

Blunt. But then you are to consider that the Money was his Master's.

Lucy. There was the Difficulty of it.—Had it been his own, it had been nothing.—Were the World his, she might have it for a Smile:—But those golden Days are done;—he's ruin'd, and *Millwood's* Hopes of farther Profits there are at an End.   20

Blunt. That's no more than we all expected.

Lucy. Being call'd, by his Master, to make up his Accounts, he was forc'd to quit his House and Service, and wisely flies to *Millwood* for Relief and Entertainment.

Blunt. I have not heard of this before! How did she receive him?   25

Lucy. As you wou'd expect.—She wonder'd what he meant, was astonish'd at his Impudence,—and, with an Air of Modesty peculiar to her self, swore so heartily, that she never saw him before,—that she put me out of Countenance.

Blunt. That's much indeed! But how did *Barnwell* behave?

Lucy. He griev'd, and, at length, enrag'd at this barbarous Treatment, was   30
preparing to be gone; when, making toward the Door, he show'd a Sum of Money, which he had brought from his Master's,—the last he's ever like to have from thence.

SCENE IV. Millwood's *House.*] SCENE II. | *A Room in* Millwood's *House.* G3–4, 7; SCENE II. |
Another Room in Thorowgood's *House.* G5–6   SD Lucy] *Enter* Lucy G3–7   12 too.] ~?
G2–7   14 in] G3–7 *omit*   20 there] G5–7; ~, G1–4   31 when] G2–7; and
G1   toward] towards G6–7   he show'd] G5–7; show'd G1–4. *See Commentary*   Sum] G2–7;
Bag G1   32 brought] G2–7; stol'n G1   Master's] G2–7; Master G1

Blunt. But then *Millwood?*

Lucy. Aye, she, with her usual Address, return'd to her old Arts of lying, 35
swearing, and dissembling.—Hung on his Neck, and wept, and swore 'twas
meant in Jest; till the amorous Youth, melted into Tears, threw the Money into
her Lap, and swore he had rather die, than think her false.

Blunt. Strange Infatuation!

Lucy. But what follow'd was stranger still. As Doubts and Fears, follow'd by 40
Reconcilement, ever increase Love, where the Passion is sincere; so in him it
caus'd so wild a Transport of excessive Fondness, such Joy, such Grief, such
Pleasure, and such Anguish, that Nature in him seem'd sinking with the
Weight, and the charm'd Soul dispos'd to quit his Breast for hers.—just then,
when every Passion with lawless Anarchy prevail'd,—and Reason was in the 45
raging Tempest lost;—the cruel, artful *Millwood* prevail'd upon the wretched
Youth to promise—what I tremble but to think on.

Blunt. I am amaz'd! what can it be?

Lucy. You will be more so, to hear it is to attempt the Life of his nearest
Relation, and best Benefactor.— 50

Blunt. His Uncle, whom we have often heard him speak of as a Gentleman of
a large Estate and fair Character in the Country, where he lives.

Lucy. The same.—She was no sooner possess'd of the last dear Purchase of
his Ruin, but her Avarice, insatiate as the Grave, demands this horrid
Sacrifice,—*Barnwell*'s near Relation; and unsuspected Virtue must give too 55
easy Means to seize the good Man's Treasure; whose Blood must seal the
dreadful Secret, and prevent the Terrors of her guilty Fears.

Blunt. Is it possible she cou'd perswade him to do an Act like that! He is, by
Nature, honest, grateful, compassionate, and generous: And though his Love,
and her artful Perswasions, have wrought him to practise what he most abhors; 60
yet we all can witness for him, with what Reluctance he has still comply'd! So
many Tears he shed o'er each Offence, as might, if possible, sanctify Theft, and
make a Merit of a Crime.

Lucy. 'Tis true, at the naming the Murder of his Uncle, he started into Rage;
and, breaking from her Arms, where she till then had held him with well 65
dissembled Love and false Endearments, call'd her cruel Monster, Devil, and
told her she was born for his Destruction.—She thought it not for her Purpose
to meet his Rage with Rage, but affected a most passionate Fit of Grief;—rail'd
at her Fate, and curs'd her wayward Stars,—that still her Wants shou'd force
her to press him to act such Deeds, as she must needs abhor as well as he; but 70
told him Necessity had no Law, and Love no Bounds; that therefore he never

---

(III. iv)   36 and wept] wept G5–7   37 amorous Youth,] G2–7 (~‿ G7); easy Fool, G1
46 cruel,] G2–7; ~‿ G1   47 promise—] G2–7; ~‿ G1   51 Uncle,] ~! G5– 7
speak of] W1; ~, G1–7   54 demands] demanded G2–7   55 Relation;] *Ed.*; ~, G1–7.
See Commentary   65 him] *Ed.*; ~, G1–7. *See Commentary*   66 Endearments,] ~‿
G2–6   her] G5–7; ~, G1–4. *See Commentary*   cruel] ~, G2–7 (Cruel G2, 7)   70 abhor]
Ed.; ~, G1–7   he;] ~? G2–4. *See Commentary*

truly lov'd, but meant, in her Necessity, to forsake her;—then kneel'd and swore, that since, by his Refusal, he had given her Cause to doubt his Love, she never wou'd see him more; unless, to prove it true, he robb'd his Uncle to supply her Wants, and murder'd him, to keep it from Discovery.   75

Blunt. I am astonish'd! What said he?

Lucy. Speechless he stood; but in his Face you might have read, that various Passions tore his very Soul. Oft he, in Anguish, threw his Eyes towards Heaven, and then as often bent their Beams on her; then wept and groan'd, and beat his troubled Breast; at length, with Horror, not to be express'd, he cry'd, Thou   80
cursed Fair! have I not given dreadful Proofs of Love! What drew me from my youthful Innocence, to stain my then unspotted Soul, but Love? What caus'd me to rob my worthy gentle Master, but cursed Love? What makes me now a Fugitive from his Service, loath'd by my self, and scorn'd by all the World, but Love? What fills my Eyes with Tears, my Soul with Torture, never felt on this   85
side Death before? Why Love, Love, Love. And why, above all, do I resolve, (for, tearing his Hair, he cry'd I do resolve) to kill my Uncle?

Blunt. Was she not mov'd? It makes me weep to hear the sad Relation.

Lucy. Yes, with Joy, that she had gain'd her Point.—She gave him no Time to cool, but urg'd him to attempt it instantly. He's now gone; if he performs it, and   90
escapes, there's more Money for her; if not, he'll ne'er return, and then she's fairly rid of him.

Blunt. 'Tis time the World was rid of such a Monster.—

Lucy. If we don't do our Endeavours to prevent this Murder, we are as bad as she.   95

Blunt. I'm afraid it is too late.

Lucy. Perhaps not.—Her Barbarity to *Barnwell* makes me hate her.—We've run too great a Length with her already.—I did not think her or my self so wicked, as I find, upon Reflection, we are.

Blunt. 'Tis true, we have all been too much so.—But there is something so   100
horrid in Murder,—that all other Crimes seem nothing when compared to that.—I wou'd not be involv'd in the Guilt of that for all the World.

Lucy. Nor I, Heaven knows;—therefore let us clear our selves, by doing all that is in our Power to prevent it. I have just thought of a Way, that, to me, seems probable.—Will you join with me to detect this curs'd Design?   105

Blunt. With all my Heart. He who knows of a Murder intended to be committed, and does not discover it, in the Eye of the Law, and Reason, is a Murderer.

Lucy. Let us lose no Time;—I'll acquaint you with the Particulars as we go.

(III. iv)   80 troubled] G2–7; *not in* G1   83 worthy] G2–7; *not in* G1   84 my self] himself G6–7   87 Uncle?] G5–7; ~. G1–4   89 Yes,] ~‸— G5–7   93 was] were G5–7 97 We've] We have G2–7   106 Heart.] G2–7; ~.—How else shall I clear my self? G1 109 go.] *after this line* G3–7 *add* SD: [*Exeunt.*

SCENE V.

A Walk at some Distance from a Country Seat.

Barnwell.

A dismal Gloom obscures the Face of Day; either the Sun has slip'd behind a Cloud, or journeys down the West of Heaven, with more than common Speed, to avoid the Sight of what I'm doom'd to act. Since I set forth on this accursed Design, where'er I tread, methinks, the solid Earth trembles beneath my Feet.—Yonder limpid Stream, whose hoary Fall has made a natural Cascade,   5 as I pass'd by, in doleful Accents seem'd to murmur, Murder. The Earth, the Air, and Water, seem concern'd; but that's not strange, the World is punish'd, and Nature feels the Shock, when Providence permits a good Man's Fall!— Just Heaven! Then what shou'd I be! for him that was my Father's only Brother, and since his Death has been to me a Father; who took me up an   10 Infant, and an Orphan; rear'd me with tenderest Care, and still indulged me with most paternal Fondness;—yet here I stand avow'd his destin'd Murderer:—I stiffen with Horror at my own Impiety;—'tis yet unperform'd.—What if I quit my bloody Purpose, and fly the Place! [*Going, then stops.*]—But whether, O whether, shall I fly!—My Master's once friendly Doors are ever shut against   15 me; and without Money *Millwood* will never see me more, and Life is not to be endured without her:—She's got such firm Possession of my Heart, and governs there with such despotick Sway;—Aye, there's the Cause of all my Sin and Sorrow:—'Tis more than Love; 'tis the Fever of the Soul, and Madness of Desire.—In vain does Nature, Reason, Conscience, all oppose it; the   20 impetuous Passion bears down all before it, and drives me on to Lust, to Theft, and Murder.—Oh Conscience! feeble Guide to Virtue, who only shows us when we go astray, but wants the Power to stop us in our Course.—Ha! in yonder shady Walk I see my Uncle.—He's alone.—Now for my Disguise.— [*Plucks out a Vizor.*] This is his Hour of private Meditation. Thus daily he   25 prepares his Soul for Heaven,—whilst I—But what have I to do with Heaven!—Ha! No Struggles, Conscience.—

> *Hence! Hence Remorse, and ev'ry Thought that's good;*
> *The Storm that Lust began, must end in Blood.*

> [*Puts on the Vizor, and draws a Pistol.*

SCENE V.] SCENE III. G3–7   SD Barnwell.] *Enter* Barnwell. G3–7   1 G3–7 *add speech-heading: Barn.*   3 I'm] I am G6–7   6 murmur,] ~,—G5–7   7 seem] seem'd G3–7   8 the Shock] a Shock G3–7   good] goods G5   10 Father;] G2–6; ~, G1, 7   14–15 whether, O whether] whether, O whither G5; whither, O whither G6–7   22 who only shows] thou . . . show'st G5–7   23 wants the Power] wantest Power G5–7   29 SD *and draws a Pistol.*] draws a Pistol, *and* [*Exit.* G3–7

SCENE VI.

A close Walk in a Wood.

Uncle.

If I was superstitious, I shou'd fear some Danger lurk'd unseen, or Death were nigh:—A heavy Melancholy clouds my Spirits; my Imagination is fill'd with gashly Forms of dreary Graves, and Bodies chang'd by Death,—when the pale lengthen'd Visage attracks each weeping Eye,—and fills the musing Soul, at once, with Grief and Horror, Pity and Aversion.—I will indulge the   5
Thought. The wise Man prepares himself for Death, by making it familiar to his Mind.—When strong Reflections hold the Mirror near,—and the Living in the Dead behold their future selves, how does each inordinate Passion and Desire cease or sicken at the View?—The Mind scarce moves;—The Blood, curdling, and chill'd, creeps slowly thro' the Veins: fix'd, still, and motionless   10
we stand, so like the solemn Object of our Thoughts, we are almost at present—what we must be hereafter; 'till Curiosity awakes the Soul, and sets it on Inquiry.—

SCENE VII.

Uncle, George Barnwell *at a Distance.*

Uncle. O Death, thou strange mysterious Power,—seen every Day, yet never understood—but by the incommunicative Dead, what art thou?—The extensive Mind of Man, that with a Thought circles the Earth's vast Globe,—sinks to the Centre, or ascends above the Stars; that Worlds exotick finds, or thinks it finds,—thy thick Clouds attempts to pass in vain, lost and bewilder'd   5
in the horrid Gloom,—defeated she returns more doubtful than before; of nothing certain, but of Labour lost.
  [*During this Speech,* Barnwell *sometimes presents the Pistol, and draws it back again.*
Barn. Oh, 'tis impossible!
  [*Throwing down the Pistol.* Uncle *starts and attempts to draw his Sword.*
Uncle. A Man so near me, arm'd and masqu'd!

SCENE VI.] SCENE IV. G3–7   SD Uncle.] *Enter* Uncle. G3–7   1 G3–7 *add speech-heading: Un.*   was] were G5–7   3 gashly] ghastly G7   4 attracks] attacks G3–4; attracts G5–7   10 Veins:] G2–7; ~,— G1   11 we stand] G2–7; *not in* G1 so] G2–7; *not in* G1   Thoughts, we] G2–7; ~.—We G1   12 hereafter;] G2–7;~, G1
SCENE VII.] G3–7 *omit*   SD Uncle, George] *Enter* George G3–7 ([~ G5–7)
1 *Uncle.*] G5–7 *omit speech-heading and run on from* IV. vi. 13   2 what] G3–7;
What G1–2   4 Worlds] G2–7; World's G1   7 certain,] ~— G5–7   7+SD *again.*]
G3–7; ~; *at last he drops it,—at which his Uncle starts, and draws* | *his Sword.* G1–2. *See Commentary*
8+SD [*Throwing . . . his Sword.*] G3–7 (∧*throwing* G3–4); *not in* G1–2

Barn. Nay, then there's no Retreat.   10

                  [*Plucks a Poniard from his Bosom, and stabs him.*

Uncle. Oh! I am slain! All gracious Heaven regard the Prayer of thy dying Servant. Bless, with thy choicest Blessings, my dearest Nephew; forgive my Murderer, and take my fleeting Soul to endless Mercy.

[*Barnwell throws off his Mask, runs to him, and, kneeling by him, raises and chafes him.*

Barn. Expiring Saint! Oh, murder'd, martyr'd Uncle! Lift up your dying Eyes, and view your Nephew in your Murderer.—O do not look so tenderly   15
upon me.—Let Indignation lighten from your Eyes, and blast me ere you die.—By Heaven, he weeps in Pity of my Woes.—Tears,—Tears, for Blood.—The Murder'd, in the Agonies of Death, weeps for his Murderer.—O, speak your pious Purpose,—pronounce my Pardon then,—and take me with you.—He wou'd, but cannot.—O why, with such fond Affection do you press my   20
murdering Hand!—What! will you kiss me!   [*Kisses him.*

Uncle. [*Groans and dies.*]

Barn. Life, that hover'd on his Lips but till he had sealed my Pardon, in that Kiss expired. He's gone for ever,—and oh! I follow.—[*Swoons away upon his Uncle's dead Body.*] Do I still live to press the suffering Bosom of the Earth?—   25
Do I still breath, and taint with my infectious Breath the wholesome Air!—Let Heaven, from its high Throne, in Justice or in Mercy, now look down on that dear murder'd Saint, and me the Murderer.—And, if his Vengeance spares,—let Pity strike and end my wretched Being.—Murder the worst of Crimes, and Parricide the worst of Murders, and this the worst of Parricides. *Cain*, who   30
stands on Record from the Birth of Time, and must to its last final Period, as accurs'd, slew a Brother, favour'd above him.—Detested *Nero*, by another's Hand, dispatch'd a Mother, that he fear'd and hated.—But I, with my own Hand, have murder'd a Brother, Mother, Father, and a Friend; most loving and belov'd.—This execrable Act of mine's without a Parallel.—O may it ever   35
stand alone,—the last of Murders, as it is the worst.—

       The rich Man thus, in Torment and Despair,
       Prefer'd his vain, but charitable Prayer.
       The Fool, his own Soul lost, wou'd fain be wise
       For others Good; but Heaven his Suit denies.   40
       By Laws and Means well known we stand or fall,
       And one eternal Rule remains for all.

           The End of the Third Act.

   12 thy] the G4–7   14 take] take away G3   16 ere] G5–7; e're G1–4
18 O,] ~! G5–7   21SD–22 *Kisses him.* | *Uncle.* [*Groans and dies.*]] *Ed.*, G1–2 (ˬ*Groans and dies.*ˬ G1; (*Groans and dies.*) G2–4; (Barnwell *kisses his Uncle, who groans and dies.*) G5–7
23 *Barn.*] G5–7 *omit speech-heading and run on from* 31   23–4 Life, that . . . Kiss expired.]
G2–7 (seal'd G7, expir'd G3–7); *not in* G1   26 breath] breathe G4–7

ACT IV.

SCENE I.

A Room in Thorowgood's *House.*

Maria.

How falsly do they judge who censure or applaud, as we're afflicted or rewarded here. I know I am unhappy, yet cannot charge my self with any Crime, more than the common Frailties of our Kind, that shou'd provoke just Heaven to mark me out for Sufferings so uncommon and severe. Falsly to accuse our selves, Heaven must abhor; then it is just and right that Innocence should   5 suffer; for Heaven must be just in all its Ways.—Perhaps by that they are kept from moral Evils, much worse than penal, or more improv'd in Virtue: Or may not the lesser Ills that they sustain, be made the Means of greater Good to others? Might all the joyless Days and sleepless Nights that I have past, but purchase Peace for thee—   10

> *Thou dear, dear Cause of all my Grief and Pain,*
> *Small were the Loss, and infinite the Gain:*
> *Tho' to the Grave in secret Love I pine,*
> *So Life, and Fame, and Happiness were thine.*

SCENE II.

Trueman *and* Maria.

Ma. What News of *Barnwell?*

Tr. None.—I have sought him with the greatest Diligence, but all in vain.

Ma. Doth my Father yet suspect the Cause of his Absence?

Tr. All appear'd so just and fair to him, it is not possible he ever shou'd; but his Absence will no longer be conceal'd. Your Father's wise; and though he   5 seems to hearken to the friendly Excuses I wou'd make for *Barnwell*; yet, I am afraid, he regards 'em only as such, without suffering them to influence his Judgment.

Ma. How does the unhappy Youth defeat all our Designs to serve him! yet I can never repent what we have done. Shou'd he return, 'twill make his   10 Reconciliation with my Father easier, and preserve him from future Reproach from a malicious unforgiving World.

SD *A Room in* Thorowgood's *House.*] G3–7; *not in* G1–2   Maria.] *Enter* Maria G3–7
1 G1, 3–7 *include speech-heading: Ma.* (*MARIA.* G6)   5 abhor;] G2–7; ~, G1
6 they] we G5–7   8 they] we G5–7   made] G2–7; *not in* G1   SCENE II.] G3–7
omit   SD Trueman *and* Maria.] *Enter* Trueman. G3–7   1 *Ma.*] G5–7 *omit speech-
heading*   3 Doth] Does G2–7   Absence] G2–7 (absence G2); absenting himself G1
6 Excuses] G2–7; ~, G1   9 him!] W1; ~, G1–4; ~? G5–7. *See Commentary*

SCENE III.

[*To them.*] Thorowgood *and* Lucy.

Thor. This Woman here has given me a sad, (and bating some Circumstances) too probable Account of *Barnwell's* Defection.

Lucy. I am sorry, Sir, that my frank Confession of my former unhappy Course of Life shou'd cause you to suspect my Truth on this Occasion.

Thor. It is not that; your Confession has in it all the Appearance of Truth. [*To* 5 *them.*] Among many other Particulars, she informs me that *Barnwell* has been influenc'd to break his Trust, and wrong me, at several Times, of considerable Sums of Money; now, as I know this to be false, I wou'd fain doubt the whole of her Relation,—too dreadful—to be willingly believ'd.

Ma. Sir, your Pardon; I find my self on a sudden so indispos'd, that I must 10 retire.—Providence opposes all Attempts to save him.—Poor ruin'd *Barnwell!*— Wretched lost *Maria!*— [*Aside.*

SCENE IV.

Thorowgood, Trueman *and* Lucy.

Thor. How am I distress'd on every Side? Pity for that unhappy Youth, fear for the Life of a much valued Friend—and then my Child—the only Joy and Hope of my declining Life.—Her Melancholy increases hourly, and gives me painful Apprehensions of her Loss.—O *Trueman!* this Person informs me, that your Friend, at the Instigation of an impious Woman, is gone to rob and murder his venerable Uncle.

Tr. O execrable Deed! I am blasted with the Horror of the Thought!

Lucy. This Delay may ruin all.

Thor. What to do or think I know not; that he ever wrong'd me, I know is false,—the rest may be so too, there's all my Hope. 1

Tr. Trust not to that, rather suppose all true than lose a Moment's Time; even now the horrid Deed may be a doing;—dreadful Imagination!—or it may be done, and we are vainly debating on the Means to prevent what is already past.

Thor. This Earnestness convinces me that he knows more than he has yet 1 discover'd. What ho! without there! who waits?

SCENE III.] G3–7 *omit* SD [*To them.*]]ˌ*Enter*ˌˌ G3–7 5 Truth.] G7; ~, G1–6
12 SD [*Aside.*] [~. *Exit* Maria. G3–7 SCENE IV.] G3–7 *omit* SD Thorowgood,
Trueman *and* Lucy.] G3–7 *omit* 3 Life.—] G2–4; ~.ˌ G1; ~!— G5–7 5 an]
am G2 7 Deed!] G2–5, 7; ~, G1; ~; G6 Thought!] G2–6; ~. G1, 7
12 Imagination!] G2–7; ~; G1 13 are] be G5–7

SCENE V.

[To them.] A Servant.

Thor. Order the Groom to saddle the swiftest Horse, and prepare himself to set out with Speed.—An Affair of Life and Death demands his Diligence.

SCENE VI.

Thorowgood, Trueman *and* Lucy.

Thor. For you, whose Behaviour on this Occasion I have no Time to commend as it deserves, I must ingage your farther Assistance.—Return and observe this *Millwood* till I come. I have your Directions, and will follow you as soon as possible.

SCENE VII.

Thorowgood *and* Trueman.

Thor. Trueman, you I am sure wou'd not be idle on this Occasion.

SCENE VIII.

Trueman.

He only who is a Friend can judge of my Distress.

SCENE V.] G3–7 *omit*   SD [*To them.*] *A Servant.*] [*Enter a Servant.*] G3–7 (∧~·∧ G3–4)
1 *Thor.*] G5–7 *omit speech-heading and run on from* IV. iv. 16 *and* SD   himself] G2–7 *omit*
2 Diligence.] *after this line* G3–7 *add* SD: [*Exit Servant.*]   SCENE VI.] G3–7 *omit*
SD Thorowgood, Trueman *and* Lucy.] G3–7 *omit*   1 *Thor.*] G3–7 *omit speech-heading and*
run on from IV. v. 2 *and* SD   4 possible.] *after this line* G3–7 *add* SD: [*Exit* Lucy.]
SCENE VII.] G3–7 *omit*   SD Thorowgood *and* Trueman.] G3–7 *omit*   1 *Thor.*] G3–7
omit speech-heading and run on from IV. vi. 4 *and* SD   wou'd] will G5–7   Occasion.] *after this*
line G3–7 *add* SD: [*Exit* Thorowgood. ([~.] G5)   SCENE VIII.] G3–7 *omit*
SD Trueman.] G3–7 *omit*   1 G3–7 *add speech-heading:* Tr.   Distress.] *after this line* G3–7
add SD: [*Exit.*

SCENE IX.

Millwood's House.

Millwood.

I wish I knew the Event of his Design;—the Attempt without Success would ruin him.—Well! what have I to apprehend from that? I fear too much. The Mischief being only intended, his Friends, in pity of his Youth, turn all their Rage on me. I should have thought of that before.—Suppose the Deed done—then, and then only I shall be secure; or what if he returns without attempting it 5 at all?

SCENE X.

Millwood, and Barnwell *bloody.*

Mill. But he is here, and I have done him wrong; his bloody Hands show he has done the Deed, but show he wants the Prudence to conceal it.

Barn. Where shall I hide me? whether shall I fly to avoid the swift unerring Hand of Justice?

Mill. Dismiss those Fears; tho' Thousands had pursu'd you to the Door, yet being enter'd here you are safe as Innocence; I have such a Cavern, by Art so cunningly contriv'd, that the piercing Eyes of Jealousy and Revenge may search in vain, nor find the Entrance to the safe Retreat; there will I hide you if any Danger's near.

Barn. O hide me from my self if it be possible; for while I bear my 1 Conscience in my Bosom, tho' I were hid where Man's Eye never saw, nor Light e'er dawn'd, 'twere all in vain. For oh! that inmate,—that impartial Judge, will try, convict, and sentence me for Murder; and execute me with never ending Torments. Behold these Hands all crimson'd o'er with my dear Uncle's Blood! Here's a Sight to make a Statue start with Horror, or turn a living Man 1 into a Statue.

Mill. Ridiculous! Then it seems you are afraid of your own Shadow; or what's less than a Shadow, your Conscience.

Barn. Tho' to Man unknown I did the accursed Act, what can we hide from Heav'ns all-seeing Eye? 2

SCENE IX.] SCENE II. G3–7   SD Millwood.] *Enter* Millwood. G3–7   1 G3–7
add speech-heading: Mill.   4 done—] G5–7; ~, G1–3; ~ₐ G4   SCENE X.] G3–7
omit   SD Millwood, *and* Barnwell *bloody.*] [*Enter* Barnwell *bloody.*] G3–7 (ₐ~·ₐ G3–4)
1 *Mill.*] G5–7 *omit speech-heading and run on from* IV. ix. 6 *and* SD   3 whether] Whether
G2–5; Whither G6–7   5 those] your G2–7   8 Retreat;] G5–7; ~, G1–4
10 me] ~— G5–7   12 oh!] G2–7 (Oh G4–5); *not in* G1   20 all-seeing] G2–7;
omniscient G1. *See Commentary*

Mill. No more of this Stuff;—what advantage have you made of his Death? or what advantage may yet be made of it?—did you secure the Keys of his Treasure,—those no doubt were about him?—what Gold, what Jewels, or what else of Value have you brought me?

Barn. Think you I added Sacrilege to Murder? Oh! had you seen him as his 25 Life flowed from him in a Crimson Flood, and heard him praying for me by the double Name of Nephew and of Murderer; alas, alas! he knew not then that his Nephew was his Murderer; how wou'd you have wish'd as I did, tho' you had a thousand Years of Life to come, to have given them all to have lengthen'd his one Hour. But being dead, I fled the Sight of what my Hands had done, nor 30 cou'd I to have gain'd the Empire of the World, have violated by Theft his sacred Corps.

Mill. Whining, preposterous, canting Villain; to murder your Uncle, rob him of Life, Natures first, last, dear Prerogative, after which there's no Injury; then fear to take what he no longer wanted, and bring to me your Penury and Guilt. 35 Do you think I'll hazard my Reputation, nay my Life, to entertain you?

Barn. Oh!—*Millwood!*—this from thee;—but I have done,—if you hate me, if you wish me dead, then are you happy,—for Oh! 'tis sure my Grief will quickly end me.

Mill. In his Madness he will discover all, and involve me in his Ruin;—we are 40 on a Precipice from whence there's no Retreat for both,—then to preserve my self.—[*Pauses.*] There is no other Way,—'tis dreadful,—but Reflection comes too late when Danger's pressing,—and there's no room for Choice.—It must be done.   [*Aside, rings a Bell.*

SCENE XI.

[*To them.*] *A Servant.*

Mill. Fetch me an Officer and seize this Villain, he has confess'd himself a Murderer; shou'd I let him escape, I justly might be thought as bad as he.

(IV. x)   23 him?—] ~;ʌ G2–7   27–8 alas, alas! . . . his Murderer;] (~ Murdererʌ) G2–7
33 Whining, preposterous,] G5–7; ~ʌ ~ʌ G1–4   Villain;] G5–7; ~, G1–4   34 Injury;]
G3–7; ~, G1–2   35 wanted,] G3–7; ~; G1–2   36 Reputation,] G2–4; ~; G1, 5–7
Life,] G2–4; ~ʌ G1, 5–7   37 Oh!—] Oʌʌ G2–7   thee;] ~! G5–7   38 dead,]
G5–7; ~; G1; ~! G4   44 SD [*Aside, rings a Bell.*] G3–7 ([~. *Rings* ~.] G5–7); [*Stamps.*
G1   SCENE XI.] G3–7 *omit*   SD [*To them.*] *A Servant.*] Ed.; ʌ*Enter a Servant.*] G3–7
(~·ʌ G3–7)   1 *Mill.*] G5–7 *omit speech-heading and run on from* IV. x. 44 *and* SD
2 Murderer;] G2–7; ~, G1   as he.] *after this line* G3–7 *add* SD: [*Exit Servant.* ([~.] G5–7)

SCENE XII.

Millwood *and* Barnwell.

Barn. O *Millwood*! sure thou dost not, cannot mean it. Stop the Messenger, upon my Knees I beg you, call him back. 'Tis fit I die indeed, but not by you. I will this Instant deliver my self into the Hands of Justice, indeed I will, for Death is all I wish. But thy Ingratitude so tears my wounded Soul, 'tis worse ten thousand times than Death with Torture.   5

Mill. Call it what you will, I am willing to live; and live secure; which nothing but your Death can warrant.

Barn. If there be a Pitch of Wickedness that seats the Author beyond the reach of Vengeance, you must be secure. But what remains for me, but a dismal Dungeon, hard-galling Fetters, an awful Tryal, and ignominious Death, justly   10 to fall unpitied and abhorr'd?—After Death to be suspended between Heaven and Earth, a dreadful Spectacle, the warning and horror of a gaping Croud. This I cou'd bear, nay wish not to avoid, had it but come from any Hand but thine.—

SCENE XIII.

Millwood, Barnwell, Blunt, *Officer and Attendants.*

Mill. Heaven defend me! Conceal a Murderer! here, Sir, take this Youth into your Custody, I accuse him of Murder; and will appear to make good my Charge.   [*They seize him.*

Barn. To whom, of what, or how shall I complain; I'll not accuse her, the Hand of Heav'n is in it, and this the Punishment of Lust and Parricide; yet Heav'n that justly cuts me off, still suffers her to live, perhaps to punish others; tremendous Mercy! so Fiends are curs'd with Immortality, to be the Executioners of Heaven.—

> *Be warn'd ye Youths, who see my sad Despair,*
> *Avoid lewd Women, False as they are Fair;*
> *By Reason guided, honest Joys pursue;* ⎫
> *The Fair, to Honour and to Virtue true,* ⎬
> *Just to her self, will ne'er be false to you.* ⎭
> *By my Example learn to shun my Fate,*
> *(How wretched is the Man who's wise too late?)*

SCENE XII.] G3–7 *omit*   SD Millwood *and* Barnwell.] G3–7 *omit*   1 thou dost] you do G3–7   2 you] you'd G4–7   10 ignominious] an ignominious G5–7   Death,] ~— G5–7   SCENE XIII.] G3–7 *omit*   SD Millwood, Barnwell, Blunt] *Enter* Blunt G3–7   4 complain;] ~? G5–7   6 others;] ~;— G3–7   10 *Fair;*] G2–7; ~, G1   11 *pursue;*] G5–7; ~, G1–4   12 *Fair,*] *Ed.*; ~ˬ G1–7   Honour] *Ed.*; ~, G1–7

Ere Innocence, and Fame, and Life be lost,—
Here purchase Wisdom, cheaply, at my Cost.

SCENE XIV.

Millwood *and* Blunt.

Mill. Where's *Lucy*, why is she absent at such a Time?

Blunt. Wou'd I had been so too. *Lucy* will soon be here, and, I hope, to thy Confusion, thou Devil!

Mill. Insolent! this to me?

Blunt. The worst that we know of the Devil is, that he first seduces to Sin, 5 and then betrays to Punishment.

SCENE XV.

Millwood.

They disapprove of my Conduct then,—and mean to take this Opportunity to set up for themselves.—My Ruin is resolv'd,—I see my Danger, but scorn both it and them.—I was not born to fall by such weak Instruments.—

[*Going.*

SCENE XVI.

Thorowgood *and* Millwood.

Thor. Where is this Scandal of her own Sex, and Curse of ours?

Mill. What means this Insolence? Who do you seek?

Thor. Millwood.

Mill. Well, you have found her then.—I am *Millwood.*—

Thor. Then you are the most impious Wretch that e'er the Sun beheld. 5

Mill. From your Appearance I shou'd have expected Wisdom and Moderation, but your Manners bely your Aspect.—What is your Business here? I know you not.

Thor. Hereafter you may know me better; I am *Barnwell's* Master.

(IV. xiii)   16 *Ere*] G3–7; *E'er* G1–2   *lost,—*] G2–4; ~,ᴧ G1, 5–7   17 *Cost.*] *after this line* G3–7 *add* SD: [*Exeunt Barnwell,* Officer and Attendants.   SCENE XIV.] G3–7 *omit* SD Millwood *and* Blunt.] G3–7 *omit*   2–3 *too. Lucy ... thou Devil!*] G3–7 (*here*; G5–7); *too, thou Devil!* G1–2   6 *Punishment.*] *after this line* G3–7 *add* SD: [*Exit* Blunt. SCENE XV.] G3–7 *omit*   SD Millwood.] G3–7 *omit*   1 G3–7 *add speech-heading:* *Mill.*   *then*] G2–7; *not in* G1   SCENE XVI.] G3–7 *omit*   SD Thorowgood *and* Millwood.] *Enter* Thorowgood. G3–7   1 *this*] the G4–7   9 *better;*] ~;— G5–7

Mill. Then you are Master to a Villain; which, I think, is not much to your 10 Credit.

Thor. Had he been as much above thy Arts, as my Credit is superior to thy Malice, I need not blush to own him.

Mill. My Arts;—I don't understand you, Sir! If he has done amiss, what's that to me? Was he my Servant, or yours?—You shou'd have taught him better. 15

Thor. Why shou'd I wonder to find such uncommon Impudence in one arriv'd to such a Height of Wickedness.—When Innocence is banish'd, Modesty soon follows. Know, Sorceress, I'm not ignorant of any of your Arts, by which you first deceiv'd the unwary Youth: I know how, Step by Step, you've led him on, (reluctant and unwilling) from Crime to Crime, to this last horrid 20 Act, which you contriv'd, and, by your curs'd Wiles, even forced him to commit.

Mill. Ha! *Lucy* has got the Advantage, and accused me first; unless I can turn the Accusation, and fix it upon her and *Blunt*, I am lost.   [*Aside.*

Thor. Had I known your cruel Design sooner, it had been prevented. To see you punish'd as the Law directs, is all that now remains.—Poor Satisfaction,— 25 for he, innocent as he is, compared to you, must suffer too. But Heaven, who knows our Frame, and graciously distinguishes between Frailty and Presumption, will make a Difference, tho' Man cannot, who sees not the Heart, but only judges by the outward Action.—

Mill. I find, Sir, we are both unhappy in our Servants. I was surpriz'd at such 30 ill Treatment, without Cause, from a Gentleman of your Appearance, and therefore too hastily return'd it; for which I ask your Pardon. I now perceive you have been so far impos'd on, as to think me engaged in a former Correspondence with your Servant, and, some Way or other, accessary to his Undoing. 35

Thor. I charge you as the Cause, the sole Cause of all his Guilt, and all his Suffering, of all he now endures, and must endure, till a violent and shameful Death shall put a dreadful Period to his Life and Miseries together.

Mill. 'Tis very strange; but who's secure from Scandal and Detraction?—So far from contributing to his Ruin, I never spoke to him till since that fatal 40 Accident, which I lament as much as you: 'Tis true, I have a Servant, on whose Account he has of late frequented my House; if she has abus'd my good Opinion of her, am I to blame? Has n't *Barnwell* done the same by you?

Thor. I hear you; pray go on.

Mill. I have been inform'd he had a violent Passion for her, and she for him; 45 but till now I always thought it innocent; I know her poor, and given to expensive Pleasures. Now who can tell but she may have influenced the

amorous Youth to commit this Murder, to supply her Extravagancies;—it must
be so. I now recollect a thousand Circumstances that confirm it: I'll have her
and a Man Servant, that I suspect as an Accomplice, secured immediately. I   50
hope, Sir, you will lay aside your ill-grounded Suspicions of me, and join to
punish the real Contrivers of this bloody Deed.   [*Offers to go.*

Thor. Madam, you pass not this Way: I see your Design, but shall protect
them from your Malice.

Mill. I hope you will not use your Influence, and the Credit of your Name, to   55
skreen such guilty Wretches. Consider, Sir! the Wickedness of perswading a
thoughtless Youth to such a Crime.

Thor. I do,—and of betraying him when it was done.

Mill. That which you call betraying him, may convince you of my Innocence.
She who loves him, tho' she contriv'd the Murder, would never have deliver'd   60
him into the Hands of Justice, as I (struck with the Horror of his Crimes) have
done.—

Thor. How shou'd an unexperienc'd Youth escape her Snares; the powerful
Magick of her Wit and Form might betray the wisest to simple Dotage, and fire
the Blood that Age had froze long since. Even I, that with just Prejudice came   65
prepared, had, by her artful Story, been deceiv'd, but that my strong Conviction
of her Guilt makes even a Doubt impossible. Those whom subtilly you wou'd
accuse, you know are your Accusers; and what proves unanswerably their
Innocence, and your Guilt: they accus'd you before the Deed was done, and did
all that was in their Power to have prevented it.   70

Mill. Sir, you are very hard to be convinc'd; but I have such a Proof, which,
when produced, will silence all Objections.

SCENE XVII.

Thorowgood, Lucy, Trueman, Blunt, Officers, &c.

Lucy. Gentlemen, pray place your selves, some on one Side of that Door, and
some on the other; watch her Entrance, and act as your Prudence shall direct
you.—This Way—[*to* Thorowgood] and note her Behaviour; I have observ'd
her, she's driven to the last Extremity, and is forming some desperate
Resolution.—I guess at her Design.—   5

(IV. xvi)   48 Extravagancies;—] G2–7; ~,∧ G1   49 so.] G2–7; ~.— G1
61 Hands] Hand G3   I (struck] ~,∧|~ G5–7   the Horror of] Horror at G3–7
Crimes)]~,∧ G5–7   63 Snares; the] ~? The G2–7   64 Form] G5–7; ~, G1–4
68 what] (which G5–7   unanswerably] G5–7; ~, G1–4   69 Guilt:] *Ed.*; ~; G1–4;
~∧) G5–7   70 have prevented] prevent G5–7   72 Objections.] *after this line* G3–7 *add*
SD: [*Exit* Millwood.   SCENE XVII.] G3–7 *omit*   SD Thorowgood, Lucy] *Enter*
Lucy G3–7

SCENE XVIII.

[To them.] Millwood *with a Pistol,*—Trueman
secures her.

Tr. Here thy Power of doing Mischief ends; deceitful, cruel, bloody Woman!

Mill. Fool, Hypocrite, Villain,—Man! thou can'st not call me that.

Tr. To call thee Woman, were to wrong the Sex, thou Devil!

Mill. That imaginary Being is an Emblem of thy cursed Sex collected. A Mirrour, wherein each particular Man may see his own Likeness, and that of all Mankind.

Thor. Think not by aggravating the Faults of others to extenuate thy own, of which the Abuse of such uncommon Perfections of Mind and Body is not the least.

Mill. If such I had, well may I curse your barbarous Sex, who robb'd me of 'em, ere I knew their Worth, then left me, too, late to count their Value by their Loss. Another and another Spoiler came, and all my Gain was Poverty and Reproach. My Soul disdain'd, and yet disdains Dependance and Contempt. Riches, no Matter by what Means obtain'd, I saw secur'd the worst of Men from both; I found it therefore necessary to be rich; and, to that End, I summon'd all my Arts. You call 'em wicked, be it so, they were such as my Conversation with your Sex had furnish'd me withal.

Thor. Sure none but the worst of Men convers'd with thee.

Mill. Men of all Degrees and all Professions I have known, yet found no Difference, but in their several Capacities; all were alike wicked to the utmost of their Power. In Pride, Contention, Avarice, Cruelty, and Revenge, the Reverend Priesthood were my unerring Guides. From Suburb-Magistrates, who live by ruin'd Reputations, as the unhospitable Natives of *Cornwall* do by Ship-wrecks, I learn'd, that to charge my innocent Neighbours with my Crimes, was to merit their Protection; for to skreen the Guilty, is the less scandalous, when many are suspected, and Detraction, like Darkness and Death, blackens all Objects, and levels all Distinction. Such are your venal Magistrates, who favour none but such as, by their Office, they are sworn to punish: With them, not to be guilty, is the worst of Crimes; and large Fees privately paid, is every needful Virtue.

Thor. Your Practice has sufficiently discover'd your Contempt of Laws, both human and divine; no wonder then that you shou'd hate the Officers of both.

SCENE XVIII.] G3–7 *omit*   SD *[To them.]*] ∧Enter∧∧ G3–4; ∧Re-enter∧∧ G5–7
2 Villain,] G2–7; ~. G1   3 thee] the G4–5   the] thy G4–7   7 *Thor.*] G2–7; *Tr.* G1.
See Commentary   Faults] G3–7; Fault G1–2   11 ere] G3–7; e'er G1–2
22 unerring] G2–7; unering G1   28 them,] *Ed.*; ~∧ G1–7   29 is] are G5–7

Mill. I know you and I hate you all; I expect no Mercy, and I ask for none; I follow'd my Inclinations, and that the best of you does every Day. All Actions seem alike natural and indifferent to Man and Beast, who devour, or are 35 devour'd, as they meet with others weaker or stronger than themselves.

Thor. What Pity it is, a Mind so comprehensive, daring and inquisitive, shou'd be a Stranger to Religion's sweet and powerful Charms.

Mill. I am not Fool enough to be an Atheist, tho' I have known enough of Mens Hypocrisy to make a thousand simple Women so. Whatever Religion is in 40 it self, as practis'd by Mankind, it has caus'd the Evils you say it was design'd to cure. War, Plague, and Famine, has not destroy'd so many of the human Race, as this pretended Piety has done; and with such barbarous Cruelty, as if the only Way to honour Heaven, were to turn the present World into Hell.

Thor. Truth is Truth, tho' from an Enemy, and spoke in Malice. You bloody, 45 blind, and superstitious Bigots, how will you answer this?

Mill. What are your Laws, of which you make your Boast, but the Fool's Wisdom, and the Coward's Valour; the Instrument and Skreen of all your Villanies, by which you punish in others what you act your selves, or wou'd have acted, had you been in their Circumstances. The Judge who condemns the poor 50 Man for being a Thief, had been a Thief himself had he been poor. Thus you go on deceiving, and being deceiv'd, harrassing, plaguing, and destroying one another; but Women are your universal Prey.

> *Women, by whom you are, the Source of Joy,*
> *With cruel Arts you labour to destroy:*
>   55
> *A thousand Ways our Ruin you pursue,*
> *Yet blame in us those Arts, first taught by you.*
> *O—may, from hence, each violated Maid,*
> *By flatt'ring, faithless, barb'rous Man betray'd;*
>   60
> *When robb'd of Innocence, and Virgin Fame,*
> *From your Destruction raise a nobler Name;*
> *To right their Sex's Wrongs devote their Mind,*
> *And future* Millwoods *prove to plague Mankind.*

The End of the Fourth Act.

(IV. xviii)   33 I know . . . Mercy, and] G2–7; I hate you all, I know you, and expect no Mercy; G1   none; I] G2–7 (~; and I G2); ~; I have done nothing that I am sorry for; G1 33–4 I follow'd] and I follow'd G2   34 does] do G4–7   35 seem] G2–7; are G1 38 sweet and] G2–7; ~, but G1   41 Evils you say] *Ed.*; ~, you say, G1–7   42 has] have G6–7   48 Valour;] ~? G5–7   58 O—] G2; ~ͅ G1; *Oh!* G3–7 (~! G5)

ACT V.

SCENE I.

A Room in a Prison.

Thorowgood, Blunt *and* Lucy.

Thor. I have recommended to *Barnwell* a Reverend Divine, whose Judgment and Integrity I am well acquainted with; nor has *Millwood* been neglected, but she, unhappy Woman, still obstinate, refuses his Assistance.

Lucy. This pious Charity to the Afflicted well becomes your Character; yet pardon me, Sir, if I wonder you were not at their Trial.

Thor. I knew it was impossible to save him, and I and my Family bear so great a Part in his Distress, that to have been present wou'd have aggravated our Sorrows without relieving his.

Blunt. It was mournful indeed. *Barnwell*'s Youth and modest Deportment, as he past, drew Tears from every Eye: When placed at the Bar, and arraigned before the Reverend Judges, with many Tears and interrupting Sobs he confess'd and aggravated his Offences, without accusing, or once reflecting on *Millwood*, the shameless Author of his Ruin; who dauntless and unconcern'd stood by his Side, viewing with visible Pride and Contempt the vast Assembly, who all with sympathizing Sorrow wept for the wretched Youth. *Millwood*, when called upon to answer, loudly insisted upon her Innocence, and made an artful and a bold Defence; but finding all in vain, the impartial Jury and the learned Bench concurring to find her guilty, how did she curse her self, poor *Barnwell*, us, her Judges, all Mankind; but what cou'd that avail? she was condemn'd, and is this Day to suffer with him.

Thor. The Time draws on, I am going to visit *Barnwell*, as you are *Millwood*.

Lucy. We have not wrong'd her, yet I dread this Interview. She's proud, impatient, wrathful, and unforgiving. To be the branded Instruments of Vengeance, to suffer in her Shame, and sympathize with her in all she suffers, is the Tribute we must pay for our former ill spent Lives, and long confederacy with her in Wickedness.

Thor. Happy for you it ended when it did. What you have done against *Millwood* I know proceeded from a just Abhorrence of her Crimes, free from Interest, Malice, or Revenge. Proselytes to Virtue shou'd be encourag'd. Pursue your proposed Reformation, and know me hereafter for your Friend.

Lucy. This is a Blessing as unhop'd for as unmerited, but Heaven that snatched us from impending Ruin, sure intends you as its Instrument to secure us from Apostacy.

Thor. With Gratitude to impute your Deliverance to Heaven is just. Many, less virtuously dispos'd than *Barnwell* was, have never fallen in the Manner he

SD Thorowgood] *Enter* Thorowgood G3–7   7 wou'd have] wou'd but have G5–7
15 *Millwood*,] G2–7; ~ ∧ G1   30 proposed] purpos'd G3–7

has done,—may not such owe their Safety rather to Providence than to themselves? With Pity and Compassion let us judge him. Great were his Faults, but strong was the Temptation. Let his Ruin learn us Diffidence, Humanity and Circumspection;—for we,—who wonder at his Fate,—perhaps had we, like him, been tryed,—like him, we had fallen too.   40

SCENE II.

A Dungeon, a Table and Lamp.

Thorowgood *at a Distance*, Barnwell *reading.*

Thor. There see the bitter Fruits of Passion's detested Reign, and sensual Appetite indulg'd. Severe Reflections, Penitence and Tears.

Barn. My honoured injured Master, whose Goodness has covered me a thousand times with Shame, forgive this last unwilling Disrespect,—indeed I saw you not.   5

Thor. 'Tis well, I hope you were better imploy'd in viewing of your self;— your Journey's long, your Time for preparation almost spent.—I sent a Reverend Divine to teach you to improve it, and shou'd be glad to hear of his Success.

Barn. The Word of Truth, which he recommended for my constant   10
Companion in this my sad Retirement, has at length remov'd the Doubts I labour'd under. From thence I've learn'd the infinite Extent of heavenly Mercy; that my Offences, tho' great, are not unpardonable; and that 'tis not my Interest only, but my Duty to believe and to rejoice in that Hope,—So shall Heaven receive the Glory, and future Penitents the Profit of my Example.   15

Thor. Proceed.

Barn. 'Tis wonderful,—that Words shou'd charm Despair, speak Peace and Pardon to a Murderer's Conscience;—but Truth and Mercy flow in every Sentence, attended with Force and Energy divine. How shall I describe my present State of Mind? I hope in doubt,—and trembling I rejoice.—I feel my   20
Grief increase, even as my Fears give way.—Joy and Gratitude now supply more Tears, than the Horror and Anguish of Despair before.

Thor. These are the genuine Signs of true Repentance, the only Preparatory, the certain Way to everlasting Peace.—O the Joy it gives to see a Soul form'd and prepar'd for Heaven!—For this the faithful Minister devotes himself to   25
Meditation, Abstinence and Prayer, shuning the vain Delights of sensual Joys, and daily dies that others may live for ever.—For this he turns the sacred

(v. i)   37 themselves?] G4–7; ~. G1–3   39 had we,] G2–7; ~, G1   SCENE II.
SD *and Lamp.* | Thorowgood . . . Barnwell *reading.*] G2; ~. | Thorowgood, Barnwell ~. G1; ~.
Barnwell *reading.* | *Enter* Thorowgood *at a Distance.* G3–7   1 There see] G3–7; See there
G1–2   2 indulg'd.   Severe] ~, severe G5–7   16 Proceed.] G2–7; Go on.—How
happy am I who live to see | this? G1   24 the certain] G2–7; certain G1. *See Commentary*

Volumes o'er, and spends his Life in painful Search of Truth.—The Love of
Riches and the Lust of Power, he looks on with just Contempt and Detestation;
who only counts for Wealth the Souls he wins; and whose highest Ambition is   3
to serve Mankind.—If the Reward of all his Pains be to preserve one Soul from
wandering, or turn one from the Error of his Ways, how does he then rejoice,
and own his little Labours over paid.

Barn. What do I owe for all your generous Kindness? but tho' I cannot,
Heaven can and will reward you.   3

Thor. To see thee thus, is Joy too great for Words. Farewell,—Heaven
strengthen thee.—Farewell.

Barn. O! Sir, there's something I cou'd say, if my sad swelling Heart would
give me leave.

Thor. Give it vent a while, and try.   4

Barn. I had a Friend,—'tis true I am unworthy, yet methinks your generous
Example might perswade;—cou'd I not see him once before I go from whence
there's no return?

Thor. He's coming,—and as much thy Friend as ever;—but I'll not anticipate
his Sorrow,—too soon he'll see the sad Effect of his contagious Ruin. This   4
Torrent of Domestick Misery bears too hard upon me,—I must retire to
indulge a Weakness I find impossible to overcome. [*Aside.*]—Much lov'd—and
much lamented Youth—Farewell—Heaven strengthen thee—Eternally
Farewell.

Barn. The best of Masters and of Men—Farewell—while I live let me not   5
want your Prayers.

Thor. Thou shalt not;—thy Peace being made with Heaven, Death's already
vanquish'd;—bear a little longer the Pains that attend this transitory Life, and
cease from Pain for ever.

SCENE III.

Barnwell.

Perhaps I shall. I find a Power within that bears my Soul above the Fears of
Death, and, spight of conscious Shame and Guilt, gives me a Taste of Pleasure
more than Mortal.

(v. ii)   29 on] upon G4–7   33 over paid.] ~? G2–3, 6–7   38 cou'd] would G2–7
41 unworthy,] ~— G5–7   43 return?] G2–7 (Return G4–7); ~. G1   54 for ever.]
after this line G3–7 *add* SD: [*Exit* Thorowgood.   SCENE III.] G3–7 *omit*   SD Barnwell.]
G3–7 *omit*   1 G3–7 *add speech-heading: Barn.*   Perhaps I shall.] G2–7; *not in* G1

SCENE IV.

[*To him.*] Trueman *and Keeper.*

Keep. Sir, there's the Prisoner.

SCENE V.

Barnwell *and* Trueman.

Barn. Trueman,—My Friend, whom I so wisht to see, yet now he's here I dare
not look upon him.   [*Weeps.*

Tr. O *Barnwell*! *Barnwell*!

Barn. Mercy! Mercy! gracious Heaven! for Death, but not for this, was I
prepared.   5

Tr. What have I suffer'd since I saw you last?—what Pain has Absence given
me?—But oh! to see thee thus!

Barn. I know it is dreadful! I feel the Anguish of thy generous Soul,—but I
was born to murder all who love me.   [*Both weep.*

Tr. I came not to reproach you;—I thought to bring you Comfort,—but I'm 10
deceiv'd, for I have none to give;—I came to share thy Sorrow, but cannot bear
my own.

Barn. My Sense of Guilt indeed you cannot know,—'tis what the Good and
Innocent, like you, can ne'er conceive;—but other Griefs at present I have
none, but what I feel for you.—In your Sorrow I read you love me still,—but 15
yet methinks 'tis strange—when I consider what I am.

Tr. No more of that,—I can remember nothing but thy Virtues,—thy honest,
tender Friendship, our former happy State and present Misery.—O had you
trusted me when first the Fair Seducer tempted you, all might have been
prevented.   20

Barn. Alas, thou know'st not what a Wretch I've been! Breach of Friendship
was my first and least Offence.—So far was I lost to Goodness,—so devoted to
the Author of my Ruin,—that had she insisted on my murdering thee,—I
think,—I shou'd have done it.

Tr. Prithee aggravate thy Faults no more.   25

Barn. I think I shou'd!—thus Good and Generous as you are, I shou'd have
murder'd you!

Tr. We have not yet embrac'd, and may be interrupted. Come to my Arms.

Barn. Never, never will I taste such Joys on Earth; never will I so sooth my

SCENE IV.] G3–7 *omit*   SD [*To him.*]] ‚Enter‚‚ G3–7   1 Prisoner.] *after this line*
G3–7 *add* SD: [*Exit Keeper.*   SCENE V.] G3–7 *omit*   SD Barnwell *and* Trueman.]
G3–7 *omit*   1 Trueman,] ~! G2–7   4 was I] I was G5–7   6 has] hath G4–7
22 Offence.—So] ~;‚ so G2–7

just Remorse. Are those honest Arms, and faithful Bosom, fit to embrace and to   3ᴄ
support a Murderer?—These Iron Fetters only shall clasp, and flinty
Pavement bear me,—[*Throwing himself on the Ground.*] even these too good for
such a bloody Monster.

Tr. Shall Fortune sever those whom Friendship join'd!—Thy Miseries
cannot lay thee so low, but Love will find thee.—Here will we offer to stern   3ᴤ
Calamity,—this Place the Altar, and our selves the Sacrifice.—Our mutual
Groans shall eccho to each other thro' the dreary Vault.—Our Sighs shall
number the Moments as they pass,—and mingling Tears communicate such
Anguish, as Words were never made to express.

Barn. Then be it so.—[*Rising.*] Since you propose an Intercourse of Woe,   4ᴄ
pour all your Griefs into my Breast,—and in exchange take mine. [*Embracing.*]
Where's now the Anguish that you promis'd?—You've taken mine, and make
me no Return.—Sure Peace and Comfort dwell within these Arms, and Sorrow
can't approach me while I'm here!—This too is the Work of Heaven, who,
having before spoke Peace and Pardon to me, now sends thee to confirm it.—O   4.
take, take some of the Joy that overflows my Breast!

Tr. I do, I do. Almighty Power, how have you made us capable to bear, at
once, the Extreams of Pleasure and of Pain?

SCENE VI.

[*To them.*] *Keeper.*

Keeper. Sir.
Tr. I come.

SCENE VII.

Barnwell *and* Trueman.

Barn. Must you leave me!—Death would soon have parted us for ever.

Tr. O, my *Barnwell*, there's yet another Task behind:—Again your Heart
must bleed for others Woes.

Barn. To meet and part with you, I thought was all I had to do on Earth!
What is there more for me to do or suffer?

(v. v)   30 those] these G5–7   31 Murderer?] G4–7; ~. G1–3   35 thee.] G2–7;
~, [*Lies down by him.*] Upon | this rugged Couch then let us lie, for well it suits| our most deplorable
Condition.— G1. *See Commentary*   36 Place] G2–7; Earth G1   40 SD [*Rising.*]] G2–7;
not in G1   41 mine.] G3–7; ~, G1–2   44 who] which G3–7   47 have you] hast
thou G5–7   SCENE VI.] G3–7 *omit*   SD [*To them.*]] ₐEnter₍₎ G3–7   2 come.]
after this line G3–7 *add* SD: [*Exit Keeper. (Exit.* G4)   SCENE VII.] G3–7 *omit*
SD Barnwell *and* Trueman.] G3–7 *omit*

Tr. I dread to tell thee, yet it must be known.—*Maria.*

Barn. Our Master's fair and virtuous Daughter!

Tr. The same.

Barn. No Misfortune, I hope, has reach'd that lovely Maid! Preserve her, Heaven, from every Ill, to show Mankind that Goodness is your Care.   10

Tr. Thy, thy Misfortunes, my unhappy Friend, have reach'd her. Whatever you and I have felt, and more, if more be possible, she feels for you.

Barn. I know he doth abhor a Lie, and would not trifle with his dying Friend.—This is, indeed, the Bitterness of Death!   [*Aside.*

Tr. You must remember, for we all observ'd it, for some Time past, a heavy   15
Melancholy weigh'd her down.—Disconsolate she seem'd, and pin'd and languish'd from a Cause unknown;—till hearing of your dreadful Fate,—the long stifled Flame blaz'd out.—She wept, she wrung her Hands, and tore her Hair, and, in the Transport of her Grief, discover'd her own lost State, whilst she lamented yours.   20

Barn. Will all the Pain I feel restore thy Ease, lovely unhappy Maid? [*Weeping.*] Why did n't you let me die and never know it?

Tr. It was impossible;—she makes no Secret of her Passion for you, and is determin'd to see you ere you die;—she waits for me to introduce her.—

SCENE VIII.

Barnwell.

Vain busy Thoughts be still!—What avails it to think on what I might have been,—I now am,—what I've made my self.

SCENE IX.

[*To him.*] Trueman *and* Maria.

Tr. Madam, reluctant I lead you to this dismal Scene: This is the Seat of Misery and Guilt.—Here awful Justice reserves her publick Victims.—This is the Entrance to shameful Death.—

Ma. To this sad Place, then no improper Guest, the abandon'd lost *Maria* brings Despair,—and see the Subject and the Cause of all this World of   5
Woe.—Silent and motionless he stands, as if his Soul had quitted her

---

(v. vii) 6 —*Maria.*] ∧~— G2; ∧~.— G3–7   19 whilst] while G7   22 did n't you]
did not you G2–3; did you not G4–7   24 ere] G3, 5–7; e'er G1–2, 4   her.—] ~.∧ G2–7;
after this line G3–7 *add* SD: [*Exit* Trueman.   SCENE VIII.] G3–7 *omit*   SD Barnwell.]
G3–7 *omit*   1 G1–7 *include speech-heading: Barn.*   2 been,] ~? G2–7   what]
W1; What G1–7   SCENE IX.] G3–7 *omit*   SD [*To him.*]] ∧*Enter*∧∧ G3–7   *and*]
with G5–7   5 Despair,—] *Ed.*; ~,∧ G1–7

Abode,—and the lifeless Form alone was left behind;—yet that so perfect, that Beauty and Death,—ever at Enmity,—now seem united there.

Barn. I groan, but murmur not.—Just Heaven, I am your own; do with me what you please.

Ma. Why are your streaming Eyes still fix'd below?—as tho' thoud'st give the greedy Earth thy Sorrows, and rob me of my Due.—Were Happiness within your Power, you should bestow it where you pleas'd;—but in your Misery I must and will partake.

Barn. Oh! say not so, but fly, abhor, and leave me to my Fate.—Consider what you are:—How vast your Fortune, and how bright your Fame:—Have Pity on your Youth, your Beauty, and unequalled Virtue,—for which so many noble Peers have sigh'd in vain. Bless with your Charms some honourable Lord.—Adorn with your Beauty, and, by your Example, improve the *English* Court, that justly claims such Merit; so shall I quickly be to you—as though I had never been.—

Ma. When I forget you, I must be so indeed.—Reason, Choice, Virtue, all forbid it.—Let Women, like *Millwood*, if there be more such Women, smile in Prosperity, and in Adversity forsake.—Be it the Pride of Virtue to repair, or to partake, the Ruin such have made.

Tr. Lovely, ill-fated Maid!—Was there ever such generous Distress before?—How must this peirce his grateful Heart, and aggravate his Woes?

Barn. Ere I knew Guilt or Shame, when Fortune smil'd, and when my youthful Hopes were at the highest; if then to have rais'd my Thoughts to you, had been Presumption in me, never to have been pardon'd,—think how much beneath your self you condescend to regard me now.

Ma. Let her blush, who, professing Love, invades the Freedom of your Sex's Choice, and meanly sues in Hopes of a Return.—Your inevitable Fate hath render'd Hope impossible as vain.—Then why shou'd I fear to avow a Passion so just and so disinterested?

Tr. If any shou'd take Occasion, from *Millwood*'s Crimes, to libel the best and fairest Part of the Creation, here let them see their Error.—The most distant Hopes of such a tender Passion, from so bright a Maid, might add to the Happiness of the most happy, and make the greatest proud.—Yet here 'tis lavish'd in vain:—Tho' by the rich Present, the generous Donor is undone,—he, on whom it is bestow'd, receives no Benefit.

Barn. So the Aromatick Spices of the East, which all the Living covet and esteem, are, with unavailing Kindness, wasted on the Dead.

Ma. Yes, fruitless is my Love, and unavailing all my Sighs and Tears.—Can they save thee from approaching Death?—from such a Death?—O terrible Idea!—What is her Misery and Distress, who sees the first last Object of her

(v. ix) 13 where] were G4   18 vain.] ~.— G5–6; ~‸— G7   19 Beauty,] G7; ~; G1–6   20 you—] G2–7; ~‸ G1   23 be] are G5–7   24 forsake.—] G3–7; ~‸— G2; ~.‸ G1   28 Ere] G3–7; E'er G1–2   32 professing] proffering G2, 4; proferring G3; prostering G5; profering G6–7

Love, for whom alone she'd live,—for whom she'd die a thousand, thousand Deaths, if it were possible,—expiring in her Arms?—Yet she is happy, when compar'd to me.—Were Millions of Worlds mine, I'd gladly give them in exchange for her Condition.—The most consummate Woe is light to mine. 50 The last of Curses to other miserable Maids, is all I ask—for my Relief, and that's deny'd me.

Tr. Time and Reflection cure all Ills.

Ma. All but this;—his dreadful Catastrophe Virtue her self abhors.—To give a Holiday to suburb Slaves, and passing entertain the savage Herd, who, 55 elbowing each other for a Sight, pursue and press upon him like his Fate.—A Mind with Piety and Resolution arm'd, may smile on Death.—But publick Ignominy,—everlasting Shame,—Shame the Death of Souls,—to die a thousand Times, and yet survive even Death it self, in never dying Infamy—is this to be endured?—Can I, who live in him, and must, each Hour of my 60 devoted Life, feel all these Woes renew'd,—can I endure this!—

Tr. Grief has impair'd her Spirits; she pants, as in the Agonies of Death.—

Barn. Preserve her, Heaven, and restore her Peace,—nor let her Death be added to my Crimes,—[*Bell tolls.*] I am summon'd to my Fate.

SCENE X.

[*To them.*] *Keeper and Officers.*

Keep. The Officers attend you, Sir.—Mrs. *Millwood* is already summon'd.

Barn. Tell 'em I'm ready.—And now, my Friend, farewell, [*Embracing.*] Support and comfort the best you can this Mourning Fair.—No more.— Forget not to pray for me,—[*Turning to* Maria.] Would you, bright Excellence, permit me the Honour of a chaste Embrace,—the last Happiness this World 5 cou'd give were mine. [*She enclines towards him; they embrace.*] Exalted Goodness!—O turn your Eyes from Earth, and me, to Heaven,—where Virtue, like yours, is ever heard.—Pray for the Peace of my departing Soul.—Early my Race of Wickedness began, and soon has reach'd the Summet:—Ere Nature has finish'd her Work, and stamp'd me Man,—just at the Time that others 10 begin to stray,—my Course is finish'd; tho' short my Span of Life, and few my Days, yet count my Crimes for Years, and I have liv'd whole Ages.—Thus Justice, in Compassion to Mankind, cuts off a Wretch like me, by one such Example to secure Thousands from future Ruin. Justice and Mercy are in

(v. ix) 51 ask—] G2–4; ~; G1; ~_∧ G5–7   for my Relief] G2–7; *not in* G1 52 that's] that G7   59 Infamy—] G2–7; ~, G1   62 impair'd] so impair'd G3–7 64 Crimes] Crime G1 (*earlier state*)   SCENE X.] G3–7 omit   SD [*To them.*]] _∧Enter_∧∧ G3–7   *Keeper and Officers.*] G3–7; *Keeper.* G1   1 The Officers attend you, Sir.] Sir, the Officers attend you; G2–7 (you, G2)   Mrs.] G2–7 *omit*   is] G3 *omits*   4 SD Maria.] G3–4, 6–7; ~_∧ G1, 5   Would] G2–7; would G1   6 mine.] G5–7; ~, G1–4   9 has] 1 G3–7   Ere] G3–7; E'er G1–2   12 Days,] *Ed.*; ~; G1–7   12–14 Thus Justice, ... future Ruin.] G2–7; G1 *omits here and prints after line 17*

Heaven the same: Its utmost Severity is Mercy to the whole,—thereby to cure   15
Man's Folly and Presumption, which else wou'd render even infinite Mercy
vain and ineffectual.

> *If any Youth, like you,—in future Times,*
> *Shall mourn my Fate,—tho' he abhor my Crimes;*
> *Or tender Maid, like you,—my Tale shall hear,*   20
> *And to my Sorrows give a pitying Tear:*
> *To each such melting Eye, and throbbing Heart,*
> *Would gracious Heaven this Benefit impart,*
> *Never to know my Guilt,—nor feel my Pain,*
> *Then must you own, you ought not to complain;*   2
> *Since you nor weep,—nor shall I die in vain.*

SCENE XI.

The Place of Execution. The Gallows and
Ladders at the farther End of the Stage.

A Crowd of Spectators. Blunt *and* Lucy.

Lucy. Heavens! What a Throng!

Blunt. How terrible is Death when thus prepar'd!

Lucy. Support them, Heaven; thou only canst support them; all other Help is
vain.

Officer within. Make Way there; make Way, and give the Prisoners Room.

Lucy. They are here: observe them well. How humble and composed young
Barnwell seems! but *Millwood* looks wild, ruffled with Passion, confounded and
amazed.

Enter Barnwell, Millwood, *Officers and Executioner.*

Barn. See, *Millwood,* see, our Journey's at an End. Life, like a Tale that's told,
is past away; that short but dark and unknown Passage, Death, is all the Space
'tween us and endless Joys, or Woes eternal.

Mill. Is this the End of all my flattering Hopes? Were Youth and Beauty given
me for a Curse, and Wisdom only to insure my Ruin? They were, they were.
Heaven, thou hast done thy worst. Or if thou hast in Store some untried Plague,
somewhat that's worse than Shame, Despair and Death, unpitied Death,
confirm'd Despair and Soul confounding Shame; something that Men and
Angels can't describe and only Fiends, who bear it, can conceive; now, pour it
now on this devoted Head, that I may feel the worst thou canst inflict and bid
Defiance to thy utmost Power.

(v. x)   26 *vain.*] *after this line* G3–7 *add* SD: [Exit *Barnwell* and Officers.   SCENE XI.] *Ed.;*
SCENE the LAST. G5–7. *The entire scene is absent from* G1–4; G5 *serves as copy-text for the present
edition*   3 canst] can G7   7 seems!] W1; ~? G5–7   8+SD *Executioner*]
Executioners G7   13 They were] G6–7; ~ Were G5   17 Fiends] Friends G6

Barn. Yet ere we pass the dreadful Gulph of Death, yet ere you're plunged in   20
everlasting Woe, O bend your stubborn Knees and harder Heart, humbly to
deprecate the Wrath divine. Who knows but Heaven, in your dying Moments,
may bestow that Grace and Mercy which your Life despised.

Mill. Why name you Mercy to a Wretch like me? Mercy's beyond my Hope;
almost beyond my Wish. I can't repent, nor ask to be forgiven.   25

Barn. O think what 'tis to be for ever, ever miserable; nor with vain Pride
oppose a Power, that's able to destroy you.

Mill. That will destroy me: I feel it will. A Deluge of Wrath is pouring on my
Soul. Chains, Darkness, Wheels, Racks, sharp stinging Scorpions, molten Lead
and Seas of Sulphur, are light to what I feel.   30

Barn. O! add not to your vast Account Despair: A Sin more injurious to
Heaven, than all you've yet committed.

Mill. O! I have sinn'd beyond the Reach of Mercy.

Barn. O say not so: 'tis Blasphemy to think it. As yon bright Roof is higher
than the Earth, so and much more does Heaven's Goodness pass our   35
Apprehension. O what created Being shall presume to circumscribe Mercy,
that knows no Bounds?

Mill. This yields no Hope. Tho' Mercy may be boundless yet 'tis free: And I
was doom'd before the World began to endless Pains and thou to Joys eternal.

Barn. O! gracious Heaven! extend thy Pity to her: Let thy rich Mercy flow in   40
plenteous Streams to chase her Fears and heal her wounded Soul.

Mill. It will not be. Your Prayers are lost in Air, or else returned perhaps with
double Blessing to your Bosom, but me they help not.

Barn. Yet hear me, *Millwood*!

Mill. Away, I will not hear thee: I tell thee, Youth, I am by Heaven devoted a   45
dreadful Instance of its Power to punish. [Barnwell *seems to pray.*] If thou wilt
pray, pray for thyself not me. How doth his fervent Soul mount with his Words,
and both ascend to Heaven! That Heaven, whose Gates are shut with
adamantine Bars against my Prayers, had I the Will to pray—I cannot bear it—
Sure 'tis the worst of Torments to behold others enjoy that Bliss that we must   50
never taste.

Officer. The utmost Limit of your Time's expired.

Mill. Incompassed with Horror, whither must I go? I wou'd not live—nor
die—That I cou'd cease to be!—or ne'er had been!

Barn. Since Peace and Comfort are denied her here, may she find Mercy   55
where she least expects it, and this be all her Hell.—From our Example may all
be taught to fly the first Approach of Vice; but if o'ertaken

> By strong *Temptation, Weakness,* or *Surprize,*
> Lament their Guilt and by Repentance rise;

(v. xi)   34 yon] you G6   45 tell thee,] G6–7; ~ₐ G5   Youth,] G6–7; ~ₐ G5
46 its] G6–7; it's G5   53 Horror,] *Ed.*; ~ₐ G5–7   59 *rise;*] *Ed.*; ~, G5–7

Th'impenitent alone die unforgiven;
To sin's like Man, and to forgive like Heaven.

SCENE XII.

Trueman, Blunt, *and* Lucy.

Lucy. Heart-breaking Sight.—O wretched, wretched *Millwood*!
Tr. How is she disposed to meet her Fate?
Blunt. Who can describe unalterable Woe?
Lucy. She goes to Death encompassed with Horror, loathing Life, and yet afraid to die; no Tongue can tell her Anguish and Despair.
Tr. Heaven be better to her than her Fears; may she prove a Warning to others, a Monument of Mercy in her self.
Lucy. O Sorrow, insupportable! break, break my Heart.
Tr. In vain

> *With bleeding Hearts, and weeping Eyes we show*
> *A human gen'rous Sense of others Woe;*
> *Unless we mark what drew their Ruin on,*
> *And by avoiding that—prevent our own.*

FINIS.

SCENE XII.] *Ed.*; SCENE XI. G1–4; G5–7 *omit*   SD Trueman, Blunt, *and* Lucy.] *Enter*
Blunt *and* Lucy. G3–4; *Enter* Trueman. G5–7   1 *Millwood*!] G2–7; ~. G1   2 How]
G5–7; You came from her then:—How G1–4   3 unalterable] unutterable G2–7
9 vain] ~. G1 (*earlier state*)   13 *that*—] G2–7; ~, G1   *FINIS.*] G6 *omits*; *The End of*
the Fifth Act. G7

EPILOGUE.

Written by COLLEY CIBBER, *Esq;*
and spoke by Mrs. CIBBER.

Since Fate has robb'd me of the hapless Youth,
For whom my Heart had hoarded up its Truth;
By all the Laws of Love and Honour, now,
I'm free again to chuse,—and one of you.

But soft,—With Caution first I'll round me peep; 5
Maids, in my Case, shou'd look, before they leap:
Here's Choice enough, of various Sorts, and Hue,
The Cit, the Wit, the Rake cock'd up in Cue,
The fair spruce Mercer, and the tawney Jew.

Suppose I search the sober Gallery;—No, 10
There's none but Prentices,—and Cuckolds all a Row;
And these, I doubt, are those that make 'em so.
                    [Pointing to the Boxes.

'Tis very well, the Jest:—But you,
Fine powder'd Sparks;—nay, I'm told 'tis true,
Your happy Spouses—can make Cuckolds too. 15
'Twixt you and them, the Diff'rence this perhaps,
The Cit's asham'd whene'er his Duck he traps;
But you, when Madam's tripping, let her fall,
Cock up your Hats, and take no Shame at all.

What if some favour'd Poet I cou'd meet? 20
Whose Love wou'd lay his Lawrels at my Feet.
No,—Painted Passion real Love abhors,—
His Flame wou'd prove the Suit of Creditors.

Not to detain you then with longer Pause,
In short, my Heart to this Conclusion draws, 25
I yield it to the Hand, that's loudest in Applause.

The Christian Hero

INTRODUCTION

SOURCES

LILLO did not attempt to repeat his success with domestic tragedy written in prose. *The Christian Hero*, first performed more than three years after the initial production of *The London Merchant*, is modelled on heroic drama, its language high-flown verse, its setting the exotic medieval East, and its subject the triumphs of Scanderbeg, 'A Pious Hero, and a Patriot King'[1] as great in political stature and moral stamina as Barnwell had been small.

The fifteenth-century Albanian liberator, George Castriot—renamed Scanderbeg by the Turks, in whose court he lived as hostage—figured prominently in popular histories of the Turkish–Christian campaigns and had been the subject of a number of adulatory if apocryphal biographies and historical romances. Remembered as the defender of public liberty as well as an exemplar of heroic virtue, he was a likely subject for a dramatist of didactic intention.

Genest complains that Lillo added to history elements of romance 'not only inconsistent with Scanderbeg's general character, but with his time of life'.[2] The process, in fact, seems to have been just the reverse: Lillo's chief source was a romantic novel, whose characters and plot he reshaped to his own didactic purposes and augmented with material, including additional characters, systematically gleaned from several historical sources.

Lillo's interest in the hero may have been stimulated by William Havard's tragedy *Scanderbeg*, performed without success in 1733. Havard's play did not, however, serve as Lillo's source or model. Nor did the late Thomas Whincop's unperformed tragedy, *Scanderbeg: or, Love and Liberty*, written before 1730 but

---

[1] Prologue, l. 28.   [2] iii. 444.

not printed until 1747, when it was published with a preface and 'List of . . . Dramatic Authors . . .' in which the anonymous editor charged that Lillo had stolen his plot from Whincop's play. No evidence supports the accusation. Davies dismisses it as an 'invidious attack'[3] and Hans Rautner, in a study of Lillo's possible sources,[4] demonstrates that the similarities between *The Christian Hero* and Whincop's tragedy indicate, at most, that the playwrights drew upon the same source, *Scanderbeg the Great*, the English translation of a novel by Anne de La Roche-Guilhem. First published in French as early as 1688,[5] this highly romanticized account of the hero's love for a Greek slave girl in the Turkish court appeared in an English version in 1690. Another translation, Lillo's source, was published in 1721 and reprinted in 1729: both editions were issued with popular collections of novels published by John Watts. Lillo's romantic plot—the capture and last-minute rescue of Scanderbeg's beloved, Althea, and her father, Aranthes—is clearly a reworking of the central action of the novel, which involves the rescue of Arianissa, the Greek slave, and her father, Aranit, who has been taken captive during the sultan's campaign against Scanderbeg. A number of Lillo's characters, situations, and scenes parallel those of *Scanderbeg the Great*.[6] The novel's heroine is the object of the unwanted love of a number of her Turkish masters, among them, as in Lillo's play, Mahomet, the son of the sultan. Like Lillo's Althea, Arianissa barely escapes sexual attack, and like Althea she urges Scanderbeg to sacrifice his concern for her to the greater cause of his own and his people's freedom. At the climax of novel and play, the sultan orders the deaths of the heroine and her father but loses the captives to Scanderbeg, and, defeated in this as in the war, rages and dies.

The central issues of the play, however, entail thematic emphases quite different from those of the novel, which rests content with its romantic plot devices. The capture of Aranit, for example, serves only to create a situation in which the sultan himself, another admirer of Arianissa's beauty, can attempt to seduce the girl by threatening to kill her father. The wider moral dimension, in which private love is opposed to public duty, love for life to love for liberty, is introduced by the playwright.

In Lillo's most extensive transformation of a situation suggested by the novel, Selimana—in the novel the chief woman of the seraglio, a vixen whose frustrated love for Scanderbeg drives her to attempt the murder of Arianissa and finally to stab herself in frenzied rage—becomes the gentle Hellena, the sultan's daughter, who sacrifices her life to warn Scanderbeg of a plot against his life.[7]

---

[3] *Life*, p. xv.

[4] *George Lillos The Christian Hero und dessen Rival Plays* (Munich, 1900), pp. 21–2 *et passim*.

[5] *Le Grand Scanderberg* [sic], *Nouvelle par Mlle.* **** (Amsterdam, 1688), is the earliest known edition.

[6] See the Commentary for comparison of details of the play with Lillo's various possible sources.

[7] Boas (p. 247) finds Hellena's farewell to Scanderbeg and her dying wish for his happy reunion with Althea 'a truly moving scene' and as 'a high tribute' to the playwright suggests 'that Hellena is

The sultan's use of Hellena as a promised prize with which to tempt Scanderbeg's traitorous kinsman, Amasie, is also Lillo's invention. Amasie, indeed, has no place in the novel and is one of the most prominent of the many elements in the play that indicate the playwright's use of additional sources. The range of historical sources available to him was wide,[8] but his characterization of Amasie indicates that he must have known Jacques Lavardin's *Historie of George Castriot, Surnamed Scanderbeg*, which appeared in an English translation in 1596. Although Amasie is mentioned in other accounts of the hero's career, he figures prominently in Lavardin's history, and only Lavardin focuses on his treachery.[9] As usual, Lillo altered his source to suit his dramatic and didactic purposes. Lavardin's Amasie genuinely repents his defection; in the play the expression of regret is pretence, a stratagem by which Amasie intends to gain the opportunity to murder Scanderbeg, and a plot device which Lillo employs to reveal the hero's only weakness, excess of human sympathy.

The playwright probably made use of other material provided by Lavardin, but a number of historical details in the play suggest that he usually referred to an unabridged edition of Richard Knolles's *Turkish History*, a compendious assemblage of facts and legend first published in 1603 and frequently reprinted in expanded editions during the seventeenth century.[10] Scanderbeg's lines at I. i. 301–2 closely parallel Knolles's version of a letter purportedly written by the hero, and Lillo's handling of Scanderbeg's confrontation with the sultan (II. i) suggests reference to other such letters given by Knolles. Minor details, such as references to Scanderbeg's brothers, his Hungarian allies, and the sultan's retirement to Magnesia, were also probably taken from the *Turkish History*.

In reconstructing the material of his various sources into a heroic drama of a

---

here of the same sisterhood as Beaumont and Fletcher's equally ill-fated Aspasia in *The Maid's Tragedy*'.

[8] Rautner refers almost exclusively to plays and works of fiction; for an extensive compilation of historical as well as fictional accounts of Scanderbeg (not, however, complete in its record of English works and translations published during the 17th and 18th cents.) see George T. Pétrovitch, *Scanderbeg . . . Essai de bibliographie raisonnée. Ouvrages sur Scanderbeg écrits en langues française, anglaise, latine . . . et publiés depuis l'invention de l'imprimerie jusqu'à nos jours* (Paris and Vienna, 1881). John Gray's advertisements for *The Christian Hero* regularly included *A Brief Account of the Life and Character of George Castriot . . . Commonly called, Scanderbeg. Inscribed to the Spectators of the Christian Hero* (1735). *A Brief Account* was also issued in his nonce collection of Lillo's works (1740). The book is almost certainly not Lillo's work, nor was it a source for his play. However, Lillo and the anonymous author of the *Brief Account* probably made use of the same historical sources (see nn. 9 and 10 below).

[9] See the Commentary on the dramatis personae and on III. i. 114. Like Lillo, the author of the *Brief Account* may well have found the story of Amasie's treachery in Lavardin's history; he seems, however, to have discovered only the report of Amasie's initial defection, and not the account of his repentance, which occurs in a later section of Lavardin's work.

[10] A sixth edition of Knolles's *Turkish History*, edited and expanded by Sir Paul Rycaut, was published in 1687. An edition abridged by John Savage appeared in 1701, but details in Lillo's play indicate that he could not have used this short version of the history. The author of the *Brief Account* (p. 19) acknowledges Knolles's history as one of his sources.

Christian hero, the paragon described by Hellena at the beginning of the play,[11] Lillo sets in the foreground a conventional conflict of love and duty. This contest is resolved, however, almost before it has begun, for it is not actually a conflict: Althea, as virtuous as Scanderbeg, urges him to hold to his cause and, like her father, prevents the hero from exposing himself to the only real threat to his valour, the excessive exercise of his own humane emotions. 'To force a Tenderness thou can'st not bear'[12] is the danger; the preventive, self-control. Emphasizing the point by contrast, Lillo makes negative examples of characters drawn from his historical and romantic sources—Amasie, driven by envy and desire, and Mahomet, on fire and ultimately shamed by 'Appetite [that] Must be appeas'd'.[13] For the superhero as for Barnwell, reining in the passions is the first and most important duty in the defence of virtue and the achievement of success.

Conflicts of forces other than love and duty move centre stage as Lillo develops his material into a broader definition of Christian heroism. The confrontation of Scanderbeg with the sultan, Amurath, is demanded by dramatic convention.[14] The scene, like the war itself, is posed as the opposition of two halves of the world; the leaders are established as contrasting figures of tyranny and liberty who, in Lillo's version, reflect in their personal as well as public lives the natures of their religions. These conflicts, in turn, are subsumed in a drama of providence, resolved in the victory of the Christian leader, whose response to adversity is to ask his God to 'Give [him] to know and to discharge [his] Duty',[15] and in the defeat of the impatient sultan, whose prayer is 'Give me Revenge, or I'll renounce thy Worship'.[16]

To dramatize the opposition of faiths in personal terms, Lillo invents the pathetic drama of Hellena, a father–daughter tragedy that for the sultan marks a crushing 'Revolution in the Source of Things', the dissolution of 'The former Chain of Beings',[17] and for the audience provides an instructive contrast to the patience of Aranthes and Althea, whose faith in providence finds joy even in the prospect of immediate death.

Lillo focuses sharply on the ideal of political liberty, especially in his final scene.[18] In other respects, *The Christian Hero* asserts values already voiced in

---

[11] I. i. 44–82.   [12] III. i. 266.   [13] II. i. 296–7.

[14] Davies (*Life*, p. xiv) suggests that the scene is an imitation of the parley between Caled and Eumenes in John Hughes's *The Siege of Damascus*, but Lillo's scene, with the Christian and Turkish soldiers symmetrically arranged on either side of the stage, is typical of the baroque heroic play.

[15] III. i. 112.   [16] I. i. 170.   [17] V. ii. 10–11.

[18] In this the play foreshadows the more direct and controversial political statement which Lillo seems to have intended to make in *Elmerick*. While a politically aware audience might have sensed a reference to the rhetoric of the opposition to Walpole in those passages in *The Christian Hero* in which the benefits of liberty are extolled, the matter of the play does not lend itself to comparison with the political situation in 18th-cent. Britain. Lillo's concern appears to have been to assert more generally the virtues of the beneficent monarch and responsible subjects in the context of what his title suggested and his contemporaries accepted to be a religious rather than political drama.

The London Merchant. It sounds them with a heroic accent, a rhetoric unfortunately more often hollow than resonant. Yet though the mixture of heroics, romance, and pathos conventional for the period proves awkward for the playwright, thematically *The Christian Hero* is as characteristically the work of Lillo as his earlier, unique, domestic tragedy, and in his design for the play history and romance, like love and true honour, are resolved in the drama of beneficent providence.

PERFORMANCE AND RECEPTION

The Christian Hero was acted at Drury Lane on Monday, 13 January 1734/5. It was repeated on the succeeding three nights, then permanently disappeared from the stage.[19] Lillo was given the customary author's benefit on the third night and had at least the satisfaction of knowing that his play had failed despite the talents of a first-rate company of actors, a number of whom had been on hand for the happier first night of *The London Merchant*. Theophilus Cibber, the original Barnwell, undertook the very different character of the hypocrite, Amasie, a part that some of his colleagues would have said was more suited to his nature. In similarly striking changes of role, Mrs Butler, the first Millwood, acted the chaste Althea while William Mills, who had played Trueman, rendered the passions of Mahomet. Amurath was played by Quin and Scanderbeg by William Milward, another Barnwell (at Lincoln's Inn Fields) and the current Thorowgood at Drury Lane.[20]

The company must have hoped that the play, brought on in the middle of the season, would match the success of Lillo's first play. The audience, however, seems to have found Lillo's hero of perfected virtue less appealing than his apprentice sinner. Davies reports that *The Christian Hero* was acted 'with tolerable success' but acknowledges that 'the muse of Lillo was more adapted to an humble than a lofty theme, to plot not so intricate, nor so overcharged with episode, to characters less elevated, and situations more familiar'.[21] The actual response the play received is no doubt more accurately reflected in Aaron Hill's remarks in the *Prompter*. Although himself an advocate of didactic drama,[22] Hill begins his comments on *The Christian Hero* with the observation that the subject of the play was less than well suited to the English theatre, which 'seems not to approve of a religious distress for tragedy'. 'The pulpit', he concludes, 'seems the properest theatre for such representations, and the clergy the properest actors in the religious drama. This then, of itself, sufficiently justified the Town in its reception of this piece.'[23]

---

[19] *London Stage, 1729–1747*. [20] *London Stage, 1729–1747*, vol. i, *passim*; deBoer, pp. 203–4.
[21] *Life*, p. xiv.
[22] Cf. the preface to *Fatal Extravagance*, *The Dramatic Works of Aaron Hill* (London, 1760), i. 288–90.
[23] Aaron Hill and William Popple, *The Prompter, A Theatrical Paper (1734–1736)*, ed. William W. Appleton and Kalman A. Burnim (New York, 1966), p. 29 (issue No. 29, 18 Feb. 1735).

THE TEXT

One authorized edition, published in 1735, soon after the play's brief appearance at Drury Lane, provides the only authoritative text of *The Christian Hero*. The edition was issued in three states: copies printed on ordinary paper, copies printed on fine paper, and a 'second edition', actually a reissue with a cancel title-gathering. A Dublin edition, also issued in 1735, has no authority but its publication may have motivated the legitimate publisher to bring out his purported 'second edition'.

First Edition

John Gray registered his copyright of *The Christian Hero* on Wednesday, 5 February 1735. Copies of his edition were probably put on sale the following day. Gray's advertisements suggest that he had intended to bring out the book somewhat earlier than this but met with problems which forced a delay. The edition itself shows evidence of some irregularity or undue haste in production.

The first announcements of the publication of *The Christian Hero* appeared on 23 January, when Gray advertised in the *Daily Post and General Advertiser* and the *Grub-Street Journal* that the play would be published 'Next Week'. That he expected to have copies available before the end of the month appears to be confirmed by his advertisement in the *Craftsman* for Saturday, 1 February, which lists the play as published 'This Day'. Such an announcement in a weekly newspaper can normally be taken to indicate that the book had been published during the preceding week.[24] However, on the following Wednesday, 5 February—the day on which Gray registered his copyright—a notice in the *Daily Courant* announced that *The Christian Hero* would be published 'Next Thursday', by which was meant not Thursday of the next week but literally the next Thursday, 6 February, when indeed a second advertisement in the *Daily Courant* announced, 'This Day is Published The Christian Hero . . .'. This advertisement was repeated on 7 February and duly followed by a similar announcement in the *Craftsman* for 8 February.

Despite the advertisements run in January, 6 February is the most likely date of publication. It is altogether unlikely that John Gray issued copies of his edition of the new Lillo play before he had protected his copyright. His concern to establish his exclusive title to the copy and to discourage the publication of unauthorized editions was such that he included a warning in the edition itself, printed on the second leaf of the original title-gathering:

---

[24] See the records of advertisements noted in the Textual Introductions to *Fatal Curiosity*, *Marina*, and *The London Merchant*. Both the *Gentleman's Magazine* and the *London Magazine*, published *c*.1 Feb., include *The Christian Hero* in their lists of books for January, providing further evidence that Gray expected to have copies ready before the end of the month.

ADVERTISEMENT.

WHEREAS the Right and Title to the Copy of this Play are enter'd in the
STATIONERS BOOK, according to the Act of Parliament, any Person or Persons,
who shall presume to print or sell any pyrated Edition of it, will be prosecuted with the
utmost Severity, as the Law directs.

Gray had had good reason to regret his oversight in failing to register his
copyright of *The London Merchant*, and during the weeks in which he was
preparing to publish *The Christian Hero* he was also seeing to the printing and
promotion of a new edition of *The London Merchant* which, with the inclusion of
a scene not previously published, was intended to thwart the competition of the
numerous unauthorized editions of the play which had appeared since its first
printing in 1731. It is clear that, in production and publication, the first edition
of *The Christian Hero* and the new edition of the *Merchant* were closely linked.
The original title-gathering of *The Christian Hero* includes an advertisement for
this 'Fifth Genuine Edition' of *The London Merchant*, which in turn contains an
announcement noting *The Christian Hero*, 'Just Published by the same Author'.
The two books were regularly advertised together in the newspapers, they share
evidence of hasty printing, and both appear to have been published somewhat
later than was expected. From the first, advertisements for *The Christian Hero*
included announcements of the new edition of the *Merchant*, worded in such a
way as to indicate that copies were already in print. However, the advertisement
printed in the title-gathering of *The Christian Hero*, which announces that the
fifth edition of *The London Merchant* is published 'This Day', is printed beneath
the dateline 'Feb. 8 1734–5', which suggests that the book was not in fact
issued until that day.[25]

The Christian Hero and the new edition of *The London Merchant* are further
linked and distinctive as the only editions of Lillo's plays which his authorized
publisher reissued with cancel title-pages altering the numbers of the editions.
Whatever problems Gray encountered in producing the original copies of the
books, he clearly continued to be concerned about the competition of piratical
editions. His decision to renumber his own editions may have been motivated
by the appearance of the Dublin edition of *The Christian Hero*. He may instead
have learnt about a spurious 'fifth edition' of *The London Merchant*, which had
been published in 1733.[26] Curiously, having taken the trouble to produce the
cancel title-pages, he did not advertise his 'new' editions in the newspapers, so
neither of the reissues can be dated precisely. However, it is clear that the two
plays were reissued virtually simultaneously and within a relatively short time of
their original publication. An advertisement for the 'sixth edition' of *The London*

---

[25] The appearance of the dateline 8 Feb. is odd in an edition presumably published on 6 Feb.,
and it might be taken to indicate that the edition of *The Christian Hero* did not in fact appear until
8 Feb. However, the dateline is clearly a part of the advertisement for the fifth edition of *The London
Merchant*, and it seems likely that it was meant to indicate the day on which the promised new
edition would finally be available. See the Textual Introduction to *The London Merchant*.

[26] 'The Fifth Edition Corrected . . . Printed for J. Green, at the King's Head', dated 1733 and set
from a copy of Gray's fourth edition (1732). See the textual introduction to *The London Merchant*.

Merchant, printed in the cancel title-gathering for the 'second edition' of *The Christian Hero*, indicates that the altered version of the edition of the *Merchant* existed or was being produced when the new title-page for *The Christian Hero* was run. The timing of the reissue of *The Christian Hero* can, in turn, be approximately established by the fact that all copies issued with the 'second edition' title-gathering (but no copies of the original issue) also include two gatherings made up of sheets reimpressed from standing type after the run of fine-paper copies. It is unlikely that the printer would long have delayed this final run, which completed the printing of sheets for copies printed on ordinary paper, and the occurrence of the reimpressed sheets in conjunction with the cancel title-gathering suggests that both were produced at about the same time.

Copies of the 'second edition' were issued again in Gray's nonce collection of Lillo's works, *c.*21 June 1740.

First issue (ordinary and fine paper)
For the title-page, see p. 223. All copies print 'Drury-lane'. The title-page is not altered for copies printed on fine paper.

> *Collation*: 8° (4's) A^2 B–I⁴ [\$2 (– A1,2) signed]; 34 leaves, pp. [*4*] *9* 10–40 49–76 *77–80* [= 68]
> *Contents*: A1 title A1ᵛ blank A2 advertisements A2ᵛ dramatis personae B1(*9*)–I2ᵛ(*76*) text (DH: [orn.] | ACT I. SCENE I.) I3(*77*)–I3ᵛ(*78*) epiloque I4(*79*) prologue I4ᵛ(*80*) blank
>
> *Note*: In one deposit copy printed on fine paper, page 13 is unnumbered and the epilogue and prologue are wrapped around or inserted between the dramatis personae and text (A^2 I4 I3 B⁴ . . .).

'Second edition'
> THE | CHRISTIAN HERO: | A | TRAGEDY. | As it is Acted at the | THEATRE ROYAL | IN | *DRURY LANE.* | [rule] | Written by Mr. LILLO. | [rule] | The SECOND EDITION. | [rule] | [orn.] | *LONDON:* | Printed for JOHN GRAY, at the *Croſs-Keys*, in the | *Poultry*, near *Cheapſide.* | [short rule] | MDCCXXXV. (Price 1*s.* 6*d.*)
>
> *Note*: The price appears to have been printed or stamped after the original printing of the title-page. In some copies '1*s.*' is damaged or prints light, and in others seems to have been removed or erased after printing, perhaps to allow sales at the more competitive price of sixpence.

> *Collation*: A^2 (±) B–H⁴ I⁴ (– I4) [\$2 (– A1,2) signed]; 33 leaves, pp. as preceding, except . . . *77–78* [= 66]
> *Contents*: As preceding, except A^2 has been cancelled and replaced by: A1 title A1ᵛ blank A2 prologue A2ᵛ dramatis personae and advertisement; I4, which originally bore the prologue, has been cancelled in all copies examined.
>
> *Note*: Prologue, dramatis personae, and advertisement, as well as title-page, are new settings.

Comments

Imposition was by half-sheets (work and turn). Press corrections, made during the run of sheets printed on ordinary paper, mark variant states of sheets C (inner and outer) and E (inner). Corrections made before printing on fine paper mark variant states of D (outer), F (inner), and G (outer and inner).[27] Additional variant states are also marked by shifting type, lost sorts, and other accidents.

The incidence of corrected sheets and comparison of copies on the Hinman Collator indicate that sheets of the same press-run of gatherings B–G were used indiscriminately to make up copies of the first and second 'editions'. Comparison on the collator sharply divides copies of sheets H and I into three groups, and the incidence of press corrections and accidents establishes the order of the printing of these groups as (1) first 'edition', (2) fine paper, and (3) 'second edition' (that is, sheets for the 'second edition' are reimpressions). The text of the edition was, then, printed in at least three press-runs: the initial run on ordinary paper, a second run on fine paper, and the reimpression of sheets H and I issued in the 'second edition'.

The format of the book as originally issued suggests that some problem or last-minute change required the printer to alter his plan for the book after at least some sheets of the text of the play had been run. The pagination of the text allows for a preliminary gathering of four leaves but only two are provided (the only instance of this inconsistency in Gray's editions of Lillo's plays). The recto of the second leaf of preliminaries, on which the prologue would normally appear, is given over to the publisher's warning against piratical editions and the dated advertisement for the fifth edition of *The London Merchant*. The prologue itself, printed on the last leaf of the final gathering (I), differs typographically from the epilogue and is less handsomely set out than the text or epilogue, evidence which suggests that it was set separately from the rest of the edition.

The cancel title-gathering for the 'second edition' includes not only a new title-page but also new settings of the dramatis personae and the prologue, which is printed in its proper place on the second leaf. The reset dramatis personae provides a new arrangement of the list of characters and the prologue includes corrections and reparagraphing which may account for its having been reset, but the use of new type for these pages could also indicate that the type for the original preliminary gathering and sheet I had been redistributed before the cancel title-gathering was made ready for the press. In all copies seen, books issued as the 'second edition' lack the last leaf of the final gathering (I⁴), an indication perhaps that the reimpressions of H and I, which completed the run of copies printed on ordinary paper, had been run, with the original setting of the prologue still in the forme, before the cancel title-gathering was printed. However, the appearance of the reimpressed sheets only in conjunction with the 'second edition' title-gathering seems clear evidence of some direct

---

[27] See the Tables of Press Corrections.

relationship between the printing of the reimpressed sheets and the decision to issue the new 'edition'. Conceivably there had been a short run not only of sheets H and I but also of the original title-gathering (normally the last sheet to be printed), and when the time came to complete the run it was decided to substitute the cancel gathering.

The edition itself—the text of Lillo's play—is handsomely designed, with rather elegant typography and many ornaments, but the state of the text gives evidence of hasty or in some way harried production and of uncertainty or inexperience on the part of the compositor(s). Analysis of corrections made during the three press-runs does not suggest systematic proof-reading by the author or an editor but, instead, the printer's efforts to improve a poorly set text when errors came to his notice. A number of obvious errors and a few infelicities of punctuation are corrected, but other obvious mistakes are allowed to stand even in formes in which some corrections are made.

One forme—inner E—is exceptional. The number and kind of corrections introduced in the two corrected pages (E2 and E4) suggest that the single example discovered of the sheet in its early state may represent a very early stage in the production of the edition and that the alterations may provide evidence of author's or proof-reader's corrections. The alterations are not numerous or extensive enough to allow firm conclusions to be drawn, but two of the substantive changes can be characterized as genuine revisions rather than simple corrections.[28] If these adjustments do represent last-minute revisions by the playwright, the forme is equally interesting for the corrections that have not been made. While the punctuation is twice corrected, in other instances pointing that comes near to destroying the sense of lines or speeches is allowed to stand, and it appears that when the author or editor made his alterations he gave the pages as a whole a cursory reading at best.

Blatant misprints on a number of sheets indicate that proof-reading was indeed a nicety for which time was not allowed. Typographical errors are relatively frequent, adding to the impression that the edition was produced in haste and probably involved the work of an inexperienced compositor. Capitalization is heavy, erratic, and occasionally incorrect. Inconsistency in the abbreviated names in speech-headings is frequent. Extreme irregularity in the use of italic and roman question marks and exclamation marks (italic pointing with roman text as well as roman pointing with italics) suggests both uncertain compositorial practice and the mixing of italic and roman sorts in the box of type. Roman text, moreover, is indiscriminately pointed with apostrophes of two sizes, one of them apparently intended for use with italic type.

Irregularity in punctuation suggests that the pointing in printer's copy was as light and casual as the compositor's pointing was hurried or uncertain. Even

---

[28] Cf. III. i. 137, 'Friendship' for 'Fondness', and also III. i. 134, 'beloved' for 'loved'. E2 and E4 include a total of ten press corrections, seven of them appearing on E4; six of the ten changes are substantive. No other corrected page in the edition includes more than three corrections, and except for the correction of one obvious misprint none of the changes is substantive.

relatively mechanical conventions, such as the use of commas to set off the names of persons addressed in vocative constructions, are inconsistently maintained. Erratically light pointing alternates with punctuation awkwardly heavy.

The vagaries in the use of commas and semi-colons can prove particularly troublesome. Frequently the heavy scattering of commas tends to obscure the sense of lines or speeches; elsewhere, however, the omission of commas is equally difficult for the reader. The pointing of relative clauses and prepositional phrases—often followed by commas but not initially set off by any pointing—is especially confusing. While some of the edition's apparently extraneous commas conceivably represent an attempt at a kind of rhetorical or histrionic pointing of the lines, commas often appear to have been set only as a convention to mark the ends of lines of verse.[29] Semi-colons, set with similar liberality, are at times more misleading than helpful, appearing to cut off the main clauses of sentences from their subordinate parts.[30]

This rather idiosyncratic punctuation cannot be called the 'usual practice' of the edition—light pointing is provided for many lines that are similar in syntax to other lines remarkable for their heavy pointing. Nor is it possible in most instances to distinguish authorial and compositorial responsibility for punctuation.

The textual peculiarities of the first edition of *The Christian Hero*, like the evidence that scheduled publication was delayed, suggest that there were problems in the production of the edition. Resemblances between the accidentals of the text and the similar if less exaggeratedly awkward punctuation characteristic of the first edition of *Fatal Curiosity* (1737) may also identify the editions as the work of the same less than skilful compositor(s), coping, as best they were able, with loosely pointed copy.

Reprints

The Dublin edition published in 1735, the only early reprint, was set from a copy of the first issue of Gray's edition and probably appeared soon after publication of the play in London. *The Christian Hero* was not again reprinted until 1759, when an edition was published as one of a series of dramas printed in Edinburgh for A. Donaldson and issued both in single copies and bound together in *A Collection of English Plays*. In 1775, Thomas Davies included the play in his collection of Lillo's works; his text was set from a copy of the 'second edition' of Gray's edition. The Dublin printer and, later, the printer or editor

---

[29] See v. iv. 84 for a specially awkward instance of the irregular punctuation of the first edition. See also IV. i. 4 and v. iv. 124. Examples of commas which separate subject and predicate for no clear reason include II. i. 251, III. i. 60, and III. i. 135. Similarly difficult divisions of predicate and object will be found at III. i. 190, IV. ii. 137a, IV. ii. 155, and IV. iv. 98. Examples of insufficient pointing include IV. iii. 65, v. iv. 41, 110, and 157–8.

[30] See I. i. 225; III. i. 22, 219; IV. ii. 129, 159; and IV. iii. 14. At III. i. 298 a semi-colon in the first edition stands between subject and predicate; portions of sentences linked by conjunctions are set off by semi-colons at II. i. 153; III. i. 17; IV. ii. 154; and IV. iv. 60.

who styled Davies's collection corrected many of the obvious errors in the text and attempted to make sense of awkward pointing, but a number of flaws passed without notice.

Editorial Procedure

The first edition serves as copy-text. Press corrections are adopted. Two necessary stage directions have been added. With one exception, variant readings of the second setting of the prologue are accepted; a number of the new readings are certainly corrections, others adjust unclear pointing, and the division of stanzas is clearly more appropriate than that of the earlier, cancelled setting.[31]

Irregular, predominantly heavy, punctuation is characteristic of the first edition and relates it to the text of Gray's edition of *Fatal Curiosity*. It has, therefore, been retained. Pointing that distorts or badly obscures the sense of lines has been emended, where possible with reference to eighteenth-century reprints, but no emendation has been made where the disputable punctuation might be taken to have a histrionic, if not strictly grammatical, function. On occasion, when the present edition retains questionable readings of the copy-text, emendations introduced in the Dublin edition and Davies's collection have been noted in the Commentary.

In vocative constructions, commas have been inserted where omitted in the copy-text since the first edition does provide such pointing in the great majority (70 per cent) of instances. In exclamatory phrases, however, commas have not been inserted; omission of pointing in such constructions is characteristic of dramatic texts of the period and of the early editions of Lillo's plays.

---

[31] The copy-text is the first edition, 'second edition' issue, a Yale University copy. Copies collated include: *first edition, original issue, ordinary paper*, CtMW, BL, MH; *first edition, fine paper*, O, DFo; *'second edition'*, O, CSmH, E, BM (2 copies), NjP, CtY, MH; *Dublin* (1735), DFo; *Edinburgh* (1759), O, E, IU; Davies, *Works* (1775), CtMW, O, BL (3 copies), CtY (2 copies).

THE
CHRISTIAN
HERO:
A TRAGEDY.

As it is acted at the

Theatre Royal in *Drury-lane.*

By His MAJESTY's Servants.

By Mr. *LILLO.*

LONDON:

Printed for JOHN GRAY, at the *Cross-Keys,* in the
Poultry, near *Cheapside.* MDCCXXXV.

Price One Shilling and Six-Pence.

PROLOGUE

spoken by Mr. *Cibber*.

Sacred to Virtue, Liberty, and Truth,
The Muses bloom in everlasting Youth.
Press'd, like the Palm, they rise beneath their Weight,
And soar above the Reach of Time, or Fate.
When Brass, or Marble, faithless to their Trust, 5
No longer bear the Name, nor guard the Dust
Of Kings, or Heroes, to their Charge consign'd,
But yield to Age, and leave no Track behind;
The Poet's Pen, with never dying Lays,
Preserves their Fame and celebrates their Praise. 10
Let Artful Maro, *or bold* Lucan *tell,*
How regal Troy, *or* Rome, *more awfull, fell;*
Nations destroy'd revive, lost Empires shine,
And Freedom glows in each immortal Line.
In vain would Faction, War, or lawless Power, 15
Which marr the Patriot's Scheme, his Fame devour;
When Bards, by their Superiour Force, can save
From dark Oblivion and defeat the Grave.

Say, Britons, *must this Art forsake your Isle,*
And leave to vagrant Apes her native Soil? 20
Must She, the dearest Friend that Freedom knows,
Driv'n from her Seat, seek Refuge with her Foes?
Forbid so great a Shame, and save the Age
From such Reproach, You Patrons of the Stage.

Since well we know, there's not a Theme so dear 25
As virtuous Freedom, to a British *Ear;*
T' indulge so just a Taste, to Night we sing
A Pious Hero, and a Patriot King;
By Nature form'd, by Providence design'd
To scourge Ambition, and to right Mankind: 30
Such Castriot *was. O might it but appear,*
That he retains the least Resemblance here!—

---

11 *Let . . . tell,*] G (*second setting*); G (*first setting*) *indents and allows space between this line and* 10
19 *Say, . . . Isle,*] G (*second setting*); G (*first setting*) *does not indent or allow space between this line and* 18

Should but the smallest Portion of that Fire,
Which fill'd his ample Breast, our Scenes inspire:
The abject Slave, to his Reproach, shall see, 35
That such as dare deserve it, may be free:
And conscious Tyranny confess, with Shame,
That blind Ambition wanders from her Aim;
While Virtue leads her Votaries to Fame.

Dramatis Personæ.

TURKS.

Amurath.	Mr. *Quin.*
Mahomet.	Mr. *W. Mills.*
Osmyn, the Visier.	Mr. *Berry.*
Kisler Aga.	Mr. *Hewit.*

5

CHRISTIANS.

Scanderbeg.	Mr. *Milward.*
Aranthes.	Mr. *Mills.*
Amasie.	Mr. *Cibber.*
Paulinus.	Mr. *Winstone.*

10

WOMEN.

Hellena.	Mrs. *Thurmond*
Althea.	Mrs. *Butler.*
Cleora.	Mrs. *Pritchard*

Guards, Mutes, Eunuchs and Attendants.

15

SCENE. *The Plain and Mountains near* Croia, *the Metropolis of* Epirus.

---

1 TURKS.] G (*second setting*) *lists characters in two groups:* TURKS (Amurath, Mahomet, Hellena, Osmyn, Kisler Aga, Cleora) *and* CHRISTIANS (Scanderbeg, Aranthes, Althea, Amasie, Paulinus). 4 *Osmyn*, the Visier.] *Ed.*; *Osmyn.* G, D, W1. *See Commentary*

ACT I.

SCENE I.

A Royal Pavilion. Hellena *on a Sofa in a Melancholy Posture.* Cleora *attending near her. Eunuchs, Mutes, Singers and Dancers.*

SONG.

    The Regent of Night with her Beams
      Had chequer'd each Valley and Grove,
    And swell'd with her Influence the Streams,
      When Fatima, *pining for Love,*
    To the Ocean, Despair for her Guide,   5
      Repaired for Relief from her Pain;
    Where plunging, receive me, she cried,
      I'm fair, young and royal in vain.

    Hellena *rises and comes forward.*

  Hel. No more, *Cleora!* I accept thy Love,
But thy officious Kindness is in vain.   10
It is not Musick, nor the sprightly Dance,
The Harmony of Motion, or of Sound,
That can asswage my Grief.
    Cle.   Let all retire.   [*Exeunt Eunuchs, &c.*
How long, my Royal Mistress! will you sooth
This secret, pining Grief? How long averse   15
To ev'ry Dawn of Joy, thus seek Retirement;
And shun the gay Delights, the Pomp and Power,
That ever wait the Daughter of our Sultan,
And first of Womankind?
    Hel.   How long shall Love
And torturing Despair, like ling'ring Fevers,   20
Feed on the Springs of Life, and drink my Blood?
How long shall *Amurath*, my awful Father,
Tho' press'd and overwhelm'd with Disappointments,
Provoke the Malice of his adverse Stars,
And urge his own Destruction; whilst in vain   25
With unrelenting Hatred he pursues,
Whom Heav'n protects, th' ever victorious Hero
of *Epirus.*
    Cle.   Thus do you always talk,
Of Love and Death, Despair and the *Epirot.*

Why will you ever strive to hide the Cause,   3
The cruel Cause of all this mighty Anguish?
Believe me, Princess! 'tis better to intrust
A faithful Slave, than keep the Secret thus
To rack your Breast; 'twill ease those Pains—
    Hel.   That Death
Alone can cure; but yet, my best *Cleora*!   3
Such is thy Truth, thy Tenderness and Love,
I can deny thee nought. Yes, thou shalt know
All thou desir'st, and share the very Heart
Of sad *Hellena.*—You must think I love.—
What else cou'd make thy Princess far more wretched   4
Than the meanest Slave, and who but *Castriot*
Cou'd merit so sublime a Flame as mine?
    Cle. 'Tis as I fear'd: She's lost beyond Redemption.   [*Aside.*
    Hel. A Royal Hostage to my Father's Court
When young he came, who loved him as a Son;
I as a Brother; so I fondly thought,
Nor found my Error, 'till the fatal Flame,
That now consumes me, cherish'd by my Weakness,
Was grown too great, too fierce to be controll'd.
O matchless Prince! who can display thy Worth?
Thou Favourite of Heav'n, and first of Men;
In Courts more soft, more lovely, more attractive
Than those fair Youths who with eternal Bloom
Injoy the fragrant Mansions of the Blest;
In Council wiser than a whole Divan;
In Anger awful; and in War as fierce
As those bright Ministers, whom Heav'n sends forth
To punish the presuming Sons of Men;
In Justice th' Image of that Sacred Power,
Whom he still serves with most unfeign'd Devotion;
Like him in Mercy too, in Bounty like him;
Excelling in Magnificence the Princes
Of th' *East*, yet temperate and self-denying
As a *Dervise.*—Who know, and Love thee not,
Avow their Malice and Contempt of Virtue.
    Cle. Think, Princess! think what 'tis you say; of whom
It is you speak. Can he, that cruel Christian,
That Enemy t'our Prophet and your Father,
Deserve such Praise from You?
    Hel.   Unjust *Cleora*!
To call him cruel—But thou know'st him not;
Or sure thy gentle Nature wou'd abhor

To wrong him thus. And wherefore dost thou urge
His diff'rent Faith to me? Love busies not
Himself with reconciling Creeds, nor heeds
The Jarrings of contentious Priests: from Courts   75
To Shades, from Shades to Courts he flies
To conquer Hearts, and overthrow Distinction,
Treating alike the Monarch and the Slave;
But shuns the noisy School, and leaves the Race
Of proud, litigious Men to their own Folly;   80
Who wise in Words alone, consume their Days
In fierce Debate, nor know the End of Life.
   Cle. Now I no longer wonder you contemn'd
Amasie and his Flame.
   Hel.   O Name him not,
The most detested Traytor; who, tho' next   85
In Blood, and late the dearest Friend of his
Indulgent Prince, without a Cause renounc'd
His Faith, his Country and his vow'd Allegiance.
   Cle. Say not without a Cause, his Love to you—
   Hel. Insolent Slave! Ambitious, bloody Traytor!   90
To claim my Love for Cruelty and Fraud!
Must I have been a Recompense for Murther!
For Regicide, the Murther of his King!
But his Defeat has freed me from that Danger:
My Father now retracts his former Promise,   95
And treats him with Aversion and Contempt.
   Cle. May Treason ever meet the like Reward.—
But see the Man we speak of comes this Way.
   Hel. I wou'd avoid him, do thou hear his Message;
His Name is hateful, but whene'er I see him,   100
My Blood runs back, my Sinews all relax,
And life itself seems ready to forsake me.   [*Exit* Hellena.

Enter Amasie.

   Cle. What wou'd you, Prince?
Ama.   I am inform'd the Sultan
Past this way, and came in Hopes to have found him
With the Princess.   105
   Cle. Your Hopes deceiv'd you, Sir.
   Ama.   May I not see
The Princess?
   Cle.   No.

Ama.   I bring her happy News.

Cle. Nor Happiness, nor Truth can come from Thee;
For ev'ry Word, and ev'ry Thought of thine
Are full of deep Deceit, and threaten Mischief.   [*Exit* Cleora.   1

Amasie *alone.*

Seen and avoided!—rated by her Slave!—
Suspected by the Sultan!—Scorn'd by all!—
Is this the Gratitude of *Turkish* Courts?
This my Reward for Heav'n and Honour lost?—
Soul poisoning Envy, eldest Born of Hell,   1
Thou Sin of Devils, and their Torment too,
To what Contempt, what Mis'ry hast thou brought Me?
Ill-tim'd Reflection!—I shall still succeed—
Love and Ambition, Hatred and Revenge—
There's not a Wish my restless Soul has form'd,   1
But shall be quickly crown'd—Then whence this Anguish?
Sure 'tis much harder to attain Perfection
In Ill, than to be truly Good.—The Sultan!—

Enter Amurath *and* Visier.

Am. Away; my Fame is lost; my Laurels won
With Pain and Toil and water'd with my Blood,
That well I hop'd wou'd flourish o'er my Grave
When I that planted them shou'd be but Dust,
Are wither'd all. O! wherefore did I tempt,
In the declining Winter of my Age,
The Vigour of a youthful Rebel's Arms?
Whose curst Success, 'gainst such prodigious odds,
Makes Credibility doubt what she sees,
And Truth appear like Falsehood.

Ama.   Mighty Sultan!—

Am. What woud'st thou, Slave! Thou Renegade, thou Spy!
Hence from my Sight: avant, perfidious Traytor.

Vis. My ever gracious Lord, you wrong the Prince;
None can be more devoted to your Service.

Am. 'Tis false. Did he not lead my Spahies forth
With Hate profest, and Boasts of sure Revenge
On *Scanderbeg*; then leave my gallant Troops
To swell the Triumph, and to glut the Rage
Of that damn'd, damn'd Destroyer of the Faithfull.

Vis. O righteous Heav'n! when will thy Judgments cease?

(1. i)   134 Slave! Thou] W1 (slave); ~! | ~ G, *which prints as two lines*

For Six revolving Moons have we in vain
Besieg'd yon City, proud, imperious *Croia*;   145
With Famine, Pestilence, and *Scanderbeg*
More terrible than both, like threat'ning Meteors,
Hov'ring o'er our Heads. Our Strengths consum'd:
By painful Watchings and incessant Toils
Do not our Numbers ev'ry Hour decrease?   150
Are we not all devoted to Destruction?
Those that escape the Plague, of Hunger die;
Or sav'd from Famine, perish by the Sword.
Yet to behold you thus, burning with Rage,
And tortur'd by Despair, afflicts us worse   155
Than all our other Griefs. Why will you still refuse
The only Help your present State admits,
That Sov'reign Balm for Minds like yours diseas'd,
And cure for ev'ry Ill—All healing Patience.
 Am. Name Patience again while th' *Epirot* lives   160
And lives victorious, and thou art thyself
A base, insulting Traytor. Hear me, *Allah*,
If thou art ought beside an empty Name,
If thou dost still exist, as Priests affirm,
Decree our Fate, and govern all below,   165
Behold, and aid a Cause so much your own.
To Slaves, to Subjects and to Priests give Patience,
But if it be within your Power to grant
Ought that is worthy of a Monarch's Prayer,
Give me Revenge, or I'll renounce thy Worship. [*Shouts.* 170
Ha! whence those loud, those joyful Acclamations.
 Ama. But that it pleas'd my Lord to strike me dumb,
I had ere this inform'd him of the Cause.
Just Heav'n, at length indulgent to your Wishes,
Has blest you with the power to end our Woes,   175
Or wreck your Vengeance on the Man you hate.
 Am. Ha! what say'st thou? take heed thou triflest not:
A second Time thou'st rais'd my Expectation;
If thou deceiv'st it now, as at the first,
Death is the lightest Ill thou hast to fear: 180
But if, beyond my Hopes, thou tell'st me Truth,
Thou shalt no longer droop beneath our Frown,
(Your Service slighted, and your Love despis'd;)
Our former lavish Grant shall be renew'd,
And my *Hellena* be thy rich Reward.   185

 (1. i) 148 Strengths] W1 (strengths); Strenghts G 185 *Hellena*] W1 (Hellena); ~, G. *See*
Commentary

Ama. [*Kneeling.*] Bounty immense! thus let—
Am.   Rise, and proceed;
Make it appear that Vengeance may be had;
Let it be merely possible,—O *Allah*!
I ask no more,—and leave the rest to me.
    Ama. Ever Invincible, you're not to learn   19█
That *Aranthes*, Prince of *Durazzo*, who derives
His high Descent from *Charlemain*, that most
Illustrious *Frank*, Santon and King; has long
Approv'd himself aspiring *Castriot*'s Friend,
And firm Ally. His Wisdom, Wealth and Power   19█
May well indear him to that haughty Rebel;
But yet a Tie much stronger binds their Friendship:
The Fair *Althea*, Daughter to *Aranthes*,
Beholds the youthful Conqueror her Slave:
Nor are his ardent Vows prefer'd in vain;   20█
With conscious Virtue, join'd with true Affection,
With Majesty and Mildness sweetly temper'd,
The charming Maid (for all who see her must
Confess her Charms,) returns his constant Flame.
This Friend and Mistress, the Partner and hoped   20█
Reward of all his Toils, are in your Power.
    Am. Prophet, thou'rt just; where are his Conquests now?
Anguish has left my Soul to live in his.
Perhaps ere this the News has reach'd his Ears.
His promis'd Joys are come to swell my Heart;   21█
I have 'em all, but doubled by his Pain.
Haste and inform us by what means, *Amasie*,
These precious Pledges came into our Hands.
    Ama. This morning from *Durazzo* they set forth,
Slightly attended for the Christian Camp,   21█
Fearing no Danger; for they knew your Army
Had been for Months immur'd within these Plains;
The Neighb'ring Mountains being all possest
By their rebellious Minion's conquering Troops.
Of this inform'd, not daring to approach   22█
Your sacred Presence, I inform'd your Son,
Your Empire's second Hope, the brave Prince *Mahomet*.
Strait with two thousand Horse guided by Me,
Who, as a Native here, best knew the Route
The little Troop must take; he left the Trenches: 22█
The Foe was quickly found; tho' few in Number

(I. i)   190 you're] D, W1; your'e G   214 *Durazzo*] D, W1; *Durrazzo* G   224 knew]
D, W1; new G   225 take;] *See Commentary*

They yet resisted long, and dearly sold
Their Liberty or Lives: *Aranthes* last
Yielded himself and Daughter to our Power.　　　　　[*Shouts.*

　　　　Enter Mahomet, Aranthes, Althea, *Lords and*
　　　　　　　Ladies in Chains.

　　Ma. Long live great *Amurath*, my Royal Father;　　　　230
O may his Days for Ages yet roll on,
And ev'ry Day encrease his Fame like this!
　　Am. Rise to my Arms; thou bring'st me Life and Fame,
And what my Soul much more desir'd, Revenge.
When from the Womb they brought thee to these Arms,　　235
The first dear Fruit of my *Maria*'s Love
And Heir to all my Kingdoms; ev'n then
I clasp'd thee with less Joy, than at this Moment.—
But let us view the Captives thou has brought.
Now by our Prophet's Head, a noble Troop;　　　　240
A fairer Purchase never grac'd my Arms.
This must be *Aranthes*, and this his Daughter.
They seem to scorn their Fortune: Conscious Majesty
Frowns on his Brow, and Beauty smiles on hers.
Proud Christian, now where is your Prophet's Power?　　245
　　Ar. Where it was ever, Sultan;—in himself.
　　Am. If it be such as vainly you suppose,
Why art thou fallen thus beneath my Power?
Whose Eyes ne'er pitied, and whose Hand ne'er spar'd
The Follow'rs of his Sect.
　　Ar.　　　　　　　　　Presumptuous Man!　　250
Shall finite Knowledge tax eternal Wisdom?
Or shameless Guilt dare, with invidious Eyes,
To search for Spots in Purity itself,
And call impartial Justice to Account?
Impious and vain! It is enough we know　　　　255
Such is his Will, who orders all Things right,
To make ev'n these thy Chains, insulting King,
Easy to us; and well content we bear 'em.
　　Am. Ill doth it suit with your reputed Wisdom
T'abet a rash rebellious Boy.
　　Ar.　　　　　　　　　Rebellious!　　260
By the heroick Virtue of the Youth,
And more th'eternal Justice of our Cause,
I must retort the Charge. Since first the Angels

By their Ambition fell; the greatest Rebels,
The most accurs'd, perfidious and ungrateful,
Are those, who have abus'd the Sovereign Power.
Why shines the Sun, why do the Seasons change,
The teeming Earth lavish her yearly Store,
And all to bless the Sons of Men in vain?
O! is it not that Tyranny prevails
And the true End of Government is lost;
That those, who shou'd defend each in his Right,
Betray their Trust, and seize upon the Whole.
This, this is to rebel against that Power,
By which Kings reign, and turn the Arms of Heaven
Against itself. Then take the Rebel back,
A virtuous Prince, the Patron of Mankind,
With just Contempt may hear a lawless Tyrant
Arraign that Conduct, which condemns his own.
　　Am. 'Tis hard to say whether thy Insolence,
Who tho' in Chains, dar'st brave me to my Face,
Or the unprincely Meanness of thy Soul,
Who wou'd by Law restrain the Will of Kings,
Amaze me most. Let *Scanderbeg* and You,
Like Fools contend, and shed your Blood in vain,
While Subjects reap the Harvest of your Toil;
O'ercome, that you may live the Slave of Slaves;
I fight to reign, and conquer for myself.
　　Ar. A gen'rous Slave wou'd scorn the abject Thought,
What shou'd a King do then?
　　Am. 　　　　　　　　Think like a King,
Whose Glory is his Power.
　　Ar. 　　　　　　　Of doing Good.
　　Am. Of doing what he will; the other's none.
　　Ar. Has Heav'n no Power because it doth no Ill?
　　Am. Were these the Thoughts of other Christian Princes,
Wou'd they stand neuter, and unmov'd behold
Th' *Epirot* and thyself sustain this War;
Nor lend you their Assistance?
　　Ar. 　　　　　　　　Foul Dishonour!
O everlasting Shame! Wou'd they unite,
Afflicted *Europe* wou'd no longer groan
Beneath your Yoke and mourn her Freedom lost:
Nor *Verna*'s nor *Basilia*'s fatal Fields
Smoke with the Blood of Christians unreveng'd:
But to the Scandal of our Holy Faith,
Some such there are, who owe their very Lives,

Their Peace and Safety to the Blood of others,   305
Yet think themselves born for themselves alone.
   Am. 'Tis time to quit a Cause so ill supported;
And your Misfortunes may inform your Friend,
What sure Destruction waits the desp'rate Wretch,
That tempts his Wrath, who rules o'er half Mankind,   310
And strikes the rest with Terror at his Name.
   Ar. Cease thy vain Boasts, and by Example learn
The frail uncertain State of human Greatness.
Where are now th' *Assyrians*, where the *Medes*;
The *Persians* and their Conquerors, the *Greeks*;   315
Or the stupendous Power of ancient *Rome*?
Has not the Breath of Time blasted their Pride,
And laid their Glory waste?
   Am.   I need not boast
T'assert my Power o'er thee. And yet perhaps
On *Scanderbeg*'s Submission we may grant   320
Your Freedom, and vouchsafe to give him Peace.
   Ar. If by Submission vainly you design
Dishonourable Terms, a shameful Peace,
Give up such Thoughts; those his great Soul must scorn;
Nor wou'd we be redeem'd at such a Price: 325
Hope not to triumph over him in us.
   Am. Where is the Majesty that us'd to awe
My trembling Slaves? Art thou in Love with Death?
   Ar. No; nor with life, when purchased at th'Expence
Of others Happiness, or my own Honour.   330
   Am. Behold this Maid, this Comfort of thy Age.
I, as a Father, know what 'tis to love
A Child like this—I have been deem'd a Man,
A brave one too—The Fair, sacred to Peace,
Have never yet been number'd with my Foes: 335
But if presumptuously thou dost dispute
Thy own and Daughter's Ransom on my Terms;
Or teach thy Pupil to oppose my Will,
Renounce me, Heav'n, if like thy bloody Priests,
Those consecrated Murtherers of thy Sect,   340
I cast not off all Bowels of Compassion,
All Pity, all Remorse—Her tender Sex,
Her Youth, her blooming Beauty shall not save her.
Away; I'll hear no more. Prudence may yet
Instruct you to avoid th'impending Ruin.   345
Amasie, we commit him to your Charge.
   Al. O my Father! tho' torn from your Embraces,

Your Precepts, your Example shall be ever
Present with *Althea*; in Doubts my Guide,
In Troubles my support.
    Ar.   This wounds indeed.   35*
'Tis hard to part and leave her thus expos'd;
But Heav'n must be obey'd. [*Aside.*] Farewell my Child!
Tho' Reason and Religion teach us Patience
Pain will be felt and Nature have her Course.   [*Aside.*
                                    [*Exit* Aranthes.
    Am. Mourn not bright Maid; you can have nought to fear: 35
A Father and a Lover rule your Fate.
    Al. I see and scorn your Arts, insidious King:
And for your Threats, pursue 'em when you dare;
Your Pride to see your Cruelty despis'd,
Shall give you greater Pain than you inflict,   36*
And turn your Rage to Shame. O Prince belov'd!
O my affianc'd Lord! let not my Danger
One Moment stop the Progress of your Arms:
I have my Wish if dying I may share
In your Renown, and justify your Choice.   36*
    Am. Osmyn, attend the Lady to *Hellena*.   [*Exit* Amurath, &c.
    Vis. Fair Princess, you shall know no more Restraint
Than what is common to the Sex with us.
    Al. Lead me to instant Death, or let me groan
Whole Years in Chains—dispose me as you please—   37*
    Tho' my lov'd Sire and Lord no more I see,
    You hope in vain to conquer them in me.   [*Exeunt.*

End of the First Act.

(I. i)   352 my Child] *Ed.*; myChild G   357 Arts,] D; ~∧ G   371 see,] ~. G (*earlier
state*)   361 Shame.] ~, G (*earlier state*)   366 *Osmyn*] *Ed.*; Osmin G
372SD [*Exeunt.*] *Ed.*; *not in* G

ACT II.

SCENE I.

*A Plain the whole Length of the Stage. One Side
lined with* Christian, *the other with* Turkish
Soldiers.

Enter Visier *and* Paulinus.

Vis. Already has the Trumpet's lofty Sound
From either Camp twice eccho'd thro' the Plain;
At the third Summons both the Kings appear.
May gracious Heav'n, in Pity to Mankind,
Incline their Breasts to sheath the Sword, to stop   5
The Tide of Blood, and give the World repose.
   Paul. What may we not expect from such a Treaty?
And yet the Caution us'd on either Side
To guard against Surprize, betrays Distrust.
   Vis. A thousand Injuries, suppos'd or real,   10
With keen Resentment whet each jealous Chief,
And seem to urge Suspicion.
   Paul.   *Scipio,*
And the fierce *African,* whom he subdu'd,
With greater Ardor never strove t'attain
For *Rome,* or *Carthage,* universal Sway;   15
Than your great Sultan to impose the Yoke
Of Arbitrary Power and make Men Slaves;
Or our brave Prince to guard their Liberties,
Or break their Chains and purchase Freedom for 'em.
   Vis. Then their known Zeal for their respective Faith   20
Must yet much farther alienate their Minds.
   Paul. 'Tis hardly to be thought a youthful Hero,
With Victories replete, will stoop to take
Abject Conditions from a beaten Foe.
   Vis. Or that an artful Prince will fail t'improve   25
Ev'ry Advantage to increase his Power.
   Paul. Fortune stands neuter, and impartial Heaven
Holds with an equal Hand the trembling Beam:
Superior Wisdom, Fortitude and Courage
Must turn the Scale. [*Trumpets.*] But see their Guards appear.   30
The great Intelligencies that inform
The Planetary Worlds, if such there be,
With all their vast Experience might attend
This Interview, and pass improv'd away.

Enter Amurath, Scanderbeg, Mahomet, Aranthes,
Amasie, *&c.*

Am. Doth it not swell thy fond, ambitious Heart?
Dost thou not burst with Pride, vain Boy, to see
The Majesty of hoary *Amurath*,
Whose numerous Years are fewer than his Conquests,
Reduc'd to Terms, and stoop to treat with thee?
    Scan. With Gratitude and Wonder I confess
Myself th' unworthy Instrument of Heaven,
To scourge thy Falshood, Cruelty and Pride,
And free a Virtuous People from thy Chains.
With Pity I behold your fierce Impatience,
Your Arrogance and Scorn; ev'n while the Hand
Of righteous Heaven is heavy on thy Crimes,
And deals thee forth a Portion of those Woes,
Which thy relentless Heart, with lawless Lust
And never sated Avarice of Power,
Has spread o'er half the habitable Earth.
    Am. And must I answer to thy bold Impeachment?
Thou Infidel relaps'd! thou very Christian!
Without Distinction and without a Name
But what implies thy Guilt. In vain thy Flatt'rers
Proclaim thee King of *Macedon*, *Epirus*,
Illyria, *Albania* and *Dalmatia*;
Gain'd by Surprize, by Treachery and Fraud;
What art thou but the more exalted Traytor?
    Scan. Let abject Minds, the Slaves of mean Ambition,
Affect vain Titles and external Pomp!
And take the Shadow for substantial Glory.
Superior Birth, unmerited Success,
The Name of Prince, of Conqueror and King,
Are Gifts of Fortune and of little Worth.
They may be, and too often are, possest
By sordid Souls, who know no Joy but Wealth;
By ri'tous Fools, or Tyrants drench'd in Blood;
A *Croesus*, *Alexander*, or a *Nero*.
The Best are sure the greatest of Mankind.
Our Actions form our Characters. Let me
Approve myself a Christian and a Soldier,
And Flatt'ry cannot add, or Envy take
Ought that I wish to have, or fear to lose.
    Am. Canst thou behold unmov'd, thou steady Traytor,

Thy most munificent and loving Patron,   75
Prest with the Weight of more than fourscore Years,
With feeble Hands compell'd to reassume
The stubborn Reins of Power, and taste again,
When Appetite is pall'd, the bitter Sweets
Of Sovereign Command? Shou'd I descend   80
To reason with thee, what cou'dst thou reply?
Have I not been a Father to thy Youth?
Did I not early form thy Mind to Greatness,
And teach thy Infant Hands the Use of Arms?
Tho' the unerring Maxims of our State,   85
(The only Rule of Right and Wrong in Courts)
Had mark'd thee for Destruction; still I spar'd thee.
Trusted, belov'd, advanc'd thou hast betray'd me:
First seiz'd the Provinces you call'd your own,
Then join'd my Foes to rob me of my Fame;   90
The perjur'd *Uladislaus*, fierce *Hunniades*,
And the *Venetians*, who have since forsook thee.
Tho' to remote *Magnesia* I retir'd,
Quitting the Toils of Empire to my Son,
To seek for Rest and find a peaceful Grave;   95
Yet there the Cries and Clamours of my Slaves,
Who fled the Terrors of thy dreadful Name,
Forbad their old o'erlabour'd King Repose;
Forc'd me once more in hostile Steel to cloth
These weary Limbs, and rouse to their Defence.   100
But that thy Soul is lost to all Remorse
Thy black Ingratitude must fright thyself.
    Scan. Can all your Kingdoms bribe the Voice of Truth?
Which, while you speak, pleads for me in your Breast;
Or Rage efface the Mem'ry of your Guilt,   105
More than ten thousand Witnesses against thee?
But Slander, like the loathsome Leper's Breath,
Infects the Healthful with its poisonous Steams,
Unless repell'd, and bids me guard my Fame.
My Ancestors for Ages fill'd this Throne,   110
A brave, a virtuous, legal Race of Princes,
No arbitrary Tyrants; the same Laws,
That made them Kings, declar'd their People free.
My Royal Father, fam'd for his Success
In War and Love of Peace, had govern'd long;   115
When with resistless Force your conquering Troops

(II. i)   88 me:] W1; ~. G   102 thyself.] W1; ~? G   113 free.] W1; ~ˌ G

Pour'd like a Deluge o'er the Realms of *Greece*:
To save his People from impending Ruin,
At your Request, the pious, gen'rous Prince
Gave up his Sons as Hostages of Peace.
He died—the best of Kings and Men. O *Castriot?*
I were unworthy of thy Race and Name
Cou'd I unmov'd remember thou'rt no more—
I wou'd have said, he died in firm Reliance
On your Promise given, your Faith and Honour;
But sure the Memory of such a Loss
May well o'er-bear, and drive me from my Purpose.
'Twas then in Scorn of ev'ry Obligation,
Of Truth and Justice, Gratitude and Honour,
Of noblest Trust and Confidence repos'd;
You like a lawless, most perfidious Tyrant,
Amidst her Griefs, seiz'd on his Widow'd Kingdom;
And to secure your lawless Acquisition.—
Oh! how shall I proceed!—My bleeding Heart
Is pierc'd anew, new Horrors wound my Soul
At every Pause; whenever I rehearse,
Whene'er I think upon thy monst'rous Crimes—
O *Reposio! Stanissa! Constantine!*
My slaughter'd Brothers, whose dear Blood still cries
Aloud to Heaven;—Your Wrongs shall find Redress.
Justice, defer'd, deals forth the heavier Blow.

Am. Shall the great monarchs of our sublime Race
Cut off their Brothers, when they mount the Throne,
Yet spare the Lives of Christians they suspect:
Their Death was wise, and I approve it yet,
But curse my Folly that preserv'd thy Life.

Scan. What was then my Life? debarr'd of my Right,
And kept t'augment the Number of your Slaves.
The only Benefit you e'er confer'd,
Was that you train'd me to the Use of Arms:
You had my Service and was overpay'd;
Yet those whom I oppos'd were, like yourself,
Tyrants, who made a Merchandize of Men;
And propagate Religion by the Sword.
Ever determin'd not to stain my Hands
With Christian Blood, when you commanded me
To turn my Arms against th'*Hungarian* King
I purpos'd from that Hour, by Heaven's Assistance,
At once t'avoid the Guilt and free my Country.

Am. O Traytor! dost thou glory in thy Shame?

Think not I have forgot thy vile Declension.
Yes on that fatal, that detested Day,
When deep *Moravia*'s Waves, died with the Blood
Of forty Thousand of my faithful Slaves,
Losing their Azure, flow'd in purple Tides;   165
Too well I know, thou didst forsake thy Charge;
And ere the News of thy Revolt arriv'd,
Surpriz'd my Bassa that commanded here;
Drove out my Garrisons, and ravish'd from me
This fair and fertile Kingdom.
  Scan.   False Aspersion!   170
The Charge impos'd was ne'er accepted by me.
I arm'd my Subjects for their common Rights.
The Love of Liberty, that fired their Souls,
That made them worthy, crown'd them with Success.
I did my Duty—'Twas but what I ow'd   175
To Heaven, an injur'd People and myself.
  Am. You will be justified in all that's past:
But I shall bend thy stubborn Temper yet—
I know the Worth of those dear Pledges now
Within my Power. Thou know'st me too—Then think   180
And yield in Time, while Mercy may be had.
  Scan. I know your Mercy by my Brothers Fate.
  Am. Then you may judge the future by the past.
  Scan. Tho' Pity be a Stranger to your Breast,
Your present dang'rous State may teach you Fear.   185
  Am. Danger and I have been acquainted long;
Full oft I'ave met her in the bloody Field,
And drove her back with Terror on my Foes:
Your other Phantom, Fear, I know her not;
Or in thy Visage I behold her now.   190
  Scan. I fear not for myself.
  Am.   Yet still thou fear'st.
Confess thyself subdu'd and sue for Favour.
  Scan. When I submit to Guilt,—I'll own your Conquest.
  Am. Think on your Friends.
  Scan.   Afflictions are no Crimes.
  Am. You wou'd redeem them!
  Scan.   Yes; on any Terms,   195
That Honour may permit, and Justice warrant.
  Am. Hear the Conditions then.
  Scan.   Why sinks my Heart?

(II. i) 167 ere] W1; e're G. *See Commentary*

Why do I tremble thus? When at the Head
Of almost twice a hundred Thousand Souls
I with a Handful charg'd this fierce old Chief,
Thou art my Witness, Heav'n, I fear'd him not.   [*Aside.*

   Am. When I look back on what you were before
Your late Revolt, charmed with the pleasing View,
I wish to see those glorious Days restor'd;
When I with Honour may indulge my Bounty,
And make you great and happy as you're brave.

   Scan. Flattery!—Nay, then he's dangerous indeed!   [*Aside.*

   Am. Renounce the Errors of the Christian Sect,
And be instructed in the Law profest
By *Ishmael's* Holy Race; that Light divine,
That darts from *Mecca's* ever sacred Fane,
T'illuminate the darken'd Souls of Men,
And fill 'em with its Brightness.

   Scan.   O *Althea!*   [*Aside.*

   Am. Break your Alliance with the Christian Princes,
And let my Foes be thine.

   Scan.   That follows well;
Th'abandon'd Wretch, that breaks his Faith with Heav'n,
Will hardly stop at any future Crime.   [*Aside.*

   Am. Forego th' Advantage, that your Arms have won,
Give up this little Part of spacious *Greece*,
Its Cities and its People to my Power:
And in Return reign thou my Substitute
O'er all my conquer'd Provinces in *Europe*,
From *Adrianople* to the Walls of *Buda.*

   Scan. Assist me, Heav'n! assist me to suppress
The rising Indignation in my Breast,
That struggles, heaves and rages for a Vent—
Aranthes! Althea! How shall I preserve you?   [*Aside.*

   Vis. He's greatly mov'd, his Visage flames with Wrath.

   Ama. Just so he looks when rushing on the Foe,
The eager Blood starts from his trembling Lips.

   Am. I wait your Resolution.

   Scan. Three Days the Truce concluded is to last;
That Space I ask to answer your Demands.

   Am. 'Tis well; enjoy your Wish—but yet remember
Honour and Int'rest, Gratitude and Love
Bleed while you pause, and press you to comply.
Farther, to favour you in all I may,

Aranthes shall attend you to your Camp:
Consult, resolve, your Interests are the same;
Althea justly claims the Care of both.   [*Exit* Amurath, &c.   240
   Scan. O thou, who art my Righteousness and Strength,
Distress'd and tempted, still in thee I trust:
The Pilot, when he sees the Tempest rise,
And the proud Waves insult the low'ring Skies,
Fix'd to the Helm, looks to that Power to lay   245
The raging Storm, whom Winds and Seas obey.   [*Exit* Scanderbeg, &c.

Amasie alone.

Shou'd he comply? as sure he's hardly press'd;
Restor'd to Favour, where is my Revenge?
He's but a Man—less tempted I fell worse;
But I'm not *Scanderbeg*—Say, he refuses;   250
It follows that the Sultan in his Rage,
Murthers the Captives, tho' we all shou'd perish.
Which Side soe'er I view, I like it not.
There is no Peace for me, while *Castriot* lives;
Plagued and distress'd, he soars above me still;   255
Insults my Hate, and awes me with his Virtue.
His Virtue! Ha! How have I dreamt till now,
How 'scap'd the Thought? His Virtue shall betray him.
Hypocrisy, that with an Angel's Likeness
May well deceive the Wisdom of an Angel,   260
Shall re-instate me in his gen'rous Heart:
Which if I fail to pierce, may all the Ill
I ever wish'd to him fall on myself.—
Th'amorous Prince—I know his haughty Soul
Ill brooks his subtle Father's peaceful Schemes.   265
He loves *Althea*, and depends on me
T'assist his Flame.

Enter Mahomet.

  Ma.   *Amasie*, what Success?
You saw the Captive Princess—
   Ama.   Yes, my Lord.
   Ma. Curse on the jealous Customs of our Court:
Why is that Privilege deny'd to me?   270
   Ama. You know why I'm indulg'd.
   Ma.   'Tis true, but say,
What hast thou done that may advance my Hopes?
   Ama. I've thought, my Lord—
   Ma.   What tell'st thou me of thoughts!

Hast thou not spoke?—what says the charming Fair?
—Shall I be blest?
   Ama.   Spoke, what? Alas! my Prince!   275
How little do you know that haughty Christian?
Bred in the rigid Maxims of her Sect,
Chaste as its Precepts, most severely vertuous,
Althea wou'd treat me with the last Contempt,
Shou'd I but name your gen'rous Passion to her;   280
And proudly term it shameful and unjust.
   Ma. Now as you wou'd avoid a Prince's Hatred,
That must one Day command you; or expect
E'er to attain my Sister's Love, the Scope
Of your Ambition, aid me with your Counsel.   285
My Blood's on Fire, and I will quench the Flame,
Tho' universal Ruin shou'd insue.
By Heaven I will; I'll plunge in Seas of Bliss,
And with repeated Draughts of Cordial Love,
Expell the raging Fever from my Veins.   29c
   Ama. Glorious Mischief!—[*Aside.*] If I judge right her Will
Is ne'er to be subdu'd, you can't possess
Her Mind, my Lord—and without that you know—
   Ma. Her Mind! a Shadow! Give me solid Joys,
And let her Christian Minion take the Rest.   29ç
I love her for myself; my Appetite
Must be appeas'd, or live my constant Plague.
Let me but clasp her in my longing Arms,
Press her soft Bosom to my panting Breast,
And crown my Wishes; tho' attain'd by Force,   30c
Tho' amidst Strugglings, Shrieks and gushing Tears;
Or while she faints beneath my strong Embrace,
And I have all my raging Passions crave.
   Am. Already I've conceiv'd the Means to serve you,
But Time must give th' imperfect Embryo Form,   30
And hail th' auspicious Birth.
   Ma.   She's justly Mine,
The Purchase of my Sword. Our Prophet thus,
   By manly Force all prior Right destroy'd;
   Power was his Claim; he conquer'd and enjoy'd:
   Beauty and Fame alike his Ardor mov'd;   31
   Fiercely he fought, and as he fought he lov'd.   [*Exeunt.*

End of the Second Act.

(II. i)   279 *Althea*] W1 (Althea); ~, G   311 SD [*Exeunt.*] *Ed.; not in* G

ACT III.

SCENE I.

The Christian Camp.

Enter Scanderbeg *and* Aranthes.

Ar. Althea mourns for this your fond Delay,
And thinks already she has liv'd too long;
Since living she protracts the Tyrant's Fate,
And clouds the matchless Lustre of your Arms.
    Scan. Justice herself would here suspend her Sword;   5
Nor with one undiscriminating Blow,
Blind as she is, destroy both Friends and Foes.
    Ar. It is appointed once for all to die:
Then what am I, or what a Child of mine,
Weigh'd with the Honour of the Christian Name,   10
To bid the Cause of Liberty attend,
While gravely you debate those very Trifles,
The Time and Circumstances of our Death:
As justly Nature might suspend her Course
To wait the Dissolution of an Insect.   15
—No, let me bear Defiance to the Sultan;
Tell him, that you already are determin'd;
And dare his worst.
    Scan.   Not for ten thousand Worlds.
Wou'd I so tempt the fretfull Tyrants Rage?
The Pangs of Death are light to those of Absence;   20
Then who can bear eternal Seperation?
Transported as you are with pious Zeal;
Look inward, search your Heart, and then confess
The Love of Heav'n excludes not sacred Friendship.
Think if my Task were your's, how you wou'd act.   25
Wou'd you not pause, conclude, retract, and pause again
To the last moment of the Time prefixt?
Wou'd you not count it Virtue to contend,
Tho' against Hope, and struggle with Despair.
I know you wou'd; for tho' your Tongue be mute,   30
Spite of yourself, your streaming Eyes confess it.
    Ar. My Weakness is no Precedent for you.
    Scan. If thus the Friend, what must the Lover suffer?
Think, good *Aranthes*, if you ever lov'd,

---

7 destroy both] D, W₁; destroy both both G   34 Think,] *Ed.*; ~ₐ G

What I endure: think on *Althea*'s Charms,   35
And judge from thence the Greatness of my Pain.
   Ar. Why will you dwell upon the dang'rous Theme?
The Strength of *Sampson* prov'd too weak for Love,
David's Integrity was no Defence;
The King, the Hero and the Prophet fell   40
Beneath the same inevitable Power:
The Wisdom of his Son was Folly here;
And he that comprehended all Things else
Knew not himself, 'till dear Experience taught
Him late Repentance, Anguish, Grief and Shame.   45
Then think no more but give us up at once;
Give up *Althea*; Heaven demands it of you;
For while she lives, your Virtue is not safe.
   Scan. Is this a Father's Voice?
   Ar.   Wou'd I had died,
Ere I was honour'd with a Father's Name;   50
Or that my Child had been less good and fair.
What was my greatest Joy, is now my Grief:
Ev'ry Perfection wrings my Heart with Pain.
For all her Charms are now so many Snares,
Which you must break, or be undone for ever.   55
—Still unresolv'd!—Forgive me if I think,
You have the Weakness now of other Men.
   Scan. If to rejoice when Virtue is rewarded;
Or mourn th' Afflictions of the Good and Brave,
Who mourn not for themselves; if Love and Friendship   60
Denote me weak, I wou'd be weaker still.
He who disclaims the Softness of Humanity,
Aspiring to be more than Man, is less.
Yet know, my Father, rev'rend good *Aranthes*!
Whatever tender Sentiments I feel;   65
Tho' as a Man, a Lover and a Friend,
I fear the Sultan's Cruelty and Malice;
Yet as a Christian, I despise 'em both.
'Tis not for Man to glory in his Strength;
The Best have fallen, and the Wisest err'd.   70
Yet when the Time shall come, when Heaven shall by
Its Providence declare, this is my Will,
And this the Sacrifice that I demand,
Why who can tell, but full of that same Energy,

Which swells your Breast; I may reply ev'n so   75
Thy will be done.
    Ar.   How have my Fears deceiv'd me?
    Scan. The careful Gard'ner turns the limpid Stream,
This Way, or that Way; as suits his Purpose best.
The Wrath of Man shall praise his Maker's Name;
The Residue, restrain'd, rest on himself.   80
Let us not rashly antedate our Woes.
Tho' I defer the Sentence of your Death,
Tho' I cou'd die ten thousand times to save you,
I do not, nay I dare not bid you live.
    Ar. Excellent Man! why did I ever doubt thee?   85
Your Zeal's no less, your Wisdom more than mine.
My Time's expir'd; Illustrious Prince,—farewel!
    Scan. My Father! My *Althea*!—
    Ar.   O my Son!
Our Part is little in this noble Conflict,
The worst is Death; your's harder, but more glorious,   90
To live and suffer. Heaven inspire thy Soul
With more than *Roman* Fortitude and Courage:
They poorly fled to Death, t'avoid Misfortunes;
May Christian Patience teach thee to o'ercome 'em.   [*Exit* Aranthes.

Scanderbeg alone.

In this Extremity shall I invoke   95
Thy awful Genius, O majestick *Rome*;
Or *Junius Brutus*, thine; who sacrificed
To publick Liberty, Paternal Love:
The younger *Brutus*; or the *Greek Timoleon*;
Of Self-Denial great Examples all: 100
But all far short of what's required of me.
These Patriots offer'd to an injur'd World
But guilty Wretches, who deserv'd their Fates.
Wou'd they have given up the best of Men,
And the most perfect of the gentler Sex   105
To Death, to worse than Death, a Tyrant's Rage?
No, Nature unassisted cannot do it.
To thee, I bow me then, Fountain of Life,
Of Wisdom and of Power,
Who know'st our Frame, and mad'st us what we are;   110
I ask not Length of Days, nor Fame, nor Empire:
Give me to know and to discharge my Duty,
And leave th' Event to thee—*Amasie* here!—

Enter Amasie, *who kneels and lays his Sword at*
Scanderbeg's *Feet.*

Ama. Well may you turn away, justly disdain
To cast one Look upon the lost *Amasie*.   115
Constant as Truth, inflexible as Justice,
Above Ambition, and the Joys of Sense,
You must abhor the Wretch, whose fatal Weakness
Betray'd him to such Crimes, as make him hateful
To Heaven, to all good Men and to himself.   120
   Scan. What com'st thou for, what canst thou hope from me?
   Ama. I come for Justice.
   Scan.   Justice must condemn thee.
   Ama. I have condemn'd myself; but dare not die,
'Till you, the proper Judge, confirm the Sentence.
   Scan. When first you fell, I deeply mourn'd your Loss;   125
But from that Moment gave you up for ever.
   Ama. Still you're my Prince! my native, rightful Prince.
   Scan. Then what art thou?
   Ama.   The blackest, worst of Traytors.
   Scan. Be that thy Punishment.
   Ama.   Dreadful Decree!
'Tis more than I can bear—leave me not thus.   130
Is not the Blood, that runs in either's Veins,
Deriv'd from the same Source? Was I not once,
Howe'er unworthy, honour'd with your Friendship,
Named your Successor? so beloved, so trusted,
That all the Envious pin'd, and all the Good   135
Look'd up with Wonder at the glorious Height,
To which your partial Friendship had advanc'd me.
   Scan. Ill judging Man, thou aggravat'st thy Crimes.
   Ama. That cannot be; I but excite your Justice.
Behold my guilty Breast; strike and maintain   140
The Honour of our House, wipe out this Stain
Of its illustrious Race and Blot of Friendship.
   Scan. If your Ambition were to fall by me,
You shou'd have met me in the Front of Battle
With manly Opposition, and receiv'd   145
The Death thou seek'st for in the Rage of War.
My Sword descends not on a prostrate Foe!

(III. i) 126 for ever.] W1; ~: G   132 Was] was G (*earlier state*)   once,] ~∧ G (*earlier state*)   134 beloved] loved G (*earlier state*)   135 Good] W1 (good); ~, G
137 Friendship] Fondness G (*earlier state*)   143 were] be G (*earlier state*)   147 Foe!]
Ed.; ~: G (*earlier state*); ~? G (*later state*). *See Commentary*

Tho' you've deserv'd to die, I've not deserv'd
To be your Executioner.
    Ama.   Just Heaven!
Are you a Christian Prince, and will you spare   150
A black Apostate?
    Scan.   Heaven can right itself
Without my Aid, nor do I know on Earth
So great, so just an Object of Compassion.
Live and repent.
    Ama.   I have and do repent,
But cannot live. The Court of *Amurath*   155
Abhors a Christian; ev'ry Christian Court
Detests a Traytor.
    Scan.   Miserable Man!   [*Aside.*
    Ama. We're taught that Heav'n is merciful and kind.
    Scan. What Wretch dares doubt of that?
    Ama.   Then why am I
Deny'd to sue for Peace and Pardon there,   160
Since I must never hope for them on Earth?
    Scan. Have I the Seeds of Frailty in my Nature?
Am I a Man, like him, and can I see,
Unpittying and unmov'd, the bitter Anguish,
The deep Contrition of his wounded Soul?   165
It will not be—O Nature take your Course,
I'll not resist your tenderest Impressions.   [*Aside.*
Suppress the Tumult of your troubled Mind;
You have o'ercome; I feel and share your Sorrows.
    Ama. O be less good, or I shall die with Shame.   170
    Scan. I have been too slow to pardon.   [*Embracing.*
    Ama.   O my Prince!
My injur'd Prince!
    Scan.   Thy Friend, thy Friend, *Amasie.*
    Ama. How have you rais'd me from the last Despair?
And dare you trust this Rebel, this Apostate?
    Scan. 'Tis Heaven's Prerogative alone to search   175
The Hearts of Men, and read their inmost Thoughts:
I wou'd be circumspect, not over wise;
Nor for one Error, lose a Friend for ever:
No, let me be deceiv'd ere want Humanity.
    Ama. The Wisdom and Beneficence of Heaven   180
Flow in your Words, and bless all those who hear 'em.
                     [*Trumpets sound a Parley.*

      (III. i)   149b Heaven] Heavens G (*earlier state*)

Scan. What means this Summons to a second Parley?
Ama. The Sultan's haste anticipates my Purpose.   [*Aside.*
Something that much concerns your Love and Honour,
I have to say; but must defer it now,   18₅
And once more join his Council; if I'm seen,
I lose the only Means that's left to serve you.
  Scan. You will return—
  Ama.   As certain as the Night;
About the Midst of which you may expect me.
  Scan. You'll find me in my Tent; The word's, *Althea.*   19₀

                    Enter Officer.

Off. The Visier with the Princess of *Durazzo,*
Demands an Audience.
  Scan.   Fly; and introduce 'em.
Can this be true?
  Ama.   Most true. The Sultan hopes
That your *Althea*'s Eyes will conquer for him:
Heaven guard your Heart. Farewell—At Night expect me.   19₅
He's well deceiv'd; Hypocrisy, I thank thee.
Dark and profound as Hell, what Line can fathom,
Or Eye explore the secret thoughts of Men?
Yet once I fear'd I shou'd betray myself
And be indeed the Penitent I feign'd;   20₀
So much his Virtue mov'd me. Curse his Virtue!
He ever will excell me—Let him die,
Tho' all my Peace die with him—Wretched Man!
When shall I rest from Envy and Remorse?   [*Aside.*
                                                        [*Exit* Amasie.

  Scan. I shall once more behold *Althea* then.   20₅
So Wretches are indulg'd the Sight of Heaven
To sharpen Pain, and aggravate their Loss.
The blended Beauties of the teeming Spring,
Whate'er excells in Nature's Works besides,
Are vile to her, the Glory of the Whole.   21₀
Flowers fade and lose their Odors, Gems their Brightness,
And Gold its Estimation in her Presence.
But see, she comes—Sure such a Form betray'd
The first of Men to quit his Paradise,
And all the Joys of Innocence and Peace,   21₅
For those he found in her: yet had the lovely,
Alas too lovely Parent of Mankind,

              (III. i)   196 Hypocrisy,] W1; ~ₐ G

Possess'd a Mind, as much Superior to
Her outward Form, as my *Althea* doth;
Mankind had never fell.   220

Enter Visier, Althea, *&c.* Scanderbeg *kneels and kisses
her Hand.*

  Scan.   O my Princess!
  Al. My ever honour'd Lord!
  Scan.   To be your Slave,
A Captive to your Charms, is more than to
Be Lord of Humankind.
  Al.   The *Visier*, Prince.— [Scanderbeg *rises.*
  Vis. Far be it, noble *Scanderbeg*, from me
To intercept my Royal Master's Bounty,   225
Who wills you to enjoy Freedom of Speech,
Uninterrupted, with the Christian Princess.
I'll with the Guards retire and wait your Leisure. [*Exit* Visier, *&c.*
  Scan. O my *Althea*!
  Al.   Speak, I'm all Attention.
  Scan. O who can raise his Thoughts to the Occasion?   230
Or doing that, reduce such Thoughts to Words?
  Al. I will assist you—we must part for ever.
  Scan. Is that, is that so easy? Righteous Heaven!
It doth amaze me, and confound my Reason
To hear thee, thus calm and serene, pronounce   235
The dreadful Sentence.
  Al.   Is it not determin'd?
  Scan. To give thee back to Slavery and Chains!
To bear the Malice of a bloody Tyrant,
Inrag'd by my Refusal!—O *Althea*!
Tho' Heav'n must be obey'd, something is due   240
To vertuous Love. We may, we must confess
A Sense of such unutterable Woe.
When in Return of my incessant Vows,
You deign'd to crown my Love, when Expectation
Of the long sigh'd for Bliss had raised my Joys   245
To that exalted Pitch, that I look'd down
With Pity on Mankind; and only griev'd
To think they stood exposed to Disappointment,
Mis'ry and Pain, while I alone was happy—
Then, then to lose thee—
  Al.   O complain no more.   250

(III. i)   224 it, noble *Scanderbeg*,] W1 (Scanderbeg); ~ˌ ~ˌ G   249 happy—] W1; ~. G

You move a Weakness here, unworthy her,
Who wou'd aspire to deserve your Love.
I wou'd have died like the mute Sacrifice;
Which goes as chearfull and as unconcern'd,
To bleed upon the Altar, as to sleep   25
Within its nightly Fold.
    Scan.   Coud'st thou do this!
    Al. Had I not seen you thus, I think I shou'd;
But at your Grief my Resolution fails me:
I'm subdued: The Woman, the weak, fond Woman
Swells in my Heart, and gushes from my Eyes.   26
    Scan. What have I done? The Greatness of thy Soul,
Not to be comprehended but by Minds
Exalted as thy own, stagger'd my Reason;
And what was Prudence and Superior Virtue,
I thought a Wrong to Love. Rash, thoughtless Man!   26
To force a Tenderness thou can'st not bear,
That stabs the very Soul of Resolution,
And leaves thee without Strength to stem a Torrent,
That asks an Angel's Force to meet its Rage.
    Al. To combat Inclination, to subdue   27
Our own Desires, and conquer by Submission;
Are Virtues, Prince, no Angel ever knew.
While these are your's, shall I indulge my Grief?
—The Storm is over, and I am calm again.
    Scan. O thou eternal Source of Admiration!   27
What new Wonder hast thou prepar'd to charm
My ravish'd Soul? where didst thou learn the Art
To stop the Tide of Grief in its full Flow,
And triumph o'er Dispair?
    Al.   In you I triumph.
Tho' rackt and torn with more than mortal Grief,   28
Amidst the Pangs of disappointed Love
And suff'ring Friendship, do I not behold thee,
Still constant as the Sun, that keeps its Course,
Tho' Storms and Tempests vex the nether Sky,
And low'ring Clouds a while obscure his Brightness.   2
    Scan. Excellent, heavenly Maid! thou rob'st thyself,
And attribut'st to me thy own Perfections.
    Al. Have you once question'd whether you should part
With two the dearest Things to Man on Earth,

(III. i)   254 *Which*] Who G (*earlier state*)   274 I am] I'm G (*earlier state*)
284 *nether*] D, W1; neither G   286 *Maid!*] W1 (maid); ~? G. *See Commentary on* III. i. 147

A Friend and Mistress; or renounce your Faith,   290
The Int'rest of Mankind and Cause of Virtue?
   Scan. That were to purchase ev'n thee too dear:
That were a Misery beyond thy Loss:
That were, my Princess! to deserve to lose thee.
   Al. That gracious Power that wrought you for this Purpose,   295
That made you great to struggle with Adversity,
And teach luxurious Princes, by Example,
What Kings shou'd be, and shame 'em into Virtue;
Beholds, with Pleasure, you discharge the Trust,
And act up to the Dignity you're form'd for.   300
   Scan. O whither wou'd thy dazzling Virtue soar?
Is't not enough we yield to our Misfortunes,
And bear Afflictions, tho' with bleeding Hearts.
Wou'd'st thou attempt to raise Pleasure from Pain,
And teach the Voice of Mourning, Songs of Joy?   305
   Al. Small is my Part and suited to my Strength.
What is dying? A Wanton *Cleopatra*
Cou'd smile in Death and Infants die in Sleep.
What tho' my Days are few and fill'd with Sorrow!
Cou'd vain Prosperity to hoary Age   310
Afford a Happiness to be compar'd
To dying now in such a glorious Cause;   .
Lamented and belov'd by thee, the best
And greatest of Mankind—Then let us haste
And close the Scene.—You, good *Paulinus*, let   315
The Visier know, I'm ready to return.
Why are you pale, why do gushing Tears
Blot the majestick Beauty of your Face?
Why is the Hero in the Lover lost?
   Scan. Let Angels, who attend in Crowds to hear thee;   320
Let all the Sons of Liberty and Fame;
Those, who still wait, and those who have obtain'd
The End of all their Labours; Heaven and Earth;
Angels and Men, the Living and the Dead;
Behold and judge if ever Man before   325
Purchas'd the Patriot's Name, or sav'd his Country,
His Faith and Honour, at a Price so dear.

Enter Visier.

   Vis. Well Prince, may we not hope that those bright Eyes
Have charm'd your Soul to Peace? Who wou'd resist,
When Honour's gain'd by being overcome?   330
To yield to Beauty, crowns the Warrior's Fame.

Scan. I'm not to learn how to esteem the Princess;
But know the Sultan over-rates his Power,
When he presumes to barter for her Love.
Her Mind is free and royal as his own;   33
Nor is she to be gain'd by doing what
Wou'd forfeit her Esteem. And I must think
This Haste to know my Mind, is Fraud or Fear.
What needs there more? The Truce is unexpired:
If your proud Master wishes for a Peace,   34
We yet may treat on honourable Terms.
In the mean Time receive the Princess back.
   Vis. Think what you do, great Sir.
   Scan.   I know my Duty.
   Al. Farewell, my Lord!
   Scan.   Farewell!—protect her Heaven!
   Al. Now let the fretful Tyrant storm and rage,   34
The only Danger we cou'd fear is past.   [*Exeunt* Althea *and* Visier.
   Scan. T'encounter Hosts of Foes is easier far,
Than to sustain this innate, Bosom War;
This one unbloody Conquest costs me more,
Than all the Battles I e'er won before.   [*Exit.*   3

End of the Third Act.

(III. i)   339 unexpired] D, W1 (unexpir'd D); unexpirsed G   346SD *Exeunt*] W1; *Exit* G
350SD [*Exit.*] *Ed.; not in* G

ACT IV.

SCENE I.

The Outward Apartment in the Womens Tent.
A Guard of Eunuchs.

Enter Kisler Aga.

Aga. 'Tis as I thought: Our Master is betray'd.
Whoever knew a Renegade sincere?
This Dog's a Christian still!

Enter Amasie.

Ama.   The Victim's prepar'd.
If Lust holds on her Course, and revels yet
In the hot Veins of rash, luxurious Youth,   5
This Christian Heroine, this second *Lucrece*, .
In *Mahomet* shall find another *Tarquin*,
As cruel and remorseless as the first.
If I shou'd fail in my Attempt to Night,
And *Scanderbeg* survive—*Althea* ravish'd—   10
He'll wish himself, I had succeeded better.   [*Aside.*
Dismiss your useless Train of prying Slaves;
I've Business that requires your Ear alone.

                    [*Exeunt* Eunuchs.

A *Grecian* Chief, who owns our Master's Cause,
Must be admitted to the Captive Princess.   15
'Tis of Importance to the Sultan's Service,
That he shou'd enter and depart unknown:
I'll introduce him, while you watch without
That none approach to give him Interruption.
   Aga. This I conceive; but why he mov'd the Lady   20
To the remotest Part of the Pavilion
I cannot comprehend.   [*Aside.*
   Ama.   You know your Duty; .
Your Life shall answer for the least Neglect.
   Aga. I shall take Care—[*Exit* Amasie.] to ruin thee, thou Traytor. [*Exit.*

---

1 *Aga.*] *Ed.*; K. A. G (*one copy*); ∧. A. G (*all other copies seen*)   24SD [*Exit.*] *Ed.*; *not in* G

SCENE II.

*Another Apartment; Stage darken'd; Table
and Lamp.*

Althea *discovered.*

Is this a Time and Place for virtuous Love?
This is the Wanton's Hour: Now she forsakes
Her Home, and, hid in Darkness, watches for her Prey:
The Soul whom Heav'n abhors, falls in her Snares;
And pierc'd with Guilt, as with an Arrow dies.
Yon sickly Lamp, that glimmers thro' my Tears,
Faintly contending with prevailing Darkness,
Spreads o'er the Place a melancholy Gloom,
That sooths the joyless Temper of my Mind.
So a pale Meteor's dull and beamless Flame
To the bewilder'd Traveller appears,
And adds new Horrors to the cheerless Night.
—Is Error then the Lot of all Mankind?
It is, it is—for *Scanderbeg* is fallen.—
O! what cou'd move him to the rash Attempt?
If he shou'd perish, as the Danger's great,
How will th' insulting Infidels rejoice?
How will the Foe, with scornful Triump, sing,
As a Fool dies, so died this mighty Chief;
His Hands unbound, no Fetters on his Feet,
But as an Ideot by his Folly falls,
So fell the Champion of the Christian Cause.

Enter Mahomet *drest like* Scanderbeg, *fast'ning the door
on the Inside.*

He's come, and all my Sorrows are compleat.
Are you pursued?—O my prophetick Fears!—
If undiscover'd you have enter'd here,
This Caution's needless; if betray'd, in vain.
   Ma. Of such a Prize who can be too secure?
   Al. 'Tis not his Voice—defend me, O defend me,
All gracious Heaven!
   Ma.   Dost thou not know me, Princess?
   Al. Alas! too well! [*Aside.*] Sure you've mistook your way,
Or came perchance to seek some other here;
Howe'er that be, permit me to retire.

(IV. ii)   4 Soul] *Ed.*; ~, G   29b me,] W1; ~‸ G

Ma. Mistaken Fair; or is this Ign'rance feign'd?
'Tis you alone I seek. Impetuous Love,
That will not be resisted, brought me here   35
To lay my Life and Fortune at your Feet.
    Al. Then I'm betray'd basely betray'd; just Heaven!
Expos'd, perhaps devoted to a Ruin,
From which the Grave itself is no Retreat,
And Time can ne'er repair—Be gracious, Sir,   40
To an unhappy Maid!—Or I'm deceiv'd,
Or you, my Lord, were pleas'd to mention Love;
Of that, alas! I am forbid to hear;
Compassion better suits my humble State,
That I intreat; have Pity on me, Prince,   45
Dispel my Fears, and send me from your Presence.
    Ma. Grant what you ask; I need Compassion too:
Your Beauty's necessary to my Peace:
Then yield, in Pity to yourself and me,
What else I'll take by Force: Consent to make me   50
Happy, and in Return, when Time shall give
The Scepter to my Hand, I'll make thee Queen
Of half the conquer'd Globe.
    Al.   Know, Impious Prince!
If one loose Thought wou'd buy the whole, I'd Scorn
It at that Price.
    Ma.   Then rifled and abandon'd,
Live thou the Scorn both of the World and me.   55
You have your Choice; I came not here to talk.
    Al. O! what were all my former Woes to this?
Under the Pain of Absence, hard Captivity
And my late Fears, Patience and Fortitude   60
Were my Support; Patience and Fortitude
Are useless now. Shame and Dishonour are
Not to be born. Father! *Aranthes*! haste,
And like *Virginius* preserve your Daughter.
Come *Castriot*, come, *Althea* calls thee now   65
To certain Death, to save her from Pollution.
    Ma. Call louder yet; your Idols do not hear.
    Al. Tho' none shou'd hear, yet Sorrow must complain.
    Ma. Your moving softness fans my am'rous Flame—
No Help can reach thee—All thy Friends are absent;   70
Wisely comply, and make a Friend of me.
    Al. All are not absent; he whose Presence fills

(IV. ii)   57 your] D, W1; you G   66 certain] *Ed.*; ccrtain G

Both Heaven and Earth; he, he is with me still;
Sees my Distress, numbers my flowing Tears,
And understands the Voice of my Complainings,   7
Tho' Sorrow drowns my Speech.
  Ma.   I'll wait no longer;
Nor ask again for that I've Power to take.
Now you may strive, as I have beg'd, in vain.
  Al. O thou, whose Hand sustains the whole Creation;
Who cloth'st the Woods, the Vallies and the Fields;   80
Who hear'st the hungry Lion, when he roars;
And feed'st the Eagle on the Mountain's Top;
Shut not thine Ear—turn not away thy Face;
Be not as one far off, when Danger's near;
Or like an absent Friend to the distress'd—   8
Assist me, save me—only thou canst save me—
O let me not invoke thy Aid in vain.
  Am. [*Without.*] Force, force an Entrance.
  Ma.   Ha! who dares do this?
                    [*The Door burst open.*

      Enter Amurath, Visier, Kisler Aga *and Guards.*

  Ma. Sham'd and prevented! O my cursed Fortune!
  Al. My Prayers are hear'd; let Virtue ne'er dispair.
  Vis. Guard well the Passage.
  Aga.   Who secures his Sword?
  Vis. Scanderbeg yeild! thou can'st not hope t'escape.
  Am. To fall so meanly after all thy Wars—
Well may'st thou hide thy Face.
  Vis.   Blinded by Love,
My Lord, he miss'd his Way.
  Am.   True, *Osmyn*, true:
That poor Excuse for Madness, Vice and Folly,
Is all this mighty Hero has to plead.
—A fair Account of Life and Honour lost.
I hoped not Triumph—Prophet, 'tis too much—
I ask'd but Vengeance—Bring him to my Tent.   10
When Mirth declining calls for something new,
We'll think upon the manner of his Death.
  Ma. Away, you Dogs! Confusion, Death and Hell!   [*Exit.*
  Al. They stand agast. Deliverance waits the just,
But short's the Triumph of deceitful Men.   1

      (IV. ii) 104 agast] aghast W1. *See Commentary*

Turn'd on themselves, their own Devices cover
Them with Shame. [*Aside.*]   [*Exit.*
   Vis.   I'm lost in Admiration!
It is the Prince *Mahomet.*
   Am.   Wonder, Rage
And Disappointment drive me to Distraction.
Kisler Aga, expect to answer this.   110
   Aga. Let not my Lord condemn his Slave unheard.
Amasie, whom I ever thought a Villain,
Going this Evening to the Captive Princess;
I follow'd unperceiv'd, and so dispos'd me
As to o'er hear him: who with many Oaths   115
Assur'd *Althea, Scanderbeg* was come;
Conceal'd by Night, and in his Faith secure,
Once more to see her and repeat his Vows.
Of this I thought myself in Duty bound
T'inform my Royal Master.
   Am.   You are clear.   120
   Aga. The Caution us'd to introduce the Prince,
Seem'd to confirm the Truth of what I heard.
   Am. Leave us—Enough; your Conduct merits Praise.
                     [*Exit* Kisler Aga.
   Vis. Th' affrighted Fair is fled to her Apartment.
   Am. Degenerate Boy? thou art my Witness, *Allah*,   125
Not so I spent my Youth, and won his Mother;
Tho' much I lov'd, and long I sigh'd in vain.
'Tis vile and base to do a private Wrong:
When Kings, as Kings, do ill; the Office then
Must justify the Man.
   Vis.   A Believing Monarch,   130
Obedient to the Messenger of Heaven,
Can never err.
   Am.   Our Prophet, by the Sword,
First taught the stubborn *Arabs* to believe,
And writ his Laws in Blood.
   Vis.   He knew Mankind.
Nay, yet the Priests of all Religions teach,   135
Whate'er is done to propagate the Faith,
Must from its End, be good.
   Am.   Thus do I stand
Acquitted to myself; and *Scanderbeg*,
Tho' by Assassination, justly falls.
To Morrow's Sun shall shine for me alone.   140

Yet, O! my faithful *Osmyn*, all's not well:
I know not how, my Spirits kindle not
As they were wont, when Glory was in View.
True, I rejoice; and yet, methinks, my Joy
Is like the Mirth wrung from a Man in Pain.   1
  Vis. Guard, righteous Heaven, thy great Vicegerent's Health.
  Am. The Body simpathizes with the Mind;
As that with what we love. My Languor may
Be the Effect of my *Hellena*'s Grief;
I live in her. My Pleasures are improv'd,   1
My Pains forgot, when I behold her Face;
The tend'rest, fondest, most belov'd of Children.
  Vis. O! what has happen'd, Sir?
  Am.   This Evening, *Osmyn*,
When I commanded her to love *Amasie*,
And look upon him, as her future Lord,
An ashy Paleness spread o'er all her Face,
And gushing Tears bespoke her strong Aversion:
But when t'inhance his Merit I disclosed
The purpos'd Murther of his native Prince;
Had I pronounc'd the Sentence of her Death,
Sure less had been her Terror and Surprize.
Kneeling, she call'd on Heav'n and Earth to witness
Her utter Detestation of the Fact,
And everlasting Hatred of *Amasie*,
His Person and Design.
  Vis.   Unhappy Princess!
To be compell'd to marry where she hates.
  Am. O! she abhors him, loaths his very Name;
Yet still her filial Piety prevail'd;
She hung upon my Neck; pray'd for my Life,
My Honour, my Success; and took her leave
In such endearing Strains, as if she never
Had been to see me more. Her moving Softness
Melted my old tough Heart—I kiss'd her—sigh'd,
And wept as fast as she. Our mingled Tears
Together flow'd down my shrunk wither'd Cheeks,
And trickled from my Beard—O! shou'd my Thirst
Of Vengeance kill my Child; shou'd she t'avoid
Amasie, fly to Death—what cou'd support me?   [*Exeunt.*

SCENE III.

A Wood, thro' which is seen the Christian *Camp.*

Enter Hellena *and* Cleora *in Mens Apparel.*

Cle. Where are we, Princess! whither will you wander?
Hel. We've gain'd the utmost Summit of the Mountain.
I hear the neigh of Horses—See'st thou not
Those Lights that glimmer thro' the Trees, *Cleora*?
The Christian Camp's before us.
    Cle.   Righteous *Allah*!   5
The Christian Camp!—
    Hel.   'Tis thither I am bound.
    Cle. Distraction!
    Hel.   I am determined.
    Cle.   Hear me, Princess!
Once take the Counsel of your faithful Slave,
And yet return before our Flight be known.
    Hel. O! no, *Cleora*! I must ne'er return.   10
    Cle. Then in your Father's Empire let us seek
Some far remote and unfrequented Village;
Where thus disguis'd, you may remain unknown
To all, but me; 'till Death shall end your Sorrows.
Why are you come to find new Dangers here?   15
Alas! I thought you only fled *Amasie*.
    Hel. Why shou'd I fly from him? in his Despite
I cou'd have died, ev'n in my Father's Arms.
Death, ever at my Call, had been a sure
Defence from his more loath'd Embraces. Gentle Maid,   20
Think it not hard, that I've conceal'd from thee
My real Intention, 'till 'twas past thy power,
Had'st thou the Inclination to prevent it.
    Cle. Break, break my Heart, for I've liv'd too long,
Since I'm suspected by my Royal Mistress.   25

(IV. iii)   1 we,] W1; ~ ∧ G   5b–6 Righteous *Allah*! . . . am bound.] *Ed.; lining in G is*
confused, giving appearance of broken metre:

                        Cle. Righteous *Allah*! The Christian Camp!—
                        Hel. 'Tis thither I am bound.

W1 *relines without restoring the metrical pattern:*

                              CLEORA.
                Righteous Allah! the Christian camp!—

                              HELLENA.
                            'Tis thither I am bound.

Hel. I fear'd thy fond Affection wou'd have weigh'd
Each Danger with too scrupulous a Hand,
I know 'twill strike thee with the last Amazement
To hear I've left the Bosom of a Father,
How e'er severe to others kind to me,
To seek his mortal Foe.
 Cle.   Your Reason's lost.
 Hel. No; I remember well the Terrors past,
And count on those to come; both worse than Death.
Conscious of my weak Sex, with all its Fears,
To pass by Night thro' Camps of hostile Men,
And urge the Presence of that awful Prince,
My Soul in secret has so long ador'd—
When I shall see him, shou'd his piercing Eye
Trace me thro' my Disguise!—O my *Cleora*!
Will not my falt'ring Tongue, my crimson Cheeks,
My panting Heart and trembling Limbs betray me?
What think'st thou? Say; shall I not die with Shame
When I wou'd speak, and leave my Tale untold.
 Cle. These and a Thousand Difficulties more
Oppose your Purpose; then in Time retire.
 Hel. No more; away; my Resolutions fixt.
The Glory and the Danger's both before me,
And both are mine—you were necessary
To my Escape—That's past—'Tis true indeed,
Your Service has by far excell'd my Bounty:
Here take these Jewels, and go seek thy Safety;
I can pursue my Purpose by myself.

Enter Paulinus, *with a Guard; who come from the farther Part of the Stage
to the Front and stand listening for some Time.*

 Cle. O how have I deserv'd this cruel Usage?
If I've discover'd any Signs of Fear,
'Twas never for myself—Go where you please,
I'll follow you to Death.
 Hel.   Kind, faithful Maid—
Wherefore shou'd I involve thee in my Ruin?
 Cle. 'Tis Ruin to forsake you.
 Hel.   Mine is certain;
Thou may'st have many happy Years to come.
 Paul. Stand, there.—Who are you?—Answer to the Guard.

(IV. iii) 52+SD *Time.*] D, W1; ~; G 60 *Paul.*] *Ed.*; *Pau.* G (*and similarly below*)

Hel. Fatal Surprize! what must we answer?

Cle.   Friends.

Paul. Make it appear—this Instant—Give the Word.

—Silent—Some Spies sent from the Sultan's Camp.

Less favour'd by the Darkness of the Night,

The Traytors shou'd Escape, guard ev'ry Passage.   65

   Hel. Scanderbeg must die.   [*Guards surround them.*

Off.   Not by thy Hand

If mine can aim aright, thou bloody Villain!   [*Wounds* Hellena.
                                   She falls.

   Hel. Untimely Fate!

Cle.   Where are you?

Hel.   Here on the Earth.

   Cle. You're wounded then?

Hel.   Alas! to Death, *Cleora.*

   Cle. Prophet, I do not charge you with Injustice;   70

But I must grieve, and wonder Things are thus.

   Hel. Too hasty Death, cou'dst thou not stay a little,

Little longer; the Business of my Life

Had soon been done, and I had come to thee.

   Paul. Moving Sounds! I fear you've been too rash.   75

Ill fated Youths, who are you, and from whence?

What dire Misfortune brought you to this Place?

   Hel. It matters not, who, or from whence we are;

But as you prize your Royal Master's Life,

Conduct me to him strait: mine ebbs apace,   80

Yet on its short Duration his depends.

   Paul. Your Adjuration is of such a Force,

His own Commands wou'd scarce oblige me more.

Sir, I'll attend you.

   Hel.   All you fleeting Powers,

Sight, Speech and Motion; O! forsake me not   85

So near my Journey's End; assist me to

Perform this only Task, and take your flight for ever.   [*Exeunt.*

SCENE IV.

Scanderbeg's *Tent*

   Scan. Degenerate *Rome*! by godlike *Brutus* freed

From *Cæsar* and his temporary Chain

Your own Ingratitude renew'd those Bonds,
Beneath whose galling Weight you justly perish'd.
If Freedom be Heaven's universal Gift,
Th' unalienable Right of Humankind,
Were all Men vertuous, there would be no Slaves.
Despotick Power, that Root of Bitterness,
That Tree of Death, that spreads its baleful Arms
Almost from Pole to Pole; beneath whose cursed Shade,
No good Thing thrives, and ev'ry ill finds Shelter;
Had found no Time for its detested Growth,
But for the Follies and the Crimes of Men.
In ev'ry Climate, and in ev'ry Age,
Where Arts and Arms and publick Virtue flourish'd,
Ambition, dangerous only to itself,
Crush'd in its Infancy, still found a Grave
Where it attempted to erect a Throne.

Enter Hellena, *supported by* Paulinus *and* Cleora, *Guards*
following.

Hel. My Blood flows faster, and my throbbing Heart
Beats with redoubled force, now I behold him;
O take me to thy Arms—I die, *Cleora!*   [*Swoons.*
   Paul. He faints; support him, while we search his Wound.
   Cle. Away; and touch him not—O gracious Prince!
If ever pity moved your Royal Breast,
Let all depart except yourself and us.
   Scan. Let all withdraw.   [*Exit* Paulinus, *&c.*
             Now, gentle Youth, inform me,
Why you oppose th' assistance of your Friend?
   Cle. She's gone, She's gone: O Heavens! She's past Assistance.
   Scan. Think what you say, and recollect your Reason.
   Cle. O mighty Prince! we are not what we seem,
But hapless women.
   Scan.   Ha!
   Cle.   Women; and sure
The most distress'd, and wretched of our Sex.
T'increase your Admiration, view this Face.
   Scan. Sure I have known these lovely Features well;
But when, or where, my Recollection fails me.
   Cle. And well it may. O! who cou'd know thee now;
Never enough deplor'd, unhappy Princess.

Scan. Fearful Suggestion! Sure my Eyes deceive me!
Forbid it Heaven, that this shou'd be *Hellena*.
    Hel. Who was it call'd upon the lost *Hellena*?   40
    Scan. Ha! she revives; fly instantly for Aid.
    Hel. It was his Voice—false Maid, thou hast betray'd me.
Stay—whether woud'st thou go? I'm past all Aid:
The friendly Hand of Death will quickly close
These ever streaming Eyes, and end my Shame.   45
O Prince! the most distinguish'd and belov'd
By righteous *Allah*, of his Works below;
You see the Daughter of relentless *Amurath*,
Sunk with her Father's Crimes, o'erwhelm'd with Shame,
Expiring at your Feet. My Weakness stands   50
Confess'd, but be it so I will no more
Lament my painfull, hopeless, fatal Flame,
Since Heaven ordain'd it for your Preservation.
    Scan. When will my Wonder and my Anguish cease?
    Hel. I'm come to save you, Prince, from falling by   55
A vile Assassin's Arm; the false *Amasie*,
Has deeply sworn your Death; ev'n now he comes
To plunge his bloody Poniard in your Breast.
    Scan. Fatal Mistake! what base Detractor has
Traduc'd my Friend; and wrought thee, gen'rous Princess   60
To thy Ruin?
    Hel.   Doth not the Traytor come
Here by Appointment?
    Scan.   Ha!
    Hel.   Whence learnt I that?
Be not deceiv'd, but guard your precious Life;
Or I shall die in vain. For me this bloody
Enterprize was form'd; my feeble Charms,   65
That wound but where I hate, the Motive to
This Crime.
    Scan.   Just Heav'n! that I cou'd longer doubt it!
    Cle. Alas! She's going, raise her, gently raise her.
    Hel. My Head grows dizzy.
    Scan.   Lean it on my Breast.
    Hel. This is indeed no Time to stand on Forms.   70
    Scan. The Pains, the Agonies of Death are on her;
And yet she suffers less, much less, than I.
What generous Heart can bear it?
    Hel.   Do not grieve:

(IV. iv)   68 going,] D, W1; ~ˌ G

And yet methinks your Pity sooths my Pain.

Scan. Why wou'dst thou give thy Life to Ransom mine?   7
Wou'd I had died, or yet cou'd die, to save thee.

Hel. I'd not exchange my Death, lamented thus
And in your Arms, for any other's Life—
Unless *Althea*'s.

Scan.   Were *Althea* here
She wou'd forget her own severe Distress,   8
And only weep for yours.

Hel.   May she be happy!
Yet had you never seen her, who can tell,
You sometimes might, perhaps, have thought on me.

Scan. He in my Place who cou'd refrain from Tears,
Unenvied let him boast of his Brutality.   8
I'm not asham'd to own myself a Man.

Hel. Farewel, *Cleora*!—Weep not, gentle Maid;
I recommend her, Sir, to your Protection.
And, O victorious Prince; if e'er hereafter
Conquest shou'd give my Father to your Sword
—Then think on me—suspend your lifted Arm,
And spare—O spare his Life—forget your Wrongs;
Or think them punished in his Daughter's Loss.   [*Dies.*

Scan. Her gentle Soul is fled; she rests in peace;
While we, methinks, like Gratitude and Grief,
Form'd by the Sculpture's Art to grace her Urn;
Moving, tho' lifeless; eloquent, tho' dumb;

    Excite incurious Mortals to explore,
    Virtues so rare, and trace the shining Store,
    That cou'd a Life so short so well supply;   1
    Yet mourn with us such Excellence shou'd die.   [*Exeunt.*

End of the Fourth Act.

(IV. iv) 101SD [*Exeunt.*] *Ed.; not in* G

ACT V.

SCENE I.

Christian Camp.

Enter Scanderbeg: Amasie *in Chains,* Paulinus, *&c.*

Scan. Cou'd Love, that fills each honest, gen'rous Breast
With double Ardor to excel in Vertue,
Conclude, thou Wretch! what Malice first begun,
And finish thee a Villain? Thou wou'dst die—
We'll disappoint thee—Live, tortur'd with Guilt,   5
A Terror to thyself: Or let the Sultan,
The vile Abettor of thy Crimes, reward thee;
We know no Punishment to suit thy Guilt.
This is a Christian Land. Our Laws were made
For Men, not Monsters.—Take him from my Sight.   10
'Tis needless to repeat that by Hostility,   [*Exit* Amasie.
Of the worst Kind, our faithless Enemies
Have broke the Truce. We're now again prepar'd
Once more to prove the Fortune of our Arms;
And try by honest Force, seeing all Treaties   15
With such Perfidious Men are vain, to free
Our Captive Friends, and drive these fierce Destroyers
From *Epirus. Paulinus*, with your Squadrons
Attack the Trenches Westward of the City,
T'amuse the Foe, and draw their Force that way;   20
Then I'll, with the remaining Troops, assault
Th' East; where doubly intrench'd the Royal Tents,
The Prison of *Althea* and her Father,
Raise their aspiring Heads. I need not say,
Acquit yourselves like Men; I know you well;   25
Nor spur you on with Hopes of promis'd Wealth.
I have no useless Stores of hoarded Gold.
My Revenues, you know, have been the Spoils
Of vanquish'd Foes; these I have shar'd amongst you.
Wou'd you have more? Our Enemies have enough: 30
Subdue your Foes, and satisfy yourselves.
Let each commit himself to that just Power,
Who still has been our Guide and sure Defence.
Be valiant, not presumptuous. Seek his Aid,
Who by our Weakness magnifies his Strength.   35

18 *Paulinus,*] *Ed.*; ~∧ G

Now follow me, my fellow Soldiers, and remember
You fight the Cause of Liberty and Truth,   [*Drawing his Sword.*
Your Native Land, *Aranthes* and *Althea.*
    All. Huzza! Liberty! Justice! *Aranthes* and *Althea!*   [*Exeunt.*

SCENE II.

The Sultan's Tent.

Amurath, K. Aga *and an Officer.*

    Am. Amasie's not return'd—shou'd he betray me
And join with *Scanderbeg* to free the Captives!—
That Officer's his Creature—*Mustapha!*
Resign *Aranthes* to the *Kisler Aga*—
Conduct him to *Althea.* Let *Amasie,*
That unauspicious Slave, be true or false,
Succeed or perish, they shall surely die:
So tell the Father—Hence, you Slaves, be gone.
Now let me think—There must have been a Change,
A Revolution in the Source of Things.
The former Chain of Beings is dissolv'd:
Effects roll backward, and direct their Causes,
And Nature is no more. Thou hoary Wretch,
Tear thy white Locks, abandon ev'ry Hope,
Renounce Humanity and all its Tyes.
Duty and Virtue, Gratitude and Love,
Forsook the World, when my *Hellena* fled.
May Order ne'er return to bless Mankind;
Let Discord rage, ne'er let Affections meet;
But Parents Curse, and Children disobey;
Or either's Kindness be repaid with Hate.
'Till ev'ry Child, and ev'ry Sire on Earth,
Be in each other curs'd, as me and mine.

               Enter Visier.

    Vis. Not yet at Rest?
    Am.   A Parent and at Rest!—
    Vis. The Christians have storm'd the Trenches toward the West,
Unless our Presence animate the Troops
All will be lost.
    Am.   *Hellena*'s lost already!
    Vis. Sure *Amasie* has fail'd, and *Scanderbeg*
Is come upon us to revenge th' Attempt.

    Am. 'Tis well. Wak'd from my Lethargy of Grief,   30
I yet may reach his Heart.
    Vis.   Regard your Health,
And leave the Business of this Night to us;
A burning Fever rages in your Blood.   [*Allarm.*
    Am. Fame calls me forth. Again I hear her Voice;
Earth shakes, and Heaven reverberates the Sound.   35
Affrighted Night sits trembling on her Throne;
Tumult has driven Silence from her Confines,
And half her Empire's lost. When Glory calls,
Shall Age or Sickness keep me from the Field?
No; in Spite of both I'll die like *Amurath* yet,   40
Like what I've liv'd, a Soldier and a King.   [*Exit.*
    Vis. He's desperate and will not be oppos'd.   [*Exit.*

SCENE III.

Turkish *Camp.*

Alarm, Soldiers flying.

Soldiers within. Fly, fly; Scanderbeg, Scanderbeg;
                Fly, fly.

Enter Amurath *and* Visier, *meeting the Rout.*

    Am. Turn back you Slaves.
    Soldiers within.   Fly, fly; *Scanderbeg,* fly!
    Am. Ah! Cowards, Villains! doth his Name affright you?
Are there such Terrors in an empty Sound?
And is my Rage contemn'd? but you shall find   5
Death is as certain from my Arm as his.
    Vis. O spare your faithful Slaves! What can Men do
Against a Power, invincible, like Heaven's?
    Am. And must it be, like Heaven's, eternal too?
    Vis. Retire, my Lord, into the inner Camp,   10
And there securely wait a better Hour:
For this is the *Epirot's.*
    Am.   Slave, thou liest!
This Hour is mine: I'll triumph o'er him yet.
This Hour his Friend and Mistress both shall die.
The Royal Brute, tho' in the Hunter's Toils,   15

  (v. ii)   36 Throne;] ~; Like G (*later state, in which catchword has been moved and appended to this*
line)   41SD [*Exit.*] W1; *not in* G   42SD [*Exit.*] W1; *not in* G   (v. iii) 12a *Epirot's*]
D; *Epirots* G   15 Hunter's] W1 (*hunter's*); Hunters G

Pierc'd with a thousand Wounds is still a Lion;
Dreadful in Death and dang'rous to the last   [*Exeunt.*

SCENE IV.

Althea*'s Apartment.*

Al. Was ever Night like this? what Terrors have
I past? and, O! what Terrors yet surround me?
A loud deaf'ning Sound, that seem'd the Voice
Of a chased Multitude, or many Waters
Vex'd to a Storm, first spread thro' all the Camp;
Then Shrieks and Cries and Yellings of Despair;
Mix'd with the Shouts of Victory and Joy.
Sure Sleep has left all Eyes, as well as mine.
Fate is at work; I sink beneath my Fears.
Since I have known a Danger worse than Death
My Courage has forsook me.

Enter Aranthes.

               Ha! who comes
At this late Hour? Protect me, righteous Heaven!
   Ar. Why, my *Althea*! dost thou fly thy Father?
   Al. Sure 'tis his Voice! O gracious Heaven! it is,
It is my Father.—Most unlook'd for Joy!
   Ar. Do I once more behold thee, my *Althea*!
   Al. To whose bless'd Bounty do we owe this Meeting?
   Ar. Thou dearest earthly Bliss, this Moment's our's,
No Matter how attain'd; I have thee now
In my fond Arms, and wou'd indulge my Joy,
Nor think how soon 'twill end. Why shou'd poor Mortals,
To trouble born, anticipate their Pains?
   Al. I can't conceal my Fears: If you again
Must leave me here, the Sun in all its Course,
Sees not a Wretch so lost as poor *Althea*.
   Ar. Alas! why will you urge me to disclose
What wou'd, tho' I were silent, soon be known.
The wrathful Sultan has pronounc'd our Death.
Yes, I am come to die with thee, my Child!
   Al. Then we shall part no more.
My Soul's at Peace—Forgive, O righteous Heaven!
My weak Distrust of thy Almighty Power,

Thy Kindness and Protection. O my Father!
I wish'd t'have died alone; yet at your Death,
I must not, dare not murmur or complain;   35
Since Heaven with you permits me to descend,
Pure and unspotted to the peaceful Grave.
    Ar. Heroick Maid! O most exalted Virtue.   [*Aside, weeping.*
    Al. Why do you hide your Face, why turn you from me?
Be not surpriz'd, nor charge me with Unkindness.   40
There is, my dearest Father! one Calamity,
Tho' sure but one, by far more dreadful
Ev'n than thy Death—O speak, speak to me, Sir!
    Ar. Good Heav'n! my Joy's too great;—I cannot speak.
Tears must relieve me, or my Heart will burst.   45
I thank thee, Heaven! I have not liv'd in vain.
This happy Hour o'erpays an Age of Sorrow.
My Child! my Life! my Soul! my dear *Althea*!
Thy bright Example fires my Emulation;
Thou hast the Start, but must not bear away   50
The Victor's Palm alone, and shame thy Father.
No, my *Althea*! to that bounteous Hand
Which made thee what thou art, and made thee mine,
Without the least Reluctance, I'll resign thee.—
And see the Tryal comes.   55

           Enter K. Aga *and Mutes.*

    Aga. Forgive, fair Princess, a devoted Slave,   [*Kneeling.*
Who know no Will, but his imperial Lord's;
No Merit, but Obedience. Cou'd my Tears
Have mov'd the Sultan, I had been excused
This fatal Visit.
    Al.   *Kisler Aga*, rise;   60
Spite of thy Office, thou hast a human Soul.
What are thy Master's Orders? Art thou come
A second Time to my Deliv'rance?
    Aga.   If
Death, sudden, violent and immature,
Be a Deliverance; you will soon be free.   65
    Al. To Minds prepar'd, Death strip'd of all its Terrors,
In any Form, at any Hour is welcome.
    Aga. Whether the Sultan, raging for the Loss
Of his lov'd Daughter, thinks that other's Pain,
In the same Kind, wou'd mitigate his own;   70

        (v. iv)   41 is,] W1; ~‸ G

Or from some other Cause, I cannot say;
But he has order'd that the Lady first
Shou'd suffer Death, her Father being present.—
I see you're mov'd.
    Ar.   I am:—But 'tis with Scorn
Of your proud Master's Impotence and Malice.
Alas! I'm not to learn my Child is mortal.
    Aga. These eager Blood Hounds growl at my Delay,
And will, perhaps, accuse me to the Sultan.
    Al. Obey the Tyrant, let them do their Office.
    Aga. I must; but Heaven can tell with what Reluctance.
The only Favour in my Power to grant,
Is the sad Choice of dying by the Bowstring,
The fatal Poynard, or this pois'nous Draught.
    Al. Give me the Bowl. Death, this Way, seems less frightful,
Than from the Hands of rude and barbarous Men.
    Ar. Farewell, my Child!
    Al.   Assist me with your Prayers.
    Ar. My Prayers have been incessant as thy own,
And both are heard—Fear not—thy Crown's prepar'd;
And Heav'n, with all its Glories, lies before thee:
Millions of Angels wait to guard the Passage;
Thou can'st not miss thy way.
    Al.   Shou'd Heav'n preserve you?—
Shou'd you live to see him?—commend me to
My Lord—Tell him, that I die his—That Heaven,
Which calls me now, is only lov'd beyond him—
That I'm not lost—That we shall meet again.—
Bid him not grieve.—   [*Allarm.*

Enter Scanderbeg, *&c.*

He flies to Althea.

    Scan. Away you sacrilegious Slaves—She lives—
I have her warm and panting in my Arms—
Lift up thy Eyes, dearer to mine than Light—
O let me hear the Musick of thy Voice,
Lest I shou'd doubt I come too late to save thee,
And Discord seize my Soul.
    Al.   Surprize is dumb.
So sudden a Transition who can bear?
My Thoughts were all just reconcil'd to Death,

(v. iv) 84 Death, this Way,] *Ed.*; ~, ~ ~_∧ G

But thou hast call'd them back. The Love of Life,   105
That seem'd extinguish'd in me, now returns.
O! if there is a Happiness on Earth,
Here I must find it, here and only here.
    Scan. Aranthes too!—he lives!—Consummate Joy!
    Ar. And lives by thee, thou glorious happy Youth!   110
O let me press thee in my longing Arms—
My Child too!—My *Althea*!—
    Al.   O my Father!
    Ar. Compleat Felicity!
    Al.   O dangerous Bliss!   [*Weeps.*
    Scan. Why weeps my Life?
    Al.   Some have their Portion here;
Flatt'ring Prosperity has ruin'd Thousands,   115
Whom Death with all its Terrors cou'd not shake.
    Scan. Thy pious Fears shall guard us from that Danger.
    Al. Is not the Glory of both Worlds too much
For frail, imperfect Mortals to expect?
    Scan. Our Happiness, tho' great, is far from perfect;   120
Since she, the fair unfortunate *Hellena*,
To whom next Heav'n we owe it, is no more.
I cannot blame your Tears; this is no time
To tell the mournful Tale, that must whene'er
Remember'd, make me sad, tho' crown'd with Victory,   125
And in thy Arms. *Croia*, reliev'd, expects us:
My grateful Subjects will for thy Deliv'rance
Express more Joy, than that their Foes are fled.

        Enter Paulinus, *and the* Sultan, *Prisoner.*

    Paul. Hail glorious King! Your Conquest is compleat;
Behold Ambitious *Amurath* your Captive.   130
    Scan. Take off his Chains.
    Am.   What Pageantry is this?
    Scan. Sound a Retreat; since none resist, let War,
And Slaughter cease. It grieves my Soul to think
The Crimes of One shou'd cost Mankind so dear.
    Paul. Sir, how will you dispose the cruel Tyrant?   135
    Scan. Give him his Liberty, and leave him here
Till he shall think it proper to retire.
Such of his Subjects as attend him now,
Or shall repair hither to do him Service,
Shall all be safe. His lovely, virtuous Daughter,   140

(v. iv)   110 Youth!] ~ᴧ G (*earlier state*)   124 whene'er] D, W1; when e'er, G

Worthy a better Race and happier Fate,
Preserv'd my Life.
    Am.   Dogs! Slaves! will none dispatch me!
Must I hear this yet be compell'd to live?
    Scan. Unhappy Man! how will he bear the rest?
When Justice strikes let guilty Mortals tremble   14
And all revere her Power, but none insult
The miserable. Her impartial Sword
Scorns to assist Man's selfish, low Revenge:
T'avoid her Anger let us shun the Thought.
Be witness, Heaven! I pity and forgive him.   [*Exeunt* Scanderbeg, 15
                                  Aranthes, *and* Althea.

    Am. Can this be true! Am I cast down from that
Majestick Height, where like an earthly God,
For more than half an Age, I sate enthron'd,
To the abhor'd Condition of a Slave?
A pardon'd Slave! What! live to be forgiven!   1^
And all this brought upon me by *Hellena*!
Shou'd our Prophet return to Earth and swear it
I'd tell him to his Face that he was perjured.
Hell wants the Power and Heaven wou'd never curse
To that Degree a doating, fond, old Man.—   1^
What make my Child! my loving, gentle Child!
The Instrument and Author of my Ruin!

           Enter Visier, *Officers and* Amasie.

    Vis. Beg them to halt; blast not a Parent's Eye
With such a Sight.
    Am.   What Sight? but 'tis no Matter;
There's nothing left for me to hope or fear.   1^
    Vis. A mourning Troop of Christians from their Camp
In solemn Pomp's arriv'd; who, bath'd in Tears,
(What En'my cou'd refrain?) attend a Chariot,
That bears *Hellena* bleeding, pale and dead.
    Am. False *Mahomet*! [*Swoons.*]
    Off.   Our Royal Master's dead!   1^
    Vis. No! he revives; Alas! he's not so happy!
    Am. I saw *Amasie.*
    Vis.   Here the Traytor stands,
By *Scanderbeg* committed to your Mercy.
    Ama. Hellena did prevent me,—
    Am.   Damn'd Apostate!

(v. iv) 162+SD Visier,] D; ~‿ G   174b Apostate!] ~‿ G (*later state*)

I've heard enough and have no time to lose.—   175
See him impal'd alive; we'll let him know
As much of Hell as can be known on Earth,   [*Exit* Amasie.
And go from Pain to Pain. Where is my Son?
   Vis. Fled towards *Adrianople*.
   Am.   He doth well:
Death has o'ertook me here. Lord of so many   180
Fair, spacious Kingdoms, in a hostile Land,
Oppress'd with Age, Misfortunes, Grief and Shame,
Amurath breaths his last; and leaves his Bones
To beg from Foes an ignominious Grave.
False or ungrateful Prophet! Have I spread   185
Fell Devastation over half the Globe,
To raise thy Crescent's Pale, uncertain Light,
Above the Christians glowing, Crimson Cross,
In hoary Age to be rewarded thus!—
When the *Hungarian* King had broke his Faith;   190
Distress'd, to his own Prophet I appeal'd,
A Stranger, and an Enemy; he did me Right;
Restor'd lost Vict'ry to my flying Troops,
And gave the perjur'd Monarch to my Sword.
But I have done—Cou'dst thou repent, there's nothing   195
In thy Power worth my Acceptance now.
Glory, to thee I've liv'd, but pining Grief
Robs thee of half the Honour of my Death.
Osmyn, and you my other faithful Chiefs,
The poor Remains of all the mighty Host   200
I brought to this curs'd Siege, this Grave of my Renown,
If you return, and live to see my Son,
Bid him remember how his Father fell;
Bid him ne'er sheath the Sword,
Till my diminish'd Fame shine forth and blaze anew   205
In his Revenge—Revenge me—Oh! Revenge.   [*Dies.*
   Vis. Eclips'd and in a Storm our Sun is set:
And now, methinks, as when our Prophet fled,
Terror shou'd seize on each believing Heart.
Let some inform the King—This was his Fate;   210
'Tis ours to be left without a Guide.
Disperse, wander, away; our Shephard's lost.   [*Exeunt.*

(v. iv)   176 know] ~! G (*later state*)   178 Pain. Where] W1 (pain); ~. | ~ G, *which prints*
as two lines   179a *Adrianople*] D; Andrianople G   199 *Osmyn*] *Ed.*; Osmin G
205 anew] D; a-new W1; a new G. *See Commentary*   206 Revenge—Revenge me—Oh!]
Ed.; ~-~-~! G   212SD [*Exeunt.*] W1; ʌ~. G, *which prints as catchword*

SCENE V.

Enter Scanderbeg, Aranthes, Althea, Paulinus, *and Guards.*

Scan. That you are free and happy I rejoice.
If I have faithfully discharged my Trust
I'm well rewarded here.
    Paul.   O royal Sir!
Your Happiness is ours; this virtuous Princess
An equal Blessing to your self and People.   5
    2d Off. To say each Subject loves you as himself,
Is less than Truth: We love you as we ought;
As a free People shou'd a Patriot King.
    Scan. This is to reign; this is to be a King.
Who can controul his Power, who rules the Will   10
Of those o'er whom he reigns? or count his Wealth,
Who has the Hearts of Subjects that abound.
Was ever Prince so absolute as I?
    Paul. Or ever Subjects so intirely free?
Whose Duty's Interest, and Obedience Choice.   15
    Scan. For this alone was Government ordain'd;
And Kings are Gods on Earth but while, like Gods,
They do no ill, but reign to bless Mankind.
May proud, relentless *Amurath*'s Misfortunes
Teach future Monarchs to avoid his Crimes.   20
    Th' impious Prince, who does all Laws disown,
    Yet claims from Heaven a Right to hold his Throne,
    Blasphemes that Power, which righteous Kings obey;
    For Justice and Mercy bound ev'n th' Almighty's Sway. [*Exeunt.*

End of the Fifth Act.

FINIS.

EPILOGUE

Spoken by

Mrs. *Clive.*

The serious Bus'ness of the Night being over,
Pray, Ladies, your Opinion of our Lover?
Will you allow the Man deserves the Name,
Who quits his Mistress to preserve—his Fame?
And what was Fame in that Romantick Age?—   5
But sure such Whims ne'er were but on the Stage.
A Statesman rack his Brains, a Soldier fight—
Merely to do an injur'd People Right.—
What! serve his Country, and get nothing by 't!
Why, ay, says Bays, George Castriot *was the Man;*   10
'Tis a known Truth—Believe him those who can.
Not but we've Patriots too, tho' I am told
There's a vast Diff'rence 'twixt the new and old:
Say, theirs cou'd fight, I'm sure that ours can—scold.
But to the Glory of the present Race,   15
No stubborn Principles their Worth debase;
Patriots when out, are Courtiers when in Place.
So, vice versa, *turn a Courtier out,*
No Weather-Cock more swiftly veers about.
His Country now, good Man! claims all his Care.—   20
Who'd see it plunder'd?—that's deny'd his Share.

   Since Courtiers and Anticourtiers both have shown
That by the Publick Good they mean their own·;
What if each Briton, *in his Private Station,*
Should try to bilk those, who imbroil the Nation;   25
Quit either Faction, and, like Men, unite
To do their King and injured Country Right:
Both have been wrong'd: Prevent their guilty Joy,
Who wou'd your mutual Amity destroy.
Wou'd you preserve your Freedom? guard his Throne,   30
Who makes your Peace and Happiness his own.
Wou'd you be grateful? let your Monarch know
Which Way you wou'd be best, and make him so.

But soft! methinks, I hear some Fops complain;
Who came prepared to give the Ladies Pain,   35
That they have dress'd and spent—Gad's Curse—three Hours in vain.
No Hints obscene, improved by their broad Stare,
Have given Confusion to the tortured Fair.
We own the Charge. Let Monsieur Harlequin
And his trim Troop your loose Applauses win: 40
Too much already has each modest Ear
Been there insulted; we'll protect them here.

Fatal Curiosity

INTRODUCTION

SOURCES

WITH *Fatal Curiosity*, Lillo turned again to domestic drama: a 'true' story, English in setting and derived from an old, moralizing tale. He did not, however, attempt to write a second *London Merchant*. His intentions were traditional rather than experimental, to create a tragedy in verse, consciously classical in shape but illustrating Christian concepts.

The original source of the plot is very probably a black-letter pamphlet, *Newes From Perin in Cornwall: Of A most Bloody and unexampled Murther very lately committed by a Father on his owne Sonne (who was lately returned from the Indyes) at the Instigation of a mercilesse Step-mother* . . . , printed in London in 1618. However, the version of this story with which Lillo must have worked is the abbreviated account given in *Sanderson's Annals*, 1656, and reprinted in *Frankland's Annals*, 1681.[1] That Lillo used one of these histories is clearly indicated by his reference to the arrest and execution of Ralegh, a report of which immediately precedes in both *Annals* the account of the 'Monstrous Murder in Cornwall'.[2] Moreover, Lillo follows Frankland and Sanderson in substituting the young man's own mother for the stepmother of the pamphlet.

---

[1] William Sanderson's compendium of events, historical and anecdotal, of the reigns of Queen Mary and James VI of Scotland, and Thomas Frankland's similar history, much of it taken from Sanderson, of the reigns of James I and Charles I, published anonymously, but usually known as *Frankland's Annals*. The account of the murder appears in Sanderson, pp. 463–5, and in Frankland, p. 33.

[2] Cf. I. i. 30–47a. In the 'Postscript' to the text of his adaptation of *Fatal Curiosity* (London, 1783), George Colman notes: 'The story, on which this tragedy is founded, is, I believe, at present no where extant, except in a folio volume, printed in the year 1681, and entitled *The Annals of King James and King Charles the First. Both of happy memory*. . . . They are published anonymously yet are generally known by the name of *Frankland's Annals*' (p. 49). After reprinting the story as it is given in the *Annals*, Colman adds: 'The historical fact, immediately preceding this dreadful narrative, is the fate of Sir Walter Raleigh, which accounts for the author's having, in the original play, introduced the mention of him in the first scene of the tragedy' (p. 52).

In his plot, Lillo follows closely the spare outline given in his source, a version of the oft-told tale of the impoverished old couple who kill and rob a young stranger only to discover, too late, that he is their long-lost son. Lillo reduces the relatively extensive account of the young wanderer's adventures to brief reports sufficient to prove the young man's good fortune in surviving unscathed a series of hazardous adventures. He alters certain details, such as the youth's service with pirates, so that there will be no queston about the generally admirable intentions of this son who has endeavoured with success to repair his family's fortune by practising 'honest commerce'[3] in a way that Barnwell's master would commend.[4] Lillo has the 'stranger' first reveal his identity not to his sister but to his fiancée, who has faithfully waited seven years for his return. And he compresses the time-scheme so that the action of the drama, occurring in the few hours between sunset and mid-evening of one day, rushes towards its awful conclusion with the unity prescribed for regular tragedy.

This onrush of events, Lillo's dramatization of the plot outlined in his source, actually makes up only the latter half of *Fatal Curiosity*. Act I and the first two scenes of Act II are given over to preparation for it. Lillo never shifts focus away from the three characters, Old Wilmot, his wife, and his son, who will enact the terrible drama of murder and suicide, but before they are brought together each is introduced and his nature, with its relation to the moral bases of the tragedy, is made clear. To accomplish this, the playwright invents a series of subsidiary characters, prominent only in the early scenes and denouement, who serve primarily as confidants and foils for the three Wilmots. The play begins with a demonstration of the misanthropy of Old Wilmot, his hopelessness and cynicism set off by the idealism of young Randal, a loyal although long unpaid servant who urges the moral values of adversity as the proof of true virtue. The pride of Old Wilmot's wife, Agnes—impatience, and a contemptuousness born of humiliation that 'increasing, aggravates [her] grief'[5]—is made clear in a scene with Charlot, the unshakeably faithful fiancée of her son. These introductions of the disillusioned elder Wilmots frame Charlot's conversation with her friend Maria[6] in a scene that is almost a mirror-image of Old Wilmot's encounter with Randal; Maria, as pessimistically sceptical as the old man, sets out to urge Charlot to accept a rich suitor's offer of marriage but is brought to recognize and admire her friend's constancy and her faith in providence. Charlot's steadfastness in adversity—'I'll not despair, Patience shall cherish hope'[7]—is the ideal by which the Wilmots are to be judged. Her regretful

---

[3] I. iii. 67.

[4] Young Randal even more strongly echoes Thorowgood's ideal of enlightened mercantilism; see II. ii. 9–15.

[5] I. ii. 222.

[6] In Lillo's original script Maria may have been Charlot's maid, and the part was so played in some later productions. At the Haymarket, the part was played by a well-known singer, Miss Karver; it seems likely that the song (I. ii. 22–37) was written for her and that her relationship to Charlot was left vague (McBurney, *FC*, p. xiii).   [7] I. ii. 51b–52.

contemplation of the distress created by proud impatience—'The tempest must prevail 'till we are lost'[8]—sets the stage for the entrance of Young Wilmot, lately escaped from a tempest at sea and about to encounter the tempest of ill-directed passion that will destroy him. Again Lillo provides a useful foil in Young Wilmot's friend, Eustace, an 'other better Wilmot'.[9] Eustace's warnings about 'torment[ing] ourselves . . . With what shall never be'[10] underscore Young Wilmot's excessive exercise of his emotions as he imagines the utmost intensities of joy and grief that might be the outcome of his search for Charlot and his parents. Lillo further demonstrates the young man's too eager 'refinement' of emotion in his reunion with Charlot, which Young Wilmot prolongs by allowing her to think he is a stranger come to tell her of her lover's death. For Young Wilmot, this sentimentally rewarding scene serves as a rehearsal for the even more intensely melodramatic reunion he plans for his parents. Lillo designs his tragedy to illustrate the danger of such indulgence, which involves, in effect, playing at being providence, a practice specifically condemned by the virtuous Randal when Young Wilmot asks his aid in arranging the homecoming drama: 'You grow luxurious in your mental pleasures.'[11]

This preparation for the tragic action is presented economically, and there is enough in the way of characterization to interest an audience. But it is primarily a matter of setting the stage. Fielding, in his prologue to the play, points accurately to the design and dynamics of the drama when he offers a special word of encouragement to the audience: 'Thro' the first Acts a kind Attention lend, The growing Scene shall force you to attend.'[12] When Lillo has carefully defined the forces that drive his major characters, he brings the trio together to play out, swiftly and with the spareness of his source, the inevitable consequences of their fatal combination.

The playwright clearly looked to classical tragedy as the model for this latter part of his play and for the intimations of catastrophe, the double-edged lines and foreboding dreams, which accent his opening scenes with irony. The power of the play's sense of fatality has regularly been noticed, and certainly the inexorable swiftness and overwhelming completeness of the catastrophe bring the drama to a dark resolution, disturbing in its implications. As early as 1781 the gentleman-scholar of Greek, James Harris, praised *Fatal Curiosity* for its evocation, unique in its era, of the pity and terror of ancient tragedy.[13] Yet Lillo

---

[8] I. ii. 223.   [9] II. i. 156.   [10] I. iii. 109–10a.   [11] II. ii. 76.
[12] ll. 19–20.
[13] James Harris, *Philological Enquiries in Three Parts* (London, 1781), i. 156–7:

'The fatal murder is *perpetrating*, or at least but *barely perpetrated*, when *Charlotte* [*sic*] arrives, *full of Joy* to inform them, that the stranger within their walls was their *long lost son*.

'What a DISCOVERY? What a REVOLUTION? How irrestibly are the *Tragic* Passions of *Terror* and *Pity* excited.

''Tis no small Praise to this *affecting Fable*, that it so much resembles that of . . . the *Oedipus Tyrannus*. In both Tragedies that, which *apparently* leads to *Joy*, *leads* on its completion to *Misery*; both Tragedies concur in the *horror* of their DISCOVERIES; and both in those great outlines of a

attempts not only the lean strength of classical tragedy, but also the instruction of Christian drama; his sources are doctrinal as well as theatrical. The elements of fatality in Lillo's drama are a function of—indeed, made possible by—the moral deficiencies of his major characters, in Lillo's terms sins. The playwright does not dramatize the wilful fatality of the gods,[14] nor does he portray the Wilmots as morality figures of unrelieved evil. Each of the three characters has his weakness—in combination fatal—and all are shown to have commendable qualities or, in the case of Agnes, to have been subject to circumstances that extenuate guilt.[15] Old Wilmot's cynicism and Agnes's pride are forms of despair.[16] The elder Wilmots, like their son, wrongly attempt to manipulate providence; providence, in turn, destroys them. Their very special hubris, if it can be so called, consists in the failure of that patience, demonstrated by Charlot, which constitutes faith.[17]

Young Wilmot's 'curiosity' is strikingly similar to the luxurious refinement of emotion characteristic of the men of feeling who figure particularly in sentimental fiction, but in this dramatic and moral context it is neither

---

truly TRAGIC REVOLUTION, where (according to the nervous sentiment of *Lillo* himself) we see

> —*the two extremes of Life,*
> *The highest Happiness, and deepest Woe,*
> *With all the sharp and bitter Aggravations*
> *Of such a vast transition—*'

(See also i. 154–8, 169–72.)

This view of the reversal in Lillo's play as comparable to the fatal catastrophe of Sophoclean tragedy has persisted, little changed, among 20th-cent. commentators, e.g. Burgess (p. 18): '[In] the immense disparity between cause and effect in the catastrophe . . . *Fatal Curiosity* is reminiscent of classical tragedy; the devastation wrought is as complete, as overwhelming, and as arbitrary as that brought about by the occasional wilful intervention of the gods in the affairs of men.'

[14] In Germany, in the latter part of the 18th cent., *Fatal Curiosity* was taken as a significant model for the heavily ironic and fatalistic *Schicksalstragödie*, and association of Lillo's play with this movement has led to considerable misunderstanding of its moral structure. Ward (p. liii) saw in the play the 'force of destiny . . . operating to all intents and purposes independently of character', an idea tacitly accepted by Nicoll (p. 121) and further developed by Bernbaum (p. 173), who describes Young Wilmot's 'virtuous life and generous hopes . . . destroyed by a calamity for which malign fate is held responsible'. Burgess (p. 18) suggests that elements of the play 'would seem to reflect a belief on Lillo's part that there is a malevolence at large which far transcends the contrived evil of the sentimentalist's world'. However, like McBurney (*FC*, pp. xxi–xxiii), who rejects interpretations of the play which stress the influence of a fatality beyond human motivation, Burgess also sees the tragedy as rooted in 'individual guilt and personal responsibility' (p. 19).

[15] In accusing her husband of responsibility for the ills which have led her to contemplate robbery and murder, Agnes recalls Millwood's confrontation with Thorowgood (see commentary, III. i. 130–4a).

[16] Lillo's characterizations and the thematic structure of his play have been analysed persuasively in terms of traditional Christian morality and Calvinistic doctrine by deBoer (pp. 74–84).

[17] McBurney (*FC*, p. xxiii) suggests that the character of Young Wilmot is flawed not only by his 'luxurious sensibility' but also by 'the classic sin of *hubris* in his presumption of continuing good fortune'. In fact, the young man errs in forecasting, alternately, the extremes of ill fortune as well as good. Lillo makes the point clear in a speech given to Eustace: 'Blind to events, we reason in the dark, And fondly apprehend what none e'er found, Or ever shall, pleasure and pain unmixt' (I. iii. 106–8).

commendable nor sympathetically portrayed.[18] Indeed, except for Charlot's use of a mournful song to complement her grief—an interlude which conceivably was inserted to show to advantage the musical talents of the actress who first played Charlot's friend, Maria[19]—the playwright restricts the outpourings of sentiment in *Fatal Curiosity* to those characters whose excesses of emotion make the tragedy. In this restraint, as in the economy of plotting and relative complexity of character, the play stands well above Lillo's other work, marking him, in Nicoll's opinion, as 'a genius of no common rank'.[20]

In composing this artistically most successful of his plays, Lillo drew directly and indirectly upon a range of theatrical traditions and playwrights. It is conceivable that he looked to specific Greek and Roman models.[21] James Harris compared the play with *Oedipus Tyrannus*,[22] and the imagery with which Charlot describes pride recalls Haemon's warning to Creon in the *Antigone*.[23] Such parallels more likely show acquaintance with a dramatic tradition than reference to a particular speech or play. Lillo is undoubtedly indebted to *Macbeth* for certain lines and situations, in particular his handling of Agnes as she urges and then observes the murder. However, other possibly Shakespearian echoes, such as Old Wilmot's Hamlet-like meditations on life and death, probably indicate only Lillo's familiarity with the conventions and rhetoric of Shakespeare's theatre. Situations recalling the plays of Otway and other Restoration dramatists are similarly unspecific.[24]

The influence of a playwright who had the opportunity to influence more directly Lillo's shaping of his play cannot now be measured. Davies, who acted

[18] Young Wilmot's resemblance to the conventional men of sentiment has led a number of commentators to misinterpret Lillo's development of the character. Bernbaum, in particular, sees Young Wilmot as the sympathetic portrait of a man whose sentimentality 'is one of the most precious virtues in a man of feeling' (pp. 174–5). Burgess, sensing an ironic intention on the part of the playwright, pursues a middle course, concluding that while 'in having Young Wilmot act as he does, Lillo may indeed have been seeking to exploit the opportunities for sentimental effects inherent in his plot . . . the weight of the evidence suggests that, through Young Wilmot, Lillo was rejecting the cult of sensibility as a practical or acceptable guide' (p. 19).

[19] See n. 6 above.

[20] p. 122.

[21] The catalogue for the sale of Lillo's books and those of 'Another Gentleman' (Bodleian Library, Mus. Bibl. III 8° 81) suggests that Lillo was familiar with Sophocles, Euripides, and Seneca. Cf. William McBurney, 'What George Lillo Read: A Speculation', *Huntington Library Quarterly*, xxix (May 1966), 275–86. Certainly the scene in which young Wilmot allows Charlot to take him for a stranger who has come to report her lover's death recalls Orestes' encounter with his sister in the *Electra* of Sophocles, though the motives that lead the young men to practise these deceptions are very different.

[22] pp. 156–8.

[23] I. ii. 224–31. McBurney (*FC*, p. xx) suggests that the couplets which end Lillo's scenes 'are vestiges of sententious choruses which comment on past and future actions'. Similar rhymed passages appear in Lillo's other plays (see *The London Merchant*, Introduction, n. 35).

[24] Cf. McBurney (*FC*, pp. xiii–xiv), who notices a number of possible references to Shakespeare and suggests parallels with various Restoration tragedies, in particular Otway's *Venice Preserved* and *The Orphan*. However, other plays—for example, Aaron Hill's *Fatal Extravagance*, given several performances during the 1730s, among them one in Feb. 1736—include characters and situations more closely matched in Lillo's play, and it seems likely that Lillo was influenced more by conventions than by particular works.

in the first performances of *Fatal Curiosity*, remarks that Henry Fielding not only carefully rehearsed the play but revised it as well.[25] The extent to which he did in fact edit or change Lillo's text is not known. Some adjustments would inevitably have been made during rehearsals, but Fielding himself gives Lillo full credit for the extraordinary power he found in the tragedy.[26] In characterization and language, *Fatal Curiosity* is clearly Lillo's own. So too is the lesson dramatized in the seemingly unavoidable catastrophe, actually the result of human error when providence intended better. Lillo's theology, and his view of the extraordinary difficulties which confront even the best of those who seek to live morally acceptable lives, are implicit in the complex if thoroughly Calvinistic mixture of hope and darkness which characterizes the resolution of his tragedy: 'Mankind may learn . . . The most will not'.[27] Indeed, this sombre truth, dramatized in the context of the society to which the playwright and his audience belonged, stands as the most intense statement of a belief fundamental to George Lillo's efforts to create an intensely moving didactic theatre.

PERFORMANCE AND RECEPTION

Fatal Curiosity was first acted at the theatre in the Haymarket on Thursday, 27 May 1736.[28] Davies, who played Young Wilmot, suggests that Lillo 'had applied to the managers of the more regular theatres, and had been rejected'.[29] Certainly Covent Garden had shown little interest in Lillo's plays: except for three performances of *The London Merchant* given in August 1733 and one performance of a shortened version of *Silvia* presented in March 1736, Lillo's work had not been seen at the theatre.[30] At Drury Lane the memory of the unsuccessful production of *The Christian Hero* was no doubt fresh in the minds of manager and actors. Lillo may well have been, as Davies reports, 'reduced to the necessity of having his play acted at an inferior Play-house, and by persons not so well skilled in their professions as the players of the established Theatres'.

This necessity can also be seen as a stroke of good fortune. At the Haymarket his play was taken in hand by Henry Fielding, an energetic manager who 'had a just sense of [the] author's merit', 'took upon himself the management of the play', instructed 'the actors how to do justice to their parts', may have had a hand in revising the script, certainly provided the prologue, and 'warmly recommended the play to his friends, and to the public'.[31] Fielding's genuine admiration of the play is attested by a piece he published in the *Champion* some four years after his production;[32] *Fatal Curiosity*, he writes, 'is a Master-Piece in

---

[25] *Life*, p. xvii.
[26] See Performance and Reception, below.
[27] III. i. 301a–301b.
[28] *London Stage, 1729–1747*.
[29] *Life*, p. xv.
[30] *London Stage, 1729–1747*, i. 311 and 561–2.
[31] Davies, *Life*, pp. xv–xvii.
[32] 26 Feb. 1739/40.

its Kind, and inferior only to Shakespeare's best Pieces [and] gives [its author] a Title to be called the best Tragick Poet of his Age'.

Lillo attended rehearsals, offering, when requested, 'his opinion how a particular sentiment should be uttered by the actor'.[33] Despite Davies's disparaging view of the company of which he was himself a member, it seems likely that some of the parts were more than adequately acted. Charlotte Charke, who played Agnes, was at this time an experienced and capable young actress, however exotic her later career: she found her part rewarding and was so confident of her performance in it that in 1742 and again in 1755 she chose to revive *Fatal Curiosity* when, in difficult straits, she staged benefit evenings for herself.[34] In her autobiography she gives no details of her own first performance in the play but does report that '*John Roberts*, a very judicious Speaker, discovered a Mastership in the Character of the Husband'.[35] Of Davies's acting she has nothing to say.

In the Haymarket's advertisements, the play was listed as *Guilt Its Own Punishment; or, Fatal Curiosity*, a title that neatly pinpoints the double moral of Lillo's play. It was described as 'a True Story in Common Life . . . the Incidents extremely affecting'; lest this and the name of the author of George Barnwell prove insufficient to draw a good house, the management also announced that 'This is much the coolest House in Town'. As a further inducement, one of Fielding's after-pieces, *Tumble Down Dick*, was included on the bill.[36]

Mrs Charke reports that the actors 'were kindly received by the Audience',[37] and on the day following the first performance the *Daily Advertiser* informed its readers that the play 'was acted . . . with the greatest Applause that has been shewn to any Tragedy for many years. The Scenes of Distress were so artfully work'd up, and so well perform'd, that there scarce remain'd a dry Eye among the Spectators at the Representation; and during the Scene preceding the Catastrophe, an attentive Silence posses'd the whole House, more expressive of an universal Approbation than the loudest Applauses.'[38] Davies, however, says that the play 'met with very little success', adding that 'the public had been satiated with a long run of Pasquin' at the Haymarket.[39] Mrs Charke confirms that *Fatal Curiosity* was brought on when '*Pasquin* began to droop'.[40] Lillo's tragedy was given five successive performances, repeated once on 21 June, then scheduled no more.[41] The playwright's publisher printed no edition of the play.

Fielding did his best to revive the tragedy during the following season, billing it with the first performances of his *Historical Register, for the Year 1736*, which began a successful run on 21 March 1737.[42] Again the *Daily Advertiser* was

---

[33] Davies, *Life*, p. xvi.
[34] *London Stage, 1729–1747*, ii. 1015, and *London Stage, 1747–1776*, i. 490. See also commentary on the dramatis personae.
[35] Charke, *Narrative*, p. 65.
[36] Advertisement quoted in *London Stage, 1729–1747*, i. 588.   [37] Charke, loc. cit.
[38] 28 May, quoted in *London Stage, 1729–1747*, i. 588.   [39] *Life*, p. xxxv.
[40] Charke, p. 64.   [41] *London Stage, 1729–1747*, i. 589–90 *et passim*.
[42] *London Stage, 1729–1747*.

enthusiastic: 'the two new Performances . . . were receiv'd with the greatest Applause ever shown at the Theatre'.[43] Ten more performances of the double bill were presented before mid-April. John Gray brought out an edition of the play, now simply entitled *Fatal Curiosity*. On 13 April, however, *The Historical Register* was announced as the main piece and the tragedy was omitted from the bill. Except for John Roberts's benefit performance on 2 May, *Fatal Curiosity* was not scheduled again, and in June the Licensing Act brought an abrupt end to Fielding's season and his company.[44]

Three performances of *Fatal Curiosity* were offered at Goodman's Fields early in 1741.[45] Mrs Charke gave her benefit performances in 1742 and 1755. The play disappeared from the London stage for more than a quarter of a century and might well have been forgotten had James Harris not published his *Philological Enquiries*, in which he singled out Lillo's drama as the one modern drama which matched in power the tragedies of ancient Greece. Harris's comments, appearing in 1781, set off a series of new editions of *Fatal Curiosity* and a pair of new productions.

The more successful of the revivals was an adaptation devised and staged by George Colman, the elder, for his summer company at the Theatre Royal, Haymarket, in 1782.[46] Colman's alterations were, for the most part, deletions. He reduced the part of Charlot in Act III, omitting altogether her final scene. He also 'hazarded an attempt to correct . . . Some *minute inaccuracies* of language . . . and even in some measure to mitigate the horror of the catastrophe, by the omission of some expressions rather too savage, and by one or two touches of remorse and tenderness'.[47] Towards that end, Agnes's account of the murder was adjusted and made shorter. Colman took heed of Harris's advice 'totally to expunge those *wretched Rhimes*, which conclude many of the Scenes; and which 'tis probable are not from *Lillo*, but from some other hand, willing to conform to an absurd Fashion, *then* practised, but now laid aside'.[48] In one instance, however, he could not bring himself to give up a couplet (I. i. 170–1) 'too beautiful to be displaced'. The production, opening late in June, was offered eleven times before the end of the summer.[49] Colman's Agnes was Katharine Sherry, whose roles at Drury Lane during the preceding season had included Lady Macbeth as well as comic parts calling for similar

[43] 22 Mar., quoted in *London Stage, 1729–1747*, ii. 651.

[44] Ibid., pp. 651–76.   [45] Ibid., pp. 889–94.

[46] If one accepts the account given in the 'Advertisement' included with the printed text of the second adaptation produced during the 1780s, Harris's book stimulated the preparation of two revivals at virtually the same time: 'The idea of this alteration of LILLO's FATAL CURIOSITY, was first conceived from a perusal of the late Mr. *Harris*'s Philological Essays, published in 1780 [*sic*]. It was communicated to Mr. *Colman*, by a friend of the Author's, in Spring 1782; but it seems Mr. *Colman* had, at that time, resolved to bring out *Lillo*'s play at his theatre; which he accordingly did the ensuing summer' (*The Shipwreck: or, Fatal Curiosity* [London, 1784], p. 5).

[47] George Colman, 'Postscript', *Fatal Curiosity . . . with Alterations* (London, 1783), p. 48. Although Colman was the first commentator to note in print (p. 52) that the *Annals* were the source of Lillo's mention of Sir Walter Ralegh, and hence were also the probable source of the story of his play, he chose to omit the Ralegh passage from his adaptation.

[48] Harris, op. cit., p. 172.   [49] *London Stage, 1776–1800*, vol. i, *passim*.

acting strength, among them Marwell and Lady Sneerwell.[50] Old Wilmot was played by Robert Bensley, for well over a decade a principal performer in serious drama in London; dubbed 'roaring Bob' by Garrick, he was none the less cited years later by Lamb as one of the most effective interpreters of high drama, and John Boaden, writing in the 1820s, recalled his portrayal of Old Wilmot in the murder scene as 'terrible and even sublime'.[51]

Covent Garden was less successful when it offered, in 1784, Henry MacKenzie's new adaptation in five acts, *The Shipwreck*. Expanding as well as altering the text, MacKenzie sought 'to remedy . . . a want of connection and increasing interest in the scenes; to afford, from the pressing necessity of the moment, a better apology for *Wilmot*'s commission of the crime, and to shew *Agnes* tempted to it by slower degrees'.[52] The remedies included characterizing Old Wilmot as a beneficent but ruinously generous man of feeling; the appearance of a treacherous one-time steward, who comes to lay claim to the couple's last possessions; and, lest the audience lack matter for tears, the introduction of another new character, the pitiful little son of the old couple's late daughter.[53] These improvements notwithstanding, the new production held the stage for a single night. For at least one member of the audience, however, the evening was not without theatrical rewards: while praising Colman's decision to revive *Fatal Curiosity*, James Boaden reported that he had seen not one but two 'great Old Wilmots in my time', Bensley in Colman's production and John Henderson at Covent Garden.[54]

Colman's production was repeated twice in each of the summer seasons of 1783 and 1784, and once in 1786.[55] The play again disappeared from the London stage, but shortly before the end of the century reappeared for a brief but significant revival. In 1797 Sarah Siddons selected *Fatal Curiosity* as the vehicle for her 'Farewell for the Present Season'. On 1 May, with Kemble in the role of Old Wilmot, she performed the play for an audience which brought the theatre (and the actress, whose benefit it was) box office revenues in the remarkable amount of £618.[56] The production, repeated once on 6 May, was

[50] *London Stage, 1776–1800*, vol. i, *passim*.

[51] *Actors, Actresses*, ii. 36–43; Charles Lamb, *Essays of Elia*, quoted in *London Stage, 1776–1800*, vol. i, p. cxxi; James Boaden, *Memoirs of Mrs. Siddons* (London, 1827), i. 270. Bensley was unquestionably an actor of the old rather than of Garrick's school. Opinions of his portrayal of older characters vary widely. In contrast to Lamb and Boaden, the *Westminster Gazette* labelled him 'the worst Old Man we ever saw', and added that 'the uniform goggle of his eyes, by which he means to express infirmity and distress, is the look of a man in anguish from the colic' (*Actors, Actresses*, ii. 41).

[52] *The Shipwreck: or, Fatal Curiosity . . . Altered from Lillo* (London, 1784), p. 4.

[53] 'The additional character of the *Boy* is introduced, not only to infuse somewhat more of pity into the calamaties of the *Wilmot* family, but to give an opportunity of shewing the distresses resulting from their poverty, on which the pride and delicacy of a more advanced age do not easily allow it to dwell' (*The Shipwreck*, pp. 5–6).

[54] Boaden, loc. cit. Boaden notes that the play was revived 'with the deep interest which formerly attended it' and that, while audiences were less ready to be moved by *The London Merchant* than they had been in former times, response to *Fatal Curiosity* continued to give evidence that 'Of human nature . . . Lillo was as profound a student as even the author of Tom Jones' (i. 268–9).

[55] *London Stage, 1776–1800*, i. 623, 625; ii. 715, 711, 897.

[56] *London Stage, 1776–1880*, iii. 1958–9.

criticized for the elegant scenery and costumes which 'destroyed much of the effect of the tragedy [in which] the characters are supposed to be "steeped in poverty to the very lips"'.[57] However, the high moments in Mrs Siddons's performance as Agnes are reported to have been strikingly effective,[58] and more than sixty years after its initial performances Lillo's drama would seem to have moved the audience with something of the tragic power which Fielding found in it in 1736.

THE TEXT

One edition of *Fatal Curiosity* was published during the author's lifetime and provides the only authoritative text.

First Edition

Lillo's publisher, John Gray, registered his copyright on 2 April 1737. Advertisements in the *Daily Post* indicate that copies of the play were to be available at three in the afternoon of the same day.[59] No fine-paper copies of the edition were advertised and none have come to light. Two issues of the edition were produced, however: the regular London edition and an Irish 'edition' clearly prepared to prevent competition by unauthorized editions actually printed in Dublin. The edition (London imprint) was reissued in Gray's nonce collection of Lillo's plays, c.21 June 1740.

(the following are printed in red: 'FATAL CURIOSITY:', 'NEW THEATRE', 'By Mr. *LILLO.*', and '*LONDON:*').

For the title-page, London issue, see p. 293.

The title-page of the 'Dublin' issue is the same except that the imprint has been reset to read:

DUBLIN: | Printed for *A. Bradly.* at the *Two Bibles* in *Dame-|Street*, and also for *J. Potts* Bookſeller in Belfaſt.

Collation: 8° (4's) A–F⁴ [$2 (− A1) signed]; 24 leaves, pp. *1–5* 6–47 *48*
Contents: A1(*1*) title A1ᵛ(*2*) blank A2(*3*) prologue A2ᵛ(*4*) dramatis personae A3(*5*)–F4(47) text (DH: FATAL CURIOSITY.) F4ᵛ(*48*) advertisement

Comments

Imposition was by half-sheets (work and turn). Collation of multiple copies reveals press corrections in sheets B (inner), D (outer and inner), and F (outer); see Tables of Press Variants. The 'Dublin' issue appears to be made up of

[57] *Monthly Mirror*, May 1797, quoted in *London Stage, 1776–1800*, iii. 1958.
[58] Cf. Henry Crabbe Robinson, *Diary, Reminiscences, and Correspondence*, quoted in *London Stage, 1776–1800*, iii. 1958.
[59] *Daily Post*, 1 Apr. 1737, 'To-morrow, at 3 o'clock will be publish'd . . .'; 2 Apr., 'This Day, at 3 o'clock will be publish'd . . .'. The announcement of 2 Apr. is repeated in the *Daily Post* on 8 and 11 Apr., and in the *Daily Journal* on 6 and 8 Apr.

sheets B–F from the regular run of the London issue. Comparison of copies indicates that except for the substitution of the reset imprint the type for gathering A was not disturbed or removed from the forme before the alternative title-page was printed.

In the main, the edition was well produced, apparently from copy that was clean though very possibly pointed loosely and at times unclear concerning the division of lines of verse. Except for the correction of two misspellings,[60] the press corrections revise punctuation, a necessary task that might well have been carried further in an edition whose rather idiosyncratic and occasionally misleading pointing presents some difficulties for the reader. Characteristically heavy, but in a few instances erratically light, this punctuation resembles the pointing of the first edition of *The Christian Hero*, though the problems are neither as numerous nor as pronounced as those to be found in that earlier edition. Frequently a comma is printed after the subject or subject phrase of a sentence, thus seeming to separate it from the predicate or adjectival phrase to which it relates. At times a semi-colon makes an inordinately heavy break, appearing to cut off a final phrase from the sentence to which it clearly belongs; since the text is marked by several examples of this sort of punctuation, it would seem that the semi-colons were not set in error but represent individualistic styling by the author, editor, or a compositor.[61] Very probably much of the pointing had to be supplied by the compositor(s). The awkwardness and inconsistency of style suggest that punctuation in the manuscript was unclear or the compositor(s) uncertain about their conventions of pointing. A number of confusing commas, for example, may have been set simply because it was customary to supply pointing at the end of a line of verse. At times, however, the heavy pointing suggests a kind of histrionic punctuation intended perhaps to guide the actors in interpreting the lines and conceivably reflects the author's approach to pointing.

The edition includes a number of obvious errors not corrected in any copies examined: a very few accidentals clearly set in error, occasional inconsistencies in speech-headings, the omission of at least one necessary stage direction,[62] a misnumbered scene,[63] and two errors in line-division.[64]

---

[60] One of the adjusted spellings—the substitution of 'Scanderbeg' for 'Scanderburg'—occurs on a page of advertisements included at the end of the edition.

[61] Examples typical of the edition's heavy pointing will be found at I. i. 70, 159; I. ii. 6, 98, 99, 139, 219; and III. i. 146. The present editor considered following the practice of W1, which regularly omits the commas set after the subjects of sentences. However, since the punctuation is characteristic of the first edition and quite regularly maintained, the commas have been retained except in four cases in which this pointing, in the context of other punctuation, markedly distorted the sense of the lines (I. i. 55, I. ii. 163, 168, and II. ii. 25). Similarly, the semi-colons of the copy-text have been reproduced, except at II. ii. 6 and III. i. 147, where the pointing was peculiarly awkward.

[62] III. i. 199SD.

[63] II. iii.

[64] I. ii. 209–10a and III. i. 162. The awkward lining at III. i. 165–71 is apparently the result of confusion in the printer's copy.

Later Reprints

A second edition, set from a copy of Gray's edition, was published by Thomas Davies in 1762. During the same year Davies published the first edition of the adaptation of *Arden of Feversham* attributed to Lillo, and it is possible that this project stimulated him to attempt a new edition of another of the playwright's domestic tragedies. Davies was familiar with *Fatal Curiosity*, having appeared in Fielding's original production at the Haymarket in 1737. He reprinted the play a second time as a part of his collection of Lillo's works (1775). The copy-text was again the first edition; reference was not made to the edition of 1762. Both Davies editions include routine corrections of obvious errors in the first edition and a good many attempts to clarify the pointing. The edition of 1762 is marked by several new errors and a number of substantive emendations introduced, apparently, as improvements.

At least three other editions of *Fatal Curiosity* appeared during the 1760s, all of them published by the itinerant printer Orion Adams: a Dublin edition (1766), probably produced to capitalize on a production of the play at the Theatre in Smock Alley; a 'seventh edition', with a Leeds imprint, dated 1767; and another 'seventh edition', purportedly published in London, dated 1768. The texts of these Adams editions derived from the first edition, bear no relation to the Davies editions, and, of course, have no textual authority. As a group, however, they are unique curiosities in the history of the book trade and of the promotion of Lillo's plays for the enjoyment of readers. All include additions to the text, which is made progressively more melodramatic and sentimental with each edition. Moreover, in the Leeds and London editions rather primitive efforts are made to transform the dramatic text mechanically into the 'affecting narrative' announced on the title-pages: act- and scene-headings are omitted, some stage directions are rewritten in the past tense of narrative fiction, and in the latest edition Lillo's verse is reset as prose.

Editorial Procedure

The present edition takes as copy-text Gray's first edition, including the later states of all sheets known to have been corrected. Comparisons have been made with the two Davies editions as an aid to analysing the pointing and occasionally imperfect lining of the first edition. I have also consulted the modernized texts edited by A. W. Ward (1906) and William McBurney (1966).[65]

---

[65] The copy-text is the first edition, a Yale University copy. Copies collated include: *first edition, London issue*, CtY (2 copies), CtMW, O, NjP (2 copies), CSmH, DFo; *first edition, 'Dublin' issue*, DFo; *second edition*, DFo; Davies, *Works* (1775), CtMW, O, BL (3 copies), CtY (2 copies).

FATAL CURIOSITY:

A TRUE

TRAGEDY

OF

THREE ACTS.

As it is Acted at the

NEW THEATRE

IN THE

HAY-MARKET.

By Mr. *LILLO.*

LONDON:
Printed for JOHN GRAY at the *Cross-Keys* in the
Poultry near *Cheapside.* MDCCXXXVII.
[Price One Shilling.]

PROLOGUE,

Written by *Henry Feilding*, Esq;

Spoken by Mr. *Roberts*.

The tragic Muse has long forgot to please
With Shakespear*'s Nature, or with* Fletcher*'s Ease:*
No Passion mov'd, thro' five long Acts you sit,
Charm'd with the Poet's Language, or his Wit.
Fine Things are said, no matter whence they fall;   5
Each single Character might speak them all.

  But from this modern fashionable Way,
To Night, our Author begs your Leave to stray.
No fustian Hero rages here to Night;
No Armies fall, to fix a Tyrant's Right: 10
From lower Life we draw our Scene's Distress:
—Let not your Equals move your Pity less!
Virtue distrest in humble State support;
Nor think, she never lives without the Court.

  Tho' to our Scenes no Royal Robes belong,   15
And tho' our little Stage as yet be young,
Throw both your Scorn and Prejudice aside,
Let us with Favour, not Contempt be try'd;
Thro' the first Acts a kind Attention lend,
The growing Scene shall force you to attend;   20
Shall catch the Eyes of every tender Fair,
And make them charm their Lovers with a Tear.
The lover too by Pity shall impart
His tender Passion to his fair One's Heart:
The Breast which others Anguish cannot move,   25
Was ne'er the Seat of Friendship, or of Love.

Dramatis Personæ.

MEN.

Old *Wilmot.*	Mr. *Roberts.*
Young *Wilmot.*	Mr. *Davies.*
Eustace.	Mr. *Woodburn.*
Randal.	Mr. *Blakes.*

5

WOMEN.

Agnes, Wife to old *Wilmot.*	Mrs. *Charke.*
Charlot.	Miss *Jones.*
Maria.	Miss *Karver.*

Visiters Men and Women.

10

SCENE, *Penryn* in *Cornwall.*

3 *Davies*] D; *Davis* G   4 *Woodburn*] D; *Wooburn* G

FATAL CURIOSITY.

ACT I.

SCENE I.

A room in Wilmot*'s house.*

Old Wilmot *alone.*

The day is far advanced; the chearful sun
Pursues with vigour his repeated course;
No labour less'ning, nor no time decaying
His strength, or splendor: Evermore the same,
From age to age his influence sustains   5
Dependent worlds, bestows both life and motion
On the dull mass that forms their dusky orbs,
Chears them with heat, and gilds them with his brightness.
Yet man, of jarring elements composed,
Who posts from change to change, from the first hour   10
Of his frail being till his dissolution,
Enjoys the sad prerogative above him,
To think, and to be wretched—What is life,
To him that's born to die! or what that wisdom
Whose perfection ends, in knowing we know nothing!   15
Meer contradiction all! A tragick farce,
Tedious tho' short, and without art elab'rate,
Ridiculously sad—

Enter Randal.

     Where hast been, *Randal?*
 Rand. Not out of *Penryn,* sir; but to the strand,
To hear what news from *Falmouth* since the storm   20
Of wind last night.
  O. *Wilm.*   It was a dreadful one.
 Rand. Some found it so. A noble ship from *India*
Ent'ring in the harbour, run upon a rock,
And there was lost.
  O. *Wilm.*   What came of those on board her?

Rand. Some few are saved, but much the greater part,
'Tis thought, are perished.

    O. *Wilm.*   They are past the fear
Of future tempests, or a wreck on shore;
Those who escaped, are still exposed to both.

    Rand. But I've heard news, much stranger than this ship-wrack
Here in *Cornwall.* The brave Sir *Walter Raleigh*,
Being arrived at *Plymouth* from *Guiana*,
A most unhappy voyage, has been betray'd
By base Sir *Lewis Stukeley*, his own kinsman,
And seiz'd on by an order from the court;
And 'tis reported, he must lose his head,
To satisfy the *Spaniards.*

    O. *Wilm.*   Not unlikely;
His martial genius does not suit the times.
There's now no insolence that *Spain* can offer,
But to the shame of this pacifick reign,
Poor *England* must submit to—Gallant man!
Posterity perhaps may do thee justice,
And praise thy courage, learning and integrity,
When thou'rt past hearing: Thy successful enemies,
Much sooner paid, have their reward in hand,
And know for what they labour'd.—Such events
Must, questionless, excite all thinking men,
To love and practise virtue!

    Rand.   Nay; 'tis certain,
That virtue ne'er appears so like itself,
So truly bright and great, as when opprest.

    O. *Wilm.* I understand no riddles.—Where's your Mistress?

    Rand. I saw her pass the *High-street* t'wards the minster.

    O. *Wilm.* She's gone to visit *Charlot*—She doth well.
In the soft bosom of that gentle maid,
There dwells more goodness, than the rigid race
Of moral pedants e'er believ'd, or taught.
With what amazing constancy and truth,
Doth she sustain the absence of our son,
Whom more than life she loves! How shun for him,
Whom we shall ne'er see more, the rich and great;
Who own her charms more than supply the want
Of shining heaps and sigh to make her happy.
Since our misfortunes, we have found no friend,
None who regarded our distress, but her;

(I. i)   55 pedants] D, W1; ~, G

And she, by what I have observed of late,
Is tired, or exhausted—curst Condition!   65
To live a burden to one only friend,
And blast her youth with our contagious woe!
Who that had reason, soul, or sense would bear it
A moment longer!—Then this honest wretch!—
I must dismiss him—Why should I detain,   70
A grateful, gen'rous youth to perish with me?
His service may procure him bread elsewhere,
Tho' I have none to give him.—Prithee, *Randal*!
How long hast thou been with me?
    Rand.   Fifteen years.
I was a very child when first you took me,   75
To wait upon your son, my dear young master!
I oft have wish'd, I'd gone to *India* with him;
Tho' you, desponding, give him o'er for lost.   [*Old* Wilmot *wipes
                                        his eyes.*

I am to blame—This talk revives your sorrow
For his absence.
    O. *Wilm.*   How can that be reviv'd,   80
Which never died?
    Rand.   The whole of my intent
Was to confess your bounty, that supplied
The loss of both my parents: I was long
The object of your charitable care.
    O. *Wilm.* No more of that: Thou'st served me longer since   85
Without reward; so that account is balanced,
Or rather I'm thy debtor—I remember,
When poverty began to show her face
Within these walls, and all my other servants,
Like pamper'd vermin from a falling house,   90
Retreated with the plunder they had gain'd,
And left me, too indulgent and remiss
For such ungrateful wretches, to be crush'd
Beneath the ruin they had helped to make,
That you, more good than wise, refused to leave me.   95
    Rand. Nay, I beseech you, sir!—
    O. *Wilm.*   With my distress,
In perfect contradiction to the world,
Thy love, respect and diligence increased;
Now all the recompence within my power,

(I. i)   70 detain,] ~∧ D, W1. *See Commentary*

Is to discharge thee, *Randal*, from my hard,   10(
Unprofitable service.
  Rand.   Heaven!, forbid.
Shall I forsake you in your worst necessity?—
Believe me, sir! my honest soul abhors
The barb'rous thought.
   O. *Wilm.*   What! canst thou feed on air?
I have not left wherewith to purchase food   10!
For one meal more.
  Rand.   Rather than leave you thus,
I'll beg my bread, and live on others bounty
While I serve you.
   O. *Wilm.* Down, down my swelling heart,
Or burst in silence: 'Tis thy cruel fate
Insults thee by his kindness—His is innocent   11(
Of all the pain it gives thee—Go thy ways—
I will no more suppress thy youthful hopes
Of rising in the world.
  Rand.   'Tis true; I'm young,
And never tried my fortune, or my genius;
Which may perhaps find out some happy means,   11
As yet unthought of, to supply your wants.
   O. *Wilm.* Thou tortur'st me—I hate all obligations
Which I can ne'er return—And who art thou,
That I shou'd stoop to take 'em from thy hand!
Care for thy self, but take no thought for me;   12
I will not want thee—trouble me no more.
  Rand. Be not offended, sir! and I will go.
I ne'er repined at your commands before;
But, heaven's my witness! I obey you now
With strong reluctance, and a heavy heart.   12
Farewel, my worthy master!   [*Going.*
   O. *Wilm.*   Farewel—Stay—
As thou art yet a stranger to the world,
Of which alas! I've had too much experience,
I shou'd, methinks, before we part, bestow
A little counsel on thee—Dry thy eyes—   13(
If thou weep'st thus, I shall proceed no farther.
Dost thou aspire to greatness, or to wealth,
Quit books and the unprofitable search
Of wisdom there, and study human kind:
No science will avail thee without that;   13
But that obtain'd, thou need'st not any other.
This will instruct thee to conceal thy views,

And wear the face of probity and honour,
'Till thou hast gain'd thy end; which must be ever
Thy own advantage, at that man's expence   140
Who shall be weak enough to think thee honest.
 Rand. You mock me, sure.
 O. *Wilm.*   I never was more serious.
 Rand. Why should you counsel what you scorned to practise?
 O. *Wilm.* Because that foolish scorn has been my ruin.
I've been an idiot, but would have thee wiser,   145
And treat mankind, as they would treat thee, *Randal*,
As they deserve, and I've been treated by 'em.
Thou'st seen by me, and those who now despise me,
How men of fortune fall, and beggars rise;
Shun my example; treasure up my precepts;   150
The world's before thee—be a knave, and prosper.
What art thou dumb?   [*After a long pause.*
 Rand.   Amazement ties my tongue.
Where are your former principles?
 O. *Wilm.*   No matter;
Suppose I have renounced 'em: I have passions,
And love thee still; therefore would have thee think,   155
The world is all a scene of deep deceit,
And he who deals with mankind on the square,
Is his own bubble, and undoes himself.   [*Exit.*
 Rand. Is this the man, I thought so wise and just?
What teach, and counsel me to be a villain!   160
Sure grief has made him frantick, or some fiend
Assum'd his shape—I shall suspect my senses.
High-minded he was ever, and improvident;
But pitiful and generous to a fault:
Pleasure he loved, but honour was his idol.   165
O fatal change! O horrid transformation!
So a majestick temple sunk to ruin,
Becomes the loathsome shelter and abode
Of lurking serpents, toads, and beasts of prey;
 And scaly dragons hiss, and lions roar,   170
 Where wisdom taught, and musick charm'd before. [*Exit.*

(I. i) 171SD [*Exit.*] Ed.; *not in* G

SCENE II.

A parlour in Charlot's *house.*

Enter Charlot *and* Maria.

   Char. What terror and amazement must they feel
Who die by ship-wrack!
   Mar.   'Tis a dreadful thought!
   Char. Ay; is it not, *Maria*! to descend,
Living and conscious, to that watry tomb?
Alas! had we no sorrows of our own,
The frequent instances of others woe,
Must give a gen'rous mind a world of pain.
But you forget you promised me to sing.
Tho' chearfulness and I have long been strangers,
Harmonious sounds are still delightful to me.
There is in melody a secret charm
That flatters, while it adds to my disquiet,
And makes the deepest sadness the most pleasing.
There's sure no passion in the human soul,
But finds its food in musick—I wou'd hear
The song composed by that unhappy maid,
Whose faithful lover scaped a thousand perils
From rocks, and sands, and the devouring deep;
And after all, being arrived at home,
Passing a narrow brook, was drowned there,
And perished in her sight.

SONG.

> *Mar. Cease, cease, heart-easing tears;*
>   *Adieu, you flatt'ring fears,*
>   *Which seven long tedious years*
>   *Taught me to bear.*
>   *Tears are for lighter woes;*
>   *Fear no such danger knows,*
>   *As fate remorseless shows,*
>   *Endless despair.*
>   *Dear cause of all my pain,*
>   *On the wide stormy main,*
>   *Thou wast preserved in vain,*
>   *Tho' still adored;*

(I. ii)   3 Ay;] ~: G (*earlier state*)

> *Had'st thou died there unseen,*
> *My blasted eyes had been*   35
> *Saved from the horrid'st scene*
> *Maid e'er deplored.*

[Charlot *finds a letter.*

Char. What's this?—A letter superscribed to me!
None could convey it here but you, *Maria.*
Ungen'rous, cruel maid! to use me thus!   40
To join with flatt'ring men to break my peace,
And persecute me to the last retreat!
   Mar. Why should it break your peace, to hear the sighs
Of honourable love, and know th' effects
Of your resistless charms? This letter is—   45
   Char. No matter whence—return it back unopen'd:
I have no love, no charms but for my *Wilmot,*
Nor would have any.
   Mar.   Strange infatuation!
Why should you waste the flower of your days
In fruitless expectation—*Wilmot*'s dead;   50
Or living, dead to you.
   Char.   I'll not despair,
Patience shall cherish hope, nor wrong his honour
By unjust suspicion. I know his truth,
And will preserve my own. But to prevent
All future, vain, officious importunity,   55
Know, thou incessant foe of my repose,
Whether he sleeps secure from mortal cares,
In the deep bosom of the boist'rous main,
Or tost with tempests, still endures its rage;
Whether his weary pilgrimage by land   60
Has found an end, and he now rests in peace
In earth's cold womb, or wanders o'er her face;
Be it my lot to waste, in pining grief,
The remnant of my days for his known loss,
Or live, as now, uncertain and in doubt,   65
No second choice shall violate my vows:
High heaven, which heard them, and abhors the perjured,
Can witness, they were made without reserve;
Never to be retracted, ne'er dissolved
By accidents or absence, time or death.   70
   Mar. I know, and long have known, my honest zeal
To serve you gives offence—But be offended—
This is no time for flatt'ry—Did your vows
Oblige you to support his gloomy, proud,

Impatient parents, to your utter ruin—   7
You well may weep to think on what you've done.
    Char. I weep to think that I can do no more
For their support—What will become of 'em!—
The hoary, helpless, miserable pair!
    Mar. Then all these tears, this sorrow is for them.   8
    Char. Taught by afflictions, I have learn'd to bear
Much greater ills than poverty with patience.
When luxury and ostentation's banish'd,
The calls of nature are but few; and those
These hands, not used to labour, may supply.   8
But when I think on what my friends must suffer,
My spirits fail, and I'm o'erwhelm'd with grief.
    Mar. What I wou'd blame, you force me to admire,
And mourn for you, as you lament for them.
Your patience, constancy, and resignation
Merit a better fate.
    Char.   So pride would tell me,
And vain self-love, but I believe them not:
And if by wanting pleasure I have gained
Humility, I'm richer for my loss.
    Mar. You have the heavenly art, still to improve
Your Mind by all events—But here comes one,
Whose pride seems to increase with her misfortunes.

                    Enter Agnes.

Her faded dress unfashionably fine,
As ill conceals her poverty, as that
Strain'd complaisance her haughty, swelling heart.
Tho' perishing with want, so far from asking,   1
She ne'er receives a favour uncompelled,
And while she ruins, scorns to be obliged:
She wants me gone, and I abhor her sight.   [*Exit* Maria.
    Char. This visit's kind.
    Agn.   Few else would think it so: 1
Those who would once have thought themselves much honoured
By the least favour, tho' 'twere but a look,
I could have shewn them, now refuse to see me.
'Tis Misery enough to be reduced
To the low level of the common herd,
Who born to begg'ry, envy all above them;
But 'tis the curse of curses, to endure
The insolent contempt of those we scorn.

            (I. ii) 104 sight.] D, W1; ~, G

Char. By scorning, we provoke them to contempt;
And thus offend, and suffer in our turns: 115
We must have patience.
    Agn.   No, I scorn them yet.
But there's no end of suff'ring: Who can say
Their sorrows are compleat? My wretched husband,
Tired with our woes, and hopeless of relief,
Grows sick of life.
    Char.   May gracious heaven support him!   120
    Agn. And, urged by indignation and despair,
Would plunge into eternity at once,
By foul self-murder: His fixed love for me,
Whom he would fain persuade to share his fate,
And take the same, uncertain, dreadful course,   125
Alone withholds his hand.
    Char.   And may it ever!
    Agn. I've known with him the two extremes of life,
The highest happiness, and deepest woe,
With all the sharp and bitter aggravations
Of such a vast transition—Such a fall   130
In the decline of life!—I have as quick,
As exquisite a sense of pain as he,
And wou'd do any thing, but die, to end it;
But there my courage fails—Death is the worst
That fate can bring, and cuts off ev'ry hope.   135
    Char. We must not chuse, but strive to bear our lot
Without reproach, or guilt: But by one act
Of desperation, we may overthrow
The merit we've been raising all our days;
And lose our whole reward—And now, methinks,   140
Now more than ever, we have cause to fear,
And be upon our guard. The hand of heaven
Spreads clouds on clouds o'er our benighted heads,
And wrapt in darkness, doubles our distress.
I had, the night last past, repeated twice,   145
A strange and awful dream: I would not yield
To fearful superstition, nor despise
The admonition of a friendly power
That wished my good.
    Agn.   I've certain plagues enough,
Without the help of dreams, to make me wretched.   150
    Char. I wou'd not stake my happiness or duty

(I. ii)   139 days;] ~, D. *See Commentary*

On their uncertain credit, nor on aught
But reason, and the known decrees of heaven.
Yet dreams have sometimes shewn events to come,
And may excite to vigilance and care,   15
In some important hour; when all our weakness
Shall be attacked, and all our strength be needful,
To shun the gulph that gapes for our destruction,
And fly from guilt, and everlasting ruin.
My vision may be such, and sent to warn us,   160
Now we are tried by multiplied afflictions,
To mark each motion of our swelling hearts,
And not attempt to extricate ourselves
And seek deliverance by forbidden ways:
But keep our hopes and innocence entire,   165
'Till we're dismist to join the happy dead
In that bless'd world, where transitory pain
And frail imperfect virtue is rewarded
With endless pleasure and consummate joy;
Or heaven relieves us here.
    Agn.   Well, pray proceed;   170
You've rais'd my curiosity at least.
    Char. Methought, I sate, in a dark winter's night,
My garments thin, my head and bosom bare,
On the wide summit of a barren mountain;
Defenceless and exposed, in that high region,   175
To all the cruel rigors of the season.
The sharp bleak winds pierced thro' my shiv'ring frame,
And storms of hail, and sleet, and driving rains
Beat with impetuous fury on my head,
Drench'd my chill'd limbs, and pour'd a deluge round me.   180
On one hand, ever gentle patience sate,
On whose calm bosom I reclin'd my head;
And on the other, silent contemplation.
At length, to my unclosed and watchful eyes,
That long had roll'd in darkness, and oft raised   185
Their chearless orbs towards the starless sky,
And sought for light in vain, the dawn appeared;
And I beheld a man, an utter stranger,
But of a graceful and exalted mein,
Who press'd with eager transport to embrace me.   190
—I shunn'd his arms—But at some words he spoke,
Which I have now forgot, I turn'd again,

(I. ii)   163 ourselves] *Ed.*; ~, G   168 virtue] D, W1; ~, G. *See Commentary on* I. ii. 70

But he was gone—And oh! transporting sight!
Your son, my dearest *Wilmot*! fill'd his place.
    Agn. If I regarded dreams, I should expect   195
Some fair event from yours: I have heard nothing
That should alarm you yet.
    Char.   But what's to come,
Tho' more obscure, is terrible indeed.
Methought we parted soon, and when I sought him,
You and his father—Yes, you both were there—   200
Strove to conceal him from me: I pursued
You with my cries, and call'd on heaven and earth
To judge my wrongs, and force you to reveal
Where you had hid my love, my life, my *Wilmot*!—
    Agn. Unless you mean t' affront me, spare the rest,   205
'Tis just as likely *Wilmot* should return,
As we become your foes.
    Char.   Far be such rudeness
From *Charlot*'s thoughts: But when I heard you name
Self-murder, it reviv'd the frightful image
Of such a dreadful scene.
    Agn.   You will persist!—   210
    Char. Excuse me; I have done. Being a Dream,
I thought, indeed, it cou'd not give offence.
    Agn. Not when the matter of it is offensive!—
You cou'd not think so, had you thought at all;
But I take nothing ill from thee—Adieu;   215
I've tarried longer than I first intended,
And my poor husband mourns the while alone.   [*Exit* Agnes.
    Char. She's gone abruptly, and I fear displeas'd.
The least appearance of advice or caution,
Sets her impatient temper in a flame.   220
When grief, that well might humble swells our pride,
And pride increasing, aggravates our grief,
The tempest must prevail 'till we are lost.
    When heaven, incensed, proclaims unequal war
    With guilty earth, and sends its shafts from far,   225
    No bolt descends to strike, no flame to burn
    The humble shrubs that in low valleys mourn;
    While mountain pines, whose lofty heads aspire
    To fan the storm, and wave in fields of fire,
    And stubborn oaks that yield not to its force,   230
    Are burnt, o'erthrown, or shiver'd in its course.   [*Exit.*

(I.ii) 209–10a image | Of such a dreadful scene.] D, W1; image of . . . G, *which prints as a single line*   231SD [*Exit.*] *Ed.; not in* G

SCENE III.

The town and port of Penryn.

Enter Young Wilmot *and* Eustace *in* Indian *habits.*

Y. *Wilm.* Welcome, my friend! to *Penryn*: Here we're safe.
  Eust. Then we're deliver'd twice; first from the sea,
And then from savage men, who, more remorseless,
Prey on shipwreck'd wretches, and spoil and murder those
Whom fatal tempests and devouring waves,
In all their fury, spar'd.
  Y. *Wilm.*   It is a scandal,
Tho' malice must acquit the better sort,
The rude unpolisht people here in *Cornwall*
Have long laid under, and with too much justice:
Cou'd our superiors find some happy means   1
To mend it, they would gain immortal honour.
For 'tis an evil grown almost inv'terate,
And asks a bold and skilful hand to cure.
  Eust. Your treasure's safe, I hope.
  Y. *Wilm.*   'Tis here, thank heaven!
Being in jewels, when I saw our danger,   1
I hid it in my bosom.
  Eust.   I observed you,
And wonder how you could command your thoughts,
In such a time of terror and confusion.
  Y. *Wilm.* My thoughts were then at home—O *England*! *England*!
Thou seat of plenty, liberty and health,   2
With transport I behold thy verdant fields,
Thy lofty mountains rich with useful ore,
Thy numerous herds, thy flocks, and winding streams:
After a long and tedious absence, *Eustace*!
With what delight we breath our native air,   2
And tread the genial soil that bore us first.
'Tis said, the world is ev'ry wise man's country;
Yet after having view'd its various nations,
I'm weak enough still to prefer my own
To all I've seen beside—You smile, my friend!   3
And think, perhaps, 'tis instinct more than reason:
Why be it so. Instinct preceded reason
In the wisest of us all, and may sometimes
Be much the better guide. But be it either;
I must confess, that even death itself   3

Appeared to me with twice its native horrors,
When apprehended in a foreign land.
Death is, no doubt, in ev'ry place the same;
Yet observation must convince us, most men,
Who have it in their power, chuse to expire   40
Where they first drew their breath.
  Eust.   Believe me, *Wilmot*!
Your grave reflections were not what I smil'd at;
I own their truth. That we're return'd to *England*
Afford me all the pleasure you can feel
Merely on that account: Yet I must think   45
A warmer passion gives you all this transport.
You have not wander'd, anxious and impatient,
From clime to clime, and compast sea and land
To purchase wealth, only to spend your days
In idle pomp, and luxury at home: 50
I know thee better: Thou art brave and wise,
And must have nobler aims.
  Y. Wilm.   O *Eustace*! *Eustace*!
Thou knowest, for I've confest to thee, I love;
But having never seen the charming maid,
Thou canst not know the fierceness of my flame.   55
My hopes and fears, like the tempestuous seas
That we have past, now mount me to the skies,
Now hurl me down from that stupendous height,
And drive me to the center. Did you know
How much depends on this important hour,   60
You wou'd not be surprized to see me thus.
The sinking fortune of our ancient house,
Which time and various accidents had wasted,
Compelled me young to leave my native country,
My weeping parents, and my lovely *Charlot*;   65
Who ruled, and must for ever rule my fate.
How I've improved, by care and honest commerce,
My little stock, you are in part a witness.
'Tis now seven tedious years, since I set forth;
And as th' uncertain course of my affairs   70
Bore me from place to place, I quickly lost
The means of corresponding with my friends.
—O! shou'd my *Charlot*! doubtful of my truth,
Or in despair ever to see me more,
Have given herself to some more happy lover!—   75

(I. iii) 65 *Charlot*;] ~, D. *See Commentary on* I. ii. 139

Distraction's in the thought!—Or shou'd my parents,
Grieved for my absence and opprest with want,
Have sunk beneath their burden, and expired,
While I too late was flying to relieve them;
The end of all my long and weary travels,　　　　　　80
The hope, that made success itself a blessing,
Being defeated and for ever lost;
What were the riches of the world to me?
　　Eust. The wretch who fears all that is possible,
Must suffer more than he who feels the worst　　　　85
A man can feel, who lives exempt from fear.
A woman may be false, and friends are mortal;
And yet your aged parents may be living,
And your fair mistress constant.
　　　　Y. *Wilm.*　　　　　　　　True, they may;
I doubt, but I despair not—No, my friend!　　　　　90
My hopes are strong and lively as my fears,
And give me such a prospect of my happiness,
As nothing but fruition can exceed:
They tell me, *Charlot* is as true as fair,
As good as wise, as passionate as chaste;　　　　　95
That she with fierce impatience, like my own,
Laments our long and painful separation;
That we shall meet, never to part again;
That I shall see my parents, kiss the tears
From their pale hollow cheeks, chear their sad hearts,　　100
And drive that gaping phantom, meagre want,
For ever from their board; crown all their days
To come with peace, with pleasure, and abundance;
Receive their fond embraces and their blessings,
And be a blessing to 'em.
　　　　Eust.　　　　　　'Tis our weakness:—　　105
Blind to events, we reason in the dark,
And fondly apprehend what none e'er found,
Or ever shall, pleasure and pain unmixt;
And flatter, and torment ourselves, by turns,
With what shall never be.
　　　　Y. *Wilm.*　　　　　I'll go this instant　　110
To seek my *Charlot*, and explore my fate.
　　Eust. What in that foreign habit!
　　　　Y. *Wilm.*　　　　　　That's a trifle,
Not worth my thoughts.
　　　　Eust.　　　　The hardships you've endured,
And your long stay beneath the burning zone,

Where one eternal sultry summer reigns,   115
Have marr'd the native hue of your complexion:
Methinks you look more like a sun-burnt *Indian*,
Than a *Briton*.
    Y. *Wilm.*   Well 'tis no matter, *Eustace*!
I hope my mind's not alter'd for the worse;
And for my outside—But inform me, friend!   120
When I may hope to see you.
    Eust.   When you please:
You'll find me at the inn.
    Y. *Wilm.* When I have learnt my doom, expect me there.
'Till then, farewel!
    Eust.   Farewel! Success attend you!   [*Exit* Eustace.
    Y. *Wilm.* 'We flatter, and torment ourselves, by turns,   125
'With what shall never be.' Amazing folly!
We stand exposed to many unavoidable
Calamities, and therefore fondly labour
T' increase their number, and inforce their weight,
By our fantastick hopes and groundless fears.   130
    For one severe distress imposed by fate,
    What numbers doth tormenting fear create?
    Deceived by hope, *Ixion* like, we prove
    Immortal joys, and seem to rival *Jove*;
    The cloud dissolv'd, impatient we complain,   135
    And pay for fancied bliss substantial pain.   [*Exit.*

ACT II.

SCENE I.

Charlot's house.

Enter Charlot *thoughtful; and soon after* Maria *from the other side.*

Mar. Madam, a stranger in a foreign habit
Desires to see you.
   Char.   In a foreign habit—
'Tis strange, and unexpected—But admit him.   [*Exit* Maria.
Who can this stranger be? I know no foreigner,

Enter Young Wilmot.

—Nor any man like this.
   Y. *Wilm.*   Ten thousand joys!—   5
                       [*Going to embrace her.*
   Char. You are rude, sir—Pray forbear, and let me know
What business brought you here, or leave the place.
   Y. *Wilm.* She knows me not, or will not seem to know me. [*Aside.*
Perfidious maid! Am I forgot or scorned?
   Char. Strange questions from a man I never knew!   10
   Y. *Wilm.* With what aversion, and contempt she views me!
My fears are true; some other has her heart:
—She's lost—My fatal absence has undone me.   [*Aside.*
—O! cou'd thy *Wilmot* have forgot thee, *Charlot*!
   Char. Ha! *Wilmot*! say! what do your words import?   15
O gentle stranger! ease my swelling heart
That else will burst! Canst thou inform me ought?—
What dost thou know of *Wilmot*?
   Y. *Wilm.*   This I know.
When all the winds of heaven seem'd to conspire
Against the stormy main, and dreadful peals   20
Of rattling thunder deafen'd ev'ry ear,
And drown'd th' affrighten'd mariners loud cries;
While livid lightning spread its sulphurous flames
Thro' all the dark horizon, and disclosed
The raging seas incensed to his destruction;   25
When the good ship in which he was embark'd,
Unable longer to support the tempest,
Broke, and o'erwhelm'd by the impetuous surge,
Sunk to the oozy bottom of the deep,
And left him struggling with the warring waves;   30

In that dread moment, in the jaws of death,
When his strength fail'd, and ev'ry hope forsook him,
And his last breath press'd t'wards his trembling lips,
The neighbouring rocks, that echoed to his moan,
Returned no sound articulate, but *Charlot*.   35
    Char. The fatal tempest, whose description strikes
The hearer with astonishment, is ceased;
And *Wilmot* is at rest. The fiercer storm
Of swelling passions that o'erwhelms the soul,
And rages worse than the mad foaming seas   40
In which he perish'd, ne'er shall vex him more.
    Y. *Wilm.* Thou seem'st to think he's dead; enjoy that thought;
Persuade yourself that what you wish is true,
And triumph in your falshood—Yes, he's dead;
You were his fate. The cruel winds and waves,   45
That cast him pale and breathless on the shore,
Spared him for greater woes—To know his *Charlot*,
Forgetting all her vows to him and heaven,
Had cast him from her thoughts—Then, then he died;
But never must have rest. Ev'n now he wanders,   50
A sad, repining, discontented ghost,
The unsubstantial shadow of himself,
And pours his plaintive groans in thy deaf ears,
And stalks, unseen, before thee.
    Char.   'Tis enough—
Detested falshood now has done its worst.   55
And art thou dead?—And wou'd'st thou die, my *Wilmot*!
For one thou thought'st unjust?—Thou soul of truth!
What must be done?—Which way shall I express
Unutterable woe? Or how convince
Thy dear departed spirit of the love,   60
Th' eternal love, and never-failing faith
Of thy much injur'd, lost, despairing *Charlot*?
    Y. *Wilm.* Be still, my flutt'ring heart; hope not too soon:
Perhaps I dream, and this is all illusion.
    Char. If as some teach, the mind intuitive,   65
Free from the narrow bounds and slavish ties
Of sordid earth, that circumscribe its power
While it remains below, roving at large,
Can trace us to our most concealed retreat,
See all we act, and read our very thoughts;   70
To thee, O *Wilmot*! kneeling I appeal,

If e'er I swerv'd in action, word, or thought
From the severest constancy and truth,
Or ever wish'd to taste a joy on earth
That center'd not in thee, since last we parted;   75
May we ne'er meet again, but thy loud wrongs
So close the ear of mercy to my cries,
That I may never see those bright abodes
Where truth and virtue only have admission,
And thou inhabit'st now.   80
  Y. *Wilm.*   Assist me, heaven!
Preserve my reason, memory and sense!
O moderate my fierce tumultuous joys,
Or their excess will drive me to distraction.
O *Charlot*! *Charlot*! lovely, virtuous maid!
Can thy firm mind, in spite of time and absence,   85
Remain unshaken, and support its truth;
And yet thy frailer memory retain
No image, no idea of thy lover?
Why dost thou gaze so wildly? Look on me;
Turn thy dear eyes this way; observe me well.   90
Have scorching climates, time, and this strange habit
So changed, and so disguised thy faithful *Wilmot*,
That nothing in my voice, my face, or mien,
Remains to tell my *Charlot* I am he?

 [*After viewing him some time, she approaches weeping, and gives him
  her hand; and then turning towards him, sinks upon his bosom.*

Why dost thou weep? Why dost thou tremble thus?   95
Why doth thy panting heart and cautious touch
Speak thee but half convinc'd? Whence are thy fears?
Why art thou silent? Canst thou doubt me still?
 Char. No, *Wilmot*! no; I'm blind with too much light:
O'ercome with wonder, and opprest with joy,   100
The struggling passions barr'd the doors of speech;
But speech enlarg'd, affords me no relief.
This vast profusion of extream delight,
Rising at once, and bursting from despair,
Defies the aid of words, and mocks description: 105
But for one sorrow, one sad scene of anguish,
That checks the swelling torrent of my joys,
I could not bear the transport.
  Y. *Wilm.*   Let me know it:
Give me my portion of thy sorrow, *Charlot*!
Let me partake thy grief, or bear it for thee.   110

 Char. Alas! my *Wilmot*! these sad tears are thine;
They flow for thy misfortunes. I am pierced
With all the agonies of strong compassion,
With all the bitter anguish you must feel,
When you shall hear your parents—   115
 Y. *Wilm.*   Are no more.
 Char. You apprehend me wrong.
 Y. *Wilm.*   Perhaps I do:
Perhaps you mean to say, the greedy grave
Was satisfied with one, and one is left
To bless my longing eyes—But which, my *Charlot*!
—And yet forbear to speak, 'till I have thought—   120
 Char. Nay, hear me, *Wilmot*!
 Y. *Wilm.*   I perforce must hear thee.
For I might think 'till death, and not determine,
Of two so dear which I could bear to lose.
 Char. Afflict your self no more with groundless fears:
Your parents both are living. Their distress,   125
The poverty to which they are reduced,
In spight of my weak aid, was what I mourned;
And that in helpless age, to them whose youth
Was crown'd with full prosperity, I fear,
Is worse, much worse, than death.
 Y. *Wilm.*   My joy's compleat! 130
My parents living, and possess'd of thee!—
From this blest hour, the happiest of my life,
I'll date my rest. My anxious hopes and fears,
My weary travels, and my dangers past,
Are now rewarded all: Now I rejoice   135
In my success, and count my riches gain.
For know, my soul's best treasure! I have wealth
Enough to glut ev'n avarice itself:
No more shall cruel want, or proud contempt,
Oppress the sinking spirits, or insult   140
The hoary heads of those who gave me being.
 Char. 'Tis now, O riches, I conceive your worth:
You are not base, nor can you be superfluous,
But when misplac'd in base and sordid hands.
Fly, fly, my *Wilmot*! leave thy happy *Charlot*! 145
Thy filial piety, the sighs and tears
Of thy lamenting parents call thee hence.
 Y. *Wilm.* I have a friend, the partner of my voyage,

Who, in the storm last night, was shipwrack'd with me.
 Char. Shipwrackt last night!—O you immortal powers!   150
What have you suffer'd! How was you preserv'd!
 Y. *Wilm.* Let that, and all my other strange escapes
And perilous adventures, be the theme
Of many a happy winter night to come.
My present purpose was t'intreat my angel,   15.
To know this friend, this other better *Wilmot*;
And come with him this evening to my father's:
I'll send him to thee.
 Char.   I consent with pleasure.
 Y. *Wilm.* Heavens! what a night!—How shall I bear my joy!
My parents, yours, my friends, all will be mine,   16
And mine, like water, air, or the free splendid sun,
The undivided portion of you all.
If such the early hopes, the vernal bloom,
The distant prospect of my future bliss,
Then what the ruddy autumn!—What the fruit!—   16
The full possession of thy heavenly charms!
  The tedious, dark, and stormy winter o'er;
  The hind, that all its pinching hardships bore,
  With transport sees the weeks appointed bring
  The chearful, promis'd, gay, delightful spring;   17
  The painted meadows, the harmonious woods,
  The gentle Zephyrs, and unbridled floods,
  With all their charms, his ravished thoughts imploy,
  But the rich harvest must compleat his joy. [*Exeunt.*

SCENE II.

A street in Penryn.

Enter Randal.

 Rand. Poor! poor! and friendless! whither shall I wander,
And to what point direct my views and hopes?—
A menial servant!—No—What, shall I live,
Here in this land of freedom, live distinguished,
And marked the willing slave of some proud subject!—
And swell his useless train for broken fragments,
The cold remains of his superfluous board?—

(II. i) 153 perilous] perillous G (*earlier state*)   161 sun,] ~. G (*earlier state*)
174SD [*Exeunt.*] *Ed.; not in* G   (II. ii) 3 What,] *Ed.;* ~∧ G, D. *See Commentary*
5 subject!—] D; ~, G 6 fragments,] D; ~; G

I wou'd aspire to something more and better—
Turn thy eyes then to the prolifick ocean,
Whose spacious bosom opens to thy view: 10
There deathless honour, and unenvied wealth
Have often crowned the brave adventurer's toils.
This is the native uncontested right,
The fair inheritance of ev'ry *Briton*
That dares put in his claim—My choice is made: 15
A long farewel to *Cornwall*, and to *England*;
If I return—But stay, what stranger's this,
Who, as he views me, seems to mend his pace?

                    Enter young Wilmot.

    Y. *Wilm. Randal!*—The dear companion of my Youth!—
Sure lavish fortune means to give me all
I could desire, or ask for this blest day,   20
And leave me nothing to expect hereafter.
    Rand. Your pardon, sir! I know but one on earth
Cou'd properly salute me by the title
You're pleased to give me, and I would not think
That you are he—That you are *Wilmot.*—   25
    Y. *Wilm.*   Why?
    Rand. Because I cou'd not bear the disappointment
Shou'd I be deceived.
    Y. *Wilm.*   I am pleased to hear it:
Thy friendly fears better express thy thoughts
Than words could do.
    Rand.   O! *Wilmot!* O! my master!   30
Are you returned?
    Y. *Wilm.*   I have not yet embraced
My parents—I shall see you at my father's.
    Rand. No, I'm discharged from thence—O sir! such ruin—
    Y. *Wilm.* I've heard it all, and hasten to relieve 'em:
Sure heaven hath blessed me to that very end:
I've wealth enough; nor shalt thou want a part.   35
    Rand. I have a part already—I am blest
In your success, and share in all your joys.
    Y. *Wilm.* I doubt it not—But tell me, dost thou think,
My parents not suspecting my return,
That I may visit them, and not be known?   40
    Rand. 'Tis hard for me to judge. You are already
Grown so familiar to me, that I wonder
I knew you not at first: Yet it may be;

(II. ii) 17 this,] ~‸ G (*earlier state*)   18 pace?] ~. G (*earlier state*)   25 think]
D; ~, G

For you're much alter'd, and they think you dead.   4
 Y. *Wilm*. This is certain; *Charlot* beheld me long,
And heard my loud reproaches, and complaints
Without rememb'ring she had ever seen me.
My mind at ease grows wanton: I wou'd fain
Refine on happiness. Why may I not   5
Indulge my curiosity, and try
If it be possible by seeing first
My parents as a stranger, to improve
Their pleasure by surprize?
 Rand.   It may indeed
Inhance your own, to see from what despair   5
Your timely coming, and unhoped success
Have given you power to raise them.
 Y. *Wilm*.   I remember,
E'er since we learned together you excelled
In writing fairly, and could imitate
Whatever hand you saw with great exactness.   6
Of this I'm not so absolute a master.
I therefore beg you'll write, in *Charlot*'s name
And character, a letter to my father;
And recommend me, as a friend of hers,
To his acquaintance.   6
 Rand.   Sir, if you desire it—
And yet—
 Y. *Wilm*. Nay, no objections—'Twill save time,
Most precious with me now. For the deception,
If doing what my *Charlot* will approve,
'Cause done for me and with a good intent,
Deserves the name, I'll answer it my self.   7
If this succeeds, I purpose to defer
Discov'ring who I am 'till *Charlot* comes,
And thou, and all who love me. Ev'ry friend
Who witnesses my happiness to night,
Will, by partaking, multiply my joys.   7
 Rand. You grow luxurious in your mental pleasures:
Cou'd I deny you aught, I would not write
This letter. To say true, I ever thought
Your boundless curiosity a weakness.
 Y. *Wilm*. What canst thou blame in this?
 Rand.   Your pardon, Sir!   8
I only speak in general: I'm ready
T' obey your orders.
 Y. *Wilm*. I am much thy debtor,

But I shall find a time to quit thy kindness.
O *Randal*! but imagine to thyself
The floods of transport, the sincere delight   85
That all my friends will feel, when I disclose
To my astonished parents my return;
And then confess, that I have well contrived
By giving others joy t' exalt my own.
    As pain, and anguish, in a gen'rous mind,   90
    While kept concealed and to ourselves confined,
    Want half their force; so pleasure when it flows
    In torrents round us more extatick grows.   [*Exeunt.*

SCENE III.

A room in old Wilmot's *house.*

Old Wilmot *and* Agnes.

    O. *Wilm.* Here, take this *Seneca*, this haughty pedant,
Who governing the master of mankind,
And awing power imperial, prates of—patience;
And praises poverty—possess'd of millions:
—Sell him, and buy us bread. The scantiest meal   5
The vilest copy of his book e'er purchased,
Will give us more relief in this distress,
Than all his boasted precepts.—Nay, no tears;
Keep them to move compassion when you beg.
    Agn. My heart may break, but never stoop to that.   10
    O. *Wilm.* Nor wou'd I live to see it—But dispatch.   [*Exit* Agnes.
Where must I charge this length of misery,
That gathers force each moment as it rolls,
And must at last o'erwhelm me; but on hope,
Vain, flattering, delusive, groundless hope;   15
A senseless expectation of relief
That has for years deceived me?—Had I thought
As I do now, as wise men ever think,
When first this hell of poverty o'ertook me,
That power to die implies a right to do it,   20
And shou'd be used when life becomes a pain,
What plagues had I prevented?—True, my wife
Is still a slave to prejudice and fear—
I would not leave my better part, the dear   [*Weeps.*
Faithful companion of my happier days,   25

SCENE III.] D; II. G   3 of—] ~_∧_ G (*earlier state*)

To bear the weight of age and want alone.
—I'll try once more—

        Enter Agnes, *and after her young* Wilmot.

  O. *Wilm.* Returned, my life! so soon!—
  Agn. The unexpected coming of this stranger
Prevents my going yet.
  Y. *Wilm.*   You're, I presume,
The gentleman to whom this is directed.   [*Gives a letter.*   3
What wild neglect, the token of despair,
What indigence, what misery appears
In each disorder'd, or disfurnished room
Of this once gorgeous house? What discontent,
What anguish and confusion fill the faces   3
Of its dejected owners?
  O. *Wilm.*   Sir, such welcome
As this poor house affords, you may command.
Our ever friendly neighbour—Once we hoped
T' have called fair *Charlot* by a dearer name—
But we have done with hope—I pray excuse
This incoherence—We had once a son.   [*Weeps.*
  Agn. That you are come from that dear virtuous maid,
Revives in us the mem'ry of a loss,
Which, tho' long since, we have not learned to bear.
  Y. *Wilm.* The joy to see them, and the bitter pain
It is to see them thus, touches my soul
With tenderness and grief, that will o'erflow.
My bosom heaves and swells, as it would burst;
My bowels move, and my heart melts within me.
—They know me not, and yet, I fear, I shall
Defeat my purpose, and betray myself.   [*Aside.*
  O. *Wilm.* The lady calls you here her valued friend;
Enough, tho' nothing more should be implied,
To recommend you to our best esteem,
—A worthless acquisition!—May she find
Some means that better may express her kindness;
But she, perhaps, hath purposed to inrich
You with herself, and end her fruitless sorrow
For one whom death alone can justify
For leaving her so long. If it be so,
May you repair his loss, and be to *Charlot*
A second, happier *Wilmot*. Partial nature,

(II. iii) 36b O. *Wilm.*] *after speech-heading,* D *adds* SD: [*Having read the letter.*]

Who only favours youth, as feeble age
Were not her offspring or below her care,
Has seal'd our doom: No second hope shall spring   65
From my dead loins, and *Agnes*' steril womb,
To dry our tears, and dissipate despair.

 Agn. The last and most abandon'd of our kind,
By heaven and earth neglected or despised,
The loathsom grave, that robb'd us of our son   70
And all our joys in him, must be our refuge.

 Y. *Wilm.* Let ghosts unpardon'd, or devoted fiends,
Fear without hope, and wail in such sad strains;
But grace defend the living from despair.
The darkest hours precede the rising sun;   75
And mercy may appear, when least expected.

 O. *Wilm.* This I have heard a thousand times repeated,
And have, believing, been as oft deceived.

 Y. *Wilm.* Behold in me an instance of its truth.
At Sea twice shipwrack'd, and as oft the prey   80
Of lawless pyrates; by the *Arabs* thrice
Surpriz'd, and robb'd on shore; and once reduced
To worse than these, the sum of all distress
That the most wretched feel on this side hell,
Ev'n slavery itself: Yet here I stand,   85
Except one trouble that will quickly end,
The happiest of mankind.

 O. *Wilm.*   A rare example
Of fortune's caprice; apter to surprize,
Or entertain, than comfort, or instruct.
If you wou'd reason from events, be just,   90
And count, when you escaped, how many perished;
And draw your inf'rence thence.

 Agn.   Alas! who knows,
But we were rendred childless by some storm,
In which you, tho' preserved, might bear a part.

 Y. *Wilm.* How has my curiosity betray'd me   95
Into superfluous pain! I faint with fondness;
And shall, if I stay longer, rush upon 'em,
Proclaim myself their son, kiss and embrace 'em
Till their souls, transported with the excess
Of pleasure and surprize, quit their frail mansions,   100
And leave 'em breathless in my longing arms.
By circumstances then and slow degrees,

They must be let into a happiness
Too great for them to bear at once, and live:
That *Charlot* will perform: I need not feign   10
To ask an hour for rest. [*Aside.*] Sir, I intreat
The favour to retire where, for a while,
I may repose my self. You will excuse
This freedom, and the trouble that I give you:
'Tis long since I have slept, and nature calls.   11

    O. *Wilm.* I pray no more: Believe we're only troubled,
That you shou'd think any excuse were needful.

    Y. *Wilm.* The weight of this is some incumbrance to me

[*Takes a casket out of his bosom and gives it to his mother.*]

And its contents of value: If you please
To take the charge of it 'till I awake,   11
I shall not rest the worse. If I shou'd sleep
'Till I am ask'd for, as perhaps I may,
I beg that you wou'd wake me.
    Agn.   Doubt it not:
Distracted as I am with various woes,
I shall remember that.   [*Exit, with Old* Wilmot.

    Y. *Wilm.*   Merciless grief!   12
What ravage has it made! how has it changed
Her lovely form and mind! I feel her anguish,
And dread I know not what from her despair.
My father too—O grant 'em patience, heaven!
A little longer, a few short hours more,   12
And all their cares, and mine, shall end for ever.
    How near is misery and joy ally'd!
    Nor eye, nor thought can their extreams divide:
    A moment's space is long, and light'ning slow ⎫
    To fate descending to reverse our woe,   ⎬   1
    Or blast our hopes, and all our joys o'erthrow. ⎭   [*Exit.*

ACT III.

SCENE I.

The scene continued.

Enter Agnes *alone, with the casket in her hand.*

Who shou'd this stranger be?—And then this casket—
He says it is of value, and yet trusts it,
As if a trifle, to a stranger's hand—
His confidence amazes me—Perhaps
It is not what he says—I'm strongly tempted   5
To open it, and see—No, let it rest.
Why should my curiosity excite me,
To search and pry into th' affairs of others;
Who have t'imploy my thoughts, so many cares
And sorrows of my own?—With how much ease   10
The spring gives way?—Surprizing! most prodigious!—
My eyes are dazzled, and my ravished heart
Leaps at the glorious sight—How bright's the lustre,
How immense the worth of these fair jewels?
Ay, such a treasure wou'd expel for ever   15
Base poverty, and all its abject train;
The mean devices we're reduced to use
To keep out famine, and preserve our lives
From day to day; the cold neglect of friends;
The galling scorn, or more provoking pity   20
Of an insulting world—Possess'd of these,
Plenty, content, and power might take their turn,
And lofty pride bare its aspiring head
At our approach, and once more bend before us.
—A pleasing dream!—'Tis past; and now I wake   25
More wretched by the happiness I've lost.
For sure it was a happiness to think,
Tho' but a moment, such a treasure mine.
Nay, it was more than thought—I saw and touched
The bright temptation, and I see it yet—   30
'Tis here—'tis mine—I have it in possession—
—Must I resign it? Must I give it back?
Am I in love with misery and want?—
To rob my self, and court so vast a loss?—
—Retain it then—But how?—There is a way—   35
Why sinks my heart? Why does my blood run cold?

Why am I thrill'd with horror?—'Tis not choice,
But dire necessity suggests the thought.

Enter old Wilmot.

O. *Wilm.* The mind contented, with how little pains
The wand'ring senses yield to soft repose,
And die to gain new life? He's fallen asleep
Already—Happy man!—What dost thou think,
My *Agnes*, of our unexpected guest?
He seems to me a youth of great humanity:
Just ere he closed his eyes, that swam in tears,
He wrung my hand, and pressed it to his lips;
And with a look, that pierced me to the soul,
Begg'd me to comfort thee: And—Dost thou hear me?—
What art thou gazing on?—Fie, 'tis not well—
This casket was deliver'd to you closed:
Why have you open'd it? Shou'd this be known,
How mean must we appear?
    Agn.   And who shall know it?
    O. *Wilm.* There is a kind of pride, a decent dignity
Due to our selves; which, spite of our misfortunes,
May be maintain'd, and cherish'd to the last.
To live without reproach, and without leave
To quit the world, shews sovereign contempt,
And noble scorn of its relentless malice.
    Agn. Shews sovereign madness, and a scorn of sense.
Pursue no farther this detested theme:
I will not die, I will not leave the world
For all that you can urge, until compell'd.
    O. *Wilm.* To chace a shadow, when the setting sun
Is darting his last rays, were just as wise,
As your anxiety for fleeting life,
Now the last means for its support are failing:
Were famine not as mortal as the sword,
This warmth might be excused—But take thy choice:
Die how you will, you shall not die alone.
    Agn. Nor live, I hope.
    O. *Wilm.*   There is no fear of that.
    Agn. Then, we'll live both.
    O. *Wilm.*   Strange folly! where's the means?
    Agn. The means are there; those jewels—
O. *Wilm.*   Ha!—Take heed:

(III. i) 45 ere] W1; e're G, D. *See Commentary*

Perhaps thou dost but try me; yet take heed—
There's nought so monstrous but the mind of man
In some conditions may be brought t'approve;   75
Theft, sacrilege, treason, and parricide,
When flatt'ring opportunity enticed,
And desperation drove, have been committed
By those who once wou'd start to hear them named.
   Agn. And add to these detested suicide,   80
Which, by a crime much less, we may avoid.
   O. *Wilm.* Th' inhospitable murder of our guest!—
How cou'dst thou form a thought so very tempting,
So advantageous, so secure, and easy;
And yet so cruel, and so full of horror?   85
   Agn. 'Tis less impiety, less against nature,
To take another's life, than end our own.
   O. *Wilm.* It is no matter, whether this or that
Be, in itself, the less or greater crime:
Howe'er we may deceive our selves or others,   90
We act from inclination, not by rule,
Or none could act amiss—And that all err,
None but the conscious hypocrite denies.
—O! what is man, his excellence and strength,
When in an hour of trial and desertion,   95
Reason, his noblest power, may be suborned
To plead the cause of vile assassination.
   Agn. You're too severe: Reason may justly plead
For her own preservation.
   O. *Wilm.*   Rest contented:
Whate'er resistance I may seem to make,   100
I am betray'd within: My will's seduced,
And my whole soul infected. The desire
Of life returns, and brings with it a train
Of appetites, that rage to be supplied.
Whoever stands to parley with temptation,   105
Does it to be o'ercome.
   Agn.   Then nought remains,
But the swift execution of a deed
That is not to be thought on, or delay'd.
We must dispatch him sleeping: Shou'd he wake,
'Twere madness to attempt it.
   O. *Wilm.*   True, his strength   110
Single is more, much more than ours united;
So may his life, perhaps, as far exceed
Ours in duration, shou'd he 'scape this snare.

Gen'rous, unhappy man! O! what cou'd move thee
To put thy life and fortune in the hands   11
Of wretches mad with anguish!
     Agn.   By what means?
By stabbing, suffocation, or by strangling
Shall we effect his death?
     O. *Wilm.*   Why, what a fiend!—
How cruel, how remorseless and impatient
Have pride, and poverty made thee?
     Agn.   Barbarous man!   12
Whose wasteful riots ruin'd our estate,
And drove our son, ere the first down had spread
His rosy cheeks, spite of my sad presages,
Earnest intreaties, agonies and tears,
To seek his bread 'mongst strangers, and to perish   12
In some remote, inhospitable land—
The loveliest youth, in person and in mind,
That ever crown'd a groaning mother's pains!
Where was thy pity, where thy patience then?
Thou cruel husband! thou unnat'ral father!   13
Thou most remorseless, most ungrateful man,
To waste my fortune, rob me of my son;
To drive me to despair, and then reproach me
For being what thou'st made me.
     O. *Wilm.*   Dry thy tears:
I ought not to reproach thee. I confess   13
That thou hast suffer'd much: So have we both.
But chide no more: I'm wrought up to thy purpose.
The poor, ill-fated, unsuspecting victim,
Ere he reclined him on the fatal couch,
From which he's ne'er to rise, took off the sash,   14
And costly dagger that thou saw'st him wear;
And thus, unthinking, furnish'd us with arms
Against himself. Which shall I use?
     Agn.   The sash.
If you make use of that, I can assist.
     O. *Wilm.* No,—'tis a dreadful office, and I'll spare   14
Thy trembling hands the guilt—steal to the door,
And bring me word if he be still asleep.   [*Exit* Agnes.
Or I'm deceiv'd, or he pronounc'd himself
The happiest of mankind. Deluded wretch!
Thy thoughts are perishing, thy youthful joys,   15

(III. i)   145 No,—'tis] W1 (No∧); No, | ∧'Tis G, *which prints on two lines*   147 word]
W1; ~; G; ~, D. *See Commentary on* I. ii. 139

Touch'd by the icy hand of grisly death,
Are with'ring in their bloom—But thought extinguisht,
He'll never know the loss, nor feel the bitter
Pangs of disappointment—Then I was wrong
In counting him a wretch: To die well pleas'd,   155
Is all the happiest of mankind can hope for.
To be a wretch, is to survive the loss
Of every joy, and even hope itself,
As I have done—Why do I mourn him then?
For, by the anguish of my tortur'd soul,   160
He's to be envy'd, if compar'd with me.

        Enter Agnes *with young* Wilmot's *dagger.*

  Agn. The stranger sleeps at present; but so restless
His slumbers seem, they can't continue long.
Come, come, dispatch—Here I've secur'd his dagger.
  O. *Wilm.* O *Agnes! Agnes!* if there be a hell,   165
'Tis just we shou'd expect it.   [*Goes to take the dagger but lets it fall.*
  Agn.   Nay, for shame,
Shake off this panick, and be more your self.
  O. *Wilm.* What's to be done? On what had we determin'd?
  Agn. You're quite dismay'd. I'll do the deed my self.   [*Takes up
                                the dagger.*

  O. *Wilm.* Give me the fatal steel.   170
'Tis but a single murther,
Necessity, impatience and despair,
The three wide mouths, of that true Cerberus,
Grim poverty, demands—They shall be stopp'd.
Ambition, persecution, and revenge   175
Devour their millions daily: And shall I—
But follow me, and see how little cause
You had to think there was the least remains
Of manhood, pity, mercy, or remorse

<hr>

  (III. i) 152 extinguisht] W1 (extin-|guisht); ex-|tinguist G; extinguish'd D. *See Commentary*
162 The stranger . . . so restless] W1; G *prints as two lines:* The stranger | Sleeps . . .
165–9 *Lining follows* W1; *metre is broken and lining confused in* G, *which reads:*

      O. *Wilm.* O *Agnes! Agnes!* if there be a hell, 'tis just
    We shou'd expect it.   [*Goes to take the dagger but lets it fall.*
      Agn. Nay, for shame, shake off this panick, and be more your self.
      O. *Wilm.* What's to be done? On what had we determin'd?
      Agn. You're quite dismay'd. I'll do
    The deed my self.   [*Takes up the dagger.*

(165 O‸ *Wilm.* G (*some copies*).) *See Commentary*   174 demands] demand D. *See Commentary*

Left in this savage breast.   [*Going the wrong way.*

   Agn.   Where do you go?   18

The street is that way.

   O. *Wilm.*   True! I had forgot

   Agn. Quite, quite confounded.

   O. *Wilm.*   Well, I recover.

—I shall find the way.   [*Exit.*

   Agn.   O softly! softly!

The least noise undoes us.

                   —Still I fear him:

—No now he seems determined—O! that pause,   18

That cowardly pause!—His resolution fails—

'Tis wisely done to lift your eyes to heaven;

When did you pray before? I have no patience—

How he surveys him? What a look was there?—

How full of anguish, pity and remorse—   1ς

—He'll never do it—Strike, or give it o'er—

—No, he recovers—But that trembling arm

May miss its aim; and if he fails, we're lost—

'Tis done—O! no; he lives, he struggles yet.

   Y. *Wilm.* O! father! father!   [*In another room.*   1ς

   Agn.   Quick, repeat the blow.

What pow'r shall I invoke to aid thee, *Wilmot*!

—Yet hold thy hand—Inconstant, wretched woman!

What doth my heart recoil, and bleed with him

Whose murther you contrived—O *Wilmot*! *Wilmot*!   [*Exit.*

Enter Charlot, Maria, Eustace, Randal *and others.*

   Char. What strange neglect! The doors are all unbarr'd,   2

And not a living creature to be seen.

Enter old Wilmot *and* Agnes.

   Char. Sir, we are come to give and to receive

A thousand greetings—Ha! what can this mean?

Why do you look with such amazement on us?—

Are these your transports for your son's return?—   2

Where is my *Wilmot*? Has he not been here?—

Wou'd he defer your happiness so long,

Or cou'd a habit so disguise your son,

That you refus'd to own him?

   Agn.   Heard you that?

What prodigy of horror is disclosing,   210
To render murther venial.
    O. *Wilm.*   Prithee, peace:
The miserable damn'd suspend their howling,
And the swift orbs are fixt in deep attention.
    Y. *Wilm.* [*Groans.*] Oh! oh! oh!
    Eust. Sure that deep groan came from the inner room.   215
    Rand. It did; and seem'd the voice of one expiring.
Merciful heaven! where will these terrors end?
That is the dagger my young master wore;
And see, his father's hands are stained with blood. [*Young* Wilmot
                                         groans again.

    Eust. Another groan! Why do we stand to gaze   220
On these dumb phantoms of despair and horror?
Let us search farther: *Randal*, shew the way.
    Char. This is the third time those fantastick forms
Have forc'd themselves upon my mental eyes,
And sleeping gave me more than waking pains.   225
O you eternal pow'rs! if all your mercy
To wretched mortals be not quite extinguish'd,
And terrors only guard your awful thrones,
Remove this dreadful vision—Let me wake,
Or sleep the sleep of death.   [*Exeunt* Charlot, Maria, Eustace,
                                      Randal, *&c.*

    O. *Wilm.*   Sleep those who may;   230
I know my lot is endless perturbation.
    Agn. Let life forsake the earth, and light the sun,
And death and darkness bury in oblivion
Mankind and all their deeds, that no posterity
May ever rise to hear our horrid tale,   235
Or view the grave of such detested parricides.
    O. *Wilm.* Curses and deprecations are in vain:
The sun will shine, and all things have their course.
When we, the curse and burthen of the earth,
Shall be absorb'd, and mingled with its dust.   240
Our guilt and desolation must be told,
From age to age, to teach desponding mortals,
How far beyond the reach of human thought
Heaven, when incens'd, can punish—Die thou first. [*Stabs* Agnes.
I dare not trust thy weakness.
    Agn.   Ever kind,   245
But most in this.
    O. *Wilm.*   I will not long survive thee.
    Agn. Do not accuse thy erring mother, *Wilmot!*

With too much rigour when we meet above.
Rivers of tears, and ages spent in howling
Cou'd ne'er express the anguish of my heart.   25•
To give thee life for life, and blood for blood,
Is not enough. Had I ten thousand lives,
I'd give them all to speak my penitence
Deep, and sincere, and equal to my crime.   [*Dies.*

Enter Charlot *led by* Maria, *and* Randal, Eustace,
and the rest.

Char. Welcome, Despair! I'll never hope again—   25
Why have you forced me from my *Wilmot*'s side?
Let me return—Unhand me—Let me die.
Patience, that till this moment ne'er forsook me,
Has took her flight; and my abandon'd mind,
Rebellious to a lot so void of mercy   2€
And so unexpected, rages to madness.
—O thou! who know'st our frame, who know'st these woes
Are more than human fortitude can bear,
O! take me, take me hence, ere I relapse;
And in distraction, with unhallow'd tongue,   2€
Again arraign your mercy—   [*Faints.*
    Eust. Unhappy maid! This strange event my strength
Can scarce support; no wonder thine should fail.
—How shall I vent my grief? O *Wilmot*! *Wilmot*!
Thou truest lover, and thou best of friends,   2⁷
Are these the fruits of all thy anxious cares
For thy ungrateful parents?—Cruel fiends!
To use thee thus!—To recompense with death
Thy most unequall'd duty and affection!
    O. Wilm. What whining fool art thou, who woud'st usurp   2
My sovereign right of grief?—Was he thy son?—
Say! Canst thou shew thy hands reeking with blood,
That flow'd, thro' purer channels, from thy loins?
    Eust. Forbid it heaven! that I should know such Guilt:
Yet his sad fate demands commiseration.   2⁴
    O. Wilm. Compute the sands that bound the spacious ocean,
And swell their number with a single grain;
Increase the noise of thunder with thy voice;
Or when the raging wind lays nature waste,
Assist the tempest with thy feeble breath;   2
Add water to the sea, and fire to *Etna*;

(III. i)   264 ere] D, W₁; e're G   254+SD Randal,] D; ~; G

But name not thy faint sorrow with the anguish
Of a curst wretch who only hopes for this   [*Stabbing himself.*
To change the scene, but not relieve his pain.
    Rand. A dreadful instance of the last remorse!   290
May all your woes end here.
    O. Wilm.   O would they end
A thousand ages hence, I then should suffer
Much less than I deserve. Yet let me say,
You'll do but justice, to inform the world,
This horrid deed, that punishes itself,   295
Was not intended as he was our son;
For that we knew not, 'till it was too late.
Proud and impatient under our afflictions,
While heaven was labouring to make us happy,
We brought this dreadful ruin on ourselves.   300
Mankind may learn—but—oh!—   [*Dies.*
    Rand.   The most will not:

Let us at least be wiser, nor complain
Of heaven's mysterious ways, and awful reign:
By our bold censures we invade his throne
Who made mankind, and governs but his own: 305
Tho' youthful *Wilmot*'s sun be set ere noon,
The ripe in virtue never die too soon.   [*Exeunt.*

FINIS.

(III. i) 306 ere] W1; e're G, D

Marina

INTRODUCTION

SOURCES

Pericles was not an obvious subject for adaptation by a playwright who sought success in the eighteenth-century theatre. Remarkable primarily for its irregularity, the play had not been performed since 1661,[1] showed the flaws of mixed authorship, and had been omitted from Pope's edition of Shakespeare.[2] Lillo acknowledged that only some of the 'whole unequal play' was Shakespeare's, but hoped, as he explains in his prologue, 'To glean and clear from chaff [the] least remains' of the great poet's 'bright inimitable lines'.[3] In fact, he based his *Marina* on Acts IV and V of *Pericles* and, where necessary for exposition, paraphrased a number of lines taken from Act III, scene i. Although modern commentators agree that Shakespeare's hand is most evident in the last two acts of *Pericles*, Lillo's decision to adapt only this part of the play almost certainly reflects not textual analysis but his concern to reduce the action to 'a single tale'[4] and to focus on those aspects of the sprawling old play that very probably first attracted him to it: a pathetic but finally triumphant heroine successful in the defence of her virtue, and an action that illustrates the proper response to a mysterious but ultimately beneficent providence. Such material was well suited to Lillo's dramatic and didactic intentions; acceptance in the contemporary theatre could come with adequate adaptation.

Compressing the action and range of settings, regularly filling out scenes with material of his own, Lillo creates a new full-length play of three acts. 'Charming *Marina*'s wrongs begin the scene; *Pericles* finding her with his lost Queen, Concludes the pleasing task.'[5] Lillo does not altogether regularize his adaptation, however; he presents his serious scenes 'With humour mix'd in your

---

[1] Hoeniger, p. lxvii.

[2] Hoeniger, p. xl. Despite Pope's rejection of the play it was printed in the supplementary volume added to his edition by Sewell.

[3] Prologue, ll. 17, 15, 20. [4] Prologue, l. 24. [5] Prologue, ll. 25–7.

fore-fathers way'.[6] While he may have intended by this only to preserve the style of Elizabethan drama, he clearly enjoys and is well able to write rough comedy.

Only one of Lillo's six scenes is not at least suggested in his source: Act III, scene i, which serves to resolve the comic element in his plot and marks a passage of time in the serious drama. To provide motivation and a dramatic beginning for his truncated story, he makes a major alteration in the plot given in his source: substituting Queen Philoten for her mother, Shakespeare's Dionyza, Lillo invents an intrigue situation in which the queen, envious of Marina's charm, arranges to have her murdered by Leonine (a courtier, now, rather than a servant), whom she entices with hints of the sexual favours she will grant and with promises of advancement at court. As in *Pericles*, Leonine does not kill Marina but releases her to a group of pirates and falsely reports her death to the queen. However, Lillo adds a highly dramatic resolution to the intrigue. In a scene of recrimination somewhat reminiscent of Middleton's *The Changeling*, Leonine demands marriage with the queen as the price of his silence about the supposed murder of Marina; when she informs him that she has already taken the precaution to poison him secretly, he stabs her, and the two schemers die together.

In other respects, Lillo follows the main outline—and many details and speeches—of his source,[7] eliminating inessential characters and achieving a degree of unity of setting as well as action by having his pirates carry Marina directly to Ephesus, the city of her special goddess, Diana, in whose temple her mother serves as chief priestess. Rescued from the bawd by Lillo's morally improved Lysimachus, his Marina is given to the protection of the priestesses, a situation that allows the playwright to stage Pericles' reunions with his daughter and his wife in a single scene. Lillo eliminates Shakespeare's Pandar, giving some of the character's lines to Bolt and the bawd. He does not, however, tone down the bawdry of the old comic scenes. Indeed, he adds new passages of low comedy and sexual jokes, written with a vigour and success that belie his traditional reputation as a prudish moralist.[8] The pirates, by contrast, are somewhat transformed in the adaptation, exhibiting an admirable rough goodness in their rescue of Marina; later on, however, their leader is eager enough to sell the girl to the bawd if offered a good price.

These adjustments of plot and character are less significant than Lillo's changes of emphasis, alterations and additions which not only make clear his particular thematic concerns but are also strongly reflected in the dramatic structure of his adaptation. Reworking the 'single' but actually episodic story in his source, he creates, in effect, two dramas, overlapping and interrelated but not always unified in their appeal to the audience: the drama of the pathetic

[6] Prologue, l. 23. Lillo also follows the earlier drama in mixing blank verse and prose in a single play, carefully maintaining the traditional distinction between characters associated with the court, who are given verse to speak, and the 'low characters', who speak only prose.

[7] See Commentary on the head-notes for each scene.

[8] Lillo had, of course, included comedy in a similar vein in his ballad opera, *Silvia* (1730).

heroine whose virtue triumphs over the envy, greed, and passion of the sensual world into which she is thrown, and the drama of her parents, whose endurance of adversity is resolved in joy as great and mysteriously worked as the tribulations they have undergone. Marina's drama, heightened by the intrigue which begins the play and by the situation of suspense in which she is involved, provides plot interest, though this plot is effectively resolved by the end of Act II. The drama of Pericles and Thaisa carries the thematic burden of the play but is not openly introduced until the first scene of Act II, and is then ignored until the reunion scene, the major focus of Act III, scene ii.

The obvious similarities between Marina and certain heroines of sentimental fiction have added to the interest that she has held for literary historians. It appears that Lillo himself was aware, and in revision made the most, of the opportunity her story provided for developing a favourite theme.[9] His heroine's encounter with Lysimachus involves not only her strong defence of her chastity but also the near destruction of a young man of exemplary virtue who, like Barnwell, is confronted with a person who stirs his sensuality beyond control. 'When sin Appears in such a form, the firmest virtue Dissolves to air before it';[10] and the young governor, who 'came hither . . . bent to detect And punish these bad people',[11] would himself succumb were it not that the maiden on whose 'luxurious charms' he would 'feast each aking sense'[12] is—in contrast to Millwood—a paragon of virtue, and just as well able as Millwood to argue her case.

Despite its theatrical excitement, this conflict of chastity and sensuality is meant to be subsumed in the larger drama of loss, forbearing endurance, and joyful reunion. Lillo suggests in his dedication and makes clear in his last act that in *Pericles* he had found, first of all, a tale that exemplified 'steady virtue, and exalted piety',[13] the faith that makes possible and is demonstrated by particular virtues but far exceeds them in a conscious acceptance of the will of providence. The doctrine needed to be set out more fully and specifically; Lillo provided this emphasis as he reshaped the action and added to the dialogue of his source. Thus, where *Pericles* has a simple dumb show, augmented by Gower's narration, to present the hero's reaction to the news of his daughter's death, Lillo writes a major scene, not only dramatizing Pericles' grief but carefully defining the moral nature of this response to so overwhelming a stroke of fortune. Before he views the monument, Lillo's Pericles is too ready to rehearse the painful details of the loss of his wife; afterwards, he prays to be given the strength not to deny the very existence of the gods, but in forswearing speech, food, and all outward signs of human dignity, he clearly yields, in Lillo's view, to despair. As contrasts, Lillo poses two figures of exemplary fortitude: Thaisa, who has 'long been learning A perfect resignation to [the gods'] pleasure',[14] and Marina, whose account of her own tribulations teaches her father the pity and humility he has preached in Tharsus but not really

---

[9] See the Textual Introduction. [10] II. ii. 46–8. [11] II. ii. 44–6.
[12] II. ii. 88–9. [13] Dedication, l. 5. [14] III. ii. 56–7.

understood.[15] The nature of the hero's error is made more than clear in the lines with which Lillo has Pericles express his reaction to rediscovering his daughter: 'I've been a sinful man; but from this hour, In darkness and distress, I'll wait [the] mercy [of the gods], And ne'er distrust them more.'[16] When Pericles has reached this new level of understanding, the gods and Lillo allow him the final joy that providence has held in store for him, his reunion with his wife.

The lesson of patience is in *Pericles*, of course.[17] Lillo reshapes it, however, in order to advocate active virtue as the characteristic of proper endurance, the quality that merits providential reward. Thaisa states the doctrine.[18] It is dramatized in the career of Marina, a 'miracle' and 'wonder' of steadfastness. Thematically, then, Lillo's two dramas are one; their connection is summed up in Marina's song: 'Tho' fortune ev'ry other triumph bars, Seek joy in Virtue that we honour most.'[19]

Philoten's intrigue is also meant to be part of the moral drama: impatient and proud, she attempts to manipulate events and in so doing loses life itself. With lucid if momentary regret, the queen herself observes the irony of her situation: 'Had I tarry'd but a little longer, Marina had been gone without my guilt.'[20]

The care with which Lillo worked out his adaptation is regularly evidenced in his efforts to relate the elements of his rather disparate action to a single theme. For effective drama, however, a different sort of calculation is required. Emphasis inevitably falls on Marina and the suspense inherent in her story. Pericles is introduced late in the action, Thaisa not until the last act. The comic scenes, while entertaining, divert attention from the succession of serious scenes linked less by dramatic action than by words.

Wordiness is a particular problem in the play. Because he adapts only the final two acts of *Pericles*, Lillo must interrupt his scenes with lengthy passages of exposition; similarly undramatic speeches are required to clarify the thematic situation. On occasion, Lillo does achieve something like the poetic strength of his source. Often, however, even the basically Shakespearian verse is weakened by revision, usually the result of Lillo's concern to explain or underscore a thematic point.[21]

---

[15] II. i. 183–4 and 192–8.

[16] III. ii. 246–248a.

[17] Cf. Hoeniger, pp. lxxix–lxxxviii. Maxwell (p. xxvii) cites a number of the commentators who have emphasized this theme of patience in adversity.

[18] III. ii. 309–12.   [19] III. ii. 164–5.   [20] II. i. 200–1.

[21] Burgess (pp. 21–3) suggests that the problem stems from Lillo's lack of facility in close adaptation: 'In every case where he adhered closely to the original, reworking line by line passages he found in *Pericles*, the results . . . were not happy. This is true even where there was margin for improvement, where Lillo was dealing with, if not bad lines, then, at least, lines which are not among Shakespeare's most successful. The few instances of genuine power, of felicitous thought and expression in the play's verse are to be found among those passages which are original with Lillo, where he added to rather than adapted from his source.' However, deBoer (pp. 170–1) feels that the influence of Lillo's Shakespearian source is evidenced in an improvement in his poetry.

Despite its defects, *Marina* has been singled out as one of the best of the eighteenth-century adaptations of Shakespeare;[22] certainly it is one of the most thoughtful, strikingly representative of its period and, even more, its author. As the dramatization of an idea, the play stands as a counterpart to *Fatal Curiosity*, Lillo's tragedy of disbelief. Although it lacks the strength of the playwright's domestic dramas, it serves not only to emphasize the importance of his particular doctrine of providence but also as a useful example against which to measure Lillo's thematically less specific if dramatically more successful plays.

PERFORMANCE AND RECEPTION

Marina was first acted at Covent Garden on 1 August 1738.[23] Performance of the new play in mid-summer suggests that Lillo had again found the managers of the Theatres Royal less than eager to risk production of his work. *Marina* was advertised as 'Alter'd . . . by the Author of George Barnwell', but it seems likely that the play was scheduled because it was based on Shakespeare. In his epilogue, Lillo praises the Shakespeare Ladies' Club, whose vigorous efforts to restore the 'manly genius' of the English stage had brought about revivals of a number of Shakespeare's plays. Whether the ladies directly influenced the writing and performance of *Marina* or Lillo simply hoped for their support is not known.[24] However, the managers of the theatres had themselves been promoting revivals of Shakespeare's plays—primarily the comedies—as a way to counter audience reaction against new plays in the months immediately following passage of the Licensing Act.[25] Perhaps at Covent Garden there was hope that the comic scenes in *Marina* would prove sufficiently entertaining to fill the house during the slack season.

Davies, in a prefatory remark to his comments on *Marina*, says 'It was the fate of Lillo to be reduced to the necessity of having his plays presented by inferior actors.'[26] Certainly the actors in the summer company at Covent Garden were not as strong as those who held the stage at the height of the season. Arthur Hallam, who played Lysimachus and whose signature on the application for licensing suggests that he managed the summer company, was not among the most notable actors on the theatre's roster.[27] The career of Samuel Stephens, who acted Pericles, had begun with a brilliant success as Othello in 1734 and mercurially descended; during the regular seasons, 1737–9, Stephens played

---

[22] Genest (iii. 567) called the adaptation 'on the whole . . . a good one', and Odell (i. 259) concedes, if somewhat grudgingly, that Lillo 'was a bigger man than your Johnsons and Millers'.

[23] *London Stage, 1729–1747*.

[24] See Commentary on the Epilogue. Burgess (p. 20) sees the play as 'a rather transparent attempt to capitalize on the interest engendered by the subscription series to Shakespeare of the season before', a series sponsored by the ladies' club. However, deBoer (p. 210) writes that 'it is clear that *Marina* was written and staged as a result of the efforts of this determined band'. The available evidence is too indefinite to support either of these conclusions.

[25] *London Stage, 1729–1747*, vol. i, p. cl.

[26] p. xxxvi. [27] See cast lists, *London Stage, 1729–1747, passim.*

second and third leads but later worked steadily down to bit parts.[28] Marina was undertaken by Miss Vincent, apparently a most accomplished young leading lady, though her talents may not have been ideally suited to Lillo's sober Marina; her roles during the summer season included Sylvia in *The Old Bachelor* and Polly in *The Beggar's Opera*. As usual in this period, a female part considered indelicate beyond the sensibilities (or reputations) of the actresses was performed by an actor in skirts. William Hallam was a popular comedian and Lillo's comic scenes must have been well served by his performance as Mother Coupler.[29]

Whatever the virtues or defects of its production, *Marina* did not succeed. The play was given a second performance on Thursday, 4 August, and acted once more on the following Tuesday—the author's benefit night—but was not scheduled again.[30] There is no record of a revival.

LILLO'S COPY OF *PERICLES*

Although Lillo frequently follows passages of *Pericles* quite closely, his alterations of the details of the text are so extensive that precise identification of the edition of the play with which he worked is not possible. The catalogue of the posthumous sale of his books and those of 'Another Gentleman . . . lately Deceased'[31] lists 'Pope's Shakespeare, 9 vol., 1728', the edition which includes Sewell's supplementary volume in which *Pericles* appears. Collation suggests that Lillo may have used this edition while writing *Marina*. However, except for a single, less than decisive, instance in which Lillo's text duplicates a reading otherwise unique to Sewell's edition,[32] the emended readings shared by the two texts are also to be found in Rowe's editions of 1709 and 1714. Moreover, Lillo's text twice includes readings found only in the edition of *Pericles* published by Tonson in 1734,[33] which, with the possible exception of Robert Walker's unauthorized edition (also 1734), was the most recent edition of the play available in 1738. However, the text of the Tonson edition agrees, in the main, with the Rowe and Sewell editions, the two distinctive readings are not decisive, and one variation between the Tonson text and *Marina* argues strongly that Lillo used some edition other than Tonson's.[34]

The printed text of *Marina*, though not the Larpent manuscript, twice includes distinctive readings paralleled in early editions of *Pericles* but

---

[28] *London Stage, 1729–1747*, vol. i, p. cxxx.

[29] See cast lists, *London Stage, 1729–1747, passim*.

[30] *London Stage, 1729–1747*, ii. 725 *et passim*.

[31] Bodleian Library, Mus. Bibl. III 8°/81. For a detailed description of the catalogue, see William McBurney, 'What George Lillo Read: A Speculation', *Huntington Library Quarterly*, xxix (May 1966), 275–86.

[32] II. ii. 137: 'sty', Lillo and Sewell; 'stue', other editions.

[33] III. ii. 365: 'preserv'd', Lillo and Tonson; 'prefer'd', other editions (see Commentary). I. i. 71: 'haling', Lillo and Tonson; 'hailing', other editions (but see n. 35 below).

[34] I. i. 29: 'purple∧', Lillo, Rowe, and Sewell; 'purple,', Tonson. Inclusion of the comma alters the sense (*Pericles*, IV. i. 15).

eliminated by emendation in the eighteenth-century texts.[35] It is possible, then, that Lillo or someone concerned with the publication of *Marina* referred to an old copy of the play.

Beyond question, however, Lillo normally worked from an eighteenth-century text of *Pericles*, and while the evidence is not decisive, it is more likely that he used Sewell's supplement to Pope's Shakespeare than any other text.

THE TEXT

Marina appeared in a single, authorized edition published less than a month after the play's brief run in the theatre. It was not reprinted until Davies issued his collection of Lillo's works in 1775. The manuscript submitted to the Lord Chamberlain closely parallels, for the most part, the text of the first edition but clearly represents an earlier state of the text. A copy, not a holograph, the manuscript has no authority.

Larpent Manuscript

Arthur Hallam's application for a licence to perform the play, written on the verso of the first leaf of the manuscript submitted to the Chamberlain's office, is dated 6 July 1738. The manuscript (Larpent MS 9 in the Huntington Library) is the work of two copyists, one of whom transcribed the title, prologue, dramatis personae, and Acts I and II in a clear, somewhat embellished, hand; the second copyist transcribed Act III and the epilogue in a rougher hand, apparently working in some haste.[36] Variations between the manuscript and the text of the first edition are noted in the Historical Collation.

First Edition

John Gray registered his copyright of *Marina* on 21 August 1738. An advertisement in the *London Daily Post and General Advertiser* indicates that his edition was published on 22 August.[37] The edition was reissued in Gray's nonce collection of Lillo's plays, c.21 June 1740.

For the title-page, see p. 343. All copies print '*CONVENT-GARDEN*'.

Collation: 8° (4's) A–G⁴ H² [\$2 (− A1, H2) signed]; 30 leaves, pp. *i–ii* iii–vi
   vii–viii 9–60 [iii, 9 centred in parentheses]
   Var: misprinting 53 as '35' (2 copies)

[35] III. ii. 243: 'imposture' (see Commentary); I. i. 71: 'haling' (the reading does appear also in Tonson's edition).

[36] Abbreviations of characters' names in speech-headings vary considerably in Act III and at times are reduced to the minimal notation required to identify the characters (e.g. 'Bo.' and 'Ba.' for 'Bolt' and 'Bawd' for most of III. i.). Speech-headings in Acts I and II vary only occasionally (e.g. 'Baw.' and 'Bawd'). The dramatis personae and normally, though not always, the text give the spelling 'Boult' for 'Bolt' ('Bou.' at times in Acts I and II, 'BOU.' and 'Bo.' in Act III).

[37] *London Daily Post and General Advertiser*, 22 Aug., 'This Day is Publish'd . . .'. The advertisement is repeated on 23 Aug., and similar announcements appear in the *Daily Gazetteer* for 26 and 28 Aug., and the *Craftsman* for 9 and 16 Sept.

Contents: A1(*i*) title A1ᵛ(*ii*) blank A2 (iii)–A3ᵛ(vi) dedication A4(*vii*) prologue A4ᵛ(*viii*) dramatis personae B1(9)–H2(59) text (DH: [double rule] | *MARINA*. | [rule]) H2(59)–H2ᵛ(60) epilogue and advertisement

Comments

Comparison of copies on the Hinman Collator reveals no press corrections or accidents, except that in two of the copies examined page 53 is misnumbered as '35'. There is no indication of reimpression. One error has been corrected by hand in all copies seen.[38] The publisher did not advertise copies printed on fine paper and none have been found.

The edition was well produced, cleanly pointed, and set in a relatively modern style with light capitalization. It is, of course, the only authoritative text of the play.

Comparison of the edition with the Larpent manuscript does reveal variants which indicate authorial revision during or after production in the theatre. A number of these adjustments simply represent the polishing of lines or phrases and the correction of slips between source and adaptation. Of greater interest are a few variants, passages several lines in length and certainly authorial, that provide significant evidence of Lillo's efforts to reshape and expand the Shakespearian material to his own intentions. The important confrontation between Marina and Lysimachus, for example, is greatly heightened and changed by two passages that appear only in the printed text.[39] In the first of these, Lillo seems clearly concerned to redefine and improve the character of Lysimachus: in the new lines the point is made that Lysimachus, though young and susceptible to temptation, has remained chaste and that even now he has no general predilection for the lewd pleasures of Mother Coupler's den but cannot resist the particular beauty of Marina. This reinterpreted Lysimachus is a young man well suited to rule his people and, in the proper setting, an appropriate suitor for Marina. More significantly, the adjustment of characterization provides Lillo with the opportunity to dramatize again the overwhelming threat of passion, which in a moment can transform and destroy even the most virtuous if they are young. Marina's stature is similarly heightened by her offer to kill herself to preserve her chastity, an incident not included in the scene as given in the Larpent text. The need to improve the character of Lysimachus could well have occurred to Lillo as he reviewed the scene in his study but might also have become evident as he observed the play in rehearsal; the threatened suicide smacks of the theatre. Whether these major additions were made before or during production, they were not isolated changes but formed a part of a careful reshaping of the entire scene, revision evidenced by a series of minor substantive variations between the printed text and the manuscript submitted to the Lord Chamberlain.[40]

---

[38] II. i. 42. In the phrase 'our own wants', 'own' is crossed out.
[39] II. ii. 81–119a and 122a–131b.   [40] See apparatus criticus and the Commentary.

A third substantial addition to the text serves primarily to supply necessary exposition, though the lines also provide an easier opening for a scene that, if played in the manuscript version, would begin with awkward abruptness.[41] The added passage includes a pair of lines[42] which in the manuscript appear later in the scene, an indication that the speech was indeed inserted late and not inadvertently omitted from the Larpent text or its source.

In the opening portion of Act III, scene ii, the omission from the printed text of a number of lines recorded in the manuscript suggests that the author attempted to shorten or speed up an episode which serves primarily to set the scene and provide exposition for the important reunion scene that follows.

The remainder of the play was not extensively revised after the Larpent manuscript was copied. Variants include fewer than ten revisions of lines and a similarly small number of lines deleted before publication. Variants that involve changes in one or two words, however, are relatively numerous. A number of these may well represent compositorial normalization—'I am' for 'I'm', and the like. Other minor substantive changes appear to be authorial and include the systematic substitution of 'Mistress' for 'Patrona', the form of address for the bawd regularly given in the Larpent text.[43]

The accidentals of the manuscript and first edition differ frequently. No evidence suggests that the author gave particular concern to this aspect of the printed text, and the variants probably indicate the individual practices of compositor(s) and copyists working with lightly pointed copy.

Later Reprint

Thomas Davies reprinted *Marina* in his collection of Lillo's works, published in 1775. His text was set from a copy of the first edition, which it follows closely.

Editorial Procedure

The first edition serves as copy-text for the present edition. The very few errors and extreme infelicities of the copy-text have been corrected, where possible with readings from the Larpent manuscript and where necessary with reference to Davies's edition (1775). In every case, a possible reading in the first edition has been accepted in preference to an alternative offered by the manuscript. As far as possible, typographical distinction is made between prose speeches and lines of verse in scenes in which the two are mixed and, at times, alternate rapidly.[44]

---

[41] II. i. 1–11. [42] II. i. 6–7. [43] See the Commentary on I. ii. 2.

[44] The copy-text is the first edition, a Huntington Library copy. Copies collated include: *first edition*, CSmH (2 copies), CtMW, CtY, O (4 copies); Davies, *Works* (1775), CtMW, O, BL (3 copies), CtY (2 copies).

MARINA:

A
PLAY

OF
THREE ACTS.

As it is Acted at the

THEATRE ROYAL

IN

CONVENT-GARDEN.

Taken from

PERICLES Prince of TYRE.

By Mr. LILLO.

LONDON:

Printed for JOHN GRAY, at the *Cross-Keys* in the *Poultry*, near *Cheapside*. M.DCC.XXXVIII.

[Price *One Shilling*.]

TO THE

RIGH T HONOURABLE the

Countess of Hertford.

MADAM,

Permit me to hope that you will pardon the honest ambition which has encourag'd me to seek a proper Patroness for *Marina* in your Ladyship; whose real character gives countenance to the imaginary one, and whose constant practice is a living example of that steady virtue, and exalted piety, which the   5 Author of the old Play from whence this is taken, has happily described in his *Princess of Tyre*.

Conscious of no mean views, and secur'd by the universal acknowledgment of your merit from the imputation of flattery, I approach your Ladyship, though a stranger, and without any previous application, with the less   10 diffidence: If this Play should appear on perusal to be designed to promote something better than meer amusement, that will effectually recommend it to the favour of the Countess of *Hertford*.

To place merit in the gifts of fortune, and happiness in what an hour may, and a few years certainly will bring to an end, is the folly and misery of too many   15 who are reputed wise and great. To be truly so is with your Ladyship to regard the finest understanding, the most fruitful invention, the happiest elocution, talents far superior to wealth and dignity, but as they subserve the interest of truth and virtue, and render the possessors of them, in the midst of affluence, moderate even in the use of lawful pleasures, humble in the most exalted   20 stations, and capable of living above the world, even in the possession of all it can bestow. I am afraid and unwilling to offend. But as universal benevolence is the perfection of virtue, your Ladyship must suffer your own to be spoken of, however painful it may be to you, that others may not want a pattern for their encouragement or reprehension, as they shall improve or neglect it. A truly   25 great mind discovers it self by nothing more than by a benign and well plac'd condescension; of which your Ladyship's known esteem for the late excellent Mrs. *Rowe*, is a noble instance, and an undoubted proof, amongst many others which you daily give, of the goodness of your heart and understanding, and cannot be mentioned but to your honour.   30

I can affirm, and I hope I shall be thought sincere, that what I have said doth not proceed from custom as a Dedicator, but from a mind fully convinc'd of its truth in every circumstance, and a heart touch'd with a character so very amiable.

Dedication is not in L

That you may long live an ornament and a support of those excellent
principles which you profess and practice, and that your influence and example
may do all the good that you your self can wish, is the earnest desire of,

Your LADYSHIP'*s*

Most obedient

Humble Servant,

GEO. LILLO.

PROLOGUE.

Hard is the task, in this discerning age,
To find new subjects that will bear the stage;
And bold our bards, their low harsh strains to bring
Where Avon's Swan has long been heard to sing:
Blest Parent of our Scene! whose matchless wit,　　　　　5
Tho' yearly reap'd, is our best harvest yet.
Well may that genius every heart command,
Who drew all nature with her own strong hand;
As various, as harmonious, fair and great,
With the same vigour and immortal heat,　　　　　10
As through each element and form she shines:
We view Heav'ns hand-maid in her Shakespear's lines.
Though some mean scenes, injurious to his fame,
Have long usurp'd the honour of his Name;
To glean and clear from chaff his least remains,　　　　　15
Is just to him, and richly worth our pains.
We dare not charge the whole unequal play
Of Pericles on him; yet let us say,
As gold though mix'd with baser matter shines,
So do his bright inimitable lines　　　　—　　　　20
Throughout those rude wild scenes distinguish'd stand,
And show he touch'd them with no sparing hand.

　With humour mix'd in your fore-fathers way,
We've to a single tale reduc'd our play.
Charming Marina's wrongs begin the scene;　　　　　25
Pericles finding her with his lost Queen,
Concludes the pleasing task. Shou'd as the soul,
The fire of Shakespear animate the whole,
Shou'd heights which none but he cou'd reach, appear,
To little errors do not prove severe.　　　　　30
If, when in pain for the event, surprize
And sympathetick joy shou'd fill your eyes;
Do not repine that so you crown an art,
Which gives such sweet emotions to the heart:
Whose pleasures, so exalted in their kind,　　　　　35
Do, as they charm the sense, improve the mind.

23 L does not indent or allow space above the line

Dramatis Personæ.

MEN.

PERICLES, *King of* Tyre. —   Mr. *Stephens.*

LYSIMACHUS, *Governor of*
Ephesus. — — —   Mr. *Hallam.*

ESCANES, *Chief Attendant*
on Pericles. — —   Mr. *Shelton.*

LEONINE, *A young Lord of*
Tharsus. — — —   Mr. *Stevens.*

VALDES, *Captain of a Crew*
of Pirates. — —   Mr. *Bowman.*

BOLT, A Pander. — —   Mr. *Penkethman.*

WOMEN.

THAISA, *Queen of* Tyre. ——   Mrs. *Marshall.*

PHILOTEN, *Queen of* Tharsus.   Mrs. *Hamilton.*

MARINA, *Daughter to* Pericles
and Thaisa. ——   Mrs. *Vincent.*

MOTHER COUPLER, *A Bawd.*   Mr. *W. Hallam.*

Gentlemen, Two Priestesses, Ladies, Officers, Guards,
Pirates, and *Attendants.*

2–12 *Character descriptions and actors' names are not in* L   7 *Below this line* L *reads:* 3 Pyrates
13–14 *Gentlemen, . . . and Attendants.*] Gentlemen, Ladies, Officers, Guards, | and Attendants.—L

MARINA.

ACT I.

SCENE I.

A Grove, *with a Prospect of a calm Sea, near*
the City of Tharsus.

Enter Philoten *and* Leonine.

Queen.

Thy oath remember, thou hast sworn to do it,
'Tis but a blow, which never shall be known.
Kind Nature hath been bounteous to thy youth:
Thy graceful person, language and address,
Are almost peerless, and thy steril fortune   5
Our favour shall improve. But let not conscience,
Which none who hope to rise in courts regard,
Disarm your hand, nor her bewitching eyes
Inflame your amorous bosom.
Leon.   I have promis'd,
And will perform. Yet she's a goodly creature.   10
Q. The fitter for the Gods. I, while she lives,
Am not a Queen. This poor, this friendless daughter
Of *Pericles*, the wretched Prince of *Tyre*,
Whom my fond Parents from compassion foster'd,
Is more belov'd, more reverenc'd in *Tharsus*   15
Than I their Sov'reign. And when foreign Princes,
Drawn by the fame of my high rank and beauty,
As suitors, throng my court; let her appear
(Such is the force of her detested charms)
And I am streight neglected; and their vows   20
And adorations all transferr'd to her.
Here she comes, weeping for my mother's death:
She had good cause to love her. Let not pity,

(I. i) SD *A* Grove] Scene a Grove L   *Sea, near* | *the City of* Tharsus.] Sea∧ | at a distance. L
Enter Philoten *and* Leonine.] Philoten Q. of Tharsus and Leonine∧ L   1 hast sworn] art
bound L   5 thy] your L   10 perform.] ~—L   11 I, while] And while L
12 Am not a] I am no L   16 Than] The{ir}n L

Which women have cast off, defeat your purpose:
There's nothing thou can'st do, live e'er so long,
Shall yield thee so much profit.

Leon. I'm determin'd.

Enter Marina *with a wreath of flowers.*

Mar. No: I will rob gay *Tellus* of her weed,
To strew thy grave with flowers. The yellows, blues,
The purple violets and marygolds
Shall, as a carpet, hang upon thy tomb,
While summer days do last. Ah me, poor maid!
Born in a tempest when my mother dy'd,
And now I mourn a second mother's loss.
This world, to me, is like a lasting storm,
That swallows, piece by piece, the merchant's wealth,
And in the end himself.

Q. Why, sweet *Marina,*
Will you consume your youth in fruitless grief,
And choose to dwell 'midst tombs and dreary graves?
You harm your self, and profit not the dead.
Give me that wreath, who have most cause to mourn,
And let your heart take comfort. I will leave you
To the sweet conversation of this Lord,
Who has the art of dissipating sadness.

Mar. Pray, let me not bereave you of his service:
I choose to be alone.

Q. You know I love you
With more than foreign heart, and will not see
The beauty marr'd that fame reports so perfect.
Shou'd your good father come at length to seek you,
And find his hopes and all report so blasted,
He may repent the breadth of his great voyage,
And blame our want of care.

Mar. You may command,
But I have no desire to tarry here.

Q. Once more be chearful, and preserve that form
That wins from all competitors the hearts
Of young and old. 'Tis no new thing for me
To walk alone, while you are well attended.

Mar. I hope you're not offended.

Q. Nothing less.
Farewell, sweet Lady. Sir, you will remember—

(I. i) 26b I'm] I am L   49 hopes] L; ~, G   58 Lady.] ~— L

Leon. Fear not, she ne'er shall vex your quiet more.   [*Exit* Queen.
Mar. I know no cause, yet think the gentle Queen   60
     Went hence in some displeasure. Is she well?
     What are your thoughts?
Leon.   That she's nor well, nor gentle.
Mar. I'm sorry for't. Is the wind westerly?
Leon. South-west.
Mar.   When I was born the wind was north.
Leon. The wind was north you say. I should not hear her,   65
     Lest I relent. The Queen's enamour'd of me,
     She prais'd my blooming youth, and good proportion:
     And shall I lose a crown for foolish pity?
Mar. My Father, as *Lychorida* hath told me,
     (My Nurse that's dead) did never fear: but then,   70
     Galling his kingly hands with haling ropes,
     And chearing the faint Sailors with his voice,
     Endur'd a sea, that almost burst the deck.
Leon. And when was this?
Mar.   I said when I was born.
     Never were waves nor winds more violent.   75
     This tempest, and my birth, kill'd my poor Mother,
     I was preserv'd, and left an Infant here.
     Now do you think I e'er shall see my Father?
Leon. Never. Come, say your prayers.
Mar.   What do you mean?
Leon. If you require a little space for pray'r,   80
     That I'll allow you; pray, but be not tedious:
     The Gods are quick of ear, and I'm in haste.
Mar. Why will you kill me, Sir?
Leon.   T' obey the Queen.
Mar. Why will she have me kill'd? I never wrong'd her.
     In all my life I never spake bad word,   85
     Nor did ill turn to any living creature:
     By chance I once trod on a simple worm,
     But I wept for it. How have I offended?
Leon. I'm not to reason of the deed, but do it.
Mar. You will not do't for all the world, I hope.   90
     You are well favour'd, and your looks bespeak
     A very gentle heart. I saw you lately,
     When you caught hurt in parting two that fought:
     Good sooth, it shew'd well in you: Do so now:
     If the Queen seeks my life, come you between,   95

(I. i)   71 haling] halling L. *See Commentary*   74b born.] ~—L   76 Mother,] ~: L
85 spake] spoke L   89 of] on L   94 you:] ~. L

And save poor me the weaker.

Leon.   I have sworn,
And will dispatch.

Mar.   Yet hear me speak once more.   [*Kneeling.*
O do not kill me, though I know no cause
Why I should wish to live who ne'er knew joy,
Or fear to die who ever fear'd the Gods;
But 'tis, perhaps, the property of youth
To doat on its new being, and depend,
Howe'er deprest, on pleasures in reversion.
You are but young your self: then, as you hope
To prove the fancy'd bliss of years to come,
Spare me, O spare me now.

Leon.   You plead in vain,
Commit your soul to heaven.

Mar.   Can you speak thus!
O can you have compassion for my soul;
Yet, at the instant, by a cruel deed,
That Heaven and Earth must hate, destroy your own?

Enter Pirate, *and interposes.*

1 *Pir.*   Hold, villain. Fear not, fair one, I'll defend thee.
Leon.   Slave, how doth her defence belong to you?
                Who, and what are you?

1 *Pir.* A man, fool. *Alexander* the Great was no more. You are a poltron, a
coward, and a rascal, to draw cold iron on a woman.

Leon.   I want not courage, base intruding villain,
                To scourge thy insolence.   [*Fight.*

Mar.   You gracious Gods!
                Must I behold, and be the cause of murder?

Enter second, and then third Pirate.

2 *Pir.* A prize! A prize!
3 *Pir.* Half part, Mate, half part.
1 *Pir.* What, are they quarrelling about my booty! Hold, Sir.
Leon.   With all my heart.
                If you increase so fast, 'tis time to fly.
                I know them now for Pirates.   [*Exit* Leonine.

1 *Pir.* Hands off. I found her first.
2 *Pir.* That's no claim amongst us.
3 *Pir.* No, none at all. Every man is to have his share of all the prizes we take.

(I. i)   97b *Mar.*] *speech-heading not in* L   111 Hold,] L; ~ ∧ G   villain. Fear] ~—fear L
114 fool.] ~— L   poltron] poltroon L. *See Commentary*   115 a coward] {&} a coward L
121 about] {for} about L   124 them] 'em L

1 *Pir.* Nay, if you come to that, she belongs to the whole ship's company.

2 *Pir.* Who denies that? But I will not quit my part in her to the Captain himself: sink me if I do.   130

3 *Pir.* Nor I, by *Neptune*.

1 *Pir.* This is no place to dispute in. We shall have the city rise upon us: therefore we must have her aboard suddenly.

Omnes. Ay; bear a hand, bear a hand.

1 *Pir.* Come, sweet Lady.   135

2 *Pir.* None shall hurt you.

3 *Pir.* We'll lose our lives before we'll see you wrong'd.

Mar.   You sacred powers! who rule the rudest hearts,
                Protect me whilst among these lawless Men
                From loath'd pollution, violence and shame;   140
                And bold blasphemers, who shall hear the wonder,
                Shall own you are, and just.

1 *Pir.* A rare prize, if a man cou'd have her to himself. A pox of all ill fortune, say I.   [*Exeunt.*

Re-enter Leonine.

Leon.   These Pirates serve the daring ruffian *Valdes*,   145
                A desperate crew they are. There is no fear
                Marina will return. They'll, doubtless, have
                Their pleasure of her first; and then, perhaps,
                According to a custom long us'd by 'em,
                Sell her where she will ne'er be heard of more: 150
                Then I may take the merit of her death,
                And claim the whole reward. It shall be so.
                I'll swear to the fond Queen, I have dispatch'd
                And thrown her in the sea.—A rare device!—
                These rogues have sav'd me from a hellish deed,   155
                And a fair wind attend them.   [*Exit* Leonine.

SCENE II.

A House in Ephesus.

Enter Bawd *and* Bolt.

Bawd. Sad times, *Bolt*.

Bolt. Ay, very sad times, Mistress.

Bawd. This new order, so much talk'd of, for suppressing publick lewdness, will be the ruin of us. All our business will fall into private hands. I must shut up my doors, I must quit my house, unless we can find some way to evade it.

Bolt. Whip Bawds and Panders! fine doings! rare Magistrates! Let 'em whip their own lubberly Sons and dough-bak'd Daughters for their idleness, and not punish people for their industry and service to the publick.

Bawd. Nay, nay, if they will return iniquity out of the high-ways, they must expect to find it in their families. Let them keep their Wives and Daughters honest if they can. The necessities of Gentlemen must be supply'd.

Bolt. There are abundance of foreign Merchants and Travellers here in *Ephesus*, that us'd to be our customers.

Bawd. And old Batchelors.

Bolt. And younger Brothers.

Bawd. And disconsolate Widowers.

Bolt. And Husbands that have old Wives.

Bawd. And Philosophers, Lawyers, and Soldiers that have none at all; and all these must be serv'd.

Bolt. And will, while Women are to be had for money, love, or importunity.

Bawd. Ay, let the Citizens, who spirited up this prosecution against our useful vocation, think of the consequence, and tremble.

Bolt. Yet, after all, these threats may come to nothing. You have weather'd many such a storm, Mother *Coupler*.

Bawd. Ay, *Bolt*, I have had my ups and my downs—no Woman more—But I will not be discourag'd, I will not neglect business for a rumour neither. The mart will fill the town, and we are but meanly finish'd.

Bolt. Never worse. Three poor wenches are all our store, and they can do no more than they can.

Bawd. Thou say'st true. And those so stale, so sunk, and so diseas'd, that a strong wind would blow 'em all to pieces. I must have others, whatever they cost me.

Bolt. Shall I search the slave market?

Bawd. Those we buy there, are mostly half worn out before we have them. There was the little *Transilvanian* you bought last, did not live above three months, and never brought in half the money she cost.

Bolt. Ay, she was quickly made meat for worms. But there are losses in all trades, and ours not being honest—

Bawd. Marry come up; I pray, what trades are honest, as they are us'd? We are no worse then others.

Enter Valdes, *and other* Pirates, *with* Marina.

Vald. Where's Mother *Coupler*? Where are you, Bawd?

Bawd. Why, how now, Roister? How now, Captain Thief? Use your

Tarpaulin language to thy own natural Mother; do, Brawn and Bristle, do, Ironface.

Vald. Let any one be judge, whether my chin, somewhat black and rough I   45
must confess, or thine, that's cover'd with grey down, like a goose's rump, be the more comely. Thy face is a *memento mori* for thy own sex, and to ours an antidote against the sin you live by. But, see what we have brought you: Here's a Paragon.

Bolt. [*Aside the Bawd.*] Mark the colour of her hair, complection, shape and   50
age.

Bawd. I have noted them all. When Nature form'd this piece, she meant me a good turn.

Vald. Here's that will repair your decay'd arras, and set you up for a Bawd of condition.   55

Bawd. I was just saying, what stale, worn out creatures are daily brought to market; and those who buy of Pirates, must expect as bad, or worse: And then I have choice enough, and those not blown on.

Vald. Nay, nay, use your pleasure: You have the first proffer of her. If she's not for your turn, there's no harm done: She's any one's money.   60

Bawd. You don't consider the dulness of the times. If men were as they have been—

Vald. A virgin too.

Bawd. A likely matter, coming from the hands of such a lawless crew!

Vald. You are deceived. We have laws amongst our selves, or I would not   65
have parted with her. However we are distinguish'd by titles and office, each man hath a right to his proportion of every prize we take; which all claiming on the sight of her, and refusing to compound with, or give place to any other, there ensued such jealousy, such fury and contention, that we were obliged, by common consent, to leave her untouch'd, and dispose of her, as soon as   70
possible, to prevent the cutting of one anothers throats.

Bawd. Well, what's your price?

Vald. What do you mean, ready rigg'd? She has excellent cloaths you see.

Bawd. If I deal for her, I take her altogether.

Vald. I won't bate one doit of a thousand pieces.   75

Bawd. What shall I give you for your conscience, *Valdes*?

Vald. Your honesty, Mother *Coupler.* We won't differ for a trifle.

Bawd. Five hundred pieces, Sir!

Vald. Four times told, Madam.

Bawd. Why, what the Devil, you said but a thousand e'en now.   80

Vald. I thought you cou'dn't hear but by halves, and was willing to come up to your understanding.

Bolt. You'll stand haggling till you lose her.

(I. ii)   45 be] *not in* L   50 *Bolt.* [*Aside the Bawd.*] Mark] (Boult to the Bawd apart | Mark L
56 what] that L   57–8 I have] I've L   65 amongst] among L   73 mean,] L; ~∧ G
74 her altogether] altogether L

Vald. Look you, I am at a word. But for the reason I just now spoke of, you shou'd not have had her for twice the sum.

Bawd. Follow me, and you shall have your money. *Bolt*, take care of my purchase.

Bolt. Never fear, Mistress, never fear.   [*Exeunt* Vald., Bawd *and* Pirates.

Mar.   Immortal Gods! to what am I reserv'd?

Bolt. Come hither, child. You are but young, and may want some instructions. Tho' she who has bought you, your Mistress and mine, knows as much as a woman can know; yet there's nothing like a man to teach you the practical part of business, take my word for it.

Mar. What are you, Sir?

Bolt. A middle aged person, as you see; and in perfect health, that you may depend upon.

Mar. Is your mind sound?

Bolt. She's mighty simple. Ay, ay, as sound as my body.

Mar.   The Gods preserve it so. Yet you talk strangely.

Bolt. I thank you heartily for your good wishes. Nay, I am the principal person in this family, after our Mistress: It may be well worth your while to make a friend of me.

Mar.   I know not, but am sure I want a friend.
          I am of maids most wretched.

Bolt. I'll quickly ease you of the wretchedness of being a maid. Yet you must pass for one, and often.

Mar. I understand you not.

Bolt. Such things are common here. But of that, and other needful arts in our profession, my Mistress will inform you.   [*Lays hold of her.*

Mar.   Why do you rudely lay your hands upon me?
          I am not to be touch'd.

Bolt. Not to be touch'd! Ha, ha, in troth a pretty jest, and will do rarely with some young gulls. To seem most fearful when you are most willing, and weep as you do now, will move the pity of your Inamoratos, and strain their purses to shower down gold upon you. Your striving will not save you: This is no place for squeamish modesty: We live by lewdness here, and you were bought to carry on the trade.

Mar.   Hence, thou detested slave, thou shameless villain. [*Breaks from him.*

Enter Bawd.

          You powers that favour chastity, defend me.

Bawd. Why how now? what's the matter here? what have you been doing with her?

___

(I. ii)   84 I am] I'm L   88SD Vald.,] *Ed.*; Vald.ₐ G; Val.ₐ L   95 and] *not in* L
96 upon] {on} upon L   103 want] ~, L   103-4 friend. | . . . maids] ~. {I am of |
maid's} | I am of maid's L   114 your] you L

Bolt. Nothing, Mistress, and I am afraid there is nothing to be done with her. She fights like a she Tyger.

Bawd. Out, you rascal. Is this a morsel for your chaps?

Bolt. Why not? Do you think I'll serve up a delicate dish without tasting it? 125

Bawd. In your turn, sirrah, in your turn. Let your betters be serv'd before you.

Bolt. Ay, but a bit of the spit, you know—

Bawd. About your business, and let Gentlemen know how we are provided for their entertainment. [*Exit* Bolt.] Don't cry, pretty one: He shall be made to know his distance, and his time. While you behave discreetly, child, you shall be 130 reserv'd for the better sort of men only. You are fallen into good hands, depend upon it.

Mar.   O why was *Leonine* so slack, so slow!
           Wou'd he had us'd his sword, and not his tongue!
           Or that the Pirates, not enough Barbarians,   135
           Had thrown me in the sea to seek my mother.

Bawd. Come, come, my rose-bud, my sprig of Jessamin, you are all beauty and sweetness—you have no cause to grieve—Heaven has done its part by you.

Mar. I accuse not Heaven.

Bawd. Here you may live, and shall.   140

Mar.   The more's my grief.
           T' have scap'd his hands, who wou'd have given me death.

Bawd. And live with pleasure.

Mar. No.

Bawd. You shall not want variety: you shall have men, and men of all 145 complexions.

Mar. Are you a woman?

Bawd. A woman! pray, what do you take me for, Madam? I have been thought a woman, and an handsome woman in my time.

Mar. Of this I'm sure, you are not what you shou'd be: A woman shou'd be 150 honest.

Bawd. O the Devil!

Mar. And modest, and religious.

Bawd. You're a sapling to talk so to one of my experience. Honest, modest, and religious, with a pox to you! I'll make you know, before I've done with you, 155 that I won't have any such thing mention'd in my house.

Mar. The gracious Gods defend me.

Bawd. What, do you offer to say your prayers in my hearing! Is this a place to pray in? Don't provoke me, don't. I find I shall have something to do with you. But you shall bend or break, I can tell you that for your comfort.   160

Enter Bolt.

(I. ii)   122 Mistress] Patrona L   127 Ay, but] Ay, Patrona, but L   148 I have]
I've L   149 an] a L   154 a] *not in* L

Bolt. Mistress, here's the lean *French* Knight, he that cowers in the hams, and the fat *German* Count.

Bawd. In good time. Here, take this stubborn fool, and carry her to them.

Bolt. To which of them?

Bawd. To him that will give most first, and to the other afterwards. She cost me a round sum, but don't refuse money. Her blushes must be quench'd with present practice: She's good for nothing as she is.

Mar. Diana, aid my purpose.

Bolt. Come your ways. What have we to do with *Diana*?

Bawd. Ay, troop, follow your Leader. We'll teach you honesty, modesty, and religion with a vengeance.

Mar.   If fires be hot, steel sharp, or waters deep,
                 Unstain'd I still my virgin fame will keep.   [*Exeunt.*

                    The End of the First ACT.

ACT II.

SCENE I.

An Apartment adjoining to a Temple at the
Court of Tharsus.

Enter Queen *and* Leonine.

Leonine.

To bury kneaded earth for dead *Marina*
Was a most quaint device. The cheated *Tharsians*
Pierced Heaven with their howlings; but suspicion,
As if Death closed her busy prying eyes
When the fair *Tyrian* died, still slumbers on.   5
The monument of *Parian* marble wrought,
And epitaph in characters of gold,
Were my contrivance too, and now are finish'd.
I have done all that your resentment ask'd,
And well secured your safety and your fame: 10
'Tis more than time you listen'd to my suit.
    Q. Can nothing but my person and my crown
Reward your service?
    Leon.   I deserve them both.
    Q. Were I sole mistress of the spacious world,
I'd give it all this murther were undone.   15
The very Wrens of *Tharsus* will betray it
To *Pericles*, who now comes to demand her.
    Leon. That's only in my power: Give me your promise
To be my bride, and seal my lips for ever.
    Q. What! wed a murtherer!
    Leon.   Who made me so?   20
Resolve in time ere ruin overtake you,
O'ertake us both. Your flatt'ries drew me in,
You taught me to be bloody and ambitious,
And I will now partake your throne, or perish—
But not alone. You know how popular   25
The injur'd Prince of *Tyre* is here in *Tharsus*.
This City, now the seat of wealth and plenty,
Whose towers invade the clouds, which never stranger
Beheld but wonder'd at, as all acknowledge,
Had but for *Pericles* been desolate,   30
Forsaken, or the grave of its inhabitants,

SD *a Temple*] the Temple L   1–11 Leonine. | To bury . . . my suit.] *not in* L
13a service] services L

A den for bats to build and wolves to howl in.
How many thousands, living now, remember,
When, famishing with hunger, Prince and people
Sat down and wept for bread; when tender mothers
Fed on their new born babes, and man and wife
Drew lots who first shou'd die, and furnish food
To lengthen out the life of the survivor.
This our distress brought *Pericles* from *Tyre*;
Who, bravely scorning to improve th' advantage,
And make a conquest of a prostrate land,
Did with a lib'ral hand supply our wants,
And turn our dying groans to songs of joy.
For this the *Tharsians* love him as a Father,
And as a God adore him.
     Q.   Be it so:
I'm still their Queen, and hold 'em in subjection.
    Leon. Yes, while they please: As we have seen a Lyon
Held with a thread, until some accident,
Or his rash keeper's folly, rous'd his fury.
They've some regard for the good line you came of,
And yet are thereby hardly held from outrage:
So hateful have the pride and other vices,
Notorious in you, made you to the million.
But shou'd they hear, or have the least suspicion
Of your foul dealing with the much lov'd daughter
Of royal *Pericles*, like flames let loose,
They'd in an instant make this lofty dome
Your fun'ral pile, and give the winds your ashes:
Or having torn you in ten thousand pieces,
With honest scorn, cast out your loath'd remains
For kites and crows to feed on.
     Q.   'Tis too true:
Shou'd this dark deed take light, my reign were ended.
I see I must comply. She who has us'd
A wicked agent in a shameful act,
Must thenceforth be his slave. You have my word.
Now your ambition's serv'd, teach me to answer
The King of *Tyre* when he demands his child.

(II. i)   39 our] their L   40 Who, bravely . . . th' advantage,] Who scorn'd to take th'
advantage their state gave him, L   42 Did] But L   supply] supply'd L   our] *Ed.*; our own
G (own *deleted by hand in all copies examined*); their L   43 turn our] turn'd their L
47 Yes, while] While L   50 for] to L   52 have] has L   59 pieces,] ~ ∧ L
62 ended.] ~ — L   63 comply.] ~ — L   65 slave.] ~ — L   word.] ~ — L

Leon. Say she dy'd suddenly, as what's more common?
That you wept o'er her hearse, and mourn her yet;
Then show the monument and epitaph   70
Procur'd at your expence; and her griev'd Sire
Shall curse the cruel fates that still pursue him
With plague on plague, but ne'er suspect that you
Have been their instrument.
Q.   The deed's not mine.—   [*Trumpets.*
Pericles comes, and I must seem content: 75
The Traytor's in the toils, and cannot 'scape me.

Enter Pericles, Escanes, *Guards and Attendants.*

Q. Welcome, great *Pericles*, to mourning *Tharsus.*
My royal parents and your faithful friends,
Cleon and *Dionysia*, are no more.
    Per. Ent'ring the port I met the fatal news.   80
The hot salt tears this unthought loss drew from me,
Are yet wet on my cheeks. O two such friends!—
But I'm a man born to adversity;
No land e'er gave me rest, and winds and waters,
In their vast tennis-court, have, as a ball,   85
Used me to make them sport.—But to my purpose.
'Tis more than twice seven years since I beheld thee
With my *Marina*, both were infants then.
Peace and security smil'd on your birth;
Her's was the rudest welcome to this world   90
That e'er was Prince's child: Born on the sea,
Hence is she call'd *Marina*, in a tempest,
When the high working billows kist the Moon,
And the shrill whistle of the boatswain's pipe
Seem'd as a whisper in the ear of Death: 95
Born when her Mother dy'd. That fatal hour
Must still live with me—O you gracious Gods!
Why do you make us love your goodly gifts,
And snatch them streight away? The waves receiv'd
My Queen. A sea mate's chest coffin'd her corpse;   100
In which she silent lies 'midst groves of coral,
Or in a glitt'ring bed of shining shells.
The air fed lamps of Heaven, the spouting whale,

(II. i)   70–1 epitaph | Procur'd] ~, | The one of choicest Parian marble wrought, | The other
penn'd in characters of gold, | Procur'd L   82–3 friends!— | But I'm ... to adversity;] ~,ʌ |
So loving, so beloved!—But I'm a man | Born to adversity, a mass of sorrow. L   84–6 No
land ... my purpose.] *not in* L   100 coffin'd] confin'd L

And dashing waters, that roll o'er her head,
Compose a monument to hide her bones,   1(
Spacious as Heaven, and lasting as the frame
Of universal Nature.
    Esc.   Royal Sir,
This sad companion, dull-ey'd Melancholy,
So long carest, shou'd now be cast aside.
    Per. O never, never: Do not interrupt me.   1
In the days glorious walk, or peaceful night,
When grief shou'd seem to sleep, a welcome guest,
She fills my anxious thoughts and broken slumbers
With the lov'd image of my lost *Thaisa*,
And prompts me to rehearse the oft-told tale   1
Of her disast'rous end; and chiefly now
I come to seek the Phenix that took life
From her dead ashes—But I've almost done—
We left my Princess in her wat'ry tomb,
And, as the winds gave way, arriv'd at *Tharsus*.   1
Here to your royal parents I committed
(Whose love I had experienc'd and deserv'd)
My only child, to give her education
Suiting her rank, and in some sort supply
Her pious mother's loss. And this the rather,   1
For that the peace of *Tyre* was sorely broken
By foreign foes, and treasons bred at home:
For I have drank the dregs of all misfortunes.
I vow'd too then, though it show'd wilful in me,
That all unsister'd shou'd this heir of mine   1
Remain till she were marry'd. Those commotions,
That long embroil'd me, being now compos'd;
I'm come to pay my thanks, and claim my daughter.
    Q. Unhappy Prince! wou'd Heaven have heard my Pray'rs,
Thy sweet *Marina* now by my lov'd side   1
Had bless'd thy longing eyes; but wretched mortals
In vain oppose the powers that rule above 'em:
Shou'd we rage loud as did the winds and seas
When she was born, things would be as they are.
Unfold those doors, and let the care-worn King   1
Behold the testimony of our love
To our fair foster Sister, and our grief
For her untimely fate.

  The Scene *draws, and discovers a Temple with the Monument.*

    Per. [*Reading.*]   'Here lieth interr'd
Marina, daughter to the Prince of *Tyre*.'
O thou who gav'st me reason and reflection,   145
Eternal *Jove*, rebuke these swelling thoughts,
That wou'd dispute your goodness or your being:
Bind them in walls of brass: Let me remember
I hold my powers from thee, that earthly man
Is but a substance made for your high pleasure: 150
Teach me, as fits my nature, to submit
To your thrice kindled wrath.
    Esc.   Let those who think.
They cou'd endure his woes, speak comfort to him;
My soul is faint with terror to behold 'em.
    Per. Fire, water, earth, and air in loud combustion   155
Herald my lost *Marina* to the light;
But dumb and speechless sorrow shall attend
Her timeless passage to the realms of death.
From this curst hour I'll never speak again,
To mock with words unutterable grief;   160
But make my manners savage as my fortunes,
And be as wretched as the Gods wou'd have me.
Sable shall be the ship henceforth that bears me;
No steel shall touch my face, no water cleanse it,
Nor comb be us'd to part my matted hair.   165
If e'er I change my raiment, galling sackcloth,
Instead of royal robes, shall gird my loins,
And ashes be my crown. I'll ne'er return,
Ne'er view thy spires again, renowned *Tyre*;
But wander through the world a wilful vagrant,   170
And ne'er taste comfort more till death relieve me,
Or *Jove* restore to my unhoping eyes
What his vindictive hand hath taken from me.
What I have been I'll study to forget:
Do you so too. Tell who I was to no man;   175
What I am now, a wretch by heav'n devoted
To all distress and by himself abandon'd,
Shall evidence it self. Come, my *Escanes*.
    Esc. O woful, woful hour! Where shall we go?
    Per. I care not, let blind fortune be our guide: 180
Shun *Tyre*, and ev'ry other place is equal.
Fair Queen, adieu. Your kindness to my child

  (II. i) 143b–144 'Here . . . *Tyre*.'] W1 ("~ . . . Tyre."); "~ . . . ~.ᴧ G; "~ . . . Tyre.—L
156 Herald] W1; Hareld G; Harold L. *See Commentary*   173 hath] has L   175 was]
am L

The Gods return you double. Yet consider
And view the frailty of your state in me.
Once Princes sate, like stars, about my throne,
And veil'd their crowns to my supremacy:
Then, like the sun, all paid me reverence
For what I was, and all the grateful lov'd me
For what I did bestow; now not a glow-worm
But in the chearless night displays more brightness,
And is of greater use, than darken'd *Pericles*.
Be not high minded, Queen, be not high minded:
Time is omnipotent, the King of Kings,
Their parent and their grave—Beware, beware—
Let those who drink of sweet prosperity
In flowing cups, mingle their draughts with pity;
    And think when they behold th' afflicted's tears,
    The misery of others may be theirs.   [*Exeunt* Pericles, Escanes, *&c.*
    Q. Unhappy Queen! detested *Leonine*!
O had I tarry'd but a little longer,
Marina had been gone without my guilt:
Or had you put me by this one bad thought,
In which perhaps I ne'er shou'd have relaps'd,
I might have bless'd you as my better genius;
But now must curse you as a cruel wretch
Who seeing me unguarded, seiz'd that moment
To blast my fame, and ruin me for ever.
    Leon. Were this repentance true, 'tis now too late:
But if, as I suspect, 'tis but assum'd
(Your purpose being serv'd) to vail your falshood
(Pretending conscience for your breach of faith)
The cheat's too gross, and you may rest assur'd,
I shall see through and scorn the thin disguise.
    Q. Then here I cast it off. Shall I, who cou'd not bear
The unmeant rivalship of sweet *Marina*,
Resign my crown, and live a slave to thee?
A wretch whom I detest, a venal villain,
One whom I fix'd on as the worst of men,
For the worst purpose.
    Leon.   Base, ungrateful Queen!
Is this all the reward I'm to expect?
    Q. Such a reward as such vile instruments
As you deserve, a murderer's reward,

(II. i)   214-15 Shall I, . . . The unmeant] Shall I, a Queen, | Who cou'd not bear the unmeant L

Thou hast already.
   Leon.   Hah!
   Q.   Yes, thou art poison'd.
The subtle potion working in thy veins
Is a more certain remedy for talking,   225
Than all my wealth, or the rich crown of *Tharsus.*
Not that I fear, now *Pericles* is gone,
The utmost of thy malice cou'd'st thou live,
As 'tis most sure thou can'st not.
   Leon.   Cursed Harpy!
The loathsome grave is better than thy bed,   230
And Death a lovelier paramour than thee.
O! I am sick at heart.
   Q.   The venom works.
How wild he looks? I will be kind, and leave him.
   Leon. Assist my feeble arm, ye righteous Gods!
Though I've offended, do not fail me now.   235
This cause is yours—'tis well—my hand is arm'd—
Now guide my weapon's point to her false heart,
And we shall both have justice.
   Q.   Thoughtless wretch!
Where are my Guards? I shall be murder'd here.
   Leon. As sure as you contriv'd *Marina*'s death,   240
As sure as you've betray'd and murther'd me.   [*Stabs her.*
I fall, but fall reveng'd. Now triumph fury.

Enter Guards and Ladies.

   Q. You come too late: The slave has pierc'd my heart.
   Leon. To wound it deeper, know, *Marina* lives.
The death intended her by you and me,   245
By Heaven is justly turn'd upon our selves.
To will or act is one at that strict audit,
Where we must soon appear—O *Radamanthus*—   [*Dies.*
   Q. Tear out his tongue, let not the traytor speak.
   Guard. It need not, Madam; he has spoke his last.   250
   Q. I shall not long survive him—Bear me hence—
Thou art the care of Heav'n, virtuous *Marina*;
Its out-casts we. The Gods are just and strong;
And none who scorn their laws, e'er prosper long.   [*Exeunt.*

(II. i)   235 now.] ~—L   236 This] The L   242 triumph] ~, L

SCENE II.

A House in Ephesus.

Enter Bawd *and* Bolt.

Bawd. Where are the Gentlemen?
Bolt. Gone.
Bawd. Gone!
Bolt. Ay, gone away, and left her untouch'd. With her holy speeches, kneeling, prayers, and tears, she has converted 'em to chastity.
Bawd. The Devil she has!
Bolt. They vow never to enter a bawdy-house again, but turn religious, and frequent the Temples: They are gone to hear the Vestals sing already.
Bawd. What will become of me? O the wicked jade, to study the ruin of a poor Gentlewoman! [*Weeping.*] I'd rather than twice the worth of her she had never   1 come here.
Bolt. She's enough to undo all the Panders and Bawds in *Ephesus*.
Bawd. Pox of her green sickness.
Bolt. Ay, if she wou'd but change one for the other, there were some hopes of her. But I have good intelligence that the Lord *Lysimachus* will be here   1 presently.
Bawd. The Governor?
Bolt. Ay, but he's a great persecutor of persons of our profession.
Bawd. Pho, those are our best customers and surest friends in private. If the peevish baggage wou'd but hear reason now, we were made for ever. Fetch her.   2 We'll try once more. [*Exit* Bolt.] She must be marble if she don't melt at the sight of so great, so rich, so young and handsome a man as the Lord *Lysimachus*.

Enter Lysimachus.

Lys.   Well, thou grave planter of iniquity,
               Whose just returns are full grown crops of shame,
               Are you supply'd with new and sound temptations?
               Such as an healthy man may venture on,
               And fear the loss of nothing—but his soul.

Bawd. I'm proud to see your Lordship here, and glad your honour is so chearfully dispos'd. *Venus* forbid a Gentleman shou'd receive an injury in my house. No, Sir, we defy the Surgeons. And for temptation, I have such an one, if she would but—
Lys. Prythee, what?
Bawd. Your Honour knows what I mean well enough.
Lys. Well, let me see her.

(II. ii)   7 enter a] enter into a L   15 her.] ~— L

Bawd. Such flesh and blood, Sir!—For red and white—Well, you shall see a 35
flower, and a flower she were indeed, had she but—
Lys.   Why dost not speak? What is there wanting in her?
Bawd. O, Sir, I can be modest.
Lys.   When such as these pretend to modesty,
           They are then most impudent.   40

Enter Bolt, *forcing in* Marina.

Bawd. Now, Sir, what do you think of her? Wou'dn't she serve after a long
voyage?—Ay, Sir—
Lys.   I'm lost in admiration—Here's your fee:
           Away, be gone and leave us. I came hither,
           O who wou'd trust his heart, bent to detect   45
           And punish these bad people; but when sin
           Appears in such a form, the firmest virtue
           Dissolves to air before it.
Bawd. I pray your Honour let me have a word with her: I'll have done
presently.   50
Lys. Do, I beseech you.
Bawd. First I wou'd have you take notice that this is a man of Honour.
Mar. Grant, Heav'n, I find him so!
Bawd. And next, that he's a great man and Governor of this country; and
lastly, one I'm bound to.   55
Mar.   If he's greatly good
           And governs well, you're bound to him indeed.
Bawd. Pray use him kindly, or—
Lys. Have you yet done?
Bawd. I'm afraid your Lordship must take some pains with her, but there's 60
nothing to be done with these unexperienc'd things without it. Come, we'll
leave his Honour and her together.   [*Exeunt* Bawd *and* Bolt.
Lys.   Thou brightest star that ever left its sphere
           (For sure you once shone in a higher region)
           For low pollution and the depth of darkness,   65
           How long hast thou pursu'd this devious course?
Mar.   What course d'ye mean, my Lord?
Lys.   I dare not name it:
           For, loving, I am fearful to offend.
Mar.   I cannot be offended at the truth.
Lys.   How long have you been what you now profess?   70
Mar.   E'er since I can remember.

(II. ii)   35 see a] see {her} a L   47 the firmest] th'{in}firmer L   62 SD *Exeunt*
Bawd and Bolt.] Bawd & Boult Exeunt. L   67a d'ye] do you L

Lys.	Gods! what pity!
	Were you a prostitute so very young?
Mar.	I ne'er was other—if I am so now.
Lys.	You are proclaim'd a creature set to sale
	By being here.
Mar.	And do you know this house

A place of such resort, yet venture in it?
I've heard you are of honourable rank,
And govern here.

Lys.   O, you have heard my pow'r,
And therefore stand aloof, but without cause;
For my authority shall here be blind,
Or look with kindness on thee. I've now learnt
What once seem'd strange, why rich men grasp at pow'r,
And the poor murmur at restrictive laws.
Passion wou'd have the means to work its ends,
And the fierce tumult of intemp'rate blood
Rages the more the more it is resisted.
I must and will, in spite of vain remorse
And what I have been, feast each aking sense
On thy luxurious charms. Why dost thou shun me?
Blushing I speak it, thou shalt never find
Amongst the herd whose only joy is lewdness,
A more devoted slave. Is wanton pleasure
What you affect? My youth, yet unimpair'd
By riot or disease, shall meet your wishes.
Art thou ambitious? Power and pomp attend thee.
Or if the love of Gold, that cursed bait
That ruins half thy sex, possess thy heart;
I will descend to gratify a passion
I should detest in any but thy self.

Mar. Cou'd you do thus! O you immortal powers,
What is your influence on the heart of Man,
If ev'ry slight temptation wins him from you?
Shall painted clay, shall white and red, less pure
Than that which decks the lilly and the rose,
Seduce you from the bright unfading joys
Your goodness yields! For sure your speech imports,
And I well hope, you have not yet renounc'd it.

Lys. Thou art so fair, so exquisitely fair,
And plead'st against thy self with so much art,

(II. ii)   72 young] {long} young L   74 sale] sail L   79 aloof, but without cause;]
aloof. But trust me, fair one, L   80 For my] My L   81–119a I've now learnt . . . guard
her own!] *not in* L

That had I known thee sooner—What a thought!—   110
But sully'd as thou art I must possess thee,
Whate'er the purchase cost.

Mar.   To think me, Sir,
A creature so abandon'd yet pursue me,
Is sure as mean and infamous, as wicked.
What! waste your youth in arms that each lewd ruffian   115
Who pays the price, may fill; lavish your wealth,
And yield your sacred honour to the hand
Of an improvident and wastful Wanton,
Who does not guard her own!

Lys.   True, I came hither,
With thoughts like these—But lead me to some place   120
Private and dark—Alas, why dost thou weep?

Mar.   Dare not come near me.

Lys.   By the raging flame
Thy eyes have kindled here, I must enjoy thee.

Mar.   Then view my last defence.   [*Draws a dagger.*

Lys.   What dost thou mean!

Mar.   To die if you pursue your hated purpose,
Vain, rash, mistaken man.   125

Lys.   O hold thy hand:
By *Jove* she doth amaze me. Rest assur'd
I will not offer violence again
Be who or what thou wilt—But let me seize
This threat'ning steel, that fill'd my soul with terror
While levell'd at thy breast.   130

Mar.   O mighty Sir,
If you were born to honour show it now;
If put upon you, make that judgment good
That thought you worthy of it.

Lys.   She's in earnest.
Here is some mystery I cannot fathom.   [*Aside.*   135

Mar.   Have pity on a maid, a friendless maid,
By fortune forc'd to this detested sty;
Where since I came, diseases have been sold
Dearer than physick. Wou'd the gracious Gods
But set me free from this unhallow'd place,   140
Though they did change me to the meanest bird
That flies in the pure air, I shou'd be happy.

Lys.   Conviction rises with each word she speaks.

(II. ii)   119b came hither,] came⌃ L   120 thoughts like these] other thoughts L
122a–131b Dare not . . . O mighty Sir,] *not in* L   134b–135 She's in . . . cannot fathom.]
Ha! how's this! L   143–4 Conviction rises . . . chaste as fair.] *not in* L

She's all a miracle, as chaste as fair.   [*Aside.*

He must indeed have a corrupted mind,   1₄

Whom thy speech cou'd not alter. Here's gold for thee:

Still persevere in the clear way thou goest,

And the Gods strengthen thee. As for my self,

The short liv'd error which thy beauty caus'd,

Thy goodness and thy wisdom have corrected.   1₅

Mar. Now you're a true and worthy Gentleman,

The gracious Gods preserve you.

Lys.   Fare thee well.

If I shou'd take thee hence, licentious tongues

May wrong my fair intentions, and thy fame.

Thou art a piece of virtue, and I doubt not   1

But that thy birth and training both were noble.

A curse upon him, die he, like a thief,

That shall again attempt to wrong thy honour.

If thou hear'st from me, as thou may'st expect it,

And quickly too, it shall be for thy good.   1

Enter Bolt.

Bolt. I beseech your Honour, one piece for me.

Lys. Avaunt, thou damn'd door keeper, pander, hence.

Your house but for this virgin that doth prop it,

Wou'd sink, and overwhelm you.   [*Exit* Lysimachus.

Bolt. I see we must take another course with you; or your peevish chastity, ›

which is not worth a breakfast in the cheapest country in the universe, will undo

a whole family. Come your ways.

Enter Bawd.

Bawd. How now! what's the matter?

Bolt. Worse and worse, Mistress. She has been talking religion to my Lord

Lysimachus.

Bawd. O abominable!

Bolt. She makes our profession stink, as it were in the nostrels of all who

come near her.

Bawd. Marry hang her.

Bolt. My Lord wou'd have us'd her as a Lord shou'd use a gentlewoman, for I

over heard 'em; but she sent him away as cold as a snow-ball; saying his Prayers

too.

(II. ii) 144 SD [*Aside.*] *not in* L   145–6 He must . . . alter. Here's] Had I brought hither
a corrupted mind, | Thy speech had alter'd it. Hold, here's L   147 clear] pure L
149 The short liv'd] As I came hither with no ill intent, | The short liv'd L   151 Now you're]
You are L   153–4 If I shou'd . . . thy fame.] *not in* L   156 thy] your L   were] are L
158 shall again . . . thy honour] shall again attempt to rob thee of thy honour L

Bawd. Take her away: use her at your pleasure.

Mar. Hark, hark, you Gods!

Bawd. She's at her pray'rs again. Away with her. I wish she had never enter'd   180
my doors.   [*Exit* Bawd.

Bolt. Come, mistress, you shall along with me.

Mar. O wither wou'd you have me?

Bolt. Into the next room, to take from you by force the jewel you are so
unwilling to part with.   185

Mar. Pray tell me one thing first.

Bolt. Propose your Question.

Mar. What wou'd you wish to your worst enemies?

Bolt. Why I wou'd wish 'em as infamous as my mistress.

Mar.   And yet that wretch is not so bad as thou art,   190
                Since she's thy better as she doth command thee.
                The place thou hold'st is such that *Cerberus*
                Wou'd not exchange his reputation with thee,
                The filthy groom, door-keeper to a brothel.
                Then to the chol'rick fist of ev'ry villain   195
                Thy ear is liable. Thy food is such
                As hath been breath'd on by infectious lungs.

Bolt. What wou'd you have me do? Go to the wars! Where a man may serve
seven years for the loss of a leg, and not have money enough in the end to buy
him a wooden one.   200

Mar.   Do any kind of thing but this thou do'st:
                Empty receptacles of common filth,
                Serve by indenture to the common hangman,
                Or herd with swine, or beg from door to door:
                The worst of these is far to be preferr'd   205
                To what you practise. If no sense of shame,
                No fear of laws, no rev'rence of the Gods
                Come near thy heart; let that which doth persuade
                Millions to evil, bribe thee to be good:
                Touch not my honour, help me to escape   210
                This house of shame, and take the shining gold
                The good Lord gave me.

Bolt. Nay, I don't see why a man mayn't as well do a good deed as a bad one,
especially when he's paid for it. And to say the truth, I think you wou'd freeze
the blood of a Satyr, and make a Puritan of the Devil, if they were to cheapen a   215
kiss of thee. Come, give me the money.

Mar.   No, first conduct me to some place of safety.

Bolt. But shall I have it then?

(II. ii)   197 breath'd] belch'd L   207 of the] to the L   208 thy] your L
217 conduct] convey L

Mar. If I deceive you, take me home again,
      And prostitute me to the vilest groom
      That doth frequent your house.

Bolt. Well, I'll trust you. I'll see you plac'd—

Mar. But among honest women.

Bolt. Troth, I've but little acquaintance amongst them. But there is one who is known to all *Ephesus* by fame, the holy priestess of *Diana*'s temple: She will be proud of such a chaste companion, and has besides the power to protect you.

Mar. O the good Gods direct me how to find her!

Bolt. But, hark, I hear my mistress. We must be gone: This way we may avoid her.

Mar. *Jove*'s virgin-best-loved daughter, bright *Diana*,
      Who shar'st with *Sol* the skies, chaste Queen of night,
      Defend my virtue, and direct my flight.   [*Exeunt* Marina *and* Bolt.

Enter Bawd.

Bawd. Bolt, Bolt, Where are you? Secure *Marina.* The Governor's officers are searching the house for her: we shall have her forc'd away. Why *Bolt*—O the Devil! the back door is open: The villain is run away with my slave, and all the money I paid for her will be lost.

Enter Officers.

1 *Off.* She's no where to be found.

Bawd. No, no, she's gone. My man had stole her away before you came, a pox confound him and you too: I am likely to be brought to a fine pass betwixt you.

Off. Then we must execute our other orders, which are to turn this Beldame out of doors, and then shut up the house.

Bawd. Turn me out of doors! how must I live?

Off. Do you take care of that. It is a favour, and a great one too, that you are not sent to prison.

Bawd. Such Governors are enough to make a woman do what she never thought of.

Off. Ay, do—work—that's what I dare be sworn you never thought of.

Bawd. No, nor ever will. A Gentlewoman, and work! I'll see you all hang'd first.

Off. Chuse, and be hang'd your self: You have long deserv'd it.

Bawd. Have I so, scoundrel? And yet you have been glad of a cast of my office before now. While such as you are trusted with authority, as sure as thieves are honest, strumpets chaste,

Or priests hate money; this same sinful nation
Is in a hopeful way of reformation.   [*Exeunt.*

The End of the Second ACT.

ACT III.

SCENE I.

A street in Ephesus.

Enter Bawd.

Bawd.

If I could but recover *Marina*, and make her pliable, I shou'd do very well still: I cou'd make an handsome living of her in any ground in *Asia*.

Enter Bolt, *singing.*

Bolt. Hah, Mother *Coupler*! How is it with thee, old flesh-monger? thou quondam retailer of stale carrion, and propagator of diseases. What, quite broke! no private practice!—I know you hate to be idle—Though your house is 5 shut up, you have some properties, I hope. Why, you'll make a good stroling bawd still. What never a new vamped up wench, just come out of an hospital, to accommodate a friend with?

Bawd. Villain, traitor, thief, runaway, how dare you look me in the face?

Bolt. I am too well acquainted with your face to be afraid of it—ugly as it is. 10

Bawd. You have the impudence of old Nick.

Bolt. Then I did not converse with you so long without learning something.

Bawd. You seduced my slave.

Bolt. That's a lye; for she seduced me.

Bawd. You deserve to be hang'd for robbing me of my property. What have 15 you done with her?

Bolt. If I had done with her what you wou'd have had me, we shou'd both have been hang'd: So take the matter right, and you are oblig'd to me.

Bawd. Not at all: For though it happen'd as you say, you intended me no good. 20

Bolt. And pray whom did you ever intend any good to?

Bawd. Where have you put *Marina*?

Bolt. No where: She was taken from me before we had gone the length of the street by the Governor's servants.

Bawd. This is your praying Lord, plague rot him for a cheating hypocrite. 25 And so after all my cost and pains about her to no manner of purpose, he has her for nothing.

Bolt. No, he has n't her neither.

Bawd. That's some comfort yet: Then perhaps I may have her again.

Bolt. When she turns strumpet, and you repent. 30

Bawd. Where is she?

1 *Marina*,] Marina again∧ L   6 you'll] you'd L   18 you are] you 're L   26 no] not in L

Bolt. Where the air is as disagreeable to a bawd, as the air of a bawdy-house is to her—in the Temple of *Diana*.

Bawd. I'm a ruin'd woman.

Bolt. You can never be long at a loss for a living: It is but removing your 35 quarters, and beginning your trade again where you are n't known—if you can find such a place.

Bawd. You're a sneering rascal. But I hope you did not let *Marina* go off with the money the Governor gave her?

Bolt. No, no, I took care to lighten her of that burthen.   40

Bawd. And where is it?

Bolt. Very safe, very safe.

Bawd. Why, you don't intend to cheat me of that too?

Bolt. I don't well understand what you mean by cheating, but am sure I shou'd deceive you most egregiously if I were to part with a single stiver. No, 45 no, I shall take care of my self: I shall keep what I have got, depend upon it.

Bawd. But what a conscience must you have in the mean time!

Bolt. Don't you and I know one another, Mother *Coupler*? Measure my conscience exactly by your own, and you'll find its dimensions to the breadth of a hair.   50

Bawd. If I ben't reveng'd, may I die of the pip without the comfort of an hospital to hide my shame and misery from the world.

Bolt. Or the pleasure of deserving it.   [*Exeunt different ways.*

SCENE II.

The Temple of Diana, *with her statue and altar.*

Near them Thaisa *is discover'd, sleeping; two
Priestesses attending, who come forward.*

  1 *Priest.* Sleeps the high Priestess yet?

  2 *Priest.*   If the suspension
Of sense without the benefit of rest
Be sleep, she sleeps: She's greatly discomposed.

  1 *Priest.* Yet trouble in her irritates devotion.
Hence day and night, before her sacred shrine,   5
She seeks with ardour the celestial maid,
Or watching waits her will; or if by chance
She slumbers, 'tis, as now, beneath her altar.

  2 *Priest.* You must have known her long?

(III. i)   34 I'm] I am L   36 quarters,] lodgings∧ L   are n't] are not L   38 rascal.
But] ~, but L   40 burthen] burden L   49 exactly] *not in* L   the breadth of] *not in* L
(III. ii) SD *altar*] her altar L   8 altar.] ~∧ | To feel her woes yet bear them as she ought— |
Wisdom & piety compose her character. L

1 *Priest.*   E'er since that morning,
When from the troubled bosom of the deep   10
The billows cast her, breathless, on the beach,
That fronts this holy temple. I was present
When the good father of *Lysimachus*
(And my kind uncle) by his art restor'd her
From her most death like trance.
    2 *Priest.*   This, though long since   15
And a known truth, is still the theme of wonder.
    1 *Priest.* I remember, when all suppos'd her dead,
This learned Lord did from the first affirm,
That death might for some hours usurp on nature,
And yet the fire of life kindle again   20
The o'er prest spirits: And she liv'd to prove it.
    2 *Priest.* 'Tis strange none e'er discover'd who she is.
    1 *Priest.* From the rich robe she'd on, and gems found with her,
We judg'd her royal: All she wou'd disclose
Was that she lost a husband, and with him   25
All hopes and all desires of earthly joys.
And choosing to devote her future days
To chastity and grief, she here retir'd;
And took with me, who then was just prepar'd
To be profest, the habit of Argentine.   30
The sacred dignity she now sustains
Was much against her will conferr'd upon her,
When sage *Euphrion* dy'd.
    2 *Priest.*   Did you not mark
How in an instant sorrow overwhelm'd her,
When news was brought from *Cyprus* of the death   35
Of the good King *Simonides*?
    1 *Priest.*   I did.
Her fortune's teeming with some great event.
    2 *Priest.* The perfect likeness too there is between
Her self and sweet *Marina*, much amaz'd her.
    1 *Priest.* And must do all that see them. But allow   40
The diff'rence time must make, and they're the same:
Just what *Marina* is, *Thaisa* was
When I beheld her first.
    Tha.   O *Pericles*!
    1 *Priest.* Did she not speak? Attend.
    Tha.   Art thou restor'd

To the long widow'd arms of thy *Thaisa!*—   45
Ha!—   [*Rises and comes forward.*
   1 *Priest.* Madam, How fare you?
   Tha.   'Twas but a dream,
A flattering dream. And what is life it self,
Being justly weigh'd, but a meer fleeting shadow?
Most like these visions now so frequent with me—
I am troubled, and trouble you, my friends.   50
   2 *Priest.* Cou'd our best service help you, we were happy.
   1 *Priest.* I fain wou'd hope your present perturbation
May prove the prelude to your lasting peace.
   Tha. The lasting'st peace is death: And that, perhaps,
Is what my dreams portend.
   1 *Priest.*   The Gods forbid.   55
   Tha. The Gods do all their will: I've long been learning
A perfect resignation to their pleasure.
My dream was this. Attending on the altar,
The Goddess seem'd to animate her statue;
And, as I view'd the prodigy with terror,   60
Took from my brow the Crescent and Tiara,
The symbols of my office, and then struck
The smoaking Censer from my trembling hand.
   1 *Priest.* 'Twas wond'rous strange.
   Tha.   And with a radiant smile
Consign'd me to the arms of my lov'd Lord,   65
Who stood confest and living to receive me.
With the surprize I wak'd.
   1 *Priest.*   A fair presage.
Our Goddess visits you as a reward
For your true piety: This dream's from her.
   Tha. We doubtless think our selves of more importance   70
Than the wise Gods allow us.
   2 *Priest.*   Sacred Madam,
The Lord *Lysimachus*—   [*Enter* Lysimachus.
   Tha.   He's ever welcome.

(III. ii)   45–6a To the . . . *Thaisa!*— | Ha!—] To these long widow'd arms?—ha!— L
46b Madam, How fare you?] How fare you, Madam? L   48 shadow?] ~, L   66 living]
willing L   70 We doubtless] We know but little, & that makes us vain. | We doubtless L
71a allow us.] allows us: L, *which continues:*

                             I revere them
       And trust their providence, yet must believe them
       Not conversible with mortality.
       Their presence would confound our feeble beings,
       Shou'd they approach too near us.

Lys. Hail, holy Priestess, whose celestial mind
Adds whiteness to the silver robe you wear,
Have you yet learnt ought of the birth and fortunes
Of that sweet virgin I commended to you?
　Tha. No, my good Lord. When e'er I question her
Who and from whence she is, she answers not,
But sits her down and weeps.
　Lys.　　　　　　　　　　I wish I knew.
　Tha. Time may reveal it. She's a miracle:
My eyes ne'er saw her peer.
　Lys.　　　　　　　　O gracious Lady,
She's such an one that were I well assur'd
Came of a gentle kind and noble stock,
I'd wish no better choice.

　　　　　　　　　　　Enter Gentleman.

Gent.　　　　　　　　　Most honour'd Sir,
There is a ship arriv'd of strange appearance,
The hull, sails, streamers, tackle, all are black;
From whence is in a chaloupe come on shoar
A person of a great but mournful mein,
Whose chief attendant asks to be admitted
To see our Governor. What is your will?
　Lys. That he have his: I pray you greet him fairly.　　　　　*[Exit
　　　　　　　　　　　　　　　　　　　　　　　Gentleman.*

　　　　Enter Escanes*; and others after him, bearing* Pericles.

　Lys. Hail, reverend Sir: The gracious Gods preserve you.
　Esc. And you, t'out-live the age that I am now,
And die as I wou'd wish.
　Lys.　　　　　　　　You greet me well.
　Esc. Our vessel is of *Tyre*, our business here,
T'implore *Diana*'s aid for one distress'd;
And such an one as in his happier days
Never forgot his duty to the Gods,
Nor let th'afflicted sue to him in vain.
　Lys. And may she prove propitious.
　Esc.　　　　　　　　　Sir, we thank you.
And further wou'd intreat that for our gold,
Your people may supply us with provisions,
Whereof we are not destitute for want,
But weary for the staleness.

    Lys.   'Tis a courtesy
Which if we shou'd deny, the most just Gods   105
For ev'ry graft wou'd send a caterpiller,
And so inflict our province. But inform me,
Who is that melancholy Gentleman.
    Esc. He is of note (I may reveal no more)
And was a goodly person, ere disasters,   110
Too great for human suff'rance, sunk him thus.
    Lys. Upon what ground is his distemperance?
    Esc. It would be now too tedious to repeat;
But his main grief springs from the timeless loss
Of a beloved wife, and only child.   115
    Lys. Good Sir, all hail: The Gods preserve you, hail.
    Esc. 'Tis all in vain, my Lord; he will not speak
To any one, nor takes he sustenance
But to prolong his grief.
    Lys.   Yet I durst wager,
We have a maid in *Ephesus* wou'd win   120
Some words from him.
    Tha.   'Tis well bethought, my Lord.
She, questionless, with her sweet harmony,
And other choice attractions, wou'd allure him,
And melt his fix'd resolves: She is most happy
In form and utt'rance.
    Lys.   Say, we wish to see her.   *[Exit Gentleman.*   125
    Esc. Sure all's effectless: Yet we'll omit nothing
That bears recov'ry's name.

Enter Marina.

    Lys.   This is the virgin.
Thrice welcome, fair one.
    Esc.   She's a gallant Lady.
    Lys. Lovely physician of distemper'd minds,
We did send for thee to exert thy skill,   130
And matchless goodness on a noble patient;
View this majestick ruin, and then judge
By what remains how excellent a pile
Grief hath defac'd: Absent to all things else,
And self resign'd to silence and despair,   135
See, he appears his own sad monument.
Now, if thy heav'nly art, so prosperous
In all attempts, can win him to attention,

  (III. ii) 117 all] *not in* L   119b durst] darest L   125a form and utt'rance] all
attractions L   133 excellent] glorious L

And draw him but to answer thee in aught;
Thy sacred physick shall receive such thanks   14
As thy desires can wish.
   Mar.   You over rate me.
But I will use my uttermost endeavours
For his recovery.
   Tha.   Succeed them, Heaven!
What strange unlikelihood assaults my mind!
My wild, ungovern'd fancy wou'd perswade   14
My memory to find some traces there,
In that marr'd face, yet unobliterated,
Of my long dead, long drowned *Pericles.*   [*Aside.*
   Lys. Mark, she will try the force of musick first.

SONG.

Mar. Let those who are in favour with their stars,   15
    Of publick honour and proud titles boast;
While we whom fortune of such triumph bars,
    Seek joy in Virtue that we honour most.

Great Princes Favourites their fair leaves spread,
    But as the marygold at the Sun's eye;   1
While ruin in their pride but hides its head:
    For at a frown their flatt'ring glories die.

The painful warriour famoused for fight,
    After a thousand victories once foil'd,
Is from the book of Honour razed quite,   1
    And all the rest forgot for which he toil'd.

Then let us bear the malice of our stars,
    And make our noble sufferance our boast;
Tho' fortune ev'ry other triumph bars,
    Seek joy in Virtue that we honour most.

   Tha. Mark'd he your musick?
   Mar.   No, nor look'd upon me.
   Lys. She'll speak to him.
   Mar.   Sir, lend me your attention,
And behold me. Indeed I am a Maid
Who ne'er before invited ears or eyes;
But have been sought too like an oracle,

(III. ii) 140 thanks] pay L   149 first.] ~. | Sh'as all attractions, & excells in all. L
SONG.] a Song by Marina‿ L   150–65 Mar. *Let . . . honour most.*] *not in* L

And gaz'd on like a comet. Sir, she speaks,
Who, may be, hath endur'd calamities
Might equal yours, if both were justly weigh'd—
Alas he heeds me not. I wou'd give o'er,
But something whispers in my ear, *Go on.*   175
   Per. What Syren have they found to force attention?
I'll steal a look, but not a word shall scape
From forth my lips.—[*Rises.*] O you immortal Gods!
   Mar. Why do you gaze so eagerly upon me?
Why spreads that burning crimson o'er your face   180
But now so pale? If you did know me, Sir,
You wou'd not do me harm.
   Per.   I do believe thee.
Nay, turn thy eyes upon me—O how like!—
Such things I've heard—Inform me what thou art.
   Mar. I am what I appear, a simple Maid.   185
   Per. My long pent sorrow rages for a vent,
And will o'erflow in tears. Such was my wife,
And such an one my daughter might have been.
My Queen's square brows, her stature to an inch,
As wand like strait, as silver voic'd, her eyes   190
As jewels like, in pace another *Juno*:
And then, like her, she starves the ears she feeds,
And makes them crave the more, the more she speaks.
Where were you born? and how did you atchieve
Endowments, that you make more rich by owning?   195
   Mar. If I shou'd tell my story it wou'd seem
Like lyes, disdaining the disguise of truth,
And found in the reporting.
   Per.   Prithee, speak.
Thou seem'st a palace for crown'd truth to dwell in:
No falshood can come from thee. Sweet, begin,   200
And I will make my senses to give credit
To points that seem impossible. I think,
Thou said'st thou had'st been toss'd from wrong to wrong,
And that thou thought'st thy griefs might equal mine,
If both were open'd.
   Mar..   Some such thing I said,   205
And said no more than what I thought was likely.
   Per. Rehearse what thou hast born: If that consider'd

(III. ii)   178 you] ye L   185 simple Maid] maid and mortal L   187 tears.] ~—L
wife,] ~— L   188 been.] ~—L   189 brows,] ~— L   inch,] ~—L
190 strait,] ~— L   voic'd,] voiced—L   191 jewels like,] {Juno} Diamond-like— L
192 ears] ear L   207 hast] has L

Prove but the thousandth part of my endurance,
I will forego my sex, thou art a man,
And I have suffer'd like a girl. Yet thou   2
Dost look like patience, gazing on Kings graves,
And wooing with her smiles resolv'd extremity,
To spare himself, and wait a better day.
My most kind virgin, come and sit down by me.
Recount, I do beseech thee, what's thy name.   2
   Mar. My name, Sir, is *Marina.*
   Per. [*Rising.*]   O! I'm mock'd,
And thou by some incensed God sent hither,
To make the world laugh at me.
   Mar.   Nay, have patience,
Or here I'll cease.
   Per.   I will, I will have patience.
   Mar. That name was giv'n me by a King and Father.   2
   Per. How! a King's daughter too! and call'd *Marina!*
   Mar. Did you not say you wou'd believe me, Sir?
But not to be a troubler of your peace,
I will end here.
   Per.   But are you flesh and blood?
Have you a working pulse? are you no spirit?—   2
Substance and motion—Well, where were you born?
And wherefore call'd *Marina?*
   Mar.   I was born
At sea, and from that circumstance so named.
   Per. Hold, hold awhile. This is the rarest dream,
That e'er dull sleep did mock sad fool withal.   2
How shou'd this be my child?—Buried and here,
Living and dead at once—It cannot be.
   Mar. 'Twere best I did give o'er.
   Per.   Yet give me leave.
Where were you bred? How came you to these parts?
   Mar. The King, my father, did in *Tharsus* leave me,   2
Till *Philoten*, the Queen, fought to destroy me;
And having won a villain to attempt it,
A crew of pirates came and rescued me,
Who brought me here.
   Per.   You Gods! if I'm deceiv'd
Ne'er let me wake again—*Marina!*—O!   [*Takes her hand.* 2
   Mar. Why do you wring my wrist? Where wou'd you draw me?

(III. ii)   209 sex,] ~— L   216b O! I'm] O ∧ I am L   229 Hold, hold awhile.] Stop a
little— L   230 withall.] withall— L   231 this be . . . and here,] this be?—my child
buried & here— L   233b leave.] ~— L   239b You] Ye L

Why do you weep, good Sir? what moves you thus?
In sooth, I'm no imposture, but the daughter
Of good King *Pericles*.
  Per.   I'll praise the Gods,
Their power, and goodness, ever while I breath.   245
I've been a sinful man; but from this hour,
In darkness and distress I'll wait their mercy,
And ne'er distrust them more.
  Tha.   You mighty Gods!
Whose boundless goodness still delights to triumph
O'er our demerits and confirm'd despair,   250
And evidence the wisdom of your counsels,
By shewing man the folly of his own;
What are you doing now to raise our wonder!
That voice and person grow familiar to me.
Doth my Lord live! hath *Pericles* a daughter!   255
It cannot, cannot be. Then who are these?
I'm deeply int'rested, yet know not how.
Some God, instruct me what to hope or fear,
To ask or deprecate. Stupid amazement
Obstructs my powers—When will these clouds disperse,   260
And day break in on my benighted mind?
 Per. But one thing more: Tell me, who was thy mother?
 Mar. She was the daughter of the King of *Cyprus*.
 Tha. O let me hear the rest.
 Mar.   Her name *Thaisa*:
Who, as *Lychorida* oft told me weeping,   265
Did end the very moment I began.
 Per. You Gods! you Gods! your present kindness makes
All my past mïs'ries sport—
I'm *Pericles* of *Tyre*.
 Mar.   My royal Father!—   *[Kneels; he raises her.*
 Tha. You gracious Gods! if now you take me hence,   270
I shall not taste the joys of your Elizium.   *[Faints.*
 Lys. What! ho! help here: The holy Priestess dies.
 Mar. The heav'nly pow'rs forbid.
 Lys.   She did observe
The progress of this strange discovery,
With strong emotions and unusual transports.   275
 Per. I pray who is this Lady?

(III. ii) 243 imposture] impostor L. *See Commentary* 245 while] whilst L breath.]
~—. L   248b You] Ye L   256 be.] ~— L   260 powers—] ~. L
267 You . . . you] Ye . . . ye L   268 sport—] ~. O bless my arms | And ease my throbbing
heart y^t faints wth fondness—L 270 You] Ye L

    Lys. A miracle of goodness, sent by Heav'n
To make this land most happy. In her bloom,
After a tempest, in the which 'twas thought
All her companions perish'd, she was cast   28
Here on our coast.
    Per.   Near it I lost the mother
Of my *Marina.*
    Tha.   Hark, what musick's that?
    Per. These very hands did cast into those seas
The treasure of my soul.
    Tha.   I know it now:
It is the harmony the spheres do make—   28
Nay do not weep—I am but overjoy'd—
I shall recover strait.
    Per.   Pray, how long since
Was this strange chance you speak of?
    Lys.   'Tis, I've heard,
About as many years as your fair daughter
Seems to be old.
    Per.   I do begin to doat;   2
And yet the Gods are mighty as they're good.
How was she found?
    Lys.   Close in a sailor's coffer.
She seem'd a breathless corpse; but my good father,
(Now with the Gods) by his superior skill
Did find it was not so, and by his art,   2
Which equall'd his humanity, restor'd her
To health and vigour.
    Tha.   Where, O where's my Lord?
    Per. Thaisa's voice!
    Tha.   Yet let me look again:
If he be none of mine, my sanctity
Shall guard me still from his licentious touch—   3
I'll none but *Pericles.*
    Per.   Her face, her stature,
That beauty that nor time nor grief cou'd change—
It is, it can be, none but my *Thaisa.*
    Tha. But dare we trust?—
    Per.   By *Jove,* I'd not be kept
A moment longer absent from thy bosom,   3
Tho' I were sure as I did press thy lips,

(III. ii) 290b doat] {doubt} doat L   294 (Now ... Gods)] ∧~ gods, ∧ L   301b face,
her stature,] ~—~— L   303 is,] ~— L

My high wrought spirits wou'd dissolve to air,
And leave me cold and lifeless in thy arms.
 Tha. You sons and daughters of adversity,
Preserve your innocence, and each light grief,   310
(So bounteous are the Gods to those who serve them)
Shall be rewarded with ten thousand joys.
 Mar. My heart bounds in me, and wou'd fain be gone
Into my mother's bosom.
 Per. See who kneels there, thy Child and mine, *Thaisa*, 315
Bought almost with thy life.
 Tha.   And cheaply purchased.
Blest and my own! Thou mak'st my joy compleat.
 Esc. Hail, royal master.
 Lys.   Happy monarch, hail.
 Per. O good *Escanes*, strike me, noble Sir,
Give me a gash, put me to present pain;   320
Lest this great sea of joys rushing upon me,
O'er bear the mounds of frail mortality,
And sweetness be my bane. O come, come both:
Thou whom the boundless ocean gave me back,
O let me bury thee a second time,   325
And hide thee in my heart; and thou who gavest
Him life who did beget thee, come thou too:
There's endless space, and as repleat with love
As the great deep with waters. Wou'd our voices
Rise with our thoughts, we'd thank the holy Gods 330
As loud as their high thunder threaten'd us,
When thou wast born, and thou did'st seem to die.
This tribute paid not to our will but power,
I do resolve for *Tharsus*; there to strike
Th' inhospitable Queen.
 Lys.   I have advice,   335
My Lord, that she is slain by *Leonine*,
One who was poison'd by her.
 Mar.   That's the wretch
She hir'd to murder me.
 Lys.   'Tis added too,
She dy'd in evil fame and unlamented.
Then, mighty Sir, repose your self awhile   340
After your weary griefs, and make our court
Proud with your presence.

 (III. ii) 311 (So ... who ... them)] ˄So ... yᵗ ... them,˄ L 315 thy Child and mine] flesh
of thy flesh L   321 joys] joy L 322 mounds] bounds L   327 who] yᵗ L
333 paid] ~, L

    Per.   You're a noble host,
And sue to purchase trouble with expence;
Injoy thy wish.
    Lys.   Herein I'm highly honour'd.
But, royal Sir, I've yet a bolder suit.   3

    Per. Your princely Sire preserv'd *Thaisa*'s life,
And you are master of as gracious parts
In mind and form, as any I e'er noted;
You shall prevail, be it to woo my daughter.
    Lys. Thanks, royal Sir. If she accept my vows,   3
I am the very happiest of mankind.
    Tha. And she, sweet maid, most happily bestow'd.
O my dear Lord, he has been noble to her;
But that and all we've proved since our sad parting,
We will rehearse at leisure. I have had   3
From sure intelligence the heavy news
Of my good Father's death, and that our subjects
In peace and loyalty do wait our coming.
    Per. Heav'n make a star of him. Yet here, My Queen,
We'll celebrate their nuptials; and our selves   3
Will in fair *Cyprus* spend our future days,
And to our children leave the crown of *Tyre*.

    To cast new light on truth, in us is seen,
    Tho' long assail'd with fortunes fierce and keen,
    Virtue preserv'd from fell destruction's blast,   3
    Led on by Heav'n, and crown'd with joy at last.   *[Exeunt.*

The END.

EPILOGUE.

When to a future race the present days
Shall be the theme of censure or of praise,
When they shall blame what's wrong, what's right allow,
Just as you treat your own fore-fathers now,
I'm thinking what a figure you will make,   5
No light concern, Sirs, where your fame's at stake.
I hope we need not urge your country's cause,
You'll guard her glory, and assert her laws,
Nor force your ruin'd race, mad with their pains,
To curse you as the authors of their chains.   10
We dare not think, we wou'd not fear, you will;
For Britons though provok'd, are Britons still.
Yet let not this kind caution give offence:
The surest friend to liberty is sense.
How that declines the drooping arts declare;   15
Are your diversions what your fathers were?
At masquerades, your wisdom to display,
You make the stupid farce for which you pay.
Musick it self may be too dearly bought,
Nor was it sure design'd to banish thought.   20
But, Sirs, what e'er's your fate in future story,
Well have the British Fair secured their glory.
When worse than barbarism had sunk your taste,
When nothing pleas'd but what laid virtue waste,
A sacred band, determin'd, wise, and good,   25
They jointly rose to stop th' exotick flood,
And strove to wake, by Shakespear's nervous lays,
The manly genius of Eliza's days.

    Be it an omen of returning sense,
Others adopt our softness and expence: 30
Well pleas'd such harmless insults we may bear,
Those follies lost we've numbers yet to spare;
Unquestion'd let 'em rob us of our shame—
We need but ask our treasure and our fame.

---

12 *though provok'd*] tho' Supine L   17 *your wisdom to display*] a Foreign Vagrant's Prey L
20 *sure*] e'er L   21–34 *the final leaf of* L, *which presumably included these lines, is missing*

Elmerick

OR

Justice Triumphant

INTRODUCTION

SOURCES

FIELDING, in a notice of the opening of *Elmerick* which warmly eulogizes its author,[1] identifies Lillo's source as the Abbé de Vertot's *History of the Knights of Malta*.[2] Vertot's collection of admiring if frequently unhistorical accounts of the crusaders, originally published in France in 1726, appeared in an English translation in 1728. In this version, set into the history of Andrew II of Hungary, Lillo discovered the brief moral anecdote of the honest regent and righteous king which provides the main outline for this play. Certain details, including the name of Lillo's hero, indicate that Lillo also dipped into other historical sources, collecting more precise or exotic information about his subject, much as he did when writing *The Christian Hero*.[3]

The medieval setting of Vertot's tale no doubt offered romantic possibilities for the stage. But, as Fielding tells his readers, Lillo's title, *Justice Triumphant*, 'is interesting and instructive'. In the story of the king whose justice extends to forgiving the execution of his wife on the order of the subject-regent whom he had commanded 'to do exact justice . . . without regard to any one's rank or condition'[4] Lillo saw first the subject for a drama designed for the 'Advancement . . . [of] the Cause of Liberty and Justice'. In particular, he would seem to have discovered in an incident of thirteenth-century history material appropriate to illustrate and argue the ideal of constitutional monarchy

---

[1] *The Champion*, 26 Feb. 1739/40.
[2] Fielding's article has frequently been cited for its account of Lillo and its praise of *Fatal Curiosity*, but his identification of the source of *Elmerick* seems not to have been noted (cf. deBoer, p. 102; Burgess, pp. 23–5).
[3] See the Commentary, in particular notes on the dramatis personae.   [4] Vertot, p. 123.

propounded in his own time by the 'patriot' opposition to the Walpole administration. The thematic emphases of the play and keywords in its vocabulary echo the rhetoric of opposition spokesmen and writers, suggesting strongly that *Elmerick* represents a concern for politics which had not come to the fore in Lillo's earlier dramas.[5] Political links of this sort would, of course, explain Fielding's support of the play and its author. An awareness that the play would be recognized as controversial would account for the first performances having been offered under the 'protection' of the Prince of Wales, who was so frequently associated with the opposition cause.[6]

In the *History* Vertot tells of an unfortunate incident that occurred in Hungary while the king was campaigning in the Holy Land. The queen, moved by the love-sick melancholy of her brother, helps to arrange his rape of the virtuous wife of the palatine who has been appointed regent of the kingdom. When the brother flees, the outraged regent kills the queen, then seeks out the king in Constantinople to report what he has done and offer to accept judgment. He reminds the king, however, that as regent he was charged to rule with unbiased justice; now, he suggests, the situation is reversed: 'by my life or death . . . your subjects will judge of your equity.'[7] The king sends him back to Hungary, asking him to remain as regent. Later, when the king has returned from the Holy Land, the regent is formally acquitted.

The story needed only to have its eighteenth-century significance made clear, and Lillo holds closely to the basic incidents of his source. His characters, except the king, are given names appropriate to the exotic setting, but only a messenger, two minor functionaries of the court, and Bathori, the heroine's father, are new in the play, and Lillo focuses sharply on the central scenes reported by Vertot. The appointment of Elmerick as regent and the king's charge that he govern with unbiased justice provide the central scene of Lillo's first act, which is made the occasion for a paean to the exemplary government of Buda, its subjects loyal and its monarch devoted to the 'perfection . . . of Publick Liberty'.[8] The test of the king's true commitment to justice is the chief action in Act V and is drawn directly from Vertot, though Lillo alters the time-scheme and introduces elements of conflict not found in his source. In Vertot's brief account, King Andrew never wavers; Lillo's monarch has to overcome his

---

[5] John Gray, dedication of *Elmerick*, ll. 7–9.

[6] Dedication, ll. 14–17. Burgess (p. 23) suggests that as Lillo's medieval Hungarians talk like 18th-cent. Englishmen so his king, 'with thoroughly unfeudal notions of a limited monarchy, anticipates by five centuries the Whig ideal of the constitutional monarch'. In the 1730s, however, limiting the power of government was the central concern of the opposition, the back-bench and defected Whigs and certain Tories who combined in the attempt to undermine Walpole and the Whig Establishment. The term 'liberty', much emphasized in *Elmerick*, was an opposition catchword. Lillo's selection of the virtuous palatine and ultimately noble monarch of the 13th cent. might also be seen to relate to the ideal of an earlier, uncorrupted state ruled by a natural aristocracy made up of peers and gentry, a view of history which informed a good many works written during the Walpole era by those who saw England in their own time as having sunk into a vice-ridden society dominated by corrupt politicians.

[7] Vertot, loc. cit.   [8] I. ii. 49–50.

private emotions before he can affirm the public justice he so easily, and rather too proudly, proclaimed before it had been put to any severe test.[9]

Lillo compresses the action, limiting the setting to the court of Buda and avoiding references to time so that events in the single plot seem to follow in a rush. He writes, in fact, a highly regular play, neo-classic in design and heroic in conception. In the major speeches, those of Elmerick in particular, he attempts the rhetorical grandeur of the heroic stage; although the regent is the representative of Buda's citizenry, Lillo portrays him as a superhero, adored by the people, unassailable in virtue, and impeccable in honour.[10]

The heroic drama of justice, however, holds the stage only at the beginning and end of the play; in terms of plotting and dramatic emphasis, it serves as a frame for Lillo's development and considerable expansion of the events that lead to the test of royal justice. In dramatizing this situation—the rape of the regent's wife by her rejected lover, the brother of the queen—Lillo adds two significant elements to Vertot's story and his own externally heroic drama: the pathetic tragedy of the victim, Ismena, and a drama of romantic intrigue that centres on the queen and her brother, Conrade.

The romantic drama is, for the most part, Lillo's own. To Conrade's pursuit of Ismena, sketched in by Vertot, the playwright adds a parallel, the queen's secret love for Elmerick; revealed and rejected, this romantic passion is transformed into fury that drives the queen to accuse the regent in public of attempted seduction and in private to contrive the violation of his wife. The queen and Conrade do have a place in Lillo's didactic drama of public good: Olmutz, the capital of their homeland, Moravia, is the seat of tyranny as Buda is the throne of liberty. In this carefully posed symbolic opposition of the two capitals, the power that ultimately threatens Buda is political tyranny, but the immediate threat is tyrannous enslavement by ungoverned sensuality. Such depravity, according to political theories popular during the early decades of the

---

[9] The scene is not the simple demonstration of ideal monarchy that it has been taken to be (cf. deBoer, p. 104): not only does it prepare for the irony of Act V, it is itself ironic, preceded as it is by Bathori's disapproving remarks about the 'rash, romantick war' (I. i. 51) and its appeal to a king 'benevolent and brave, But covetous of Glory to excess' (I. i. 55–6). Nor does Lillo laud the crusades, as Burgess implies (p. 23); the campaigns are 'Begot by hot-brained bigots' (I. i. 52). The focus of this criticism of the king's campaign may be the activities of the pope and Roman Catholic Church in attempting to manipulate national leaders and to interfere in the affairs of their countries. While it is conceivable that Lillo intended to make a statement against war in general or at least against campaigns begun in too great haste, such a view related to events in his own times would mark him as one who did not in all things sympathize with the opposition or, indeed, with the merchant interests he is usually taken to represent: in 1738–9 Walpole was struggling to maintain his peace policy while the opposition, strongly supported by commercial interests, clamoured for war with Spain. For Lillo to take a stand against a Spanish campaign would also appear to be out of keeping with the outspoken anti-Spanish sentiments he expresses in *The London Merchant* (I. i. 1–18, 24–41) and *Fatal Curiosity* (I. i. 30–40). It should be noted, however, that in the *Merchant* Lillo's particular point is to praise Elizabeth for having frustrated the Spanish without going to war, and the London merchants whose influence made it possible for her to do so.

[10] Cf. Burgess (pp. 23–7), who details the heroic and neo-classical aspects of *Elmerick*: 'In most of the essentials, it adheres to the pseudo-Aristotelian rules for the drama which preoccupied critics and theorists during the first half of the eighteenth century.'

eighteenth century, opens the way for tyranny in the government of the state. And in the arguments of those writing in opposition to Walpole the point is made that moral corruption is fostered in a Machiavellian way by those who seek to bring the people to give up their liberty.[11] From such a point of view, the sensual evil that comes to Buda from Moravia threatens not only those in direct contact with the queen and Conrade but the state itself. Thus the political elements of the play, relatively new matter for Lillo, could be merged with the moral theme which regularly provides a central focus for his dramas.

Certainly the playwright sees again and makes full use of an opportunity to dramatize the 'vassalage To passions'.[12] Buda, to the queen, is a place of that 'grave grimace that's call'd Religion here',[13] Olmutz the happy court where 'constant revels, feastings, mirth and musick Sooth'd every sense'.[14] With her 'warm passions . . . she follows Each gust of inclination',[15] while her brother, 'the willing slave of every youthful passion',[16] brings to Hungary an infectious sickness, 'the soft poison'[17] of sensuality, and 'stain[s] *Buda* With his *Moravian* riot'.[18] Lillo allows both queen and Conrade moments of regretful self-recognition, but their intrigues of sensuality must lead inexorably to their own destruction, a crisis in the government of Buda, and the tragic ruin of a guiltless heroine.

Ismena, whose pathos provides the emotional peaks of the play, owes her place in the drama and much of her characterization to the luckless ladies of Rowe and Otway, though she eschews a mad scene and with heroic decorum dies (of anguish) off-stage. Her chastity and the honour that will not permit her to return to the arms of her husband when she has been 'polluted'[19] are suggested by Vertot and made absolute by Lillo, who introduces as the force that works her destruction—and makes his plot workable—not injustice but ill fortune. He begins his play with Ismena's expression of vague apprehension: 'bless'd even to our utmost wish . . . yet [I] fear, I know not why, some fatal change.'[20] The queen's schemes are founded on an accident of timing.

[11] Drawing in particular on *Cato's Letters* (Nos. 18, 26, 31, 107), written between 1720 and 1722 by Thomas Gordon and John Trenchard, W. A. Speck sums up these opposition themes as follows: 'They got from Machiavelli the notion that kings inevitably exploited every opportunity to increase their power and sought to be absolute. Only the vigilance of the people to preserve their liberties could prevent this from happening. They agreed with Hobbes that unfortunately human nature was base and that a skilful prince could easily prey on man's depravity to corrupt him. Algernon Sydney was quoted for the view that "Liberty cannot be preserved, if the manners of the people are corrupted", since corrupt politicians would sell liberty to an absolute monarch. The tendency for monarchs to aim at absolutism and for corrupt human nature to aid and abet them was exemplified in the fall of Rome, which "fell a victim to ambition and faction, to base and unworthy men, to parricides and traitors; and every other nation must run the same fortune, expect the same fatal catastrophe, who suffer themselves to be debauched with the same vices, and are actuated by the same principles and passions." . . . Corruption not only eroded the constitutional safeguards against unlimited power, it also rotted the social fabric, since there was a deliberate conspiracy to debauch the people in order to make them surrender their freedom and become slaves.' (*Stability and Strife: England, 1714–1760* [Cambridge, Mass., 1977], pp. 223–4, 226.)

[12] II. ii. 19–20. [13] II. i. 23–4. [14] II. i. 22–3. [15] I. i. 67–9.
[16] v. i. 337. [17] II. i. 132. [18] I. i. 78–9. [19] Cf. IV. ii. 32.
[20] I. i. 1–10.

References to fortune are regularly planted, like signposts, to mark the turnings of the plot. And when the messenger has wrung the pathos out of his account of Ismena's death and Conrade has stabbed himself in guilty grief, Elmerick, in a last flow of rhetoric, equates fortune with providence and both with eternal, if humanly incomprehensible, justice, while Lillo labours to draw together the disparate elements of his play.

Lillo was aware of some at least of the difficulties he faced in attempting to blend three dramas into one, and of the special demands of his theme of political justice. In particular, he forces the characterization of Elmerick as dispassionate figure of justice rather than injured husband. To accomplish this, he adjusts Vertot's story so that the regent does not himself kill the queen but orders her death, he inserts intense invocations of justice for his hero, and in revising the play, he thoroughly reworks the beginning of the confrontation scene in which Elmerick's unquestionable purity of motive (and the didactic level of the play) must be unshakably confirmed.

These efforts help to hold the play together thematically. The pathos of Ismena provides an emotional centre for audience involvement in the action, and the story of the crime of which she is the victim provides a sharp focus for the development of the plot. Lillo handles his exposition economically. Trusting character and situation to carry the moral argument, he avoids, for the most part, interrupting the drama to make or explain a didactic point, and once the situation has been established he moves his action forward with a directness that achieves considerable momentum and dramatic intensity. It is skilful writing for the theatre. It may also reflect the author's concern to write a play which would adhere closely to the neo-classical rules for the drama so much discussed by his contemporaries. Lillo does not, however, attempt to emulate some earlier form of drama. *Elmerick* is an amalgam of dramatic types; the playwright, typical of the serious dramatists of his time, draws on a range of earlier plays but is specifically indebted to none. It is also an amalgam of Lillo's particular concepts of the function of tragedy, applied to Vertot's story, often effectively realized in theatrical terms and, at the end of the author's career, significant in exposing more fully than before the thematic convictions by which he wrote.

PERFORMANCE AND RECEPTION

Elmerick was first acted at Drury Lane on Saturday, 23 February 1739/40. John Gray, in dedicating his edition of the play to Frederick, Prince of Wales, speaks of 'the Protection which [his] Royal Highness was graciously pleas'd to afford this Piece during the Performance of it',[21] and Davies suggests 'it is but reasonable to believe that the play was acted at Drury-Lane Theatre through the influence' of the prince.[22] The third performance—a benefit for 'the

---

[21] ll. 15–17. [22] *Life*, p. xl.

Author's Poor Relations' given on 26 February—was presented 'by Command' of the prince and princess.[23] A member of the prince's circle, James Hammond, composed the prologue while another, Lord Lyttelton, probably provided the epilogue.[24] It seems likely that concern for politics as well as the theatre stimulated this interest in high places. Davies reports that the play was felt to be 'bold as well as hazardous [in introducing] a scene where [Elmerick] makes use of his delegated power against the consort of his royal master'.[25] But the drama as a whole could be taken to have clear political implications, and it is quite possible that the management of Drury Lane sought the reassurance of the prince's support before scheduling the production.

The management's hopes for the play appear to have been high. It was performed six times within a period of nine days, at least once (25 February) at advanced prices.[26] A strong cast was headed by Mrs Butler, a favourite Millwood, as the passionate queen, and Quin, whom Davies remarks upon as a peculiarly appropriate Elmerick since he was 'unacquainted . . . with passion, and incapable to express it, [but] always gave weight and dignity to sentiment'.[27]

Fielding gave the play a strong recommendation in the *Champion* on 26 February, the day of the first of two benefits for the 'Poor Relations'. Davies reports that the play's success 'was much greater than was expected from a tragedy written on so simple a plan, and with so antiquated, though so excellent a moral, as the necessity of universal and impartial justice'.[28] However, despite the advantageous circumstances of its production, *Elmerick* did not find a place in the repertory of the Drury Lane company. Except for a production offered at some time in 1740 by the company of actors at the White Swan in Norwich,[29] the play is not known to have been acted after its initial London performances.

THE TEXT

No edition of *Elmerick* was published before the author's death in September 1739. The manuscript submitted to the Lord Chamberlain by the manager of the playhouse early in 1740 cannot be precisely dated but provides a record of two stages of composition, a transcript of an apparently early text of *Elmerick* to which has been added a set of revisions. A copy, not a holograph, and therefore not itself authoritative, the manuscript does appear to offer significant evidence about the text of the authoritative manuscript(s) from which it and the printed text were derived. The first edition, published in March 1740, has also a certain

---

[23] *London Stage, 1729–1747.* [24] See Commentary on the prologue and epilogue.

[25] Loc. cit. Lillo's depiction of the queen and her execution could well have had a particular and certainly controversial interest for the audience in 1739/40. For more than a decade, Queen Caroline had been a close ally and supporter of Walpole, especially in his dealings with the king. So important was this collaboration that when the queen died in 1737 Walpole, according to the Duke of Newcastle, felt it 'the greatest Blow that ever he received' and considered retiring (quoted by Basil Williams, *The Whig Supremacy* [Oxford, 1939], p. 193).

[26] *London Stage, 1729–1747.* [27] Loc. cit.

[28] Loc. cit. Ibid. [29] Sybil Rosenfeld, *Strolling*, p. 59.

claim to authority in that it was produced by John Gray, an executor of Lillo's will and his regular publisher, who seems to have discussed the disposition of the play with the author before he died.

Larpent Manuscript

Charles Fleetwood's application for a licence to perform *Elmerick* is written on the verso of the last leaf of the manuscript submitted to the Lord Chamberlain and dated 'Janry 3d 1739' (i.e. 1739/40). The date 'Janry 1739' has also been written below the title on the first leaf, but was clearly added after the play was first copied, probably by the copyist who inserted revisions.

In its initial state, the manuscript (Larpent MS 19 in the Huntington Library) was a professional transcription of a version of *Elmerick* earlier than that reproduced in the first edition. This text may well represent a version of the play submitted for consideration by the management of Drury Lane, and it is conceivable that this version came to the theatre before the author's death.[30] Beyond question, however, Lillo continued to work on the play after he had completed this version, and a series of alterations inserted in the Larpent manuscript provide a record of his revision.

The original transcription is a good, clear copy, apparently taken from an easily followed manuscript. It was the work of two copyists, one of whom ('A') copied the dramatis personae and the text as far as IV. i. 41b, while the other ('B') completed the transcription. There is evidence of sophistication, especially in the transcription of copyist B, whose pointing is normally heavy; at times however, apparently working in haste, he omits obviously necessary punctuation. On occasion the work of copyist B is marked also by incorrect pointing, and he consistently writes 'Elmeric' for 'Elmerick'. Final punctuation is omitted not infrequently by both copyists, and they often fail to point the ends of stage directions. Both made occasional slips in transcription, nearly all of which appear to have been corrected immediately. Capitalization is erratic.

The alterations and additions later inserted in the Larpent manuscript were entered systematically and all at one time.[31] One addition is purely mechanical: lines 294–311 of Act III, scene i, are inserted, having been inadvertently omitted from the original transcription. The other changes clearly represent revisions. Many of these alter only one or two words or adjust half-lines to regularize the metre, but others involve the addition or deletion of passages several lines in length. In one instance a portion of a central scene has been

[30] Davies (*Life*, p. xv) suggests that the manuscript of *Fatal Curiosity* had been the rounds of 'the more regular theatres' before Fielding chose to produce it at the Haymarket. Submission of *Elmerick* as early as the summer of 1739—the time for considering plays for the upcoming season—seems not unlikely.

[31] Changes were inserted in Act I by copyist A, and in Acts II–V either by another copyist (not B) or, more likely, copyist A working at so fast a pace that he abandoned the elegancies of his professional hand.

thoroughly reworked.[32] The number of minor adjustments, the shifting of emphasis in the more extensive revisions, the effort to define more precisely character and situation, and the style of writing identify the alterations as authorial, as does comparison with Lillo's revisions in the texts of *The London Merchant* and *Marina*.[33] No evidence suggests that while some of the revisions are the work of the author others represent adjustments made in the theatre. The prologue and epilogue were transcribed separately on loose sheets not bound with the manuscript of the play.

The historical collation appended to the present edition provides a record of variations between the initial and later versions of the manuscript and a comparison with the text of the first edition.

First Edition

John Gray registered the copyright of *Elmerick* on 3 March 1739/40, exactly six months after the author's death. On 5 March he advertised publication of the play, which he issued in fine-paper as well as ordinary copies.[34] He reissued copies of the edition printed on ordinary paper in his nonce collection of Lillo's works, *c.*21 June 1740.

Gray's dedication makes it clear that he had discussed the disposition of *Elmerick* with the author and indicates that Lillo had come near enough to completing his work on the play to be able to talk with certainty about publication and presumably performance. Gray had been the playwright's only authorized publisher since the publication of *The London Merchant* in 1731. He is one of three executors named in Lillo's will.[35] It seems likely that he had access to the author's papers after Lillo's death, and one would expect his edition of *Elmerick* to have the authority of a completed draft of the play and any revised version or notes for revision left by the playwright. Questions about the authority of the first edition arise, however, when the text is compared with the Larpent manuscript.

For the title-page, see p. 401. For the run of copies on fine paper the type of the title-page was altered to include a different ornament and omit the price.

Collation: 8° A–D⁸ E⁴ [$4 (– A1,E3,4; misprinting D1–4 as 'E', 'E2', 'E3', 'E4') signed]; 36 leaves, pp. *1–11* 12–71 *72*

Contents: A1(*1*) title A1ᵛ(*2*) blank A2(*3*)–A4ᵛ(*8*) dedication A5(*9*) prologue A5ᵛ(*10*) dramatis personae A6(*11*)–E4(71) text (DH: ELMERICK.) E4ᵛ(*72*) epilogue

[32] v. i. 160–205a; see also footnotes to text, in particular I. iii. 73–89, II. i. 20, II. ii. 59–60, III. i. 55–60, 65–73, 294–311, and IV. i. 210–14.
[33] See textual introductions to *The London Merchant* and *Marina*.
[34] *London Daily Post and General Advertiser*, 5 Mar. 1739/40: 'This Day is published . . . There are a few printed on a super-fine Royal Paper . . .' The advertisement is repeated on 7 Mar. Similar announcements appear in the *Daily Gazetteer* for 8 Mar. and the *Craftsman* for 8, 15, and 29 Mar.
[35] Bodleian Library, MS Rawl. J fol. 4, item 43.

Note: An errata slip containing three corrections is pasted below the prologue in all but one copy examined. At least three settings have been distinguished.

Comments

In copies printed on fine paper, D1 and D3 are correctly signed.

The edition provides a clean text, well set and marred by few typographical errors. Comparison of copies reveals no press corrections or evidence of reimpression except for the run of copies on fine paper. The errata slip, apparently issued regularly with copies of the edition, includes the correction of one misprint and gives the text of a passage of six lines omitted from the printed text. Variations in the styling of stage directions identify the work of probably two compositors.[36] Analysis of accidentals indicates sophistication of punctuation, especially in the quite extensive use of colons, though there is evidence that this characteristic of the edition represents the exaggeration of an idiosyncrasy of the printer's copy. Heavy pointing parallels the punctuation of several early editions of Lillo's plays, but is much less troublesome here than in the first edition of *The Christian Hero*. There are a number of obvious errors and some infelicities of pointing, in particular the awkward but relatively frequent setting of full stops at the end of rhetorical questions. As in the Larpent manuscript, capitalization is irregular at best.

The text of the edition includes most of the revisions recorded in the manuscript submitted to the Chamberlain's office. It is clear that the two texts stem from the same authorial source. However, a number of substantive variants indicate that the edition and revised manuscript cannot have shared an immediate common ancestor. Gray may well have had access to Lillo's papers and it is conceivable that he provided Drury Lane with the late author's revisions of *Elmerick*, but at least one witness intervened between the manuscript which actually served as copy for his edition and the revised text or list of changes on which the Larpent manuscript revisions were based. Moreover, certain variants call into question the authority of the printed text. The edition fails, for example, to print a few of the later readings inserted into the Larpent text, though these readings must have the same authority as other insertions made at the same time, emendations which the first edition does reproduce. In a number of instances, the edition omits a line or lines included in the original Larpent text and not deleted when revisions were recorded in the manuscript;[37] since it seems most unlikely that the copyist who meticulously entered the many revisions in the Larpent manuscript would have overlooked these deletions of a line or more in length, the passages would seem to have the same authority as the revisions themselves.

---

[36] Act I, Act II, and the first two-thirds of Act V (pp. 59–67) were set by a compositor whose regular practice, with the single exception of a direction in the middle of a line, was to set a square bracket before directions that required setting off. The compositor(s) who set the remainder of the text used parentheses only and were erratic in practice, at times enclosing directions in parentheses, at times setting only a single parenthesis to the left.

[37] See the Commentary, especially on IV. i. 59–64 and V. i. 162–3.

On the whole, while the printed text does include one passage not recorded in the Larpent manuscript,[38] it is most improbable that the edition represents authorial revision later than that recorded in the Larpent text, and analysis of the omissions suggests that some are the result of unclear or defective copy while others are changes made during rehearsal or when the text was prepared for publication.[39] Variation in the ordering of the last lines of the play also argues for revision in the theatre reflected in the printed text and can be compared with similar rearrangements made in *The London Merchant*.[40]

That the printer at times found it difficult to follow his copy and so misconstrued the text is indicated in a number of instances. The heavily revised portion of Act V, scene i, in particular, presented problems which were not fully untangled even when the errata slip was run. In the Larpent manuscript, the changes recorded in this section of the scene include revisions within lines, the deletion of a block of twelve lines (some of them transferred to other speeches), and the addition of lines to substitute for the cancelled text. The copyist who entered these changes in the Larpent text seems to have followed them with no great difficulty, though he may have made a false start in marking the major deletion. In the printed text, the required deletion is made but the six lines which follow are also omitted and the text resumes with a one-line speech transposed from its proper position three lines above the deletion. In the errata slip, the printer restores the six lines mistakenly omitted, but, unable to append them to the transposed speech and apparently unaware that this line is out of place, he directs that the line be deleted. Only reference to the Larpent manuscript makes possible the restoration of the passage to conform to the author's probable intentions.

Such relatively obvious solutions are not available for a number of textual questions raised by comparison of the first edition with the Larpent manuscript. Certain probabilities, however, do emerge and suggest procedures for the editor. Despite Gray's close association with Lillo, analysis indicates that the copy on which his edition was based was not more accurate than that represented in the Larpent text, that it failed to record some minor authorial revisions, and that it was subject to contamination with theatrical or editorial revision or both. The Larpent manuscript is not invariably reliable, but in the main must be accepted as the most accurate extant record of the revised text left by the author at his death. Finally, while textual analysis focuses primarily on the differences between the edition and the manuscript, the two texts do, for the most part, agree and together indicate that the author left the play in a state orderly enough to make possible posthumous copies of considerable authority.

One aspect of the text as represented in both the printed and manuscript versions does suggest that Lillo had not given the script of *Elmerick* a final polish before his death. Short lines are more than thirty in number. In Lillo's earlier

---

[38] See the Commentary on V. i. 241–5.
[39] See the Commentary on IV. i. 59–64 and V. i. 146b–148.
[40] *The London Merchant*, V. x, 12–17.

verse dramas, examples of broken metre are relatively rare. On occasion, the playwright does make use of a truncated line for dramatic effect in these plays, and a number of the short lines in *Elmerick* can be read in this way. In a good many instances, however, the indication of rhetorical intent is ambiguous at best. Other half-lines are merely awkward.[41] Moreover, it is impossible to tell if certain short lines, occurring one after the other, were meant to stand alone or to form parts of single lines of blank verse.[42] These problematical lines may represent details that the author meant to deal with in a final revision which he did not live to complete.

Later Reprint

Elmerick was not reprinted until Thomas Davies published his collected edition of Lillo's works in 1775. The copy-text was, of course, Gray's first edition.

Editorial Procedure

The editor has sought to provide a printed text which, in its substantive readings, provides the most nearly authoritative text which the evidence allows and, in its handling of accidentals and typography, retains the authenticity of the early texts by avoiding excessive emendation or editorial invention. The following editorial procedures have therefore been adopted:

1. The first edition serves as copy-text. The first printed version of the play, it was produced by the publisher to whom Lillo clearly entrusted its publication and, in its typography and other mechanical details, closely parallels the authoritative editions of the author's work produced during his lifetime.[43]

2. Where the Larpent manuscript and first edition differ, serious consideration is always given to variant substantive readings in the manuscript, and when no strong reason for rejecting these readings can be found, they are adopted.

3. The accidentals of the copy-text are, for the most part, accepted, including inconsistencies of heavy and light pointing. Regular reference has been made to the pointing in the Larpent manuscript, and variants which suggest alternative interpretations of lines are recorded in the footnotes to the text. In the rare instances in which such variants strikingly alter the sense, these are treated as substantive variants and are adopted. Obvious errors in the copy-text are corrected, where possible with readings from the Larpent text, where necessary with reference to Davies's edition (*Works*, 1775), and in a very few cases with

---

[41] Examples of short lines employed for rhetorical effect include, among others, I. iii. 15; IV. i. 77, 94, 161, 178; V. i. 102, 289, 339. Among the many examples of broken metre with no clear dramatic intention are lines I. i. 73, II. i. 104–5, III. i. 214. Short lines which interrupt otherwise regular passages of verse include I. iii. 52; III. i. 13, 160; IV. i. 127, 147.

[42] Cf. IV. i. 192–3, V. i. 23–4.

[43] The copy-text is the first edition, a Yale University copy. Copies collated include: *first edition, ordinary paper*, O (2 copies), CtY (4 copies), NjP, CSmH; *first edition, fine paper*, O; Davies, *Works* (1775), CtMW, O, BL (3 copies), CtY (2 copies).

pointing introduced by the editor. The frequent use of colons, apparently exaggerated by the compositor(s) but characteristic of the manuscript as well as the printed text, is followed except where a series of colons clouds the meaning of lines or negates the rhetorical effect apparently indicated by certain colons in the series; emendation is normally supported by the pointing of the Larpent text. Dashes in the copy-text are regularly retained; in a vew few instances where dashes in the Larpent manuscript have a clear, emphatic effect appropriate to the passages in question, these dashes have been adopted.

The pointing in the copy-text represents, at best, a style characteristic of the early editions of Lillo's other plays. Given the indications of sophistication in the punctuation of the Larpent manuscript as well as the first edition, an attempt to recreate an approximation of the author's pointing would be fruitless. Taking the Larpent text as the copy-text for accidentals, on the probability that it is less sophisticated than the first edition, would involve such extensive emendation to supply missing pointing and to adjust speech-headings and other mechanical details to the requirements of a readable printed edition that the result would be an editorial invention.

ELMERICK:

OR,

Justice Triumphant.

A

TRAGEDY.

As it is Acted at the

THEATRE ROYAL

IN

DRURY-LANE.

By Mr. *LILLO.*

LONDON:

Printed for JOHN GRAY at the *Cross-Keys* in the *Poultry* near *Cheapside.* MDCCXL.

[Price One Shilling and Six-Pence.]

TO HIS
ROYAL HIGHNESS
THE
PRINCE
OF
WALES.

SIR,

The Author of these Scenes always propos'd to himself the Honour of address-
ing them to the Prince of *Wales*: And when he perceiv'd himself just quitting the
Stage of this Life, and retiring beyond the Reach of the Smiles or Frowns of
Princes; his Veneration even then of your Royal Highness's exalted and most   5
amiable Qualities was so intense and strong, that he solemnly enjoin'd me to
perform this Duty for him. For as he was always remarkably devoted to the
Cause of Liberty and Justice, (for the Advancement of which the following
Piece was written) he thought it would be a kind of Injury, not to consecrate it to
the most illustrious Patron of Justice, Heroick Virtue, and the Rights of   10
Mankind. Your Royal Highness's great Condescension in permitting me to
execute the Will of my departed Friend, and in patronizing his Orphan Play, is a
Circumstance that is very glorious to him, and gives a Sanction to his Fame.

All true *Englishmen* in general, as well as the Friends of Mr. *Lillo* in
particular, have great Reason to congratulate one another on the Protection   15
which your Royal Highness was graciously pleas'd to afford this Piece during
the Performance of it. For to see the Heir Apparent of these Kingdoms so
generously countenancing a Tragedy, in which the Character of a Righteous
King, who founds all his Glory on the Liberty and Happiness of his Subjects, is
drawn in such strong and lively Colours, must give a very sensible Pleasure to   20
the whole Nation: It serves to keep alive the Hopes which the Publick has long
since conceiv'd, and is an undoubted Pledge, of many future Blessings from
your auspicious Influence.

Your Elegancy of Taste, and Illustrious Virtues render you the most
generous Protector and the noblest Theme of all who cultivate the politer Arts;   25
as the continual Overflowings of your Bounty towards all Objects of Distress
daily endear you to every Heart that has any Feelings of Humanity: This your
Princely Heavenly Disposition is universally felt and acknowledged, and
consider'd with all its Circumstances without a Parallel.

Dedication is not in L

That your Royal Highness may long continue the Munificent Encourager of 30
Arts and Letters, an Example to Princes of public Spiritedness, Humanity, and
Condescension, is the ardent Wish of every honest *Briton*: For notwithstanding
all our Divisions, the Voice of the whole Nation is unanimous in praying for
your Life, Honour, and Prosperity: And this we should do from Motives of
Interest and Self-love, were we not impell'd to it by Gratitude and Duty. 35

I am,

SIR,

Your Royal Highness's

Most Devoted

Humble Servant

JOHN GRAY.

PROLOGUE.

Spoken by Mr. QUIN.

No labour'd Scenes to Night adorn our Stage,
Lillo's plain Sense wou'd here the Heart engage.
He knew no Art, no Rule; but warmly thought
From Passion's Force, and as he felt he wrote.
His Barnwell *once no Critick's Test cou'd bear,*   5
Yet from each Eye still draws the natural Tear.
With generous Candour hear his latest Strains,
And let kind Pity shelter his Remains.
Deprest by Want, afflicted by Disease,
Dying he wrote, and dying wish'd to please.   10
Oh may that Wish be now humanely paid,
And no harsh Critick vex his gentle Shade.
'Tis yours his unsupported Fame to save,
And bid one Laurel grace his humble Grave.

2 *engage.*] engage: L

Dramatis Personæ.

MEN.

Andrew II. King of *Hungary*: Commonly called *Andrew* of *Jerusalem*.	Mr. *Mills*.
Conrade, Prince of *Moravia*.	Mr. *Millward*.
Elmerick.	Mr. *Quin*.
Bathori, Father to *Ismena*.	Mr. *Wright*.
Belus, Secretary to *Elmerick*.	Mr. *Winstone*.

WOMEN.

Matilda, Queen of *Hungary*.	Mrs. *Butler*.
Ismena, Wife to *Elmerick*.	Mrs. *Mills*.
Zenomira, Attendant on the Queen.	Miss *Bennet*.

Lords, Deputies, and Guards.

SCENE the King's Palace at *Buda*.

ELMERICK.

ACT I.

SCENE I.

Scene Ismena's *Apartment in* Elmerick's *House.*

Enter Ismena *alone.*

When we are bless'd even to our utmost wish,
Is it the nature of the restless mind
To work its own disquiet, and extract
Pain from delight? O *Elmerick*! my life,
My lord, my husband! when I count with transport   5
Thy amiable virtues, when I think
How fair a treasure I possess in thee,
I'm lost in scenes of soft, bewild'ring bliss;
Yet fear, I know not why, some fatal change
May rob me of my happiness.   10

Enter Bathori.

  Bath. So early musing, and alone, my daughter?
  Ism. My Lord is with some Nobles of the States,
And I can ne'er be gay while he is absent.
  Bath. You shou'd remember 'tis the greatest honour
To be so oft consulted, so rever'd   15
By men who stand the foremost in their country.
  Ism. Remember too, how dear a sacrifice
My *Elmerick* made, when he forsook retreat,
And chang'd our solid peace for courts and senates.
We knew no want, no avarice, no ambition: 20
Intruding business and corroding cares,
Though hid beneath the pomp of wealth and power,
Must take from our felicity; who find,
Each in the other, what the world besides
Is much too poor to give.

---

11 early musing] L; melancholy G   daughter?] L; ~! G   12 States,] L; ~. G
13 And I . . . is absent.] L; G *omits*

Bath.　　　　　　You must not weigh　　　　2
Your single quiet with the good of millions.
Your noble husband's rank and high abilities
Have destin'd him the servant of his country:
For *Elmerick* has every gift of Heaven
That renders publick care a debt to virtue,　　　3
And soft retirement poor, unmanly baseness.
　　Ism. Still you forget the graces that have made
Your only child, your lov'd *Ismena*, happy.
　　Bath. Thou dearest comfort of thy father's age!
My heart is pleased that thou art mindful of them.　　3
Your well placed love, this tender gratitude,
Are proofs you merit, what you justly boast of,
To have the hand and heart, to be the wife
Of *Elmerick*—I cannot praise thee higher.
　　Ism. The highest praise my vainest wish aspires to,　　4
Is that my ardent love bears some proportion
To its exalted object.
　　Bath.　　　　　　Both are happy;
And Heaven preserve you so!—I judge that now
The States may be assembling in the Palace,
As summon'd by the King. He has not met them　　4
Since they elected *Elmerick* their Palatine,
Pursuant to the grant he gave his people.
He means this morning to appoint a Regent,
Then to set forth for *Palestine*.
　　Ism.　　　　　　What dangers
He generously meets!
　　Bath.　　　　　　For me, I own,　　5
I ne'er approv'd this rash, romantick war,
Begot by hot-brained bigots, and fomented
By the intrigues of proud, designing priests.
All ages have their madness, this is ours.
The King is wise, benevolent and brave,　　5
But covetous of Glory to excess;
And if he steer amiss, 'tis in a torrent
That bears down all before it.
　　Ism.　　　　　　His fair Queen,
No doubt, will greatly mourn so long an absence.
　　Bath. Perhaps she may.—Yet—I cou'd wish, *Ismena*,　　6
(I speak in confidence and with concern)
The Queen were wise, and gentle like thy self.

Ism. My place and near attendance on her person
Have given me means to know her, and, 'tis sure,
To Nature none owes more.
    Bath.   Yes, I confess,   65
Matilda wants not charms, sharp female wit,
And dignity of form; but her warm passions,
And the wild eagerness with which she follows
Each gust of inclination, may, I fear,
Prove dangerous to herself, the King and Realm.   70
    Ism. You're too severe.
    Bath.   She is too loose of conduct.
    Ism. Detraction cannot say she e'er transgrest
The strictest bounds of virtue.
    Bath. Suppose her chaste, 'tis pride, not virtue in her.
Can she be virtuous, who beheld, unmoved,   75
The treacherous arts of her licentious brother
To tempt your virgin honour, while he stay'd
To grace his sister's nuptials, and stained *Buda*
With his *Moravian* riot?
    Ism.   I reveal'd
Her thoughtless conduct, which indeed amazed me,   80
Only to you, my Father.—Let it die:
Be all her errors mended and forgot,
Her worth improv'd and honour'd.
    Bath.   Nay, I wish it:
Wou'd I cou'd add, with truth, I hop'd it too!—
Thou dearest pleasure of my ebbing life,   85
With thee conversing, I forgot the hours
Were passing on—I go: The States demand me. *[Exeunt separately.*

SCENE II.

The Assembly of the States.

    1st Ld. That the King means this day to join the army
Is then no longer doubted?
    Elm.   No, my Lord.
    1st Ld. May health and safety wait upon his person!
    2nd Ld. May fortune never cross his generous labours,
But victory and triumph bring him home!   5
    Elm. So please just Heaven! 'Tis the devoutest wish
Of every honest heart in *Hungary*.

  (I. i) 71a–71b *Ism.* You're ... of conduct.] L; G *omits*   73 The strictest ... virtue.] *Short line, breaking the metre. See introduction, pp. 398–9*

To them enter King, Bathori, *Attendants.*
King *taking a Seat of State.*

K. You Nobles, and you Deputies of *Hungary*,
And you confederate States that own our scepter,
Know, I this day depart for *Palestine*:   10
Where, like a mourning matron, by her sons
Neglected, or forgot in her distress,
Lyes sacred *Sion*, captived and profaned.
But ere I name the Regent of my Kingdoms,
Which you shall witness and, I trust, applaud;   1
I greet, with heart-felt joy, your wise election
Of *Elmerick*, first Palatine of *Hungary*:
The Conservator of your laws and rights,
Guardian of Liberty, and Judge of Power.
His manly virtues answer my big thought,   2
And give full vigour to the awful title:
Wisdom consummate in the fire of youth,
The hardiest valour join'd with soft compassion,
And justice never to be brib'd or awed—
    Elm. My life's poor labours never can deserve   2
My Country's favour, or my Sov'reign's praise.
And, O perpetual source of bounteous virtue,
Who but a King, whose wide expanding heart
Feels a whole people's bliss, humanely great,
Wisely ambitious, e'er, benignant, plan'd,   3
In his high soaring thought, so large a gift;
Gave to a subject right to judge his acts,
And say to sov'reign power—Here shalt Thou stay?
    K. What we have thought of Regal Government,
Its bounds and end, I hope our reign has witness'd.   3
To make a People wretched, to entail
The curse of bondage on their drooping race,
Can add no joy to sense, can sooth no passion
That hath its seat in nature—May reproach
Sound through the loathing world his guilty name   4
Who dares attempt it.—What can be his motive,
Whom long descent, or a free People's love,
Has raised an earthly God, so to degrade
Himself, and take the office of a Fiend!—
Too foul mistake!—Let me aspire to glory   4
By glorious means! To have my reign illustrious,

(I. ii)   12 Neglected,] L; ~ ∧ G   15 witness] L; ~, G   27 And,] L; ~ ∧ G
virtue,] ~! L   30 e'er,] *See Commentary*   33 shalt] shall L   44–5 Fiend!— |Too
foul mistake!—] fiend? ∧ | ~! ∧ L

The theme of loud-tongued fame and ecchoing Nations,
May it give birth to an eternal Æra,
And be the happy date when Publick Liberty
Receiv'd its last perfection!
    Bath.   Matchless King!   50
How shall thy subjects pay this God-like gift!
    K. Defend it as your lives—Said I your lives?
That's poor, and far unworthy its importance;
Defend it as you wou'd your fame and virtue.
And if, hereafter, some ill-judging Monarch   55
Invade your rights with bold, oppressive power;
Under the conduct of your Palatine,
Repel by Legal Force the known injustice,
And place the sacred crown of holy *Stephen*,
Thus forfeited and impiously prophaned,   60
On some more worthy head. [*Pauses.*]—All gracious Heaven!
Affection melts their hearts—There's not an eye
But swells with tears in all this great Assembly.
The active warmth of youth, the cool experience
Of venerable age, the statesman's wisdom,   65
And hardy soldier's courage, overcome
By obligation, melt to infant softness,
And speechless tears.
    Bath.   O gracious Monarch!
    1st Ld.   Father!
    Elm. Glory, and Guardian Angel of our country!
    K. Why, let the envious call this flattery,   70
Unmanly art! to which unhappy slaves
Are forced to form their lips—You need it not—
My last, just care has made it useless to you.
    Elm. When gratitude o'erflows the swelling heart,
And breaths in free and uncorrupted praise   75
For benefits received; propitious Heaven
Takes such acknowledgement as fragrant incense,
And doubles all its blessings.
    K.   'Tis enough—
The powerful theme had sway'd my glowing thought
From the important business of this day,   80
Which claims your high attention—I shall now
Repose the Sov'reign Power in proper hands,
During the war I wage in *Palestine*.

  (I. ii)   56 bold,] L; ~ ‸ G   oppressive] injurious L   power;] ~, L²; ~, ⸍ (Be he my son) I give
it you in charge, L¹   62 hearts] ~! L   63 swells] flows L   68a tears.] ~! L

Elm. May Heaven direct your choice!
For what is law more than the breathless form
Of some fall'n Hero, spiritless and cold,
To be despis'd and trampled on at pleasure
By every bold offender; unless steady
And vig'rous execution give it life?

   K. 'Tis justly urged, my Lord, and you yourself
Shall in my absence guard it from contempt
By vigorous execution. Take the sword,
And bear it not in vain.—Shou'd any dare,
Presuming on their birth or place for safety,
Disturb my subjects peace with bold injustice;
Let no consideration hold your hand,
As you shall answer it to me and Heaven:
Think well how I would act, or ought to act,
Were I in person here, and do it for me.

   Elm. An awful trust, my Liege, and strongly urged:
And while I rule your realm, shou'd some bold crime
Demand the righteous rigour you enjoin;
May Heaven deal with me, as I shall discharge
With faithfulness and courage, or neglect
Through treachery or fear, the painful duty.

   K. Unbless'd a King, whose self-reproaching heart
Ne'er, calm, reposes on a subject's virtue!
Thank Heaven, I am not such: I taste the safe,
The generous joys of confidence well placed.
With you, brave *Elmerick*, the States have lodg'd
Their noblest right, and I dare trust my crown.
But there is yet a dearer, tenderer charge,
And let me recommend, ere I dismiss you,   [*Turning to the States.*
More than my crown, my Queen to your affections.
I go, once more, to take my last adieu,
Then lead my hallow'd banners to the East.   [*Exeunt.*

85

90

95

100

105

110

115

        Elm. I wou'd shun this great and arduous trust—
        K.   I will bear no excuse—I know thee worthy
             And equal to all trust—Take thou the sword,

93 vain.] ~ˌ L   104 neglect] L; ~ˌ G   111 crown.] ~— L

SCENE III.

Queen *and* Zenomira.

Q. To stoop beneath a constant weight of cares
To purchase ease for others!—Poor and senseless!
Injurious to himself, and base to me!
   Zen. The King is held by all most wise and just.
   Q. For me, I cannot think so—Then this start   5
To *Palestine*, this warlike pilgrimage,
This holy madness will bear no excuse.
Need he regard whether the line of *Baldwin*,
Or *Saladin*, be victors in a clime
So far remote, who might enjoy repose   10
And pleasure here? I tell thee, *Zenomira*,
I'm not, by far, so happy as *Ismena*.
For *Elmerick*, the theme of every tongue,
Can love: And to our sex, love crowns all merit.
   Zen. Madam, the King—   15
   Q. He comes to take his leave. Ungrateful man!
He merits not my heart, who vainly dares
To rate his pride above it.   [*Exit* Zenomira.

Enter King.

   K. The urgent business of this day, *Matilda*,
How has it robb'd me of thy dear society!   20
   Q. You will have constant business, Sir—The camp
Detains you from me now, and now the senate;
And when your court receives you, restless still,
And fired with some bright phantom of ambition,
You mix with hoary heads, and plan new glories.   25
   K. If, faithful to the trust imposed by Heaven,
I oft have born with grief thy painful absence;
O think me not less thine, my lov'd *Matilda*,
But pity my sad duty.
   Q.   Said you duty?—
Your idol Honour rather—that you worship—   30
That sends your banners to the distant East,
To fruitless wars, and visionary triumphs.
   K. Honour's a duty, Madam, and the noblest;
And ardent I pursue the powerful impulse.
There are (with shame I speak it) those who loiter   35

(I. iii)   12 *Ismena.*] Ismena— L   14 love:] ~:— L   22 you from me] me from you L

In this religious warfare. The Emperor
Cannot unite his *Germans*; *France* delays;
Grim death has forced the slaught'ring battle-axe
From *Cœur de Lion*'s strong unerring hand;
And *John* of *England*, his unthrifty brother,
Repell'd abroad, prepares his luckless sword
To wound the liberties, rescind the laws,
And sheath it in the bowels of his kingdom.
Our troops are ready: *Sion*'s mournful cries
Call loud for instant succour—and I go.
  Q. Then I must learn to bear my King's neglect,
And endless solitude.
  K.   No, my *Matilda*;
The time will come when war's rough labours ended
Shall give me up devoted to thy beauties,
And all our days to come shall blended flow
In one pure stream of calm, unruffled love.
  Q. Our days to come
Are dark uncertainties; and doating age,
Shou'd we attain it, painful or insipid.
  K. Do not distract me, call back these reproaches.
Urge not, my Queen, thy soft'ning power too far,
But think thy husband's triumphs will be thine.—
Mean-time, to soften my unwilling absence,
Thy brother comes, the partner of thy heart:
Each day my Court expects him from *Moravia*.
His sprightly temper, his engaging converse,
Will steal all sorrow from thee.
  Q.   In my brother
I still have found a friend; and friendship now
Is all the good my widow'd heart must hope for.—
But in your absence, Sir, the Sovereign Power
To whom intrust you? Whom must I obey?
  K. Lord *Elmerick*, as you know was my fix'd purpose,
I have appointed Regent of my Kingdoms.
  Q. The world talks loud of *Elmerick*'s fair merits,
And I, unused to think on such grave subjects,
Congratulate your choice.—
  K.   You're just and kind
To crown with your auspicious praise the man

(I. iii) 37 delays;] L; ~: G. *See Commentary* 48 war's] wars G 58–66 Mean-time
...I obey?] *so* L² (*variants noted below and in collation*); *not in* L¹ 58 absence,] L²; ~ₐ G
63 friend;] ~—L² 64 for.—] ~.ₐ L² 71b just] L; ~; G

Whom I so love and honour.—May I hope
That all those lips have dropt less gentle to me,
Was but the tender fears of love alarm'd?   75
Oh say but this! and I will think it kinder
That all th' endearments of affected fondness.
    Q. Think what will please you best, and that I said it,—
And may the shining Fame you seek so far
Pay your long labours!
    K.   One embrace, *Matilda*!   80
May Heaven on all thy days shed sweetest comfort,
And peace with angel wings o'ershade thy slumbers!
Eager for Fame, and zealous to chastize
The foes of Heav'n, I thought I could resist
This heart-invading softness—Fond mistake!   85
Call'd to begin the task by leaving thee,
I find my fancy'd heroism vain,
And all the feeble, tender man returns.—
I must not give it way.—Once more, farewel.   [*Exeunt separately.*

                     End of the First Act.

(I. iii)   73–89 May I hope . . . more, farewel.] *so* L² (*variants noted in collation*); L¹ *reads:*

         But now, Matilda, how shall I discharge
         The hardest part of duty leaving thee?
         Eager for fame, and zealous to chastise
         The foes of Heaven, I thought I cou'd resist
         This heart-invading softness. Fond mistake!
         Call'd to begin the task by quitting thee,
         I find my fancy'd heroism vain,
         And all the tender man return upon me.
     Q. The swelling hopes of some important victory,
         Will soon efface my image from your heart,
         And give you all to Sion, arms & triumphs‸
     K. May I hope
         These thoughts are but yᵉ fears of love alarm'd?
         O say but this, and I will think it kinder
         Than all the tender things that tongue e'er utter'd.
     Q. Think what will please you best, and that I said it—
         And may the shining fame you seek so far,
         Pay your long labours.
     K. One embrace, Matilda,
         May Heaven on all thy days shed sweetest comfort,
         And peace, with angel-wings, o'ershade thy slumbers,
         Till I return from my hard task of war,
         And victory shall take its noblest lustre
         From thy approving smiles—Once more—farewell.

ACT II.

SCENE I.

Queen *and* Ismena.

Q. Yes, I resent the King has left me thus!—
Thus in the bloom of youth to be forsaken!—
I'll have revenge.
   Ism.   Forgive your servant, Madam;
Grief and impatience interrupt your reason:
You think not what you speak, or will not think it,
When time shall give you leisure to reflect.
The King, howe'er in this—
   Q.   Excuse him not;
I never lov'd him, and now never will.—
You seem amaz'd! Is it so very strange,
A lady should not love the man she weds?
   Ism. My happy fortune, Madam, makes me think so,
Nor wou'd I lose that thought to be a Queen.
   Q. I wou'd I were no Queen!—at least not here!
When in *Moravia*, at my father's court,
The only daughter and the darling joy
Of my fond Parents love; officious Fame
Proclaim'd me as a miracle of beauty:
Justly or not is now of small importance,
'Twas then thought true, and Princes came in crouds
To love and be refus'd. The noblest triumphs
Our sex can boast, charm'd my aspiring thoughts;
And constant revels, feastings, mirth and musick
Sooth'd every sense. No grave grimace, that's call'd
Religion here; no visionary schemes
To set the Rabble free, and fetter Kings;
No anxious cares for what regards not us,
Remote posterity; obscur'd the lustre,
Or damp'd the joys of *Olmutz'* gallant court:
Soft am'rous sighs were all the mournful sounds,
And deep intrigues to gain some haughty Fair
Were all the business of that happy place

---

10 should not . . . she weds?] *so* L² (shou'd); weds the man she does not love? L¹
11–12 My happy . . . a Queen.] *so* L² (so. | . . . loose); Indeed it seems so. Witness Heav'n! | Had I
not lov'd, wou'd I, to be a Queen— L¹   13 Queen!—] ~!ₐ L   20 love] *so* L²; sigh L¹
The noblest triumphs] *so* L²; Triumph on triumph | O'er vanquish'd hearts, the noblest acquisition L¹
23 Sooth'd] *so* L²; Charm'd L¹   26 regards not us] *so* L²; may never be L¹

I left for this proud, solemn seat of dulness,
This pompous grave of pleasure, hated *Buda*.
   Ism. What wit and charm has education marr'd!   [*Aside.*
   Q. Then judge, *Ismena*,   35
Who know'st this formal Court, and sober King,
My hopeless, lost condition.
   Ism.   May I hope
Your Majesty's forgiveness, should I ask,
The absence of your royal Lord excepted,
What more cou'd kind, indulgent Heaven bestow?   40
Power, wealth, and honour wait upon your will.
   Q. Power, wealth and honour feed man's high ambition;
But for our humbler sex, we're true to nature,
And rest content with pleasure. But to me
Pleasure's impossible, whilst my grave Master   45
More than forbids it by his wise example.
And then this last injurious slight has mov'd me
Beyond the power to pardon.
   Ism.   Shou'd my Lord
Have left me thus, I might, I must gave griev'd—
I think to death; but sure no angry thought   50
Had ruffled my sad bosom.
   Q.   You, *Ismena*,
Are a rare instance of felicity,
A happy, marry'd woman.
   Ism.   Marriage, Madam,
Is happiness or misery compleat
To our soft hearts. 'Tis true, indeed, my Lord,   55
Or I am partial, has not many equals:
The manly beauty of his pleasing face,
His perfect symmetry and noble mein,
His tender language, and his soft address—
   Q. I am no stranger to them—Wou'd I were!   [*Aside.* 60
   Ism. But then the matchless beauty of his mind—
Ne'er were the great and tender so united
As in the soul of *Elmerick.*
   Q.   Rash creature!   [*Aside.*
   Ism. How happy were our sex if more were like him!
   Q. Why was not I reserv'd for such a lover?   65
My passions must have vent. [*Aside.*] Gentle *Ismena*!
Wait for me near the fountain in the garden.   [*Exit* Ismena.

(II. i)   34 marr'd!] L; ~‸ G   44 pleasure. But] ~: but L   53b–55 Marriage,
Madam . . . my Lord,] L²; O what pity | That shou'd be thought so rare! 'Tis true, my lord, L¹; 'Tis
true, my Lord, G   61 mind] ~! L

When murm'ring at my fate, to set before me,
And in so full a light, those very graces
That long have charm'd me! Vain, officious woman!—   7
Why have you, Heaven, so form'd this heart for love,
With no more reason than you must foresee,
Subservient to that love, will make me wretched?

Enter Elmerick.

Elm. Hail to the Queen! and may the news I bear,
Prove a glad omen of my future service   7
From this auspicious hour! Your royal brother,
The valiant *Conrade*, is arriv'd at *Buda*.
  Q. Now by the joys my soul has long been lost to,
This kind, this gen'rous haste to bring relief
To a forsaken, solitary Queen,   8
Does justice to your character. My thanks—
But that's a poor reward, current at courts
For want of something better.—I wou'd find
Some solid favour to engage your service,
Worthy of me, and worthy your acceptance.   8
  Elm. Is there a man so venal or so vain,
As not to think the happiness to serve
So good and great a Queen, a full reward
For all he can perform?—And then the honour
Done to my wife!—Your favour to *Ismena*
Exceeds all gratitude.
  Q.   Gall, gall and poison!   [*Aside.*
  Elm. Madam, I take my leave. The Prince is ent'ring.
  Q. My Lord, when our first interview is over,
We shall expect your presence.   [*Exit* Elmerick.

Enter Conrade.

Conr.   My *Matilda*!
Long let me press thee to my joyful breast,
I who have often mourn'd thy tedious absence,
Thou dear, dear object, both by choice and nature,
Of my fond love, my sister and my friend!
  Q. And was it tedious? Did you think it long?
Why should I doubt it? When was you not kind?   1
When did thy active genius let me want
New pleasures to repel intruding thought,

(II. i)   72 reason] L; ~, G   80 forsaken,] L; ~ˌ G   91b poison!] L (poyson); ~. G

And lash the lazy minutes into swiftness?
Our Parents—
    Conr. Are well. There is no sorrow in *Moravia*   105
But from the want of thee.
    Q.   I have not known,
'Till now, a joyful moment since I left it.
    Conr. We have been happy: And shou'd Fortune prove
Once more propitious to me, those gay fires
That shone so bright at *Olmutz*, may revive   110
And blaze at *Buda*.
    Q.   What, my dearest *Conrade*,
Has *Hungary* to give worth thy desiring?
    Conr. Forgive, *Matilda*, while I own my Heart:
Though I have ever lov'd and fondly love thee,
I had, besides the joy of seeing thee,   115
Another powerful hope that fired my soul,
And wing'd my haste to *Buda*.
    Q.   You surprize me!
    Conr. When first I led you here to warlike *Buda*,
And gave you blooming to your royal husband,
You must remember, during my short stay,   120
I saw and lov'd the daughter of *Bathori*.
    Q. I know it well, and all her rigors to you;
But thought your am'rous and inconstant heart
(Lost often, and as many times retriev'd
Since I beheld you last) had not retain'd   125
The least impression of *Ismena*'s charms.
    Conr. Not all the gaudy pleasures I once courted,
Can cure the rooted passion, raging still,
Invincible as ever. It has cost me,
While distant from her charms I pin'd in absence,   130
A sickness almost fatal to my life;
Which though my youth recover'd, the soft poison
Still preys upon thy brother's heart, *Matilda*,
And makes me hate my being—I will die
Or find relief, and therefore am I come,   135
Determined to attempt my fate one more.
My state cannot be worse.—That she is wedded
To *Elmerick*, I know: Yet he's a subject;
And were he more, his greatness shou'd not awe me.
    Q. This favours my design on *Elmerick*'s heart,—   140

(II. i) 113 Heart:] L (heart); ~. G   134 being] L; ~: G   134–5 die | Or find
relief, and] L; ~, | ~. And G   136 Determined] L; ~, G   my fate] *so* L²; her heart L¹
more.] L; ~: G

If he should gain *Ismena*, *Elmerick*'s mine.   [*Aside.*
Let me dissuade you from a wild attempt
Your rashness must defeat. Lord *Elmerick*,
Who now resides, as Regent, in the Palace,
Must soon perceive your love, and will find means   1
To guard his honour, and secure *Ismena*
From bold solicitation.
   Conr.   I'm convinc'd
That course were wrong; do you direct me better,
Or see me die the victim of despair.
   Q. How, *Conrade*! can you think I would assist   1
In such a purpose?—But were virtue silent,
A thousand difficulties rise before me:
Lord *Elmerick* is Palatine and Regent—
Terms must be kept with him. And then *Ismena*,
Fond of her Lord, and vain of such a choice,   1
Will hear you with disdain. For happy *Elmerick*
Fills all her tender wishes, all her heart.—
Yet should some accident disturb their loves,
There might be hope: For she who once has lov'd,
May love again. The softness in our frame,   1
That has dispos'd us first to the fond passion,
Is ready to betray us ever after.
   Conr. This distant glimpse of hope, this poor reversion,
To one that loves as I do, is despair—
But 'tis from her alone, who rules my fate,
That I can learn my doom. Where may I find her?
   Q. I gave her charge to wait me in the garden,
And soon shall meet her there.
   Conr.   Unkind *Matilda*,
Cou'dst thou know this, and yet detain me here?
I wou'd not lose the present, lucky moment
For ages in reversion.   [*Exit* Conrade.
   Q.   Yes, my *Conrade*,
Though you was ever dearly welcome to me,
I now behold you with unusual transport.
O! may your sighs, your vows, your importunities
Subdue *Ismena*'s heart; as *Elmerick*,   1
Without their pleasing aid, has conquer'd mine:

(II. i)   142 attempt] L; ~, G   144 resides, as Regent,] ~ ∧ ~ ∧ L   148 wrong; . . .
better,] *Ed.*, G, L² (wrong, G, L²); ~, . . . ~. L¹   149 Or see . . . of despair.] *so* L²;
not in L¹   150 can] Can L   152 thousand] L²; cloud of L¹, G   167 gave] *so* L²;
have L¹   168a And soon . . . her there.] *so* L²; *not in* L¹   168b *Matilda*,] Matilda! L

At least divide, break, and confound their peace:
Raise storms of jealousy, and fill their souls
With darkness and despair: 'Till in the tempest
Love be for ever lost, and the wild wreck   180
Compel abandon'd *Elmerick* to seek
For shelter in some near and friendly port,
And find the blest asylum in my arms.   [*Exit* Queen.

SCENE II.

A Garden.

Conrade *and* Ismena.

Conr. Her charms are still the same, and at her sight
Love burns with double fury: Yet I want
My former resolution: I am aw'd,
And scarce have courage left me to approach her.   [*Aside.*   5
—Be not surpriz'd, adorable *Ismena*,
To see me here, and see me still your slave:
Yes, those all-powerful beauties, that subdu'd
My ranging heart to constancy and truth,
Still hold the binding charm: To love *Ismena*
Is, as I feel too well, to love for ever.   10
    Ism. As you are brother to my royal mistress,
I'm not surpriz'd to see you here, Prince *Conrade*;
But as I'm wife to noble *Elmerick*,
To hear you hold this language does surprize me.
    Conr. Nor time, nor absence, nor the last despair,   15
For I have prov'd them all, can cure my passion,
A mortal passion, that must soon consume me,
Unless you bid me live.
    Ism.   Live, and be wise;
Live, and be noble: break your vassalage
To passions that debase the name of Prince,   20
While that of Man is forfeited and lost.
    Conr. This high disdain, this counsel urg'd in scorn,
Is cruel and unjust.—Too haughty Fair!
Wilt thou ne'er learn compassion? Never melt
At my long tender sorrows? Let me hope—   25
    Ism. What have I done to raise your vanity
To this presumptuous heigth?

Conr.   O call it love,
And I'll confess it soars to all the heigths
Of fond, distracted passion.
     Ism.   Impious trifles!
Are these the arts by which false man betrays?—
Unhappy women! do they yield to guilt
Because a madman raves, a traitor flatters?—
I thought, vain Prince, I had been better known;
And that your rash attempt when here before,
At least had taught you wisdom.
     Conr.   I confess
My love was then to blame, so to expose
Your virgin honour: You have now a husband—
     Ism. You sink beneath my scorn—I have a husband—
And such an one as loose incontinence
Would want the will to wrong. Sir, if I bear
This insult unreveng'd, 'tis to my prudence,
Not to your birth and name, you owe your safety.
     Conr. My safety!—Hell!—let the proud *Palatine*
But dare to threaten thus—
     Ism.   Take my advice,
And dare not to provoke him. Thus far, Prince,
I judge my scorn sufficient.
     Conr. Oh! 'tis too much, and all that I can fear:—
I'll conquer it or perish.
     Ism.   Since your reason
Is wholly lost in this impetuous frenzy,
To shun your madness shall be all my care.
     Conr. Fly where you will, honour, as well as love,
Compels me now for ever to pursue you.
     Ism. The light, vain Libertine grows formidable!—
His insolence may lay a scene of ruin,
That chills my blood with horror but to think on.
     Conr. Her Cynick father!—There's another champion.
What with her innate pride and high alliances
She makes a strong resistance; and my passion,

(II. ii)   30 betrays?—] ~?∧ L   35a least] L; ~, G   45–50 Thus far, Prince, . . . all
my care.] *so* L² (*variants noted in collation*); L¹ *reads:*

                                Thus far then,
         Presumptious Prince, I judge my scorn sufficient.
            Conr. O 'tis too much, and all that I can fear—
         I'll conquer it or perish.
            Ism. Since you're quite lost in error, all my care
         Shall be to shun your uncorrected madness.

53 formidable!—] ~!∧ L   57 high] *so* L²; proud L¹

Enter Bathori.

By opposition irritated, burns
More fiercely to attempt the noble conquest.   [*Exit* Conrade.   60
    Bath. Prince *Conrade* just now leaves you?
    Ism.   Let him go.
    Bath. You seem disorder'd.
    Ism. Howe'er misplac'd by Fortune, Nature form'd me
For the domestick joys of calm retreat:
I'm sick of court already.
    Bath.   For what cause?   65
You know your Lord, by his high trust compell'd,
Here must reside: It cannot be dispens'd with.
    Ism. 'Tis true, and all our happy days are past:
For insolence and *Conrade* still pursue me.
Then judge, when this shall reach my husband's ear,   70
As soon it must, how will his soul endure
This outrage on my virtue and his honour?
Shall I not see his hands stain'd with the blood
Of the Queen's brother, or the noble *Elmerick*
(A thousand, thousand deaths are in the thought)   75
Bleed by the rage of impious, desperate *Conrade*?
    Bath. Unheard-of insolence! He shall be taught
The difference between the passive slaves
Of loose *Moravia*, and our free *Hungarians*.
Your Lord must never learn this daring insult: 80
For know, my Child, I hold myself sufficient
To shield a daughter from this princely Libertine,
And awe him into silence and respect.
    Ism. You know him not: He is not to be aw'd:
There is but one, one only way to shun him: 85
Let me forsake the court, with you retire
'Till *Conrade* quits the kingdom.
    Bath.   Rightly judg'd.
Thy prudence is thy guard; safer in that
From being made the theme of busy rumour,
Ever injurious to a woman's fame,   90
Than in an army rais'd for thy defense.
My house and arms are ready to receive thee.   [*Exeunt.*

End of the Second Act.

(II. ii)   59–60 By opposition . . . noble conquest.] *so* L² (fiercly); Collects new force as her disdain increases. L¹   62 disorder'd.] ~! L   85 one, one only] *so* L²; one, only L¹
90 woman's] *so* L²; lady's L¹

ACT III.

SCENE I.

Queen *and* Zenomira.

Q. Be dumb, vain, busy wretch: Because thou'rt trusted,
Dost thou presume to offer thy advice?
Wou'd'st thou be hated too?
    Zen.   Think, royal Madam,
To whom I, undeserving, owe my fortune.
My gratitude—
    Q.   A servant's gratitude!—   5
Consider well your interest and your safety.
Remember I, who made you what you are,
Can make you more, or speak you into nothing.
If *Elmerick* return the love I proffer,
I shall employ you often: Shou'd he not,   10
(Do not my eyes dart ruin while I speak it)
My first command in this shall be my last.
Seek him now,
And bring him hither.—No, I see my brother:
Wait in the anti-chamber 'till he's gone,   1
Then do as I directed.   [*Exit* Zenomira.

Enter Conrade.

    Conr.   Curst be the hour,
When, sated with delight, I quitted *Olmutz*,
Where all my vows were heard with extasy,
And beauty took its value from my breath,
To meet contempt, despair and death at *Buda*.   2
Ismena at this instant leaves the court:
No hope is left, no patience—I'm distracted.
The subtle tyrant Love, who led me long
Through flow'ry paths, and spread elysium round me;
Whose fires, 'till now, serv'd but to heighten pleasure,   2
And quicken it to transport; has betray'd me
To plagues and torments not to be supported.
Ismena is essential to my being. O *Matilda*!
Assist me with your counsel, or I'm lost.
    Q. Alas! he knows not it too much imports me.   [*Aside.*
Do not abandon hope, but leave despair
To fools and cowards. Know, exalted souls

---

9 the love I proffer] the love I {offer} proffor L²; my amorous flame L¹   10 you] *so* L²;
thee L¹

Have passions in proportion violent,
Resistless, and tormenting: They're a tax
Imposed by nature on preheminence,   35
And fortitude, and wisdom must support them.
   Conr. Who but *Matilda* e'er cou'd flatter misery,
And prove superior merit from our weakness?
At thy awak'ning voice my hope revives.
Coud'st thou but stop *Ismena*'s purpos'd flight   40
(An nothing is too hard for wit like thine)
I yet may triumph o'er her pride and virtue.
   Q. By stratagem to keep *Ismena* here
Can serve no end: When she perceives the fraud,
She'll fly more irritated than before.   45
   Conr. But I shall see her first.
   Q.   What can you hope
From such an interview? While *Elmerick*
Continues kind, he'll prove too strong a rival.
Her pride and virtue are meer accidents:
She chanc'd to marry where she chanc'd to like;   50
But should he, touch'd with some new flame, neglect her,
As time is fruitful of more strange events,
Her pride wou'd make her hate him.—You must wait.
   Conr. You talk of ease whole ages hence to one
Stretch'd on the rack of violent desire.   55
By Heav'n I will pursue to her retreat,
And bear her thence in spite of Father, Husband,
And every sword that dares oppose my purpose.
She shall return to court, she shall behold
And hear my raging love: She shall be mine.   60
   Q. Forbear such wild and unbecoming thoughts:
The *Palatine* is Regent, you a stranger,
And I, perhaps, have reasons of my own
To keep his good opinion. If to see her
Within this Palace, with the due respect   65
You owe her birth and rank, may satisfy

(III. i) 33–4 passions . . . Resistless,] ~, in proportion, violent, | Resistless∧ L   47 While]
L; while G   56–60 By Heav'n . . . be mine.] *so* L² (*variants noted below and in collation*); L¹
reads:

> Let me but once have her in my power!—
> She shall not mock my love—When these nice dames
> Have rashly boasted their exalted virtue,
> The forward lover is their truest friend.

60 love: She] L; ~, she G   65–73 Within this . . . may yield.] *so* L² (*variants noted below and
in collation*); *not in* L¹, *which reads:*

> May satisfy your ardor, I'll assist you.

For once your present ardour, I'll assist you.
Love may perhaps inspire your soothing tongue
With eloquence to soften and persuade
The melting Fair to break her resolution,
And hear at least, if not return your Love:
The firmest purpose of a Woman's heart
To well-tim'd, artful flattery may yield.
  Conr. And shall I see again my lov'd *Ismena?*
Oh say what pow'r, what art can bring her hither?
  Q. Belus, chief secretary to the Regent,
Shall be, unknowingly, a proper agent:
He has been *Zenomira's* lover long—
But see! she comes. She must not see you now:
Trust in a sister's love, and wait th' event.   [*Exit* Conrade.

Enter Zenomira.

  Zen. Madam, my Lord the Regent will attend you.
  Q. Is *Belus* still thy lover, *Zenomira?*
  Zen. So he professes, Madam.
  Q. Then shou'd you feign a message from his Lord,
He'd not distrust you?
  Zen.   His believing passion
Ne'er yet has seem'd to doubt whate'er I utter'd.
What must I say?
  Q.   Say that her Lord intreats
Ismena, some time hence, to meet him here.
I think she has conceiv'd some slight disgust
Which I wou'd fain remove. This artifice
I shall so well account for when I see her,
You and your lover shall incur no blame.
  Zen. ·What dangers wou'd I meet, cou'd I improve
Your friendship for that Lady! May I hope
Your thoughts of *Elmerick* are chang'd already?
  Q. The plague of confidents!—Do as directed. [*Exit* Zenomira.
And yet this wretch, this little busy wretch,
Whose love, whose care and counsel I despise,
Is infinitely wiser than *Matilda!*
I've sent for *Elmerick*—But let me think—
Ere yet my sliding feet forego the shore,
That quitted once can never be recover'd—

(III. i) 69 soften] L²; ~, G 72 of] {in} of L² 74–80 And shall . . . wait th' event.]
so L¹; L² *deletes, then restores with insertion of lines* 65–73, *above* (*variants,* L¹ *and* L², *noted below and in*
collation) 75 bring her hither] *so* L²; change her purpose L¹ 79 see! she comes. She]
L², L¹ (see, L¹); ~∧ ~, she G 93 meet] *so* L²; face L¹ 99 *Matilda!*] Matilda: L
100 think—] L; ~. G 102 recover'd–] L; ~, G (recovered G)

In what a boundless ocean am I plunging,
With only one uncertain light to guide me!—
If that should fail, I sink o'erwhelm'd for ever.—   105
But shou'd the grateful *Elmerick* stretch forth
His saving hand, and snatch me from the billows,
Love will return a thousand solid joys
For every transient pain.—But O the hazard!—
A woman and a Queen to offer love,   110
And hear herself refus'd!—'Tis misery!
'Tis everlasting shame! 'Tis death and Hell!—
I will not think so poorly of my fate,
My self, or *Elmerick*—My present lot
Is cheerless and forlorn—Impetuous gusts   115
Of stormy passions drive me through the gloom,
Unsteady and uncertain. All before me
Is the profound, unfathomable deep;
And all behind a dark and boundless waste—
But he appears, the star that must direct me   120
To peace and joy—or light me to my ruin.

                    Enter Elmerick.

I fear, my Lord, this importunity
May interrupt your labours for the Publick,
I shall become your trouble.
        Elm.   I serve the King,
I serve the publick, Madam, serving you: 125
My pride and joy is to attend your person.
        Q. And are you pleas'd, most noble *Elmerick*,
To hear a woman's talk, and sooth my cares?
But you are wond'rous good: And let me boast
That I've a heart susceptible of kindness,   130
In all its various forms, ev'n to a fault.
        Elm. How infinitely bountiful is Nature!
Giving such softness to the pleasing sex,
As well rewards the toils she lays on ours.
If we excel, 'tis when the glorious hopes   135
Of serving or delighting you inspire us:
And to obtain your smiles is to be happy.
        Q. If happiness be in our pow'r to give,
'Tis hard to want the blessings we bestow:
To love and to be lov'd is to be happy.   140

(III. i) 105 ever.—] ~.ᴧ L   112 Hell!—] L; ~!ᴧ G   115 forlorn—] ~! L
132 Nature!] L; ~? G   136 serving] *so* L²; pleasing L¹

Elm. Your sex by nature form'd to merit love,
Can rarely want it.
    Q.   Possibly the brave,
Who hate ingratitude, wou'd not despise
A lady who renounced her native pride,
The painful'st proof our sex can give of love.   14
    Elm. A generous man must think it double grace,
When love and virtue condescend to chuse him.
    Q. My Lord, shou'd fate reduce some hapless woman,
Trembling and almost dying with confusion,
To make an offer of her love to you;   15
And such a love as instant death or madness
Were certain to ensue, shou'd you refuse it;
How wou'd you act? How treat a suppliant heart,
Whose weakness you had caus'd?
    Elm.   Your pardon, Madam;
'Tis what I can't suppose, and ask no answer.   15
    Q. Why not suppose? Is it impossible?
Say—I—shou'd love; and trusting to your honour,
Have laid this fair occasion in your way
To break my fall, and spare me half my shame.
    Elm. What vanity   16
Have I betray'd, what baseness, what presumption,
To need so strange a trial? If you doubt
My loyalty, and think I entertain
Designs injurious to my Sov'reign's honour,
And your fair virtue—
    Q.   'Tis too much, my Lord,   16
This diffidence, this cold reserve—You urge me
To what I wou'd avoid, beyond the bounds
I had prescrib'd myself: Yes, I cou'd die
Ere speak more plain; but must not have you think
I wou'd betray you. Heavens! what feign a passion   1⁊
My soul ne'er knew! No, rather let me bear
Your utmost cruelty, your scorn and hatred
For what I am, a lost unhappy Queen,
Than once be thought so mean and so perfidious.
    Elm. Confounded and amaz'd, my fault'ring tongue   1⁊
Scarce does its office.—Whither wou'd you urge me?
'Tis too severe a proof!—As you are fair;
As charms like yours, may warm the coldest heart,

(III. i) 141 sex] ~, L   nature] Nature L   142b Possibly] *so* L²; But suppose they
shou'd. Perhaps L¹   149 Trembling]~, L   159 shame.] ~— L   170 you.] ~! L
172 hatred] L; ~, G

And shake the most resolv'd; what if my senses
Should mutiny against my weaker reason,   180
And tempt me to betray you,—horrid thought!—
To sure and endless ruin!
    Q.   What do you see
That looks like ruin here?
    Elm.   Guilt:—That is ruin.
    Q. Why be it so, your love shall make it glorious.
    Elm. No, shame and just remorse must still pursue   185
Foul, trust-betraying love. And shou'd I say
Ev'n that were in my power, I must deceive you.
Shou'd wild desire, in an unguarded moment,
Rifle your charms, and lay your virtue waste;
The first return of thought wou'd bear me back   190
To her, who claims me by the dearest ties
Of virtuous, grateful love. Oh then return,
With recollected powers o'ercome this weakness,
And rise more glorious from this short decline.
    Q. This short decline!—No, let victorious love   195
Here end a Queen's confusion, or your scorn
Sink my despairing and indignant soul
Where calm repose and hope shall never find it,
And your repentance come too late to save me.
    Elm. I must assert your honour and my own.   200
Remember who I am, my trust, and office—
Almighty power! Shall I who bear the sword
To punish bold offenders, break the laws
Your providence has call'd me to defend?
Doth the least subject look to me for justice,   205
And shall my King, my ever-gracious master,
In recompence for his unbounded favour,
Receive the highest, most opprobrious wrong
A King or man can suffer?
    Q.   Shame and ruin!
    Elm. Not to deceive you, Madam, not to flatter   210
Views so unworthy of yourself and me;
I must avow the ample power I hold,
Each thought, each toil, my life, devoted all
To gratitude and justice.
    Q. Enough my Lord—your gratitude has charm'd me—   215
Who shall oppose your justice? Here display it:
Rise by my ruin to the height of glory,

And let fame deaffen the astonish'd world
With your triumphant virtue.
    Elm.   I wou'd triumph
But o'er your weakness, not your peace and fame: 220
So may you triumph too.—Oh hear me, Queen—
    Q. I have heard too much,
I've heard my love refused.—Death! horror!—shame
And burning indignation!—Pierce my heart,
Dispatch me, give me death. Is that too much?—   225
Is pity to the wretched, is compassion
Of every kind among the hateful crimes
The gen'rous, valiant *Elmerick* abhors?—
Then give me this, afford the means of death,
And leave me to apply them.   [*Going to seize his sword.*
    Elm.   Heavens! what frenzy   230
Possesses you!—Yet hear me—
    Q.   Off, be gone,
And let me die!
    Elm.   Safe as my soul the secret
Shall be preserv'd.
    Q.   What! be olig'd to you!—
Owe my precarious honour to your silence!—
But keep your sword, I shall not want even that—   235
    Elm. She is not to be trusted with her life—
Royal, unhappy Fair, what can I say
To calm this raging tempest in your bosom?
For though I dare not be, what you must hate,
False to my trust and Sov'reign; I wou'd die   240
To save your life and honour, to restore
Your peace of mind, and raise declining virtue—

Enter Conrade.

Shame and confusion!—Madam, see, the Prince—
    Conr. Well may'st thou start, proud Lord: The Queen's disorder,
And your confusion, must import some rudeness.   245
    Q. Rudeness!—that word suggests an happy thought—
Yes, let despair and shame give way to vengeance.   [*Aside.*
O brother! if I dare to call you brother
After the vile indignity I've suffer'd;
That wretch, presuming on his boundless power,   250
Has talk'd to me of love.

<hr>

(III. i) 222 I have] I've L   223–4 —Death! . . . indignation!—] ∧~! horror!∧
shame | ~!∧ L   232b–233a my soul . . . | Shall be preserv'd.] my soul | The secret shall be
preserv'd. L   237 say] ~! L   246 an] a L

  Elm.   What can I answer?
When accidents concur with calumny,
Her pois'nous breath obscures the brightest fame,
And conscious virtue only can support us.
  Conr. I saw and heard too much. The traitor's life   255
Is a mean sacrifice.
  Elm.   To plead my cause
Before a judge like thee, were mean and vain;
Yet be advis'd, young Prince, nor rashly draw
A sword that can't avail you.
  Q.   Will you hear him?
Think on the affront done to our royal house:—   260
Remember who he is, think on *Ismena*:
Who, if he 'scapes your sword, is lost for ever. [*To* Conrade.
  Conr. Then love inspire me.   [*They fight.*
  Q.   Ha! my brother!—
Elmerick has th' advantage.   [Conrade *disarm'd.*
  Elm.   Take your life,
Young Prince. The false appearance that misled you,   265
Withholds my hand from punishing your rashness;
But as the King's authority lives in me,
It may be fatal to repeat these insults,
Which nor my spirit, nor my place will bear.
Remember you are warn'd.—For you, proud Queen,   270
I pity and forgive your groundless hatred,
And still have that attention to your happiness,
To wish, even from my soul, you wou'd review,
With an impartial eye, our different conduct.
Wou'd you atone for error, make it short;   275
Reproach yourself, and use this as a motive,
That he, whom you have wrong'd, scorns to approach you.
             [*Exit* Elmerick.

  Q. Most exquisite! Legions of plagues and curses!
Has Heaven nor Hell no vengeance in reserve,
No bolts to strike, no light'ning to consume   280
This overbearing traitor; who has dar'd
To talk of wrongs, reproach, and teach us fear!
  Conr. Vain of th' advantage fortune gave him o'er me,
He us'd me with the last indignity,
Gave me my life in scorn, check'd, rated, threaten'd.—   285
But may my sword ne'er do me right in battle,

(III. i) 259b him?] ~? (To Conrade) L 260 house:] ~‸ L 261 is,] ~: L
Ismena:] Ismena‸ L 262SD [*To* Conrade.] *not in* L (*see* 259, *above*) 263b Ha] L; Ah G
270 warn'd.—] L; ~.‸ G 281 traitor;] traytor, L

May I be blasted with a coward's name,
If I forget to pay him this foul outrage
With double weight of vengeance.

                  Enter Zenomira.

   Zen. Madam, *Ismena*—
   Q.   Ha!—*Ismena*, say'st thou!—   290
Say, *Zenomira*, that her Lord expects her.   [*Exit* Zenomira.
   Conr. *Ismena* in my power! O Fortune, Fortune!
From this blest hour I'll worship none but thee.
I might have rack'd my thoughts in vain for ages,
And ne'er have found the thousandth, thousandth part   29
Of this complete, this most luxurious vengeance.
   Q. Revenge, thou com'st too sudden;
And risest to my view in such a form,
So shocking, so tremendous, that my soul
Shrinks back with horror now I shou'd embrace thee.—   30
I justify thy scorn, proud *Elmerick*,
By this degenerate pity.—Let it be—
The haughty Regent's heart shall know such anguish,
That his complaints shall move ev'n Fiends to pity,
And vengeance to repent.—Retire, my *Conrade*,   30
And watch till I have sent *Ismena* hence.   [*Conrade retires.*
I am so lost, that only horror, ruin,
Can cover my disgrace.

              Enter Ismena *looking round.*

   Ism.   Lord *Elmerick* not here!—
Have my unheeded steps mistook their way?—
The Queen!—and deep in thought!
   Q.   She has not wrong'd me—   3
But misery is cruel and remorseless.—
   Ism. Forgive me, gracious Queen, if I am rude,
In vent'ring thus to press on your retirement;
I was inform'd Lord *Elmerick* was here.
   Q. Yes,—no,—he was—Good Heavens! how shall I frame   3
My tongue to this vile office.   [*Aside.*
   Ism.   Are you well?—
Pray Heaven preserve the Queen!—You're strangely alter'd
—The blood forsakes your cheeks—you start, and tremble.
   Q. You'd see your Lord, seek him in those apartments.

(III. i)   294–311 I might . . . and remorseless.] *so* L² (*variants noted below and in collation*);
not in L¹   295 ne'er have] {not have} ne'er have L²   310b me—] ∼: L²
311 remorseless.—] L²; ∼.∧ G   317 Pray] L; ∼, G

Ism. For that I came; but dare not leave you thus.　　　320
　Q. It was a short disorder, and 'tis past—
Go, you're expected—　　　　　　　　　　[*Exit* Ismena.
　　　　　　　She is gone, and ruin,
Inevitable ruin meets her there.
The mean, perfidious, barb'rous task is done.
My heart is adamant, or Heaven-born pity　　　325
Had melted my resentments. Poor *Ismena*!
To be so plac'd by fate, that love or vengeance
Cou'd find no passage to the stubborn breast
Of *Elmerick*, but through thy breaking heart.

End of the Third Act.

ACT IV.

SCENE I.

Belus *and* Zenomira.

Bel. Then you confess that I've been made the tool
Of some vile purpose, that my Lord ne'er sent
The message you deliver'd?—Faithless woman!
How shall I meet my Lord's just indignation,
Or make my conduct clear?
    Zen.   Prepare to curse,
Prepare to kill me, *Belus*; or my fears
Will quickly end me, and prevent your justice.
    Bel. False woman! you've betray'd me into ruin.
    Zen. O we are both betray'd, and both are ruin'd:
Both made t'assist in such a villainy
As Hell would blush to own, and Heav'n and Earth
Must join to see reveng'd. O cruel Queen!
Curst *Conrade!* lost *Ismena!*
    Bel.   *Conrade!*—Queen!
    Zen. I say the Queen, and *Conrade*, and *Ismena*.
I saw her pass to the Queen's own apartment,
And cursed *Conrade* follow her soon after.
The rooms were bar'd.—But O the dismal cries,
The lamentations and the shrieks that followed!—
    Bel. O lost *Ismena*! O unhappy Lord!—
Yes they become thee well, these gushing tears—
    Zen. But danger presses on us—What's our duty
In this extreme?
    Bel.   To be both just and cautious:
Not rashly to proclaim what we have heard,
But boldly dare to evidence the truth,
And justify our selves, whenever call'd on.—
But see, *Ismena* comes. Merciful Heav'ns!
Who that beholds her now, can doubt her suff'rings!
    Zen. Heart-breaking spectacle!
    Bel.   She thinks us guilty:
We must avoid her sight. [*Going.*] Her Father's here!—

    Enter at opposite doors Bathori *and* Ismena.

O what a woful greeting! Now, by Heaven,
I know not which demands compassion most.   [*Exeunt* Belus *and*
                                       Zenomira.

    Bath. The Regent sent to see *Ismena* here?—

Perhaps, then—
 Ism.   Oh!—
 Bath.   From whence that mournful sound!
 Ism. Since life is but a witness of my shame,
Why do I longer bear it?
 Bath.   Some sad child   35
Of sorrow and despair, hiding her face,
And bending t'wards the earth, seems to bewail,
In bitterness of soul, some dire misfortune.
 Ism. Why is the grave, the hospitable grave,
The silent seat of darkness, closed to me?   40
Almighty power!   [*Raising her face.*
     My Father! ha!—   [*Seeing* Bathori.
 Bath.   Impossible!—
Art thou *Ismena?*—Let me doubt it still—
To see thee thus, and know thee for my child,
Must split my brain with horror.
 Ism.   Since my woes
Renounce all cure, and, told, must blast the hearer; 45
O let me pour them out to wilds and deserts,
Shun all mankind, but chiefly those I love!
 Bath. Come, my *Ismena*, to my sheltring bosom—
Close, closer still—and while I thus weep o'er thee,
Tell me, my child,—I know 'twill break my heart, 50
But let it break—come, tell me all thy suff'rings.
 Ism. Think where I am, remember what I told you
Of the detested rage of brutal *Conrade.*
 Bath. Then art thou ruin'd, past redemption ruin'd!
 Ism. Past, past redemption! every other ill   55
May be reliev'd by hope, or born with patience;
Here hope's impossible, and patience guilt.
 Bath. Then the last sacred business is revenge—
Give me some circumstances of thy wrongs.
 Ism. O shame! O horror! spare my loathing tongue 60
The painful task: Be it enough to say,
The Queen betray'd me, *Conrade* wrought my ruin.
 Bath. May curses, equal to their crimes, o'ertake 'em,
The monstrous, fiend-like, execrable pair!
 Ism. Look down, all-pitying Heaven, on these my woes, 65
Woes undeserv'd, and guiltless misery:
They plead my cause, the cause of innocence,

35a it?] L; ~; G 41a ff. *A second hand takes over transcribing* L *at this line and continues to the*
end of the play 59–64 Give me . . . execrable pair!] L (Conrade); G *omits* 65 Heaven,]
Heav'n! L

An injur'd, violated matron's cause;
And shall they plead in vain?
   Bath.   Yes, my dear child,
In whom thy Father's secret soul rejoic'd;   7
Whose goodness and whose happiness was such,
He found old age delightfull; let thy foes,
Those kindred fiends, to this thy just appeal
Plead their high rank, and try its weight with Heaven.
   Ism. Or *Elmerick*, whose wrath perhaps they fear   7
Much more than Heaven's.
   Bath.   And therefore may avoid.
This asks some thought—
For who can answer for thy husband's transport,
Wise as he is, when he shall hear thy wrongs?
   Ism. O what a scene of horror have you rais'd!   8
He'll rush, unarm'd, on our insidious foes,
Fall in their toils, and perish. Yes, my woes,
My miseries, enormous as they are,
Admit of aggravation.
   Bath. His danger wou'd be great—Some hand less fear'd   8
May make revenge more certain—Nay, 'twere kind
To spare thy Lord such anguish and despair.
   Ism. O Heaven! and Earth! to whom shall I complain,
Where pour my sorrows forth, if not to him?
   Bath. Think you expose his life.
   Ism.   Death seal my lips!
   Bath. Retire, and trust our vengeance to my prudence.
Compose thy self, and when thou seest thy Lord—
   Ism. Madness will seize me,
Or raging grief disclose the horrid secret.   [*Exit.*
   Bath. Suspence was ease to this confirm'd despair.
Would thou wert dead, *Ismena!*—O my child!
Thou art so lost beyond the reach of hope,
That love itself compels thy wretched Father
To wish thee dead; and in the bitterness
Of anguish mourn that ever thou wert born.
May one kind grave soon hide thy woes and mine,
Ismena!—oh!—But while I weep thy wrongs,
The spoiler lives.—Those are the Queen's apartments,
And, doubtless, there her brutal brother lurks.
Nor courts, nor shrines and altars shall protect him.

(IV. i)   68 violated] L; ~, G   85 great—] L; ~. G   88 Heaven!] Heav'n, L
101 mine,] L; ~. G

What, ho! within! Prince of *Moravia*! *Conrade*!
If thou'rt a man, stand forth, appear and answer.

Enter Conrade.

Conr. What insolence is this!—*Ismena*'s Father!—
Bath. Yes, impious Prince, the Father of *Ismena*.
Conr. Forbear, rash man; this foul reproach I pardon.   110
Somewhat, I grant, is due to thy first transports
Of jealous honour, and much more from me
To fair *Ismena*'s father.
  Bath.   Yes, thy blood.
  Conr. Yet hold; I've that to say may calm thy fury.
  Bath. Coward!
  Conr.   I smile, old man,   115
And will be heard. Your daughter has been wrong'd,
But most by her ungrateful, faithless Lord;
Whose rude attempt upon the Queen, my sister,
Makes what I've done a just, though bold, reprisal.
Let him atone his treasonous presumption,   120
Which, be assur'd, he answers with his life;
And let me perish, if I not restore
The injur'd honour of your lov'd *Ismena*
With vast increase, and seat her on a throne.
  Bath. I'd rather see her in the arms of death   125
Than reigning o'er the universe with thee.
Mark thy progression,
From rape to subornation, thence to murther.
Long-suffering Heaven, whose patience thou hast tir'd,
Calls loud for vengeance on thee.   [*Draws.*
  Conr.   Frantick man!   130

Enter Queen, *Lords and Guards, who interpose.*

  Q. You Lords of *Hungary*, behold this sight,
And vindicate your hospitality.
Is this fit treatment for a royal guest?
Will you endure this more than barb'rous outrage,
And share the guilt of him and his confed'rates?   135
Who twice this day, and for a cause too vile
For me to name, have sought my brother's life.
  1st Ld. How shall we reconcile what we have seen
With your known wisdom, and consummate virtue?
  Bath. Believe me, friends, there is, there is a cause   140

(IV. i) 111 thy] the L

For what you saw—for, what I fain wou'd hide,
These eyes still swelling with unmanly tears—
Which when you know, you'll join with me to curse
The chance that brought you to prevent my justice.

   1st Ld. The great, good man! so long, so often prov'd   145
The fearless advocate of injur'd innocence,
Wou'd he shed tears,
And call for justice when no wrong was done him?
Judge others as they please, I will not think it.

2nd Ld. Nor I.

   3rd Ld.   Nor I.

   4th Ld.   Why is that wrong conceal'd?   150

   Bath. For most important reasons: Though I fear
It will too soon be known.

   4th Ld.   'Till then, my Lord,
Excuse me, if I think our country's honour
Must suffer by your conduct.

   5th Ld.   That's my judgment.

   Bath. If your long knowledge of me cannot gain   155
Some credit to my word, at least suspend
Your hasty censures.   *[Going.*

   1st Ld.   We accept your word,
And vow to share your counsels, and your fortune.

   Bath. You're truly noble. And be well assur'd
That 'tis an honest cause, and worth espousing. *[Exeunt* Bathori, 1*st,*   160
                                         2*d,* 3*d Lords.*

   Q. Unmanner'd Traitors!
From you, my Lords, who think and act more nobly,
What may insulted Majesty expect?

   4th Ld. All that becomes good subjects, who will guard
The venerable rights of hospitality.   165

   5th Ld. Bathori, whose rash conduct we condemn,
At our joint charge, shall answer to the Regent
His bold attempt.

   Q.   The Regent!—
His daughter's husband! his confed'rate!—

   5th Ld. No kindred, Madam, will prevail with *Elmerick*   170
To stop the course of justice.

   Q.   Left to him,
Whose daring insolence has been the source
Of these fierce discords! Lords, if you regard
The publick safety, if you love the King,

(IV. i)   141 saw—for,] L; ~, ~_∧_ G   142 tears—] L; ~; G   143 you know] *so* L²;
reveal'd L¹   144 you] L; ~, G   167 Regent] L; regent G

Or dare defend your Queen from foulest insult;   175
Go find him now, attack him unprepar'd,
Stand not on forms, the least delay is fatal.
    4th Ld. Your pardon, Madam—
    5th Ld. Our zeal shall never make assassins of us.
    Q. Nor men, tame Lords. You who have seen my brother   180
Assaulted with a murderous intent,
Is this your boasted loyalty and honour?
    4th Ld. These bind us to respect the character,
The dignity and person of the Regent.
    5th Ld. If you, my Queen, or you, great Prince, are wrong'd,   185
The King will do you justice.   [*Exeunt Lords.*
    Conr.   Canting traitors!
They go to join our foe, and swell his power:
This shrub of one day's growth, this idol Regent
Attracts their ready worship.
    Q.   Let them go.
Now by the burning rage that drinks my blood,   190
The fools spoke true: The King shall do us justice.
    Conr. Elmerick,
His Influence—
    Q.   We will accuse him first.
The King has not yet reach'd *Alba-Regalis,*
You soon will overtake him. What you saw   195
Of *Elmerick*'s base purpose strongly urg'd,
Join'd with the earnest letters I shall write,
Will so alarm and prepossess the King;
That all complaints of their *Ismena*'s sufferings
Will be regarded as an after feint,   200
A mean device to screen her guilty lord.
What are your thoughts?
    Conr.   That thou wast born to triumph.
This traitor, when unmask'd, shall fall unpitied
By all mankind, and hated by *Ismena.*
    Q. Still your *Ismena!*
    Conr.   O my best *Matilda!*   205
The hopes that freed by death from her false husband,
And of his crimes convinc'd, she then may deign
To bless my vows, and share my future throne,
Are more than safety, life or vengeance to me.

    (IV. i) 179 *5th Ld.*] *Ed.*; 5 *Ld.* G; L *omits speech-heading, giving the speech to* 4*th Ld.*
186a will] *so* L²; shall L¹   190 blood,] L; ~∧ G

My blind impetuous passion once desir'd   21(
Those charms alone which violence cou'd gain;
But now the avarice of love aspires
To mutual bliss, and more refin'd disdains
Th'imperfect pleasures which her will denied.
    Q. She may be wholly and for ever yours.   21
You mark'd with how much care the cautious sire
Preserv'd the secret of his daughter's wrongs.
    Conr. Oh may I live to make her reparation
By gentlest love for wrongs which now my soul
Detests, and sickens at the vile remembrance.   22(
    Q. Live and be bless'd. I do not hate *Ismena*:
Cut off that source of both our wrongs, her husband,
And my tormenting thirst of vengeance ceases.
    Conr. Prepare your letters. I'll be instant ready.   [*Exit* Conrade.
    Q. Yes, I will humble that exalted mein,   22
And teach this new made Regent's pride submission.
He is secure, and let him be so still;
'Till my revenge, a slighted Queen's revenge,
Burst forth, and blast him with unthought of ruin.   [*Exit Queen.*

SCENE II.

Ismena's Apartment.

Enter Elmerick *running to embrace her.*

  Elm. Thou hast too long been absent, my *Ismena*!
A thousand anxious cares have fill'd my heart
Since I beheld thee last. But thou art found,
Who ne'er appear'd to my desiring eyes
But peace and comfort and delight came with thee.
O take me to thy arms, and quite extinguish
The memory of pain.
    Ism.   O misery!   [*Refusing to embrace him.*
Unequal'd misery! I am excluded
For ever from those arms.
    Elm.   All-gracious Heaven!

(IV. i) 210–14 My blind . . . will denied.] *so* L² (*variants noted in collation*); L¹ *reads:*

        My high enamour'd fancy once aspir'd
        But to the charms my ravish'd eye captor'd,
        Oh! avarice of Love!—now I aspire
        And languish for the joys of mutual passion.

216 sire] L; Sire G   218 Oh] ~! L   222 off] L; ~, G

What mean these broken thoughts, this lab'ring anguish,　　10
My soul, thou sum of all my joys, my wife!
　　Ism. Thou hast no wife.
　　Elm.　　　　　　　Distraction!
　　Ism.　　　　　　　　　　　　I'm a wretch
Without a name, and fain would quit my being.
　　Elm. Protect me, Heaven! *Ismena*! what dire thought
Shakes thy sweet soul with such tempestuous agony?　　15
What ill so sudden, since we parted last,
Preventing even my fears, has burst upon thee?
Say, tell me—
　　Ism.　　　　No, I cannot, dare not tell you:—
You cannot bear it. Though I ne'er conceal'd
A thought before, I must be silent now.　　20
　　Elm. What can this mean? And yet I dread to know—
Perhaps the envious Queen has wrong'd my truth,
Can you suspect my love?
　　Ism.　　　　　　　You love too well:
O that 'twere in your power to love me less!
　　Elm. Nay, then I'm lost indeed—Pronounce my doom;　　25
But let me hear it folded in thy arms.
　　Ism. Avoid me, fly, and think of me no more.
　　Elm. What! shun my arms, *Ismena*!
　　Ism.　　　　　　　　　　There's my misery,
I must for ever shun 'em—Now, my Father,
Where is your prudence? Must I seem a monster,　　30
Ungrateful, false to *Elmerick*; or bring
—Detested thought—pollution to his arms?
　　Elm. Pollution! madness!
　　Ism.　　　　　　　　I have been betray'd,
Basely betray'd to infamy and ruin,
Render'd unworthy of thy chaste embraces:　　35
That execrable fiend, that monster *Conrade*
Has robb'd me of my honour.
　　Elm.　　　　　　　　Hear me, Heaven!
Let not this whirlwind of overwhelming passion
Tear up my being—Let me live whole ages
Though raging with despair, rather than die　　40
And leave her unreveng'd.
　　Ism.　　　　　　　Had not religion
Withheld my hand, whose law forbids self-murder,

(That short and easy cure for shame and anguish)
These sorrows ne'er had reach'd you.
  Elm.   Talk not thus,
Talk not of dying; thou art innocent,   4
Thy mind unstain'd; thy wrongs shall be reveng'd,
And thou still bless my days.
  Ism.   It cannot be:
My power to bless is lost. I am the blot,
The only blot of *Elmerick*'s fair honour.—
O! why was it committed to the charge   5
Of one so heedless, so improvident,
Guardian unworthy of a trust so noble.
  Elm. O my *Ismena*!
  Ism.   O my dearest Lord!
Alas you weep—I cannot bear your tears,
They melt my firmest purpose—but Adieu--   5
One last embrace, as on a dying friend,
It will not stain your glory to bestow
On your undone *Ismena*—
  Elm.   To my bosom
With tenderer fondness did I never press thee.
Here rest, my love, a while, and lose thy woes.   6
  Ism. The greatness of my woes will make 'em short:
I feel my vital powers decay apace.
To part with thee, was all that e'er appear'd
Dreadful to me in death—that's past already—
And all to come is ease and soft repose.   6
When I'm no more, remember, *Elmerick*,
My reverend Father—comfort and support him
The best you can—my loss will touch him nearly—
I see you burn for vengeance—but beware—
The cruel, treach'rous Queen conspir'd with *Conrade*. 7
  Elm. Alike remote from rashness and from fear,
I'll trace this hellish mystery to its source,
And deal to each, with an inflexible
And equal hand, the portion they deserve:
I'll weigh it as the action of my life
That must give name and value to the whole;
And raise a monument to thee and justice

(IV. ii) 43 (That . . . anguish)] ₋~ . . . ~,₋ L   49 honour.—] honor.₋L
51 improvident,] ~! L   53b Lord!] ~!—L   54 weep] ~! L   55 Adieu] L;
Farewell G 61 greatness] G (*errata slip*), L; greatest G 67 Father—] L (father); ~; G
68 can—my] L; ~: My G nearly—] L; ~. G 69 vengeance—] L (vengance); ~, G
beware—] L; ~; G

Shall strike exalted wickedness with terror,
And freeze the boiling blood of future *Conrades*.
Adieu, be patient, and expect th'event.   [*Exeunt.*   80

End of the Fourth Act.

(IV. ii)   80 Adieu] L; Farewell G   80SD [*Exeunt.*] *not in* L

ACT V.

SCENE I.

Queen *alone.*

To recollect and judge our actions past,
May yield instruction—I approve my caution,
And bless the fortune that conceal'd my weakness
For the proud Regent, even from my brother.
My seeming innocence preserves respect,
And gives him life and vigour to pursue
My daring scheme to crush the man I hate.
Shou'd it succeed, secure from all reproach,
Life may be worth my care.

Enter Zenomira.

               I had forgot—
This woman knows too much—her lover too—   1
They may be dangerous—that too shou'd be thought on,
And shall be so hereafter—What's your business?
  Zen. Madam, the Regent asks to be admitted.
  Q. Why shou'd I be alarm'd?—No, 'tis not fear
That gives this sudden sickness to my heart:—   1
This tremor, these convulsive starts proceed
From strong aversion only—I contemn him.   *[Apart.*
Yes, let him enter.   *[Exit* Zenomira.
            I'll enjoy his anguish:
Safe in my sex and dignity, I'll tell him,
That 'tis my pride and glory to have made him   2
The very wretch he is.

Enter Elmerick *and* Zenomira.

  Zen.   Madam, the Regent—
  Elm. I've orders, Madam, from your Lord and mine
Fit only for your ear.
  Q. What gloomy grandeur he assumes!
What insolent tranquillity he bears?   2
You may withdraw.   *[Exit* Zenomira.
  Elm.   I hear *Conrade* is fled.
  Q. You've bad intelligence, the state must suffer
While you're no better serv'd: He scorns to fly,
And will confront you soon.

11 on,] ~—L   15 heart:] ~ˌL   17 him.] ~—L   26b hear] L; ~, G

Elm.   'Till then, let guilt
And fear attend, and keep the villain waking.   30
  Q. You come to rail: Begin, I stand collected,
Nay, will assist you. You refus'd my love,
And in my turn, I have undone *Ismena*.
  Elm. You do confess it then?
  Q.   I glory in it.
To wound you where I knew you most secure,   35
To taint your Heaven, to curse you in *Ismena*,
Was my contrivance: *Conrade*'s desperate passion
Subservient to my vengeance, wrought her ruin.
  Elm. This I had charg'd you with; but, self-convicted,
My pains are spar'd, and here your process ends.   [*A pause.*   40
Thou awful power, whose bright tremendous sword
Rules Heaven and Earth, while Hell resists in vain,
Inexorably firm, eternal Justice;
Fearless I offer up this high delinquent
To you and to *Ismena*: Deign t' accept   45
No common sacrifice, and may it prove
A solemn lesson and a dreadful warning,
T' instruct and to alarm a guilty world.
  Q. Dost thou presume, the subject of our throne,
To menace me with justice?
  Elm.   You're no Sov'reign,
Your King's authority resides in me.   50
  Q. Not to assassinate his Queen. Help! Treason!   [*Calls.*
  Elm. Cease your vain clamour, and prepare to die;
I've taken measures not to be prevented.
  Q. Traitor, think who I am, respect my rank.   55
  Elm. That you shou'd have respected.
The blackest aggravation of your guilt
Is from your rank, and other benefits
Receiv'd from Heaven: Not to have done much good
With your advantages, forfeits them all,   60
And leaves you debtor to a vast account;
But their abuse—
  Q   And who shall judge of that?
  Elm. All may, and must, who feel and suffer by it;
But I've a double right to judge and punish.
The ignominy of a bar and scaffold,   65
Which our strict laws, and your high crimes demand;
For the King's honour, here I take upon me

(v. i)   41 power,] Pow'r! L   43 Justice;] ~! L   48 world.] ~! L   52 Help!
Treason!] L (treason); ~. ~. G   62a their] L; there G

At my own peril to remit, and make
Myself your only judge, and this your scaffold.
If you've not sin'd beyond the hopes of pardon,
But wou'd in pray'r and penitential tears
Employ a few short moments, they are yours—
The utmost of my mercy.

    Q.   So determin'd!
The King's arrival yet wou'd change our fates.   [*Aside.*
Cruel man!
Blame your own scorn for what I've rashly done,
And let us now exchange mutual forgiveness.   [*Weeps.*

    Elm. I have not gone thus far without consulting
Reason and Justice, with the extent and end
Of that great Power and Trust impos'd upon me:
No, had the wrong you've basely done my wife,
Been done the meanest peasant's wife in *Hungary*,
Nor rank, nor vain intreaties shou'd protect you.

    Q. Conrade is gone t' accuse you to the King—
You know how well the strong appearance won
My brother's credit to th' imputed crime;
My death wou'd be so full a confirmation
Of all I charg'd you with, that certain ruin,
And everlasting infamy, must follow.

    Elm. And do you thus atone for your offences?
Is this the use you make of my indulgence,
To boast new crimes?

    Q.   To warn you of your danger.
I tell you once again, you dare not kill me.

    Elm. I dare not let you live, for that's injustice,—
The only thing I fear: And had you fear'd it,
You had been safe and happy.—Enter now,
Ye ministers of justice: Do your office.

      Enter the Executioners. While they prepare to strangle
                 her, she speaks.

    Q. Is there no help then? Must I fall his victim?—
Almighty power, who gav'st me my existence,
And with it strong affections and aversions,
Why hast thou dealt so very hardly with me?
If you have mercy— [*They pull her into the Recess in the back Scene, and*
                                      strangle her.

    (v. i) 72 yours—] your's; L   87 full] *so* L²; strong L¹   94 injustice,—] ~,ᴧ L
96 happy.—] L; ~.ᴧ G   now,] L; ~ᴧ G   97+SD *Enter the Executioners.*] The Executioners
enter. L   99 power,] Pow'r! L

Elm. O let her life atone for all its errors!—
Thus I supply the interrupted pray'r
That death breaks off, and may it find acceptance!   105
The fiercest anger in the human mind
Shou'd reach but to the grave—*Belus.*

Enter Belus.

Bel.   My Lord,
What is your pleasure?
    Elm.   We must seek the King.
    Bel. My Lady's father, and th' assembled Peers—
    Elm. 'Tis true, I had forgot. Behold within there.   [*Pointing to the*   110
                                           Recess in the back Scene.
    Bel. Alas! my Lord!—   [*Seeing the Queen.*
    Elm.   At what are you surpriz'd?
    Bel. The Queen is dead!
    Elm.   She is, and by my sentence.
Have I done ought unjust?
    Bel.   I dare not say it,
Yet stand astonish'd at the rigorous deed.
    Elm. So do not I that wickedness abounds,   115
When justice is a wonder. Seek the Peers,
And bring 'em to behold what thou hast seen.
    Bel. You wou'd not have this known?
    Elm.   Not have it known!
The business of my life is to proclaim it.   [*Exit* Belus.
O thou impartial, universal power,   120
Wise Nature's eldest law, wrote by herself
Upon the heart of man, eternal Justice;
Inspired by thee, with one determin'd blow
I have redrest my poor *Ismena's* wrongs,
(As far as wrongs like hers can be redress'd)   125
And wip'd dishonour from my house and name:
And now if I am call'd to be thy martyr,
My race will end with glory.

Enter Bathori *and Lords.*

Bath.   I have declared
To these right noble Lords, as you commanded,
The Queen and *Conrade's* most inhuman guilt.   130
    Elm. Then judge, my Lords, whether this dreadful act
Merits reproach or praise.   [*Pointing to the Queen.*

(v. i)   103   errors!—] ~!ᴧ L   106   the human] *so* L² (yᵉ); a human L¹
122   Justice;] ~! L   123   blow] L; ~, G   131   dreadful] *so* L² (dredful); noble L¹

1st Ld.   Speak he that can.

2d Ld. Astonishingly bold—

3d Ld.   But righteous vengeance:
Unprecedented Justice!

   Bath. Yes, this transcends example. Gracious Heaven!   1
May I but live to see her brother thus!—

   1st Ld. Sir, your interest
May make you partial: Not that we condemn
Or justify the Regent: To the King
We must refer his sentence.

   Elm.   'Tis but just.   1
And so may Heaven deal with my soul hereafter,
When I shall stand at that all-seeing bar;
As I will render up a strict account,
Urge to the King himself his Queen's misdoing,
And seek my judge with his wife's blood upon me.   1

   1st Ld. Heard you that trumpet?   [*Flourish of trumpets.*

2d Ld.   'Tis the King. [*Enters Gentleman.*

   Gent. His Majesty is ent'ring.

   1st Ld.   Let us meet him.

   2d Ld. We are prevented: see! the King appears.

Enter King, Conrade, *and Attendants.*

   K. Where is this Patriot who defies all law,
And uses our authority for treason?
I ask for *Elmerick.*

   Elm.   Your loyal subject,
The *Palatine* and Regent of your kingdom,
Who bears that name, is here.

   K. Doth not the presence of thy King confound thee?

   Elm. I burnt with strong impatience 'till I saw him.

   K. Where is *Matilda?* Go and call the Queen:
Let her appear and strike the Traitor dumb.
—What means this gloomy silence? Are you motionless?
Why am I not obey'd?

   Elm.   I pray, give back—
Behold, unhappy King, to what my Justice
Has brought thy guilty Queen.

   K.   Heavenly powers!
For what unknown offence am I condemn'd

(v. i)   132b can.] ~— L   138 partial:] ~; L   146b–148 'Tis the . . . King
appears.] L (Enters Gentleman); See, the King appears. G   149 who] *so* L²; that L¹
156 Go and] *so* L² (go); someone L¹   157 appear] L; ~, G   160–161a to what . . .
guilty Queen.] *so* L²; the poor remains | Of her that was Matilda. L¹   162–3 For what . . .
barb'rous Villain—] L; G *omits*

To bear this murth'ring sight?—barb'rous Villain—
Matilda! Am I come, though on the wings
Of love, too late to save thee?   [*Runs to the body in the Recess.*
    Conr.   O my sister!   165
Are these our promis'd joys? Is this our triumph?
    Elm. Suspend the Husband, and exert the King.
    K. Inhuman wretch! I will exert the King,
And give new majesty and double terror
To that important name, for thy destruction.   170
    Elm. Condemn'd on circumstances, and unhear'd!—
Yet, I resign my life without reluctance;
Take, if you please, my head. But know, your fame
Is in the balance, and your conduct now
Must fix your character to all posterity;   175
Must place you in the list of lawless tyrants,
Or Kings, whose virtue dignify'd the office,
And honour'd human nature. If you think
The abject fear of death, not a regard
To your yet spotless virtue and renown,   180
Inspires my tongue, you've my compassion, Sir.
Monarchs are men—I've said—and use your pleasure.
    K. I thought I knew thee well: hence my amazement
Is equal to my grief and indignation.
Had'st thou the tongue of Angels, cou'd'st thou hope   185
To clear thyself of my *Matilda*'s death?
    Elm. Nor was it e'er my purpose to attempt it.
    K. A murderer confess'd dare talk of Justice?
    Elm. Yes, I've a right to justify myself
If innocent, and to be heard with patience.   190
But if, through passionate and blind prevention,

(v. i)   171–2 Condemn'd on . . . Yet, I resign] L; Sir, I resign G   173 head. But] ~;
but L   187 attempt it.] L; ~; G   188 *K.* A murderer . . . of Justice?] L (justice); G
prints after 190; G (*errata slip*) *directs that the line be deleted* (*see* 191–6a, *below*)   189 Yes,] L;
But∧ G   190 with patience.] *after this line* L¹ *reads:*

             K. You shall be heard: a seat—O! my Matilda,
                Forgive this short delay. Let the rash man
                Endev'ring to defend, convict himself,
                And fall the more abhorr'd—You may proceed—
             Elm. To pay my life for daring to be just,
                Is buying glory at a small expence—
             K. To the charge—
                My patience is abus'd, I will not keep it
                To hear a traytor glory in his guilt
             Elm. My guilt is yet unprov'd.
             K. The horrid fact is plain, and asks no proof.
             Elm. I ask but to be heard and that's no favour.

191–6a But if . . . my country.] L (*without italics*), G (*errata slip; variants noted below*); G *omits these*

You do refuse to hear, I wou'd not live
To bear the unavailing name of Palatine,
First guardian of the rights of freeborn *Hungary*,
And be a witness to an innovation   19
So fatal to my country.
   K.   Thou hast touch'd
My inmost soul. I'd rather thou shou'dst 'scape,
Than fix a precedent which may be urged
Hereafter, to suppress the voice of truth;
Lose the benignant character of King,   20
And change my glories for a tyrant's shame.—
You shall be heard: A seat—O my *Matilda*,
Forgive this short delay. Let the rash man,
Endeavouring to defend, convict himself,
And fall the more abhorr'd.
   Elm.   You may remember,   20
When you appointed me your substitute,
You did pronounce, in presence of your states,
The worst abuse of law and all just power,
Is when the great offend and pass unpunish'd.
This you injoin'd me strongly not to suffer,   2
Nor bear the sword in vain. You've been obey'd—
The Queen transgress'd—and I have done my duty.
  K. Your duty, Sir! Dare you affirm the Queen—
  Elm. Deserv'd the death I gave her. Hear me out.
If, with deep fore-thought and deliberate malice,   2
To plot and to effect a matron's ruin,
To give her up to a lewd spoiler's rage,
By laws, divine and human, be pronounc'd
A crime deserving death, the guilty Queen
Drew on herself the justice I inflicted.   2
Her wicked agent *Conrade*, her vile brother,
Who stain'd the purity of my *Ismena*,
Is left to prove your justice.   [*King rises.*

lines and prints: K. A murderer confess'd dare talk of Justice! (*errata slip restores* 191–6a *and directs that this line be deleted*)

 (v. i) 192 wou'd not live] L; had rather die G (*errata slip*)   193 To] L; Than G (*errata slip*) 195 be] L; live G (*errata slip*) 201 shame.—] ~._∧ L 202–5a You shall . . . more abhorr'd.] *so* L² (*variants noted below and in collation*); L¹ *includes these lines after* 189, *above, and here reads:*

> No, live and mock attention, talk whole days,
> I will, if possible, be calm and hear you.
> Elm. I thank you for the honor done yourself,
> And shall be brief.

205b remember,] L²; ~, Sir, L¹, G 210 suffer,] ~. L 211 vain. You've] ~—you've L
213 Sir!] sir. L 218 laws,] L; ~_∧ G human] humane L 221 vile] *so* L²; lewd L¹

    K.   Can it be!
Thy lovely chaste *Ismena*!
    Elm.   She, my wife.
Lovely she was, and chaste; and not less worthy   225
That just regard the meanest may pretend to,
I trust, for being mine.
    Conr.   Evasive traitor!
Say for what cause, with impious prophanation,
You dar'd attempt your master's sacred bed;
And I may deign to answer to your charge.   230
    K. Is this the court of *Buda?* This vile stage
Of lewdness, death, and black recrimination?
Of what a sudden growth is rank corruption!
That, during my short absence, hath infected
My house and throne, those I most loved and trusted.   235
—But bring the clearest proof of this foul charge
Against my Queen and brother, or expect
The self same mercy thou hast shewn to her:
Whom, if thy accusation be unjust,
Thou'st basely murder'd twice.
    Elm.   I have the strongest proofs,   240
My wife's accusing tears, who cou'd not forge
To her own ruin and to my dishonour
A tale so full of shame. But more, the Queen,
The Queen herself, triumphant in her malice,
Confest it to my face, and gloried in it.   245
    K. And will *Ismena* vouch it?—I think highly
Of your Wife's truth;—so did I of *Matilda*'s—
I'll not condemn her on a single witness:
Ismena is but one, thy word is nothing.
    Elm. I have yet farther Proofs. Peruse this scroll, [*Giving the King*   250
                                     a Paper.
This full avowal of the hellish deed,
Witness'd by these who both were actors in it [*Pointing to* Belus *and*
                                             Zenomira.
Without designing ill, which I produce
With strong reluctance, as it speaks a weakness
Of the lost Queen, which I wou'd fain conceal.   255
    K. Why shou'd I tremble thus? Let truth appear,
And shame light where it will. [*Reads.*] Madness and death!
Confess a guilty passion for the Regent!—

  (v. i) 241–5 who cou'd . . . Confest it] the Queen's confession, | Who own'd it L
252 it] L; ~, G   257 will. [*Reads.*] Madness] *Ed.*; will. (*Reads*ᴧ) | Madness G, L (Reads L),
which treat as two lines   death!] ~!— L   258 Regent!—] ~!ᴧ L

Can these things be!—That dignity of spirit,
That high demeanour stoop to such dishonour!—   2(
How shall I credit—what I can't reject?
How root out fixt ideas from a heart
Matilda fill'd, and bend it to conviction?—
O *Elmerick*! I see the pois'nous source
Of our united woes.
    Elm.   Her will refus'd,   2(
She offer'd at her Life—
    Conr.   This claims attention.   [*Aside.*
    Elm. Which while I strove to save, her brother enter'd;
And, by her art deceiv'd, attempted mine:
The rest that paper speaks.
    Conr.   Too fatal truth!
'Twas gallant in him then not to accuse her.   2(
I see my fate, and am prepar'd to meet it.   [*Aside.*
    K. You do acknowledge, and confirm for truth
All that is here contain'd?   [*To* Belus *and* Zenomira.
    Both.   So Heaven deal with us.
    K. 'Tis all too plain: Her lawless love, fierce malice,
Conrade's foul rage, and poor *Ismena*'s ruin—   2
To find her guilty, is to find her hateful:
And I wou'd hate—what once I dearly lov'd.
No blood—but tears, and those too weakly shed,
Must stream o'er thy dishonourable hearse,
Unhappy, false *Matilda*!—But no more.—   2
I will dismiss this weak unworthy softness.
Let *Elmerick* go weep.—*Ismena*'s wrongs
May call forth tears that manhood may be proud of.
To weep *Ismena* is to feel for virtue.
How is it with her sorrows? From this hour   2
My tenderest care shall be to give them comfort.
    Elm. I fear her sorrows ne'er will taste of comfort.
But see, the messenger I sent returns.

               Enter Messenger.

    Mess. I come, my Lord—
    Elm. Be brief: how fares my wife?
    Mess.   As Angels fare,   2
With whom she now inhabits. When you sent me,
I found her in the arms of her attendants—
Fainting she seem'd—But when I told my message

(v. i) 261 credit—] ~ₐ L   270 then not to accuse her] *so* L²; not to accuse her then L¹
289–90b *Mess.* I come, . . . Angels fare,] *lineation Ed.; see Commentary*

She rais'd her head, and lifting up her eyes,
'Till then just clos'd, propitious Heaven! she cried,   295
Defend this noblest pattern of your justice,
Nor let his matchless love go unrewarded.
Then with an heavenly smile addrest me thus:
Assure my Lord I die without reluctance.
My soul, that melts with gratitude, presages   300
Unequal'd blessings shall attend him here,
While I enjoy—and then her speech forsook her,
And she, without one painful sigh, expir'd.
     K. Too sure a testimony hast thou given
Of thy foul wrongs, *Ismena—Elmerick!*—   305
Quite speechless and o'erwhelm'd!—her father too!—
Turn not away—I do not offer comfort—
I mean but to mourn with you.
     Elm.   So to die!—
Her delicately chaste and heavenly soul
Forsook its earthly temple when prophan'd   310
Without the steel or poison's lawless aid—
And lives the man who wrong'd me in *Ismena?*
Hear then, O righteous King, my high appeal
To thee, and to the law of warlike *Hungary.*
Give me to meet this impious Prince in battle;   315
There, in the crouded lists, dread scene of justice,
There only can I sue for retribution,
Wrong'd as I am, without a soldier's shame.
And thou, *Ismena*, from thy sainted seat,
Where high thou sit'st crown'd with the starry wreaths   320
That angels weave for purity like thine,
Look down propitious on me, and accept
This high, this second sacrifice of vengeance.
     Conr. Then I have murder'd thee, ador'd *Ismena.*
These mourn thy fate with tears, but what's the sorrow   325
That streaming eyes can utter and relieve!
Though thou disdain'st my grief, yet learn this truth   [*Turning to
                                                            Elmerick.*

From him thou most abhor'st:—The innocent
Are not the fittest objects of compassion:
O there's no pain, no misery like guilt—   330
Nor do I fall thy sacrifice: For know,
Had I been plac'd above the power of vengeance;

Ismena's fate, th'effect of my rash love,
Had been lamented thus, and thus reveng'd—   [*Stabs himself.*
   K. This is t'atone one error by another.   33
   Conr. Nothing but error: I was born to err:
The willing slave of every youthful passion.
'Tis now too late to learn—my day is past—
'Tis night—*Ismena*—oh—   [*Dies.*
   Elm. Unerring power! whose deep and secret counsels   34
No finite mind can fathom and explore;
It must be just to leave your creatures free,
And wise to suffer what you most abhor:
Supreme and absolute of these your ways
You render no account—We ask for none.   34
For mercy, truth, and righteous retribution
Attend at length your high and awful throne.
Ismena is aveng'd—Let me be wretched!
   K. Our sorrows must be felt. Yet, O! brave *Elmerick*,
Let not the Publick suffer! Thou'st done greatly.   3:
The face of justice as she shines in Heaven,
In native purity, unclouded splendor,
Alone can charm beyond thy virtuous daring.
That be Thy praise—be mine that I approve it.
Still hold the Sov'reign Power till I return   3:
From *Jordan*'s sacred stream and holy *Sion*;
My Substitute till then, my Friend for ever.

End of the Fifth Act.

(v. i)   349 O!] ~‿∧ L   350 done greatly.] *after this line* G *prints lines* 355–7
351 justice . . . Heaven,] ~, as she shines in Heaven∧ L   354 be mine . . . approve it] L; that
I approve it mine G   355–7 Still hold . . . for ever.] L (*variants noted below and in collation*);
G *prints after* 350, *above*   357 for ever] forever L

EPILOGUE.

Spoken by Mr. MILWARD.

You, who supreme o'er ev'ry work of Wit,
In Judgment here unaw'd, unbiast sit,
The Palatines *and* Guardians *of the Pit;*
If to your minds this meerly-modern Play,
No useful sense, no gen'rous warmth convey;   5
If Fustian *here, thro' each unnat'ral Scene,*
In strain'd conceits sound high, *and* nothing mean;
If Lofty Dulness *for your Vengeance call;*
Like Elmerick Judge, *and let the* Guilty Fall.
But if Simplicity with Force and Fire,   10
Unlabour'd thoughts and artless words inspire;
If, like the Action which these Scenes relate,
The whole appear irregularly Great;
If master-strokes the nobler Passions move,
Then, like the King, acquit *us, and* approve.   15

The END.

Britannia and Batavia

INTRODUCTION

COMPOSITION

BRITANNIA AND BATAVIA was the last of Lillo's works to appear in print, in a posthumous edition published in June 1740. It had been written some seven years earlier, a topical masque intended to celebrate the marriage of Princess Anne, the eldest daughter of George II, and William Charles Henry, Prince of Orange.[1] The royal wedding was scheduled to occur on 12 November 1733, but the ill health of the prince forced a series of postponements and the marriage ultimately took place on 14 March 1733/4. Lillo may well have completed his masque during the autumn of 1733, in time for it to be considered for the special performances that the theatre managements then expected to offer in November, though he could have offered it to the theatres as late as January 1733/4.[2]

The work derives from no specific source. Lillo drew on history and the perceived significance of the marriage itself as the basis for his allegorical

---

[1] William IV of Orange-Nassau, 1711–51. He was of another branch of the Orange family than William III, whose line had become extinct with his death in 1702.

[2] The wedding scheduled for 12 Nov. was postponed first to 15 Nov., then to 1 Dec., again to 1 Mar., and ultimately to 14 Mar. The theatres, having invested in the preparations for special celebrations, variously persisted with or rescheduled these entertainments. It appears that pieces performed when the wedding finally took place were, in the main, those that had been in preparation in November. However, some new offerings had also been mounted when it became clear that the wedding would not occur until February or March. On 11 Feb. Giffard and his company at Goodman's Fields offered *Britannia: or, The Royal Lovers*, not really a new work but an extensive revision of *The Happy Nuptials*, first presented on 12 Nov. 1733. On 21 Mar. Drury Lane introduced *Britannia: or, Love and Glory*, a new serenata written by Thomas Phillips with music by Dr Arne. Both theatres had enjoyed successful runs of *The London Merchant*, and it is not impossible that Lillo submitted his own Britannia masque to one or both managements to be considered for this second round of nuptial celebrations, but submission in time for the productions expected to be performed in November seems more likely. Despite the similar titles, Lillo's masque bears no relation to the pieces presented at Drury Lane and Goodman's Fields or to any other of the wedding celebrations known to have been staged in London's theatres. (*London Stage, 1729–1747*, vol. i, *passim*; Emmett L. Avery, 'A Royal Wedding Royally Confounded', *Western Humanities Review*, x [1956], 153–64.)

episodes and in form followed the conventions of the short musical masque. This eighteenth-century version of the masque, ideally suited to the requirements for afterpieces and affording full opportunity for theatrical spectacle, had become increasingly popular as English writers and managers sought to compete with the Italian opera—an effort, as Colley Cibber described his first attempt at a work of this sort, to bring to the town 'a little good music in a language they understood'.[3] Lillo chose the mythological, rather than the pastoral, mode of the masque as more appropriate to the occasion and his subject, and in the main adopted the structure characteristic of the genre in his time. Three brief serious episodes alternate with two briefer musical interludes or anti-masques and are followed by a spectacular finale. Each episode recalls, through transparent allegory, a historical situation selected to demonstrate the appropriateness and significance of the union of the Princess Royal with the Prince of Orange and the strengthened ties between the nations they represent. In the first scene, England in the character of Britannia is called upon to save her Dutch counterpart Batavia from 'proud *Hispania*'s fierce and cruel Power'[4]—an allusion to Elizabethan Britain's support of the northern provinces of the Netherlands in their ultimately successful rebellion against Phillip II. Episode two celebrates the accession of William and Mary in the glorious revolution of 1688; Britannia, herself oppressed by Tyranny, Slavery, Superstition, and other papish powers, receives aid from Batavia, who sends the kingly Liberto to free Britannia from her bonds and remain to 'guard the Freedom he restor'd'.[5] The betrothal of Anne and the young William is the subject of the third episode in which still grateful Britannia, to ease Batavia's grief at the death of Liberto, gives 'the First-born Princess of her Royal House'[6] as bride for Liberto's heir. Guardian angels guide the course of these events, and under their aegis the masque concludes with the marriage procession, '*as near as possible with the same Magnificence, as it was really perform'd*'.[7] The piece is designed to make full use of the stage machinery and spectacular effects that drew crowds to London's theatres. In concept, verse, and the lyrics for the songs, it is at best typical of a form of drama undistinguished in this period.

It is hardly remarkable that Lillo, himself of Dutch and English descent and staunchly Protestant in his religion, should have decided to compose a work to commemorate the dynastic marriage intended to provide a new link between the two peoples and to strengthen the Protestant succession in Britain. More notable are the indications that this topical piece—an apparent 'patriotic gesture'[8] to compliment a joyful occasion in the royal household—in fact serves

---

[3] Preface to *Venus and Adonis*, 1715, quoted by Nicoll, p. 259.

[4] i. 20. [5] ii. 63. [6] iii. 20. [7] iii. 33+SD.

[8] As Burgess notes (p. 11), the masque has been taken as 'a natural patriotic gesture on the part of Lillo', a slight if effusive occasional piece of little interest. Davies (pp. xxxix–xl), in the only reference to *Britannia and Batavia* in his biography of the playwright, misremembers the occasion for which it was written: 'Lillo had a great veneration for the prince [of Wales], and had, in a masque . . . , exerted his poetical skill on the marriage of his Royal Highness to the Princess of

as a vehicle to voice two controversial political themes, contemporary issues of
the sort reflected in the author's full-length plays: in episode one, justification
of military action to curb Spanish imperialism and the evils of the papacy or
Inquisition; in episode two (and, by implication, the final scenes of the masque),
the glorification of 'liberty' in the person of a patriot king. These themes are
appropriate, of course, to the historical situations figured in the allegory. They
might also be taken to express, in general, anti-Jacobite sentiments of the kind
encouraged by Walpole and his government. Both, however, relate directly to
issues central to the opposition case against the Ministers. The pillaging and
confiscation of British trading vessels by the Spaniards and the government's
reluctance to take strong action against the marauders had for more than two
decades roused increasing anger among English merchants, providing ammunition
for Walpole's opponents in Parliament. In 1738 these pressures would force the
government to undertake a war with Spain.[9] The rhetoric of the opposition
focused, however, on the ideal of constitutional monarchy, exemplified in the
figure of a capable and generous king who 'would use his royal prerogative to
regain powers the Ministers had usurped and would reanimate his people to a
jealous concern for the preservation of their liberties'.[10] Lillo's Liberto
represents of course precisely such an idealized monarch, and it is unlikely that
Lillo's contemporaries, had they been given the opportunity to see *Britannia and
Batavia*, would have failed to recognize the echoes of current political themes
that sounded through the high-flown verse of a little masque to celebrate a royal
occasion. The name Liberto would itself have been sufficient to signal that a
double interpretation was to be drawn.

Saxe-Gotha.' Given the political point of view on which the work appears to be based, Davies's slip
in associating it with the Prince of Wales is understandable. Modern commentators seem not to
have noticed this political dimension of the masque; John Loftis does not cite the work in his helpful
analysis of the elements of opposition doctrine and rhetoric to be found in such plays of Lillo's as
The Christian Hero and *The London Merchant* (cf. *The Politics of Drama in Augustan England* [Oxford,
1963], pp. 121–2 and 125–7).

[9] Allusions to Spanish hostility, which link Lillo with the cause of the merchants and opposition
politicians, are also to be found in *The London Merchant* (I. i. 2–8, I. iii. 20–2, and III. i. 1–7) and
Fatal Curiosity (I. i. 38–40). Walpole's policy of peace was a particular grievance to British merchant
interests affected by Spain's sometimes stringent measures to discourage clandestine trade with
Spanish America, efforts which included search and confiscation of British cargoes and, it was
reported, the taking of British seamen to be handed over to the torturers of the Inquisition. Lillo's
unrestrained portrayal of the viciousness and cruelty of figures representing the papacy as well as
Spain may also reflect the anger raised by Walpole's policy that Britain should not intervene in the
War of Polish Succession, which began late in 1733 and in which Catholic France was seen as the
primary aggressor (see the commentary on i. 23–32). (Paul Langford, *Modern English Foreign Policy:
The Eighteenth Century 1688–1815* [New York, 1976], pp. 104–15.)

[10] Loftis, op. cit., p. 119. This theme and the lessons to be learnt from the careers of such
exemplary rulers are developed more fully in *Elmerick* and *The Christian Hero*. It seems likely that, as
Loftis suggests (p. 121), Lillo's ideas relate to, if they do not stem directly from, Bolingbroke's *Idea
of a Patriot King*, versions of which were known in manuscript during the 1730s (see *The Christian
Hero*, commentary on the prologue, l. 28). 'Liberty' was, of course, a catchword of special
significance in anti-Walpole propaganda and its political resonances were certain to be recognized
by London audiences of the period.

For this reason, perhaps, the masque was never performed. The managers who read Lillo's manuscript—if, indeed, it was submitted for their consideration— were concerned primarily to capitalize on the excitement surrounding the royal wedding and, despite the fervent patriotic sentiments that characterize the surface of the work, may have judged it as something less than appropriate to the occasion and hardly likely to win the approbation of the king. They may simply have seen no great promise in the piece as popular entertainment. No evidence suggests that the masque was scheduled for performance but withdrawn and not rescheduled during the months in which the theatres scrambled to alter their calendars to adjust to the several postponements of the royal marriage.[11] There is no indication that the necessary music was composed for the piece.[12] However, the text published seven years later appears to be that of a completed work, not a work in progress or an editor's attempt to polish up an early draft. It seems likely therefore that Lillo meant the work to be performed and had some hope that it would be taken up by one of the theatres. That did not come about. The work is known only because it came into the hands of Lillo's publisher, who printed it, perhaps to add the appeal of a new piece to his nonce collection of the playwright's works. In so doing, he provided one further if slight example of Lillo's readiness to experiment with a variety of theatrical genres and intriguingly suggestive evidence of the political views that inform his more significant dramas.

THE TEXT

The single separate edition of *Britannia and Batavia* was published some nine months after the author's death. It is authoritative to the extent that it was produced by the bookseller who had published the authorized editions of all but the first of Lillo's works and who, as an executor of the playwright's will, can be presumed to have had access to manuscripts left when he died. No evidence suggests that the work itself is not authentic.

Britannia and Batavia was not reprinted until Davies published his collected edition of Lillo's works in 1775.

---

[11] Although the rescheduling of the wedding created confusion and indecision in the theatres, it appears that all of the celebratory performances planned for the occasion were presented, some of them on the dates originally announced, others at later times (cf. Avery, loc. cit.).

[12] It has been erroneously reported, on occasion, that Henry Carey composed a score for Lillo's masque (cf. *The National Union Catalog: Pre-1965 Imprints* [London and Chicago, 1974], xcv. 236 and cccxxxiii. 269; Elisabeth A. Heisch, 'A Selected List of Musical Dramas and Dramas with Music from the 17th and 18th Centuries', *Restoration and Eighteenth Century Theatre Research*, xi. 1 [May 1972], 38). The error probably came about through the confusion of *Britannia and Batavia* with *Britannia: or, The Royal Lovers*, the revised version of *The Happy Nuptials*, the Goodman's Fields wedding celebration for which Carey provided music (cf. Roger Fiske, *English Theatre Music in the Eighteenth Century* [London, 1973], p. 173).

First Edition

Advertisements in *The Craftsman* indicate that John Gray published his edition of *Britannia and Batavia* on or about 21 June 1740.[13] Almost certainly this edition of a minor work that had never been performed was printed to form a part of and to help promote the sale of Gray's nonce collection, *The Works of the Late Mr. George Lillo*, which was probably issued at the same time that *Britannia and Batavia* was first offered for sale.[14] Advertisements for *Britannia and Batavia* include the note that 'all Mr. Lillo's other Works' will also be found at the bookseller's shop; the list of titles that follows includes *Silvia*, published by John Watts and never before advertised by John Gray, suggesting that Gray had recently obtained Watts's stock of the ballad opera in order to be able to issue a complete collection.[15]

It is not known if Lillo had asked that *Britannia and Batavia* be published or whether Gray obtained a manuscript of the piece before or after the author's death. Lillo's choice of the bookseller as an executor of his will suggests that he was a trusted friend as well as a business associate; it seems unlikely that Gray would have made public a work which for artistic or other reasons the playwright had wished to have suppressed.

For the title-page, see p. 463.

Collation: 8° A⁸ [$4 (– A1, 2) signed]; 8 leaves, pp. *1–4* 5–15 *16* (5 centred in parentheses)

Contents: A1 (*1*) half-title A1ᵛ (*2*) blank A2 (*3*) title A2ᵛ (*4*) dramatis personae A3 (*5*)–A8 (15) text (DH: *Britannia* and *Batavia*: | A | MASQUE. | [rule]) A8ᵛ (16) blank

> *Note*: The half-title (*1*) reads as follows: Britannia and Batavia: | A | MASQUE. | [Price Six-Pence]

Comments

There is no indication of press corrections or reimpressions.

The text is clean and set out well. Except for possible confusion in the method of heading the three episodes or scenes—the first is given a scene-

---

[13] *The Craftsman*, 21 June 1740: 'This day is publish'd . . .'; repeated 28 June. The newspaper came out once a week, on Saturday, and it is likely that *Britannia and Batavia* was published during the week preceding 21 June; when Gray ran advertisements for his editions of Lillo's plays in the daily papers as well as the weekly, he regularly used the phrase 'This day is published' in the notices in *The Craftsman* even though the editions had been issued a few days earlier.

[14] Given the apparent political slant of *Britannia and Batavia*, it is also possible that Gray published the piece in the hope that the edition and nonce collection would gain the support of the Prince of Wales and his followers. Earlier in the year Gray had dedicated his edition of Lillo's last play, *Elmerick*, to the prince. That the edition was advertised only in *The Craftsman*, an opposition periodical, may also suggest the audience of readers whom the bookseller expected to take a particular interest in the publication.

[15] As late as 5 Mar. 1740, when Gray advertised his publication of *Elmerick*, he omitted *Silvia* from the list of Lillo's plays available at his shop. The issuing of the nonce collection would seem, then, to date from June 1740 and to coincide with the publication of *Britannia and Batavia*.

number while the second and third are unnumbered[16]—there is every indication that the printer worked from clear copy, a good transcription of a finished work. The pointing is consistent, appropriate, easily followed, and rarely incorrect, suggesting not only that the compositor worked from good copy but also that before it came to him the manuscript had been edited well. While the punctuation may well represent the work of an editor, nothing indicates that the author had left the text in a rough state or incomplete. The pattern of blank verse is varied by the use of shorter lines, in most cases clearly chosen for purposes of dramatic effectiveness. However, on occasion the lineation intended by the playwright is ambiguous. Perhaps for this reason the printer made no effort to distinguish typographically the few pairs of half-lines, given to different speakers, that together form single lines of blank verse.[17] Despite this, the edition is in general cleaner and presents fewer editorial problems than most of the first editions of Lillo's plays that were printed while the playwright was alive and able to correct copy or proofs.

Editorial Procedure

The first edition serves as copy-text for the present edition. The second and third episodes have been headed as scenes, following the convention established by the heading of scene one. The very few errors in the accidentals of the copy-text have been corrected. Where this was necessary, reference has been made to Davies's reprint of 1875, which has also been followed in the setting of half-lines, spoken by different characters, that can appear to combine into single lines of blank verse.[18]

[16] Scene one is headed 'SCENE the FIRST'; the second episode has a centred heading, 'SCENE', but no scene-number; the shift to the third episode is treated simply as a stage direction.

[17] See i. 10 and 18, ii. 21 and 55.

[18] The copy-text is the first edition, a Princeton University copy. Copies collated include: *first edition*, NjP, CtY, CSmH, BL (2 copies), O; Davies, *Works* (1775), CtMW, O, BL (3 copies), CtY (2 copies).

Britannia and *Batavia:*

A

MASQUE.

Written on the MARRIAGE of the

PRINCESS ROYAL

With his HIGHNESS the

PRINCE of *ORANGE.*

By the late Mr. *LILLO.*

LONDON:

Printed for JOHN GRAY, at the *Cross-Keys* in the
Poultry near *Cheapside.* MDCCXL.

Dramatis Personae.

Ithuriel.
Eliphas.
Britannia.
Batavia.
Liberto.   5
Tyranny.
Superstition.
Chorus of Country Lads and Lasses.
Chorus of Sailors and their Lasses.
Landlady.   10
Chorus of Spectators.
The Procession.
Slavery *and* Poverty, *Attendants on*
    Tyranny.
Pride *and* Cruelty, *Attendants on*
    Superstition.

Mutes {

Britannia and *Batavia*:

A

MASQUE.

SCENE the First.

A Pleasant Country.

Britannia *asleep under a small, but rich Pavilion. Her Sword and Shield lying by her.* Ithuriel *her Guardian Angel with a drawn Sword, leaning on a Cloud, and suspended in the Air near her.*

> *Ith.* Sleep, fair *Britannia*, sleep secure;
> Thy own *Ithuriel*, happy in his Charge,
> Thy Guardian Angel wakes.

AIR I.

> Rest is the Recompence of Toil,
> The noblest Fruit of Conquest, Peace;   5
> Learn but Content, high-favour'd Isle,
> And nothing can your Bliss increase.
> What Splendor rises in the East,
> Now when the Sun has measured half the Day?
> Some alien Spirit sure—

Descends, and stands before Britannia *in a Posture of Defence.* Eliphas, *the Guardian Angel of* Batavia, *descends with an Olive Branch in his Hand.*

>   *Eliphas*, as I think,   10
> The vigilant Protector of *Batavia*.
>   *El.* Exalted Seraph, powerful and benign,
> Thou judgest right, I am indeed *Eliphas*.
>   *Ith.* Distinguish'd as thou art,
> Prudent, and brave, and of approv'd Integrity,   15
> Thou can'st not doubt thy Welcome:
> Yet let me wonder, high and friendly Guest,
> Why thou hast left thy Charge.

El.   Not so, bright Chief;
Unable to defend her
From proud *Hispania*'s fierce and cruel Power,   20
I've brought her here,
To seek Protection from *Britannia*'s Arms.
  Ith. For others Dangers
I may not interrupt her calm Repose;
Her Peace and Safety are my Care,   2[
Her Virtue is her own.

AIR II.

  El. 'Tis great to succour the distrest!
  Ith. Britannia's Bounty stands confest,
    Unequal'd and alone.
  El. Can lost *Batavia* sue in vain?   30
  Ith. Must *Britain* endless Wars maintain
    For Causes not her own?

El. Behold the mourning Fair.

> *Enter* Batavia *in Mourning, supported; her Hair*
> *dishevel'd, and her Coronet falling.*

Bat. Ah! me, ah! wretched, wretched lost *Batavia*.

Britannia *wakes.*

  Brit. Whoe'er thou art, thy Groans have wak'd *Britannia*.
  Bat. [*Kneeling.*] Thou great and just Defender of th'opprest,
See at your Feet poor and distrest *Batavia*:
Her Cities ras'd, her sacred Rights destroy'd,
Her Nobles slaughter'd, and her Sons enslav'd.

AIR III.

O whither shall I turn me, whither fly,   4[
  If you refuse your Aid?
  By Friends forsaken,
  By my Foes betray'd,
There's not on Earth so lost a Wretch as I.
O! whither, &c.

  Brit. Arise, afflicted Fair, my Sister, rise;
Believe, I feel and will redress thy Wrongs;

Deceitful bloody *Rome*, and haughty *Spain*,
Shall be compell'd to render back their Prey.

AIR IV.

Brit. Let Tyranny devour,   50
       And build in Blood her Throne;
       Britannia holds her Power
       For righteous Ends alone.
Bat. While Heaven refers to you the Fate
       Of *Europe*; while you hold the Scale,   55
       And may dispense the casting Weight,
       Justice and Virtue must prevail.

       [*Both repeat the first Stanza.*]

       End of the first serious Interlude.

———————————

Enter a Chorus of Country Lads and Lasses.

AIR V. *Under the Greenwood Tree.*

1st Lad. Let envious Faction call me Slave,
            I know and feel I'm free.
1st Lass. 'Tis well, brisk Sir, that you're so brave;   60
            I thought you bound to me.
1st Lad.   Such lovely Eyes,
1st Lass.   Must tyrannize,
            And you their Captive be.
1st Lad.   Love's Chains alone,   65
            True Britons own,
            Nor wou'd from them be free.
Chorus. Love's Chains alone, &c.
                    [*Dancing suitable to the Occasion. Exeunt.*]

SCENE II.

A Palace.

Britannia on a Couch in a Posture expressive of Distress. On her Right Hand,
Tyranny *attended with* Slavery *and* Want; *on her Left,* Superstition *attended*
with Cruelty *and* Pride. Ithuriel *at a Distance weeping.*

SCENE II. | *A Palace.*] Ed.; SCENE‸ | *A* ~. G

Brit. Surpriz'd! betray'd! no Help, no Succour near!
O most undone! O ruin'd, lost *Britannia*!
    Tyr. Stubborn, ungrateful Fair,
Blinded by Error will you ever scorn
The friendly Hand that offers at your Cure?
Behold thy Soul's Physician.
    Sup. Taste of this Cup, and be enlighten'd:
Thou hast lost no Freedom,
Except the fatal Liberty to err;
And Riches are but Snares;
Those we'll remove:
But in return the Church
Shall pour forth all her Benedictions on thee:
Thou shalt abound in Grace.
    Brit. Detested Superstition! Bloated Monster!—
Drunk with the Blood of Nations,—from my Sight.
I'll have no more to do with thy Inchantments.
Hence, Sorcerer, hence, and let me die in Peace.
    Sup. Consult not Reason, close the Eye of Sense;
So shall you judge aright, and see the better.
We are your Friends.
    Brit.   I know and I abhor you.
    Sup. Poor wand'ring Soul!
She must be driven back into the Fold:
Wholesom Severities may set her right,
And save her from Destruction.
    Tyr. I trust your pious Skill.
    Sup. Whips, Chains and Racks,
Those gentler Methods,
May first be tried;
If these shou'd seem too mild,
You must impute it to our tender Mercy.
    Ith. Now, *Batavia*, if thou hast Gratitude,
Assert it now, and save distrest *Britannia*.   [*Aside and Exit.*
    Sup. Heresy is indeed a rank Disease,
But then the Fire's a never failing Cure.
    Tyr. Take your own Way.
    Sup. Nay, nay, I but advise;
The Church expects that you shou'd do her Justice:
She but condemns—She never deals in Blood—
She damns, 'tis true, the Wretch who spares her Foes;
But begs, by me, your Mercy

For this poor Heretick relapsed.
Touch not her Life, singe not a single Hair,
Nor shed one Drop of Blood.
 Tyr. I understand the Church, and know my Duty.   45
[*To his Attendants.*] Seize her, and bind her strait.

AIR VI.

 Brit. [*Kneeling.*] Just Heaven! if e'er
     The Wretched's Prayer
   I hear'd, and eas'd his Pain;
    Now in return,   50
    Let me not mourn,
   Nor ask Relief in vain.

Loud Shouts without, mixt with martial Musick, Cries of Liberty, &c. Scene changes
to the Prospect of a calm Sea with a Fleet of Ships at Anchor. Enter Ithuriel,
Eliphas, *and* Batavia, *ushering in* Liberto, *richly habited and attended. At whose*
Appearance, Tyranny, Superstition, *and their Followers run off in Confusion.*
Liberto *unbinds* Britannia.

 Brit. Grateful *Batavia*! generous *Liberto*!
Bounteous Heaven! O how shall I express
My Wonder, or my Thanks?
 Lib.   Fair Queen of Isles,   55
Guardian of Liberty and sacred Truth,
In saving you we have preserv'd ourselves;
Our Interest is the same.
 Brit. Most Godlike Prince! O how shall I reward thee!
 Lib. To serve *Britannia* is its own Reward.   60
 Brit. —It shall be so—
Prudence and Gratitude demand it of me—
He best can guard the Freedom he restor'd,
And well deserves to wear the Crown he sav'd.   [*Aside.*
What think'st thou of me Prince?   65
 Lib. All must confess your Charms:
Fair and majestick, happy in your Offspring.
Europe sees few so great, and none so blest:
Freedom, and Wealth and Power are in your Hand.
 Brit. Then here I place them all. [*Giving her Hand.* 70
  Lib. And I with Joy accept 'em.   [*Kissing it.*
'Twere Folly to refuse so great a Blessing.
Whether Ambition, or the Love of Virtue,
Sway most with me, my Actions must declare.
 Brit. By me you are not doubted, brave *Liberto*: 75
And let inveterate Malice do her worst,

Grateful Posterity shall clear your Fame.
Bat. O happy Change! O glorious Revolution!

AIR VII.

Lib.	To conquer without Blood;
Brit.	To reign for others Good;
Bat.	Lost Freedom to restore;
Brit.	This is the Hero's Praise:
Bat.	For this we Temples raise,
Lib.	And justly Heav'n adore.
All three.	To conquer, &c.

End of the second serious Interlude.

———————

A Chorus of Sailors.

AIR VIII. *When the Stormy,* &c.

1st Sail. You Terror of *Britannia*'s Foes,
    Whose Valour does maintain
    Her Power, where'er the Ocean flows,
      Or stormy Tempests reign;
    For Liberty restor'd,
    Now let your Joys o'erflow:
      As on the Shore
      The Billows roar,
    When the stormy Winds do blow.

Enter Landlady, follow'd by a Train of young Women.

AIR IX.

Land. Well fare your Hearts, my jovial Boys,
    You ranting, roaring Sons of Noise,
    See who are come to aid your Joys,
      And hail you safe to Shore:
    See here the Treasure of our Isle,
    Here reap the Fruits of all your Toil,
    And all your future Cares beguile,
      With fal, lal, &c.
Chorus. See here, &c.   [*Dancing.*

SCENE III.

A magnificent Monument in the Front of the Stage, at the Foot of which Batavia *is discovered, leaning on an Urn.*

AIR X.

> *Bat.* Tho' hopeless, I must ever languish:
> Nor Time, nor Fate, can ease my Anguish,
> Still adoring,
> Still deploring
> Lost *Liberto*: endless Grief!   5
> Will the cruel Grave return him,
> Can I ever cease to mourn him?
> Will my Sorrows bring Relief?

> *Enter* Eliphas.

El. Arise, *Batavia*, and with Wonder hear
How generous *Britannia* has devised   10
To pay her Tribute to *Liberto*'s Fame,
And make her Gratitude, like that, immortal.
She on the Princely Youth,
In whom *Liberto*'s Name
Must live or be extinguished,   15
Does Wisdom, Beauty, Majesty bestow,
Domestick Happiness, Wealth, Fame, and Power;
To sum up all that may be said or thought
She gives,—
The First-born Princess of her Royal House,   20
Replete with ev'ry Virtue, for his Bride.
Her joyful Sons
With acclamations rend the Skies;
Assist, *Batavia*, and increase their Joys:
Now prove how you regard your Princely Charge,   25
And what you owe *Liberto*,
Pay to his dear Remains.

AIR XI.

> Hark, from *Britannia*'s Shore
> The Cannons loudly roar;
> The Horizon how bright?   30

SCENE III. | *A*] *Ed.; Scene a* G; *SCENE a* W1   SD *Stage, at*] *Ed.;* ~, | *At* G

> Ten thousand Piles of Fire,
> Waving to Heaven aspire,
> And turn to Day the Night.

> [*Chorus of Spectators.*

Scene the Procession of the Marriage of the Princess Royal with his Highness the Prince of Orange in the same Order, and as near as possible with the same Magnificence, as it was really perform'd.

AIR XII.

Spec. Ten thousand Joys
  Attend the Princely Pair,   35
 Whilst ev'ry grateful *Briton*
  Applauds his Sovereign's Care;
 Who on *Nassau* bestows,
  (A Name to *Britons* dear,
 Whence ev'ry Blessing flows,   40
  And we with Transport hear)
 Anna, that Royal Dame,
  Our Blessings to insure;
 That Freedom like his Fame,
  May evermore endure.   45
Chorus. Ten thousand, &c.

THE END.

Arden of Feversham

INTRODUCTION

AUTHORSHIP: THE EXTERNAL EVIDENCE

THE version of *Arden of Feversham* believed to have been written by George Lillo was first acted in 1759, some twenty years after the playwright's death. It was later reported that the script performed and subsequently published (1762) had been 'completed' by Dr John Hoadly. That the adaptation was initially Lillo's work and, in large or small measure, finished or revised by Hoadly has never apparently been questioned.

Evidence to confirm Lillo's and Hoadly's association with *Arden* is spare. The earliest known record of the adaptation is the Larpent manuscript, submitted to the Chamberlain's office on 29 June 1759; no author is noted on the title-page or elsewhere in the manuscript. Advertisements for the first performance, offered at Drury Lane on 12 July, announce the play as 'written by the late Mr. Lillo, author of *George Barnwell*'.[1] The first edition, published about three years later, similarly ascribes the work to Lillo, makes no reference to Hoadly, and provides no explanation as to how the drama came to light two decades after the death of the author. The publisher of the first edition, Thomas Davies, does offer minimal information about Lillo's work on the play in the *Life of Lillo* included in his collection of the playwright's works, published in 1775: 'I have heard from Roberts, the old comedian, who was well acquainted with Mr. Lillo, that his tragedy of Arden of Feversham was written before the year 1736. How it came to lie dormant till 1762 [*sic*], when it was first acted in the summer season, I have not been able to learn.'[2] Davies would seem to have forgotten or did not credit the information which had been provided by the *Monthly Review* when, in 1762, it commented on the publication of the play: 'the manuscript . . . was long in the possession of . . . Mr. Theophilus Cibber, who first brought [Lillo's] Barnwell on the stage: but whether this edition is printed from

---

[1] *London Stage, 1747–1776*.   [2] *Life*, p. xliii.

Cibber's or some other copy, we are not informed.'[3] That the version of the play which reached the public included material written by anyone other than Lillo is not mentioned in print until 1782, when the second edition of the *Biographia Dramatica*, updated and expanded by Isaac Reed, notes that 'Arden of Feversham was left imperfect by Mr. Lillo, and finished by Dr. Hoadly.'[4] This note, the basis for attributing the play to Hoadly as well as Lillo, was among a number of comments and criticisms incorporated into the second edition of Lillo's collected works and was thus established as an accepted element in the history of the composition of the tragedy.

These pieces of external evidence—more suggestive than concrete, and none of them directly linked with Lillo himself—are individually plausible. None contradicts another, and they can be fitted together to form a plausible conjectural reconstruction of the process of composition, disappearance, rediscovery, and revision which ultimately resulted in the performance and publication of the play. But certain gaps remain unfilled, and there are puzzling details which pose questions concerning the accuracy or authenticity of the reports that make up the story.

The actor John Roberts could have been well acquainted with Lillo, as Davies reports, during the years in which the author was active as a playwright. A veteran of many seasons at Drury Lane, Roberts played the uncle in the first performance of *The London Merchant* and later, as a member of Fielding's company at the Haymarket, played Old Wilmot in the original production of *Fatal Curiosity*.[5] In recalling that Lillo wrote *Arden of Feversham* 'before 1736', Roberts may simply have remembered that the project evolved during the time when both he and Lillo were associated with Drury Lane and Theophilus Cibber—i.e. the period extending from the production of *The London Merchant* (1731) to the less than successful première of *The Christian Hero* (1735) or to Lillo's eventual association with Fielding and the Haymarket (1736).[6] After the success of the *Merchant*, it seems not unlikely that the management of Drury Lane encouraged Lillo to attempt a second domestic tragedy based on an old, true story with a strong moral theme. *Arden of Feversham* would have served as an ideal basis for such a project. And while the old play had not been acted in

[3] *Monthly Review*, Dec. 1762, excerpt reprinted in *The Works of Mr. George Lillo* (1810), ii. 177.

[4] *Biographia Dramatica* (1782), ii. 20. The entry for John Hoadly includes the note 'He also revised Lillo's *Arden of Feversham*' (i. 238).

[5] *London Stage, 1729–1747*, i. 147 and 588. Roberts joined the company at Drury Lane in the season of 1721–2 and, except for two seasons (1726–8), continued to act regularly at the theatre until 1734. As one of the actors who remained loyal to the theatre in 1733–4, when many of the company's leading actors joined Theophilus Cibber in the revolt against the patentees, Roberts moved to Covent Garden as soon as Cibber and the others returned to Drury Lane (Apr. 1734). He was a member of Fielding's company during its two seasons at the Haymarket (1735–7), then returned to Covent Garden. His last recorded performances in London were occasional appearances at Goodman's Fields and Covent Garden in the season of 1745–6. (*London Stage, 1700–1729, 1729–1747, passim.*)

[6] Roberts's association with Drury Lane ended nine months before the production of *The Christian Hero*. However, as a member of the rival company at Covent Garden he would have been well aware of the première of a new play by Lillo.

London for many years, it continued to be popular, in various forms, in Faversham and the surrounding towns, an area frequently visited in summer by companies made up of actors from the London theatres. John Roberts was one of such a group which played the 'Kentish Circuit' in 1733.[7]

If Lillo did begin work on an adaptation of *Arden* after the production of *The London Merchant* and before he turned to *The Christian Hero*, any draft of all or a portion of the play which he wished to have considered at the theatre would probably have been submitted to Theophilus Cibber, who had been instrumental in bringing the *Merchant* successfully to the stage. As his father's presumed successor in the Drury Lane partnership, Theophilus was taking an increasing interest in the management of the theatre. For the season of 1732–3 he served in Colley Cibber's stead as co-manager of the company, but his own illness and the death of his wife kept him away from the theatre for at least two months during the winter of 1733. The following season, owing to disputes with the new partners, one of whom had purchased Colley's share of the patent, Theophilus led a group of dissident Drury Lane actors in setting up a rival company which played at the Haymarket for much of the year.[8] Had the younger Cibber taken an interest in staging a new drama by Lillo, these events might well have disrupted his plans and discouraged the playwright from continuing his work on the project. Such a situation would not only account for the report that a manuscript of the *Arden* adaptation had come into the possession of Theophilus Cibber, it would also explain the considerable lapse of time between the successful première of *The London Merchant* and the appearance of Lillo's next play.

It must be noted, however, that when a new play by Lillo—*The Christian Hero*—did reach the stage in 1735, it was presented at Drury Lane by Theophilus Cibber. If Lillo had earlier completed an adaptation of *Arden*, would Cibber not have staged it? One can at best conjecture either that the theatre management felt that the play was not ready or appropriate for production, or that Lillo for some reason lost interest in the project. On the other hand, the playwright could have proposed the *Arden* adaptation soon after, rather than before, the Drury Lane performances of *The Christian Hero*. If so, the relative failure of that play might well have discouraged Cibber from scheduling another of Lillo's plays.[9] Either of these conjectured timetables accords with Lillo's having worked on *Arden* before 1736, though the earlier schedule is more persuasive in confining the project to a period when he seems to have had no other play in hand (mid-1731 to 1734).

---

[7] Extant records show that Roberts played what Rosenfeld has termed the 'Kentish Circuit' in the summer of 1733, acted in Norwich in the summer of 1734, and was active in other provincial companies (Rosenfeld, *Strolling Players*, pp. 58 and 225). Rosenfeld stresses the frequency of performances of *Arden c.*1730 and also notes the announcement of puppet performances of the play in 1736 (pp. 219 and 226).

[8] *Actors, Actresses*, iii. 245–7.

[9] No new play by Lillo was again attempted at Drury Lane until 1740, by which time Cibber had removed himself to Covent Garden.

A version of *Arden of Feversham* did reach the London stage in January 1736.[10] It was not Lillo's. Offered for a single night at the Haymarket, the production featured, as Mrs Arden, the popular writer of fiction Eliza Haywood, who may herself have written the adaptation.[11] The very little that is known about the performance suggests nothing that would link Lillo, or those associated with him in the theatre, to this particular revival of the old play. However, during the following season Mrs Haywood was a member—as were John Roberts and Thomas Davies—of Fielding's company at the Haymarket, which continued to offer performances of *Fatal Curiosity*, first performed in the preceding year.[12] It is unfortunate that the version of *Arden* acted by Mrs Haywood was not published and has not survived in manuscript. Her association, in the year following that production, with a theatre in which Lillo was active and with actors who would later be a source of information about his work on an adaptation of *Arden* is, at least, an intriguing coincidence, as is the fact that Mrs Haywood's performance of *Arden* occurred in the year mentioned by Roberts in his attempt to date Lillo's work on the play. It would be useful to be able to compare the two eighteenth-century versions of the old tragedy and reassuring to confirm that, after the passing of more than twenty years, Haywood's adaptation had not, through some misrecollection, been attributed to Lillo.[13]

Theophilus Cibber died in 1758. The first performance of the Arden play ascribed to Lillo was offered in 1759. This chronology could indicate that Cibber did, as the *Monthly Review* reports, possess a manuscript of the play and

---

[10] 21 Jan. 1736 (*London Stage, 1729–1747*).

[11] Advertisements for the performance are worded ambiguously: 'Arden of Feversham. Mrs Arden—by Mrs Eliza Haywood, the Author.' However, the piece is announced as 'Never Acted before'; this suggests that it had, to some extent at least, been revised, and the lack of other credit for the writing would seem to indicate that Haywood herself was responsible for the revision.

[12] Almost certainly Mrs Haywood did not act in *Fatal Curiosity* (advertisements do not announce the cast, but nearly all those who acted in the original production in 1736 were members of the company in 1737). However, she did perform regularly with Roberts and Davies in *The Historical Register*, which on several evenings was offered on the same bill as Lillo's play. (*London Stage, 1729–1747*, ii. 651–7 and 665.)

[13] It is unlikely that such a mistake was made, and no extant evidence indicates a link between the two 18th-cent. versions of *Arden*. It must be noted, however, that after Mrs Haywood's death in 1756 new and revised works presumably of her composing appeared in 1768 and later, which suggests that at least some of her papers were preserved and considered for publication or other use. If she did write an adaptation of *Arden*, it is not impossible, then, that a manuscript of the work was discovered after 1756. It would, in any case, be useful to know if there was any relation between Mrs Haywood's production of some version of *Arden* and Lillo's adaptation based on the same old play. For example, if Mrs Haywood's performance was less than successful, as the evidence suggests, that failure could well have discouraged interest in Lillo's version of the play. On the other hand, despite Roberts's report that Lillo worked on his adaptation before 1736, it is not beyond possibility that in fact the revival of *Arden* in 1736 by an author-actress who, like Lillo, was associated with the Haymarket company in 1737 could have stirred Lillo's interest in attempting his own revision of the play (such a chronology would, however, seem to preclude Theophilus Cibber's association with the Lillo adaptation). It is altogether unlikely that the version of *Arden* acted by Mrs Haywood was itself the Lillo adaptation; had the play been his, his name would certainly have been well publicized in advertisements for the performance. (George Frisbie Whicher, *The Life and Romances of Mrs. Eliza Haywood* [New York, 1915], pp. 71, 169, and 204.)

that it was unearthed among his effects after his death.[14] Such a reconstruction of events will account nicely for the late discovery of the play. It assumes, however, that Cibber had the only copy extant at the time of Lillo's death or that no one took an interest in the manuscripts of unperformed works found among the playwright's papers after he died. The posthumous publication of two other Lillo dramas, brought out by John Gray in 1740, calls into question both of these assumptions.

Lillo's authorized publisher since 1731, John Gray was also an executor of the playwright's estate. In his nonce collection of Lillo's works, issued some ten months after the author's death, Gray included not only the edition of *Elmerick* which he had published soon after its posthumous production at Drury Lane but also *Britannia and Batavia*, an unperformed occasional piece written in 1733 but never before printed.[15] Publication of this minor work would seem to indicate that, as one would expect, Gray had access to Lillo's papers and that he was concerned to publish any previously unknown work which was in a state to be published and might be of interest to the public.[16] Since Gray issued his collection with no preface or other account of Lillo's career as playwright, one cannot know what he may have found among the author's papers but elected not to print.[17] However, had Lillo completed a draft of a full-length drama—a domestic tragedy certain to be compared with his *London Merchant*—it seems most unlikely that Gray would not have published it for the nonce collection. It is possible, of course, that while a forgotten manuscript of the play was in Cibber's possession, no copy was found among the playwright's own papers. However, if Lillo had indeed worked on an adaptation of *Arden*, it seems more probable either that he had informed Gray that he did not wish the play to be

[14] Given the relative turmoil of his personal and professional life during his last twenty years, and his frequent shifting of residences in order to escape his creditors, Theophilus Cibber seems a most unlikely person to have preserved for an extended period of time the manuscript of a dead playwright's possibly unfinished, certainly unproduced, play. Conceivably, papers dating back to his time at Drury Lane remained at the theatre or had been left in the keeping of someone associated with it and so came to light after his death.

[15] See introduction to *Britannia and Batavia*. Although published as a separate edition, the work was advertised in conjunction with announcements promoting 'all of Mr. Lillo's works', issued at this time in the nonce collection. The certain date of the composition of *Britannia and Batavia*, a work which after 1734 could have been of no interest to the theatre managers, suggests that at least some manuscripts dating from the period in which Lillo is reported to have worked on the *Arden* adaptation were indeed preserved and available to John Gray.

[16] Apparently a trusted friend as well as a business associate, Gray would surely have been aware of the playwright's work on any project for a full-length drama. It seems probable also that he would have made an effort to locate a copy of the *Arden* adaptation if he found no manuscript among the author's papers but knew that Lillo had substantially completed such a play. Had the whereabouts of a copy been known at Drury Lane, Gray would probably have learnt about it; his edition of *Elmerick* makes it clear that he was in contact with the theatre during the winter of 1739–40, when the play was prepared for its first performance.

[17] Davies's reported search for a copy of *The Regulators*, an unpublished and unperformed comedy said to have been written by Lillo, may lend credence to the account of Cibber's possession of a manuscript of *Arden* when apparently no copy was available to John Gray (cf. *Biographia Dramatica* [1812], p. 455). In reviewing the alternatives, one must also acknowledge the possibility that Lillo had not in fact written or begun an adaptation of *Arden* at all.

made public or that he had left the work in so incomplete or fragmentary a state
that publication was out of the question.

If one accepts the report of the *Biographia Dramatica*, a manuscript of the
adaptation of *Arden*, in some way 'imperfect', found its way to John Hoadly. It is
impossible to assign a date to this occurrence. Hoadly, a clergyman fascinated
by the stage, was associated with the London theatre as early as 1731. No
evidence suggests that he was acquainted with George Lillo or John Gray, nor
does there seem to have been a link between him and Theophilus Cibber which
would suggest that he obtained the manuscript directly from the actor.
However, Hoadly was later in close touch with Drury Lane through his good
friend David Garrick, and it is possible that this association lies behind his
apparent acquisition of a copy of the *Arden* adaptation.

John Hoadly's enthusiasm for the theatre and his interest in revising old plays
are well documented. While still a Cambridge undergraduate, he had written an
original satirical comedy, *The Contrast*, which was given three performances at
Lincoln's Inn Fields in 1731.[18] This adventure in the professional theatre
ended abruptly when the play, a spoof of living poets, was withdrawn at the
request of Hoadly's father, the Bishop of Winchester. In 1735 the opportunity
to take advantage of the profitable livings at the disposal of the bishop led
Hoadly to commit himself to a career in the Church. Appointed chaplain to the
household of the Prince of Wales and secure in the incomes from several
rectories, Hoadly had money and time to pursue his theatrical interests and, as
amateur actor, aspiring playwright, and friend of prominent performers, did so
until his death in 1776.[19] His correspondence with Garrick, carried on for more
than thirty years, is filled with plans for writing plays, some of them original
ideas but more of them proposals for reworking old dramas which Garrick
might revive at Drury Lane. In 1744, Hoadly provided the fifth act for Garrick's
première of *Mahomet the Imposter*, adapted from Voltaire by James Miller,
whose illness prevented his completing the piece.[20] Two years later, Garrick,

---

[18] *The Contrast: A Tragi-Comical Rehearsal of Two Modern Plays: Match Upon Match: or, No Match
at All, and the Tragedy of Epaminondas* was first acted on 30 Apr. 1731 (*London Stage, 1729–1747*). In
writing the play, John Hoadly may have been assisted by his brother Benjamin; John, in turn, may
have had a hand in the composition of Benjamin's very successful comedy *The Suspicious Husband*,
first performed, with Garrick in a leading role, in Feb. 1747 (*London Stage, 1729–1747*, ii. 1287;
DNB).

[19] Hoadly took the degree of LL B in 1735. On 29 Nov. of that year he was appointed chancellor
at Winchester, ordained as a deacon on 7 Dec., and as a priest on 21 Dec. His appointment as
chaplain in the household of the Prince of Wales followed immediately and continued until the
death of the prince. Hoadly was then made chaplain in the household of the Princess Dowager. His
several livings included five rectories, one of them at Alresford in Hampshire, where he lived for
much of his life. (*DNB*.)

[20] *Biographia Dramatica* (1782) notes that Miller, 'being unable to put the finishing hand to
[*Mahomet*], . . . received some assistance in the completing of it from Dr. John Hoadly' (ii. 123).
The entry for Hoadly is more specific in reporting that he 'wrote the fifth act of Miller's *Mahomet*'
(i. 238). The play was first performed on 25 Apr. 1744; Miller died the following day (*London
Stage, 1729–1747; DNB*).

proposing a possible new production of *The London Merchant*, suggested that Hoadly alter the play for him. Hoadly seems not to have taken up the project, though on at least one occasion he had discussed with Garrick a new scene to be added to Lillo's play. Instead, he undertook to revise *Cymbeline* and, encouraged by Garrick, seems frequently to have proposed similar projects for adapting old plays.[21]

There is no evidence that Garrick actually staged one of Hoadly's adaptations. However, had a Lillo manuscript of the sort said to have been in the possession of Theophilus Cibber come into Garrick's hands, he might well have thought of his friend Hoadly as the person to revise or complete the play for performance. Certainly such a project would have appealed to Hoadly himself.

Again the plausible reconstruction must be weighed in terms of significant gaps in the evidence. The surviving letters of Garrick and Hoadly include no reference to *Arden of Feversham*. Although the adapted *Arden* was acted at Drury Lane, nothing indicates that Garrick took a active interest in the production.[22] And while it is not surprising that Hoadly's name is omitted from advertisements for the performance and from the title-page of the first edition of the play announced as a new work by George Lillo, it is curious that Davies fails to allude to him when writing about the rediscovery of the play in his *Life of Lillo*.

That Hoadly's association with *Arden* is not mentioned in print until after his death might well be explained by the restrictions imposed upon him by his position in the Church. As a clergyman, he had to be cautious about involving himself with the public theatre. He made this clear in a letter written to Garrick in 1765: expressing his regret at having decided not to have one of his plays acted at Drury Lane because Garrick himself could not be available to play in it, Hoadly wrote, 'Nothing but my entire friendship for you, your conduct of the [play], and your inimitable performance, could induce me to break through the prudery of my profession, and the fantastical decency of my (too) exalted station in it, and bring the name of Hoadly again upon the public stage.'[23] Dr Hoadly

---

[21] On 19 Aug. 1746 Garrick wrote to Hoadly:

I was thinking if George Barnwell was alter'd in some places & the Scene You mention'd introduc'd I could make some figure in that Character; what think you Sir? Could you amuse Y^{r}self that Way, or spend Y^r Time better upon Another Plan? I beg You would invoke y^r Tragic Muse, and bring the produce of Your Amour in Y^r Pocket—don't dare to look me in ye face without a Couple of Acts at least & keep it a Secret from Every body but myself. (Garrick, *Letters*, i. 84.)

Hoadly's decision to pursue another project is reflected in Garrick's letter of 14 Sept., which in part reads:

I am glad to hear You have dock'd & alter'd Cymbeline & beg You will send it up immediately directed for Me, at my Lodgings in James Street, Cov^t Garden; You will give me great Pleasure & may do me Service by it . . . (Garrick, *Letters*, i. 85.)

Additional letters reprinted in Garrick, *Letters*, and *Correspondence* indicate that it was Hoadly's habit over the years to send Garrick sketches and scenes for his proposed play-writing projects.

[22] See discussion of performances, below.

[23] Garrick, *Correspondence*, i. 191 (21 July 1765). The play was an original tragedy based on history, *Lord Cromwell*. In another letter, written at about the same time to an unknown

may also have felt it inappropriate to make public his association with the production or publication of *Arden*, despite the play's moralizing conclusion. Conceivably, Davies and the other commentators who wrote about the play while Hoadly was alive were aware of his work in preparing the final version but respected his wish for anonymity.[24]

As suggested above, if one accepts the available pieces of evidence as essentially accurate and further agrees to the conjectured explanations required to fill the gaps or to deal with such problematical issues as John Gray's failure to print the play in 1740, one can propose a history of the composition of the *Arden* adaptation which reasonably assumes that a substantial portion of the work was initially written by George Lillo. However, the external evidence relating to the authorship of the adaptation must finally be described as inconclusive. The first edition of the play and advertisements for the first performance are unambiguous in ascribing the work to George Lillo; there is no evidence of any attempt by the theatre management or publisher to gull the public with a false attribution.[25] On the other hand, the evidence which remains to support this assumption or to detail Lillo's actual association with the play is relatively slight and dependent on recollections dating some twenty years after the fact; John

correspondent, Hoadly states again his concern about the propriety of his associating himself with the theatre in a public way, noting that only Garrick's interest and talent and 'the religious subject of the drama . . . could have persuaded me to break through the prudery of my profession and (in my situation in the church) produce a play upon the stage' (quoted in *Biographia Dramatica* [1812], i. 351). Hoadly's immediate reason for withdrawing the play was that Garrick, who was talking of retiring from the stage, would not be available to act in it. However, writing again to Garrick in Sept. 1765, Hoadly seems to suggest that his friend had expressed reservations about the quality of the play itself as well as the appropriateness of the clergyman's associating himself with the theatre: 'I think myself highly obliged to you and Mrs. Garrick, in speaking so plainly to me, as it will have saved me the infinite mortification I must have met with, finding it not approved.' (Garrick, *Correspondence*, i. 199.) Hoadly's cautiousness may reflect his recollection of the bitter experience of James Miller, whose *Mahomet* he completed. Having had an early success (and scandal) with his play *The Humours of Oxford*, Miller determined to resume writing for the theatre when the small income from his appointments as a clergyman proved inadequate to support his family. In so doing he roused the wrath of the bishop from whom he had expected to receive preferment. His refusal to accept the bishop's demand that he quit the theatre, which he unwisely made public in a satirical poem, doomed Miller to years of near poverty while advancement in the Church was denied him.

[24] Hoadly may well have intended that his contributions to the theatre become known after his death. When agreeing to withdraw his tragedy of *Cromwell* he also expressed his concern to have Garrick's comments about the play in order 'that I may leave that (and one or two other things) behind me in as perfect a state as the nature of them will admit of, whatever I may resolve concerning them hereafter' (Garrick, *Correspondence*, i. 191). That Hoadly's association with both *Mahomet* and *Arden* is reported in the first edition of the *Biographia Dramatica* to be published after his death suggests that those who knew the circumstances of the plays' composition allowed (or encouraged) the truth of his involvement to become public at this time because they also knew that he would not have regretted receiving posthumous credit for his work with the dramas.

[25] That the play is an adaptation rather than a totally original work based on historical sources was nowhere mentioned in print until 1770, when Edward Jacob published a reprint of the *Arden* quarto of 1592 and in his preface (p. iv) noted 'that a Play lately written by Mr. *Lillo*, with the Title of *Arden of Feversham*, contains many Sentiments, Expressions, and even whole Speeches taken from this very Performance'. The *Biographia Dramatica* included an entry describing the old play, but none of the editors who prepared the original and updated editions of the compendium noted this work as the source of the tragedy ascribed to Lillo.

Hoadly's involvement is similarly documented only in a report of unknown authority printed more than two decades after the first performance of the play. In short, the evidence available to the modern editor is neither complete enough nor sufficiently concrete to substantiate beyond question the tradition which with such confidence attributes the adapted *Arden* to Lillo; at the same time, no external evidence persuasively refutes that tradition. The effort to assess Lillo's contribution to the play must also, then, include analysis of evidence of authorship provided by the text.

THE SOURCE AND INTERNAL EVIDENCE OF AUTHORSHIP

The version of *Arden* attributed to George Lillo was adapted from *The Lamentable and True Tragedie of Master Arden of Feversham*, first printed in 1592.[26] Although the title-page of the first edition of the eighteenth-century *Arden* describes the play as 'taken from Holinshed's Chronicle', the adaptation regularly follows the adjustments in historical details made by the anonymous author of the old tragedy, and there is virtually no evidence to suggest additional reference to Holinshed or another of the early accounts of the famous murder in Kent.[27] Frequent verbal echoes and, on occasion, near word-for-word quotation of lines make clear the extent to which the adapter(s) worked directly from a copy of the original play.[28]

Arden had not been reprinted since the quarto of 1633. However, Lillo's interest in early drama could well have led him to discover the play, which in his time continued to be known and acted in Kent if not in London. If he was concerned to repeat his success with the domestic tragedy of *The London Merchant*, *Arden* would have provided material ideally suited to his purpose.

[26] Feversham is the form of the town name printed in the titles of the first and third quartos (1592 and 1633). The second quarto prints 'Feuersham'. The accepted spelling in modern times is 'Faversham'.

[27] In a reference to Saint Valentine's Fair, the adaptation recalls a historically accurate detail not specifically mentioned in the original play (see IV. ii. 131 and n.). In no other instance does the text of the adaptation indicate possible reference to any source other than the old tragedy of Arden. This apparent reliance exclusively on a primary source when other accounts of the historical event were available is notably different from Lillo's approach to gathering material and background information for *The Christian Hero* and *Elmerick* (see introductions to these plays).

[28] While close reference to the text of the original *Arden* is evidenced in many passages of the adaptation, the treatment of material borrowed from the old play differs markedly from Lillo's practice in adapting Shakespeare's *Pericles*. *Marina* includes full lines and on occasion extended passages adopted from Shakespeare with minimal alteration. In the adapted *Arden*, phrases, words, images, and ideas are taken from the original text but almost always rearranged into new lines and speeches. Adoption of full lines is rare. The greater liberties taken with *Arden* may indicate that the adapter was intrigued by the subject-matter of the 16th-cent. play but saw little virtue in preserving the anonymous author's verse, while in adapting *Pericles* a primary concern was to 'save' the best of Shakespeare contained in a play thought to have been roughly made and contaminated by passages written by other writers. The situation might also indicate an extensive second level of adaptation— i.e. that Hoadly, working primarily from the manuscript of the early version of the adaptation and not from the original *Arden*, thoroughly edited the text, obliterating a closer reliance on the rhetoric of the old play.

Like the ballad of George Barnwell, it was based on an actual event of the Tudor era;[29] its characters were drawn from the lower and emerging middle classes; its highly dramatic situation—a murder motivated by passionate lust, ambition, and malice—lent itself readily to illustrating a strong moral lesson.

The adaptation follows quite closely the general outline and frequently the details of the murder drama which provides the earlier tragedy with its framework of plot. In both versions of the play the central figures in the conspiracy to kill Arden are his wife Alice (Alicia in the adaptation) and her lover Mosby, a poorly born young man who has risen in social standing through his service to a local lord. In *Arden I*,[30] Alice is the chief instigator of the schemes to kill Arden, the deviser of plots and employer of assassins, a relentless force driving herself and others on to murder. In *Arden II*, however, this role is given to Mosby, while Alicia, initially persuaded by him to agree to the murder, soon repents and strives to save her husband. Despite this fundamental alteration, the mechanics and essential sequence of events of the murder drama are changed minimally in the adaptation. The action is compressed, the range of settings reduced—no scene takes place away from Feversham and as many of them as logic will allow are set in Arden's house.[31] The series of unsuccessful attempts on Arden's life is concentrated into a few representative incidents, but the emphasis on the providential nature of his escapes is, in this phase of the drama, retained. As in *Arden I*, the chief conspirator draws a number of other characters into the plot to kill Arden: Michael, Arden's servant, who agrees to assist the murderers in return for the promise that he will marry Mosby's sister, another servant in the household; Green, whose patrimony of land has been granted to Arden by royal fiat; the hired ruffians, Black Will and Shakebag; and the hapless townsman, Bradshaw, unwittingly implicated as an accomplice in the murder conspiracy. The adaptation retains and intensifies Michael's struggles with his conscience, but eliminates the extended subplot involving his rivalry with a painter who devises exotic means for poisoning Arden. Black Will and Shakebag are as prominent in *Arden II* as they are in the old play and portrayed with the same combination of grisly horror and low comedy.[32] Green, whose case against Arden's rapacity in acquiring land at his neighbours' cost is presented strongly in *Arden I*, is transformed in the adaptation into a wastrel whose threatened impoverishment is, for the most part, the result of his own improvidence. The alteration seems clearly intended to improve the character of Arden. So does the adaptation's

---

[29] Although the date of the actual events on which the ballad of George Barnwell was said to have been based is not known, Lillo makes it a point to set his play in the Elizabethan period.

[30] For clarity and convenience, the original and 18th-cent. versions of the play are referred to by the short titles *Arden I* and *Arden II*.

[31] The action of *Arden I* moves freely through a variety of locales in Faversham and the Kentish countryside, and for a time to settings in London.

[32] While Black Will and Shakebag are not made tamer or bowdlerized in the adaptation, their scenes lack the vigour and low comic invention which characterizes Lillo's treatment of similar figures in *Marina*.

total omission of Reede, the young sailor whose family's suffering stands as unambiguous evidence of Arden's wrongful acquisitiveness, and whose curse lends an air of inevitability as well as justness to Arden's violent death.

In dramatizing the murder itself and the discovery of the conspirators, the adaptation duplicates not only the general action but also many of the particulars of *Arden I*, except of course that Mosby directs the assassins while Alicia is present to protest at rather than participate in the killing of her husband. The resolution of the drama is considerably tightened, with the action adjusted to limit the setting for the final scenes to Arden's house and to bring the conspirators together to face their accusers in a neatly rounded-off and morally satisfying finale. All of the criminals are brought to justice at one time, and there are no loose ends of the sort which in the historically more accurate *Arden I* require an epilogue to report the ultimate punishment and deaths of those conspirators who escape the authorities in Feversham.[33]

In this concentrated form the adaptation maintains the fundamental action of the original play of the murder of Arden. But this drama is the subject for little more than half of the text of *Arden II*. A considerable portion of the revised tragedy is devoted to the development of material in large measure invented by the adapter(s).

In its essential dramatic structure, the tragedy of Arden—original version and adaptation—can be seen as composed of two dramas: the murder of Arden, which gives the play its framework of plot, and, within this, a second drama in which character, social background, and ethical significance are developed. In the sixteenth-century *Arden*, this inner play is a drama of complex, ambivalent characters in a society ambivalent in its evolving social values. 'Harsh, complicated and totally unsentimental', it defies didactic interpretation despite its homiletic character, evoking, as Wine suggests, 'contradictory responses regarding its aim', though it is clearly concerned to convey 'the feeling of the larger powers of destiny operating on the anarchic lives of ordinary men and women'.[34]

Little of this is preserved in the eighteenth-century adaptation, which departs radically from the old play in developing the drama of character and idea contained in the plot drama of Arden's murder. New scenes and situations are invented, the nature and motivations of central characters altered, to create a thematic structure not suggested by *Arden I*—a drama of domestic virtue. At the centre of this major interpolation is the drastically revised characterization of Alice/Alicia, developed in new monologues, adjusted scenes with Mosby, and a greatly expanded series of confrontations with Arden, all of them providing opportunity for exercising intensely the emotions of characters and audience.

---

[33] For details of the correlation of scenes in *Arden I* and *Arden II*, see head-notes in the commentary.
[34] Wine, pp. lxxiv, lviii, and lxxix.

Bernbaum, contrasting the ethical standards of the Elizabethan and eighteenth-century versions of *Arden*, notes that Alicia has undergone a great 'reformation' in the adaptation.[35] In fact, this 'reformation'—progressive, and detailed in its various stages—is made a central action of *Arden II*. The original play portrays Alice as an evil woman, without explanation driven unremittingly in her adulterous passion for Mosby and detestation of her husband.[36] Reversing this characterization, the adaptation supplies motivation and a sympathetic explanation for Alicia's attachment to Mosby. He was the love of her youth, whom she gave up to marry a suitor more appropriate to her social position and the expectations of her family.[37] Her naïve assumption that with marriage would come affection for the husband who loves her has not been realized. When Mosby urges 'the ardor of our youthful passion', a 'heroic love' greater than marital duty,[38] Alicia is for a time persuaded. But the moral values of *Arden II* are not ambivalent, the apparent conflict between the equal demands of love and duty is deceptive,[39] and in place of Alice's implacability the adaptation substitutes the edifying transformation of Alicia. By stages shifting her affections from Mosby to Arden, she learns first the necessity of domestic virtue, then its rewards in peace of mind, and at last the joy in loving truly the husband to whom she is, in any case, bound by honour and law.

Parallel growth in wisdom is invented for Arden. No longer culpable in his acquisition of land (indeed, 'much belov'd | By all degrees of men'[40]), in *Arden II* he remains entirely, as in *Arden I* he was in part, the jealous husband. Aided by good advice from his friend Franklin—the figure of reason in both versions of the play—Arden must learn to forgive and to overcome the doubts which too readily accept suspicion as certainty and, in their disruption of domestic tranquillity, may even incite the infidelities he so fears.[41]

Liberally interpolating situations and details, drawing minimally on the original play, the adaptation introduces a series of new scenes in which the drama of husband and wife is played out.[42] Alicia's attempt to murder Arden in his sleep, an incident invented by the adapter(s), provides an episode of high drama and a critical turning-point as the wife drops her dagger, struck by the horror of the deed she was ready to commit, a surge of feeling for a generous and guiltless husband, and an awakened sense of 'those chaster pow'rs that

---

[35] p. 35.   [36] Cf. Wine, p. lxxii.
[37] See III. ii. 25–31.   [38] III. ii. 38 and 12b.
[39] Alicia's situation bears some similarity to the dilemma falsely posed for Barnwell when Millwood forces him to choose either the dishonour of stealing from his master or the apparently equal ignominy of turning his back on a beloved lady in distress (cf. *The London Merchant*, II. xi–xiv).
[40] II. i. 123–4.
[41] Although the adapter makes the point strongly in his scenes for Arden and Franklin, he omits to provide support for it in his development of Alicia's scenes with Mosby, which contain no suggestion that Arden's jealousy has had a causal relation to her continuing passion for Mosby. Later in the play, however, the jealous fears which prevent Arden from accepting Alicia's change of heart are posed as real are posed as a critical hindrance to their reconciliation.
[42] Cf. the extended initial confrontation in I. ii; the solo scene for Alicia (II. ii); her attempt to murder Arden (II. iii); and the reconciliation scene (IV. ii).

guard the nuptial bed'.[43] The reconciliation (IV. ii) affords a scene of extended emotional intensity matched only by the murder itself. The moral lesson in the situation is fully underscored:

> *Arden.* I will not doubt my happiness. . . .
> *Alicia.* The wandering fires that have so long misled me,
> Are extinguished. . . .
> The flowering path of innocence and peace
> Shines bright before, and I shall stray no longer.[44]

These alterations and additions require corresponding adjustments in Alicia's scenes with Mosby. In their first encounter (*Arden II*, I. iii) she is as frantic to see him as Alice is in the comparable scene in *Arden I* (i. 105–41 and 178–223), but she can be moved to agree to Arden's murder only by Mosby's plea that his own life is at stake if their affair is discovered. At the midpoint of the revised drama (III. ii) Alicia rejects Mosby, determined 'no longer [to] live the abject slave | Of loose desire',[45] although his impassioned protestations of love bring her to allow that she would reconsider 'shou'd chance or nature | Lay *Arden* gently in a peaceful grave' (a concession she withdraws in Act IV, when she renounces Mosby forever).[46] The scene contrasts sharply with the parallel confrontation in *Arden I*, in which Alice's attack of bad conscience is overcome not by Mosby's lovemaking but by his threat to leave her, at which point she commits herself utterly to him and to the murder.

It is clear that considerable attention was given to reshaping the character of Mosby himself, now the play's villain, but the effect of these changes is problematic. Mosby is given a new soliloquy, the opening scene of the adaptation, in which to announce his 'horrid . . . purpose'.[47] An introspective and remorseful solo speech found in scene viii of *Arden I* is revised and shifted to a spot later in the play (V. ii), where it can provide a major dramatic moment for Mosby after the murder. His initial confrontation with Arden is much altered,[48] and in all of his scenes adjustments are made for reasons of character as well as plot. Yet the result of these efforts is a curiously confusing or incomplete characterization, unclear at best and at times apparently contradictory.

The adaptation is unambiguous in portraying the overriding concern which shapes Mosby's actions throughout the play: he is determined to bring about the death of Arden. The disparities emerge in the development of the motivations which explain and give force to this commitment to murder. 'Love,

---

[43] II. iii. 48. There is also a suggested element of providential intervention to prevent the murder—a voice, either supernatural or 'fancy' stemming from Alicia's awakened conscience, which seems to cry '*Alicia*, hold!' (cf. ll. 9–12).

[44] IV. ii. 126 and 137–40.   [45] III. ii. 82–3.

[46] III. ii. 69–70. To intensify the situation, the adaptation places the scene for Mosby and Alicia at a point in the action when Mosby, without informing Alicia, has hired the pair of assassins and has good reason to believe that Arden has already been killed.

[47] I. i. 1.

[48] The balance of the scene is effectively reversed in the adaptation by having Arden, rather than Mosby, draw his sword to attack his rival.

interest, and self-defence, all ask his death,' Mosby tells his hired assassins.[49] Recalling his motives in the soliloquy after the killing, he offers a similar list adjusted in tone, 'Ambition, av'rice, lust, | That drove me on to murder'.[50] The speeches nicely summarize three motivations for Mosby's villainy: his love or desire for Alicia, his avarice or his ambition for advancement (or both), and his concern for self-preservation in the face of Arden's anger. The portrayal of Mosby in certain other scenes[51] implies a fourth element in the characterization, an inherent maliciousness or inclination to villainy, to some extent a counterpart to Alice's unexplained malice in *Arden I*. The four motivations could well have been combined to create a coherent, persuasive characterization appropriate to the role Mosby is required to fill in the adaptation. Instead, they are variously stressed in different scenes, apparently forgotten in other episodes, and seem ultimately to represent alternative rather than complementary aspects of Mosby's character.

The problems relate in part to the extensive alterations in the thematic structure of the play. In *Arden I* Mosby is characterized primarily by his ambition or, in the opinion of Arden and his friends, his presumptuousness. Any love he feels for Alice is subsumed in his concern to acquire her husband's property and, with it, advancement. Arden's fury is roused less by his wife's apparent infidelity than by her involvement with 'such a one as he',[52] a peasant 'Who . . . Crept into service of a nobleman'.[53] In turn, as Wine notes, Mosby stabs Arden 'not as a lover eliminating his rival but as a scorned inferior taking revenge'.[54] In *Arden II* this ambitious Mosby is recalled in the late soliloquy: 'O! happiest was I in my humble state'.[55] The moralizing tag which ends the adaptation makes him the 'dread instance . . . of Avarice'.[56] However, except in his conversation with Black Will and Shakebag, noted above, this is nowhere dramatized in the earlier action or dialogue of the adaptation.[57]

An evolving society's ambivalent view of ambition, which has been seen to provide thematic material for the sixteenth-century *Arden*,[58] would of course have had less meaning for an audience of eighteenth-century Londoners, the City men and ladies for whom ambition, rightly pursued, was a virtue and George Barnwell's 'history' the more tragic because he could have earned his

---

[49] II. i. 119. He is more explicit in saying that '[Arden] once dead, [I] might with her share his fortunes' (l. 116). This motive is not mentioned again, and conveivably is introduced here less as an explanation of Mosby's intentions than as an argument likely to move Black Will and Shakebag, who presumably will be the readier to assist Mosby if they know he will be able to reward them well for their services. In any case, the next line gives nearly equal emphasis to Mosby's concern for self-preservation: 'He's jealous too of late, and threatens me.'

[50] V. ii. 44–5.   [51] I. i, IV. iii, and v. iii.   [52] *Arden I*, i. 22.
[53] *Arden I*, i. 26–7.   [54] p. lxxi.   [55] v. ii. 14.   [56] V. iii. 141.

[57] In inviting Green to join the conspiracy, Mosby, playing down his affair with Alicia, presents himself as concerned to deal with the man who has 'accus'd, insulted, struck me' (II. i. 31) and ill-treated his wife. 'Insulted' may recall the derisive epithets thrown at Mosby by Arden and his friends in *Arden I*; echoes of these derisive descriptions of Mosby can be found elsewhere in *Arden II* (e.g. 'base mechanic slave', I. ii. 35b), but no point is made of them and those who speak them do not mention Mosby's ambition.

[58] Cf. Wine, pp. lxi–lxv, lxix–lxx.

way to become a Thorowgood. In the adapted *Arden*, the central moral issue is not ambition but domestic virtue, judged for the most part in terms of sexual fidelity.[59] In this context Mosby is presented as moved first by his passion for Alicia and by its counterpart, his intense jealousy of the man she has married (an element minimally developed in *Arden I*). This is the focus of his first scene with Alicia, and in the moments immediately following the murder the adaptation does characterize Mosby as the lover who has taken vengeance on a rival:

> *Arden.* Why have you drawn my blood upon your souls?
> *Mosby.* Behold her there, to whom I was betrothed,
> And ask no further—[60]

Given this altered characterization, it is puzzling to discover that Mosby's soliloquy in the next scene deals not with the regrettable outcome of excessive or misdirected passion but with the hollow rewards of misguided ambition.

A similar discontinuity marks the solo speech invented to begin the adaptation and introduce Mosby. Neither his ambition nor his passionate love for Alicia is suggested here. The soliloquy presents instead the double portrait of a would-be murderer, three times unsuccessful, deeply afraid for his life—'I am not safe: The living may revenge'[61]—and, in a manner recalling the villains of Renaissance drama, a self-proclaimed scoundrel activated by instinctive malice and a delight in the skilful manipulation of those he would use. These characteristics do reappear, at times, later in the adaptation. Self-preservation emerges as a motive for murder second only to Mosby's passion for Alicia as the action of the play develops (I. iii–IV. i); if she is lost to him, Arden must still be killed that Mosby may 'not live in fear'.[62] In the latter part of the play, as Mosby dupes Arden with the false street fight (IV. iii), the fearful Mosby is replaced by the clever scoundrel. This air of bravado seems also to characterize Mosby's efforts, in the final scene of the drama, to persist in his deceptions even as the evidence of his guilt is uncovered.[63]

These odd variations in the characterization of Mosby are worth pursuing in some detail for what they may suggest about the composition of *Arden II*. Some lack of coherence might simply reflect the difficulty of integrating the new drama of domestic virtue with the old murder plot—Mosby is the one character

---

[59] As in *The London Merchant*, sexual indulgence can be seen as a moral offence leading automatically to other crimes and ultimately to murder. But in *Arden II* this theme is developed minimally and never emphasized.

[60] V. i. 105–7a. See also IV. i. 19–23.   [61] I. i. 3–4.

[62] III. ii. 75. Presented first as an argument to persuade Alicia to agree to her husband's murder (cf. I. iii. 26–40a), fear for his own life becomes at times Mosby's overriding concern later in the play, when Alicia repents and rejects him. In III. ii his impassioned efforts to win her back focus on their old love, and underlying this may be a hint of concern to acquire her husband's fortune; but it is clear that his first interest is to save his skin.

[63] Curiously, the characterization of Mosby in this scene reflects none of the anguish of guilt he is shown to suffer at the end of the preceding scene. And when cornered by his accusers his reaction is terse and virtually uncharacterized: 'I freely yield me to my fate' (v. iii. 99).

who must function actively in both contexts throughout the play.[64] However, the more awkward inconsistencies might well bear witness to the contributions of two writers not only separated in time but also at variance in their understanding of the intentions of the adaptation. In particular, the two soliloquies, neither of which relates easily to the other scenes of *Arden II*, might be taken as late additions inserted by someone other than the writer who devised the basic approach to the adaptation.[65]

The treatment of the resolution of the play also raises questions which may provide clues to the unusual circumstances of the composition of *Arden II*. During the first four acts, the two dramas developed in the adaptation rarely overlap; they are played out alternately in separate scenes. In Act V the strands must be drawn together. The mechanics of the murder are handled in much the same way as they were in *Arden I*, but the scene is expanded to include Alicia's frantic efforts to prevent the killing and an extended death scene for Arden, in which the happy resolution of the drama of husband and wife is tragically and ironically undercut. Modern commentators have been quick to notice the contrast between the original scene—harsh, unsentimental, and spare—and the eighteenth-century revision, in which the episode is taken as an opportunity for wringing out the emotional responses, a situation exacerbated by the alterations in character which reduce Alicia to the role of passive victim capable only of emotive reaction.[66] What seems not to have been noticed is the adapter's failure to realize, either through the exercise of feeling or open didactic statement, the thematic resolution prepared for by the interpolation of the new Arden–Alicia drama into the framework of the old play's murder plot. The instructive irony is, of course, implicit in the adaptation's version of the murder scene—the process set in motion by Alicia's old passion and Arden's excessive jealousy cannot be halted by love and trust that come too late. But the lack of explicit statement pointing up the moral lesson is at least curious in a play in which the thematic aspects of the Arden–Alicia situation have earlier been developed so thoroughly and with such emphasis. Moreover, in the final scene of the play, the adaptation omits and does not replace the moralizing speeches provided for the leading characters at the end of *Arden I*. The adapter's concern, clearly, is to tie up the loose ends of plot neatly and as rapidly as

[64] Until their reconciliation has been accomplished, the domestic drama of Arden and Alicia is effectively removed from the murder drama, which is developed in scenes which feature Mosby, Michael, Green, and the hired assassins. Although Arden appears in the scenes which involve the unsuccessful attempts on his life, his role as unsuspecting intended victim is passive, requiring no character development that might conflict with his characterization in the scenes centred on his relationship with Alicia.

[65] It must be noted, however, that the two speeches themselves appear to be contradictory in portraying Mosby's motivations. Moreover, they differ strikingly in their relation to the text of *Arden I*: the first introduces material almost entirely new in the adaptation while the second represents one of the very few passages in *Arden II* heavily dependent on words and ideas borrowed from the original play.

[66] Cf. Wine, p. xlviii; Bernbaum, pp. 34–5.

possible, not to expound a final thematic argument.[67] Exceptions are Mosby's soliloquy on ambition and the pat tag given to Franklin; neither relates meaningfully to the central drama of Arden and Alicia, and both appear to contradict ideas and characterizations developed during the first four acts of the adaptation.

Taken together, these oddities or shortcomings in the latter part of the play seem less to indicate the ineptitude of a single adapter or the excesses often attributed to the sentimental drama of the period than to suggest that portions at least of the text of Act V as it now stands reflect some misunderstanding of the original intentions of the adaptation—that is, that the play does indeed represent at least two or more phases of composition and the work of more than one writer. It is tempting to interpret the situation as indicating simply that for Lillo's *Arden*, as earlier for Miller's adaptation of *Mahomet*, John Hoadly supplied a fifth act for a work otherwise substantially completed by the original author. However, the inconsistencies in the characterization of Mosby suggest that, whatever the state of the unfinished adaptation said to have been left by George Lillo, a second adapter's efforts almost certainly involved additions or changes in earlier scenes of the play. Hoadly's revisions of material completed by Lillo may have been extensive,[68] or the manuscript from which he worked may have represented an early draft of the adaptation in which some scenes or speeches had been fully developed while others were merely sketched in. Efforts to reconstruct the process of composition can at best be highly conjectural.

While certain passages in the text can appear to echo Lillo rhetorically, one cannot with certainty identify any portion of *Arden II* as his, nor indeed determine through textual analysis that the adaptation at its first level of composition was beyond question the work of George Lillo. The domestic subject and setting of *Arden I* and the adapter's concern to develop an emotionally heightened, morally instructive drama within the framework of the murder story do recall Lillo's approach to selecting and treating the sources of his most successful plays. However, the adaptation as it now stands lacks the thoroughly developed, fully articulated didactic framework characteristic of every play of Lillo's that was performed and published during his lifetime or immediately after his death. The new approach to the drama of Alicia and Arden does introduce a strong moralizing element at the centre of *Arden II*, but

---

[67] Except for brief speeches defending Mosby's sister's innocence (necessary to resolve an element of plot), even Alicia and Mosby subside into silence when the details of the murder have been uncovered.

[68] Hoadly's correspondence with Garrick indicates that he saw no harm in adding a new scene to *The London Merchant* and revising the original text of the play. As noted above, the very free treatment of words and phrases borrowed from the text of *Arden I* may stand as evidence of substantial revision by the second adapter responsible for *Arden II* (see n. 28 above). Conceivably the omission of explanatory speeches emphasizing the didactic framework of *Arden II* might also reflect the work of a later adapter who took his cue from the theatre: during the latter part of the 18th cent. the moralizing speeches seem regularly to have been deleted when *The London Merchant* was acted.

this is not integrated into a thematic structure encompassing the entire play.[69] Moreover, the drama of domestic virtue resolved in tragedy has no doctrinal dimension, no context in religious thought. This is the more remarkable in that the original tragedy emphasizes the providential nature of Arden's series of escapes from his would-be murderers: the play is infused throughout with a sense of destiny working in the confused lives of individual men and women. In the adaptation, this influence of providence, pointed up in certain early scenes, is forgotten halfway through the play. In the view of the present editor, it is inconceivable that Lillo, provided with this theme by his source, would not have developed it and made it central to the resolution of the tragedy; indeed, if one is to judge by the plays of which he is certainly the author, had the old play not included this thematic element Lillo would have added it in writing his version.

Did Lillo write all or a portion of an adaptation of *Arden of Feversham*, and was his work somehow preserved in a forgotten manuscript, discovered, polished up, and performed in 1759? The published text of the play does not provide evidence that Lillo did not undertake and complete at least a part of such a project. It does suggest, however, either that the manuscript which came to light years after his death represented an uncompleted adaptation of *Arden* or that his work was subject to substantial revisions and additions by another writer, presumably John Hoadly. It seems likely that Hoadly literally 'completed' the adaptation, providing much or all of the fifth act, and that he at least edited the earlier acts, making alterations and on occasion interpolating new material into the text. The textual evidence does not indicate that *Arden* should be excluded entirely from the Lillo canon, and external evidence argues, if unemphatically, for its inclusion. At the same time, it is clear that the play cannot be taken to have authority at all comparable to that of the other dramas assigned to the playwright. The adaptation stands as probable evidence of Lillo's interest in an early domestic tragedy and to some degree his perceptions about how that old play could be made meaningful in his own time. However, to make use of the play in any detailed way as illustrative of George Lillo's ideas, his rhetorical style, or his craftsmanship in the theatre is clearly inappropriate.

PERFORMANCE AND RECEPTION

Advertised as 'An Historical Play, taken from Holinshead's Chronicles, and written by the late Mr Lillo, Author of *George Barnwell*', the adaptation of *Arden of Feversham* was first acted at Drury Lane on 12 July 1759.[70] David Garrick,

---

[69] That Act V lacks a fully stated thematic resolution appropriate to the moral drama developed earlier in the play might be taken as evidence that a first version of the adaptation was left incomplete and the final scenes were provided by a second adapter. However, study of Lillo's plays makes it clear that it was not his practice simply to state a moral at the end of the drama. He established his moral patterns while developing his action, and such clear thematic groundwork is missing, along with the resounding moralizing conclusion, from the *Arden* adaptation as it now exists.

[70] *London Stage, 1747–1776*.

co-manager of the theatre company and its leading actor, was a long-time friend of John Hoadly. He had encouraged Hoadly's proposed revisions of old plays, and on occasion had suggested that he would himself stage and act in one of these adaptations.[71] Accepting Hoadly's involvement in preparing the *Arden* adaptation for production, one would expect Garrick to have been instrumental in the decision to perform the play at Drury Lane. Possibly he was. However, Garrick may well have been away from London at the time of the first performance; he did not appear in the play and no evidence suggests that he took a hand in the production.[72] Indeed, neither the scheduling of the performance—in midsummer—nor the cast assembled for it suggests great interest or support by the theatre's management.

In 1759 there were no summer companies playing at the patent theatres as there had been when *The London Merchant* and *Marina* were given off-season trials. At Drury Lane the regular season had ended on 4 June. Two performances to benefit 'some distressed Actors who formerly belonged to the theatres' were scheduled later in the month.[73] Following these, nothing except the single performance of *Arden* was offered until the company opened its new season in September. Announced 'For one night only' and 'By Particular Desire', the production of *Arden* must have come about through some special sponsorship. Conceivably it was a project developed to indulge the theatrical enthusiasms of Dr Hoadly, a persistent promoter of amateur theatricals;[74]

---

[71] Garrick and Hoadly were on the most genial and easy terms. Their correspondence, extending over a period of more than three decades, indicates that it was Hoadly's habit to send copies of his playwrighting efforts to Garrick, ostensibly for the actor's amusement and comment but also clearly in the hope that one of the pieces would be selected for production at Drury Lane (Garrick, *Correspondence, passim*; and see n. 21 above). None of the extant letters makes reference to the *Arden* adaptation. However, if one of Hoadly's projects was actually being prepared for performance in London, it is inconceivable that he would not have shown a manuscript to Garrick.

[72] Garrick was certainly at his Hampton villa on 29 June, the day on which his partner, James Lacy, submitted the manuscript of *Arden* to the Chamberlain's office. A letter written to Garrick on 12 July, in which the correspondent seeks to arrange a time to meet with him when he returns to London, seems clear evidence that he was not in town on the day of the performance; this is confirmed by a reference in one of Garrick's own letters to a message, dated 13 July, having to do with a matter of Drury Lane business which he would have dealt with in person had he been in town at that time. On 3 Aug. Garrick writes that he was in London on the first day of the month, apparently not having been there for some weeks, and in this letter he refers to Dr Hoadly in a way that clearly implies that he had not seen him for some time. (Garrick, *Letters*, pp. 310 and 315; Garrick, *Correspondence*, i. 100 and 102.) It is puzzling that Garrick would seem to have avoided or ignored the *Arden* production if it was indeed a project in which Hoadly had an interest. Conceivably he felt that the play would not succeed and so stayed away rather than be present on an occasion that might prove an embarrassment for his friend. However, Garrick was not shy about expressing his opinions of Hoadly's work, and at least once seems to have advised his friend that a play he proposed for production should not be exposed on the professional stage. (Garrick, *Correspondence*, i. 191 and 199.)

[73] Tues., 19 June, and Thurs., 28 June. Garrick appeared in neither performance. (*London Stage, 1747–1776*.)

[74] 'So great . . . was the Doctor's fondness for theatrical exhibitions, that no visitors were ever long in his house before they were solicited to accept a part in some interlude or other' (*Biographia Dramatica* [1812], p. 351).

perhaps it was hoped that a successful trial performance would encourage the management of the threatre to schedule the play during the regular season. The production might also have been designed to show off the talents of the actress who played Alicia, a 'Young Gentlewoman, who never appeared on any stage'.[75]

Neither the aspiring actress or the adapted drama fared well. Tom Davies, who was a member of the Drury Lane company and may have seen the performance, characterizes the young lady as 'a raw young actress, unacquainted with the stage, and utterly incapable of comprehending, much less representing a character which required the strongest expression of violent and conflicting passions'.[76] The evening was to some extent saved, Davies reports, by William Havard, who acted the part of Arden 'with great judgment'. A reliable and quite accomplished actor of featured and sometimes leading roles, Havard was at the mid-point of his thirty-year career at Drury Lane and well experienced in playing Elizabethan drama. Roles currently his included Iago, Edgar in *King Lear*, Horatio to Garrick's Hamlet, and Angelo in *Measure for Measure*.[77] The rest of the cast for *Arden* was made up of Drury Lane regulars of considerably less reputation and one actor borrowed from Covent Garden. Astley Bransby, who played Mosby, normally appeared in supporting roles—serious older men and eccentric comic characters—to which his great height could lend presence. Popular opinion held him to be more careful than remarkable on stage, an unlikely approach to carrying off the intense Mosby, virtually the only leading role assigned to Bransby during his London career.[78] John Packer (Green), Henry Scrase (Franklin), and Edmund Burton (Mayor) were drawn from the corps of actors who supplied the theatre with its Guildensterns and Montagues.[79] Low comedy and country characters were the specialty of Mr Phillips and Mr Vaughan, not inappropriately cast as Black Will and Shakebag.[80] Michael was played by John Wignell, whose assignments at Covent

---

[75] *London Stage, 1747–1776*, ii. 735. [76] *Life*, p. xliii.

[77] Havard was cast as Thorowgood when Garrick revived *The London Merchant* in 1765 and continued to play the part at Drury Lane until 1768. Early in his career he had played Barnwell for a single performance at Lincoln's Inn Fields. (*London Stage, 1729–1747; 1747–1776*, ii, *vol. passim.*)

[78] Bransby 'Avoids all censure, if he meets no praise', said Kelly in *Thespis* (1766), summing up the actor's characteristic approach to his roles. Francis Gentleman, writing in 1772, was less generous; Bransby and Edmund Burton, he reported, were 'gentle opiates' of the stage. But Bransby was a useful actor and his appearances on the Drury Lane stage were frequent. During the regular season of 1758–9 his assignments included Don John (*Much Ado About Nothing*), Escalus (*Measure for Measure*), the Ghost (*Hamlet*), Lovwit (*The Alchemist*), and Kent (*King Lear*), a role in which he did achieve some reputation. (*London Stage, 1747–1776*, vol. ii, *passim; Actors, Actresses*, ii. 312.)

[79] Scrase appears to have been called on to act very few times during the regular season, with Montague as his most significant assignment. Packer was cast more frequently, in supporting roles ranging from Rosencrantz to Albany in *King Lear*. Burton was regularly assigned a variety of secondary parts, among them Montague, the Player King in *Hamlet*, a witch in *Macbeth*, and Barnwell's Uncle in *The London Merchant*. He achieved greater reputation as Subtle in Garrick's many performances of *The Alchemist* and, later in his career, as Gloucester in *King Lear*. (*London Stage, 1747–1776*, vol. ii, *passim; Actors, Actresses*, ii. 436–7.)

[80] Among Phillips's assignments during the regular season were Corin in *As You Like It*, Ananias in *The Alchemist*, and Sir Tunbelly in *The Relapse*. Vaughan was a more sprightly comedian, a dancer as well as an actor, a popular Harlequin in provincial theatres, and at Drury Lane cast in such parts

Garden included Guildenstern but also such featured parts as Bardolph (*Merry Wives*) and Lodovico in *Othello*.[81] Maria was a final apprentice role for Frances Barton, who, as Mrs Abington, would become one of the leading actresses on the London stage.[82]

For Davies, the performance by this rather unbalanced cast stood as another instance that it was Lillo's 'fate . . . to have several of his plays acted to disadvantage'. Except for Havard's performance, 'we cannot say that much justice was done to this pathetic tragedy'. In later years, some would recall that the audience had been greatly moved. 'However,' as Davies sums it up, 'it is certain that *Arden*, though much applauded, was acted but one night.'[83]

Perhaps reflecting the general reception of the play, Davies also noted some flaws in the adaptation itself. 'The story of Arden's murder is not an improper subject for the stage, and many scenes of the play are happily written'; however, 'perhaps in adhering too strictly to our old chronicles, the writer has deprived himself of advantages which he might have obtained from a slight deviation from them'. Such deviation would have been in aid of a tighter and more persuasive plot, 'a probable story, well contrived, and artfully conducted'. Davies also suggests that 'Detested characters, the perpetrators of low villainy, murderers and assassins, should be sparingly introduced upon the stage. . . An audience will not long endure their company.'[84] In this Davies was wrong: over the years, Black Will, played with comic bravura, became the favourite character in the play and on occasion threatened to overwhelm the tragedy.[85]

Davies regretted that, before the first performance, 'some friend of the author had not applied to Mr. Garrick to revise, correct, and amend this play'.[86] In 1790 another enterprising actor, Joseph George Holman, undertook the task of revision and gave the play its first London production since its unsuccessful trial in 1759. Holman reduced the adaptation to three acts, provided 'material Alterations', and offered the new version of the drama for his benefit night at Covent Garden. The *European Magazine* reported that the tragedy 'was well performed by Mr. Holman [Arden], Mr. Hartley, and Mrs. Pope, who represented Mosby, and Mrs. Arden'.[87] But no additional performances were scheduled.

---

as Stephano in *The Tempest*, Dapper in *The Alchemist*, and Launcelot in *The Merchant of Venice*. (*London Stage, 1747–1776*, vol. ii, *passim*; Rosenfeld, *Strolling Players*, p. 239.)

[81] *London Stage, 1747–1776*, vol. ii, *passim*.   [82] *Actors, Actresses*, i. 13.

[83] *Life*, pp. xlii–xliv. Davies notes that the 'writer of the Companion to the Theatre' (i.e. David Erskine Baker, *Biographia Dramatica* [1764]) speaks 'with rapture of the effects produced by the representation of' *Arden*.

[84] *Life*, p. xliv.

[85] As late as 1954 Kenneth Tynan, writing about a production of the original version of *Arden*, noted 'the natural tendency to overact the role of Black Will' (Wine, p. liii). In 1852, however, the critic of a London revival of the adaptation praised both the writing and performance of Will and Shakebag as 'the most effective parts in the representation . . . both [are] character parts—and first-rate of their class' (*The Athenaeum*, No. 1301, 2 Oct. 1852).

[86] *Life*, pp. xliv–xlv.   [87] Apr. 1790, quoted by Wine, p. xlix.

Away from London, the Lillo–Hoadly adaptation persisted and enjoyed considerable success, as it appears to have done during most of the three decades following its first performance. The few extant records of presentations by touring companies of actors indicate that *Arden of Feversham* was a popular favourite during the 1760s, especially in the towns in and near Kent. It is impossible to know if the play regularly offered was the Lillo–Hoadly adaptation or some other version of the old tragedy. However, the Lillo version was specifically announced in advertisements published in 1765 by the Chatham Company of Comedians when it offered a series of plays in Maidstone during a tour which also included Canterbury, Faversham, and other towns of the region.[88] Until a seventeenth-century text of the original play was reprinted in 1770, Davies's edition of the adaptation (1762) was the only recently printed text of *Arden* to which actors could refer, and it seems likely that the adaptation served as script for many of the apparently frequent performances of the play given in provincial towns. Holman's revision was taken up by at least one touring company, which announced a production of *Arden* based on the manuscript of Holman's benefit 'five seasons before', to be performed 'for Rochester, Chatham, Strood, and the Vicinity'.[89] But it was the adaptation credited to Lillo which was regularly reprinted during the first half of the nineteenth century and thus would seem to have been accepted as the standard version of the play. No fewer than eight such reprints appeared between 1804 and 1850, most of them in collections of popular plays, although occasional single editions were published.[90] The adaptation held the stage in provincial theatres well past the middle of the nineteenth century, and in Faversham was the basis for frequent productions which continued into the 1880s or later.[91] That the play depicted a sensational incident in local history was, no doubt, in large measure responsible for its popularity. However, its special appeal was its power to wring the emotions of an audience with a 'scene of domestic distress'.[92] *Arden* was promoted, acted, and received in much the

[88] Rosenfeld, *Strolling Players*, pp. 263–4.

[89] Wine, p. xlix, quoting from a fragmentary handbill in the Harvard Theatre Collection, which announces a benefit for Mr Keys.

[90] The play appeared regularly in such collections as *The British Drama* (1804 and ? 1824), *The Modern British Drama* (1811), *The London Stage* (182?), and a similar collection published in Philadelphia in 1850. At least two single editions of the play were published by D. S. Maurice (1819 and ? 1821).

[91] In his edition of the original version of *Arden*, published in 1887, A. H. Bullen notes that 'In recent years the play has been frequently acted, doubtless in Lillo's wretched version, at the Faversham Theatre' (p. xix, quoted by Wine, p. l).

[92] The play was so described in the handbill announcing the provincial production of Holman's revision (see n. 89 above), which offered a description of the performance of Alicia as an enticement to playgoers:

[She] displays great feeling for [Arden's] approaching fate, and endeavours to frustrate the designs of his murderers, and though, in many instances, she was culpable, yet in viewing this sad scene, every human breast must feel for her situation, and drop a tear at her untimely fate. In short, the whole piece forms such a scene of domestic distress, as is scarcely to be equalled in the annals of the British Drama.' (Quoted by Wine, p. xlix.)

Bullen also reports that 'wretched as is Lillo's recast of the old play, it produced on one occasion,

same way as 'the natural and affecting tragedy of George Barnwell',[93] which it was felt to resemble. And, like *The London Merchant*, it persisted despite the disapprobation of those critics who pronounced it outdated and inept. When the play was revived at Sadlers Wells in 1852, *The Athenaeum* predicted that 'this unfortunate play has now probably found its last trial; as notwithstanding that on occasion it was efficiently acted, it yet proved powerless to excite the least manifestation of feeling on the part of the audience'.[94] In fact, the play seems never to have fared well in its London trials, possibly because, for a sophisticted audience, it lacked the skilful shaping which Davies felt that a Garrick could have given it. The adapted *Arden* found its public among the patrons of provincial acting companies and, apparently, those who read plays. With their support, it continued as the accepted version of the old play until the twentieth century, when a revival of interest in Elizabethan theatre encouraged a return to original texts and attempts at more authentic representations of sixteenth-century drama.[95]

THE TEXT

The first edition of the version of *Arden of Feversham* ascribed to George Lillo was published in 1762, some two years after the single performance of the first production of the adaptation. A manuscript of the play, submitted to the Lord Chamberlain in June 1759, is a professional copy and provides no evidence about revisions or stages of composition. Comparison of the manuscript with the first edition indicates that both texts derive ultimately from a common source and that copy for the printed text was, to some extent at least, emended to included alterations made during production in the theatre. Neither text can be said to be authoritative, but the first edition does appear to represent the text of the adaptation as it was acted in 1759.

according to Campbell, so magnetic an effect of terror on the audience that the representation [at the Faversham Theatre] had actually to be suspended' (p. xix, quoted by Wine, p. l).

[93] *Monthly Review* (Dec. 1762), which judges 'this melancholy tale of Arden' to be 'of the same rank and moral turn' as *The London Merchant*. The comment is quoted in the reprint (1810) of Davies's collection of Lillo's works, ii. 177.

[94] The reviewer takes a position opposite to that of Davies, whom he quotes, in identifying the flaws in the play. In addition to praising the parts of Black Will and Shakebag (see n. 85 above), he finds that the drama's greatest strength is its story or plot:

The expedients by which the premeditated murder is procrastinated from act to act are amongst the most skillful contrivances for prolonging an interest ever exhibited. As a piece of mechanical arrangement, the drama is perfect;—but the mediocrity of Lillo's genius in the delineation of character, in the expression of sentiment, and in poetic diction could not enable him to lift up either his theme or his persons to the proper dramatic elevation . . . An interest was felt in the story—but none in the persons, the two murderers aforesaid excepted.' (*The Athenaeum*, No. 1301, 2 Oct. 1852.)

[95] The first revivals of complete or nearly complete versions of the original play were staged in 1921 by the Marlowe Society and in 1925 by William Poel (Wine, p. li).

Larpent Manuscript

James Lacy's request for licence to act the play at Drury Lane is written on a slip of paper apparently pasted on to the recto of the second leaf—the title-page—of the manuscript submitted to the Chamberlain's office and is dated 29 June 1759. The manuscript (Larpent MS 160 in the Huntington Library) is the work of a single copyist. The transcription is clean and punctuated quite carefully, though on occasion pointing is omitted at the ends of lines and especially at the ends of stage directions. In capitalization the copyist held firmly to the old style; virtually every noun is capitalized, and not a few adjectives and verbs. The manuscript does not include the prologue or epilogue.

First Edition

The edition, published by Thomas Davies, is dated 1762. In typography and design it can be paired with Davies's edition of *Fatal Curiosity*, also dated 1762, which includes *Arden of Feversham* among the plays by Lillo listed in an advertisement printed on the verso of its final leaf.[96] No newspaper advertisement announcing publication of these editions has been found, and neither play is among the titles of new books listed by the *Gentleman's Magazine* and *London Magazine* during 1762. However, in 1761 Davies, who with his wife had acted with the company at Drury Lane since 1752, was stung greatly by the scathing comment about his acting included in Charles Churchill's *Rosciad*; at the end of the season of 1761–2 he seems to have curtailed his theatrical activities, and after the following season withdrew from the stage altogether to devote his time to the bookshop he had opened in 1760.[97] In 1762, concerned to draw greater income from bookselling, Davies might well have remembered the unpublished play attributed to George Lillo and thought it a likely project. Possibly his friendship with Garrick, or Garrick's close acquaintance with John Hoadly, gained him access to a manuscript of the work.[98]

For the title-page, see p. 503.

Collation: 12° (6's) A–E⁶ F² [\$3 (− F2, 3) signed]; 32 leaves, pp. *1–5* 6–63 *64*

---

[96] The ornament made up of flowers, which appears on the title-page of Davies's edition of *Arden*, was used also for his edition of *Fatal Curiosity*. Davies would have had good reason to remember *Fatal Curiosity* when planning an edition of another of Lillo's plays: he had acted Young Wilmot in the first production of the play. Publication of the list of Lillo's plays, including *Arden*, in the edition of *Fatal Curiosity* but not in the edition of *Arden* suggests that *Fatal Curiosity* was the second of the two to be printed. The list itself may indicate Davies's first interest in reprinting all of the playwright's works.

[97] Both Garrick and Doctor Johnson reported that Churchill's ridicule had driven Davies from the stage. After 1763 Davies did not act again until 1778, and then only to raise money in a time of financial stress. He had first ventured into bookselling in 1737, when passage of the Licensing Act ended his engagement with Fielding's company at the Haymarket, and had maintained his shop for some eight years before returning to the stage. (*Actors, Actresses*, iv. 205–7.)

[98] See 'Authorship: The External Evidence', above.

Contents: A1(*i*) title A1ᵛ(*2*) blank A2(*3*) prologue A2ᵛ(*4*) dramatis personae A3(*5*)–F2ʳ(*63*) text (DH; ARDEN of FEVERSHAM.) F2ᵛ(*64*) epilogue

Comments

Comparison of copies reveals no press corrections and only one press accident.[99] There is no evidence of reimpression. No copies printed on fine paper have been found.

The edition was adequately set out and printed, though designed to fit as much type as possible on to the duodecimo pages. It was set in a relatively modern style with light capitalization. The pointing, much of it probably contributed by the compositor, is lavish in the use of commas but at times omits essential punctuation or provides punctuation which obscures or distorts the sense of the lines (see below).

Comparison of the edition with the Larpent manuscript indicates that, while the two texts are very similar and stem ultimately from the same manuscript, they clearly did not share a common copy-text. The edition represents a somewhat later state of the text than the version copied for submission to the Chamberlain and, in a few instances, records alterations made during production in the theatre.[100] Minor substantive variants, more than sixty in number, suggest that the copy-texts for the edition and Larpent manuscript derived separately from their common ancestor. The great majority of these minor variants—e.g. 'not' for 'nor', 'were' for 'was', 'I've had' for 'I'd have', 'shall' for 'may'—alter the sense of the lines minimally at most and appear to be slips on the parts of compositor and copyist, perhaps in following a manuscript less than clear, or to reflect their efforts to polish up the text.[101] Three such variants which materially affect the meaning of lines could well represent mistranscription, not conscious emendation.[102] Two variants do indicate authorial or editorial alteration.[103] The omission from the printed text of one full line preserved in the Larpent manuscript is clearly an error.[104]

In the Chamberlain's manuscript, V. i–ii, treated as two scenes in the edition, is transcribed as a single scene. The manuscript and edition agree in failing to number II. ii, though it is set off as a new scene in both, and in misnumbering III. iii as III. iv. Both texts omit a number of necessary stage directions, but in some cases directions not given in the printed text are included in the

---

[99] III. ii. 85a will.] ~∧ (DFo copy).

[100] At IV. iii. 47–51, lines not included in the Larpent manuscript may represent a later addition to the text. In V. iii, lines and stage business have been altered to allow the search of Alicia's person to be done off-stage, almost certainly an adjustment made in the theatre (see commentary on V. iii. 70SD). See also V. iii. 99 and n.

[101] The occurrence of errors gives no indication about the relative accuracy of manuscript and printed text; the number of obvious if minor mistakes is about the same in each.

[102] I. iii. 91, IV. ii. 75a, and V. i. 102.

[103] III. ii. 31 and III. iii. 54. Another considered editorial change was several times made by the printer or the person who prepared his copy-text: Black Will's oath—'Blood' in the manuscript—is regularly printed as 'S'blood' (see commentary on II. i. 60).

[104] I. ii. 23; see also V. ii. 42.

manuscript, and vice versa.[105] The relation of dialogue and stage directions is sometimes handled awkwardly in the edition, in particular when an entrance signals a strong reaction by one or more characters already on stage. The different ordering of such directions and exclamations given in the manuscript is less confusing.[106] In general, it is clear that an effort was made to normalize the presentation of stage directions in the printed text but that the compositor was uncertain about the conventions for setting such material.

The compositor or editor who prepared the text for printing had equal difficulty in determining the proper division of lines of verse, and in distinguishing between passages of verse and prose in scenes in which the two alternate.[107] The copyist who transcribed the Larpent manuscript was at times similarly confused, evidence that the copy from which both texts derive was not always clear. However, irregular or problematic versification in *Arden* is not always a matter of printer's error or poor copy; throughout the adaptation, long and short lines occur much more frequently than in the blank verse characteristic of the plays known certainly to have been written by George Lillo. Truncated lines, which may be intended to stand alone for rhetorical effect or may represent the first part of a verse line continued in the next speech, are a special problem.

Variations among the accidentals of the edition and manuscript suggest that copyist and compositor were required to supply much of the pointing. The frequent appearance of dashes in the printed text, but not in the manuscript, suggests also that dashes may have served in lieu of other punctuation in the casually pointed copy from which later texts were taken.[108]

The pointing of the edition is marked by the very frequent use of commas, often set apparently only to denote the ends of verse lines. At the same time, the lack of heavier punctuation such as semi-colons to set off effectively separate sentences in a linked series, confuses or misrepresents the sense of some passages. The omission of commas in some vocative constructions creates additional problems. The compositor had special difficulty in handling pointing in association with parentheses; often in such situations his punctuation is redundant, misplaced, or incorrect.[109] The setting of exclamation marks is at best erratic.[110]

---

[105] Cf. II. ii. 9SD, III. ii. 76SD, IV. ii. 136SD, V. ii. 12SD, and V. iii. 19SD.

[106] See commentary on I. ii. 59+SD. The printer also appears to have been uncertain about the conventions for handling directions that mark asides or indicate the manner in which a line is to be spoken. [107] e.g. V. i. 147b–148a, 163b–164, and 173–4.

[108] The compositor was uncertain and at times incorrect in setting additional punctuation with or in place of the dashes, in particular in providing full stops when the dashes indicate speeches broken off or interrupted (cf. I. ii. 39a, 95a, 113a, and III. i. 94a).

[109] Most often, an unnecessary or unwanted comma precedes the phrase in parentheses (e.g. I. ii. 16–17, I. ii. 60–1, I. iii. 81–3, II. ii. 6–7, III. ii. 50–1, III. iii. 4–5, IV. i. 8, IV. iii. 68 and 70). However, on rare occasions pointing required by the sense of the speech is omitted (e.g. III. ii. 40).

[110] While exclamation marks are used freely in some portions of the text, in other, extended, passages full stops and question marks are set where exclamation marks seem clearly called for, as though the compositor had exhausted his supply of exclamation marks (e.g. I. ii. 36b, I. iii. 41, II. iii. 26, III. iii. 15, IV. ii. 67, and V. i. 91).

The pointing of the Larpent text is rather more regular than that of the edition, and helpful as a reference when the printed text is difficult to follow. An exception is the occasional omission of pointing at the ends of lines and stage directions.

Later Reprints

The adaptation was reprinted in a Dublin edition, dated 1763, 'Printed for T. and J. WHITEHOUSE, Book-|sellers; at the *State-Lottery-Office in Nicholas* | *street*'. The edition was set from a copy of the first edition, which it follows closely though the printer made efforts to correct and improve the pointing of his copy-text. Davies himself reprinted the text of his edition of 1762, with corrected and emended accidentals, when he published the collected edition of Lillo's works in 1775.

Editorial Procedure

The first edition serves as copy-text for the present edition. The line and another half-line recorded in the Larpent manuscript but omitted from the first edition have been adopted. Readings clearly incorrect have been emended, usually with reference to the Larpent text. Where the edition and manuscript disagree, if the reading in the edition is possible it has been retained. However, on rare occasions, when the manuscript variants correctly maintain the metre of lines of verse and there appears to be no persuasive rhetorical reason for retaining the broken metre of the copy-text, the manuscript versions have been adopted. An effort has been made to correct apparent errors in the lining of verse, and to distinguish verse and prose in scenes which include both, but it is not always possible to ascertain beyond question what the author's intentions may have been in such situations. Necessary stage directions have been supplied, when possible with directions given in the manuscript. The awkward ordering of related entrances and exclamations in the first edition has been adjusted. The punctuation of the copy-text has been retained except where it is obviously incorrect, seriously distorts the sense of lines, or is certain to mislead the reader; as often as possible, such emendations follow alternatives provided by the manuscript; reference has also been made to the texts of the Dublin edition and Davies's *Works* as suggestive of eighteenth-century responses to problems presented by the accidentals of the first edition. The characteristic pointing associated with parentheses has normally been accepted, but emended in a very few instances in which this punctuation is markedly misleading. Similarly, where a question mark set in lieu of an exclamation mark effetively contradicts the meaning of a line, the pointing has been emended.[111]

[111] The copy-text is the first edition, a Yale University copy. Copies collated include: first edition, CtY, DFo, O, BL; Davies, *Works* (1775), CtMW, O, BL (3 copies), CtY (2 copies). The Dublin edition (1763) has also been collated but, like the *Works*, is mentioned in textual footnotes and historical collation only when it has been consulted for contemporary responses to problems in the copy-text. Because they are so very numerous and of minimal editorial interest, the variants in the Larpent manuscript which involve only capitalization have not been recorded in the historical collation except when they could be said to affect the sense of the text.

Arden of Feversham.

John Genest Dec.r 22. 1804.

AN HISTORICAL
TRAGEDY:

TAKEN FROM

HOLINGSHEAD's CHRONICLE,
In the Reign of King EDWARD VI.

ACTED AT THE

THEATRE-ROYAL, in DRURY-LANE.

By the late Mr. L I L L O.

L O N D O N,

Printed for T. DAVIES, at *Shakespear's Head*, in
Russell-Street, Covent-Garden. 1762.

PROLOGUE,

By a FRIEND.

Spoken by Mr. HAVARD.

THE piece is Lillo's—*He, long since in dust:*
Criticks far hence; or spare his urn's sad trust,
Kind to his Muse, and to his memory just.

 His Muse resembles him, and knows no art;
She speaks not to the head, but to the heart.   5
The artless maid, by no false seal impress'd,
Bears but an honest copy of his breast:
And ev'ry eye has own'd, his natural lay,
Sprung from the heart, wings to the heart its way.

 The Tragic Bard apes not the Epick fire,   10
On Fancy's wing still aiming to aspire:
In Nature's palace, simple, great, and plain,
Inrich'd and crowded ornament were vain:
Embellishment does but distract the mind,
Which Art should never to minuteness bind.   15
Tho' honey'd language she from Hybla steal,
Your ears applaud—your hearts no ardours feel.
With labour'd art tho' the sad tale be told,
The melting tear, mean while congeal'd, grows cold.
When Passion speaks immediate to the soul,   20
Parts she o'erlooks, to grasp at once the whole.

 To night, your Bard, from your own annals shews,
A dreadful story of domestic woes:
From facts he draws (his picture's from the life)
The injur'd husband, and the faithless wife,   25
Doom'd all the train of bosom pangs to prove,
Pangs, which must always wait on lawless love.

 Ye generous, who feel for other's woe,
Ye fair, whose tears for injur'd virtue flow,
In justice to yourselves, applaud his plan,   30
And judge the poet, as ye lov'd the man.

PROLOGUE] L *does not include prologue*   3 *just.*] WI; ~; D   9 its] I; it's D
16 Hybla] *Ed.*; *Hybla* D   28 generous,] I; ~ᴧ D

Dramatis Personæ.

MEN.

The Mayor of *Feversham*.	Mr. *Burton*.
Arden, a gentleman of *Feversham*.	Mr. *Havard*.
Franklin, his friend.	Mr. *Scrase*.
Michael, Arden's servant.	Mr. *Wignell*.
Green.	Mr. *Packer*.
Mosby.	Mr. *Bransby*.
Bradshaw.	Mr. *Johnston*.

Black Will,
George Shakebag,⎫ Ruffians. ⎧ Mr. *Phillips.*
⎩ Mr. *Vaughan.*

Lord *Cheyney*.

Adam Fowl, an inn-keeper.

Officers, *&c.*

A servant to *Arden*.

WOMEN.

Alicia, wife to *Arden*.—A young gentlewoman.

Maria, sister to *Mosby*.   Miss *Barton*.

SCENE, *Feversham*, in *Kent*.

2 The Mayor] *Ed.*; The mayor G; Mayor L   Mr. *Burton.*] *Actors' names are not in* L
4 *Franklin,*] L (Franklin); ~ ∧ D   9.5 Ruffians.] I; ~ ∧ D; *not in* L   11 Lord *Cheyney*] L
begins list of men with this entry   12 *Adam . . .* inn-keeper] L *includes this entry immediately before*
line 9   18 in *Kent*] *not in* L

ACT I.

SCENE I.

The street before Arden*'s door.*

Mosby *alone.*

The morning's dark, and horrid, as my purpose.—
Thrice have my snares been laid for *Arden*'s life,
And thrice hath he escap'd.—I am not safe:
The living may revenge.—Oh! cou'd I win
Alicia to conspire her husband's fall,   5
Then might I say, security, thou'rt mine,
And laugh at all to come.—For other instruments,
There's *Green*: he bears him hard about this suit
For th'abbey-lands, to which the hot youth pleads
Some fancy'd right.—*Michael*, the trencher-fav'rite;   10
A bastard, bred of *Arden*'s charity:
He has been privy to our secret joys,
And, on that trust presuming, loves my sister—
Winks at adultery, and may at murder.
Maria is his price. I've plac'd her here,   15
Companion of my sweet *Alicia*'s hours,
To spread her charms for ever in his eye:
To her are all my visits. But *Alicia*—
She must, she shall comply: when to my arms
Her honour she resign'd, her fond reluctance whisper'd,   20
She cou'd deny me nothing.—This to try. [*Exit into* Arden*'s house.*

SCENE II.

A chamber.
Arden *in his night-gown.*

Unhappy *Arden*, whither canst thou wander
To lay thy heavy load of sorrows down!
Will change of place relieve th'afflicted mind,
Or does all nature yield a balm to cure
The pangs of slighted love and broken faith?   5
Ungrateful false *Alicia*! false with *Mosby*,
The vile dependent of my foe profess'd,
Lord *Clifford*'s full-fed flatt'rer!—O damn'd!—

SD Mosby] Enter Mosby L   7 come.—] ~.ˌ L   (I. ii) SD Arden] Enter Arden L
6 Ungrateful] ~, L

Come, *Franklin*, come: *Arden* thy friend invites thee;
And let me pour my griefs into thy bosom,   1c
And find in friendship what I've lost in love.

Enter Alicia.

    Alic. Why, *Arden*, do you leave your bed thus early?
Have cold and darkness greater charms than I?
There was a time when winter-nights were short,
And *Arden* chid the morn that call'd him from me.   1§
    Ard. This deep dissembling, this hypocrisy,
(The last worst state of a degen'rate mind)   [*Aside.*
Speaks her in vice determin'd and mature.
    Alic. What maid, that knows man's variable nature,
Wou'd sell her free estate for marriage bonds?   2c
From vows and oaths, and every servile tye,
The tyrant man at pleasure is set free;
Himself th'offender and himself the judge.
The holy nuptial bond leaves him at large;
Yet vests him with a power that makes us slaves.   2§
'Tis heav'nly this—
    Ard.   To stop my just reproach
Art thou the first to tax the marriage state?
    Alic. Are you not jealous? do you not give ear
To vain surmises and malicious tongues,
That hourly wound my yet untainted fame?   3c
    Ard. And wou'dst thou make me author of the shame
Thy guilt has brought on us!—I'll bear no longer.
The traitor *Mosby*, curs'd, detested *Mosby*,
Shall render an account for both your crimes.
    Alic. What do I hear!   [*Aside.*
    Ard.   That base mechanic slave   3
Shall answer with his blood.
    Alic.   O hear me speak!
    Ard. No, I am deaf: As thou hast ever been
To fame, to virtue, and my just complaints.
    Alic. Thus on my knees—
    Ard.   Adult'ress! dost thou kneel
And weep, and pray, and bend thy stubborn heart   4
(Stubborn to me) to sue for him?—Away,
Away this instant, lest I kill thee too.   [*Recovering himself.*
No—Not the hell that thou'st kindled in this bosom
Shall make me shed thy blood.

    (I. ii) 9 *Arden*] L (Arden); ~, D   23 Himself th'offender ... the judge.] L (& ... Judge);
not in D   26a this—] This. L   32 us!—] ~?∧ L   33 curs'd] curst L
35b slave] Slave! L   36b speak!] L; ~. D   39a knees—] L (Knees); ~. D

Alic.   I do not hope it.
Ard. For me, be as immortal as thy shame.   45
  Alic. I see your cruel purpose: I must live,
To see your hand and honour stain'd with blood,
Your ample fortune seiz'd on by the state,
Your life a forfeit to the cruel laws.
O *Arden*, blend compassion with your rage,   50
And kindly kill me first.
      Ard.   Not for my sake
Are all thy tears, (then had you felt them sooner).
Plead not the ruin you have made; but say
Why have you driven me to these extremes?
Why sacrific'd my peace, and your own fame,   55
By corresponding with a menial slave?
  Alic. Thou canst not think, that I have wrong'd thy bed?
  Ard. Wou'd I cou'd not!
  Alic.   By heav'n!—
  Ard.   No perjuries.
But now, as you lay slumb'ring by my side,
I still awake, anxious and full of thought,   60
(For thou hast banish'd sleep from these sad eyes)
With gentle accents thrilling with desire,
You call'd on *Mosby*. Love made me doubt my ears,
And question if the dark and silent night
Conspir'd not with my fancy to deceive me: 65
But soon I lost the painful pleasing hope;
Again you call'd upon your minion *Mosby*.
Confirm'd, I strove to fly your tainted bed,
But, wanting strength, sunk lifeless on my pillow.
You threw your eager arms about my neck,   70
You press'd my bloodless cheeks with your warm lips,
Which glow'd, adult'ress, with infernal heat;
And call'd a third time on the villain *Mosby*.
  Alic. A dream indeed, if I e'er call'd on him.
  Ard. Thy guilty dreams betray thy waking thoughts.   75
  Alic. I know I'm simple, thoughtless, and unguarded;
And what is carelesness, you construe guilt.
Yet were I weak as those fantastic visions,
Sure I cou'd never have condemn'd you, *Arden*,
On circumstances and an idle dream.   80
  Ard. But such a dream.—
  Alic.   Yet was it but a dream,

(I. ii)   47 blood,] I; ~. D, L (Blood L)   52 tears,] *Ed.*; ~ ͏ D, L   sooner).] *Ed.*;
~,) ͏ D; ~ ͏ L   63 *Mosby*. Love] L (Mosby); ~, love D   72 glow'd,] L; ~ ͏ D
77 carelesness] Carelessness L

Which, tho' I not remember, I abhor;
And mourn with tears, because it gives you pain.
Arden, you do not wish me innocent,
Or on suspicions cou'd you doom me guilty!
    Ard. Not with thee innocent! do sinking mariners,
When struggling with the raging seas for life,
Wish the assistance of some friendly plank?
'Tis that, and that alone, can bring me comfort.
    Alic. O jealousy! thou fierce remorseless fiend,
Degen'rate, most unnatural child of love;
How shall I chace thee from my *Arden*'s bosom?
    Ard. There is a way, an easy way, *Alicia*.—
    Alic. O name it—speak.
    Ard.   What's past may be forgotten.
Your future conduct—
    Alic.   You distract me, *Arden*.
Say, how shall I convince you of my truth?
    Ard. I ask but this: never see *Mosby* more.   [*He starts.*
By heav'n, she's dumb!
    Alic.   O how shall I conceal
My own confusion, and elude his rage?   [*Aside.*
    Ard. Thou'rt lost, *Alicia*!—lost to me—and heav'n.
    Alic. Indeed I'm lost, if you unkindly doubt me.
    Ard. Wilt thou then ne'er converse with *Mosby* more?
    Alic. If e'er I do, may heav'n, and you, forsake me!
    Ard. You'll keep your word, *Alicia*!—Prithee, say—
    Alic. You'll break my heart.
    Ard.   I'd rather break my own.
Then thou art innocent, and lov'st me still.
    Alic. And ever will.
    Ard.   Give me thy hand—thy heart,
O give me that!
    Alic.   That always was your own.
    Ard. Thou flatterer—then whence this cruel strife?
Still art thou cold: nor warm are thy embraces,
Nor sparkle in thine eyes the fires of love:
Cold, cold, and comfortless.
    Alic.   Indeed you fright me.
    Ard. 'Tis possible—
    Alic.   What?
    Ard.   That thou may'st yet deceive me.
    Alic. O! I am wretched!

    (I. ii)   86 thee] the L   93 *Alicia.*—] Alicia.ᴧ L   95a conduct—] L (Conduct);
~.— D   113a possible—] L; ~. D

Ard.   Both perhaps are so.
But if thou ever lov'dst, thou'lt not despise me,   115
And wilt forgive me, if indeed I've wrong'd thee,
As I've forgiven thee—Pity, I'm sure, I need.   [*Exit* Arden.
     Alic. Thou hast it, *Arden*, ev'n from her that wrongs thee.
All, all shall pity thee, and curse *Alicia*.
Can I feel this, and further tempt the stream   120
Of guilty love! O whither am I fallen!
                    Enter Maria.

     Mar. An happy day, *Alicia*—and may each morn
Of coming life be usher'd with like joy.
Franklin, from court return'd, has brought the grant
Of the abbey-lands confirm'd by the young king,   125
To *Arden* for his life: nor will deliver
But to himself the Deed.
     Alic.   A worthy friend!
The grant is not more welcome to my husband,
Than *Franklin*'s company.
     Mar.   He's flown to meet him.

                    Enter a servant.

     Serv. Madam, your brother *Mosby*—
     Alic.   Where is *Mosby*?   130
     Serv. He waits below.—
     Alic.   O haste, and lead me to him.
     Serv. Madam, he but desires to see his sister.
     Alic. His sister! what! did he not ask for me?
     Mar. Perhaps—
     Alic.   Pray, give me leave—looks he in health?—
     Serv. He seems in health—
     Alic.   Here, and not ask for me!   135
Seems he or angry then, or melancholy?—
Answer me, stock, stone.—
     Serv.   Truly, I can't say.
     Alic. Thou canst say nothing—Get thee from my sight.
Yet stay—no matter. I'll myself go seek him.   [*Exeunt* Alicia *and servant.*
     Mar. Where reason is, can passion thus prevail!   [*Exit* Maria.   140

(I. ii)   122 *Alicia*] Alicia! L   130a *Mosby*—] Mosby. L   133 what!] What, L
135a health—] Health. L   136 melancholy?—] Melancholy?‸ L   137a me, stock,
stone.—] ~! Stock! Stone!‸ L   138 nothing—] ~. L

SCENE III.

A parlour in Arden*'s house.*

Enter Alicia *meeting* Mosby.

Alic. Mosby, that brow befits our wayward fate.
The evil hour, long fear'd, is fallen upon us,
And we shall sink beneath it. Do not frown—
If you're unkind, to whom shall I complain!
   Mosby. Madam, it was my sister I expected—
   Alic. Am I forgotten then! Ungrateful man!
This only cou'd have added to my woes.
Did you but know what I have borne for you,
You wou'd not thus, unmov'd, behold my tears.
   Mosby. Madam, you make me vain.
   Alic.   Insult not, *Mosby*.
You were the first dear object of my love,
And cou'd my heart have made a second choice,
I had not been the object of your scorn:
But duty, gratitude, the love of fame
And pride of virtue, were too weak t'erase
The deep impression of your early vows.
   Mos. Therefore you kindly chose to wed another.
   Alic. Reproach me not with what I deem'd my duty.
Oh! had I thought I cou'd assume the name,
And never know the affection of a wife,
I wou'd have died ere giv'n my hand to *Arden*.
   Mos. You gave him all.—
   Alic.   No, no, I gave him nothing:
Words without truth—an hand without an heart.
But he has found the fraud—the slumb'ring lion
At length hath rous'd himself—
   Mos.   —And I must fall
The victim—
   Alic.   —No, he knows not yet his wrongs.
   Mos. But quickly will.
   Alic.   That, that's my greatest fear.
   Mos. Then, branded with a strumpet's hated name,
The cause abhorr'd of shame, of blood, and ruin,
Thou'lt be expos'd and hooted thro' the world.

(I. iii) 3 frown—] ~. L   5 expected—] ~. L   14 fame] L (Fame); ~, D
22a all.—] All.ᴧ L   24 fraud—the] Fraud. The L   25a himself—] ~. L
25b —And] ᴧ~ L   25b–26a fall | The] fall the L, *incorrectly writing as one line*
26a victim—] Victim. L   26b —No] ᴧ~ L

Alic. O hide the dreadful image from my view!
Chaste matrons, modest maids, and virtuous wives,
Scorning a weakness which they never knew,
Shall blush with indignation at my name.
   Mos. My death—but that—tho' certain.—
   Alic.   Labour not   35
To drive me to despair. Fain wou'd I hope—
   Mos. You may—and be deceiv'd. For me I know
My fate resolv'd—and thee the instrument;
The willing instrument of *Mosby*'s ruin.
Inconstant, false *Alicia!*
   Alic.   False indeed,   40
But not to thee, cruel, injurious *Mosby!*
   Mos. Injurious! false one! might not all these dangers
That threaten to involve us both in ruin,
Ere this have been prevented?
   Alic.   Ha!—say on.
   Mos. And not preventing, art not thou the cause?   45
   Alic. Ah! whither, *Mosby*—whither wou'dst thou drive me?
   Mos. Nay, didst thou love, or wou'dst secure thy fame,
Preserve my life, and bind me yours for ever;
'Tis yet within your power.—
   Alic.   By *Arden*'s death!
Mean'st thou not so? speak out, and be a devil.   50
   Mos. Yes, 'tis for thee I am so.—But your looks
Declare, my death wou'd please you better, Madam.
   Alic. Exaggerating fiend! be dumb for ever.
His death! I must not cast a glance that way.
   Mos. Is there another way?—O think, *Alicia.*   55
   Alic. I will, for that will make me mad: And madness
Were some excuse. Come, kind distraction! come,
And *Arden* dies—my husband dies for *Mosby.*   [*Shrieks, and runs to*
                                                       Mosby.

He's here! O save me! tell me, did he hear?

                Enter Arden *and* Franklin.

   Ard. [*Starting.*] *Franklin,* support your friend. I shake with horror.   60
   Frank. What moves you thus?
   Ard.   See—*Mosby*—with my wife!

(I. iii) 33 they] the L   35a certain.—] ~.ₐ L   41 thee,] ~; L   *Mosby!*] L
(Mosby); ~. D   44b Ha!—] ~!ₐ L   46 *Mosby*—] Mosby, L   49a power.—]
Power.ₐ L   55 way?—] ~?ₐ L   57 distraction!] Distraction, L   59+SD *Enter*
Arden *and* Franklin.] L (*italics* Ed.); D *prints immediately before line* 59.   61b *Mosby*—]
Mosby, L

Mos. But, Madam, I shall spare your farther trouble;
In happy time behold my neighbour here.   [*As taking leave of* Alicia.
    Alic. Mischief and wild confusion have begun,
And desolation waits to close the scene.   [*Exit* Alicia.
    Mos. Sir, I wou'd gladly know, whether your grant
Of the rich abbey-lands of *Feversham*
Be yet confirm'd or not?
    Ard.   What if I tear
Her faithless heart, ev'n in the traitor's sight,
Who taught it falshood.   [*Aside.*
    Frank.   He is lost in thought.
But I can answer that: It is confirm'd—
I brought the deed, with the great seal annex'd,
Sign'd by our pious *Edward*, and his council.
    Mos. I'm satisfied.—
    Ard.   So am not I—By hell,
There's justice in the thought.—I'm strangely tempted.   [*Aside.*
    Mos. My friend seems wrapt in thought—I came to advise him,
That *Green*, by virtue of a former grant
His father long enjoy'd—
    Ard.   For my estate
The law, and this good seal, is my security;
To them I leave *Green* and his groundless claim.
But my just right to false *Alicia*'s heart,
(So dearly purchas'd with a husband's name,
And sacred honour of a gentleman)
I shall assert myself, and thus secure
From further violation.   [*Draws.*
    Mos.   Her known virtue
Renders the injury your fancy forms,
A thing of air.
    Frank.   Impossible to thought.
Whence, *Arden*, comes this sudden madness on thee.
That your *Alicia*, ever dear esteem'd,
And deeply lov'd—
    Ard.   Out on the vile adult'ress!
But thou demure, insinuating slave,
Shalt taste my vengeance first. Defend thyself.
    Mos. I scorn to take advantage of your rage.
    Ard. A coward too! O my consummate shame!
    Mos. This I can bear from you.
    Ard.   Or any man.

Why hangs that useless weapon by thy side,
Thou shame to manhood?—Draw.—Will nothing move thee?

                                            [*Strikes him.*

    Frank. Hold. Whither wou'd your mad revenge transport you?
    Ard. Shall shameful cowardise protect a villain?
    Mos. You chuse a proper place to shew your courage!   100
    Ard. Go on. I'll follow to the ocean's brink,
Or to the edge of some dread precipice,
Where terror and despair shall stop thy flight,
And force thy trembling hand to guard thy life.
    Mos. What I endure to save a lady's honour!   [*To* Franklin.   105
    Frank. Your longer stay will but incense him more;
Pray quit the house.
    Mos.   Sir, I shall take your counsel.   [*Exit* Mosby.
    Ard. He hath escap'd me then—But for my wife—
    Frank. What has she done?
    Ard.   Done! must I tell my shame?
Away, begone—lest from my prey withheld   110
I turn, and tear th'officious hand that lets me.
Soft! art thou *Franklin?* Pardon me, sweet friend;—
My spirits fail—I shake—I must retire.
    Frank. To your *Alicia.*
    Ard.   To my lonely couch;
For I must learn to live without her, *Franklin.*   115
    Frank. Pray heaven forbid!
    Ard. To hate her, to forget her—if I can:
No easy task for one who doats like me.
From what an height I'm fallen! Once smiling love
    Of all its horrors robb'd the blackest night,   120
    And gilt with gladness ev'ry ray of light.
    Now tyrant-like his conquest he maintains,
    And o'er his groaning slave with rods of iron reigns.   [*Exeunt.*

The end of the first act.

(I. iii)   97 manhood?—] Manhood!∧ L   Draw.—] ~!∧ L   110 begone—] ~! L
113 shake—] ~, L   121 light.] L (Light); ~, D   123SD [*Exeunt.*] *Ed.; not in* D, L
The end] End L

ACT II.

SCENE I.

The Street.

Green. Mosby.

Gr. You pity me, and know not my estate.
　　I'm ruin'd, *Mosby*; thoughtless and ill-advised,
　　My riotous youth will leave my age a beggar.
　　These abbey-lands were all the hopes I'd left;
　　My whole support.

Mos. 　　　　　　　　Base and ungen'rous *Arden*,
　　To force a man, born equal to himself,
　　To beg, or starve.

Gr. 　　　　　　　　By heaven, I will do neither:
　　I'll let the proud oppressor know—

Mos. 　　　　　　　　　　　How blind is rage!
　　Who threats his enemy, lends him a sword
　　To guard himself.—

Gr. 　　　　　　　　Robb'd of the means of life,
　　What's life itself? an useless load, a curse:
　　Which yet I'll dearly sell to my revenge.

Mos. You mean to kill him then?

Gr. 　　　　　　　　　I do, by heaven.

Mos. Suppose you fail—

Gr. 　　　　　　　　I can but lose my life.

Mos. Then where is your revenge, when he, secure,
　　Riots unbounded in his ill-got wealth?

Gr. What can I do?

Mos. 　　　　　　　'Tis plain you wish him dead.

Gr. Each moment of his life is to my soul
　　A tedious age of pain; for while he lives,
　　Contempt and all the ills a lazar knows,
　　Must be my wretched lot, and lengthen out
　　The miserable hours. What groveling wretch
　　Wou'd wish to hold his life on such conditions?

Mos. But change the scene: suppose but *Arden* dead,
　　Your land restor'd, and fortune in your pow'r;
　　Honour, respect, and all the dear delights
　　That wait on wealth, shall wing the joyful hours,
　　And life contracted seem one happy day.

SD *Green. Mosby*.] Enter Green & Mosby∧ L　　　　　　2 *Mosby*;] L (Mosby); ~, D
5b *Arden*,] Arden! L　　　7b neither:] ~! L　　　14a fail—] ~? L

I hate this *Arden*, and have stronger motives
Than any you can urge to wish his death;   30
He has accus'd, insulted, struck me, sir—
Nay, his fair, virtuous wife, on my account—
Gr. If fame speaks true, you're to be envy'd there.
Mos. The world will talk—But be that as it may:
I want not cause, nor will, not means, nor friends—   35
Gr. Nor opportunity shall long be wanting.
Mos. Enough: his fate is fixt—See! *Bradshaw*'s here.

Enter Bradshaw.

Brad. Save, save you, gentlemen.
Mos.   We thank you, neighbour.
But whither in such haste?
Brad.   To the isle of *Shippey*,
To wait on good lord *Cheyney*. As he holds   40
In high esteem our worthy townsman *Arden*,
I shall first call on him.—'Tis well I met you,
For yonder two were but bad road-companions.
Gr. They seem of desp'rate fortunes.
Mos.   Have they names?
Brad. One I know not: But judge him from his comrade.   45
The foremost of the two I knew at *Boulogne*,
Where in the late king's reign I serv'd myself.
He was a corporal then, but such a villain—
Beneath a soldier's name.—A common cut-throat,
That preys on all mankind, and knows no party.   50
Mos. An horrid character you give him, *Bradshaw*.
Brad. No worse than he deserves.
Mos. [*Aside.*]   (An useful hint:
He shall not want employment) What's his name?
Brad. *Black Will.* His family-name I never heard.
Mos. [*To* Green.] A word—write you a letter to *Alicia*:   55
Disguise your hand.—This honest fool may bear it.
Hint at these men.—In case her courage fail,
She will be glad to shift the deed on them.
Gr. I am instructed.

Enter Black Will *and* Shakebag.

B. Will. What, comrade *Bradshaw*! How fare you, man? S'blood! dost not   60
remember honest *Black Will*? Why, thou'rt grown purse proud sure.

(II. i)   31 sir—] L (Sir); *not in* D   35 not cause . . . not means] nor Cause . . .
nor Means L   37 fixt—] ~. L   See] Good L   49 name.—] Name.ᴧ L
53 employment] L (Employment); ~: D   56 hand.—] Hand.ᴧ L   60 not] *not in* L

Brad. Why, you're not easily forgotten, *Will.* But, prithee, what brings thee to *Feversham?*

B. Will. A soldier, you know, is at home wherever he comes. *Omne solum forti patria.* There's *Latin*—Give's a tester.

Brad. In time of peace we should apply to some honest creditable business, and not turn the name of soldier into vagabond.

B. Will. Yes, as you have done. I'm told you keep a goldsmith's shop here in *Feversham*, and, like a mechanical rogue, live by cheating. I have more honour.

Brad. Wou'd thou had'st honesty.

B. Will. Where do our honesties differ? I take a purse behind an hedge, and you behind a counter.

Brad. Insolent slave!

B. Will. You *cent. per cent.* rascal! I may find a time to teach you better manners.

Brad. Go, mend thy own.

B. Will. Thou wert always a sneaking fellow, *Bradshaw*, and cou'dst never swear, nor get drunk. Come, shall I and my comrade *Shakebag* taste your ale?

Brad. My house entertains no such guests. Farewel, gentlemen.

Mos.	Along with *Bradshaw*,
	And leave the management of these to me.　　　　　[*Aside to* Green.
Gr.	It shall be done.—*Bradshaw*, a word with thee.
Brad.	Your pardon, gentlemen.　　[*Exeunt* Green *and* Bradshaw.

B. Will. He was a cadet in the last *French* war, like other soldiers then; but now he has got a nest, and feather'd it a little, he pretends to reputation. S'blood! had this been a fit place, he had not scap'd me so. You have survey'd us well. [*To* Mosby.] How do you like us?

Mos.	Methinks I read truth, prudence, secrecy,
	And courage writ upon your manly brows.

B. Will. What hellish villany has this fellow in hand, that makes him fawn upon us?　　　　　　　　　　　　　　　　　　　　　　　[*Aside.*

Mos.	I fear the world's a stranger to your merit.
	If this may recommend me to your friendship—　[*Gives a purse.*
B. Will.	Of what damn'd deed is this to be the wages?
Shake.	Hast ever an elder brother's throat to cut?
B. Will.	Or an old peevish father to be buried?
Mos.	Neither of these.
Shake.	A rival then mayhap—
Mos.	There you come nearer to me.
Shake.	Then speak out.
	We're honest, sir.
B. Will.	Trusty, and very poor.

(II. i)　62 Why,] L; ~, D　　　　　68 told] L; ~, D　　　　71 an hedge] a Hedge L
81SD [*Aside to* Green.] L *includes immediately after line* 80　　　　　82 done.—] ~., L
85 little, he] ~. He L　　86 S'blood] Blood L　　93 friendship—] Friendship. L

   Mos.   Metal too fit for me. [*Aside.*] Then hear me, sir.—   100
       But you must both, ere I disclose my purpose,
       Promise and bind that promise by your oaths—
       Never—[*They both laugh.*] Why this unseasonable mirth?
 B. Will.   You'd have us swear?—
   Mos.   Else why did I propose it?

 B. Will. There's the jest. Are men who act in despite of all law, honour, and 105
conscience; who live by blood (as it is plain you think we do); are we free-
thinkers, like silly wenches and canting priests to be confin'd by oaths?

 Shake. Wou'd you bind us, let the price equal the purchase, and we'll go to
hell for you with pleasure.

   Mos.   Horrid! they shock ev'n me who wou'd employ 'em.   [*Aside.* 110
       I apprehend—The business then is this:
       In *Feversham* there lives a man, call'd *Arden*;
       In general esteem, and ample means;
       And has a wife, the very pride of nature.
       I have been happy long in her affections,   115
       And, he once dead, might with her share his fortunes.
       He's jealous too of late, and threatens me.
       Love, int'rest, self-defence, all ask his death.—
 B. Will. This man you'd have dispatch'd?
 Mos. I wou'd.   120
 B. Will. Rich, you say?
 Mos. Immensely so.
 B. Will. And much belov'd?
 Mos. By all degrees of men.
 B. Will. George! this will be a dang'rous piece of work.   125
 Shake. Damn'd dangerous. A man so known; and of his reputation too.
 B. Will. And then the pow'r and number of his friends must be consider'd.
   Mos.   What! does your courage shrink already, sirs?
 Shake. No.

 B. Will. This is ever the curse of your men of true valour; to be the tools of 130
crafty cowardly knaves, who have not the heart to execute what their heads have
projected. It is a damn'd ungrateful world—What money have you more about
you?

 Mos. Ten pieces.
 B. Will. I've had as much for stealing a dog.   135
   Mos.   I give you that as a retaining fee:
       When the deed's done, each shall have twice that sum,
       And a good horse to further his escape.
 B. Will. Sir, will you have him murder'd in a church?

(II. i) 100 sir] Sirs L   102 oaths—] Oaths, L   104a swear?—] Swear?ᴧ L
108 purchase, and] Purchaseᴧ | And L, *writing as two lines of verse* 125 *George!*] George, L
132 world—] World. L   135 I've had] I'd have L   137 that] the L

Shake. Or on the altar; say the word, and it shall be done.   1
    Mos. Some safer place, the street, highway, or fields
         Will serve my turn as well.
Shake.   Just as you please.
    Mos. Where may I find you, gentlemen?
B. Will. At *Adam Fowl's*, the *Flower-de-luce.*
    Mos. I have confederates in this design;
         When we've contriv'd the manner of his death,
         I'll send you word.
B. Will. You'll find us always ready.
    Mos. And determined?
B. Will. Ay, fear it not. Farewel.   [*Exeunt several ways.*

SCENE II.

A room in Arden*'s house.*

Enter Alicia *with a letter.*

He doubts me; yet he dares not tell me so,
But thus, by *Green*, whets my unsettled mind.   [*Reads.*
    'Strike home, or not at all. In case you fail,
       We have found instruments by means of *Bradshaw*.'
He shall not find me undetermined now.
Hark!—*Michael's* on the watch.—If *Arden* sleeps,
(For so he seem'd dispos'd,) he'll bring me word.
That, that's the safest time. This promis'd marriage
With *Mosby's* sister, has remov'd his qualms.   [Alicia *starts.*

Enter Michael.

Why dost thou break upon me unawares?
What of your master?
    Mich.   He's scarce sunk to rest,
But full of meditated rage 'gainst *Mosby.*
    Alic. He'll sleep in peace ere long.—
    Mich.   Think not on that.
O did *Maria* bless me with her smiles,
As you do *Mosby*, had I twenty lives,
I'd risque 'em all to win her to my arms.
    Alic. I prithee leave me, *Michael.* [*Exit* Michael.] What is nature!
There is a pow'r in love, subdues to itself
All other passions in the human mind.

(II. i)   146 we've] L; w'have D   SCENE II. | *A*] *Ed., following* W1; SCENE, *a* D;
Scene a L   7 dispos'd] L; ~, D   9SD [Alicia *starts.*] L (Alicia Starts.); *not in* D
13a long.—] ~_{∧∧} L

This wretch, more fearful than the lonely murderer,   20
Whom with inquiring eyes some stranger views,
Wou'd meet the king of terrors undismay'd,
For her he loves, and dare him to the combat.
And shall not I preserve my *Mosby*'s life,
And shall not I—A husband!—What's a husband?   25
I have a soul above th'unnatural tie,
That tells me, I'm his right, and only his,
Who won my virgin heart.—Ye tender parents,
Whose cruel kindness made your child thus wretched,
Turn not your eyes towards earth to view this scene;   30
'Twill make you sad in heav'n.   [*Exit.*

SCENE III.

Another room. Arden *sleeping on a couch.*

Enter Alicia *with a dagger in her hand.*

Alic. See!—Jealousy o'erwatch'd is sunk to rest,
While fearful guilt knows no security,
But in repeated crimes. My weary eyes,
Each moment apprehensive of his vengeance,
Must seek for rest in vain 'till his are clos'd.   5
Then for our mutual peace, and *Mosby*'s love— [*Approaching to stab
                                                                him, starts.*

He wakes—Defend me from his just revenge!
And yet he sees me not, nor moves a finger
To save his threaten'd life. Then whence that voice,
That pierc'd my ears, and cry'd, *Alicia*, hold!   10
Can mimic fancy cheat the outward sense,
And form such sounds? If these heart-racking thoughts
Precede the horrid act, what must ensue?
Worse plague I cannot fear from *Arden*'s death,
But from his life—the death of him I love.   15
Perish the hated husband.—Wherefore hated!
Is he not all that my vain sex cou'd wish?
My eyes, while they survey his graceful form,
Condemn my heart, and wonder how it stray'd.
He sighs—he starts—he groans. His body sleeps,   20
But restless grief denies his mind repose.
Perhaps he dreams of me; perhaps he sees me.

(II. ii)   25 —What's] ‸~ L   (II. iii)   6 love—] Love. L   6SD [*Approaching . . .*
starts.] L *includes* SD *after line* 5   17 cou'd] can L   22 me.] ~, L

Thus like a fury, broke from deepest hell,
Lust in my heart, and murder in my hand— [Alicia *drops the dagger.*
             Arden *starts up.*

 Ard. Her dagger, *Michael*—seize it, and I'm safe.   2
How strong she is!—Oh!—what a fearful dream!
Before me still! speak, vision—art thou *Alicia,*
Or but the coinage of my troubled brain?
 Alic. O *Arden*—husband—lord—
 Ard.   Art thou my wife?
Thou'rt substance—I am wrap'd in wonder—Hence!   3
Hast lost all sense of fear, as well as shame,
That thou durst haunt me thus, asleep and waking,
Thou idol, and thou torment of my soul?
 Alic. My bleeding heart—
 Ard.   Away, begone and leave me:
Lest, in the transports of unbounded rage,   3
I rush upon thee, and deface those charms
That first enslav'd my soul; mangle that face
Where, spite of falshood, beauty triumphs still;
Mar that fair frame, and crush thee into atoms.
Avoid me, and be safe—Nay, now you drive me hence. [Alicia *kneels,*   4
                he turns away.

Cruel and false as thou hast been to me,
I cannot see thee wring thy suppliant hands,
And weep, and kneel in vain.—   [*Exit* Arden.
 Alic.   This, this is he
I came prepar'd to murder. Curst *Alicia!*   [*Takes up the dagger.*
In thy own bosom plunge the fatal steel,   4
Or his, who robb'd thee of thy fame and virtue—
It will not be—Fear holds my dastard hand:
Those chaster pow'rs that guard the nuptial bed
From foul pollution, and the hand from blood,
Have left their charge, and I am lost for ever.   [*Exit.*   5

The end of the second act.

(II. iii) 24 hand—] Hand. L 25 dagger, *Michael*] ~! Michael! L 26 is!] L; ~? D
27 thou] *not in* L 30 Hence!] L; hence— D 32 durst] darst L 36 charms] L
(Charms); ~, D 46 virtue—] Virtue. L *The end*] End L

ACT III.

SCENE I.

A road or highway near Feversham.

Black Will *and* Shakebag.

Shake. Damnation! posted as you were, to let him 'scape!

B. Will. I pray thee, peace.

Shake. Green and I beheld him pass carelesly by within reach of your dagger. If you had held it but naked in your hand, he wou'd have stabbed himself as he walk'd. 5

B. Will. I had not power to do it: a sudden damp came over me;—I never felt so in my life—A kind of palsy seized me.

Shake. Palsy! when you're upon your duty! Go, go and sleep, or drink away your fears. You tremble still.—

B. Will. I tremble! my courage was never yet call'd in question, villain. When 10 I fought at *Boulogne* under the late king, both armies knew, and fear'd me.

Shake. That might be, because they did not know you. Dog, I'll shake you off to your old trade of filching in a throng—Murder's too genteel a business for your capacity.—Sirrah, I have taken more gold at noon-day, than ever you filch'd copper by candlelight. 15

B. Will. Cowardly slave, you lye.

Shake. A coward! S'blood! that shall be proved. Come on.

B. Will. To thy heart's blood.

Shake. To thine.   [*They fight.*

Enter Green.

   Gr. What! are you mad! For shame put up your swords. 20

  Shake. Not till I've had his life.

B. Will.   Fool, guard thy own.

   Gr. Pray hear me, gentlemen.

B. Will.   Stand farther off.

Shake. Away.

Gr. This broil will ruin all.

Shake. He begun it. 25

B. Will. Ay, and will end it too.

   Gr. Arden, you know, returns, and will you let him
      Escape a second time?

Shake. Who did the first?

Gr. No matter, that may be repair'd. 30

B. Will. Brand me with cowardice!

SD Black Will] Enter Black Will L   2 thee,] ~ʌ L   7 life—] Life. L
9 still.—] ~.ʌ L   11 at] a L   12 you. Dog,] ~, ~! L   13 throng—] Throng. L
14 capacity.—] Capacity.ʌ L   17 S'blood] Blood L

Gr.   Come, come, you're both to blame.
             Speak, will you lay aside this senseless broil?
B. Will. Nay, let him speak.
Shake. Why, rather than lose this opportunity—   [*Puts up his sword.*   3
B. Will. Ay—We'll defer it 'till *Arden*'s dead. I'm for doing business first, and
then for play—
Shake. Challenge me when thou darest.
Gr.   The night draws on. Are you resolv'd?
Shake.   We are.
Gr.   Enough.—See where he comes. I must withdraw;   4
             But when you've done the deed, and sent his soul—
             No matter where—I'll come to you again.   [*Exit* Green.
B. Will. Something rises in my throat—I can scarce breathe—I'd rather
poison half a dozen cardinals, than kill this honest man, but—I'll do't, for my
reputation.   4
Shake. He comes. Retire a little. Let him advance, then bury your dagger in
his heart. If you fail, I'll second you.
B. Will. Stand further off, I shall not need your aid.
Shake. Now strike—

                 Enter Arden *first, and then Lord* Cheyney *attended.*

B. Will. Again prevented! Ten thousand devils take them all!   5
L. Chey.   *Arden*, well met. You're to the isle of *Shippey*
             Grown quite a stranger. Shall we see you there?
Ard.   I purpos'd soon t'have waited on your lordship.
L. Chey.   Well, will you sup with me to night at *Shorlow*?
Ard.   *Franklin*, my lord, who is my guest at present,   5
             Expects me at my house.
L. Chey.   Then will you dine with me tomorrow?
Ard.   I'll not fail your lordship.
L. Chey.   Believe me, worthy friend, I'm glad to see you.
             Walk you towards *Feversham*?
Ard.   So please your lordship.   6
                              [*Exeunt Lord* Cheyney, *and* Arden.
B. Will. Just as I'd taken aim too!—S'blood I cou'd kill myself for vexation.

                              Enter Green.

Gr. Well, *Arden* is at last dispatch'd?
Shake. Yes, safe to *Feversham*.
Gr.   Safe, say you! his good fortune mocks us all.

(III. i)   36 Ay—] ~; L   37 play—] Play. L   40 Enough.—] ~.ₐ L
49 strike—] ~. L   60ᵒᵇˢᴅ *Lord* Cheyney, *and* Arden] Lᵈ Cheyn: Arden L   61 too!—]
~!ₐ L   S'blood] Blood! L

These strange escapes have almost stagger'd me;   65
But thinking of my wrongs, I'm more confirm'd.
B. Will. Well said, my man of resolution! A gentleman commits a murder
with double the satisfaction for such a heart.—We must lay our snares more
cunning for the future.

Gr.   We shou'd consult with *Michael*, *Arden*'s man—   70
     The pigmy-hearted wretch, though long ago
     He swore his master dead, acts with reluctance.
Shake. The coward must be spurr'd.—He does it, or he dies.
Gr.   I wonder at his absence, as he knew
     Of this attempt, and promis'd to be here.   75

       Enter Michael.

Mich.   I saw my master and lord *Cheyney* pass,
     And my heart leap'd for joy.   [*Apart.*
B. Will.   What says the villain?
Mich.   Would I were gone. [*Aside.*] Sir, if I give offence— [*Going.*
Gr.   *Michael*, come back; you must not leave us so.
Mich.   What is your pleasure?
Gr.   Why, we understand   80
     You are in love with *Mosby*'s beauteous sister.
Mich. Suppose I am.
B. Will. You deal too mildly with the peasant. You swore to kill your master,
villain. Be an honest man of your word, and do't then, white liver.
Mich. Sir, I repented.   85
B. Will. Repented! what's that? Dog, know your rank, and act as we
command, or your heart's blood—
Mich. What must I do?   [*Frighted.*
B. Will. Do! you must shew us the house, appoint the time and place, and
lure your master thither—We'll take care of him without your trouble.   90
Gr.   So shall you purchase noble *Mosby*'s friendship,
     And, by his friendship, gain his sister's love.
Mich.   They'll murder me too, shou'd I not comply— [*Aside.*
Gr.   Think on your love, your interest—
B. Will.   Or your death.
Mich.   To night, soon as the abbey-clock strikes ten, [*Trembling.* 95
     Come to his house: I'll leave the doors unbarr'd:
     The left-hand stairs lead to my master's chamber;
     There take him, and dispose him as you please.
Gr. This cannot fail.

(III. i) 67 A] a L 68 heart.—] ~.ʌ L 70 man—] Man. L 73 spurr'd.—]
~.ʌ L 84 villain.] Villain: L white liver] White-Liver L 87 command] command
you L 90 thither—] ~. L 93 comply—] Comply. L 94a interest—] L
(Interest); ~. D

Shake. Unless this love-sick coward thinks to deceive us.   1
Mich. I will not, by heaven!
B. Will. I believe thee; for by hell thou darest not.   [*Exeunt*
Mich.   Master, thy constant love and daily bounty
                    Deserve more grateful offices from *Michael*.   [*Exit weeping.*

SCENE II.

A room in Arden*'s house.*

Alicia *alone.*

When vice has spread her poison thro' the soul,
How lifeless, slow, confus'd, and insincere
Are our resolves in the pursuit of virtue!
What wonder then heaven shou'd refuse its aid
To thoughts, that only blossom for a time;
Look blooming to the eye, but yield no fruit.

Enter Mosby.

    Mos. I come, *Alicia*, to partake thy griefs;
For fire divided burns with lesser force.
    Alic. I know thee: thou art come to fan the flame,
Thy breath hath kindled here, till it consume us.
But tears and sighs shall stifle in my heart
The guilty passion—
    Mos.   —Is heroic love,
That form'd the bright examples of thy sex,
Made their lives glorious, and their fame immortal,
A crime in thee? Art thou not mine by oaths,
By mutual sufferings, by contract mine?
    Alic. Why do you urge a rash, a fatal promise,
I had no right to make, or you to ask?
Why did you practise on my easy heart?
Why did I ever listen to your vows?
In me 'twas foolish guilt and disobedience;
In you 'twas avarice, insolence, and pride.
    Mos. 'Twas love in me, and gratitude in you.
    Alic. 'Twas insolence in you, meanness in me,
And madness in us both. My careful parents,
In scorn of your presumption and my weakness,
Gave me in marriage to a worthy gentleman,
Of birth and fortune equal to my own.

(III ii.)   12a passion—] Passion. L   12b —Is] ∧~ L   , 28 fortune] L (Fortune); ~, D

Three years I liv'd with him without reproach,
And made him in that time the happy father   30
Of two most lovely babes. I too was happy;
At least I liv'd in hopes I might be so:
For time, and gratitude, and *Arden*'s love,
I hop'd might quench my guilty flame for you,
And make my heart a present worthy him.   35
    Mos. And dost thou glory in thy perjuries?
In love, inconstancy alone's a crime.
Think on the ardor of our youthful passion,
Think how we play'd with love; nor thought it guilt,
Till thy first falshood, (call it not obedience)   40
Thy marriage with this *Arden* made me desperate;
Think on the transports of our love renew'd,
And—
    Alic. Hide the rest, lest list'ning winds shou'd hear,
And publish to the world our shameful tale.
Here let remembrance of our follies die.   45
    Mos. Shall our loves wither in their early bloom?
    Alic. Their harvest else will be to both our shames.
Hast thou not made a monster of me, *Mosby*?
You shou'd abhor me, I abhor myself.
When unperceiv'd I stole on *Arden*'s sleep,   50
(Hell steel'd my heart, and death was in my hand)
Pale anguish brooded on his ashy cheek,
And chilly sweats stood shivering on his brow.
Relentless murder, at a sight so sad,
Gave place to pity; and as he wak'd, I stood   55
Irresolute, and drown'd in tears.
    Mos.   She's lost,
And I in vain have stain'd my soul with blood.   [*Aside.*
    Alic. Give o'er in time: in vain are your attempts
Upon my *Arden*'s life; for heaven, that wrested
The fatal weapon from my trembling hand,   60
Still has him in its charge.
    Mos.   Little she thinks,   [*Aside.*
That *Arden*'s dead ere now.—It must be so;
I've but that game to play, ere it be known.
    Alic. I know our dang'rous state; I hesitate;
I tremble for your life; I dread reproach.   65
But we've offended, and must learn to suffer.

(III. ii)   31 babes] L (Babes); children D   40 falshood, (call] *Ed.*; ~ ∧ (~ D; Falshood.
'Call L   49 me,] ~; L   57SD [*Aside.*] L *includes* SD *at end of line* 56b   61a its] his L
'5 reproach.] Reproach: L

Mos. Then *Arden* live in his *Alicia* blest,
And *Mosby* wretched. Yet shou'd chance or nature
Lay *Arden* gently in a peaceful grave,
Might I presume to hope? *Alicia*, speak.

   Alic. How shall I look into my secret thoughts,
And answer what I fear to ask myself?   [*A long pause.*

   Mos. Silence speaks best for me. His death once known,
I must forswear the fact, and give these tools
To public justice—and not live in fear.   [*Aside.*
Thy heart is mine. I ask but for my own.   [*To her.*
Truth, gratitude, and honour bind you to me,
Or else you never lov'd.

   Alic.   —Then why this struggle?
Not lov'd! O had my love been justly plac'd,
As sure it was exalted and sincere,
I should have gloried in it, and been happy.
But I'll no longer live the abject slave
Of loose desire—I disclaim the thought.

   Mos. I'll ask no more what honour should deny;
By heaven, I never will.

   Alic.   Well then remember,
On that condition only, I renew
My vows. If time and the event of things   [*Giving her hand.*
Should ever make it lawful, I'll be yours.

   Mos. O my full joys!—

   Alic.   Suppress thy frantic transports;
My heart recoils, I am betray'd; O give me back
My promised faith.

   Mos.   First, let the world dissolve.

   Alic. There is no joy, nor peace for you, or me:
All our engagements cannot but be fatal.

   Mos. The time may come when you'll have other thoughts.
'Till then, farewel.—[*Aside.*] Now, Fortune, do thy worst.   [*Exit.*

   Alic. *Mosby*, return—He's gone, and I am wretched.
I shou'd have banish'd him my sight for ever.
You happy fair ones, whose untainted fame
Has never yet been blasted with reproach,
Fly from th'appearance of dishonour far.
Virtue is arbitrary, nor admits debate:
To doubt is treason in her rigid court;
But if ye parley with the foe, you're lost.   [*Exit.*

(III. ii) 75 justice—] Justice, L   76SD [*To her.*] *not in* L   78b —Then] ~ L
85a will.] ~ (*DFo copy*); ~! L   85b then] ~, L   89a joys!—] Joys! L
89b transports;] L (Transports); ~, D   90 betray'd;] L; ~, D   91b First,] ~ L
94 thoughts.] *Ed.*; ~ D, L (Thoughts L)   95 farewel.—] ~! L   103 ye] you L

SCENE III.

Another room in Arden*'s house.*

Arden *and* Franklin *sitting together on a couch:*
Arden *thoughtful.*

  Frank. Nay, wonder not.—Tho' ev'ry circumstance
Thus strangely met to prove the lady false,
And justify the husband's horrid vengence;
Yet it appears to ev'ry honest eye,
(Too late for the poor lady) she was wrong'd.   5
  Ard. Is't possible?
  Frank.   —Ay, very possible:
He lives that proves it so. Conceal'd from justice,
He pines with ceaseless sorrow for his guilt,
And each hour bends him lower towards his grave.
  Ard. I know thy friendship, and perceive its drift. 10
I'll bear my wrongs—for sure I have been wrong'd.
Do I but think so then? What fools are men
Whom love and hatred, anger, hope, and fear,
And all the various passions, rule by turns,
And in their several turns alike deceive!   15
  Frank. To cast away, and on suspicion only,
A jewel, like *Alicia,* were to her
Unjust, and cruel to yourself. [*Clock strikes ten.*] Good night,
The clock has strucken ten.
  Ard.   I thought it more.
  Frank. I thought it not so much.
  Ard.   Why, thus it is: 20
Our happy hours are few, and fly so swift,
That they are past ere we begin to count 'em:
But when with pain and misery opprest,
Anticipating Time's unvarying pace,
We think each heavy moment is an age.   25
  Frank. Come, let's to rest. Impartial as the grave,
Sleep robs the cruel tyrant of his pow'r,
Gives rest and freedom to the o'erwrought slave,
And steals the wretched beggar from his want.
Droop not, my friend, sleep will suspend thy cares, 30
And time will end them.

 SCENE III. | *Another*] *Ed., following* W1; SCENE, *another* D; Scene_∧ Another L
SD *thoughtful*] very thoughtful L   1 not.—] ~·_∧ L   6b —Ay,] *Ed.;* —~_∧ D; _∧~, L
11 wrongs—] Wrongs; L wrong'd.] Wrong'd: L 12 then?] L; ~! D 15 deceive!]
L; ~? D   18 + 18SD yourself.... night,] yourself. Good Night! (Clock strikes 10. L
19a strucken] striken L 26 rest.] Rest: L

Ard.   True, for time brings death,
The only certain end of human woes.
Sleep interrupts, but waking we're restor'd
To all our griefs again. Watching and rest
Alternately succeeding one another,
Are all the idle business of dull life.
What shall we call this undetermin'd state,
This narrow isthmus 'twixt two boundless oceans,
That whence we came, and that to which we tend?
Is it life checker'd with the sleep of death?
Or death enliven'd by our waking dreams?
But we'll to bed. Here, *Michael*, bring the lights.

Enter Michael *with lights.*

Heaven send you good repose.   [*Gives* Franklin *a candle.*
Frank.   The like to you.
Mich. Shall I attend you, sir?
Frank. No, no, I choose to be alone. Good night.   [*Exit* Franklin.

Michael *attends his master with the other
light, and returns.*

Mich. I, who shou'd take my weapon in my hand,
And guard his life with hazard of my own,
With fraudful smiles have led him, unsuspecting,
Quite to the jaws of death—But I've an oath.
Mosby has bound me with an horrid vow,
Which if I break, these dogs have sworn my death.
I've left the doors unbar'd—Hark! 'twas the latch.
They come—I hear their oaths, and see their daggers
Insulting o'er my master's mangled body,
While he for mercy pleads.—Good master, live:
I'll bar the doors again. But shou'd I meet 'em—
What's that?—I heard 'em cry, Where is this coward?
Arden once dead, they'll murder me for sport.
Help! call the neighbours—Master, *Franklin*!—Help!

Enter Arden *and* Franklin, *undress'd, at several
doors.*

Ard. What dismal outcry's this?
Frank.   What frights thee, *Michael*?

(III. iii)   32 woes.] Woes: L   40 death?] Death, L   45SD–45+SD [*Exit* Franklin. |
Michael . . . *returns.*] *Ed., following* L *and* W1; D *prints as a single, bracketed* SD   52 unbar'd] L
(unbarr'd); ~. D   54 mangled body] Murder'd Corse L   59 Help! call] L; ~—call D
Master, *Franklin*!—Help!] L (Franklin); ~—~ˌ—help. D

Mich. My master!—*Franklin*!
Ard.   Why do'st tremble so?
Mich. I dream'd the house was full of thieves and murderers.
                                        [*Trembling.*
Ard. Dream'd! what, awake! Are all the doors made fast?
Mich. I think they are.
Ard.   I'll go and see myself.   [*Exit* Arden.
Frank. You made a fearful noise.
Mich.   Did I?—   65
Ard. [*Within.*]   Why, *Michael*!
Frank. You tremble still.—Has any one been here?
Mich. No, I hope not. My master will be angry.

                    Enter Arden.

Ard. This negligence not half contents me, sir:
The doors were all left open.
    Mich.   Sir—
    Ard.   To bed,
And as you prize my favour be more careful.   [*Exit* Michael.   70
Frank. 'Tis very cold. Once more, my friend—
Ard.   —Good night.
                                        [*Exeunt.*

    Scene changes to the street before Arden's *door, the
                    door shut.*

            Enter Black Will, *and* Shakebag.

B. Will. Zounds! *Michael* has betray'd us—
The doors are fast. Away, away—Disperse.   [*Exeunt.*

        The end of the third act.

(III. iii)   62 dream'd] dreamt L   65b I?—] ~?ₐ L   65c Why,] L; ~ₐ D
66 still.—] ~.ₐ L   69b Sir—] ~, L   71b —Good night.] ₐ~ Night—L
71bSD *Exeunt.*] L (Exeunt); *Exit* Arden. D. *See Commentary*   71b+SD *door,*] House: L
72 us—] Us. L   73 Away, away—] ~, ~, L   SD *The end*] End L

ACT IV.

SCENE I.

An Inn, the Flower-de-Luce.

Mosby *and* Michael.

Mich. Tho' I with oaths appeal'd to conscious heav'n,
That *Arden* rose and shut the doors himself,
Yet, but for *Green*, these bloody rogues had kill'd me.
We must desist—*Franklin* and sweet *Maria*
Have promis'd, at *Alicia*'s own request,
To interfere—
   Mos.   —Such ever be the employ
Of him I hate.
   Mich.   —The mourning fair, all chang'd,
By me conjures you, (and with tears she spake it)
Not to involve yourself and her in ruin,
By seeking to renew a correspondence,
She has renounced for ever.
   Mos.   How! confusion!
   Mich. And hopes, as heaven, in answer to her prayers,
Hath reconcil'd her duty and affection,
You will approve her resolution—
   Mos.   Doubtless!
   Mich. And learn by her example, to subdue
Your guilty passion—
   Mos.   Ha, ha, ha, exquisite woman!
So! rather than not change, she'll love her husband!
But she will not persevere.
   Mich.   Yes, shure, she will.
   Mos. Have I then slighted her whole sighing sex,
Bid opportunity and fortune wait;
And all to be forsaken for an husband!
By heaven, I am glad he has so oft escap'd,
That I may have him murder'd in her sight.

Enter Green.

Green. How strange a providence attends this man!
'Tis vain to strive with heaven—Let's give it o'er.

SD *An Inn, the*] The L   6b —Such] ∧~ L   7b —The] ∧~ L   8 (and . . .
spake it)] *Ed.*; (~,) D; ∧& with Tears she speaks it,∧ L   13 affection,] L (Affection); ~; D
14a resolution—] Resolution. L   16a passion—] Passion. L   18a she will] she'll L
18b shure] sure L   20 wait;] ~, L   25 heaven—] Heav'n. L

Mos. No: when I do, may I be curst for ever,
Hopeless to love, and hate without revenge:
May I ne'er know an end of disappointment,
But prest with hard necessity, like thee,
Live the contempt of my insulting foe.   30
   Green. I scorn the abject thought—Had he a life
Hung on each hair, he dies!—[*To* Michael.] If we succeed,
This very night *Maria* shall be thine.
   Mich. I am a man again.
   Mos.   I've thought a way—
That may be easy under friendship's mask,   35
Which to a foe suspected may be hard.
   Green. Friendship! impossible—
   Mos.   —You know him not.
You, with your ruffians, in the street shall seek him.
I follow at some distance. They begin
(No matter how) a quarrel, and at once   40
Assault him with their swords.—Straight I appear,
Forget all wrongs, and draw in his defence;
Mark me, be sure, with some slight wound; then fly,
And leave the rest to me.
   Mich.   —I know his temper.
This seeming benefit will cancel all   45
His former doubts, and gain his easy heart.
   Green. Perhaps so—yet—
   Mos.   —Further debates are needless. [*Exeunt.*

SCENE II.

A room in Arden's *house.*

Franklin *and* Maria.

Frank. Well, in what temper did you find *Alicia*?
   Mar. Never was anguish, never grief like hers:
She eats, nor sleeps. Her lovely, downcast eyes,
That us'd to gladden each beholder's heart,
Now wash the flinty bosom of the earth.   5
Her troubled breast heaves with incessant sighs,

(IV. i) 29 necessity,] Necessity∧ L   31 thought—] Thought! L   32 dies!] L; ∼∧ D
32+32SD [*To* Michael.] If we succeed,] *Ed.*; If we succeed, [*To* Michael. D, L (succeed∧ [to ∼∧ L);
W1 *prints after line* 31   37a impossible—] Impossible! L   37b —You] ∧∼ L
38 shall] may L   39–40 begin | (No matter how)] ∼, | ∧∼,∧ L   41 swords.—]
Swords:∧ L   47a so—] ∼: L   (IV. ii) 1 Well,] L; ∼∧ D

Which drink the purple streams of life, and blast
Her bloom, as storms the blossoms of the spring.
But sure her prayers must quickly reach high heaven,
Relenting *Arden* kindly sooth her sorrows,   10
And her lost peace restore.
    Frank.   Their mutual peace, *Maria*!
For his can ne'er be found but in *Alicia*.
Asham'd to view the face of man or day,
As *Mosby*'s name was written on his brow,
He cheerless wanders; seeks the darkest gloom   15
To hide his drooping head, and grieve alone.
With a full heart, swoln eyes, and faltring tongue,
He sometimes, seeking to beguile his grief,
Begins a mournful tale: But straight a thought
Of his imagin'd wrongs crossing his memory,   20
Ends his sad story ere the half be told.
O may our pains with wish'd success be crown'd.

Enter Arden.

    Ard. No, *Franklin*, no; your friendly cares are vain:
Were I but certain she had wrong'd my bed,
I then might hate her, and shake off my woes;   25
But thus perplex'd, can never taste of comfort.
    Frank. O jealousy! thou bane of social joys!
Oh! she's a monster, made of contradictions!
Let truth in all her native charms appear,
And with the voice of harmony itself   30
Plead the just cause of innocence traduc'd;
Deaf as the adder, blind as upstart greatness,
She sees nor hears. And yet let slander whisper,
Or evil-ey'd suspicion look oblique,
Rumour has fewer tongues than she has ears;   35
And *Argus*'s hundred eyes are dim and slow,
To piercing jealousy's.—
    Ard.   —No more, no more—
I know its plagues, but where's the remedy?
    Mar. In your *Alicia*.
    Frank.   She shall heal these wounds.
    Ard. She's my disease, and can she be my cure?   40
My friends shou'd rather teach me to abhor her,
To tear her image from my bleeding heart.
    Mar. We leave that hateful office to the fiends.

(IV. ii) 10 *Arden*] L (Arden); ~, D   sooth] sooth's L   28 Oh!] ~, L   36 *Argus*'s]
Argus' L   37a jealousy's.—] Jealousy's.ʌ L   37b —No more, no more—] ʌ~, ~! L

Frank. If you e'er lov'd, you'll not refuse to see her:
You promis'd that.
  Ard.   Did I?
  Frank.   Indeed you did.   45
  Ard. Well then, some other time.
  Frank.   No, see her now.
  Ard. Franklin, I know my heart, and dare not see her.
I have an husband's honour to maintain,
I fear the lover's weakness may betray.
Let me not do what honour must condemn,   50
And friendship blush to hear.
  Frank.   That *Arden* never will.
  Mar. Did you but know her grief—
  Ard.   Am I the cause?
Have I, just heaven, have I e'er injur'd her!
Yet I'm the coward.—O prepost'rous fear!
See where she comes—Arm'd with my num'rous wrongs, 55
I'll meet with honourable confidence
Th' offending wife, and look the honest husband.
  Frank. Maria, we'll withdraw—even friendship here
Wou'd seem impertinence.—   [*Exeunt* Franklin *and* Maria.
  Ard.   Be still my heart.
      [Alicia *enters, not seeing* Arden.
  Alic. How shall I bear my *Arden's* just reproaches! 60
Or can a reconcilement long continue,
That's founded on deceit! Can I avow
My secret guilt!—No—At so mean a thought
Abandon'd infamy herself would blush.
Nay, cou'd I live with public loss of honour,   65
Arden would die to see *Alicia* scorn'd.
He's here, earth open—hide me from his sight!
  Ard. Guilt chains her tongue. Lo! silent self-condemn'd,
With tearful eyes and trembling limbs she stands.
  Alic. Fain would I kiss his footsteps—but that look, 70
Where Indignation seems to strive with grief,
Forbids me to approach him.
  Ard.   Who wou'd think
That anguish were not real?
  Alic.   I'm rooted here.
  Ard. Those tears, methinks, ev'n if her guilt were certain,
Might wash away her stains.

(IV. ii) 58 withdraw—even] ~. Ev'n L 63 No—At] ~; at L 67 here, earth] ~.
Earth L sight!] L (Sight); ~. D 74 were] was L 75a stains] L (Stains); pains D.
See Commentary

Alic.   Support me, heaven!   7

Ard. Curse on the abject thought. I shall relapse
To simple dotage. She steals on my heart,
She conquers with her eyes. If I but hear her voice,
Nor earth nor heaven can save me from her snares.
O! let me fly—if I have yet the pow'r.   8

   Alic. O *Arden!* do not, do not leave me thus. [*Kneels, and holds him.*
   Ard. I pray thee loose thy hold.
   Alic.   O never, never.
   Ard. Why should I stay to tell thee of my wrongs,
To aggravate thy guilt, and wound thy soul?
Thyself, if all these agonizing struggles   8
Of tears, of sighs, of groans, of speechless sorrow
Be but sincere—thyself will do it better.
One thing I'll tell thee, (for perhaps 'twill please thee)
Thou'st broke my heart, *Alicia.*
   Alic.   —Oh!   [*She falls to the ground.*
   Ard.   And canst thou,
Can woman pity whom she hath undone?   9
Why dost thou grasp my knees? what woud'st thou say,
If thou cou'dst find thy speech?
   Alic.   O! mercy, mercy!
   Ard. Thou hast had none on me, let go my hand:
Why dost thou press it to thy throbbing heart,
That beats—but not for me?
   Alic.   Then may it ne'er beat more.   9
   Ard. At least, I'm sure it did not always so.
   Alic. For that my soul is pierc'd with deep remorse,
For that I bow me to the dust before thee,
And die to be forgiven. O *Arden! Arden!*
   Ard. Presumptuous fool! what business hast thou here?   10
Did I not know my weakness, and her pow'r!
Rise—rise—*Alicia.*
   Alic.   No: here let me lie
On the bare bosom of this conscious earth,
'Till *Arden* speak the words of peace and comfort,
Or my heart break before him.
   Ard.   O *Alicia,*   1
Thou inconsistent spring of grief and joy,
Whence bitter streams and sweet alternate flow,

(IV. ii) 79 heaven] L (Heav'n); ~, D   80 O!] ~ʌ L   fly] ~! L   86 sorrow]
Sorrows L   88 tell thee,] L; ~ʌ D   (for . . . thee)] ʌ~,ʌ L   89b —Oh] ʌ~ L
89bSD *to*] on L   93 me, let] ~. Let L   hand:] Hand! L   100 hast] hadst L
102a Rise—rise—] ~, ~, L   107 streams] L (Streams); ~, D

Come to my arms, and in this too fond bosom
Disburden all the fulness of thy soul.
    Alic. Let me approach with awe that sacred temple,   110
Resume my seat, and dwell for ever there.
    Ard. There ever reign, as on thy native throne,
Thou lovely wanderer.
    Alic.   Am I at last,
In error's fatal mazes long bewilder'd,
Permitted here to find my peace and safety!   115
    Ard. Dry up thy tears; and tell me, truly tell me:
Has my long-suffering love at length prevail'd,
And art thou mine indeed?
    Alic.   Heaven is my witness,
I love thee, *Arden*; and esteem thy love
Above all earthly good. Thy kind forgiveness   120
Speaks to my soul that peaceful calm confirm'd,
Which reason and reflexion had begun.
    Ard. Thou'rt cheaply purchas'd with unnumber'd sighs,
With many a bitter tear, and years of patience,
Thou treasure of more worth than mines of gold.   125
I will not doubt my happiness. Thou art,
Thou wilt be mine, ever, and only mine.
    Alic. I am, I will. I ne'er knew joy 'till now.
    Ard. This is our truest, happiest nuptial day.
To-night, thou knowest according to my custom,   130
Our yearly fair returning with *St. Valentine*,
I treat my friends. I go to countenance
Their honest mirth, and chear them with my bounty.
'Till happy night, farewel. My best *Alicia*,
How will our friends rejoice, our foes repine,   135
To see us thus?
    Alic.   —Thus ever may they see us!   [*Exit* Arden.
The wandering fires that have so long misled me,
Are now extinguish'd, and my heart is *Arden*'s.
The flow'ry path of innocence and peace
Shines bright before, and I shall stray no longer.   140
Whence then these sighs, and why these floods of tears?
Sighs are the language of a broken heart,
And tears the tribute each enlighten'd eye
Pays, and must pay, for vice and folly past.
And yet the painful'st virtue hath its pleasure: 145
Tho' dangers rise, yet peace restor'd within,

  (IV. ii)   127 ever, and only mine.] ever$_\wedge$ ~? L   134 night,] L (Night); ~$_\wedge$ D
136bsp [*Exit* Arden.] L (Exit); *not in* D

My soul collected shall undaunted meet them.
Tho' trouble, grief, and death, the lot of all,
On good and bad without distinction fall;
The soul which conscious innocence sustains,   15◦
Supports with ease these temporary pains;
But stung with guilt and loaded by despair,
Becomes itself a burden none can bear.

[*Exit* Alicia.

SCENE III.

The street. People at a distance as at a Fair.

Enter Arden *on one side, and* Black Will *and*
Shakebag *on the other,* Green *directing them.*

B. Will. Shakebag, you'll second me—S'blood, give the way.   [*Jostles* Arden.
Shake. May we not pass the streets?
Ard. I saw you not.
B. Will. Your sight perhaps is bad, your feeling may be better.   [*Strikes him.*
Ard. Insolent villains!   [*Draws.*
B. Will. Come, we'll teach you manners.
Ard. Both at once! barb'rous cowards!

Enter Mosby.

Mos.   O bloody dogs! attempt a life so precious!—
B. Will. This is a fury, *George*.   [Black Will *and* Shakebag *beaten off.*   ¹
Shake. —I've pink'd him tho'—
Ard.   Villains come back, and finish your design.
Mos.   Shall I pursue them, sir?
Ard.   Not for the world—
          Mosby! amazing generosity!
Mos.   I hope you are not hurt.
Ard.   Pierc'd to the heart—
Mos.   Forbid it, heaven! quick, let me fly for help.
Ard.   With sharp reflexion:—*Mosby*, I can't bear
          To be so far oblig'd to one I've wrong'd.
Mos.   Who wou'd not venture life to save a friend?
Ard.   From you I've not deserv'd that tender name.
Mos.   No more of that—wou'd I were worthy of it!

(IV. ii)   148 Tho'] L *does not indent*   153SD [*Exit* Alicia.] L (Exit ~ ∧); *not in* D
SCENE III] *Ed.*; SCENE IV D; Scene 4ᵗʰ L.   1 me—] ~. L   S'blood,] Blood! L
way.] Way! L   9SD Will] L; ~. D   *beaten off*] are beaten off L   10 tho'—] ~. L
12b world—] World. L   16 reflexion:—] Reflection.∧ L

Ard. I own my heart, by boiling passions torn,
  Forgets its gentleness—yet is ever open
  To melting gratitude. O say what price
  Can buy your friendship?

Mos.   —Only think me yours.

Ard. Easy indeed. I am too much oblig'd.   25
  Why reek'd not your good sword its justice on me,
  When mad with jealous rage, in my own house,
  I urg'd you to my ruin?

Mos.   —I lov'd you then
  With the same warmth as now.

Ard.   —What's here! you bleed.
  Let me bind up your wound.

Mos.   —A trifle, sir—   30

Ard. Your friendship makes it so.—See, *Franklin*, see

                    Enter Franklin.

  The man I treated as a coward, bleeding,
  (Wretch that I am!) for his defence of me.
  Look to your wound. And, *Mosby*, let us hope
  You'll sup with me. There will be honest *Bradshaw*,   35
  And *Franklin* here, and—

Mos.   —Sir, I will not fail.

Frank. I shall not come.

Ard.   —Nay, *Franklin*, that's unkind.
  Prithee—

Frank.   —Nay, urge me not.—I have my reasons.

Mos. Avoids my company!—So much the better.
  His may not be so proper. [*Aside.*]—An hour hence,   40
  If you are not engag'd, we'll meet at *Fowl*'s.

Ard. I will be there.

Mos.   Till then I take my leave.   [*Exit* Mosby.

Ard. How have I been mistaken in this man?

Frank. How are you sure you're not mistaken now?

Ard. No doubt he loves me; and I blush to think   45
  How I've suspected him, and wrong'd *Alicia*.

Frank. May you be ever happy in your wife:
  But—

(IV. iii) 23 say] ~, L   24b —Only] ∧~ L   28b —I] ∧~ L   29b —What's]
∧~ L   30b —A] ∧~ L   sir—] Sir. L   31 so.—] ~.∧ L   33 (Wretch . . . am!)]
∧~!∧ L   36b —Sir] ∧~ L   37b —Nay] ∧~ L   38b —Nay] ∧~ L   not.—]
~;∧ L   39 company!—] Company!∧ L   40 —An] ∧~ L   41 you are] you're L
44 sure] L; ~, D   45–51 *Ard.* No doubt . . . then ever.] *not in* L   47 your] *Ed.*; you D

Ard.	Speak—But what? Let's have no riddles here.
	Can she be innocent, and *Mosby* guilty?
Frank.	To speak my thoughts, this new officious fondness 50
	Makes me suspect:—I like him worse than ever.
Ard.	Because I like him better. What a churl!
Frank.	You're credulous, and treat my serious doubts
	With too much levity. You vex me, *Arden.* [*Exit.*
Ard.	Believe me, friend, you'll laugh at this hereafter. [*Exit the other way.* 55

Mosby, *having watch'd* Franklin *out, re-enters
with* Green.

Mos.	The surly friend has left him—As I wish'd—
	You see how eagerly the foolish fowl
	Flies headlong to our snare: now to inclose him.
	At eight the guests are bidden to his banquet,
	And only *Michael*, of his numerous train, 60
	Keeps home with his *Alicia*. He'll secure
	The keys of all the doors, and let you in
	With my two trusty blood-hounds. *Alicia* seems
	Averse at present—
Gr.	—She'll not dare betray us.
Mos.	Not when the deed is done. We know too much. 65
	She'll be our prisoner, and shall be observ'd.
	Towards evening, then, upon a slight pretence
	To pass an hour at draughts, (a game he loves)
	I'll draw this husband home. You'll be prepar'd
	In th' inner room, (*Michael* will shew it you) 70
	'Till at a signal given, you all rush forth,
	And strangle him.
Gr.	Good—'tis a death that leaves
	No bloody character to mark the place.
Mos.	Howe'er, come all provided with your daggers.
	Do you seek *Michael*, I'll instruct the rest. 75
Gr.	What shall the signal be?
Mos.	—These words in th' game,
	I take you now.
Gr.	—*Arden*! thou'rt taken now indeed.
Mos.	His body, thrown behind the abbey-wall,
	Shall be descried by th'early passenger

(IV. iii) 52 What a churl!] ~, a Churl? L 54SD [*Exit.*] *not in* L 55SD [*Exit the other way.*] (Exeunt severally∧ L 55+SD Mosby . . . Green.] Mosby reenters with Green having watch'd Franklin out. L 58 our] the L 64a present—] ~. L 64b —She'll] ∧~ L 68 (a game he loves)] ∧a Game ~, ∧ L 70 (*Michael* . . . you)] ∧Michael~,∧ L 72b Good—] ~! L 76b—These] ∧~ L 77b —*Arden*!] ∧Arden, L 79 th'early] the' early L

   Returning from the Fair.—My friend, thy hand—   80
   Shakes it?—Be firm, and our united strength
   With ease shall cast dead *Arden* to the earth.
 Gr. Thanks to his foolish tenderness of soul.
 Mos. True, he who trusts an old invet'rate foe,
   Bares his own breast, and courts the fatal blow. [*Exeunt.* 85

    The end of the fourth act.

ACT V.

SCENE I.

Arden's house.

Alicia *alone.*

What have I heard! Is this the house of *Arden*!
O! that the power which has so often sav'd him,
Wou'd send his guardian angel to him now,
To whisper in his ear his present danger!
Fly, *Arden*, fly, avoid this fatal roof,
Where murder lurks, and certain death awaits thee:
Wander—no matter where—Turn but from hence,
Thou canst not miss thy way.—The house is theirs.—
I am suspected—*Michael* guards the door—
And ev'n *Maria's* absent. Bloody *Mosby*,
These are the fruits of thy detested lust.
But hark, the fiends approach.—*Green* had humanity,

Enter Green, Black Will, Shakebag, Michael.

Cou'd I prevail on him!—O sir—   [*Talks apart with* Green.
B. Will. What a fair house! rich furniture! what piles of massy plate! And then
yon iron chest. Good plunder, comrade.
Shake. And madam *Arden* there—A prize worth them all to me.
B. Will. And shall that fawning, whiteliver'd coward, *Mosby*, enjoy all these?
Shake. No doubt he wou'd, were we the fools he thinks us.

Gr.	Had he as many lives as drops of blood,
	I'd have them all.— [*To* Alicia.
Alic.	But for one single night—
Gr.	I'd not defer his fate a single hour,
	Tho' I were sure myself to die the next.
	So, peace, irresolute woman—and be thankful
	For thy own life.
Alic.	—O mercy, mercy—
Gr.	Yes,
	Such mercy as the nursing lioness,
	When drain'd of moisture by her eager young,
	Shews to the prey that first encounters her.

B. Will. Who talks of mercy, when I am here?

Gr. She wou'd prevent us; but our steady courage
    Laughs at her coward arts. [*Knocking gently at the gate.*] Why, *Michael.* 30

Mich.   —Sir!

Gr. Thou bloodless coward, what dost tremble at?
    Dost thou not hear a knocking at the gate?   [*Exit* Michael.
    Mosby, no doubt. How like a sly adulterer,
    Who steals at midnight, and with caution gives
    Th'appointed signal to his neighbour's wife.   35

B. Will. Which is the place where we're to be conceal'd?

Gr. This inner room.

B. Will. 'Tis well.—The word is, Now I take *you*. [*Knocking louder than before.*

Gr. Ay, there's authority. That speaks the master.
    He seems in hast: 'Twere pity he shou'd wait,   40
    Now we're so well prepar'd for his reception.   [Green,
                    Black Will, *and* Shakebag *go into the inner room.*

                    Alicia *remains alone.*

Alic. Now whither are they gone?—The door's unbar'd.
    I hear the sound of feet. Shou'd it be *Arden*,
    And *Mosby* with him—I can't bear the doubt,
    Nor wou'd I be resolv'd. Be hush'd my fears,   45
    'Tis *Mosby*, and alone. [*Enter* Mosby.] Sir; hear me, *Mosby.*

Mos. Madam, is this a time?

Alic.   —I will be heard,
    And mark me, when I swear, never hereafter,
    By look, word, act—

Mos.   Be damn'd—your husband—

Alic.   Ha!—

                                          [*She screams.*

                    Enter Arden *and* Michael.

Ard. Am I a monster, that I fright thee thus?   [*To* Michael. 50
    Say, what has happen'd since I left the house?
    Thou look'st, *Alicia*, as if wild amazement
    Had chang'd thee to the image of herself.

Alic. Is *Franklin* with you?

Ard.   No.

Alic.   Nor *Fowl*, nor *Bradshaw*?

(v. i)   30aSD *Knocking*] a knocking L   30b —Sir] ∧~ L   34 with] at L
38SD *Knocking*] a Knocking L   40 hast] haste L. *See Commentary*   41SD Shakebag]
L; ~, D   41+SD *Alicia . . . alone.*] *not in* L   46 Sir;] Alic: Sir, L, *beginning a new line*
47b —I] ∧~ L   49b damn'd—] ~!— L   husband—] Husband. L
49c Ha!—] ~!∧ L   49c+SD *Enter . . . Michael.*] L *includes before line* 49c
54a *Franklin*] L (Franklin); *Frankland* D

Ard. Neither, but both expected.—

Alic.   Merciful heav'n!   5.

Ard. I meant to dedicate this happy night

To mirth and joy, and thy returning love.   *[She sighs.*

Make me not sad, *Alicia*: For my sake

Let discontent be banish'd from your brow,

And welcome *Arden*'s friends with laughing eyes.   6.

Amongst the first let *Mosby* be enroll'd—

Alic. The villain!

Ard.   Nay, I am too well convinc'd

Of *Mosby*'s friendship, and *Alicia*'s love,

Ever to wrong them more by weak suspicions.

I've been indeed to blame, but I will make thee   6.

A large amends, *Alicia*.—Look upon him,

As on the man that gave your husband's life.

Alic. Wou'd take my husband's life!—I'll tell him all,

And cast this load of horror from my soul:

Yet, 'tis a dreadful hazard. Both must die.   7

A fearful thought! *Franklin* may come, or *Bradshaw*—

O let me not precipitate his fate!   *[Aside.*

Mos. I see my presence is offensive there.   *[Going.*

Ard. Alicia! No—She has no will but mine.

Mos. It is not fit she shou'd:—and yet—perhaps—   7

'Twere better, sir—Permit me to retire.

Ard. No more—Our friendship publickly avow'd

Will clear her injur'd virtue to the world.

Mos. Something there is in that—

Ard.   —It is a debt

I owe to both your fames, and pay it freely.   8

Mos. For her sake then, not for my own.

Alic.   —O damn'd dissembler.

                                   [Aside.

Ard. Come, take your seat; this shall not save your money.

Bring us the Tables, *Michael*—   *[They sit and play.*

Alic.   —O just heaven!   *[Aside.*

Wilt thou not interpose?—How dread this pause!

Ten thousand terrors crowd the narrow space.   8

Ard. Your thoughts are absent, *Mosby*.

B. Will. Blood! why don't *Mosby* give the word?

Mich. Give back, the game's against him.

(v. i)   55a expected.—] ~.∧ L   56 meant] mean L   59 your] thy L   67 that]
who L   husband's] Husband L. *See Commentary*   75 yet—] ~, L   79b —It] ∧~ L
81b–81bSD dissembler. [*Aside.*] Ed., *following* L; D ([~.]) *prints immediately after speech-heading*
83b–83bSD heaven! [*Aside.*] Ed., *following* L; D ([~.]) *prints immediately after speech-heading*

Alic. Fly, *Franklin*! fly, to save thy *Arden*'s life!
 Murder herself, that chases him in view,   90
 Beholding me starts back, and for a moment
 Suspends her thirst of blood.   [*Apart.*
Ard. Come, give it up; I told you I shou'd win.   [*Rises.*
Mos. No, I see an advantage; move again.
Ard. There.
Mos.   Now I take *you*.   95

[Black Will *throws a scarf over* Arden*'s head, in order to strangle him; but* Arden
 disengages himself, wrests a dagger from Shakebag, *and stands on his defence, 'till*
 Mosby *getting behind and seizing his arm, the rest assassinate him.*

Alic. O pow'r omnipotent! make strong his arm,
 Give him to conquer. Ha! my prayers are curses,
 And draw down vengeance where they meant a blessing.
Ard. Inhospitable villain!
Alic.   O! he dies.
Ard. O hold your bloody—*Mosby* too! Nay, then   [*Falling.* 100
 I yield me to my fate.—Is this, *Alicia*,
 This the return for my unequall'd love?
Alic. Or death, or madness, wou'd be mercies now,
 Therefore beyond my hopes.
Ard.   O *Mosby, Michael, Green*,
 Why have you drawn my blood upon your souls?   105
Mos. Behold her there, to whom I was betroth'd,
 And ask no further—
Gr.   —Think on thy abbey-lands
 From injur'd *Green*.
Ard.   —You now are your own judges,
 But we shall meet again where right and truth—
 Who—who are these? But I forgive you all.   110
 Thy hand, *Alicia*—
Alic.   —I'll not give it thee.
Ard. O wretched woman! have they kill'd thee too?
 A deadly paleness, agony, and horror
 On thy sad visage sit. My soul hangs on thee,
 And tho' departing—just departing—loves thee: 115
 Is loth to leave, unreconcil'd to thee,
 This useless mangled tenement of clay.
 Dismiss her pleas'd, and say thou'rt innocent.

(v. i) 89 life!] L (Life); ~. D   92SD *Apart*] aside L   95b *you.*] you! L
96 arm,] Arm! L   100 Nay,] L; ~∧ D   102 unequall'd] L; unequal D
107a further—] ~. L   107b —Think] ∧~ L   108b —You] ∧~ L   110 Who—
who] ~? ~ L these?] ~?— L   111a *Alicia*—] Alicia. L   111b —I'll] ∧~ L

Alic. All hell contains not such a guilty wretch.
Ard. Then welcome death! tho' in the shape of murder.   12
     How have I doated to idolatry!
     Vain, foolish wretch, and thoughtless of hereafter,
     Nor hop'd, nor wish'd a heaven beyond her love.—
     Now, unprepar'd, I perish by her hate.
Alic. Tho' blacker, and more guilty than the fiends,   12
     My soul is white from this accursed deed.
     O *Arden*! hear me—
Ard.   —Full of doubts I come,
     O thou Supreme, to seek thy awful presence.
     My soul is on the wing. I own thy justice.
     Prevent me with thy mercy.   [*Dies.*
Alic.   —Turn not from me: 1
     Behold me, pity me, survey my sorrows.
     I who despis'd the duty of a wife,
     Will be thy slave.—Spit on me, spurn me, sir,
     I'll love thee still.—O couldst thou court my scorn,
     And now abhor me, when I love thee more,   1
     If possible, than e'er thou lov'dst *Alicia*.
Mos. Mad fool, he's dead, and hears thee not.
Alic.   —'Tis false—
     He smiles upon me, and applauds my vengeance.   [*Snatches a*
            dagger, and strikes at Mosby.—*A knocking at the gate.*
Mos. Damnation!—
B. Will. 'Sdeath! we shall leave our work unfinish'd, and be betray'd at last.— 1
Let's hide the body.
Mos.   —Force her away.
Alic.   Inhuman bloody villains!   [*She swoons, as she*
                       is forc'd from the body.

              Enter Maria.

Mar. Mosby here!—
     My sliding feet, as they move trembling forwards,
     Are drench'd in blood. O may I only fancy   1
     That *Arden* there lies murder'd—
Mos.   —How fares *Alicia?*—
Alic.   As the howling damn'd:

(v. i)   123 love.—] Love: ∧ L   127a me—] ~! L   127b —Full] ∧~ L
128 Supreme,] Supreem! L   129 justice.] Justice: L   130a mercy.] Mercy— L
130b —Turn] ∧~ L   133 slave.—] Slave. ∧ L   me, spurn] ~! Spurn L   137a fool,]
Fool! L   137b —'Tis] ∧~ L   138sd *Snatches*] She snatches L   139 Damnation!—]
~! ∧ L   140 last.—] ~. ∧ L   142a —Force] ∧~ L   143 here!—] ~! ∧ L
146 murder'd—] Murder'd! L   147a —How . . . *Alicia?*—] ∧~Alicia? ∧ L
147b–148a As the . . . hell—] *line-division follows* L; D *prints as one line*

And thou my hell—

Mar.   *Mosby*! Unhappy brother!

If thou hast done this deed, hope not to 'scape:

Mercy herself, who only seeks for crimes,   150

That she may pardon and reform the guilty,

Wou'd change her nature at a sight like this.

Enter Michael.

Mich. The guests are come—the servants all return'd.

Mos.   *Alicia*, be thyself; and mask thy heart   [Mosby *lifts up* Alicia.

From ev'ry prying eye with courteous smiles.   155

Alic. Thou canst not think me mean enough to live.

Mos.   You wou'd not choose an ignominious death?

Alic. That's all I dread—Might but the silent grave,

When it receives me to its dark abode,

Hide, with my dust, my shame!—O might that be,   160

And *Arden*'s death reveng'd.—'Tis my sole prayer.

If not, may awful justice have her course.   [*Exit* Alicia.

Mos.   Sister! Our lives are thine—

Mar.   Tho' *Mosby* has shook off

Humanity, I can't be his accuser.   [*Exit* Maria.

Mos.   Follow them, *Green*, and watch *Alicia*'s conduct.   165

Gr.   I will, but cannot answer for my own.

O *Arden*! *Arden*! cou'd we change conditions!   [*Exit* Green.

B. Will. Why, what a crew of cowards! In the same moment murdering
and repenting.

Mos.   Give me the ring that is on *Arden*'s finger.   170

Shake. There. Will you have his purse too?

Mos.   No, keep that.

B. Will. Thanks for our own: we shou'd have kept the ring, were it not
too remarkable. But how must we dispose of the body?

Mos.   Convey it thro' the garden, to the field   175

Behind the abbey-wall: *Michael* will shew the way.

The night is dark and cloudy—yet take heed—

The house is full of company.

B. Will. Sir, if you doubt our conduct, do't yourself.

Mos.   Nay, gentlemen—

Shake.   Pretend to direct us!   180

Mos.   For your own sakes—*Arden* will soon be mist.

(v. i) 148a hell—] Hell. L   148b *Mosby*!] L (Mosby); *not in* D. *See Commentary*
154SD Mosby] *not in* L   158 dread—] ~. L   160 be,] ~! L   161 reveng'd.—]
~!ᴧ L   163a thine—] ~. L   163b–164 off | Humanity] L; off humanity D, *printing*
speech as prose   170 the ring] ring L   173–4 kept . . . body?] *Ed., arranging as prose:* D
and L *treat as verse (see collation)*   179 conduct,] L (Conduct); ~; D

Shake.	We know our business, sir.
Mos.	I doubt it not.

There's your reward. The horses both are saddled,
And ready for your flight.

B. Will. Use them yourself:
I hope we're as safe as you.   1

Mos. Why, gentlemen—*Arden*, I us'd thee worse.   [*Aside.*

B. Will. We shall take care however for our own sakes.

Mos. 'Tis very well—I hope we all are friends.
So—softly—softly—*Michael*, not that door—   [Michael *going
out at the wrong door.*
So—make what speed you can: I'll wait you there.   [*Exeunt.* 1

SCENE II.

A hall in Arden*'s house.*

Mosby *alone.*

They must pass undescry'd: gardens and fields
Are dreary deserts now. Night-fowls and beasts of prey
Avoid the pinching rigour of the season,
Nor leave their shelter at a time like this.
And yet this night, this ling'ring winter night,
Hung with a weight of clouds that stops her course,
Contracts new horrors, and a deeper black,
From this damn'd deed.—*Mosby*, thou hast thy wish.
Arden is dead; now count thy gains at leisure.
Dangers without, on every side suspicion;
Within my starting conscience, mark such wounds
As hell can equal, only murderers feel.   [*A pause.*
This, this the end of all my flatt'ring hopes!
O! happiest was I in my humble state:
Tho' I lay down in want, I slept in peace:
My daily toil begat my night's repose,
My night's repose made day-light pleasing to me.
But now I've climb'd the top-bough of the tree,
And sought to build my nest among the clouds:
The gentlest gales of summer shake my bed,

(v. i)   185 we're] we are L   188 well—] ~. L   189 So—softly—softly] ~,
~, ~! L   door—] Door: L   189SD [Michael . . . *door.*] *not in* L   190 So—] ~; L
SCENE II. *A hall . . . alone.*] Scene shuts. Mosby alone. L, *continuing scene* i   8 wish.] Wish, L
11 starting] staring L   conscience,] L (Conscience);   ~_∧ D. *See Commentary*   wounds] L
(Wounds); ~, D   12 hell] Hell alone L   12SD [*A pause.*] *not in* L   15 lay] laid L

And dreams of murder harrow up my soul.
But hark!—Not yet:—'Tis dreadful being alone.
This awful silence, that unbroken reigns
Thro' earth and air, awakes attention more,
Than thunder bursting from ten thousand clouds: 25
S'death!—'tis but *Michael*—Say—

Enter Michael.

Mich.   Dead *Arden* lies
Behind the abbey—'tis a dismal sight!
It snow'd apace while we dispos'd the body.
   Mos. And not as you return'd?
Mich.   No, sir—
Mos.   That's much—
Shou'd you be question'd as to *Arden*'s death,   30
You'll not confess?
   Mich.   No, so *Maria*'s mine.
Mos. She's thine, if all a brother can—
   Mich.   —What's if?
I bought her dear, at hazard of my soul,
And force shall make her mine.—
   Mos.   —Why, how now, coward!

Enter Maria.

   Mar. The guests refuse to take their seats without you.   35
Alicia's grief too borders on distraction.
Thy presence may appease—
   Mos.   Increase it rather.
Mar. Michael, your absence too has been observ'd.
Mos. Say we are coming.   [*Exit* Maria.
   Mich.   One thing I'd forgot.   [*Returning.*
Soon as the company have left the house,   40
The ruffians will return.
   Mos.   What wou'd the villains?
 Mich. They mutter'd threats and curses twixt their teeth,
And seem'd not satisfied with their reward.   [*Exit* Michael.
   Mos. Let them take all. Ambition, av'rice, lust,
That drove me on to murder, now forsake me.   45
O *Arden*! if thy discontented ghost

(v. ii)   22   —Not yet:] ∧~! L   23   awful] aweful L   27   abbey—] Abbey. L
28   apace] L; a pace D. *See Commentary*   29b   sir—] Sir. L   29c   much—] ~! L
32b   —What's] ∧~ L   34a   mine.—] ~.∧ L   34b   —Why] ∧~ L   now,] ~! L
34b+SD   *Enter* Maria.] Enter ~∧ L, *which includes after line* 34a   39b   I'd] I had L
42   twixt their teeth] L (Teeth); *not in* D   44   them] 'em L

Still hovers here to see thy blood reveng'd,
View, view the anguish of this guilty breast,
And be appeas'd.   [*Exit.*

SCENE III.

A room in Arden's *house.*
A table spread for supper.

Green, Bradshaw, Adam Fowl, Alicia, Maria, *&c.*

Brad. Madam, be comforted.
A. Fowl. Some accident, or business unforseen,
          Detains him thus.
Brad.   I doubt not of his safety.
Alic. I thank you, gentlemen; I know you lov'd
       My *Arden* well, and kindly speak your wishes.

Enter Mosby.

Mos. I am asham'd I've made you wait: be seated.
Gr. Madam, first take your place.
Alic.   Make me not mad—
       To me henceforth all places are alike.   [*Sits.*
Mos. Come, since we want the master of the house,
       I'll take his seat for once.
Alic.   Dares he do this?   [*Aside.*
Mos. I'm much afflicted that he stays so late;
       The times are perilous.
Gr.   And he has enemies.
       Tho' no man, sure, did e'er deserve them less.
Mos. This day he was assaulted in the street.
Gr. You sav'd him then.
Mos.   Wou'd I were with him now!
Mar. She starts, her looks are wild. [*Aside.*]—How fare you, madam?
Alic. I'm lost in admiration of your brother.
Mar. I fear her more than ever. [*Aside.*]—Madam, be merry.
Mos. Michael, some wine. Health and long life: to *Arden.*   [*Drinks.*
Alic. The good you wish, and have procur'd for *Arden,*   [*Rising.*
       Light on thyself.
Mar.   For heaven's sake!—

(v. ii)   48 View, view] View L   SCENE III.] Scene 2ᵈ. L   SD *A room . . . house.*]
not in L   3a Detains] L; detains D   6 I've] I L   7b mad—] ~! L   13 no]
not in L   16 starts, her] ~ʌ are L   18 —Madam] ʌ~ L   19SD [*Drinks.*] *not in* L
20SD [*Rising.*] L *includes* SD *after line* 21a   21a thyself] yourself L   21b sake!—]
Sake!ʌ L

Alic.	Give me way. *[Comes forward.*
	Let them dispatch, and send me to my husband: *[All rise.*
	I've liv'd too long with falshood and deceit. *[Knocking at the gate.*
A. Fowl.	What noise is that? *[Exit* Michael.
Brad.	Pray heaven, that all be right.
Mos.	Bar all the doors.

Enter Michael.

Mich.	We are discover'd, sir. *[To* Mosby.	25
	The mayor with officers, and men in arms.	

Enter Mayor, *&c.*

Mayor.	Go you with these, and do as I directed. *[Exeunt officers and others.*	
	I'm sorry that the duty of my office	
	Demands a visit so unseasonable.	
Mos.	Your worship doubtless were a welcome guest	30
	At any hour; but wherefore thus attended?	
Mayor.	I have received a warrant from the council	
	To apprehend two most notorious ruffians;	
	And information being made on oath,	
	That they were seen to enter here to-night,	35
	I'm come to search.	
Gr.	I'm glad it is no worse. *[Aside.*	
Mos.	And can you think that *Arden* entertains	
	Villains like those you speak of? Were he here,	
	You'd not be thank'd for this officiousness.	
Mayor.	I know my duty, sir, and that respect,	40
	So justly due to our good neighbour's worth.—	
	But where is *Arden*?	
Alic.	Heavens! where indeed!	
Mar.	*Alicia,* for my sake— *[Aside.*	
Alic.	If I were silent,	
	Each precious drop of murder'd *Arden*'s blood	
	Wou'd find a tongue, and cry to heaven for vengeance.	45
Mayor.	What says the lady?	
Mos.	Oh! sir, heed her not:	
	Her husband has not been at home to-night,	
	And her misboding sorrow for his absence,	
	Has almost made her frantic.	
Mayor.	Scarce an hour,	
	Since I beheld him enter here with you.	50

(v. iii)   21CSD   *Comes forward.*] (Comes forward∧) They all rise∧) L   22 them] 'em L
dispatch,] ~∧ L   22SD *[All rise.]* not in L *(see* 21CSD, *above)*   23SD *Knocking*] A Knocking L
27SD *and others*] &c. L   28 I'm] I am L   33 apprehend] L.; appprehend D
41 worth.—] Worth.∧ L   43a sake—] Sake. L   46b Oh! sir,] Oh, Sir! L

Mos. The darkness of the night deceiv'd you, sir:
It was a stranger, since departed hence.
Mayor. That's most surprising. No man knows him better.
Frank. [*Without.*] Within there—ho—bar up your gates with care,
And set a watch—Let not a man go by—   5

Franklin *and others enter with lights.*

And ev'ry tongue, that gave not its consent
To *Arden*'s death, join mine and cry aloud
To heaven and earth for justice. Honest *Arden*,
My friend—is murder'd!
Mayor.   Murder'd!
Gr.   How?
Mos.   By whom?
Frank. How shall I utter what my eyes have seen!   6
Horrid with many a gaping wound he lies
Behind the abbey, a sad spectacle!
O vengeance! vengeance!
Mayor.   Justly art thou moved.
Passion is reason in a cause like this.
Frank. Eternal Providence, to whose bright eye   6
Darkness itself is as the noon-day blaze,
Who brings the midnight murd'rer and his deeds
To light and shame, has in their own security
Found these.
Mayor.   Here seize them all—this instant: [Alicia *faints.*
Look to the lady. This may be but feign'd.   [Alicia *is carried out.*   7
Your charge but goes along with my suspicions.
Brad. And mine.
A. Fowl.   And mine.
Frank.   First hear me, and then judge,
Whether on slight presumptions I accuse them.
These honest men (neighbours and townsmen all)
Conducted me, dropping with grief and fear,
To where the body lay;—with them I took these notes,
Not to be trusted to the faithless memory.
'Huge clots of blood and some of *Arden*'s hair

(v. iii)   53 most] more L   him] L; *not in* D   better.] ~. Enter Franklin & others, with
Lights. L. *See Commentary*   54SD [*Without.*]] *not in* L (*see* 53, *above*)   54 there—ho—]
~, ~! L   55 watch—] Watch! L   55+SD Franklin . . . *lights.*] *Ed.*, D (~—D); *not in* L
(*see* 53, *above*)   59a friend—] Friend, L   murder'd!] L; ~. D   63b art] are L
69b all—] ~ ∧ L   70 lady] Woman L   70SD [Alicia *is carried out.*] *Ed.*; *not in* D, L.
See Commentary   71 along] L; a long D   74 men (neighbours and townsmen all)] *Ed.*,
following W1, D (men,); men ∧Neighbours & Townsmen all, L   76 lay;—with] ~.
∧With L

       May still be seen upon the garden-wall;
       Many such rushes as these floors are strew'd with,   80
       Stick to his shoes and garments: and the prints
       Of several feet may in the snow be trac'd,
       From the stark body to the very door.'
     These are presumptions he was murder'd here,
     And that th'assassins having borne his corse   85
     Into the fields, hither return'd again.
Mos. Are these your proofs?
Gr.   These are but circumstance,
     And only prove thy malice.
Frank.   —And this scarf,
     Known to be *Arden*'s, in the court was found,
     All blood.—   90
Mayor. —Search 'em—
Mich.   I thought I'd thrown it down the well.   [*Aside.*
Mayor. —[*To an officer.*] Enter that room, and search the lady there;
     We may perhaps discover more.

             *Officer goes out and re-enters, in the mean time
                 another officer searches* Mosby *and* Green.

1st Officer. On *Arden*'s wife I found this letter, sir.
2d Officer. And I this ring on *Mosby*.
Mayor.   —Righteous heaven!   95
     Well may'st thou hang thy head, detested villain:
     This very day did *Arden* wear this ring,
     I saw it on his hand.—
Mos. I freely yield me to my fate.

                 Enter another officer.

Officer. We've seiz'd two men behind some stacks of wood.   100
Mayor. Well, bring 'em in.—   [Black Will *and* Shakebag *brought in.*
                 —They answer the description:
     But let them wait 'till I have done with these.
     Heavens! what a scene of villany is here!   [*Having read the letter.*
B. Will. Since we're sure to die, tho' I cou'd wish 'twere in better company,
(for I hate that fawning rascal, *Mosby*) I'll tell the truth for once. He has been 105

(v. iii)   88b —And] ∧~ L   91a *Mayor.*—Search 'em—] *not in* L   92SD [*To an
officer.*] *not in* L   92–3 Enter . . . more.] Search 'em: we may perhaps discover more. L. *See
Commentary*   93+SD *Officer . . .* Green.] The Officers search Mosby, Green & Alicia. L
94 letter, sir.] L (Letter, Sir); letter. D   95b —Righteous] ∧~ L   96 villain:] Villain! L
98 hand.—] Hand.∧ L   99 *Mos.* I freely . . . my fate.] *Ed.*, D (fate∧ D); *not in* L
99+SD *another*] *not in* L   100 We've] Worshipful Sir, | We've L. *See Commentary*
101aSD Black . . . in.] Enter Black Will; Shakebag &c. L   101b —They] ∧~ L
102 them] 'em L   105 (for . . . *Mosby*)] *Ed.*, D (Mosby, D); ∧for . . . Rascal∧ Mosby,∧ L

long engaged in an affair with *Arden*'s wife there, but fearing a discovery, and
hoping to get into his estate, hired us to hide him.—That's all.

Mayor. And you the horrid deed perform'd?

Shake. We did, with his assistance, and *Green*'s and *Michael*'s.

Mayor. This letter proves *Alicia*, from the first,   11
   Was made acquainted with your black design.

B. Will. I know nothing of that: but if she was, she repented of it afterwards.
So, I think, you call that a change of mind.

Mayor. That may avail her at the bar of heav'n,
   But is no plea at our's. [*Alicia brought in.*] Bear them to prison;   11
   Load them with irons, make them feel their guilt,
   And groan away their miserable hours,
   Till sentence of the law shall call them forth
   To publick execution.—

Alic.   —I adore
   Th'unerring hand of justice; and with silence   12
   Had yielded to my fate, but for this maid,
   Who, as my soul dreads justice on her crimes,
   Knew not, or e'er consented to this deed.

Mayor. But did she not consent to keep it secret?

Mos. To save a brother, and most wretched friend.—   1

Mayor. She has undone herself—Behold how innocence
   May suffer in bad fellowship.—And *Bradshaw*,
   My honest neighbour *Bradshaw* too—I read it
   With grief and wonder.—

Brad.   —Madam, I appeal
   To you; as you are shortly to appear   1
   Before a judge that sees our secret thoughts,
   Say, had I knowledge, or—

Alic.   You brought the letter,
   But well I hope, you knew not the contents.

Mayor. Hence with them all, 'till time and farther light
   Shall clear these mysteries.

A. Fowl.   If I'm condemn'd,   1
   My blood be on his head that gives the sentence.
   I'm not accus'd, and only ask for justice.

Frank. You shall have justice all, and rig'rous justice.
   So shall the growth of such enormous crimes,
   By their dread fate be check'd in future times.   1
   Of Avarice, *Mosby* a dread instance prove,
   And poor *Alicia* of unlawful Love.   [*Exeunt.*

(v. iii) 107 him.—] ~.ₐ L 115SD [Alicia *brought in.*]] *not in* L 119a execution. —]
~.ₐ L 119b —I] ₐ~ L 129a wonder.—] Wonderₐ—L 129b —Madam]
ₐ~ L 142 And poor *Alicia*] And, poor Alicia, L 142SD [*Exeunt.*] *Ed.*; *not in* D, L

EPILOGUE,

By a FRIEND.

Spoken by the young Gentlewoman who
performed ALICIA.

An ancient bard, vers'd in dramatick laws,
Has said, (and well he knew to gain his cause)
'The seasoning of a play, is the applause*.'
Within these walls, this truth no doubt will bear,
Without such seasoning, there's no 'biding here.—   5
First for our author: for his play, I mean,
(For he's beyond the reach of critick-spleen);
If he has touch'd your hearts, your tears will show it,
And your hands echo back, you acquit the poet.
Next, our performance; there, we've done our best: 10
And where ought's wanting, you'll supply the rest:
I know you will, you must; from hence I spy,
Good nature sparkling in each generous eye.
Last for my humble self,—thus low I sue;   [Curstying.
Do not too rigid give me all my due: 15
What's wanting, pardon: and if ought appears,
That may be ripen'd by theatrick-years:
Kindly protect the plant, your smiles now raise:
Be mine, obedient thanks; yours, all the praise.

* Ben Jonson's Volpone.

EPILOGUE] L *does not include epilogue*   6 *mean,*] Ed.; ~; D   7 *critick-spleen);*]
Ed.; ~)ᴧ D   18 *raise:*] W1; ~, D

COMMENTARY

SILVIA

NOTE. The music has a separate commentary, pp. 568 ff.

Dedication

Mrs. *Harriott Janssen*] Harriet—formally Henrietta—Janssen was the fourth of the eight children and the eldest daughter of the financier Sir Theodore Janssen (*c.*1658?–1748), a director of the South Sea Company, and a founder and thrice-elected director of the Bank of England. Of Flemish descent, as was Lillo, he had arrived in England with a fortune of £18,000 or more, which by 1720 had grown to *c.*£250,000. In the forfeiture of directors' estates that followed the South Sea collapse Janssen lost something on the order of £200,000, though it should be noted that his allowance of £50,000 was the highest granted. His case in mitigation of liability was apparently a strong one; Sir Richard Steele was among his proponents in the Commons. A different view—evidence that his wealth had become legendary—was expressed by Swift, who wrote of him that he 'amassed such vast sums of money that he settled upon each of his six [sic] children *only* sixty thousand pounds; and yet pleaded poverty, to the House of Commons, when under examination.' (See the Twickenham Edition of the *Poems of Alexander Pope* iii/2. 4 n. 1, concerning l. 158 in the Dublin edition of the *Epistle to Cobham*.) By his own account (*The Case of Sir Theodore Janssen*, 1721) he pleaded not so much poverty as futile probity, and remarked of his children's settlements that he had 'made no such Provision for any of them, but what must be submitted to the pleasure of Parliament.' Swift's figure of £60,000 per child, whether multiplied by eight or six, appears in fact to represent an exaggeration of Janssen's considerable wealth.

Janssen married, in January 1697 (i.e. 1697/8?) according to his *Inventory* (1721), Williamsa, daughter of Sir Robert Henley of the Grange and sister of Anthony Henley. It would appear, by his reckoning in *The Case of Sir Theodore Janssen* as well as in his *Inventory*, that the eight children were born between 1698 and 1710 inclusive, from which one would guess that Henrietta, the fourth child, was born in 1702 or 3. It has not been possible to establish the date of her death, though according to her father's obituary in the *Gentleman's Magazine* all eight children were still living at the time of his death (22 Sept. 1748). She seems never to have married.

One contemporary reference to Henrietta occurs in Lord Hervey's *Memoirs*, where it is related that in 1735 'Miss Janssen, sister to Lord Baltimore's wife', was recruited as a go-between in the business by which, in anticipation of his wedding, the Prince of Wales was separated from his mistress, Anne Vane. Hervey characterizes Miss Janssen as 'a very dexterous lady'. (John, Lord Hervey, *Some Materials Towards Memoirs of the Reign of King George II*, ed. Romney Sedgwick [London, 1931], ii. 482. The reference can only be to Henrietta, whose two sisters, Mary, Lady Baltimore, and Barbara Bladen, were both married by 1735: see below, 1. 19 n.)

A female dedicatee was quite appropriate for *Silvia*, and in addressing Harriet Janssen, Lillo was clearly making a bid for support from the City, as he was later and more successfully to do in dedicating *The London Merchant* to Sir John Eyles. What other considerations Lillo may have had in mind lie within reach only of the purest speculation. It is not even certain when he solicited Miss Janssen's 'Generosity and Condescention in permitting this Address', which was almost certainly printed some six months later than the text (Introduction, pp. 21–2). By her sister's marriage to Lord Baltimore on 20 July 1730—between the printing of the text and that of the dedication—Henrietta Janssen was situated at least on the edge of the Prince of Wales's circle, a connection that might have proved attractive to a playwright (Introduction, p. 15). Whether court gossip concerning Baltimore's earlier amorous conduct had reached Lillo's ears is quite beyond knowing (see below, l. 19 n.).

For details, see *DNB*, s.v. 'Janssen, Sir Theodore'; *Sir Theodore Janssen, Kt. Bart. His Particular and Inventory* (London 1721; issued with *The Particulars and Inventories of the Late Sub-Governor, Deputy-Governor, and Directors of the South-Sea Company . . .* [London, 1721]), which lists his children in birth order; *Verses to the Memory of the Late Sir Theodore Janssen, Bart.* (London, 1754; unique [?] copy in the Bancroft Library, University of California); *The Case of Sir Theodore Janssen, One of the Late Directors of the South-Sea Company* (London, 1721); John Burke and John Bernard Burke, *A Genealogical and Heraldic History of the Extinct and Dormant Baronetcies of England, Ireland, and Scotland*, 2nd edn. (London, 1844); GEC, *Baronetage*. See also indexed references to Janssen in George Rudé, *Hanoverian London 1714–1808* (London, 1971).

9 Interest] influence due to personal connection; power of influencing the actions of others (*OED*).

13 Condescention] affability to one's inferiors, with courteous disregard of difference of rank or position (*OED*).

19 The Noble Lord to whom you are so happily Ally'd] Mary Janssen (*c*.1710–70), Henrietta's youngest sister, married on 20 July 1730 Charles Calvert, fifth Baron Baltimore (1699–1751), hereditary proprietor of the American province of Maryland and Lord of the Bedchamber to Frederick, Prince of Wales. He appears, by contemporary accounts, to have had a rather undistinguished reputation as a courtier. As a bachelor he was himself—ironically enough in the present context—something of a Sir John. Edward Young, writing to Thomas Tickell on 5 June 1727, remarked that 'Ld. Baltamore has been near Death by a Blow from a Tennis Ball to ye great affliction of the Fair, who find no consolation under their misfortune but being beggard at ye Card Table; Money is all the Dear man has left many of them to lose' (*The Correspondence of Edward Young 1683–1765*, ed. Henry Pettit [Oxford, 1971], pp. 56–7). Even more Sir John-like was his conduct in December 1729 towards the widow Mrs Pendarves (later Mrs Delany), whom he had been courting:

> He said he was determined never to marry, unless he was assured of the affection of the person he married. My reply was, can you have a stronger proof (if the person is at her own disposal) than her consenting to marry you? He replied that was not sufficient. I said he was *unreasonable*, upon which he started up and said, 'I find, madam, this is a point in which we shall never agree.' He looked piqued and angry, made a low bow and went away immediately. (Quoted from Mrs Delany's autobiography in R. Brimsley Johnson [ed.], *Mrs. Delany at Court and among the Wits* [London, 1925], p. 78.)

Henrietta's other sister Barbara married in 1731 Col. Thomas Bladen (1698–1780), born at Annapolis in Maryland, who was governor of the province (1742–7) and the executor of Baltimore's will in 1751.

22 Ornament] a person who adorns or adds lustre to his sphere, time, etc. (*OED*). Cf. Note on Alterations, ll. 16–17 and n.; *Marina*, Dedication, l. 35.

23 Admiration] object of admiration or wonder (*OED*).

Table of Songs

Air 47 *stern*] No evidence has been found by which to ascertain whether O's reading *'vain'* is erroneous or based on a variant manuscript source.

Prologue

15 *Toast*] a figurative application of 'toast', the name of the lady being supposed to flavour a bumper like a spiced toast in the drink; thus, any person whose health is proposed and drunk to (*OED*).

33 *Brave*] in this context 'an indeterminate word, used to express the superabundance of any valuable quality in men or things' (Johnson's *Dictionary*, quoted by *OED*).

36 *ere*] O prints *'e'er'*, a common 18th-cent. form of the word characterized as erroneous by *OED*; according to Johnson's *Dictionary* the word 'is sometimes vitiously written *e'er*, as if from *ever*'. The form occurred again in O in the Table of Songs (first line of Air LV), in the present edition silently emended and at III. xvi. 4, but elsewhere (I. ix. 99, II. iv. 50) another erroneous form, *'e're'*, appears. The correct spelling does not occur in O; D and E follow O, except that D substitutes *'e're'* for *'e'er'* at III. xvi. 4. *OED* does not include *'e're'* in its list of earlier forms of 'ere', though it appears in two quotations dated 1647 (edition of 1702) and 1649. ('Er e're'—i.e. 'ere ever'—is found in a quotation dated 1630, though *'e're'* is not listed among the variant forms of 'ever'.) Both *'e'er'* and *'e're'* are corrected to 'ere' throughout this edition to avoid confusion with 'ever'; W1 also routinely corrects the spelling. See also notes to *London Merchant*, Prologue, l. 24; *The Christian Hero*, II. i. 167; *Fatal Curiosity*, III. i. 45. The correct form is used exclusively in early editions of *Marina*, *Elmerick*, and *Arden of Feversham*.

Dramatis Personæ

5 Gaffer] in 17th–18th cent. the usual prefix, in rustic speech, to the name of a man below the rank of those addressed as 'Master' (*OED*). The reading 'Geffer' in O2 appears to be a misprint; the word does not appear in that form in *OED*.

13 Goody] shortened from 'goodwife'. A term of civility formerly applied to a woman, usually a married woman, in humble life; often prefixed as a title to the surname (*OED*).

Note on Alterations

For remarks on the relation of these alterations to the printed text see Introduction, pp. 10 and III. xv n.

SD *Sir* John *discover'd at a Table, reading.*] i.e. the stage shutters are drawn aside to reveal the new scene. Cf. *London Merchant*, I. viiiSD.

5–9 'Tis hard . . . A Poem on a Dwarf!] See III. x. 1–5 n.

5 dispossess] See III. x. 1 n.

16–17 the most shining Ornament of thy Sex] i.e. 'the most shining ornament peculiar to thy sex'. *OED* defines 'ornament' in a figurative sense as 'a quality or circumstance that confers beauty, grace, or honour', quoting 1 Pet. 3: 4, 'the ornament of a meek and quiet spirit'. See Introduction, pp. 8–9, for a discussion of the applicability of 1 Pet. 3: 1–7 to prominent themes in *Silvia*.

An antithesis similar to that in ll. 16–17 is found in Shakespeare, Sonnet 54, ll. 1–2: 'O how much more doth beauty beauteous seem | By that sweet ornament which truth doth give!'

I. ii

8 nearly] in a special degree; particularly (*OED*).

12 Discoveries] revelations, disclosures (*OED*). The once usual meaning of the verb 'to discover'—to disclose, reveal—was gradually superseded by the modern meaning in the 19th cent. Cf. III. i. 44, 'Discovery'.

14 improve] to make profitable or advantageous use of (*OED*). Cf. I. iv. 30 n.

17 Family] servants of a house; the body of persons who live in one house or under one head (*OED*). In this period the word did not necessarily imply blood relationship or a married household (cf. III. v. 21, 'Batchelors Families').

I. iii

1 discover] See I. ii. 12 n.

I. iv

24–26 Long we suspect, and hardly are con-|vinc'd . . . attain'd] The meaning of this sentence is clear in general, but the details of its construction are ambiguous, owing in part to the placing of a comma after 'suspect' and the lack of one after 'convinc'd', and in part to the ambiguous meaning of the verb 'suspect'. The following analyses seem equally plausible:

(1) 'Suspect' is used absolutely, meaning 'to be in a state of doubt' (the object of doubt being unexpressed or indicated by the context). 'Convinc'd' is a participial adjective, and 'hardly' means 'barely'.

(2) 'Suspect' is used absolutely. 'Are convinc'd' is a passive verb, and 'hardly' means 'not easily', a meaning later eclipsed by the modern meaning 'barely'; in the 18th c. the word was regularly used in both senses.

(3) The two verbs 'suspect' and 'are convinc'd' govern the object clause 'that . . . attain'd'. In this case 'suspect . . . that' must be taken to mean 'doubt whether', the modern sense ('to imagine something to be possible') being quite opposite. Though the meaning thus suggested is a rare one according to *OED*, which specifies it only in the construction 'suspect whether', with a single supporting quotation dated 1698, it does not seem implausible. 'Suspect' is often used with a direct object, meaning 'to have doubts about' or 'to doubt the genuineness of something', and might easily have taken a clause as object at a time when the range of possible constructions was wider than it now is.

A comma after 'convinc'd' would tend to favour the third interpretation; while the punctuation as it stands seems to favour the first two, it is not necessarily authoritative, and should not be taken to preclude the third, which seems the most dynamic and dramatically effective.

30 *improve*] to increase, augment, make greater in amount (*OED*). The sense of ll. 30–1 is therefore that virtue increases the magnitude of love and truth increases its duration. Only later was the word restricted to the sense of making something better, though that sense is here supplied by the context. The word has a certain resonance in

this scene: it is used again by Sir John (l. 37) and by Silvia (l. 55). Cf. II. ix. 23 and n., II. ix. 29.

45 discover] See I. ii. 12 n.

55 improv'd to] increased, developed into (*OED*). Cf. I. iv. 30 n.

61 Imprecate] invoke evil (upon a person) (*OED*), referring to Sir John's lines immediately preceding. Cf. II. xv. 160, 'Imprecations'.

Wave] variant spelling of 'waive', 15th–19th cent. (*OED*).

65–7 Each Day I shall a happy Bridegroom be . . . verify'd in us] 'It was the Islamic paradise which more than any other theme seemed to sum up the Christian idea of Islam. . . . the flowing waters, the mild air in which neither heat nor cold could afflict, the shady trees, the fruits, the many-coloured silken clothing and the palaces of precious stones and metals, the milk and wine served in gold and silver vessels by angels, saying, "eat and drink in joy"; and beautiful virgins, "untouched by men or demons". . . . With this garden of material delights it was usual to contrast the concept of a purely spiritual apprehension of God, the Beatific Vision of Christian tradition.' (Norman Daniel, *Islam and the West* [Edinburgh, 1960], p. 148.) Though this very general contrast is certainly apposite, Sir John has specifically in mind the perpetually renewed virginity of Believers and of the houris given them as wives in Paradise. See the *Encyclopaedia of Islam*, new edn., ed. B. Lewis *et al.* (Leiden; London, 1960–), s.v. 'Djanna', 'Hur'.

73 blasting] blowing or breathing on balefully or perniciously. Said of a malignant wind (*OED*).

87 *treat*] discuss terms of settlement, bargain, negotiate (*OED*).

I. viii

SD *Gaffer . . . Goody*] Both words are titles, like 'Sir' and 'Mrs.' (see Dramatis Personæ, nn. on ll. 5 and 13), and are so treated by the editor in stage directions (silently) and in the text. In stage directions O consistently sets the two words in roman, as if they were proper names. In the text of Act I (ix. 28, 31, 150) 'Goody' is always italic; in the text of Act III (ii. 3, iii. 23, 25, v. 34, xxii. 1, 16) it is always roman, with one exception at III. v. 5. 'Gaffer' does not occur anywhere in the text.

Sexton] The word represents an occupation, not a name. Here, in line 2, and in I. ixSD, the typography is accordingly emended. O sets the word in roman at I. ix. 87.

1–5 A very pretty Fancy . . . Cloaths?] 'I am further advised, That several of the Defunct, contrary to the Woollen Act, presume to dress themselves in Lace, Embroidery, Silks, Muslins, and other Ornaments forbidden to Persons in their Condition' (*The Tatler*, No. 118 [1710]). The 'Woollen Act' (30 Charles II, c. 3) required that burial-clothes should be made of English wool. The Act, frequently circumvented, is also alluded to in Steele's *The Funeral*, v. iii. 58–60, and in Pope's *Epistle to Cobham*, ll. 242–7.

5–7 But the Truth . . . Drinking] By 'good Eating and Drinking' the sexton means parish feasts and other entertainments for parish officers. Responsibility for poor relief was till 1782 confined to individual parish vestries and appointed overseers. The summary of chapter II in the contents of Dorothy Marshall's *The English Poor in the Eighteenth Century* (London, 1926), p. vi, suggests some of the results:

. . . overseers . . . were appointed annually and . . . were forced to seve or pay a fine. In practice the Justices [*to whom they were nominally answerable*] exercised very little influence over them. Type of man chosen not suitable—untrained—unwilling [*surely this varied from parish to parish*]—also economy not forced on them—therefore easy attitude towards expenditure and accounts—in many parishes not noticeably corrupt but careless and inefficient—and accounts neglected. But London parishes notoriously corrupt because the size of the out parishes offered more opportunities for peculation. Chief ways were by juggling with contracts—by falsifying disbursements to the casual poor—by spending unnecessary amounts on parish feasts. Methods of collection were also open to suspicion. Abuse of communion money highly probable.

21–2 *No matter, so . . . be sold*] The comma is added after '*matter*' to clarify the sense of '*so*': 'No matter, so long as you fill your purse.' The words '*Living and Dead*' seem to refer to the sexton's entire speech, with its reference to parish officers, as well as to the first quatrain of the song. If he were referring only to the latter, 'so' could well mean 'thus', in which case a comma would be extraneous.

I. ix

4 *long Home*] a metaphor for 'grave' first cited by *OED* in a passage dated 1303. Cf. Eccles. 12: 5: '. . . man goeth to his long home, and the mourners go about the streets'.

32 spare to speak, and spare to speed] The proverb is addressed to Timothy, and means 'if you don't speak up, you won't get anywhere' (with Goody Costive). 'Spare' is used in the obsolete sense 'refrain from doing', 'speed' in the obsolete sense 'succeed, prosper' (*OED*).

67 sad] deplorably bad; chiefly (as here) as an intensive qualifying terms of depreciation (*OED*). With the same sense, the word stands alone at II. ix. 8 and III. v. 19, 24.

94 If he ben't] Though O's reading 'been't' could represent a contraction of the pseudo-dialectical 'been not' (for which see *OED*), nothing else in the 'country' characters' lines supports the possibility. It is almost certainly a contraction of the subjunctive 'be not', and is accordingly emended. I. ix. 13, 'I ben't', is, however, an example of a form, 'I be', said by *OED* to be a common first-person singular indicative in southern and Midland dialects, the negative contraction being variously spelt 'ben't', 'beant', 'baint'. Cf. III. xv. 26 n.

104 pretend] intend; perhaps with the additional sense of venture, presume (*OED*).
118 withal] often substituted for 'with' in postposition (*OED*).
177 *wind*] to wrap a corpse in a shroud or winding-sheet (*OED*).

I. x

SD Dorothy *in the Grave*] Though not at first visible, Dorothy is on stage in this scene. She has accordingly been added to the direction, as in O in I. ixSD. Cf. II. iSD: in that scene Timothy remains off-stage, though his voice is heard.

4 Howlet] dialectical form of 'owlet' (*OED*).

6 Flock-bed] a bed the mattress of which is stuffed with wool (*OED*). The word seems meant to indicate Timothy's modest prosperity: feather-beds were for the well-to-do; the poor slept on straw.

14 *Dor.*] '*Dol.*', in O, is an abbreviation of 'Dolly', a common pet-form of the name 'Dorothy' (*OED*). In the present edition '*Dor.*' is used in this scene (as 'Dorothy' for 'Dolly' in line 21SD) for the sake of consistent reference.

50 *Ambo*] Latin: both.

I. xi

3 Style] variant spelling of 'stile' (*OED*). In its list of historical forms *OED* notes this

as a 15th-cent. spelling only, though the latest quotation in which it occurs is dated 1675. The word is again thus spelt at I. xii. 93.

I. xii

6 Laud] noted by *OED* as an 18th-cent. form of 'lord'.

25+ Air XVIII] The erroneous numbering in O of this and the following air could easily have come about through scribal or compositorial omission of the final 'I' of 'XVIII' and reversal of the 'IX' of 'XIX'. There is no evidence in the text that points to anything other than these two isolated errors.

36 Pimp in ordinary] a satirical phrase. 'In ordinary' is added to various official titles, meaning 'ordinary' as opposed to 'extraordinary' (*OED*).

37+ Air XIX] See I. xii. 25+ n.

44 palms] strokes with the hand, though the verb can also mean 'to take or grasp the hand of' (*OED*). Swift, in *The Tatler*, No. 230 (1710), included 'palming' in a list of deplorable 'modern Terms of Art'. Cf. II. xiv. 4 n.

59–60 the Thoughts of a Husband] The modern equivalent would be 'the thought of a husband'; it is highly unlikely that Lettice is speaking in this context of a husband's own thoughts. None of *OED*'s definitions or quotations is specifically relevant, and the text has been left unemended on the ground that the phrase as it stands would not have been ambiguous for an 18th-cent. reader. Cf. III. xxiii. 4, 'the Fears of Poverty', where modern usage would prefer the singular 'fear'.

85 Justice of Peace] 'Justices of the peace exercised a . . . variety of functions. . . . A single justice could practise summary jurisdiction on the basis of informations against offenders allegedly breaking the laws on vagrancy, drunkenness, profaneness and Sunday trading, hearing those charged and sentencing them to a small fine or even to public chastisement. In conjunction with one other magistrate they could execute justice in a "petty" sessions over such offenders as unlicensed alehouse keepers, unmarried mothers, runaway servants and apprentices. Three justices could even sentence a person to seven years' transportation for rickburning. Groups of neighbouring justices could supervise affairs in a particular part of a county. . . . Besides acting as judges they also administered the laws covering a whole gamut of activities, such as repairing highways, licensing alehouses and implementing the poor laws. They even assumed a legislative role, making their own laws to keep the peace, for instance by regulating fairs and other methods of buying or selling. They also appointed the constables of hundreds who were responsible for law and order in the county at large.' (W. A. Speck, *Stability and Strife* [Cambridge, Mass., 1977], pp. 28–9; see also Basil Williams, *The Whig Supremacy*, 2nd edn., rev. C. H. Stuart [Oxford, 1965], pp. 49–56.)

93 Style] See I. xi. 3 n.

II. vi

7 Drab] harlot (*OED*). Etymologically distinct from 'drab' meaning 'of a dull light-brown or yellowish-brown'.

II. vii

34, 39, 40 *admire*] view with wonder or surprise; to wonder or marvel at (*OED*). The word did not till the 19th cent. automatically connote approbation. Cf. *London Merchant*, III. iv. 2.

II. viii

12 Holland] a linen fabric originally called Holland cloth (*OED*).

II. ix

5 Kind Innocent, yet charming Creature] 'Kind, innocent, yet charming Creature' might be a better reading here: a scribe or compositor could simply have been misled into thinking 'innocent' a noun rather than an adjective, owing to the lack of a comma after 'Kind'. But there may be an intended antithesis between 'Kind Innocent' and 'charming Creature', since 'Creature', in this context, is probably meant to be taken, even if it is not given, in a derogatory sense; the word was often so used (*OED*; that it could be used without derogatory implication is evident at III. xxi. 32). It seems best, therefore, to let O's reading stand.

8 sad] See I. ix. 67 n.

23 *improving*] See I. iv. 30 n.

29 *improv'd*] in the same sense as '*improving*' in l. 23, but perhaps with a glance at another sense, 'making profitable use of' (*OED*). Cf. I. ii. 14, I. iv. 30 nn.

II. xiii

2 *Minks*] noted by *OED* as a 17th/18th-cent. form of 'minx', for which it gives two senses: pert girl, hussy—now often used playfully (modern); and lewd or wanton woman (obsolete). The phrase 'mistress minx' is separately noted, with a number of quotations dating from the late 16th to the mid-18th cent.

II. xiv

1 Trapes] opprobrious name for a woman or girl slovenly in person or habits (*OED*).

2 huff'd] offended by discourtesy (*OED*).

4 poz.] This abbreviation of 'positive' was included by Swift in a 'letter', part of his essay in *The Tatler*, No. 230 (1710), illustrating the use of unfortunate 'late Refinements crept into our Language'. Cf. I. xii. 44 n.

II. xv

This scene must have been considerably modified or heavily cut in performance. According to the note on alterations that was originally printed, as in the present edition, immediately preceding the text of the play, Air XL (ll. 126–47) was to be sung in Act III in a new scene that would replace III. x–xiv; ll. 149–53, with some variation, were incorporated into the new scene as well (Note on Alterations, ll. 23–5). See Introduction, p. 10.

SD *Another . . . House*] The change of scene, not provided for in O, is called for in Sir John's instructions to Jonathan at II. x. 3: 'Tell [Welford], I am coming down.' Scenes vi–xiv clearly take place in an upper-floor room, either in Sir John's bedchamber or, better suited to the action, in an antechamber or dressing-room of his private apartment. The latter interpretation allows for the entrances and exits of Betty, Jonathan, Lettice, and Sir John, with Lettice—and possibly Sir John—presumed to be coming in from the bedchamber of the apartment in scenes viii and ix, after Betty and Jonathan have exited through opposite proscenium doors. Lettice would exit to the bedchamber after scene xiii, leaving Betty to come downstage away from her, again towards a proscenium door. The 'Chamber' referred to by Lettice at II. xiii. 5–6 would therefore mean either the bedchamber, off-stage, or, more loosely speaking, the apartment in general. See Mark Girouard, *Life in the English Country House* (New Haven and London, 1978), pp. 120–62, for an account of the architectural arrangement of such a house as one would presume Sir John's to be—something on the order of Coleshill House (pp. 122–5).

11 a Matter of Courtesy, not Right] Since Welford's farm is his apparently by

leasehold for a fixed term, Sir John might renew the lease or refuse to do so at will. The legal point is not profound, and seems more importantly to be a prelude to Welford's insistence that it is Sir John who has forfeited any rights—to Silvia.

39 *Phœnix*] a person (or thing) of unique excellence or of matchless beauty; a paragon (*OED*). Lillo here makes no apparent reference to the self-immolation and rebirth of the mythical phœnix, as he does in *Marina*, II. i. 117.

100 chast] variant spelling of 'chaste'. The latest passage quoted by *OED* in which this spelling occurs is dated 1673. Cf. III. xxii. 82, 'tast' for 'taste', and *Arden of Feversham*, v. i. 41, 'hast' for 'haste'.

110 Fortune,] The comma, added by W1, precludes the rhythmically awkward though not impossible reading in which 'Fortune with Fame on Earth' is but another element in a list that ends with 'Everlasting Happiness'. With the comma the sentence points up an antithesis between 'Fame on Earth' and 'Everlasting Happiness' hereafter, with the implication that no happiness in this life is everlasting, and that fame—i.e. reputation—is irrelevant in the life to come, an implicit theological statement of a kind that is found throughout Lillo's work.

II. xvi

17 complain] in the obsolete sense, to mourn or lament (*OED*); as opposed to the kind of complaining that Betty here indulges in.

29–30 Cabinet-Counsellor] private counsellor (*OED*), i.e. confidant, the cabinet being the innermost and most private room in a private apartment (cf. II. xvSD n.). This is the origin of the political term 'cabinet'. The use of the term is perhaps a mild satirical touch (cf. I. xii. 36 n.).

50 out of Conceit with] dissatisfied with, no longer pleased with (*OED*).

62 Rubs] wounds or chafes given to the feelings of another (*OED*).

III. i

42, 44 discover'd . . . Discovery] See I. ii. 12 n.

52 *prove*] experience, 'go through', suffer (*OED*).

III. ii

SD *To them . . . Goody* Gabble.] In Act III the stage directions are frequently rather vague—and in III. viiiSD simply mistaken—in specifying the characters on stage. In this case, as is clear from ll. 1–4, only the three 'Goodies' have entered; they are correctly listed in III. ivSD. The phrase '*To them*' is required by the conventions of French scenes as they are used in O, to indicate that Silvia and Welford remain after scene i.

III. iii

The division of scenes in O places Welford's exit too early. The first part of Goody Busy's speech (III. ii. 7–10 in the present edition) is obviously addressed to him, the change of address, to Silvia, having been indicated originally by the dash before 'Dost not know me, pretty one?' (III. iii. 1).

SD *and Goody* Gabble.] See III. iiSD n.

8 enow] dialectical form of 'enough' (*OED*).

12 careful] fraught or attended with sorrow, trouble, or anxiety (*OED*).

34 Lyings-in] To 'lie in' is 'to be brought to bed of a child' (*OED*). The second word in the compound is invariably the preposition 'in', and *OED* lends no support to O's reading 'Lyings-|Inn'. D also corrects the error, at the same time omitting the hyphen. Cf. III. xxii. 19, 'lay-in'.

38 Christening] It is at this time, presumably, that a midwife could expect gifts of money from those present.

III. v

SD *and Goody* Gabble.] See III. iiSD n.

8 salute] kiss or greet with a kiss (*OED*).

14 As you see] Jonathan is dressed in the servants' livery of Sir John's household.

17 Family] i.e. 'family of servants' (*OED*). See I. ii. 17 n.

19, 24 sad] See I. ix. 67 n.

21 Batchelors Families] See I. ii. 17 n.

28 She has something to bring you to] i.e. her husband has left her an estate which would be Jonathan's upon his marrying her.

31 kill'd her with Kindness] The context of this phrase does little to relieve its ambiguity. That the wife had *formerly* 'brought . . . a Child every Year' indicates that the husband finally gave up relations with her and succumbed to the effects of his own abstinence. On the other hand, Jonathan concludes that the widow must be a wanton, in which case the husband might have succumbed to the effects of over-indulgence. Unfortunately Goody Busy does not state her views on the aetiology of 'Consumption'— which in the 18th cent. could mean any wasting disease. Perhaps Lillo had in mind the title of Thomas Heywood's *A Woman Killed with Kindness*, in which a wife is sent into comfortable exile by her husband; but if there is a play on the title, then the 'Kindness' here in question could as well mean the opposite.

36 withal] See I. ix. 118 n.

38 make with] have to do with, used chiefly in collocation with 'meddle' (*OED*).

46 Pack] applied to a person of low or worthless character; almost always with 'naughty' (*OED*).

54 *Whip and stitch with a Jerk*] 'Whip' is a term in needlework, meaning to sew with an overcast stitch, and possibly to trim or ornament with embroidery (*OED*). It appears from the quotations in *OED* that 'whip and stitch' was a frequent verbal combination. *OED* gives no meaning for 'jerk' other than the ones still in common usage; in this context it seems simply to indicate quickness of movement.

III. vi

Goody Busy's speech refers to Welford in the third person, and is clearly not addressed to him. The interposition of this scene implies that Welford and Silvia appear on stage at some distance from the group already present.

SD *and Goody* Gabble.] See III. iiSD n.

III. viii

SD Silvia] Though the reading in O—'Jonathan' instead of 'Silvia'—is obviously erroneous, it was followed in all other editions, including W1.

III. ix

This scene was originally the conclusion of III. viii. It is separately numbered in the present edition to maintain consistency in the use of French scenes. The original deviation from convention may indicate revision in the printer's copy, though this is by no means certain. See Introduction, p. 23.

III. x–xiv

According to the note on alterations immediately preceding the text of the play, these scenes were never performed as printed.

III. x

1–5 'Tis hard . . . A Poem on a Dwarf!] I have not been able to identify the poem referred to.

1 dispossess] cast out (the evil spirit by which any one is possessed); exorcise (*OED*).

III. xi

20 O Fathers!] Neither *OED* nor the dictionaries of colloquial usage seen by me mention this oath.

III. xii

2 *prove*] know by experience (*OED*). Cf. III. i. 52.

III. xv

6 outstood your market] stood out about terms till the opportunity was lost (*OED*).

26 Sure you be'nt] This is almost certainly a contraction of 'be not', and could be taken either as a subjunctive expressing doubt or as a dialectical use of 'be' in the indicative. Though it might more properly be printed 'ben't', it is just possible that O's reading, followed in all subsequent editions, represents the pronunciation 'beënt'. Cf. I. ix. 94 n.

III. xviii

SD Lettice *Singing*] Since Lettice does not sing for very long, no separate song is provided for her here. Two of her songs in Act II—Air XXXIII (II. viii. 1–11) or Air XXXVI (II. xii. 7–12)—would seem to be appropriate choices, both being expressive of the fragile triumph that is now to be abruptly shattered.

11 Justice] i.e. Sir John, who is a justice of the peace (see I. xii. 85 n.).

16 *Goose*] a tailor's smoothing-iron, so called from the resemblance of the shape of the handle to a goose's neck (*OED*).

22 *surprizing*] overcoming, overpowering the mind, will, heart, etc. (*OED*).

36–7 May-game] object of jest or ridicule (*OED*).

40 all along of] in archaic or dialectic usage: on account of (*OED*).

III. xix

SD *whispers*] whispers to (*OED*).

III. xxi

21 Wealth or Power, or Love] The comma after 'Wealth' printed in O and followed in all other editions tends to obscure the antithesis, clearly intended in ll. 21–2, between wealth and power on the one hand, and love on the other, which alone is 'more tempting to a generous Mind'.

34 *wooe*] variant spelling of 'woo'. Though *OED* gives a range of 15th–17th cent., 'wooes' appears in a quotation dated 1792.

III. xxii

SD *Sir* John . . . *&c.*] In the present edition, to avoid unnecessary ambiguity, '*&c.*' is here and in III. xxiiiSD limited to unnamed supernumeraries, as in I. viiiSD and I. ixSD. The named characters are listed in related groups. Those on stage in this and the following scene, in addition to the named characters, are the 'rest of my Friends who came with me' referred to by Welford in III. xxii. 1—that is, the 'Neighbours' whom Goody Busy had conducted to Welford's house before III. ii, a group which would naturally include Goody Costive, Goody Gabble, and Gaffer Gabble. The 'Tenants' who are summoned for the final dance (III. xxiii. 19–24) would most likely have been the dancers of the Lincoln's Inn Fields company.

19 lay-in] See III. iii. 34 n. The hyphenated form of the verb was apparently uncommon: the quotations in *OED* include only one example, 'lies-in'. The hyphen might have misled a scribe or compositor into capitalizing the verb as if it were a noun. D drops the hyphen, though it does retain the capital L.

39–42 Soon after . . . Voluntier.] The chronology of Welford's account, and his specifying Flanders, indicates that he served in one or more of Marlborough's campaigns in the War of the Spanish Succession. It was one of the earliest of these that culminated in the Battle of Blenheim (13 Aug. 1704); the campaigns continued till 1711, when Marlborough was dismissed from all his offices.

By 'an honourable Post in the Army' it is probably meant that the elder Sir John was a colonel. In the 17th and 18th cents. the colonelcy of a British regiment implied a proprietary right in the organization. Whether or not the colonel commanded the regiment in the field, he always superintended its finances and internal economy, usually to his profit. Armies were raised for each campaign, and the regiments were made up from qualified volunteers ('voluntier' is an archaic variant spelling [*OED*]), though this system underwent considerable modification with the institution of standing armies towards the end of the 17th cent. Besides the profits resulting from economical—and sometimes parsimonious or fraudulent—discharge of his proprietary rights, the officer could sell his proprietary interest when he retired (*Enc. Brit.* [1969], iii. 83 and xvi. 878).

82 tast] variant spelling of 'taste'. The latest passage quoted by *OED* in which this spelling occurs is dated 1700. Cf. II. xv. 100 n.

III. xxiii

SD *Sir* John . . . Ploughshare.] See III. xxiiSD n.

Epilogue

29 *attone*] Though 'atone' is etymologically correct, more than two-thirds of the passages dated before 1730 quoted by *OED* have 'attone', a spelling which appears in only one quotation of later date, taken from a 1761 edition of Dryden's dramatic works.

34 *undistinguish'd*] in which no distinction is made or can be observed (*OED*, quoting, *inter alia*, James Thomson, *Summer* [1727], ll. 347–8: 'A dazling deluge reigns; and all | From pole to pole is undistinguish'd blaze'). As here applied to '*Light*', in conjunction with '*spotless and bright*' (l. 33), it means 'alike throughout, of uniform brightness'. There is also an antithetical play, against '*Superior*' in the same line, on the now more usual meaning 'not . . . elevated above others' (*OED*), with the implication that those who are undistinguished in social position may none the less be regarded as superior in the brightness of their virtue.

Commentary on the Songs and their Music

Introduction

John Watts used two different kinds of woodcut music in the printing of *Silvia*. Most of the pieces are fairly compact, having from one to four or occasionally five lines, and are printed from a single block. A smaller number (Airs IV, V, XVII, XXI, XXIX, XXX, XXXVI, XLVII, LVII, LVIII, and LIX) are printed from composite blocks made up of separate lines; these had been prepared for and first used in Watts's six-volume song collection, *The Musical Miscellany*, in which the words of the first verses and, in volumes iii–vi, bass lines were set between the lines of vocal music.

It was the use of woodcuts that allowed Watts, in a single printing operation, to 'prefix' the music to the songs within the text. Though it seems an obvious and inexpensive format for a printer of ballad operas to employ, Watts was virtually alone in doing so, and he dominated the ballad-opera market. Only the printer of Charles Coffey's *The Female Parson* (published by Lawton Gilliver in 1730) used woodcuts in similar fashion. Thomas Odell's *The Patron* (1729) was printed by W. Pearson—the printer of *Pills to Purge Melancholy*—with typeset music prefixed to the songs, but this is an isolated and rather unattractive example. In all other cases ballad-opera texts were printed without music, though almost always with tune-titles; engraved music might be appended to the text or published under separate cover.

It should not be assumed that the music printed in *Silvia* represents the tunes exactly as they were sung. It would have been the responsibility of the musical director to arrange the tunes for accompaniment by the instrumental ensemble, or at least to assemble a score from previous arrangements. The peculiarities of these performance versions of the tunes are by no means necessarily reflected in Watts's woodcuts. Those which had been used before in *The Musical Miscellany* or in earlier ballad operas cannot have derived from the score used for the performances of *Silvia*. The woodcuts first used in the text of *Silvia* may in some cases reflect the score (see below, List of Abbreviated References, n. 3); but they could as well have been copied from existing printed or manuscript sources, which often vary in melodic and rhythmic detail, sometimes to the extent of representing rather different tunes altogether. It must also be borne in mind that singers were accustomed to embellish melodies, the vocal line as printed being a basic melodic guide. In short, this largely popular music was as fluid in character as the popular music of the present day; even 'sacred' music was not always held sacred—see for example the note to Air LIII. For contemporary theatre-goers the printed music probably served more than anything else as an *aide-mémoire* by which to recall the performance, and for readers as a means to get a tune in their heads, if they did not already know it from the tune-title. For the modern reader it provides access to tunes as distant from us as 'Stardust', 'Keep the Home Fires Burning', or 'I Wanna Hold your Hand' will most likely be for anyone living in the 23rd cent.

Since ballad-opera songs were frequently written with some degree of reference to the words with which the borrowed tunes were associated, it was the purpose of the research undertaken for the following notes to discover the songs so used by Lillo, and to make some of them available for immediate comparison. In some cases it has been found that Lillo wrote with previous ballad-opera songs in mind; in other cases he wrote with little or no regard to earlier lyrics; and in still other cases he adopted a tune used so often that only a general tone, rather than a particular lyric or ballad, was associated with it. He drew, as most ballad-opera writers did, from a wide range of sources: ballad-tunes recorded as long as two centuries before, theatre-songs in vogue at the time of writing, operatic arias, political songs set to tunes used again and again in the streets, country dances and minuets, tender love lyrics, and bawdy tavern songs.

Wherever possible, the following notes are heavily dependent on the work of Claude Simpson, Harold Gene Moss, and occasionally William Chappell (see the List of Abbreviated References, below). It was thought at first that bare reference to appropriate entries in Moss, supplemented by references to Simpson, would suffice. Simpson, however, was chiefly concerned with supplying music for ballads most often published without it, using the music to relate the ballads to one another. The result is an excellent work of scholarship, but only incidentally related to ballad opera, and no texts are reprinted. Moss's dissertation was intended, according to his abstract, to present 'a detailed history of each piece of music used by the authors of ballad operas between 1728 and 1733. Not only does it record the ballad-opera songs set to each tune, it also contains other lyrics set to the same music that had some popularity during these years.' It is indeed a useful compilation, and has served as an indispensable reference; but the treatment of underlying sources, and especially of their music, can be rather cursory, and is in some cases mistaken or incomplete. Moss does not reproduce the texts of source-songs used only once during the period surveyed, a category which includes fully a third of Lillo's sources. For these reasons, a brief narrative account of each song's background seemed the only possible way of dealing with this important element of the play, if it was to be dealt with at all.

These accounts are mainly based on the following, in addition to Simpson and Moss: examination of the music found in early editions of nearly all the ballad operas that were published, reprinted in W. H. Rubsamen's twenty-eight-volume facsimile collection, *The Ballad Opera* (New York, 1974); a survey of the contents of *The Musical Miscellany* and the 1719–20 edition of *Pills to Purge Melancholy*, which between them contain versions of just above half of Lillo's sources; explorations, following secondary references or simple hunch, in the printed collections of broadside ballads listed below; a search of the contents of the *British Union Catalogue of Early Music*; and use of the full range of indexes in the *National Tune Index*.

It was not possible to undertake direct examination of contemporary sources—broadsides, song-sheets, and printed and manuscript collections of songs and music—found in certain major libraries, many of which are noted from the work of others. A thoroughgoing survey of those materials might have brought to light some of the sources 'not found' and obviated a good deal of conjecture in the attempt to relate Watts's woodcuts to other versions of the tunes. Any purely musical analysis of the songs would take one well beyond the concerns of the present edition, involving matters for which Lillo was not directly responsible. Both the rudimentary nature of the printed music and my own very elementary grasp of musicology would at any rate have precluded it; but it has in most cases been possible, using the resources to hand, to establish whether or not a given piece of music properly represents the tune indicated. Those who wish to know more about ballad-opera music and musicians should begin by consulting ch. 3 of Roger Fiske's *English Theatre Music in the Eighteenth Century*.

Musical settings included in the present text are reproduced exactly as found in Watts's edition. No attempt has been made to emend or note in detail the occasional minor errors in accidentals, dotting, etc., since none of these errors renders the music unintelligible. Only in the music for Air LV has an error in transcription made it impossible to fit the words: a reconstruction of the appropriate measures is included in the note to the song.

As noted in the Introduction (p. 24), stanza divisions of the song texts are reproduced as they stand in the copy-text ('O'). To avoid ambiguity, all page breaks occurring within the texts of songs, whether in the copy-text or in the present edition, are accounted for in the reference lines of notes to the affected songs.

List of Abbreviated References
Works and collections marked with an asterisk have not been seen by the present editor.

Actors, Actresses: see List of Abbreviated References, p. x.

BB: J. W. Ebsworth, ed., *The Bagford Ballads*, 2 vols., London, 1878.

Bronson, *Traditional Tunes*: Bertrand H. Bronson, *Traditional Tunes of the Child Ballads*, 4 vols., Princeton, 1959–72.

BUCEM: *The British Union Catalogue of Early Music*, 2 vols., London, 1957. Parenthetical references give the composer's name or keyword under which an item is found.

*CD: Book 1—*The Compleat Country Dancing Master*, London, J. Walsh and J. Hare, 1718; Book 2—*The Second Book of the Compleat Country Dancing Master*, London, J. Walsh and J. Hare, 1719. Later editions and further books published after *Silvia* are surveyed in *NTI*.

Chappell, *PMOT*: William Chappell, *The Ballad Literature and Popular Music of the Olden Time*, 2 vols., London, 1859.

Day and Murrie: Cyrus Lawrence Day and Eleanore Boswell Murrie, *English Song Books, 1651–1702: A Bibliography with a First-line Index of Songs*, London, 1940.

*DM: *The Dancing Master* (1st edn., *The English Dancing Master*), London, many editions and two later volumes: 1st–18th edns., 1651–*c.*1728; vol. ii, 1st–4th edns., *c.*1713–28; vol. iii, 1st and 2nd edns., *c.*1719, *c.*1727. See Margaret Dean-Smith, *Playford's English Dancing Master 1651* (London, 1957), a facsimile reprint of the 1st edn. with a descriptive bibliography and census of known copies of all editions; see also Margaret Dean-Smith and E. J. Nichol, '"The Dancing Master": 1651–1728', *Journal of the English Folk Dance and Song Society*, iv. 4 (1943), 131–45; iv. 5 (1944), 167–79; iv. 6 (1945), 211–31.

EB: *The Euing Collection of Broadside Ballads in the Library of the University of Glasgow*, Glasgow, 1971.

Fiske: see List of Abbreviated References, p. xi.

London Stage: see List of Abbreviated References, p. xi.

MM: *The Musical Miscellany*, 6 vols., London, J. Watts, 1729–31. Advertisements in newspapers and in books printed by Watts indicate the following dates of publication: vols. i and ii, 13 Jan. 1728/9; vols. iii and iv, 12 Nov. 1729; vols. v and vi, 12 Nov. 1730.

Moss: see List of Abbreviated References, p. xi.

New Grove: Stanley Sadie, ed., *The New Grove Dictionary of Music and Musicians*, 20 vols., London, 1980.

NTI: Carolyn Rabson and Kate Van Winkle Keller, *The National Tune Index: 18th-century Secular Music*, New York, 1980, 78 microfiches. Cross-references indexes to the texts (titles, first lines, refrains) and/or musical incipits of approximately 40,000 examples of Anglo-American secular tunes found in over 500 chiefly 18th-cent. sources, including ballad operas and other British theatre works, manuscript music compilations, and British instrumental and song collections, song-sheets, and dance collections (including all extant editions of *DM*). Abbreviated references to collections surveyed in *NTI*:

    *DFo–C.42.1–4: 'A Collection of Eighteenth Century Single Sheet Songs' in the Folger Shakespeare Library, M1497.C42, vols. i–iv Cage. Parenthetical references give page numbers as in the collection.

    *MH Marshall Coll.: Marshall Collection of Song Sheets in the Houghton Library, Harvard University (three boxes of loose song-sheets, alphabetized by title, not catalogued at time of writing). Parenthetical references give the item-numbers assigned in *NTI*.

OPB: *Broadside Ballads of the Restoration Period from the Jersey Collection known as The Ostley Park Ballads*, London, 1930.

Orpheus Caledonius: William Thomson, *Orpheus Caledonius: or, A Collection of Scots Songs*, 2nd edn., 2 vols., London, 1733 (*1st edn., 1 vol., London, 1726).

*Pepys: A six-volume collection of 17th- and 18th-cent. broadsides in the Pepysian Library, Magdalene College, Cambridge.

Pills: *Wit and Mirth: or Pills to Purge Melancholy*, 6 vols., London, W. Pearson for J. Tonson, 1719–20 (first five vols. also issued as *Songs Compleat, Pleasant and Divertive*, 1719). All quotations are from an undated (*c*.1876) page-for-page reprint. Parenthetical references specify the initial appearance of songs in earlier editions, as given in Day and Murrie. See Cyrus L. Day, '*Pills to Purge Melancholy*', *Review of English Studies*, viii (1932), 177–84.

Ramsay, *Works*: Burns Martin and John W. Oliver (vols. i–iii), Alexander M. Kinghorn and Alexander Law (vols. iv–vi), eds., *The Works of Allan Ramsay*, 6 vols., London and Edinburgh, 1945–74 (Scottish Text Society, 3rd ser. 19, 20, 29, 4th ser. 6–8).

RB: William Chappell and J. W. Ebsworth, eds., *The Roxburghe Ballads*, 8 vols., London, 1871–99.

Rollins, *Analytical Index*: Hyder E. Rollins, *An Analytical Index to the Ballad-entries (1557–1709) in the Registers of the Company of Stationers of London*, Chapel Hill, NC, 1924.

Simpson: Claude M. Simpson, *The British Broadside Ballad and its Music*, New Brunswick, NJ, 1966.

*Stuart, *Musick*: Alexander Stuart, *Musick for Allan Ramsay's Collection of Scots Songs*, Edinburgh, Allan Ramsay, n.d. (*c.*1724).

William C. Smith, *Handel*: William C. Smith, *Handel: A Descriptive Catalogue of the Early Editions*, 2nd edn., London and New York, 1970.

TTM: Allan Ramsay, *The Tea-table Miscellany: A Collection of Choice Songs Scots and English*, Glasgow, 1871 (a reprint of the 14th edn., 4 vols. in 2). Reference is made to vols. i–iv, with page-numbers as they appear in the reprint, in which vol. i = i. 1–111, vol. ii = i. 133–239, vol. iii = ii. 1–108, vol. iv = ii. 109–266.

Notes

1. References to ballad operas as a rule give the title, date of the first edition, and number of the song under discussion. These references are not meant to be exhaustive, being generally confined to the appearance elsewhere of a given woodcut, other versions of the music, or song-texts of particular interest. References to Charles Johnson's *The Village Opera* take into account the two states in which it was printed by Watts: 1729*a*, the first state, contains sixty-three numbered songs, and an additional song printed in the preliminaries; 1729*b* contains fifty-three numbered songs. Charles Coffey's *The Devil to Pay* was printed by Watts in a number of editions, the first of which is the only printing of the three-act version, with forty-two songs. Later editions contain various one-act versions, with anywhere from fifteen to eighteen songs. Only the three-act version is noted; in all cases the same woodcut was used for a song included in the shortened versions. Henry Fielding made some alterations to *The Lottery* in the second and later editions, some involving the addition or deletion of songs. The resulting changes in numbering are not systematically accounted for in the references.

2. Quotations from Fielding's *The Grub-Street Opera* are taken from Edgar V. Roberts's modernized edition (Lincoln, Nebr., 1968; London, 1969). His notes and appendices enable the reader to reconstruct the earlier versions, called *The Welsh Opera* (the version actually performed) and *The Genuine Grub-Street Opera*.

3. It is usually possible to determine whether a given woodcut was first used in the printing of *Silvia*, but there is some question with respect to those used in other ballad operas printed by Watts in 1730. The third edition of *The Lover's Opera* (the first to include music) is included among the books advertised in *Silvia*, and must therefore have been printed earlier. *The*

Chambermaid was probably printed later, but all the woodcuts had been used in *The Village Opera* (1729), of which *The Chambermaid* is a reduction. *Damon and Phillida* shares no woodcuts with *Silvia*. In the introduction to the text (pp. 21–2) it is argued that *Silvia* was very likely printed before *Patie and Peggy*, *The Fashionable Lady*, and *Robin Hood*, and it would appear that *The Generous Freemason* was printed at about the time of its performance in Dec. 1730. If this is true, Airs X, XVI, XXXIII, XLI, XLVIII, and L are among those whose woodcuts were first used in *Silvia*.

Air I (I. i. 9–19; Moss 628)

The music renders, with minimal simplification, the melodic line of the first part of the da capo aria 'Il tricerbero humiliato' from Handel's opera *Rinaldo* (1711). Watts used the same woodcut in *The Lover's Opera* (3rd edn., 1730; Air 19). The tune-title refers to a song adapted to the aria by Thomas D'Urfey, originally called 'The Whim' but reprinted, without music, in *Pills*, i. 110–11, as 'The Happy Country Gentleman'. *BUCEM* ('All') lists two single-sheet editions of 'The Whim', dating both *c.*1711; Moss cites BL H.1601.(34). William C. Smith (*Handel*, p. 60) dates these editions *c.*1716, but the political events alluded to by D'Urfey belong to the late years of Queen Anne's reign. The song actually begins 'All the World's in Strife and Hurry'; no example of a version beginning 'Since' has been seen (the tune-title in *The Lover's Opera* begins 'All').

D'Urfey's song is for the most part a catalogue of political upheavals, but Lillo may nevertheless have had it in mind: Welford's inward agitation stands in direct contrast to the contentment of the country gentleman:

> How blest is the happy he
> Who from Town, and the Faction that is there, is free;
> For Love and no ill ends,
> Treats his neighbours and his Friends,
> He shall ever in the Book of Fame,
> Fix with Honour a glorious Name.
>
> (*Pills*, i. 110)

Lillo's song also contains an echo, perhaps coincidental or unconscious, of Chetwood's song in *The Lover's Opera*, which reads in full:

> O cruel Maid to slight me!
> I'll tear thee from my Breast.
> No more thy Charms delight me,
> But rob me of my Rest.

It is possible that the heroic character of Air I derives from the original aria, which reads, in the English version by Aaron Hill:

> Three headed Cerberus in chains
> My sword shall triumph o'er;
> I'll shake the realms where Pluto reigns
> And make his devils feel the pains
> Alcides taught them once before.

The tune was called for in Air 3 of Fielding's *Grub-Street Opera* by the alternative title 'Let the Drawer Bring Clean Glasses', the first line of a song written to the music of 'Il tricerbero humiliato', *c.*1714. See William C. Smith, *Handel*, pp. 57–60, for a list of song-sheets and collections that include it; it was sometimes called, after the last line,

'The Founder of the Feast'. It is reprinted in Joseph Ritson, *A Select Collection of English Songs*, 2nd edn., rev. Thomas Park, 3 vols. (London, 1813), ii. 93, iii. 247–50; the three quatrains are set to the music of the entire aria, rather than the first part only.

Though Fielding adapted much from *Silvia*, he seems in this case to parody Chetwood's song:

> How curst the puny lover!
> How exquisite the pain,
> When love is fumbled over,
> To view the fair's disdain!
> But oh, how vast the blessing,
> Whom to her bosom pressing,
> She whispers, while caressing,
> Oh, when shall we again.

(ed. Roberts, p. 10)

Fielding may also have been capitalizing on the revival of *Rinaldo* on 6 Apr. 1731: *The Welsh Opera* (the version of *The Grub-Street Opera* actually performed) opened on 22 Apr. (*London Stage, 1729–1747*).

Air II (I. iii. 3–11; Moss 231)

Source not found. Moss, suggesting that the music is that of a 'rural dance', claims not to have found it in 'any of the usual collections of such music'; it does not at any rate appear under that title in *DM* or *CD*. The tune had been called for earlier in *The Patron* (1729; Air 17) and *Chuck* (1729; Air 6). Watts's music differs little from that printed in *The Patron* and in the later *Devil of a Duke* (1732; Air 11). Only Lillo's song includes the refrain indicated by the tune-title; the tune-title in *Chuck* is 'Gameorum, Game'.

Though the two earier ballad-opera songs contain elements of social satire similar to that in Lillo's song, he does not directly imitate either one. 'Priests and Lawyers, by the Throng' were traditional objects of opprobrium; Lillo might, however, have been partly inspired by the much harsher Air 1 of *The Beggar's Opera*, which was also sung by Hippisley, in the role of Peachum.

Air III (I. iv. 28–35; Moss 75)

Moss writes: 'Richard Leveridge's tune, composed around 1700, seems to have gained predominance over the older, folk-song music originally used for the song's traditional lyrics. (Compare Leveridge's music . . . to the older tune, [BL G.306. (195)].)' The woodcut used in *Silvia* was also used in *The Village Opera* (1729*a*, Air 48; not in 1729*b*) and *The Chambermaid* (1729; Air 19); it differs in a few melodic details from the music printed in *Polly* (1729; Air 63) and *The Beggar's Wedding* (1729; Act II, Air 11), which in turn differs slightly from the music in *Pills*, iv. 271 (*Pills*, Part 2 [1700], p. 248). Moss cites three single-sheet editions in BL: G.306.(234), G.304.(26), and H. 1601.(67). The earliest such edition listed in *BUCEM* ('Leveridge') is there dated 1700; *NTI* indexes a song-sheet, DFo-C.42.4 (129), which bears the title 'A Scotch Song'. The song originally had two verses; the second and third of the four verses printed in *TTM* i. 158 were added presumably by Allan Ramsay.

'Blithe Jockey young and gay' is the simplest of love songs:

> Blith *Jockey* Young and Gay,
> Is all my Soul's Delight,

> He's all my Talk by Day,
>   And all my Dreams by Night:
>   If from the Lad I be,
>   'Tis Winter still with me,
>   But when he's with me here,
>   'Tis Summer all the Year.
>
> I'm Blith when *Jockey* comes,
>   Sad when he gangs away,
> 'Tis Night when *Jockey* Glooms,
>   And if he Smiles, 'tis Day:
>   When our Eyes meet, I pant,
>   I Colour, Sigh, or Faint,
>   What Lass that would be kind
>   Can better tell her Mind?
>   (*Pills*, iv. 271)

Lillo's song seems to derive indirectly from 'Blithe Jockey' by way of Gay's song in *Polly* (quoted from Moss):

> Can Words the Pain express
>   Which absent lovers know?
> He only mine can guess
>   Whose Heart hath felt the Woe.
> 'Tis Doubt, Suspicion, Fear,
>   Seldom Hope, oft' Despair;
> 'Tis Jealousy, 'tis Rage, in brief,
>   'Tis every Pain and Grief.

It is possible that Lillo was also writing a deliberate corrective to Coffey's song in *The Beggar's Wedding*:

> That Maid ne'er knows her Heart,
>   But by one Spark caress'd;
> The Pain is small to part,
>   When in another blest:
> 'Tis sweet Variety
>   That Beauty does controul,
> But Interest still should be
>   Ascendant o'er the Soul.

Air IV (I. iv. 85–92. Moss 737)

'Tweed Side' is one of the tunes most often used by the ballad-opera writers. The song associated with it, beginning 'What beauties does Flora disclose', is identified as the work of Robert Crawford in *BUCEM* ('What') and in Ramsay, *Works*, iv. 143–4; the editors of the latter add that the song was 'set to the old tune "Twide Syde" (first heard of in 1692)'. The three single-sheet editions of the song listed in *BUCEM* are there dated *c*.1725; the first of these is called only 'Charming Moggy', while the other two include 'Tweed Side' as a title or subtitle. A number of song-sheets are listed in *NTI*; those which include 'Tweed Side' as a title have four verses (DFo-M1497.C52.Cage [199], MH Marshall Coll. [183, 1260], New York Public Library Mus. Res. +MN

C695); those called only 'Charming Moggy' have two verses (DF0-C.42.2 [195], DF0-C.42.3 [395], MH Marshall Coll. [184], Huntington Library 291705, vol. i [9]). It would appear that those versions called only 'Tweed Side' refer to the girl as 'Mary' rather than 'Moggy', as in the song-sheet quoted in full by Moss (BL G.313. [71]). 'Tweed-Side' appears in *TTM* i. 4–5, with four verses, and differs little from the song-sheet quoted by Moss. 'Charming Moggy', with two verses, is reprinted in *MM* ii. 160–1: the first verse is nearly identical to that of the longer version, while the second verse consists of the first four lines of its fourth verse, followed by the last four lines of its third verse.

Both versions of the song are typical pastoral celebrations of the charms of a shepherdess. Lillo may well have had in mind the second verse of the longer version, which reads (in *TTM*):

> The warblers are heard in the grove,
>   The linnet, the lark, and the thrush,
> The blackbird, and sweet-cooing dove,
>   With music enchant ev'ry bush.
> Come, let us go forth to the mead,
>   Let us see how the primroses spring,
> We'll lodge in some village on Tweed,
>   And love while the feather'd folks sing.

Another possible influence on Lillo is Ramsay's song in the ballad-opera version of *The Gentle Shepherd* (reprinted in *TTM* ii. 218–19; presumably brought into the 'fifth edition' [1729] of vol. ii—see Ramsay, *Works*, vi. 11), which appears as Air 18 of *Patie and Peggy* (1730). Set to 'Tweed-side', it concludes:

> Nor age, nor the changes of life,
>   Can quench the fair fire of love,
> If virtue's ingrain'd in the wife,
>   And the husband have sense to approve.

Lillo's song, however, most strongly recalls Air 49 of *The Village Opera* (1729*a*; 1729*b*, Air 42), which is set to a different tune (see Air XLIV n.):

> Deluded by her Mate's dear Voice,
> The wanton Bird pursues her Joys,
> 'Till now, alas! and now too late
> She finds her Fault, and meets her Fate;
> Intangled in the fatal Clue,
> Bids Love and Life at once Adieu.

Watts produced two different woodcuts for the music of 'Tweed Side'. The earlier one was used in *MM* and *Silvia*, and in *Robin Hood* (1730; Air 17). The later woodcut, which presents a more syncopated version of the tune, was used in *Patie and Peggy* (1730; Air 18), *The Highland Fair* (1731; Air 21), *Don Quixote in England* (1734; Air 2), and *An Old Man Taught Wisdom* (1735; Air 7). The music given in Edgar Roberts's edition of *The Grub-Street Opera* corresponds to that found in *Polly* (1729; Air 67) in key (A) and melodic detail, not to the second Watts version in *Don Quixote in England* cited as the source on p. 148. The versions of the tune, both in A, in *Orpheus Caledonius*, i. 32–3, and, to judge from the incipit given in *NTI*, in Stuart, *Musick*, i. 8–9, more nearly resemble the earlier Watts version than they do the later one.

Air 20 of Fielding's *Grub-Street Opera* (included in *The Welsh Opera*), set to 'Tweedside', is an obvious burlesque of Lillo's song, though Fielding could also have had Ramsay's song in mind. See Introduction, p. 14.

Air V (I. vii. 12–17; Moss 117 [= Moss 114])

The music of Lillo's source, 'The Polish Minuet, or Miss Kitty Grevil's Delight', was from its first publication in musical collections attributed to Handel, an attribution accepted as probable in the *New Grove*. It first appeared in single-sheet editions in 1720, and was included in *The Monthly Mask of Vocal Musick* for Nov. 1720; it later appeared in *A Choice Collection of English Songs Set to Musick by Mr. Handel* (London, 1731), No. 17. (See William C. Smith, *Handel*, p. 171, for a list of single-sheet editions in BL; *NTI* lists DFo-C.42.4 [168], MH Marshall Coll. [923, 924, 925].) The first line of the song is properly 'Charming is your Shape and Air', but the version printed in Richard Neale's *A Pocket Companion for Gentlemen and Ladies* (London, 1724) does begin 'Charming is your Face'. The song was reprinted in *MM* ii. 90–1 as 'The Reproof', with the music unattributed. Lines 1, 2, and 5 of the music in *MM* were printed from the same woodcuts later used in *Silvia* and *The Jovial Crew* (1731; Air 22); lines 3 and 4 present a different version of measures 2–9 of the second strain.

Lillo's song reads like a continuation of the original two verses:

> Charming is— your Shape and Air,
> And your Face as Morning fair! As morn—ing fair!
> Coral Lips, and Neck of Snow;
> Cheeks, where op'ning Roses blow! Ro—ses blow!
> When you speak, or smile, or move,
> All is Rapture, all is Love.
>
> But those Eyes, alas, I hate!
> Eyes, that heedless of my Fate,
> Shine with undiscerning Rays;
> On the Fopling idly gaze;
> Watch the Glances of the Vain;
> Meeting mine with cold Disdain.
>
> (*MM* ii. 90; first verse printed line by line with
> music.)

The single-sheet text reprinted by Moss (from BL H.1601.[91]) repeats the whole of the fourth line as well as the final phrase, indicating that the music corresponds to that in Watts's ballad-opera printings as opposed to *MM*. (Moss provides separate entries for 'Charming is your Shape' and 'Charming is your Face', despite the identical music.) The other versions of the music have not been examined and the source of the variation in Watts's woodcuts cannot be accounted for here.

Air VI (I. viii. 15–22; Moss 681 [incorrect])

Source not found. Moss includes this air in his entry for 'There was a Jovial Beggar' (discussed by Simpson, pp. 40–2, as 'A-begging We Will Go'), but the tune printed in *Silvia*—to which Lillo's words can be easily fitted—bears no relation to that of 'The Jovial Beggar'. Moreover, Lillo's song lacks any reference to the refrain 'And a Begging we will go, | We'll go, we'll go, | And a Begging we will go', which was quoted or closely adapted by all the ballad-opera writers who used the tune.

'There was a jovial beggar-man' is the first line of 'The Politicke Beggar Man' (1656), No. 2131 in Rollins, *Analytical Index*. Rollins notes that the ballad is in Pepys, iii. 73 (not seen). It may very well be the basis for Lillo's song.

Air VII (i. ix. 1–4; Moss 66)

Source not found.

Air VIII (i. ix. 21–4; Moss 526)

Source not found. Lillo's song may well be related to 'The Fond Lovers Friendly Advice. To a Pleasant New Tune', beginning 'Hi-ho, I've lost my Love, Toll la ra, Toll la ra ra' (Pepys, v. 170), mentioned by Simpson, p. 480, in connection with D'Urfey's 'Make Your Honours Miss' (*Pills*, ii. 170–1), which has a similar refrain, though it is set to a quite different tune. D'Urfey's song is written in six-line stanzas; the four-line stanza, noted by Simpson, of 'The Fond Lovers Friendly Advice' relates it more closely to Lillo's song, the music of which may then represent the 'Pleasant New Tune'. The music printed with the ballad is characterized by Simpson as 'corrupt'.

Air IX (i. ix. 33–46; Moss 368)

Source not found.

Air X (i. ix. 76–86; Moss 306)

The dance-tune called 'Hunt the Squirrel' appears in *DM*, 14th edn. (1709) and in all subsequent editions (in all cases on p. 357); it also appears in *CD*, Book 1 (1718), p. 16. The identity of the tune is clear from the incipits in *NTI*, all identical with each other and all in the key of A. The tune appears to have remained popular throughout the 18th cent., and appears in manuscript as late as *c*.1790 (BL Add. MS 29371, fo. 52^v; the manuscript is so dated in *NTI*, which calls it 'Hammersley MS'), but the disparate tunes for 'Hunting the Squirrel', in Cecil J. Sharp and Herbert C. MacIlwaine, *Morris Dance Tunes*, Set III, and 'Hunt the Squirrel', in the same authors' *Country Dance Tunes*, Set II, do not much resemble the 18th-cent. tune. The woodcut used in *Silvia*, which differs in melodic and rhythmic detail as well as in key from the music in *Polly* (1729; Air 34), was also used in *The Fashionable Lady* (1730; Air 33), *The Generous Freemason* (1730; Air 22), and *The Lottery* (1st edn., 1732; Air 15—but omitted from the 2nd edn., 1732, and later editions). The music in *Polly*, like that of *DM* and *CD*, is in A, and may have been directly transcribed from one or the other.

No evidence has been found of a song associated with the tune before it was used in ballad operas. Lillo's song is clearly based on Air 34 of *Polly* (quoted from Moss):

> The world is always jarring;
>   This is pursuing
>   T'other man's Ruin,
> Friends with Friends are warring
>   In a false cowardly way.
> Spurr'd on by Emulations,
>   Tongues are engaging,
>   Calumny, raging
> Murthers Reputations,
>   Envy keeps up the Fray.

> Thus, with burning Hate,
> Each, returning Hate,
> Wounds and robs his Friends.
> In civil Life,
> Every Man and Wife
> Squabble for selfish Ends.

Fielding used the tune for Air 52 of *The Grub-Street Opera*, but his subject-matter is unrelated to Lillo's. Air 37, set to 'Dainty Davy', does, however, recall Lillo's words ('What the devil mean you thus | Scandal scattering, | Me bespattering . . .'). Fielding may have had Lillo's song in mind, as well as Gay's, when he wrote Air 15 of *The Lottery* (quoted from Moss):

> Whom do not Debts enthral?
> People of Quality, People of Quality.
> Who are proud of nothing at all?
> People of Quality.
> At Church, and Court,
> Who dares to sport?
> At Park, at Play, at Ball,
> Who rattle, prattle, tattle all?
> People of Quality.

Air XI (I. ix. 97–103; Moss 285)

The source for this song is found in a single-sheet edition headed (quoting *BUCEM* ['Boarding School']) 'Hey ho! Who's There. *A Dialogue in the comedy call'd the Boarding-Schooll*, sung by Mr. Ray and Miss Willis . . .'. In *BUCEM* this is dated *c*.1733; two other editions with similar headings are dated 1733 and 1735. *BUCEM* notes, however, that 'Coffey's "Boarding-School" was first produced in 1733. Neither Miss Willis nor Mr. Ray was in the cast, and this song seems of an earlier date. The words are not in D'Urfey's "Love for Money", from which Coffey's opera was adapted.' In fact, 'the Boarding-Schooll' is D'Urfey's play, referred to by its subtitle. It was performed at Drury Lane on 11 July 1718 ('Not Acted these Ten Years') with Miss Willis in the role of Molly. Ray is not listed in the play-bill, but he was at the time a singer with the company. The play was repeated occasionally in the ensuing seasons, with Miss Willis listed in the cast till her departure from the company in 1723. Ray was not listed till 1725 (Drury Lane, 21 Apr.), when he was noticed as the 'Singing Master'. (See *London Stage, 1700–1729*.) It seems likely that he performed the role in the 1718 revival, and that both the role and the song had been added to the play at that time. The earliest song-sheets must therefore date from 1718–23, the period during which Miss Willis was in the cast; 1718, when the song was probably first heard, is the most likely date. The song is not in *Pills*, and may well not be by D'Urfey.

The song-sheets have not been seen, and Moss is unaware of their existence; but it is reasonable to conclude with Moss that Coffey simply incorporated the song into his ballad-opera version of *Love for Money*, as he did another song from the original play, in this case written by D'Urfey and included in the 1691 text, beginning 'Make your Honours Miss' (see Simpson, pp. 479–80, and Air VIII n.). Lillo's song echoes the words that appear in *The Boarding-School* (Air 19, here quoted from Moss):

HE. Hey ho! Who's there?
SHE. No body but I, my Dear.
  H. Hey ho! Who's above?
  S. No body but I, my Love.
  H. Shall I come up, and see how you do?
  S. Ay, marry, and thank you too.
  H. Where's your Governess?
  S.   She is a-Bed.
  H. Where are the Keys, my Love?
  S.   Under her Head.
  H. Go, go, fetch them hither,
     That you and I may be merry together.
  S. The Dog it will bark, and I dare not, I'll swear;
  H. Take then a Halter, and hang up the Cur.
  S. Oh! no.
  H.   Why, why?
  S. I'd not for a Guinea my Dog shou'd die.
  H. Then farewel, my Dearest, for I must be gone.
  S. Tarry, sweet Tom, I'll be with you anon.
  H. Oh! no.
  S.   Why, why?
  H. Your Dog is much better belov'd than I.

The music that accompanies the song is printed from the same woodcut used in *Silvia*. The opening phrases correspond to the incipits of the two single-sheet editions listed in *NTI* (DFo-C.42.4 [381] and MH Marshall Coll. [313], probably copies of the two editions listed in *BUCEM*); the three versions differ slightly, but all represent the same basic melody, in the same key.

The line 'Ay, marry, and thank you too' echoes the refrain of an earlier ballad: see Air XVI n.

Air XII (I. ix. 127–32; Moss 527)

The source for this song (not identified by Moss) is almost certainly 'The Unconstant Shepherd; or, The Forsaken Lass's Lamentation. To an Excellent new Tune', beginning 'Oh, how can I be merry or glad' (broadside, *c.*1685–90, reprinted in *EB*, No. 365, pp. 607–8, and *BB* ii. 981–3, from the Euing copy). This is discussed by Simpson, pp. 314–15, as 'How Can I Be Merry or Glad'. Simpson reproduces the tune printed with that title in *Youth's Delight on the Flagelet*, 11th edn. (1697) (first included in 9th edn., *c.*1690). It differs considerably in melodic and rhythmic detail from the music printed in *Silvia*, but the identity of the tunes is clear from their general contour, especially in the final measures of each strain; the music in *Silvia* seems like a rather sophisticated recasting of the music in *Youth's Delight*.

The tune-title for Air XII is drawn from the third line of the fourth and fifth of the ballad's fifteen quatrains. The ballad itself is rather odd: the first five verses, which conclude with the lines paraphrased by Lillo—including the rhyme 'eyes/lies'—read like part of a ballad that was taken up and continued in a different vein by another writer; this impression is reinforced by the fact that these verses are printed on the obverse, and the remainder on the reverse, of the broadside. Ebsworth (*BB* ii. 978–80) rejects this conclusion on shaky evidence, but it is at least clear from his account that the first five verses were often treated as a separate song in themselves, which is further evidenced in the tune-title 'Oh that I was . . .':

> Oh, how can I be merry or glad,
>   or in my mind contented be;
> When the bonny bonny Lad whom I love best,
>   is banish'd out of my Company?
>
> Tho' he was banish'd it was for my sake,
>   and his true Love I still remain;
> He has caus'd me many a night for to wake,
>   and adieu to my true Love once again.
>
> I dare not come where my Love is,
>   I dare not for to sport nor play,
> For their evil tongues they are so glib,
>   I must take a kiss and go my way.
>
> Kissing is but a silly fancy,
>   it brings true Lovers into sin;
> O that I were, and I wish that I were,
>   for to see my true Love once again.
>
> As I was walking through the Hall,
>   I 'spy'd the twinkling of my Love's eyes;
> O that I were, and I wish that I were
>   in the Chamber where my true Love lies.

The second part begins:

> Away fond Fool, call home thy heart,
>   and in thy mind contented be;
> For thou spend'st thy time, and gets no gain,
>   by loving a Lover that loves not thee.
>
> If I do spend my time in vain,
>   oh, it is no loss to none but me;
> I'll set it as light as the wavering wind,
>   that daily blows from tree to tree.

The introduction of the man's voice in the sixth verse turns the song in a different direction. The remaining verses continue the lass's avowals of love; there is no further reference to banishment, and the song concludes:

> Unto the *Elizium* Shades I'll go,
>   where hovering Spirits do remain;
> Repeating their killing griefs and woe,
>   who by their hard-hearted Lovers was slain.
>
> Of my little Lambs I take my leave,
>   and every Creature in the Grove;
> Young *Phaon* he won't my Life reprieve,
>   therefore, alas! I die for love.

Lillo appears to have had the entire broadside ballad in mind: the idea of dying for love seems to underlie his changing the 'Chamber' of the original to the 'cold Grave', and the first two lines of his song epitomize the feelings expressed in the second part of the ballad.

A later broadside issued by the same publisher is 'An Answer to the Unconstant Shepherd . . . To an excellent New Tune', beginning 'My Dear let nothing trouble thy Heart'; Simpson notes that the copy in the collection of the Earl of Crawford (No. 832) contains the music. He cites a number of other ballads to the tune, most on roughly the same subject, but no occurrence of songs or music in books other than *Youth's Delight*.

Air XIII (I. ix. 167–80; Moss 68)

Source not found. The correspondence between the tune-title and the first line of Lillo's 'Chorus' certainly suggests that he adapted some part—perhaps the burden—of his source.

Air XIV (I. x. 8–13; Moss 654)

Source not found.

Air XV (I. x. 44–50; Moss 738)

Source not found. The date 23 Apr., apart from being St George's Day, was also the Coronation Day of Charles II (1661) and Anne (1702), and the source indicated by the tune-title may therefore be a political or patriotic ballad. A version of the same tune, in E minor, is included with the music for *The Beggar's Wedding* (1729; Act I, Air 16) for a song that calls for 'Once I had a Sweet-heart'. No source has been found for this song, which reads:

> Oh! how can I think from my True-Love to part,
> Oh! how can I think from my True-Love to part,
> The Moment I lose him, the Moment I lose him,
> The Moment I lose him, 'twill break my fond Heart.

Air XVI (I. x. 59–70; Moss 312)

This tune is discussed by Simpson, pp. 25–7, as 'Aye, Marry, and Thank You Too'. Moss wrongly identifies the source as 'The Maid of Lyn', beginning 'On *Brandon* Heath, in sight of *Methwold* Steeple' (in *Pills*, iv. 343–5), a song which, though it was quite probably inspired by 'Aye, Marry', is written in a quite different metrical pattern to an unrelated tune.

Lillo's source is a song beginning 'I met with a Country Lass' (reprinted in *The Amanda Group of Bagford Ballads*, ed. J. W. Ebsworth [1880], p. 542). He may have been put in mind of it by the sixth line of 'Hey ho! who's there?' (see Air XI n.). The original song, which inspired a number of 'replies' and imitations, describes the encounter of a man with a 'Country Lass' whose reiterated reply to his dishonourable entreaties is 'Aye [*or* 'I'], marry, and thank you too'. 'I live in the town of *Lynn* | Next door to the *Anchor* blew' (the source of the often used alternative tune-title) begins the tenth verse, in which she extends an open invitation. She is, in all respects, the antithesis of Silvia and the embodiment of Lettice:

> [HE.] 'I never intend to wed,
>   for fear my heart should rue;
>   Yet shall I have thy Maiden-head?'
> [SHE.]   'I, marry, and thank you too.'

A sequel, 'The Lass of *Lynn's* sorrowful Lamentation for the Loss of her Maiden-Head', is contained in *Pills*, v. 59–61, with music much more distantly related to the tune in *Silvia* than the version in *Youth's Delight on the Flagelet*, 9th edn. (*c*.1690) (reproduced by Simpson, fig. 17).

There is a distinct group of ballads written to the same tune to which Lillo might also have been responding: 'The Henpeckt Cuckold' and 'The Cuckold's Complaint', recounting the indignities to which a husband is subjected by a shrewish wife, and a reply, 'The Wife's Answer to the Hen-peckt Cuckold's Complaint' (all three reprinted in *RB* vii. 431–3). The 'Lass of Lynn' songs were probably better known. One could speculate that Lillo was aware of both groups of ballads, the one related to Timothy and Dorothy, the other to Lettice and Sir John. The tune's ribald associations tend to undercut the reconciliation of the Stitches, and it is possible, though by no means certain, that Lillo intended the irony.

Though Lillo borrowed the refrain associated with the tune, his song seems to owe a great deal to Airs 10, 'I, like a ship in storms, was tost' (set to 'Thomas I cannot') and 16, 'Were I laid on *Greenland's* coast' (set to 'Over the hills and far away') in *The Beggar's Opera*.

The same woodcut was used in *Robin Hood* (1730; Air 15) with a tune-title, 'The Bark in Tempests tost', drawn from the first line of Lillo's song. Of the 19 numbered airs in *Robin Hood*, five were set to tunes found also in *Silvia*, though in most cases the tune-titles differ and the songs appear to be unrelated. There is also an unnumbered song, printed without music, that follows almost immediately after Air 15 in *Robin Hood*. (Since it was clearly to be sung a cappella, it was probably felt that it did not qualify as a song on a level with the others.) Though Moss regards it as a continuation of Air XV, it is quite different in metre and cannot be sung to the same tune. It looks as if it could well have been meant for the shortened form of 'Greensleeves' to which Lillo wrote his Air XXVIII, q.v. The song is a *double-entendre* lullaby:

> Thy dainty high Forehead, and high *Roman* Nose,
> And that pretty Mark that lies under thy Cloaths;
> Before that I rock thee to sweet Lullaby,
> Give me thy sweet Lips—for to kiss, kiss, kiss, kiss.

Assuming that 'Greensleeves' was the intended tune, the nature of the song, and its immediate context—the singer intones 'Bye, bye, bye' before and after—connect it with the 'Father Peter' song that is the source of the tune-title of Air XXVIII. If this is indeed the case, it constitutes the only other reference to the 'Father Peter' song in ballad opera.

It is uncertain how much can be inferred from all this. *Silvia* was almost certainly in print, though not yet published, by the time *Robin Hood* was performed in Aug. and Sept. at Bartholomew Fair and Southwark Fair, and the association of the tune with Lillo's song may have had to do only with the organization of Watts's printing office. On the other hand, someone connected with its production may have had access to *Silvia* in printed or manuscript form, and used it as a source of tunes in the course of hasty writing. The cast of *Robin Hood* included Hulett (Welford), Ray (sexton), Mrs Egleton (Betty), and Chapman, another member of the regular-season company at Lincoln's Inn Fields. Lillo's play must have been submitted to Lincoln's Inn Fields during the preceding season (see Introduction, p. 15; *London Stage, 1729–1747*). That Lillo himself had anything to do with *Robin Hood* seems highly unlikely, though it is not inconceivable, especially in the case of the blank-verse scenes. The evidence presented here is, however, too tenuous to bear further speculation.

Air XVII (I. xi. 14–19; Moss 651 [= Moss 778])

The tune-title is the first line of a song discussed by Simpson, pp. 681–3, as 'The Spinning Wheel'. By his account it was first published as a broadside *c.*1685–8 as 'The bony Scot: Or, the Yielding Lass, To an excellent new Tune' (reprinted in *BB* i. 19). It appears in *Pills*, iii. 88–9, entitled 'A Scotch Song', with a tune that appears also in *Pills*, ii. 176, with a related song by Thomas D'Urfey beginning 'Upon a sunshine Summers Day', in which the refrain, modified in succeeding verses, is 'And still she turn'd her Wheel about'. The two songs were first collected together in *Pills*, 1699, pp. 113–14, 115–16, and were thus printed together in succeeding editions of the first volume of *Pills* up to and including the fourth (1714). A different tune appears with D'Urfey's song in a single-sheet edition dated *c.*1715 in *BUCEM* ('Upon'); the incipits given for this tune in *NTI* (DFo-C.42.3 [358] and MH Marshall Coll. [1146]) show that, as Simpson implies, it is not related to the music printed in *Silvia*.

'As I sat at my Spinning Wheel' was called for by various titles in a number of late 17th-cent. ballads (see Simpson), and the words of the original song are clearly Lillo's model for Air XVII:

> As I sat at my Spinning-Wheel,
> A bonny Lad there passed by,
> I kenn'd him round, and I lik'd him weel,
> Geud Feth he had a bonny Eye:
> My Heart new panting, 'gan to feel,
> But still I turn'd my Spinning-Wheel.

> (*Pills*, iii. 88, first verse)

There is, however, no evidence that the tune printed in *Silvia*, quite different from the one in *Pills*, had been previously associated with any 'spinning wheel' song. Watts had used this woodcut music in two earlier publications. It first appears in *MM* ii. 92 with 'The Inconstant', a song of quite different character found, as *BUCEM* notes, in Act III of Robert Gould's *The Rival Sisters* (London, 1696), a play whose only recorded performance(s) took place at Drury Lane in October 1695 (*London Stage, 1660–1700*). The two single-sheet editions of the song listed in *BUCEM* are there dated *c.* 1730. *NTI* lists three song-sheets (DFo-C.42.1 [125], DFo-C.42.4 [268], MH Marshall Coll. [528]) and a number of appearances in mid-century collections with identical incipits that differ slightly from Watts's version, and correspond rather to the music printed with the song in *The Gentleman's Magazine*, viii (May 1738), 270. The song may thus have been in the early stages of its eventual popularity when *Silvia* was written and printed.

Watts used the music again—its first use in a ballad opera—in *Momus Turn'd Fabulist* (1729; Air 8) under the tune-title 'A Scotch Tune' (Moss 778, 'source unknown'). Though this is appropriate to the nature of the tune, it had not been previously called 'Scotch'. The song itself gives one no reason to suppose that the tune is not the one intended: the text recalls neither the spinning-wheel songs nor 'The Inconstant', though in general character, and perhaps in stanza form, it has a closer affinity with the latter.

The music next appears in *Silvia*. Perhaps Lillo simply preferred it to the tune printed in *Pills* with the song beginning 'As I sat at my Spinning-Wheel'. It is also conceivable that he intended to set words that recalled one popular song to music associated with another. Lettice, who at this point in the play is not about to let herself be tied to one man, might indeed wish to emulate the 'inconstant' charmer:

> But long I had not been in view,
> Before her Eyes their Beams withdrew;
> Ere I had reckon'd half her Charms,
> She sunk into another's Arms.
> But she that once cou'd faithless be,
> Will favour him no more than me:
> He too, will find himself undone,
> And that she was not made for One.
>
> (*MM* ii. 93, third verse)

It seems, however, at least equally possible that the use of this music might have resulted from a printing-house confusion between 'A Scotch Song', as the spinning-wheel song was called in *Pills*, and a woodcut labelled, after the printing of *Momus*, 'A Scotch Tune'.

The *MM/Momus/Silvia* woodcut appears again, almost certainly in error this time, in *The Jovial Crew* (1731; Air 14), where the tune-title, 'Still I turn'd my Wheel about', clearly refers to D'Urfey's song 'Upon a sunshine Summers Day'. (Watts never did print a version of the spinning-wheel tune.) The woodcut was used for the last time in Coffey's *The Merry Cobler* (1735; Air 9) for a song that closely paraphrases Lillo's.

Two anonymous late ballad operas, printed without music, call for the tune by titles drawn from the first line of 'The Inconstant', 'Fair, and soft, and gay, and young': *Court and Country* (1743; Air 10) and *The Sailor's Opera* (1745; Air 26). The songs are both obviously based on 'The Inconstant', with its refrain 'made for [more than] One'. *NTI* records that the tune of 'The Inconstant' was printed, without words, under the title 'The Spinning Wheel', in James Aird, *A Selection of Scotch, English, Irish, and Foreign Airs*, ii (Glasgow, 1785). Perhaps by that time a misnomer had evolved into an alternate name.

Moss includes Air 31 of *The Footman* (1732) in his discussion of the 'spinning-wheel' songs, but the tune-title, 'The bony Scot', actually refers to a song known also as 'The canny boatman' (Moss 101; reprinted in *MM* ii. 129–30), not to the original title of 'The Spinning Wheel'. Neither Moss nor Simpson connects the tune in *Silvia* with 'The Inconstant' or the song in *Momus*, though Moss does conjecture that the music in *Silvia* may be erroneous, at the same time using it as his one musical example.

Air XVIII (I. xii. 26–9; Moss 555)

The tune is discussed by Simpson, pp. 563–4, whose account begins: 'A late seventeenth-century broadside "The Constant Lady and False-hearted Squire . . . To a New Tune," beginning "Near Woodstock town in Oxfordshire, | As I walk'd forth to take the air" (Pepys, v. 285; reprinted in *RB* viii. 635–6) was known in eighteenth-century editions as "The Oxfordshire Tragedy: Or, The Death of Four Lovers."' To the two parts of the earlier version the later one merely adds a pair of ballads that need not be dealt with here (see *RB* viii. 637–8). The 'Oxfordshire Tragedy' itself is the story of a 'fair Lady' courted, seduced, and cruelly rejected by a 'Wealthy Squire'. The second part relates how 'she mourning broke her heart, and dy'd', returning afterwards to haunt her lover:

> Soon after this he was possest with various thoughts, that broke his rest;
> Sometimes he thought her groans he heard, sometimes her ghastly ghost
>   appeared,
>
> With a sad visage, pale and grim, and ghastly looks she cast on him;
> He often started back and cried: 'Where shall I go, my self to hide?
>
> .   .   .   .
>
> 'Since my unkindness did destroy my dearest love and only joy,
> My wretched life must ended be: now I must die and come to thee.'
>
> His rapier from his side he drew, and pierc'd his body thro' and thro';
> So he dropt down in purple gore, just where she did some time before.
>
> (RB viii. 636)

Though the parallel is by no means exact, it is natural that Lillo's Jonathan, seeing his master in the company of an apparition in a churchyard, should recall the fate of the false squire.

The tune had been used previously in *The Cobler's Opera* (1728; Air 22) and *The Village Opera* (1729*a*, Air 46; 1729*b*, Air 41). The music in each of these varies to some degree, but the music in *A Sequel to Flora* (1732; Air 13) follows that in *Silvia* note for note. Since Watts printed *The Village Opera*, the new version in *Silvia* may represent reworking or preference for another version.

According to Ebsworth (*RB* viii. 69) the tune direction in 'The Oxfordshire Tragedy; Or, The Death of Four Lovers' (the later edition noted by Simpson, who says nothing about a tune direction) names 'As our King lay musing on his bed', which is Child Ballad No. 164, 'King Henry Fifth's Conquest of France'. Bronson (*Traditional Tunes*, iii. 127), remarking on the music, notes that this 'group of tunes is so steeped in the common stuff of British folk-melody that it is very difficult to follow it back with any assurance. It may have a not too distant relative in the tune of "The Oxfordshire Tragedy," which Chappell found in several ballad operas of around 1730. He was "strongly impressed" that it might be an old minstrel tune, and he prints it among tunes of the Elizabethan era.' The link seems to be established in the tune direction just noted, and in the resemblance between some of the traditional tunes reproduced by Bronson and the music in the ballad operas. It is even possible that the ballad-opera tunes are versions of 'As our King lay musing on his bed', which had prevailed over the 'New Tune' called for in the 17th-cent. broadside—if it was indeed new—taking on the name of a more popular ballad. Any such speculation must, however, take into account a number of other ballads and tunes, more than can be dealt with here. See Simpson, pp. 104, 563–4; *RB* vi. 744, viii. 68–9, 635–6; Chappell, *PMOT* i. 190–1.

Air XIX (I. xii. 38–43; Moss 831 [= Moss 413])

Watts used the woodcut earlier in *The Quaker's Opera* (1728; Air 7), where the tune is called 'Lovely, Charming Woman' (Moss 413). No source has been found for the tune by either title. The one would seem to reflect the first line, the other the refrain—both echoed by Lillo—of a song associated with the music.

The last four lines of Lillo's song fit the second strain of the tune quite easily; fitting the first two lines to the first strain appears to be much more difficult. Perhaps, however, the humour of the song, apart from the falsetto singing, consists in a burlesque of the highly melismatic fitting of words in the arias of Italian opera, in which case the first strain could be repeated for each of the first two lines. On the other hand, if phrases are repeated in those lines, the first strain need be sung only once—e.g. 'Charming, lovely Woman, lovely Woman, I am in love with thee; | Nay Sir, pish Sir, fye Sir, sure that ne'er can be, sure that ne'er can be.'

Air XX (I. xii. 65–72; Moss 839)

The tune-title is the first line of a song by Dryden, in Act V of his *Love Triumphant* (1694); the music was composed by John Eccles: see Cyrus Lawrence Day, *The Songs of John Dryden* (Cambridge, Mass., 1932), pp. 110–12, 181, who reproduces the song as it appears with Eccles's music in *The Gentleman's Journal* (Jan. and Feb. 1694), 35. The song was reprinted in *Pills*, iii. 227–8 (*Pills*, 1699, p. 238), with music that exactly reproduces the version in *The Gentleman's Journal*. The music in *Silvia* is in a different key (originally B flat) and, along with minor variants in phrasing, presents a quite different version of the fifth and sixth measures. According to Day the music is also found in *Thesaurus Musicus* (1694), ii. 2, and BL Add. MS 35043, fo. 6ᵛ, which have not been seen for comparison with the music in *Silvia*.

Day notes that Lillo's song was reprinted in *The Musical Companion* (1741), p. 35; his first two lines were reused in Air 37 of Isaac Bickerstaffe's *Love in a Village* (1762) (set to B. Galuppi's aria 'Son troppo vezzose' from *Enrico* [1743]).

The original song by Dryden reads:

> Young I am, and yet unskill'd
> How to make a Lover yield;
> How to keep, or how to gain,
> When to love; and when to feign:
>
> Take me, take me, some of you,
> While I yet am Young and True;
> E're I can my Soul disguise;
> Heave my Breasts, [heave my Breasts] and roul my Eyes.
>
> Stay not till I learn the way,
> How to lye, and to Betray:
> He that has me first, is blest,
> For I may deceive the rest.
>
> Cou'd I find a blooming Youth:
> Full of Love, and full of Truth,
> Brisk, and of a janty meen,
> I shou'd long to be fifteen.

(Day, *Songs of Dryden*, pp. 110–12.)

Air XXI (I. xii. 73–81 [no stanza break in O]; Moss 218)

The tune-title is the first line of a 'Pastoral' by Henry Carey, who almost certainly wrote both words and music. The earliest single-sheet edition listed in *BUCEM* ('Carey, Henry') is there dated *c.*1720: 'Flocks are sporting. *A Pastoral.* . . . By Mr. Carey. Sung by Mr. Randal at the Theatre.' A 'Randal' (or 'Randall') appears in bills for Drury Lane in the summer of 1715 and for Lincoln's Inn Fields in the season of 1715–16, which provides a likely date for the earliest song-sheets (*London Stage, 1700–1729*). This is corroborated by the title given the song in Carey's *The Musical Century*, vol. i (1737), 'Pastoral Made in the Year 1715'. Later song-sheets are listed in *BUCEM* (Moss cites

BL H.1601.[150]); *NTI* lists a song-sheet (DFo-C.42.4[290]) with an incipit that matches the music in *Silvia*. Watts's woodcut music had been used earlier in *The Village Opera* (1729*a*, Air 28; 1729*b*, Air 24). The vocal line for Carey's song in *MM* iii. 20–1 was printed from different woodcuts—those designed for 'prefixing' were not suitable for fitted words—but it represents the same version of the tune.

Carey's 'pastoral' is a simple celebration of spring:

> Flocks are Sporting, Doves are Courting,
> Warbling Linnets sweetly sing.
> Joy—Joy and Pleasure, without Measure,
> [K]ind—ly Hail the Glorious Spring;
> Kindly Hail the glorious Spring.
>
> Flocks are Bleating, Rocks Repeating,
> Valleys eccho back the Sound;
> Dancing, Singing, Piping, Springing,
> Nought but Mirth and Joy go round.
>
> (*MM* iii. 20–1; first verse printed
> line by line with music.)

As the words are fitted in *MM*, the word 'Joy' in line 3 is sung to the first four measures of the second strain. Lillo has altered this pattern in repeating the whole line 'Fans the Fire | Of Desire' (the song in *The Village Opera* differs from both in this respect). The writer of *The Footman* (1732; Air 24) followed Lillo's pattern, and appears to have borrowed his imagery as well:

> If a Lover
> You'd discover,
> Jealousy detects his Ways;
> If he's roving,
> That will prove him,
> If he's knowing
> The least glowing,
> That's the Gale which bids it blaze.
>
> (Quoted from Moss.)

Air XXII (I. xii. 99–110 [no stanza break in O]; Moss 543)

Two single-sheet editions of 'The Bashfull Maid' are listed in *BUCEM* ('Much'): one, dated *c*.1720, that begins 'Much I lov'd . . .', and another, dated *c*.1725, that begins 'Much I love . . .' (Moss reprints the text of the apparently earlier edition, BL H.1601[300]). The song was reprinted in *MM* iii. 172–3, where it begins 'Once I lov'd . . .'.

Watts produced two woodcuts, each representing a version of the music that is rhythmically and melodically distinct. The one used in *Silvia* had been used in *Momus Turn'd Fabulist* (1729; Air 19, tune-title 'Much . . .'); it has a much more flowing rhythm than the version in *MM*. Since the vocal-line woodcuts of the latter would seem to have been available, the ballad-opera music may represent an adaptation of the tune better suited to the song in *Momus*, which is by far less bawdy than 'The Bashful Maid'. The music printed in *The Female Parson* (1730; Air 3, tune-title 'Once . . .'), in 6/4 time, sounds like a hybrid of the two Watts versions with melodic variants of its own. The ultimate source of all these versions is uncertain: the incipits given for the song-sheets listed in *NTI* (DFo-C.42.3[68] and MH Marshall Coll. [92], which may both be copies of the earlier edition listed in *BUCEM*) appear to represent a different tune in C major. The tune is called for in the text of *The Mock Lawyer* (1733; Air 19, tune-title 'Once . . .'), but is among those omitted from the printed music.

The original song is an unabashed account of a seduction:

> Once I lov'd a charming Creature,
>> But the Flame with which I burn,
> Is not for each tender Feature,
>> Nor for her Wit nor sprightly Turn,
> But for her Down, down, der—ry down;
>> but for her down, down, derry Down.
>
> On the Grass I saw her lying,
>> Strait I seiz'd her tender Waist;
> On her Back she lay complying,
>> With her lovely Body plac'd
> Under my *Down, down,* &c.
>
> But the Nymph being young and tender,
>> Cou'd not bear the dreadful Smart,
> Still unwilling to surrender,
>> Call'd Mamma to take the Part
> Of her *Down, down,* &c.
>
> Out of Breath Mamma came running,
>> To prevent poor *Nancy*'s Fate,
> But the Girl, now grown more cunning,
>> Cry'd, *Mamma, you're come too late,*
>> For I am *Down, down,* &c.

Lillo's song, without the refrain, was expropriated by Allan Ramsay for Air 1 of his 1733 Edinburgh edition of Robert Drury's *The Devil of a Duke* (1732). This is one of fifteen songs not in the London edition, reprinted in Ramsay, *Works*, iv. 264–9. In the editor's notes (vi. 191) these are all attributed to Ramsay, but a cursory examination, using Moss's index, shows that seven of them, including Lillo's song, were taken from other ballad operas; to some of them Ramsay assigned different, Scottish tunes (in the case of Lillo's song, 'What should a Lassie do with an old man').

Air XXIII (II. i. 1–8, 11, 15–22 [page break in O before l. 17]; Moss 507)

The tune-title is the first line of a song first published in a single-sheet edition *c.*1713, according to *BUCEM* ('O'): 'Oh the charming month of may. *A New song* out of the Guardian.' A later song-sheet also listed is dated *c.*1720. (Moss cites BL H.1601.[328].) It was reprinted in *Pills*, vi. 344–5 (*Pills*, 1714, v. 270–1), with music, in A minor, that corresponds to the incipits given for the song sheets listed in *NTI* (DFo-C.42.2[20] and MH Marshall Coll. [807]). The music in *Silvia* has a rather more flowing rhythm. It closely resembles the version in G minor printed in *The Cobler's Opera* (1729; Air 8), which includes an eight-measure instrumental introduction and appears, from the anacrusis at the beginning of the song proper, to reflect adaptation for lyrics that begin 'And dare you thus my Faith upbraid?'

The original song does not appear in any printed editions seen of Abraham Cowley's

The Guardian, or the later version, *Cutter of Coleman-Street,* nor does it appear among his poems. Almost certainly, given the date of the earlier song-sheet, it was inserted when the play was revived at Drury Lane on 1 Aug. 1712, the first performance since 1702 (*London Stage, 1700–1729*). It celebrates various pleasant features of the countryside in May, the last of these being 'the Country Lass' who 'leaves her Milking | For a green Gown upon the Grass'. The first and last of the eight verses read:

> Oh the Charming Month of *May,*
> When the Breezes fan the Trees, is
> Full of Blossoms fresh and gay,
> Full of Blossoms fresh and gay:
> Oh the Charming Month of *May,*
> Charming, Charming Month of *May.*

> . . . .

> Oh the Charming Curds and Cream,
> When all is over she gives her Lover,
> Who on her Skimming-dish carves her Name,
> Oh the Charming Curds and Cream,
> Charming, Charming Curds and Cream.

> (*Pills,* vi. 344–5.)

The repeats necessary for the singing of Air XXIII are not indicated in the music. Measures 1–4 repeat for lines 1 and 2, and measures 5–8 for the repetition of line 4. Timothy's echo must be sung to measures 9–12, repeating Silvia's preceding line verbally and musically, so that the 'something more' (II. i. 12) is his singing of the final cadence.

It is possible that Lillo was influenced by Lacy Ryan's song in *The Cobler's Opera,* which likewise calls for a repetition of the first strain of music not found in the *Pills* reprinting of the original song (Ryan's song also repeats the last four measures, as well as the intervening measures). The context in which Air XXIII is sung also recalls Ryan's song:

> And dare you thus my Faith upbraid?
> Were I to ask all
> If you're a Rascal,
> Yes, is the Answer would be made.

> (Quoted from Moss.)

Cf. II. i. 23–4: 'that false, deceitful Sex, which only seems unhappy, when it would make ours so indeed'. Thus Ryan's song seems to be intermediate musically and in subject-matter between the original and Air XXIII.

Air XXIV (II. ii. 21–31 [no stanza break in O]; Moss 558)

The tune is discussed by Simpson, pp. 658–9, as 'The Shepherd's Daughter'. It appears in all editions except the first of *DM* (as 'Parson upon Dorothy', or a variation of that title, in the 2nd, 3rd, and 6th–18th edns., and as 'Shepherd's Daughter' in the 4th–8th edns.—i.e. the tune was duplicated under different titles in the 6th–8th edns.). The alternative title is taken from a ballad called 'The Knight and Shepherd's Daughter' (Child Ballad No. 110), but the connection is not apparent in the ballad-opera songs set to the tune (see Simpson; Chappell, *PMOT* i. 126–7; Bronson, *Traditional Tunes*, ii. 535–46, where two of the Playford versions are among those reproduced). The tune underwent a gradual evolution through editions of *DM*; it appears in its final form in the 17th and 18th edns. (1721, 1728), followed exactly in Watts's music except for the descending quavers of the first measure, which are peculiar to his version. The woodcut had been used earlier in *Momus Turn'd Fabulist* (1729; Air 42). The music in *Polly* (1729; Air 59) follows that of the fifteenth and sixteenth editions of *DM*, transposed into A minor. Lillo's song makes no reference to either of the previous ballad-opera songs.

Air XXV (II. ii. 53–60; Moss 573)

'Polwart *on the Green*' is the title of a song that appears in *Poems by Allan Ramsay* (1721; in Ramsay, *Works* i. 171–2, and *TTM* i. 67). *BUCEM* ('At') lists three single-sheet editions dated *c*.1720, *c*.1725, and *c*.1730, all entitled 'The Kind Lass of Polwart' (Moss cites BL G.306.[47]; *NTI* lists DFo-C.42.4 [92], MH Marshall Coll. [584, 585]). It was sung between acts according to the bills of Lincoln's Inn Fields for 21 and 25 May and 1 June 1730 (*London Stage, 1729–1747*). Watts used two blocks, representing slightly different versions of the music, in his ballad-opera printings. The one in *Silvia* was also used in *The Village Opera* (1729*a*, Air 12; 1729*b*, Air 8), *The Chambermaid* (1730; Air 5), *Patie and Peggy* (1730; Air 4), and *The Highland Fair* (1731; Air 45). The other was used in *Robin Hood* (1730; Air 16), *The Intriguing Chambermaid* (1734; Air 9), and *An Old Man Taught Wisdom* (1735; Air 11). The second version corresponds to the music printed in *Polly* (1729; Air 20), *The Beggar's Wedding* (1729; Air 5), and to the music printed with the original song in *Orpheus Caledonius* (1733, i. 49–50). Incipits in *NTI* link the second version also with the music of the song-sheets and with Stuart, *Musick*, i. 8–9.

The original song, in three verses, is addressed by the kind lass to 'the lad and lover you', and ends (Ramsay, *Works*, i. 172):

> At *Polwart* on the Green,
>   Amang the new mawn Hay,
> With Sangs and Dancing keen
>   We'll pass the heartsome Day.
> *At Night if Beds be o'er thrang laid,*
>   *And thou be twin'd of thine,*
> *Thou shalt be welcome, my dear Lad,*
>   *To take a Part of mine.*

Though this was probably the best known of the songs set to the tune, Ramsay included another in *TTM* i. 3–4. The first of the three verses of this song, called simply 'An Ode', reads:

> Tho' beauty, like the rose
>   That smiles on Polwart green,
> In various colours shows,
>   As 'tis by fancy seen;
> Yet all its diff'rent glories ly,
>   United in thy face,
> And virtue, like the sun on high,
>   Gives rays to ev'ry grace.

The song continues in this vein, and it is possible that Lillo borrowed the image of the rose from it; he may also have been influenced by Johnson's song in *The Village Opera*:

> The trembling Pulse discovers
> The Fever in the Blood;
> Such is the State of Lovers,
> Inconstant as the Flood.
>
> Now swelling flows the Tide in,
> Again it ebbs as low;
> So Love my Soul dividing,
> From Pleasure, sinks to Woe.

Lillo's own song was reprinted in Joseph Ritson, *A Select Collection of English Songs*, 3 vols. (London, 1783), ii. 103.

Air XXVI (II. iv. 15–22; Moss 486)

The tune-title is the first line of a song, discussed by Simpson, pp. 521–3, first printed in a single-sheet edition of 1709, 'Now comes on, the glorious year. *A Song on the Ensuing Campaign*. Design'd to be sung between the acts in The Modern Prophets. Written by Mr. Durfey' (listed in *BUCEM* ['Modern Prophets']; Moss cites BL H.1601.[315]; *NTI* lists DFo-C.42.2 [17], DFo-C.42.3 [107]). It was reprinted in *Pills*, i. 27 (*Pills*, 1714, v. 285–6), along with another song set to the same tune, '*Britains* now let Joys increase', in celebration of the accession of George I. Some minor, mainly rhythmic, variations in the music seen seem to reflect the phrasing of the different songs: the song-sheet version (Simpson, fig. 332) is clearly right for 'Now, now comes on the glorious Year', while the music in *Pills* has been adapted for the later song.

Watts's version of the music reflects the phrasing of the song-sheet music; the woodcut was also used in *The Lover's Opera* (3rd edn., 1730; Air 30), *The Fashionable Lady* (1730; Air 5), and *The Generous Freemason* (1730; Air 6). The version that appears in *Flora* (1729; Air 18) corresponds more nearly to the *Pills* music, as is appropriate for Hippisley's song.

The original song, and the many others set to the tune and noted by Simpson, are all expressions of nationalistic or party fervour. It is to be wondered whether the moral fervour displayed in Lillo's song would not have seemed faintly ridiculous to his audience, especially to those who were familiar with the immensely popular *Flora*: Lillo echoes, perhaps coincidentally or unconsciously, Hippisley's song, sung by the bumpkin Hob after he has cudgelled Roger to win a 'Hat and Favour':

> Now, brave Boys, the Fight is done,
> And I the Prize have fairly won;
> For I knew I cou'd beat'n four to one,
> And that he'll sore remember.
>   Fal, lal, &c.

This song is in turn closely based on the third and final verse of 'Now, now comes on the glorious Year' (*Pills*):

> Beat up the Drum a new Alarm,
> The foe is cold, and we are warm;
> The Monsieur's Troops can do no harm,
> Tho' they abound in Numbers:

Push then once more and the War is done,
Old Men and Boys will surely run;
And we know we can beat 'em if four to one;
Which he too well remembers.

Air XXVII (II. iv. 29–36; Moss 547)

The tune-title is the first line of 'Love in the Groves'; *BUCEM* ('One') lists two single-sheet editions, dated *c.*1710 and *c.*1720 (Moss cites BL H.1601.[337]). It was reprinted in *TTM* ii. 60–2, with seven verses; the song sheet listed in *NTI* (MH Marshall Coll. [634]) contains ten verses.

The woodcut used in *Silvia* was used again in *The Jovial Crew* (1731; Air 30). It differs very slightly from the music in *Polly* (1729; Air 68), the first few measures of which correspond to the incipit given for the song-sheet listed in *NTI*.

The original song finds the singer in a grove, where he meets a 'nymph':

> One evening as I lay
>   A-musing in a grove,
> A nymph exceeding gay
>   Came there to seek her love;
> But finding not her swain,
>   She sat her down to grieve,
> And thus she did complain,
>   How men her sex deceive.
>
> Believing maids, take care
>   Of false, deluding men,
> Whose pride is to ensnare
>   Each female that they can:
> My perjur'd swain he swore
>   A thousand oaths to prove
> (As many have done before)
>   How true he'd be to love.
>
> Then, virgins, for my sake,
>   Ne'er trust false man again;
> The pleasure we partake,
>   Ne'er answer half the pain;
> Uncertain as the seas,
>   Is their unconstant mind,
> At once they burn or freeze,
>   Still changing like the wind.

At this point the singer goes on to tell how he proposed 'For grief a Remedy'; his proposal is accepted, and the song concludes:

> I courted her with care,
>   Till her soft soul gave way,
> And from her breast so fair,
>   Stole the sweet heart away:

> Then she with smiles confess'd,
> Her mind felt no more pain,
> When she was thus caress'd,
> By such a lovely swain.
>
> (*TTM* ii. 60–2.)

Apart from the fact that his scene takes place in a grove, Lillo may have been influenced in his choice of a tune by Gay's song in *Polly*, beginning 'My Heart forebodes he's dead'. The parallel is less evident in the words of the two songs than in the predicaments of the characters who sing them. Just as Silvia mourns that she must 'love where [she] should hate', Polly mourns the possible death of Macheath, having a short time earlier said of him, 'He ran into the madness of every vice. I detest his principles, tho' I am fond of his person to distraction. Could your commands for search and enquiry restore him to me, you reward me at once with all my wishes. For sure my love still might reclaim him.' (*Polly*, III. xii. 76–9, in *The Poetical Works of John Gay*, ed. G. C. Faber [Oxford, 1926].) Silvia is more inclined to abandon Sir John to his vices and herself to mourning.

Air XXVIII (II. iv. 55–8 [no stanza break in O]; Moss 796)

The music represents one of the many variants of 'Greensleeves', in this case the abbreviated form usually called 'Which nobody can deny', the tune-title that appears with the same woodcut in *The Jovial Crew* (1731; Air 42) and *The Merry Cobler* (1735; Air 15). The use of 'Greensleeves' for a large number of ballads is discussed by Simpson, pp. 268–78, who traces this version of the tune to James Smith's poem 'The Blacksmith' (in *Wit and Drollery* [1656]), with its refrain 'Which no body can deny': 'The tune, which was vastly popular for a century or more, consists of the first strain of "Greensleeves," sometimes lengthened from eight to ten measures to accommodate a repetition of the refrain.' (Simpson, p. 274.)

The tune-title in *Silvia* paraphrases or quotes a variant of the first line, 'In *Rome* there is a most fearful Rout', of an anti-Catholic ballad of 1688 called, in broadside, 'A New Song of Lulla By, or Father Peter's [Petre's] Policy Discovered', to be sung to 'Greensleeves, or, My Mistriss is to Bulling Gone'. *Silvia* is the only ballad opera in which this song is explicitly referred to (see, however, note to Air XVI), but Lillo's song contains no apparent reference to it as seen in *A Supplement to the Collection of Miscellany Poems against Popery and Slavery* [i.e. *The Muses Farewel to Popery and Slavery* (1689)] (1689), pp. 91–3, where it has ten verses and is called '*A New Song*. To the Tune of, *Lulla by Baby*.' The only early ballad calling for the tune by the first line of 'Father Peter's Policy' is 'The Frightened People of Clerkenwell . . . 1689', beginning 'In Clerkenwell-Church there was a Rout' (see Simpson, p. 276). Unless Lillo borrowed something from the 'Clerkenwell' ballad, his song is very much his own, though consistent in tone with many others set to the tune. An intended connection between the 1688 ballad, which questions the identity of the son—the 'Old Pretender'—born to James II in that year, and the exchange of Sir John and Silvia in their infancy, seems rather far-fetched, but cannot be ruled out entirely.

Air XXIX (II. v. 8–15 [2 stanzas in O]; Moss 219)

'Fond Echo, forbear thy light strain' is the first line of a song by Lewis Theobald, included in his play—which he claimed was based on a Shakespeare manuscript—

called *The Double Falshood; or, The Distrest Lovers*, first performed at Drury Lane on 13 Dec. 1727 (*London Stage, 1700–1729*). *BUCEM* ('Double Falsehood') lists a song sheet dated *c.*1728, entitled 'The Forsaken Maid. A new song in the tragedy call'd "Double Falsehood" by Shakespeare', with music credited to Gouge. It was reprinted in *MM* ii. 124 (*'Sung in the* Distrest Lovers. The Words by Mr. Theobald. Set by Mr. Gouge.'), with music printed from woodcuts later used in *Silvia, The Generous Freemason* (1730; Air 16), and *Trick for Trick* (1735; Air 5). Identical incipits for the single-sheet editions listed in *NTI* (DFo-C.42.1 [149 + 173], DFo-C.42.4 [297], MH Marshall Coll. [410, 411], and Huntington Library 291705, vol. i [50]) correspond to Watts's music, though indicating that the two notes of the third measure were distributed as in the sixth and seventh measures.

Lillo's song is one of the most obvious examples of his 'moralizing' a tune, since it is something like the original song that one would expect at a similar point in any other play of the period:

> Fond Echo, forbear thy light Strain,
> And heedfully hear a lost Maid;
> Go, tell the false Ear of the Swain,—
> How deeply his Vows have betray'd;
> Go, tell him what Sorrows I bear;
> 'Tis now he must heal my Despair,
> Or Death will make Pi—ty too slow.

> > (*MM* i. 124; words printed line by
> > line with music.)

Fielding, in Air 62 of *The Grub-Street Opera*—set to 'Fond Echo' and heard on the stage in *The Welsh Opera*—does not so much burlesque Lillo's song as play off his theme, while reverting to more natural subject-matter (Molly, who sings the first verse, and Owen, who sings the second, are trying to persuade Sir Owen to accept their marriage—see Introduction, pp. 12–13):

> Oh think not the maid whom you scorn,
> > With riches delighted can be!
> Had I a great princess been born,
> > My Owen had been dear to me.
> On others your treasure bestow,
> > Given Owen alone to these arms,
> In grandeur and wealth we find woe,
> > But in love there is nothing but charms.

> In title and wealth what is lost,
> > In tenderness oft is repaid;
> Too much a great fortune may cost,
> > Well purchased may be the poor maid.
> While fancy's faint dreams cheat the great,
> > We pleasure will equally prove;
> While they in their palaces hate,
> > We in our poor cottage may love.

> > (*Grub-Street Opera*, ed. Roberts,
> III. xv. 6–21.)

Air XXX (II. vi. 9–16; Moss 841)

Lillo's song simply reverses the import of its source, the first of the 'Songs and Dialogues In the First and Second Part of *Massaniello*. The First Song Set by Mr. Daniel Purcell', in *Pills*, i. 265–6 (*Pills*, 1706, iv. 32–3):

> Young *Philander* woo'd me long,
>   I was peevish and forbid him;
> Nor would hear his loving Song,
>   And yet now I wish, I wish I had him.
> For each Morn I view my Glass,
>   I perceive the Whim is going;
> For when Wrinkles streak the Face,
>   We may bid farewel to Wooing.
> For when Wrinkles streak the Face,
>   We may bid farewel to Wooing.
>
> Use your time ye Virgins fair,
>   Choose before your days are Evil;
> Fifteen is a Season rare,
>   Five and Forty is the Devil:
> Just when Ripe consent to do't,
>   Hug no more the lonely Pillow;
> Women like some other Fruit,
>   Loose their relish when too Mellow.

    The source of the music is harder to trace. 'Young *Philander*' was not printed in the play *Massaniello*, and was apparently first published in D'Urfey's *The Second Collection of New Songs and Ballads. With the Songs and Dialogues in* . . . Massaniello. (1699), pp. 1–2 (Day and Murrie, p. 399), where the music is credited to Daniel Purcell, presumably the same tune that later appears in editions of *Pills*. The single-sheet edition listed in *NTI* (DFo-C.42.3[527]), which contains two verses, also credits the music to Daniel Purcell; the incipit in *NTI* corresponds exactly to the music in *Pills*. The song-sheet listed in *BUCEM* ('Purcell, Daniel') is dated *c*.1710 (Moss cites BL H.1601. [543]). The Purcell tune is entirely distinct from the tune printed in *Silvia* from woodcuts that were first used with an expanded version of 'Young Philander' found in *MM* ii. 46–8, entitled 'Clelia's *Reflections on her Self for slighting* Philander's *Love*'; here the song has six verses, D'Urfey's song, with frequent substantive alteration, being the first and third. The *MM* woodcut music was also used in *The Jovial Crew* (1731; Air 23). A Scottified *rifacimento* of this longer version of the song appears in *TTM* ii. 199–200, with the title as in *MM* (except 'Celia's') and a tune direction calling for 'The gallant shoemaker' (not identified); the first three verses were reprinted in *Orpheus Caledonius*, ii. 67–8, entitled '*Peer* of Leith' in the text and 'Young Philander' in the engraved music, which presents a recognizable variant of the tune in *MM* and *Silvia*. '*Peer* of Leith' is very possibly a tune-title, indicating a Scottish or pseudo-Scottish origin consistent with the tune's decidedly Scottish flavour. Another version of this tune was printed in *The Village Opera* (1729*a*, Air 6; not in 1729*b*); the first strain is identical to that of the *Silvia* version, but the second strain differs considerably, and lacks the F sharp to F natural modulation found in the second strains of both the *Silvia* and *Orpheus Caledonius* versions.

Air XXXI (II. vii. 13–20 [2 stanzas in O]; Moss 407)

The tune-title clearly refers to Thomas D'Urfey's song beginning 'Great Lord Frog to Lady Mouse', entitled 'A Ditty on a high Amour at St. *James's*. Set to a Comical Tune', in *Pills*, i. 14–16 (*Pills*, 1714, v. 298–300). It was first printed in single-sheet editions, one of which is dated *c*.1710 (*BUCEM* ['Great']); the identical incipits given for the copies listed in *NTI* (DFo-C.42.1[190, 200], DFo-C.42.4[346], and MH Marshall Coll. [761]) correspond to the tune printed in *Pills*.

Watts's woodcut music had been used earlier in *Momus Turn'd Fabulist* (1729; Air 37), where it is called 'Cockamycari She' after one of D'Urfey's refrain lines, and it was later used in *Achilles* (1733; Air 41), as 'Lord *Frog* and Lady *Mouse*'; the music called 'Cockymycary She' in *The Decoy* (1733; Air 47) follows this tune exactly. Watts's version of the tune is, however, quite different from that in *Pills*, though they are similar in their general contour and rhythm; both have the sudden drop of an octave in the second line of the song. All the ballad-opera songs just mentioned, as well as Lillo's, could be sung to the *Pills* tune. It is notable that in spite of their tune-titles none of the four ballad-opera songs printed with music—in all cases representing the Watts version—contains a refrain, while those printed without music, in *The Humours of the Court* (1732; Air 24), *The Sturdy Beggars* (1733; Air 25), and *The State Juggler* (1733; Air 13), all use the three refrains found in D'Urfey's song:

> Great Lord Frog to Lady Mouse,
> Croakledom hee Croakledom ho;
> Dwelling near St. *James's* house,
>   Cocky mi Chari she;
> Rode to make his Court one day,
> In the merry Month of *May*,
> When the Sun Shon bright and gay,
>   Twiddle come Tweedle twee.
>
>   (*Pills*, i. 14.)

Ballads about the courtship of the frog and the mouse date back at least as far as 1549 (see Chappell, *PMOT* i. 88, where the music, from *Melismata* [1611], is that of a G major tune that only vaguely resembles the tunes in *Pills* and the ballad operas). Chappell discusses D'Urfey's song and the ballad-opera derivatives in connection with 'The Northern Lass' and 'Muirland Willie', treating these tunes as a single one with diverse forms (*PMOT* ii. 559–61, 786). Of 'The Northern Lass' he notes (p. 786):

The Scotch sing the song of *Muirland Willie* to this tune,—not the slow version, which is evidently the original,—but to the air in its abbreviated dancing form. We do not find *Muirland Willie* sung to it until after it had been turned into a lively air by D'Urfey, and, although the words of the Scotch song are old, we have no indication of any tune to which they were to be sung in early copies. They seem to have been intended for *Green Sleeves*, more likely than any other air. *Muirland Willie* was first printed to this tune by Thomson, in his *Orpheus Caledonius*, folio, entered at Stationers' Hall on 5th January, 1725–6. The tune had then been published, as *Great Lord Frog*, in Walsh's 24 *New Country Dances for the year* 1713; with words in vol. i of *The Merry Musician*, dated 1716, and in vol. i of *Pills to Purge Melancholy*, 1719.

(The words of 'Muirland Willie', marked 'Z.' for an old song, are in *TTM* i. 7–9; the music alone is in Stuart, *Musick*, i. 14–15; the words and music appear in *MM* i. 78–82, with the title 'Scotch Wedding'.) While Chappell's account may be correct—there is enough similarity between 'Muirland Willie' and 'Great Lord Frog' to justify it— 'Muirland Willie' seems to have been regarded as a quite separate song; there is some variation among the different versions, but all of them much more closely resemble the tune Chappell reproduces for 'The Northern Lass' (*PMOT* ii. 560) than they do 'Great Lord Frog'. Nevertheless, the song itself recalls the still familiar 'A Frog he would a-wooing ride':

> On his gray yade as he did ride,
> With durk and pistol by his side,
> He prick'd her on wi' meikle pride,
>   Wi' meikle mirth and glee.
> Out o'er yon moss, out o'er yon muir,
> Till he came to her daddy's door.
>   *With a fal, dal,* &c.
>
>   (*TTM* i. 7, verse 2.)

Watts's version, however, appears to have greater affinity with a tune called 'Goddesses' in all editions of *DM*, and associated with a ballad, distinct from 'The Northern Lass', called 'The Northern Lass's Lamentation' (see Chappell, *PMOT* ii. 456–8, 782, 794, and Simpson, pp. 351–3). How Watts's tune came to be printed under the title 'Great Lord *Frog*, and Lady *Mouse*', etc., is hard to say. It might represent a separately developed tune which Watts simply reprinted, or, more likely, an adaptation made for the song in *Momus* with dual reference to D'Urfey's tune and a version of 'Goddesses'. (If Pepusch worked on *Momus*, as he may well have done, this is not altogether unlikely: the tune later called 'Goddesses' appears as 'Quodling's Delight' in *The Fitzwilliam Virginal Book*, which Pepusch owned. See Charles W. Hughes, 'John Christopher Pepusch', *Musical Quarterly*, xxi. 1 [Jan. 1945], 54–70, and Fiske, pp. 114–15, 125–6.)

It is at any rate very likely that the four ballad-opera songs printed with the Watts version of the tune were all indeed meant to be sung to it, and not to the *Pills* version. The first of these, in *Momus*, is an allegory in which a 'learned Sage' dangles a 'curious Sugar-Plumb' before a crowd in the market-place of Athens. When a 'brisk Youth' at last seizes the prize and taunts the sage, he is told:

> Let stay, and hear me tell a Tale,
>   I shall show
>   A propos,
> Says the Sage, 'twill sure prevail,
> It is the Female's Doom:
> This prize resembles Virgin Hearts,
> Which Man his utmost Power exerts
> To gain—then soon the Fair deserts,
> Cloy'd with the Sugar-Plumb.
>
>   (Quoted from Moss.)

Lillo's song seems to be based on this one. The song in *The Decoy* refers to 'children, pleas'd with Sugar-Plumbs'. The song in *Achilles* is minimally related to the subject-matter of its predecessors, but it is at least consistent with them in lacking a refrain.

Air XXXII (II. vii. 29–44; Moss 170)

The tune is discussed in Simpson, p. 168. The original song, 'Dear Pinkaninny', by Thomas D'Urfey, occurs in Act IV of the Third Part of his *Don Quixote*, and was reprinted in *New Songs in the Third Part of Don Quixote* (1696; according to Simpson it is found only in 'some copies'). It was later included in *Pills*, i. 282–3 (*Pills*, 1699, pp. 305–6) with music identical with that of the first printing (Simpson, fig. 106, noting that the tune was 'identified only as a minuet'). The music in *Silvia* differs very little from that in *Pills*; Watts reused the woodcut in the three-act version of *The Devil to Pay* (1731; Air 20) with the same tune-title.

D'Urfey's song is a dialogue 'Intended to be Sung by 2 Poppets one representing a Captain tother a Town Miss'. Though Lillo did not adapt D'Urfey's words in his song, they are reflected in exchanges between Jonathan and Betty in this scene (ll. 10–13) and in III. xv. 5–6.

> Dear Pinckaninny, if half a Guinny,
> To Love will win ye,
>   I lay it here down;
> We must be Thrifty,
> 'Twill serve to shift ye,
> And I know Fifty,
>   Will do't for a Crown.
>
> Dunns come so boldly,
> King's Money so slowly,
> That by all things Holy,
>   'Tis all I can say;
> Yet I'm so rapt in,
> The Snare that I'm trapt in,
> As I'm a true Captain,
>   Give more than my Pay.
>
> Good Captain Thunder,
> Go mind your Plunder,
> Ods—ns I wonder,
>   You dare be so bold;
> Thus, to be making,
> A Treaty so sneaking,
> Or Dream too of taking,
>   My Fort with small Gold.
>
> Other Town Misses,
> May gape at Ten Pieces,
> But me who possesses,
>   Full Twenty shall Pay;
> To all poor Rogues in Buff,
> Thus, thus I strut and huff,
> So Captain kick and cuff,
>   March on your way.
>
>   (*Pills*, i. 283.)

Air XXXIII (II. viii. 1–11; Moss 451 [= Moss 801])

'Mrs. Le Gard' was actually Mary Laguerre, wife of John Laguerre, the singer-actor who played Timothy Stitch. The name Laguerre was variously spelt, 'Legar' being the most common variant; it is possible that the spelling in the tune-title reflects confusion with 'Delagarde', the name of a dancer, and his sons, at Lincoln's Inn Fields, whose wife appeared only briefly on the stage early in the century (*Actors, Actresses*). '*Perseus* and *Andromeda*' can thus be identified as the extraordinarily successful pantomine, subtitled *The Spaniard Outwitted*, first performed at Lincoln's Inn Fields on 2 Jan. 1729/30 (*London Stage, 1729–1747*). It is discussed by Fiske (pp. 75, 84–7), who conjectures that it was written by Lewis Theobald, with music by J. E. Galliard. Moss incorrectly identifies the source as *Perseus and Andromeda: With the Rape of Columbine: or, The Flying Lovers*, with music by J. C. Pepusch, first performed at Drury Lane on 15 Nov. 1728 (*London Stage, 1700–1729*).

This tune was not included in *The Comic Tunes in Perseus and Andromeda*, published by Walsh in 1763 (Fiske, p. 83), but since Mrs Laguerre played an Amazon—a classical character—her dance would not have been part of the Harlequin scenes that the comic tunes were meant to accompany. On 18 Apr. 1730 Walsh advertised *The Tunes, Aires, and Dances in the Entertainment, call'd Perseus and Andromeda. As they are perform'd at the Theatre Royal in Lincoln's Inn-Fields*, which may well have included the music of her dance, but no copy is known to have survived (William C. Smith and Charles Humphries, *A Bibliography of the Musical Works Published by the Firm of John Walsh during the Years 1721–1766* (London, 1968), No. 1197; the *Comic Tunes* are No. 1200). The tune came to be known as 'The White Joak' by analogy with a popular dance-tune in the same style called 'The Black Joak' or 'The Coal Black Joak': 'The White Joke' was billed as a new dance, by Eaton, at Goodman's Fields, 28 Apr. 1730. Eaton introduced a new dance called 'The Yellow Joke' on 29 June, and in Aug. 1730 Walsh published *The Third Book of The most Celebrated Jiggs . . . To which is added the Black Joak the White Joak, the Brown, the Red, and the Yellow Joaks* (Smith and Humphries, No. 866).

On 2 June 1730 Goodman's Fields advertised a 'New Song, called *Myra's Choice*, to the Tune of the White Joke' (*London Stage, 1729–1747*). This song, beginning 'Gay Myra, Toast of all the Town', was published in single-sheet editions headed 'The White Joak. Sung by Mrs. Roberts at the Theater in Drury Lane. The Words by Mr. Davis' (quoted from Moss 801 [BL G.308.(12)]). *BUCEM* ('Gay') dates the earliest of the three editions listed *c*.1725, but this is, in view of the references to the dance and song as new in 1730, too early; at any rate Mrs Roberts did not join the Drury Lane company till the season of 1728–9. Five copies of single-sheet editions, the incipits for which correspond to the music in *Silvia*, are listed in *NTI* (DFo-C.42.1[195], DFo-C.42.4[322], MH Marshall Coll. [1307, 1308, 1309]).

Lillo sold his copy of *Silvia* to Watts on 23 Jan. 1729/30, and the edition was almost certainly printed within two months of that date (see Introduction, pp. 21–2). He was therefore the first to write words for the tune, even before it had acquired the name by which it was always later known. Watts reused the woodcut in other ballad operas, where it is always called 'White Joak': *Robin Hood* (1730; Air 14), which was probably printed in late Aug., *The Generous Freemason* (1730; Air 3), *The Lottery* (2nd edn., 1732; Air 14), and *The Livery Rake* (1733; Air 9). A slightly different version of the tune was printed in *MM* vi. 82–5 with 'The White Joak', i.e. 'Gay Myra'. Another version with only slight variations is printed in *The Decoy* (1733; Air 30), which contains three other tunes labelled 'In Perseus and Andromeda'.

Air XXXIV (II. ix. 9–14; Moss 10)

The tune is discussed by Simpson, pp. 530–1. The song beginning 'Oh fie, what mean I foolish Maid' appears in Act II of John Crowne's *The Married Beau* (1694). Simpson (fig. 337) reproduces the music as it is found in a single-sheet of 1694, 'A Song in the last New Comedy call'd the Married Beau or the Curious Impertinent. Sung by Mr. Doggett & Sett by Mr. John Eccles.' (*BUCEM* ['Eccles, John'] dates this edition *c*.1700, but the play was performed only in Apr. 1694 [*London Stage, 1660–1700*].) A broadside of the same date, 'An Excellent New Song, Called The Private Encounter Between Two Loyal Lovers', contains Crowne's first three verses (as verses 1, 2, and 5), with three new verses, ending 'My love shall still be firm and pure, | And . . . in thy arms I'll lye' (reprinted in *OPB*, pp. 13–14). The song was reprinted in *Pills*, iii. 243–4 (*Pills*, 1699, pp. 261–2), with music that follows exactly that of the song-sheet. The music in *Silvia* is transposed down a fourth and has a more flowing rhythm, with twelve measures in the second strain as opposed to the original fifteen.

The version in *Pills* omits the last two of the five verses printed in the play. Lillo's song epitomizes the whole of the song, specifically the last verse (bracketed portions from *Pills*, corrected, show the original repetitions):

> Oh fie! What mean I, foolish Maid,
> In this remote and silent Shade,
> To meet with you alone?

> My Heart does with the place combine,
> [And both are more your Friends than mine,]
> And both are more your Friends than mine:
> [Oh! oh! oh! I shall, I shall, I shall be undone,]
> Oh! [oh! oh! oh!] I shall be undone.

> A Savage Beast I wou'd not fear,
> Or shou'd I meet with Villains here,
> I to some Cave wou'd run.

> But such inchanting Arts you shew,
> I cannot strive, I cannot go:
> Oh! I shall be undone.

> Ah! give your sweet Temptations o're,
> I'll touch these dangerous Lips no more:
> What, must we yet Fool on?

> Ah! now I yield! Ah! now I fall!
> And now I have no Breath at all;
> And now I'm quite undone.

> I'll see no more your tempting Face,
> Nor meet you in this dangerous place,
> My Fame's for ever gone.

> But Fame, to speak the truth, is vain,
> And every yielding Maid does gain,
> By being so undone.

In such a pleasing Storm o' Bliss,
To such a Bank o' *Paradise*,
Who wou'd not swiftly run?

If you but truth to me will swear,
I'll meet you again; nor do I care,
How oft I be undone.

(*The Married Beau*, 1694.)

The music printed in *Silvia* likewise demands a repetition of the fifth line; the final line would be sung 'To be by you undone, | To, to, to, to be by you undone'.

Lillo clearly based his words on a version of the original beginning 'Oh fie'; no version beginning 'Alas', as in the tune-title, has been seen.

Air XXXV (II. ix. 20–9; Moss 812 [= Moss 88])

This tune was known by two different titles in the ballad operas in which it was used: 'Brisk Tom and Jolly Kate', from a song that I have not been able to trace, and 'Windsor Terras', from a song written to the tune by Thomas D'Urfey, beginning 'Musing I late, | On *Windsor* Tarrass sate', in *Pills*, i. 232–3 (*Pills*, 1714, v. 289–91). D'Urfey's song was published in a single-sheet edition dated *c*.1715 in *BUCEM* ('Musing'); the incipit for the copy listed in *NTI* (DFo-C.42.3[73]) corresponds exactly to the music in *Pills*. Day and Murrie (p. 290) note the occurrence of the song in *Musa et Musica* (1710). Moss finds it also in a 'later manuscript' (BL Add. MS 35043, fo. 122), where the tune is identified as a 'Welch air'. As 'Windsor Terras' the tune appears in *DM*, vol. ii (3rd and 4th edns., 1718, 1728), p. 239, and in *CD*, Book 2 (1719), p. 261.

D'Urfey's song has four verses, the first and third of which are to be sung to the first strain, repeated (the repeat is indicated in the *Pills* music). Lillo's song appears to be designed for the second strain only. The same is true of Air 54 of *The Fashionable Lady* (1730), with music printed from the same block used in *Silvia* under the tune-title 'Windsor Terras'; yet the first line of the song, 'Pert Tom and modish Sue', recalls 'Brisk Tom and Jolly Kate'. Another such song is Air 2 of *The Harlot's Progress* (1733), beginning 'Brisk Wine and Women are', with the tune-title 'Brisk Tom and Jolly Kate'. Watts's woodcut was first used in *The Quaker's Opera* (1728; Air 6, with the tune-title 'Windsor Terras') for a song meant to be sung to both strains without repeats, as is Air 12 of *Bays's Opera* (1730), with the tune-title 'Windsor Terrace'. Air 9 of *The Cobler's Opera* (1728), in which the music is called 'Brisk Tom and Jolly Kate', looks as if it should be sung to the first strain without a repeat, the whole of the second strain being repeated for the rest of the song. There is a slight degree of variation among the versions of the music in Watts's woodcut, *Pills*, and *The Cobler's Opera*. Moss overlooks the basic identity of all these tunes, and treats 'Brisk Tom and Jolly Kate' separately.

In D'Urfey's song the singer overhears a 'blund'ring Country Beau' propose marriage to a 'Nymph', boasting of his 'thousand Pound a Year'. The 'Art' that figures in her refusal is played on in Lillo's song.

Mony the crew
Of Sots think all must do;
And now this Fool,
Unlearn'd at School,
It seems believes so too:

> But the rare Girl,
> More worth than Gold or Pearl,
> Was Nobly got,
> And brought, and Taught,
> To slight the sordid World.

> She then brisk and gay,
> That lov'd a Tuneful Lay,
> In hast pull'd out,
> Her little Flute,
> And bad him Sing or Play;
> He both Arts defy'd,
> And she as quickly cry'd;
> Who learnt no way,
> To Sing nor Say,
> Shou'd ne'er make her a Bride.

> (*Pills*, i. 233.)

Air XXXVI (II. xii. 7–12; Moss 777)

The tune-title is the first line of 'The Artifice', a song for which *BUCEM* ('When') lists three single-sheet editions, dated *c.*1720 (two editions) and *c.*1725 (Moss cites BL H.1601.[522]). Incipits given for the song-sheets listed in *NTI* (DFo-C.42.2[193], DFo-C.42.2[417], and MH Marshall Coll. [63]), all identical, correspond exactly to the music in *Silvia*, printed from the woodcuts used with 'The Artifice' in *MM* iii. 81–3.

   Lillo's song is a close adaptation of the second verse of the original song:

> The Maidens are shy,
> Cry—Pish! and cry—Fye!
> And vow if you're rude they will call:
> But whisper so low,
> That they let us know,
> It is all Artifice, all;
> It is all Ar—ti—fice, Ar—ti—fice all.

> (*MM*; burden from verse 1.)

The other three verses separately consider the 'Artifice' displayed by the suitors of one 'Cloe'; by wives who promise never, as widows, to remarry; and by those who cry loudly and publicly 'For Church and for Justice'.

Air XXXVII (II. xiv. 11–26; Moss 597)

The tune is discussed by Simpson, p. 617. The tune-title is the first line (lacking one 'Room') of Thomas D'Urfey's song called 'The Blackbird', in *Pills*, ii. 204–6 (*Pills*, 1700, ii. 1–2 [first sequence]). Simpson notes a song-sheet of *c.*1705, which identifies the tune as 'y^c new Dance' and credits it to James Paisible. The song-sheet music (Simpson, fig. 400) is nearly identical to the music printed in *Silvia* from a woodcut later used in *The Jovial Crew* (1731; Air 49). Incipits given in *NTI* for 'The English Pasby' in *DM*, beginning with the eleventh edition of 1701 (p. 276), appear to represent this tune, as do those for 'The English Paspy' in *CD*, Book 1 (1718), p. 289 ('Pasby' and 'Paspy' presumably mean 'passepied'). It appears that all versions of the music are in 3/2 time, except *Pills*, in 6/4.

D'Urfey's song is a generalized look at politics from the perspective of the country;
Lillo's song reflects the tone of the original as a whole, adopting the birds of the first
verse:

> Room, room, room for a Rover,
>   Yonder Town's so hot;
> I a Country Lover
>   Bless my Freedom got:
> This Celestial Weather
>   Such enjoyment gives,
> We like Birds flock hither,
>   Browzing on green leaves:
> Some who late sate Scowling,
>   Publick Cheats to mend;
> Study now with Bowling,
>   Each to Cheat his Friend:
> *Whilst on the Hawthorn Tree, Terry rerry, rerry, rerry, rerry,*
> *rerry, rerry, sings the Blackbird, Oh what a World have we.*

Air XXXVIII (II. xv. 22–30 [page break in O before l. 26]; Moss 541)

'On yonder high Mountain' is referred to in Simpson's discussion of 'Love will find
out the way', the refrain of a ballad called 'Truth's Integrity, Or, A curious *Northern* Ditty
Called, Love will find out the Way. To a pleasant new tune' (see Simpson, pp. 472–4;
also Chappell, *PMOT* i. 304–5, ii. 681–2). The ballad is reprinted in *RB* ii. 639–43
(*c.*1630) and *EB*, No. 358, pp. 594–5 (1656), and in *Pills*, vi. 86–9 (*Pills*, 1714, v. 34–5
[first part only?]), with an elaborate version of the tune found in *A Musicall Banquet*
(1651; Simpson, fig. 295). Simpson notes a number of musical variants, finding in the
tune called 'On yonder high Mountain' a 'family likeness to the tune of "Love will find
out the way," despite a good deal of difference in harmonic and melodic detail'. It has a
rather Scottish flavour that may have to do with the original ballad's putative 'Northern'
provenance.

'On yonder high Mountain' was called for in three other ballad operas: *Momus Turn'd
Fabulist* (1729; Air 29), in which Watts first used this woodcut; the earlier *Cobler's Opera*
(1728; Air 21), with music that is melodically almost identical; and *The Fancy'd Queen*
(1733; Air 15), printed without music. Despite the tune-title, both Ryan's song in *The
Cobler's Opera* and Lillo's recall one verse in particular of 'Truth's Integrity':

> Well may the eagle
>   Stoope downe to the fist;
> Or you may inveagle
>   The Phenix of the east;
> With feare the tiger's moved
>   To give over his prey,
> But never stop a lover,
>   *He will poast on his way.*

> (*RB* ii. 640, verse 5.)

Ryan's song reads:

> Ah, foolish Peg Wellfleet,
> How could'st thou e'er believe
> That on Land, or in the whole Fleet,
> Is the Man that won't deceive?
>   'Tis the Nature
>   Of the Creature,
> As of Wolves, to seek for Prey;
>   So 'tis common
>   In the Woman,
> To throw herself away.

(Quoted from Moss.)

No song beginning 'On yonder high Mountain' has survived, but these resemblances may provide a clue to its content. The short version of 'Truth's Integrity' found in *TTM* ii. 171 and in Percy's *Reliques* ends with the verse quoted above, thus omitting the whole of the second part and the last two verses of the first part (the latter, concerning Guy of Warwick and Bevis, were probably not to 18th-cent. taste); the verse thereby gains a prominence that it lacks in the full-length version. Ryan's song also recalls the penultimate verse of 'The Wandring Virgin', set to 'Over Hills and High Mountains' (in *RB* ii. 575–6):

> I'le search over *England*,
> to see if 't contain;
> If not, i'le turn Sailor,
> to search on the Main,
> The Ocean, so boundless,
> i'le travel about,
> *I'le range the wide world,*
> *but i'le find my Love out.*

This ballad is a 'reply' to 'The Wandring Maiden', which begins 'Over hills and high mountains', and is itself set to 'an excellent new Tune'. Both Chappell and Simpson regard 'The Wandring Maiden' as a 'paraphrase' of 'Truth's Integrity', and suggest that the tune 'Over hills and high mountains', cited in a number of later ballads, may be the one that came to be known as 'On yonder high mountain'. There is, however, no verse in 'The Wandring Maiden' that resembles verse 5 of 'Truth's Integrity': apparent references to it in the ballad-opera songs, and the consistency of the tune and its title, combine to suggest that 'On yonder high Mountain' may well have been, both in words and music, an 18th-cent. variant or reworking of 'Truth's Integrity', perhaps in short form, and perhaps incorporating elements of 'The Wandring Virgin' (Ryan could of course have referred to the latter on his own). This supports Moss's conclusion, which is based on more general evidence:

> If we assume that the original song was similar in content to ['Truth's Integrity'], three of the authors who use the music then simply reverse the sentiment of the original . . . a common practice in ballad operas. In other instances we find that Lillo refers to the traditional lyrics for the tone and idea he communicates in his songs, a fact which supports my supposition about the contents of the original, 'On Yonder High Mountain.'

The general character of Lillo's song recalls the *Pills* version of 'Truth's Integrity', in which 'Tears' rather than 'fear' move the tiger. In *TTM* and Percy's *Reliques* this becomes 'The lioness, ye may move her | To give o'er her prey'.

Air XXXIX (II. xv. 70–82; Moss 157)

The tune-title is the first line of Lillo's source, a song published in a single-sheet edition with the title 'The Country Delight', the text of which is reprinted by Moss (BL G.316.d.[29.], dated '1730?'). A version of the same song, containing a number of variant words and lines, appears as Air 5 of Coffey's *Southwark Fair* (1729), with a tune-title calling for 'The Country Wake'. The relationship between the two songs is uncertain, but Coffey may well have simply incorporated the song into his play, making changes of his own or referring to an edition other than the one found by Moss (*BUCEM* ['Country'] lists only one other edition, dated *c.*1750; cf. note to Air XI). Neither Moss nor the present editor has found an appropriate tune called 'The Country Wake', which could simply be an alternative title for 'The Country Delight': the last two of the song's four verses concern the pleasures of country wakes and fairs. Moss unfortunately says nothing about the music of the song-sheet; it is not found in the collections surveyed for *NTI*.

It is nevertheless clear that Lillo worked from some version of this song, as evidenced by the versification and the use of the word 'plow', the key word of the original refrain. The music is appropriate, and demands the repetition of the final line indicated in the song-sheet. The text of the song-sheet contains some rather incoherent passages; the first verse of the version in *Southwark Fair* reads:

> A Country Life is sweet,
> In moderate Cold or Heat,
> To walk in the Air so pleasant and fair,
> In every Field of Wheat;
> The Goddess of Flowers,
> Adorn'd in their Bowers,
> And every Maid a Bow,
> Therefore I say, no Courtier may,
> Compare with they, that's cloath'd in Grey,
> Do follow the painful Plough.

> (Quoted from Moss.)

Air XL (II. xv. 126–47; Moss 188)

BUCEM ('Motley, Richard') lists three editions, the earliest dated *c.*1705, of a song beginning 'Draw, Cupid, draw' (Moss cites BL G.304.[44.] and G.307.[133.]). Identical incipits for the two copies listed in *NTI* (DFo-C.42.1[119] and DFo-C.42.4[258]) correspond exactly to the music in *Silvia* and to that printed with the original song in *Pills*, vi. 305–6, which varies slightly in only a few measures. The tune was included in *DM*, vol. ii (four editions, 1713–28), p. 47, and in *CD*, Book 2 (1719), p. 66 (not seen— the incipits in *NTI* are identical to those for the song-sheets). The music is attributed to Motley in the song-sheets and in *Pills*; Moss mistakes the name of the song-sheet publisher, D. Wright, for that of the anonymous author of the words. Watts used the woodcut music also in *The Merry Cobler* (1735; Air 7). The untitled music for Air 18 of *The Devil of a Duke* (1732), a song clearly based on 'Draw, Cupid, draw' beginning 'Fly, Cupid, fly', is a new composition (though quoting the four-measure descending figure in the second strain of the original tune) almost certainly by Seedo (see Fiske, p. 115). It is of interest as demonstrating the elaborate treatment, with instrumental introduction and coda, that might be accorded a climactic song of this kind.

Lillo's song is a close reworking of the original, which Moss speculates may have 'influenced Lillo's choice of a name for his heroine', Silvia—and perhaps suggested 'Angelica' as well:

> Draw *Cupid* draw, and make fair *Sylvia* know;
> The mighty Pain her suff'ring Swain does for her undergo;
> Convey this Dart into her Heart, and when she's set on Fire,
> Do thou return and let her burn, like me in chast desire;
> That by Experience she, may learn to pity me,
> Whene'er her Eyes do tyrannize o'er my Captivity:
> But when in Love we jointly move, and tenderly imbrace,
> Let Angels shine, and sweetly join to one another's Face.

(Pills, vi. 306.)

BUCEM ('Reign') lists a single-sheet edition of a song beginning 'Reign Silvia reign', dated *c.*1770, which may be a reprinting of Lillo's song. If so, the incipit given for the copy listed in *NTI* (in Boston Public Library, Brown Collection, ++M.Cab.1.3, vol. i [187]) indicates that it was provided with new music.

Air XLI (ii. xv. 172–80; Moss 446)

This country dance tune is discussed under its earlier title, 'Mall Peatly', by Simpson (pp. 481–2), who traces it to D. P. Pers's *Bellerophon* (Amsterdam, 1633), where the first and second strains are in common time and 'the modern equivalent of 6/4' respectively (cf. note to Air LXIII). Both Simspon and Chappell (*PMOT* i. 289–90) note that all English versions of the tune are in triple time throughout. It was included in *DM*, 4th edn. (1665) and in all subsequent editions. Chappell quotes *Round about our coal-fire, or Christmas Entertainments* (7th edn., 1734) on the dance: '*Moll Peatly* is never forgot;— this dance stirs the blood and gives the males and females a fellow-feeling for each other's activity, ability, and agility: Cupid always sits in the corner of the room where these diversions are transacting, and shoots quivers full of arrows at the dancers, and makes his own game of them.' The tune-title in *Silvia* is taken from 'Gillian of Croyden, a new Ballad: The Words made to the Tune of a Country Dance, call'd Mall Peatly', by Thomas D'Urfey, in *Pills*, ii. 46–8 (*Pills*, 1699, pp. 236–9). The music reproduced by Simpson (fig. 301) from D'Urfey's *Choice Collection of New Songs and Ballads* (1699), p. 2, is identical to the tune in *Pills*; the incipit given for a single-sheet edition listed in *NTI* (MH Marshall Coll. [1060]) corresponds to it exactly. The *Pills* version is in 3/4 time, and extends the second strain to fit the song, but none of the ballad operas which name 'Gillian of Croydon' rather than 'Mall Peatly' (the spelling varies) follows it: all are in the swifter 6/4 time of the *DM* versions, and of the same length (those with which no music is printed do not appear to reflect D'Urfey's extended refrain). Watts used the same woodcut in *The Fashionable Lady* (1730; Air 46, 'Gillian of Croydon') and *Achilles* (1733; Air 18, 'Moll Peatly'); the music in *The Jealous Clown* (1730; Air 6, 'Gilline of Croydne' [*sic*]) and *The Decoy* (1733; 'Moll Peatly') is melodically quite similar.

Both the dance and D'Urfey's song, with its broad political satire and verbal horseplay, make a very odd background for Lillo's song; it is, however, quite possible that Lillo intended Sir John to seem ridiculous in his choice of a tune. The first verse of 'Gillian of Croyden' reads (in *Pills*, ii. 47):

> One Holiday last Summer,
>   From four to seven by *Croyden Chimes*,
> Three Lasses toping Rummers,
>   Were set a prating of the Times,
>   A Wife call'd *Joan* of the Mill,
>   A Maid they call'd bonny brown *Nell*,
>   A Widow mine Hostess *Gillian* of *Croyden*, *Gillian* of
> *Croyden*, *Gillian*, young *Gillian*, *Jolly Gillian* of *Croyden*,
> Take off your Glass, cry'd *Gillian* of *Croyden*,
>   A Health to our Master *Will*.

Air XLII (ii. xv. 181–90; Moss 284)

This tune is discussed in Simpson, pp. 304–8. The tune-title originates with the refrain found in the 1682 broadside version of Thomas D'Urfey's Tory song 'The Whigs Exaltation; A Pleasant New Song of 82. To an Old Tune of 41'. The song, a close adaptation of an anti-Puritan ballad of 1641 by Francis Quarles, first appeared in D'Urfey's play *The Royalist* (1682), Act IV, with the refrain as in Quarles's song, 'Hey then up go we'.

The early history of the tune is complicated by the fact that Quarles's ballad, originally printed without a tune direction, was finally directed, in *The Rump* (1662), to be sung to a tune called 'Cuckolds all a-row', distinct from, though interchangeable with, the tune under discussion here (Simpson, p. 146). Simpson can find no record of the latter earlier than the broadside printing—with music—noted above, though he surmises that it 'seems doubtful that the tune was new in 1682'; he notes that it was incorporated into *DM* in 1682 (Supplement to the 6th edn. [1679]), 'originally in common time [as is the music in the broadside (Simpson, fig. 190)] but in 6/4 beginning with the 9th ed., 1695' (Simpson, p. 306). The intersection of the histories of the two tunes is not confined to the ballads: in a note on the dance-tune known as 'Hit or Miss' Margaret Dean-Smith and E. J. Nichol state that 'Playford consistently gives [the] name ["Cuckolds all a-row"] to this tune and dance, and that of "Hey Boys up we go" [*sic*] (as we call the dance) to the tune and dance we know as "The Way to Norwich"' ('The Dancing Master', *Journal of the English Folk Dance and Song Society*, iv. 6 [Dec. 1945], 222).

Nevertheless, after 1682 the history of the tune 'Hey Boys up go we' is perfectly straightforward, its popularity evidenced by the large number of ballads noted by Simpson—predominantly but by no means exclusively political—that were written to it. Two versions of the tune are found in *Pills*: one, printed with D'Urfey's song, in cut time, a syncopated version of the broadside music (ii. 286); and another in 6/4 time, containing a newly composed second strain (Simpson, p. 308), printed with a political song beginning 'Your Melancholy's all a Folly' (vi. 334). The source of the music in *Silvia* is very likely *DM*; the tune was also included in *CD*, Book 1 (1718). Watts used the woodcut again in *The Devil to Pay* (1731; finale). Quite similar music is also found in *The Patron* (1729; Air 2) and *The Prisoner's Opera* (1730; Air 10).

Despite the tune's mostly political associations, none of the ballad-opera songs set to it follows suit. Lillo's song is the only one to recall in any way the partisan triumphalism exemplified in the first verse of D'Urfey's song (*Pills*, ii. 286):

> Now, now the *Tories* all shall stoop,
>> Religion and the Laws,
> And *Whigs* and *Commonwealth* get up,
>> To tap the GOOD OLD CAUSE:
> *Tantivy-boys* shall all go down,
>> And haughty *Monarchy*,
> The *Leathern Cap* shall brave the *Throne*,
>> Then hey Boys up go we!

Air XLIII (II. xvi. 22–7; Moss 836)

The tune-title is the first line of a song, perhaps by Sir Charles Sedley (Day and Murrie, p. 398), set by Jeremiah Clarke. *BUCEM* ('Clarke, Jeremiah') lists three single-sheet editions dated *c.*1695, *c.*1705, and *c.*1710. A list of single-sheet copies in Thomas F. Taylor, *Thematic Catalogue of the Works of Jeremiah Clarke* (Detroit, 1977), 367, includes BL G.304.(190) (*c.*1695), H.1601.(538) (*c.*1705), G.305.(9) (*c.*1710), and CSmH (Huth) 81013.v.53 (*c.*1705). The song was included in *Pills*, v. 126–7 (*Pills*, 1707, iii. 205–6). Watts's woodcut music differs only in details of notation from the music in *Pills*, and both correspond to the incipit in the *Thematic Catalogue*.

   Lillo adopted the refrain from his source, but in other respects his song is quite his own. The original begins (in *Pills*, v. 126):

> Young *Coridon* and *Phillis*
>> Sate in a lovely Grove;
> Contriving Crowns of Lilies,
>> Repeating Tales of Love:
> *And something else, but what I dare not, &c.*

The refrain recalls Air 4 of *The Beggar's Opera*, which ends with the same phrase. Gay's song is, however, based on 'Why is your faithful Slave disdained', written *c.*1689 (see Day and Murrie, p. 387) and set to a different tune (Moss 804, with the music from *Pills*, iii. 211, though Gay used another tune altogether).

Air XLIV (II. xvi. 44–9; Moss 176)

A song beginning '*Strephon*, when you see me fly', entitled simply 'Song, *to* Denoye's *Minuet*', is found in *MM* ii. 65–7; this is a reprint, with a different tune and a few trifling textual variants, of 'The shy Shepherdess', an anonymous lyric first published *c.*1720 in single-sheet editions with a musical setting credited to Anthony Young (*BUCEM* ['Young, Antony'] lists two editions dated *c.*1720 and another dated *c.*1725; *NTI* lists DFo-C.42.3[230]; the present commentary is based on Huntington Library, Huth Collection, 81013.i.28). Single-sheet versions of the song begin '*Shepherd* when thou see'st me fly'. The words of Lillo's Air XLIV are clearly based on this song, being essentially a moralized extrapolation applicable to the fallen women in his play, Lettice and Betty. The dilemma of the singer in the original reminds one also of Silvia's passionate ambivalence towards Sir John:

> *Strephon*, when you see me fly,
>> Why shou'd that your Fear create?
> Maids may be as of—ten shy
>> Out of Love, as out of Hate:

When from you I fly away,
'Tis because I fear to stay.

.   .   .   .   .

Cruel Duty bids me go;
   Gentle Love commands my Stay:
Duty's still to Love a Foe;
   Shall I This, or That, obey?
Duty frowns, and *Cupid* smiles;
That defends, and This beguiles.

.   .   .   .   .

If you love me, *Strephon*, leave me;
   If you stay, I am undone:
Oh, you may with Ease deceive me;
   Pr'ythee, charming Boy, be gone:
The Gods decree that we must part;
They have my Vow, but you my Heart.

              (*MM* ii. 65–6, verses 1, 3, 5.)

   The derivation of the music printed in *Silvia*, from a woodcut not used elsewhere by Watts, is less straightforward. Though the minuet credited to Denoyer, a leading dancing master of the early 18th cent. (see *Actors, Actresses*), replaced Young's tune in *MM*, the latter appears with 'Advice to Phillis', beginning '*Phillis* has such charming Graces', in *MM* iv. 196–7. Apparent references to the two tunes in ballad operas predating *Silvia* are of little help. The music called 'Monsr. *Denoyer*'s Minuet' in the *The Village Opera* (1729*a*, Air 49; 1729*b*, Air 42) was retitled '*Handell*'s Minuet' in *The Chambermaid* (1730; Air 20). It is similar to the uncredited 'Minuet' setting of Benjamin Griffin's song beginning 'As on a Sunshine Summer's Day', in *MM* ii. 39–41; with the same tune the song is also included in a number of collections of songs set to Handel's music, and the attribution of the tune to Handel is accepted as 'probably authentic' in the *New Grove* (see also William C. Smith, *Handel*, p. 167). In the second edition (1729) of *The Lover's Opera*, Air 29 calls for 'Denoyer's Minuet', though in the first edition (1729) Air 33—the same song—calls for 'Sawney was tall', an entirely distinct tune. The song was omitted from the third edition (1730), printed, by Watts, with music. The final song of *The Lover's Opera*—numbered 43, 39, and 32 in the first, second, and third editions respectively—originally bore the tune-title 'Shepherd when thou seest', probably referring to Young's tune. In the second and third editions, however, this was changed to 'Come Brave Boys', another tune. Though the version of the song included in the first edition has not been seen, it would appear from the description in *NTI* that it was rewritten for the later editions.

   One might suppose that Lillo wrote his song to either the Young or Denoyer tune, the music printed in *Silvia* being therefore incorrect. Nevertheless, comparison of the three suggests that the music in *Silvia* is a hybrid product in which Young's first measure—i.e. the first two measures of Air XLIV—has been grafted to a composition based on the phrasing and harmonic structure of the Denoyer tune. This is particularly evident in the first strain, the third, fourth, seventh and eighth measures of which reproduce in all but one minor detail the corresponding measures of Denoyer's minuet. The ascent to the octave in the fifth and sixth measures reflects the Denoyer ninth measure, which begins a new passage to which the third and fourth lines of the verses are sung—the repetition of the first eight measures is peculiar to the *Silvia* music; the indicated repeat of the second strain corresponds to 'dal Segno' markings in the Young setting. The combined resemblances are enough to indicate that the printed music is correct, having perhaps been composed for *Silvia*, though it is not impossible that it was originally intended for the first of the songs in *The Lover's Opera* discussed above before it was decided to omit it from the third edition.

Air XLV (ii. xvi. 65–72 [page break as in O; probably 2 stanzas]; Moss 761)

Source not certain. A possible source is 'An excellent Ballad of the Mercers Son of *Midhurst*, And the Cloathiers Daughter of *Guilford*', in eight-line trimeter stanzas, beginning 'There was a Wealthy man, | in *Sussex* he did dwell', with a tune direction naming 'Dainty come thou to me'. The last verse begins 'As after you shall hear, | in the old mans Complaint', i.e. 'A Ballad, entituled the Old mans Complaint against the Wretched Son, who to advance his Marriage did undo himself. To the same Tune', beginning 'All you that Fathers be'. The two ballads, obviously related despite their separate titles, are found together as *EB*, No. 90, pp. 133–4; the first stands alone as No. 91, p. 135, the second twice as Nos. 12 and 13, pp. 17, 18. They are reprinted together in *RB* ii. 189–97, with notes on other copies, some paired and some separate. All these broadsides date from the second half of the 17th cent., but the ballads themselves date from considerably earlier: 'Mercers sonne of Medhurst' is No. 1705 in Rollins, *Analytical Index*, entered 14 Dec. 1624; 'Old man and his sonne', No. 2006, was entered 1 June 1629. Even earlier, a manuscript ballad of *c.*1609, 'Pride's fall', beginning '*England's* fayre daintye dames', printed in *The Shirburn Ballads 1585–1616*, ed. Andrew Clark (Oxford, 1907), No. 33, pp. 134–9, called for the tune of 'All yow that fathers bee'. Broadside versions of 'Pride's Fall' of 1656 and 1675 (Rollins, *Analytical Index*, Nos. 2194, 2195; reprinted in *RB* viii. 20 and *EB*, No. 269, pp. 439–40) call for 'All you that love Goodfellows', but Simpson notes (pp. 15–16) that the 'trimeter lines of the ballad fit that lost tune ['Dainty come thou to me', the tune named for 'All you that fathers be'] far better than they do the music of ' "All you that love good fellows" '. Elsewhere, in his discussion of the tune 'Phillida flouts me' (pp. 576–8), he questions the tune direction 'Dainty come thow to me' for the earliest extant version of the original 'Phillida' ballad (*Shirburn Ballads*, p. 297): 'Ballads to this popular lost tune are uniformly in a different meter from those to "Phillida"; hence there appears to be a mistake in directing the Shirburn ballad to be sung to "Dainty come thou to me." ' Among those that name the tune is the ballad of 'Sir Richard Whittington', discussed by Chappell (*PMOT* ii. 515–17), who reproduces a tune known also as 'Turn again, Whittington' and—indicative of the tune's character—'The Bells of Osney' and possibly 'Whittington's Bells'. Chappell speculates that '*Dainty, come thou to me . . . may* be another name for the same [tune]', but it seems more likely that the tune (found also with 'An Epitaph' in *Pills*, iv. 328–9, as '*Turn again* Whittington, &c.') was originally composed with bells in mind, and proved therefore especially well suited to the Whittington ballad. A variation of the name 'Dainty come thou to me' appears in a passage from *A Navy Land of Ships* (1627; quoted in Chappell, *PMOT* i. 82): 'Nimble-heel'd mariners, like so many dancers, capering a morisco [morris dance] or *Trenchmore* of forty miles long, to the tune of "Dusty, my dear," "Dirty, come thou to me," "Dun out of the mire," or "I wail in woe and plunge in pain:" all these dances have no other music.'

'Dainty, come thou to me!' ends the refrain of 'A new Northern Jigge, called Daintie, come thou to me', reprinted in *RB* i. 629–31, from a broadside bearing the imprint of the 'Assignes of Thomas Symcocke', and therefore dating most likely from the 1620s. The *Silvia* tune, which implies a trimeter quatrain followed by one in Poulter's measure, does correspond with some exactness to the basic metrical pattern of that ballad, exemplified in the second verse (a failure of the rhyme in the first verse indicates corruption of it in this printing):

> Were my state good or ill
>   rich, or in misery,
> Yet would I love thee still,—
>   prove me, and thou shalt see!
> *Cast no care to thy heart,*
>   *from thee I will not flee,*
> *Let them all say what they will,*
>   *Dainty, come thou to me!*

Though the lines of the 'Mercer's Son' ballads as read do not in general demand an initial stress, they can easily sustain it in singing; some verses of the second ballad correspond metrically to the verses of 'Daintie, come thou to me', though most are trimeter throughout. The content of Lillo's song provides no compelling evidence for a connection by which to suggest that the music of Air XLV might represent a version of the 'lost' tune 'Daintie, come thou to me', though Betty's promise of revenge is comparable in tone to the story told in 'The Mercers Son of *Midhurst*' and 'The Old mans Complaint'. In the first, seeing his son pining for the clothier's daughter, the mercer conveys all his property to him to enable the marriage. As the second ballad relates, he soon comes to regret his action: 'Each day they wish me dead, | yet say I'le never dye.' In the end he outlasts them. The daughter, unable to bear children, tries a number of horrific treatments: 'She strangled at the laste | her self within the bed.' As for the son,

> E're thirteen years were past,
>   dy'd he without a will,
> And by this means at last,
>   the old man living still;
> Injoy'd his land at last,
>   after much misery.
> Many years after that
>   liv'd he most happily[.]

(EB, p. 134.)

The first three measures of 'The Cordwainer's March' (in James Aird, *A Collection of Scotch, English, Irish, and Foreign Airs*, vol. i [Glasgow, 1782], p. 61) appear, from the incipit given in *NTI*, to be nearly identical to those of this tune. No words are printed with it, as Aird's collection is entirely instrumental.

Air XLVI (II. xvii. 8–15 [2 stanzas in O]; Moss 799)

The tune is discussed in Simpson, pp. 772–3. The song beginning 'Whilst I gaze on Cloe trembling' inspired a number of settings, of which Simpson reproduces two (figs. 514, 515): a 17th-cent. setting by Thomas Overbury, and an early 18th-cent. setting that superseded it. The latter first appeared in single-sheet editions *c.*1720, in which the song is called 'Cloe's Admirer' and a new verse has been inserted between the original two; it was originally entitled 'The Jealous Lover's Complaint' and began 'While I gaze on Cloris . . .' (reprinted in *OPB*, p. 79). Identical incipits for the song-sheets listed in *NTI* (DFo-C.42.2[207], DFo-C.42.3[464], and MH Marshall Coll. [205, 206]) correspond exactly to Simpson's fig. 515 (Moss cites BL H.1601.[482] and G.316.a.[56]). This version was followed exactly in *Polly* (1729; Air 65). The music in *Silvia* represents an elaborated version of this tune first used in *MM* ii. 76–7, where the song is called 'The Lukewarm Lover'. The music was printed anonymously in the song-sheets—the words being credited only to a 'Parson of Quality'—but in *MM* the song is said to be 'Set by Mr. [Lewis] *Ramondon*'. It is not clear whether Ramondon composed the tune or was responsible only for the recasting. Watts used the same woodcut music in *The Fashionable Lady* (1730; Air 52) and *The Devil to Pay* (three-act version, 1731; Air 26). The music in *The Mock Lawyer* (1733; text, Air 12, music, Air 14) is simpler than the Watts version, but incorporates some of its features.

Lillo's song is essentially a heightened condensation of the content of the original:

> Whilst I gaze on *Chlo—e* trembling,
>   Strait her Eyes my Fate declare;
> When she smiles, I fear dis-sembling;
>   When she frowns, I then despair:
> Jealous of some rival Lover,
>   If a wand'ring Look she give;
> Fain I wou'd re—solve to leave her,
>   But can soon—er cease to live.
>
> Why shou'd I conceal my Passion,
>   Or the Torments I endure?
> I'll disclose my Inclination;
>   Awful Distance yields no Cure:
> Sure it is not in her Nature
>   To be cruel to her Slave;
> She is too divine a Creature
>   To destroy, what she can save.
>
> Happy's he, whose Inclination
>   Warms but with a gentle Heat,
> Never flies up to a Passion;
>   Love's a Torment, if too great:
> When the Storm is once blown over,
>   Soon the Ocean quiet grows;
> But a Constant Faithful Lover
>   Seldom meets with true Repose.
>
>   (*MM* ii. 76–7; first verse printed line
>   by line with music.)

Lillo's song also to some degree resembles Gay's song in *Polly* (sung by Cawwawkee upon hearing Polly's continuing protestations of love for Macheath):

Whilst I gaze in fond desiring,
    Every former thought is lost.
Sighing, wishing and admiring,
    How my troubled soul is tost!
Hot and cold my blood is flowing,
How it thrills in every vein!
Liberty and life are going,
    Hope can ne'er relieve my pain.

Air XLVII (III. i. 1–8; Moss 442)

The general history of Air XLVII is in many ways parallel to that of Air XLVI. It too is printed from woodcut music first used in *MM* (i. 69–71), representing an elaborated version of a simpler melody, by Henry Carey, found in single-sheet editions. *BUCEM* ('Carey, Henry') lists three single-sheet editions, all dated *c.*1725 (Moss cites BL G.316.f.[60]). Only the incipits given for the song-sheets listed in *NTI* have been seen (DFo-C.42.2[188] and DFo-C.42.3[386]); these correspond exactly, except in key, to the music printed in *The Jealous Clown* (1730; Air 13). It appears that the simpler version was printed in subsequent collections listed in *NTI*, of 1740, 1746, and 1754, and finally in Joseph Ritson, *A Select Collection of English Songs*, 3 vols. (London, 1783), ii. 218–19 (text), iii. 107–8 (music), where the music is melodically identical to that in *The Jealous Clown*, apart from a few erroneous accidentals. The version of 'Midsummer Wish' in *The Mock Lawyer* (1733; text, Air 8, music, Air 9) is analogous to that of 'Whilst I gaze on Cloe' in the same work, a simplified treatment of the music as it appears in *MM*.

The original song was by 'the Author of the Fair Circassian [Samuel Croxall]. *Written when he was at* Eton *School.*' (The poem was reprinted in *The Gentleman's Magazine*, i [Feb. 1731], 74, where it is for some reason credited to Stephen Duck. Moss notes the general resemblance of Croxall's poem to Gray's 'Ode on a Distant Prospect of Eton College', which contains a number of verbal echoes of Croxall's second and third stanzas; the 'Ode' could be regarded as a response to Croxall's youthful complacency.) Lillo's song borrows from the imagery of Croxall's poem, while quite reversing its emotional tone:

Waft me, some soft and cooling Breeze,
    To *Windsor*'s sha—dy kind Retreat,
Where *Sylvan* Scenes, wide-spread—ing Trees,
    Re—pel the Dog-Star's raging Heat:
Where tufted Grass, and mossy Beds,
    Afford a Rural calm Repose;
Where Woodbines hang their dew—y Heads,
    And fra—grant Sweets around disclose.

Old oozy *Thames*, that flows fast by,
    Along the smiling Valley plays;
His glassy Surface chears the Eye,
    And thro' the flow'ry Meadow strays.
His fertile Banks with Herbage green,
    His Vales with golden Plenty swell;
Where-e'er his purer Streams are seen,
    The Gods of Health and Pleasure dwell.

Let me thy clear, thy yielding Wave
　　With naked Arm once more divide;
In thee my glowing Bosom lave,
　　And cut the gently-rolling Tide.
Lay me, with Damask-roses crown'd,
　　Beneath some Osier's dusky Shade;
Where Water-Lilies deck the Ground,
　　Where bubbling Springs refresh the Glade.

Let dear *Lucinda* too be there,
　　With azure Mantle slightly drest:
Ye Nymphs, bind up her flowing Hair;
　　Ye *Zephyrs*, fan her panting Breast.
O haste away, fair Maid, and bring
　　The Muse, the kindly Friend to Love;
To Thee alone the Muse shall sing,
　　And warble thro' the vocal Grove.

　　(*MM* i. 69–70; first verse printed line by line
　　with music.)

Also set to 'Midsummer Wish' is Air 42 of *The Grub-Street Opera*, at the end of a scene (II. viii) in which Owen and Molly have disagreed on the necessity of marriage (see Introduction, pp. 12–14). Molly, left alone by Owen, proves to be less adamant than Silvia: 'Should Owen ever return, should he renew his entreaties, I fear his success; for I find every day love attains more and more ground of virtue.' She then sings the following song, in which the metaphor of Lillo's first four lines is burlesqued:

　　When love is lodged within the heart,
　　Poor virtue to the outworks flies,
　　　　The tongue in thunder takes its part,
　　And darts in lightning from the eyes.

　　From lips and eyes with gested grace,
　　In vain she keeps out charming him,
　　　　For love will find some weaker place,
　　To let the dear invader in.

　　(*Grub-Street Opera*, ed. Roberts, II. viii.
　　63–70.)

Fielding used the words of the song again as Air 8 of *The Lottery* (1732), set to a tune newly composed by Seedo.

Air XLVIII (III. i. 32–9; Moss 300)

Chappell (*PMOT* ii. 597) quotes only the first two verses of the apparent source, a ten-verse ballad called 'The Distracted Sailor', beginning 'O how happy are young lovers'. The entire ballad has not been seen; Chappell mentions two broadside editions, in the Douce collection—now in the Bodleian Library—and in the personal collection of J. M. Gutch. The latter bears the tune direction 'What is greater joy and pleasure', which is also the tune-title of Air 11 in *The Rape of Helen* (1737), printed without music. The music (marked '*slow*') is found in *The Wedding* (1729; Air 7), in which the tune-title is 'Oh how pleasant are young Lovers'. Watts's woodcut differs in key, in melodic detail, and in barring (anacrustic in *The Wedding*); it was also used in *Robin Hood* (1730; Air 11) with the tune-title as in *Silvia*. The version of the tune printed by Chappell, barred as in *The Wedding*, differs yet again in detail, but the melody is substantially the same in all three versions. Incipits given in *NTI* for 'The Sailor's Complaint' (see below) correspond to the music as printed in *PMOT* and *The Wedding*.

The tune, at one point falsely attributed to Handel (see the *New Grove*), was a popular one in the 18th cent.: Chappell notes a number of ballads written to it, all on nautical or naval themes. Of these 'The Storm', beginning 'Cease rude Boreas', appears to have had the widest circulation. Though the earliest ballads, 'What is greater joy and pleasure' and 'The Distracted Sailor', have not been seen, it would seem, to judge by the consistency of later songs set to the tune, that storms figured importantly in at least the second of them; the two verses of 'The Distracted Sailor' quoted by Chappell are, however, irrelevant in a discussion of Lillo's song.

Chappell does quote in full a song called 'The Sailor's Complaint', beginning 'Come and listen to my ditty', the earliest editions of which are dated *c.*1730 in *BUCEM* ('Come'). The penultimate verse can be compared to Lillo's Air XLVIII:

> On a rocky coast I've driven,
>   Where the stormy winds do rise,
> Where the rolling mountain billows
>   Lift a vessel to the skies:
> But from land, or from the ocean,
>   Little dread I ever knew,
> When compared to the dangers
>   In the frowns of scornful Sue.
>
>   (Chappell, *PMOT*, ii. 598.)

Air XLIX (III. i. 49–56; Moss 550)

Simpson (pp. 557–9) traces the words of the song beginning 'One night when all the village slept', by Sir Carr Scrope, to Act IV, scene i, of Nathaniel Lee's *Mithridates, King of Pontus* (1678). He reproduces three tunes, the first of which, by Grabu, is here irrelevant. The second appeared with Scrope's song in *MM* ii. 42–3, there entitled 'Despairing Myrtillo', and in *The Merry Musician*, vol. iii (1731), 166. The third tune is that which appears in *Silvia*; Watts used the woodcut only once. Simpson cannot trace the source of the second or third, but remarks that, despite the 6/8 time of the *MM* tune, 'there are points of similarity to suggest that both may derive from a melody now lost to us'. (See Simpson for notes on broadside amplifications and later settings of the song.)

Scrope's song is a not very remarkable pastoral of unrequited love. Though Lillo probably had it in mind, his own song is a characteristic moralization of the theme. In Air XLVII Silvia too has welcomed death—as the abode of innocence, be it noted—but her emergent fortitude may be contrasted, in attitude and circumstance, with the self-indulgent resignation of Myrtillo:

> One Night, when all the Village slept,
>   *Myr*—*tillo*'s sad Despair
> The wand'ring Shepherd waking kept,
>   To tell the Woods his Care:
> Be gone, said he, fond Thought, be gone,
>   Eyes give your Sor—rows o'er;

Why shou'd you waste your Tears for One
  That thinks on you no more?

Yet all the Birds, the Flocks, the Powers,
  That dwell within this Grove,
Can tell how many happy Hours,
  We here have pass'd in Love:
The Stars above (my cruel Foes)
  Have heard how she has sworn
A thousand times, that like to Those
  Her Flame shou'd ever burn.

But, since she's lost, oh! let me have
  My Wish, and quickly die:
In this cold Bank I'll make a Grave,
  And there for ever lie:
Sad Nightingales the Watch shall keep,
  And kindly here complain;
Then down the Shepherd lay to sleep,
  And never wak'd again.

       (*MM* ii. 42–3; first verse printed line
       by line with music.)

Air L (III. iii. 15–22 [2 stanzas in O]; Moss 164)

The tune is discussed in Simpson, pp. 155–7. *BUCEM* ('Kingdom of the Birds') lists two single-sheet editions, the earlier dated *c*.1706, of 'The Dame of Honnour, or Hospitallity. Sung by Mrs. Willis in the opera call'd [The Wonders in the Sun, or] the Kingdom of the Birds'. (Simpson notes BL H.1601.[388]; *NTI* lists DFo-C.42.3[237] and MH Marshall Coll. [269].) D'Urfey's comic opera was first performed at the Queen's Theatre on 5 Apr. 1706 (*London Stage, 1700–1729*). The song was reprinted in *Pills*, i. 212–14 (*Pills*, 1706, iv. 146–8), with the tune exactly as it appears in the song-sheet (the latter reproduced by Simpson as fig. 99). Incipits given in *NTI* for 'Queen Bess's Dame of Honour' in *DM* ii. 107 (four edns., 1713–28) and 'Dame of Honour' in *CD*, Book 2 (1729), p. 126, correspond exactly to the song-sheet/*Pills* music. The music for the tune in *Polly* (1729; Air 33) and *The Decoy* (1733; Air 19) follows this version very closely, except for the second measure, in which the third note, as in Watts's music, is the same as the first; in earlier versions it was the third above the tonic. Watts's music differs from all these versions in key (originally D), and in a number of rhythmic details; the woodcut was also used in *The Fashionable Lady* (1730; Air 3), *The Jovial Crew* (1731; Air 4), *The Devil to Pay* (1731; Air 29), *The Lottery* (1732; Air 11), and *The Lover His Own Rival* (1735; Air 1). Moss includes Air 2 of *The Beggar's Wedding* in his discussion of 'Dame of Honour'; but it was set to a quite different tune, called 'Since all the World is distracted in Wars', and could not be sung to 'Dame of Honour'. Simpson notes that D'Urfey's song was reprinted in many poetical miscellanies of the 18th cent., and its popularity may be gauged from the parodies and imitations it inspired. He counts sixteen ballad operas in which it was used.

  D'Urfey's song is a general satire on modern manners, which the singer compares unfavourably with her own conduct in earlier days. Lillo's song recalls the original only in the most general way: Goody Busy, like the original Dame, is an advocate of old-fashioned virtues. The first and sixth of D'Urfey's seven verses read:

> Since now the world's turn'd upside down,
>   And all things chang'd in Nature;
> As if a doubt were newly grown,
>   We had the same Creator:
> Of ancient Modes and former ways,
>   I'll teach you, Sirs, the manner;
> In good Queen *Besses* Golden Days,
>   When I was a Dame of Honour.
>
> .   .   .   .   .
>
> My Curling Locks I never bought
>   Of Beggar's dirty Daughters:
> Nor prompted by a wanton thought,
>   Above Knee ty'd my Garters;
> I never glow'd with Painted Pride,
>   Like Punk when the Devil has won her:
> Nor prov'd a cheat to be a Bride,
>   When I was a Dame of Honour.
>
> (*Pills*, i. 213–14.)

Fielding used the tune for Airs 31 and 50 of *The Grub-Street Opera*, but in this case his songs have nothing to do with *Silvia* (see Introduction, pp. 12–14).

Air LI (III. v. 52–63; Moss 426)

The tune is discussed in Simpson, pp. 84–5. The tune-title is the first line of 'Another Scotch Song, by way of Dialogue, Set to a very pretty Northern Tune', which Simpson traces to *A Compleat Collection of Mr. Durfey's Songs and Odes* (1687), printed without music; the song was not included in *Pills*. According to Simpson the song, 'which may be an adaptation of an earlier text, was expanded into a broadside of about the same date'; in this form it is entitled 'Chastities Conquest, Or, No Trusting before Marriage. A New Song, To the Tune of, Canst Thou not weave Bone-lace', i.e. to its own tune (reprinted in *RB* iii. 497–9, and *EB*, No. 28, p. 39). Simpson continues, 'No contemporary copy of the music has been found, but it appears as a spirited dance tune in . . . *Silvia*.'

In his note to 'Chastities Conquest' (*RB* iii. 496) Chappell prints the tune from *Silvia*, equating it with 'A Trip to Marrowbone', to which D'Urfey wrote a song that begins 'Maiden fresh as a Rose' (in *Pills*, i. 56–7). Chappell notes the occurrence of 'A Trip to Marrowbone' in *DM*; Simpson specifies the twelfth (1703) and later editions, but *NTI* indicates that in fact it is found under that name only in *DM*, vol. ii (1st–4th edns., 1713–28), p. 112, as well as in *CD*, Book 2 (1719), p. 131, and later collections. Chappell (*PMOT* ii. 792) claims to have found it in *Appollo's Banquet* (1669) as a 'Scotish jig'. Comparing 'Canst thou not weave Bone-lace' and 'A Trip to Marrowbone', Simpson remarks that the 'two tunes are similar in their basic rhythm [slip jigs, nine beats to a measure] and in their final cadence, but they differ melodically'. Moss, ignoring his own reference to Simpson's account, perpetuates Chappell's erroneous equation of the two tunes, and infers that the source of Lillo's song is 'a folk ballad which is not extant'. As 'Maidens as fresh as a Rose', in *Momus Turn'd Fabulist* (1729; Air 6), with music, and in later ballad operas without it, the tune used by D'Urfey has a separate history; it also appears in the music of *The Decoy* (1733; Air 39) under the tune-title 'Maggy's Tocher'.

A tune that more closely resembles the music of Air LI is 'Nobe's Maggot', found in *DM*, 12th–13th edns., p. 346, 14th–18th edns., p. 302; in *CD*, Book 1 (1718), p. 174, it is called 'Tobe's Maggot' (but 'Nobe's' in the edition of 1731). The tune is reprinted and briefly discussed in Chappell, *PMOT* ii. 595. Simpson's remarks about the relation between 'A Trip to Marrowbone' and 'Canst thou not weave Bone-lace' are equally applicable to that between the latter and 'Nobe's Maggot'; but the resemblances seem too close to be coincidental, amounting, in the first strains of the two tunes, to nothing more than different deployment of the same melodic elements. The two tunes share rhythmic characteristics not found in 'A Trip to Marrowbone'.

Apart from these considerations Lillo's debt to 'Canst thou not weave Bone-lace' is not in question. The first verse reads:

> Canst thou not weave Bonelace,
>   yea by Lady that I can,
> Canst thou not lisp with Grace
>   yea as well as any one,
> Canst thou not Card and Spin
>   yea by Lady that I can
> And do the other thing
>   wee I'se do what I can
> Come then and be my sweet
>   To Bed I'l carry thee
> No in Geud faith not a bit
> Unless you marry me.

> (*EB*, p. 39.)

In the expanded version, over the course of the remaining five verses, the man at last consents to marry, much to the young woman's delight.

Air LII (III. ix. 4–13 [page break in O before l. 8]; Moss 781)

Source uncertain. Moss states unequivocally that the source is the ballad of 'Sir Andrew Barton', in *RB* i. 10, which begins:

> When Flora with her fragrant flowers
>   bedect the earth so trim and gay,
> And Neptune with his dainty showers
>   came to present the month of May . . .

There is no apparent connection between Lillo's song and the words of the ballad. As for the music—if it has anything at all to do with 'Sir Andrew Barton'—it has proved impossible to go beyond Bronson's summary (*Traditional Tunes*, iii. 133):

> Apparently 'Sir Andrew Barton' was already a very popular song in the sixteenth century; and this favor it retained, as many broadsides remain to testify, throughout the seventeenth, and well into the eighteenth, century.
>   The earlier copies are all in tetrameter quatrains or double quatrains. Where a direction for a tune is given, it is always, 'Come follow my Love, &c.,' which, I believe,

can only be the tune of the 'Fair Flower of Northumberland' ([Child] No. 9), a song
that Deloney liked well enough to include in his *Jacke of Newbrie*, c. 1597. The musical
tradition for the 'Fair Flower,' so far as it is now known, is late and Scottish, but quite
consistent and uniform. Its metre is 6/8, and perfectly suited to 'Barton.' But no copy
of the tune as early as the seventeenth century appears to have survived.

Other broadsides of the seventeenth century are extant, directed to be sung to the
tune of 'Sir Andrew Barton,' which would suggest that the present song supplanted
the other in familiar use and in turn gave its name to the tune. . . . White-letter copies
of 'Sir Andrew' carry no indications of a tune.

'The Fair Flower of Northumberland' tells the story of a lady betrayed by the Earl of
Northumberland, whom she has rescued from imprisonment and followed on a difficult
journey. Unhappy love is the subject of some other ballads written to the tune: see *RB*
viii. 120, where 'The Pining Maid' and 'The Unfortunate Love of a Lancashire
Gentleman, and the Hard Fortune of a fair young Bride' are discussed. Lillo's song
seems at least consistent with this tradition, and the tune printed in *Silvia* may then
represent a version, or perhaps more properly a treatment, of 'Come follow my Love'.

Air LIII (III. xii. 1–8; Moss 341)

The tune-title is the first line of Thomas D'Urfey's song 'Conjugal Love. *Made on a Man
of Quality and his Lady, to an air in* Pyrrhus' (in *Pills*, i. 44–6). The music is that of
Handel's aria 'Ho un non so che nel cor', written for his oratorio *La Resurrezione*.
D'Urfey's song is listed with other English songs written to the tune in Smith, *Handel*,
pp. 133–4, citing a song-sheet of *c.*1711 (BL H.1601.[219]); *NTI* lists DFo-C.42.4
(465). Of the aria Smith notes that it 'was afterwards used by Handel in "Agrippina"
(Venice, 1709) and inserted in Alessandro Scarlatti's opera "Pirro e Dimetrio" . . . for
the 1710–11 performance of the work in London. It was the first of Handel's songs to be
sung upon the English stage. . . . The tune became very popular in a number of English
versions . . .'

In D'Urfey's song the singer overhears an amorous couple and draws a wrong
conclusion; the ending contains the lesson that Sir John is about to learn.

> In *Kent* so fam'd of Old,
> Close by the famous *Knoll*,
> A Swain a Goddess told
>   An Am'rous story:
>   [*first four lines are repeated*]
>
> Cry'd he, these Jarring Days,
> When Kings contend for Bays,
> Your Love my Soul does raise,
>   Beyond their Glory;
>
>   ['Cry'd . . . Bays' *repeated*]
>   ['Cry'd . . . Glory' *repeated*]
>
> My Life my Lovely dear,
> Whil'st you are Smiling here,
> The Plants and Flow'rs appear,
>   More Sweetly charming:

The Sun may cease to Shine,
And may his pow'r resign,
Your Eyes give rays Divine,
  All nature warming: . . .

She made a kind return,
That nothing had of scorn,
This Youth, thought I, does burn,
  To bring her under:
But as they homeward mov'd,
And walk'd, and talk'd, and Lov'd,
I found his Spouse she prov'd,
  That was his wonder; . . .

(Pills, i. 45–6.)

The music printed in *Pills* contains a two-measure melodic figure not found in the Watts woodcut, to which the first repetition of the words 'Cry'd . . . Bays' etc. is to be sung. Watts used his woodcut first in *Momus Turn'd Fabulist* (1729; Air 20) for a song of two verses, each a double quatrain. The version of the tune printed in *Love in a Riddle* (1729; Act I, Air 12) corresponds to the music in *Pills*, as the song demands.

Moss reprints the text of a single-sheet edition of a song called 'The Expiring Lover' (BL G.316.e.[44.]) that he does not differentiate from 'Conjugal Love'. In *BUCEM* ('In') this edition is dated *c.*1745; the song consists of D'Urfey's first two verses, to which are added two new ones that conclude the song in more conventional fashion: the couple, not married, retire to 'a Grove'.

Air LIV (III. xv. 15–28; Moss 682)

The traditional ballad of 'The Baffled Knight' (Child Ballad No. 112) exists in many versions, some dating back to the early 17th cent. The tune is discussed by Simpson (pp. 27–8), who reproduces the music in *Silvia* (fig. 19). The best musical survey is found in Bronson, *Traditional Tunes*, ii. 547–63. 'There was a Knight was drunk with Wine' is the first line of a version traced by Simpson to a broadside of 1693, 'The Lady's Policy; or, The Baffled Knight'; an 18th-cent. broadside reprint, with three additional parts, is found in *RB* vii. 439–41. Simpson also identifies the source of the music, a tune called 'There was a Knight' in *Youth's Delight on the Flagelet*, 9th edn. (*c.*1690); this tune is reproduced in Bronson, ii. 549, and in Chappell, *PMOT* ii. 520. The music in *Silvia* varies slightly from the melody in *Youth's Delight*, but reproduces its essential features, including the ending on the dominant.

In Lillo's song it is the 'lady' who is baffled. In the original the lady, met 'along the way' by the knight and immediately propositioned, submits a counter-proposal: that he should accompany her to her father's house, where, she says, 'you shall have your will of me, within, Sir, and without, Sir'. He goes with her,

But when she came to her father's house, which was moated all round about, Sir,
She slipt herself within the gate, and lock'd the Knight without, Sir.

  .   .   .   .

'We have a flower in our garden, some calls it Marygold, Sir,
And he that would not when he might, he shall not when he would, Sir.

But if you chance to meet a maid, a little below the town, Sir,
You must not fear her gay clothing, nor the wrinkling of her gown, Sir.

(*RB* viii. 439.)

Air LV (II. xvi. 4–16; Moss 662)

The tune-title is taken from the first line of 'A New Song' written and composed by Richard Leveridge; *BUCEM* ('Leveridge, Richard') lists two single-sheet editions, the earlier dated *c*.1700 (Moss cites BL G.312.[28]). The incipit given for the song-sheet listed in *NTI* (DFo-C.42.3[313]) corresponds to the music found with the song in *Pills*, iii. 235–7 (*Pills*, 1699, pp. 252–3), which is melodically all but identical to the music in *Silvia*, but in 3/4 time. The music is credited to Leveridge in the song-sheets, but the song is printed anonymously in *Pills*. The first measure of the incipit given for a 6/4 tune called 'Jane Shore' in Rosamond E. M. Harding, *A Thematic Catalogue of the Works of Matthew Locke* (Oxford, 1971), p. 121, is melodically identical to that of this tune, though the remainder of the incipit is quite different; Harding considers the attribution to Locke doubtful. The tune bears no resemblance to those associated with the ballads on Jane Shore in Simpson (pp. 120–2) and Chappell (*PMOT* i. 213–15).

Leveridge's song recounts the experiences of a country lass who cannot escape the attentions of '*Dick* of our Town', an 'old Justice', the Justice's clerk, and the Parson. The first verse reads:

> The Sun was just Setting, the Reaping was done,
> And over the Common I tript it alone;
> Then whom should I meet, but young *Dick* of our Town,
> Who swore e'er I went I shou'd have a Green-gown:
> *He prest me, I stumbl'd,*
> *He push'd me, I Tumbl'd,*
> *He Kiss'd me, I Grumbl'd,*
> *But still he Kiss'd on,*
> *Then rose and went from me as soon as he'd done.*
> If he be not hamper'd for serving me so,
> May I be worse Rumpl'd,
> Worse Tumbl'd, and Jumbl'd,
> Where ever, where ever I go.

(*Pills*, iii. 236.)

'Dal segno' markings in the *Pills* music indicate that the second and third measures of the third line in Watts's woodcut must be repeated to accommodate repetition of the line 'But . . . undone'. The rebarring of the tune into the quicker 6/4, and a few other adjustments, suggest that Watts's version may be taken from a dance set (cf. Air LVI). In addition, the barring of the second line is incorrect, one of the measures having nine beats; and in the same passage a portion of the melody is omitted, so that the words cannot be fitted to the music as it stands. The passage can be reconstructed, with reference to the music in *Pills*, as follows:

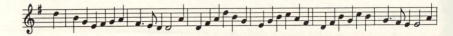

Air LVI (III. xviii. 15–22; Moss 276)

The tune-title is the first line of a song called 'The Broken South-Sea Taylor's Ditty', which, according to a single-sheet edition listed in *BUCEM* ('Harlequin Director'), was 'made to ye slow air in ye Magician or Harlequin Director'. This edition is dated *c.*1720 in *BUCEM*, but Rich's pantomime was first performed at Lincoln's Inn Fields on 16 Mar. 1721 (*London Stage, 1700–1729*). Two later editions listed in *BUCEM* ('Hear'), dated *c.*1722 and *c.*1725, do not mention the pantomime, but are headed 'Sung by Mr. Platt at Sadler's Wells'. Identical incipits given for two copies of song-sheets of the second type in *NTI* (DFo-C.42.4[371] and MH Marshall Coll. [155]) correspond melodically to Watts's woodcut music, but in 3/4 time. Virtually the same tune is printed in *The Lover's Opera*, 3rd edn. (1730; Air 24—Air 30 in earlier editions), with the tune-title 'Quaker's Wedding'. Like the tune in *Silvia*, it is in 6/4 time, but transposed up a third and lacking the third and fourth measures of the first strain. The source for this version of the tune has not been traced.

Air LVII (III. xviii. 29–34; Moss 614)

John Donne's poem 'The Message', with verbal alterations and a new title, 'The Reproach', was set to music in the early 18th cent. by Anthony Young and again by Richard Leveridge. A song-sheet dated *c.*1720 in *BUCEM* ('Young, Antony') contains both tunes. Such an edition is listed in *NTI* (DFo-C.42.3[227, 228]; neither of the incipits corresponds to the beginning of the tune in *Silvia*, printed from the same woodcuts used in *MM* i. 52–3, where both the words and the music are anonymous. Watts used this music again in *The Devil to Pay* (1731; Air 15); the versions of the tune in *Love in a Riddle* (1729; Act III, Air 9) and *The Wedding* (1729; Air 9), both in 6/8 time, are virtually identical. Though this tune appears to differ from the Leveridge setting, in 3/4 time, in the song-sheets, the first strain strongly resembles that of his setting, also in 3/4, of Gay's ballad 'Sweet William's Farewell to Black-ey'd Susan', though the second strains differ considerably.

'The Reproach', as printed in *MM* reads:

> Send back my long-stray'd Eyes to me,
> Which, Oh! too long have dwelt on thee;
>   Send home my long-stray'd Eyes to me,
> Which, Oh! too long have dwelt on thee:
> But if from you they've learnt such Ill,
>   To sweetly Smile,
>   and then Beguile,
> Keep the Deceivers, keep them still.

> Send home my harmless Heart again,
> Which no unworthy Thought cou'd stain:
> But if it has been taught by thine
>   To forfeit both
>   Its Word and Oath,
> Keep it, for then 'tis none of mine.

>   Yet send me back my Heart and Eyes,
> For I'll know all thy Falsities;

> That I one Day may laugh, when thou
> Shalt grieve and mourn;
> For one will scorn,
> And prove as False as thou art now.

Air LVIII (III. xviii. 44–52; Moss 491)

'The Jolly Young Swain' is found in *MM* ii. 36–8, with music printed from the same woodcuts later used in *Silvia*. *BUCEM* ('Nymph') lists three single-sheet editions, the earliest of which is dated *c.*1710, the others *c.*1715 (Moss cites BL H.1601.[27]). Identical incipits given for two song-sheets in *NTI* (DFo-C.42.4[10] and MH Marshall Coll. [573]) correspond exactly to the music in *Silvia*. The words appear with slight alterations in *TTM* iii. 1–2.

The first verse of 'The Jolly Young Swain' as printed in *MM* reads:

> A Nymph of the Plain
> By a Jolly young Swain,
> By a Jolly young Swain,
> Was addrest to be kind;
> But relentless I find,
> To his Pray'rs she appear'd,
> Tho' him—self he endear'd
> > In a manner so soft, so en—gaging and sweet,
> > As soon might perswade her his Passion to meet.

Over the course of the remaining four verses the 'Nymph' proves to be not so relentless as she at first appeared.

Air LIX (III. xviii. 57–66; Moss 842)

The tune-title is the first line of a song written by Wilks, with music by Henry Carey, published in single-sheet editions *c.*1720 and *c.*1725 (*BUCEM* ['Carey, Henry']) Moss cites BL H.1601.(549). Identical incipits given for the song-sheets listed in *NTI* (DFo-C.42.2[227], DFo-C.42.3[528], MH Marshall Coll. [1142]) correspond exactly to the music in *Silvia*, printed from woodcuts first used in *MM* iii. 68–9; the same music appears in *The Fashionable Lady* (1730; Air 62). Words and music are also found in *The Pocket Companion* (1725), p. 63. The tune as printed in *The Beggar's Wedding* (1729; Air 3) is, apart from details of notation and a few melodic variants, identical to that in *Silvia*.

In the first verse of the original Philoret uses all his arts of flattery to win the favours of Celia; his failure is described in the second and concluding verse (*MM* iii. 69):

> With skilful Tongue
> The Shepherd sung,
> And told a melting Tale;
> > But all his Art,
> > To touch her Heart,
> Prov'd vain, nor cou'd prevail.
> > Th' insulting Fair
> > With scornful Air
> Still mock'd the love-sick Swain;
> > And while he sigh'd,
> > She still reply'd,
> *I've Pleasure in your Pain.*

Air LX (III. xx. 10–14; Moss 326)

The source is not altogether certain, but Moss cites a ballad reprinted in W. Walter Wilkins, *Political Ballads of the Seventeenth and Eighteenth Centuries*, 2 vols. (London, 1860), ii. 168–9. The words can indeed be sung to the tune of Air LX, though some adjustment would be needed to fit the refrain. The first and last of the ballad's five verses read:

> I am Ormond the Brave—did you ever hear of me?
> A man lately banish'd from his own country,
> I fought for my life, and pawn'd my estate,
> For being so loyal to the Queen and the great.
> > You know I am Ormond, I am Ormond the Brave;
> > You call me Jemmy Butler, but I am Ormond the Brave!
>
> . . . .
>
> 'I never was a traitor, as you have been saying:
> I never damn'd Queen Anne, as her grave she lay in;
> But I was Queen Anne's darling, and Old England's delight,
> And for the crown of England so boldly I did fight.'
> > And sing hey, &c.

No reference to contemporary copies has been found. Wilkins notes: 'This is a traditionary ballad, and was taken down by Mr. Roach Smith in 1841, from the mouth of an itinerant fisherman in the Isle of Wight, who knew no more about it than that it had been sung by his father and grandfather before him. I have transcribed it from the pages of *England under the House of Hanover*, by . . . Thomas Wright . . .' Wilkins quotes Wright to the effect that the ballad 'is evidently much corrupted, as here given from the mouth of the singer'. If, however, the ballad belongs to the tune printed in *Silvia*, the fact that it fits fairly well may indicate that this version of it is relatively uncorrupted.

Air LXI (III. xxi. 27–34; Moss 816)

Source not found. According to L. J. Morrissey ('Henry Fielding and the Ballad Opera', *Eighteenth-century Studies*, iv. 4 [Summer 1971], 393) this 'undifferentiated "Minuet"' is to be found somewhere in *MM*. Neither direct survey nor cross-checking of the incipit for Air LXI in *NTI* has revealed it there or elsewhere. The compact woodcut is not of the type that Watts used in *MM* for printing above words, and it is too low in register to be music 'for the flute', which was appended to each of the songs.

Air LXII (III. xxii. 95–116; Moss 6)

'*An* Ode *on* Musidora, *walking in the* Spring-Garden. *The Tune by Mr.* [William] Croft', written by Thomas D'Urfey, is included in *Pills*, i. 136–7 (*Pills*, 1706, iv. 56–67), and in *Mercurius Musicus . . . for January and February* (1701), pp. 34–5 (not seen). *BUCEM* ('Croft, William') lists three single-sheet editions, dated *c.*1700, *c.*1705, and *c.*1710 (Moss cites BL H.1601.[42]).

Watts reprinted the ode, reproducing the melody exactly as it appears in *Pills*, in *MM* v. 198–9. The music in *Silvia* is a fourth lower and contains minor variation in rhythmic and melodic detail. The repetitions of words in Lillo's song correspond to those in the original, which reads (*MM*, repetitions here omitted):

> Oh how sweet are the cooling Breeze,
>   And the blooming Trees,
> When into his Bower Love guides *Musidora*:
> When we meet there the Nightingales
>   Sing pretty Tales,
> Mistaking my Dear for the Goddess *Aurora*.
>   Jessamine and Roses,
>   A thousand pretty Posies
>   the Summer's Queen discloses,
>   And strews as she walks.
>   Passion, Devotion
>   She gains with each Motion,
>   Lutes too, and Flutes too,
>   are heard when she talks, Oh *Venus* . . .

Air LXIII (III. xxiii. 25–45; Moss 193)

'Dutch Skipper' was one of the most frequently advertised theatre dances of the quarter century preceding the performance of *Silvia*, and the popularity of this tune lasted at least to the end of the century. The dance first appears by name in the Drury Lane bill for 7 June 1704; the dance-title 'Dutch Skipper and Wife' (Drury Lane, 21 May 1711), probably for a different dance, seems to indicate that 'Dutch Skipper' referred to a personage rather than a type of dance (*London Stage, 1700–1729*). It is not certain that any one piece of music invariably accompanied it. The D minor tunes called '*Dutch* Skipper' and 'Second part of *Dutch* Skipper' in *Damon and Phillida* (1729; Airs 14 and 15) are entirely distinct from the tunes of Air LXIII. Neither set of songs could be easily sung to the other pair of tunes, but the structure is the same: two parts, each binary, the first in common time and the second in 6/4. (The *Damon and Phillida* woodcuts had been used in *Love in a Riddle* [1729; Act III, Airs 16 and 17] for the same songs, but, like all the other tunes in the play, they were labelled, not with tune-titles, but with Cibber's first lines.) It is possible that Drury Lane, where Cibber's plays were performed, and Lincoln's Inn Fields used different music for the dance; but it is at least as likely that Henry Carey, the musical arranger for Drury Lane at the time (see Fiske, p. 122), composed the tunes for *Love in a Riddle*.

The tunes used by Cibber do not correspond to any others found in *NTI*. Incipits in *NTI* show that the tunes used in *Silvia* were those named 'Dutch Skipper' in *DM*, vol. ii (four editions, 1713–28), p. 102, and in *CD*, Book 1 (1718), p. 120, and that the same tune and name appear in three later manuscripts and in James Aird, *A Selection of Scotch, English, Irish and Foreign Air's*, vol. iii (Glasgow, 1788), p. 180. Two later tunes are specifically entitled 'New Dutch Skipper' and 'Auretti's Dutch Skipper'.

To the tunes used by Lillo, Thomas D'Urfey had earlier written a song called 'The British Toper. Made in honour of a bowle of punch occasioned by the intollerable price of bad clarret', its two 'movements' beginning 'Come aid me ye muses' and 'Then merrily merrily, fill away boys'. The earlier of the two single-sheet editions listed in *BUCEM* ('Come') is there dated 1710; the later edition, dated *c*.1715, includes the tune name in its title, 'The Dutch Skipper or British Toper in Praise of Punch'. Moss cites the later of these editions, BL G.307.(10); incipits given for copies of the earlier edition in *NTI* (DFo-C.42.4[182] and MH Marshall Coll. [154]) correspond to the music printed by Watts. Moss, having found only the later song-sheet, and citing no performance of the dance earlier than 1717, concludes that D'Urfey's song 'could have been sung along with the dancing in theatres, and these lyrics then would have been as popular as the tune itself'. 'Dutch Skipper' was, however, always billed as a dance, and D'Urfey's words were ignored by all the ballad-opera writers who used the music.

The bipartite structure of the music, with its change in time signature—and thus almost certainly in tempo—places it in a class with a small number of tunes, some of them apparently quite old, often associated with game or kissing dances. Two examples are discussed by Chappell: 'The Cushion Dance' (*PMOT* i. 153–7), for which he reproduces two tunes, 'Galliard Sweet Margaret' and 'Joan Sanderson' (the latter in *DM*, 7th and later edns.); and 'Barley-break', with a tune from *Lady Neville's Virginal Book* (1591). These tunes are all in two sections, in 3/4 and 6/8. A tune called 'Gray's Inn Masque, or Mad Tom' (*PMOT* i. 328–32; see also Simpson, pp. 263–6) has five sections in common time, concluding with a sixth in 6/4, with a change of key from minor to major. 'Mall Peatly'—i.e. 'Gillian of Croydon', the tune of Air XLI—appears to have begun as such a tune as well, changing from common time to 6/4. Analysis of these dances and tunes is a study in itself, which cannot be undertaken here. Interested readers should consult the sources noted above, and the second and third parts of Margaret Dean-Smith and E. J. Nichol, 'The Dancing Master', *Journal of the English Folk Dance and Song Society*, iv. 5 (1944), 167–79, and iv. 6 (1945), 211–31, which contain extensive bibliographies in addition to the information presented in the articles.

It is possible that Lillo was influenced in his choice of 'Dutch Skipper', despite the different tunes, by the songs in *Love in a Riddle* and its shortened version, *Damon and Phillida*. These come at the resolution of the sub-plot in the former and constitute the finale of the latter. After Phillida has dismissed her philandering Damon's two ridiculous rivals, 'Damon *presents himself to* Phillida, *singing*'. In this stage direction, and in the text of the song, there is a hint of something like 'Joan Sanderson, or The Cushion Dance' as it is described in *DM* (quoted by Chappell, *PMOT* i. 154). In the *New Grove* ('Cushion Dance') the description is summarized:

> . . . a man (or woman, if she initiates the proceedings) dances round the room holding a cushion (or sometimes a handkerchief) which he places before a chosen member of the opposite sex. She kneels on it and they kiss; she takes the cushion and the two dance hand-in-hand round the room. She in the same way chooses a man and the three dance in a ring. The action is repeated until all, men and women alternately, have been drawn into the ring. The process is then reversed, and one by one they leave the ring.

In the *DM* description the dance is accompanied by a sung dialogue.

The texts of Cibber's songs, which culminate the reform of Damon, read (in *Damon and Phillida*, Scene xi):

> DAM. See! behold, and see!
> With an Eye kind, and relenting,
> *Damon*, now, repenting,
> Only true to thee;
> Content to love, and love for Life!
>
> PHILL. If you, now sincere,
> With an honest Declaration
> Mean to prove your Passion,

> To the Purpose swear,
> And make, at once, a Maid a Wife.

DAM. Thus, for Life, I take thee,
> Never to forsake thee,
> Soon or late,
> I find our Fate,
> To Hearts astray,
> Directs the way,
> And brings, to lasting Joys, the Rover home.

PHILL. Ever kind, and tender,
> Conquer'd, I surrender:
> Prove but true,
> As I, to you,
> Each kindling Kiss
> Shall add a Bliss,
> That only, from the constant Lip, can move.

DAM. To the Priest away, to bind our Vows,
> With our Hands and Hearts united.

PHILL. To reduce the Rover to lawful Spouse,
> Is a triumph, my Heart has delighted.

DAM. If I never could fix,
> 'Twas the Fault of the Sex,
> Who easily yielding, were easy to cloy,

BOTH. But in Love we still find,
> When the Heart's well inclin'd,
> In One, only One, is the Joy.
> But in love, &c.

If the finale of *Silvia* was influenced, directly or indirectly, by the earlier plays and/or the dance, the result could well have been staging in which the four singers of the first part of the tune 'present' themselves to Silvia, followed by a celebratory dance linked to that action. One wonders whether the choreography of 'Dutch Skipper', which could at any rate have varied from one performer to another, exerted any influence on the staging of Cibber's or Lillo's scenes.

More generally, the pairing of tunes of different measures recalls the frequent pairing of the slow, usually duple-time, pavan with the triple-time galliard (see the *New Grove* articles on those two dances, and Chappell, *PMOT* i. 155–7). Watts used the woodcut of 'Dutch Skppper' as a unit only in *Silvia*. The first section was reused in *Achilles* (1733; Air 10). In *The Fashionable Lady* (1730; Air 49), where the song is written to the second part only, a different woodcut, melodically almost identical but in the key of C, was used; it reappears with Air 11 of *Achilles*, which is separated by dialogue from Air 10, and in revised editions of *The Lottery* (1732; Air 19).

Fielding wrote Air 7 of *The Grub-Street Opera* to both parts of 'Dutch Skipper'. The song, in which Parson Puzzletext extols the pleasures of sporting after a 'brushing hare' and Owen those of courting a 'brushing lass', is perhaps a response to, but not directly a burlesque of, the moral tendencies of Cibber's and Lillo's songs (see Introduction, pp. 12–14). The metrical patterns of Fielding's songs correspond to those of Lillo's Air LXIII, and were clearly intended to be sung to the tune found in *Silvia*.

THE LONDON MERCHANT

Motto

Learn to be wise . . . full well.] A variation of the final lines of the ballad 'The Lady's Fall', which appears in several collections, including the third edition of *A Collection of Old Ballads*, printed for J. Roberts, 1727, edited by A. Philips. In this reprint, as in all versions seen, the first of the lines in question reads 'By others Harm learn to be wise'. Although the epigraph underscores Lillo's didactic purpose, as McBurney remarks, and summarizes Barnwell's conclusion concerning the possible significance of his downfall, the ballad itself—the tale of a well-born girl who dies in childbirth, deserted by her lover—bears no relation to Lillo's play.

Dedication

Sir John Eyles] Lillo could have chosen no more suitable dedicatee than Sir John, a highly respected merchant and member of a prominent City family. A Member of Parliament for Chippenham (1713–27) and for London (1727–34), he had served as Lord Mayor in 1726–7, an honour that had also been accorded to his uncle, and in 1719–20 as Sheriff of London. Lillo remarks on Sir John's services to the South Sea Company; he was also a director and sometime governor of the Bank of England, as was his father, Sir Francis, who served many years as a director of the East India Company and was created a baronet by George I (Cokayne, *Baronetage*, v. 22; Ward, p. 114).

1–3 as Mr. *Dryden . . . of its Kind.*] This statement has not been found in Dryden's work, but Dryden argues in a similar way in the *Essay of Dramatic Poesy* (1668). Ward, followed by McBurney, notes that in the *Discourse concerning the Original and Progress of Satire* (1693) Dryden quotes 'our master Aristotle' as saying that 'the most perfect work of Poetry is Tragedy'.

6–8 the End of Tragedy . . . their Excess.] Lillo's concept of the 'End of Tragedy', as Ward notes, is hardly Aristotelian. However, the statement here does focus on a major theme of Lillo's plays and a central source of motivation for many of his characters: the dangerous potency of the passions and the need to rein them in. Moreover, Lillo's definitions of the two sorts of 'criminal' passions—those inherently evil and those by nature good but dangerous in excess—point towards significant elements in his plays and their meaning. Passion of the first kind, for example, drives the villainous characters of *Elmerick* and provides the springs of action of the play, while in *The Christian Hero* the rousing of an essentially benevolent passion to too intense a pitch threatens, as nothing else can, the hero's commitment to courage and his cause. In all of the plays, restraint of the passions and an awareness of their dangerous power are posed as the keys to a happy and prosperous as well as virtuous life; any yielding to 'inclination' is the certain way to catastrophe (see I. viii. 8–9 n.).

26 *Tamerlane . . . Bajazet*] The spellings of the names indicate reference not to Marlowe's play but to Rowe's *Tamerlane* (1702), in which the contrast between benevolent ruler and tyrant was taken to illustrate a similar disparity between William III and Louis XIV (Ward, N & C, McBurney).

30–4 The Sentiments . . . or Revenge.] The statement effectively sets out the central argument of Lillo's last play, *Elmerick*, although the concern for responsible kingship reflected in a defence of the liberties of individual subjects is regularly voiced in Lillo's plays. Like the reference to the passions (ll. 6–8, above), this brief statement can serve as a significant point of reference for the interpreter of Lillo's plays.

31 *Cato*] Addison's play, first performed in 1713, regularly held the stage in Lillo's time.

43–48 *Had he . . . and Ears.*] McBurney notes that this quotation and those at lines 50–4 and 61–2 are 'Lillo's versions of' *Hamlet* (II. ii). Some departures from the now usual readings of Shakespeare's lines may indeed be Lillo's, but others reproduce the readings of 18th-cent. editions. '*I've*' and '*Creatures at*' (for 'creatures sitting at') in line 50, for example, follow Pope's text, although Lillo and Pope vary at other points.

46 *appale*] G2, apparently not recognizing Shakespeare's word, emends to 'appall' and is followed by subsequent editions.

78–83 The Proprietors . . . greatest Danger.] Eyles was appointed Sub-Governor on 31 Jan. 1721 in the general reorganization of the company which followed the over-speculation and panic of 1720 (N & C, McBurney).

83 Neither] So G2 and subsequent editions; G1 prints 'Nor'. A stylistic nicety, perhaps intended to contrast with 'Nor' of line 77, above; the emendation is possibly, though not necessarily, authorial.

83–4 the Court] McBurney notes that '*The Political State of Great Britain* for December, 1729, reported that Eyles, accompanied by other directors of the South-Sea Company, had been "received with great Distinction by his Majesty", to whom Eyles delivered "a very Dutiful and Loyal Address".'

84–5 a Character so well known] So G5 and subsequent editions; G1–4 print 'your Character'. An additional nod in compliment to the dedicatee, the emendation is so substantial—and unnecessary except as an added courtesy—that it seems doubtful that anyone other than the author can have been responsible.

Prologue

Mr. CIBBER, *Jun.*] Theophilus Cibber, who, as stage manager or under-manager in charge of the summer company at Drury Lane, produced Lillo's play (*London Stage, 1729–1747*, vol. i, p. xcvii).

17 *Brillant*] a form of 'brilliant' (from French; current in England 17th–18th cent.), meaning 'shining' and also 'diamond of finest cut and brilliancy' (*OED*).

22 *fam'd old Song*] the ballad of George Barnwell; see Introduction.

24 *ere*] So G3–7; G1–2 print '*e'er*'. See *Silvia*, Prologue, l. 36 n.; cf. also *The Christian Hero*, II. i. 167 n., and *Fatal Curiosity*, III. i. 45 n. The word is so spelt throughout G1 (I. i. 6, IV. xiii. 16, IV. xviii. 11, V. vii. 24, V. ix. 28, V. x. 9), except at III. vii. 16, where the spelling is 'e're'. G2 follows G1, correcting 'e'er' to 'ere' only at I. i. 6; G3 corrects 'e'er' in all cases, but does not correct 'e're'; G5 corrects 'e're', and prints 'ere' in V. xi (l. 20), a scene first printed in G5. In conformity with these later authoritative editions of the play, the word is routinely emended to 'ere'.

26 *thousand-thousand*] Ward notes *The Tempest*, III. i. [9]. Cf. *The London Merchant*, V. ix. 47, and *Elmerick*, II. ii. 75.

29 *insure*] So G2 and subsequent editions; G1 prints '*secure*'. The nature of the change suggests intentional emendation, very possibly authorial. While there is some possibility of confusion as to the meaning of 'secure'—'acquire' or 'obtain' as well as 'make secure'—the two words are essentially synonymous in this context. The change may well have been meant to eliminate the inelegant rhyme 'secure/cure'.

31 *Crimes*] An emendation, very likely authorial, introduced in G2 for '*Guilt*' (G1 only). Like a number of textual adjustments made in the second edition, this change may have been intended to make precise (or to avoid) a theological nicety: Millwood's crimes are obvious; her guilt, in the context of a predestined world (a concept clearly of concern to Lillo), is less clear-cut. A simpler explanation for the emendation is possible, however: '*Guilt*' appears in line 30, the emendation to '*Crimes*' avoids repeating the word in line 31.

Dramatis Personæ

6 *Wetherilt*] So G1–2; G3–4 print '*Witherhilt*'; G5–7 print '*Witherhile*'. Robert Wetherilt's name is found variously spelt, but the version printed in G1–2 is accepted as standard by the *London Stage, 1729–1747* (vol. i, pp. cxxvi, clix).

I. i

4 disappointed of . . . from *Genoa*] Modern editors regularly note that this story, which Thorowgood expands in detail in ll. 24–33, lacks historical foundation; Spain was dominant in Genoa at the time in question. Leo Hughes suggests that Lillo's audience may have seen topical allusions in the story inasmuch as 'the House of Hanover was quite aware of its debt of gratitude to the City' (*The Drama's Patrons* [Austin, Tex., and London, 1971], pp. 151–2). Lillo's primary purpose in inventing, or at any rate including, the tale—his concern to establish the merchant's merit and value to his nation—is clear enough. Of greater critical interest is Lillo's posing of the English merchants in opposition to villainous Spaniards, a contrast developed into a metaphor when Millwood compares her approach to her victims with the Spaniards' treatment of conquered natives (I. iii. 20–2) and continued in Thorowgood's discussion of the benefits of humane colonization (III. i. 1–7).

20 complement] an accepted spelling of 'compliment' (*OED*).

27 *Walsingham*] Sir Francis Walsingham (*c.*1530–90), who from 1573 until his death served as a Secretary of State under Elizabeth.

35–6 those Princes, who make] So G2 and subsequent editions; G1 prints 'to former Princes, who made'. Almost certainly authorial, the emendation in G2 generalizes Trueman's remark, maintaining the contrast already established between English and foreign kings while preventing any interpretation that might suggest a slur against particular English monarchs.

41 Sir] G1 prints as the beginning of a new speech and includes a speech-heading for Trueman. While this could suggest that a speech of Thorowgood's was omitted, it is most unlikely that so obvious an omission would have gone unnoticed during the preparation of G2. Conceivably an earlier version of the scene included a speech for Thorowgood. It is also possible that the first portion of Trueman's speech ('On these terms . . . our Acceptance') was given originally to Thorowgood but reassigned in order to create a greater sense of dialogue in a rather heavy passage of historical and moral exposition. Throughout this part of the scene the two characters are virtually undifferentiated in style of speech.

43–4 Only look . . . if there are, send] So G2 and subsequent editions; G1 prints 'Only to look . . . and if there are, to send'. These minor emendations appear to have been intended, like a number of probably authorial adjustments in G2, to eliminate rather stiffly formal syntax in order to make the speech more direct and natural. Editorial nicety would more likely have had an opposite effect.

I. ii

3 the Courtiers may at least commend] So G2 and subsequent editions; G1 prints 'the Courtiers, tho' they should deny us Citizens Politeness, may commend'. The phrase omitted by G2 could have proved offensive to either courtiers or merchants, and it seems probable that the author deleted it.

7 at present] Omitted by G2 and subsequent editions. G2 also introduces a semi-colon after 'Conversation' (l. 7), which in G1 completes a line of type; possibly the compositor or an editor misinterpreted 'at present', associating it with the phrase which follows, and, when this seemed awkward, made the deletion. No explanation of editorial niceness or adjustment of meaning seems possible.

10 dispense with] excuse, indulge (*OED*).

29–46 Thou know'st . . . immediately concern'd.] In their concern for the happiness of one another rather than for themselves in the matter of the selection of a son-in-law and husband, Thorowgood and Maria—or their author—would seem to know and emulate the scrupulosity of Steele's Sir John Bevil and Bevil Junior.

I. iii

2 A little more Red] The allusion to Lady Wishfort and the toilet-table scene in Congreve's *The Way of the World* is unmistakable here, as it is later in Millwood's rehearsal of the manner in which she will greet her expected lover (I. iv. 3 ff.).

40 and has a good Face] So G2 and subsequent editions; not in G1. The emendation is almost certainly authorial.

46–7 sooner. Having . . . him,] So G5 and subsequent editions; G1–4 print 'sooner, having long had a Design on him;'. The punctuation of G1, clearly incorrect, may well evidence the extent to which the pointing of the play, minimal or difficult to interpret in the manuscript, was left to the invention of the less than skilful compositor(s) of the first edition.

I. v

8 I may . . . you think] So G3 and subsequent editions; G1–2 print 'All my apprehensions proceed from my Fears of your thinking'. The emendation eliminates convoluted if genteel complexities which perhaps became peculiarly apparent on the stage.

15 simple] So G3 and subsequent editions; G1–2 print 'silly'. Since it is improbable that the change came about through error or as an editorial nicety, it may well be authorial, although accounting for it is difficult. 'Simple' retains the meaning 'innocence' while avoiding strong connotations of 'foolishness' or 'imbecility', which, in context, Millwood clearly would not intend.

22 Subject] So G3 and subsequent editions; G1–2 print 'Affair'. The emendation eliminates a possible *double entendre* that would be unfortunate at this point in the scene.

28 the Love of Women] McBurney cites 2 Sam. 1: 26—'thy love to me was wonderful, passing the love of women'—and remarks, 'Here Lillo begins a series of verbal echoes of the Biblical story of David and Jonathan.' Lillo's style, especially in Barnwell's farewell to Trueman (Act V), does appear to attempt a biblical resonance, and one could expect him to draw on the story or language of the biblical model in dramatizing the friendship of Barnwell and Trueman. However, despite the clear verbal allusion in this line, very few genuine echoes of the language of the Old Testament story are to be found in the play, and the elements of Lillo's plot bear almost no similarity to the story of David and Jonathan. Lillo's model, surely, was the conventional conflict of

friendship and love (or passion), a plot device so common to Restoration tragedy that it can be called a formula. His concern about the moral implications of Barnwell's downfall leads him to emphasize other aspects of his drama, but the elements of this conventional plot—commitment to friendship, counter-attraction, betrayal, realization, and reunion—are present in *The London Merchant* and developed in the conventional sequence.

45 Master] So G3 and subsequent editions; G1–2 print 'Master as you are'. Again adjustment of the text serves to eliminate rather stiff syntax, which, while precise, in this case interrupts the rush of an impassioned speech.

63 with] So G2 and subsequent editions; G1 prints 'wish'. The emended reading seems more appropriate to the sense of the line, the situation, and Millwood's character; however, compositorial error in G2 is easily possible as an explanation for the change.

65–6 Blushes (this . . . declare] So G2 and subsequent editions; G1 prints 'Blushes speak.—This Flood of Tears to that will force their way, and declare—'. The alterations in G2 tighten, clarify, and add impetus to a passage which, as originally printed, may have proved awkward. G1 is neither incorrect nor lacking in sense. The emendations alter the meaning of the speech to the extent that 'declare' takes 'Blushes' rather than 'Flood of Tears' as its subject—a reading which different punctuation would have produced in G1. The changes made in G2 may well have been intended to eliminate this ambiguity as well as to sharpen the conclusion of a speech which must have a strong effect on Barnwell. While the decision to adopt one reading or the other is finally arbitrary, the pattern of authorial emendations in G2 and heightened dramatic effectiveness argue for acceptance of the emended version of the lines.

I. vii

1 What, is] *Ed.*; G1 prints 'what is'; G2 and subsequent editions print 'What's'. Lucy's speech—'So it seems' (l. 3)—indicates that G2's reading is impossible and that only pointing similar to that provided in the present edition is feasible, even though this means that Blunt must begin two speeches in precisely the same way, which is rhetorically unfortunate at best (l. 4 clearly requires pointing similar to that of line 1, although none is supplied in G1). Ward, followed by N & C, accepts this interpretation of the two speeches but prints exclamation marks instead of commas. McBurney, perhaps striving to minimize the echo between lines 1 and 4, punctuates Blunt's first speech as two questions: 'What is all . . . music? For the . . . young fellow?' No early edition suggests this interpretation.

15 Patridge] an accepted spelling of 'Partridge', 17th–19th cent. (*OED*). G6 and subsequent editions print 'Partridge'.

I. viii

SD *Scene draws . . . they come forward.*] The expanded direction, first printed in G3, almost certainly describes staging developed in the theatre (see textual introduction).

Millwood's 'entertainment' lent itself, of course, to the theatre managers' concern to meet the popular demand for interludes of music and dancing, and advertisements for performances of the play frequently include announcements of the selections and performers to be presented 'in Act I'. Offerings range from 'a Piece of Musick, compos'd by Signior Vivaldi, call'd *The Cuckow*, by Charke [in the character of Lucy?] and others' (Drury Lane, 23 July 1731) to 'Signora Merigghi's Favourite Song in *Porus* by Miss Raftor' (Drury Lane, 27 July 1731) and 'An *English Cantata*, by Mrs. Clive' performed at Drury Lane on Boxing Day, 1735 (*London Stage, 1729–1747*, dates cited).

8–9 The Law . . . our Passions.] The first dramatic statement of a unifying motif in

Lillo's plays, one which, according to the dedication (ll. 6–8), he held to be central to the function of tragedy. Millwood's reply, that self-denial is unnatural, is a dangerous rationale, to which most of Lillo's erring characters subscribe.

20 *Woman kind*] In G6 emended to '*Woman-kind*', an easily possible compositorial slip and almost certainly misinterpretation of the meaning of the line.

II. i

4 Breach of Trust] 'Apparently Barnwell gave Millwood the money which he had at the end of the previous day's transactions' (McBurney).

9–11 Sure such . . . Hell about him.] McBurney is clearly correct in seeing in Lillo's 'grand Apostate' a reference to *Paradise Lost*; however, the passage seems to relate less directly to book II, which McBurney cites, than to book IV, ll. 20–3:

> for within him Hell
> He brings, and round about him, nor from Hell
> One step no more than from himself can fly
> By change of place:
>
> (ed. Merritt Y. Hughes [New York, 1957].)

The subjects of Milton's next lines—Satan's despair wakened by conscience, his 'bitter memory | Of what he was, what is, and what must be | Worse', worse deeds and suffering to ensue—similarly find parallels in Barnwell's speech. Lillo may also have known, as Milton did, Marlowe's Mephistophilis, although the modern reader is more likely to be sensitive to possible echoes of *Dr. Faustus* than Lillo's contemporaries would have been. Ward credits Lillo's own inventiveness for 'an apparently original, and a profoundly conceived, refinement upon the thought which . . . Mephistophilis expresses in the line of which there are many *analoga*: "Why this is hell, nor am I out of it."' Whatever the analogues, Lillo's image involves a nice theological point: to the orthodox Christian, Satan 'bore his future hell about him' only from the moment at which he conceived of rebellion—the idea implied in Barnwell's speech—and Milton, in fact, makes no reference to hell in his descriptions of Satan in heaven; to the Calvinist, the 'future hell' was about the sinner from the moment of his creation—a possibility raised, and it appears not entirely resolved, in Lillo's attempt at the end of his play to define the nature, extent, and origins of Barnwell's guilt.

II. ii

66–71 We have heard . . . consuming Flames;] Barnwell cites a series of miracles, the biblical sources of which have been variously identified by modern editors: 'the glorious Sun'—Josh. 10: 13 (Ward, McBurney, N & C [as 10: 12–14]), Isa. 38: 8 (Ward, McBurney), 2 Kgs. 20: 9–11 (N & C); 'The Dead have risen'—1 Kgs. 17: 17–22 (McBurney, N & C [as 17: 17–24]), Luke 7: 12–15 (McBurney [as 7: 15]), John 11: 37–44 (McBurney [incorrectly as 11: 22]), and elsewhere in the Gospels; 'parched Rocks pour'd forth . . .'—Num. 20: 11 (McBurney), Exod. 17: 5–7 (N & C); 'The Sea divided'—Exod. 14: 21 (Ward, N & C [as 14: 21–31], McBurney [incorrectly as 16: 21]); 'Hungry Lions have refus'd their Prey'—Dan. 6: 16–23 (N & C, McBurney [as 6: 22]); 'Men have walk'd amidst consuming Flames'—Dan. 3: 19–27 (N & C, Ward and McBurney [as 3: 25]).

76 we ought] So G2 and subsequent editions; G1 prints 'he who trusts Heaven ought'. Intended, apparently, to eliminate in Trueman's speech any suggestion that men,

trusting heaven or not, ought ever to yield to despair, the emendation is almost certainly authorial.

II. iii

1 ingaged him to apply . . . to repair] Emendations in G2 and G3 correct the ambiguity and syntactical awkwardness of G1, which prints 'to have applied . . . to have repaired'. The problem hinges on the meaning of 'trusted'; in the text as first printed, Barnwell can mean either that he should have expected (counted on) Trueman to seek help from the uncle or, as Lillo clearly intends, that he should have placed his trust in Trueman and employed him to ask the uncle's aid. G2 attempts clarification by substituting 'who wou'd apply' for 'to have applied' and eliminates the awkwardness of 'to have repaired'. G3 improves on G2, making the meaning indisputable by inserting 'and ingaged him' before the readjusted 'to apply'.

10 Inclination] disposition, propensity (*OED*). In Lillo's plays the word is regularly given stronger force, as 'natural drive' or 'passionate impulse'. Cf. II. iv. 16, IV. xviii. 34; *Elmerick*, I. i. 69; and *Fatal Curiosity*, III. i. 91.

II. iv

15–16 best when oppos'd] G2, followed by subsequent editions, emends to 'best, oppos'd', a change that obscures the syntactical relationships of 'oppos'd'. If the word is taken as parallel to 'weak', 'form'd', and 'unassisted', the syntax suggested by G2's pointing, then the emendation forces a mistaken interpretation of the meaning of the line. The adjustment may represent mistaken editorial niceness intended to eliminate repetition of 'when', which occurs twice previously in the sentence.

21 I never will.] So G2 and subsequent editions, omitting a phrase found in G1, which prints '. . . will; so Heav'n confirm to me the Pardon of my Offences'. The change appears to be another nice adjustment by the author concerned to do away with any suggestion that Thorowgood's generosity is motivated, even in part, by self-interest. The original line reiterates a fundamental doctrine of the Gospels: as God in his greatness pardons man, so man, in emulation and in the hope of that forgiveness, should forgive his fellows; as first printed, however, the line is unfortunately ambiguous.

22 now,] G2 and subsequent editions omit. The inclusion of 'now' (G1) makes clear and emphatic the antithesis on which the speech is constructed, and it seems likely that the word was deleted in error. Occurring at the end of a line of type in G1, the word follows a semicolon at the end of a syntactically complete sentence, is not essential to the sense of the next part of the speech, and might well have been overlooked by a compositor. It is also possible that the compositor or editor who reviewed the details of the text for the second edition mistook lines 21–2 ('when the Sense . . . strongest Curb;') as a clause dependent on 'this . . . Season' (l. 21) and struck out 'now' as awkward.

25 me] So G2 and subsequent editions; G1 prints 'me then'. Compositorial error is unlikely in this instance and, taken with the emendation in l. 26, the deletion in G2 appears to be intentional and probably authorial. The change could have been made to ensure that Barnwell's speech would not be mistakenly read to refer to the time 'When Vice becomes habitual' (l. 24), but can be more simply explained as meant, like the emendation in l. 26, to produce a speech more direct and less formal.

26 Not a Syllable] So G2 and subsequent editions; G1 prints 'I will not hear a'. The emendation gives the speech greater directness and is very probably authorial, perhaps influenced by an actor's reading of the line.

II. vii

1–2 Now every Thing . . . made me?] So G3 and subsequent editions; in G1–2 the order of the two sentences is reversed. The later version of the speech represents a pattern of ideas more logical and natural in their succession and, given the emphatic concluding sentence, is certainly more dramatic. The rearrangement is the sort of change that one would expect to come about—and to meet with the author's approval—while a play took shape in a theatre. In either version the line echoes *Macbeth* (II.ii.56), 'How is't with me when every noise appals me?' (See also IV.ix.1 n. and 14–15 n., below.)

II. viii

SD *Another Room in* Thorowgood's *House*.] There appears to be no logical reason for a change of setting at this point in the play, and it is possible that none was called for in Lillo's original text. Scene viii itself is possibly a late addition to the play. It serves a purely mechanical purpose, providing an entrance for Millwood and Lucy. Moreover, without this scene, Barnwell would be required to exit (scene vii) and enter (scene ix) all but simultaneously, no dialogue having been provided for the ladies while they wait for him to appear. The ladies' entrance with the footman could, then, have been devised in the theatre to cover an awkwardness in the work of an inexperienced playwright, but it seems at least as likely that the awkwardness developed *in* the theatre: except for the change of setting, not actually required by the situation, scene ix could follow directly and easily after scene vii—that is, the ladies could enter the room where Barnwell waits. Barnwell's reaction to seeing them would fit this action exactly, and it seems very possible that the change of setting was added for production, perhaps to allow for an interlude of music or simply to avoid playing the entire act in one setting. The direction at the head of I. viii indicates that for this production the stage equipment was set up to effect rapid shifts of scene by 'drawing' the flats.

A new reading at II. ix. 9, introduced in the third edition, suggests that some adjustment of the action occurred after copies of the author's final version of the play had been made. In G1 and G2, Millwood describes herself and Lucy as having been 'directed' to the room; in G3, 'directed' is emended to 'conducted'. Strictly interpreted, 'directed' is an error if the ladies have been brought to the room by the footman. However, if they simply enter the room in which the earlier scenes of the act have been played and there discover Barnwell, they have indeed been 'directed here', Barnwell's reaction is altogether appropriate, and the awkwardness in the printed text—the necessity for Barnwell to enter almost while the footman is announcing that he will come, there being nothing for the ladies to say until he appears—does not exist.

The minor discrepancy eliminated by the emendation in G3 is of the kind likely to occur when details of staging are added or changed and easily overlooked when the altered business and the line it affects occur at different places in the text. The emendation itself looks like the work of a sharp-eyed and rather fussy editor, but it may well belong with the many adjustments in G3 that seem clearly to record details of performance.

II. ix

9 conducted] So G3 and subsequent editions; G1–2 print 'directed'. See II. viiiSD n., above.

27 indulgent] So G2 and subsequent editions; G1 prints 'kind'. The change cannot

have come about through error and it seems unlikely that anyone other than the author was responsible for it.

II. xi

11 whether] G3, followed by subsequent editions, emends to 'whither'. *OED* records 'whether' as an alternative spelling for 'whither', 15th–18th cent., and cites, among others, Defoe, *Journal of the Plague Years* (1722), 'In Heaven, whether I hope we may come.' Cf. III. v. 14–15, IV. x. 3, and *The Christian Hero*, IV. iv. 43.

18 Wiles] So G1–5; G6–7 print 'Wilds'. While 'wiles' in its usual sense—deceptions, delusions, slynesses—is not nonsensical here, it is at least very odd in context. 'Wilds', nearly synonymous with and, as here, regularly linked in phrases with 'desarts', is a much more probable reading (cf. 'wilds and deserts', *Elmerick*, IV. i. 46; *OED* cites many examples of this pairing). No variant form of 'wild(s)' without the 'd' is given by *OED*; no example of 'wiles' as denoting a place, even in figurative usage, is cited. A citation from *The Comedy of Errors* (IV. iii. 10–11) suggests such an extension or play of meaning, but seems to be unique: 'Sure these are but imaginarie wiles, | And lapland Sorcerers inhabite here.' The word in G1 could represent a misreading or mis-setting of 'wiles' for 'wildes', a spelling common in the 18th cent.; since 'wiles' is a highly familiar word and moreover readily associated with Millwood, such an error in a phrase which appears to make good enough sense unless one stops to think about it might well have passed unnoticed until picked up by the editor or compositor of G6. However, the word survived the scrutiny of those who corrected and emended a series of editions, it forms a part of an intelligible if curious phrase, and it has been retained in the present edition.

II. xii

7 *Mill.* Leave that to me.] First printed in G2. Lucy's speech (ll. 5–6) requires some comment from Millwood and leaves the scene unresolved. It seems likely that the line was inadvertently omitted from the first edition or from the manuscript from which it was set.

II. xiii

12 least] variant form of 'lest' (*OED*).

II. xiv

1–9 What have I . . . how or why—] In Lillo's view Barnwell's dilemma—the problem that arises when an act of evil is required in an apparently good cause—is, of course, much less paradoxical or insoluble than the young man supposes. He has not, it is true, 'sought the Occasion' by which he is tested; however, like several of the playwright's characters, he is led (i.e. deceived) by his 'Heart' rather than by 'Reason'. The situation is clarified and answers to the questions posed by Barnwell are given at III. i. 1–7 and 24–6.

III. i

SD *A Room in* Thorowgood's *House.*] So G3 and subsequent editions; G1–2 give no setting for the scene.

1–7 Methinks I wou'd . . . from Pole to Pole.] Thorowgood's speech and the scene itself may well seem to be little more than extraneous moralizing on the merits of the merchant class and the business in which it engaged. In part, no doubt, they are so, and 'prompt-book' editions of the play indicate that after 1775, if not before, much of the scene was omitted in performance. However, the scene does have a legitimate place in

Lillo's moral history of Barnwell, providing, in effect, the answers to the young man's dilemma, dramatized in the preceding scene, and pointing to the alternative to his (and Millwood's) passion-driven course of action. The lesson Thorowgood teaches is the function of 'method' (reason) in shaping nature towards useful, moral, and fulfilling ends and in harnessing that which is savage (in the moral as well as anthropological sense) or evil.

The adjustment in G2 (l. 4) of 'promoted Humanity' to 'promotes Humanity' suggests concern on the part of the author to make it clear that the benefits of 'Merchandize', great in the past, are equally significant in the present.

9–15 I have observ'd . . . in need of.] The passage is clearly intended to stand in sharp contrast to Millwood's remark about her emulation of the vicious greed of Spanish conquerors (cf. I. iii. 20–2).

24–6 Method in Business . . . and in Danger.] The application of 'Method', founded in reason (l. 3), is surely not meant to be limited to business alone. Thorowgood's assertion provides an answer to the moral perplexities of Barnwell, whom the audience has just seen 'uncertain, and in Danger'.

III. iii

50 only Witnesses] So G3 and subsequent editions; G1–2 print 'Judges'. Like a number of changes introduced in early editions, the emendation appears to involve theological niceness, a careful distinguishing of men as witnesses rather than judges of one another's actions. Despite a possible ambiguity, 'Witnesses' almost certainly refers to 'Heaven' and 'you', not to 'you' alone; in the present edition, the pointing has been adjusted to make this clear.

III. iv

SD Millwood*'s House*.] G5–6—clearly in error—place the scene in Thorowgood's house (see apparatus criticus).

2 admire] in context, 'to be astonished, wonder'.

31–2 a Sum . . . brought from] So G2 and subsequent editions; G1 prints 'a Bag . . . Stol'n from'. The emendation appears intended to relieve Barnwell of the blame for overt criminal intent in bringing the money from Thorowgood's, or at any rate to leave the situation ambiguous. It may also relate to the characterization of Lucy, whose sympathies are shifting to Barnwell. (See apparatus criticus for minor changes made necessary by the emendation.)

37 amorous Youth] So G2 and subsequent editions; G1 prints 'easy Fool'. Again, the alteration in G2 attempts to improve, to a degree, the character of Barnwell as he is described in this scene. Emendations apparently similarly motivated occur at ll. 80 and 83.

65–6 held him . . . Endearments, call'd] The pointing of G1 leaves the speech awkward and ambiguous; various adjustments were attempted in subsequent editions (see apparatus criticus). Ward's deletion of the comma after 'held him' is the simplest solution and is followed in the present edition.

66 call'd her cruel Monster] So G5 and subsequent editions; G1–4 print a comma after 'her', which is not incorrect syntactically but almost certainly obscures the intended meaning. G2's insertion of a comma after 'cruel' does not really help and may, in fact, distort the sense (although, again, the pointing is valid syntactically). The present editor, like Ward, follows G5 in omitting the comma after 'her' and adheres to G1's 'cruel

Monster'. McBurney and N & C reproduce the pointing of G5, including the comma after 'cruel' introduced by G2.

70 he;] G2–4 print 'he?', clearly in error. This mistaken emendation may be taken as an indication that at least some of the many question marks introduced by G2 are not authorial emendations, even though a good number of them are necessary and most are useful rhetorically.

106 all my Heart.] Following this sentence, G1 prints 'How else shall I clear my self?' The omission by G2 and subsequent editions excludes explicit self-concern as the primary motivation for Blunt's change of heart, thus dramatically changing the emphasis of the speech and, indeed, the situation.

III. v

9 Then what . . . for him] Ward notes, 'For he (elliptically)'. McBurney, capitalizing 'for', finds Lillo's meaning 'obscure here' and suggests that 'the emendation of the two piratical editions ["then what should I feel for him" (Cooper "7th" and all Cooper "8th" edns.)] is plausible'. In fact, the sentence is without syntactical irregularity and makes sense as it stands, if 'for' is understood to be a preposition, not a conjunction, and the exclamation mark is recognized as interjected punctuation not marking the conclusion of a sentence. The speech, then, asks 'What should I be for him that was my Father's only Brother . . .'; the reply, in part implicit, is 'I should not be, but am, avowed his destined murderer.'

11 indulged] 'Indulges' seems a very possible emendation, but has been found in no edition examined.

III. vi

3 gashly] ghastly, horrid (*OED*, which records this as perhaps an altered form of 'ghastly').

4 Visage] N & C note, 'i.e. of the corpse awaiting burial'.

7 Reflections] Ward remarks, 'The ill-chosen word "reflections" can here only mean "thought."' It seems likely, however, that an ambiguity, happy or not, was intended.

9–13 The Blood . . . on Inquiry.—] The passage, as printed in G1, is notably awkward, suggesting that the printer's copy was minimally or ambiguously pointed, perhaps merely with dashes: 'The Blood, curd-|ling, and chill'd, creeps slowly thro' the Veins,— | fix'd, still and motionless, like the solemn Object | of our Thoughts.—We are almost at present— | what we must be hereafter, 'till Curiosity awakes | the Soul, and sets it on inquiry.—' Difficulties in sorting out the proper relation of phrases are compounded by unhelpful or incoherent punctuation. Is 'fix'd, still and motionless' to be taken as modifying 'Veins' or as autonomous? Must the next phrase also be taken to qualify 'Veins', as the pointing in G1 requires, or does it relate to 'fix'd, still and motionless', or is neither construction intended? With the insertion of three words, G2 provides a comprehensible, effective reading of the line: '. . . fix'd, still, and motionless we stand, so like the solemn Object . . .'; adjustment of the pointing further clarifies the passage. The substantive emendations may well be authorial, certainly they serve to make clear the ideas clouded by the text of G1. Authority for the emended accidentals cannot be ascertained, and some details can be questioned (e.g. the very light pointing after 'Thoughts'); the adjusted pointing has been accepted as perhaps associated with the substantive changes and, overall, an essential improvement on the misleading pointing of G1. Reference to G1 is helpful, however, in confirming that 'so', added by G2, should be taken to mean 'utterly, very' rather than 'thus'.

III. vii

6 she] 'The antecedent of "she," as well as of the preceding "it," is "the mind of man"' (N & C). The contradictory pronouns are awkward and seemingly beyond explaining.

8+SD *Throwing . . . his Sword.*] So G3, emending a stage direction which, in G1, is printed as a continuation of the direction which follows l. 7. The alteration brings lines and action into proper relation. In having Barnwell throw down rather than merely drop his pistol, the revised direction serves also to strengthen the action and clarify its motivation—i.e. Barnwell does not weakly fail in his attempt at murder but, until threatened (or frightened) by his uncle's sword, emphatically rejects it. Like other stage directions adjusted or introduced in G3, the emendation may reflect practice in the theatre.

16 ere] So G5–7; G1–4 print 'e're', an incorrect form of the word, and presumably a variation of 'e'er', a common variant form, which appears elsewhere throughout G1 to the exclusion of the correct form 'ere'. See Prologue, l. 24 n.

23–4 Life, that . . . Kiss expired.] First printed in G2. The added lines, almost certainly authorial, serve to inform the audience that Barnwell's uncle is indeed dead, and they may have been added simply for this reason; but the author may also have felt it necessary to heighten the moment rhetorically.

26 breath] breathe (*OED*, which notes the spelling as current during the 18th cent.).

37–40 *The rich Man . . . his Suit denies.*] The reference is to the parable of the rich man and Lazarus, Luke 16: 19–31 (Ward [as 16: 27–8], N & C, McBurney). McBurney finds 'the reference . . . unfortunate since the parable concludes with Abraham telling the rich man (Dives) that his brother [*sic*] would not profit by a messenger from beyond the grave'; however, while Lillo later emphasizes the usefulness of Barnwell's example to others tempted to err as he does, the final couplet of this scene reiterates precisely the more severe conclusion of the parable, with Lillo's 'Laws and Means well known' standing in exact parallel to the biblical 'Moses and the Prophets'. Ward suggests the rich man of Luke 12: 20 as the reference for the 'Fool' of ll. 39–40, but, as McBurney notes, it is more likely that Lillo's 'rich Man' and 'Fool' both refer to the parallel in Luke 16.

38 *Prefer'd*] probably 'proffered', a sense the *OED* records for this spelling, 16th–19th cent.

IV. i

SD *A Room in* Thorowgood*'s House.*] G1–2 include no reference to the setting.

6–8 they are . . . they sustain] G5 emends to 'we are . . . we sustain'd'; strictly correct, but more likely an editorial nicety than an emendation introduced by the author, who, in G2, almost certainly did revise a part of l. 8 (see below).

7 penal] Qualifying 'Evils', apparently 'misdeeds associated with punishment' (*OED*); in context, 'misdeeds for which one suffers openly or through law', in contrast to 'moral Evils', which, while more comprehensive and serious, are judged and punished by the laws of heaven, not of man.

8 be made] So G2 and subsequent editions; G1 prints 'be'. A nicety, theological rather than syntactical, that indicates authorial emendation. The later version suggests that Heaven may *elect* to turn 'ills' to good use rather than that this occurs automatically or by fortunate accident; there is also, perhaps, the suggestion that Maria herself may turn her suffering to some good for someone else.

IV. ii

9 him!] W1; G1–4 print 'him,'; G5–7 print 'him?' The characteristically light pointing of G1 is awkward for the reader and weakens the emphatic statement it is meant to set off. G5 and subsequent editions confusingly suggest an interrogatory rather than an exclamatory reading (compositors of the period seem frequently to have used '!' and '?' interchangeably).

IV. ix

1 Event] outcome (*OED*, which cites, among others, Steele, *Spectator*, No. 113 [1711], § 3, 'A beautiful Creature in a Widow's Habit sat in Court, to hear the Event of a Cause concerning her Dower').

1–2 the Attempt . . . ruin him.] Cf. Lady Macbeth (II. ii. 10–11), 'Th' attempt, and not the deed, Confounds us.'

4 done—] So G5 and subsequent editions; G1–3 print 'done,'; G4 prints 'done‸'. The punctuation in G5 makes clear the only possible meaning of the line, which G1 obscures and G4 mistakes.

IV. x

3–4 Where shall . . . Hand of Justice?] The biblical echoes are obvious; Ward, followed by McBurney, cites Ps. 139: 7 ff., Hos. 10: 8, and Rev. 6: 16. Comparison with the opening lines of Faustus's final speech in Marlowe's play is also possible, as Ward suggests.

6 Cavern] McBurney remarks that 'Millwood's cavern may be a property common to enchantresses (no specific source has been found), or simply an oblique reference to a grave'. Mention of the cavern does suggest a new aspect of Millwood's character, but surely this cavern is to be compared with the hideaways of thieves, smugglers, and other figures of a criminal rather than a supernatural underworld; and although the suggestion that Millwood may ironically refer to a grave is ingenious, such a reference would be appropriate for Barnwell but not for Millwood: the scene focuses on the contrast between Millwood's insistence that hiding is possible and Barnwell's certainty that no hideaway is secure because he is himself the accuser-discoverer.

14–15 Behold these . . . Uncle's Blood!] Comparison with *Macbeth* is difficult to avoid, as it is at IV. x. 1–2. Lillo's clear indebtedness to *Macbeth* for certain elements of the language and plot of *Fatal Curiosity* indicates that he was well acquainted with Shakespeare's play.

20 all-seeing] So G2 and subsequent editions; G1 prints 'omniscient'. The emendation is very probably authorial but could have been suggested by a precise editor who noted that 'omniscient' in its literal sense is an inappropriate adjective for 'Eye'.

44SD *Aside, rings a Bell*.] So G3 and subsequent editions; G1–2 print '*Stamps*.' The emended direction may well describe stage business as it was performed in the theatre.

IV. xiii

9–17 *Be warn'd . . . at my Cost*.] The lines are an expansion of the tag at the end of the old ballad of George Barnwell. However, the focus of the moralizing—the emphasis on reason and the posing of Barnwell as a conscious example to others—is Lillo's own; the moral in the last verse of the ballad is simply a warning against consorting with harlots.

10–13 *are Fair; . . . false to you*.] The meaning of these lines is all but obscured by the punctuation of G1 (see apparatus criticus). In subsequent early editions, efforts, not entirely successful, are made to make sense of the passage by adjustments in the pointing. The present edition follows Ward, as do McBurney and N & C.

IV. xiv

2–3 *Lucy* will . . . to thy Confusion] So G3 and subsequent editions; not in G1–2 (see apparatus criticus). The added sentence is probably intended to make more credible Millwood's realization (scene xv) that Blunt and Lucy have begun to work against her. The need for this change might well not have become evident until the play reached the theatre, a hypothesis strengthened by the appearance of the emendation in the third edition. However, an emendation at IV. xv. 1 (see apparatus criticus) suggests that the author was concerned with this problem when G2 was in preparation.

IV. xvi

11 Credit] 'reputation for trustworthiness' (N & C); 'in the wider sense of "honour, reputation"' (Ward).

21 commit.] So G2 and subsequent editions, which omit an additional phrase included in G1: 'and then betray'd him'. The phrase is paraphrased at 58 (an indication, perhaps, that the scene was reworked and expanded from an earlier, shorter version); it seems likely that the deletion in G2 was made in order to eliminate the awkward repetition.

22 the Advantage] So G2–7; G1 prints 'Advantage of me'. Another of the minor deletions by which G2 apparently intended to sharpen the dialogue and make it easier or more natural.

27 Frame] natural disposition (*OED*).

31 without Cause . . . your Appearance,] So G2 and subsequent editions; G1 prints 'without Cause,' after 'Appearance,'. Whether corrected by the author or an editor, the awkwardness in G1 is obvious.

63–7 How shou'd . . . Doubt impossible.] W1 sets off this portion of Thorowgood's speech as an aside, inserting a stage direction to that effect after 'Doubt impossible'—an indication perhaps of how the speech was spoken in the theatre (or had come to be spoken by 1775). The earlier texts, of course, allow but do not insist on this interpretation.

IV. xviii

7 *Thor.*] So G2 and subsequent editions; G1 gives the speech to Trueman, almost certainly incorrectly. Concern for the 'Abuse' of Millwood's 'uncommon Perfections of Mind and Body' (l. 8) is characteristic of Thorowgood but out of keeping with Trueman's mood in this scene. Ward, N & C, and McBurney appear not to have observed the variant; although they normally accept readings of the fifth edition, N & C give the speech to Trueman, as do Ward and McBurney, for whom the first edition served as copy-text.

7 aggravating] probably 'magnifying'; but note v. i. 7, 12, and v. v. 25, where 'aggravate' appears to have the meaning 'excite to greater intensity' (*OED*).

22 Suburb-Magistrates] 'Magistrates in the environs of London, i.e. outside the "City", had no regular salary, but subsisted upon their fees; many of them therefore encouraged vice in order to increase their profits' (N & C; similarly McBurney and Ward). 'Suburb', as a hyphenated prefix, means 'belonging to or characteristic of the suburbs (of London) as a place of inferior, debased, and especially licentious habits of life' (*OED*, which cites no example after 1688). Cf. 'suburb Slaves', v. ix. 55.

23–4 unhospitable Natives . . . by Ship-wrecks] Cf. *Fatal Curiosity*, I. iii. 2–13.

33–4 I know . . . my Inclinations,] So G3–7, following and in one word correcting G2 (see apparatus criticus). G1 prints the passage as follows: 'I hate you all, I know you, and expect no | Mercy; nay, I ask for none; I have done nothing | that I am sorry for, I follow'd my Inclinations . . .' Substantial revision of a speech marking a critical moment in Thorowgood's confrontation with Millwood strongly suggests revision by the author. It can at least be argued, however, that in some aspects the speech is rhetorically more effective in G1 than in the altered version. And an apparent error in G2 may be taken to indicate some uncertainty in the incorporation of revisions into the printed text, a situation which could cast doubt on the accuracy of other changes introduced here by G2.

On analysis, the emendations involve a series of primarily interpretative rather than mechanical questions. Initially, reordering of the three phrases which begin the speech as it was originally printed negates the dramatic impact of the retort with which Millwood responds to Thorowgood in the G1 text:

> *Thor.* . . . you . . . hate the officers of both.
> *Mill.* I hate you all . . .

However, the revised text does eliminate an ambiguity; in G1, 'I know you' can be read to relate to and qualify either 'I hate you' or 'I expect no mercy'. G2 settles the question—'I know you and [therefore] I hate you all'—and in the emended text Millwood's reply thus represents an extension of the accusations and the rationale for her behaviour which are central to her preceding long speech.

The emendation also eliminates, of course, the alternative possible reading in G1—'I know you and [therefore] I expect no mercy.' And in G2 the latter phrase is linked with the next element in the speech—'I expect no mercy and I ask for none.' The performer may regret the loss of the emphatic 'nay' provided by the text of G1, but the revision again clarifies a thematic point. In the resolution of Lillo's moral drama, Millwood, in sharp contrast to Barnwell, cannot (i.e. will not) ask for mercy and so can expect none; conversely, expecting no mercy, she cannot ask for it. The emended speech allows Millwood to declare this explicitly at an earlier point in the play, when her concern is the judgement and generosity of men rather than of God. Moreover, the rearrangement of phrases avoids any suggestion, even on the part of Millwood, that to 'know' Thorowgood is to 'expect no mercy'; in the didactic structure of the play, Thorowgood is, of course, the exemplification of mercy to those able to recognize and respond to his generosity.

The revision further involves deletion of 'I have done nothing I am sorry for'. If this change relates to the clarification of the speech itself or of ideas central to the play, the rationale is obscure. The line seems entirely in keeping with Millwood's character and her place in the play. Immediately following the deletion, G2 inserts 'and' before the next portion of the speech, an awkward addition, apparently made in error and corrected in G3 and subsequent editions. This seeming mistake could be taken as evidence that the editor's or compositor's copy for the revision was difficult to follow, a possible basis for arguing that the deletion was also made in error. However, the line was not restored when the extraneous 'and' was cancelled by G3. If neither thematic nor mechanical evidence provides persuasive reasons for retaining or omitting the line, the apparently calculated effectiveness of the rhetorical structure of the entire revised passage (ll. 33–4) does suggest that the emendations, including the deletion, should be accepted as an integrated group of improvements of the text. Taken together, the revisions create a series of three parallel sentences, set off by semicolons rather than full stops and each balanced by 'and'; the first two elements in the sequence are nearly isocolic while the third expands for a rolling climax, underscoring both rhetoric and the accusation with which Millwood resolves the series. In actors' terms, the speech 'builds' to very good effect. Given the ambiguities of the text in G1 and clear indications of author's revision in those emendations which relate to thematic concerns, it seems best to accept the apparently rhetorical adjustment as also authorial, and to adopt the altered version of the passage as a whole.

34 Inclinations] Cf. II. iii. 10, II. iv. 16; *Elmerick*, I. i. 69; and *Fatal Curiosity*, III. i. 91.

34–6 All Actions . . . than themselves.] A statement of the Hobbesian conception of man in its vulgarized form, a point of view central to much Restoration comedy. Lillo vehemently rejects the philosophy and, in his dedication to *The London Merchant* and by the example of his plays, the dramas based upon it. Emendation of 'are' to 'seem' (G2 and subsequent editions) could have resulted from compositorial error, but may well have involved the nice sort of distinction characteristic of several apparently authorial changes introduced in G2.

38 sweet and] So G2 and subsequent editions; G1 prints 'sweet, but'. Again an emendation apparently based upon a very nice distinction (that there is nothing contradictory in religion's 'Charms' being both 'sweet' and 'powerful').

V. ii

1 There see] So G3 and subsequent editions; G1–2 print 'See there'. The change has a purely rhetorical effect and may well be authorial.

16 Proceed.] So G2 and subsequent editions; G1 prints 'Go on.—How happy am I who live to see this?' The emendation is almost certainly authorial and intended perhaps to increase the pace of the scene.

23–4 Preparatory, the certain] The capitalization of 'Preparatory' indicates that it is to be construed as a noun (N & C); the insertion of 'the' before 'certain' (G2 and subsequent editions) is clearly intended to eliminate the possible ambiguity.

27 daily dies] Ward cites 1 Cor. 15: 31, 'I protest by your rejoicing which I have in Christ Jesus our Lord, I die daily.' In the context of Paul's description of his ministry founded on belief in the resurrection, Lillo's otherwise rather puzzling phrase does take on a specific and appropriate meaning.

42–3 from whence there's no return?] Ward cites *Hamlet*, III. i. 70–80.

V. iii

2 conscious] consciousness attributed to a personal quality (*OED*). Cf. *The Christian Hero*, I. i. 201, 243, and *Elmerick*, III. i. 254.

V. v

22 devoted] 'dedicated', but also with the sense of 'given over to the powers of evil, doomed' (*OED*, McBurney). Cf. v. ix. 61, v. xi. 18; *The Christian Hero*, IV. ii. 38; and *Fatal Curiosity*, II. iii. 72.

26 thus] Ward emends, inserting a comma after 'thus'.

35 Love will find thee.] So G2 and subsequent editions, which add the stage direction '*Rising*' for Barnwell at l. 40; in G1, Trueman lies down beside Barnwell and is given the line (omitted by G2 and subsequent editions) 'Upon this rugged Couch then let us lie, for well it suits our most deplorable Condition.' One cannot avoid the conjecture that in performance (or rehearsal) the business called for in the original script

proved ludicrous even to audiences (or actors) accustomed to the fulsomeness of sentimental drama histrionically performed. It is also possible that sensible theatre practice argued against playing a major scene with the actors lying on the stage floor, where many in the audience might have difficulty seeing them.

37 eccho] an archaic form that persisted through the 18th cent. (*OED*). Cf. *The Christian Hero*, II. i. 2, 'eccho'd'.

V. ix

2 reserves] detains (Ward), sets apart (N & C).

32 professing] So G1; G2, 4 print 'proffering'; G3 prints 'proferring'; G5 prints 'prostering'; and G6–7 print 'profering'. The possibility of compositorial error in G2 is obvious, and borne out by the variations introduced in subsequent editions. Moreover, 'professing' is clearly appropriate in context. One curious piece of evidence, however, may argue for G2's emendation: the appearance of 'proffered', in a context relatively parallel to the line in the play, in the old ballad of George Barnwell:

> All blithe and pleasant then,
> To banqueting we go;
> She proffered me to lie with her,
> And said it should be so.
>
> (Pt. I, ll. 161–4 as reprinted by
> Ward and McBurney.)

55 suburb] See IV. xviii. 22 n.

55 passing] N & C suggest that the intended meaning is 'dying', not 'going past, passing through'.

61 devoted] doomed; see V. v. 22 n.

V. x

1 The Officers . . .—Mrs.] The nature of the changes in G2 (see apparatus criticus) marks them almost certainly as the result of compositorial carelessness.

12–17 Thus Justice . . . and ineffectual.] So G2 and subsequent editions; G1 prints the two sentences in reverse order. The emendation, very probably authorial and perhaps influenced by rehearsal or performance, appears to have been made for rhetorical reasons, the general statement about justice and mercy following resoundingly the particular example of Barnwell and his place in justice's compassionate scheme for mankind.

14 Justice and Mercy] Ward refers to *The Merchant of Venice*, IV. i. 194–5, 'earthly power doth then show likest God's, | When Mercy seasons justice'. However, in interpreting the conventional concept of the fusion of justice and mercy in heavenly wisdom, Lillo's emphasis is the reverse of Shakespeare's; for Lillo, godlike mercy must be seasoned with severe justice. Central to this idea is Lillo's statement of the particular doctrine (essentially, though not exclusively, Calvinist) of a kind of double standard in predestination: severity to the erring individual (Barnwell) which, at the same time, is mercy to the generality of mankind.

V. xi

The scene is first printed in G5, where it is headed, as in subsequent editions, 'Scene the Last' (see textual introduction). The numbering of the scene in the present edition conforms to the French scene-divisions of the copy-text for the earlier portion of the act.

18 devoted] See v. v. 22 n.

22 deprecate] pray to avert (*OED*). Cf. *Fatal Curiosity*, III. i. 237, 'deprecations'; and *Marina*, III. ii. 259.

25 I can't . . . to be forgiven.] Comparison with *Dr Faustus* is more tempting here than at the lines cited above as possibly yielding Marlovian echoes or analogues. Millwood's ultimate sin, the pride of despair, is Faustus's also, though Lillo needed no reference to Marlowe for the doctrine, which had long been conventional. Further echoes of Faustus's final scene, however, seem to sound clearly in Millwood's outburst at the gallows, 'How doth his fervent Soul mount with his words, and both ascend to Heaven!' (v. xi. 47–8, cf. *Dr Faustus*, xix. 145).

29–30 Chains, Darkness . . . what I feel.] Ward suggests yet another reference to *Dr Faustus*: 'Adders and serpents, let me breathe awhile!' (xix. 188). It seems more likely, however, that Lillo simply drew on a general tradition of stage rhetoric for the speech, which might, for example, be compared, not with Marlowe, but with Otway or even Webster: cf. *The Duchess of Malfi*, IV. ii. 25–6 (Revels edition, ed. J. R. Brown [London, 1964]), 'Th' heaven o'er my head seems made of molten brass, | The earth of flaming sulphur, yet I am not mad.'

50–1 Sure 'tis . . . never taste.] Ward refers again to the parable of the rich man and Lazarus, Luke 16: 23 (see III. vii. 37–40 n.).

61 *To sin's . . . like Heaven.*] The aphorism is conventional, but reference to Pope (*Essay on Criticism* [1711], ii. 325) is unavoidable.

V. xii

2 How] So G5 and subsequent editions, an emendation required by the addition of scene xi (see apparatus criticus).

3 unalterable] G2, followed by subsequent editions, emends to 'unutterable'. 'Unutterable woe' is possible, of course, but could well represent a compositorial slip in setting the familiar rather than the less obvious phrase. Moreover, Lillo's characterization emphasizes the extent to which the woe Millwood faces is, for her, unalterable.

Epilogue

Mrs. CIBBER.] The actress delivers the epilogue in her character of Maria.

8 *cock'd up in Cue*] His hair spruced up in a fashionable queue or pigtail (*OED*, N & C, McBurney).

9 *tawney*] probably a reference to the yellow head-dress which Jews had been compelled to wear (Ward, McBurney).

20–3 *What if . . . of Creditors.*] The stanza can be read, as McBurney points out, as a complicated family joke: Mrs Cibber, who spoke the epilogue, was the daughter-in-law of its author, the Poet Laureate (since 1730) and a patentee of Drury Lane Theatre.

23 *wou'd prove . . . of Creditors.*] 'would prove to be no more disinterested than the suit of creditors' (N & C; similarly Ward, McBurney).

THE CHRISTIAN HERO

Prologue

28 *a Patriot King*] Bolingbroke's treatise, *The Idea of a Patriot King*, sets out the opposition theory of 'an able and unselfish king . . . [who] would use his royal prerogative

to regain powers the Ministers had usurped and . . . reanimate his people to a jealous concern for the preservation of their liberties' (John Loftis, *Politics of Drama in Augustan England* [Oxford, 1963], p. 119). Lillo's prologue not only emphasizes a key phrase of those who spoke out against the Walpole government but also reflects their ideal of a monarch '*By Nature form'd, by Providence design'd | To scourge Ambition, and to right Mankind*' (ll. 29–30). While Bolingbroke's treatise was not published until 1738, Loftis reports that it was 'known in preliminary statements much earlier', and he suggests (p. 121) that the history of Scanderbeg having 'provided the basis for three tragedies [Lillo's, Havard's, and Whincop's] in the space of a few years may be attributed to its usefulness as a symbol of resistance to tyranny'. (Cf. *Britannia and Batavia*, Introduction, p. 459, n. 10.)

Dramatis Personæ

2 *Amurath*] Murad II (1403–51), Sultan of Turkey from 1421. The son of Mohammed I, who had recovered the kingdom lost by his father, Bajazet, to Tamerlane, Murad II was particularly successful in extending Turkish conquests in Asia and Europe. In histories popular during the 17th and 18th cents., Murad was a central figure—'the great Establisher of [the Turkish] Kingdom' (Knolles, p. 173). Although he became the subject of many apocryphal reports and tales, he was in general treated with considerable respect by those who wrote about him.

3 *Mahomet*] Mohammed II (1430–81), Murad's son and successor. On two occasions, when Murad retired from active participation in his government, Mohammed acted as regent (see II. i. 93 n.).

4 *Osmyn, the Visier*] In the dramatis personæ, G lists only 'Osmyn', although the character is referred to as 'Visier' in stage directions and speech-headings throughout the play. The name itself, a variant of the European form (Osman) of the Arabic Othman and familiar as the name of the founder of the Ottoman (or Osmanlis) dynasty, would seem to have been adopted late, when Lillo's dialogue required that the Visier be addressed directly by other Turks. This might account for the uncertainty about the proper spelling of the name, which G twice prints as '*Osmyn*' (dramatis personæ and IV. ii. 95) and four times as '*Osmin*' (I. i. 366, IV. ii. 141 and 153b, and V. iv. 199).

5 *Kisler Aga*] The character, a functionary in the Turkish court, appears to have been Lillo's invention. No source has been found for the name, which is authentically Near Eastern in form. 'Aga' is the familiar title, originally applied to chief officers in the Ottoman empire but later used more generally to lend distinction to civil officers and others. It is not clear if 'Kisler' is intended as a personal name or forms an additional part of the title. The character is once addressed simply as 'Kisler Aga' (IV. ii. 110) but at V. ii. 4 is referred to as 'the Kisler Aga'. 'Kisler' is conceivably derived from 'Kizil' (or 'Kizyl'), meaning 'red', and found in such relatively well-known place-names as Kizil-Irmak, the 'Red River' of Asia Minor, and Kizyl-Kum, a major desert in the region.

7 *Scanderbeg*] George Castriot (Georgias Kastriotes; 1403–67), king of Epirus (Albania) from 1443. In fulfilment of the terms of a treaty made between his father, John Castriot, and Murad II, he went as hostage to Turkey in 1423. During his more than twenty years in the Turkish court, he so distinguished himself for courtliness and for prowess on the battlefield that he was made an officer in the Sultan's army and honoured with the name Scanderbeg (Iskender Bey, or Prince Alexander). A favourite of Murad's and apparently loyal to the Turkish throne, he was spared when, at the death of his

father, his brothers, also hostages, were executed. In 1443, however, he took advantage of an opportunity to flee the Turks, gained entrance to the capital of Epirus by means of a counterfeit letter from the Sultan, and reclaimed the kingdom which, since his father's death, had been treated as a Turkish possession. For nearly twenty-five years he led his people in sporadic campaigns against the Turks, but his style of battle, dictated by the terrain of his country and the small numbers of his men, was more that of guerrilla warfare than of the grand campaigns implied in the early histories and dramatized by Lillo. As a defender of Christian lands against Turkish encroachment, and a figure whose life story lent itself to romance, Scanderbeg was an ideal subject for the pens of moralizing historians and romantic novelists. By the 18th cent. his virtues and his exploits, on the battlefield and off, were matters of popular legend.

8 *Aranthes*] 'Scanderbeg . . . married the Daughter of Aranthes Conino, Prince of *Durazzo*' (*Brief Account*, p. 31); the girl's father was, in fact, a local chieftain (*Enc. Amer.* xxiv. 878). The name, like the report of Scanderbeg's marriage, is probably based on historical fact; Aranthes is not mentioned by Knolles, but Moore (p. 211), following Lavardin, gives his name as 'Ariamnites Comminat'. In the novel *Scanderbeg the Great*, Aranthes (called 'Aranit') figures prominently and, in character and action, may well have served as Lillo's model. Durazzo is Albanian Dourtz, the province of Dyrrachium.

9 *Amasie*] Scanderbeg, escaping from the Turks, took 'with him his nephew Amesa' (Knolles, p. 193). Amasie's defection is included by Lavardin and Moore, who report the incident as having occurred in the years after the death of Murad II; in this account, Amasie ('Amese')—in courage and brilliance second only to Scanderbeg but 'withal possessing great power of dissimulation' (Moore, p. 211)—is captured by Scanderbeg's forces, turns again to the Christian cause, and returns to Mohammed's court as Scanderbeg's spy. The reversal of this situation and Amasie's plot against the life of Scanderbeg appear to be Lillo's invention.

12–14 *Hellena . . . Althea . . . Cleora*] The names were almost certainly chosen by Lillo, not adopted from one of the sources of his story. The character of Althea appears to have been suggested by a similar character, Arianissa, in *Scanderbeg the Great*, while Hellena seems to be, in effect, a portrait-in-reverse of the novel's Selimana, the jealous first woman of the seraglio.

16–17 *Croia, the Metropolis of* Epirus] Kroïa, the capital of the Castriots. The kingdom, as the author of the *Brief Account* (pp. 4–5) reports, included 'some parts of the ancient Kingdoms of *Epirus* and *Macedon*, and of the Provinces of *Liburnia, Dalmatia*, and *Illyria*. . . . The *Castriots* . . . were generally called Kings of *Epirus*, but *Albania* was certainly the most powerful and wealthy part of their Dominions, and *Croia*, it's [*sic*] Metropolis, the Seat of their Residence.' W1 adjusts the geographical reference, substituting 'Albania' for G's 'Epirus'. The siege of Croia by Murad II, the historical incident behind the play, occurred in 1449.

I. i

1–8 SONG] In the novel *Scanderbeg the Great*, a similar song of grief in love is sung by the waiting-woman, Arianissa, to Selimana, first of the Sultan's women, who then reveals her secret love for Scanderbeg.

55 Divan] an oriental council of state (*OED*).

60 he still serves] So G, followed by D and W1. 'He' can refer only to Scanderbeg, but the shift from apostrophizing him in the second person to describing him in the third person is awkward at best. It is most unlikely that the problem represents scribal

or printing-house error; the awkwardness would seem to derive from the manuscript copy, perhaps authorial, behind G.

64 *Dervise*] dervish; a Mohammedan friar, who has taken vows of poverty and austere life (*OED*). Lillo's association of temperance and self-denial with the term indicates that he was aware of its particular meaning.

76 Shades] retired spots, abodes sheltered from the world (*OED*).

79 School] presumably 'a troop, crowd', a sense derived by transference from 'school of fish' (*OED*).

101 My Blood runs back] apparently 'blood draws back towards the heart from skin and limbs, creating paleness and weakness'. The phrase is not cited by the *OED*.

138 Spahies] horsemen of a body of cavalry, an important part of the Turkish army and to some extent organized on a feudal basis (*OED*, citing 'spahi, -is; spahee; spahei; spahy'; but not 'spahies').

148 Strengths] So W1; G prints 'Strenghts', a spelling not recorded later than 16th cent. by the *OED*.

170SD *Shouts*] Line 171 makes it clear that the stage direction, ambiguous in reference since it is printed on the line with the end of Amurath's speech, in fact refers to voices off-stage.

176 wreck] wreak. *OED* cites Goldsmith, *History of England in a Series of Letters* . . . [1772], ii. 231, 'There was no object on whom to wreck their vengeance.'

185 *Hellena*] So W1; G prints a comma after '*Hellena*', pointing typical of the first edition's irregular, sometimes awkward, use of commas. See Textual Introduction.

192 high Descent from *Charlemain*] Lillo's authority for linking Aranthes to the line of Charlemagne is not known.

193 *Frank*] the name given by nations bordering on the Levant to an individual of Western nationality (*OED*, citing North, *Lives* [1734], ii. 456, 'All European nations that live among them . . . are called Franks').

193 Santon] European designation for a kind of monk or hermit among the Mohammedans (*OED*), though Lillo may simply have intended 'saint'.

197–9 Friendship: . . . Slave:] Similar series of colons will be found at I. i. 225–9, 300–2, III. i. 176–8, 258–9, 292–3, and IV. ii. 47–50. Somewhat disconcerting to the modern reader and perhaps indicative of the uncertainties (or lack of regular practice) in the use of semicolons and colons in 18th-cent. printing-houses, the pointing does, on analysis, appear to be employed for deliberate rhetorical effect. This impression is supported by the number of examples of such series and by the particular dramatic demands of the text in those places at which the colon sequences appear. Punctuation of this sort will also be found in *Elmerick* (see II. i. 176–7 and n.).

201 conscious Virtue] the faculty of consciousness attributed to a personal quality rather than to a person (*OED*); here, virtue so endowed, a sense of the word—and a concept—that Lillo frequently found useful and significant (cf. I. i. 243; *The London Merchant*, v. iii. 2; and *Elmerick*, III. i. 254).

224 knew] G prints 'new', a spelling not given by the *OED* and almost certainly an error.

225 take;] Characteristic of the first edition's heavy punctuation, the semicolon here can appear to cut off the main clause of the sentence from its subordinate parts. See the Textual Introduction for discussion of these problems in the pointing of the copy-text.

228–9 *Aranthes* last . . . our Power.] The story of the capture of Scanderbeg's intended bride and her father has been found in no historical account of Scanderbeg's wars with the Turks. This element of Lillo's plot and, to a certain extent, its development later in the play appear to have been based on the novel *Scanderbeg the Great* (see Introduction).

284 Amaze] 'Amaze' fits the metre, though the syntax would seem to require 'amazes'.

301–2 Nor *Verna*'s . . . Christians unreveng'd] '. . . *neither should the Fields of* Varna *or* Basilia *so often smoke with the Blood of the Hungarians* . . .' (Knolles, p. 201, purportedly quoting a letter written by Scanderbeg to Uladislaus of Hungary on 3 Aug. 1444). King Uladislaus, campaigning to drive the Turks back to Gallipoli, was killed at a disastrous battle at Varna in Bulgaria on 10 Nov. 1444; the catastrophè was in part due to the failure of the Venetians to live up to their pledge to cut off a large portion of Murad's army at the Bosporus. Although Lillo's debt to Knolles for this pair of lines is clear, Lillo's play is set at a time after the death of Uladislaus. Aranthes' sharp words about those Christians who have failed to join the war against the Turks (ll. 303–6) may refer specifically to the Venetians or more generally to the various Christian monarchs whom the Pope had tried to rouse to action and who the papal legate had led Uladislaus to believe would support his campaign. Scanderbeg alone had attempted to join Uladislaus, but, cut off by a force of Turks, he had not been able to do so. Knolles and the other historians placed much of the blame for the Varna disaster on the Pope and on the legate who had persuaded Uladislaus not only to break the oath of peace he had given Murad but also to campaign without proper support; Lillo here ignores this aspect of the event, preferring to focus on the good cause to which too few gave aid. (See II. i. 91 n.)

341 Bowels] seat of the sympathetic emotions (*OED*). Cf. *Fatal Curiosity*, II. iii. 49. McBurney (*FC*, p. 37) cites Col. 3: 12, 'bowels of mercies'.

II. i

The scene, the confrontation of Amurath and Scanderbeg, may well have been inspired by two passages in Knolles: a letter addressed to Scanderbeg (pp. 204–5), in which Amurath pretends great love for the Christian leader and offers to pardon him if he will yield the towns of Epirus; and Scanderbeg's reply, also a letter (pp. 205–6), in which he rejects the Sultan's offers.

12b–13 *Scipio,* | And the fierce *African*] The Roman general Publius Cornelius Scipio, later surnamed Africanus, defeated the forces of Carthage under Hannibal at Zama in 202 BC. Famous not only for this victory but also as a young commander who avenged the death of his father by campaigning against a great and seemingly undefeatable opponent, Scipio provides a useful analogue for Lillo's hero. The fact that Scipio was defending a republic was also no doubt intended to make its point.

55–6 *Macedon, Epirus* . . . and *Dalmatia*] Territories all or in part ruled by the Castriots (see dramatis personæ, 16–17 n.).

91 The perjur'd *Uladislaus*] King of Hungary (Ulászló I, 1440–4) and Poland (Wladyslaw III, 1434–44). In 1443 he successfully campaigned against the Turks, his victory at Nish making possible Scanderbeg's escape and return to Croia. He agreed to terms with Murad II in 1444, swearing a holy oath not to break peace. Shortly thereafter, however, he allowed the papal legate to persuade him that the Pope could free him from this pledge and that it was his duty as a Christian to resume the fight against the Mohammedans. In the new campaign he was killed, and it was said that this was God's judgement upon him for breaking his oath.

91 *Hunniades*] Janos Hunyadi (? 1407–56), a brilliant young Hungarian officer, chief

of Uladislaus's commanders and famous for his campaigns against the Turks. He was in command of the king's victorious troops at the battle of Nish.

92 the *Venetians* . . . forsook thee] Lillo may refer to the Venetians' failure to provide support promised to Uladislaus (see I. i. 301–2 n.) or to the fact that Scanderbeg and the Venetians engaged for a time in a territorial dispute. At the time of the siege of Croia, however, the Venetians and the Albanians appear to have been on good terms.

93 to remote *Magnesia* I retir'd] Probably Magnesia ad Sipylum, in Lydia at the foot of Mt. Sipylum. Murad twice attempted to abdicate in favour of his son Mohammed. Deeply affected by the death of another, older, son, he withdrew to Magnesia after making his treaty with Uladislaus. However, with the resumption of the Hungarians' campaigns he returned to command his armies. After the Turkish victory at Varna in 1444 he again withdrew to Magnesia, but was soon called back to put down a revolt of his janizaries (*Enc. Brit.* xix. 14).

138 *Reposio! Stanissa! Constantine!*] Elder brothers of Scanderbeg, held hostage by the Turks and, after the death of their father, executed as threats to Turkish domination of Albania (Knolles, p. 177).

153–4 who made . . . the Sword.] The semicolon notwithstanding, the two lines clearly stand parallel syntactically although their verbs do not, an awkwardness that may represent an error in transmission of the text or possibly an error in the author's manuscript. 'Make' is a possible emendation—correct if not easy syntactically, and the correction of a conceivable scribal or compositorial error. The requirements of the metre will not, of course, allow 'propagated.'

156–7 when you commanded . . . th'*Hungarian* King] Scanderbeg was, it appears, among the forces sent to hold back the Hungarians. In the *Brief Account* (p. 13) he is described as leading his men—Epirots—in fleeing the battle. Earlier accounts, probably more authentic, do not bear this out. Knolles (p. 191) reports merely that some Turks thought that Scanderbeg had provided Hunyadi with secret instructions which markedly affected the course of the battle.

163–4 When deep . . . faithful Slaves] The battle of Nish, in which Hunyadi's Hungarians routed the Turkish forces, occurred near the River Moravia (Savage, p. 163). The account of Turkish casualties has been exaggerated more than tenfold by Lillo or his source: although the *Brief Account* (p. 13) also gives the number as 40,000, Knolles (p. 191) lists 3,000 Turks killed and 4,000 captured.

167 ere] So W1; G prints 'e're'. The correct form occurs at I. i. 173, 209, and III. i. 50, 179. See *Silvia*, Prologue, l. 36 n.; cf. also *The London Merchant*, Prologue, l. 24 n.

168 Bassa] pasha.

187 I'ave] W1 retains the unusual form of the contraction; cf. *Arden of Feversham*, II. i. 146: 'W'have' (printed text; the Larpent manuscript reads 'we've').

222–3 my conquer'd . . . Walls of *Buda.*] During the last six years of his life, Murad's forces campaigned in Europe, frequently against the Hungarians under Hunyadi.

289 Cordial] restorative, as of medicinal beverages; perhaps combined with a second meaning, 'heartfelt, from the heart' (*OED*).

III. i

79–80 The Wrath . . . on himself.] 'Man's wrathfulness, his passionate anger, should be employed only in the service of God; his other qualities, controlled by reason, are his to use as he sees fit.' This sentiment appears to sum up a neat, if rather too nice, resolution of Lillo's views, at times apparently conflicting, about man's innate passionateness, his duty to rein in his passions, and his acknowledgement of himself as the subject of a providential and good creator (see *The London Merchant*, Dedication, 6–8 n., I. viii. 8–9 n.; and III. i. 1–7 n.).

96–9 Thy awful . . . *Greek Timoleon*] The Roman spirit invoked is commitment to opposing tyranny even beyond the claims of kinship. Junius Brutus tried and condemned his sons for conspiring to restore the tyranny of the Tarquins. The 'younger *Brutus*' was, of course, among the murderers of Caesar and served Pompey, who had ordered the death of his father. Timoleon is said to have murdered his brother when he attempted to make himself absolute in Corinth, and later to have rid Syracuse and the smaller states of Sicily of tyrants. The theme is a favourite of Lillo's and, in large measure, the subject of *Elmerick* (see also Lillo's remarks about *Cato* in the dedication of *The London Merchant*, ll. 30–4).

114 ff. *Ama.* Well may you turn away . . .] The situation and scene may have been contrived by Lillo; neither is suggested by *Scanderbeg the Great* or Knolles. Both, however, could have been derived from Lavardin's history, in which Amasie, captured by the Christians, is brought back to Epirus and, after a time, repents his defection and entreats Scanderbeg's forgiveness. Amasie's hypocrisy is almost certainly Lillo's invention; in Lavardin's account, Amasie's protestations to Scanderbeg are genuine, and though he returns to the Turkish court (of Mohammed, not Murad), he does so to serve as Scanderbeg's spy and to protect the lives of his wife and children, still resident in the Sultan's domain.

147 Foe!] G, in the earlier state of this forme, prints a colon after 'Foe', pointing not inappropriate to the line. In the later state, this is replaced by a question mark; while clearly at odds with the sense of the line and speech, this may still represent a printer's response to a request that the colon be replaced. G is characteristically imprecise in its use of question marks and exclamation marks, either because type for the two had been mixed in the case or because the two were to a considerable extent used interchangeably—cf. the pointing of rhetorical questions and, in particular, III. i. 286, where a question mark in G clearly distorts the meaning. Neither page nor forme gives evidence of accidental disturbance of the type.

The present editor has accepted that a change in punctuation was intended in the corrected state of G and has substituted the exclamation mark that may well have been intended and does suit the sense of the line.

266 To force a Tenderness] to labour to stir up compassionate emotions. As at III. i. 79–80 and elsewhere, Lillo labours to differentiate his Christians and Mohammedans in terms of emotions reined in and exorbitant.

IV. ii

Although greatly transformed to suit Lillo's plot and purpose, incidents in the novel *Scanderbeg the Great* almost certainly provided the basis for this scene. A portion of the novel is told by Arianissa, Althea's counterpart, who has safely returned to Scanderbeg and the Christian court; she recounts her adventures in the Sultan's seraglio and tells of the night when Mahomet, the Sultan's son, and Musulman, a favourite though treacherous adviser to the Sultan, came to woo her in the garden of the women's quarters, neither expecting the other to be there and both disguised as women. Earlier in the book (though late in the plot of the romance), the Sultan himself, certain that Scanderbeg is about to overwhelm his camp, seeks to rape Arianissa, only to discover that she has been spirited away by Musulman, from whose lustful imprisonment she has then to be rescued by Scanderbeg and a chagrined Mahomet. The episodes may well have suggested to Lillo his own scene of attempted seduction and rape, and it seems clear that he drew on them for a number of his details.

18 Triump] Perhaps a conscious archaism, or a compositorial slip; the *OED* records the spelling no later than 16th cent. D and W1 emend to 'Triumph'.

21 Ideot] an ignorant, unlearned person, simple man, clown (*OED*). This spelling was standard during the 18th cent.

38 devoted] doomed, given over or consigned to the powers of evil or destruction (*OED*). Cf. *The London Merchant*, v. v. 22, v. ix. 61; and *Fatal Curiosity*, ii. iii. 72.

55b rifled] despoiled, plundered (*OED*, which gives no specifically sexual application of the word). Perhaps an echo of Shakespeare's Lucrece, l. 692, 'Pure chastity is rifled of her store'; Lillo may also have had the poem in mind at iv. i. 6–7.

64 *Virginius*] A centurion, Virginius killed his daughter rather than allow her to be violated by a Roman official who, by false means, had gained possession of her as a slave. Again Lillo has chosen his example with care, for Virginius was famous not as the defender of sexual virtue but as one who exposed the evils of tyranny.

90 hear'd] *OED* does not record this form, a false nicety which W1 corrects to 'heard'.

104 agast] The form, more accurate historically than 'aghast', continued standard during the 18th cent. (*OED*).

146 Vicegerent's] one appointed by a ruler to act in his place; applied to rulers or magistrates as representatives of the Deity (*OED*).

IV. iv

43 whether] whither (see *The London Merchant*, ii. xi. 11 n.).

94–101 Her gentle . . . shou'd die.] The speech is a notable example of the heavy use of commas and semicolons characteristic of G—pointing in this instance intelligible to the 18th-cent. reader to the extent that neither D nor W1 elected to alter it.

96 the Sculpture's Art] presumably 'the art of sculpture'. The phrase is odd, however, and *OED* cites no similar examples. There is no evidence that 'sculpture' could be taken as an alternative form for 'sculptor'.

V. i

20 amuse] to divert the attention from the facts at issue; to beguile, deceive (the usual sense during the 18th cent.); in military tactics, to divert the enemy from one's real designs (*OED*).

V. iv

30 Then we . . . no more.] Broken metre, a rare occurrence in this play; perhaps intended for dramatic effect, which may also be the case in l. 55, below.

84 Death, this Way,] editor's punctuation. The first edition omits the comma after 'Way', thereby suggesting that the speech is addressed to a personified Death; the syntax required by l. 85, however, makes this an impossible reading.

205 anew] G prints 'a new', a form not given by the *OED* and not followed by D or W1; it may represent an echo of the origin of the word, a corruption of 'of new'. Emendation seems essential for clarity.

Epilogue

39 *Monsieur* Harlequin] Harlequinades enjoyed great success at the theatres. The managers, not slow to capitalize on such popularity, produced a series of new versions of the frequently less than virtuous adventures of Harlequin and his friends. The playlets became a focus of criticism and annoyance for those concerned to preserve or restore the moral and literary standards of the English stage. (See commentary notes to *Marina*, Dedication and Epilogue.)

FATAL CURIOSITY

Prologue

Henry Feilding] This spelling is frequently found in contemporary references to Fielding, who staged the first performances of *Fatal Curiosity* with his company at the Haymarket (see introduction).

16 *our little . . . be young*] Fielding's company at the New Haymarket (frequently called 'the little theatre') was relatively young, its first performance having been given on 5 Mar. 1736. The theatre itself had been in use since 1720 (*London Stage, 1729–1747*, vol. i, pp. xx, 558).

Dramatis Personæ

2 Old *Wilmot*] The name, like those of the other characters in the play, appears to have been Lillo's invention.

3 Mr. *Davies*] Thomas Davies (*c.*1717–85), who, in 1775, edited and published the first proper collection of Lillo's works, for which he also wrote a biography. Best known as the biographer of Garrick and a friend of Dr Johnson, to whom he introduced Boswell, Davies seems to have begun his London acting career with his appearance in *Fatal Curiosity*. Later, in 1737, Davies turned to bookselling when imposition of the licensing act forced Fielding's company to close. Although he returned to the stage some years later and for ten seasons (1752–62) performed with Garrick's company at Drury Lane, he left the theatre in 1762 and gave his time fully to the bookshop he had opened some two years earlier—a decision not unrelated to certain verses, included by George Churchill in *The Rosciad* (1761), in which Davies's acting powers were savagely ridiculed. Davies's publications in 1762 included an edition of *Fatal Curiosity* and the first edition of the adaptation of *Arden of Feversham* attributed to Lillo. (*Actors and Actresses*, iv. 203–8.)

7 Mrs. *Charke*] Charlotte Charke (d. 1760), the daughter of Colley Cibber, who was manager of Drury Lane when Charlotte, not long on the stage, played Lucy in the first production of *The London Merchant*. Later, in the course of the extraordinary career that followed estrangement from her father and included performances with every sort of trumped-up company, she acted Millwood and, in breeches, Barnwell. Lillo's Agnes, however, appears to have been a role she particularly favoured—or one that she felt an audience would pay to see her play—and she was responsible for two of the three London revivals of *Fatal Curiosity* that occurred between 1737 and the introduction of Colman's revision of the play in 1782. In Nov. 1742 (*London Stage, 1729–1747*) Mrs Charke appeared as Agnes in a performance announced as a 'Benefit [for] a Person who

has a mind to get money' (almost certainly the actress herself). In Sept. 1755 (*London Stage, 1747–1776*), hoping to capitalize on the notoriety gained by the publication of her memoirs, she took the theatre in James Street and staged a performance as a benefit for herself; for this financially important occasion she again chose *Fatal Curiosity*, and in a segment of her *Life* (issued in weekly parts) she carefully prepared the way for this revival:

> Mr. *Lillo*, the Author of *George Barnwell*, brought Mr. *Fielding* a Tragedy of Three Acts, called, *The* [sic] *Fatal Curiosity*, taken from a true tragic Tale . . . In this Play are two well-drawn Characters, under the Denominations of old *Wilmot* and his Wife *Agnes*, an aged Pair; who had, from too much Hospitality on the Husband's Part, and unbounded Pride on the Wife's, out-ran a vast Estate, and were reduced to extreamest Poverty.
>
> The late Mr. *John Roberts*, a very judicious Speaker, discovered a Mastership in the Character of the Husband, and I appeared in that of the Wife. We were kindly received by the Audience; the Play had a fresh Run the Season following; and if I can obtain a Grant for ONE NIGHT ONLY, I intend to make my Appearance once more as Mrs. *Agnes*, for my own Benefit, at the *Hay-Market* Theatre [*the James Street theatre was near the Haymarket, although Mrs Charke may have hoped to use the New Theatre in the Haymarket*]; on which Occasion, I humbly hope the Favour and Interest of my worthy Friends. (*Life*, pp. 64–5.)

The extent to which the actress's worthy friends favoured her with the price of a ticket of admission is not recorded, but it is beyond question that in enacting the distresses of extremest poverty she could call on a wealth of personal experience. (*London Stage, 1729–1747*, vol. i, pp. xx, xxxiv–xxxvi; Charke, *Life*, intro. by L. R. N. Ashley, p. vii.)

I. i

   10 posts] hastens (*OED*, Ward, McBurney).

   12 above him] beyond him, to which he is unequal (Ward).

   30–36a Sir *Walter Raleigh* . . . the *Spaniards*.] In 1617 Ralegh planned an expedition to Guiana, promising James I to find a gold-mine for him and to do so without violating Spanish territory. The Spanish ambassador protested to the king, asserting that since Spain had already established settlements along the coast of Guiana Ralegh's promises could not be kept. The king preferred not to stop the expedition, but gave the ambassador his word that if Ralegh should be guilty of piracy he would be executed on his return to England. The expedition was a disastrous failure, Ralegh's men were indeed involved in bloody altercations with the Spanish, and soon after Ralegh landed at Plymouth, in June 1618, he was arrested by Sir Lewis Stukeley, his cousin, who held the office of vice-admiral of Devonshire. Late in October, after an unsuccessful attempt to escape to France, Ralegh was executed (*Enc. Brit.*, xxii. 871). Lillo, of course, reiterates the popular, anti-Spanish view of these events (see 38–40 n.). Both Frankland and Sanderson, whose annals for the year 1618 include the story upon which Lillo's play is based, print accounts of Ralegh's last expedition and his death in their records for 1617–18, and Lillo's reference to Ralegh may well be traced to this juxtaposition.

   38–40 There's now . . . submit to—] There can be little doubt that Lillo's caustic reference to Spain relates less directly to 1618 than to 1736, a time when 'powerful Court and City factions felt that Spain's "insolence" was forcing the "pacific reign" of George II and Walpole toward open hostilities' (McBurney, pp. 7 (ll. 38–40 n.) and 55;

cf. Ward, pp. xlvi–xlvii). Lillo may well have felt sympathy for these factions, in part because his family was Dutch. He had portrayed the Spaniards as types of vicious greed in *The London Merchant* (I. iii. 20–3).

43–5 Thy successful . . . they labour'd.] 'Between the stories of Raleigh's betrayal and the Penryn murder, Sanderson and Frankland have a short item labeled "4 Earls created for mony": "Having paid the price, a good sum for their honours; so earnest some are, and so ambitious of preferment, as what they cannot get by merit, they covet to purchase with money." Old Wilmot, or Lillo, seems to connect this event with the Raleigh debacle' (McBurney).

51 the *High-street* . . . the minster.] Lillo is unfamiliar with his Cornish setting: Penryn is the site of a parish church, which can never have been referred to as the 'minster', and it stands about a mile away from the High Street (Ward, p. xlviii).

66 one] a not impossible reading, but awkward; 'one's' (or 'ones') seems a plausible alternative and is adopted in Adam's Leeds edition.

70 detain,] The comma here is typical of the copy-text's irregular, often heavy, sometimes awkward use of commas. See Textual Introduction, p. 291.

158 bubble] one who may be or is 'bubbled'; a dupe, a gull (*OED*).

163 High-minded] possessing or characterized by a haughty, proud, or arrogant spirit (*OED*). The phrase, as McBurney suggests, is probably used in this pejorative sense, given the antithetical balance of lines 163–4: Old Wilmot is proud and 'improvident', but full of pity for others and excessively 'generous'. Cf. *Marina*, II. i. 192, where 'high-minded' is clearly used in this sense.

I. ii

11–15 There is . . . in musick—] 'The idea is much the same as that of the opening lines of *Twelfth Night*' (Ward).

21 And perished in her sight.] One of the very few metrically short lines in the play. The only other examples will be found at I. iii. 122, III. i. 170–1 (see apparatus criticus, ll. 165–9), and III. i. 266.

139 days;] Characteristic of the copy-text's often heavy punctuation, the semicolon here can appear to separate the main clause of the sentence from its final subordinate part. See Textual Introduction (p. 291) for discussion of these problems in the pointing of the copy-text.

152 aught] *OED* cites no example of this spelling later than the 17th cent.

I. iii

2–13 Then we're deliver'd . . . hand to cure.] Lillo's sharp condemnation of Cornish marauders may well have been intended, as McBurney suggests, to serve an ironic purpose: Young Wilmot is exposed to savagery and remorselessness at the hands not of the overt plunderers, whom he avoids, but of people of 'the better sort'—his parents—to whom he entrusts himself. However, Lillo had earlier made reference to Cornish raiders in *The London Merchant* (IV. xviii. 23), and the length and intensity of the reference in *Fatal Curiosity*, as well as Lillo's strong injunction to the authorities, suggest that the subject itself concerned him.

133–6 Deceived by . . . substantial pain.] Versions of the story of Ixion vary, but all agree that he was brought to heaven by Jove and that, when he attempted to seduce Juno, Jove banished him, condemning him to be fastened to a wheel endlessly whirling in hell. Line 135 indicates that Lillo recalled the version of the tale in which Jove tricks Ixion with an image of Juno made from a cloud. The reference to Ixion seems clearly intended to forecast ironically the dissolving of Young Wilmot's dreams of homecoming into the actual horror of his murder, but unlike the images drawn from mythology for *The London Merchant*, this reference appears to have no more than a surface appropriateness to character and situation; indeed, the story of Ixion's insolence, treachery, and punishment could more readily be applied to the elder Wilmots than to their son.

II. i

102 enlarg'd] almost certainly in the sense of 'set at large, released from confinement' (*OED*).

132–3 From this . . . my rest.] The sentence is ambiguous: either, 'I'll count my remaining hours of life from this happiest hour', the sense towards which the reader is led, despite the tortured syntax ('my' rather than 'the'), by the presence of 'date' following 'this . . . hour' (an ultimate, definitive moment); or, 'This happiest hour marks the beginning of relief from weariness and anxiety', an interpretation easy syntactically and, it can be argued, supported by the line that follows. Either interpretation allows the irony for which the speech is primarily designed and which includes a play on 'rest' in the sense of 'death'.

153 perilous] G, in the earlier state of the sheet, prints 'perillous', a spelling not given by the *OED*, although 'perill' is cited, 15th–17th cent.

168 hind] servant, especially a farm servant, an agricultural labourer (*OED*).

II. ii

3–7 What, shall . . . superfluous board?—] With one exception ('What,' *Ed.*), accidentals in this passage have been emended to follow D, which recognized and effectively adjusted the incorrect pointing of G. It seems likely that the problems in G represent not the heavy punctuation frequently characteristic of the edition but misinterpretation of lines 5 and 6 ('And . . . | And . . .' mistakenly read as parallel). D seeks further to avoid this misreading by substituting 'To' for 'And' in line 6.

4 distinguished] clearly synonymous with and syntactically parallel to 'marked'.

83 quit] make return for (*OED*).

II. iii

1–4 this *Seneca* . . . praises poverty—] McBurney, noting that 'the "Discovered, reading" scene was a dramatic commonplace', suggests that Lillo may have had in mind Addison's *Cato*, whose hero 'is discovered reading Plato and debating the morality of suicide'. Lillo's dedication of *The London Merchant* (l. 31) makes it clear that he was familiar with Addison's play. McBurney further suggests that the book Old Wilmot holds is L'Estrange's translation of Seneca's *Morals of a Happy Life*, first published in 1693. 'Part II, Chapter XXV, entitled "Poverty to a Wise Man, is rather a Blessing than a Misfortune," includes the following statements: "Shall I call him Poor that wants nothing, though he may be beholden for it to his Patience, rather than to his Fortune," and "Bread, when a Man is hungry, does his Work, be it never so coarse." The sale catalogue of Lillo's library [and that of "Another Gentleman"] lists "Seneca's Morals. 1720"' (McBurney, footnote to this line).

2 master of mankind] Seneca's pupil, Nero.

4 millions] by repute, 300 million sesterces (Ward, McBurney).

12 charge] in the sense of 'lay blame upon' (*OED*, McBurney).

49 bowels] considered as the seat of the sympathetic emotions and hency 'pity, compassion, feeling' (*OED*). Cf. *The Christian Hero*, I. i. 341, 'Bowels of Compassion'.

McBurney cites various biblical references, including Phil. 2: 1, 'bowels and mercies'; Col. 3: 12, 'bowels of mercies'; and 1 John 3: 17, 'bowels of compassion'.

72 devoted] given over or consigned to the powers of evil or destruction; doomed (*OED*, McBurney). Cf. *The London Merchant*, v. v. 22, v. ix. 61, and *The Christian Hero*, IV. ii. 38.

80–5 At Sea twice . . . slavery itself] Lillo considerably revises Young Wilmot's history, describing him as the victim of pirates; in the Sanderson and Frankland versions of the story he is himself a pirate. Two escapes from sea disasters—an explosion and a shipwreck on the Cornish coast—and service among the slaves on a Turkish galley are included in the old accounts. The two robberies and three plunderings are, as McBurney notes, Lillo's reversal and expansion of the brief account of the young man's piratical career given in Sanderson and Frankland.

82 once] *Ed.*, following W1 and McBurney; G, D print 'one', a barely possible reading if 'one' is taken to parallel 'me' of l. 79. Emendation appears to be required for sense and syntax as well as to allow effective culmination of the rhetorical sequence 'twice . . . thrice . . . once' (ll. 80–2), which is underscored by G's pointing, in this instance uncharacteristically sharp and clear.

120aSD *Exit, with Old* Wilmot] *Ed.*; G, D print '*Exit*'. Although the stage direction follows Agnes's speech and, as given in G, appears to relate only to her, it is clear that Young Wilmot's next speech is a soliloquy and that Old Wilmot must exit at l. 120 if he has not done so earlier. It is possible that a direction for Old Wilmot to exit was omitted after l. 112 (for an example of a similar omission see III. i. 199). That the problem stems from omission in the printer's copy is suggested by the incorrect '*Exeunt*' printed at the end of the scene—a mistake likely to have been made by an editor or compositor who was routinely supplying an end-of-scene stage direction and who noticed that his copy had provided an exit for only one of the three characters in the scene. The required exit for Old Wilmot was not included in a printed text until Thomas Cadell's edition of George Colman's 'altered' version of the play was published in 1783.

III. i

45 ere] So W1; G prints 'e're', as it does at III. i. 264 and 306, while printing the correct form 'ere' at III. i. 122 and 139. 'E're' is routinely corrected to 'ere' in this edition. See *Silvia*, Prologue, l. 36 n.; cf. also *The London Merchant*, Prologue, l. 24 n., and *The Christian Hero*, II. i. 167 n.

91 inclination] For Lillo the word appears to carry a stronger meaning—'intense inborn desire' or 'passionate impulse'—than the usual 'tendency or bent of the mind, will, or desire towards a particular object' (*OED*); cf. *The London Merchant*, II. iii. 10 and n. Moreover, Old Wilmot's cynicism is a trait common to the playwright's erring characters, who regularly preface indulgence of their passions with statements asserting the primacy of man's emotions over his reason. Although Lillo never underestimates the potency of passion, he treats such assertions and the cynicism they involve as being in themselves errors of indulgence, certain indications that the characters have yielded already in the war between passion and reason.

123 presages] probably 'predictions, prognostications', although an alternative sense—'presentiments, forebodings'—is not impossible (*OED*).

130–4a Thou cruel . . . thou'st made me.] Cf. *The London Merchant*, IV. xviii. Agnes, defending herself against accusations made by the man she holds responsible both for her condition and for the desperate actions to which she has been driven, bears a remarkable resemblance to Millwood, although, as Davies implies in his biography of Lillo and as modern critics have regularly remarked, the scene and situation are clearly inspired by Shakespeare's *Macbeth*.

152 extinguisht] G's reading 'extinguist' is not supported by *OED*, where 'sh' occurs in all the recorded historical forms.

165–71 O *Agnes!* . . . single murther,] The arrangement of the lines follows W1, which reconstructs the blank verse patterns (ll. 165–9) in a passage badly confused in G and D (see apparatus criticus). The lines which follow (170–1) are short. They could be set out as making up a single verse line or, alternatively, line 170 could be interpreted as being the second half of the preceding line in G's reading. But the present arrangement underscores a crucial moment in the drama and could well have been intended for rhetorical effect. (See *Elmerick*, Textual Introduction, for reference to a number of ambiguous line-divisions in that play.)

171–4 'Tis but . . . be stopp'd.] D prints 'demand' for 'demands', an emendation which makes clear the meaning all but obliterated by the awkward syntax of the speech: 'The three mouths—of necessity, impatience and despair—of that true Cerberus, grim poverty, demand but a single murder; they shall be stopped.'

199SD *Exit*] Ed.; not in G or D. Agnes's re-entrance (201+SD) requires that she earlier make an exit.

211a to render murther venial] Ward's reading is clearly correct: 'to make mere ordinary murder (as distinct from the murder of a son) venial'.

213 orbs] planets. Ward's suggested alternative reading, 'the tortured and roving eyes of the damned', seems strained at best; the speech is intended, surely, to balance hell and the heavens, both 'fixed [halted] in deep attention'.

231 perturbation] mental agitation or disquietude; trouble (*OED*). Association of the word with feelings of anguished shame seems intended, as in Milton, *Paradise Lost*, x. 111–14, 'Love was not in thir looks, . . . but apparent guilt, | And shame, and perturbation, and despaire.'

237 deprecations] prayers for the removing (of evil, disaster) (*OED*). Although the word, balanced against 'curses', clearly suits Lillo's meaning, the editor or compositor of the *Works* (1775) found it difficult: 'depredations' was set, then corrected in the list of errata to 'imprecations'. Cf. *Marina*, III. ii. 259, and *The London Merchant*, V. xi. 22, 'deprecate' with the sense 'seek to avert by prayer'.

MARINA

NOTE. Correspondence between scenes of *Marina* and Shakespeare's *Pericles* is briefly described in a head-note for each scene. Scene- and line-numbers for *Pericles* refer to the revised Arden edition, edited by F. D. Hoeniger (London, 1962).

Dedication

Countess of Hertford] Frances Thynne (1699–1754), wife of Algernon Seymour, Lord Hertford, later (1748) seventh Duke of Somerset. A lady of the bedchamber to Queen Caroline, the countess was a conscientious patron of poetry and learning. Lillo's selection of her as the dedicatee of *Marina* may indicate that she was a member of the 'Shakespeare Ladies Club', a group formed in 1736 and active as late as 1738, whose purpose was to reform the English stage by persuading the managers of the theatres to offer more performances of Shakespeare's plays. Lillo's adaptation of Shakespeare was almost certainly produced as a result of the ladies' campaign (see notes on the epilogue, below). In writing in his dedication that he hopes his play will appear 'to be designed to promote something better than meer amusement' (ll. 11–12), Lillo echoes the sentiments of the ladies' club, whose particular concern seems to have been to drive from the stage harlequinades and similar light entertainments. The countess's lifelong friendship with the pious poetess Elizabeth Rowe may also have recommended her to Lillo as a likely patroness for his play. (*DNB* xvii.1237; Cokayne, *Peerage* [1953], xii. 80–1; Avery, 'The Shakespeare Ladies Club', pp. 153–8.)

3 countenance] credit or repute; also, perhaps, in the related sense, 'moral support' (*OED*).

17 elocution] probably 'eloquence', as well as the more usual sense, 'way or manner of speaking' (*OED*).

28 Mrs. *Rowe*] Elizabeth Rowe (1674–1737), an author whose works in poetry and prose were much admired for their moral strength and intense sensibility; her evocations of pathos were particularly remarked.

In seeking the favour of the Countess of Hertford, Lillo was well advised to cite Mrs Rowe. She had been a close acquaintance of the countess's family since 1696, when publication of her first collection of poems brought her the patronage of the countess's grandfather, Lord Weymouth of Longleat. Moreover, Mrs Rowe, her husband, and Lillo shared common religious views and political concerns as well as a belief in the moral efficacy of literature. The daughter of a Nonconformist minister who had served in prison for his beliefs, Mrs Rowe held firmly to her family's religion after her verse-writing brought her literary success and a place with the family at Longleat. Her husband Thomas combined classical studies with a fervent concern for political and religious liberty, and before his early death had begun writing a series of homiletic lives of ancient heroes omitted from Plutarch's *Lives*. Lillo may have taken particular interest in Mrs Rowe's *Letters Moral and Entertaining*, three collections of prose pieces (1729, 1731, and 1733) by which she set out to awaken religious feelings in the careless and dissipated, and in which she did not shrink from portraying the excesses of dissipation with considerable frankness. A similar intention to expose licentiousness may account for the openly bawdy elements in Lillo's *Marina*. Although no evidence suggests that Lillo and Mrs Rowe were acquainted, he clearly knew her reputation and he could expect that those to whom her books appealed would look with favour on his own not dissimilar efforts. (*DNB* xvii. 338; Boswell, *Life of Johnson*, ed. G. B. Hill, rev. L. F. Powell [Oxford, 1934], i. 312.)

Dramatis Personæ

3 *Governor of* Ephesus] In *Pericles*, Governor of Mytilene (see I. iiSD n.).

5 LEONINE, *A young Lord of* Tharsus] In *Pericles* the character is simply a servant to the queen.

6 VALDES] Shakespeare's pirates are identified as men 'who serve the great pirate Valdes' (IV. i. 96), but Valdes himself does not appear in *Pericles* (see I. i. 145 n.).

7 BOLT, *A Pander*] Lillo conflates Shakespeare's Pandar and Boult, his servant.

10 PHILOTEN, *Queen of* Tharsus] In the place of Dionyza, the queen who plots Marina's death, Lillo introduces Philoten, Dionyza's daughter. The change is essential,

of course, to Lillo's major addition to the plot, the jealousy and death of the queen of Tharsus.

12 MOTHER COUPLER, *A Bawd*] Shakespeare's bawd has no name.

I. i

The scene is based on *Pericles*, IV. i, which it frequently follows closely despite Lillo's substitution of Philoten for Dionyza.

27 *Tellus*] the earth. Cf. *Pericles*, IV. i. 13, 'I will rob Tellus of her weed'.

28 grave] So *Pericles*, IV. i. 14, third folio, Rowe, and Sewell; the quarto prints 'green'.

71 haling] drawing, pulling (*OED*). Lillo takes the word from Shakespeare (IV. i. 54), apparently recognizing its meaning (unlike those editors who have wrongly emended *Pericles* at this point). This spelling is not reproduced in Sewell's supplement (1728) to Pope's Shakespeare, which prints 'hailing'—an indication that Lillo worked from some other edition of the play.

93–4 that fought: . . . so now:] The series of colons appears to represent punctuation intended for rhetorical purposes, not uncertainty as to the intentions of the copy-text or confusion about the conventional use of colons and semicolons. Similar sequences will be found at I. ii. 115–16 and II. i. 147–50. L employs different pointing in all three passages, which could suggest that the sequences in the printed text are compositorial and without authority. Whether they stem from the author or the printing-house, such series of colons apparently used for dramatic effect are characteristic of the first editions of several of Lillo's plays, especially *Elmerick* (cf. II. i. 176–7 and n.).

114 poltron] L writes 'poltroon'. The spelling 'poltron', introduced into English in the 16th cent., persisted until the 19th cent. and here may still indicate pronunciation with the accent upon the first syllable (*OED*).

145 *Valdes*] Unlike Shakespeare, Lillo brings Valdes on stage (I. ii). He makes no point of the pirate's being Spanish, and it seems improbable that he was aware of the associations which the name Valdes, especially in the context of piracy, may have had for Shakespeare and his audience (Hoeniger (IV. i. 96), following Malone, notes that the Spanish Armada may have furnished Shakespeare with the name; Don Pedro de Valdés, an admiral, was captured by Drake in July 1588). Given the openly anti-Spanish sentiments expressed in *The London Merchant* (I. i. 3–8 and I. iii. 20–2) and in *Fatal Curiosity* (I. i. 30–6), it is remarkable, perhaps, that Lillo bypasses a similar opportunity here.

I. ii

The scene is based on *Pericles*, IV. ii, although the episode in which the bawd bargains with the pirates (ll. 41–87) and the dialogue for Marina, the bawd, and Bolt (ll. 89 ff.) have been much expanded.

SD Ephesus] In *Pericles*, Mytilene. By changing the setting Lillo brings his characters to the city famous as a centre for the worship of Diana, the goddess who presides over the resolution of the play.

2 Mistress] L regularly gives 'patrona' when the bawd is addressed. It seems clear that Lillo wrote 'patrona' in his earlier version(s) of the play, perhaps as a device to add to the exotic or foreign colour of his setting, but that he changed his mind during or after production of the play.

7 dough-bak'd] deficient, especially in intellect or sense; feeble, 'soft'; from 'imperfectly baked, so as to remain doughy' (*OED*).

16 Widowers] L writes 'widows', a form which was still acceptable as an alternate for

'widowers' in the 18th cent. (*OED*). The context, of course, leaves no doubt as to the gender of the bereaved persons described here.

35–7 the little . . . meat for worms.] Lillo reverses the details of the anecdote. In *Pericles*, the Transylvanian, one of the bawd's male clients, is said to have been infected by one of her girls and so 'made . . . roastmeat for worms' (IV. ii. 20–3).

39 Marry come up] expression of indignant or amused surprise or contempt; 'hoity-toity' (*OED*).

43 Tarpaulin language] obviously 'seaman's language'; the *OED* records the use of 'tarpaulin' as an adjective, but not in this particular derogatory sense.

43 Brawn and Bristle] an epithet open to a variety of interpretations, none of them complimentary: like a boar or hog; brawny and bristling (sharp-tempered); and, probably, tough-skinned and unshaven.

54–5 arras . . . condition] In the context of the scene, the puns are surely as intentional as obvious.

58 blown on] with the bloom taken off, made stale (*OED*).

75 bate one doit] deduct one quarter of a farthing or any other trifling sum (*OED*).

127 bit of the spit] Cf. *Pericles*, IV. ii. 130, 'Thou mayst cut a morsel off the spit'. Shakespeare's bawd, more generous if less cautious than Lillo's, offers rather than denies Bolt this sample.

137 sprig of Jessamin] jasmine; the *OED* gives no figurative use of this phrase.

161 *French* knight . . . in the hams] 'Cowers' with the meaning 'bends, squats' (*OED*)? Cf. *Pericles*, IV. ii. 103, 'French knight that cowers i' the hams'. Hoeniger, following Deighton (Arden edn., 1907), suggests 'here, apparently, in consequence of his diseased condition'. Lillo's context, however, does not demand this interpretation and the word may simply be intended to be associated with the knight's thinness.

173 Unstain'd I . . . will keep.] Cf. *Pericles*, IV. ii. 146, 'Untied I still my virgin knot will keep'. Lillo's emendation of Shakespeare, a matter of two words, shifts the emphasis from physical fact to concern for reputation, an alteration which exposes strikingly the contrasts between the moral sensibilities of the eras in which the two playwrights worked.

II. i

The scene draws on several passages in *Pericles*, although much of it is Lillo's invention. The turns of plot involving Leonine and the queen recall Deflores' confrontation with Beatrice in Middleton's *The Changeling* (III. iv). Their opening dialogue does draw heavily on *Pericles*, IV. iii (Dionyza and her husband, Cleon), and two short passages in I. iv. Pericles' discovery of the monument and his reaction are based on Gower's narration and the dumb show of *Pericles*, IV. iv, and on a brief passage in II. i. In Pericles' tale of Marina's birth, Lillo makes use of lines and images drawn from *Pericles*, III. i. and iii.

1–11 To bury . . . my suit.] Not in L. The only major variation between G and L in this scene, the speech was probably added—perhaps during rehearsal—to fill a gap in exposition. It also provides a less abrupt opening for the scene than does the queen's line (12) which stands at the head of the scene in L. In the manuscript, lines similar to 6 and 7 appear between ll. 70 and 71.

6 *Parian*] from the island of Paros, one of the Cyclades; in ancient times famous for fine white marble (*OED*).

14–15 *Q.* Were I . . . were undone.] The comparable line in *Pericles* (IV. iii. 5–6) is spoken by the king, Cleon, rather than by the queen. Throughout the scene, Lillo freely reorders and adjusts Shakespeare to suit his quite different purposes in this confrontation following the supposed murder.

70–1 epitaph | Procur'd] See II. i. 1–11 n.

103 air fed lamps] presumably the heavenly bodies—sun, moon, and stars; but a puzzling phrase which almost certainly represents Lillo's attempt to interpret the even more puzzling 'ayre remaining lamps' of *Pericles*, III. i. 62. Modern editors have seen 'ayre', the quarto reading, as an odd spelling for 'e'er' (Hoeniger), but the word was variously interpreted by earlier editors. Rowe (1709, 1714), Sewell (1728), and Tonson (1734) print 'Air'; accepting this reading and taking 'remaining' in a sense obscure but acceptable in Shakespeare's time, and elsewhere used by him, will allow 'which abide or dwell in the air' as a viable interpretation of the phrase in *Pericles* (*OED*).

156 Herald] G misprints 'Hareld', a form not given by the *OED*. The error may be a variation of 'Harold', the reading found in L; the *OED* records 'harolde' and 'harald' as spellings current in 16th–17th cent.

192 high minded] haughty, proud, arrogant (*OED*). Cf. *Fatal Curiosity*, I. i. 163.

202 put me by] prevented me from carrying out, or diverted me from (*OED*).

223c Yes, thou art poison'd.] Nowhere does Lillo indicate when, how, or by whom the poison was administered. The theatrical momentum of the scene—and, by this point in the play, readiness to accept the poisoning as yet another of the queen's acts of deviousness and treachery—perhaps kept audience and actors from noticing this apparent gap in action or exposition.

246–8 By Heaven . . . O *Radamanthus*] Christian judgement and pagan judge—the most severe judge-figure among those associated with the Greek Hades—are here combined in a manner characteristic of the adaptation as a whole.

II. ii

The scene is based on *Pericles*, IV. vi, which it frequently follows closely. The bawd's encounter with the officers is Lillo's invention.

13 green sickness] *Pericles*, IV. vi. 13. Hoeniger notes, 'literally an anaemic disorder to which young women are subject; but here obviously a metaphor for excessive squeamishness in sexual matters, attributed to inexperience'.

14 change one for the other] a play on 'pox' (l. 13) with the meaning 'syphilis'.

23 grave planter of iniquity] Cf. *Pericles*, IV. vi. 23–4, 'wholesome iniquity'. Sewell prints 'wholesome impurity', another indication that Lillo was not working with this edition of Shakespeare's play.

50 presently] immediately, instantly (as Hoeniger notes, IV. vi. 45).

79 aloof] So Rowe (1709, 1714), whom Hoeniger and Maxwell (*Pericles*, IV. vi. 86) credit with introducing the emendation; also Sewell (1728) and Tonson (1734); the quarto prints 'aloft'.

81–119a I've now learnt . . . her own!] Not in L; perhaps inserted during or after production, although the lines speak less to theatrical demands than to the author's concern to improve the moral character of Lysimachus to a degree appropriate to his position as just ruler and, ultimately, the successful suitor of Marina (see Textual Introduction).

122a–31b Dare not . . . mighty Sir,] Not in L. While here, as in the late addition noted above, the playwright has added lines that develop the scene's thematic content, the new material centres on the highly dramatic situation of Marina's threatened suicide, a revision that strongly suggests the influence of the theatre.

143–50 Conviction rises . . . have corrected.] Lines 143–4 are not in L, and the entire speech has been revised (see apparatus criticus). The changes seem clearly to have been associated with the insertions noted above. The earlier version (L) of ll. 145–6 follows exactly *Pericles*, IV. vi. 103–4.

147 clear] pure. So *Pericles*, although this meaning for the word was well known in Lillo's time (*OED*; Hoeniger, IV. vi. 105).

153–4 If I should . . . thy fame.] Not in L. Perhaps added at the same time as the insertions noted above (81–119a, 122a–31b), these lines supply an explanation for Lysimachus' not removing Marina from the bawd's house as soon as he knows her true character and situation—a necessary detail of exposition, the need for which could well have become evident during rehearsal or performance.

165 peevish] perverse (Hoeniger, IV. vi. 122); another sense—'silly, foolish'—could also apply (*OED*, which gives no examples of the word used with either of these meanings later than the 1670s).

174 Marry] corruption of Mary; here an expression of indignation (Hoeniger, IV. vi. 137). The *OED* suggests that the word in such constructions be taken as an interjection having the general sense, 'why, to be sure' and cites, among others, Goldsmith, *Vicar of Wakefield*, 'Marry, hang the idiot . . .'

195–6 Then to . . . is liable.] So *Pericles*, IV. vi. 166–7. In context the sense is clear: 'As doorkeeper you are obliged to respond to the angry knocking of every rogue.' Unlike some editors of Shakespeare's text cited by Hoeniger, Lillo seems not to have been troubled by 'fisting' (literally, 'punching') nor to imply their alternate interpretation of the line, 'The meanest fellow in the world would not hesitate, if angry, to box your ears.'

215 cheapen] bargain for, ask or offer the price (*OED*, which cites the word used in this sense in *Pericles* (IV. vi. 10)).

253 a cast of my office] a taste or sample of my business (*OED*).

III. i

The action and dialogue of the scene are Lillo's invention.

45 stiver] coin of small value (*OED*).

51 the pip] disease of poultry and other birds, applied vaguely (usually humorously) to various diseases in human beings (*OED*).

III. ii

The first part of the scene—Thaisa and the priestesses (ll. 1–71a)—is Lillo's invention; brief references to *Pericles*, III. ii and III. iv, are to be found in the priestesses' account of Thaisa's mysterious arrival in Ephesus. The rest of the scene (ll. 71b ff.) is based on *Pericles*, V. i; occasional lines and one brief passage are drawn from V. iii, and the final speech is a reworking of four lines of Shakespeare's epilogue.

4 irritates] excites to greater intensity, heightens (*OED*, citing this line). Compare Lillo's use of 'aggravates', in a similar sense, in *The London Merchant*, IV. xviii. 7, V. i. 7, V. i. 12, and V. v. 25.

8 altar.] Following this line, L includes two lines not in G (see apparatus criticus). G's omission of these and several other lines which L includes in this scene suggests revision (not compositorial error), perhaps intended to increase the pace of the scene. See apparatus criticus at ll. 71a, 80, 149, 268.

30 habit Argentine] silver (or white) costume of a vestal of Diana; appropriate to one 'choosing to devote her future days | To chastity' (27–8) as well as to the 'goddess Argentine' (*Pericles*, V. i. 248). Cf. *Pericles*, V. iii. 5–7, 'At sea on childbed died she, but

brought forth | A maid-child call'd Marina; who, O goddess, | Wears yet thy silver livery' (Hoeniger, following J. D. Wilson, notes *The Merchant of Venice*, II. vii. 22, 'the silver with her virgin hue').

33a *Euphrion*] not in *Pericles*, nor is the name traditionally associated with the rites or Ephesian temple of Diana.

71a allow us.] Following this line, L includes four lines not in G (see apparatus criticus). Various reasons for deletion in G suggest themselves (it is altogether unlikely that the passage can have been overlooked by a compositor). In writing the lines originally, Lillo perhaps intended merely to stress Thaisa's humility. It is possible, however, that he meant to underscore the difference between the pagan story and the doctrine of Christian providence—a cautionary reminder to the audience not to take too seriously the mythical element in the play. In either case, the lines do, in a sense, contradict the situation in the play: in the story which Lillo follows, the goddess does communicate with mortals. Perhaps the passage was deleted for this reason. But, more simply, Lillo's excursion into a nice theological point may have proved to be an unworkable intrusion into the action of the scene.

80 miracle:] Here and at l. 149 L includes lines, omitted by G, which emphasize Marina's physical and spiritual qualities (see apparatus criticus). At 149 the line is clearly extraneous, but here it fits well enough and it is not possible to establish a rationale for its omission from the printed text.

87 chaloupe] shallop, shore-boat (French 'sloop'; *OED*).

92 reverend] so Rowe (1709, 1714), whom Hoeniger and Maxwell credit with introducing the emendation, and Sewell (1728) and Tonson (1734), *Pericles*, v. i. 14; the quarto prints 'reuerent'. In Shakespeare's time the spellings were interchangeable.

119a prolong] so Rowe, Sewell, and Tonson, *Pericles*, v. i. 26; the quarto prints 'prorogue', which has the same meaning. Neither Hoeniger nor Maxwell records emendations.

119b durst] the past subjunctive, which was often used indefinitely of present time (*OED*). Cf. *Arden of Feversham*, II. iii. 32, where the Larpent manuscript reads 'darst' while the printed text reads 'durst'.

158 *painful*] painstaking, diligent (*OED*).

158 *famoused*] made famous (an obsolete form; *OED*, which cites several 17th- but no 18th-cent. examples).

199 palace] Cf. *Pericles*, v. i. 121, 'Pallas'; Rowe, Sewell, and Tonson print *'Pallas'*, the italics perhaps indicating a reference to Athena. Hoeniger and Maxwell print 'palace' and record Lillo as the originator of the emendation.

231 be my child?—Buried] L writes 'be?—my child buried'. Lillo, like Shakespeare's editors, appears to have had difficulty making up his mind about the pointing of the line (*Pericles*, v. i. 162–3). The quarto prints 'be my daughter, buried', while the third folio prints 'be my daughter; buried!' The version printed in G parallels those given by the early 18th-cent. editions ('be my daughter; buried!'—Sewell substitutes a comma for the semi-colon). The variation in L follows no known edition of the period (Hoeniger and Maxwell cite Steevens (1793) as the originator of a closely parallel emendation). It is possible that Lillo tried one version of the line (L), then referred again to his source-text and revised his line to conform more closely to that text. Error in the copying of L, although possible, is unlikely.

243 imposture] L writes 'impostor', the sense of the word commonly accepted by editors of *Pericles* and the spelling given by all early 18th-cent. editions of the play (v. i.

177). The spelling in G is that of the quarto, a form which allows a different interpretation: 'a thing (or person) which is pretended to be what it is not' (*OED*). If the word is read in this sense, Marina protests not only that she is who she claims to be but also that she is a human creature and not an illusory being foisted on Pericles by some external power (cf. III. ii. 216b–218a and 224b–225 (*Pericles*, v. i. 142b–144a and 152b–154)). While it would not have been improbable for the transcriber copying L to have written 'impostor' for the less familiar 'imposture', it seems virtually impossible that the compositor working on G would have set the unusual word if his copy had read 'impostor'. If 'imposture', then, can be taken as the more probably authoritative reading, one is led to wonder if Lillo made use of an early edition of Shakespeare's play when he wrote his adaptation.

245 breath] an alternative form for 'breathe' (the reading in L), still current in the 18th cent. (*OED*). Cf. 'breaths', *The Christian Hero*, v. iv. 183.

259 deprecate] pray for evil to be averted or removed (*OED*). Cf. *The London Merchant*, v. xi. 22, and *Fatal Curiosity*, III. i. 237.

268–9 All my . . . *Pericles of Tyre*.] The broken metre in G results from the omission of one and a half lines included in L (see apparatus criticus). Compositorial error seems all but impossible, given the typography of the lines in G (followed in the present edition). At this high moment of the scene, the metrical irregularity creates rather than destroys dramatic effect and surely came about through revision.

322 mounds] embankment or dam (*OED*, citing Rowe, translation of *Lucan* [1718], i. 193, 'But if the mound gives way, strait roaring loud | In at the breach the rushing torrents croud'), a sense that suits well Lillo's source in *Pericles*, v. i. 193, 'O'erbear the shores of my mortality'. L provides an alternate reading, 'bounds'.

333 This tribute . . . but power] 'Having paid this tribute to give honour not to achievements determined or carried out by us but to the power of the holy gods to bring about good . . .'

345 suit] Cf. *Pericles*, v. i. 259a; the quarto prints 'sleight', as does Rowe (1709); Rowe (1714), Sewell, and Tonson print 'slight'. Hoeniger and Maxwell record no emendation to 'suit' until Malone, and it appears that Lillo in fact introduced the emendation; as the word occurs in a Shakespearian scene from which Lillo borrowed very little, modern editors may well have overlooked its appearance in *Marina*. Lillo's l. 349 is taken directly from *Pericles* (259b–260), so it seems certain that the phrase in question in l. 345—'a bolder suit/sleight'—is indeed a paraphrase of Shakespeare's line 259a, not a coincidental parallel.

354 proved] learnt by experience, gone through (*OED*). Cf. *Elmerick*, II. ii. 16.

365 preserv'd] So Tonson in *Pericles*, epilogue, 5; Rowe (1709 and 1714) and Sewell follow the quarto reading, 'preferd'. This may well stand as evidence that Lillo worked from the Tonson edition, although the emendation seems an easy one which Lillo might himself have introduced, especially since it so clearly echoes the resolution of the central action of his play.

Epilogue

17 *your wisdom to display*] L reads 'a Foreign Vagrant's Prey', probably a reference to Harlequin, against whom the Shakespeare Ladies Club and their supporters in the press directed particular vituperation (see ll. 25–8 below, and nn. on the dedication; cf. *The*

Christian Hero, epilogue, 39–42 and n.). That this reference proved less than clear in context seems the best of the possible explanations for its having been emended.

25–8 *A sacred band . . . Eliza's days.*] a reference to the Shakespeare Ladies Club and, as Avery suggests (p. 157), evidence perhaps that production of Lillo's adaptation came about through the efforts of the group.

27 *nervous*] vigorous, forcible; free from weakness and diffuseness (*OED*).

29–30 *Be it . . . and expence:*] 'softness' in the sense of 'easy, voluptuous living'; 'expence' as 'wasteful extravagance' (*OED*). Given the emphasis of the main body of the epilogue, 'others' is best read as referring to other peoples or nations rather than to other individuals, and the couplet to mean 'Let us take it as a sign of good sense returning to Britain (or Britons) that other peoples are laying claim to our luxuries and extravagancies.' The couplet which follows develops the conceit to make it clear that the 'adopted' follies are being carried off or stolen.

ELMERICK

Dedication

THE PRINCE OF *WALES*] Frederick, Prince of Wales (1707–51).

15–17 the Protection . . . during the Performance of it.] Advertisements announce the third performance of the play, 26 Feb. 1739/40, as a 'Benefit [for] the Author's Poor Relations. By Command of Their Royal Highnesses the Prince and Princess of Wales' (*London Stage, 1729–1747*).

Prologue

The prologue has regularly been attributed to James Hammond (1710–42), a minor political figure, sometime poet, and friend of Cobham, Lyttelton, Chesterfield, and Pit. Hammond was appointed an equerry to the Prince of Wales in 1733, and Davies (*Life*, p. xli), who attributes the epilogue as well as the prologue to Hammond, suggests that 'it may . . . be reasonably supposed that his interest with the Prince . . . was employed to the advantage of ELMERICK'. The epilogue may, in fact, have been the work of Lord Lyttelton (see n.). Hammond's authorship of the prologue, however, has not been questioned. The piece is included among his poems in the *English Poets* (1780) and mentioned by Dr Johnson in the accompanying 'Life'. (*DNB*, viii. 1130–1; Johnson, *Lives*, ed. G. Birkbeck Hill [Oxford, 1905], ii. 312–16; Cibber, *Lives* [1735], i. 307.)

9–10 *Deprest to . . . to please.*] The author of the prologue appeals here more to sentiment than to truth. As Davies notes, and Lillo's will affirms, the playwright 'so far from being poor . . . died in very easy circumstances, and rather in affluence than in want' (*Life*, p. xlvi). Hammond's exaggeration may perhaps have stemmed from a concern to contribute to the success of the two benefit performances (26 Feb. and 3 Mar. 1739/40) given to aid 'the Author's Poor Relations'. Offering a different explanation for the belief that Lillo died impoverished, Davies (*Life*, pp. xlvi–xlvii) cites a story of the playwright's 'odd kind of stratagem' in testing the affections of his friends and relations—in particular his nephew, John Underwood—by applying to them for a loan of money, offering as security only his note of hand. Davies's tale cannot, of course, be confirmed. Underwood, who is reported to have responded generously to his uncle's request for help, is the major beneficiary named in Lillo's will.

Dramatis Personæ

2–4 *Andrew* II. King of *Hungary:* | Commonly called *Andrew* | of *Jerusalem.*] Andrew (1175–1235) succeeded to the throne of Hungary in 1205. In 1217, at the strong urging of Pope Innocent III, he led a crusade to the Holy Land. Returning to Hungary *c.*1218, he found his kingdom under the control of a group of feudal barons, who forced him to agree to certain curtailments of his powers set out in the 'Golden Bull', a document which came to be considered as comparable to Magna Charta (*Enc. Brit.* i. 972; vii. 941; xiii. 903). Lillo's characterization of the king conforms, in the main, to the description of Andrew, often implicit rather than spelt out, in Vertot's *History of the Knights of Malta* (1728), pp. 121–5. Certain details, however, suggest reference to other sources or an awareness of aspects of Andrew's character not made explicit or suggested by Vertot. Vertot, for example, nowhere refers to the king as 'Andrew of Jerusalem'. Nor does he speak of the ambitiousness, a matter of concern in Lillo's first act, which appears to have been generally attributed to Andrew (it was said, indeed, that he led his crusade in the hope of becoming Emperor of Constantinople). The conventional view of the king as weakened by improvident good nature, despite his admirable energy and valour, could also have influenced Lillo's characterization of the king.

5 *Conrade*, Prince of *Moravia.*] The name of the character is probably Lillo's invention, but the Count of Moravia figures prominently in Vertot's history, and there is no question that Vertot provided the model for Lillo's portrait of the prince and his actions.

6 *Elmerick.*] The just and honest palatine who serves as regent during Andrew's absence is borrowed from Vertot, in whose account he is called 'Bancbannus'. Lillo's name for his hero again strongly suggests reference to some source in addition to Vertot: 'Elmerick' almost certainly is derived from 'Emerich', the name of King Andrew's brother, who is not mentioned by Vertot. Emerich died in 1204 and, except for his name, appears to bear no relation to Lillo's plot or characters.

7 *Bathori*] The character appears to be Lillo's invention, as do Belus and Zenomira.

10 *Matilda*, Queen of *Hungary.*] The name appears to be Lillo's invention, as is the plot centring on the queen's passionate love for the regent. The character is drawn from Vertot, who gives her no name but depicts her, as Lillo does, as the accomplice of her brother, Conrade, in his rape of the regent's wife. Vertot (pp. 122–4) reports that the queen was killed by the regent, and gives as his source 'Bonsinius, the historian of Hungary'; he also notes, however, that 'Duglos, commonly called Longinus, pretends that the death of the princess [i.e. queen] was caused by a conspiracy of some Hungarian lords, who were incensed at the queen for bringing some German princes, her relations, to court, and giving them principal posts in the kingdom' (p. 124). This second account is, in fact, historically accurate, and Vertot, or his source, has further confused matters by conflating the events in the Hungarian court: Andrew's first queen, Gertrude, was murdered in 1213, three years before the king left on his crusade. Lillo, in the main, follows Vertot's chronology, but compresses the action following the death of the queen (see IV. ii. 8–9a and v. i. 148+SD nn.).

11 *Ismena*] The character is based on Vertot's description of the regent's wife, 'a lady of admirable beauty . . . who was yet more virtuous than she was beautiful'. The name is Lillo's invention.

I. i

12 States] the Estates of the realm, forming a constitutional assembly; the princes, dukes, nobles, etc. together with delegates or representatives of the several ranks, orders, cities, etc. of a country assembled in a parliament (*OED*, which cites the Hungarian assembly as an example). Lillo's awareness of the organization of the 'states' again suggests reference to some source or tradition other than Vertot, who does not mention this assembly—which in fact post-dates the events about which he writes.

13 And I . . . is absent.] One of a few short passages, one or two lines in length, omitted from the printed text but included in L and not deleted by the corrector of the manuscript (cf. I. i. 71). Compositorial error or deletion during theatrical production are possible, although not strongly persuasive, reasons for the omission of this line from G.

40 praise] so G; L writes 'prize'. 'Praise' appropriately echoes the preceding line, while 'prize' is a not unlikely scribal error in the context of the line itself but inappropriate to the speech as a whole.

46 Palatine] a lord having sovereign power over a province or dependency of an empire or realm (*OED*, which includes the rulers of Hungary in a brief list of those to whom the term especially applied in the Middle Ages). Election of the Palatine is not mentioned by Vertot, and presumably would not have been the practice until a later period.

51–6 I ne'er approv'd . . . Glory to excess;] Bathori's description of the king and the situation, although exaggerated through Protestant bias, appears to match the traditional view of Andrew (see dramatis personæ, ll. 2–4 n.). Condemnation of the 'rash' war 'Begot by . . . bigots' is not based on Vertot, whose depiction of the crusades might well be described as romantic.

51 romantick] presumably in the sense of 'extravagant, quixotic, going beyond what is customary or practical' (*OED*).

69 inclination] Lillo associates the word with indulgence of the feelings or passions—response to desires, natural but reprehensible—against moral restraint and reason. Cf. *Fatal Curiosity*, III. i. 91, and *The London Merchant*, II. iii. 10, II. iv. 16, and IV. xviii. 34.

75–8 Can she . . . sister's nuptials] Cf. Vertot (p. 122), 'the queen, out of a complaisance, natural to women for this sort of malady [i.e. her brother's distress in love] . . . made use of various pretences to keep the regent's wife about her, or to send for her whenever she removed from the palace'. Lillo heightens the queen's 'complaisance'. He also adjusts the chronology of the story; Vertot includes no earlier visit of the prince but describes his falling in love, unsuccessful wooing, and final resort to violence as occurring during a single stay in the Hungarian court.

79a *Moravian* riot] The distinction between Hungarian sobriety and the excesses of Moravia is Lillo's (cf. II. ii. 78–9, 'The difference between the passive slaves | Of loose *Moravia*, and our free *Hungarians*'); Vertot writes of the queen's and Conrade's predilection for 'plays, diversions', and other 'vain amusements' simply as characteristic of 'the great world' (cf. II. i. 127–31 n.).

i. ii

9 own] in the sense of 'acknowledge'.

12 Neglected,] so L; G provides no pointing after 'Neglected'. The different punctuation of L and G suggests different interpretations of the lines. Here, as in other similar instances (e.g. IV. i. 101), the present edition follows L.

20 answer my big thought] 'fulfil the requirements of my great conception'. Whether

the king's expectations focus on the great job to be done or the extraordinary man needed to perform the task is unclear.

30 e'er, benignant, plan'd] With 'e'er' an adverb modifying the verb 'plan'd' (i.e. planned), the heavy pointing is precisely correct and necessary, although it can do little to clarify a complex and difficult line. W1, mistaking the sense of the word, prints 'ere'. The construction is paralleled, in a somewhat less tortuous sentence, at I. ii. 106–7: 'Unbless'd a King, whose self-reproaching heart | Ne'er, calm, reposes on a subject's virtue!'

55–61 And if . . . worthy head.] Here, as elsewhere in the play, Lillo's depiction of the king's concern for the rights and liberties of his subjects, and the limitations to which he voluntarily subjects his power, far exceed the generosity in justice suggested by Vertot.

56 oppressive] so G; L writes 'injurious'. The reading in G suits the sense of the line and speech, and prevents an unfortunate near-echo of 'injustice' in l. 58; it has been retained in the present edition. It is possible that here and at I. ii. 63, where a similar situation pertains (see apparatus criticus), the corrector of the manuscript overlooked emendations involving single words.

59 holy *Stephen*] patron saint of Hungary.

93–6 Shou'd any . . . your hand] Cf. Vertot (p. 122), '[The king] recommended to [his regent] at parting to preserve peace with the princes his neighbours, and particularly to administer exact justice to all his subjects, without regard to the birth or dignity of any person whatsoever.'

I. iii

8–9 *Baldwin . . . Saladin*] Lillo refers to the rulers of the Latin kingdom of Jerusalem—Baldwin IV (1174–83) and Baldwin, V a child ruler, titular ruler from 1183 to 1186—and to Saladin, Sultan of Egypt (1171–93), who consolidated the power of the Moslems. In the time of Baldwin IV Jerusalem was little threatened by its Mohammedan neighbours, but the reign of Baldwin V was marked by great dissension in the kingdom and the weakening of its defences at a time when Saladin, earlier occupied in establishing himself over the other Mohammedan princes, could turn his full attention and military power against the Christian kingdom. The city of Jerusalem fell to Saladin's forces in 1187, and by 1191 only a few ports of the former state of Jerusalem, together with the small states of Tripoli and Antioch, remained in Christian hands (*Enc. Brit.* iii. 247).

32 visionary] in a derogatory sense, 'imaginary, incapable of being carried out' (*OED*).

36–43 The Emperor . . . of his kingdom.] At the time of the Hungarian king's eastern campaign, Frederick II, the grandson of Frederick Barbarossa, was labouring to consolidate his power over the German principalities after a civil war in which he was opposed by Otto of Brunswick, a rival claimant to the imperial throne. Lillo's catalogue of rulers refers to the disintegration of the Third Crusade late in the 12th cent. The crusade had been led by the old emperor Barbarossa, with Richard I and the King of France, Philip II (Philip Augustus). The emperor was drowned attempting to cross a stream in Asia Minor on his way to the Holy Land (1190). Richard achieved several victories but was unable to recover Jerusalem; with his death in 1199, England's troubles at home and in France made impossible any royal expeditions to the East. Philip retained life and throne until 1223, but early in the crusade he had pleaded illness as an excuse to return to France and he was disinclined to venture forth again. (*Enc. Brit.* vii. 538–9; xii. 46–7.)

Lillo may have intended an element of irony in King Andrew's sharp criticism of King John, who, Vertot remarks (p. 121), was 'odious to his subjects': before the play is done, Andrew will come dangerously close to affronting civil liberty in a manner clearly similar to that of the English monarch whose tyranny he here condemns.

37 *France* delays;] so L; G, printing a colon after 'delays', is clearly in error, perhaps as the result of the compositor's having associated the French sobriquet for Richard (l. 38) with '*France*'. Although an argument could be made for retaining the colon, noting that Richard had been king of half of France, the rhetorical development of the speech (ll. 36–43) indicates that '*France* delays' is one of a straightforward series of parallel examples requiring parallel punctuation.

II.i

1 I resent . . . me thus!] Vertot (p. 122) hints at the queen's distress at the departure of her husband, noting that the regent's wife 'endeavoured, by her constant attendance about the queen, to divert the melancholy which the absence of the king her husband might occasion'. The queen's melancholy vanishes, however, with the arrival of her brother at court.

28 *Olmutz*] an Austrian town; until 1640, the capital of Moravia. The town is not mentioned by Vertot.

53b–55 Marriage, Madam . . . my Lord] so L^2; L^1 writes 'O what pity | That shou'd be thought so rare! 'Tis true, my lord'; G prints ''Tis true, my Lord'. Comparison of G and L^1 suggests that the deletion required by the revision (L^2) was made by the compositor of G, or in the manuscript he followed, but that the lines to be substituted were overlooked or not available. It is also possible, although less likely given the evidence of L^2, that the revised lines were later deleted, perhaps in the theatre in order to increase the pace of the scene. In either case, the revised reading in L appears to represent the latest version of the speech in which the author can be thought to have had a hand.

58 symmetry] regularity or beauty of form, comeliness (*OED*).

100 was you] 'was', an acceptable alternative form for 'were', and, 16th–18th cent., almost universal with 'you' when used as a singular (*OED*).

101 active genius] turn of mind or disposition for action (*OED*).

122 rigors to] instances of severity or harshness in dealing with (*OED*).

127–31 Not all . . . to my life;] Vertot (p. 122) emphasizes the violence of the prince's 'passion, which was gaining ground continually, [and] threw him at last into a deep melancholy: He cared no more for plays, diversions, shows, and all those vain amusements, with which the great world so seriously idle away their time: Solitude was his only pleasure.'

132 the soft poison] Cf. Vertot (p. 122), 'the flattering poison of love'.

148 wrong;] *Ed*.; ~, G, L^1, L^2. Emendation supplies the heavier pointing required by the insertion of l. 149 (L^2, G) but not provided by the revised manuscript or printed text.

148 do you] the archaic imperative.

152 thousand] so L^2; G, like L^1, reads 'cloud of'. Retention of the clearly earlier reading in G appears to stand as evidence that at least on occasion the compositor, or the manuscript he was following, overlooked or lacked some apparently authorial revisions.

176–7 conquer'd mine: . . . their peace:] Sequences of colons such as this appear a number of times in the text, in at least several instances clearly used with rhetorical purpose. See also II. ii. 1–3, 84–5; III. i. 260–1; V. i. 138–9, 328–31, 336. Colon series are characteristic also of the first edition of *The Christian Hero* (see I. i. 197–9 and n.).

II. ii

16 prov'd] learnt by experience, gone through (*OED*). Cf. *Marina*, III. ii. 354.

27a heigth] so G and L; recorded as an obsolete form by the *OED*. Cf. II. ii. 28, 'heigths', but III. i. 217, 'height'.

56 Cynick] despite capitalization, almost certainly not intended in the particular, philosophical sense, but the more general sense of 'fault-finding' or 'fault-finder' (*OED*).

III. i

13 Seek him now,] The half-line, breaking an otherwise regular verse speech, is odd at best and suggests possible confusion in the transmission of the text. However, neither the manuscript nor the printed text shows other signs of confusion in this passage, and the line was not touched when details of the speech were adusted by L^2. The line follows a natural break and possible dramatic pause in the speech, and the short line could have been intended to provide emphasis. Deliberate isolation of 'Seek him now' for purposes of dramatic emphasis would seem to be negated by the run-on required by 'And' at the start of the line which follows. (For discussion of the frequent occurrence of short lines in this text, see Textual Introduction, pp. 398–9.)

30 imports] relates to, has to do with (cf. III. i. 245); also, very possibly, 'is of consequence to' (*OED*).

67 I'll assist you.] Vertot's queen similarly devises strategies to aid her brother, although her motive for doing so is simply sympathy for his distress (see I. i. 75–8 n.).

189 Rifle] despoil, plunder (*OED*). Cf. *The Christian Hero*, IV. ii. 55b.

232b–233a my soul . . . | Shall be preserv'd.] so G, which retains the metrical regularity of the lines. L writes 'my soul | The secret shall be preserv'd.'

254 conscious virtue] the faculty of consciousness attributed to a personal quality—virtue—rather than to a person (*OED*). Here the significance appears to lie in the distinction between virtue engendered (and functioning) of itself and virtue dependent on external support. Cf. *The London Merchant*, V. iii. 2, and *The Christian Hero*. I, i. 201, 243.

319 seek him in those apartments] Cf. Vertot (pp. 122–3), 'the queen, under pretence of talking to [the regent's wife] in private, led her into a by-place of her apartment, where shutting her in, she abandoned her to the criminal desires of her cruel brother, who, by concert with the queen, was hid in the closet'.

322a–323 Go, you're . . . her there.] The lines make it clear that G rather than L (see apparatus criticus) has set the stage direction at the appropriate place.

IV. i

59–64 Give me . . . execrable pair!] so L; not in G, an omission difficult to account for. The passage could seem redundant, reiterating the distress of Ismena and her father, a subject more than adequately developed elsewhere in the scene; and there is a rather awkward repetition in 'fiend-like . . . pair' (l. 64) and 'kindred-fiends' (l. 73). However, the lines also include Ismena's revelation that the queen as well as Conrade has conspired against her, information which must be given to Bathori before he can inveigh against both royal villains. This practical requirement would seem to preclude deletion of the passage during production in the theatre; indeed, Bathori's first line here has the ring of an insertion made to provide opportunity for needed exposition (for an example of such revision see *Marina*, II. i. 1–11). That l. 65 does follow easily from l. 58 further suggests the possibility of a late addition to the text. Inadvertent omission of so many lines is most unlikely, and the scene as a whole presents few textual problems, an indication that the printer's copy was not markedly defective or difficult to follow. Conceivably the situation resulted from an earlier stage of revision than that evidenced by the changes recorded by L²—an adjustment made to supply necessary exposition, included in the manuscript behind L but omitted from the manuscript(s) from which the printer's copy was derived. Whatever led to the omission in G, the text as it has come down to us requires the exposition which the lines provide, and they are therefore included in the present edition.

194 *Alba-Regalis*] Latin name (also Alba-Regia) for Székesfehérvár, the town which, from the 10th to the 16th cent., was the coronation and burial place of the kings of Hungary.

198 prepossess] prejudice beforehand (*OED*).

IV. ii

8–9a I am excluded . . . those arms.] Although Lillo compresses the action, the situation, Ismena's reaction, and the conversation with her husband are suggested by Vertot (p. 123):

> The regent's wife went thence [i.e. from Conrade] with confusion in her looks, and resentment in her heart; she immured herself in her house, where she did nothing but bewail in private the count's villainy and her own dishonour. But the regent being one day about to take his place in her bed, the secret broke from her, and carried away by the excess of her anguish, 'Don't come near me, sir, says she, shedding at the same time a torrent of tears, but quit a wife that is no more worthy of the chaste embraces of her husband; a wild wretch has violated your bed, and the queen his sister was not ashamed to betray and deliver me up to his violence; I had before now taken vengeance on my self for their crime, if religion had not restrained me from making away with my self. But that prohibition of the law does not regard an injured husband: I am too criminal, since I am deflowered; I ask my death of you as a favour, to keep me from surviving my shame and my dishonour.'

44b–47a Talk not . . . my days.] Vertot's regent responds to his wife's distress in part as Lillo's hero does (p. 123):

> though in the height of affliction, and in all the fury of resentment, [he] told her, 'That an involuntary fault was rather a misfortune than a crime, and that the violence done to her body did not sully the purity of her soul; that he begg'd of her to be easy, or, at least, to take care to conceal the occasion of her sorrow. A common interest, adds he, obliges us both to dissemble so horrible an outrage, till we can revenge it in a manner suitable to the enormity of the offence.'

Vertot implies, but does not make explicit, that the wife accepts the arguments and comfort offered by her husband, a detail sharply altered by Lillo.

V. i

22–3 I've orders . . . your ear.] The scene is based on Vertot (p. 123):

> [The regent's] design was to make the count feel the first effects of [his revenge]; but hearing that he was gone away privately to return to his own countrey, the regent, enraged that his victim was escaped, turned all his resentment against the queen her

self; he went to the palace, and persuading the queen to go into her closet, under pretence of shewing her some letters, which, he said, he had just received from the king, as soon as he saw himself alone with her, after reproaching her with the criminal correspondence she had held with the count, and her treachery to his wife, the furious palatine plunged his dagger in her heart; and going out of the cabinet in a rage, he publickly, before the whole court, proclaimed his shame and vengeance.

146b–148 'Tis the . . . King appears.] so L; G prints only 'See, the King appears.' The lines in L, which in effect describe stage business, may have been deleted in the theatre as unnecessary and, indeed, as weakening the drama of the king's entrance. 'His Majesty is ent'ring' is in any case a peculiar line. It seems likely, however, that the passage was in the author's latest version of the play.

148+SD ff. *Enter King . . .*] The scene is derived from Vertot, but for reasons of dramatic convenience and intensity (and, it appears, a concern for unity of time and place) Lillo again compresses the action. Vertot notes that 'there are other authors . . . who maintain that this princess died before her husband quitted Hungary to go to the holy land' (p. 124), but, citing Bonsinius, he provides a different chronology of events in which the king is already in Palestine when the queen is killed. The regent, against whom no one in the court takes any action ('Whether it was surprize or respect that hinder'd them' [p. 123]), rides to the Holy Land in the company of some nobles, presents himself to the king, and 'with an intrepidity hardly to be parallel'd' confesses the murder of the queen. As in the play (cf. ll. 189–96), kingly justice, not the regent, is on trial in this confrontation (p. 123):

'Sir, says [the regent] to him, when I received your last orders at your leaving Hungary, you recommended to me, in a particular manner, to do exact justice to all your subjects, without regard to any one's rank or condition: I have done it so my self; I have killed the queen your wife, who had prostituted mine; and, far from seeking my safety in an unworthy flight, I here bring you my head; dispose as you please of my life; but remember that it is either by my life or death that your subjects will judge of your equity, and whether I am guilty or innocent.'

The violent reaction of the king, and the acts of injustice to which this passion nearly leads him, have no counterpart in Vertot's story, which continues:

The king heard this surprizing discourse without interrupting him, and even without changing colour; and when the regent had ended, 'If the case be as you say, replies the prince to him, return into Hungary, continue to administer justice to my subjects, with as much exactness and severity as you have done it to your self; I shall stay a short while in the Holy Land, and at my return I'll examine upon the spot whether your action deserves commendation or punishment.'

Upon the king's return to Buda, 'his first care . . . was to have the affair of Bancbannus tried before him; and after hearing the witnesses himself, and examining the various circumstances of that unhappy affair, he was equitable enough to declare the regent acquitted of the queen's death' (p. 125).

162–3 For what . . . barb'rous Villain—] so L; G omits. The lines involve Lillo's characteristic questioning of the functioning of providence (cf. *The London Merchant*, IV. i. 1–6), and one is inclined to retain them for this reason. The next lines (164–5), however, follow rather awkwardly. Lines 160–1a, above, have been revised (see apparatus criticus), and the lines omitted by G relate more appropriately to the earlier than to the revised text. It is possible, then, that L² made the required change at 160–1a but neglected to delete 162–3. However, while the manner of his writing suggests that the corrector of L was working in haste in this act, is it likely that he would accurately insert new text yet overlook a deletion immediately below? Perhaps the more probable explanation is that Lillo revised ll. 160–1, but did not touch ll. 162–3, and that later an editor or someone at the theatre noticed the difficulty and deleted accordingly.

171–2 Condemn'd on . . . I resign] so L; G prints 'Sir, I resign'. Nothing in the logic or sequence of the speeches argues strongly for either reading. Again, it is possible that a deletion was overlooked by the corrector of L. It is at least as likely, however, that the speech was pruned for greater directness in the theatre.

188 *K.* A murderer . . . of Justice?] so L; G prints after line 190, then in an errata slip directs that the line be deleted. Confusion about this line, probably associated with difficulties in following major revisions in ll. 191–6a and 202–5a, suggests that G was working with poor copy (see Textual Introduction).

191–6a But if . . . my country.] so L; G omits, printing instead l. 188 (see note above), then restores the passage in an errata slip. The situation confirms the accuracy of L and again indicates that G, at least in this act, was set from poor copy. Variants indicate that L, or its manuscript source, was not the copy-text for the errata slip in G. Where L and G (errata slip) differ, the present edition follows L.

218 human] so G; L writes 'humane', almost certainly an error since the balance of 'human' and 'divine' was clearly intended.

240a–240b Thou'st basely . . . strongest proofs,] The typography indicating line-division follows W1. In G, in which the layout of speeches does not make distinction between half-lines and short lines, the passage can be taken either as two truncated lines of three stresses each or as a single verse line of six stresses. The latter reading allows the dramatic effect, paralleled elsewhere in Lillo's dramas, which comes from casting Elmerick's quick, strong response to the king's accusation as a three-stress hemistich which echoes the measure and beats of the concluding line of the king's speech.

241–5 who cou'd . . . Confest it] so G; L writes 'the Queen's confession, | Who own'd it'. The single example of a passage of several lines included in G but not in L. The lines serve to strengthen Elmerick's case to the king and to emphasize the guilt of the queen, and also to obviate the awkwardness and possible ambiguity of the version of the speech given by L. While it is possible that the alteration was made in the theatre, the revision involves more than an easy or convenient adjustment for clarity or rhetorical effectiveness. Given the indications that the source for authorial revisions of the text was difficult to follow (see 191–6a n.) and the apparent haste with which the corrector of L appears to have worked in this act, it is possible that the corrector overlooked these revised lines or that the change was not in the manuscript or notes from which he worked.

289–90b *Mess.* I come . . . Angels fare,] Given three half-lines, W1 set them out as follows:

MESSENGER.

I come, my lord—

ELMERICK.

Be brief: how fares my wife?

MESSENGER.

As angels fare,

The present edition opts for the rhetorically more viable alternative.

290b–303 As Angels . . . sigh, expir'd.] Ismena's death is Lillo's invention. Vertot gives no account of the lady after reporting her conversation with her husband, in which it appears that she accepts forgiveness and lives.

324–34 *Conr.* Then I have . . . thus reveng'd—] In Vertot's history the queen's brother disappears from Hungary immediately after his assault on the regent's wife and is not referred to again. His repentance and suicide, like Ismena's death, are Lillo's additions to the story.

355–7 Still hold . . . for ever.] so L; G prints after l. 350, above. Revision in the theatre for rhetorical effect could account for the rearrangement in the printed text (cf. *The London Merchant*, V. x. 12–14, where a similar change appears to have been made). Very probably the reading in L represents the author's ordering of the lines.

Epilogue

Davies (*Life*, p. xli) says, with 'authority from a gentleman, who stands foremost in the first class of living authors', that the epilogue as well as the prologue was written by James Hammond. However, the poem is included in the collected *Works* of George Lord Lyttelton (3rd edn., 1776, iii. 201). It is also printed among Lyttelton's poems in the *English Poets* (1810 [Chalmers], xiv. 188), although the editor appends a cautionary note to Hammond's prologue (xi. 146) remarking Davies's confident ascription of the epilogue to Hammond. Lyttelton (1709–73) was a close acquaintance of Hammond's and one of the men closely associated with the Prince of Wales; it would not have been unlikely for him to have written the epilogue for a play in which Hammond and the prince had taken an interest. Davies was not the most meticulous or accurate of literary historians; it is quite possible that he, or his eminent gentleman of letters, erred in assigning the epilogue to Hammond.

BRITANNIA AND BATAVIA

Dramatis Personæ

1 Ithuriel] guardian angel of Britannia. The name does not occur in the Bible but religious tracts of the 16th cent. identify Ithuriel as an angel (sarim) (Gustav Davidson, *A Dictionary of Angels* [New York, 1967], p. 152). Lillo probably took the name from Milton's *Paradise Lost* (iv. 788 ff.), in which Gabriel sends Ithuriel, a cherub, and Zephon to search for Satan in the Garden of Eden; discovering the tempter 'Squat, like a Toad, close at the ear of *Eve*' (iv. 800), Ithuriel touches him with his spear, causing him to resume his own shape. This incident and the meaning of Ithuriel—'discovery of God'—may have prompted Lillo to choose this name for the angel who advises and enlightens Britannia. He may also have remembered Dryden's opera, *The State of Innocence*, adapted from Milton, in which Ithuriel appears as one of two angels 'commission'd . . . From heaven the guardians of Adam and Eve' (III. i).

2 Eliphas] guardian angel of Batavia. Not traditionally the name of an angel, Eliphas (Eliphaz) occurs in two biblical contexts. In Genesis (36: 4 and 10–12) Eliphaz is the son of Esau and his wife Adah, and the ancestor of several Edomite clans. In Job (2: 11, 4: 1–21, and 15: 1–35) Eliphaz the Temanite is one of the three comforters of Job. Possibly Lillo felt that the allusion to Job was appropriate to his guardian angel's role as comforter

of Batavia when she is oppressed by Spain and, later, grief-stricken at the loss of her people's hero, Liberto. He may, however, have had in mind some parallel between the Eliphaz of Genesis as progenitor of the Edomite tribes and the stadtholders of Orange as protector-fathers of the Dutch provinces. Or perhaps he simply found the meaning of the name—'God is victorious'—appropriate to his view of the role of William III in English history.

4 Batavia] a name long associated with the Netherlands. The Batavi were people of Germany who in ancient times inhabited modern Holland, then called *Batavorum insula* (J. Lemprière, rev. by F. A. Wright, Jr., *Lemprière's Classical Dictionary* [London, 1949], p. 103).

5 Liberto] in Lillo's allegory, the figure representing William III of Orange-Nassau, in particular in his role as the Protestant leader who rid Britain of the Catholic James II in the 'bloodless revolution' of 1688.

i

The episode represents, in allegorical summary, the assistance provided by Elizabethan Britain to the Protestant Dutch provinces that rebelled against Catholic Spain and Phillip II during the latter half of the 16th cent. The extent and decisiveness of British military aid is overemphasized to create the dramatic situation appropriate to Lillo's idealized version of a mutually beneficial Dutch and British friendship.

SD *leaning on . . . the Air*] Here, as elsewhere, Lillo designs his masque to take full advantage of stage machinery available for flying the actors and set pieces, and transforming the stage with scenery moved in the view of the audience.

23–32 For others . . . her own?] Taken in a general historical context, Ithuriel's reluctance to 'interrupt [Britannia's] calm repose' to go to war 'For Causes not her own' represents sound policy and restraint in international affairs. However, to a London audience in 1733 the scene would have had a different, contemporary significance. Ithuriel's speeches and song can be interpreted to mimic the foreign policy and rhetoric of Walpole, whose strategy for Britain in the 1730s lived up to a remark he had made to George I in 1723: 'My politics are to keep free from all engagements as long as I possibly can' (W. Coxe, *Memoirs of the Life and Administration of Sir Robert Walpole, Earl of Orford* [London, 1798], ii. 263, quoted by Paul Langford, *The Eighteenth Century 1688–1815* [New York, 1976], p. 104). Lillo may intend only a general comment on the Minister's policy of peace at all costs, or he may refer more specifically to Walpole's refusal to accept what some felt to be Britain's legal and moral obligations to become involved in the War of Polish Succession, which had begun in Oct. 1733 (Langford, op. cit., p. 107).

38 ras'd] razed; an accepted variant spelling in the 18th cent. (*OED*).

54–7 While Heaven . . . must prevail] Batavia's song in praise of British justice and prestige may contain a topical political comment: in 1733–4 Britain could well have been seen to hold the 'casting Weight' in the War of Polish Succession, and in avoiding the war on the Continent to stand in danger of losing her position of power and influence in world affairs.

AIR V. *Under the Greenwood Tree.*] The tune, used frequently in ballad operas in the 18th cent., derives ultimately from the 17th-cent. ballad 'The West-Country Delight, or Hey for Zommerset-Shire', which begins 'In Summer time when flowers do spring, | and Birds sit on a Tree' (Claude M. Simpson, *The British Broadside Ballad and its Music* [New Brunswick, NJ, 1966], pp. 224–7). Fielding twice made use of the tune for mock love-songs—in *The Author's Farce* (1730) and *The Grub-Street Opera* (1731). Lillo is likely to have known these and other theatrical versions of the song, which, in some thirteen ballad operas, was used increasingly as a vehicle for satiric commentary on city life (cf. Moss, *Opera Songs*, iv. 135). He may also have had in mind Henry Potter's recent version of the song, which appeared in *The Decoy* (Feb. 1733) and satirized corrupt politicians. However, in writing his own lyrics, Lillo appears to have recalled the early words associated with the tune, which describe the pleasures of country life as contrasted with city vice, and in his song he offers a tongue-in-cheek comparison of the virtues of love's tyranny and, by implication, the vice of tyranny in government.

58 Faction] 'Party' in the abstract; factious spirit or action; dissension (*OED*, which cites Bolingbroke, *On Parties* [1735–8], 'But Faction hath no regard to national interests'). See also *The Christian Hero*, Prologue, l. 28 n., and Epilogue, ll. 24–7. Monarchy free from party division was an ideal propounded by Bolingbroke and opposition writers, and a plea for Englishmen to rise above faction could be taken as a call to dismiss Walpole (cf. John Loftis, *Politics of Drama in Augustan England* [Oxford, 1963], pp. 121–2). Throughout the comic interlude Lillo plays, in a light-hearted context, with words and ideas central to the themes of his serious episodes.

ii
The opening portion of the episode (1–52) portrays a thoroughly Protestant vision of the reign of James II, 1685–9, whose Catholicizing policy led many to believe that he 'was determined to impose on his kingdoms a Roman Catholic despotism similar to that exercised by King Louis XIV in France' (Maurice Ashley, *England in the Seventeenth Century* [Baltimore, 1952], p. 177). The latter half of the scene (53–85) celebrates the invasion of Britain by the Protestant forces of William III in Nov. 1688, and the ensuing 'bloodless revolution' which culminated in the accession of William and Mary, eldest daughter of James II, who were declared king and queen by a Convention Parliament on 6 Feb. 1689. Lillo's uncompromisingly harsh, if at times ironic, portrayal of the figures representing the evils of the Roman Catholic Church suggests not only that he shared fully the Protestant view of the religious and political oppression intended by James II but also that he meant to awaken his audience to the danger of Catholic attempts at international dominance in their own time. Certainly the scene represents the playwright's most passionate expression of his Protestant loyalties and feelings.

27–31 Whips, Chains . . . tender Mercy.] Physical tortures, long associated with the Inquisition, were also the stuff of horrific tales told about outrages in the treatment of British seamen taken by Spaniards during the late 1720s and early 1730s. Brought to national attention by a parliamentary enquiry in 1738, such reports did much to fuel the indignation that forced Walpole to take military action against Spain (cf. Basil Williams, rev. by C. H. Stuart, *The Whig Supremacy 1714–1760* [Oxford, 1962], pp. 207–10).

52+SD *Prospect of . . . at Anchor*] the fleet of William III, which reached Torquay on 5 Nov. 1688 and later anchored at Exeter.

AIR VIII. *When the Stormy*, &c.] In writing his joyful ballad to celebrate Britain's sailors and power at sea, Lillo may well have chosen this tune—'When the Stormy Winds do Blow'—because it had regularly been used for ballads in praise of seamen and life at sea—e.g. the earliest version, 'Saylors for my money, A new Ditty . . . To the tune of the Iouial Cobler'; a later version of this ballad provided the refrain from which the tune took its name. Ballads set to the tune in the latter half of the 17th cent. were topical and patriotic. Examples include a recruiting ballad dating from the 1660s and 'The Valiant Seamans Congratulations to his sacred Majesty King Charls [*sic*] the second'.

However, Lillo may have had in mind especially, and hoped his audience would recall, a ballad probably composed in Apr. 1691, which made the tune most appropriate to follow his Liberto episode, 'Englands Welcome to King William'. (Simpson, op. cit., pp. 768–9.)

iii

5 Lost *Liberto*] William III had died in 1702. His death was followed by a 'stadtholderless regime', a less than effective republican government for the five provinces William had led. William IV, hereditary stadtholder of two other Dutch provinces, was asked to rule them all in 1747.

10–11 How generous . . . *Liberto*'s Fame] Britain's generosity in selecting the Dutch prince as husband for the Princess Royal is exaggerated to suit the requirements of a festive presentation. Eligible princes were, in fact, very few in number, and, as Lord Hervey summed up the search to make a royal alliance, the princess's 'option was not between this Prince and any other, but between a husband and no husband' (quoted by Emmett L. Avery, 'A Royal Wedding Royally Confounded', *Western Humanities Review*, x [1956], 153).

33+SD *Scene the Procession . . . really perform'd*] The procession, a spectacle by which the theatres' managers competed for audiences, attempting to outdo one another in the numbers of persons involved and the splendour of their costumes, had grown from an interlude depicting the coronation of Anna Bullen, which was added to a series of performances of *Henry VIII* offered by Drury Lane in the autumn of 1727. Processions became a frequent feature of performances mounted to mark royal weddings, births, and coronations. (Cf. *London Stage, 1700–1729*, vol. i, p. cxix.)

38 *Nassau*] The princes of Orange-Nassau represented one line of descent from Walram, Count of Nassau (d. 1188). They continued to carry the name though the duchy was given up to another branch of the family in 1544, when William the Silent, ancestor of William III and leader of the Dutch provinces in their rebellion against Spain, inherited the principality of Orange.

ARDEN OF FEVERSHAM

NOTE. In the commentary the original version of the play is referred to as *Arden I*, the adaptation as *Arden II*. Correspondence between scenes or major incidents of the two versions is briefly described in a head-note for each scene. Scene- and line-numbers for *Arden I* refer to the Revels Plays edition, edited by M. L. Wine (London, 1973).

Prologue

By a FRIEND] The author of the prologue has not been identified. Lines 10–21 echo the sense though not the language of ll. 14–18 of the epilogue of *Arden I*, which could indicate that the author was someone closely associated with the adaptation of the play itself, possibly John Hoadly. However, the idea behind the lines is proverbial (as Wine notes in commenting on the passage in *Arden I*). Such apologies were offered regularly at the end of early domestic tragedies and, after the success of *The London Merchant*, became a commonplace in the prologues and epilogues of Lillo's plays.

Mr. HAVARD] William Havard, who played Arden in the first performance of the adaptation.

1 Lillo's] The focus on Lillo throughout the prologue and the assertion in its first line of his authorship of the play (without reference to John Hoadly) suggests, as do newspaper advertisements, the extent to which the producers based their hopes for the play's success on its association with the author of *The London Merchant.*

1 *long since in dust*] When the play was first presented Lillo had been dead for nearly twenty years.

4 *knows no art*] Here and throughout, the prologue serves as a virtual catalogue of the qualities that critical and popular opinion of the period associated with Lillo's writing.

15 minuteness] attention to precision, critical detail (*OED*).

16 Hybla] a Sicilian mountain (later called Megara), famous for its honey.

26 *bosom pangs*] heartfelt anguish; a combining form of 'bosom' as the seat of thoughts and feelings (*OED*).

Dramatis Personæ

6 *Green*] in *Arden I*, Greene.

11 Lord *Cheyney*] in *Arden I*, Lord Cheyne; in Holinshed, Sir Thomas Cheinie. See II. i. 40 n.

12 *Adam Fowl*] in *Arden I*, Adam Fowle.

16 *Alicia*] in *Arden I*, Alice.

16 A young gentlewoman] Her identity is not known. See Introduction, Performance and Reception.

17 *Maria*] Susan in *Arden I*, in which the character is created by combining Mosby's sister and Alice's maid; their names are not reported in Holinshed but they have elsewhere been identified as 'Cicely Pounder and Elizabeth ("Elsabeth") Stafford' (Wine, p. xxxix, referring to the official account of the murder given in the Wardmote Book of Faversham). Maria, the name given to the character in *Arden II*, appears also in *The London Merchant* and *Fatal Curiosity.*

I. i

The scene—a soliloquy in which Mosby announces his villainous schemes—has no direct parallel in *Arden I*, which begins with a conversation in which Arden and Franklin discuss the grant of Abbey lands to Arden and his suspicions about Alice's affair with Mosby. Mosby's soliloquy serves something of the same expository function, but it also demonstrates the adaptation's major reversal of character motivations: in *Arden II*, Mosby, not Alice/Alicia, will be the primary instigator of the murder while she, in sharp contrast to her counterpart in *Arden I*, will waver and require coercion. In spirit, the soliloquy bears some relation to a briefer solo speech, early in *Arden I* (i. 93–104), in which Alice makes clear her determination that Mosby 'shall be mine | In spite of him [Arden], of Hymen, or of rites'.

2–3 Thrice have . . . he escap'd.] *Arden II* includes four unsuccefful attempts on Arden's life. There are several more such efforts in *Arden I*, which the tightened structure of the adaptation did not allow. The reference here to earlier murder schemes is probably intended to make up for the omitted episodes and so to maintain the effect of Arden's remarkable series of fortunate escapes.

3 I am not safe:] In its presentation of Mosby's motives, the soliloquy is curious, and to some extent in contradiction to the scenes which follow. See Introduction, Sources.

8–10 There's *Green* . . . fancy'd right.] See II. i. 2–3 n.

10 trencher-fav'rite] parasite, toady (*OED*).

11 bastard, bred of *Arden*'s charity] In context, 'bred' surely must be taken to mean 'reared', not 'sired'. Michael's bastardy and Arden's goodness in providing him home and upbringing are inventions of the adaptation, an instance early in the play of a concern to improve the character of Arden.

I. ii

The scene draws on a number of details included in *Arden I*, i. 1–104, but rarely follows the earlier text closely. A brief confrontation between Arden and Alicia is much expanded. The intensity of Arden's feelings, Alicia's promise not to see Mosby again, her pity and self-recrimination—the beginning of her change of heart—are inventions of the adapter.

8 Lord *Clifford*'s full-fed flatt'rer] Cf. *Arden I*, i. 32, 'the Lord Clifford, he that loves me not'; through 'servile flattery and fawning' (28), Mosby, a tailor, has been made steward of Clifford's house. In *Arden II* Mosby's particular situation as the nobleman's 'dependent' is left unclear. Holinshed and other sources agree that Mosby was 'seruant' to Lord North. Wine, following Cust, suggests that there being 'no Lord Clifford at the date of the murder', an alteration was 'probably made to prevent scandal in the North family'.

9–11 Come, *Franklin* . . . in love.] Cf. *Arden I*, i. 9–12, 'Franklin, thy love prolongs my weary life; | And but for thee, how odious were this life, | That shows me nothing but torments of my soul, | And those foul objects that offend mine eyes—'. In *Arden II* Arden's solo speech is substituted for a conversation in which Arden and Franklin discuss Alice's infidelity.

12–15 Why, *Arden* . . . from me.] Cf. *Arden I*, i. 57–61:

> ALICE. Husband, what mean you to get up so early?
> Summer nights are short, and yet you rise ere day.
> Had I been wake, you had not rise so soon.
> ARDEN. Sweet love, thou know'st that we two, Ovid-like,
> Have often chid the morning when it 'gan peep,

The passage suggests the freedom with which the adapter adjusts the original text when he elects to echo at all the lines of *Arden I*.

18 determin'd] fixed, resolute (i.e. not 'ordained') (*OED*).

19–24 What maid . . . at large] The comparable passage in *Arden I* (i. 98–102) is markedly different in import:

> Sweet Mosby is the man that hath my heart;
> And he usurps it, having nought but this,
> That I am tied to him by marriage.
> Love is a god, and marriage is but words;
> And therefore Mosby's title is the best.

In *Arden II* Alicia's strong protest against the inequities forced on women by the laws and customs relating to marriage bears comparison with Millwood's condemnation of the hypocrisies of society and the inequitable treatment of women by men (*The London Merchant*, IV. xviii). However, Alicia, unlike Millwood, very much alters her opinion in these matters later in the play. See also I. iii. 10a–23 and II. ii. 25–8, which more closely parallel the sense of the lines of *Arden I* quoted above.

23 Himself th'offender and himself the judge'] The line is included in L, omitted by D. Neither the syntax nor the sense of the speech is made awkward by the omission, and l. 24 follows easily after l. 22, since they are effectively statements of the same idea. Thus accidental omission might easily have passed without notice. In context, the line left out of the printed text is of some importance since it expresses the essence of Alicia's complaint against Arden, her anger (genuine or trumped up to divert attention from her own guilt) at his haste to judge and condemn her, a woman, for purportedly indulging in peccadilloes of a kind that men engage in with impunity. The line has therefore been restored.

35b base mechanic slave] 'mechanic' in the sense of 'working at a trade', but also 'of the lower classes, vulgar, low' (*OED*, which cites a number of 18th-cent. examples). The disparity between Mosby—an ambitious servant who began life as a 'botcher' (tailor)— and Arden—a landowner, by birth a gentleman—is given minimal emphasis in the adaptation. In *Arden I* Mosby's lower-class background is the element in his relation with Alice which most angers Arden, rousing him to threaten violence and murder; except for this, the husband is quite ready to accept Franklin's worldly approach to Alice's suspected dalliance with Mosby: 'Comfort thyself, sweet friend; it is not strange | That women will be false and wavering' (i. 20–1). In *Arden II* Arden's great distress and the romantic plot of the play focus almost exclusively on the issue of sexual infidelity, although epithets attached to Mosby's name recall his lower social status.

56 corresponding] communicating in a secret or illicit way; also committing sexual intercourse (*OED*). Cf. 'correspondence', IV. i. 10.

63 You call'd on *Mosby*] Cf. *Arden I*, i. 66, 'I heard thee call on Mosby in thy sleep.' The situation further developed in the lines which follow in *Arden II*, including Alicia's calling for Mosby a second and third time, is the invention of the adapter.

77 carelesness] *OED* cites no example of this spelling later than 1613, but notes 'carelesly' as late as 1667. Cf. 'carelesly', III. i. 3.

81b Yet was it but a dream] In *Arden I* Arden follows Franklin's politic advice not to display excessive jealousy and accepts this explanation readily, saying 'there is no credit in a dream. | Let it suffice I know thou lovest me well' (i. 74–5).

92 chace] a spelling interchangeable with 'chase' until the 19th cent. (*OED*).

97SD *He starts.*] D and L agree that the direction refers to Arden, and it is not entirely illogical that his exclamatory line, which follows, be preceded by some sharp gesture. It is conceivable, however, that the direction was intended to refer to Alicia (i.e. '*She Starts*'); this would emphasize her silent reaction and motivate Arden's next line. As Alicia's aside (ll. 98b–99) makes clear, she reacts extremely to Arden's command that she not see Mosby again and is concerned that she may not be able to hide these feelings.

124–6 the grant . . . his life] 'the young king' is Edward VI, aged 13 in 1551, the time of Arden's murder. The adaptation does not follow *Arden I* in naming the Duke of Somerset as the actual arranger of the transfer of Abbey lands to Arden, an omission that may well reflect a concern to improve the character of Arden. As Wine notes (i. 2), association with Somerset provides 'an apt commentary' on Arden as he is characterized in *Arden I*; the Lord Protector is remembered for 'his rapacity in profiting by the dissolution of the monasteries . . . and the sale of church lands' (*DNB*, cited by Wine). Extant documents make it clear that the lands in question were in fact sold to Arden by Lord Cheyne, who in turn had been granted them by Henry VIII in 1540 (see II. i. 40 n.).

130–9 Madam, your . . . seek him.] The episode is a reworking of a scene in *Arden I* in which the innkeeper, Adam Fowle, reports to Alice that Mosby has come to town but does not wish her to visit him. Although their words are different, Alice and Alicia are equally frantic in their concern to see Mosby (cf. *Arden I*, i. 116–19).

I. iii

The scene is based on two episodes in scene i of *Arden I*, Alice's first scene with Mosby (185–226), in which the plot to kill Arden is initiated, and Arden's first confrontation with Mosby (290–359). Both episodes are substantially altered in the adaptation. Alicia's girlhood romance with Mosby, which predates her dutiful marriage to Arden, is a circumstance introduced by the adapter and reverses the sequence of events described in *Arden I*. In having Mosby initiate the plan to murder Arden, the adaptation also reverses the situation presented in the original drama, in which it is Alice who urges that Arden be killed and spurs Mosby on to assist in planning possible ways to bring this about. In reworking the Arden–Mosby scene, the adapter begins by following the situation and to some extent the words of *Arden I*. However, in the development and resolution of the confrontation, major elements of the action and characterization are again turned around—e.g. in *Arden I* Mosby, not Arden, attempts to resort to his sword to settle the argument about Alice; Arden accepts rather than rejects Mosby's assertion of his own and Alice's innocence, and he ends the scene by offering Mosby his friendship and trust. The brief concluding scene, in which Arden expresses his anguished jealousy, is for the most part new in the adaptation but bears some relation to *Arden I*, i. 9–14.

41 thee,] The different pointing in L—'thee;'—indicates an emphatic pause and perhaps more effective reading of the line.

59+SD *Enter* Arden *and* Franklin.] so L; D prints the direction before Alicia's exclamation (59). Situations in which an exclamation breaking off a scene and the entrance of other characters which occasions this reaction occur simultaneously clearly presented problems for those who prepared the text for publication (see Textual Introduction). Here the stage direction for the entrance of Arden and Franklin is awkwardly inserted between the direction characterizing Alicia's reaction (58SD) and the line in which it is verbalized (59). For clarity, the present edition accepts the ordering of directions and dialogue given by L, an arrangement which, in fact, D adopts (effectively emending L) at v. i. 49CSD.

77–8a That *Green . . . long* enjoy'd] The adaptation draws on *Arden I*, i. 292–7, in which Mosby reports that Green has offered to sell him the Abbey lands granted to Arden and asks if the lands do indeed belong to Arden. See II. i. 2–3 n.

78b–85a For my . . . further violation.] Cf. *Arden I*, i. 300–3:

> As for the lands, Mosby, they are mine
> By letters patent from his majesty.
> But I must have a mandate for my wife;
> They say you seek to rob me of her love.

II. i

The scene is derived from a portion of scene i and the whole of scene ii of *Arden I*. The episodes and the shape of the drama are significantly altered by the adapter's substitution of Mosby for Alice and for Greene in situations in which, in *Arden I*, they act as the instigators in plots against the life of Arden. Green's conversation with Mosby (originally with Alice) and his involvement in the murder plot parallel *Arden I*, i. 450–533. The introduction of Black Will and Shakebag, and Will's old acquaintance with

Bradshaw, are based on *Arden I*, ii. 1–80. The hiring of Will and Shakebag to perform
the murder (ll. 84–150) is a thorough revision of *Arden I*, ii. 80–111, in which Greene
(not Mosby) strikes a bargain with the cutthroats, using money given him for the purpose
by Alice.

2–3 thoughtless and . . . a beggar.] That Green has squandered his inheritance and
thus is in large measure responsible himself for his desperate situation is the invention of
the adapter. This change, like many others, serves to absolve Arden of blameful
responsibility in the situation. In *Arden I* Greene is presented as genuinely ill-treated and
Arden as clearly at fault in his rapacious schemes to acquire land. Cf. *Arden I*, i. 470–7:

> GREENE. . . . Your husband doth me wrong,
> To wring from me the little land I have.
> My living is my life; only that
> Resteth remainder of my portion.
> Desire of wealth is endless in his mind,
> And he is greedy-gaping still for gain;
> Nor cares he though young gentlemen do beg,
> So he may scape and hoard up in his pouch.

9 threats] threatens; an alternative form regularly in use during the 18th cent. (*OED*).

20 lazar] poor, diseased person, usually one afflicted with a loathsome disease,
especially leprosy (*OED*).

31 sir—] so L; D omits. The word is required to complete the line of verse.

39b isle of *Shippey*] Isle of Sheppey. Cf. *Arden I*, x. 9–10, 'to go | To the Isle of
Sheppey, there to dine with my Lord Cheyne'.

40 lord *Cheyney*] Sir Thomas Cheyne (first spelling in *DNB*), ?1485–1558. 'Never
actually Lord Cheyne, [although] his son was raised to the peerage. There is probably
some confusion here with his titles of Lord Warden of the Cinque Ports and Lord
Lieutenant of Kent. The *D.N.B.* records that . . . he was one who "profited largely by the
dissolution of the monasteries in Kent"' (Wine, ix. 94+SD n.).

46 I knew at *Boulogne*] Cf. *Arden I*, ii. 8, 'At Boulogne he and I were fellow soldiers.'
The detail is taken from Holinshed. The seaport of Boulogne was captured by Henry
VIII in 1544, but was surrendered 'back to the French in the Treaty of Boulogne,
29 March 1550, almost a year before Arden's murder' (Wine, ii. 7–32 n.).

50 party] side in a contest or dispute; cause, interest (*OED*).

55–8 A word . . . on them.] In *Arden I* Greene himself devises the letter and the plan
to have it carried by Bradshaw (cf. ii. 74–6).

60 S'blood] Here and throughout the text D prints the oath in this form while L
regularly writes 'Blood' (cf. III. i. 17, 61, IV. iii. 1). *OED* lists the two forms as
interchangeable. It seems unlikely that any concern for propriety dictated the use of one
form or the other. Conceivably someone associated with D or its source felt that
'S'blood', which more closely reflects the origin of the oath ('Christ's blood', 'God's
blood'), was more correct, though *OED* citations indicate that 'Blood' was current in
printed texts during the latter half of the 18th cent.

64–5 *Omne solum forti patria*.] Literally, 'Every land is for a brave man his homeland.'
Black Will's gloss is not inaccurate.

65 tester] name for the 'teston' of Henry VIII, especially as debased and depreciated;
subsequently a colloquial or slang term for a sixpence (*OED*).

69 mechanical] See I. ii. 35b n.

74 *cent. per cent.*] a hundred for every hundred; interest equal in amount to the principal (*OED*).

84 cadet] a gentleman who entered the army without a commission, to learn the military profession and find a career for himself (*OED*). Here the implication is clearly that one signed on as a cadet because one lacked money.

106–7 free-thinkers] The phrase would seem to have had much the same meaning that it has today, referring to those who refuse to submit their reason to the control of authority in matters of religious belief; at the beginning of the 18th cent. the designation was claimed especially by rejectors of Christianity (*OED*).

134 Ten pieces] 'Twenty angels' (ten pounds) is the price for which Black Will and Shakebag settle in *Arden I* (ii. 86–8). When their attempts at murder go awry, they regret the bargain:

> WILL. . . . were my consent to give again, we would not do it under ten pound more. I value every drop of my blood at a French crown. I have had ten pound to steal a dog . . . (iii. 71–4)

144 at *Adam Fowl's*, the *Flower-de-luce*] Cf. *Arden I*, xii. 59–60 (Alice to Black Will and Shakebag), 'Get you to Faversham to the Flower-de-Luce, | And rest yourselves until some other time.'

146 We've] so L; D prints 'w'have'. *OED* cites 'w'' for 'we' as occurring rarely before a vowel or 'h' in the 17th cent.; no examples of 'w'have' are cited under 'we' or 'have'.

II. ii

In its development of the character of Alicia and as preparation for her attempt to kill Arden in his sleep, an incident invented by the adapter, the scene has no counterpart in *Arden I*. Certain details, including the reading of the letter (its contents much revised), do draw on material in the original play. See the commentary below.

3–4 'Strike home . . . of *Bradshaw*.'] In *Arden I* the letter is delivered much later in the play, following a series of unsuccesful attempts on Arden's life; except for implicating Bradshaw in the conspiracy, the message differs markedly from that given in *Arden II* and serves a different purpose in the plot of the play: 'We have missed of our purpose at London, but shall perform it by the way. We thank our neighbor Bradshaw' (viii. 157–60).

8–9 This promis'd . . . his qualms.] These lines, and ll. 14–16 below, recall an episode in *Arden I* (i. 143–75) in which Alice promises Mosby's sister to Michael if he successfully carries out a pledge he has made to her to kill Arden.

9SD [*Alicia* starts.] so L; D omits. Alicia's next line makes clear the appropriateness of the direction, which matches those included by D as well as L in a number of similar situations in the play.

17–31 What is . . . in heav'n.] Alicia's soliloquy is invented by the adapter (see Introduction, Sources). Lines 25–8 may relate to *Arden I*, 98–102 (see I. ii. 19–24 n.).

II. iii

The situation and its development in the scene—critically important in the structure of *Arden II*—are invented by the adapter.

11 mimic fancy] imitative delusion or imagination (imitative as opposed to real) (*OED*).

30 wrap'd] *OED* notes occasional use of this form during the 18th cent., though 'wrapp'd' and 'wrapt' are usual.

30 Hence!] so L; D prints 'hence—'. The accidentals of the two texts indicate very different readings. As set out in D, 'hence' has the meaning 'thus, therefore', relates to the sentence and idea which precede it, and, as the dash indicates, must be followed by a pause indicating a break in thought. As pointed by L, 'hence' has the sense of 'go away' and relates to the lines which follow. While D is not demonstrably incorrect, the context seems clearly to demand the interpretation signalled by the pointing in the manuscript, a reading supported also by Arden's next speech (34–40): 'Away, begone and leave me . . . Nay, now you drive me hence.' The variant may well indicate that the ultimate common source of L and D was casually pointed with dashes which in this case the compositor or his copy failed to adjust.

III. i

The scene is based primarily on scene ix of *Arden I*, which includes the fight between Black Will and Shakebag interrupted by Green and the attempt at murder thwarted by Arden's appearance in the company of Lord Cheyne. The opening dialogue for Will and Shakebag bears some relation to *Arden I*, v. 1–33, and may also have been influenced by III. 64–113. The characterization of Michael, repentant but forced to continue his involvement with the would-be assassins, may well have been suggested by the latter part of scene iii of *Arden I* (especially ll. 191–209), though the situations on which this scene and III. i of *Arden II* are built are quite different.

1 posted as . . . him 'scape!] The episode to which Black Will and Shakebag refer corresponds to no single incident in *Arden I*, but instead represents the general situation of the villains frustrated in a series of attempts at murder.

6–7 I had . . . seiz'd me.] Cf. *Arden I*, v. 15–17:

> I tell thee, Shakebag, would this thing were done;
> I am so heavy that I can scarce go.
> This drowsiness in me bodes little good.

54 *Shorlow*] Shurland Castle ('Shorlow' in *Arden I*), Lord Cheyne's establishment on the Isle of Sheppey (Wine, ix. 144 n.).

95–8 To night . . . you please.] Michael's description of his plan, in its details and many of its words, closely follows *Arden I*, iii. 179–85.

103–4 Master, thy . . . from *Michael*.] Cf. *Arden I*, iii. 195–9:

> Ah, harmless Arden, how, how hast thou misdone
> That thus thy gentle life is levelled at?
> The many good turns that thou hast done to me
> Now must I quittance with betraying thee.

In contrast to his counterpart in the adaptation, the Michael of *Arden I* reverts to his commitment to kill his master before his soliloquy is done. While continuing to voice privately some regret about Arden's impending death, he does not again consider or attempt refusing to play his part in the plots against Arden.

III. ii

The scene is derived from a portion of scene viii of *Arden I*, a similarly intense confrontation between Mosby and Alice. Both versions begin with pensive expressions of repentance by Alice/Alicia and her wish to be able to return, innocent, to her husband. However, in developing the situation the adapter again departs radically from his source. In *Arden I* Mosby responds to Alice's apparent change of heart not with appeals to youthful love but with recriminations, curses, and the threat to leave her; Alice's passion for Mosby instantly reasserts itself; and the episode ends with his yielding to her plea that he forget the quarrel. In *Arden II* the scene is thoroughly revised to centre on Alicia's desperate struggle to maintain her commitment to 'the pursuit of virtue', and the adapter introduces such significant new elements as Mosby's belief that Arden has already been killed, his consequent effort to bring Alicia to agree to allow a renewal of their romance if Arden should die, and her moralizing soliloquy, which ends the scene.

4–6 What wonder . . . no fruit.] Cf. *Arden I*, viii. 66–7, 'I pray thee, Mosby, let our springtime wither; | Our harvest else will yield but loathsome weeds.'

7–10 I come . . . consume us.] Cf. *Arden I*, viii. 46–9:

> MOSBY. Make me partaker of thy pensiveness;
> Fire divided burns with lesser force.
> ALICE. But I will dam that fire in my breast
> Till by the force thereof my part consume.

22 avarice, insolence, and pride] As in Mosby's earlier confrontation with Arden (I. iii), the adaptation retains a suggestion but makes little point of Mosby's ambitions and lower-class origin (see I. ii. 35b n., and ll. 25–8 below). In *Arden I* Alice's angriest accusation, against herself as well as Mosby, is that he 'bewitched' her to love a 'mean artificer' (viii. 77–8), and this becomes a central theme of the quarrel.

31 babes] so L; D prints 'children'. The variant does not appear to involve an alteration in the sense of the line. While it seems unlikely that the substitution of 'children' for 'babes' occurred through scribal or compositorial slip, it is also difficult to explain the change as a late improvement. Such detailed editorial adjustment is not characteristic of D; since Arden and Alicia have been married only three years, it is not inappropriate to call their children 'babes' (cf. l. 29); and there is no indication elsewhere of a concern to alter words that might be taken as archaic or self-consciously poetical. The reading in L maintains the metre, made awkward by the variant in D, and has therefore been followed.

58 in time] 'soon enough (before it is too late)' is the probable meaning, but 'soon' or 'quickly' is also possible (*OED*).

80 exalted] in context, 'intense, carried to a high degree' (with reference to feelings, sentiments) seems the appropriate sense; however, in conjunction with 'sincere', the more usual sense of 'elevated, lofty in character, noble' could have been intended (*OED*).

III. iii

The scene is based on scene iv of *Arden I*, which, in the sequence of events and especially in Michael's decision to prevent the intended murder, it follows quite closely. The import of the opening dialogue concerning jealousy has been altered in the adaptation; in *Arden I* Arden at this point confirms and Franklin accepts the certainty of Alice's infidelity. The shift of scene (71b+SD) and the pair of lines in which Black Will and Shakebag react to discovering the door shut against them are a condensation of *Arden I*, v, a scene of some 63 lines.

SD *Another room in* Arden's *house.*] In *Arden I* the setting is Franklin's house in London.

12–15 What fools . . . alike deceive!] The lines summarize a soliloquy on jealousy spoken by Franklin (*Arden I*, iv. 39–54).

16–18 To cast . . . to yourself.] Franklin takes a very different view of the situation in *Arden I*, iv. 22–6:

> She will amend, and so your griefs will cease;
> Or else she'll die, and so your sorrows end.
> If neither of these two do haply fall,
> Yet let your comfort be that others bear
> Your woes twice doubled all with patience.

19a strucken] *OED* cites this form as used regularly during the 16th to 19th cents.; 'striken', the form given by L, is noted as in use during the 14th to 17th cents.

54 Insulting] contemptuously exulting, scornfully delighting (*OED*, which notes the regular use of the construction 'to insult over'). The usage here—with 'daggers' apparently to be taken as the subject for 'Insulting'—is odd. The lines in the adaptation closely echo but also condense and rearrange a passage in *Arden I*:

> Methinks I see them with their bolstered hair,
> Staring and grinning in thy gentle face,
> And in their ruthless hands their daggers drawn,
> Insulting o'er thee with a peck of oaths
> Whilst thou, submissive, pleading for relief,
> Art mangled by their ireful instruments.

(iv. 72–7)

The syntax and punctuation of these lines will allow 'daggers' as subject for 'Insulting', and conceivably the adapter read them in this way. However, the syntactical parallel between 'Staring' (73) and 'Insulting' strongly suggests that both refer back to 'them', a less strained interpretation. This situation could, in turn, suggest that the adapter meant to recreate the sense and structure of the line in his source (75), and that in the text of *Arden II* a comma has been omitted after 'daggers'—if inserted, the comma would allow 'Insulting' to relate to 'oaths' or an implicit 'them' (the murderers rather than their weapons). However, the reading of the copy-text is supported by L, and it has a clear and not undramatic sense. Moreover, if 'daggers insulting' compares oddly with the most closely related phrasing in *Arden I*, in its rhetorical effect the construction does have something of a parallel in 'ireful instruments', which appears a few lines later in the passage.

54 mangled body] The phrase given by L, 'Murder'd Corse', presumably represents an earlier version of the line, which required alteration since the following line describes the victim as still able to call for mercy.

71b+SD *Scene changes . . . door shut.*] The change could be effected quickly by the closing of the shutters (painted scene-panels which moved in grooves to close off or reveal the upstage area). The shutters, probably a stock street scene, may have included a house front and door, but one of the proscenium doors could also have been used for Black Will's and Shakebag's brief scene.

IV. i

The scene has no precise counterpart in *Arden I*. It is, in a sense, a composite in which a substantial amount of material introduced by the adapter is combined with glancing references to several scenes in the original play. Such references include Michael's excuses about the locked doors (*Arden I*, vii), Mosby's response to Alicia's rejection of him (viii), Green's view of Arden's providential escapes (ix), and Mosby's new scheme to prove that he is Arden's friend by defending him in a contrived street fight (a variation of a plot devised by Alice in scene xii and revised by her in scene xiii).

1–3 Tho' I . . . kill'd me.] The lines summarize scene vii of *Arden I*.

18b shure] *OED* notes this variant of 'sure' as current only during the 17th cent.

19–21 Have I . . . an husband!] Verbal echoes link this portion of Mosby's speech with *Arden I*, viii. 83–9. See headnote to III. ii.

24–5 How strange . . . it o'er.] Cf. *Arden I*, ix. 142, '*Greene*. The Lord of Heaven hath preservèd him.' Greene makes nothing more of this, nor does he suggest that the plot to kill Arden should be abandoned. The variation between *Arden I* and *Arden II* exemplifies the greater explicitness with which the adaptation assigns Arden's escapes to providential intervention.

32SD [*To* Michael.]] Ed. In D and L the direction is placed at the end of l. 32, the position usual for directions indicating actions but which in this instance inserts into the middle of a sentence the instruction indicating how it is to be spoken.

34b–46 I've thought . . . easy heart.] In *Arden I*, xii. 65–73, Alice proposes that she and Mosby present themselves to Arden in the street in such a way that he will draw on Mosby in anger, providing occasion for Black Will and Shakebag to intervene in Mosby's defence and give Arden a fatal wound. Attempted in scene xiii, the scheme goes awry when Arden wounds both Mosby and Shakebag. However, since Alice has had the wit to call for help for her husband at the start of the fight, she is able to deceive Arden doubly, first convincing him of her own innocence and his excessive, unfounded jealousy, then persuading him to accept Mosby as a well-meaning friend who has been wrongfully injured.

IV. ii

The scene—the reconciliation of Arden and Alicia—is the invention of the adapter(s) and has no precedent in *Arden I*.

36 *Argus's*] In mythology (e.g. Ovid, *Metamorphoses*, book I), Argus Panoptes, who had 100 eyes, only two of which slept at any one time. A jealous Juno set him to watch Io, a mistress of Jupiter whom the god, in an effort to deceive his wife, had turned into a heifer.

68 silent self-condemn'd] self-condemned by her silence.

75a stains] so L; D prints 'pains', a reading which, in context, is awkward at best and conceivably was set in error as a parallel to 'anguish', the key word in Alicia's preceding speech. Clearly it is the stain of Alicia's guilt, not the pain of her distress, which her tears might wash away.

89c canst] earlier the standard form, second person present indicative; *OED* notes no examples later than 1610.

103 conscious] in a figurative sense, attributed to inanimate things as sharing in or witnessing human actions or secrets (*OED*). See l. 150, 'conscious innocence' and n.

127 mine.] L reads 'mine?', pointing which would inappropriately alter the sense of the line and dramatic situation.

131 yearly fair . . . *St. Valentine*] *Arden I*, xiv. 42, refers to 'the fair' but mentions neither its date nor St Valentine. The detail in *Arden II* might be taken to suggest reference to Holinshed, 'But now saint Valentines faire being at hand . . .' (reprinted by Wine, p. 153). However, there is minimal evidence elsewhere to suggest that the adapter consulted Holinshed, and the adaptation, like *Arden I*, omits any reference to the

chronicler's account of Arden's having taken over the fair, 'so reaping all the gains to himself'. Conceivably the association of the murder with the St Valentine's holiday was a part of the popular tradition of the Arden drama which, in a variety of forms, was frequently produced in Kent throughout the 18th cent. (Rosenfeld, *Strolling Players*, p. 219).

133 chear] cheer. *OED* notes the form as current 16th–18th cents.

136bSD [*Exit* Arden.] The direction, included in L, is omitted by D. Arden's lines (130–6a) are clearly intended as an exit speech and, while it might be argued that in her lines which follow Alicia says nothing that could not be heard by her husband, the tone as well as the dramatic situation identify them as a solo speech comparable to II. ii. 17–31, iii. 43b–50, and III. ii. 96–103. Since D also fails to give a stage direction at the end of the scene, it is impossible to know whether the compositor thought that Alicia was alone for her speech or overheard by Arden.

147 collected] in a figurative sense, having one's thoughts or feelings at command or in order; composed, self-possessed (*OED*).

150 conscious] in the sense of being endowed by the faculty or presence of consciousness; said of persons or their attributes (*OED*). Cf. *The London Merchant*, v. iii. 2; *The Christian Hero*, I. i. 201, 243; *Elmerick*, III. i. 254.

IV. iii

The scene has two sources in *Arden I*. The street fight and Arden's acceptance of Mosby as his friend are based on *Arden I*, xiii. 77–155. The adapter's substantial alterations include omitting Alice from the episode, substituting Mosby for Alice as the person chiefly responsible for contriving and carrying out the scheme to dupe Arden, and changing the details of the scheme itself (see IV. i. 34b–46 n.). The final portion of the scene in *Arden II* (ll. 56–85) draws on *Arden I*, xiv, especially ll. 78–140, in which Alice, assisted by Mosby, Greene, Will, and Shakebag, contrives the ultimately successful plan for murdering Arden.

16 reflexion] thought or idea occurring to the mind (*OED*). Arden's speech continues an idea and sentence begun in l. 14b.

26 reek'd] wreak'd (and so printed in W1). *OED* lists 'reak', but not 'reek', as a variant form current during the 18th cent.

45–51 *Ard.* No doubt . . . than ever.] not in L. Possibly the lines represent a late addition intended to underscore Arden's credulousness and Franklin's suspicions about Mosby. Arden's speech at l. 52 is a not inappropriate response to the question posed by Franklin in l. 44, and variants in the pointing of a portion of l. 52 further suggest that the line may originally have followed l. 44: in L 'What, a churl?' clearly refers to Mosby and serves well as a response to Franklin's initial question about him; in D 'What a churl!' must refer instead to Franklin and is appropriate only if it follows the extended discussion of Mosby not included in L. It must, however, be noted that the rhetorically effective echo of l. 51 in the first half of l. 52 could be taken to indicate that the lines were written at the same time and therefore that the passage omitted by L was not an afterthought.

68 draughts] See v. i. 83a n.

V. i

The scene is based on *Arden I*, xiv. 112–271 and 328–50. The sequence of actions leading to and following the murder of Arden and the details of the murder itself are much the same in the adaptation as in *Arden I*. The action is condensed, and *Arden II* omits an episode in which the dinner guests arrive and are sent away while the conspirators remove the body from the house. Reactions to the central events and the nature of the scene itself are greatly altered, primarily as a result of the fundamental changes in the character and motivation of Arden's wife. Where Alicia (*Arden II*) opposes and would prevent the murder if she could, Alice (*Arden I*) plans, supervises, and finally takes a hand in the killing. Alicia's opening soliloquy and the scene in which she begs Black Will, Shakebag, and Green to spare Arden's life are essentially inventions of the adapter, as is Arden's extended death scene. The adapter also adds the pangs of guilt which afflict the conspirators immediately after the murder, although *Arden I* does include an episode in which the horror of the killing and her part in it are made real for Alice by her discovery of bloodstains which cannot be washed from the floor (a possibly supernatural detail omitted from the adaptation). A number of other variations between original and adaptation have less effect on the structure or intentions of the scene—e.g. in *Arden I* Greene is not present at the murder, though he arrives in time to assist in disposing of the body; in *Arden II* Mosby's sister (Maria) is involved with the conspirators only to the extent of trying to protect her brother after the murder, but the text of *Arden I* makes it clear that the girl (Susan) would be a willing accomplice, though in fact she does not know about the murder until it has been done; in *Arden I*, Black Will and Shakebag do not plan to return and plunder the house but, satisfied with the payment given them by Alice, make speed to leave the country.

17 whiteliver'd] cowardly; according to an old notion a light-coloured liver was the result of a deficiency of bile or 'choler' and thus indicated a lack of spirit or courage (*OED*). The term normally appears in hyphenated form or as a phrase of two words; *OED* cites no example of the term printed as a single word.

19–27 Had he . . . encounters her.] Green's expressions of furious hatred are introduced by the adapter, as is his presence in this portion of the scene. They serve to establish and heighten the desperateness of the situation confronting Alicia. They also substitute for similarly vindictive speeches spoken by Alice before the murder in *Arden I*.

40 hast] haste; *OED* citations indicate that 'hast' was in frequent use during the 17th and early 18th cents. but became uncommon by the middle of the 18th.

67 husband's] so D; L gives 'Husband'. D is not easy syntactically, and 'husband's' may represent the erroneous printing of the word in the form in which it appears in the line which follows. However, the reading is not strictly incorrect; it strengthens the rhetorically effective parallel with l. 68 and may well have been intended.

81a–81b For her . . . dissembler.] The verse is irregular, two short lines or a single, over-long line. Lineation of the present edition follows D and W1.

83a the Tables] In *Arden I* Alice, preparing for Arden to arrive with Mosby, calls for Michael to 'Fetch in the tables' (xiv. 157). 'Tables' was the ordinary name for backgammon (*OED*), and the dialogue which accompanies the game in *Arden I* calls for the dice-throwing that characterizes backgammon. In the adaptation the game is draughts (cf. IV. iii. 68), and the use of 'tables' here is curious since 'tables' seems not to have served as an alternative name for games other than backgammon. The phrase 'to play at tables' did come to apply to a variety of board-games, including draughts. Possibly the adapter understood 'tables' in this broader sense. Nothing in the text, however, suggests a reason for the choice of draughts in place of backgammon in *Arden II*.

95b Now I take *you*.] The phrase is also used to signal the murder in *Arden I* (cf. xiv. 104 ['Now I take you.'] and 232 ['Now I can take you.']).

102 unequall'd] so L; D prints 'unequal', a reading which at first glance may seem clear, at least in its implication, but which proves on analysis to be puzzling at best. *OED* notes 'unequal' in the sense of 'disproportionate, excessive' as an obsolete use of the word employed only during the early 18th cent.; the examples cited do not provide persuasive parallels with the construction in the *Arden I* text. Other senses of the word used with single subjects involve elements of inadequacy or negative excess, inappropriate in the context of Arden's speech, which calls for a word emphasizing the generosity of his love (e.g. 'greater', 'unmatched'). While it is possible that the reading in D represents a rare use of 'unequal' in a special and unusual sense, it seems best to adopt the clear and unambiguous alternative provided by L.

104b–124 *Ard. O Mosby . . . her hate.*] The extended, highly emotional development of Arden's death scene in the 18th-cent. adaptation contrasts sharply with the spareness of the 16th-cent. original: pulled down by Will, Arden cries out, 'Mosby! Michael! Alice! What will you do?' (xiv. 233); Mosby, Shakebag, and Alice stab him in turn, and he dies without speaking again.

130a Prevent] in a now archaic theological sense, to go before with spiritual guidance and help; said of God, or his grace anticipating human action or need (*OED*, which includes a citation from Bishop Thomas Ken, 'Divine Love' [pre-1711], *Works* [1838], p. 303, 'O let thy grace . . . ever prevent, accompany, and follow me').

148b *Mosby!*] so L; D omits. L maintains the metre in a passage (147a–148b) in which D mistakes the lineation of the verse.

170 Give me the ring] The use of the ring, which serves to incriminate Mosby (cf. v. iii. 95a), is an invention of the adapter but may have been suggested by *Arden I*, i. 17–18 (Arden), 'Nay, on his finger I did spy the ring | Which at our marriage day the priest put on.'

181 mist] an alternative form for 'missed', current during the 14th to 19th cents. (*OED*, which cites a number of 18th-cent. examples).

v. ii

The scene is for the most part the work of the adapter. It provides an opportunity to introduce a key scene for Mosby late in the play and to sort out certain essential plot details, some of which are drawn from *Arden I*, xiv, while others are invented for the adaptation. Mosby plays a relatively small part in the episodes which immediately follow the murder in *Arden I*, and at this stage of the play he shows no sign of remorse. For the soliloquy which opens the scene in *Arden II* and the speech with which it closes, the adapter made considerable use of ideas and language found in *Arden I*, viii. 1–22, a soliloquy in which Mosby, in a quite different context, regrets the troubles and dangers which have come to him through his ambitious efforts to better himself.

9–21 now count . . . my soul.] Cf. *Arden I*, viii. 11–18:

> My golden time was when I had no gold;
> Though then I wanted, yet I slept secure;
> My daily toil begat me night's repose;
> My night's repose made daylight fresh to me.
> But, since I climbed the top bough of the tree
> And sought to build my nest among the clouds,
> Each gentle starry gale doth shake my bed
> And makes me dread my downfall to the earth.

While echoing the original text much more extensively than is usual in the adaptation, the passage in *Arden II* is notable also in focusing on Mosby's ambition, a theme of which much is made in *Arden I* but which has been developed minimally in the earlier scenes of *Arden II*.

11 starting] the participial adjective, literally 'that starts'—i.e. leaping, energized, making sudden movement (*OED*). The reading in D seems preferable to 'staring' in L, though 'staring' in the now obsolete sense of 'frantic' or 'wild' is conceivable (*OED*).

11 conscience, . . . wounds] so L; D provides no pointing after 'conscience' but prints a comma following 'wounds'. The line is at best awkward to interpret. L's punctuation, which treats 'my starting conscience' as an apostrophe, does make sense syntactically. Emending 'mark' to 'marks' would allow D's pointing to stand, and provide an easier reading of the passage. The additional variant in this line (noted above) suggests that at this point the manuscript from which both L and D derived was difficult to follow.

28 It snow'd] The adaptation follows *Arden I*, xiv. 357–9, in establishing carefully the timing of the snowfall, a situation which will be important in the discovery of the murderers.

28 apace] so L; D prints 'a pace', an older form reflecting the origin of the word ('of pace', later 'a pace'); *OED* cites no example of 'a pace' later than 1553, though one 18th-cent. example of 'a-pace' is given. It seems likely that the reading in D represents not reversion to the obsolete form but an error, perhaps a misreading of 'a pace' as the noun preceded by an article.

31b–34a *Maria*'s mine . . . her mine.—] In *Arden I*, xiv. 292–3, Michael makes his claim directly to Susan (Maria), rather than to her brother, and she seems ready to accept him, thus resolving a subplot in which she, Alice, and Mosby have played him off against a rival suitor. Subplot and rival are omitted from *Arden II*, and only Mosby encourages Michael in his hope to have Maria. In adjusting the situation, the adapter may have seen an opportunity to provide an additional instance of Mosby's duplicity. The frustration of Michael's hopes also contributes to the morally edifying pattern of conspirators who fail to achieve the ambitions for which they were ready to commit murder. In any case, the outcome of the situation as presented in *Arden II* is in accord with the altered characterization of Maria: an innocent used by her brother, she neither flirts with Michael nor plays a part in the plot to kill Arden; it would be inappropriate for her to be handed over or to give herself to one of those who co-operated in the murder.

42 twixt their teeth] so L; omitted by D, thereby destroying the metre in an otherwise regular passage of verse. The omission produces no alteration in meaning that might indicate a deliberate deletion. It seems best to restore the verse line on the assumption that the final phrase was dropped inadvertently by D or its source.

V. iii

The scene is based on a portion of scene xiv and on scenes xvi and xviii of *Arden I*. Except for condensing and occasionally adjusting the order of events, the adaptation follows quite closely the series of actions which leads to the discovery of the murderers, the evidence which confirms their guilt, and the resolution of the play. However, the adapter draws these elements together in a single scene and location, and contrives to bring all of the conspirators on stage to be arrested and led away together. *Arden I* is less neatly rounded off; it is left to the epilogue to tie up loose ends of plot and make it clear that all of the conspirators eventually were punished or otherwise came to appropriately bad ends. The tense situation created by Alicia's frantic distress and the possibility that she will reveal the murder is suggested by the characterization of Alice in *Arden I*, though Alice, unlike Alicia, does not fully repent her part in the conspiracy until she is taken to look at Arden's body (xvi), an incident omitted from the adaptation.

SD Green, Bradshaw, Adam Fowl] The adaptation differs from *Arden I* in bringing these characters on stage for the denouement of the drama. In the original play Greene disappears after he exits to assist with the disposal of the body (xiv. 350SD). Bradshaw and Fowle arrive at Arden's house as guests (xiv. 271+SD), but they exit before the discovery of the body. Fowle is not seen again. Bradshaw reappears briefly as the conspirators are led off at the end of the play (xviii).

10a I'll take his seat] Cf. *Arden I*, xiv. 287 (Alice), 'Master Mosby, sit you in my husband's seat.'

17 admiration] astonishment, surprise (*OED*). Cf. *The London Merchant*, III. iv. 2.

19 Health and . . . to *Arden*.] Mosby offers a similar toast in *Arden I*, xiv. 299.

22 dispatch] Two interpretations of the word are possible: (1) dispose of, dismiss (me); (2) make haste (*OED*). The comma set after 'dispatch' suggests the second as the easier interpretation. However, 'me' (after 'send') can stand as the object of the transitive verb and, in context, this is the more persuasive reading.

48 misboding] to forebode (something evil) (*OED*, which cites this line).

53 him] so L; omission by D is clearly an error.

54SD [*Without*.]] L omits and instead, before Franklin's speech, gives the stage direction for him and the others to enter (55+SD). Franklin's words—'Within there— ho . . .'—indicate that he calls from off-stage and that the sequence of directions in D is correct.

68 security] sense of assurance, confidence (*OED*).

70SD [Alicia *is carried out*.] The stage direction is supplied by the editor; neither D nor L provides an exit for Alicia, but at l. 115 D calls for her to be '*brought in*', indicating that at some point earlier she must have exited or been carried out. The problem appears to reflect late adjustments in the staging, very possibly introduced during production in the theatre and incompletely recorded by D. The changes themselves seem to have stemmed from a concern, perhaps as a matter of propriety, that the search of Alicia's person be done off-stage rather than in front of the audience. The text of L calls for Alicia to remain on stage throughout the scene and, at an order from the mayor (92–3), 'The officers search Mosby, Green & Alicia.' (93+SD). In D, the mayor's speech (92–3) is revised to have him order an officer to enter another room to 'search the lady there'. In the absence of a direction indicating Alicia's exit, the mayor's line is in itself ambiguous, meaning either 'take the lady there and search her' or 'search the lady you will find there'. However, the stage direction which follows is unambiguous in calling for one officer to go out and re-enter while another officer '*in the mean time searches* Mosby *and* Green'. Alicia must then have exited or been carried out earlier in the scene, and the present editor has inserted a stage direction which takes her off-stage at what appears to be the one point in the action at which dramatic logic will allow this to be done. The situation has clearly the characteristics of theatrical patchwork, especially the too-quick sequence of the officer's exit, supposed off-stage search of Alicia, and re-entrance, all of which is to be covered on stage only by the searches of Mosby and Green for which no lines are supplied. Minor variations between D and L at 21cSD, 54SD and 55+SD also suggest that D or its source to some extent incorporated adjustments in stage directions made during or after production.

71 along] so L; D prints 'a long', clearly an error (*OED* notes no such form except in the sense of 'lengthwise', current in the 15th cent.).

76 these notes] Franklin's notes, the blood and hair seen on the garden wall, and the rushes found stuck to Arden's clothes are details invented by the adapter. Other items of evidence, however, are taken from *Arden I*, xiv—e.g. the footprints in the snow (394–5) and the scarf (a 'hand-towel', 383b).

92–3 Enter that . . . discover more.] L reads 'Search 'em: we may perhaps discover more.' See v. iii. 70SD n.

94 this letter] *Arden I* does not dramatize the discovery of the letter, but reference is made to it in the accusation against Bradshaw (xviii. 4).

95a this ring] See v. i. 170 n.

99 *Mos.* I freely . . . my fate.] not in L. Almost certainly the line was inserted late, perhaps even in the theatre, when it was realized that the text had provided no opportunity for Mosby to speak or otherwise react to the discovery of evidence certainly condemning him as the chief among Arden's murderers. The alteration involved the deletion of a half-line—'Worshipful sir'—which in L begins the officer's speech that now follows Mosby's line and originally completed the truncated line of verse at the end of the mayor's speech above (98). That the inserted line is peculiarly abrupt and undramatic, and that apparently no effort was made to relate it to the relatively regular verse of the passage into which it was dropped, are further indications that it represents an afterthought.

It is puzzling that the potential drama of the unmasking of the play's villain was seemingly ignored by the adapter(s) (see Introduction, Source). However, except for this one, interpolated line, neither D nor L provides evidence that the text of this portion of the scene was incomplete or in some way problematic.

100–9 *Officer.* We've seiz'd . . . and *Michael's.*] In *Arden I* Black Will and Shakebag are not immediately apprehended. They are last seen in brief monologues (xv and xvii) as they prepare to flee the country, and their deaths are described in the epilogue. Their confessions, which in *Arden II* neatly set out the list of conspirators and the ways in which each has been involved in the murder plot, are inventions of the adapter.

100 We've seiz'd] so D; L writes 'Worshipful Sir, | We've seiz'd'. See above, n. 99.

103 villany] the regular form of the word in the 18th cent.; 'villainy', a rare form before the 18th cent., did not become established until the 19th cent.

107 to hide him] i.e. to act in secret on his behalf in order that his own involvement in the scheme should not be discovered.

115 our's] a form regularly interchangeable with 'ours' during the 17th to 19th cents.

126–9a She has . . . and wonder.] The adaptation follows *Arden I* in including Maria (Susan) and Bradshaw among those who are condemned for the murder. Adam Fowle is not among those accused in *Arden I*, although he is so included (or fears that he is) in *Arden II* (cf. 135b–7). In the adaptation Fowl is at Arden's house when the mayor and the watch arrive; all others there are certainly implicated in the murder, and the adapter may have felt that it would be logical for the mayor to arrest the entire group. The situation could also suggest reference to Holinshed's *Chronicles*, which reports that Fowle was arrested and released, some time later, when he had proved his innocence. (Holinshed, reprinted by Wine, p. 159.)

Epilogue

By a FRIEND.] The author of the epilogue has not been identified.

3 *The seasoning . . . the applause*] The quotation, as the footnote in D indicates, is taken from Ben Jonson's *Volpone*. It is the first line of the epilogue, spoken by Volpone.

HISTORICAL COLLATIONS

A LIST of sigla will be found at the head of this volume. In each entry, the reading of the present edition appears first, followed by the variant readings and the sigla of the texts in which they appear. A consecutive series of editions is indicated by an en-dash between the sigla for the first and last: e.g. G2–5 means all editions from the second to the fifth. A caret (∧) indicates the omission of pointing or a letter. Angle-brackets (⟨ ⟩) indicate that material missing from copies collated has had to be inferred or omitted. Material crossed out in manuscripts is enclosed in curly brackets ({ }). 'Ed.' stands for 'Editor'.

The swung dash (~) represents one or more identifying words that do not vary, usually in entries recording variant accidentals. Thus:

well;] G5–7; ~, G1–4

The entry reports that, like the present edition, the fifth, sixth, and seventh editions print a semicolon after 'well' but the first, second, third, and fourth editions print a comma. Similarly:

(That . . . anguish)] ∧~ . . . ~,∧ L

The entry reports that the Larpent manuscript differs from the present edition in omitting the parentheses and including a comma at the end of the quoted phrase; there is no variation in the words of the phrase.

When a group of texts agree in a variation of some length but differ in minor details, the sub-variants, with appropriate sigla, follow the record of the major variant and are enclosed in parantheses. Thus:

over paid.] ~? G2–3, 6–7 (over-paid G7)

The entry indicates that the second, third, sixth, and seventh editions print a question mark where the present edition prints a full stop, but the seventh edition also hyphenates the words quoted. Similarly, when one or more texts match the present text in all but one detail while the other texts vary extensively, the minor variant is given in parentheses after the reading of the present text and immediately followed by the citation of the more extensive variant:

Crimes,—] (Crime G1, *earlier state*) ~.∧ G2–7

The entry indicates that the earlier state of the first edition varies from the present edition in misprinting 'Crime' for 'Crimes' while the second to seventh editions correctly print 'Crimes' but alter the text by substituting a full stop for the comma and omitting the dash.

Editorial parentheses and square brackets are not stylistically distinguished from those that occur in the texts of editions quoted in the notes. In the rare instances in which editorial and original parentheses or brackets do coincide, context and the spacing of the type should help the reader to avoid confusion.

THE LONDON MERCHANT

Dedication

G7 *omits the dedication*   2 some where] somewhere G6   9 Scenes] Scene G6
Deference,] ~_∧ G3–6 (Defference G5)   10 wou'd] would G2–6   12 wou'd] would G6
13 Dignity,] ~_∧ G2–6   18 liable] liablc G5   19 wou'd] would G6   23 instructive]
Instructive G5   24 or a] or G3–6   Fable] Fables G3–6   25 introduced] iutroduced G5
26 Contrast] Contract G1 (*earlier state*)   27 its] irs G5   28 former,] ~; G5–6
33 Constitution] Constitu-|on G5   Liberties] Libetties G5   42 Lines,] *Ed.*; ~. G1–6
44 *Tears*] ~, G2–6   46 *appale*] *appall* G2–6   47 *Ignorant*] *Ign'rant* G2–6   *amaze*
indeed] *amazeindeed* G1 (*earlier state*)   49 farther,] ~_∧ G5–6   Speech,] ~; G5–6
52 *Been so*] *Beenso* G1 (*some copies*)   55 perswaded] persuaded G3–6   58–9 *noble*
Father's Form] G2–6; noble Father's Form G1   59 *Spirit*] G2–6; Spirit G1   *I'll have*]
G2–6; I'll have G1   60 *Grounds more relative*] G2–6 (re-|*lative* G2; ~: G5–6); Grounds
more | relative G1   64 would] wou'd G3–5   69 Sir, I] SIR, | I (*indent*) G2–6
72 my self] my-|self G5–6   74 inferior] inferiour G5   77 declared] declar'd G6
78 confined] confin'd G6   79 Persons,] G2–6; ~; G1   82 Sub-Governor] Sub-
Governour G5   83 Neither] G2–6; Nor G1   84–5 a Character so well known,]
G5–6; your | Character, G1–4   91–2 *obedient humble*] *Obedient* | *Humble* G3–6

Prologue

PROLOGUE.] ~, G6   Spoke] Spoken G5–7   *Jun.*] jun. G6; Jun. G7   4 *Heroe's*]
Hero's G6–7   5 *know*] ~, G7   9 *Supream*] Supreme G6; supreme G7   11 *Foreign*]
foreign G2–7   12 *Grandure*] Grandeur G2–7   13 *Stage*] ~, G5–7   14 a] an G6–7
16 Rowe's] Row's G6   17 *Drops,*] ~_∧ G7   18 *Jems*] Gems G6–7   19 *Forgive*]
G3–7 indent   24 *moral*] *mortal* G5   *ere*] G3–7; e'er G1–2   26 *thousand-thousand*]
~_∧~ G5–7   27 *If*] G2–7 indent   29 *insure*] G2–7; secure G1   30 *Prevent*]
Prevents G1 (*earlier state*)   31 Millwood's] Milwood's G7   Crimes] G2–7; Guilt G1
32 *Fair;*] G5–7; ~, G1–4   33 *wanting,*] ~_∧ G4   34 *th' Attempt*] the ~ G5–7

Dramatis Personæ

2 Thorowgood,] ~. G6–7   3 *Uncle to* George] ~, G3–6; ~. G7   4 Barnwell,] ~. G7
5 Trueman,] ~. G6–7   6 Blunt,] ~. G6–7   *Wetherilt*] *Witherhilt* G3–4; *Witherhile* G5–7
8 Maria,] ~. G6–7   9 Millwood,] ~. G6–7   *Butler*] G2–7; Butler G1   10 Lucy,]
~. G6; Lucia. G7

Title

London] London G6; LONDON G7   Merchant] MERCHANT G7   *GEORGE BARNWELL*]
GEORGE BARNWELL G6–7

I.i

SD Thorowgood] *Enter* Thorowgood G3–7   1 arriv'd] arrived G5–7 (arriv-|ed G5)
2 Heav'n] Heaven G6–7   praised,] prais'd, G2–7 (~! G5–7)   the] The G5–7   threaten'd]
threatn'd G5–7   3 Liberty,] ~_∧ G5   5 return] Return G3–6 (Re-|turn G3–4, 6)
6 ere] e'er G1; e'er G6–7   Island;] ~, G4   7 means] Means G3–7   10 means] Means
G2–4; Means? G5–7   bold—] ~.— G2–4   13 Country,] ~; G3–4   times] Times
G3–7   15 on] upon G2–7   16 may] ~, G2–7   Scorn] ~, G2–7   18 Conduct] ~,
G2–7   19 excuse] Excuse G2–7   20 complement] compliment G7   Man.] ~_∧ G7
22 means] Means G2–7   heed] Heed G2–6   23 Complaisant] complaisant G7
24 Question,—] ~._∧ G5–7   Interest] ~, G2–7   25 Money] ~, G2–7
26 Armado,—] ~;_∧ G2–7   *Elizabeth*] ~, G2–6   28 City,] ~; G2–7   30 done,] ~;
G5–7   31 weigh'd] weighed G2–7 (~, G4–6; weigh-|ed, G7)   32 *London,*] ~_∧ G7
33 stiles] styles G7   both *Indies*] both*Indies* G3   34 Councils!] G2–7; ~. G1
35 —Excellent] _∧~ G2–7   those] G2–7; to former G1   36 make] G2–7; made G1

foreign] Foreign G6–7   Subjects,] ~ ₍∧₎ G5–7   38 Queen,] ~; G5–7   Peoples] People's
G3–7   40 us,] ~ ₍∧₎ G7   41 —Sir] G5–7; ₍∧₎~ G2–4; *Tr.* Sir G1, *printing as beginning of*
a new speech   43 look] G2–7; to look G1   Files] ~, G2–7   43–4 Trades-|mens]
Tradesmens G2–7   44 if] G2–7; and if G1   send] G2–7; to send G1   46 Attendance.]
after this line G3–7 *add* SD: [*Exit* Trueman.

I. ii

SCENE II.] G3–7 *omit*   SD Thorowgood *and* Maria.] *Enter* Maria. G3–7 (~.] G5–7, *which*
run on from SD *after* I. i. 46)   1 Thor.] G5–7 *omit speech-heading and run on from* SD *following*
I. i. 46   Maria,] ~ ₍∧₎ G4   2 plenty] Plenty G4–7   3 Courtiers] G3–7; ~, tho' they
should deny us Citizens Politeness, G1–2   4 endeavoured] endeavour'd G4–7
6 Caution,] ~; G5–7   cause] Cause G4–7   7 Sir!] ~, G2–7   my self] myself G5–6
Conversation] ~; G2–7   at present,] G2–7 *omit*   9 Child,] ~! G5–7   indulged.] ~, G6
10 it.] ~: G2–7   16 He] ~, G5–7   17 is] ~, G2–7   18 chuses] chooses G7
22 Disrespect] disrespect G7   27 Your's no doubt] Your's, ~, G2–7   29 thee;] ~:
G5–7   30 thine;] G5–7; ~, G1–4   Pleasure] ~, G5–7   31 Love,] ~ ₍∧₎ G7
32 leave] Leave G2–7   you,] ~, G2–7   33 that] ~, G5–7   Observation] ~, G3–7
34 for] ~, G2–7   38 Parents:] ~? G5–7   39 Croud] Crowd G4–7
40 Courtiers,] ~ ₍∧₎ G7   41 observed] observ'd G4   43 sacrificed] sacrifice G6–7
45 wou'd] would G4–7   Byass] Biass G7   48 but] G2–7; ~, G1   50 wou'd]
would G3–7   shou'd] should G4–7   53 Inclinations,] ~; G3–7   55 love] Love G6
so] G3–7 *omit*   Duty.] ~—G5–7   56 retire?] G2–7; ~. G1   57 Chamber.] *after this*
line G3–7 *add* SD: [*Exeunt.*

I. iii

SCENE III.] SCENE II.   SD Millwood's] Millwood's G4   *at her Toilet*] G3–7; *not in* G1–2
waiting] G2–7; *Waiting* G1   2 Madam!—] ~!, G5–7   5 Conquest] G2–7; ~, G1
wou'd] would G6–7   6 me.] ~ ₍∧₎ G2–7   7 am:] ~! G5–7   13 And] ~, G5
sure] ~, G5–7   hav'n't] ha'n't G3–5; ha'nt G6; han't G7   15 Men.] ~.— G3–4
18 themselves.—] ~. ₍∧₎ G5–7   Victors] Victor's G5–7   20 compleat] complete G7
21 New World] new World G3   24 politick,] ~ ₍∧₎ G3–4   25 Imployment]
Employment G4–7   31 so?] G5–7; ~. G1–3; ~ ₍∧₎ G4   —But] ₍∧₎~ G5–7
33 injured] injur'd G6–7   35 Ay,] ~ ₍∧₎ G6–7   36 Such] such G6   think,] ~ ₍∧₎ G3–4
37 Money;] ~: G7   40 made,] G2–7; ~. G1   and has a good Face.] G2–7; *not in* G1
42 Eighteen—] ~.— G2–3; ~. ₍∧₎ G5–7   43 Eighteen.—] ~! G2–7   44 your self]
yourself G5–7   46 sooner.] G5–7; ~, G1–4   Having] G5–7; having G1–4
47 him,] G5–7; ~; G1–4   48 blush'd,] ~ ₍∧₎ G6   51 Place.] ~: G5–7
52 named] nam'd G6–7   talk'd] talked G3–5   54 him.] G5–7; ~, G1–4   Some Body]
Some body G7   knocks,] ~; G5–7   hear;] ~, G3–7   55 no Body] no body G7
to Day] to day G7   him.—] ~. ₍∧₎ G2–7; *after this line* G3–7 *add* SD: [*Exit* Lucy.] (₍∧₎~ *Lucy.* ₍∧₎ G3;
₍∧₎~. ₍∧₎ G4; *Lucy* G5–6)

I. iv

SCENE IV.] G3–7 *omit*   SD Millwood.] G3–7 *omit*   1 G1, 3–4 *include speech-heading:*
Mill.; G5–7 *run on from* SD *after* I. iii. 55   Way] way G7   2 too,] ~ ₍∧₎ G6–7   3 Now,]
~ ₍∧₎ G3–7   4 receive?] ~ ₍∧₎ G7   —He] ₍∧₎~ G2–7   5 bashful;] ~: G3–7   put him
out of Countenance,] G3–7; shock him G1–2   6 Phisiognomy] Physiognomy G7
amorous,] amorous; G5–7   7 Modesty.] ~, G6–7   e'en] G3–7; *not in* G1–2
8 one] G7 *omits*   9 liked] lik'd G6–7   10 Woman,] ~— G3–7

I. v

SCENE V.] G3–7 *omit*   SD [*To her.*]] ₍∧₎*Enter* ₍∧∧₎ G2–7   Barnwell] ~, G3–7   low.]
G2–7; ~, G1   1 Joy!—] ~!, G7   2 Madam.] ~, G3–4; ~! G5–7   3 Favour,]
~! G5–7   4 Madam,] ~! G5–7   5 for,—] ~!— G5; ~! G6; ~. ₍∧₎ G7
5+SD–6 Confusion.] | To see] Ed.; ~. ₍∧₎ | Mill. To see G1–7, *which repeat speech-heading*
6 here.] ~! G5–7   Confusion.] Confusion! G7   8 Alas] Alass G3–4   I may...
you think] G3–7; All my Apprehensions proceed from my Fears of your thinking G1–2
10 confering] conferring G3–7   11 me—] ~: G2–7   promis'd] promised G5–7
(promis-|ed G5)   15 another:—] ~;, G2–7   But] but G2–7   simple] G3–7; silly G1–2
18 Heaven] Heavens G5–7   22 Subject] G3–7; Affair G1–2   28 thought] tho't G5

at] G3–7; *not in* G1–2   all.—] ~.ₐ G2–7   29 yet:] ~; G7   31 my self]
myself G5–7   —I don't] ₐ~ G2–7   World] ~, G2–7   32 wou'd n't] wou'dn't G6–7
Power.—] ~.ₐ G5–7   33 manner] Manner G3–7   Master,] ~; G5–7   but,] ~ₐ G6–7
34 then,] ~ₐ G7   35 me,] ~ₐ G7   36 Conversation.—] ~.ₐ G2–7   37 House]
G2–7; House together G1   38 Youth!—] ~!ₐ G2–7 (youth G3)   who e'er] whoe'er G6–7
39 Youth.—] ~.ₐ G5–7   Woman!—] ~—! G3–4; ~!ₐ G5–7   40 my self] myself G5–7
might,] ~ₐ G6–7   perhaps,] ~ₐ G6–7   41 it:—] ~:ₐ G3–7   43 Sex.] G5–7;
~, G1–4   45 Things] things G3–7   impossible:—] ~.— G3–4; ~.ₐ G5–7   Servant,]
~ₐ G7   Master] G3–7; Master as you are G1–2   47 are!—] G2–4; ~?— G1; ~!ₐ
G5–6; ~;ₐ G7   And] and G7   49 gone,] ~ₐ G6–7   Power] power G6–7   go.] G5–7;
~, G1–4   50 Leave.—] ~.ₐ G2–7   52 Indeed] ~, G5–7   53 cruel!—]
~!ₐ G2–7   54 my self] myself G5–6   55 that] G2–7 *omit*   —But] ₐbut G2–7
56 hence.—] ~.ₐ G2–7   58 my self] myself G5–7   60 ask?—] ~?ₐ G5–7   Youth.]
~ₐ G4–7   61 would] wou'd G7   62 do!—] ~!ₐ G5–7   63 do not,—do not]
G2–4; ~,ₐ ~, G1; ~,ₐ ~ₐ G5–7   me.—] ~.ₐ G5–6; ~,ₐ G7   with] G2–7; wish G1
64 —But] ₐbut G5–7   you,—] ~,ₐ G5–7   When] when G2–7   65 Blushes (this]
G2–7 (Blushes— G5–7); Blushes speak.— | This G1 its] G2–7; their G1   Way] G2–7;
way,ₐ G1   66 declare] G2–7 (~—G5–7); and declare— G1   67 Heavens] Heaven's
G6; Heav'ns G7 am; her] ~. Her G5–7   68 it:—] ~.ₐ G5–7   Oh,] ~ₐ G3–7
68–9 never,—never.] ~.— G5–6; ~,—~ₐ G7   69 those] your G2–7   Tears.—]
~.ₐ G5–7   always;—] ~;.ₐ G5–7   70 ever,] ~ₐ G6–7   71 wheedled] weedled G3–6
72 'till] till G2–4, 7   73 my self] myself G5–7   74 indeed;] ~: G7
75 Master;—] ~;ₐ G2–7   77 Aye] Ay G6–7   78 End,] ~ₐ G7

I. vi

SCENE VI.] G3–7 *omit*   SD [*To them.*]] ₐ*Enter*ₐ G3–7   2 you'll] G2–7; You'll G1
Defects.—] ~.ₐ G2–7   3 Entertainment.] *after this line* G3–7 *add* SD: [*Exeunt* Barnwell *and*
Millwood.

I. vii

SCENE VII.] G3–7 *omit*   SD Lucy *and* Blunt.] G3–7 *omit*   1 What, is] *Ed.*; ~ₐ ~ G1;
What's G2–7   2 Fellow!] ~? G2–7   4 What,] *Ed.*; ~ₐ G1–7   last!] ~? G2–7
6 not,] ~ₐ G4–7   Love] love G7   8 that?:] ~; G5   10 thing,] ~ₐ G7
12 her self] herself G5–7   13 Consequence;—] ~;ₐ G2–7   14 there] their G3
15 Yes,] ~ₐ G6–7   Patridge] Partridge G6–7   17 Why,] ~ₐ G3–7   18 our selves]
ourselves G5–7 (our-|selves G6)   that] ~, G5–7   say] ~, G5–7   21 by,] ~ₐ G3
23 that,] ~; G5–7   28 upon't.] *after this line* G3–7 *add* SD: [*Exeunt.* (ₐ~. G3–5)

I. viii

SCENE VIII.] G3–7 *omit*   SD *Scene draws . . . come forward.*] G3–7 (SCENE G6–7); Barnwell
and Millwood *at an Entertainment.* G1–2   1 answer!] ~; G4; ~? G5–7   3 our selves]
our-|selves G5–7   4 Anguish,] ~ₐ G7   6 great: If] ~; if G2–7   8 Heaven]
Heav'n G7   10 Beauty] ~, G3–6   11 Cruelty] a cruelty G6–7 Nature.—] ~.ₐ G5–7
us!] ~? G5–7   12 talk,—] ~,ₐ G5–7   Vice,—] ~;ₐ G5–7   13 Beauty,—] ~;ₐ G5–7
Hand,—] ~,ₐ G3–7   14 fall,—] ~;ₐ G5–7   Wishes;—] ~;ₐ G5–7   high,—] ~;ₐ G5–7
15 Desire;] ~. G2–7   yet] Yet G2–7   18–19 Chimeras all,— | —Come] Chimeras
all! ₐCome G5–7, *printing*   18 *as beginning of the couplet*   19 prove,] ~ₐ G5–7
20 Joy's] Joys G6–7   Woman kind] Woman-kind G6–7   nor] no G2–7   21 wou'd]
would G3–5 not,] ~. G7   I must] must G3–7   26 come,—] G2–7; ~,ₐ G1   behind.]
after this line, G3–7 *add* SD: [*Exeunt.   The End of the First Act.*] G6 *omits*

II. i

SD Barnwell.] *Enter* Barnwell. G3–7   1 G1, 3–7 *include speech-heading: Barn.* (BARNWELL.
G6)   Like] like G6–7   2 Ground,] ~ₐ G5–6   and fain wou'd lurk unseen,] G2–7;
not in G1   3 House.] ~.— G5–7   was] were G3–7   4 Breach] breach G3–6
Thing] thing G6–7   5 injured] injur'd G5–7   Face?—] ~?, G5–7   8 Crimes]
~, G2–7   10 Purity;] ~: G5–7   me disconsolate] ~, ~, G5–7   wander'd,] ~; G5–7
and] ~, G5–7   11 Heaven] Heav'n G6–7

II. ii

SCENE II.] G3–7 *omit*　　　　SD Barnwell *and*] *Enter* G3–7　　　1 O] Oh G3–7
2 Daughter,] ~; G3–7　who] ~, G2–7　Absence] ~, G2–6　inquir'd] enquir'd G2–7
3 gone,] ~; G5–7　　　6 belov'd; but] ~: But G4; ~:—But G5–7　when] When G5–7
8 done?] ~; G5　alter'd] altered G2–5　rather] ~, G6–7　　9 done?] ~; G7　changed]
chang'd G6–7　　11 speak] ~, G4; ~!— G5–7　me!—] G6–7; ~.‸ G1–4; ~;—G5
12 Face] ~, G3–4　wou'd] would G6–7　　14 Friend,] ~; G5–7　　15 love,] ~; G5–7
tho'] though G4–6　　17 well;] G5–7; ~, G1–4　Eyes] eyes G7　　20 forebode]
forbode G6–7　Night] ~, G5–7　　22 ingages] engages G4–7　　23 alone,] ~; G5–7
24 give] to give G6–7　　26 Grief] ~, G5–7　　28 Return;] ~: G5–7　　　30 thus:]
Ed.; ~, G1–4; ~. G5–7　all] ll G5　　32 both] ~, G3–7　　33 thus?—] G4–7;
~,‸ G1–3　　34 Youth,] G3–7; ~‸ G1–2　farewell,] ~; G5–7　　35 Advice,] ~. G5–7
SD *Going.*] ~‸ G3–5　　38 Part] part G6–7　reduc'd] reduced G6–7　act?—] ~:—G2–4;
~?‸ G5–7　'tis] 'Tis G5–7　　　40 prithee] pr'ythee G5–7　me] ~, G6–7　—Try]
‸~ G2–7　　41 your Self] your self G2–4; yourself G5–7　　45 labouring] la'bring G7
Breast,] ~; G5–7　vent] ~, G7　　46 Grief;] G5–7; ~, G1–4　shou'd] shon'd G4; should
G6–7　cure,] G5–7 (Cure G5–7); ~; G1–4　　48 observ'd,] ~; G5–7　　shou'd]
should G4–7　　49 known] ~, G2–7　wou'd] would G2–7　　52 excluded,] ~? G5–7
you?] G2–7; ~. G1　　54 again.] ~.— G3; ~‸— G4　　57 continue?] G2–7; ~. G1
59 it.] ~? G4　　61 shou'd] should G6–7　　65 Heav'n] Heaven G3–7　　66 return?]
G2–7; ~. G1　　67 stopp'd] stop'd G7　　68 parched] parch'd G6–7　　69 Peoples]
People's G5–7　　70 safety] Safety G2, 6–7　　Lions] Lyons G6　　72 past,] ~‸ G7
75 Heav'n] Heaven G3–7　　　76 we ought] G2–7; he who trusts Heaven ought G1
despair.—] *Ed.*; ~.‸ G1; ~‸— G5–7　　　　77 ill] Ill G2–7　　Snares.] ~— G5–7
79 you.] *after this line* G3–7 *add* SD: [*Exit* Trueman.] (‸~.‸ G3; [~.‸ G4)

II. iii

SCENE III.] G3–7 *omit*　　SD Barnwell.] G3–7 *omit*　　1 G3–4 *add speech-heading: Barn.*;
G5–7 *run on from* II. ii. 79　Trueman] ~, G3–7　and ingaged him to apply] G3–7; to
have applied G1; who wou'd apply G2　repair] G2–7; have repaired G1　　3 Heav'n]
Heaven G6–7　not.] ~‸ G6–7　　4 that,] ~? G6–7　　5 Heav'n] Heaven G3–7
7 fall] ~, G4–7　again.—] G3–7; ~.‸ G1; ~. G2　　8 Passion;—] G2–4; ~;‸ G1;
~.—G5; ~!— G6–7　　9 can] Can G3–7　　10 indure.—] G2–3; ~.‸ G1;
en-|dure‸— G4; endure.‸ G5–7　love] Love G6–7　Life] ~, G4–7　fear] Fear G6
12 doubt.—] ~:‸ G5–7　determine?] G2–7 (~. G7); determines. G1

II. iv

SCENE IV.] G3–7 *omit*　　SD Thorowgood *and* Barnwell.] *Enter* Thorowgood. G3–7
1 assign'd,] ~‸ G7　your self] yourself G5–6　　2 Fault,] ~‸ G7　　3 prevented; that]
~. That G5–7 (pre-|vented G5, 7)　　5 appease:] ~:—G5; ~?— G6–7　　7 o'er come]
o'ercome G2–7　Sir!] ~, G7　　9 'em] it G2–7　　11 convinc'd] convinced G7
12 Mind;—] ~?— G2–7　　15 Reason,] ~‸ G5–7　　15–16 best when oppos'd] best,
oppos'd G2–4; best‸ oppposed G5–7 (oppos-|ed G5)　　18 so] ~, G4–7　not;] ~, G5–7
being] G2–7; they being G1　　19 danger] Danger G2–7　　SD [*Aside.*] G2–7; *not in* G1
21 will.] G2–7; ~; so Heav'n confirm to me the Pardon of my Offences. G1　　22 now,]
G2–7 *omit*　　23 Appetites] ~, G5–7　fierce] ~, G5–7　　25 me] G2–7 (~, G5–7);
me then G1　Knees] ~, G5–6　confess.] ~— G4–7　　26 Not a] G2–7; I will not
hear a G1　Mercy,] ~‸ G3–7　　27 Torment to reveal] Tormen Oreveal G3
30 offended;] ~, G4　certain,] ~; G7　　31 pardon.] *after this line* G3–7 *add* SD: [*Exit*
Thorowgood. (‸~. G3)

II. v

SCENE V.] G3–7 *omit*　　SD Barnwell.] G3–7 *omit*　　1 G1, 3–7 *include speech-heading:*
Barn.　Villain, Villain,] ~! ~! G5–7　Man:] ~; G4; ~. G5–7　　　2 Folly] ~, G2–4;
~? G5–7　　3 up;—the] ~.—The G5–7　　4 unlook'd for] unlook'd-for G6–7

II. vi

SCENE VI.] G3–7 *omit*　　　　SD [*To him.*] A] *Ed.*; ‸~‸‸ a G1–2; ‸*Enter*‸‸ a G3–7
1 Ladies,] ~‸ G7　Country,] ~‸ G7　you.] ~‸ G4　　2 shou'd] should G2–7　'em.]
after this line G3–7 *add* SD: [*Exit Footman.*] (‸~.‸ G3; [~.‸ G4–6)

II. vii

SCENE VII.] G3–7 *omit*   SD Barnwell.] G3–7 *omit*   1 G1, 3–6 *include speech-heading:*
Barn.; G7 *runs on from* SD *after* II. vi. 2   1–2 Now every . . . made me?] G3–7 (alarms me∧
G4); Guilt, | what a Coward hast thou made me?—Now every | Thing alarms me. G1–2 (a |
Coward . . . made me?∧ . . . ev'ry . . . a-|larms G2)

II. viii

SCENE VIII.] SCENE II. G3–7   SD Millwood *and . . . to them*] Millwood *and* Lucy
discover'd. Enter G3–7 (*discovered* G5–7)   2 you.] *after this line* G3–7 *add* SD: [*Exit Footman.*
(*Foot.* G5–6)

II. ix

SCENE IX.] G3–7 *omit*   SD Barnwell, Millwood, *and* Lucy.] (Millwood∧ G2) *Enter*
Barnwell. G3–7   1 *Millwood.*] ~! G2–4, 7; ~!— G5–6   3 much,] ~; G5–7
5∖ my self] myself G5–7   8 suspicion] Suspicion G3–7   respect] Respect G2–7
(Re-|spect G5, 7)   9 conducted] G3–7 (con-|ducted G6); directed G1–2   11 more,]
~; G2–5; ~: G6–7   13 left me.] left. G5–7   16 so;—yet] ~.∧ Yet G5–7   ever
shall] shall ever G2–7   20 weigh'd,] ~.∧ G7   22 came] ~, G2–7
23 Confusion!] ~!— G5–7   25 Part,] ~; G2–7   26 relief] Relief G2–7
27 indulgent] G2–7; kind G1   28 resolv'd] resolved G6–7   off.] ~.∧ G4–7   29 me]
G2–7; ~, G1   33 met?] G6–7; ~. G1–5   34 me,] G5–7; ~∧ G1–4   *Barnwell,*]
~; G5–7   35 again,] ~; G5–7   36 Hand,] ~.∧ G7   37 Extacy] Extasy G6–7
38 delight] Delight G6–7   39 more;] G5–7; ~, G1–4   48 indeed,] ~.∧ G2–7
51 Favour,—] G2–7; ~,∧ G1   52 last?] ~. G3–7   farewell,—] G2–6; ~∧∧ G1; ~,∧ G7
53 ever.] *after this line* G3–7 *add* SD: [*Exeunt Millwood* and *Lucy.*

II. x

SCENE X.] G3–7 *omit*   SD Barnwell.] G3–7 *omit*   1 G1, 3–7 *include speech-heading:*
Barn.   conquer,—] G2–7; ~,∧ G1   conquer'd.—] G2–7; ~.∧ G1

II. xi

SCENE XI.] G3–7 *omit*   SD Barnwell, Millwood] *Re-enter* Millwood G3–7   1 thing]
Thing G3–5   forgot,] ~; G5–7   7 thing] Thing G3–7   danger] Danger G2–7 (Dan-
|ger G2)   8 If] if G4–7   otherwise?] ~. G5–7   10 find,] ~; G5–7   Cue] Cure G6
11 Ah;] ~! G5–7   whether] whither G3–7   12–13 your|self] yourself G5–7
14 immediately,] ~; G4–7   15 Matter] ~, G3–7   18 Wheree'er] Whene'er G2–7
Wiles] Wilds G6–7   19 Desarts,] ~,∧ G4–7 (Deserts G7)   comfort] Comfort G2–7
20 Sake!] ~!— G5–6   curs'd] curs d G3   22 matter,—] G2–3; ~,∧ G1, 4–7
25 Undoing?] Un-|doing. G7   26 To know it will] G2–7; 'Twill G1   32 Why]
~, G2–7   33 Fortune,] ~∧ G2–7   34 Care] care G7   35 —but] ∧~ G5–7
36 compared] compar'd G3–7   38 Servants;] G5–7   manner] Manner G3–7
41 wish,] ~; G5–7   42 love] Love G7   44 was,] G2–7; ~∧ G1
45 Executorship,] ~; G5–7   47 it self] itself G5–7   whom,] ~∧ G7   this] his G2–7
48 stripp'd] strip'd G7   50 her self] herself G5–7   54 raving,] ~∧ G3–7
Madman] G3; Madman∧ G1–2, 4–7   55 Marriage,] *Ed.*; ~; G1–7   59 in,] ~; G2–7
61 Seasons,] *Ed.*; ~; G1–7   62 Cold;] G5–7; ~, G1–4   unhous'd] ~, G3–7   wander]
~, G2–7   Friendless] friendless, G2–7   64 Revenge;] G5–7; ~, G1–4   woud'st]
wou'dst G2–3, 7   65 nothing,—nothing] G2–5; ~,∧ ~ G1, 7   66 Pity,] ~∧ G7
Way] way G4–6   67 now;] ~? G2–7   70 Gentleman;] *Ed.*; ~, G1–7   72 Fiend,]
~∧ G7   away.] ~∧ G7   perish, nay] ~; ~ G5–7   73 him;] ~, G7   my self]
myself G5–7   Ruin,] ~; G7   74 Patience,—] G2–7; ~,∧ G1   immediately.] G2–7
(im-|mediately G2); ~.— G1; *after this line* G3–7 *add* SD: [*Exit Barnwell.*

II. xii

SCENE XII.] G3–7 *omit*   SD Millwood *and* Lucy.] G3–7 *omit*   1 came,] ~; G5–7
perceive,] ~∧ G5–6   4 without Expence] G2–7; with no-|thing G1   5 shou'd]
should G2–7   7 *Mill.* Leave that to me.] G2–7; *not in* G1

II. xiii

SCENE XIII.] G3–7 *omit*   SD Barnwell *with . . . and* Lucy.] *Ed.*; Barnwell, Millwood, *and*
Lucy. G1–2 (Millwood∧ G2); *Re-enter* Barnwell, *with a Bag of Money.* G3–7   1 do!—] ~?—

G2–6; ~?‸ G7   2 your selves] yourselves G5–6   6 but] But G4–7   common;]
common: G7 (com-|mon G7)   8SD [*Aside.*] G3–7; *not in* G1–2   9 Here] ~, G3–7
10 House,] ~‸ G3–6   11 again.] again— G4; again? G6–7   12 not,—] ~,‸ G5–7
fly,—] ~,‸ G5–7   least] lest G2–7   14 come.—] ~.‸ G2–7   16 please.] *after this*
line G3–7 *add* SD: [*Exeunt* Millwood *and* Lucy.] ([~.‸ G3–6)

II. xiv

SCENE XIV.] G3–7 *omit*   SD Barnwell.] G3–7 *omit*   1 G3–6 *add speech-heading:*
Barn.; G7 *runs on from* SD *after* II. xiii. 16   done?] G2–7; ~. G1   2 made,—] ~?‸ G5–7
why] Why G3–7   3 and,] ~,‸ G3–7   4 —Is] ‸~ G5–7   it self] itself G5–7
5 Accidents,] ~‸ G7   6 prevent,—] ~;‸ G5–7   8 Remorse;—] ~.‸ G5–7
9 plung'd] plunged G3–7   know] known G3   why—] ~. G2; ~: G3–7   11 *Darkness*,]
~‸ G5–7   Pain.] *after this line* G3–7 *add* SD: [*Exit.*   *The End of the Second Act.*] ~ ACT. G6

III. i

SD *A Room in* Thorowgood's House.] G3–7; *not in* G1–2   SD Thorowgood] *Enter*
Thorowgood G3–7   2 Wealth.—'Twill] ~;‸ 'twill G2–7   3 Science.—See] ~,‸ to
see G2–7   4 Things.—How] ~;‸ how G2–7   promotes] G2–7; has promoted G1
opened] open'd G2–7   9 farther.—] ~.‸ G2–7   11 Mankind,—] ~;‸ G2–7
Friendship,] ~‸ G5–7   12 savage,—] ~;‸ G2–7   Traffick,—] ~,‸ G2–4; ~‸ G5–7
13 Superfluities,] Superfluities; G5–7   14 manual] mutual G6–7   15 Accident,]
G2–7; ~‸ G1   16 observ'd:—] ~.‸ G2–7 (observed G6)   18 World's rich Earth]
G2–7; World G1   19 Ore.—] ~.‸ G2–7   20 it self.—] ~.‸ G2–7 (itself G6–7)
21 Climate,] ~; G5–7   25 He,] ~‸ G3–7   it,] ~‸ G7   27 Inspection?] G2–7; ~; G1
28 Confusion.] ~‸ G2   29 has n't] hasn't G6–7   31 I'm] I am G7   32 ready.]
after this line G3–7 *add* SD: [*Exeunt.*

III. ii

SCENE II.] G3–7 *omit*   SD Maria] *Enter* Maria G3–7   Book] ~, G3–7   1 G1, 3–7
include speech-heading: Ma.   The] the G6–7   that,—] ~,‸ G2–7   2 it self,—] ~,‸ G2–7
(it-|self G5, 7; itself G6)   beholds—] ~.‸ G2–7   5 Heaven.—Small] ~;‸ small G2–7
Reward;—not] ~:‸ Not G2–7   6 dissolved] dissolv'd G2–7   7 hopeless] ~, G2–7

III. iii

SCENE III.] G3–7 *omit*   SD Trueman *and* Maria.] *Enter* Trueman. G3–7   1 Friend,]
~! G5–7   fallen?] ~! G5–7   2 say] ~, G7   Barnwell.] ~! G5; ~! G6–7
3 conceal'd.—] ~:‸ G2–7   I've] G2–7; Iv'e G1   4 your self] yourself G5–7   knew]
know G5–7   5 Heaven!] ~!—G5–7   6SD–7 [*Gives . . . reads.* | Trueman,] (*letter*; G5)
[Trueman *gives a Letter*, Maria *reads.* G6–7, *misprinting salutation of letter as part of* SD (*Gives* G6)
7 Ma.] *Ed.*; G1–7 *do not include speech-heading*   8 your self] yourself G5–7   12 yet,]
~‸ G3–7   13 lost] ~, G6   15 Yes] yet G7   shou'd] should G5–7   17 Virtue—]
~; G2–7   19 open,] ~‸ G4   generous] G2–7; ~, G1   manliness]
Manliness G3–7 (Manli-|ness G3–4)   21 Truth.—] ~.‸ G2–7   22 delight]
Delight G2–7   26 do] G5–7; Do G1–4   31 lost.—A] ~.‸~ G2; ~,‸ a G3–7
32 never.—] ~.‸ G2–7   though] tho' G2–7   34 much,—] ~,‸ G2–7
35–6 *Tr.* That's . . . the Sum?] G5 *prints both lines, including speech-headings, on one line*
37 considerable.—] ~:‸ G2–7   39 shou'd] should G2–7   40 Father?] G2–7; ~.—G1
41 easy:] ~. G3–7   42 Virtue] G2–7; ~, G1   Maria's.] ~‸ G4–7   45 Price.—But]
~;‸ but G2–4; ~:—but G5–7   46 that.—] ~.‸ G2–7   time] Time G3–7
48 suspected.] ~? G7   50 Heaven] *Ed.*; ~, G1–7   only Witnesses] G3–7; Judges G1–2
51 do] G2–7; have done G1   thing] Thing G3–7   53 succeed] succeeds G2–7
54 slightest] lightest G3–7   Breath;] ~: G5–7   55 Father,] ~‸ G5–7   sake,] G2–4;
~; G1   mine] ~, G5–7   him.] *after this line* G3–6 *add* SD: [*Exeunt.*

III. iv

SCENE IV. Millwood's House.] (Milwood's G1) SCENE II. | *A Room in* Millwood's House. G3–4,
7; SCENE II. | *Another Room in* Thorowgood's House. G5–6   SD Lucy] *Enter* Lucy G3–7
2 surprizing:—] ~:‸ G2–7   3 feign'd,] ~,‸ G4–7   tho'] though G2–4   4 her:—
But] ~;‸ but G2–7   7 Understanding;] Understanding. G6–7 (Understand-|ing G7)
imposed] impos'd G4–7   8 believe.—] ~.‸ G2–7   9 all,] ~‸ G7   12 too.]
~? G2–7   14 in] G3–7 *omit*   15 well.—] ~.‸ G2–7   17 it.—] ~.‸ G2–7

18 nothing.—] ~.ₐ G2–7   his,] ~ₐ G7   Smile:—] ~:ₐ G2–7   19 done;—] ~;ₐ G2–7
20 there] G5–7; ~, G1–4   26 expect .—]~.ₐ G2–7   27 Impudence,—] ~,ₐ G2–7
and,] ~ₐ G3–7   her self] herself G5–7   28 before,—] ~,ₐ G2–7   29 indeed!] ~?
G4–5; ~: G6–7   30 and,] ~ₐ G7   31 gone;] ~: G7   when] G2–7; and
G1 toward] towards G6–7   he show'd] G5–7; show'd G1–4   Sum] G2–7; Bag G1
32 brought] G2–7; stol'n G1   Master's] G2–7; Master G1   —the] ₐ~ G2–7
34 *Millwood*?] ~?— G3–5   35 Aye] Ay G3–7   36 swearing,] ~ₐ G3–7
dissembling.] ~: G2–7   —Hung] ₐ~ G2–7 (hung G5–7)   and wept] wept G5–7
37 till] 'till G5–7   amorous Youth,] G2–7 (~ₐ G7); easy Fool, G1   38 die,] ~ₐ G4–7
40 Fears,] ~ₐ G3–7   41 Love,] ~ₐ G2–7   44 hers,] ~. G2–6   just] Just G2–5
45 prevail'd,—] ~,ₐ G2–7   46 lost;—] ~,ₐ G2–7   cruel,] G2–7; ~ₐ G1
47 promise—] G2–7; ~,ₐ G1   51 Uncle,] ~! G5–7   speak of] W1; ~, G1–7
52 Estate] ~, G6–7   53 same.—] ~.ₐ G2–7   possess'd] possessed G6–7
54 demands] demanded G2–7   55 Sacrifice,] ~ G2–5; ~. G6–7   Relation;] *Ed.*;
~, G1–7   56 Treasure;] ~: G6–7   58 perswade] persuade G6–7   that!] ~? G2–7
58–9 is, by Nature,] ~ₐ ~ₐ G7   59 though] tho' G5–7   60 Perswasions] Persuasions
G6–7   61 comply'd! So] ~: ~ G2–7 (so G6–7)   64 Rage;] ~, G4   65 till]
'till G7   him] *Ed.*; ~, G1–7   66 Endearments,] ~ₐ G2–6   her] G5–7; ~, G1–4
cruel] ~, G2–7 (Cruel G2, 7)   67 Destruction.] ~ₐ G4–7 (De-|struction G4)
68 Grief;—] ~;ₐ G2–7   69 Stars,—] ~,ₐ G2–7   shou'd] should G7   70 abhor]
Ed.; ~, G1–7   he;] ~? G2–4   72 meant,] ~ₐ G5–7   Necessity,] ~ₐ G7
74 robb'd] rob'd G7   80 troubled] G2–7; *not in* G1   Horror,] ~ₐ G2   81 Fair!]
~? G3   Love!] ~? G4–7   82 Soul,] ~; G3–4   caus'd] caused G3–7   83 worthy]
G2–7; *not in* G1   84 my self] myself G5; himself G6–7   86 Why] ~, G2–6
resolve,] resolveₐ G2–3   87 for,] ~ₐ G3–7   Uncle?] G5–7; ~. G1–4   88 mov'd]
moved G6–7   89 Yes,] ~ₐ G3–4; ~ₐ— G5–7   93 was] were G5–7   Monster.—]
~.ₐ G2–7 (Mon-|ster G3–4)   97 not.—] ~.ₐ G5–7   her.—] ~.ₐ G2–7   We've] We
have G2–7   98 my self] myself G5, 7   100 true,] ~ₐ G5–6   101 Murder,—]
~,ₐ G2–7   nothing] ~, G2–7   103 our selves] ourselves G5–7   104 that,] ~ₐ G2
105 probable.—] ~.ₐ G2–7   Design?] ~. G6–7   106 Heart.] G2–7; ~.—How else shall
I clear my self? G1   109 Time;—] ~;ₐ G2–7   go.] *after this line* G3–7 *add* SD: [*Exeunt.*

III. v

SCENE V.] SCENE III. G3–7   SD Barnwell.] *Enter* Barnwell. G3–7   1 G3–7 *add*
speech-heading: Barn.   dismal] Dismal G7   slip'd] slipt G6–7   2 Speed,] ~ₐ G6–7
3 I'm] I am G6–7   accursed] accurs'd G2–7   5 Feet.—] ~.ₐ G2–7   6 murmur,]
~,— G5–7   7 seem] seem'd G3–7   8 the Shock] a ~ G3–7   good] goods G5
9 shou'd] should G2–7   10 Father;] G2–6; ~, G1, 7   13 What] ~, G7
14–15 whether, O whether,] whether, O whither, G5; whither, O whither, G6–7 (~,~ₐ G7)
15 Master's] Mas-|ters G3   18 Aye] Ay G7   21 Theft,] ~ₐ G7   22 Conscience!]
Con-|science; G4   Virtue,] ~; G5–7   who only shows] thou . . . show'st G5–7   23 wants
the Power] wantest Power G5–7   24 Uncle.] ~ₐ G5–7   Disguise.] ~ₐ G5–7
25 private] Private G6–7   26 Heaven,] ~ₐ G4–7   27 Heaven!—] ~!ₐ G4–7
Struggles, Conscience.] ~ₐ~ ~ₐ G7   28 Hence! Hence] ~! hence, G7   29SD *and draws*
a Pistol.] draws a Pistol, and [*Exit.* G3–7

III. vi

SCENE VI.] SCENE IV. G3–7   SD Uncle.] *Enter* Uncle. G3–7   1 G3–7 *add speech-*
heading: Un.   was] were G5–7   2 night:—] ~;— G4; ~.ₐ G5–7   3 gashly]
ghastly G7   Death,—] ~;ₐ G2–7   4 pale] ~, G5–6   attracks] attacks G3–4; attracts
G5–7   Eye,—] ~,ₐ G2–7   4–5 Soul, at once,] ~ₐ ~ₐ G7   5 Aversion.—] ~.ₐ G2–7
7 Mind.—] ~.ₐ G2–7   near,—] ~,ₐ G2–7   8 selves] Selves G2–7   9 cease]
~, G5–7   View?—] ~?ₐ G2–7   moves;—The] ~;ₐ the G2–7   10 curdling,] curdlingₐ
G5–7   Veins:] G2–7; ~,— G1   fix'd] Fix'd G2–7   11 we stand] G2–7; *not in* G1
so] G2–7; *not in* G1   Thoughts, we] G2–7; ~.—We G1   12 hereafter;] G2–7; ~, G1
'till] till G2–4   13 Inquiry.—] ~.ₐ G5–7

III. vii

SCENE VII.] G3–7 *omit*   SD Uncle, George] *Enter* George G3–7 ([~ G5–7)   *a Distance.*]
~.] G5–7   1 Uncle.] G5–7 *omit speech-heading and run on from* IV. vi. 13   Power,] ~; G7

—seen] ∧~ G2–7   2 understood—] ~∧ G2–7   what] G3–7; What G1–2   —The]
∧~ G5–7   3 Globe,—] ~,∧ G2–7   4 Stars;] ~, G6–7   Worlds] G2–7; World's G1
finds,—] ~,∧ G2–7   5 vain,] ~; G2–4; ~: G5–7   6 Gloom,—] ~;∧ G2–3;
~,∧ G4–7   7 certain,] ~— G5–7   7+SD *again.*] G3–7; ~; *at last he drops it,—at*
which his Uncle starts, and draws | his Sword. G1–2   8+SD [*Throwing . . . his Sword.*] G3–7
(∧*throwing* G3–4; [*throwing* G5–7; *Pi-|stol* G5); *not in* G1–2   9 masqu'd!] ~!— G3–7
10 Retreat] retreat G7   10+SD *Bosom,*] ~∧ G7   12 Servant.] ~: G5–7   thy]
the G4–7   Nephew;] ~: G4–7   13 take] take away G3   13+SD *and,*] ~∧ G7
chafes him.] ~, G6   16 me.] ~∧ G4–7   ere] G5–7; e're G1–4   17 Heaven,]
~∧ G2–7   18 Murder'd] mur-|der'd G7   O,] ~! G5–7   19 Purpose,] ~; G5–7
then,—] ~,∧ G2–7   20 wou'd,] ~∧ G7   21 Hand!] ~? G2–7   me!] ~? G2–7
21SD–22 *Kisses him. | Uncle.* [*Groans and dies.*]] Ed., G1–4 (∧*Groans and dies.*∧ G1; (*Groans and*
dies.) G2–4); (Barnwell *kisses his Uncle, who groans and dies.*) G5–7   23 *Barn.*] G5–7 *omit*
speech-heading and run on from 21   23–24 Life, that . . . Kiss expired.] G2–7 (seal'd G7;
expir'd G3–7); *not in* G1   24 follow.] ~∧ G3–7   26 breath] breathe G4–7
wholesome] wholesom G7   Air!] ~? G2–7   27 Justice] justice G4   28 murder'd]
murdered G3–6 Murderer.—] ~;∧ G2–7   And] and G2–7   spares,—] ~,∧ G5–7
32 Brother,] ~∧ G2–7   him.] ~: G2–7   33 hated.] ~: G2–7   36 alone,—] ~,∧
G2–7   worst.—] ~.∧ G2–7   37 rich] Rich G4–7   41 fall,] ~; G2–7   *The End*
of the Third Act.] ~ *ACT.* G6

IV. i
SD *A Room in Thorowgood's House.*] G3–7; *not in* G1–2   Maria] *Enter* Maria G3–7
1 G1, 3–7 *include speech-heading: Ma.* (*MARIA.* G6)   judge] ~, G5–7   2 here.] ~? G5–7
3 shou'd] should G7   4–5 our selves] ourselves G5–6   5 abhor;] G2–7; ~, G1
6 suffer;] ~, G7   they] we G5–7   7 moral] Moral G7   8 they sustain,] we sustain∧
G5–7   made] G2–7; *not in* G1   10 thee—] ~.∧ G2, 4; ~,∧ G3, 5–7   12 *Gain:*]
~; G4–7   13 *Grave*] ~, G2–7   *Love*] ~, G2–6   14 *Life,*] ~∧ G4–7

IV. ii
SCENE II.] G3–7 *omit*   SD Trueman *and* Maria.] *Enter* Trueman. G3–7   1 *Ma.*]
G5–7 *omit speech-heading*   2 None.—] ~.∧ G5–7   3 Doth] Does G2–7   Absence]
G2–7 (absence G2); *absenting himself* G1   5 though] tho' G7   6 Excuses] G2–7;
~, G1   9 him!] W1; ~, G1–4; ~? G5–7   11 Reproach] ~, G6–7
12 malicious] ~, G5–6

IV. iii
SCENE III.] G3–7 *omit*   SD [*To them.*]] ∧*Enter*∧∧ G3–7   1 (and bating] ∧and (~ G2–7
4 shou'd] should G7   5 Truth.] G7; ~, G1–6   7 Times,] ~∧ G5   10 my self]
myself G5–6   12 Maria!—] ~!∧ G2–6; ~.∧ G7   SD [*Aside.*] [~. *Exit* Maria. G3–7

IV. iv
SCENE IV.] G3–7 *omit*   SD Thorowgood, Trueman *and* Lucy.] G3–7 *omit*   2 Friend]
~, G2–7   3 Life.—] G2–4; ~.∧ G1; ~!— G5–7   4 Loss.] ~∧ G5–7   5 an]
am G2   7 Deed!] G2–5, 7; ~, G1; ~; G6   Thought!] G2–6; ~. G1, 7   10 false,—]
~;∧ G2–7   too,] ~; G5–7   12 Imagination!] G2–7; ~; G1   13 are] be G5–7
16 What] ~, G5–7   ho!] ~? G2–7   there!] ~? G2–7

IV. v
SCENE V.] G3–7 *omit*   SD [*To them.*] *A Servant.*] [*Enter a Servant.*] G3–7 (∧~.∧ G3–4)
1 *Thor.*] G5–7 *omit speech-heading and run on from* IV. iv. 16 *and* SD   himself] G2–7 *omit*
2 Speed.] ~; G5–7   —An] ∧~ G2–7 (an G5–7)   Diligence.] *after this line* G3–7 *add* SD: [*Exit*
Servant.]

IV. vi
SCENE VI.] G3–7 *omit*   SD Thorowgood, Trueman *and* Lucy.] G3–7 *omit*   1 *Thor.*]
G3–7 *omit speech-heading and run on from* IV. v. 2 *and added* SD   2 ingage] engage G2–7 (en-
|gage G2)   Assistance.—] ~.∧ G2–7   3 till] 'till G5–7   4 possible.] *after this line*
G3–7 *add* SD: [*Exit* Lucy.]

IV. vii
SCENE VII.] G3–7 *omit*   SD Thorowgood *and* Trueman.] G3–7 *omit*   1 *Thor.*] G3–7

omit speech-heading and run on from IV. vi. 4 *and added* SD   wou'd] will G5–7   Occasion.] *after this line* G3–7 *add* SD: [*Exit* Thorowgood. ([~.] G5)

IV. viii
SCENE VIII.] G3–7 *omit*   SD Trueman.] G3–7 *omit*   1 G3–7 *add speech-heading:* Tr. only who is a Friend] ~, who is a Friend, G2–7   Distress.] *after this line* G3–7 *add* SD: [*Exit.*

IV. ix
SCENE IX.] SCENE II. G3–7   SD Millwood.] Enter Millwood. G3–7   1 G3–7 *add speech-heading: Mill.*   2 him.] ~‿ G7   4 have] ~, G4   done—] G5–7; ~, G1–3; ~‿ G4   5 only] ~, G3–7   6 all?] ~. G4–7

IV. x
SCENE X.] G3–7 *omit*   SD Millwood, *and Barnwell* bloody.] [Enter *Barnwell* bloody.] G3–7 (‿~·‿ G3–4)   1 Mill.] G5–7 *omit speech-heading and run on from* IV. ix. 6 *and* SD   show] shew G7   2 show] shew G7   3 whether] Whether G2–5; Whither G6–7   4 Justice?] ~. G4–5   5 those] your G2–7   Fears;] ~? G3–5   tho'] though G2–7   pursu'd] pursued G3–7 (pur-|sued G3–4)   6 here] ~, G2–7   Innocence;] ~. G5–7   Art] ~, G2–7   8 Retreat;] G5–7; ~, G1–4   10 me] ~— G5–7   my self] myself G4; myself, G5–7   11 tho'] though G3–4   12 oh!] G2–7 (Oh G4–5); *not in* G1   inmate] Inmate G4–7 (In-|mate G5)   —that] ‿~ G2–7   13 convict,] ~‿ G5–7   Murder;] ~, G2–7   17 or] ~, G2–7   20 Heav'ns] Heaven's G2–7   all-seeing] G2–7; omniscient G1   21 advantage] Advantage G2–7 (Ad-|vantage G2)   Death?] ~, G5–7   22 advantage] Advantage G2–7 (Ad-|vantage G2)   it?—did] ~?‿ Did G2–7   23 Treasure,—those] ~?‿ Those, G2–7 (Those‿ G5; those, G7)   him?—] ~;‿ G2–7   25 Sacrilege] Sacriledge G5   27 Murderer;] ~: G7   27–28 alas, alas! . . . his Murderer;] (~ Murderer‿) G2–7   28 tho'] though G2–6   29 come,] ~‿ G5–7   30 Hour.] ~? G7   done,] ~; G2–7   31 I] ~, G2–7   violated by Theft] ~, by theft, G2–7   33 Whining, preposterous,] G5–7; ~‿ ~‿ G1–4   Villain;] G5–7; ~, G1–4   34 Natures] Nature's G2–7   Prerogative] Perrogative G5   Injury;] G3–7; ~, G1–2   35 wanted,] G3–7; ~; G1–2   36 Reputation,] G2–4; ~; G1, 5–7   nay] ~, G3–7   Life,] G2–4; ~, G1, 5–7   37 Oh!—] O‿‿ G2–7   thee;] ~! G5–7   38 dead,] G5–7; ~; G1; ~! G4   Oh] oh G2–7   40 all,] ~‿ G5–7   Ruin;—] ~;‿ G2–7   41–2 my self.] ~‿ G4   42 There] —There G4–7   43 pressing,] ~‿ G4–7   room] Room G7   44SD [*Aside, rings a Bell.*] G3–7 ([~. Rings ~.] G5–7); [*Stamps.* G1

IV. xi
SCENE XI.] G3–7 *omit*   SD [*To them.*] A Servant.] Ed.; (~‿) ~. G1–2; ‿Enter a Servant. G3–7 (Ser-|vant.] G5, 7; Servant‿] G6)   1 Mill.] G5–7 *omit speech-heading and run on from* IV. x. 44 *and* SD   2 Murderer;] G2–7; ~, G1   shou'd] should G3–7   as he.] *after this line* G3–7 *add* SD: [*Exit Servant.* ([Exit | Servant.] G5–7)

IV. xii
SCENE XII.] G3–7 *omit*   SD Millwood *and* Barnwell.] G3–7 *omit*   1 thou dost] you do G3–7   Messenger,] ~; G2–3   2 Knees] ~, G2–6   you,] ~‿ G2–3; you'd‿ G4–7   3 my self] myself G4–6   Justice,] ~; G2–4   will,] ~; G5–7   4 wish.] ~: G2–7   6 will,] ~; G5–7   live;] ~, G2–7   secure;] ~, G2–7   10 Tryal] Trial G3–7   ignominious] an ignominious G5–7   Death,] ~— G5–7   11 abhorr'd?] ~‿ G2; ~. G3–7 (abhor'd G7)   12 warning and horror] Warning and Horror G2–7   Croud.] Crowd.—G7   14 thine.—] ~.‿ G2–7

IV. xiii
SCENE XIII.] G3–7 *omit*   SD Millwood, Barnwell, Blunt] Enter Blunt G3–7   1 here,] ~‿ G4–7   2 Custody,] ~. G6–7   Murder;] ~, G2–7   4 complain;] complain? G5–7   5 Parricide;] ~. G5–7   yet] Yet G5–7   6 Heav'n] ~, G2–7 (Hea-|ven G6–7)   live,] ~;   G5–7   others;] ~;— G3–7   8 Heaven.—] ~.‿ G2–7   9 warn'd] ~, G7   10 lewd] lew'd G5   False] false G7   Fair;] G2–7; ~, G1   11 pursue;] G5–7; ~, G1–4   12 Fair,] Ed.; ~‿ G1–7   Honour] Ed.; ~, G1–7   13 her self] herself G5–7   14 Example] ~, G2–7   16 Ere] G3–7; E'er G1–2   lost,—] G2–4; ~,‿ G1, 5–7   17 Cost.] *after this line* G3–7 *add* SD: [Exeunt *Barnwell*, Officer and Attendants.

IV. xiv

SCENE XIV.] G3–7 *omit*   SD Millwood *and* Blunt.] G3–7 *omit*   1 *Lucy*,] ~; G2;
~? G3–7   2–3 too. *Lucy . . . thou Devil!*] G3–7 (here; G5–7); too, thou Devil! G1–2
4 this] This G3–7   6 Punishment.] *after this line* G3–7 *add* SD: *[Exit* Blunt.

IV. xv

SCENE XV.] G3–7 *omit*   SD Millwood.] G3–7 *omit*   1 G3–7 *add speech-heading:*
Mill.   then] G2–7; *not in* G1   —and] ∧~ G3–7   2 resolv'd,] ~; G3–7 (resolved G4–6)
Danger,] ~; G7   3 them.—] ~;∧ G5–7   Instruments.—] ~.∧ G2–7

IV. xvi

SCENE XVI.] G3–7 *omit*   SD Thorowgood *and* Millwood.] *Enter* Thorowgood. G3–7
1 this] the G4–7   4 *Millwood.*—] ~.∧ G2–7   6 Appearance] ~, G2–7
7 Aspect.—] ~.∧ G2–7   9 better;] ~;— G5–7   13 blush] have blush'd G3–7
14 Arts;] ~! G2–7   If] if G7   17 arriv'd] arrived G7   Wickedness.—] ~.∧ G2;
~?∧ G3–7   18 your] the G3–4; thy G5–7   21 curs'd] cursed G3–7   commit.]
G2–7; ~, and then betray'd him. G1   22 Advantage,] G2–7; Advantage of me, G1   first;]
G2–7; ~, G1   24 prevented. To] ~; to G5–7   25 directs,] ~.∧ G7   remains.—]
~.∧ G2–7   Satisfaction,—] Satisfaction!∧ G2–7 (Satis-|faction G2)   26 compared]
compar'd G3–7   28 cannot,] ~; G5–7   29 Action.—] ~.∧ G2–7   30 Servants.]
~, G4   31 without Cause, . . . Appearance,] G2–7; from a Gentleman of your Appearance,
without | Cause, G1   32 it;] ~: G6–7   34 Servant,] ~; G5–7   35 Undoing]
undoing G7   37 Suffering,] ~; G2–7   39 —So] ∧~ G2–7 (so G6–7)   43 Has
n't] Hasn't G6–7   46 till now] G3–7; *not in* G1–2   47 Pleasures. Now] ~: now G5–7
48 Extravagancies;—] G2–7; ~,∧ G1   49 so.] G2–7; ~.— G1   56 Sir!] ~, G2–7
perswading] persuading G4–7 (per-|suading G5, 7)   61 Hands] Hand G3   I (struck] ~,∧
~ G5–7   the Horror of] Horror at G3–7   Crimes)] ~,∧ G2–7   63 unexperienc'd]
unexperien'd G5   Snares; the] ~? The G2–7   64 Form] G5–7; ~, G1–4
65 Prejudice] perjidice G4   66 prepared] prepar'd G3–7   had,] ~,∧ G7   Story,] ~∧ G7
67 subtilly] subtlely G7   68 what] (which G5–7   unanswerably] G5–7; ~, G1–4
69 Innocence,] ~,∧ G5–7   Guilt:] *Ed.*; ~; G1–4; ~,∧ G5–7   70 have prevented]
prevent G5–7   72 Objections.] *after this line* G3–7 *add* SD: *[Exit* Millwood.

IV. xvii

SCENE XVII.] G3–7 *omit*   SD Thorowgood, Lucy] *Enter* Lucy G3–7   1 your selves]
yourselves G5–7   3 you.—This Way—] ~. ∧~∧ G5–7   Behaviour;] ~: G5–6
5 Resolution.—] ~.∧ G5–7   Design.—] ~.∧ G4–7

IV. xviii

SCENE XVIII.] G3–7 *omit*   SD *[To them.]*] ∧*Enter*∧ G3–4; ∧ *Re-enter*∧ G5–7   Pistol,—]
~.∧ G5–7   2 Villain,] G2–7; ~. G1   can'st] canst G6–7   3 thee] the G4–5
Woman,] ~∧ G5–7   the] thy G4–7   Sex,] ~; G5–7   5 Mirrour] Mirror G7
7 *Thor.*] G2–7; *Tr.* G1   Faults] G3–7; Fault G1–2   own,] ~; G5–7   10 robb'd]
rob'd G7   11 ere] G3–7; e'er G1–2   Worth,] ~; G5–7   me,] ~,∧ G5–7
22 unerring] G2–7; unering G1   24 Ship-wrecks] Shipwrecks G4–7   26 suspected,]
~; G2–7   28 them,] *Ed.*; ~∧ G1–7   29 Fees] ~, G5–7   is] are G5–7
33 I know . . . Mercy, and] G2–7; I hate you all, I know you, and expect no Mercy; G1
none; I] G2–7 (~; and I G2); ~; I have done nothing that I am sorry for; G1
33–4 I follow'd] and I follow'd G2   34 does] do G4–7   35 seem] G2–7; are G1
Beast,] ~; G2–7   38 sweet and] G2–7; ~, but G1   39 Atheist,] ~; G2–6; ~! G7
tho'] though G2–4   41 it self] itself G5–7   Evils you say] *Ed.*; ~, you say, G1–7
42 has] have G6–7   48 Valour;] ~? G5–7   49 Villanies,] Villainies; G5–7
(Villanies G5)   your selves] yourselves G5–7   50 Judge] ~, G2–7   51 himself]
him-self G2   52 deceiv'd] deceived G7   57 *Arts*,] ~∧ G7   58 O—] G2; ~∧
G1; Oh! G3–7 (~! G5)   59 flatt'ring] flat'ring G7   60 robb'd] rob'd G7   *The End
of the Fourth Act*.] ~ ACT. G6

V. i

SD Thorowgood] *Enter* Thorowgood G3–7   1 *Thor.*] THOROWGOOD. G6   5 me,]
~∧ G5   6 him,] ~; G5–7   7 wou'd have] wou'd but have G5–7   10 past] pass'd

G4–7   Eye:] ~. G5–7   15 *Millwood*,] G2–7; ~∧ G1   18 guilty] Guilty G4–7   her
self] herself G5–7 (her-|self G5, 7)   19 avail?] ~; G3–4   21 on,] ~; G5–7
25 ill spent] ill-spent G4–7   confederacy] Confederacy G2–7 (Confe-|deracy G5)
29 shou'd] should G3–7   encourag'd. Pursue] ~; pursue G5–7   30 proposed] purpos'd
G3–7   31 unmerited,] ~; G5–7 (unmeri-|ted G5; unme-|rited G7)   Heaven] ~, G7
33 Apostacy] Apostasy G7   36 done,] ~; G2–7   37 themselves?] G4–7; ~. G1–3
39 —for we,—who wonder at his Fate,—] ∧~,∧ ~,∧ G2–7   we,] G2–7; ~∧ G1
40 tryed,—] tried,∧ G2–7   him, we] ~∧ ~ G7

v. ii

SD *and Lamp.* | Thorowgood . . . Barnwell *reading.*] G2; ~. | Thorowgood, Barnwell ~. G1; ~.
Barnwell *reading.* | *Enter* Thorowgood *at a Distance.* G3–7   1 There see] G3–7; See
there G1–2   Reign,] ~∧ G5–7   2 indulg'd. Severe] ~, severe G5–7   4 times]
Times G2–7   Disrespect,—] ~;∧ G5–7   6 imploy'd] imployed G4–5; employed G6–7
your self;—] ~:∧ G2; ~;∧ G3–7 (yourself G4–7)   7 your Journey's] Your Journey's
G2–3   preparation] Preparation G2–7   spent.—] ~.∧ G2–7   8 shou'd] should G4–7
12 labour'd] laboured G4–7 (la-|boured G5)   learn'd] learned G4–6   14 Hope,—] ~.—
G2, 4; ~∧— G3; ~:∧ G5–7   16 Proceed.] G2–7; Go on.—How happy am I who live to see
| this? G1   17 wonderful,—] ~,∧ G2–3; ~∧ G4–7   18 Conscience;—] ~;∧ G2–3,
5–7; ~,∧ G4   20 doubt,—] ~,∧ G2–7   rejoice.—] rejoice;∧ G2–7 (re-|joice G5)
21 way.—] ~.∧ G2–7   23 Repentance,] Repentance; G5–6 (Repen-|tance G5)
24 the certain] G2–7; certain G1   25 Heaven!—For] ~!∧ ~ G2–6; ~;∧ for G7
26 shuning] shunning G2–7 (shun-|ning G3–4)   27 for ever.—] ~.∧ G2–7
28 —The Love] ∧~ G2–7   29 Riches] ~, G2–7   on] upon G4–7
31 Mankind.—] ~.∧ G2–7   33 over paid.] ~? G2–3, 6–7   36 thus,] ~∧ G7
Words,] ~∧ G4–5   38 cou'd] would G2–7   39 leave] Leave G4–7
41 unworthy,] ~— G5–7   42 perswade;] persuade, G3–7 (per-|suade G5)   cou'd]
Cou'd G2–7   once] ~, G2–7   43 return?] G2–7 (Return G4–7); ~. G1
44 coming,—] ~,∧ G2–7   ever;—] ~;∧ G2–7   45 Sorrow,—] ~,∧ G2–4; ~;∧ G5–7
46 me,—] ~,∧ G2–7   53 vanquish'd;—] ~;∧ G2–7   54 for ever.] *after this line* G3–7
add SD: [*Exit* Thorowgood.

v. iii

SCENE III.] G3–7 *omit*   SD Barnwell.] G3–7 *omit*   1 G3–7 *add speech-heading:*
Barn.   Perhaps I shall.] G2–7; *not in* G1   2 spight] spite G7   3 Mortal] mortal
G3–7

v. iv

SCENE IV.] G3–7 *omit*   SD [*To him.*]] ∧*Enter*∧∧ G3–7   1 Sir,] ~. G6   there's]
There's G4–6   Prisoner.] *after this line* G3–7 *add* SD: [*Exit Keeper.*

v. v

SCENE V.] G3–7 *omit*   SD Barnwell *and* Trueman.] G3–7 *omit*   1 Trueman,] ~! G2–7
wisht] wish'd G4–7   4 was I] I was G5–7   6 has] hath G4–7   7 thus!]
~!— G3–7   13 know,—] ~;∧ G2–7   'tis] tis G5   14 conceive;—] ~;∧ G2–7
Griefs at present] ~, at present, G2–7   15 you.—] ~.∧ G2–7   still,—] ~;∧ G2–7
16 yet methinks] ~, methinks, G2–7   strange—] ~,∧ G2–7   17 that,—] ~,∧ G2–4;
~;∧ G5–7   Virtues,—] ~,∧ G2–7   19 Fair] fair G2–7   21 Alas,] ~∧ G4–7
know'st] knowest G4–7   Wretch] Wreth G5   been!] ~. G5–7   22 Offence.—So] ~;∧
so G2–7   Goodness,—] ~,∧ G2–7   23 of] o G3   Ruin,—] ~,∧ G2–7
25 Prithee] ~, G2–7   26 shou'd] should G2–4   27 murder'd] murdered G4–5
28 embrac'd] embraced G5–7   30 those] these G5–7   Arms,] ~∧ G4–7   Bosom,]
~∧ G5–7   31 Murderer?] G4–7; ~. G1–3   —These] ∧~ G2–7   32 me,—] ~,∧
G2–4; ~;∧ G5–7   34 join'd!—] (joined G4) joined!∧ G5–7   35 thee.] G2–7; ~,
[*Lies down by him.*] Upon | this rugged Couch then let us lie, for well it suits | our most deplorable
Condition.— G1   Here] here G2–4   36 Calamity,] ~; G5–7 (Calami-|ty G7)   Place]
G2–7; Earth G1   our selves] ourselves G4–7   37 eccho] echo G7   Vault.—] ~.∧
G2–3; G4–6   Our] our G4–7   38 —and] ∧~ G2–7   40 so.—] ~.∧ G2–7
~,∧ G3–7   SD [*Rising.*]] G2–7; *not in* G1   41 Breast,—] ~, ∧ G2–7   mine.] G3–7;
~, G1–2   42 promis'd?—] ~?∧ G2–7 (promised G4–5)   43 Return.—] ~.∧ G2–7

(return G6–7) 44 here!—] ~;— G3–4; ~.ᴧG5–7 Heaven,] ~; G5–7 who,] which, G3–7 (~ᴧG5–6) 45 it.] ~ᴧG3 47 have you] hast thou G5–7 48 Extreams] Extremes G7 Pain?] ~. G2–6; ~! G7

V. vi

SCENE VI.] G3–7 *omit* SD [*To them.*]] ᴧ*Enter*ᴧᴧ G3–7 Keeper] Keeper G5–7 2 come.] *after this line* G3–7 *add* SD: [*Exit Keeper* (*Exit.* G4)

V. vii

SCENE VII.] G3–7 *omit* SD Barnwell *and* Trueman.] G3–7 *omit* 1 me!] ~? G2–7 2 O,] ~ᴧG4–7 Barnwell,] ~! G5–7 Task] task G3 4 you,] ~ᴧG5–7 Earth!] ~. G5–7 6 known.] ~, G2–4 —*Maria.*] ᴧ~— G2; ᴧ~.— G3–7 7 Daughter!] ~!— G3–5; ~?— G6–7 10 show] shew G7 11 Friend,] ~ᴧG5 12 felt,] ~ᴧG5–7 13 Lie] Lye G4–6 14 is, indeed,] ~ᴧ~, G4; ~ᴧ~ᴧG5–7 Death!] ~. G5–7 15 observ'd] observed G4–7 16 Melancholy] Melancholly G4–5 weigh'd] weighed G4–7 down.—] ~. G2–3; ~, G4; ~;ᴧG5–7 17 unknown;—] ~; G2–7 till] 'till G5–7 Fate,—] ~,ᴧG2–7 18 out.—She] ~.ᴧ— G2–4; ~,ᴧshe G5–7 19 Hair,] ~; G5–7 discover'd] discovered G4–7 whilst] while G7 21 lovely] ~, G5–7 22 did n't you] did not you G2–3; did you not G4–7 24 determin'd] determined G4–7 ere] G3, 5–7; e'er G1–2, 4 her.—]~.ᴧG2–7; *after this line* G3–7 *add* SD: [*Exit* Trueman.

V. viii

SCENE VIII.] G3–7 *omit* SD Barnwell.] G3–7 *omit* 1 G1–7 *include speech-heading:* Barn. Vain] ~, G5–7 2 been,] ~? G2–7 am,] ~ᴧG5–7 what] W1; What G1–7 my self] myself G4–7

V. ix

SCENE IX.] G3–7 *omit* SD [*To him.*]] ᴧ*Enter*ᴧᴧ G3–7 and] with G5–7 3 Death.—] ~.ᴧG2–7 5 Despair,—] *Ed.*; ~,ᴧG1–7 6 Woe.—] ~.ᴧG5–7 7 Abode,—] ~,ᴧG2–7 behind;—] ~;ᴧG2–7 8 Death,—] ~,ᴧG2–7 —now] ᴧ~ G2–7 9 Heaven,] Heavenᴧ G7 11 below?—as] below?ᴧ As G2–7 (be-|low G5) 12 Due.—] ~.ᴧG2–7 Happiness] happiness G6 13 where] were G4 pleas'd;—] ~;ᴧG2–7 15 Fate.] ~ᴧG7 16 are:] ~; G7 17 Virtue,—] ~,ᴧG2–4; ~;ᴧG5–7 18 vain.] ~.— G5–6; ~;ᴧ— G7 19 Lord.—] ~.ᴧG2–4; ~,ᴧ— G5–7 Beauty,] G7; ~; G1–6 20 Merit;] ~: G5–7 you—] G2–7; ~,ᴧG1 though] tho' G5–7 21 been.—] ~.ᴧG2–7 22 indeed.—] ~.ᴧG2–3, 5–7; ~,ᴧG4 23 be] are G5–7 24 forsake.—] G3–7; ~,ᴧ— G2; ~.ᴧG1 26 Maid!—] ~!ᴧG2–7 27 before?—] ~?ᴧG2–7 peirce] pierce G2–7 28 Ere] G3–7; E'er G1–2 Fortune] fortune G7 30 pardon'd,—] ~,ᴧG2–7 31 your self] yourself G4–7 32 who,] ~ᴧG4–7 professing] proffering G2, 4; proferring G3; prostering G5; profering G6–7 Love,] ~ᴧG7 34 vain.] ~ᴧG3 36 shou'd] should G7 Occasion,] ~ᴧG4–7 Crimes,] ~ᴧG5–7 37 Error.—] ~.ᴧG2–7 38 Passion,] ~ᴧG5–7 39 —Yet] ᴧ~ G2–7 40 vain:—] ~:ᴧG2–7 Present,] ~ᴧG5–7 undone,—] ~,ᴧG2–7 46 Idea!] ~ᴧG4 47 live,—] ~,ᴧG2–7 48 possible,—] ~,ᴧG2–7 51 ask—] G2–4; ~; G1; ~ᴧG5–7 for my Relief] G2–7; ~ᴧ(Re-|lief G3–4); *not in* G1 52 that's] that G7 54 her self] herself G5–7 abhors.] ~, G2 55 suburb] suburd G1 (*earlier state*) Herd,] ~; G5–7 56 Fate.] ~ᴧG6 57 arm'd,] ~ᴧG7 58 Shame,] ~: G3–7 59 it self] itself G5–7 Infamy—] G2–7; ~, G1 60 him,] ~; G5–7 61 can] Can G7 this!] ~? G2–7 62 impair'd] so impair'd G3–7 Spirits;] ~, G3–7 Death.—] ~.ᴧG2–7 63 her,] ~ᴧG6–7 Peace,—] ~,ᴧG2–7 64 Crimes,—] Crime G1 (*earlier state*); ~.ᴧG2–7

V. x

SCENE X.] G3–7 *omit* SD [*To them.*]] ᴧ*Enter*ᴧᴧ G3–7 Keeper and Officers.] G3–7; Keeper. G1 1 The Officers attend you, Sir.] Sir, the Officers attend you; G2–7 (you, G2) Mrs.] G2–7 *omits* is] G3 *omits* 2 farewell,] ~. G3–7 3 more.] ~ᴧG5–7 4 me,] ~. G4–7 SD Maria.] G3–4, 6–7; ~ᴧG1, 5 Would] would G1 5 Embrace,—] ~,ᴧG2–7 6 mine.] G5–7; ~, G1–4 SD enclines] inclines G3–7 7 —where] ᴧ~ G2–7 9 has] I G3–7 Summet:] ~; G2; ~! G3–7 (Summit G5–7) Ere] G3–7; E'er G1–2 10 Man,—] ~,ᴧG2–7 11 stray,—] ~,ᴧG5–7 finish'd;]

~. G5–7   tho'] though G3–4; Though G5–7   Life,] ~∧ G5–7   12 Days,] *Ed.*; ~; G1–7
12–14 Thus Justice, . . . future Ruin.] G2–7; G1 *omits here and prints after line 17*
13 Justice,] ~∧ G4–6   me,] ~; G5–7   15 whole,] ~; G5–7 (Whole G7)   —thereby]
∧~ G5–7   17 ineffectual.] G2–7; ~.— G1, *which then prints lines 20–2:* Thus Justice, . . .
future Ruin.   18 *you,*—] ~,∧ G2–7   19 *Fate,*—] ~,∧ G2–7   20 *you,*—]
~,∧ G3–7   24 *Guilt,*—] ~,∧ G2–7   25 *own,*] ~.∧ G7   *complain;*] ~, G7
26 *vain.*] *after this line* G3–7 *add* SD*:* [Exit *Barnwell* and Officers.

v. xi

SCENE XI.] *Ed.*; SCENE the LAST. G5–7   G1–4 *do not include this scene;* G5 *serves as
copy-text for the present edition*   3 canst] can G7   7 seems!] W1; ~? G5–7
8+SD *Executioner*] Executioners G7   13 They were] G6–7; ~ Were G5   17 describe]
describe, G6–7   Fiends] Friends G6   29 Lead] ~, G6–7   33 sinn'd] sin'd G7
34 yon] you G6   39 doom'd] ~, G6–7   began] ~, G6–7   Pains] ~, G6–7
42 Prayers] Prayes G7   45 tell thee,] G6–7; ~∧ G5   Youth,] G6–7; ~∧ G5
46 its] G6–7; it's G5   53 Horror,] *Ed.*; ~∧ G5–7   59 rise;] *Ed.*; ~, G5–7
60 Th'impenitent] Th' impenitent G6–7

v. xii

SCENE XII.] *Ed.*; SCENE XI. G1–4; G5–7 *omit*   SD Trueman, Blunt, *and* Lucy.] *Enter*
Blunt *and* Lucy. G3–4; *Enter* Trueman. G5–7   1 *Millwood!*] G2–7; ~. G1   2 How]
G5–7; You came from her then:—How G1–4 (then:∧ G2–4)   3 unalterable] unutterable
G2–7   7 her self] herself G5–7   8 Sorrow,] ~∧ G2–7   9 vain] ~. G1 (*earlier
state*)   13 *that*—] G2–7; ~, G1   FINIS.] FINIS. G5; G6 *omits; The End of the Fifth
Act.* G7

Epilogue

EPILOGUE.] ~, G2–6   *Esq;*] ~; *Poet Laureat.* G2–7 (*Esq, G3*)   and] And G2–7   spoke]
spoken G5–7   1 robb'd] rob'd G7   hapless] hopeless G1 (*earlier state*)   4 chuse]
choose G7   you.] ~, G3   5 soft,] ~; G5–7   6 shou'd] should G4–7   look,] ~∧ G5–7
7 enough,] ~∧ G7   9 tawney] tawny G6–7   10 Gallery;—] ~;∧ G6–7   11 *Row;*]
~, G7   13 *'Tis*] Tis G4–5   16 *'Twixt*] Twixt G3–7   21 *Lawrels*] Laurels G7
24 *Not*] Nor G6–7   25 *draws,*] ~∧ G6   26 *Hand,*] ~∧ G3–7

THE CHRISTIAN HERO (*preliminary gathering*)

Prologue

1 Liberty,] ~∧ G (*second setting*)   2 everlasting] G (*second setting*); Everlasting G (*first
setting*)   11 Let . . . tell,] G (*second setting*); G (*first setting*) *indents and allows space between this
line and* 10   17 Superiour] G (*second setting*); Superior G (*first setting*)   save] G (*second setting*);
~, G (*first setting*)   19 Say, . . . Isle,] G (*second setting*); G (*first setting*) *does not indent or allow
space between this line and* 18   20 Apes] G (*second setting*); ~, G (*first setting*)   30 scourge]
G (*second setting*); Scourge G (*first setting*)   32 here!—] G (*second setting* [~!]); ~!∧ G (*first setting*)

Dramatis Personæ

1 TURKS.] G (*second setting*) *lists characters in two groups:* TURKS (*Amurath, Mahomet, Hellena,
Osmyn, Kisler Aga, Cleora*) *and* CHRISTIANS (*Scanderbeg, Aranthes, Althea, Amasie, Paulinus*)
4 Osmyn, the Visier.] *Ed.*; Osmyn. G (*both settings*)

MARINA

Dedication

Dedication is not in L

Prologue

PROLOGUE] Prologue L   6 *Tho'*] Tho L   *reap'd*] reapt L   12 *hand-maid*]
handmaid L   14 *Name*] name L   19 *though*] tho' L   *mix'd*] mixt L
21 *Throughout*] Thro' out L   *wild*] L *inserts above the line*   stand,] stand, L   22 *touch'd*]
toucht L   23 L *does not indent or allow space between this line and 22*   *mix'd*] mixt L
fore-fathers] forefathers L   28 *whole*,] whole; L   31 *If*,] If, L   *surprize*] surprise L
36 *Do*,] Do, L

Dramatis Personæ

1 MEN.] Men, L   2–12 *Character descriptions and actors' names are not in* L   7 BOLT]
Boult L   *Below this line* L *reads:* 3 Pyrates   8 WOMEN.] Women , L
13–14 *Gentlemen, . . . and Attendants.*] Gentlemen, Ladies, Officers, Guards, | and Attendants.
—L

I. i

SD *A Grove*] Scene a Grove L   *Prospect*] prospect L   *Sea, near* | *the City of Tharsus.*] Sea, | at a
distance. L   *Enter* Philoten *and* Leonine.] Philoten Q. of Tharsus and Leonine, L
1 remember,] ~: L   has sworn] art bound L   do it,] ~. L   4 graceful] gracefull L
address,] ~, L   5 peerless,] ~; L   thy] your L   9a amorous] amourous L
9b *Leon.*] Leo. L (*and similarly below*)   10 perform.] ~—L   11 I, while] And while L
12 Am not a] I am no L   14 Parents] parents L   16 Than] The {ir}n L
20 neglected;] ~, L   21 her.] ~.— L   22 mother's] Mother's L   death:] ~, L
23 pity] pitty L   24 purpose:] ~. L   26b I'm] I am L   27 No:] ~, L
weed,] ~, L   31 Ah me,] ~! L   32 mother] Mother L   dy'd,] ~; L
33 mother's] Mother's L   34 world, to me,] ~, ~, L   44 Pray,] ~, L
49 hopes] L; ~, G   53 chearful] cheerfull L   57a you're] your L   58 Lady.]
~— L   59 Fear not,] ~: L   59SD Queen.] Q. L   65 should] shou'd L   her,]
~, L   66 Lest] Least L   me,] ~: L   67 youth,] ~, L   proportion:] ~. L
71 haling] halling L   73 sea] Sea L   74b born.] ~—L   76 tempest,] ~, L
birth,] ~, L   kill'd] killd L   Mother,] ~: L   79a prayers] pray'rs L   80 pray'r,]
~, L   81 you;] ~: L   82 ear,] ~, L   85 spake] spoke L   86 creature:]
~. L   89 of] on L   deed,] ~, L   92 lately,] ~, L   94 you:] ~. L
97b *Mar.*] speech-heading not in L   99 should] shou'd L   live] ~, L   joy,] ~; L
100 die] ~, L   101 'tis,] ~, L   103 Howe'er] How e'er L   104 your self:] ~; L
then,] ~, L   106b vain,] ~: L   107b thus!] ~? L   108 soul;] ~, L
109 Yet, . . . deed,] ~, . . . ~, L   110+SD Pirate] 1ˢᵗ Pyrate L   111 1 *Pir.*]
First P.—L   Hold,] L; ~, G   villain. Fear] ~—fear L. thee.] ~, L   112 defence]
defense L   114 1 *Pir.*] 1 Pyr. L (*and similarly below*)   man] Man L   fool.] ~—L
poltron] poltroon L   114–15 a coward] {&} a coward L   rascal,] ~, L   118 cause
of] ~, L   118+SD *Enter second, and then third* Pirate] Enter 2ᵈ & 3ᵈ Pyrates L
119 2 *Pir.*] 2 Pyr. L (*and similarly below*)   prize! A prize!] ~, a prize. L   120 3 *Pir.*] 3 Pyr. L
(*and similarly below*) part,] ~, L   121 What,] ~, L   quarrelling] quarreling L about]
~, L   127 man] Man L   128 ship's company] Ship's Company L   129 denies]
deny's L   130 sink] Sink L   131 Nor I,] ~, L   132 city] City L   134 Ay;]
~, L   140 loath'd] loth'd L   violence] ~, L   143 man] Man L   145 Pirates]
Pyrates L   146 crew] Crew L   147 return.] ~— L   They'll, doubtless,] ~, ~, L
148 first; and then,] ~, ~, L   150 more:] ~. L   152 reward. It . . . so.]
~—It . . . ~— L   153 Queen,] ~, L   154 sea.] Sea, L   device!—] devise,— L
155 sav'd] saved L   156 them] h'em L   156SD Leonine.] ~, L

I. ii

SCENE II.] Scene 2ᵈ L   1 *Bawd.*] Baw. L (*and similarly throughout this scene*)   *Bolt*] Boult L
2 Mistress] Patrona L   3 publick] Publick L   4 shut] shutt L   5 house,] ~, L
6 *Bolt*] Boult L (*and similarly through this scene, except* Bolt *at* 28, 33, 90, 100, 112, 164, *and* 169, *and*
Bou *at* 161)   Panders!] ~. L   Magistrates] magistrates L   9 high-ways] high-|ways L
10 them] 'em L   keep their] keep their {keep thei} L   Wives] wifes L   Daughters]

daughters L   12 Merchants] merchants L   Travellers] Travel-|ers L   14 Batchelors]
batchelors L   15 Brothers] brothers L   16 Widowers] widows L   17 Husbands
... Wives] husbands ... wives L   18 Lawyers ... Soldiers] lawyers ... soldiers L   at all;]
~, L   20 Women] women L   love,] ~_∧ L   21 useful] usefull L   23 Yet,
after all,] ~_∧ ~ ~_∧ L   24 storm,] ~_∧ L   Mother *Coupler*] Mother-Coupler L
25 Woman] woman L   But] but L   26 discourag'd] discouraged L   28 store,] ~; L
31 would] wou'd L   34 them] 'em L   35 *Transilvanian*] Transylvanian L
39 pray,] ~_∧ L   honest,] ~_∧ L   40+SD Valdes, ... Pirates,] ~_∧ ... Pyrates_∧ L
41 *Vald.*] Val. L (*and similarly below*)   you,] ~_∧ L   42 how now,] ~_∧ L   Roister]
Royster L   How now,] ~_∧ L   43 Mother;] ~, L   do, ... do,] ~_∧ ... ~_∧ L
45 be] *not in* L   judge,] ~_∧ L   whether] wether L   46 down,] ~_∧ L   48 But,] ~_∧ L
you:] ~. L   50 *Bolt.* [*Aside the Bawd.*] Mark] (Boult to the Bawd apart | Mark L
52 piece,] ~_∧ L   54 Bawd] bawd L   56 saying,] ~_∧ L   what stale,] that stale_∧ L
57 market;] markett, L   Pirates,] Pyrates_∧ L   bad,] ~_∧ L   57–8 I have] I've L
59 her.] ~: L   62 been—] ~._∧ L   64 matter,] ~_∧ L   65 deceived] deceiv'd L
amongst] among L   our selves,] ~; L   68 with,] ~_∧ L   69 obliged,] oblig'd_∧ L
70 consent,] ~_∧ L   her,] ~_∧ L   71 possible,] ~_∧ L   72 Well,] ~_∧ L
73 mean,] L; ~_∧ G   74 her altogether] altogether L   75 bate] bait L   a thousand]
a 1000 L   77 trifle] triffle L   80 a thousand] 1000 L   81 cou'dn't] couldn't L
83 haggling] hagling L   84 I am] I'm L   86 money.] ~— L   88 *Bolt*] Boult L
fear,] ~_∧ L   Mistress] mistress L   88SD *Exeunt* Vald.,] *Ed.*; ~ ~._∧ G; Ex. Val._∧ L
89 Gods!] ~_∧ L   90 hither,] ~_∧ L   child.] Child_∧ L   You] you L   91 Mistress]
mistress L   92 know;] ~, L   95 and] *not in* L   96 upon] {on} upon L
99 strangely] strangly L   100 Nay,] ~_∧ L   principal] principle L   101 family,] ~_∧ L
103 want] ~, L   103–4 friend. | ... maids] ~. {I am of | maid's} | I am of maid's L
108 needful] needfull L   109 inform you. [*Lays hold of her.*] inform you_∧ | {Mar. Why
do you rudely I} (lays hold of her_∧ L   112 Ha] ha L   113 fearful] fearfull L
114 your] you L   Inamoratos] inamouratos L   115–16 you: ... modesty:] ~. ... ~. L
118SD–118+SD *him.* | *Enter* Bawd.] him_∧) Enter Bawd. L   120 what's] What's L   what]
What L   122 Nothing,] ~_∧ L   Mistress] Patrona L   her.] ~: L   124 Out,] ~_∧ L
126 turn.] ~: L   127 Ay, but] Ay, Patrona, but L   spit,] ~_∧ L   128 we] We L
129SD *Exit* Bolt.] Ex Bou. L   130 child] Child L   131 men] Men L
134 Wou'd] Woud L   135 Pirates] Pyrates L   Barbarians] barbarians L
136 mother] Mother L   137 sprig] sprigg L   Jessamin] Jesamine L   142 T' have]
scap'd] T'ave 'scap'd L   hands,] ~_∧ L   given] giv'n L   145 you] You L   have men]
have Men L   146 complexions] complections L   148 pray,] ~_∧ L   for,] ~_∧ L
I have] I've L   149 an] a L   150 sure,] ~; L   are] are {ar} L   153 modest,
and religious.] ~_∧ ~ ~_∧ L   154 a] *not in* L   155 know,] ~_∧ L   157 me.] ~! L
158 prayers] pray'rs L   161 Mistress] Patrona L   *French*] french L   hams,] ~; L
162 *German*] german L   163 Here,] ~_∧ L   165 that] who L   167 practice]
Practice L   169 ways. What] ~, what L   170 Leader] leader L

II. i

ACT II. SCENE I.] Act. 2. Scene 1. L   SD *a Temple*] the Temple L   1–11 Leonine. |
To bury ... my suit.] *not in* L   13a service] services L   22 flatt'ries] flatteries L   in,]
~; L   24 throne,] ~_∧ L   29 Beheld ... acknowledge,] L *writes the line twice, then deletes
the repetition*   32 den] Den L   bats] batts L   33 thousands] Thousands L
38 survivor] survivour L   39 This] ~, L   our] their L   *Tyre;*] Tyre_∧ L   40 Who,
bravely ... th' advantage,] Who scorn'd to take th'advantage their state gave him, L   41 land,]
~; L   42 Did] But L   supply] supply'd L   our] *Ed.*; our own G (own *deleted by hand in all
copies examined*); their L   wants,] ~_∧ L   43 turn our] turn'd their L   47 Yes, while]
While L   50 for] to L   52 hateful] hatefull L   have] has L   56 flames] L
inserts above the line   57 dome] Dome L   58 fun'ral] funeral L   59 ten thousand]
10 Thousand L   pieces,] ~_∧ L   60 loath'd] loth'd L   62 light,] ~_∧ L ended.]
~— L   63 comply.] ~— L   64 agent] Agent L   shameful] shamefull L
65 slave.] ~— L   word.] ~— L   67 *Tyre*] Tyre, L   70–1 epitaph | Procur'd] ~, |
The one of the choicest Parian marble wrought, | The other penn'd in characters of
gold, | Procur'd L   73 on plague] L *inserts above the line*   74b mine.] ~_∧ L
74bSD *Trumpets.*] Trumpets_∧ L   75 content:] ~. L   77 Welcome, great *Pericles*,] ~_∧

~ Pericles‸ L   78 faithful] faithfull L   80 Ent'ring port] Entring porte L
news.] ~: L   81 unthought loss] unthought-loss L   82–3 friends!— | But I'm ... to
adversity;] ~‸ | So loving, so belov'd!—But I'm a man | Born to adversity, a mass of sorrow. L
84–6 No land ... my purpose.] *not in* L   87 thee] ~, L   90 Her's] Hers L
94 boatswain's] Boatswain's L   95 Death] death L   96 dy'd] dyed L   97 me—]
~. L   99 receiv'd] receivd L   100 coffin'd] confin'd L   101 coral] corral L
104 waters,] ~‸ L   roll] rowl L   106 Heaven] heaven L   107a Nature] nature L
108 Melancholy] Melancholly L   110 never: ... me.] ~— ... ~— L   111 peacefull]
peacefull L   117 Phenix] phenix L   119 Princess] princess L   wat'ry] watry L
125 mother's] mothers L   127 foreign] forreign L   128 dregs] dreggs L
129 wilful] wilfull L   132 long embroil'd me,] long-embroyl'd me‸ L   134 Heaven]
Heav'n L   136 eyes; but] ~. But L   139 would] wou'd L   140 care-worn] care
worn L   142 Sister] sister L   143a+SD *draws,*] draws‸ L   143b–144 'Here ...
Tyre.'] W1 ("~ ... Tyre."); "~ ... ~.‸ G; "~ ... Tyre.— L   147 being:] ~, L
148 brass:] Brass. L   150 pleasure:] ~— L   153 cou'd] coud L   156 Herald]
W1; Hareld G; Harold L   162 wou'd] woud L   163 me;] ~. L   166 sackcloth]
sackcloath L   167 loins] loyns L   168 crown.] ~, L   170 world] ~, L   wilful]
wilfull L   vagrant,] ~‸ L   173 hath] has L   175 was] am L   177 and by
himself] L *writes twice, then deletes the repetition*   178 Come,] ~‸ L   179 woful, woful]
woful, wofull L   181 ev'ry] every L   185 sate] sat L   188 grateful] gratefull L
189 glow-worm] glowworm L   191 use,] ~‸ L   192 minded:] ~— L   197 th'
afflicted's] the afflicted's L   198 theirs.] ~‸ L   198SD *Exeunt* Pericles, Escanes, &c.]
Ex: Per: Esc: &c‸ L   207 for ever] forever L   209 assum'd] asum'd L
212 assur'd,] ~‸ L   214–15 Shall I, ... The unmeant] Shall I, a Queen, | Who cou'd not
bear the unmeant L   218 fix'd] fixt L   219b ungrateful] ungratefull L
223a already.] ~‸ L   223c poison'd] poyson'd L   224 subtle] subtil L   veins] ~, L
226 crown] Crown L   228 cou'd'st] coudld'st L   232a O!] O‸ L   233 kind,]
~‸ L   235 Though] Tho' L   now.] ~— L   236 This] The L   237 weapon's]
weapons L   241 murther'd] murder'd L   242 triumph] ~, L   242+SD *Ladies.*]
Ladies‸ L   246 our selves] ourselves L   249 tongue, let] ~‸ ~, L   traytor] traitor L
250 *Guard.*] Gua. L   Madam;] ~, L   252 Heav'n] heaven L   253 out-casts]
outcasts L

II. ii

SCENE II.] Scene 2. L   SD Bolt] Boult L (*and similarly in* SD *in this scene*)   1 *Bawd.*]
Baw. L (*and similarly in this scene*)   2 *Bolt.*] Bou. L (*and similarly in this scene, except* Bolt *at* 7,
12, 14 *and* 18)   5 prayers] prayrs L   7 enter a] enter into a L   bawdy-house] bawdy‸
house L   religious,] ~‸ L   8 Vestals] vestals L   10 Gentlewoman] gentlewoman L
12 Panders] panders L   Bawds] bawds L   15 her.] ~— L   21SD *Exit* Bolt.] Ex‸
Boult‸ L   22+SD Lysimachus.] ~‸ L   23 Well,] ~‸ L   27 soul] Soul L
29 Gentleman] gentleman L   30 Surgeons.] ~— L   temptation] temptations L
31 would] woud L   32 Prythee,] ~‸ L   33 Honour] honour L   35 Sir!—For]
~!‸ For L   Well,] ~‸ L   see a] see {her} a L   39 modesty,] ~‸ L   40+SD Bolt,]
Boult‸ L   41 Wou'dn't] Wou'd L   46 but when] {wh} but when L   47 the
firmest] th' {in} firmer L   49 Honour] honour L   52 Honour] honour L
53 Heav'n] Heaven L   so!] ~. L   54 Governor] Governer L   54–5 country; and
lastly,] Country. ~‸ L   60 her,] ~; L   61 Come,] ~‸ L   62 Honour] honour L
62SD *Exeunt* Bawd *and* Bolt.] Bawd & Boult Exeunt. L   66 pursu'd] pursued L
67a d'ye] do you L   68 fearful] fearfull L   72 young] {long} young L   74 sale]
sail L   79 aloof, but without cause;] aloof. But trust me, fair one, L   80 For my] My L
81–119a I've now learnt ... guard her own!] *not in* L   119b came hither,] came‸ L
120 thoughts like these] other thoughts L   But] but L   122a–131b Dare not ... O mighty
Sir,] *not in* L   132 honour] ~, L   now;] ~: L   134b–135 She's in ... cannot
fathom.] Ha! how's this! L   137 sty;] ~: L   138 came,] ~‸ L   139 physick]
Physick L   142 flies] flys L   143–4 Conviction rises ... chaste as fair.] *not in* L
144SD [*Aside.*] *not in* L   145–6 He must ... alter. Here's] Had I brought hither a corrupted
mind, | Thy speech had alter'd it. Hold, here's L   146 thee:] ~. L   147 clear] pure L
149 The short liv'd] As I came hither with no ill intent, | The short liv'd L   caus'd,] ~‸ L
151 Now you're] You are L   Gentleman] gentleman L   153–4 If I shou'd ... thy fame.]

not in L   156 thy] your L   were] are L   158 shall again . . . thy honour] shall again
attempt to rob thee of thy honour L   159 it,] ~₍ₐ₎ L   161 Honour,] honour ₍ₐ₎ L
164 sink, . . . you.] ~₍ₐ₎ . . . ~₍ₐ₎ L   166 country] countrey L   172 nostrels] nostrils L
175 as a Lord] L *reproduces twice, then deletes repetition*   176 snow-ball;] ~, L   Prayers]
pray'rs L   179 hark,] ~₍ₐ₎ L   184 room,] ~₍ₐ₎ L   194 brothel] brothell L
195 ev'ry] every L   197 breath'd] belch'd L   203 indenture] {the} indenture L
207 of the] to the L   208 thy] your L   persuade] perswade L   212 me.] ~₍ₐ₎ L
215 Satyr . . . Puritan] satyr . . . puritan L   Devil] devil L   217 conduct] convey L
220 And] and L   224 Troth,] ~₍ₐ₎ L   them.] ~— L   225 temple:] Temple. L
227 her!] ~. L   228 mistress.] ~— L   This] this L   230 -loved] -lov'd L
Diana,] Diana₍ₐ₎ L   233 *Bolt, Bolt,*] Bolt, Boult, L   235 Devil!] ~₍ₐ₎ L   is run] has ~ L
237 1 *Off.*] 1ˢᵗ Of. L   238 had] hath L   244 favour,] ~₍ₐ₎ L   that you] that *not in* L
247 of] on L   249 of] on L   250 Gentlewoman,] gentlewoman₍ₐ₎ L   252 your
self] yourself L   254 thieves] {thief} thieves L   255 honest,] ~₍ₐ₎ L   strumpets]
Strumpets L (*at beginning of prose line, perhaps inadvertently capitalized*)   chaste,] ~₍ₐ₎ L
256 sinful] sinfull L   257 hopeful] hopefull L   257SD [*Exeunt.*] *not in* L   The
End of the Second ACT.] End of 2ᵈ Act. L

III. i

ACT III. SCENE I.] Act 3 Scene 1. L   1 *Marina*,] Marina again₍ₐ₎ L   3 Hah] Ha L
Mother] mother L   flesh-monger] Flesh₍ₐ₎ monger L   4 propagator] propogator L
5 practice!—] ~!₍ₐ₎ L   idle—Though] ~; tho L   6 you'll] you'd L   stroling] strolling L
7 vamped] vamp'd L   wench,] ~₍ₐ₎ L   hospital,] Hospital₍ₐ₎ L   8 accommodate]
accomodate L   with?] wᵗʰ! L   9 traitor] traytor L   10 it—] ~, L   11 Nick]
nick L   13, 15 *Bawd.*] B. L   14 *Bolt.*] Bo. L (*and similarly in this scene*)   lye;] ~— L
15 hang'd] hanged L   17 we] We L   18 hang'd:] hanged, L   So] so L   you are
oblig'd] you 're obliged L   19 *Bawd.*] Ba. L (*and similarly in this scene*)   For though] for tho' L
23 She] she L   24 Governor's] Governour's L   servants.] serᵗˢ₍ₐ₎ L   26 no] *not in* L
29 yet:] ~₍ₐ₎ L   32 bawd] Bawd L   bawdy-house] bawdy₍ₐ₎ house L   33 Temple]
temple L   34 I'm] I am L   36 quarters,] lodgings₍ₐ₎ L   are n't] are not L
38 rascal. But] ~, but L   39 Governor] Governour L   her?] ~. L   40 burthen]
burden L   43 Why,] ~₍ₐ₎ L   45 egregiously] egriously L   if] If L (*at beginning of a line*)
47 time!] ~? L   48 Mother] mother L   49 exactly] *not in* L   you'll] {the} find L
its] it's L   the breadth of] *not in* L   51 reveng'd] revenged L   53SD *Exeunt*] Ex. L

III. ii

SCENE II.] Scene. 2 L   SD *altar*] her altar L   *discover'd*,] discover'd₍ₐ₎ L   1a 1 *Priest.*]
1 Pr. L (*and similarly below*)   1b 2 *Priest.*] 2 Pr. L (*and similarly below*)   4 devotion.] ~: L
5 night,] ~₍ₐ₎ L   8 slumbers, 'tis, as now,] ~₍ₐ₎ ~₍ₐ₎ ~₍ₐ₎ L   altar.] ~₍ₐ₎ | To feel her woes yet
bear them as she ought— | Wisdom & piety compose her character. L   9a long?] ~. L
11 her, breathless,] ~₍ₐ₎ ~₍ₐ₎ L   12 this] the L   14 (And . . . uncle)] ₍ₐ₎~ . . . unckle,₍ₐ₎ L
restor'd] restored L   15b This, though] ~₍ₐ₎ tho' L   16 wonder.] ~₍ₐ₎ L
17 suppos'd] supposed L   18 affirm,] ~₍ₐ₎ L   21 spirits:] ~; L   And] & L   liv'd]
lived L   24 judg'd] judged L   royal: All] ~. all L   25 Was] ~, L   she] she'd L
husband,] ~₍ₐ₎ L   26 joys.] ~: L   27 And choosing] Chusing L   28 retir'd;]
retired₍ₐ₎ L   29 prepar'd] prepared L   31 sustains] ~, L   32 her,] ~₍ₐ₎ L
33a dy'd] died L   39 *Marina*,] Marina₍ₐ₎ L   amaz'd] amazed L   40 that] who L
44a Attend] attend L   44b restor'd] restored L   45–6a To the . . . *Thaisa!*— | Ha!—]
To these long widow'd arms?—ha!— L   46b Madam, How fare you?] How fare you,
Madam? L   47 dream. And] ~! & L   it self,] itself₍ₐ₎ L   48 shadow?] ~, L
49 me—] ~. L   54 death: And] ~, and L   56 will] Will L   58 altar,] ~₍ₐ₎ L
59 statue;] ~, L   61 Crescent] crescent L   64a wond'rous] wondrous L
65 Consign'd] Consigned L   lov'd] loved L   Lord] lord L   66 living] willing L
me.] ~; L   67a wak'd] waked L   69 This dream's] this Dream's L
70 We doubtless] We know but little, & that makes us vain. | We doubtless L   71a allow us.]
allows us: L, *which continues:*

> I revere them
> And trust their providence, yet must believe them
> Not conversible with mortality.

Their presence would confound our feeble beings,
Shou'd they approach too near us.

74 wear,] ~ₐ L   76 virgin] ~, L   you?] ~. L   80 miracle:] ~ₐ | Of wisdom, as of
innocence & beauty: L   82 assur'd] assured, L   84a+SD *Gentleman*.]
Gentlemanₐ L   84b honour'd] honoured L   85 appearance,] ~: L   86 tackle,]
~ₐ L   87 shoar] shore L   88 great] ~, L   mournful] mournfull L
90 Governor] Governour L   91SD *Exit*] Ex. L   91+SD Escanes;] ~, L   him,] ~ₐ L
92 The] yᵉ L   gracious] Gracious L   93 you,] ~ₐ L   t'out-live] t'outlive L
95 *Tyre*,] Tyre: L   here,] ~ₐ L   96 distress'd;] ~, L   97 his] is L
99 th'afflicted] the afflicted L   101 further] farther L   gold,] ~ₐ L   104b courtesy]
~, L   105 deny,] ~ₐ L   106 ev'ry] every L   caterpiller] caterpillar L
108 Gentleman] gentleman L   109 note (I] ~ {:} (~ L   more)] ~ {:)) L
110 person,] ~ₐ L   113 repeat;] ~, L   115 wife,] ~ₐ L   116 the Gods] The
Gods L   you, hail] ~, Hail L   117 all] *not in* L   Lord;] ~: L   118 one, nor] ~:
Nor L   119a grief.] ~ₐ L   119b durst] darest L   wager,] ~ₐ L   124 fix'd] fixt L
resolves:] ~. L   125a form and utt'rance] all attractions L   125b her.] ~ₐ L
125bSD *Exit Gentleman*.] Ex. Gent. L   126 effectless: Yet] ~; yet L   127b virgin.] ~: L
128b Lady] lady L   129 physician] Physician L   131 patient;] ~. L
133 excellent] glorious L   134 defac'd:] defaced. L   135 despair] dispair L
137 heav'nly] heavenly L   139 aught;] ~, L   140 physick] physic L   thanks] pay L
141b *Mar*.] Ma. L (*and similarly below*)   over rate] overate L   143b Heaven!] ~. L
145 wild,] ~ₐ L   perswade] persuade L   147 unobliterated,] ~ₐ L   148SD [*Aside*.]
not in L   149 first.] ~. | Sh'as all attractions, & excells in all. L   SONG.] a Song by
Marinaₐ L   150–65 Mar. *Let . . . honour most*.] *not in* L   168 Maid] maid L
169 eyes;] ~, L   170 too] to L   171 gaz'd] gazed L   172 Who, may be,] ~ₐ ~ₐ L
endur'd] endured L   173 yours,] ~ₐ L   weigh'd—] ~. L   174 not.] ~: L
175 *Go on*] go on L   176 attention?] ~! L   177 look,] ~ₐ L   scape] 'scape L
178 lips.—] ~ₐₐ L   you] ye L   Gods!] ~!— L   179 eagerly] egerly L
183 Nay,] ~ₐ L   185 simple Maid] maid and mortal L   187 tears.] ~— L
wife,] ~—L   188 been.] ~—L   189 Queen's] queen's L   brows,] ~—L   inch,]
~—L   190 strait,] ~—L   voic'd,] voiced— L   191 jewels like,] {Juno} Diamond-
like— L   *Juno*:] Juno. L   192 then, . . . her,] ~ₐ . . . ~ₐ L   ears] ear L
193 crave the more,] ~ₐ L   194 born?] ~ₐ L   197 lyes] lies L   198a reporting.]
~ₐ L   198b Prithee] Prythee L   199 in:] ~. L   200 falshood] falsehood L
Sweet,] ~ₐ L   202 think,] ~ₐ L   203 said'st . . . had'st] saidst . . . hadst L
204 thought'st] thoughtest L   205a open'd.] ~ₐ L   207 hast] has L   born:] born. L
208 endurance,] ~ₐ L   209 forego] forgo L   sex,] ~—L   210 girl. Yet] ~: yet L
211 patience,] ~ₐ L   212 wooing] woing L   resolv'd] resolved L   extremity,] ~ₐ L
214 virgin, come] ~ₐ ~, L   me.] ~: L   216a name, Sir,] ~ₐ ~ₐ L   *Marina*.] Marinaₐ L
216b O! I'm] ~ₐ I am L   219a cease.] ~ₐ L   220 giv'n] given L   224b blood?]
~! L   225 are] Are L   226 motion] ~! L   229 Hold, hold awhile.] Stop a
little— L   230 withal.] withall— L   231 this be . . . and here,] this be?—my child
buried & here— L   232 once—It] ~, it L   be.] ~!— L   233b leave.] ~—L
235 King,] ~ₐ L   father,] ~ₐ L   236 *Philoten*,] Philotenₐ L   Queen,] ~ₐ L
238 pirates] pyrates L   came] ~, L   239b You Gods!] Ye ~ₐ L   deceiv'd] deceived L
240 O!] Oh!— L   242 what] What L   243 sooth,] ~ₐ L   imposture] impostor L
245 goodness,] ~ₐ L   while] whilst L   breath.] ~—. L   246 sinful] sinfull L
man;] ~, L   hour,] ~ₐ L   247 distress] ~, L   248b You] Ye L   Gods!] ~, L
250 despair] dispair L   251 counsels,] ~ₐ L   252 shewing] showing L   own;] ~, L
253 wonder!] ~? L   255 live! hath] ~? Hath L   daughter!] ~? L   256 be.] ~—L
258 God,] godₐ L   260 powers—] ~. L   disperse,] ~? L   262 me,] ~: L
mother?] ~. L   264a rest.] ~!— L   264b *Thaisa*:] Thaisa. L   267 You Gods!
you Gods!] Ye ~, ye ~! L   268 sport—] ~. O bless my arms | And ease my throbbing heart
yᵗ faints wᵗʰ fondness— L   269a *Tyre*.] Tyreₐ L   269bSD *Kneels*;] kneels: L
270 You] Ye L   hence,] ~ₐ L   271 Elizium] Elyzium L   272 here: The . . .
Priestess] ~! {She} The . . . priestess L   273a heav'nly pow'rs] heavenly powers L
274 discovery,] ~ₐ L   275 emotions] ~, L   276 pray] ~, L   277 Heav'n]
Heaven L   279 tempest,] ~ₐ L   282b Hark,] ~! L   286 Nay . . . weep—] ~,

... ~: L   287b Pray,] ~∧ L   290b doat;] {doubt} doat!— L   293 corpse;]
corps∧ L   294 (Now ... Gods)] ∧Now ... gods,∧ L   295 so, ... art,] ~; ... ~∧ L
296 humanity,] ~∧ L   restor'd] restored L   297b O] o L   298a voice!] ~!— L
298b again:] ~. L   300 touch—] ~: L   301a *Pericles.*] Pericles∧ L   301b face,
her stature,] ~——— L   303 is, it can be,] ~∧——∧ L   304b *Jove,*] Jove∧ L
307 air,] ~∧ L   310 innocence,] ~∧ L   311 (So ... who ... them)] ∧So ...
yᵗ ... them,∧ L   312 ten thousand] 10,000 L   313 me,] ~∧ L   315 thy Child
and mine] flesh of thy flesh L   316a life.] ~∧ L   317 own! Thou mak'st] ~!—thou
makest L   319 me,] ~∧ L   Sir,] ~— L   320 pain;] ~, L   321 joys] joy L
me,] ~∧ L   322 mounds] bounds L   323 both:] both, L   325 time,] ~∧ L
326 heart; and] ~: And L   327 who] yᵗ L   328 space,] ~∧ L   repleat] replete L
love] ~, L   332 did'st] didst L   333 paid] ~, L   334 *Tharsus;*] Tharsus, L
338a hir'd] hired L   339 dy'd] died L   343 expence;] ~: L   344b honour'd]
honoured L   346 preserv'd] preserved L   348 noted;] ~: L   350 royal Sir. If]
Royal Sir, if L   352 she, ... maid,] ~∧ ... ~∧ L   353 Lord] lord L   her;] ~. L
354 parting,] ~. L   355 We] I L   357 Father's] father's L   359 Heav'n]
Heaven L   him.] ~: L   Queen,] ~⟨,⟩ L (*edge of MS broken away*)   363 truth,] ~∧ L
364 Tho' long] Altho L   365 preserv'd] preserved L   destruction's] distruction's L
366 Heav'n] Heaven L   366SD [*Exeunt.*] Ed.; *not in* G, L

Epilogue

EPILOGUE.] Epilogue∧ L   2 *censure ... praise*] Censure ... Praise L   4 *fore-fathers*]
Forefathers L   6 *fame's*] Fame's L   7 *country's*] Country's L   9 *race*] Race L
pains,] pains∧ L   10 *authors*] Authors L   *chains.*] chains: L   12 Britons *though*
provok'd] ~, tho' Supine L   13 *caution*] Caution L   *offence:*] offence; L   14 *liberty is*
sense] Liberty is Sense L   15 *arts*] Arts L   *declare;*] declare. L   16 *fathers*] Father's L
17 *your wisdom to display*] a Foreign Vagrant's Prey L   18 *farce*] Farce L
19 *Musick it self*] Musik itself L   20 *sure design'd*] e'er designed L   21–34 *Final leaf*
of L, which presumably included these lines, is missing

ELMERICK

Dedication

Dedication is not in L

Prologue
PROLOGUE.] Prologue∧ L   1 *Night*] night L   *Stage,*] Stage; L   2 *engage.*] engage: L
4 *Force*] force L   *felt*] felt, L   5 *Critick's*] critick's L   *Test*] test L   6 *Eye*] eye L
Tear] tear L   7 *Strains*] strains L   8 *Pity*] pity L   *Remains*] remains L
9 *Disease*] Desease L   11 *Wish*] wish L   12 *Critick*] Critic L   13 *yours*] yours, L

Dramatis Personæ

1 MEN.] Men∧ L   2 *Andrew* II.] Andrew 2ᵈ. L   3 Commonly] commonly L   called]
call'd L   Mr. *Mills.*] *actors' names are not in* L   4 *Jerusalem.*] Jerusalem∧ L
5 *Moravia.*] Moravia∧ L   7 *Ismena*] Ismena L   9 WOMEN.] Women∧ L
13 Queen.] ~∧ L   14 SCENE ... at *Buda.*] *not in* L

I. i
ACT I. SCENE I.] Act 1ˢᵗ. scene 1ˢᵗ. L   1 bless'd] blest L   even] ev'n L   5 when]
When L   8 bewild'ring] bewildring L   11 early musing] L; melancholy G
alone,] ~∧ L   daughter?] L; ~! G   12 Nobles] nobles L   States,] L; ~. G
13 And I ... is absent.] L; G *omits*   16 country] Country L   17 sacrifice] sacrafice L
18 made,] ~∧ L   20 avarice] av'rice L   23 find,] ~∧ L   33 *Ismena,*] Ismena∧ L
35 pleased] pleas'd L   mindful] mindfull L   36 well placed] well-plac'd L
40 praise] prize L   to] to{o} L   41 Is] ~, L   48 Regent] regent L   50b own,]
~∧ L   52 hot-brained] hot-brain'd L   55 brave,] ~∧ L   56 Glory] glory L
excess;] ~: L   60 may.] ~∧ L   63 place] ~, L   65a Nature] nature L

65b confess,] ~∧ L   70 herself] her self L   71a–71b *Ism.* You're ... of conduct.] L;
G *omits*   75 virtuous,] ~∧ L   unmoved] unmov'd L   78 stained] stain'd L
87 The] the L   87SD *separately*] seperately L

I. ii

SCENE II.] Scene 2. L   1 *1st Ld.*] *Ed.*; *1st* L. G; 1 Ld. L   7 *Hungary.*] Hungary! L
7+SD *enter*] Enter L   8 Nobles] nobles L   Deputies] deputies L   9 confederate]
confed'rate L   States] states L   10 Know,] ~∧ L   11 matron] Matron L
12 Neglected,] L; ~∧ G   13 Lyes] Lies L   captived] captiv'd L   profaned] profan'd L
14 ere] e'er L   Kingdoms] kingdoms L   15 witness] L; ~, G   applaud;] ~, L
17 *Hungary:*] Hungary, L   18 Conservator] conservator L   19 Liberty] liberty L
Judge of Power] judge of power L   21 vigour] vigor L   awful] awfull L
22 consummate] consumate L   24 awed] aw'd L   26 Country's] country's L
27 And,] L; ~∧ G   virtue,] ~! L   31 high soaring] high-soaring L   33 shalt] shall L
34 Regal Government] regal government L   36 People] people L   37 race,] ~; L
42 People's] people's L   love,] ~∧ L   43 raised] rais'd L   44–5 Fiend!— | Too
foul mistake!—] fiend?∧ | ~!∧ L   47 Nations] nations L   48 Æra] aera L
49 Publick] publick L   51 gift!] ~? L   53 poor,] ~∧ L   54 virtue.] ~: L
55 Monarch] monarch L   56 bold,] L; ~∧ G   oppressive] injurious L   power;] ~, L²;
~, | (Be he my son) I give it you in charge, L¹   58 Legal Force] legal force L
59 holy] Holy L   60 forfeited] ~, L   prophaned] profaned L   61 head. [*Pauses.*]—
All] ~.—(pauses∧) | ∧~ L   62 hearts] ~! L   63 swells] flows L   tears] ~, L
Assembly] assembly L   67 softness,] ~∧ L   68a tears.] ~! L   68b Monarch]
monarch L   69 Guardian Angel] guardian angel L   72 forced] forc'd L   You] you L
76 received;] receiv'd, L   79 powerful] powerfull L   82 Sov'reign Power] sov'reign
power, L   hands,] ~∧ L   88 offender;] ~, L   89 life?] L; ~. G   90 urged]
urg'd L   yourself] your self L   91 Shall in my absence] Shall, | ~, L   92 Take the
sword,] *so* L²; L¹ *reads*:

> Elm. I wou'd shun this great and arduous trust—
> K.   I will bear no excuse—I know thee worthy
>   And equal to all trust—Take thou the sword,

93 vain.] ~∧ L   95 subjects] subject's L   injustice;] ~, L   98 would] wou'd L
100 awful] awfull L   Liege] leige L   urged] urg'd L   101 realm] Realm L
102 rigour] rigor L   104 faithfulness] faithfullness L   neglect] L; ~, G
105 painful] painfull L   106 King,] ~! L   108 Heaven,] ~! L   111 crown.]
~— L   114 crown] Crown L   115 adieu] Adieu L

I. iii

SCENE III.] Scene yᵉ Third. L   9 *Saladin,*] Saladin∧ L   12 *Ismena.*] Ismena— L
14 love:] ~:— L   And] and L   sex,] ~∧ L   16 Ungrateful] Ungratefull L
man] Man L   17 heart] Heart L   20 society!] ~. L   21 Sir] ~. L
22 you from me] me from you L   24 fired] fir'd L   26 faithful] faithfull L
imposed] impos'd L   27 painful] painfull L   absence;] ~, L   30 Honour] honour L
31 East] east L   34 powerful] powerfull L   37 delays;] L; ~: G   38 forced]
forc'd L   40 brother,] ~; L   44 mournful] mournfull L   45 loud] lou'd L
succour] succor L   47b *Matilda;*] Matilda, L   48 come] ~, L   war's] L; wars G
ended] ~, L   49 beauties] {beat} beauties L   50 shall] ~, L   blended] blendid, L
54 painful] painfull L   55 reproaches.] ~, L   58–66 Mean-time ... I obey?] *so* L²
(*variants noted below*); *not in* L¹   58 Mean-time] Mean time L²   absence,] L²; ~∧ G
59 brother] Brother L²   partner] part'ner L²   heart:] ~; L²   60 day] Day L²   Court]
court L²   62a thee.] ~∧ L   62b brother] Brother L²   63 friend;] ~— L²
64 for.—] ~.∧ L²   65 Sovereign Power] sov'reign pow'r L²   66 Whom] whom L²
70 unused] unus'd L   subjects,] ~∧ L   71a choice] ~∧ L   71b just] L; ~; G
73–89 May I hope ... more, farewel.] *so* L² (*variants noted below*); L¹ *reads* (*numbers in parentheses*
refer to lines in the present edition):

> But now, Matilda, how shall I discharge
> The hardest part of duty leaving thee?
> Eager for fame, and zealous to chastise   (83)
> The foes of Heaven, I thought I cou'd resist   (84)

This heart-invading softness. Fond mistake! (85)
Call'd to begin the task by quitting thee, (86)
I find my fancy'd heroism vain, (87)
And all the tender man return upon me. (88)

Q. The swelling hopes of some important victory,
Will soon efface my image from your heart,
And give you all to Sion, arms & triumphs∧

K. May I hope
These thoughts are but yᵉ fears of love alarm'd? (75)
O say but this, and I will think it kinder (76)
Than all the tender things that tongue e'er utter'd.

Q. Think what will please you best, and that I said it— (78)
And may the shining fame you seek so far, (79)
Pay your long labours.

K. One embrace, Matilda, (80)
May Heaven on all thy days shed sweetest comfort, (81)
And peace, with angel-wings, o'ershade thy slumbers, (82)
Till I return from my hard task of war,
And victory shall take its noblest lustre
From thy approving smiles—Once more—farewell.

74 me,] ∼∧ L² 76 Oh] o L¹ this!] ∼, L¹ 77 th' endearments of affected
fondness.] the tender things that tongue e'er utter'd. L¹ 78 best,] ∼∧ L² it,] ∼∧ L¹, L²
79 Fame] fame L¹, L² far] ∼, L¹ 80a labours!] ∼. L¹ 80b *Matilda*!] Matilda, L¹
82 peace] ∼, L¹; Peace, L² angel] Angel L² wings] ∼, L² 83 Fame] fame L¹, L²
chastize] chastise L¹, L² 84 Heav'n] Heaven L could] cou'd L¹, L² 85 softness—]
∼. L¹ 86 leaving] quitting L¹ thee,] ∼. L² 87 heroism] Heroism L² 88 all
the] all yᵉ L² (*inserted above the line*) feeble,] L²; ∼∧ G; *not in* L¹ man] Man L² returns.—]
return upon me,∧ L¹; ∼∧— L² 89 way.] ∼∧ L² more,] ∼— L¹; ∼∧ L² farewel]
farewell L² *End*] *The End.* G

II. i

ACT II. SCENE I.] Act 2. Scene 1. L 4 reason:] ∼. L 5 it,] ∼∧ L 7a King,]
∼∧ L 8 will.] ∼∧ L 10 should not . . . she weds?] *so* L² (shou'd); weds the man she
does not love? L¹ 11–12 My happy . . . a Queen.] *so* L² (so. | . . . loose); Indeed it seems so.
Witness Heav'n! | Had I not lov'd, wou'd I, to be a Queen— L¹ 13 Queen!—] ∼!∧ L
14 father's] Father's L 15 daughter] ∼, L 16 Parents] parents L love;] ∼, L
Fame] fame L 17 beauty:] ∼, L 19 Princes] princes L 20 love] *so* L²; sigh L¹
The noblest triumphs] *so* L²; Triumph on triumph | O'er vanquish'd hearts, the noblest
acquisition L¹ 23 Sooth'd] *so* L²; Charm'd L¹ call'd] calld L 25 Rabble] rabble L
free,] ∼∧ L Kings] kings L 26 cares for] cares{,} for, L regards not us] *so* L²; may
never be L¹ 27 posterity;] ∼, L 28 *Olmutz*'] Olmutz's L court:] ∼. L
29 mournful] mournfull L 30 Fair] fair L 32 dulness] dullness L
33 pleasure,] ∼∧ L 34 marr'd!] L; ∼∧ G 36 Court] court L 38 should]
shou'd L 40 kind,] ∼∧ L 41 wealth,] ∼∧ L 44 pleasure. But] ∼: but L
45 Master] master L 46 wise] wi{z}se L 53b–55 Marriage, Madam . . . my Lord,]
L²; O what pity | That shou'd be thought so rare! 'Tis true, my lord, L¹; 'Tis true, my Lord, G
60SD *Aside.*] Aside∧ L 61 his] L *inserts above the line* mind] ∼! L 66 vent.] ∼∧ L
66SD *Aside.*] Aside∧ L 67 garden] Garden L 68 fate,] ∼∧ L 72 reason] L; ∼, G
73 love,] ∼∧ L wretched?] ∼. L 77 valiant] valient L *Conrade*,] Conrade∧ L
78 Now] ∼, L 79 gen'rous] generous L 80 forsaken,] ∼∧ G Queen,] ∼∧ L
83 better.] ∼∧ L 86 venal] ∼, L 91b poison!] L (poyson); ∼. G 93 over,] ∼, L
95 joyful] joyfull L 96 I] I, L 97 object,] ∼∧ L nature,] ∼∧ L 98 sister] ∼, L
friend!] ∼. L 100 should] shou'd L 102 pleasures] ∼, L 107 joyful] joyfull L
108 Fortune] fortune L 113 Heart:] L (heart); ∼. G 115 joy] {hop} joy L
116 powerful] powerfull L fired] fir'd L 121 lov'd] loved L 131 life;] ∼, L
132 Which] ∼, L poison] ∼, L 134 being] L; ∼: G 134–5 die | Or find relief,
and] L; ∼, | ∼. And G 136 Determined] L; ∼, G my fate] *so* L²; her heart L¹
more.] L; ∼: G 138 *Elmerick*,] Elmerick∧ L 140 heart,—] ∼.∧ L 141 If] —— L
should] shou'd L mine.] ∼∧ L 141SD *Aside.*] Aside∧ L 142 dissuade] disswade L

attempt] L; ~, G   143 *Elmerick,*] Elmerick_∧ L   144 resides, as Regent,] ~_∧ ~ ~_∧ L
Palace,] Pallace_∧ L   147a solicitation] sollicitation L   147b *Conr.*] L (Conr.); *Con.* G
148 wrong; ... better,] *Ed.*, G, L² (wrong, G, L²); ~, ... ~. L¹   149 Or see ... of despair.]
so L²; *not in* L¹   150 How,] ~_∧ L   can] Can L   would] wou'd L   152 thousand]
L²; cloud of L¹, G   me:] ~. L   157 wishes,] ~_∧ L   heart.] ~_∧ L   158 should]
shou'd L   159 lov'd,] loved_∧ L   161 dispos'd] disposed L   167 gave] so L²;
have L¹   garden,] Garden. L   168a And soon ... her there.] so L²; *not in* L¹
168b *Matilda,*] Matilda! L   169 Cou'dst] Coud'st L   170 lose] loose L
173 transport.] ~_∧ L   174 O!] ~_∧ L   175 heart;] ~, L   176 aid,] ~_∧ L
177 peace!] ~; L   179 despair:] ~, L   'Till] 'till L   183SD Queen.] Queen.) L

II. ii
SCENE II.] Scene 2. L   SD Ismena.] ~_∧ L   3 resolution:] ~. L   aw'd] awed L
4 her.] ~_∧ L   6 here,] ~_∧ L   slave:] ~. L   7 all-powerful] all-powerfull L
subdu'd] subdued L   9 charm:] ~. L   14 language] ~, L   18b Live] ~_∧ L
wise;] ~, L   19 Live,] ~_∧ L   21 Man] man L   23 unjust.] ~_∧ L   Fair] fair L
24 Wilt] Will't L   Never] never L   29b trifles] triffles L   30 betrays?—] ~?_∧ L
31 women] Women L   32 traitor] traytor L   34 before,] ~_∧ L   35a least] L; ~, G
39 one] ~, L   40 Would] Wou'd L   43 let] Let G   45 far, Prince,] so L²
(Prince_∧); far then, L¹   46 I judge] so L²; Presumptious Prince, I judge L¹   47 Oh!]
O_∧ L   fear:] ~_∧ L   48b–50 Since your ... my care.] so L² (frenzy_∧); Since you're quite
lost in error, all my care | Shall be to shun your uncorrected madness. L¹   53 formidable!—]
~!_∧ L¹   56 father] Father L   57 high] so L²; proud L¹   58 passion,] ~_∧ L
59–60 By opposition ... noble conquest.] so L² (fiercely); Collects new force as her disdain
increases. L¹   62 disorder'd.] ~! L   63 Fortune, Nature] fortune, nature L
68 true,] ~; L   74 brother,] ~! L   77 He] he L   80 insult:] ~; L
81 For] ~, L   know,] ~_∧ L   myself] my self L   85 one, one only] so L²; one, only L¹
88 guard;] ~: L   89 rumour] rumor L   90 woman's] so L²; lady's L¹
91 defense] defence L   92 house] House L   arms] Arms L   thee] Thee L

III. i
ACT III. SCENE I.] Act 3. Scene 1. L   1 wretch:] ~. L   thou'rt] thour't L
3a Wou'd'st] Woud'st L   5b servant's] servants L   9 the love I proffer,] the love I
{offer} proffor_∧ L²; my amorous flame_∧ L¹   10 you] so L²; thee L¹   14 hither.] ~_∧ L
15 anti-chamber] Anti-chamber L   16aSD [*Exit*] _∧Exit L   18 extasy] extacy L
19 breath,] ~_∧ L   23 Love] love L   24 elysium] elizium L   me;] ~. L
26 transport;] ~, L   30 me] ~_∧ L   33–4 passions ... Resistless,] ~, in proportion,
violent, | Resistless_∧ L   34 tormenting:] ~. L   35 Imposed] Impos'd L
37 Who but *Matilda*] ~, but Matilda, L   40 flight] ~, L   41 too] to L
42 virtue.] ~_∧ L   44 fraud,] ~_∧ L   47 While] L; while G   51 should] shou'd L
52 fruitful] fruitfull L   56–60 By heav'n ... be mine.] so L² (*variants noted below*); L¹ *reads:*

> Let me but once have her in my power!—
> She shall not mock my love—When these nice dames
> Have rashly boasted their exalted virtue,
> The forward lover is their truest friend.

56 Heav'n] Heaven L   retreat,] ~_∧ L   57 spite] spight L   Husband,] ~_∧ L
58 purpose.] ~_∧ L   60 love: She] L; ~, she G   61 Forbear] For bear L
65–73 Within this ... may yield.] so L² (*variants noted below*); *not in* L¹, *which reads:* May satisfy
your ardor, I'll assist you.   65 Palace] Pallace L²   67 ardour] ardor L²   68 may
perhaps] ~, ~, L²   69 soften] L²; ~, G   persuade] perswade L²   70 Fair] fair L²
71 Love:] love. L²   72 of] {in} of L²   Woman's] woman's L²   73 artful] artfull L
74–80 And shall ... wait th' event.] so L¹; L² *deletes, then restores with insertion of lines 65–73, above*
(*variants,* L¹ *and* L², *noted below*)   75 Oh] O L¹, L²   pow'r] power L¹, L²   bring her
hither] so L²; change her purpose L¹   76 secretary] Secretary L²   Regent,] ~_∧ L²
77 agent:] ~. L¹, L²   78 long] ~. L¹, L²   79 see! she comes. She] L², L¹ (see, L¹);
~_∧ ~, she G   now:] ~. L¹, L²   80 love,] ~_∧ L   event.] ~_∧ L   80SD [*Exit
Conrade.*] (Exit Conrade.) L¹; _∧Exit Conrade_∧ L²   81 Lord] ~, L   82 lover,] ~_∧ L
86 utter'd] utterd L   91 for] ~, L   93 meet,] ~_∧ L²; face, L¹   94 Lady] lady L
98 care] ~, L   99 *Matilda!*] Matilda: L   100 think—] L; ~. G   102 That

quitted once] ~, quitted once, L   recover'd—] L; ~, G (recovered)   104 one] ~, L
105 should] shou'd L   ever.—] ~.ˌ L   106 grateful] gratefull L   107 hand,] ~ˌʌ L
billows,] ~ˌ L   109 hazard] hazzard L   111 herself] her self L   'Tis] Tis L
112 Hell!—] L; ~!ˌ G   115 forlorn—] ~! L   118 deep;] ~, L   119 waste] ~. L
121 joy—] L *appears to write a comma, then change to a dash*   123 Publick] publick L
125 you:] ~. L   128 talk,] ~ʌ L   129 good:] ~. L   131 ev'n] even L
132 bountiful] bountifull L   Nature!] L; ~? G   133 such softness] suchs oftness L
134 ours.] ~ˌ L   135 excel,] excellʌ L   136 serving] so L²; pleasing L¹   us:] ~, L
138 pow'r] power L   give,] ~ʌ L   139 'Tis] Tis L   140 lov'd] loved L
141 sex] ~, L   nature] Nature L   142b Possibly] so L²; But suppose they shou'd.
Perhaps L¹   144 lady] Lady, L   renounced] renounc'd L   145 painful'st] painfull'st L
146 grace,] ~ʌ L   147 condescend] condessend L   149 Trembling] ~, L
150 you;] ~, L   153 heart,] ~ʌ L   154b pardon,] ~ʌ L   Madam;] ~, L
157 and] ~, L   honour] honnour L   159 shame.] ~— L   162 trial] tryal L
164 honour,] ~ʌ L   168 myself:] my self. L   170 you.] ~! L   172 hatred] L; ~, G
176 office.] ~ʌ L   177 fair;] ~, L   178 charms] ~, L   179 resolv'd] resolvd L
180 Should] Shou'd L   181 you,] ~ʌ L   182a ruin!] ~? L   183b Guilt:] ~ʌ L
185 pursue] purs{e}ue L   186 shou'd] shoud L   187 Ev'n] Even L
189 charms,] ~ʌ L   192 grateful] gratefull L   Oh] O! L   201 trust,] ~ʌ L
202 I] I, L   206 master] Master L   211 yourself] your self L   me;] ~, L
212 hold,] ~ʌ L   213 life,] ~ʌ L   221 Oh] O L   222 I have] I've L
223–4 —Death!... indignation!—]ʌ~! horror!ʌ shame |~!ʌ L   225 me,] ~ʌ death]
Death L   227 hateful] hatefull L   228 valiant] valient L   230ASD *sword.*]
Sword.) L   231b be gone] begone L   232b–233a my soul ... | Shall be preserv'd.] my
soul | The secret shall be preserv'd. L   237 Fair] fair L   say] ~! L   240 Sov'reign;]
sov'reign, L   242 virtue] ~. L   244 may'st] mayst L   disorder,] ~ʌ L
245 confusion,] ~ʌ L   246 that] That L   an] a L   249 suffer'd;] ~ʌ L
252 concur] concurr L   255 traitor's] traytor's L   256a sacrifice] sacrafice L
256b cause] ~, L   257 vain;] ~: L   259b him?] ~? (To Conrade) L   260 the
affront] th'affront L   house:] ~ʌ L   261 is,] ~: L   *Ismena:*] Ismenaʌ L
262 Who,] ~ʌ L   sword,] ~ʌ L   262SD [*To* Conrade.] *not in* L (*see* 259b, *above*)
263a me.] ~ʌ L   263b Ha] L; Ah G   264ASD disarm'd.] disarm'dʌ L
270 warn'd.—] L; ~.ʌ G   275 atone] attone L   short;] ~, L   276 yourself] your
self L   277 he,] ~ʌ L   wrong'd,] ~ʌ L   280 light'ning] lightning L
281 overbearing] over bearing L   traitor;] traytor, L   284 indignity,] ~ʌ L
285 threaten'd.] ~ʌ L   290b thou!] ~? L   294–311 I might ... and remorseless.]
so L² (*variants noted below*); *not in* L¹   295 ne'er have] {not have} ne'er have L²
296 complete] compleat L²   297 Revenge,] ~ʌ L²   298 form,] ~ʌ L²
300 thee.—] ~ʌ— L²; ~.ʌ G   301 proud] prou'd L²   302 pity.] ~ʌ L²
303 haughty] Haughty L²   anguish,] ~ʌ L²   304 That] Th{e}at L²   ev'n] even L²
Fiends] fiends L²   pity,] ~ʌ L²   305 repent.] ~ʌ L²   *Conrade,*] ~ʌ L²
306 till] 'till L²   307 ruin,] ~ʌ L²   308a disgrace.] ~ʌ L²   308a+SD Ismena]
~, L²   310a Queen!—] ~,ʌ L   310b me—] ~: L²   311 remorseless.—]
L²; ~.ʌ G   312 rude,] ~ʌ L   313 retirement;] ~. L   315 Yes,] ~ʌ L
316ASD [*Aside.*] (Asideʌ) L   317 Pray] L; ~, G   alter'd] ~. L   318 start,] ~ʌ L
321 disorder,] ~; L   322ASD [*Exit* Ismena.] (Exit ~ʌ L, *which includes the* SD *following
line* 323   325 heart] Heart L   *End*] The End. G

IV. i

ACT IV. SCENE I.] Act 4. Scene 1. L   1 *Bel.*] L (Bel.); *Belus.* G   11 Hell] hell L
would] wou'd L   Heav'n] Heaven L   Earth] Eath L   13a lost] Lost L
13b Queen!] ~!— L   15 Queen's] Queens L   16 follow] follow{d} L
17 bar'd.] barr'dʌ L   18 followed] follow'd L   20 Yes] ~, L   22a extreme]
extream L   25 our selves] ourselves L   on.] ~ʌ L   26 see,] ~! L   Merciful]
Mercifull L   Heav'ns] heavens L   27 now,] ~ʌ L   30 woful] wofull L
31SD Belus *and* Zenomira.] *Ed.*; ~, G; Bel. & Zen. L   32 here?] ~! L
33a Perhaps,] ~ʌ L   33c mournful] mournfull L   35a it?] L; ~; G
40 darkness,] ~ʌ L   closed] clos'd L   41a ff. *A second hand takes over transcribing* L *at this
line and continues to the end of the play*   42 Let] let L   45 hearer;] ~, L

46 deserts] desarts L 47 mankind,] ~ˏₐ L 48 sheltring] shelt'ring L
50 child,] ~ₐ L 55 every] Ev'ry L 57 Here] ~, L 58 business] bus'ness L
59–64 Give me . . . execrable pair!] L (Conrade); G *omits* 65 all-pitying] all pitying L
Heaven,] Heav'n! L 68 violated] L; ~, G matron's] Matron's L 70 Father's]
father's L rejoiced;] rejoic'd, L 71 goodness] ~, L 72 delightfull;] delightful, L
74 its] it's L Heaven.] heav'nₐ L 75 *Elmerick*] Elmeric L wrath perhaps] ~, ~, L
76a Heaven's] Heav'n's L 81 rush, unarm'd,] ~ₐ ~ₐ L 82 toils,] ~ₐ L
85 great—] L; ~. G hand less fear'd] ~, less fear'd, L 87 Lord] lord L
88 Heaven!] Heav'n, L Earth] earth L 90a life.] ~, L 91 vengeance] vengance L
92 thy self] thyself L 96 Would] wou'd L 98 Father] father L 99 and] ~, L
100 Of] of L anguish] ~, L 101 mine,] L; ~. G 106 What,] ~ₐ L
108 insolence] Insolence L Father] father L 109 Yes,] ~ₐ L Prince] prince L
Father] father L 111 thy] the L 112 honour,] honor; L 116 heard] hear'd L
117 Lord;] lord, L 119 though] tho' L bold,] ~ₐ L 120 atone] attone L
121 life;] ~, L 122 And] ~, L 125 death] ~, L 130a vengeance] vengance L
130b Frantick] Frantic L man] Man L 130b+SD Lords] Lords, L *Guards*,] Guardsₐ L
interpose.] interposeₐ L 131 Lords] lords L 138 *1st Ld.*] L (1st Ld.); 1 *Ld.* G (*and
similarly in this scene*) 141 saw—for,] L; ~, ~ₐ G 142 tears—] L; ~; G
143 Which] ~, L you know] *so* L²; reveal'd L¹ 144 you] L; ~, G
150a *2d Ld.*] *Ed.*; 2 Ld. G; 2 Ld. L 150b *3d Ld.*] *Ed.*; 3 Ld. G; 3 Ld. L
150c *4th Ld.*] *Ed.*; 4 Ld. G (*and similarly in this scene*); 4 Ld. L (*and similarly in this scene*)
151 Though] tho' L 152a known.] ~ₐ L 152b 'Till] Till L Lord] lord L
153 country's] Country's L honour] honor L 154b *5th Ld.*] *Ed.*; 5 *Ld.* G (*and similarly in
this scene*); 5 Ld. L (*and similarly in this scene*) 155 knowledge] Knowledge L
157b word,] word, {and vow to share} L 160 cause,] ~ₐ L 160SD *1st, 2d, 3d
Lords.*] *Ed.*; 1, 2, 3 ~. G; 1. 2. 3. Lordsₐ L 161 Traitors] traytors L 162 Lords]
lords L 167 Regent] L; regent G 170 *Elmerick*] Elmeric L 174 publick]
public L 175 insult;] ~, L 179 *5th Ld.*] *Ed.*; 5 *Ld.* G; L *omits, giving the speech to*
4th Ld. zeal] Zeal L assassins] assasins L 180 men] Men L You] ~, L
182 honour?] honor! L 185 or you,] ~ₐ L 186a will] *so* L²; shall L¹ justice.] ~ₐ L
186b traitors] Traytors L 187 power;] pow'r; L 190 blood,] L; ~ₐ G
191 The] the L justice] Justice L 192 *Elmerick*,] Elmericₐ L 193a Influence]
influence L 196 *Elmerick's*] Elmeric's L 198 King;] ~, L 199 sufferings]
suff'rings L 200 after feint] after-feint L 201 Lord] Lord L 203 traitor]
traytor L 206 hopes] ~; L 209 life] ~, L vengeance] vengance L
210–14 My blind . . . will denied.] *so* L² (*variants noted below*); L¹ *reads*:

> My high enamour'd fancy once aspir'd
> But to the charms my ravish'd eye captor'd,
> Oh! avarice of Love!—now I aspire
> And languish for the joys of mutual passion.

212 love] Love L² aspires] aspires {to mutual bliss} L² 213 and more refin'd] ~, more
refind, L² 214 denied] deny'd L² 216 sire] L; Sire G 218 Oh] ~! L
220. remembrance.] remical'ranceₐ L 222 off] L; ~, G 223 vengeance] vengance L
224 ready] read{d}y L 226 new made] new-made L 229 forth,] ~ₐ L ruin]
Ruin L

IV. ii
SCENE II.] Scene 2.ᵈ L SD Elmerick] Elmeric, L 1 absent,] ~ₐ L 3 last.] ~: L
5 peace] ~, L comfort] ~, L 9b Heaven] Heav'n L 13 would] wou'd L
14 Heaven] Heav'n L 15 tempestuous] tempest'ous L 17 even] ev'n L
18b you:] Youₐ L 19 Though] Tho' L 21 mean?] ~! L 23b well:] ~. L
24 power] pow'r L 25 doom;] ~, L 28a arms,] ~ₐ L 29 Father] father L
31 *Elmerick*] Elmeric L 32 —Detested thought—] ₐ~, L 34 ruin,] ~; L
35 chaste] chast L embraces:] L; ~, L 37a honour] honor L 37b Heaven]
Heav'n L 38 overwhelming] o'erwhelming L 39 ages] ~, L 42 Withheld]
Witheld L 43 (That . . . anguish)] ₐ~ . . . ~, ₐ L 44a you.] ~ₐ L
44b thus,] thus, {tal} L 46 unstain'd;] ~: L 48 power] pow'r L 49 *Elmerick's*]
Elmeric's L honour.—] honor.ₐ L 51 improvident,] ~! L 53a O] Oh L

53b O] Oh L   Lord!] ~!— L   54 weep] ~! L   55 Adieu] L; Farewell G
58b bosom] ~, L   59 tenderer] tender{ly}er L   60 a while] awhile L
61 greatness] G (*errata slip*), L; greatest G   62 powers] pow'rs L   66 *Elmerick*]
Elmeric L   67 reverend] rev'rend L   Father—] L (father); ~; G   him] ~, L
68 can—my] L; ~: My G   nearly—] L; ~. G   69 vengeance—] L (vengance); ~, G
beware—] L; ~; G   71 rashness] ~, L   72 mystery] myst'ry L   its] it's L
74 deserve:] ~; L   76 whole;] ~: L   80 Adieu] L; Farewell G   80SD [*Exeunt.*]
not in L

V. i

ACT V. SCENE I.] Act 5. Scene 1. L   1 G *adds speech-heading*: Queen.   4 even] ev'n L
6 vigour] vigor L   11 dangerous] dang'rous L   on,] ~— L   14 'tis] tis L
15 heart:] ~∧ L   17 him.] ~— L   21a+SD Elmerick *and* Zenomira] Zenomira and
Elmeric L   26b hear] L; ~, G   27 intelligence,] ~; L   30 attend,] ~∧ L
31 Begin] begin L   collected,] ~. L   33 turn,] ~∧ L   34b in it] in't L
36 Heaven] Heav'n L   37 desperate] desp'rate L   39 with;] ~, L   but,] ~∧ L
41 power,] Pow'r! L   42 Heaven] Heav'n L   Earth] earth L   Hell] hell L
43 Justice;] ~! L   45 Deign] deign L   47 lesson] ~, L   48 T' instruct]
T'instruct, L   world.] ~! L   50b Sov'reign,] sov'reign; L   52 assassinate] assasinate L
Help! Treason!] L (treason); ~. ~. G   53 die;] dye. L   55 Traitor] Traytor L
59 Heaven:] Heav'n. L   61 account;] ~: L   62a their] L; there G   63 it;] ~: L
66 laws,] ~∧ L   demand;] ~, L   67 honour] honor L   70 sin'd] sinn'd L
72 yours—] your's; L   74SD [*Aside.*] *not in* L   79 Justice] justice L   extent] ~, L
80 Power] pow'r L   Trust] trust L   me:] ~; L   83 shou'd] shoud L   87 full] *so*
L²; strong L¹   89 infamy,] ~∧ L   90 atone] attone L   93 again,] ~∧ L
94 injustice,—] ~,∧ L   95 And] and L   96 happy.—] L; ~.∧ G   now,] L;
~∧ G   97 justice:] ~; L   Do] do L   97+SD Enter the Executioners.] The Executioners
enter. L   *While*] while L   her,] her∧ L   speaks.] speaks ∧ L   98 Must] must L
99 power,] Pow'r! L   102SD *Recess*] recess L   *back Scene,*] back-scene∧ L
103 atone] attone L   its] it's L   errors!—] ~!∧ L   106 the human] *so* L² (yᵉ); a
human L¹   110 true,] ~∧ L   Behold] behold L   there.] ~∧ L   113b it,] ~; L
114 rigorous] rig'rous L   115 abounds,] ~∧ L   119 business] bus'ness L
120 power] pow'r L   121 Nature's] nature's L   122 Justice;] ~! L
123 Inspired] Inspir'd L   blow] L; ~, G   125 hers] her's L   126 dishonour]
dishonor L   name:] ~; L   128b declared] declar'd L   131 dreadful] *so* L² (dredful);
noble L¹   132aSD *Queen.*] Queen ⟨ ⟩ L(*edge of MS missing*)   132b can.] ~— L
134 Justice] justice L   135 Bath.] L (Bath.); *Ba.* G   Heaven] Heav'n L   137 interest]
int'rest L   138 partial:] ~; L   141 Heaven] Heav'n L   142 bar;] ~, L
146a *Ld.*] L (Ld.); *L.* G   146b–148 'Tis the . . . King appears.] L (Enters Gentleman); See,
the King appears. G   148+SD Conrade,] ~∧ L   149 who] *so* L²; that L¹
151a *Elmerick*] Elmeric L   156 Go and] *so* L² (go); someone L¹   157 appear] L; ~, G
Traitor] traytor L   159b pray,] ~∧ L   160–1a to what . . . guilty Queen.] *so* L²; the
poor remains | Of her that was Matilda. L¹   161b Heavenly powers] Heav'nly pow'rs L
162–3 For what . . . barb'rous Villain—] L; G *omits*   164 Am] am L   165aSD *Recess*]
L (Recess); *recess* G   166 Is] is L   167 Husband] husband L   171–2 Condemn'd
on . . . Yet, I resign] L; Sir, I resign G   173 head. But] ~; but L   178 honour'd]
honor'd L   think] ~, L   181 Sir.] ~: L   183 well:] ~; L   184 indignation.] ~: L
185 cou'd'st] coud'st L   187 attempt it.] L; ~; G   188 *K.* A murderer . . . of
Justice?] L (justice); G *prints after* 190 (Justice!); G (*errata slip*) *directs that the line be deleted* (*see*
191–6a, *below*)   189 Yes,] L; But∧ G   190 heard] hear'd L   with patience.] *after*
this line L¹ *reads* (*numbers in parentheses refer to lines of the present edition; variants also noted at*
appropriate lines below):

K. You shall be heard: a seat—O! my Matilda,   (202)
    Forgive this short delay. Let the rash man   (203)
    Endev'ring to defend, convict himself,   (204)
    And fall the more abhorr'd—You may proceed—   (205a)
Elm. To pay my life for daring to be just,
      Is buying glory at a small expence—

K. To the charge—
　　My patience is abus'd, I will not keep it
　　To hear a traytor glory in his guilt
Elm. My guilt is yet unprov'd.
K. The horrid fact is plain, and asks no proof.
Elm. I ask but to be heard and that's no favour.

191–6a But if . . . my country.] L (*without italics*), G (*errata slip; variants noted below*); G *omits these lines and prints:* K. A murderer confess'd dare talk of Justice! (*errata slip restores* 191–6a *and directs that this line be deleted*)　　191 if,] L; ~∧ G (*errata slip*)　　through] G (*errata slip*); thro' L prevention,] L; ~∧ G (*errata slip*)　　192 wou'd not live] L; had rather die G (*errata slip*) 193 To] L; Than G (*errata slip*)　　Palatine] palatine G (*errata slip*)　　194 *Hungary*] G (*errata slip*); Hungary L　　195 be] L; live G (*errata slip*)　　197 shou'dst] shoud'st L 'scape,] ~∧ L　　198 urged] urg'd L　　199 Hereafter,] ~∧ L　　201 shame.—] ~.∧ L　　202–5a You shall . . . more abhorr'd.] *so* L² (*variants noted below*); L¹ *includes these lines after* 189, *above, and here reads:*

　　No, live and mock attention, talk whole days,
　　I will, if possible, be calm and hear you.
Elm. I thank you for the honor done yourself,
　　And shall be brief.

202 heard:] ~. L²　　A seat] a seat L¹; a Seat L²　　O] ~! L¹　　*Matilda,*] Matilda∧ L² 203 man,] ~∧ L¹; Man∧ L²　　204 Endeavouring] Endev'ring L¹　　himself,] ~∧ L² 205a abhorr'd.] ~—You may proceed— L¹　　205b remember,] L²; ~, Sir, L¹, G 208 power,] pow'r∧ L　　210 suffer,] ~. L　　211 vain. You've] ~—you've L 213 Sir!] sir. L　　Dare] dare L　　affirm] ~. L　　215 fore-thought] forethought, L deliberate] delib'rate L　　216 plot] ~, L　　217 lewd] leud L　　218 laws,] L; ~∧ G human] humane L　　219 death,] ~; L　　221 agent] ~, L　　vile] *so* L²; lewd L¹ 224a *Ismena!*] Ismena!— L　　227b traitor] traytor L　　228 prophanation,] ~∧ L 229 bed;] ~{?}. L　　235 loved] lov'd L　　240b proofs,] ~; L　　241–5 who cou'd . . . Confest it] the Queen's confession, | Who own'd it L　　　　　　245 in it] in't L 247 Wife's] wife's L　　truth,] ~∧ L　　250 Proofs] proofs L　　scroll,] scrol∧ L 250SD *Paper*] paper L　　251 deed,] ~∧ L　　252 it] L; ~, G　　253 ill,] ~; L 256 Let] let L　　257 will. [*Reads.*] Madness] *Ed.*; will. (*Reads.*) | Madness G, L (Reads L), *which treat as two lines*　　death!] ~!— L　　258 Regent!—] ~!∧ L　　259 That] that L 260 dishonour] dishonor L　　261 credit—] ~∧ L　　262 fixt] fix'd L　　ideas] Ideas L 264 pois'nous] poisonous L　　266a Life] life L　　266bSD *Aside*] aside L 267 Which] ~, L　　enter'd;] ~, L　　270 then not to accuse her] *so* L²; not to accuse her then L¹　　271 fate,] ~∧ L　　271SD *Aside.*] Aside∧ L　　272 acknowledge,] ~∧ L truth] ~, L　　273aSD Belus *and* Zenomira] L (&); Bel. *and* Zen. G　　273b Heaven] Heav'n L us.] ~∧ L　　274 Her] her L　　276 her . . . her] {s}her . . . {s}her L　　guilty,] ~∧ L hateful:] ~; L　　278 shed,] ~∧ L　　280 more.] ~∧ L　　282 *Elmerick*] Elmeric L weep.] ~∧ L　　284 *Ismena*] Ismena, L　　288 messenger] Messenger L　　sent] ~, L 288+SD *Enter*] Enters L　　290a brief:] ~; L　　293 message] ~, L　　295 Heaven] Heav'n L address] address'd L　　thus:] *Ed.*; ~, L; ~. G　　299 Lord] ~, L　　reluctance.] ~: L 302 then] ~, L　　303 sigh,] ~∧ L　　306 o'erwhelm'd] oerwhelm'd L　　308b die] dye L　　311 poison's] poyson's L　　312 man] Man L　　314 thee,] ~∧ L warlike] war like L　　315 Prince] prince L　　316 justice,] Justice! L 317 retribution,] ~∧ L　　319 seat,] ~∧ L　　320 sit'st] ~, L　　wreaths] wreath L 321 angels] Angels L　　323 sacrifice] sacr{a}ifice L　　326 relieve!] ~?— L 328 abhor'st:] ~∧ L　　329 compassion:] ~. L　　331 sacrifice:] sacrafice. L know,] ~∧ L　　332 power] pow'r L　　vengeance;] ~, L　　334 reveng'd—] ~. L 335 t'atone] t'attone L　　336 error:] ~. L　　err:] ~; L　　337 youthful] youthfull L 340 power!] ~, L　　341 explore;] ~, L　　343 abhor:] ~. L　　346 truth,] ~∧ L 347 awful] awfull L　　348 aveng'd] avengd L　　349 O!] ~∧ L　　350 Publick] publick L　　suffer!] ~. L　　done greatly.] *after this line* G *prints* 355–7　　351 justice] ~, L Heaven,] ~∧ L　　352 purity,] ~∧ L　　354 Thy] thy L　　be mine . . . approve it] L; that I approve it mine G　　355–7 Still hold . . . for ever.] L (*variants noted below*); G *prints after*

350, *above*   355 Sov'reign Power] sov'reign power L   till] 'till L   356 *Sion;*] Sion, L
357 Substitute] substitute L   till] 'till L   Friend] friend L   for ever] forever L

Epilogue

EPILOGUE.] Epilogue∧ L   Spoken by Mr. MILWARD.] *not in* L   1 *supreme*] supream L
2 *unbiast*] unbias'd, L   4 *Play,*] Play∧ L   5 *gen'rous*] generous L
7 high,] ~∧ L   8 *Vengeance*] vengeance L   9 Judge] judge L   Guilty Fall] Guilty fall L
11 *thoughts*] thôts, L   12 *If,*] If∧ L   *Action*] action L   13 *irregularly*] Irregularly L
14 *master-strokes*] master∧ strokes L   *Passions*] passions L   *move,*] move; L   15 *Then,*]
Then∧ L   King,] ~∧ L

ARDEN OF FEVERSHAM

Prologue

PROLOGUE] L *does not include prologue*   3 *just.*] W1; ~; D   9 its] I; it's D
16 Hybla] *Ed.*; *Hybla* D   28 generous,] I; ~∧ D

Dramatis Personæ

1 MEN.] ~∧ L   2 The Mayor] *Ed.*; The mayor D; Mayor L   Mr. *Burton.*] *Actors' names are
not in* L   4 *Franklin,*] L (Franklin); ~∧ D   9 *Will,*] Will. L   9.5 Ruffians.] I; ~∧
D; *not in* L   10 *Shakebag*] Shakebag. L   11 Lord *Cheyney.*] ~ Cheyney∧ L, *which
begins list of men with this entry*   12 *Adam* . . . inn-keeper.] Adam Fowl∧ an Innkeeper. L, *which
includes this entry before line* 9   18 in *Kent*] *not in* L

I. i

ACT I. SCENE I.] Act 1ˢᵗ Scene 1ˢᵗ L   door.] *Door*∧ L   SD Mosby] Enter Mosby L
1 dark,] ~∧ L   horrid,] ~∧ L   purpose.—] Purpose∧— L   7 come.—] ~.∧ L
10 fancy'd] fancied L   *Michael,*] Michael∧ L   trencher-fav'rite] Trencher-Favourite L
13 And,] ~∧ L   15 here,] ~; L   17 for ever] forever L   20 whisper'd,]
Whisper'd∧ L

I. ii

SCENE II. *A chamber.*] Scene 2ᵈ A Chamber∧ L   SD Arden . . . night-gown] Enter Arden in
his night-gown L   2 down!] ~? L   4 yield] yeild L   6 Ungrateful] ~, L
9 *Arden*] L (Arden); ~, D   19 nature,] Nature∧ L   21 every] ev'ry L   23 Himself
th'offender . . . the judge.] L (& . . . Judge); *not in* D   25 power] Pow'r L   26a heav'nly]
heavenly L   this—] This. L   29 surmises] Surmises, L   32 us!—] ~?∧ L
33 curs'd,] curst∧ L   35a hear!] ~? L   35b slave] Slave! L   36b speak!] L; ~. D
39a knees—] L (Knees); ~. D   39b kneel] ~, L   47 blood,] I; ~. D, L (Blood L)
50 *Arden,*] Arden! L   52 tears,] *Ed.*; ~∧ D, L   sooner).] *Ed.*; ~,)∧ D; ~∧)∧ L
55 sacrific'd] sacrificed L   peace,] Peace∧ L   fame,] Fame∧ L   57 think,] ~∧ L
58b heav'n] Heaven L   62 accents] Accents, L   63 *Mosby.* Love] L (Mosby); ~, love D
66 painful] ~, L   72 glow'd,] L; ~∧ D   77 carelessness] Carelessness L
85 cou'd] could L   guilty!] Guilty? L   86 thee] the L   87 life,] Life∧ L
89 alone,] ~∧ L   90 fierce] ~, L   93 *Alicia.*—] Alicia.∧ L   94a it—] ~, L
speak.] ~! L   95a conduct—] L (Conduct); ~.— D   98a heav'n,] Heav'n∧— L
100 heav'n] Heaven L   103 heav'n,] Heaven∧ L   you,] ~∧ L   104 Prithee,] ~∧ L
107b heart,] Heart∧ L   108b own.] ~∧ L   113a possible—] L; ~. D
117 Pity,] ~∧ L   sure,] ~∧ L   121 love!] Love? L   122 *Alicia—*] Alicia!— L
125 the abbey-lands] th'Abbey-Lands L   128 husband,] Husband∧ L   130a *Mosby—*]
Mosby. L   131a below.—] ~.∧ L   131b haste,] ~∧ L   133 what!] What, L
135a health—] Health. L   135b Here,] ~; L   136 melancholy?—] Melancholy?∧ L
137a me, stock, stone.—] ~! Stock! Stone!∧ L   137b Truly,] ~∧ L   138 canst] can'st L
nothing—] ~. L   140 prevail!] ~? L

I. iii

SCENE III.] Scene 3.^{d} L   2 hour,] Hour$_\wedge$ L   fallen] fall'n L   3 frown—] ~. L
4 complain!] ~? L   5 sister] Sister, L   expected—] ~. L   6 then!] ~? L
8 borne] born L   10a Madam,] ~$_\wedge$ L   12 choice,] Choice$_\wedge$ L   14 fame] L
(Fame); ~, D   19 name,] Name$_\wedge$ L   20 the affection] th'affection L   21 ere]
'ere L   giv'n] given L   22a all.—] All.$_\wedge$ L   22b No, no,] ~, ~$_\wedge$ L
24 fraud—the] Fraud. The L   25a himself—] ~. L   25b —And] $_\wedge$~ L
25b–26a fall | The] fall the L, *incorrectly writing as one line*   26a victim—] Victim. L
26b —No] $_\wedge$~ L   wrongs.] Wrongs$_\wedge$ L   28 Then,] ~$_\wedge$ L   29 abhor'd] abhor'd L
blood,] Blood$_\wedge$ L   30 expos'd] ~, L   32 maids,] Maids$_\wedge$ L   33 weakness]
Weakness, L   they] the L   35a certain.—] ~.$_\wedge$ L   37 may—] ~$_\wedge$ L   deceiv'd]
deceived L   me] ~, L   38 instrument;] Instrument, L   41 thee,] ~; L   *Mosby*!] L
(Mosby); ~. D   44a Ere] 'Ere L   44b Ha!—] ~!$_\wedge$ L   46 *Mosby*—] Mosby, L
wou'dst] wou'd'st L   48 for ever;] forever. L   49a power.—] Power.$_\wedge$ L
51 so.—] ~$_\wedge$— L   52 Declare,] ~$_\wedge$ L   53 for ever] forever L   55 way?—] ~?$_\wedge$ L
56 will,] ~; L   57 distraction!] Distraction, L   58SD *Shrieks,*] Shrieks$_\wedge$ L
59+SD *Enter* Arden *and* Franklin.] L (*italics Ed.*); D *prints immediately before* 59   61b *Mosby*—]
Mosby, L   62 Madam,] ~$_\wedge$ L   65 scene.] Scene$_\wedge$ L   66 know,] ~$_\wedge$ L
whether] whither L   69 sight,] Sight$_\wedge$ L   70a falshood.] Falshood! L   71 that:]
~. L   72 deed,] Deed$_\wedge$ L   73 *Edward*,] Edward$_\wedge$ L   74a satisfied.—] ~.$_\wedge$ L
75 thought.—] Thought.$_\wedge$ L   76 thought—] Thought. L   to advise] t'advise L   him,]
~$_\wedge$ L   77 *Green*,] Green$_\wedge$ L   79 seal,] Seal$_\wedge$ L   86 forms,] ~$_\wedge$ L
89 esteem'd,] ~$_\wedge$ L   91 insinuating] insulting L   93 your] thy L   94 consummate]
consummate L   96 side,] ~$_\wedge$ L   97 manhood?—] Manhood!$_\wedge$ L   Draw.—] ~!$_\wedge$ L
98 Hold.] ~! L   100 chuse] choose L   101 on.] ~! L   brink,] Brink$_\wedge$ L
103 flight,] Flight$_\wedge$ L   110 begone—] ~! L   111 th'officious] the officious L
112 me,] ~$_\wedge$ L   friend;—] Friend$_\wedge$— L   113 shake—] ~, L   119 fallen] fall'n L
121 light.] L (Light); ~, D   122 tyrant-like] Tyrant like L   maintains,] ~$_\wedge$ L
123SD [*Exeunt.*] *Ed.*; *not in* D, L   *The end*] End L

II. i

ACT II. SCENE I.] Act 2.^{d} Scene 1st. L   SD *Green. Mosby.*] Enter Green & Mosby$_\wedge$ L
1 estate.] Estate; L   2 *Mosby*;] L (Mosby); ~, D   5b *Arden*,] Arden! L
6 himself,] ~$_\wedge$ L   7a beg,] Beg$_\wedge$ L   7b neither:] ~! L   9 enemy,] Enemy$_\wedge$ L
10a himself.—] ~.$_\wedge$ L   13b heaven.] Heaven! L   14a fail—] ~? L   15 secure,]
~$_\wedge$ L   19 pain;] ~: L   20 Contempt] ~, L   26 respect,] Respect$_\wedge$ L
30 urge] ~, L   death;] Death: L   31 sir—] L (Sir); *not in* D   33 envy'd] envied L
35 not cause . . . not means] nor Cause . . . nor Means L   37 Enough:] ~; L
fixt—] ~. L   See] Good L   38a gentlemen.] Gentlemen! L   42 him.] ~$_\wedge$ L
you,] ~$_\wedge$ L   46 *Boulogne*,] Boulogne; L   47 Where] ~, L   myself.] ~: L
49 name.—] Name.$_\wedge$ L   50 mankind,] Mankind$_\wedge$ L   52b (An] $_\wedge$~ L   hint:] ~. L
53 employment] L (Employment); ~: D   54 *Black Will*] Black-Will L   56 hand.—]
Hand.$_\wedge$ L   60 you,] ~$_\wedge$ L   not] *not in* L   61 Why,] ~$_\wedge$ L   62 Why,] L; ~$_\wedge$ D
forgotten,] ~$_\wedge$ L   64 soldier, you know,] ~$_\wedge$ ~$_\wedge$ L   wherever] whereever L
66 business,] Business; L   68 told] L; ~, D   69 and,] &$_\wedge$ L   rogue,] Rogue$_\wedge$ L
cheating] Cheating: L   70 had'st] hadst L   71 an hedge] a Hedge L   74 *cent. per*
cent.] Cent$_\wedge$ per Cent$_\wedge$ L   79 gentlemen.] Gentlemen! L   80 *Bradshaw*] Bradshaw$_\wedge$ L
81SD [*Aside to* Green.] L *includes after* 80   82 done.—] ~.$_\wedge$ L   *Bradshaw*,] Bradshaw$_\wedge$ L
84 war,] War; L   85 nest,] Nest$_\wedge$ L   little, he] ~. He L   86 S'blood] Blood L
scap'd] 'scap'd L   87 well.] ~$_\wedge$ L   us?] ~. L   88 secrecy,] Secrecy$_\wedge$ L
90 hand,] ~$_\wedge$ L   93 friendship—] Friendship. L   100 sir.] Sirs, L   101 ere]
'ere L   102 Promise and] ~, ~ L   oaths—] Oaths, L   103SD *laugh.*] Laugh$_\wedge$ L
104a swear?—] Swear?$_\wedge$ L   106 blood] Blood; L   do);] ~)$_\wedge$ L   108 purchase, and]
Purchase$_\wedge$ | And L, *writing as two lines of verse*   112 call'd] called L   116 And, he]
~$_\wedge$ ~, L   117 late,] ~$_\wedge$ L   118 int'rest] Inte'rest L   death.—] Death.$_\wedge$ L
125 *George*!] George, L   dang'rous] dangerous L   126 known;] ~: L   127 pow'r]
Power L   130 valour;] Valour, L   131 crafty] Crafty, L   132 world—] World. L

135 I've had] I'd have L 137 that] the L 143 you,] ~∧ L gentlemen?]
Gentlemen. L 146 we've] L; w'have D 151SD ways.] Ways∧ L

II. ii

SCENE II. | A] Ed., *following* W1; SCENE, a D; Scene a L SD Alicia] ~, L 3 fail,]
fail∧ L 5 undetermined] undetermin'd L 6 watch.—] Watch∧— L
7 dispos'd] L; ~, D 9SD [Alicia *starts*.] L ((Alicia Starts); *not in* D 13a ere] 'ere L
long.—] ~∧∧ L 17 nature!] Nature? L 18 love,] Love∧ L 23 loves,] Loves∧ L
24 life,] Life? L 25 —What's] ∧~ L 30 towards] t'wards L 31 heav'n]
Heaven L

II. iii

SCENE III.] Scene 3.ᵈ L SD *room*.] room; L 6 love—] Love. L
6SD [*Approaching . . . starts*.] L (him∧) *includes* SD *immediately after* 5 10 cry'd] cried L
hold!] ~? L 11 mimic] mimick L sense,] Sense∧ L 17 cou'd] can L
18 form,] Form∧ L 22 me.] ~, L 24 hand—] Hand. L 25 dagger, *Michael*]
~! Michael! L 25 it,] ~∧ L 26 is!] L; ~? D 27 vision—] Vision!— L
thou] *not in* L 29a *Arden*—] Arden!— L husband—] Husband!— L lord—] Lord! L
30 wonder] Wonder! L Hence!] L; hence— D 32 durst] darst L thus,] ~∧ L
34b me:] ~! L 35 Lest,] ~∧ L rage,] Rage∧ L 36 thee,] ~∧ L charms]
(Charms); ~, D 37 soul;] ~! L face] Face, L 38 falshood] Falsehood L still;]
~: L 39 atoms.] Atoms! L 40 me,] ~∧ L 40SD *kneels*,] kneels∧ L
43a weep,] Weep∧ L vain.—] Vain.∧ L 46 his,] ~∧ L virtue—] Virtue. L
50 for ever] forever L *The end*] End L

III. i

ACT III. SCENE I. A] Act 3.ᵈ Scene 1ˢᵗ. a L SD Black Will] Enter Black Will L
1 were,] ~∧ L 2 thee,] ~∧ L 3 carelessly] carelessly L 6 a] A L me;] ~: L
7 life—] Life. L seized] Seiz'd L 9 still.—] ~.∧ L 10 villain.] Villain! L
11 at] a L *Boulogne*] Boulogne, L knew,] ~∧ L 12 you. Dog,] ~, ~! L
13 throng—] Throng. L 14 capacity.—] Capacity.∧ L 15 candlelight] Candle-light L
16 lye.] ~! L 17 S'blood] Blood L 18 blood.] Blood! L 19 thine.] ~! L
20 What!] ~, L mad!] ~? L 21a till] 'till L 23 Away.] ~! L 30 matter,] ~: L
36 Ay—] ~; L 37 play—] Play. L 39a on.] ~; L 40 Enough.—] ~.∧ L
withdraw;] ~. L 44 man,] Man: L do't,] ~∧ L 48 off,] ~: L
49 strike—] ~. L 49+SD *then*] then, L 51 met.] ~! L 57 tomorrow]
to-morrow L 60bSD *Lord* Cheyney, *and* Arden] L.ᵈ Cheyn: Arden L 61 too!—] ~!∧ L
S'blood] Blood! L 64 you!] ~? L 67 A] a L 68 heart.] ~! L
70 man—] Man. L 71 though] tho' L 73 spurr'd.—] ~.∧ L it,] ~∧ L
75 attempt,] Attempt∧ L 78 Would] Wou'd L gone.] ~∧ L 79 back;] ~: L
84 villain.] Villain: L white liver] White-Liver L 87 command] command you L
90 thither—] ~. L 92 And,] ~∧ L 93 comply—] Comply. L 94a interest—]
L (Interest); ~. D 96 unbarr'd] unbar'd L 98 take him,] ~∧ L 102 thee;] ~: L
not.] ~! L

III. ii

SCENE II.] Scene 2.ᵈ, L 5 thoughts,] Thoughts∧ L 6 yield] yeild L 7 griefs;]
Griefs: L 9 flame,] Flame∧ L 10 till] 'till L us.] Us: L 12a passion—]
Passion. L 12b —Is] ∧~ L heroic] heroick L 14 immortal,] ~∧ L
17 promise,] Promise∧ L 21 me] ~, L 22 you] ~, L avarice] Av'rice L
insolence,] Insolence∧ L 28 fortune] L (Fortune); ~, D 31 babes] L (Babes);
children D 33 gratitude,] Gratitude∧ L 34 hop'd] hoped, L 38 passion,]
Passion; L 40 Till] 'Till L falshood, (call] Ed.; ~∧ (~ D; Falshood. (Call L
41 desperate;] ~: L 43 hear,] ~∧ L 49 me,] ~; L 55 wak'd,] ~∧ L
57SD [*Aside*.] L ((aside∧)) *includes at end of* 56b 61a its] his L 62 ere] 'ere L
now.—] ~∧— L so;] ~. L 63 ere] 'ere L 65 reproach.] Reproach: L
66 offended,] ~∧ L 73 known,] ~∧ L 75 public] publick L justice—] Justice, L
76SD [*To her*.] *not in* L 77 gratitude,] Gratitude∧ L 78b —Then] ∧~ L
81 should] shou'd L 83 thought.] Thought! L 84 should] shou'd L
85a heaven,] Heaven∧ L will.—] ~∧ (*DFo copy*); ~! L 85b then] ~, L 88 Should]

Shou'd L   89a joys!—] Joys!∧ L   89b transports;] L (Transports); ∼, D
90 betray'd;] L; ∼, D   91a promised] promis'd L   91b First,] ∼∧ L   dissolve.] ∼! L
92 you,] ∼∧ L   94 thoughts.] *Ed.*; ∼∧ D, L (Thoughts L)   95 then,] ∼∧ L   farewel.
—] ∼!∧ L   Now,] ∼∧ L   Fortune,] ∼∧ L   worst.] ∼! L   96 *Mosby,*] Mosby∧ L
97 for ever] forever L   98 fair ones,] Fair Ones∧ L   100 far.] ∼: L
101 debate:] ∼; L   103 ye] you L

III. iii

SCENE III. *Another*] *Ed., following* W1; SCENE, *another* D; Scene ∧ Another L   SD *thoughtful*]
very thoughtful L   1 not.—] ∼.∧ L   3 vengence] Vengeance L   6b —Ay,] *Ed.*;
—∼∧ D; ∧∼, L   7 so.] ∼: L   11 wrongs—] Wrongs; L   wrong'd.] Wrong'd: L
12 then?] L; ∼! D   13 hatred] Hat'red L   14 passions,] Passions∧ L   15 deceive!]
L; ∼? D   16 only,] ∼∧ L   17 jewel] Jewel∧ L   18+18SD yourself. . . . night,]
yourself. Good Night! (Clock strikes 10. L   19a strucken] striken L   20b Why,] ∼∧ L
22 ere] 'ere L   26 rest.] Rest: L   32 woes.] Woes: L   40 checker'd] chequer'd L
death?] Death, L   43a repose.] Repose! L   45 night.] Night! L
45SD–45+SD [*Exit* Franklin. | Michael . . . *returns.*] *Ed., following* L *and* W1 (Light∧ L); D *prints as*
a single, bracketed SD   52 unbar'd] L (unbarr'd); ∼. D   54 mangled body] Murder'd
Corse L   55 live:] ∼! L   56 'em—] ∼?— L   57 Where] where L
59 Help! call] L; ∼—∼ D   Master,] L; ∼— D   *Franklin!*—Help!] L (Franklin); ∼∧—help. D
59+SD *and* Franklin, *undress'd,*] & Franklin∧ ∼∧ L   62 dream'd] dreamt L
65b I?—] ∼?∧ L   65c Why,] L; ∼∧ D   66 still.—] ∼.∧ L   68 sir:] Sir. L
69b Sir—] ∼, L   71a more,] ∼∧ L   71b —Good night.] ∧∼—Night— L
71bSD *Exeunt.*] L (Exeunt); *Exit* Arden. D   71b+SD door,] House: L   Black Will,] ∼∧ L
72 us—] Us. L   73 Away, away—] ∼, ∼, L   Disperse.] ∼! L   *The end*] End L

IV. i

ACT IV. SCENE I. *An Inn, the*] Act 4ᵗʰ. Scene 1ˢᵗ.—The L   1 heav'n] Heaven L
4 *Franklin*] Franklin, L   5 request,] Request∧ L   6b —Such] ∧∼ L
7b —The] ∧∼ L   8 (and . . . spake it)] *Ed.*; (∼,) D; ∧& with Tears she speaks it,∧ L
11a renounced] renounc'd L   for ever] forever L   12 heaven] Heav'n L
13 affection,] L (Affection); ∼; D   14a resolution—] Resolution. L   16a passion—]
Passion. L   16b Ha, ha, ha,] ∼, ∼, ∼! L   18a she will] she'll L   18b shure]
sure L   20 wait;] ∼, L   22 heaven] Heav'n L   25 heaven—] Heav'n. L
o'er] over L   26 No:] ∼; L   for ever] forever L   27 revenge:] Revenge! L
28 disappointment,] Disappointment∧ L   29 prest] press'd L   necessity,] Necessity∧ L
30 foe.] Foe! L   31 thought—] Thought! L   32 dies!] L; ∼∧ D   32+32SD [*To*
Michael.] If we succeed,] *Ed.*; If we succeed, [*To* Michael. D, L (succeed∧ [to ∼∧ L); W1
prints after 31   37a impossible—] Impossible! L   37b —You] ∧∼ L   38 You,
. . . ruffians,] ∼∧ . . . Ruffians∧ L   shall] may L   him.] ∼; L   39–40 begin | (No matter
how)] ∼, | ∧∼, ∧ L   41 swords.—] Swords:∧ L   42 defence;] Defence. L
44b temper.] Temper, L   47a so—] ∼: L

IV. ii

SCENE II.] Scene 2ᵈ L   1 Well,] L; ∼∧ D   4 gladden] gladen L   5 earth.]
Earth; L   9 prayers] Pray'rs L   heaven] Heav'n L   10 *Arden*] L (Arden); ∼, D
sooth] sooth's L   11b *Maria!*] Maria. L   17 eyes,] Eyes∧ L   faltring] Falt'ring L
18 grief,] Grief∧ L   21 ere] 'ere L   22 crown'd.] Crown'd! L   23 vain:] ∼∧ L
25 her,] ∼∧ L   26 perplex'd,] ∼∧ L   28 Oh!] ∼, L   monster,] Monster∧ L
32 greatness,] Greatness∧ L   33 sees] ∼, L   hears.] ∼; L   36 *Argus's*] Argus' L
slow,] ∼∧ L   37a jealousy's.—] Jealousy's.∧ L   37b —No more, no more—] ∧∼,∼! L
44 lov'd,] ∼∧ L   46a then,] ∼∧ L   47 heart,] Heart∧ L   48 maintain,] ∼; L
53 heaven] Heav'n L   54 coward.] Coward∧ L   55 wrongs,] Wrongs: L
58 withdraw—even] ∼. Ev'n L   59a impertinence.—] Impertinence.∧ L
59aSD Franklin *and*] Frank: & L   60 reproaches!] Reproaches? L   61 continue,] ∼∧ L
62 deceit!] Deceit? L   63 guilt!] Guilt? L   No—At] ∼; at L   64 would] wou'd L

65 public] publick L   66 would] wou'd L   67 here, earth] ~. Earth L   sight!] L
(Sight); ~. D   70 would] wou'd L   but] But L   74 were] was L   certain,] ~∧ L
75a stains] L (Stains); pains D   76 thought.] Thought! L   77 heart,] Heart; L
78 eyes.] Eyes! L   voice,] Voice∧ L   79 heaven] L (Heav'n); ~, D   80 O!] ~∧ L
fly] ~! L   81 thus.] ~∧ L   82a thee] ~, L   82b never, never.] ~, ~! L
83 should] Shou'd L   86 sorrow] Sorrows L   88 tell thee,] L; ~∧ D   (for . . .
thee)] ∧~ . . . ~,∧ L   89b —Oh] ∧~ L   89bSD to] on L   89c canst] can'st L
91 woud'st] wou'dst L   say,] ~∧ L   92b O! mercy, mercy!] ~, ~! Mercy! L   93 me,
let] ~. Let L   93 hand:] Hand! L   97 remorse,] Remorse; L   100 hast] Hadst L
101 weakness,] Weakness∧ L   pow'r!] Pow'r? L   102a Rise—rise—] ~, ~, L   *Alicia.*]
Alicia! L   107 streams] L (Streams); ~, D   111 for ever] forever L   116 tears;]
Tears, L   tell me:] ~, L   117 long-suffering] long suffering L   118b witness,]
Witness∧ L   122 reflexion] Reflection L   125 gold.] Gold! L   127 ever, and
only mine.] ever∧~? L   128 will.] ~! L   130 knowest] know'st, L   131 *St.
Valentine*] *Ed.*; St. Valentine D, L   133 chear] cheer L   134 night,] L (Night); ~∧ D
136b —Thus] ∧~ L   136bSD [*Exit* Arden.] L (Exit); *not in* D   137 wandering]
wand'ring L   me,] ~∧ L   148 Tho'] L *does not indent*   grief,] Grief∧ L
152 despair,] Despair∧ L   153SD [*Exit* Alicia.] L (Exit ~∧); *not in* D

IV. iii

SCENE III] *Ed.*; SCENE IV D; Scene 4.ᵗʰ L   street. People] Street— | People L   1 me—]
~. L   S'blood,] Blood! L   way.] Way! L   8 precious!—] ~!∧ L   9SD Will] L; ~. D
beaten off] are beaten off L   10 tho'—] ~. L   11 back,] ~∧ L   12b world—]
World. L   14b heart—] Heart.— L   15 heaven] Heav'n L   16 reflexion:—]
Reflection.∧ L   19 name.] Name; L   21 heart,] Heart∧ L   torn,] ~∧ L   23 say] ~, L
24b —Only] ∧~ L   27 rage,] Rage∧ L   28b —I] ∧~ L   29b —What's] ∧~ L
here!] ~? L   bleed.] ~! L   30b —A] ∧~ L   sir—] Sir. L   31 so.—] ~.∧ L
Franklin, see] Franklin, ~, L   33 (Wretch . . . am!)] ∧~ . . . ~!∧ L   34 hope] ~, L
35 me.] ~; L   36b —Sir] ∧~ L   37b —Nay] ∧~ L   38b —Nay] ∧~ L
not.—] ~;∧ L   39 company!—] Company!∧ L   better.] ~: L   40 —An] ∧~ L
hence,] ~∧ L   41 you are] you're L   engag'd,] Engag'd∧ L   42b then] ~, L
44 sure] L; ~, D   45–51 *Ard.* No doubt . . . than ever.] *not in* L   47 your] *Ed.*; you D
52 What a churl!] ~, a Churl? L   54 *Arden.*] Arden∧ L   54SD [*Exit.*] *not in* L
55SD+ [*Exit the other way.*] (Exeunt severally∧ L   55+SD Mosby . . . Green.] Mosby reenters
with Green having watch'd Franklin out. L   58 our] the L   60 *Michael,*] Michael∧ L
train,] Train∧ L   62 doors,] Doors∧ L   64a present—] ~. L   64b —She'll] ∧~ L
67 evening, then,] Evening∧ ~∧ L   68 (a game he loves)] ∧a Game ~,∧ L
70 (*Michael* . . . you)] ∧Michael . . . ~,∧ L   71 given,] ~∧ L   forth,] ~∧ L
72b Good—] ~! L   74 Howe'er,] ~∧ L   76b —These] ∧~ L   game,] Game. L
77b —*Arden*!] ∧Arden, L   78 body,] Body∧ L   abbey-wall,] Abbey-Wall∧ L
79 th'early] the' early L   80 —My friend, thy hand—] ∧~ Friend, ~ Hand. L
81 it?—] ~?∧ L   firm,] ~∧ L   84 True, he] ~. He L   foe,] Foe∧ L
85SD [*Exeunt.*] *Ed.*; *not in* D, L   The end] End L

V. i

ACT V. SCENE I.] Act 5.ᵗʰ Scene 1.ˢᵗ L   1 *Arden*!] Arden? L   2 O!] ~, L   sav'd]
saved L   7 hence,] ~∧ L   8 way.—] Way.∧ L   theirs.—] ~.∧ L   10 *Mosby,*]
Mosby! L   12 hark,] ~! L   approach.—] ~.∧ L   12+SD Shakebag,] ~∧ L
13 him!—] ~!∧ L   13+13SD O sir— | [*Talks* . . . Green.] (talks . . . Green. | Alic.
O Sir— L   15 chest.] Chest— L   17 fawning,] ~∧ L   whiteliver'd] white-Liver'd L
18 wou'd,] ~∧ L   19–20a blood, | I'd have them] Blood∧ I'd have | them L
20a all.—] ~! L   20b night—] Night. L   22 next.] ~! L   23 So,] ~∧ L
woman—] Woman; L   24b —O . . . mercy—] ∧O Mercy, Mercy! L   25 lioness,]
Lioness∧ L   26 young,] ~∧ L   29 us;] ~∧ L   30a arts.] Arts∧ L
30aSD *Knocking*] a Knocking L   30b —Sir] ∧~ L   33 *Mosby,*] Mosby∧ L
34 midnight,] Midnight∧ L   with] at L   38 well.] ~∧ L   38SD *Knocking*] a
Knocking L   40 hast] haste L   wait,] ~∧ L   41SD Will] ~, L Shakebag] L; ~, D
go] goe L   41+SD Alicia . . . *alone*.] *not in* L   46 Sir;] Alic: Sir, L, *beginning a new line*
47a Madam,] ~∧ L   47b —I] ∧~ L   heard,] ~; L   48 hereafter,] ~∧ L

49b damn'd—] ~!— L   husband—] Husband. L   49c Ha!—] ~!∧ L
49c+SD *Enter . . . Michael.*] L *includes before* 49c   50 monster,] Monster∧ L
54a *Franklin*] L (Franklin); *Frankland* D   55a expected.—] ~.∧ L   55b heav'n]
Heaven L   56 meant] mean L   57 joy,] Joy∧ L   58 *Alicia:*] Alicia; L
59 your] thy L   60 eyes.] Eyes! L   63 friendship,] Friendship∧ L   67 that] who L
husband's] Husband L   68 life!—] Life∧— L   70 Yet,] ~? ∧ L   75 yet—] ~, L
76 sir—] Sir,— L   79b —It] ∧~ L   80 freely.] ~,∧ L   81bSD [*Aside.*] *Ed.,
following* L; D ([~.]) *prints immediately after speech-heading*   83bSD [*Aside.*] *Ed., following* L;
D ([~.]) *prints immediately after speech-heading*   89 *Franklin!*] Franklin, L   fly,] ~∧ L
life!] L (Life); ~. D   90 herself,] ~∧ L   view,] ~∧ L   91 me] ~, L
92SD *Apart.*] aside∧ L   93 up;] ~: L   94 advantage;] Advantage: L   95b you.]
you! L   95b+SD *himself,*] himself; L   *defence,*] defence; L   96 pow'r] Power L
arm,] Arm! L   97 conquer.] Conquer! L   prayers] Pray'rs L   curses,] Curses,]
98 blessing.] Blessing! L   99b O!] ~, L   100 Nay,] L; ~∧ D   101 fate.] Fate! L
102 unequall'd] L; unequal D   103 death,] Death∧ L   now,] ~∧ L   104b *Green,*]
Green! L   107a further—] ~. L   107b —Think] ∧~ L   abbey-lands] Abbey Lands L
108b —You] ∧~ L   judges,] Judges: L   110 Who—who] ~? ~ L   these?] ~?— L
all.] All: L   111a *Alicia*—] Alicia. L   111b —I'll] ∧~ L   113 agony,] Agony∧
115 thee:] ~! L   117 useless] ~, L   clay.] Clay: L   118 pleas'd,] ∧~ L
122 wretch,] Wretch! L   123 heaven] Heav'n L   love.—] Love:∧ L   125 blacker,]
~∧ L   fiends,] Fiends; L   127a me—] ~! L   127b —Full] ∧~ L
128 Supreme,] Supreem! L   129 wing.] Wing! L   justice.] Justice: L   130a mercy.]
Mercy— L   130b —Turn] ∧~ L   me:] ~! L   131 sorrows.] Sorrows! L
132 wife,] Wife∧ L   133 slave.—] Slave.∧ L   me, spurn] ~! Spurn L   134 still.—]
Still∧— L   136 lov'dst] ~, L   137a fool,] Fool! L   137b —'Tis] ∧~ L
138 me,] ~∧ L   138SD *Snatches*] She snatches L   *dagger, . . . Mosby.*—] Dagger∧ & strikes
at Mosby: L   139 Damnation!—] ~!∧ L   140 unfinish'd,] unfinish'd∧   last.—]
~.∧ L   142a —Force] ∧~ L   142b Inhuman] ~, L   142bSD *swoons,*] swoons∧ L
143 here!—] ~!∧ L   144 feet,] Feet∧ L   forwards,] ~∧ L   146 murder'd—]
Murder'd! L   147a —How . . . *Alicia?*—] ∧~ . . . Alicia?∧ L   147b–148a As the . . .
hell—] *line-division follows* L; D *prints as one line*   147b damn'd:] damned; L
148a hell—] Hell. L   148b *Mosby!*] L (Mosby); *not in* D   154 thyself;] ~, L
154SD *Mosby*] *not in* L   158 dread—] ~. L   160 Hide,] ~∧ L   dust,] Dust∧ L
be,] ~! L   161 reveng'd.—] ~!∧ L   prayer.] Prayer: L   163a Sister!] ~∧ L
thine—] ~. L   163b–164 off | Humanity] L; off humanity D, *printing speech as prose*
166 will,] ~; L   170 the ring] ring L   172 No,] ~: L   173–4 kept . . . body?]
Ed.; D *and* L *treat as verse, with line-division after* ring, *and initial capital on* Were   175 garden,]
Garden∧ L   179 conduct,] L (Conduct); ~; D   185 we're] we are L
188 well—] ~. L   189 So—softly—softly] ~, ~, ~! L   door—] Door: L
189SD [*Michael . . . door.*] *not in* L   190 So—] So; L

V. ii

SCENE II. | *A hall . . . house.* | *Mosby alone.*] Scene shuts. Mosby alone. L, *continuing scene i*
2 Night-fowls] Night Fowls L   5 winter night] Winter-Night L   7 horrors,] Horrors∧ L
black,] Black∧ L   8 wish.] Wish, L   10 every] ev'ry L   11 starting] staring L
conscience,] L (Conscience); ~∧ D   wounds] Wounds; ~, D   12 hell] Hell alone L
12SD [*A pause.*] *not in* L   13 This, this] ~, ~, L   15 lay] laid L   17 repose]
Repose, L   day-light] Daylight L   me.] ~: L   19 clouds:] Clouds; L   22 —Not
yet:] ~∧~! L   23 awful] aweful L   24 more,] ~∧ L   26a *Michael*—] Michael.—
27 abbey—] Abbey. L   28 apace] L; a pace D   29b sir—] Sir. L   29c much—]
~! L   32a thine,] ~∧ L   32b —What's] ∧~ L   34a mine.—] ~.∧ L
34b —Why] ∧~ L   now,] ~! L   34b+SD *Enter* Maria.] Enter ~∧ L, *which includes
after* 34a   39b I'd] I had L   forgot.] ~: L   42 twixt their teeth] L (Teeth); *not in* D
44 them] 'em L   lust,] Lust∧ L   48 View, view] View L

V. iii

SCENE III.] Scene 2ᵈ L   SD *A room . . . house.*] *not in* L   3a Detains] L; detains D
6 I've] I L   7b mad—] ~! L   11 late;] ~: L   13 no] *not in* L   16 starts,
her] ~∧ are L   wild.] Wild∧ L   18 —Madam] ∧~ L   19 wine.] Wine! L   *Arden.*]

Arden! L 19SD [*Drinks.*] *not in* L 20 *Arden,*] Arden∧ L 20SD [*Rising.*] L
includes SD *after* 21a 21a thyself] yourself L 21b sake!—] Sake!∧ L
21CSD [*Comes forward.*] (Comes forward∧) They all rise∧) L 22 them] 'em L dispatch,]
~∧ L 22SD [*All rise.*] *not in* L 23SD *Knocking*] A Knocking L 24b heaven,]
Heav'n∧ L right.] ~! L 25b sir.] Sir; L 26 officers,] Officers∧ L 27SD *and*
others] &c. L 28 I'm] I am L 30 worship] Worship, L 31 hour;] Hour: L
33 apprehend] L; appprehend D 35 to-night,] to Night∧ L 40 respect,] Respect∧ L
41 worth.—] Worth.∧ L 42b Heavens] Heav'ns L indeed!] ~? (aside) L
43a sake—] Sake. L 45 heaven] Heav'n L 46b Oh! sir,] Oh, Sir! L
47 to-night] to Night L 48 absence,] Absence∧ L 49b Scarce] Scarse L
53 most] more L surprising] Surprizing L him] L; *not in* D better.] ~. Enter Franklin &
others, with Lights. L 54SD [*Without.*]] *not in* L 54 there—ho—] ~, ~! L
55 watch—] Watch! L by—] ~: L 55+SD Franklin . . . lights.] *Ed.*, D (lights— D);
not in L 58 heaven] Heav'n L 59a friend—] Friend, L murder'd!] L; ~. D
60 seen!] ~? L 63b art] are L moved] mov'd L 65 eye] Eye. L
67 murd'rer] Murderer L 69b all—] ~∧ L instant:] ~. L 69bSD Alicia] Alic: L
70 lady] Woman L 70SD [*Alicia is carried out.*] *Ed.*; *not in* D, L 71 along] L; a long D
72c judge,] ~∧ L 74 men (neighbours and townsmen all)] *Ed., following* W1, D (men,); men
∧Neighbours & Townsmen all, L 76 lay;—with] ~.∧ With L notes,] Notes∧ L
78 blood] Blood, L 80 rushes] Rushes, L 81 garments:] Garments; L
82 trac'd,] ~∧ L 85 borne] born L 88b —And] ∧~ L 91a *Mayor.*—Search
'em—] *not in* L 92SD [*To an officer.*]] *not in* L 92–3 Enter . . . more.] Search 'em: we
may perhaps discover more. L 93+SD *Officer* . . . Green.] The Officers search Mosby,
Green, & Alicia. L 94 letter, sir.] L (Letter, Sir); letter. D 95b —Righteous] ∧~ L
heaven] Heav'n L 96 villain:] Villain! L 97 ring,] Ring; L 98a hand.—]
Hand.∧ L 99 *Mos.* I freely . . . my fate.] *Ed.*, D (fate∧ D); *not in* L 99+SD another] not
in L 100 We've] Worshipful Sir, | We've L 101a in.—] ~.∧ L 101aSD Black
. . . in.] Enter Black Will; Shakebag &c. L 101b —They] ∧~ L 102 them] 'em L
104 die,] ~; L 105 (for . . . *Mosby*)] *Ed.*, D (Mosby, D); ∧for . . . Rascal∧ Mosby,∧
106 engaged] engag'd L discovery,] Discovery∧ L 107 him.—] ~.∧ L
109 assistance,] Assistance∧ L *Green's*] Greens L 112 that:] ~; L afterwards.]
Afterwards: L 113 So,] ~∧ L think,] ~∧ L 114 heav'n] Heaven L
115 our's] ours L 115SD [*Alicia* brought in.]] *not in* L 118 Till] 'Till L forth] ~, L
119a publick] {P}publick L execution.—] ~.∧ L 119b —I] ∧~ L 120 justice;]
Justice∧ L 121 yielded] yeilded L maid,] Maid; L 126 innocence] innocen{t}ce L
127 fellowship.] Fellowship∧ L 129a wonder.—] Wonder∧— L 129b —Madam] ∧~ L
135b condemn'd,] Condemn'd∧ L 136 sentence.] Sentence! L 138 rig'rous]
rigorous L justice.] Justice! L 139 crimes,] Crimes∧ L 141 prove,] ~; L
142 And poor *Alicia*] And, poor Alicia, L 142SD [*Exeunt.*] *Ed.*; *not in* D, L

Epilogue

EPILOGUE] L *does not include epilogue* 6 *mean,*] *Ed.*; ~; D 7 *critick-spleen);*] *Ed.*; ~)∧ D
18 *raise:*] W1; ~, D

TABLES OF PRESS VARIANTS

THE LONDON MERCHANT (*first edition*)
Press Variants

Sig.	Line	Uncorrected	Corrected
A3	dedication 26	Contract	Contrast
A4	dedication 47	*amazeindeed*	*amaze indeed*
	dedication 52	*Beens o*	*Been so*
A6	prologue 30	*Prevents*	*Prevent*
F1	v. ix. 55	suburd	suburb
	v. ix. 64	Crime	Crimes
F2ᵛ	epilogue 1	*hopeless*	*hapless*

THE CHRISTIAN HERO (*first and 'second' editions*)
Press Variants

Sig.	Line	Uncorrected	Corrected
C1	I. i. 287	Stave	Slave
	I. i. 291a	Power;	Power.
	I. i. 292	will,	will;
C2	I. i. 361	Shame,	Shame.
C2ᵛ	I. i. 371	see.	see,
C3ᵛ	II. i. 29	Fortitude, aud	Fortitude‸ and
D3	II. i. 266	depeuds	depends
E2	III. i. 132	was	Was
	III. i. 132	once‸	once,
	III. i. 134	loved	beloved
	III. i. 137	Fondness	Friendship
	III. i. 143	be	were
	III. i. 147[1]	Foe:	Foe?
	III. i. 149b	Heavens	Heaven
E4	III. i. 254	Who	Which
	III. i. 268	steem	stem
	III. i. 274	I'm	I am
G4ᵛ	IV. iv. 92	Aud	And

[1] Emended in the present edition to read: Foe!

Press Accidents

Only those press accidents which occur in the text are recorded. Those involving only catchwords or page numbers are not included.

Sig.	Line	1st State	2nd State	3rd State
E3^v	III. i. 239	*Althea!*	*Althea*$_\wedge$	
F1^v	III. i. 350	Battles	Ba ttles	Battles
F2	IV. i. 1^1	*K. A.*	$_\wedge$. *A.*	
H2	v. ii. 25^2	[the West,	$_\wedge$the West,	
	v. ii. 36^3	Throne;	Throne; Like	
H3^v	v. iv. 31	Heaven!	Heaven$_\wedge$	
H4^v	v. iv. 110	Youth!	Youth$_\wedge$	
I1^v	v. iv. 171	he's not so	he'$_\wedge$ not so	he'snot so
	v. iv. 174b	Apostate!	Apostate$_\wedge$	
	v. iv. 176^4	know$_\wedge$	know!	

[1] Emended in present edition to read: *Aga.*
[2] Bracket set before run-over.
[3] In later state catchword has been moved and appended to this line.
[4] Exclamation mark moved from line 174b to line 176.

FATAL CURIOSITY (*first edition*)
Press Variants

Sig.	Line	Uncorrected	Corrected
B2	I. ii. 3	Ay:	Ay;
D1	II. i. 65	intuitive	intuitive,
	II. i. 68	large	large,
D2	II. i. 114	feel	feel,
D2^v	II. i. 153	perillous	perilous
D3	II. i. 161	sun.	sun,
D3^v	II. ii. 17	this	this,
	II. ii. 18	pace.	pace?
D4^v	II. iii. 3	of$_\wedge$	of—
F4^v	advertisement, item III^1	*Scanderburg*	*Scanderbeg*

[1] See textual introduction, p. 291 n. 60.

HYPHENATIONS AT THE ENDS OF LINES

END-OF-THE-LINE HYPHENATION IN THE PRESENT EDITION

[NOTE: No hyphenation of a possible compound appears at the end of a line in the present edition except the following readings, which are hyphenated within the lines in the copy-text.]

Silvia

I.xii.93–4   Church-yard
II.ii.49–50   Fellow-Creatures
II.xvi.29–30   Cabinet-Counsellor
III.i.23–4   when-e'er
III.v.11–12   ill-bred
III.xi.3–4   to-day
III.xviii.36–7   May-game

The London Merchant

I.i.43–4   Trades-mens
II.xiii.1–2   all-sufficient

Arden of Feversham

II.i.106–7   free-thinkers

END-OF-THE-LINE HYPHENATION IN THE COPY-TEXTS

[NOTE: The following compounds or possible compounds are hyphenated at the ends of lines in the copy-text. The form in which they have been transcribed represents the general practice of the copy-texts as evidenced by other appearances or parallels.]

Silvia

I.iv.66   Bridegroom
I.viii.6   Parish-Officers
I.x.24   Church-yard
I.x.30   to-night
I.xii.57   himself
I.xii.84   scot-free
II.xv.61   Eye-witness
III.iii.34   Lyings-in (Lyings-Inn O)

The London Merchant

Dedication 82   Sub-Governor
I.v.30, III.i.11, V.x.13   Mankind
II.xi.54   Madman

Elmerick

Dedication 11   Mankind

Arden of Feversham

I.i.10   trencher-fav'rite
IV.ii.68   self-condemn'd

TITLE AND FIRST-LINE INDEX TO SONGS AND MUSIC FOR *SILVIA*

An index to individual songs and pieces of music included in *Silvia* or mentioned in the commentary on songs and music for that play. Songs from other ballad operas are indexed (under first line, though some are referred to only by ballad-opera title and song number) only if they have been quoted or otherwise specially noted in the commentary. The ballad operas themselves and other related works are included, along with authors and composers, in the general index.

Entries are for the most part modernized in spelling and typography, and may not therefore precisely match corresponding text in *Silvia* or other sources.

GENERAL INDEX